SHOW MUSIC ON RECORD

SHOW MUSIC ON RECORD

from the 1890s to the 1980s

A comprehensive list of original cast and studio cast performances issued on commercial phonograph records, covering
music of the American stage, screen, and television, with composer performances and other selected collateral recordings

With photographs

JACK RAYMOND

FREDERICK UNGAR PUBLISHING CO./NEW YORK

Library of Congress Cataloging in Publication Data

Raymond, Jack, 1923-
  Show music on record.

  Bibliography: p.
  Includes index.
  1. Musical revues, comedies, etc.—Discography.
I. Title.
ML156.4.046R4   016.7899'12281   81–40471
ISBN 0–8044–5774–3
ISBN 0–8044–6672–6 (pbk.)

The author and the publishers acknowledge with gratitude the kind assistance of the following in supplying photographs and other illustrative
material: RCA Records, CBS Records, Andrew Velez, Walter Hampden
Memorial Library of The Players Club.

Contents

Introduction

It is difficult to imagine what it would be like if we could go to the phonograph and put on a record of the voice of George Washington or Shakespeare. The original cast of *Hamlet*. Or Christ or Mohammed. Bach playing his organ. The chamber orchestra of Haydn.

In the year 3000, people will be able to listen to speeches by Franklin Roosevelt and Theodore Roosevelt, but not to Lincoln's Gettysburg Address. They will be able to hear Cole Porter playing and singing his songs, but not Stephen Foster.

In the cultural history of mankind, there are certain crucial dates of technological advance such as the invention of the printing press. The invention of sound recording is one such date. Mark it well: December 1877. It is so recent that the significance may be blurred in our eyes, but the date will go down in history as a knife edge—before which voices spoke, sang, and vanished, and after which some of the voices remained.

Centuries from now, people will look upon the early phonograph records as we look upon the early cuneiform tablets, or incunabula in the field of printing. The sounds of the 1890s will forever remain the earliest sounds anyone can hear.

The phonograph records issued in this first century of recorded sound constitute a priceless resource for studying the cultural life of the era. Sadly, libraries and other institutions have not done a good job of cataloguing and preserving those records. In the field of show music, which is the subject of this book, no library or other institution has anything approaching a comprehensive collection of the records listed in this book. Furthermore, the indexing and cataloguing of institutional collections are in many cases practically nonexistent, and storage conditions are often terrible.

Private collectors have in some respects done a better job. The best collections of show music are in private hands, and it would have been impossible to assemble the information in this book without the cooperation of those private collectors. In particular, I would like to thank Bradley Bennett of Los Angeles; Larry Warner of New Orleans; Richard C. Norton, Hilary Knight, and Dan Langan of New York; and William C. Caffrey of Chicago. I am also indebted to Daniel G. Dietz of Washington; Warren A. Seamans of Boston; Gary MacMillan of Rochester; Richard C. Lynch and Andrew Velez of New York; and James L. Limbacher of Detroit. Dorothy M. Jones provided encouragement and assistance when it was most needed. Finally, to the staffs of the Recorded Sound and Motion Picture Division of the Library of Congress and to the Rodgers & Hammerstein Collection and the Performing Arts Division of the New York Public Library, I extend warm thanks for their help and forbearance during my hours spent at those institutions.

In general terms, the book lists all commercially issued recordings of show music from the American stage, screen, and television as performed by members of the original cast and subsequent casts, including studio productions. Performances by composers are also listed, as are certain recordings of related interest.

The listings have been arranged chronologically by year to put each show in historical context. The musical show buff may enjoy browsing through the years, marveling perhaps at the wealth of material that has been recorded.

Robin Hood is apparently the first American musical show from which original cast recordings exist. Jessie

Bartlett Davis, Eugene Cowles, and W. H. MacDonald, all of whom appeared in the original production in Chicago in 1890 and in New York the following year, recorded one song apiece from the show between 1898 and 1911.

Chauncey Olcott recorded "My Wild Irish Rose" and "When Irish Eyes Are Smiling," two songs which he helped write and which he personally introduced in musical shows in 1899 and 1913 respectively.

The seventeen-year-old Kate Smith can be heard singing two songs from *Honeymoon Lane*, the show in which she made her debut in 1926.

Tastes of the times are revealed in some odd material that was recorded. *The Bird of Paradise*, a show which opened in 1912, had twenty-one numbers recorded by its performers—Ben Waiaiole, S. M. Kaiawe, W. B. J. Aeko, E. K. Rose, and the Hawaiian Quintette. That is more records than were in the original cast album of *Oklahoma!* Songs from *The Bird of Paradise* include titles like "Press Me to Thee," "I Love but Thee," and "My Love Is Like a Blooming Rose," but the material was clearly popular in its time.

The British did a consistently better job than the Americans in recording show music. A few London shows at the turn of the century were recorded almost as fully as shows are recorded today. *Florodora* opened in London in 1899. The following year, members of the original cast recorded twelve numbers from the show. (None of those records has been reissued on LP, incidentally, and what an interesting album the complete set would make!) In America, only one song from *Florodora* was recorded, despite the show's popularity: three Florodora Girls of the 1900 New York cast sang "Tell Me, Pretty Maiden" for Columbia Records.

In 1943, the original cast album became a commerical success with the issue of *Oklahoma!* by Decca. Six years earlier, however, Musicraft had issued virtually the complete score of *The Cradle Will Rock* performed by the original performers with composer Marc Blitzstein at the piano. The material on that album is nearly twice the length of Decca's *Oklahoma!* And to go back even further, in 1932 and 1933 Brunswick issued original cast albums (albeit reconstituted) of *Blackbirds of 1928* and *Show Boat*.

Some show material recorded by original cast members was never released, and most of those unissued recordings have been lost. Nora Bayes and Jack Norworth recorded "Shine On, Harvest Moon," a song they wrote and which they sang in the *1908 Ziegfeld Follies*. The master was never issued, and no copy of the recording exists today. Irene Bordoni recorded the Cole Porter song "Two Little Babes in the Wood," which she introduced in *Paris* in 1928. It too has been lost. Evelyn Herbert recorded "Wanting You" from Sigmund Romberg's *The New Moon*, in which she starred on stage. It was not issued, and no copy remains.

Although the material here has never been published in this form, a few specialized discographies have been especially helpful in its preparation. In particular, I would like to mention the works of Brian Rust, Allen Debus, Jim Limbacher, and Steve Smolian. Books published by these men are listed in the bibliography, together with other reference books which made my job easier.

Record producers whose recordings belong in future editions of this book are asked to send review copies to the author at 3709 George Mason Drive #1011, Falls Church, VA 22041. Readers are invited to correspond with the author concerning corrections and additions. With their help, it may be possible to publish a revised edition at a later time.

CRITERIA FOR INCLUDING RECORDS

The objective of the book is to provide a list of commercial recordings of music from American shows and foreign shows which played in America—music of the stage, screen, and television in original cast and studio cast performances. It also includes records of composers performing their own show songs, as well as certain collateral material assumed to be of interest to readers in this field.

Which Shows Qualify?

If it is a United States stage show with songs, it qualifies for inclusion—whether operetta, book musical, or revue. Even a concert-type revue is included if it was produced as a show rather than as a cabaret entertainment and if the stars were essentially stars of the stage or screen. Thus *Judy Garland at the Palace* is included, as is *An Evening with Beatrice Lillie*. On the other hand, the Cotton Club revues are not, nor are Broadway engagements by Tony Bennett or Bette Midler. Anna Russell is not included, on the grounds that her material is not really "show music."

INTRODUCTION

Obviously a line must be drawn somewhere this side of grand opera. Shows which are generally thought of as "operettas" are included, since the operetta was the popular "musical" of its day. But the works of Menotti will not be found here, nor will Bernstein's *Trouble In Tahiti*. On the other hand, you will find Sondheim's *Sweeney Todd*.

In general, foreign shows—including London shows—are not included unless they played in the United States or were written by American composers. Among the few exceptions are the shows of Noel Coward, Ivor Novello, and Sandy Wilson, which are somewhat arbitrarily included.

Any United States motion picture or television show qualifies for inclusion if it has songs. Obviously *Singin' in the Rain* is included, as are the Elvis Presley films. But so is a film like *Casablanca*—certainly not a "movie musical" but a film in which Dooley Wilson's singing of "As Time Goes By" is an important moment. And *High Noon*, in which the only song is sung under the title of an off-camera singer. And *The Notorious Landlady*, which had no songs at all but was publicized by a "title song" recorded by Fred Astaire, who was in the film. Recordings from all such films are included in the book, and the same broad criteria are applied to television shows.

Records of movie musicals from England and other English-speaking countries are also included, on the assumption that most of those films were released at one time or another in the United States. Recordings from foreign-language films are included only if the records, as well as the films, were released here. No foreign television material is included.

It should perhaps be emphasized that the book does not include the multitudinous commercial recordings of motion picture and television soundtracks that consist only of background music. Unless it has songs, the show is not listed.

College shows, amateur shows, and industrial shows are included only if they are of special interest—usually because of well-known composers or performers. "Record productions" that are really book musicals are included, and so are puppet shows with songs, popular oratorios, pageants, and cantatas—but only if they are in the mainstream of "show music."

Which Records Qualify?

In general, any English-language recording that contains representative selections from a show's score is included in the book. Strictly orchestral versions are not included, however, nor are jazz and dance-tempo versions. Demonstration records are not included unless they later had a commercial release, although an exception has been made occasionally in the case of a demo record of unusual interest. Foreign-language recordings (the German production of *My Fair Lady*, for example) are not included, although again there are exceptions. The Paris production of *Man of La Mancha* is included because Joan Diener of the New York cast was also in the Paris production. The original Berlin production of *The Three-Penny Opera* is listed, as are the Rome productions of *Rugantino*.

Studio cast albums of shows are included if they contain a truly representative sample of songs from the score, even if as many as two or three scores are sampled on a single LP record. But studio cast "samplers" which hop from show to show are not listed.

Prior to the introduction of the modern LP record, there were efforts to provide the score of a show on 78rpm records. In the late 1930s and 1940s, this usually took the form of 78rpm show albums. But prior to that time, it was common practice to issue a vocal medley of songs from a show, usually on a 12" record, and often performed by one of the "Light Opera Companies" which were put together by recording companies. Dance bands also occasionally came out with medleys of songs from a particular show, sung by the vocalists of the band. All such recordings are included in this book, provided the intent of the record producer was to give a representative selection of songs from the score of a particular show.

In addition to the type of show records discussed up to now, another category of recording qualifies for inclusion in the book, namely an individual song recorded by a person who was in a stage, screen, or television production of the show. The distinction is that we are now talking about individual songs, not medleys or albums. Medleys and albums are included regardless of who the singers are, provided they meet the other criteria. Recordings of individual songs are included only if they are sung by persons who were in a stage, screen, or television production of the show, or if they are performed by the composer.

The book does not include individual show songs performed by people who had nothing to do with a production of the show. A Tommy Dorsey record with Frank Sinatra singing a song from a Broadway show will not be listed, even if it is the only recording ever made of the song.

It should be pointed out that any song from a show recorded by a person who was in the show is eligible for inclusion, whether or not that person sang the particular song in the show. For example, Ginger Rogers's recording of "The Way You Look Tonight" is included in the book, although it was Fred Astaire who sang the song in *Swing Time*.

Frequently a performer or composer will record a medley of his well-known songs. No song from such a medley is listed in the book unless at least one full chorus of the song is sung.

Finally, let me recognize a few of the book's anomalies:

● All records by Gertrude Lawrence of songs from her shows are included in the book, even though some of the shows were not produced in the United States and would therefore not otherwise qualify for inclusion. The same goes for Beatrice Lillie, Maurice Chevalier, and a few other internationally famous stars.

● If a well-known American star made records of songs he sang in a London show, those records are listed—even though the show does not otherwise qualify for inclusion, and even though other songs from the show are not listed. For example, Raymond Hitchcock starred in *Mr. Manhattan* in London and recorded a number from the show. It is listed, even though another song from the show, recorded by an English performer, is not.

● When a song from an "artist album" or an "anthology" qualifies for listing in the book, all other original cast songs on that album are also listed, even though the shows they are from do not otherwise qualify to be listed in the book.

● Although practically all of the original cast material listed in the book are songs, there are a few sketches of special interest. From *At Home Abroad* you'll find Reginald Gardiner's records of his "Trains" monologue; from *Set To Music* there is Richard Haydn's "Fish Mimicry"; and from *My Dear Public*, Willie Howard's "Comes the Revolution!"

● A few original cast recordings issued in limited pressings for members of the production have been included, despite the fact that they are not "commercial" records.

In short, the author has exercised his prerogative to include any material he thinks may be of interest, even if it fails to meet the formal criteria of the book.

HOW TO USE THE BOOK

Key Numbers. To facilitate the indexing of artists whose records are included in this book, each show is identified by a key number of six digits, derived from the date when the show was first produced. The first two digits of the key number represent the year, the next two the month, and the last two the day of the month. Since *Roberta* opened on November 18, 1933, it bears the key number 331118. To differentiate the key numbers of two shows which opened on the same date, an asterisk is added to one of them. Thus the key number of *Funny Face* is 271122 and that of *Take The Air* is 271122*. For shows produced in the nineteenth century, the first two digits of the key numbers are underscored. Thus *Robin Hood*, which opened on September 28, 1891, bears the key number 910928.

The opening date of a musical show is taken to be its opening in New York or in London, Vienna, Paris, or another foreign capital. If it did not play in New York or a foreign capital, its opening in another major city is used to establish the key number.

The date chosen is the date of the "official" premiere of the musical show—usually the performance which the critics reviewed. Since the opening date of a film musical is seldom so easily established, those musicals are assigned key numbers in which the first two digits represent the year, the middle two digits are always "00," and the last two digits are arbitrarily assigned for the purpose of giving each film its own distinctive key number. The film *The Alamo* bears the key number 600012, which indicates that it was released in 1960. The "12" is an identifying number to distinguish this film from all other films released in that year. There is no significance at all to the sequence in which identifying numbers are assigned to films of any given year.

"LP" Album Numbers. In addition to relatively complete albums of show scores, the book also lists individual show songs that were recorded at one time or another by performers who sang them in stage, screen, or television productions. If such a record was released only in a 78rpm or 45rpm format, the record manufacturer and label number are shown in parentheses after the title of the song.

INTRODUCTION

In the case of songs issued in albums, however, the record manufacturer and label number would not be enough to identify the album properly: the title of the album would also have to be given, and such lengthy record identification would make the book awkward to use.

Therefore each album which is an anthology, and each album of songs by a particular artist, is given an identifying "LP" number to identify the provenance of songs from that album which appear in the show listings. The album *Bing Crosby and Fred Astaire: A Couple of Song and Dance Men*, issued in England as United Artists 29888, is identified in this book as "LP-396," the number being randomly assigned. Any song on that album which apears in the show listings bears the reference "LP-396." By looking up the "LP" number, the reader can get detailed information on the album, including the title, the record manufacturer, and the record number.

The Sections of the Book. The book is divided into six principal sections:

1. An alphabetical list of shows and their key numbers.

2. A chronological list of shows and recordings from the shows.

3. A numerical list of "LP" numbers.

4. An alphabetical list of artist albums, with more detail than is given in the "LP" numbers list.

5. An alphabetical list of anthologies, with the same detail as in the list of artist albums.

6. An index to artists mentioned in the chronological list of shows.

To Look Up Records by a Particular Artist

1. Look up the artist's name in the index (last name first).

2. Note the six-digit key numbers that follow the artist's name. (The six-digit numbers are often remembered more easily if they are thought of as two groups of three digits.)

3. Refer to those key numbers in the chronological list of shows.

4. If a record in the show listings is identified by an "LP" number, refer to the numerical list of "LP" numbers to determine the title, manufacturer's name, and number of the album.

5. If you want more information on the album, look it up in the alphabetical listing of artist albums or anthologies.

To Look Up Records of a Particular Show

1. Obtain the key number from the list of shows and their key numbers.

2. Look up that key number.

HOW TO READ THE SHOW LISTINGS

Look at listings in the chronological list of shows. You will notice that a letter follows each key number. *There is no significance to the sequence in which these letters are assigned.* They are assigned arbitrarily, the only purpose being to identify the various recordings of a given show. The key number for all listings of a show is the same; the letter that follows the key number provides specific identification for indexing purposes.

The words that precede the title of a show indicate the show's original format. The words "film," "TV show," "puppet show," or "record prod" indicate that the work was originally in that medium. An exception is made in the case of certain material that started out as a record production and then became a stage production. *Evita, Jesus Christ Superstar,* and *Archy and Mehitabel* are examples. Such shows are treated as the stage productions they became and bear key numbers based on the opening dates of the stage productions.

The words that follow the title indicate the production with which the particular listing is concerned. For example—

● "SHOW BOAT 1936 film soundtrack" indicates that this particular listing is of soundtrack recordings from the 1936 film.

● "Film ROBIN AND THE SEVEN HOODS orig prod" indicates that this is not a soundtrack, but rather a contemporary recording of music from the film by members of the original film production.

• "Film THE WIZARD OF OZ 1941 studio prod" indicates that this particular listing is of a 1941 studio production of the score of the film.

When the term "album" is used in the place of "studio prod," it indicates that the material is more a collection of songs from the show than full-fledged studio production with overture, chorus, etc.

"Orig prod" always refers to a New York production unless otherwise specified—for example, "orig (Los Angeles) prod" or "orig (South Africa) prod."

After the show's title (and the words that precede and follow the title) come the names of the persons who wrote the songs for the show. "MUSIC" and "WORDS" precede the names of the composer and lyricist. Rather than include the composer and lyricist in every listing of the show, however, the names are given as a rule only in the first (or "a") listing.

The orchestrator ("ORCH") and conductor ("COND") come next, and then the "CAST."

If no song titles are given, that particular listing is of a relatively complete recording of the show's score. If certain songs are listed, it means that only those songs are included. This is an important point to note. Song titles are listed *only* if the recording of the score is incomplete.

Identification of the recordings is given in parentheses. Any such record identification applies to all songs that precede it, going back to the previous record identification.

The names of record manufacturers are abbreviated in some instances (see list of abbreviations), and prefixes and suffixes to the label numbers are omitted if they are not significant. Generally speaking, it is the first LP edition that is listed. No attempt is made to include all editions. Original 78rpm, 45rpm, tape cassette, and cylinder references are given only when the material has not been reissued on LP.

The focus of the book is on the material that has been recorded from the various shows rather than on details of the record issues. For any particular performance, only one prime edition is generally given. Occasionally, however, it happens that one edition is complete whereas another lacks certain material. The book will alert the reader to such a situation, with appropriate notations as to the completeness of the editions. Excerpts from show albums (issued on artist albums and anthologies) are also listed, as an aid to keeping track of them and knowing the various sources of material.

In the case of 78rpm singles that have been reissued on artist albums and anthologies, *all* reissues are listed.

Unless otherwise indicated, LPs are 12" and 45s and EPs are 7". The size of 78rpm single records is not specified. 78rpm albums are 10" unless specified as 12".

"78/Bruns 4069" refers to a 78rpm Brunswick record. "45/Col 4-40784" refers to a 45rpm Columbia record. "Dec 10" 5108" refers to a 10" Decca LP record. "RCA 7" LL-201" refers to a 7" RCA record that plays at LP speed (33rpm). "CYL/Edison 4M-136" refers to a four-minute Edison cylinder. "Unnamed label mx 3075/6" refers to an LP with no manufacturer's name, no label number, and with master numbers 3075 and 3076 for the two sides. "78/Dec 12" album 130" refers to a 12" Decca 78rpm album. "45/RCA album EPB-581" refers to an RCA 45rpm album.

EPs are considered as single records unless they have been issued in sets of two or more records, in which case they are listed as "albums".

When the designation "(E)" follows the manufacturer's name, it indicates an English pressing. France, Germany, Italy, Japan, and Canada are similarly abbreviated. The names of other countries are written out in full.

"LP" numbers have been discussed above, but an additional point should be made: Artist albums and anthologies that are in a 78rpm or 45rpm format are also assigned "LP" numbers if the material on them has never been issued on LP.

ABBREVIATIONS

Record Manufacturers

ABC	ABC/Paramount
Cap	Capitol
Col	Columbia
Dec	Decca
HMV	His Master's Voice
Monmouth	Monmouth/Evergreen
RCA	RCA Victor (applied only to 45rpm and 33rpm records)
Vic	Victor, or RCA Victor (applied only to 78rpm records)

Countries of Origin

C	Canada
E	England
F	France
G	Germany
I	Italy
J	Japan

General Abbreviations

cond	conductor or conducted
contemp	contemporary
incl	including
orch	orchestrator or orchestrated
orig	original
prod	production
rec	recorded
CAS	tape cassette
CYL	cylinder

BIBLIOGRAPHY

Baral, Robert. *Revue: The Great Broadway Period.* New York: Fleet, 1962.

Barr, Steven C. *The (Almost) Complete 78rpm Record Dating Guide.* 1979.

Blum, Daniel. *A Pictorial History of the Talkies.* New York: Grosset, 1958.

Blum, Daniel. *A Pictorial History of the American Theatre, 1860–1976.* New York: Crown, 1977.

Bordman, Gerald. *American Musical Theatre.* New York: Oxford, 1978.

Bordman, Gerald. *Jerome Kern: His Life and Music.* New York: Oxford, 1980.

Brooks, Tim, and Earle Marsh. *The Complete Directory to Prime Time Network TV Shows, 1946–1979.* New York: Ballantine, 1979.

Brown, T Allston. *A History of the New York Stage, 1732–1901.* New York, 1964.

Burton, Jack. *The Blue Book of Broadway Musicals.* New York: Century, 1969.

Burton, Jack. *The Blue Book of Hollywood Musicals.* New York: Century, 1953.

Burton, Jack. *The Index of American Popular Music.* New York: Century, 1957.

Dimmitt, Richard B, and Andrew A Aros. *An Actor Guide to the Talkies, 1949–1974.* New Jersey: Scarecrow, 1967 & 1977.

Dimmitt, Richard B, and Andrew A Aros. *A Title Guide to the Talkies, 1927–1974.* New Jersey: Scarecrow, 1965 & 1977.

Ewen, David. *American Popular Songs.* New York: Random House, 1966.

Ewen, David. *The Book of European Light Opera.* New York: Holt, 1962.

Ewen, David. *New Complete Book of the American Musical Theater.* New York: Holt, 1970.

Farnsworth, Marjorie. *The Ziegfeld Follies.* New York: Crown, 1956.

Gifford, Denis. *British Cinema.* New York: Barnes, 1968.

Gifford, Denis. *The British Film Catalogue, 1895–1970.* Devon: David & Charles, 1973.

Gilbert, Douglas. *American Vaudeville: Its Life and Times.* New York: Dover, 1963.

Graham, Peter J. *A Dictionary of the Cinema.* New York: Barnes, 1968.

Green, Stanley. *Rodgers and Hammerstein Fact Book.* New York, 1980.

Green, Stanley. *Encyclopaedia of the Musical Theatre.* New York: Dodd Mead, 1976.

Green, Stanley. *Ring Bells! Sing Songs!* New York: Arlington, 1971.

Green, Stanley. *Encyclopaedia of the Musical Film.* New York—Ofxord, 1981.

Green, Stanley. *The World of Musical Comedy.* New York: Barnes, 1968.

Halliwell, Leslie. *The Filmgoer's Companion.* New York: Hill and Wang, 1977.

Hummel, David. *The Collector's Guide to the American Musical Theatre.* Michigan, 1977–1979.

Jay, Dave. *The Irving Berlin Songography, 1907–1966.* New York: Arlington, 1969.

Kimball, Robert. *Cole.* New York: Holt, 1971.

Kimball, Robert, and Alfred Simon. *The Gershwins.* New York: Atheneum, 1973.

Kinkle, Roger D. *The Complete Encyclopedia of Popular Music and Jazz, 1900–1950.* New York: Arlington, 1974.

Kobal, John. *Gotta Sing Gotta Dance: A Pictorial History of Film Musicals.* London: Hamlyn, 1970.

Kreuger, Miles. *The Movie Musical from Vitaphone to 42nd Street.* New York: Dover, 1975.

Kreuger, Miles. *Show Boat.* New York: Oxford, 1977.

Lewine, Richard, and Alfred Simon. *Songs of the American Theatre.* New York: Dodd Mead, 1973.

Limbacher, James L. *Theatrical Events: A Selected List of Musical and Dramatic Performances on Long-Playing Records.* 1968.

Loewenberg, Alfred. *Annals of Opera, 1597–1940.* New Jersey, 1978.

Lubbock, Mark. *The Complete Book of Light Opera.* London: Putnam, 1962.

Maltin, Leonard. *The Disney Films.* New York: Bonanza, 1973.

Mattfeld, Julius. *Variety Music Cavalcade, 1620–1969.* New Jersey: Prentice-Hall, 1971.

McSpadden, J Walker. *Operas and Musical Comedies.* New York: Crowell, 1951.

McVay, Douglas. *The Musical Film.* New York: Barnes, 1967.

Michael, Paul. *The American Movies Reference Book: The Sound Era.* New Jersey: Prentice-Hall, 1969.

Parish, James Robert. *Actors' Television Credits, 1950–1976.* New Jersey: Scarecrow, 1973 & 1978.

Parish, James Robert. *The Paramount Pretties.* New York: Arlington, 1972.

Pitts, Michael, and Louis H Harrison. *Hollywood on Record.* New Jersey: Scarecrow, 1978.

Rigdon, Walter. *The Biographical Encyclopaedia & Who's Who of the American Theatre.* New York, 1966.

Rust, Brian. *The American Dance Band Discography, 1917–1942.* New York: Arlington, 1975.

Rust, Brian. *The Complete Entertainment Discography.* New York: Arlington, 1973.

Rust, Brian. *Jazz Records, 1897–1942.* New York: Arlington, 1978.

Rust, Brian. *London Musical Shows on Record, 1897–1976.* Middlesex, 1977.

Rust, Brian. *The Victor Master Book, Volume 2 (1925–1936).* Middlesex, 1969.

Scheuer, Steven H. *Movies on TV.* New York: Bantam, 1974.

Shapiro, Nat. *Popular Music, 1920–1969.* New York: Adrian, 1964–1973.

Smolian, Steven. *A Handbook of Film, Theater, and Television Music on Record, 1948–1969.* New York, 1970.

Taylor, John Russell, and Arthur Jackson. *The Hollywood Musical.* New York: McGraw-Hill, 1971.

Thomas, Lawrence B. *The MGM Years.* New York: Columbia, 1971.

Toll, Robert C. *On with the Show.* New York: Oxford, 1976.

Vallance, Tom. *The American Musical.* New York: Barnes, 1970.

Weaver, John T. *Forty Years of Screen Credits, 1929–1969.* New Jersey: Scarecrow, 1970.

The American Film Institute Catalog of Motion Pictures: Feature Films 1921–1970. New York: Bowker, 1971 & 1976.

The ASCAP Biographical Dictionary. New York: Crowell, 1952 & Schirmer, 1966.

ASCAP: 40 Years of Show Tunes, 1917–1957. New York, 1959.

INTRODUCTION

The Best Plays of 1894–1979. New York: Dodd Mead.

Enciclopedia dello Spettacolo. Rome, 1954–1968.

Die Musik in Geschichte und Gegenwart. Basel, 1949–1979.

New York Theatre Critics' Reviews, 1940–1980. New York.

New York Times Film Reviews, 1913–1976. New York: Arno, 1970–1977.

New York Times Theatre Reviews, 1920–1978. New York: Arno, 1971–1979.

Notable Names in the American Theatre. New Jersey: James T White, 1976.

Screen World, 1949–1980. New York: Crown.

Theatre World, 1944–1979. New York: Crown.

Theatre World Annual, 1949–1966. London.

U S Copyright Office: Motion Pictures, 1912–1969. Washington: Library of Congress, 1951–1971.

Who Was Who in the Theatre, 1912–1976. Detroit, 1978.

Shows and Their Key Numbers

A 5-6-7-8 760709
A TO Z 211011
AARON SLICK FROM PUNKIN CREEK
 520005
ABOUT FACE 520023
ABOUT MRS. LESLIE 540025
ABOVE SUSPICION 430018
ABSENT MINDED PROFESSOR, THE
 610011
ABYSSINIA 060220
ACE OF CLUBS 500707
ACROSS AMERICA 760324
ACT, THE 771029
ADAM'S RIB 490025
ADELE 130828
ADVENTURES OF BULLWHIP GRIFFIN,
 THE 670005
ADVENTURES OF MARCO POLO, THE
 560414
AFFAIR IN TRINIDAD 520020
AFFAIR TO REMEMBER, AN 570012
AFFAIRS OF DOBIE GILLIS, THE 530030
AFGAR 190917
AFRICANA 270711
AFTER THE BALL 540610
AIN'T MISBEHAVIN' 780509
AIN'T SUPPOSED TO DIE A NATURAL
 DEATH 711020
ALADD 760215
ALADDIN 580221
ALADDIN 791221
ALAKAZAM THE GREAT! 610007
ALAMO, THE 600012
ALEXANDER'S RAGTIME BAND 380009
ALGERIA 080831
ALI BABA AND THE 40 THIEVES 40 570003
ALI BABA GOES TO TOWN 370042
ALIAS JESSE JAMES 590008
ALICE IN WONDERLAND See 410031
 "Scenes from 'Alice in Wonderland' and
 'Through the Looking Glass' "
ALICE IN WONDERLAND 321212
ALICE IN WONDERLAND 510013
ALICE IN WONDERLAND 660330
ALICE THROUGH THE LOOKING GLASS
 661106*
ALICE'S ADVENTURES IN WONDERLAND
 720002
ALIVE AND KICKING 500117
ALL ABOUT LIFE 630011
ALL AMERICAN 620319
ALL HANDS ON DECK 610003
ALL IN LOVE 611110
ALL NIGHT STRUT!, THE 791004
ALL THAT JAZZ 790004
ALL THE KING'S HORSES 350023
ALLEGRO 471010
ALMA, WHERE DO YOU LIVE? 100926
ALONE AT LAST 140130
ALONG FIFTH AVENUE 490113
ALONG THE NAVAJO TRAIL 450013

ALWAYS LEAVE THEM LAUGHING 490021
AMAZING ADELE, THE 551226
AMAZING MRS. HOLLIDAY, THE 430010
AMBASSADOR 711019
AMERICAN BEAUTY, AN 961228
AMERICAN IN PARIS, AN 500001
ANCHORS AWEIGH 440012
AND THE ANGELS SING 440021
ANDROCLES AND THE LION 671115
ANDY HARDY MEETS A DEBUTANTE
 400002
ANGEL 780510
ANGEL IN THE WINGS 471211
ANIMAL CRACKERS 281023
ANKLES AWEIGH 550418
ANNA 510014
ANNA LUCASTA 580018
ANNE 560304
ANNE OF GREEN GABLES See 560304
 "Anne"
ANNIE 770421
ANNIE GET YOUR GUN 460516
ANOTHER EVENING WITH FRED ASTAIRE
 591104
ANYA 651129
ANYONE CAN WHISTLE 640404
ANYTHING GOES 341121
APPLAUSE 290009
APPLAUSE 700330
APPLE BLOSSOMS 191007
APPLE SAUCE 400827
APPLE TREE, THE 661018
APRIL IN PARIS 520021
APRIL LOVE 570007
ARABIAN NIGHTS 540624
ARC DE TRIOMPHE 431109
ARCADIANS, THE 090428
ARCHY AND MEHITABEL See 570413
 "Shinbone Alley"
ARE YOU WITH IT? 451110
AREN'T WE ALL? 320007
ARGENTINE NIGHTS 400017
ARISTOCATS, THE 690007
ARMS AND THE GIRL 500202
AROUND THE WORLD IN EIGHTY DAYS
 460531
AROUND THE WORLD IN EIGHTY DAYS
 570019
ART OF LOVE, THE 650011
ARTHUR GODFREY'S TV CALENDAR
 SHOW 530023
ARTISTS AND MODELS 370029
ARTISTS AND MODELS 550017
ARTISTS AND MODELS OF 1924 241015
ARTISTS AND MODELS OF 1925 250624
ARTISTS AND MODELS OF 1927 271115
ARTIST'S MODEL, AN 950202
AS LONG AS THEY'RE HAPPY 540021
AS THE GIRLS GO 481113
AS THOUSANDS CHEER 330930
AS YOU WERE 180803

ASTAIRE TIME 600928*
AT HOME ABROAD 350919
AT LONG LAST LOVE 750002
AT THE CIRCUS 390013
AT THE DROP OF A HAT 570124
AT THE DROP OF ANOTHER HAT 631002
AT WAR WITH THE ARMY 500016
ATHENA 540011
ATHENIAN TOUCH, THE 640114
AUNT SALLY 330016
AVEC LE SOURIRE 360048

BABES IN ARMS 370414
BABES IN TOYLAND 031013
BABES ON BROADWAY 410004
BABETTE 031116
BABY, TAKE A BOW 340019
BACK AGAIN 190902
BAJOUR 641123
BAKER STREET 650216
BAKER'S WIFE, THE 760511
BALALAIKA 361222
BALALAIKA 390017
BALKAN PRINCESS, THE 100219
BALLAD FOR AMERICANS See 390424
 "Sing For Your Supper"
BALLAD FOR BIMSHIRE 631015
BALLROOM 781214
BALLYHOO 321222
BAMBI 420009
BAND CONCERT, THE 350057
BAND WAGON, THE 310603
BAND WAGON, THE 530001
BANJO EYES 411225
BANJO ON MY KNEE 360031
BAR MITZVAH BOY 781031
BARBARIAN, THE 330020
BARKLEYS OF BROADWAY, THE 490002
BARNEY 'N ME 560400
BARNUM 800430
BARRICADE 380030
BARRY OF BALLYMORE 110130
BAT, THE See 740405 "Die Fledermaus"
BATHING BEAUTY 440031
BATTLE OF PARIS, THE 290040
BE KIND TO PEOPLE WEEK 750323
BE MY GUEST 590121
BE YOURSELF 300003
BEATLEMANIA 770531
BEAU HUNKS 310018
BEAU JAMES 570009
BEAUTY AND THE BEAST 720612
BEAUTY SHOP, THE 140413
BEAUTY SPOT, THE 090410
BECAUSE OF HIM 450010
BECAUSE THEY'RE YOUNG 600015
BECAUSE YOU 'RE MINE 520006
BEDKNOBS AND BROOMSTICKS 710001
BEDTIME STORY, A 330046

BEG, BORROW OR STEAL 600210
BEHIND THE FRIDGE 721121
BEI MIR BISTU SCHOEN 611021
BELIEVERS, THE 680509
BELLE OF BRITTANY, THE 081024
BELLE OF NEW YORK, THE 970928
BELLE OF NEW YORK, THE 510002
BELLE OF THE NINETIES, THE 340042
BELLE OF THE YUKON, THE 440024
BELLE PAREE, LA 110320
BELLS ARE RINGING 561129
BELLS OF ST. MARY'S, THE 450007
BELOVED VAGABOND, THE 360026
BELOW THE BELT 660623
BEN FRANKLIN IN PARIS 641027
BENNY GOODMAN STORY, THE 550011
BEOWULF 771201
BERLIN TO BROADWAY WITH KURT
   WEILL 721001
BERNARDINE 570016
BEST FOOT FORWARD 411001
BEST LITTLE WHOREHOUSE IN TEXAS,
   THE 780417
BEST THINGS IN LIFE ARE FREE, THE
   560004
BETJEMANIA 761206
BETSY 261228
BETTY 150424
BETWEEN THE DEVIL 371222
BEYOND THE FRINGE 610510
BEYOND THE FRINGE '64 640108
BEYOND THE RAINBOW 781109
BIFF, BING, BANG 191001
BIG BEAT, THE 580024
BIG BOY 250107
BIG BROADCAST, THE 320010
BIG BROADCAST OF 1936, THE 350010
BIG BROADCAST OF 1937, THE 360047
BIG BROADCAST OF 1938, THE 380013
BIG BUSINESS 340043
BIG CIRCUS, THE 590020
BIG CITY 480008
BIG FELLA 370035
BIG MAN 750006
BIG POND, THE 300008
BIG STORE, THE 410008
BILLBOARD GIRL 320015
BILLIE 281001
BILLIE 650014
BILLION DOLLAR BABY 451221
BILLY 740501
BILLY BARNES' L.A. 621010
BILLY BARNES REVUE 590609
BILLY BISHOP GOES TO WAR 800529
BILLY NONAME 700302
BILLY ROSE'S DIAMOND HORSESHOE
   450016
BILLY ROSE'S JUMBO See 351116 "Jumbo"
BING BOYS ARE HERE, THE 160419
BIRD OF PARADISE, THE 120108
BIRDS AND THE BEES, THE 560022
BIRTH OF THE BLUES, THE 410016
BIRTHDAY GARLAND FOR MR. JAMES
   CASH PENNEY, A 600900
BISTRO CAR ON THE C N R, A 780323
BITTER SWEET 290718
BLACK AND TAN 290039
BLACK EAGLE, THE 780001

BLACK MIKADO, THE See 850314 "The
   Mikado"
BLACK NATIVITY 611211
BLACK VANITIES 410424
BLACK VELVET 391114
BLACKBIRDS 260911
BLACKBIRDS OF 1928 280509
BLACKBIRDS OF 1930 301022
BLACKBIRDS OF 1936 360709
BLESS THE BRIDE 470426
BLESS YOU ALL 501214
BLONDE VENUS 320018
BLOOD AND SAND 410009
BLOOD RED ROSES 700322
BLOOMER GIRL 441005
BLOSSOM TIME 160115
BLUE ANGEL, THE 300001
BLUE BIRD, THE 760005
BLUE EYES 280427
BLUE GARDENIA, THE 530028
BLUE HAWAII 620009
BLUE KITTEN, THE 220113
BLUE MAZURKA, THE 200528
BLUE MONDAY See 220828 "George
   White's Scandals of 1922"
BLUE OF THE NIGHT 330038
BLUE RHYTHM 310016
BLUE SKIES 270624
BLUE SKIES 460004
BLUEBIRD, THE 400011
BLUES, BALLADS AND SIN-SONGS See
   541004 "Libby Holman's 'Blues, Ballads
   and Sin-Songs'"
BLUES IN THE NIGHT 410005
BLUES OPERA See 460330 "St. Louis
   Woman"
BOBBY, GET YOUR GUN 381007
BODY BEAUTIFUL, THE 580123
BODY IN THE SEINE, THE 550025
BOHEMIAN GIRL, THE 431127
BOLERO 340036
BOMBO 211006
BONANZA BOUND 471226
BONGO See 470016 "Fun and Fancy Free"
BOODLE 250310
BORN TO DANCE 360018
BOTTOMLAND 270627
BOTTOMS UP 340055
BOW BELLS 320104
BOY, THE 170914
BOY FRIEND, THE 540114
BOY MEETS BOY 750917
BOY NAMED CHARLIE BROWN, A 690006
BOY ON A DOLPHIN 570037
BOYS FROM SYRACUSE, THE 381123
BOY'S OWN McBETH 810411
BRAIN CHILD 740325
BRAN PIE 190828
BRAVO GIOVANNI 620519
BREAKFAST AT TIFFANY'S 610006
BREAKFAST AT TIFFANY'S 661214
BREAKFAST IN HOLLYWOOD 460022
BREAKING THE ICE 380020
BREWSTER'S MILLIONS 350016
BRIC-A-BRAC 150918
BRIDE WORE RED, THE 370039
BRIGADOON 470313
BRIGHAM! 760414

BRIGHT EYES 340013
BRING ON THE GIRLS 450023
BRING YOUR SMILE ALONG 550030
BRITANNIA OF BILLINGSGATE 330019
BROADWAY BREVITIES OF 1920 200929
BROADWAY GONDOLIER 350002
BROADWAY HOSTESS 350039
BROADWAY MELODY 290005
BROADWAY MELODY OF 1936 350027
BROADWAY MELODY OF 1938 370007
BROADWAY MELODY OF 1940 400012
BROADWAY RHYTHM 440025
BROADWAY THRU A KEYHOLE 330040
BROKEN IDOL, A 090816
BUBBLING BROWN SUGAR 760302
BUCCANEER, THE 530908
BUCK BENNY RIDES AGAIN 400023
BUCK PRIVATES 410013
BUDDIES 191027
BUGSY MALONE 760004
BULLWHIP GRIFFIN See 670011 "The
   Adventures of Bullwhip Griffin"
BUNDLE OF BLUES, A 330044
BUNDLE OF JOY 560010
BUS STOP 560018
BUSINESS AS USUAL 141116
BUTTERFLIES ARE FREE 691021
BUZZ-BUZZ 181220
BY JUPITER 420602
BY THE BEAUTIFUL SEA 540408
BY THE LIGHT OF THE SILVERY MOON
   530003
BY THE WAY 250122
BYE BYE BIRDIE 600414

CAB CALLOWAY'S HI-DE-HO 330043
CABARET 661120
CABARET GIRL, THE 220919
CABARET TAC 380043
CABIN IN THE SKY 401025
CADDY, THE 530018
CAIN AND MABEL 360054
CAIRO 420025
CALAMITY JANE 530004
CALIFORNIA 490010
CALL IT LOVE 600622
CALL ME MADAM 501012
CALL ME MISTER 460418
CALL OF THE FLESH 300015
CALYPSO HEAT WAVE 570034
CAMELOT 601203
CAMELS ARE COMING, THE 340020
CAN HEIRONYMUS MERKIN EVER
   FORGET? 690001
CANADA 770708
CAN-CAN 530507
CANDIDE 561201
CAN'T HELP SINGING 440002
CANTERBURY PILGRIMS, THE See 680320
   "Canterbury Tales"
CANTERBURY TALES 680320
CANYON PASSAGE 460007
CAPTAIN CRASH VERSUS THE ZZORG
   WOMEN 810001
CAPTAIN JANUARY 360009
CAPTAIN OF THE GUARD 300018
CAPTAIN'S KID, THE 360049
CAR OF DREAMS 350047

CAREER 590019
CAREFREE 380003
CARELESS RAPTURE /360911
CARIB SONG 450927
CARMELINA 790408
CARMEN JONES 431202
CARMINETTA 170822
CARNEGIE HALL 470028
CARNIVAL See 200405 "Ed Wynn Carnival"
CARNIVAL! 610413
CARNIVAL IN COSTA RICA 470013
CAROLINA BLUES 440029
CAROLINE 230131
CAROUSEL 450419
CASABLANCA 430006
CASBAH 480004
CASINO DE PARIS See 350011 "Go into Your Dance"
CASINO GIRL, THE 000319
CASTLES IN THE AIR 260906
CAT AND THE FIDDLE, THE 311015
CAT BALLOU 650008
CATCH MY SOUL 680305
CATS 810511
CAUGHT IN THE ACT See 531002 "Comedy in Music"
CAVALCADE 311013
CAVIAR 340607
CELEBRATION 690122
CELEBRATION OF RICHARD RODGERS, A 720326
CENTENNIAL SUMMER 460014
CERTAIN SMILE, A 580021
CHAMPAGNE CHARLIE 440032
CHAMPAGNE WALTZ 370033
CHANGE OF HABIT 700005
CHANGING OF THE GUARD 360059
CHAPERONS, THE 020605
CHARLOT SHOW OF 1926, THE 261005
CHARLOT'S MASQUERADE 300904
CHARLOT'S REVUE OF 1924 240109
CHARLOT'S REVUE OF 1925 250330
CHARLOT'S REVUE OF 1926 251110
CHARRO! 690009
CHASING RAINBOWS 300022
CHECK AND DOUBLE CHECK 300023
CHEE-CHEE 280925
CHEEP 170426
CHEER UP AND SMILE 300029
CHEYENNE SOCIAL CLUB, THE 690010
CHICAGO 750603
CHILD IS BORN, A 551225
CHILDREN OF PLEASURE 300038
CHIMES OF NORMANDY, THE 770419
CHINA GATE 570029
CHIN-CHIN 141020
CHINESE HONEYMOON, A 011005
CHITTY CHITTY BANG BANG 680005
CHOCALONIA 810201
CHOCOLATE DANDIES, THE 240901
CHOCOLATE SOLDIER, THE 081114
CHORUS LINE, A 750521
CHRISTINE 600428
CHRISTMAS CAROL, A 541224
CHRISTMAS HOLIDAY 440017
CHRISTMAS RAPPINGS 691214
CHRISTY 751014
CHU-CHIN-CHOW 160831

CIAO, RUDY 660107
CINDERELLA 470027
CINDERELLA 490011
CINDERELLA 570331
CINDERELLA 660010
CINDERFELLA 600003
CINDY 640319
CINGALEE, THE 040305
CIRCUS GIRL, THE 961205
CITY CHAP, THE 251026
CLAMBAKE 670010
CLARA See 600210 "Beg, Borrow or Steal"
CLOCHES DE CORNEVILLE, LES See 770419 "The Chimes of Normandy"
CLOSE HARMONY 290043
CLOWNAROUND 720427
CLOWNS IN CLOVER 271201
COCA-COLA GRANDE, EL 730213
COCHRAN'S 1930 REVUE 300327
COCHRAN'S 1931 REVUE 310319
COCKEYED TIGER, THE 770113
COCO 691218
COCOANUT GROVE, THE 380038
COCOANUTS, THE 251208
COHAN REVUE OF 1918 171231
COLE 740702
COLE PORTER: A REMEMBRANCE 651007
COLE PORTER IN PARIS 730117
COLETTE 700506
COLLEEN 360063
COLLEGE COACH 330004
COLLEGE HOLIDAY 360056
COLLEGE HUMOR 330023
COLLEGE RHYTHM 340011
COLLEGE SWING 380041
COLLEGIATE 360029
COME BLOW YOUR HORN 630016
COME FLY WITH ME 630018
COME OF AGE 340112
COME OUT OF THE PANTRY 350007
COME SEVEN 200719
COME TO ME 571204
COMEDY IN MUSIC 531002
COMIN' ROUND THE MOUNTAIN 510031
COMPANY 700426
CONEY ISLAND 430013
CONGRESS DANCES, THE 310007
CONNECTICUT YANKEE, A 271103
CONNECTICUT YANKEE IN KING ARTHUR'S COURT, A 490009
CONTINENTAL VARIETIES 341003
CONTINENTAL VARIETIES OF 1936 351226
CONVERSATION PIECE 340216
COOL MIKADO, THE See 850314 "The Mikado"
CO-OPTIMISTS, THE 210627
CO-OPTIMISTS, THE See 280130 "The Optimists"
COPACABANA 470029
COPPER AND BRASS 571017
CORONADO 350050
COTTON CLUB REVUE 1958 580004
COUNT OF LUXEMBOURG, THE 091112
COUNTESS MARITZA 260326
COUNTRY GIRL, A 940101
COUNTRY GIRL, THE 540002
COURT JESTER, THE 560008
COVER GIRL 440028

COWARDY CUSTARD 720710
COWBOY FROM BROOKLYN 380005
CRADLE WILL ROCK, THE 380103
CRANKS 560301
CREST OF THE WAVE 370901
CRICKET ON THE HEARTH 671218
CROSSROADS 420024
CROWNING EXPERIENCE, THE 580616
CRY FOR US ALL 700408
CRYSTAL HEART, THE 570219
CUBAN LOVE SONG 310002
CUBAN PETE 460024
CUCKOOS, THE 300035
CUE MAGAZINE'S SALUTE TO ASCAP 660501
CURLEY McDIMPLE 671122
CURLY TOP 350014
CYRANO 580513
CYRANO 730319*

DADDY GOODNESS 790913
DADDY LONG LEGS 550005
DAMES 340021
DAMES AT SEA 681220
DAMN YANKEES 550505
DAMSEL IN DISTRESS, A 370005
DANCE AND GROW THIN 170119
DANCE GIRL DANCE 400032
DANCE OF LIFE, THE 290044
DANCING AROUND 141010
DANCING CO-ED 390030
DANCING LADY 330027
DANCING ON A DIME 410032
DANCING YEARS, THE 390323
DANDELION WINE 720310
DANGEROUS CHRISTMAS OF RED RIDING HOOD, THE 651128
DANGEROUS NAN McGREW 300027
DANNY AT THE PALACE See 530118 "Danny Kaye's International Show"
DANNY KAYE'S INTERNATIONAL SHOW 530118
DARLING LILI 690003
DARLING OF THE DAY 680127
DATE WITH JUDY, A 480013
DAVY CROCKETT 541215
DAWN, THE 641225
DAY IN HOLLYWOOD/A NIGHT IN THE UKRAINE, A 790328
DAY OF THE LOCUST, THE 740007
DAYS OF WINE AND ROSES 620012
DEAR WORLD 690206
DEAREST ENEMY 250918
DECLINE AND FALL OF THE ENTIRE WORLD, THE 650330
DEEP IN MY HEART 540010
DELICATE DELINQUENT, THE 570043
DELICIOUS 310014
DELIGHTFULLY DANGEROUS 450015
DELIVERY BOY 310015
DEMI-DOZEN 581011*
DESERT SONG, THE 261130
DESIGNING WOMAN 570025
DESIRE 360055
DESTRY RIDES AGAIN 390004
DESTRY RIDES AGAIN 590423
DEVIL MAY CARE 290042
DEVIL'S HAIRPIN, THE 570038

DIAMOND HEAD 620011
DIAMOND HORSESHOE See 450016 "Billy
  Rose's Diamond Horseshoe"
DIAMOND LIL 280409
DIAMOND STUDS! 750114
DICK TRACY IN B-FLAT 450215
DIME A DOZEN 621018
DIMPLES 360011
DINO 570035
DISC JOCKEY 510028
DISTRICT LEADER, THE 060430
DIVORCE ME DARLING! 650202
DIXIANA 300006
DIXIE 430017
DO I HEAR A WALTZ? 650318
DO NOT DISTURB 650002
DO RE MI 601226
DO WHAT YOU WILL! 690724
DO YOU LOVE ME? 460013
DOCTOR DOLITTLE 670006
DOCTOR RHYTHM 380019
DOCTOR SELAVY'S MAGIC THEATRE
  721123
DOLL FACE 450019
DOLL GIRL, THE 130825
DOLLAR PRINCESS, THE 090906
DOLLY SISTERS, THE 450003
DONNYBROOK! 610518
DON'T BOTHER ME, I CAN'T COPE 720419
DON'T FENCE ME IN 450014
DON'T GET PERSONAL 360052
DON'T GO NEAR THE WATER 570039
DON'T PLAY US CHEAP 720516
DOROTHY 860925
DOUBLE DYNAMITE 510015
DOUBLE OR NOTHING 370022
DOUBLE TROUBLE 670007
DOWN ARGENTINE WAY 400009
DOWN IN THE VALLEY 480715
DOWN TO EARTH 470017
DOWNRIVER 751219
DR. JAZZ 750319
DREAM HOUSE 320011
DREAMBOAT 620006
DREAMING OUT LOUD 400027
DRESSED TO THE NINES 600929
DUBARRY, THE 310814
DUBARRY WAS A LADY 391206
DUCHESS OF DANTZIC, THE 031017
DUCHESS OF IDAHO, THE 500015
DUDE 721009
DUEL See 770322 "Pageant in Exile"
DUFFY'S TAVERN 450018
DUMBO 410024

EADIE WAS A LADY 450022
EARL AND THE GIRL, THE 031210
EARL CARROLL'S SKETCH BOOK 290701
EARL CARROLL'S VANITIES (INTER-
  NATIONAL EDITION) 270101
EARL CARROLL'S VANITIES OF 1926
  260824
EARL CARROLL'S VANITIES OF 1928
  280806
EARL CARROLL'S VANITIES OF 1932
  320927
EARL OF RUSTON 700004
EARLY TO BED 430617

EARTHQUAKE 731217
EAST SIDE OF HEAVEN, THE 390009
EASTER PARADE 480002
EASY COME, EASY GO 670008
EASY MONEY 470032
EASY TO LOVE 530025
ECLIPSE, THE 191112
ECSTASY OF RITA JOE, THE 671100
ED WYNN CARNIVAL 200405
EDDIE CANTOR STORY, THE 540007
EDDIE FISHER AT THE WINTER GARDEN
  621002
EDDIE DUCHIN STORY, THE 560007
EILEEN 170319
ELEPHANT CALF, THE 630122
ELVIS 681203
EMPEROR WALTZ, THE 480007
EMPEROR'S NIGHTINGALE, THE 650222
ENCORE BREL 800507
ERMINIE 851109
ERNEST IN LOVE 600504
ESCAPE FROM FORT BRAVO 530033
EUBIE! 780920
EUROPEAN HOLIDAY 560027
EVENING WITH BEATRICE LILLIE, AN
  521002
EVENING WITH FRED ASTAIRE, AN
  581017
EVENING WITH MICHAEL BROWN AND
  HIS FRIENDS, AN 660207
EVENING WITH W. S. GILBERT, AN
  800228
EVER GREEN 301203
EVERY NIGHT AT EIGHT 350004
EVERY SUNDAY 360060
EVERYBODY, EVERYBODY 760229
EVERYBODY SING 380023
EVERYBODY'S DOING IT 120214
EVERYBODY'S WELCOME 311013*
EVERYTHING I HAVE IS YOURS 520007
EVERYTHING IS RHYTHM 360046
EVITA 780621
EXCHANGE 700208

F. P. I. 330033
FABULOUS DORSEYS, THE 470014
FACE IN THE CROWD, A 570015
FACE THE MUSIC 320217
FADE OUT, FADE IN 640526
FALLING FOR YOU 330013
FAMILY AFFAIR, A 620127
FANCY PANTS 500013
FANNY 541104
FANTASTICKS, THE 600503
FARMER TAKES A WIFE, THE 520003
FARMER'S DAUGHTER, THE 400035
FASHIONS OF 1934 340040
FATHER GOOSE 640004
FEATHERTOP 611019
FESTIVAL 790517
FEUDIN' RHYTHM 490026
FIDDLER ON THE ROOF 640922
FIFTH OF JULY, THE 801105
FIFTY MILES FROM BOSTON 080203
FIG LEAVES ARE FALLING, THE 690102
FINGS AIN'T WOT THEY USED T'BE
  600211

FINIAN'S RAINBOW 470110
FIORELLO! 591123
FIREBRAND OF FLORENCE, THE 450322
FIREFLY, THE 121202
FIREMAN'S FLAME, THE 371009
FIRST A GIRL 350009
FIRST IMPRESSIONS 590319
FIRST LOVE 390002
FIRST NUDIE MUSICAL, THE 760003
FISHERMAN'S WHARF 390014
FIVE AFTER EIGHT 791127
FIVE CARD STUD 680014
FIVE PENNIES, THE 590003
5-6-7-8, A See 760709 "A 5-6-7-8"
FLAHOOLEY 510514
FLAME AND THE FLESH, THE 540014
FLAME OF NEW ORLEANS, THE 410037
FLAME OF THE ISLANDS 550015
FLAMING STAR 600007
FLAMINGO ROAD 490017
FLEDERMAUS, DIE 740405
FLEET'S IN, THE 420017
FLEET'S LIT UP, THE 380817
FLIGHT AT MIDNIGHT 390024
FLIGHT TO HONG KONG 570032
FLIRTATION WALK 340004
FLOODLIGHT 370623
FLORA BELLA 160911
FLORA, THE RED MENACE 650511
FLORODORA 991111
FLOWER DRUM SONG 581201
FLOWERS FOR ALGERNON 790614
FLUSH LEFT, STAGGER RIGHT 660325
FLY BLACKBIRD 620205
FLY WITH ME 200324
FLYING COLORS 320915
FLYING DOWN TO RIO 330005
FLYING HIGH 300303
FOLIES BERGERE 350021
FOLIES BERGERE 640602
FOLLIES 710404
FOLLOW A STAR 300917
FOLLOW ME 161129
FOLLOW THAT DREAM 620008
FOLLOW THE BOYS 440010
FOLLOW THE BOYS 630006
FOLLOW THE CROWD See 151225 "Stop!
  Look! Listen!"
FOLLOW THE FLEET 360012
FOLLOW THE GIRLS 440408
FOLLOW THE LEADER 300032
FOLLOW THE SUN 360204
FOLLOW THRU 290109
FOOLS RUSH IN 341225
FOOTLIGHT PARADE 330002
FOOTLIGHT SERENADE 420016
FOOTSTEPS IN THE DARK 410028
FOR GOODNESS' SAKE 220220
FOR ME AND MY GAL 420002
FOR THE FIRST TIME 590004
FOR THE LOVE OF MARY 480015
FOR THE LOVE OF MIKE 311008
FORBIDDEN MELODY 361102
FORD 50TH ANNIVERSARY TELEVISION
  SHOW 530615
FOREIGN AFFAIR, A 480006
FOREVER, DARLING 560024
FORTUNE TELLER, THE 980926

FORTY LITTLE MOTHERS 400006
42ND STREET 330021
42ND STREET 800825
FORWARD MARCH 300039
FOUR BELOW STRIKES BACKS 600103
FOUR JILLS IN A JEEP 440022
1492 930515
FOX MOVIETONE FOLLIES OF 1929 290035
FOXFIRE 550024
FOXY 640216
FRANKIE AND JOHNNY 340009
FRANKIE AND JOHNNY 570005
FRANKIE AND JOHNNY 660008
FREDERICA 281004
FREE AND EASY See 460330 "St. Louis Woman"
FREE FOR ALL 310908
FREE TO BE . . . YOU AND ME 720004
FREEDOMLAND U.S.A. 600619
FRENCH LINE, THE 540012
FRESH FROM PARIS 550028
FRIENDLY PERSUASION 560009
FRITZ IN TAMMANY HALL 051016
FRONT STREET GAIETIES 801111
FULL OF LIFE 570033
FUN AND FANCY FREE 470016
FUN IN ACAPULCO 630012
FUN OF THE FAYRE, THE 211017
FUNNY FACE 271122
FUNNY FACE 570001
FUNNY GIRL 640326
FUNNY LADY 750001
FUNNY THING HAPPENED ON THE WAY TO THE FORUM, A 620508

G. I. BLUES 600008
GALA TRIBUTE TO JOSHUA LOGAN, A 750502
GANG'S ALL HERE, THE 430004
GANGWAY 370006
GARDEN OF THE MOON 380016
GARRICK GAIETIES (THIRD EDITION), THE 300604
GAY DECEIVERS 350523
GAY DESPERADO, THE 360044
GAY DIVORCE 321129
GAY LIFE, THE 611118
GAY PURR-EE 620001
GAY ROSALINDA See 740405 "Die Fledermaus"
GAY SENORITA 450021
GAY'S THE WORD 510215
GEISHA, THE 960425
GENE AUSTIN STORY, THE 570421
GENE KRUPA STORY, THE 600004
GENERAL ELECTRIC PRESENTS SAMMY 731116
GENERAL MOTORS 50TH ANNIVERSARY TELEVISION SHOW 571117
GENTLEMEN MARRY BRUNETTES 550002
GENTLEMEN PREFER BLONDES 481208
GEORGE M! 680410
GEORGE WASHINGTON, JR. 060212
GEORGE WHITE'S MUSIC HALL VARIETIES 321122
GEORGE WHITE'S SCANDALS 340005
GEORGE WHITE'S SCANDALS OF 1920 200607
GEORGE WHITE'S SCANDALS OF 1921 210711
GEORGE WHITE'S SCANDALS OF 1922 220828
GEORGE WHITE'S SCANDALS OF 1923 230618
GEORGE WHITE'S SCANDALS OF 1924 240630
GEORGE WHITE'S SCANDALS OF 1926 260614
GEORGE WHITE'S SCANDALS OF 1928 280702
GEORGE WHITE'S SCANDALS OF 1929 290923
GEORGE WHITE'S SCANDALS OF 1931 310914
GEORGE WHITE'S SCANDALS OF 1935 350003
GEORGE WHITE'S SCANDALS OF 1936 351225
GEORGE WHITE'S SCANDALS OF 1939 390828
GERTRUDE STEIN'S FIRST READER 691215
GIDGET 590018
GIDGET GOES HAWAIIAN 610009
GIFT OF GAB, THE 340025
GIFT OF LOVE, THE 580029
GIFT OF THE MAGI, THE 581209
GIGI 580001
GILDA 460018
GIRL BEHIND THE COUNTER, THE 060421
GIRL CRAZY 301014
GIRL FRIEND, THE 260317
GIRL FROM KAY'S, THE 021115
GIRL FROM UTAH, THE 140824
GIRL HAPPY 650005
GIRL IN PINK TIGHTS, THE 540305
GIRL IN THE TAXI, THE 101024
GIRL IN THE TRAIN, THE 081223
GIRL MOST LIKELY, THE 570006
GIRL OF THE GOLDEN WEST, THE 380001
GIRL ON THE FILM, THE 130405
GIRL RUSH, THE 550009
GIRL WHO CAME TO SUPPER, THE 631208
GIRLS, LES 570002
GIRLS AGAINST THE BOYS, THE 591102
GIRLS! GIRLS! GIRLS! 620010
GIROFLE-GIROFLA 741111
GIVE A GIRL A BREAK 530021
GIVE ME A SAILOR 380042
GIVE MY REGARDS TO BROADWAY 480024
GIVE OUT SISTERS 420007
GLAMOROUS NIGHT 350505
GLAMOUR GIRL 480026
GLASS BOTTOM BOAT, THE 660005
GLENN MILLER STORY, THE 540008
GLOBE REVUE 520710
GLORIFYING THE AMERICAN GIRL 290010
GO FLY A KITE 660920
GO INTO YOUR DANCE 350011
GODSPELL 710517
GOIN' TO TOWN 350018
GOING GREEK 370916
GOING HOLLYWOOD 330022

GOING MY WAY 440006
GOING PLACES 380015
GOING UP 171225
GOLD DIGGERS IN PARIS 380039
GOLD DIGGERS OF BROADWAY 290019
GOLD DIGGERS OF 1933 330001
GOLD DIGGERS OF 1935 350001
GOLD DIGGERS OF 1937 360006
GOLDEN APPLE, THE 540311
GOLDEN BOY 641020
GOLDEN CIRCLE, THE 591125
GOLDEN DAWN, THE 271130
GOLDEN GIRL, THE 090200
GOLDEN GIRL 510018
GOLDEN KNIGHT, THE 621004
GOLDEN RAINBOW 680204
GOLDEN SCREW, THE 670130
GOLDILOCKS 581011
GOLDILOCKS 700303
GOLDWYN FOLLIES 380014
GONE WITH THE WIND 700103
GOOD BOY 280905
GOOD COMPANIONS, THE 310514
GOOD COMPANIONS, THE 330012
GOOD COMPANIONS, THE 570011
GOOD COMPANIONS, THE 740711
GOOD EVENING See 721121 "Behind The Fridge"
GOOD MORNING, BOYS 370016
GOOD MORNING, JUDGE See 170914 "The Boy"
GOOD NEWS 270906
GOOD NEWS ABOUT OLDS 580002
GOOD OLD BAD OLD DAYS, THE 721220
GOODBYE, MR. CHIPS 690004
GOODNIGHT VIENNA 320008
GOODTIME CHARLEY 750303
GRACIE ALLEN MURDER CASE, THE 390026
GRAND STREET FOLLIES OF 1928 280528
GRAND TOUR 590430
GRAND TOUR, THE 790111
GRANDE DE COCA-COLA, EL See 730213 "El Coca-Cola Grande"
GRANDMA MOSES 500025
GRANDPA 770123
GRASS HARP, THE 711102
GRASSHOPPER AND THE ANTS, THE 340038
GREASE 720214
GREAT AMERICAN BACKSTAGE MUSICAL, THE 761202
GREAT AMERICAN BROADCAST, THE 410027
GREAT CARUSO, THE 510007
GREAT LOVER, THE 490012
GREAT MAN, THE 570030
GREAT RUPERT, THE 500014
GREAT VICTOR HERBERT, THE 390018
GREAT WALTZ, THE See 301030 "Waltzes from Vienna"
GREAT WALTZ, THE 380024
GREAT ZIEGFELD, THE 360003
GREATEST SHOW ON EARTH, THE 520024
GREEK SLAVE, A 980608
GREEN GROW THE LILACS 310126
GREENWICH VILLAGE FOLLIES OF 1919 190715

15

GREENWICH VILLAGE FOLLIES OF 1920
   200830
GREENWICH VILLAGE FOLLIES OF 1921
   210831
GREENWICH VILLAGE FOLLIES OF 1922
   220912
GREENWICH VILLAGE FOLLIES OF 1924
   240916
GREENWICH VILLAGE FOLLIES OF 1928
   280409*
GREENWICH VILLAGE, U.S.A. 600928
GREENWILLOW 600308
GROSSE VALISE, LA 651214
GROUNDS FOR MARRIAGE 500018
GUNMAN'S WALK 580014
GUNS OF THE PECOS 370041
GUNS OF THE TIMBERLAND 600014
GUYS AND DOLLS 501124
GYPSY 590521
GYPSY BARON, THE 851024
GYPSY LOVE 100108

HAIR 671029
HALF A SIXPENCE 630321
HALF-PAST WEDNESDAY 620406
HALLELUJAH 290027
HALLELUJAH, BABY! 670426
HALLELUJAH, I'M A BUM 330006
HAM TREE, THE 050828
HAND IS ON THE GATE, A 660921
HANGING TREE, THE 590017
HANS ANDERSEN See 520001 "Hans
   Christian Andersen"
HANS BRINKER OR THE SILVER SKATES
   580209
HANS CHRISTIAN ANDERSEN 520001
HANSEL AND GRETEL 931223
HANSEL AND GRETEL 580427
HAPPIEST GIRL IN THE WORLD, THE
   610403
HAPPIEST MILLIONAIRE, THE 670004
HAPPINESS AHEAD 340003
HAPPY 340049
HAPPY ANNIVERSARY 590011
HAPPY DAY, A 160513
HAPPY DAYS 300037
HAPPY GO LUCKY 430015
HAPPY HUNTING 561206
HAPPY LANDING 380033
HAPPY ROAD, THE 570027
HAPPY TIME, THE 680118
HARD DAY'S NIGHT, A 640017
HARD JOB BEING GOD 720515
HARD TO GET 380037
HARK! 720522
HAROLD ROME'S GALLERY 640006
HAROLD TEEN 340046
HARUM SCARUM 650006
HARVEY GIRLS, THE 460006
HAVANA 080425
HAVE A HEART 170111
HAVE A HOLIDAY 570045
HAVE I GOT ONE FOR YOU! 680107
HAWAII CALLS 380021
HAZEL FLAGG 530211
HEAD OVER HEELS 360005
HEADS UP 300016
HEAR! HEAR! 550727

HEART O' TH' HEATHER, THE 160228
HEART OF NEW YORK See 330006
   "Hallelujah, I'm a Bum"
HEARTS DIVIDED 360007
HEATHEN! 720521
HEIDI 370024
HEIDI 681117*
HELEN 320130
HELEN MORGAN STORY, THE 570004
HELEN MORGAN STORY, THE 570516
HELLO DADDY 281226
HELLO, DOLLY! 640116
HELLO, EVERYBODY 330009
HELLO, 'FRISCO, HELLO 430003
HELLO, GOODBYE See 700002 "Hello-
   Goodbye"
HELLO, SOLLY! 670404
HELLO, YOURSELF! 281030
HELLO-GOODBYE 700002
HELP! 650010
HEN-PECKS, THE 110204
HENRY, SWEET HENRY 671023
HER FAMILY TREE 201227
HER FIRST ROMAN 681020
HER JUNGLE LOVE 380026
HER MAJESTY, LOVE 300014
HER SOLDIER BOY 161206
HERE COME THE WAVES 440004
HERE COMES THE BRIDE 300220
HERE COMES THE GROOM 510011
HERE IS MY HEART 340022
HERE'S HOWE 280501
HERE'S LOVE 631003
HERE'S PAT O'BRIEN 640020
HERE'S TO ROMANCE 350033
HERS TO HOLD 430001
HI DIDDLE DIDDLE 341003*
HIDE AND SEEK 371014
HIDEAWAY GIRL 370046
HIGH BUTTON SHOES 471009
HIGH JINKS 131210
HIGH KICKERS, THE 411031
HIGH NOON 520015
HIGH SOCIETY 560001
HIGH SOCIETY BLUES 300042
HIGH SPIRITS 640407
HIGH TIME 600009
HIGH TOR 560310
HIGH, WIDE AND HANDSOME 370037
HIGHER AND HIGHER 400404
HIGHWAY LIFE, THE See 721009 "Dude"
HIP-HIP-HOORAY 150930
HIPS, HIPS HOORAY 340030
HIS BUTLER'S SISTER 430009
HIS KIND OF WOMAN 510025
HIS MONKEY WIFE 711220
HIT PARADE OF 1937, THE 360028
HIT PARADE OF 1941, THE 400024
HIT THE DECK 270425
HITCHY-KOO 170607
HOEDOWN 500026
HOKEY-POKEY 120208
HOLD EVERYTHING! 281010
HOLD ON TO YOUR HATS 400911
HOLD THAT GHOST 410014
HOLE IN THE HEAD, A 590014
HOLIDAY IN FASHION 590024
HOLIDAY IN HAVANA 490005

HOLIDAY IN MEXICO 460009
HOLIDAY INN 420001
HOLLYWOOD CANTEEN 440015
HOLLYWOOD HOTEL 361218
HOLLYWOOD HOTEL 370023
HOLLYWOOD ON PARADE 310009
HOLLYWOOD OR BUST 560016
HOLLYWOOD PARTY 340044
HOLLYWOOD REVUE 290020
HOME AND BEAUTY 370202
HOMME DU JOUR, L' 360021
HONEY 300012
HONEY GIRL 200503
HONEYMOON EXPRESS 130206
HONEYMOON LANE 260920
HONG KONG AFFAIR 580030
HONKY TONK 290002
HONOLULU 390029
HOORAY FOR WHAT 371201
HOOT MON 270507
HORSE FEATHERS 320013
HOT CHOCOLATES 290629
HOT HEIRESS 310011
HOT MIKADO, THE See 850314 "The
   Mikado"
HOT RHYTHM 300821
HOT-CHA! 320308
HOTEL SAHARA 510006
HOUND-DOG MAN 600013
HOUP-LA 161123
HOUSE I LIVE IN, THE 450009
HOUSE OF FLOWERS 541230
HOUSE OF LEATHER, THE 700318
HOUSE THAT JACK BUILT, THE 291108
HOUSEBOAT 580028
HOUSEWIFE-SUPERSTAR! 760708
HOW NOW, DOW JONES 671207
HOW THE WEST WAS WON 620003
HOW TO MARRY A MILLIONAIRE 530022
HOW TO STEAL AN ELECTION 681013
HOW TO STUFF A WILD BIKINI 650003
HOW TO SUCCEED IN BUSINESS
   WITHOUT REALLY TRYING 611014
HOW'S ABOUT IT? 430011
HUCKLEBERRY FINN 740008
HULLO AMERICA 180925
HULLO RAGTIME 121223
HULLO TANGO 131223
HUMAN JUNGLE, THE 540023
HURLEY BURLEY 980908
HURRICANE, THE 370017
HUSH . . . HUSH, SWEET CHARLOTTE
   640009
HYDE PARK CORNER 350015

I AND ALBERT 721106
I CAN GET IT FOR YOU WHOLESALE
   620322
I COULD GO ON SINGING 630001
I DO! I DO! 661205
I DREAM TOO MUCH 350048
I HAD A BALL 641215
I LIVE FOR LOVE 350034
I LOVE MELVIN 530007
I LOVE MY WIFE 770417
I MARRIED AN ANGEL 380511
I SURRENDER DEAR 310012
I WONDER WHO'S KISSING HER NOW

470020
ICE CAPADES OF '53 See 470313
    "Brigadoon"
ICE FOLLIES OF 1939 390025
ICE FOLLIES OF 1949 481116
ICE FOLLIES OF 1951 510029
ICE FOLLIES OF 1956 560026
ICE FOLLIES OF 1967 670110
ICE SHOW, THE See 770517 "Toller
    Cranston's The Ice Show"
ICELAND 420030
ICHABOD AND MR. TOAD 490015
I'D RATHER BE RICH 640014
IDIOT'S DELIGHT 390008
IDOL'S EYE, THE 971025
IF A MAN ANSWERS 620016
IF I HAD MY WAY 400018
IF I'M LUCKY 460017
IF YOU FEEL LIKE SINGING See 500002
    "Summer Stock"
IF YOU KNEW SUSIE 480009
I'LL BE SEEING YOU 440003
I'LL CRY TOMORROW 560012
I'LL GET BY 500019
I'LL SEE YOU IN MY DREAMS 520010
I'LL TAKE ROMANCE 370025
ILLYA DARLING 670411
I'M GETTING MY ACT TOGETHER 780516
I'M NO ANGEL 330008
IN CALIENTE 350038
IN CIRCLES 671013
IN OLD CHICAGO 380029
IN PERSON 350049
IN SEARCH OF THE CASTAWAYS 630008
IN THE GOOD OLD SUMMERTIME 490001
IN THE NAVY 410015
IN TROUSERS 790221
INCENDIARY BLONDE 450017
INCREDIBLE MR. LIMPET, THE 640018
INDISCREET 310006
INN OF THE SIXTH HAPPINESS, THE
    580032
INNER CITY 711219
INNOCENT EYES 240520
INNOCENTS OF PARIS 290007
INSIDE U.S.A. 480430
INSPECTOR GENERAL, THE 490020
INTERNATIONAL HOUSE 330030
INTERNATIONAL REVUE See 300225 "Lew
    Leslie's International Revue"
INTERNATIONAL SOIREE 580312
INTERRUPTED MELODY 550012
INVISIBLE DRAGON, THE 741215
IOLE 131229
IPI-TOMBI 740322
IRENE 191118
IRENE 310020
IRISH EYES ARE SMILING 440027
IRMA LA DOUCE 561112
IRVING BERLIN TRIBUTE, AN 380803
IS EVERYBODY HAPPY? 290018
IS EVERYBODY HAPPY? 430005
ISABEL'S A JEZEBEL 701215
ISLAND IN THE SUN 570017
ISLE O' DREAMS, THE 130127
IT ALL CAME TRUE 400037
IT HAPPENED AT THE WORLD'S FAIR
    630013

IT HAPPENED IN BROOKLYN 470006
IT HAPPENED IN NORDLAND 041205
IT HAPPENED TO JANE 590015
IT STARTED WITH A KISS 580009
IT'S A BIRD IT'S A PLANE IT'S SUPERMAN
    660329
IT'S A DATE 400008
IT'S A GREAT FEELING 490016
IT'S A GREAT LIFE 290012
IT'S A GREAT LIFE 360032
IT'S ALWAYS FAIR WEATHER 550007
IT'S HOLIDAY TIME 580033
IT'S LOVE AGAIN 360004
IT'S MAGIC See 480010 "Romance on the
    High Seas"

JACK AHOY 330015
JACK AND JILL 230322
JACK AND THE BEANSTALK 561112*
JACK AND THE BEANSTALK 670226
JACK O' LANTERN 171016
JACK OF ALL TRADES 360014
JACK'S THE BOY 320005
JACQUES BREL IS ALIVE AND WELL AND
    LIVING IN PARIS 680122
JAILHOUSE ROCK 570020
JAMAICA 571031
JAZZ SINGER, THE 270001
JAZZ SINGER, THE 530014
JEANNE EAGELS 570031
JEEVES 750422
JENNY 631017
JERICHO 370036
JESSICA 620002
JESUS CHRIST SUPERSTAR 711012
JIMMIE 201117
JIMMY 691023
JITTERBUG PARTY 340050
JOAN 720619
JOAN OF ARKANSAS 250404
JOEY 560325
JOHN BROWN'S BODY 530214
JOHN GOLDFARB, PLEASE COME HOME
    650012
JOHN MURRAY ANDERSON'S ALMANAC
    See 290814 "Murray Anderson's Almanac"
JOHN MURRAY ANDERSON'S ALMANAC
    531210
JOHNNY ANGEL 450026
JOHNNY APOLLO 400020
JOHNNY APPLESEED See 480019 "Melody
    Time"
JOHNNY CONCHO 560020
JOHNNY JOHNSON 361117
JOKER IS WILD, THE 570010
JOKER OF SEVILLE, THE 741128
JOLLY BACHELORS, THE 100106
JOLSON REVUE, THE 741007*
JOLSON SINGS AGAIN 490003
JOLSON STORY, THE 460005
JOSEPH AND THE AMAZING TECHNI-
    COLOR DREAMCOAT 721108
JOSEPH McCARTHY IS ALIVE AND
    LIVING IN DADE COUNTY 770808
JOURNEY BACK TO OZ 740009
JOURNEY TO THE CENTER OF THE EARTH
    600006
JOY 700127

JOY OF LIVING, THE 380032
JOYCE GRENFELL REQUESTS THE
    PLEASURE OF YOUR COMPANY 540602
JUBALAY See 780323 "A Bistro Car on the
    C N R"
JUBILEE 351012
JUDY GARLAND AT THE PALACE 511016
JUDY GARLAND AT THE PALACE 670731
JUKE BOX JENNY 420035
JULIE 560013
JULIE AND CAROL AT CARNEGIE HALL
    620611
JULIE AND CAROL AT LINCOLN CENTER
    710701
JUMBO 351116
JUMP FOR JOY 410804
JUNE DAYS 250806
JUNE LOVE 210425
JUNGLE BOOK, THE 680007
JUNGLE FIGHTERS See 610010 "The Long
    and the Short and the Tall"
JUNGLE PRINCESS 360019
JUNIOR MISS 571220
JUNO 590309
JUST A GIGOLO 790001
JUST AROUND THE CORNER 380006
JUST FOR OPENERS 651103
JUST FOR YOU 520012

KA-BOOM! 801120
KARL MARX PLAY, THE 730316
KATINKA 151223*
KATJA, THE DANCER 230105
KEAN 611102
KEEP 'EM FLYING 410020
KEEP OFF THE GRASS 400523
KEEP SHUFFLIN' 280227
KEEP SMILING 380017
KELLY 650206
KID BOOTS 231231
KID FROM SPAIN, THE 320001
KID GALAHAD 640012
KID MILLIONS 340010
KILL THAT STORY 340829
KING AND I, THE 510329
KING CREOLE 580012
KING DODO 020512
KING OF BURLESQUE 350005
KING OF HEARTS 781022
KING OF JAZZ, THE 300005
KING OF THE ENTIRE WORLD, THE
    781007
KING SOLOMON OF BROADWAY 350042
KING SOLOMON'S MINES 370034
KING STEPS OUT, THE 360022
KINGS GO FORTH 580022
KING'S RHAPSODY 490915
KISMET 531203
KISS AND MAKE UP 340056
KISS ME DEADLY 550027
KISS ME KATE 481230
KISS ME, STUPID 640016
KISS THE BOYS GOODBYE 410006
KISSIN' COUSINS 640013
KISSING BANDIT, THE 480011
KISSING TIME 190520
KITTIWAKE ISLAND 601012
KITTY GREY 010907

KLONDIKE ANNIE 360045
KNICKERBOCKER HOLIDAY 381019
KNIGHT OF THE BURNING PESTLE, THE
   741115
KNOCK ON WOOD 540016
KURT WEILL CABARET, A See 630606 "The
   World of Kurt Weill in Song"
KWAMINA 611023

LA LA LUCILLE 190526
LADIES FIRST 181024
LADIES' MAN 470015
LADIES OF THE CHORUS 480021
LADIES THEY TALK ABOUT 330025
LADY AND THE TRAMP 550018
LADY, BE GOOD! 241201
LADY FROM PHILADELPHIA, THE See
   571230 "See It Now: The Lady From
   Philadelphia"
LADY IN RED, THE 190512
LADY IN THE DARK 410123
LADY LUCK 270427
LADY MADCAP 041217
LADY MARY 280223
LADY OF BURLESQUE 430020
LADY OF THE PAVEMENTS 290004
LADY OF THE SLIPPER, THE 121028
LADY ON A TRAIN 450011
LADY SINGS THE BLUES 740003
LAND OF JOY, THE 171101
LAND OF SMILES, THE 291010
LAS VEGAS NIGHTS 410019
LAS VEGAS STORY, THE 520013
LAST SWEET DAYS OF ISAAC, THE 700126
LAST TIME I SAW PARIS, THE 540024
LAST WALTZ, THE 200212
LATIN LOVERS 530029
LAUGH PARADE, THE 311102
LAUGHING ANNE 530032
LAUGHING HUSBAND, THE 131002
LAUGHING IRISH EYES 360034
LEAD THE CARE-FREE LIFE . . . IN THE
   HOLIDAY MOOD 561107
LEAVE IT TO JANE 170829
LEAVE IT TO ME 381109
LEGEND 760513
LEGEND OF SLEEPY HOLLOW, THE See
   490015 "Ichabod and Mr. Toad"
LEMMINGS 730125
LEND AN EAR 481216
LET 'EM EAT CAKE 331021
LET FREEDOM RING 390016
LET FREEDOM SING 421005
LET IT RIDE! 611012
LET MY PEOPLE COME 740108
LET'S BE HAPPY 560011
LET'S DANCE 500021
LET'S DO IT AGAIN 530015
LET'S FACE IT 411029
LET'S FALL IN LOVE 340014
LET'S HAVE FUN 351022
LET'S LIVE TONIGHT 350058
LET'S MAKE LOVE 600001
LET'S MAKE MUSIC 400034
LET'S SING AGAIN 360024
LETTER, THE 590021
LEW LESLIE'S INTERNATIONAL REVUE
   300225

LIBBY HOLMAN'S "BLUES, BALLADS,
   AND SIN-SONGS" 541004
LIDO LADY 261201
LIEBER AUGUSTIN, DER 120203
LIEUTENANT, THE 750309
LIFE AND ADVENTURES OF NICHOLAS
   NICKLEBY, THE 800622
LIFE BEGINS AT 8:40 340827
LIFE OF THE PARTY, THE 370048
LIGHTS UP 400209
LI'L ABNER 561115
LILAC DOMINO, THE 141028
LILAC TIME See 160115 "Blossom Time"
LILACS IN THE SPRING 550023
LILI 530009
LILLIAN RUSSELL 400016
LILY OF KILLARNEY, THE 620208
LIMELIGHT 350041
LIMELIGHT 520018
LISBON STORY, THE 460028
LISTEN DARLING 380002
LISTEN LESTER 181223
LISZTOMANIA 750005
LITTLE BIT OF HEAVEN, A 400026
LITTLE BOY LOST 530006
LITTLE CAFE, THE 131110
LITTLE COLONEL, THE 350028
LITTLE DAMOZEL, THE 330017
LITTLE DOG LAUGHED, THE 391011
LITTLE JESSIE JAMES 230815
LITTLE JOHNNY JONES 041107
LITTLE MARY SUNSHINE 591118
LITTLE ME 621117
LITTLE MICHUS, THE 971116
LITTLE MISS BLUEBIRD 230828
LITTLE MISS BROADWAY 380007
LITTLE MISS FIX-IT 110403
LITTLE MISS MARKER 340054
LITTLE NELLIE KELLY 221113
LITTLE NELLIE KELLY 400004
LITTLE NIGHT MUSIC, A 730225
LITTLE PRINCE, THE 740002
LITTLE SHOW, THE 290430
LITTLE WILLIE JR'S RESURRECTION
   781113
LITTLE WOMEN 581016
LITTLEST ANGEL, THE 691206
LITTLEST CLOWN, THE 680012
LITTLEST REBEL, THE 350019
LITTLEST REVUE, THE 560522
LIVE A LITTLE, LOVE A LITTLE 680013
LIVELY SET, THE 640007
LIVING IN A BIG WAY 470031
LIVING IT UP 540020
LIZA 221127
LIZA 740106
LIZA WITH A "Z" 720910
LIZZIE 560023
LOCK UP YOUR DAUGHTERS 590528
LONDON CALLING 230904
LONDON TOWN 460027
LONELY MAN, THE 570036
LONESOME TRAIN, THE 440321
LONG AND THE SHORT AND THE TALL,
   THE 610010
LOOK FOR THE SILVER LINING 490024
LOOK MA, I'M DANCIN'! 480129
LOOK UP AND LAUGH 350059

LOOKING ON THE BRIGHT SIDE 320020
LORD BYRON OF BROADWAY 300044
LORD DON'T PLAY FAVORITES, THE
   560917
LORELEI See 481208 "Gentlemen Prefer
   Blondes"
LOST HORIZON 730001
LOST IN THE STARS 491030
LOUISIANA PURCHASE 400528
LOVE AND LET LOVE 680103
LOVE COMES ALONG 300024
LOVE FINDS ANDY HARDY 380004
LOVE FROM JUDY 520925
LOVE HAPPY 490022
LOVE IS A MANY SPLENDORED THING
   550029
LOVE LETTER, THE 211004
LOVE LIFE 481007
LOVE, LIFE AND LAUGHTER 340032
LOVE ME FOREVER 350026
LOVE ME OR LEAVE ME 550003
LOVE ME TENDER 560017
LOVE ME TONIGHT 320004
LOVE O' MIKE 170115
LOVE PARADE, THE 290011
LOVE SONG, THE 250113
LOVE SONG OF BARNEY KEMPINSKI, THE
   660914
LOVELY TO LOOK AT See 331118
   "Roberta"
LOVER COME BACK 460016
LOVER COME BACK 610005
LOVERS 750127
LOVE'S LOTTERY 041003
LOVESONG 761005
LOVING YOU 570023
LUCKEE GIRL 280915
LUCKY 270322
LUCKY BOY 290003
LUCKY IN LOVE 290023
LUCKY LADY 760002
LUCKY ME 540018
LULLABY LAND 330042
LULLABY OF BROADWAY 510009
LULU BELLE 480032
LUTE SONG 460206
LUXURY LINER 480030
LYRIC REVUE, THE 510524

MACK AND MABEL 741006
MACUSHLA 120205
MAD ABOUT MEN 550031
MAD ABOUT MUSIC 380010
MAD SHOW, THE 651223
MADAME POMPADOUR 220302
MADAME SHERRY 031223
MADCAP DUCHESS, THE 131111
MADEMOISELLE COLOMBE 770207
MADEMOISELLE MODISTE 051225
MAGGIE FLYNN 681023
MAGGIE MAY 640922*
MAGIC GARDEN OF STANLEY SWEET-
   HEART, THE 700006
MAGIC NIGHT See 320008 "Goodnight
   Vienna"
MAGIC OF LASSIE, THE 780004
MAGIC SHOW, THE 740528
MAGYAR MELODY 390120

18

MAID IN AMERICA 150218
MAID OF THE MOUNTAINS, THE 170210
MAIN STREET TO BROADWAY 530024
MAKE A WISH 370028
MAKE A WISH 510418
MAKE IT SNAPPY 220413
MAKE MINE MANHATTAN 480115
MAKE MINE MUSIC 460011
MAMBA'S DAUGHTERS 390103
MAME 660524
MAMMY 300010
MAN ABOUT TOWN 390012
MAN CALLED ADAM, A 660006
MAN FROM BROADWAY, THE 630021
MAN FROM CHINA, THE 040502
MAN FROM THE FOLIES BERGERE, THE
See 350021 "Folies Bergere"
MAN I LOVE, THE 460026
MAN IN THE MOON 630411
MAN OF LA MANCHA 651122
MAN OF MAYFAIR, A 310004
MAN OF THE HOUR See 360021
"L'Homme du Jour"
MAN OF THE WEST 580023
MAN ON FIRE 570026
MAN ON THE MOON 750129
MAN WHO KNEW TOO MUCH, THE
560019
MAN WITH A LOAD OF MISCHIEF 661106
MAN WITH THREE WIVES, THE 080121
MAN WITHOUT A STAR 550013
MANHATTAN MELODRAMA 340045
MANHATTAN MERRY-GO-ROUND 370031
MANHATTAN TOWER 480014
MANNEQUIN 380036
MAN'S A MAN, A 620919
MAN'S CASTLE, A 330036
MANY HAPPY RETURNS 340048
MARACAIBO 580025
MARDI GRAS 580007
MARDI GRAS 650626
MARIANNE 290026
MARIE GALANTE 340033
MARINELLA 350060
MARINKA 450718
MARITANA 451115
MARITZA See 260326 "Countess Maritza"
MARJOE 720003
MARLENE DIETRICH 641123*
MARRIAGE MARKET, THE 130922
MARRY ME 320021
MARY 201018
MARY C. BROWN AND THE HOLLY-
WOOD SIGN 721112
MARY LOU 480031
MARY POPPINS 640001
MASCOTTE, THE 801229
MASQUERADE IN MEXICO 450002
MASTERS OF MELODY 290036
MATA HARI 671118
MATING GAME, THE 590007
MATTER OF TIME, A 760008
MAURICE CHEVALIER 320209
MAURICE CHEVALIER 470310
MAURICE CHEVALIER 480229
MAVERICK QUEEN, THE 560025
MAVOURNEEN 910928*
MAX MORATH AT THE TURN OF THE

CENTURY 691230
MAYFAIR AND MONTMARTRE 220309
MAYFLOWER 751210
MAYFLOWERS 251124
MAYOR OF 44TH STREET, THE 420027
MAYTIME 170816
MAZURKA 350035
ME AND BESSIE 751022
ME AND JULIET 530528
ME AND MY GIRL 371216
ME NOBODY KNOWS, THE 700518
MEET DANNY WILSON 520017
MEET ME AFTER THE SHOW 510030
MEET ME IN LAS VEGAS 560005
MEET ME IN ST. LOUIS 440001
MEET THE PEOPLE 440030
MELBA 530019
MELODY FOR TWO 370021
MELODY TIME 480019
MEMBER OF THE WEDDING 530002
MERCENARY MARY 250413
MERRY ANDREW 580008
MERRY COUNTESS, THE See 740405 "Die
Fledermaus"
MERRY MALONES, THE 270926
MERRY MERRY See 250924 "Merry-Merry"
MERRY WIDOW, THE 051230
MERRY WIDOW AND THE DEVIL, THE
090118
MERRY-MERRY 250924
MERTON OF THE MOVIES 411117
MESSENGER BOY, THE 000203
MESSIN' AROUND 290422
METROPOLITAN 350030
MEXICAN HAYRIDE 440128
MICHAEL TODD'S PEEP SHOW 500628
MICKEY 480017
MICKEY AND THE BEANSTALK See 470016
"Fun and Fancy Free"
MICKEY'S FOLLIES 290041
MICKEY'S GALA PREMIERE 330045
MICKEY'S GRAND OPERA 360038
MIDNIGHT GIRL, THE 140223
MIDNIGHT ROUNDERS, THE 200712
MIDNIGHT ROUNDERS OF 1921, THE
210205
MIDNIGHT SONS, THE 090522
MIDSHIPMAID, THE 320009
MIDSUMMER NIGHT'S DREAM, A 731120
MIGHTY HERCULES, THE 620014
MIKADO, THE 850314
MILK AND HONEY 611010
MINNIE'S BOYS 700326
MIRACLE CAN HAPPEN, A 480034
MIRACLE OF THE BELLS, THE 480012
MISS CAPRICE See 120203 "Der Lieber-
Augustin"
MISS DAISY 140909
MISS HOOK OF HOLLAND 070131
MISS LIBERTY 490715
MISS MOFFAT 741007
MISS 1917 171105
MISS SADIE THOMPSON 540003
MISS SPRINGTIME 160925
MISSISSIPPI 350024
MIXED DOUBLES 661019
MOCKING BIRD, THE 021110
MODERN EVE, A 150503

MONKEY BUSINESS 310019
MONKEYS, GO HOME! 670009
MONSIEUR BEAUCAIRE 190419
MONSIEUR DE POURCEAUGNAC 780300
MONTANA MOON 300025
MONTE CARLO 300009
MONTE CARLO STORY, THE 570041
MONTE CRISTO JR. 190212
MOON OVER BURMA 400022
MOON OVER LAS VEGAS 440008
MOON OVER MIAMI 410021
MOON PILOT 620015
MOONEY SHAPIRO SONGBOOK, THE See
790725 "Songbook"
MOONLIGHT AND CACTUS 440013
MOONLIGHT IS SILVER 340919
MOROCCO 300002
MORRIS GEST MIDNIGHT WHIRL 191227
MOSKAU-SHANGHAI 360053
MOST HAPPY FELLA, THE 560503
MOTHER EARTH 721019
MOTHER GOOSE 031202
MOTHER OF PEARL 330127
MOTHER WORE TIGHTS 470010
MOTHER'S BOY 290022
MOULIN ROUGE 340027
MOUNTAIN MUSIC 370045
MOVE OVER DARLING 630009
MOVIE MOVIE 780002
MOVING DAY 360039
MOZART 260621
MR. BROADWAY 570511
MR. CINDERS 290211
MR. HAMLET OF BROADWAY 081223*
MR. IMPERIUM 510005
MR. MANHATTAN 160330
MR. MUSIC 500012
MR. PRESIDENT 621020
MR. WHITTINGTON 340201
MR. WONDERFUL 560322
MR. WOOLWORTH HAD A NOTION
650616
MRS. PATTERSON 541201
MUPPET MOVIE, THE 790002
MURDER AT THE VANITIES 330908
MURDER AT THE VANITIES 340028
MURRAY ANDERSON'S ALMANAC 290814
MUSIC BOX REVUE OF 1921, THE 210922
MUSIC BOX REVUE OF 1922, THE 221023
MUSIC BOX REVUE OF 1923, THE 230922
MUSIC BOX REVUE OF 1924, THE 241201*
MUSIC FOR MILLIONS 440009
MUSIC FROM SHUBERT ALLEY 591113
MUSIC GOES ROUND, THE 360036
MUSIC IN MY HEART 400028
MUSIC IN THE AIR 321108
MUSIC IS MAGIC 350045
MUSIC MAN, THE 571219
MUSICAL CHAIRS 800514
MUSICAL JUBILEE, A 751113
MY BLUE HEAVEN 500003
MY COUSIN JOSEFA 690806
MY DEAR PUBLIC 430909
MY DREAM IS YOURS 490014
MY FAIR LADY 560315
MY FAIRFAX LADY 590023
MY FAVORITE BRUNETTE 470009
MY FAVORITE SPY 420029

MY FRIEND IRMA 490023
MY FRIEND IRMA GOES WEST 500020
MY FUR LADY 570207
MY GAL SAL 420021
MY LADY MOLLY 030314
MY LADY'S MAID See 041217 "Lady Madcap"
MY MAGNOLIA 260708
MY MAN 280002
MY MARYLAND 270912
MY PEOPLE 630816
MY SIX LOVES 630005
MY SQUARE LADDIE 550016
MY WILD IRISH ROSE 470022
MYRA BRECKINRIDGE 700003

NACHT DER ENTSCHEIDUNG, DIE 380040
NANCY BROWN 030216
NANCY GOES TO RIO 500008
NASHVILLE 750003
NASHVILLE NEW YORK 791106
NAT GONELLA AND HIS GEORGIANS 350051
NATIONAL LAMPOON'S LEMMINGS See 730125 "Lemmings"
NAUGHTY BUT NICE 390020
NAUGHTY CINDERELLA 251109
NAUGHTY MARIETTA 101107
NAVY BLUES 410029
NED WAYBURN'S GAMBOLS 290115
NEFERTITI 770920
NEPTUNE'S DAUGHTER 490004
NERVOUS SET, THE 590512
NEVER BE AFRAID 580019
NEVER SAY DIE 390032
NEVER TOO LATE 621127
NEVER TROUBLE TROUBLE 310021
NEW ALICE IN WONDERLAND, THE See 660330 "Alice in Wonderland"
NEW FACES 340315
NEW FACES OF 1937 370047
NEW FACES OF 1952 520516
NEW FACES OF 1956 560614
NEW FACES OF 1962 620201
NEW FACES OF 1968 680502
NEW GIRL IN TOWN 570514
NEW MOON, THE 280919
NEW ORLEANS 470021
NEW YORK, NEW YORK 770002
NEW YORK SUMMER!, A 790531
NEW YORKERS, THE 301208
NIAGARA 530023
NICE GIRL? 410002
NICHOLAS NICKLEBY See 800622 "The Life and Adventures of Nicholas Nickleby"
NIFTIES OF 1923 230925
NIGHT AND DAY 460010
NIGHT AT THE OPERA, A 350022
NIGHT BOAT, THE 200202
NIGHT IN SPAIN, A 270503
NIGHT IN VENICE, A 831003
NIGHT IS YOUNG, THE 350017
NIGHT OF FATE See 380040 "Die Nacht der Entscheidung"
NIGHT OF THE QUARTER MOON 590022
NIGHT OUT, A 200918
NIGHT SONG 470030
NIGHT THAT MADE AMERICA FAMOUS, THE 750226
NIGHT THEY RAIDED MINSKY'S, THE 680006
NINA See 760008 "A Matter of Time"
NINA ROSA 300920
NINA, THE PINTA AND THE SANTA MARIA, THE 590016
9-SHARP 380126
NO FOR AN ANSWER 410105
NO LEAVE, NO LOVE 460025
NO MAN CAN TAME ME 590201
NO, NO, NANETTE 250311
NO SKY SO BLUE 380608
NO STRINGS 620315
NO TIME FOR SERGEANTS 551020
NOBODY HOME 150420
NORA PRESTISS 470025
NORTHWEST OUTPOST 470018
NORWOOD 690005
NOT AS A STRANGER 550019
NOTEWORTHY OCCASION, A 710606
NOTHING BUT THE TRUTH 290028
NOTORIOUS LANDLADY, THE 620013
NOW I'LL TELL 340039
NOW IS THE TIME FOR ALL GOOD MEN 670926
NOW, VOYAGER 420022
NYMPH ERRANT 331006

O MISTRESS MINE 361203
O SAY CAN YOU SEE! 621008
OCEAN'S ELEVEN 600010
ODDS AND ENDS OF 1917 171119
OF THEE I SING 311226
OFFICE BLUES 290033
OFFICE GIRL See 300034 "Die Privat Sekretaerin"
OH, BOY! 170220
OH! CALCUTTA! 690617
OH CAPTAIN! 580204
OH, COWARD! 721004
OH, I SAY! 131030
OH, JOY! See 170220 "Oh, Boy!"
OH, KAY! 261108
OH, LADY! LADY! 180201
OH, LOOK! 180307
OH! OH! DELPHINE 120930
OH, PLEASE! 261217
OH, ROSALINDA! See 740405 "Die Fledermaus"
OH! SAILOR BEHAVE 300026
OH WHAT A LOVELY WAR 630319
OH, YOU BEAUTIFUL DOLL 490027
OIL TOWN, U.S.A. 530026
OKLAHOMA! 430331
OLD DUTCH 091122
OLD TOWN, THE 100110
OLD-FASHIONED WAY, THE 340052
OLIVER! 600630
OLIVETTE 791113
OLYMPUS 7-0000 660928
OMAHA! 580010
ON A CLEAR DAY YOU CAN SEE FOREVER 651017
ON AN ISLAND WITH YOU 480027
ON MOONLIGHT BAY 510012
ON THE AVENUE 370001
ON THE FLIP SIDE 661207
ON THE OLD SPANISH TRAIL 470023
ON THE RIVIERA 510001
ON THE TOWN 441228
ON THE TWENTIETH CENTURY 780219
ON WITH THE DANCE 250430
ON WITH THE SHOW 290001
ON YOUR TOES 360411
ONCE UPON A MATTRESS 590511
ONCE UPON A TOUR 710814
ONE AND ONLY GENUINE ORIGINAL FAMILY BAND, THE 680003
ONE DAM' THING AFTER ANOTHER 270520
ONE HEAVENLY NIGHT 300045
ONE HOUR LATE 350036
ONE HOUR WITH YOU 320002
100 MEN AND A GIRL 370003
101 DALMATIONS 610008
110 IN THE SHADE 631024
135TH STREET See 220828 "George White's Scandals of 1922"
ONE IN A MILLION 360058
ONE LITTLE GIRL 601103*
ONE MO' TIME 791020
ONE MORE CHANCE 310013
ONE NIGHT OF LOVE 340012
ONE NIGHT WITH YOU 480020
ONE STAR RISING 760408
$1000 A TOUCHDOWN 390033
ONE TOUCH OF VENUS 431007
ONE-WAY TICKET TO BROADWAY, A 790005
ONLY GIRL, THE 141102
OPERATOR 13 340035
OPERETTE 380316
OPTIMISTS, THE 280130
ORCHESTRA WIVES 420008
ORCHID, THE 031026
ORPHANS' BENEFIT, THE 340037
OUR LITTLE GIRL 350029
OUR LOVE IS HERE TO STAY 760009
OUR LOVE LETTER See 590021 "The Letter"
OUR MISS GIBBS 090123
OUR TOWN 550919
OUT OF THE BOTTLE 320611
OUT OF THIS WORLD 450006
OUT OF THIS WORLD 501221
OUTLAW BLUES 770003
OUTSIDE OF PARADISE 380028
OVER HERE! 740306

PACIFIC 1860 461219
PACIFIC OVERTURES 760111
PADDY O'DAY 350046
PAGAN, THE 290016
PAGAN LOVE SONG 500009
PAGANINI 251030
PAGEANT IN EXILE 770322
PAINT YOUR WAGON 511112
PAINTING THE CLOUDS WITH SUNSHINE 510017
PAJAMA GAME, THE 540513
PAL JOEY 401225
PALEFACE, THE 480022
PALM SPRINGS 360030
PALM SPRINGS WEEKEND 630003
PALMY DAYS 310005

PALOOKA 340023
PANAMA HATTIE 401030
PANDORA AND THE FLYING DUTCHMAN 510008
PAPA'S DELICATE CONDITION 630007
PAPER MOON 740005
PARADE 600120
PARADISE, HAWAIIAN STYLE 660009
PARAMOUNT ON PARADE 300004
PARAPLUIES DE CHERBOURG, LES See 640003 "The Umbrellas of Cherbourg"
PARDNERS 560015
PARDON MY ENGLISH 330120
PARDON MY SARONG 420013
PARDON US 310017
PARENT TRAP, THE 610002
PARIS 281008
PARIS HOLIDAY 580027
PARIS HONEYMOON 390010
PARIS '90 520304
PARISIAN MODEL, THE 061127
PARISIENNE, LA 590005
PARTY WITH BETTY COMDEN AND ADOLPH GREEN, A 581223
PASSING FAIR 650009
PASSING SHOW, THE 140420
PASSING SHOW OF 1914, THE 140610
PASSING SHOW OF 1917, THE 170426*
PAUL SILLS' STORY THEATRE 701026
PEACE 690127
PEARL AND THE PUMPKIN, THE 050821
PEEP SHOW See 500628 "Michael Todd's Peep Show"
PEG OF OLD DRURY 350055
PEGGY 110304
PEGGY-ANN 261227
PELL-MELL 160605
PENNEY PROUD 620205*
PENNIES FROM HEAVEN 360015
PEPE 600002
PERCHANCE TO DREAM 450421
PERFECT UNDERSTANDING 330018
PERILS OF PAULINE, THE 470011
PERSONAL COLUMN See 390028 "Pieges"
PERSPECTIVE FOR THE SEVENTIES 690200
PETE KELLY'S BLUES 550004
PETER PAN 500424
PETER PAN 530010
PETER PAN 541020
PETE'S DRAGON 770005
PHANTOM OF THE PARADISE 740006
PHANTOM PRESIDENT, THE 320014
PHILEMON 750408
PHOENIX '55 550423
PIANO BAR 780608
PICKWICK 630704
PIECES OF EIGHT 590924
PIED PIPER, THE 081203
PIED PIPER OF HAMELIN, THE 571126
PIEGES 390028
PIGSKIN PARADE 360040
PILLOW TALK 590009
PINK LADY, THE 110313
PINOCCHIO 400001
PINOCCHIO 570018
PINOCCHIO 571013
PINOCCHIO 651226
PINOCCHIO 710003

PINS AND NEEDLES 371127
PIN-UP GIRL 440026
PIPE DREAM 551130
PIPPIN 721023
PIRATE, THE 480003
PIRATES OF PENZANCE, THE 791231
PLAIN AND FANCY 550127
PLANTATION REVUE 220717
PLATINUM 781112
PLAYBOY OF PARIS 300007
PLAYGIRL 540022
PLAYMATES 410023
PLEASE 331116
PLEASE DON'T EAT THE DAISIES 600005
PLEASE TEACHER 351002
PLEASURE BOUND 290218
PLEASURE SEEKERS, THE 650001
PLUME DE MA TANTE, LA 581111
POINTED HEELS 290017
POLICY PLAYERS, THE 000402
POLLYANNA 600011
POLONAISE 451006
POMEGRANADA 660304
POM-POM 160228*
POOR LITTLE RICH GIRL 360010
POPEYE CARTOONS 330032
POPPY 240904
PORGY AND BESS 351010
POSSESSED 310010
POT O' GOLD 400030
POUPEES DE PARIS, LES 640422
POUSSE CAFE 971202
PRESENTING LILY MARS 420023
PRIMROSE 240911
PRINCE AND THE PAUPER, THE 620311
PRINCE AND THE SHOWGIRL, THE 570022
PRINCE OF ARCADIA 330031
PRINCE OF PILSEN, THE 030317
PRINCE OF TONIGHT, THE 090208
PRINCESS CAPRICE See 120203 "Der Lieber Augustin"
PRINCESS CHARMING 261021
PRINCESS FLAVIA 251102
PRINCESS PAT, THE 150929
PRINCESS TAM-TAM 350052
PRIVATE BUCKEROO 420006
PRIVATE LIVES 300924
PRIVAT SEKRETAERIN, DIE 300034
PRODIGAL, THE 310001
PROMENADE 690604
PROMISE, THE 790003
PROMISES, PROMISES 681201
PROUD VALLEY, THE 400029
PUBLIC NUISANCE NO. 1 360042
PURLIE 700315
PURPLE ROAD, THE 130407
PUSS IN BOOTS 680222*
PUT AND TAKE 210823
PUTTIN' ON THE RITZ 300013

QUAKER GIRL, THE 101105
QUEEN, THE See 340047 "The Queen's Affair"
QUEEN HIGH 260908
QUEEN O' HEARTS 221010
QUEEN OF HEARTS 360057
QUEEN OF THE MOVIES, THE 140112

QUEEN'S AFFAIR, THE 340047
QUEEN'S LACE HANDKERCHIEF, THE 801001

R.S.V.P. 260223
R.S.V.P. THE COLE PORTERS 740004
RACHAEL LILY ROSENBLOOM 731126
RACHEL AND THE STRANGER 480005
RAGGED ROBIN 100124
RAGGEDY ANN & ANDY 770001
RAGTIME YEARS, THE 771221
RAIN 221107
RAINBOW 281121
RAINBOW GIRL, THE 180401
RAINBOW ON THE RIVER 360016
RAINBOW 'ROUND MY SHOULDER 520016
RAINTREE COUNTY 570013
RAISIN 731019
RAISING THE FAMILY FOR FUN AND PROFIT 630020
RAMONA 280001
RANG TANG 270712
REACHING FOR THE MOON 310008
READY, WILLING AND ABLE 370052
REALLY ROSIE 801014
REAP THE WILD WIND 420031
REBECCA OF SUNNYBROOK FARM 380008
REBEL WITHOUT A CAUSE 550021
RECKLESS 350031
RECORD CITY 770004
RED GARTERS 540009
RED, HOT AND BLUE! 361029
RED, HOT AND BLUE! 490013
RED MIKADO, THE See 371127 "Pins and Needles"
RED MILL, THE 060924
REDHEAD 590205
RELUCTANT DRAGON, THE 410033
RESCUERS, THE 770006
RETURN TO OZ, THE See 740009 "Journey Back to Oz"
REVENGE WITH MUSIC 341128
REVEREND JOHNSON'S DREAM 400031
REX 760425
RHAPSODY IN BLACK 310504
RHAPSODY IN BLACK AND BLUE 320017
RHAPSODY IN BLUE 450008
RHYTHM ON THE RANGE 360027
RHYTHM ON THE RIVER 400025
RICH, YOUNG AND PRETTY 510004
RIDING HIGH 430022
RIDING HIGH 500011
RIGHT THIS WAY 380105
RIO BRAVO 590025
RIO RITA 270202
RISE AND SHINE 360507
RISE AND SHINE 410036
RIVER OF NO RETURN 540005
RIVERSIDE NIGHTS 260410
RIVERWIND 621212
ROAD IS OPEN AGAIN, THE 330003
ROAD TO BALI, THE 530011
ROAD TO HONG KONG, THE 610001
ROAD TO MOROCCO, THE 420012
ROAD TO RIO, THE 470002
ROAD TO SINGAPORE, THE 400019

ROAD TO UTOPIA, THE 460003
ROAD TO ZANZIBAR, THE 410017
ROADHOUSE 340017
ROADHOUSE NIGHTS 300020
ROAR OF THE GREASEPAINT, THE 650516
ROB ROY 941029
ROBBER BRIDGEGROOM, THE 761010
ROBERTA 331118
ROBIN AND THE SEVEN HOODS 640002
ROBIN HOOD 910928
ROBIN HOOD See 520019 "The Story of
   Robin Hood"
ROBIN HOOD 730003
ROBINSON CRUSOE· JR. 160217
ROCK-A-BYE BABY 180522
ROCK-A-BYE BABY 580017
ROCKABYE HAMLET 760217
ROCKY HORROR SHOW, THE 730619
ROGUE SONG, THE 300017
ROI, LE 490018
ROLL ON TEXAS MOON 460012
ROMAN SCANDALS 330028
ROMANCE IN THE DARK 380045
ROMANCE OF ATHLONE, A 990109
ROMANCE ON THE HIGH SEAS 480010
RONDE, LA 500027
ROSALIE 370020
ROSE OF ALGERIA, THE 090920
ROSE OF PERSIA, THE 991129
ROSE OF WASHINGTON SQUARE 390005
ROSELAND 300040
ROSE-MARIE 240902
ROSY RAPTURE, THE PRIDE OF THE
   BEAUTY CHORUS 150322
ROTHSCHILDS, THE 701019
ROUND THE MAP 170719
ROUSTABOUT 640012
ROYAL AFFAIR, A See 490018 "Le Roi"
ROYAL WEDDING 510003
RUFUS LEMAIRE'S AFFAIRS 270328
RUGANTINO 621215
RUGGLES OF RED GAP 570203
RUMPELSTILTSKIN 650327
RUMPELSTILTSKIN See 620406 "Half-Past
   Wednesday"
RUN, LITTLE CHILLUN! 330301
RUNAWAY GIRL, A 980521
RUNAWAYS 780513
RUNNIN' WILD 231029

'S WONDERFUL, 'S MARVELOUS,
   'S GERSHWIN 720117
SADDLE THE WIND 580026
SADIE McKEE 340016
SAFETY IN NUMBERS 300030
SAGA OF THE DINGBAT, THE 630019
SAIL AWAY 611003
SAILING ALONG 380027
SAILOR BEWARE 510023
SAILORS THREE 400014
SALE AND A SAILOR, A 260425
SALLY 201221
SALLY IN OUR ALLEY 020829
SALLY IN OUR ALLEY 310003
SALLY, IRENE AND MARY 220904
SALLY, IRENE AND MARY 380031
SALUDOS AMIGOS 420018
SALUTE TO ASCAP See 660501 "Cue

Magazine's Salue to ASCAP"
SALVATION 690924
SAMMY See 731116 "General Electric
   Presents Sammy"
SAMMY CAHN SONGBOOK, THE See
   740416 "Words and Music"
SAN FERNANDO VALLEY 440019
SAN FRANCISCO 360013
SAN TOY 991021
SANDERS OF THE RIVER 350043
SANDHOG 541129
SANDY WILSON THANKS THE LADIES
   710610
SANTA CLAUS IS COMING TO TOWN
   711203
SARATOGA 591207
SARAVA 790213
SARI 121010
SATINS AND SPURS 540912
SAY, DARLING 580403
SAY IT WITH SONGS 290015
SAY ONE FOR ME 590006
SAY WHEN 280626
SAY WHEN 341108
SCARLETT See 700103 "Gone With the
   Wind"
SCENES FROM "ALICE IN WONDER-
   LAND" 410031
SCRAMBLED FEET 790611
SCROOGE 700001
SCROOGE 781222
SEA LEGS 300046
SEARCH FOR PARADISE 570040
SEASIDE SWINGERS 650007
SECOND BEST BED 460604
SECOND CHORUS 400007
SECOND FIDDLE 390015
SECOND GREATEST SEX, THE 560021
SECOND SHEPHERD'S PLAY, THE 761215
SECRET LIFE OF WALTER MITTY, THE
   470001
SECRET LIFE OF WALTER MITTY, THE
   641026
SEE HERE, PRIVATE HARGROVE! 430021
SEE IT NOW: THE LADY FROM PHILA-
   DELPHIA 571230
SEE YOU LATER 511003
SEESAW 730319
SELMA 751121
SEND ME NO FLOWERS 601205
SENIOR PROM 590013
SERENADE, THE 970316
SERENADE 560006
SERGEANT BRUE 040614
SET TO MUSIC 390118
SEVEN BRIDES FOR SEVEN BROTHERS
   540001
SEVEN COME ELEVEN 611005
SEVEN DAYS' LEAVE 420028
SEVEN DREAMS 530020
SEVEN HILLS OF ROME 580005
SEVEN LITTLE FOYS 550008
SEVEN LIVELY ARTS 441207
SEVEN SINNERS 400013
SEVEN SWEETHEARTS 420020
SEVENTEEN 510621
1776 690316
SEVENTH HEAVEN 550526

70, GIRLS, 70 710415
SHALL WE DANCE 370004
SHAMEEN DHU 140202
SHAMUS O'BRIEN 960302
SHANGRI-LA 560613
SHE DONE HIM WRONG 330007
SHE LEARNED ABOUT SAILORS 340006
SHE LOVES ME 630423
SHE LOVES ME NOT 331120
SHE LOVES ME NOT 340015
SHE MARRIED A COP 390023
SHE SHALL HAVE MUSIC 590122
SHELTER 730206
SHENANDOAH 750107
SHEPHARD'S PIE 391221
SHE'S A GOOD FELLOW 190505
SHE'S MY BABY 280103
SHINBONE ALLEY 570413
SHIP AHOY 420011
SHIP CAFE 350032
SHIPMATES FOREVER 350040
SHIPYARD SALLY 390007
SHIRLEY MacLAINE 760419
SHOCKING MISS PILGRIM, THE 470003
SHOESTRING '57 571105
SHOESTRING REVUE 550228
SHOP GIRL, THE 941124
SHOPWORN ANGEL, THE 290037
SHOW BOAT 271227
SHOW BUSINESS 440016
SHOW GIRL 290702
SHOW GIRL 610112
SHOW GOES ON, THE 370050
SHOW IS ON, THE 361225
SHOW OF SHOWS, THE 290021
SHUFFLE ALONG 210523
SIDE BY SIDE BY SONDHEIM 760504
SIGH NO MORE 450822
SILK STOCKINGS 550224
SILKS AND SATINS 200715
SILVER SLIPPER, THE 010601
SIMPLE SIMON 300218
SIMPLY HEAVENLY 570521
SINBAD 180214
SING AS WE GO 340026
SING, BABY, SING 360017
SING, BING, SING 330037
SING BOY SING 570024
SING FOR YOUR SUPPER 390424
SING ME A LOVE SONG 360033
SING MUSE! 611206
SING OUT, SWEET LAND! 441227
SING OUT THE NEWS 380924
SING YOU SINNERS 380018
SINGIN' IN THE RAIN 520002
SINGING FOOL, THE 290014
SINGING GIRL, THE 991023
SINGING GUNS 500024
SINGING KID, THE 360020
SINGING MARINE, THE 370011
SINGING NUN, THE 660001
SIS HOPKINS 410030
SITTING PRETTY 330029
SKIRTS AHOY 520011
SKY HIGH 250302
SKY'S THE LIMIT, THE 430002
SKYSCRAPER 651113
SLEEPING BEAUTY 590010

SLEEPLESS NIGHTS 320016
SLIM PRINCESS, THE 110102
SLINGS AND ARROWS 481117
SLIPPER AND THE ROSE, THE 760006
SMALL TOWN GIRL 530013
SMARTEST GIRL IN TOWN, THE 360041
SMASHING TIME 670002
SMASH-UP 470026
SMILE, SMILE, SMILE 730404
SMILIN' THROUGH 410011
SMILING THE BOY FELL DEAD 610419
SNAPSHOTS OF 1921 210602
SNOOPY!!! 751209
SNOOPY, COME HOME 720001
SNOW WHITE AND THE SEVEN DWARFS 370012
SNOW WHITE AND THE SEVEN DWARFS 651218
SO DEAR TO MY HEART 480029
SO THIS IS COLLEGE 290025
SO THIS IS LOVE 530016
SO THIS IS PARIS 550006
SOLDIER BOY See 161206 "Her Soldier Boy"
SOLDIERS OF THE KING 330014
SOME CAME RUNNING 580015
SOME LIKE IT HOT 390021
SOME LIKE IT HOT 590002
SOMEBODY LOVES ME 520009
SOMEBODY'S SWEETHEART 181223*
SOMETHING FOR EVERYBODY'S MOTHER See 720522 "Hark!"
SOMETHING FOR THE BOYS 430107
SOMETHING IN THE AIR 430923
SOMETHING IN THE WIND 470005
SOMETHING TO SHOUT ABOUT 430023
SOMETIME 181004
SON OF PALEFACE 520014
SONDHEIM: A MUSICAL TRIBUTE 730311
SONG IS BORN, A 480025
SONG O' MY HEART 300031
SONG OF FREEDOM 360037
SONG OF LOVE, THE 290032
SONG OF NORWAY 440821
SONG OF SCHEHERAZADE 470012
SONG OF SOHO, A 300011
SONG OF SONGS 330010
SONG OF THE FLAME 251230
SONG OF THE FLAME, THE 300021
SONG OF THE ISLANDS 420015
SONG OF THE OPEN ROAD, THE 440020
SONG OF THE SOUTH 460020
SONG OF THE WEST See 281121 "Rainbow"
SONGBOOK 790725
SONS O' FUN 411201
SONS O' GUNS 291126
SONS OF HAM 020303
SONS OF THE DESERT 340053
SOPHIE 630415
SOPHISTICATED LADIES 810301
SOUL KISS, THE 080128
SOUND OF MUSIC, THE 591116
SOUTH PACIFIC 490407
SOUTHERN MAID, A 200515
SPARKLES 810605
SPEEDWAY 680008
SPICE OF 1922 220706

SPINOUT 660007
SPIRIT OF ACHIEVEMENT, THE 760400
SPIRIT OF '66 See 660207 "An Evening with Michael Brown and His Friends"
SPRING IS HERE 290311
SPRING MAID, THE 090123*
SPRING PARADE 400005
SPRINGTIME IN THE ROCKIES 420014
ST. BENNY THE DIP 510022
ST. LOUIS BLUES 290038
ST. LOUIS BLUES 390019
ST. LOUIS BLUES 580006
ST. LOUIS WOMAN 460330
STAGE DOOR CANTEEN 430012
STAGE FRIGHT 500007
STAGE STRUCK 360008
STAGES 781006
STAND UP AND CHEER 340018
STAND UP AND SING 310305
STAR! 680001
STAR GAZER, THE 171126
STAR IS BORN, A 550001
STAR IS BORN, A 760007
STAR MAKER, THE 390011
STAR SPANGLED RHYTHM 420004
STARLIFT 510024
STARLIGHT ROOF 471023
STARS AND STRIPES FOREVER 520008
STARS ARE SINGING, THE 530005
STARS IN YOUR EYES 390209
STARS OVER BROADWAY 350012
START CHEERING 380022
STARTING HERE, STARTING NOW 770307
STATE FAIR 450001
STEAMBOAT WILLIE 280003
STEP LIVELY 400036
STEP THIS WAY 160529
STEPHEN FOSTER STORY, THE 590626
STINGIEST MAN IN TOWN, THE 561223
STOOGE, THE 520022
STOP FLIRTING See 220220 "For Goodness' Sake"
STOP! LOOK! LISTEN! 151225
STOP THE WORLD, I WANT TO GET OFF 610720
STOP, YOU'RE KILLING ME 520025
STORK CLUB, THE 450012
STORMY WEATHER 430007
STORY OF ROBIN HOOD, THE 520019
STORY OF VERNON AND IRENE CASTLE, THE 390034
STORY THEATRE See 701026 "Paul Sills' Story Theatre"
STOWAWAY 360001
STRAIGHT, PLACE AND SHOW 380034
STRANGE LADY IN TOWN 550026
STRAW HAT REVUE, THE 390929
STRAWS IN THE WIND 750221
STREAMLINE 340928
STREET SCENE 470109
STREETS OF NEW YORK, THE 631029
STREETS OF PARIS, THE 390619
STRICTLY DISHONORABLE 510021
STRICTLY DYNAMITE 340031
STRICTLY IN THE GROOVE 420034
STRIKE ME PINK 330304
STRIKE ME PINK 360043
STRIKE UP THE BAND 300114

STRIKE UP THE BAND 400003
STRIP, THE 510026
STRIP FOR ACTION 560317
STRIPPER, THE 630015
STUDENT GYPSY, THE 630930
STUDENT PRINCE, THE 241202
STUDENT TOUR 340051
SUBTERRANEANS, THE 600016
SUBWAYS ARE FOR SLEEPING 611227
SUGAR 720409
SULTAN OF SULU, THE 021229
SUMMER HOLIDAY 460019
SUMMER HOLIDAY 630010
SUMMER MADNESS See 550022 "Summertime"
SUMMER MAGIC 620004
SUMMER STOCK 500002
SUMMER WIDOWERS, THE 100604
SUMMERTIME 550022
SUN COMES UP, THE 490019
SUN NEVER SETS, THE 380609
SUN VALLEY SERENADE 410012
SUNBONNET SUE 450025
SUNNY 250922
SUNNY SIDE OF THE STREET 510016
SUNNY SIDE UP 290029
SUNNY SKIES 300043
SUNSHINE GIRL, THE 120224
SUNSHINE SUSIE See 300034 "Die Privatsekretaerin"
SUPERMAN See 660329 "It's a Bird It's a Plane It's Superman"
SURVIVAL OF ST. JOAN, THE 710228
SUSAN SLEPT HERE 540026
SUZY 630023
SWANEE RIVER 390027
SWEATER GIRL 420032
SWEENEY TODD 790301
SWEET ADELINE 290903
SWEET CHARITY 660129
SWEET INNISCARRA 970125
SWEET MUSIC 350044
SWEET ROSIE O'GRADY 430014
SWEETHEART OF SIGMA CHI, THE 460015
SWEETHEART OF THE CAMPUS, THE 410034
SWEETHEARTS 130908
SWEETIES 290008
SWING HIGH 300036
SWING HIGH, SWING LOW 370009
SWING TIME 360002
SWING WHILE YOU'RE ABLE 370032
SWINGER, THE 660002
SWINGIN' THE DREAM 391129
SWINGTIME JOHNNY 440014
SWISS MISS 380044
SWORD IN THE STONE, THE 630014
SYBIL 160110
SYMPHONY HOUR 420033
SYMPHONY IN BLACK 350056
SYNCOPATION 290024

TABS 180515
TAIL SPIN 390022
TAKE A CHANCE 321126
TAKE FIVE 571010
TAKE ME ALONG 591022
TAKE ME OUT TO THE BALL GAME

490007
TAKE MY TIP 370013
TAKE THE AIR 271122*
TAMALPAIS EXCHANGE See 700208
    "Exchange"
TAMMY AND THE BACHELOR 570008
TANGERINE 210809
TANGO NOTTURNO 370043
TATOOED MAN, THE 070218
TEA FOR TWO See 250311 "No, No,
    Nanette"
TEACHER'S PET 580031
TELL HER THE TRUTH 320614
TELL ME LIES 670003
TELL ME MORE! 250413*
TELL ME ON A SUNDAY 800128
TEN THOUSAND BEDROOMS 570021
TENDER TRAP, THE 550014
TENDERLOIN 601017
TEXAS CARNIVAL 510019
TEXAS, LI'L DARLIN' 491125
THANK YOUR LUCKY STARS 430016
THANKS A MILLION 350013
THANKS FOR THE MEMORY 380012
THANKS FOR THE MEMORY See 610302
    "25 Years of Life"
THAT CERTAIN AGE 380011
THAT CERTAIN FEELING 560003
THAT GIRL FROM PARIS 360051
THAT GOES DOUBLE 330041
THAT LADY IN ERMINE 480023
THAT MIDNIGHT KISS 490006
THAT NIGHT IN RIO 410007
THAT'S A GOOD GIRL 280605
THAT'S ENTERTAINMENT 740001
THAT'S ENTERTAINMENT, PART 2 760001
THAT'S RIGHT, YOU'RE WRONG 390031
THAT'S THE TICKET 480924
THEODORE AND CO. 160919
THERE GOES THE BRIDE 320003
THERE'S NO BUSINESS LIKE SHOW
    BUSINESS 540004
THEY GOT ME COVERED 430019
THEY LEARNED ABOUT WOMEN 300028
THEY MET IN ARGENTINA 410035
THEY'RE PLAYING OUR SONG 790211
THIEF OF BAGDAD, THE 680222
THIN ICE 370038
THINGS ARE LOOKING UP 350020
THIRD LITTLE SHOW, THE 310601
13 DAUGHTERS 610302
THIS COULD BE THE NIGHT 570014
THIS GUN FOR HIRE 420026
THIS IS MY LOVE 540013
THIS IS OLDSMOBILITY 570044
THIS IS THE ARMY 420704
THIS TIME FOR KEEPS 470004
THIS WAY PLEASE 370044
THIS WEEK OF GRACE 330026
THIS YEAR OF GRACE 280322
THIS'LL MAKE YOU WHISTLE 370019
THOROUGHLY MODERN MILLIE 670001
THOSE REDHEADS FROM SEATTLE
    530031
THOUSAND MILES OF MOUNTAINS, A
    640019
THOUSANDS CHEER 430008
THREE BILLION MILLIONAIRES 630002

THREE CABALLEROS, THE 440023
THREE CHEERS FOR LOVE 360062
THREE COINS IN THE FOUNTAIN 540019
THREE DARING DAUGHTERS 480016
THREE FOR THE SHOW 550010
3 FOR TONIGHT 550406
365 NIGHTS IN HOLLYWOOD 340007
THREE LITTLE GIRLS IN BLUE 460023
THREE LITTLE MAIDS 020510
THREE LITTLE PIGS, THE 330035
THREE LITTLE WOLVES, THE 360061
THREE LITTLE WORDS 500004
THREE MUSKETEERS, THE 280313
THREE SAILORS AND A GIRL 530008
THREE SISTERS, THE 340409
THREE SMART GIRLS 370018
THREE SMART GIRLS GROW UP 390003
THREE TO MAKE MUSIC 581227
THREE TWINS 080615
THREE WALTZES 351005
THREE WISHES FOR JAMIE 520321
THREEPENNY OPERA, THE 280828
THREE'S A CROWD 301015
THRILL OF A LIFETIME, THE 370040
THRILL OF A ROMANCE 450004
THUNDER ROAD 580016
TICKLE ME 650004
TILL THE CLOUDS ROLL BY 460002
TIMBUKTU! See 531203 "Kismet"
TIME FOR SINGING, A 660521
TIME OUT FOR RHYTHM 410025
TIME REMEMBERED 571112
TIME, THE PLACE AND THE GIRL, THE
    070805
TIME, THE PLACE AND THE GIRL, THE
    460021
TIME TO SING, A 680010
TIMES SQUARE LADY 350054
TIN PAN ALLEY 400015
TINSELTOWN 810328
TIP TOP 201005
TIP-TOES 251228
TO BEAT THE BAND 350037
TO BROADWAY WITH LOVE 640429
TO HAVE AND HAVE NOT 440007
TO LIVE ANOTHER SUMMER, TO PASS
    ANOTHER WINTER 711021
TOAST OF NEW ORLEANS, THE 500006
TOGETHER ON BROADWAY 770515
TOGETHER WITH MUSIC 551022
TOLLER CRANSTON'S THE ICE SHOW
    770517
TOM JONES 070417
TOM JONES 600428*
TOM JONES 640005
TOM SAWYER 561121
TOM SAWYER 730002
TOM THUMB 580003
TOMFOOLERY 800605
TOMMY THE TOREADOR 590012
TONI 240512
TONIGHT AND EVERY NIGHT 450020
TO-NIGHT AT 8:30 360109
TONIGHT WE SING 530017
TONIGHT'S THE NIGHT 141224
TOO MANY GIRLS 391018
TOO MUCH HARMONY 330024
TOP BANANA 511101

TOP HAT 350006
TOP O' THE MORNING 490008
TOP OF THE TOWN 370008
TOPSY AND EVA 241223
TORCH SINGER 330034
TORCH SONG 530012
TOREADOR, THE 010617
TOUCH 701108
TOUCH AND GO 491013
TOVARICH 630318
TRAILIN' WEST 360025
TRANSATLANTIC MERRY-GO-ROUND
    340029
TRANSATLANTIC RHYTHM 361001
TRAVELING SALESWOMAN, THE 500022
TREASURE GIRL 281108
TREE GROWS IN BROOKLYN, A 510419
TREEMONISHA 751021
TRESPASSER, THE 290006
TRIBUTE TO GEORGE GERSHWIN, A
    380710
TRILBY 950415
TROIS VALSES, LES See 351005 "Three
    Waltzes"
TROPIC HOLIDAY 380025
TROPICANA HOLIDAY 580013
TROUBLE WITH GIRLS, THE 690008
TROUBLE WITH WOMEN, THE 470024
TRUE TO LIFE 430024
TUNNEL OF LOVE 580011
TUPPENCE COLOURED 471015
TURN OFF THE MOON 370030
TURNABOUT! 750004
TUSCALOOSA'S CALLING ME . . . BUT I'M
    NOT GOING! 751201
25 YEARS OF LIFE 610302*
TWENTY MILLION SWEETHEARTS 340002
20,000 LEAGUES UNDER THE SEA 540017
TWIRLY WHIRLY 020911
2 780117
TWO BY TWO 701110
TWO FOR TONIGHT 350025
TWO GENTLEMEN OF VERONA 711201
TWO GIRLS AND A SAILOR 440011
TWO GUYS FROM TEXAS 480028
TWO HEARTS IN WALTZ TIME 300019
TWO ON THE AISLE 510719
TWO SISTERS FROM BOSTON 460008
TWO TICKETS TO BROADWAY 510010
TWO TICKET TO PARIS 630004
TWO WEEKS WITH LOVE 500005
TWO WHITE ARMS 320006
TWO'S COMPANY 521215
TYPHOON 400021

UMBRELLAS OF CHERBOURG, THE
    640003
UNCLE REMUS See 460020 "Song of the
    South"
UNCLE TOM'S CABIN 650013
UNDER YOUR SPELL 360050
UNDERPUP, THE 390006
UNFINISHED DANCE, THE 470019
UNSINKABLE MOLLY BROWN, THE
    601103
UNTAMED 290034
UP AND DOING 400419
UP IN ARMS 440005

UP IN CENTRAL PARK 450127
UP WITH PEOPLE! 660627
UP WITH PEOPLE! III 730419*
UPPER WORLD 340041
UPS-A-DAISY 281008*
UTTER GLORY OF MORRISSEY HALL, THE 790513

VAGABOND KING, THE 250921
VAGABOND LOVER, THE 290013
VALLEY OF THE DOLLS 680011
VALMOUTH 581002
VANITY FAIR 161106
VARIETY GIRL 470007
VARSITY SHOW 370010
VERA VIOLETTA 111120
VERONIQUE 981210
VERY GOOD EDDIE 151223
VIA GALACTICA 721128
VINTAGE '60 600912
VIVA LAS VEGAS 640011
VIVACIOUS LADY 380035
VOGUES OF 1938 370051

W. T. GRANT'S 50TH ANNIVERSARY SHOW 560200
WABASH AVENUE 500017
WAGON MASTER, THE 290045
WAIKIKI WEDDING 370027
WAIT A MINIM! 620005
WAKE UP AND DREAM 290327
WAKE UP AND DREAM 340008
WAKE UP AND LIVE 370002
WALKING HAPPY 661126
WALKING MY BABY BACK HOME 530027
WALTZ DREAM, A 070302
WALTZES FROM VIENNA 301030
WARRIOR, THE See 740322 "Ipi-Tombi"
WATCH YOUR STEP 141208
WATER GIPSIES, THE 550831
WATERSHIP DOWN 780003
WAY OUT WEST 300033
WAY OUT WEST 370049
WAY TO LOVE, THE 330047
WAYWARD WAY, THE 530903
WE THINK THE WORLD IS ROUND See 590016 "The Nina, The Pinta and the Santa Maria"
WE'D RATHER SWITCH 690502
WEEKEND AT THE WALDORF 450024
WEEK-END IN HAVANA, A 410010
WELCOME, STRANGER 470008
WE'RE NOT DRESSING 340024
WEST POINT STORY, THE 500023
WEST SIDE STORY 570926
WESTWARD HO THE WAGONS! 560014
WHAT IS WAS, WAS LOVE 690002
WHAT MAKES SAMMY RUN? 640227
WHATEVER HAPPENED TO BABY JANE? 620007
WHAT'S A NICE COUNTRY LIKE YOU DOING IN A STATE LIKE THIS? 730419
WHAT'S COOKIN'? 420010
WHAT'S NEW PUSSYCAT? 680002
WHEN DREAMS COME TRUE 130818
WHEN JOHNNY COMES MARCHING HOME 021216
WHEN KNIGHTS WERE BOLD 350008

WHEN LADIES MEET 410026
WHEN MY BABY SMILES AT ME 480033
WHEN THE BOYS MEET THE GIRLS See 301014 "Girl Crazy"
WHEN YOU'RE IN LOVE 370026
WHERE DO WE GO FROM HERE? 450005
WHERE'S CHARLEY? 481011
WHIRL OF SOCIETY, THE 120305
WHIRL-I-GIG 990921
WHISPERS ON THE WIND 700603
WHISTLE AT EATON FALLS, THE 510027
WHITE CHRISTMAS 540006
WHITE HEN, THE 070216
WHITE HORSE INN 301108
WHO COULD ASK FOR ANYTHING MORE 590001
WHO KILLED COCK ROBIN? 350053
WHOOPEE 281204
WHOOPEE PARTY, THE 320019
WHOOP-UP 581222
WHO'S GOT THE ACTION? 630017
WIDOW JONES, THE 950916
WILD BLUE YONDER, THE 510020
WILD IN THE COUNTRY 610004
WILD IS THE WIND 570028
WILD ROSE See 201221 "Sally"
WILDCAT 601215
WILDFLOWER 230207
WILL O' THE WHISPERS 280404
WILLY WONKA & THE CHOCOLATE FACTORY 710002
WINGED VICTORY 431120
WINNIE THE POOH AND THE BLUSTERY DAY 680009
WINNIE THE POOH AND THE HONEY TREE 660004
WISH YOU WERE HERE 520625
WITH A SMILE See 360048 "Avec le Sourire"
WITH A SONG IN MY HEART 520004
WITH LOVE AND KISSES 360035
WITNESS FOR THE PROSECUTION 580020
WIZ, THE 750105
WIZARD OF OZ, THE 390001
WIZARD OF THE NILE, THE 951104
WOLF SONG, THE 290030
WOMAN COMMANDS, A 320012
WOMAN OF THE RIVER 570042
WOMAN OF THE YEAR 810329
WOMEN EVERYWHERE 300041
WONDER BAR, THE 301205
WONDER BAR 340001
WONDER OF WOMEN 290031
WONDERFUL TOWN 530226
WONDERFUL WORLD OF CHEMISTRY, THE 640008
WORDS AND MUSIC 320916
WORDS AND MUSIC 480001
WORDS AND MUSIC 740416
WORKING 780514
WORLD OF KURT WEILL IN SONG, THE 630606
WORLD OF SUZIE WONG, THE 581014

YANK IN THE R.A.F., A 410022
YANKEE CONSUL, THE 040222
YANKEE DOODLE DANDY 420005
YANKEE GIRL, THE 100210

YANKEE PRINCESS, THE 221002
YANKEE TOURIST, A 070812
YEARLING, THE 651210
YELLOW ROSE OF TEXAS, THE 440018
YELLOW SUBMARINE 680015
YES, MADAM 340927
YES! MR. BROWN 330011
YIP YIP YAPHANK 180819
YOKEL BOY 390706
YOLANDA AND THE THIEF 450027
YOU BELONG TO ME 340034
YOU CAN'T HAVE EVERYTHING 370014
YOU CAN'T RUN AWAY FROM IT 560002
YOU SAID IT 310119
YOU WERE MEANT FOR ME 480018
YOU WERE NEVER LOVELIER 420003
YOU'LL FIND OUT 400033
YOU'LL NEVER GET RICH 410003
YOUNG ABE LINCOLN 610425
YOUNG AT HEART 540015
YOUNG GIRLS OF ROCHEFORT, THE 680004
YOUNG MAN FROM BOSTON, THE 650524
YOUNG MAN WITH A HORN 500010
YOUNG PEOPLE 400010
YOUR ARMS TOO SHORT TO BOX WITH GOD 761222
YOUR CHEATIN' HEART 640015
YOUR OWN THING 680113
YOU'RE A GOOD MAN, CHARLIE BROWN 660003
YOU'RE A SWEETHEART 370015
YOU'RE IN LOVE 170206
YOU'RE NEVER TOO YOUNG 550020
YOU'RE THE ONE 410018
YOURS IS MY HEART See 291010 "The Land of Smiles"
YOUTH ON PARADE 420019
YVONNE 260522

ZEN BOOGIE 760506
ZIEGFELD FOLLIES 460001
ZIEGFELD FOLLIES OF 1909 090614
ZIEGFELD FOLLIES OF 1910 100620
ZIEGFELD FOLLIES OF 1911 110626
ZIEGFELD FOLLIES OF 1912 121021
ZIEGFELD FOLLIES OF 1913 130616
ZIEGFELD FOLLIES OF 1914 140601
ZIEGFELD FOLLIES OF 1915 150621
ZIEGFELD FOLLIES OF 1917 170612
ZIEGFELD FOLLIES OF 1919 190623
ZIEGFELD FOLLIES OF 1920 200622
ZIEGFELD FOLLIES OF 1921 210621
ZIEGFELD FOLLIES OF 1922 220605
ZIEGFELD FOLLIES OF 1923 231020
ZIEGFELD FOLLIES OF 1924 240624
ZIEGFELD FOLLIES OF 1927 270816
ZIEGFELD FOLLIES OF 1931 310701
ZIEGFELD FOLLIES OF 1934 340104
ZIEGFELD FOLLIES OF 1943 430414
ZIEGFELD FOLLIES OF 1958 570912
ZIEGFELD GIRL 410001
ZIEGFELD'S MIDNIGHT FROLIC 160001
ZIEGFELD'S MIDNIGHT FROLIC 280004
ZIG-ZAG 170131
ZORBA 681117
ZULU AND THE ZAYDA, THE 651110

Chronological List of Shows

PRE-1890

431127a THE BOHEMIAN GIRL 1968 album. MUSIC: William Michael Balfe. WORDS: Alfred Bunn. VOCALS: Eric Hinds, Veronica Dunne, Uel Deane, Una O'Callaghan. (HMV(E) CSD-3651, with Maritana & The Lily of Killarney)

431127b THE BOHEMIAN GIRL medleys by Victor Light Opera Company. (1909: 78/Vic 31761)(1916: 78/Vic 35603)(1927: 78/Vic 35819)

431127c THE BOHEMIAN GIRL medley by Brunswick Light Opera Company. (78/Bruns 20020)

431127d THE BOHEMIAN GIRL medleys by Light Opera Company. (1927: 78/HMV(E) C-1382)(1933: 78/HMV(E) C-2605)

431127e THE BOHEMIAN GIRL medley by Zonophone Light Opera Company. (78/Zonophone(E) A-349)

431127f THE BOHEMIAN GIRL 1914 record by Henri Scott of 1918 New York prod. "Heart Bowed Down" (78/Col A-5500)

431127g THE BOHEMIAN GIRL 1929 medley by Columbia Light Opera Company. (78/Col(E) 9579)

451115a MARITANA 1968 album. MUSIC: William Vincent Wallace. WORDS: Edward Fitzball. VOCALS: Eric Hinds, Uel Deane, Veronica Dunne. (HMV(E) CSD-3651, with The Bohemian Girl & The Lily of Killarney)

451115b MARITANA 1911 medley by Victor Light Opera Company. (78/Vic 31804)

451115c MARITANA 1929 medley by Light Opera Company. (78/HMV(E) C-1693)

451115d MARITANA 1930 medley by Columbia Light Opera Company. (78/Col(E) DB-9872)

451115e MARITANA 1931 studio prod. COND: Clarence Raybould. CAST: Miriam Licette, Dennis Noble, Clara Serena, Heddle Nash, chorus. (78/Col(E) DB-613/8)

620208a THE LILY OF KILLARNEY 1968 album. MUSIC: Julius Benedict. WORDS: John Oxenford, Dion Boucicault. VOCALS: Eric Hinds, Uel Deane, Veronica Dunne. (HMV(E) CSD-3651, with The Bohemian Girl & Maritana)

740405a DIE FLEDERMAUS studio prod. MUSIC: Johann Strauss Jr. WORDS: Norman Sachs, Mel Mandel. ORCH: Henri Rene. COND: Lehman Engel. CAST: Anna Moffo, Jeanette Scovotti, Rosalind Elias, William Lewis, Robert Nagy, Lee Cass, William Chapman. (Reader's Digest 40-1, with Mademoiselle Modiste)

740405b DIE FLEDERMAUS soundtrack of 1955 film (entitled "Oh, Rosalinda!"). VOCALS: Walter Berry (for Anton Walbrook), Michael Redgrave, Sari Barabas (for Ludmilla Tcherina), Alexander Young (for Mel Ferrer), Annelise Rothenberger, Anthony Quayle, Dennis Dowling (for Dennis Price). (Mercury 20145)

740405c DIE FLEDERMAUS Metropolitan Opera (New York) prod. WORDS: Howard Dietz. COND: Tibor Kozma. CAST: Heidi Krall, Laurel Hurley, Mildred Miller, Brian Sullivan, John Brownlee, Clifford Harvuot. (Metropolitan Opera 518)

740405d DIE FLEDERMAUS 1945 records by members of 1945 London prod, entitled "Gay Rosalinda." COND: Richard Tauber. Overture (78/Col(E) DX-1203) Irene Ambrus: "Laughing Song," "Audition Song" (78/Col(E) DB-2187) Orchestra: Overture (78/Col(E) DX-1203)

740405e DIE FLEDERMAUS 1912 medley by Victor Light Opera Company. MUSIC & WORDS: Johann Strauss. Arthur Anderson, others. (78/Vic 31875, entitled "The Merry Countess," as was the 1912 New York prod)

740405f DIE FLEDERMAUS studio prod. WORDS: Howard Dietz. COND: Eugene Ormandy. CAST: Lily Pons, Ljuba Welitch, Richard Tucker, Charles Kullman, Martha Lipton, John Brownlee. (Col SL-108)

740405g DIE FLEDERMAUS 1964 studio prod. COND: Oscar Danon. CAST: Anna Moffo, Sergio Franchi, Rise Stevens, Jeanette Scovotti, Richard Lewis, George London, John Hauxvell. (RCA LSC-2728)

740405h DIE FLEDERMAUS 1959 London prod. WORDS: Christopher Hassall. COND: Vilem Tausky. CAST: John Heddle Nash, Alexander Young, Victoria Elliott, Marion Studholme, Rowland Jones, Frederick Sharp, Anna Pollak. (EMI(E) CSD-1266)

741111a GIROFLE-GIROFLA 1911 medley by Victor Light Opera Company. MUSIC: Charles Lecocq. WORDS: Harry B Smith. (78/Vic 31827)

770419a THE CHIMES OF NORMANDY 1912 medley by Columbia Light Opera Company. MUSIC: Robert Jean Planquette. WORDS: M Cooney. (78/Col A-5339)

770419b THE CHIMES OF NORMANDY 1910 medley by Victor Light Opera Company. (78/Vic 31788)

770419c THE CHIMES OF NORMANDY medley by Brunswick Light Opera Company. (78/Bruns 20020)

770419d THE CHIMES OF NORMANDY medley by Columbia Light Opera Company, entitled "Les Cloches de Corneville." (78/Col(E) DX-235)

770419e THE CHIMES OF NORMANDY 1930 medley by Light Opera Company, entitled "Les Cloches de Corneville." (78/HMV(E) C-2039)

770419f THE CHIMES OF NORMANDY medley by Zonophone

Light Opera Company, entitled "Les Cloches de Corneville." (78/ Zonophone(E) A-384)

770419g THE CHIMES OF NORMANDY medley by Zonophone Operatic Party, entitled "Les Cloches de Corneville." (78/ Zonophone(E) A-43)

770419h THE CHIMES OF NORMANDY medley by New York Light Opera Company. (78/Edison 80722)

791113a OLIVETTE 1909 medley by Victor Light Opera Company. MUSIC: Edmond Audran. WORDS: Henri Chivot, Alfred Duru. (78/Vic 31801)

791231a THE PIRATES OF PENZANCE 1981 New York prod. MUSIC: Arthur Sullivan. WORDS: William Gilbert. ORCH & COND: William Elliott. CAST: Kevin Kline, Estelle Parsons, Linda Ronstadt, George Rose, Rex Smith, Tony Azito, Stephan Hanan, Alexandra Korey, Marcie Shaw. (Elektra VE-601)

801001a THE QUEEN'S LACE HANDKERCHIEF 1912 medley by Victor Light Opera Company. MUSIC: Johann Strauss. WORDS: Louis C Elson. (78/Vic 31880)

801229a THE MASCOTTE 1910 medley by Victor Light Opera Company. MUSIC: Edmond Audran. WORDS: Alfred Duru, Henri Chivot. (78/Vic 31813)

831003a A NIGHT IN VENICE 1952 New York (Jones Beach) prod. MUSIC: Johann Strauss. WORDS: Ruth & Thomas Martin. COND: Thomas Martin. CAST: Enzo Stuarti, Thomas Tibbett Hayward, Norwood Smith, Guen Omeron, Jack Russell, Nola Fairbanks, Laurel Hurley, David Kurlan, Kenneth Schon. (Everest 3028)

831003b A NIGHT IN VENICE studio prod. WORDS: Norman Sachs, Mel Mandel. ORCH: Henri Rene. COND: Lehman Engel. CAST: Anna Moffo, Jeanette Scovotti, William Lewis, Peter Palmer, Stanley Grover, George Gaynes. (Reader's Digest 40-3, with Babes in Toyland)

850314a THE MIKADO 1960 TV prod. MUSIC: Arthur Sullivan. WORDS: William Gilbert. ORCH: Arthur Sullivan. COND: Donald Voorhees. CAST: Groucho Marx, Robert Rounseville, Stanley Holloway, Dennis King, Helen Traubel, Barbara Meister, Sharon Randall, Melinda Marx. (Col OS-2022)

850314b THE MIKADO 1939 radio performance by members of 1939 New York prod entitled "The Hot Mikado." Robert Parrish: "A Wand'ring Minstrel" Eddie Green: "Tit Willow" Bill Robinson, Rose Brown: "His Daughter-in-Law Elect" Robinson: "A More Humane Mikado" (LP-311)

850314c THE MIKADO soundtrack of 1963 film, entitled "The Cool Mikado." ORCH & COND: Martin Slavin. CAST: Stubby Kaye, Frankie Howerd, Tsai Chin, Kevin Scott, Dennis Price, Jill Mai Meredith, Jacqueline Jones. (Parlophone(E) PMC-1194)

850314d THE MIKADO 1975 London prod entitled "The Black Mikado." CAST: Michael Denison, Derek Griffiths, Val Pringle, Norman Beaton, Anita Tucker, Patricia Ebigwei. (Transatlantic(E) TRA-300)

851024a THE GYPSY BARON studio prod. MUSIC: Johann Strauss Jr. WORDS: Norman Sachs, Mel Mandel. ORCH: Henri Rene. COND: Lehman Engel. VOCALS: Jeanette Scovotti, Rosalind Elias, William Lewis, John Hauxvell. (Reader's Digest 46-N1, with No, No, Nanette)

851109a ERMINIE 1915 medley by Victor Light Opera Company. MUSIC: Edward Jacobowski. WORDS: Harry Paulton. (78/Vic 31818)

851109b ERMINIE 1911 medley by Columbia Light Opera Company. (78/Col A-5243)

851109c ERMINIE medley by New York Light Opera Company. (78/Edison 80689)

860925a DOROTHY 1911 medley by Light Opera Company. MUSIC: Alfred Cellier. WORDS: B C Stephenson. (78/HMV(E) C-515)

1891

910928a ROBIN HOOD records by members of orig cast. MUSIC: Reginald DeKoven. WORDS: Harry B Smith. Jessie Bartlett Davis: "O Promise Me" (1898: LP-778) Eugene Cowles: "The Armorer's Song" (1906: 78/Vic 4737) W H MacDonald: "The Armorer's Song" (1911: 78/Col A-963)

910928b ROBIN HOOD medleys by Victor Light Opera Company. (1909: 78/Vic 31768)(1912: 78/Vic 31868)(1915: 78/Vic 35413)(1926: 78/Vic 35784)

910928c ROBIN HOOD 1913 medley by Columbia Light Opera Company. (78/Col A-5402)

910928d ROBIN HOOD records by Wilfred Glenn of 1944 prod. "Armorer's Song" (1913: 78/Vic 17268)(1928: 78/Col 1439-D)

910928e ROBIN HOOD 1924 medley by Brunswick Light Opera Company. (78/Bruns 20016)

910928f ROBIN HOOD contemp records by members of 1919 prod. Herbert Waterous: "The Armorer's Song" Chorus: " The Tinkers' Chorus" (78/Pathe 50007) James Stevens, chorus: "Brown October Ale" Sextet: "Oh, See the Little Lambkins Play" (78/Pathe 50005) Waterous, chorus: "The Crow Song" Cora Tracey, chorus: "The Legend of the Chimes" (78/Pathe 50010) Ivy Scott: "The Forest Song" Tracey: "O, Promise Me" (78/Pathe 50009)

910928g ROBIN HOOD studio prod by Liverpool Light Opera Company. (REM 10" LP-9)

910928*a MAVOURNEEN 1913 record by Chauncey Olcott of 1895, 1896, & 1897 prods. "Molly O" (78/Col A-1309)

1893

930515a 1492 contemp records by Edward M Favor of orig cast. MUSIC: Carl Pflueger. WORDS: Robert Ayres Barnet. "Whisper Love" (CYL/Edison 972) (Excerpt: LP-571) "The King's Song" (CYL/ Col 6544)

931223a Opera HANSEL AND GRETEL 1954 film soundtrack. MUSIC: Engelbert Humperdinck. WORDS: Adelheid Wette, Padraic Colum. COND: Franz Allers. VOCALS: Anna Russell, Constance Brigham, Mildred Dunnock, Frank Rogier, Delbert Anderson, Helen Boatwright. (RCA LXA-1013)

931223b Opera HANSEL AND GRETEL 1946 record prod. COND: Carmen Dragon. NARRATOR: Basil Rathbone. VOCALS: Jane Powell, Rece Saxon. (Col 10" ML-2055)

931223c Opera HANSEL AND GRETEL album by Jane Pickens, narration & vocals. COND: Harry Sosnik. (78/Vic BY-14)

1894

940101a A COUNTRY GIRL 1911 medley by Victor Light Opera Company. MUSIC: Lionel Monckton, Paul Rubens. WORDS: Adrian Ross, Percy Greenbank. (78/Vic 31838)

940101b A COUNTRY GIRL 1902 records by members of 1902 London prod. Evie Greene: "Try Again, Johnny" (LP-524) "Not the Little Boy She Knew" (78/G&T(E) GC-3419) Isobel Jay: "Coo" (78/ G&T(E) GC-3530) Henry Lytton: "Peace, Peace" (78/G&T(E) 2-2111) "Me and Mrs Brown" (78/G&T(E) 2-2136) Lytton & Louie Henri (not of 1902 cast): "Two Little Chicks" (78/G&T(E) 4062) "Quarrelling Duet" (78/G&T(E) 4084)

940101c A COUNTRY GIRL 1930 medley by Columbia Light Opera Company. (78/Col(E) DX-73)

941029a ROB ROY 1912 medley by Victor Light Opera Company. MUSIC: Reginald De Koven. WORDS: Harry B Smith. (78/Vic 31858)

941029b ROB ROY 1913 record by Frank Pollock & Henrietta Wakefield of 1913 prod. "Who Can Tell Me Where She Dwells?" (78/Vic 70101)

941029c ROB ROY 1914 medley by Columbia Light Opera Company. (78/Col A-5508)

941029c ROB ROY 1914 medley by Columbia Light Opera Company. (78/Col A-5508)

941124a THE SHOP GIRL 1932 record by Seymour Hicks of orig (London) & 1895 New York prods. MUSIC & WORDS: Ivan Caryll, H J Dam, Adrian Ross, Lionel Monckton. "And Her Golden Hair Was Hanging Down Her Back" (78/HMV(E) C-2432)

1895

950202a AN ARTIST'S MODEL records by Maurice Farkoa of orig (London) & 1896 New York prods. "Laughing Song" (1896, in English: 78/Berliner 1302)(1898, in French: 78/Berliner(E) 2125. Excerpt: LP-531)(1898, in English: 78/Berliner(E) 2128)(1899, in French: 78/Berliner(E) 32111, 32654)(1905, in French: G&T(E) GC3-2261)

950415a TRILBY 1915 records by George MacFarlane of 1915 prod. "To the Lass We Love, a Toast," "A Breath o' Blooming Heather" (78/Vic 45068)

950916a THE WIDOW JONES 1907 record by May Irwin of orig cast. "The Bully" (78/Vic 31642)

951104a THE WIZARD OF THE NILE 1911 medley by Victor Light Opera Company. MUSIC: Victor Herbert. WORDS: Harry B Smith. (78/Vic 31834)

951104b THE WIZARD OF THE NILE Schenectady, N Y, prod. COND: Edward J Hatfield Jr. CAST: Emerson Smith, Sylvia Horovitz, Dick Babbitt, Julie Shirk, Ed Curry, Peggy Coe. (Schenectady Light Opera Company 101/102)

1896

960302a SHAMUS O'BRIEN 1916 recording of the Overture by orchestra cond by the composer. MUSIC & WORDS: Charles Stanford. (78/HMV(E) 2-0699)

960302b SHAMUS O'BRIEN 1901 record by Joseph O'Mara of orig (London) & 1897 New York casts. "Ochone! I When Used to Be Young" (78/G&T(E) GC2-2567)

960425a THE GEISHA records by members of orig (London) prod. MUSIC & WORDS: Sidney Jones, Harry Greenbank, others. Marie Tempest, 1901: "The Jewel of Asia" (LP-524) Conway Dixon, 1903: "Jack's the Boy" (78/Zonophone(E) X-2291)

960425b THE GEISHA 1931 medley by Light Opera Company. (78/HMV(E) C-2144)

960425c THE GEISHA 1930 medley by Columbia Light Opera Company. (78/Col(E) DX-256)

961205a THE CIRCUS GIRL 1903 record by Ellaline Terriss of orig (London) cast. "Just a Little Piece of String" (78/G&T(E) GC-3440)

961228a AN AMERICAN BEAUTY 1900 record by Edna May of 1900 London prod. MUSIC: Gustave Kerker. WORDS: C M S McLellan ("Hugh Morton"). "Dear Little Baby" (78/ Berliner(E) 3191)

1897

970125a SWEET INNISCARRA 1913 record by Chauncey Olcott of orig cast. "Sweet Inniscarra" (78/Col A-1309)

970316a THE SERENADE 1910 medley by Victor Light Opera Company. MUSIC: Victor Herbert. WORDS: Harry B Smith. (78/Vic 31811)

970316b THE SERENADE medley by Columbia Light Opera Company. (78/Col A-5520)

970316c THE SERENADE 1898 record by W H MacDonald & Jessie Bartlett Davis of orig cast. "Don Jose of Sevilla" (78/Berliner 3020)

970928a THE BELLE OF NEW YORK records by members of 1898 London cast. MUSIC: Gustave Kerker. WORDS: C M S McLellan ("Hugh Morton"). Edna May (also of orig (New York) cast), 1900: "They all Follow Me," "The Purity Brigade" (LP-524) Frank Lawton, 1898: "She Is the Belle of New York'" (78/Berliner(E) 2265)

970928b THE BELLE OF NEW YORK 1929 medley by Columbia Light Opera Company. (78/Col(E) 9925)

970928c THE BELLE OF NEW YORK 1958 album. COND: Michael Collins. VOCALS: Barry Kent, Mary Thomas, chorus. (Encore(E) 178, with The Maid of the Mountains, No, No, Nanette, & others)

970928d THE BELLE OF NEW YORK 1913 medley by Victor Light Opera Company. (78/Vic 31887)

971025a THE IDOL'S EYE 1910 medley by orchestra cond by Victor Herbert, composer. (LP-629)

971116a THE LITTLE MICHUS 1905 records by members of 1905 London prod. MUSIC: Andre Messager. WORDS: Percy Greenbank. Louis Bradfield: "This Little Girl and That" (78/G&T(E) GC-2364) (78/G&T(E) 3-2626) Robert Evett: "It's No Use Crying for the Moon" (78/Odeon(E) 44055) Denise Orme, Gladys Roberts: "Prayer to St Valentine" (78/G&T(E) GC-4385)

971202a POUSSE CAFE 1912 record by Weber & Fields of orig cast. Skit "Contract Scene" (78/Col A-1219)

1898

980521a A RUNAWAY GIRL 1911 medley by Victor Light Opera Company. MUSIC: Ivan Caryll, Lionel Monckton. WORDS: Aubrey Hopwood, Harry Greenbank. (78/Vic 31845)

980521b A RUNAWAY GIRL records by members of orig (London) cast. Ellaline Terriss, 1903: "The Boy Guessed Right," "For There's No One in the World like You" (78/G&T(E) 03006)(78/G&T(E) GC-3457) Connie Ediss, 1900: "Oh! I Love Society" (LP-524)

980608a A GREEK SLAVE contemp records by Scott Russell of orig (London) cast. MUSIC: Sidney Jones. WORDS: Harry Greenbank, Adrian Ross. "Saturnalia" (78/Berliner(E) 2338) "The Girl of My Heart" (78/Berliner(E) 2984)

980908a HURLEY BURLEY 1912 record by Weber & Fields of orig cast. Skit "Hypnotic Scene" (78/Col A-1159)

980926a THE FORTUNE TELLER records by members of orig cast. MUSIC: Victor Herbert. WORDS: Harry B Smith. Eugene Cowles: "Gypsy Love Song" (1898: 78/Berliner 1909)(1906: LP-628) Alice Nielsen: "Always Do as People Say You Should" Chorus: "Opening Chorus of Schoolgirls" (1898: LP-628)

980926b THE FORTUNE TELLER 1911 medley by Victor Light Opera Company. (LP-628)

980926c THE FORTUNE TELLER medleys by orchestra cond by Victor Herbert, composer. (1903: LP-628)(1910: LP-629)

980926d THE FORTUNE TELLER medley by New York Light Opera Company. (78/Edison 80823)

981210a VERONIQUE medleys by Light Opera Company. MUSIC: Andre Messager. WORDS: Lilian Eldee, Percy Greenbank. (1913: 78/HMV(E) C-520)(1929: 78/HMV(E) C-1684)

981210b VERONIQUE 1931 medley by Columbia Light Opera Company. (78/Col(E) DX-303)

1899

990109a A ROMANCE OF ATHLONE 1913 record by Chauncey Olcott of orig & 1901 casts. MUSIC & WORDS: Chauncey Olcott. "My Wild Irish Rose" (LP-324)

990921a WHIRL-I-GIG 1912 record by Weber & Fields of orig cast. Skit "Drinking Scene" (78/Col A-1159)

991021a SAN TOY 1910 medley by Victor Light Opera Company. MUSIC: Sidney Jones, Lionel Monckton. WORDS: Adrian Ross, Harry Greenbank. (78/Vic 31778)

991021b SAN TOY contemp records by members of orig (London) prod. Scott Russell: "When You Are Wed to Me" (78/Berliner(E) 4082-X) "The One in the World" (78/ Berliner(E) 2960) "Love Has Come from the Lotus Land" (78/Berliner(E) 2985) "Little Chinee Maid" (78/Berliner(E) 4078) Conway Dixon: "Lotus Land" (78/Zon-ophone(E) X-2290) Chorus: "I Mean to Introduce It into China" (78/Berliner(E) 4518) "The Emperor's Own" (78/Berliner(E) 4519) "The Moon" (78/Berliner(E) 4520)

991023a THE SINGING GIRL medley by Columbia Light Opera Company. MUSIC: Victor Herbert. WORDS: Harry B Smith. (78/Col A-5423)

991023b THE SINGING GIRL 1910 medley by orchestra cond by Victor Herbert, composer. (LP-629)

991111a FLORODORA 1930 medley by Columbia Light Opera Company. MUSIC & WORDS: Leslie Stuart, others. (78/Col(E) DX-126)

991111b FLORODORA 1902 record by three unidentified Floro-dora girls of 1900 New York cast & three men. "Tell Me, Pretty Maiden" (78/Col 647)

991111c FLORODORA 1911 medley by Victor Light Opera Company. (78/Vic 31817)

991111d FLORODORA medleys by Columbia Light Opera Company, (1911:78/Col A-5326) (1920:78/Col A-6158)

991111e FLORODORA medley by Brunswick Light Opera Company. (78/Bruns 20021)

991111f FLORODORA medleys by Light Opera Company. (1913: 78/HMV(E) 04534)(1931: 78/HMV(E) C-2253)

991111g FLORODORA 1900 records by members of orig (London) cast. Louis Bradfield: "I Want to Be a Military Man" (78/Berliner(E) 4521)(1903: 78/Zonophone(E) X-2289) "Phrenology" (78/Berliner(E) 4522) "Burlesque on 'Pretty Maidens'" (78/Berliner(E) 2935) Bradfield, Kate Cutler: "Galloping" (78/Berliner(E) 4119) Cutler: "Willie Was a Gay Boy" (78/Berliner(E) 3205) "Whistling" (78/Berliner(E) 3204) Ada Reeve: "Tact" (78/Berliner(E) 3210) "Queen of the Phillipine Islands" (78/Berliner(E) 3209) "I've an Inkling" (78/Berliner(E) 3211) Florence St John: "He Loves Me, He Loves Me Not" (78/Berliner(E) 3200) Chorus: "Tell Me, Pretty Maiden" (78/Berliner(E) 4524) "Opening Chorus" (78/Berliner(E) 4523)

991129a THE ROSE OF PERSIA 1912 record by C H Workman of orig (London) cast. MUSIC: Arthur Sullivan. WORDS: Basil Hood. "The Small Street Arab" (78/Odeon(E) 0851)

1900

000203a THE MESSENGER BOY records by members of orig (London) prod. MUSIC: Ivan Caryll, Lionel Monckton. WORDS: Adrian Ross, Percy Greenbank. Connie Ediss, 1900: "Comme ci, comme ca" (78/Berliner(E) 3161) "It All Comes Out in the Wash" (78/Berliner(E) 3160) Fred Wright Jr, 1904: "Captain Potts" (78/G&T(E) GC-3-2039)

000319a THE CASINO GIRL 1907 records by Marie George of 1900 London prod. MUSIC: Ludwig Englander. WORDS: Harry B Smith. "Mam'selle," "De Voodoo Man" (78/ Favorite(E) 1-66034)

000402a THE POLICY PLAYERS 1901 record by Bert Williams of orig cast. "The Ghost of a Coon" (78/Vic 998)

1901

010601a THE SILVER SLIPPER contemp records by members of orig (London) cast. MUSIC: Leslie Stuart. WORDS: W H Risque. Louis Bradfield: "The Detrimental Man" (78/G&T(E) GC-2433) "A Happy Day" (78/G&T(E) GC-2414) "Clytie" (78/Col(E) 25155) Connie Ediss: "Good Behaviour" (78/G&T(E) GC-3266) "Class" (78/ G&T(E) GC-3267)

010617a THE TOREADOR records by members of orig (London) cast. Connie Ediss, 1903: "Maud" (78/G&T(E) GC-3447) Gertie Millar, 1938: "Keep Off the Grass" (LP-524)

010617b THE TOREADOR 1902 records by William H Thompson of 1902 New York prod. "In the Moonlight with the Girl You Love" (CYL/Edison 8044) "Toreador's Song" (CYL/Edison 8245)

010907a KITTY GREY 1901 record by Maurice Farkoa of orig (London) cast. MUSIC & WORDS: Lionel Monckton, Howard Talbot, Adrian Ross, others. "Kitty Grey" (78/G&T(E) GC-2-2528)

011005a A CHINESE HONEYMOON 1902 records by members of orig (London) prod. MUSIC: Howard Talbot. WORDS: George Dance. Marie Dainton: "The A La Girl" (78/G&T(E) GC-3409) "That's All" (78/G&T(E) GC-3415) "Sweet Little Sing-Sing" (78/G&T(E) GC-3416) "Mary Was a Housemaid" (78/G&T(E) GC-3417) Louie Freear: "I Want to Be a Laidy" (78/G&T(E) GC-3412)

1902

020303a SONS OF HAM 1901 records by members of orig cast. Bert Williams: "All Going Out and Nothing Coming In" (78/Vic 994) "The Phrenologist Coon" (78/Vic 992) "My Little Zulu Babe" (78/Vic 1084) Williams, George Walker: "My Little Zulu Babe" (78/Vic 1086)

020510a THREE LITTLE MAIDS 1902 records by members of orig (London) prod. MUSIC & WORDS: mostly by Paul Rubens. Madge Crichton (also of 1903 New York prod): "My Gal Sal" (78/G&T(E) GC-3425) "Men" (78/G&T(E) GC-3426) "Something Sweet about Me" (78/G&T(E) GC-3427) G P Huntley (also of 1903 New York prod): "Algy's Simply Awf'lly Good at Algebra" (78/G&T(E) GC2-2762) Huntley, George Carroll: skit "The Golf Scene" (78/G&T(E) GC-1233) (1907: 78/G&T(E) GC-1372)

020512a KING DODO 1912 medley by Victor Light Opera Company. MUSIC: Gustav Luders. WORDS: Frank Pixley. (78/Vic 31884)

020605a THE CHAPERONS contemp records by members of orig cast. Walter Jones: "Somehow It Made Me Think of Home" (78/

Vic Monmouth M-3622) Joseph C Miron: "My Low C" (78/Vic Monmouth M-3621)

020829a SALLY IN OUR ALLEY 1917 record by Marie Cahill of orig cast. "Under the Bamboo Tree" (78/Vic 45125)

020911a TWIRLY WHIRLY 1912 record by Lillian Russell of orig cast. "Come Down, Ma Evenin' Star" (LP-323) (LP-579) (Incomplete: LP-20)

021110a THE MOCKING BIRD 1915 medley by Victor Opera Company. MUSIC: A Baldwin Sloane. WORDS: Sydney Rosenfeld. (78/Vic 35473)

021115a THE GIRL FROM KAY'S 1903 records by Louis Bradfield of orig (London) prod. MUSIC & WORDS: Ivan Caryll, Adrian Ross, others. "Matilda and the Builder" (78/Zonophone(E) X-2283) (78/Col(E) 25152) "I Don't Care" (78/Zonophone(E) X-2284) (78/G&T(E) 02041) (78/Col(E) 25157) "The Customers at Kay's" (78/Zonophone(E) X-2285) (78/G&T(E) GC2-2931) (78/Col(E) 25156) "Mr Hoggenheimer" (78/G&T(E) GC2-2932) "Remorse" (78/G&T(E) 02042) "A Little Thing like That" (78/G&T(E) 02033) "Glass, Glass" (78/G&T(E) GC2-2946) "The Philosopher" (78/G&T(E) GC2-2999) "Mr Mosenstein" (78/G&T(E) 25151) "A High Old Time" (78/Col(E) 25160)

021216a WHEN JOHNNY COMES MARCHING HOME contemp records by William H Thompson. "Katie, My Southern Rose" (CYL/Edison 8315) "My Own United States" (CYL/Edison 8329)

021229a THE SULTAN OF SULU 1911 medley by Victor Light Opera Company. MUSIC: Alfred G Wathall. WORDS: George Ade. (78/Vic 31850)

1903

030216a NANCY BROWN 1917 record by Marie Cahill of orig cast. "Under the Bamboo Tree" (78/Vic 45125)

030314a MY LADY MOLLY 1907 record by Walter Hyde of orig (London) prod. MUSIC: Sidney Jones. WORDS: George H Jessup, others. "There's a Little Maid I Know" (78/Odeon(E) 0222)

030317a THE PRINCE OF PILSEN medley by Columbia Light Opera Company. MUSIC: Gustav Luders. WORDS: Frank Pixley. (78/Col A-5411)

030317b THE PRINCE OF PILSEN 1911 medley by Victor Light Opera Company. (78/Vic 31795)

030317c THE PRINCE OF PILSEN medley by Brunswick Light Opera Company. (78/Bruns 20012)

031013a BABES IN TOYLAND studio prod. MUSIC: Victor Herbert. WORDS: Glen MacDonough. COND: Lehman Engel. CAST: Mary Ellen Pracht, Jeanette Scovotti, Sara Endich, Patricia Kelly, Peter Palmer, Mallory Walker. (Reader's Digest 40-3, with A Night in Venice)

031013b BABES IN TOYLAND 1946 studio prod. COND: Alexander Smallens. CAST: Kenny Baker, Karen Kemple, chorus. (Dec 10" 7004. Incomplete: Dec 8458, with The Red Mill)

031013c BABES IN TOYLAND 1961 film prod. MUSIC: Victor Herbert, George Bruns. WORDS: Mel Leven. CAST: Ray Bolger, Tommy Sands, Annette Funicello, Ed Wynn, Henry Calvin, Ann Jilliann, Mary McCarthy. (Disneyland 1219)

031013d BABES IN TOYLAND 1910 medley by Victor Light Opera Company. (78/Vic 31814)

031013e BABES IN TOYLAND c. 1930 medley by Victor Light Opera Company. COND: Nathaniel Shilkret. (LP-304)

031013f BABES IN TOYLAND 1938 medley. COND: Nathaniel

Shilkret. VOCALS: Ann Jamison, Gladys Rice, chorus. (LP-305) (LP-767)

031013g BABES IN TOYLAND soundtrack of 1934 film, with interpolated material. VOCALS: Felix Knight, Charlotte Henry. (Mark 56 Records 577)

031013h BABES IN TOYLAND records by orchestra cond by Victor Herbert, composer. 1911: "March of the Toys" 1912: "The Toymaker's Shop," "Kiss Me Again" (LP-628) 1909: Medley (LP-629)

031013i BABES IN TOYLAND studio prod. VOCALS: Jane Conners, Bill Anders, Jack Mitchell. (Happy Time 1002)

031013j BABES IN TOYLAND studio prod. ORCH & COND: Jim Timmens. VOCALS: The Sandpipers. (Golden 78)

031013k BABES IN TOYLAND soundtrack of 1979 stage prod. Adaptations & new music & lyrics by Shelly Markham & Annette Leisten. ORCH: Bob Christianson, Kirk Nurock. COND: Bob Christianson. VOCALS: uncredited. (Babes in Toyland 91550)

031017a THE DUCHESS OF DANTZIC medleys by Light Opera Company. MUSIC: Ivan Caryll. WORDS: Henry Hamilton. (1913: 78/HMV(E) 04535) (1931: 78/HMV(E) C-2262)

031026a THE ORCHID contemp records by Fred Wright Jr of orig (London) cast. "Bunny at the Bun Shop" (78/Col(E) 25203) (78/G&T(E) GC3-2044) "Little Mary" (78/G&T(E) GC3-2022) "Liza Ann" (78/G&T(E) GC3-2023) "The Emperor of Sahara" (78/G&T(E) GC3-2038)

031116a BABETTE 1931 medley by Victor Salon Group. MUSIC: Victor Herbert. WORDS: Harry B Smith. COND: Nathaniel Shilkret. (LP-767) (LP-777)

031202a MOTHER GOOSE 1911 records sung by the composer. MUSIC & WORDS: George M Cohan. "I Want to Hear a Yankee Doodle Tune" (LP-214) (LP-758) (Incomplete: LP-20, LP-365, LP-542) "Hey There! May There!" (78/Vic 60049) (Incomplete: LP-365)

031210a THE EARL AND THE GIRL 1904 records by members of orig (London) cast. MUSIC: Ivan Caryll. WORDS: Percy Greenbank. Henry Lytton: "My Cosy Corner Girl" (78/G&T(E) 2-2462) "By the Shore of the Mediterranean" (78/G&T(E) 2-2463)

031223a MADAME SHERRY 1911 medley by Victor Light Opera Company. MUSIC: Karl Hoschna. WORDS: Otto Harbach. (78/Vic 31824)

1904

040222a THE YANKEE CONSUL 1910 records by Raymond Hitchcock of orig cast. MUSIC: Alfred G Robyn. WORDS: Henry Blossom. "Ain't It Funny What a Difference Just a Few Hours Make?" (78/Col A-5231) "In the Days of Old" (78/Col A-5257)

040305a THE CINGALEE contemp records by members of orig (London) cast. MUSIC & WORDS: Lionel Monckton, Paul Rubens, Adrian Ross, Percy Greenbank. Louis Bradfield: "The Ladies" (78/G&T(E) GC3-2589) "Four Little Girls of Ceylon" (78/G&T(E) GC3-2244) Bradfield, Isobel Jay: "A Marriage Has Been Arranged" (78/G&T(E) GC-4372) "You and I" (78/G&T(E) GC-4373)

040502a THE MAN FROM CHINA record by Stella Mayhew of orig cast. "Fifty-seven Ways to Catch a Man" (78/Edison D-23)

040614a SERGEANT BRUE 1904 records by Olive Morrell of orig (London) cast. MUSIC: Liza Lehman. WORDS: J Hickory Wood. "Under a Panama" (78/Pathe(E) 50220) "The Sweetest Girl in Dixie" (78/Pathe(E) 50221)

040614b SERGEANT BRUE 1905 record by Harry MacDonough of 1905 New York prod. "Dearie" (CYL/Edison 9054)

041003a LOVE'S LOTTERY contemp record by Ernestine Schumann-Heink of orig cast. MUSIC: Julian Edwards. WORDS: Stanislaus Stange. "Sweet Thoughts of Home" (LP-748)

041107a LITTLE JOHNNY JONES records by George M Cohan of orig cast. MUSIC & WORDS: George M Cohan. "I'm Mighty Glad I'm Living, That's All" (1911: LP-214) "Life's a Funny Proposition after All" (1911: LP-44, LP-214, LP-323, LP-365, LP-539, LP-711) "Give My Regards to Broadway," "The Yankee Doodle Boy" (1938?: LP-467)(1941 radio performance: LP-38, LP-321, LP-365, LP-467)

041205a IT HAPPENED IN NORDLAND 1912 medley by Victor Light Opera Company. MUSIC: Victor Herbert. WORDS: Glen MacDonough. (78/Vic 31851)

041205b IT HAPPENED IN NORDLAND 1911 record by orchestra cond by Victor Herbert, composer. "Al Fresco" (LP-628)

041217a LADY MADCAP records by members of orig (London) prod(retitled "My Lady's Maid" for 1906 New York Prod). MUSIC & WORDS: Paul Rubens, Percy Greenbank. Maurice Farkoa: "I Like You in Velvet" (1905: 78/G&T(E) GC3- 2254) (1908: 78/HMV(E) 4-2016) (1910: 78/Pathe(E) 694) "Do I Like Love" (1905:78/G&T(E) GC3-2255) Farkoa, Delia Mason: "My Portuguese Princess" (1905: 78/G&T(E) GC-4374)

1905

050821a THE PEARL AND THE PUMPKIN 1905 records by Harry MacDonough of orig cast. "Honeymoon Hall" (CYL/Edison 9126) "Lily White" (CYL/Edison 9151)

050828a THE HAM TREE 1905 records by Harry Tally of orig cast. "Good-bye, Sweet Manhattan Isle" (78/Col 3277) "On an Automobile Honeymoon" (78/Vic 4592)

051016a FRITZ IN TAMMANY HALL 1910 record by Stella Mayhew of orig cast. "I'm a Woman of Importance"(CYL/Edison 4M-374)

051225a MADEMOISELLE MODISTE studio prod. MUSIC: Victor Herbert. WORDS: Henry Blossom. ORCH: Henri Rene. COND: Lehman Engel. CAST: Jeanette Scovotti, Sara Endich, Patricia Kelly, Evelyn Sachs, Arthur Rubin, Robert Nagy, Kenneth Smith. (Reader's Digest 40-1, with Die Fledermaus)

051225b MADEMOISELLE MODISTE 1953 album. COND: Jay Blackton. CAST: Doretta Morrow, Felix Knight, Robert Roecker. (RCA 10" LPM-3153, with Naughty Marietta)

051225c MADEMOISELLE MODISTE 1910 medley by Victor Light Opera Company. (LP-628)

051225d MADEMOISELLE MODISTE 1909 record of ballet music. COND: Victor Herbert, composer. (LP-629)

051230a THE MERRY WIDOW 1952 studio prod. MUSIC: Franz Lehar. WORDS: Adrian Ross. COND: Lehman Engel. CAST: Dorothy Kirsten, Robert Rounseville, Genevieve Warner, Clifford Harvuot, Wesley Dalton, Betty Bartley. (Col ML-4666)

051230b THE MERRY WIDOW records by Jeanette MacDonald of 1934 film cast. 1934: "Vilia" (LP-71) (LP-536) "I Love You So" (LP-77) "Tonight Will Teach Me to Forget" (LP-536) 1949: "Vilia" (45/RCA 49-0773)

051230c THE MERRY WIDOW studio prod. COND: Al Goodman. CAST: Donald Richards, Elaine Malbin, Nino Ventura. (RCA LK-1020)

051230d THE MERRY WIDOW 1952 film soundtrack. WORDS: Paul Francis Webster. ORCH & COND: Jay Blackton. CAST: Fernando Lamas, Trudy Erwin (for Lana Turner), Richard Haydn. (MGM 10" 157)

051230e THE MERRY WIDOW studio prod. WORDS: Norman Sachs, Mel Mandel. ORCH: Henri Rene. COND: Lehman Engel. CAST: Anna Moffo, Mary Ellen Pracht, William Lewis, Arthur Rubin, Robert Nagy, Kenneth Smith. (Reader's Digest 40-2, with A Waltz Dream).

051230f THE MERRY WIDOW 1953 studio prod. COND: George Greeley. CAST: Gordon MacRae, Lucille Norman, chorus. (Cap 10" L-335)

051230g THE MERRY WIDOW 1944 studio prod. COND: Isaac van Grove. CAST: Kitty Carlisle & Wilbur Evans of 1943 Boston prod; Lisette Verea of 1944 New York prod; Felix Knight. (Dec 8004)

051230h THE MERRY WIDOW 1949 album by Rise Stevens & Dennis Morgan. COND: Max Rudolf. (Col 10" ML-2064)

051230i THE MERRY WIDOW 1962 studio prod. WORDS: Merl Puffer, Deena Cavalieri. COND: Franz Allers. CAST: Lisa Della Casa, John Reardon, Laurel Hurley, Charles K L Davis, Paul Franke, Howard Kahl, Paul Richards. (Col OS-2280)

051230j THE MERRY WIDOW 1932 record by Carl Brisson of 1932 English touring prod. "Maxim's" (LP-122)

051230k THE MERRY WIDOW 1964 New York prod. WORDS: Forman Brown. COND: Franz Allers. CAST: Patrice Munsel, Bob Wright, Sig Arno, Frank Porretta, Joan Weldon, Mischa Auer, Joseph Leon, Robert Goss, Rudy Vejar. (RCA LSO-1094)

051230l THE MERRY WIDOW 1959 studio prod. WORDS: Christopher Hassall. COND: William Reid. CAST: Thomas Round, June Bronhill, Howell Glynne, Marion Lowe, William McAlpine, Denis Dowling, John Kentish. (Angel 35816)

051230m THE MERRY WIDOW 1910 medley by Victor Light Opera Company. (78/Vic 31805)

051230n THE MERRY WIDOW medley by Light Opera Company. (78/Vic 36101)

051230o THE MERRY WIDOW 1968 studio prod. WORDS: Christopher Hassall. COND: Vilem Tausky. CAST: June Bronhill, Jeremy Brett, David Hughes, Ann Howard, Leslie Fyson, Neil Howlett, Edgar Fleet. (Col(E) TWO-234)

051230p THE MERRY WIDOW studio prod. WORDS: Christopher Hassall. COND: John Hollingsworth. CAST: Jacqueline Delman, John Larson, John Wakefield, Barbara Elsy, Edward Brooks, Robert Bowman, David Price, Geoffrey Shaw, Geoffrey Walls. (World Record Club(E) TP-60)

051230q THE MERRY WIDOW 1907 records by members of 1907 London prod. Robert Evett, Elizabeth Firth: "A Dutiful Wife" (78/Odeon(E) A-122) "Love In My Heart Awakening" (78/Odeon(E) A-128) Evett: "Home" (78/Odeon(E) A-140)

051230r THE MERRY WIDOW medley by Columbia Light Opera Company. (78/Col(E) DX-159)

051230s THE MERRY WIDOW 1978 New York prod. WORDS: Sheldon Harnick. COND: Julius Rudel. CAST: Beverly Sills, Alan Titus, Glenys Fowles, Henry Price, James Billings, David Rae Smith, chorus. (Angel S-37500)

051230t THE MERRY WIDOW 1977 Scottish prod. COND: Alexander Gibson. CAST: Catherine Wilson, Jonny Blanc, Patricia Hay, David Hillman, chorus. (Music for Pleasure (E) CFP-40276)

051230u THE MERRY WIDOW 1934 medley. COND: H Leopold Spitalny. VOCALS: Bernice Claire, Henry M Shope, Walter Preston, chorus. (78/Dec 15001)

051230v THE MERRY WIDOW 1934 film soundtrack. WORDS: Lorenz Hart, Gus Kahn. COND: Herbert Stothart. CAST: Jeanette MacDonald, Maurice Chevalier. (Nadine 260, with The Love Parade)

051230w THE MERRY WIDOW medley by Zonophone Light Opera Company. (78/Zonophone(E) A-367)

1906

060212a GEORGE WASHINGTON, JR. 1941 radio performance by George M Cohan of orig cast. MUSIC & WORDS: George M Cohan. "You're a Grand Old Flag" (LP-365) (LP-467)

060220a ABYSSINIA records by members of orig cast. Bert Williams: "Nobody" (1906: LP-639) (1913: LP-20, LP-157, LP-323, LP-758) "Let It Alone" (1906: 78/Col 3504) Williams, George Walker: "Pretty Desdemona" (1906: 78/Col 3410)

060421a THE GIRL BEHIND THE COUNTER 1906 records by members of orig (London) prod. MUSIC & WORDS: mostly Howard Talbot, Arthur Anderson. Fred Allandale: "Enid, the Vicar's Daughter" (78/Favorite(E) 1-65030) "If It Wasn't for the Apple on the Tree" (78/Favorite(E) 1-67001) Isobel Jay: "I Want to Marry a Man" (78/ Favorite(E) 1-66015) Jay, E Gordon Cleather: "Won't You Buy?" (78/Favorite(E) 1-69003)

060430a THE DISTRICT LEADER 1947 record sung by the composer, who was also in the orig prod. MUSIC & WORDS: Joe Howard. "What's the Use of Dreaming?" (LP-369)

060924a THE RED MILL 1955 studio prod. MUSIC: Victor Herbert. WORDS: Henry Blossom. COND: Carmen Dragon. CAST: Gordon MacRae, Lucille Norman. (Cap 10" L-530)

060924b THE RED MILL 1946 studio prod. COND: Al Goodman CAST: Earl Wrightson, Mary Martha Briney, Donald Dame, the Mullen Sisters. (RCA LK-1016)

060924c THE RED MILL studio prod. ORCH: Henri Rene. COND: Lehman Engel. CAST: Mary Ellen Pracht, Jean Sanders, Evelyn Sachs, Richard Fredericks, Williams Chapman, Stanley Grover. (Reader's Digest 40-6, with The Student Prince)

060924d THE RED MILL 1946 studio prod. COND: Jay Blackton. CAST: Wilbur Evans, Eileen Farrell, Felix Knight. (Dec 8016, with Up in Central Park)

060924e THE RED MILL 1911 medley by Victor Light Opera Company. (78/Vic 31794)

060924f THE RED MILL 1930 medley by Victor Light Opera Company. COND: Nathaniel Shilkret. (LP-304)

060924g THE RED MILL 1938 medley. COND: Nathaniel Shilkret. VOCALS: Anne Jamison, Thomas L Thomas, Jan Peerce, chorus. (LP-305) (LP-767)

060924h THE RED MILL 1909 medley by orchestra cond by Victor Herbert, composer. (LP-629)

060924i THE RED MILL 1979 studio prod. ORCH: Gregg Smith. COND: Carl Eberl. CAST: Rosalind Rees, Leonard Van Camp, Michael Wilson, Kimball Wheeler, Samantha Genton, Mukund Marathe, William Powell, Walter Richardson, chorus. (Turnabout 34766)

061127a THE PARISIAN MODEL 1907 record by Henri Leoni of orig cast. "I Love You, Ma Cherie" (78/Vic 5201)

1907

070131a MISS HOOK OF HOLLAND 1930 medley by Light Opera Company. MUSIC & WORDS: Paul Rubens. (78/HMV(E) C-1989)

070216a THE WHITE HEN 1908 record by Ralph C Herz of orig cast. "Very Well, Then" (78/Vic 5661)

070218a THE TATTOOED MAN 1909 medley by orchestra cond by Victor Herbert, composer. (LP-629)

070302a A WALTZ DREAM studio prod. MUSIC: Oscar Straus. WORDS: Norman Sachs, Mel Mandel. ORCH: Henri Rene. COND: Lehman Engel. CAST: Jeanette Scovotti, Mary Ellen Pracht, Evelyn Sachs, Mallory Walker, William Chapman, George Gaynes. (Reader's Digest 40-2, with the Merry Widow)

070302b A WALTZ DREAM 1960 studio prod. WORDS: Adrian Ross. COND: Michael Collins. CAST: June Bronhill, David Hughes, Marion Grimaldi, chorus. (HMV(E) CSD-1321)

070302c A WALTZ DREAM 1908 records by Robert Evett of 1908 London prod. WORDS: Adrian Ross. "The Dream Waltz," "My Dear Little Maiden" (78/Odeon(E) 0413)

070417a TOM JONES 1967 studio prod. MUSIC: Edward German. WORDS: Charles M Taylor. COND: Gilbert Vinter. CAST: Frederick Harvey, Cynthia Glover, Shirley Minty, Stanley Riley, chorus. (HMV(E) CSD-3628)

070417b TOM JONES 1907 record by Ruth Vincent of orig (London) prod. "Waltz Song" (78/Col(E) 6009)

070805a THE TIME, THE PLACE AND THE GIRL records by Joe Howard, composer & member of 1942 cast. MUSIC: Joe Howard. WORDS: Will Hough, Frank Adams. 1929: "Honeymoon," "Blow the Smoke Away" (78/Bruns 4340) 1936: "Honeymoon" (78/Vocalion 3357)

070812a A YANKEE TOURIST 1910 record by Raymond Hitchcock of orig cast. MUSIC: Alfred G Robyn. WORDS: Wallace Irwin. "So What's the Use?" (78/Col A-5165)

1908

080121a THE MAN WITH THREE WIVES 1913 medley by Victor Light Opera Company. MUSIC: Franz Lehar. WORDS: Various. (78/Vic 31883)

080128a THE SOUL KISS 1908 records by Ralph C Herz of orig cast. "Very Well, Then" (78/Vic 5661) "That Wasn't All" (78/Vic 5654)

080203a FIFTY MILES FROM BOSTON 1911 record by George M Cohan of orig cast. MUSIC & WORDS: George M Cohan. "The Small Town Gal" (LP-214) (LP-365)

080425a HAVANA contemp medley by Victor Light Opera Company. MUSIC: Leslie Stuart. WORDS: Adrian Ross, George Arthurs. (78/Vic 31744)

080425b HAVANA 1908 record by Jessie Broughton of orig (London) cast. "Zara" (78/Col(E) 26461)

080615a THREE TWINS contemp medley by Victor Light Opera Company. MUSIC: Karl Hoschna. WORDS: Otto Harbach. (78/Vic 31809)

080831a ALGERIA contemp medley by Victor Light Opera Company. MUSIC: Victor Herbert. WORDS: Glen MacDonald (78/Vic 31766)

081024a THE BELLE OF BRITTANY contemp medley by Victor Light Opera Compant. MUSIC & WORDS: Various. (78/Vic 31765)

081114a THE CHOCOLATE SOLDIER 1949 studio prod. MUSIC: Oscar Straus. WORDS: Stanislaus Stange. COND: Al Goodman. CAST: Ann Ayars, Charles Fredericks, Jimmy Carroll, John Percival, chorus. (RCA LK-1006)

081114b THE CHOCOLATE SOLDIER 1959 studio prod. COND: Lehman Engel. CAST: Rise Stevens (of 1941 film cast & 1955 TV cast), Robert Merrill, Jo Sullivan, Peter Palmer, Sadie McCollum,

Michael Kermoyan, Eugene Morgan. (RCA LSO-6005. Excerpts: LSO-1506)

081114c THE CHOCOLATE SOLDIER 1941 album, with a song by Bronislau Kaper & Gus Kahn written for the 1941 film. COND: Robert Armbruster. VOCALS: Nelson Eddy & Rise Stevens of 1941 film cast; chorus. (Col ML-4060, with The Student Prince. Excerpt: Eddy, Stevens: "My Hero" (LP-432).)

081114d THE CHOCOLATE SOLDIER 1910 medley by Victor Light Opera Company. (78/Vic 31780)

081114e THE CHOCOLATE SOLDIER studio prod. COND: Lehman Engel. CAST: Jeanette Scovotti, Rita Williams, Jean Allister, William Lewis, John Hauxvell. (Reader's Digest 46-2, with White Horse Inn)

081114f THE CHOCOLATE SOLDIER 1963 studio prod. ORCH & COND: Alan Braden. CAST: Laurie Payne, Stephanie Voss, Barbara Elsy, Pauline Stevens, chorus. (World Record Club(E) T-210, with The Firefly)

081114g THE CHOCOLATE SOLDIER medley by Brunswick Light Opera Company. (78/Bruns 20021)

081114h THE CHOCOLATE SOLDIER c 1965 cabaret performance by Nelson Eddy of 1941 film cast & Gale Sherwood. "My Hero" (LP-499)

081114i THE CHOCOLATE SOLDIER medleys by Light Opera Company. (1910: 78/HMV(E) 04509) (Later: 78/HMV(E) C-1705)

081114j THE CHOCOLATE SOLDIER contemp records by members of 1910 London prod. Evelyn d'Alroy: "Sympathy" d'Alroy, Lempriere Pringle, Tom Shale, C H Workman, Amy Augarde: Finale, Act 2 (78/Odeon(E) 0703) "The Tale of a Coat" Pringle: "Bulgarians" (78/Odeon(E) 0705) d'Alroy, Workman: "That Would Be Lovely," "The Letter Song" (78/ Odeon(E) 0704)

081114k THE CHOCOLATE SOLDIER medley by Columbia Light Opera Company. (78/Col(E) DX-284)

081203a THE PIED PIPER 1909 records by Grace Cameron of orig prod. "Adam and Eve" (CYL/Edison 4M-136) "Whose Baby Girl Are You?" (78/Edison 10265)

081223a THE GIRL IN THE TRAIN 1910 medley by Light Opera Company. MUSIC: Leo Fall. WORDS: Adrain Ross. (78/HMV(E) 04508)

081223b THE GIRL IN THE TRAIN 1910 record by Phyllis Dare of 1910 London prod. "The Sleeping Car Song" (78/HMV(E) 03189)

081223*a MR. HAMLET OF BROADWAY 1909 records by Maude Raymond of orig cast. "Goodbye, Molly Brown" (78/Vic 5715) "The Dusky Salome" (78/Vic 5671)

1909

090118a THE MERRY WIDOW AND THE DEVIL 1909 record by Blanche Ring of orig cast. 'Yip! I Adee! I Aye!" (LP-20)(LP-323)

090123a OUR MISS GIBBS contemp records by members of orig (London) cast. MUSIC: Ivan Caryll, Lionel Monckton, WORDS: Adrian Ross, Percy Greenbank. Gertie Millar: "Moonstruck," "In Yorkshire" (LP-227) George Grossmith Jr: "Yip! I-Addy! I-Ay!" (LP-227)(78/Jumbo(E) 415) "Angelina" (78/HMV(E) 02253)(78/Jumbo(E) 520) "Bertie the Bounder" (LP-227)(78/Jumbo(E) 520) "Ou-la-la" (78/HMV(E) 02285)(78/Jumbo(E) 569)

090123b OUR MISS GIBBS 1910 medley by Victor Light Opera Company. (78/Vic 31802)

090123*a THE SPRING MAID 1911 records by members of 1910 New York cast. MUSIC: Heinrich Reinhardt. WORDS: Harry B

Smith, Robert B Smith. Tom McNaughton: "The Three Trees"(recitation with music) (LP-323) Christie MacDonald: "Day Dreams, Visions of Bliss" (78/Vic 60061) MacDonald (with Reinald Werrenrath, not of orig cast): "Two Little Love Bees" (78/Vic 60060)

090123*b THE SPRING MAID 1911 medley by Victor Light Opera Company. (78/Vic 31833)

090200a THE GOLDEN GIRL contemp medley by Victor Light Opera Company. MUSIC: Joseph E Howard. WORDS: Will Hough, Frank R Adams. (78/Vic 31758)

090208a THE PRINCE OF TONIGHT records sung by Joe Howard (composer). MUSIC: Harold Orlob (although long credited to Joe Howard). WORDS: Will Hough, Frank Adams. "I Wonder Who's Kissing Her Now" (1936: 78/Vocalion 3357)(1947: LP-369)

090208b THE PRINCE OF TONIGHT 1909 medley by Victor Light Opera Company. (78/Vic 31748)

090410a THE BEAUTY SPOT contemp medley by Victor Light Opera Company. MUSIC: Reginald DeKoven. WORDS: Joseph W Herbert. (78/Vic 31745)

090428a THE ARCADIANS 1969 studio prod. MUSIC: Lionel Monckton, Howard Talbot. WORDS: Arthur Wimperis. COND: Gilbert Vinter. CAST: Cynthia Glover, Shirley Minty, Robert Bowman, John Lawrenson, Stanley Riley, Leslie Fyson. (Music for Pleasure(E) 1323)

090428b THE ARCADIANS 1941 records by Julia Sanderson of 1910 New York cast. "The Girl with a Brogue," "Bring Me a Rose" (LP-57)

090428c THE ARCADIANS 1968 studio prod. COND: Vilem Tausky. CAST: June Bronhill, Ann Howard, Andy Cole, Peter Regan, Michael Burgess, Jon Pertwee, chorus. (Col(E) TWO-233)

090428d THE ARCADIANS contemp medley by Victor Light Opera Company. (78/Vic 31775)

090428e THE ARCADIANS records by members of orig (London) cast. Phyllis Dare, 1910: "The Girl with a Brogue" (78/ HMV(E) 03191) "Bring Me a Rose" (78/HMV(E) 03190) "The Sleeping Car Song" (78/HMV(E) 03189) Alfred Lester, 1915: "I've Got a Motter" (LP-524) Florence Smithson, 1915: "The Pipes of Pan," "Arcady Is Ever Young" (78/Col(E) 542) "Come Back to Arcady," "Light Is My Heart" (78/Col(E) 543

090428f THE ARCADIANS 1929 medley by Light Opera Company. (78/HMV(E) C-1684)

090522a THE MIDNIGHT SONS 1909 records by Blanche Ring of orig cast. "I've Got Rings on My Fingers" (LP-18) (LP-711) "The Billiken Man" (78/Vic 5731)

090614a ZIEGFELD FOLLIES OF 1909 1922 record by Eva Tanguay, who joined the show in July. "I Don't Care" (Rare Records 7"' V-203)(LP-1)(Incomplete: LP-20, LP-324)

090816a A BROKEN IDOL contemp medley by Victor Light Opera Company. MUSIC: Egbert Van Alstyne. WORDS: Harry Williams. (78/Vic 31757)

090906a THE DOLLAR PRINCESS contemp medley by Victor Light Opera Company. MUSIC: Edmund Eysler. WORDS: George Grossmith Jr, Adrian Ross. (78/Vic 31751)

090906b THE DOLLAR PRINCESS 1909 studio prod by "The Dollar Princess Operatic Party." VOCALS: Peter Dawson, Eleanor Jones-Hudson, Stanley Kirkby, Ernest Pike, Carrie Tubb, Harold Wilde. Opening Chorus (78/HMV(E) GC-4621)"Ring o' Roses" (78/HMV(E) 04039) "And Now Assemble/Finale, Act 1" (78/HMV(E) 04501) "The Dollar Princesses" (78/HMV(E) GC-4622) "How Do You Do?" (78/ HMV(E) 04502) "Chewska" (78/HMV(E) GC-4623) "A Self-Made

Maiden" (78/HMV(E) GC-3815) "Many a Lover" (78/HMV(E) GC-3814) "Lady Fortune" (78/HMV(E) GC4-2026) "Riding Lesson" (78/HMV(E) GC2-4003)

090920a THE ROSE OF ALGERIA 1931 medley by Victor Salon Group. MUSIC: Victor Herbert. WORDS: Glen MacDonough. COND: Nathaniel Shilkret. (LP-767)(LP-777)

091112a THE COUNT OF LUXEMBOURG 1912 medley by Victor Light Opera Company. MUSIC: Franz Lehar. WORDS: Adrian Ross, Basil Hood. (78/Vic 31856)

091112b THE COUNT OF LUXEMBOURG 1969 studio prod. COND: Vilem Tausky. CAST: June Bronhill, Neville Jason, Neilson Taylor, Leslie Fyson, James Lewington, chorus. (Col(E) TWO-246)

091112c THE COUNT OF LUXEMBOURG medley by Columbia Light Opera Company. (78/Col A-5434)

091112d THE COUNT OF LUXEMBOURG 1911 records by members of 1911 London prod. May de Sousa: "Pierrette and Pierrot" (78/HMV(E) 03248) de Sousa, W H Berry: "A Carnival for Life" (78/HMV(E) 04087) "In High Society " (78/HMV(E) 04086)

091122a OLD DUTCH 1909 medley by orchestra cond by Victor Herbert, composer, (LP-629)

1910

100106a THE JOLLY BACHELORS contemp records by members of orig cast. MUSIC & WORDS: Nora Bayes, Jack Norworth, others. Nora Bayes, Jack Norworth: "Come Along, My Mandy" (78/Vic 70016) "Rosa Rosetta" (78/Vic 70019) Bayes: "Has Anybody Here Seen Kelly?" (LP-1) (LP-157)(LP-323) "Young America" (78/Vic 70015) Stella Mayhew: "Savannah" (CYL/Edison 4M-467) Norworth: "College Medley" (78/Vic 60014)

100108a GYPSY LOVE 1912 medley by Light Opera Company. MUSIC: Franz Lehar. WORDS: Adrian Ross. (78/HMV(E) 04550)

100108b GYPSY LOVE 1911 records by members of 1911 New York cast. Marguerite Sylva: "Melody of Love " (CYL/Edison 28001) "I Will Give You All for Love" (CYL/Edison 28003) Sylva, Arthur Albro: "Love Is like the Rose" (CYL/Edison 28002) Sylva, Carl Hayden: "There Is a Land of Fancy " (CYL/Edison 28004)

100110a THE OLD TOWN 1911 records by David Montgomery & Fred Stone of orig cast. "Travel, Travel, Little Star" (LP-323)(LP-7ll) "Moriah: A Scotch Medley " (LP-20)

100110b THE OLD TOWN 1933 radio performance by Fred Stone of orig cast & Will Rogers. "Travel, Travel, Little Star" (LP-740)

100124a RAGGED ROBIN 1913 record by Chauncey Olcott of orig cast. "I Used to Believe in Fairies" (78/Col A-1308)

100210a THE YANKEE GIRL contemp records by Blanche Ring of orig cast. "I've Got Rings on My Fingers" (LP-18) (LP-711) "Nora Malone" (78/Vic 60024) "The Top o' the Morning" (78/Vic 60025)

100219a THE BALKAN PRINCESS contemp medley by Victor Light Opera Company. MUSIC: Paul Rubens. WORDS: Arthur Wimperis, Paul Rubens. (78/Vic 31821)

100219b THE BALKAN PRINCESS 1910 medley by Light Opera Company. (78/HMV(E) 04507)

100604a THE SUMMER WIDOWERS records by Irene Franklin of orig cast. MUSIC: Burton Green. WORDS: Irene Franklin. "Redhead" (l915: LP-20)(1917: 78/Emerson 7165)

100620a ZIEGFELD FOLLIES OF 1910 records by Bert Williams of orig cast. "Nobody" (1906: LP-639)(1913:LP-20, LP-157, LP-323, LP-758) "I'll Lend You Anything" (1910: LP-324, LP-639) "Play That

Barber-Shop Chord," "Something You Don't Expect" (1910:78/Col A-929)

100926a ALMA, WHERE DO YOU LIVE? 1911 records by Truly Shattuck, who joined orig cast in Dec 1910. MUSIC & WORDS: Jean Briquet. "Alma," "Sail Home" (78/Col A-1092)

101024a THE GIRL IN THE TAXI 1912 medley by Light Opera Company. (78/HMV(E)04545)

101105a THE QUAKER GIRL contemp records by members of orig (London) cast. MUSIC: Lionel Monckton. WORDS: Adrian Ross, Percy Greenbank. Gertie Millar: "A Quaker Girl," "Tony from America," "I Wore a Little Grey Bonnet" George Garvey: "Come to the Ball" Joseph Coyne: "I'm a Married Man" (LP-227) Gracie Leigh: "Come to the Ball" (78/HMV(E) 03298)

101105b THE QUAKER GIRL contemp medley by Victor Light Opera Company. (78/Vic 31847)

101105c THE QUAKER GIRL 1912 medley by Columbia Light Opera Company. (78/Col A-5388)

101105d THE QUAKER GIRL medleys by Light Opera Company. (1911: 78/HMV(E) C-521)(1930, cond by Ray Noble: 78/HMV(E) C-2015)

101105e THE QUAKER GIRL 1932 medley by Columbia Light Opera Company. (78/Col(E) DX-413)

101107a NAUGHTY MARIETTA 1954 studio prod. MUSIC: Victor Herbert. WORDS: Rida Johnson Young. ORCH & COND: George Greeley. CAST: Gordon MacRae, Marguerite Piazza, Katherine Hilgenberg. (Cap l0" L-468)

101107b NAUGHTY MARIETTA records by members of 1935 film cast. Jeanette MacDonald: "Italian Street Song" (1935: LP-4, LP-71) (1944: LP-378)(1945: LP-77)(1958: LP-134) "Ah! Sweet Mystery of Life" (1935: LP-536)(1950: LP-77, LP-119) Nelson Eddy: "Tramp! Tramp! Tramp!" (1935: LP-4, LP-117, LP-462) "Ah! Sweet Mystery of Life" (1935: LP-117, LP-462) "'Neath the Southern Moon" (1935: LP-4)(1948: LP-756) "I'm Falling in Love with Someone" (1935: LP-4) MacDonald, Eddy: "Ah! Sweet Mystery of Life" (1936: LP-4, LP-462, LP-539)(1958: LP-134)

101107c NAUGHTY MARIETTA 1950 studio prod. COND: Al Goodman. CAST: Earl Wrightson, Elaine Malbin, Jimmy Carroll. (RCA LK-1005)

101107d NAUGHTY MARIETTA studio prod. ORCH: Henri Rene. COND: Lehman Engel. CAST: Anna Moffo, Rosalind Elias, William Lewis. (Reader's Digest 40-4, with The Desert Song)

101107e NAUGHTY MARIETTA 1949 album by Nelson Eddy of 1935 film cast & Nadine Conner, chorus. COND: Robert Armbruster. (Col 10" ML-2094. Excerpts: Eddy: "Tramp, Tramp, Tramp" (LP-432) "I'm Falling in Love with Someone" Conner: "Italian Street Song" Eddy, Conner: "'Neath the Southern Moon," "Ah! Sweet Mystery of Life" (LP-268).)

101107f NAUGHTY MARIETTA 1953 album. COND: Jay Blackton. CAST: Doretta Morrow, Felix Knight. (RCA 10" LPM-3153, with Mademoiselle Modiste)

101107g NAUGHTY MARIETTA medleys by Victor Light Opera Company. (1911: LP-628)(1923: 78/Vic 35736)(c.1930: LP-304)

101107h NAUGHTY MARIETTA 1944 radio prod with members of l935 film cast, Jeanette MacDonald: "Prayer," "Italian Street Song" Nelson Eddy: "'Neath the Southern Moon," "I'm Falling in Love with Someone" Eddy, chorus: "Tramp, Tramp, Tramp" MacDonald, Eddy:"Ah! Sweet Mystery of Life" (Pelican 117)

101107i NAUGHTY MARIETTA medley by Brunswick Light Opera Company. (78/Bruns 20012)

101107j NAUGHTY MARIETTA 1938 medley. COND: Nathaniel Shilkret. VOCALS: Anne Jamison, Tom Thomas, Jan Peerce, chorus. (LP-305)

101107k NAUGHTY MARIETTA studio prod. COND: Paul Britten. VOCALS: uncredited. (MGM 3080, with The Firefly)

101107l NAUGHTY MARIETTA 1961 studio prod. ORCH & COND: Alan Braden. CAST: Stephanie Voss, Peter Regan, chorus. (World Records(E) TP-88, with No, No, Nanette)

101107m NAUGHTY MARIETTA 1911 record by orchestra cond by Victor Herbert, composer. "Intermezzo" (LP-628)

101107n NAUGHTY MARIETTA 1965 studio prod. COND: Colin Beaton. CAST: Mary Thomas, John McNally, chorus. (Fontana(E) SFL-13025, with The Student Prince)

101107o NAUGHTY MARIETTA 1935 film soundtrack. WORDS: Rida Johnson Young, Gus Kahn, ORCH & COND: Herbert Stothart. CAST: Jeanette MacDonald, Nelson Eddy, Charles Bruins, Delos Jewkes, Zaruhi Elmassian, chorus. (Hollywood Soundstage 413)

1911

110102a THE SLIM PRINCESS records by members of orig cast. Elsie Janis, 1912: "Fo' de Lawd's Sake, Play a Waltz" (LP-18)(LP-20) "When Antelo Plays the 'Cello" (78/Vic 60093) Charles King, Elizabeth Brice, 1911: "Let Me Stay and Live in Dixieland" (78/Vic 5843) "That's Ever-Loving Love" (78/Vic 5847)

110130a BARRY OF BALLYMORE 1913 records by Chauncey Olcott of orig prod. MUSIC: Ernest Ball. WORDS: Chauncey Olcott. "I Love the Name of Mary" (78/Col A-1310) "Mother Machree" (78/Col A-1337)

110204a THE HEN-PECKS records by Blossom Seeley of orig cast. "Toddling the Todalo" (1952: LP-479) "June" (1957: LP-764)

110304a PEGGY 1911 records by members of orig (London) prod. MUSIC: Leslie Stuart. WORDS: C H Bovill. Phyllis Dare: "Ladies, Beware!" (78/HMV(E) 03230) Dare, George Grossmith: "You're the Only Girl" (78/HMV(E) 04083) Connie Ediss: "What He Didn't Expect from a Lady" (78/HMV(E) 03251) "I Like to Have a Little Bit On" (78/HMV(E) 03252) Grossmith, Edmund Payne: "I Beg Your Pardon" (78/HMV(E) 04082) Grossmith: "Don't Forget You're a Lady" (78/HMV(E) 02316) "Mr. Edison" (LP-524) Robert Hale: "Whistle and the Girls Come 'Round" (78/HMV(E) 02344) Olive May: "The Lass with the Lasso" (78/HMV(E) 03231)

110304b PEGGY 1911 medley by Light Opera Company. (78/HMV(E) 04517/8)

110313a THE PINK LADY contemp medley by Victor Light Opera Company. MUSIC: Ivan Caryll. WORDS: C M S McClellan. (78/Vic 31823)

110320a LA BELLE PAREE records by Al Jolson of orig cast. "That Lovin' Traumerei" (1912: LP-290, LP-323)(1947: LP-478)

110403a LITTLE MISS FIX-IT 1911 records by members of orig cast. MUSIC & WORDS: Nora Bayes, Jack Norworth. Bayes: "Strawberries" (78/Vic 60041) Bayes, Norworth: "Turn Off Your Light, Mister Moon-Man" (LP-18)(LP-148)(LP-711) Norworth: "For Months and Months and Months" (LP-324)

110626a ZIEGFELD FOLLIES OF 1911 1913 record by Bert Williams of orig cast. MUSIC & WORDS: Irving Berlin. "Woodman, Spare That Tree" (LP-639)

111120a VERA VIOLETTA 1911 records by Al Jolson of orig cast. "That Haunting Melody" (by George M Cohan) (LP-18)(LP-290)(LP-470) (LP-539)(LP-626)(LP-711) "Rum Tum Tiddle" (LP-290)(LP-470)(LP-550)

1912

120108a THE BIRD OF PARADISE contemp records by members of orig prod. VOCALS & ACCOMPANIMENT: Ben Waiaiole, S M Kaiawe, W B J Aeko, E K Rose, W K Kolomku (guitar), the Hawaiian Quintette. Hawaiian Quintette: "One-Two-Three-Four" (78/Vic 65344) "Song of the Lonesome Forest" ("Kumukahi") (78/Vic 65349) "Press Me to Thee" ("Tomi Tomi"), "Forget Me Not" ("Mai Poina oe Ia'u") (78/Vic 65340) "I Love but Thee" ("Akahi Hoi"), "My Love Is like a Blooming Flower" ("Pau i Mohala") (78/Vic 65346) "Farewell to Thee" ("Aloha oe") (78/Vic 65348) "Sparkling Waters" ("Waialae") (78/Vic 65345) "Maui Girl" (78/Vic 65440) "Honolulu Boy" ("Sonny Cunha") (78/Vic 65343) "The Bubbling Spring" ("Kaua i ka Huahuai"), "Drowsy Waters" ("Wailana") (78/Vic 65339) W K Kolomku (guitar solo): "Hawaiian Melodies" (Incidental Music) (78/Vic 65341) S M Kaiawe & Hawaiian Quintette: "Native Plantation Song" ("Kuu Home") (78/Vic 65348) "Sacred Dancing Hula Song" ("Mauna Kea") (78/Vic 65345) "Maid of Honolulu" W B J Aeko & Hawaiian Quintette: "The Whirling Waters" ("Kawiliwiliwai") (78/Vic 65338) Ben Waiaiole & Hawaiian Quintette: "Hawaiian Hula Dance Song" ("Moanalua") (78/Vic 65341) E K Rose & Hawaiian Quintette: "My Honolulu Hula Girl" (78/Vic 65344) "Farewell to Thee" ("Aloha oe") (78/Vic 35622) "Fragrance of the Lehua Wreath" ("Sweet Lei Lehua") (78/Vic 65343)

120108b THE BIRD OF PARADISE 1919 records by The Hawaiians of 1919 London prod. "Aloha oe" (78/HMV(E) B-1077) "On the Beach at Waikiki," "Mona Kiea/One-Two-Three" (78/HMV(E) B-1068)

120203a DER LIEBER AUGUSTIN (later retitled "Miss Caprice") contemp medley by Victor Light Opera Company. MUSIC: Leo Fall. WORDS: Edgar Smith, (78/Vic 35332)

120203b DER LIEBER AUGUSTIN 1914 record by George MacFarlane of 1913 New York prod. "Look in Her Eyes" (by Jerome Kern & Michael E Rourke) (78/Vic 60120)

120203c DER LIEBER AUGUSTIN 1912 medley by Light Opera Company, entitled "Princess Caprice." (78/HMV(E) 04531/2)

120205a MACUSHLA 1920 records by Chauncey Olcott of orig & 1920 casts. MUSIC: Ernest Ball. WORDS: Rida Johnson Young. "That's How the Shannon Flows," "I'll Miss You, Old Ireland, God Bless You, Goodbye" (78/Col A-3525) "'Tis an Irish Girl I Love," "Macushla Asthore" (78/Col A-2988)

120208a HOKEY-POKEY 1912 records by members of orig cast. Lillian Russell: "Come Down, Ma Evenin' Star" (LP-323) (LP-579) (Incomplete: LP-20) Weber & Fields: Skit "Drinking Scene" (78/Col A-1159)

120214a EVERYBODY'S DOING IT contemp record by Robert Hale and Ida Crispi of orig (London) prod. MUSIC & WORDS: Irving Berlin. "Everybody's Doing It Now" (LP-158)

120224a THE SUNSHINE GIRL contemp records by members of orig (London) cast. MUSIC & WORDS: Paul Rubens, Arthur Wimperis. George Grossmith Jr: "Little Girl, Little Girl" (78/HMV(E) 02404) "The Other Chap" (78/HMV(E) 02406) Violet Essex: "Here's to Love" (78/Polyphon(E) 5628)

120224b THE SHUNSHINE GIRL 1913 record by Joseph Cawthorn of 1913 New York prod. "You Can't Play Every Instrument in the Band" (by Joseph Cawthorn, John Golden) (LP-323)

120224c THE SUNSHINE GIRL contemp medley by Victor Light Opera Company. (78/Vic 31889)

120224d THE SUNSHINE GIRL 1912 medley by Light Opera Company. (78/HMV(E) C-522)

120305a THE WHIRL OF SOCIETY records by members of orig cast. Stella Mayhew: "A Songologue" (1912: CYL/Edison 4M-987) Mayhew, Billie Taylor: "My Lou" (1912: CYL/Edison 4M-995) Blosson Seeley: "Toddlin' the Todalo" (1952: LP-479)

120930a OH! OH! DELPHINE contemp medley by Victor Light Opera Company. MUSIC: Ivan Caryll. WORDS: C M S McClellan. (78/Vic 31878)

120930b OH! OH! DELPHINE medley by Columbia Light Opera Company. (78/Col A-5445)

120930c OH! OH! DELPHINE 1913 record by Dorothy Jardon of 1913 London prod. "The Venus Waltz" (78/HMV(E) 03326)

121010a SARI 1914 medley by Victor Light Opera Company. MUSIC: Emmerich Kalman. WORDS: C C S Cushing, E P Heath. (78/Vic 35365)

121021a ZIEGFELD FOLLIES OF 1912 1913 records by Bert Williams of orig cast, "My Landlady" (78/Col A-1289) "On the Right Road" (78/Col A-1354)

121028a THE LADY OF THE SLIPPER contemp medley by Victor Light Opera Company. MUSIC: Victor Herbert. WORDS: James O'Dea. (LP-767)

121202a THE FIREFLY 1951 studio prod. MUSIC: Rudolf Friml. WORDS: Otto Harbach, Gus Kahn, Robert Wright, George Forrest. COND: Al Goodman. CAST: Allan Jones of 1937 film cast; Elaine Malbin, Martha Wright, Hayes Gordon, the Guild Choristers. (RCA 10" LM-121)

121202b THE FIREFLY records by members of 1937 film prod. Allan Jones: "The Donkey Serenade" (1937: LP-126, LP-183) (1966: LP-586) "Giannina Mia" (1937: LP-126)(1966: LP-586) Jeanette MacDonald: "Giannina Mia" (1946: LP-210, LP-249) (1958: LP-134) "The Donkey Serenade" (1946: LP-210, LP-249)

121202c THE FIREFLY studio prod. COND: Paul Britten. VOCALS: uncredited. (MGM 3080, with Naughty Marietta)

121202d THE FIREFLY records by Rudolf Friml (composer), piano. "Giannina Mia," "Sympathy," "Donkey Serenade," "When a Maid Comes Knocking" (Later: LP-733)(1963: LP-354)

121202e THE FIREFLY 1963 studio prod. ORCH & COND: Alan Braden. CAST: Stephanie Voss, Laurie Payne, chorus. (World Record Club(E) T-210, with The Chocolate Soldier)

121202f THE FIREFLY 1912 record by Craig Campbell of orig cast. "A Woman's Smile" (78/Col A-1274)

121202g THE FIREFLY 1929 medley by Victor Salon Group. COND: Nathaniel Shilkret. (LP-590)

121223a HULLO RAGTIME contemp records by members of orig (London) prod. MUSIC & WORDS: Louis Hirsch, Harold Atteridge, others. Lew Hearn & Bonita: "Hitchy Koo" (LP-158) "Snooky Ookums" (78/HMV(E) 04100) "You're My Baby" (78/HMV(E) 04108) Shirley Kellogg, Gerald Kirby: "The Wedding Glide" (78/HMV(E) 04097) Ethel Levey: "How Do You Do, Miss Ragtime?" (78/HMV(E) 03377)

121223b HULLO RAGTIME contemp records by the Ragtime Orch. COND: Louis Hirsch, composer. Medley (LP-700) "The Wedding Glide," "How Do You Do, Miss Ragtime?" (78/HMV(E) B-188) "My Honolulu Honey Lou," "Ragging the Baby to Sleep" (78/HMV(E) B-187)

121223c HULLO RAGTIME 1913 medley by the Ragtime Quintet. COND: Louis Hirsch, composer. (78/HMV(E) 04558)

1913

130127a THE ISLE O' DREAMS contemp records by Chauncey Olcott of orig prod. MUSIC: Ernest Ball. WORDS: Chauncey Olcott, George Graff. "When Irish Eyes Are Smiling" (78/Col A-1310) "Mother Machree" (78/Col A-1337)

130206a HONEYMOON EXPRESS records by Al Jolson of orig cast. "My Yellow Jacket Girl" (1913: LP-44, LP-290) "The Spaniard That Blighted My Life" (1913: LP-44,LP-290)(1946: LP-682)(1947: LP-245, LP-383) "You Made Me Love You" (1913: LP-290)(1946: LP-145, LP-245, LP-739)(1946: LP-682)(1947: LP-409)(1948:LP-677) "Who Paid the Rent for Mrs. Rip Van Winkle?" (1946: LP-682)

130405a THE GIRL ON THE FILM 1914 medley by Victor Light Opera Company. MUSIC & WORDS: Albert Sirmay, Willy Bredschneider, Walter Kollo, Adrian Ross. (78/Vic 35363)

130405b THE GIRL ON THE FILM 1913 record by George Grossmith of 1913 London & 1913 New York prods. "Tommy, Won't You Teach Me How to Tango?" (78/HMV(E) 02500)

130407a THE PURPLE ROAD contemp medley by Victor Light Opera Company. MUSIC & WORDS: Heinrich Reinhardt, others. (78/Vic 35349)

130616a ZIEGFELD FOLLIES OF 1913 contemp records by members of orig cast. Jose Collins: "Just You and I and the Moon" (LP-1) Nat M Wills: "If a Table at Rector's Could Talk" (LP-1)(LP-157) "New York, What's the Matter with You?" (78/Vic 17461)

130818a WHEN DREAMS COME TRUE contemp medley by Victor Light Opera Company. MUSIC: Silvio Hein. WORDS:Philip Bartholomae. (78/Vic 35336)

130825a THE DOLL GIRL contemp medley by Victor Light Opera Company. MUSIC: Leo Fall, Jerome Kern. WORDS: Harry B Smith. (LP-606)

130828a ADELE contemp medley by Victor Light Opera Company. MUSIC: Jean Briquet. WORDS: Adolph Philipp, Edward Paulton. (78/Vic 35339)

130908a SWEETHEARTS 1913 records by Christie MacDonald of orig cast & Reinald Werrenrath. MUSIC: Victor Herbert. WORDS: Robert B Smith. MacDonald: "Sweethearts" MacDonald & Werrenrath: "The Cricket on the Hearth," "The Angelus" (LP-628)

130908b SWEETHEARTS 1947 studio prod. COND: Al Goodman. CAST: Earl Wrightson, Frances Greer, Jimmy Carroll, Christina Lind. (RCA LK-1015)

130908c SWEETHEARTS 1945-46 records by Jeanette MacDonald of 1938 film cast. "Sweetheart Waltz" (LP-4)(LP-210) "Summer Serenade" (LP-4)

130908d SWEETHEARTS medleys by Victor Light Opera Company. (1913: LP-628)(1923: 78/Vic 35736)(c.1930: LP-304)

130908e SWEETHEARTS 1946 radio prod. VOCALS: Jeanette MacDonald & Nelson Eddy of 1938 film cast. (Pelican 143, with additional MacDonald/ Eddy radio material)

130908f SWEETHEARTS 1938 medley. COND: Nathaniel Shilkret. VOCALS: Anne Jamison, Jan Peerce, chorus, (LP-305)(LP-767)

130908g SWEETHEARTS 1923 medley by orchestra cond by Victor Herbert, composer. (LP-628)

130922a THE MARRIAGE MARKET contemp medley by Victor Light Opera Company. MUSIC & WORDS: Victor Jacobi, Jerome Kern, others. (LP-606)

131002a THE LAUGHING HUSBAND contemp medley by Victor Light Opera Company. MUSIC: Edmund Eysler, Jerome Kern. WORDS: Arthur Wimperis, Harry B Smith. (LP-606)

131030a

131030a OH, I SAY! contemp medley by Victor Light Opera Company. MUSIC: Jerome Kern. WORDS: Harry B Smith. (LP-606)

131110a THE LITTLE CAFE contemp medley by Victor Light Opera Company. MUSIC: Ivan Caryll. WORDS: C M S McClellan. (78/Vic 35349)

131111a THE MADCAP DUCHESS contemp medley by Victor Light Opera Company. MUSIC: Victor Herbert. WORDS: David Stevens, Justin McCarthy. (LP-767)

131210a HIGH JINKS contemp medley by Victor Light Opera Company. MUSIC: Rudolf Friml. WORDS: Otto Harbach. (78/Vic 35382)

131210b HIGH JINKS records by members of 1916 London prod, with additional songs by others. Marie Blanche: "The Bubble" Peter Gawthorne: "Something Seems Tingle-ingleing" (78/HMV(E) C-720) W H Berry: "It's Wonderful How Trouble Clings to Me" (78/HMV(E) 4-2784) "I Could Love a Nice Little Girl" (78/HMV(E) 4-2785) "What Is Life Without Love?" (78/HMV(E) 02679) Blanche, Berry: "It Isn't My Fault" (LP-430) Berry, Violet Blyth: "Spaniards' Duet" (78/HMV(E) 04:75) Gawthorne, Maisie Gay: "Love's Own Kiss" Gay, W H Rawlins: "She Says It with Her Eyes" (78/HMV(E) C-721) Gawthorne, Nellie Taylor: "Love's Own Kiss" (78/HMV(E) C-737) Gay: "Jim," "I'm Through with Roaming Romeos" (78/HMV(E) B-712) Adelphi Theatre Orch: "Overture," "Oyra's Dance" (78/HMV(E) C-713) "Finale, Act 2," "Something Seems Tingle-ingleing" (78/HMV(E) C-719)

131210c HIGH JINKS records by Rudolf Friml (composer), piano. "The Bubble" (Later: LP-733)(1963: LP-354) "Something Seems Tingle-ingleing" (Later: LP-733)

131210d HIGH JINKS 1929 medley by Victor Salon Group. COND: Nathaniel Shilkret, (45/Camden CAE-253, with The Vagabond King) (LP-590)

131223a HULLO TANGO 1914 records by members of orig (London) prod. Gerald Kirby: "Get Out and Get Under" Frank Carter & Isobell d'Armond: "Love Me While the Lovin' Is Good" (LP-158) Morris Harvey, Eric Roper: "Wilkinson, the Ledger Clerk" (78/HMV(E) 01106) Ethel Levey: "My Tango Girl" (LP-700)

131229a IOLE contemp medley by Victor Light Opera Company. MUSIC: William F Peters. WORDS: Robert W Chambers, Ben Teal. (78/Vic 35385)

1914

140112a THE QUEEN OF THE MOVIES contemp medley by Victor Light Opera Company, MUSIC: Jean Gilbert. WORDS: Glen MacDonough. (78/ Vic 35365)

140130a ALONE AT LAST contemp medley by Victor Light Opera Company. MUSIC: Franz Lehar. WORDS: Matthew Woodward. (78/Vic 35517)

140130b ALONE AT LAST 1915 record by Roy Atwell of 1915 New York cast. "Some Little Bug Is Going to Find You" (78/Col A-1926)

140202a SHAMEEN DHU 1913 record by Chauncey Olcott of orig cast. "Too-Ra-Loo-Ra-Loo-Ral" (78/Col A-1410)

140223a THE MIDNIGHT GIRL 1914 record by Margaret Romaine & George MacFarlane of orig cast. MUSIC: Jean Briquet. WORDS: Adolph Philipp, Edward Paulton. "Oh! Gustave" (78/Vic 60118)

140223b THE MIDNIGHT GIRL contemp medley by Victor Light Opera Company. (78/Vic 35379)

140413a THE BEAUTY SHOP contemp medley by Victor Light Opera Company. MUSIC: Charles J Gebest. WORDS: Rennold Wolf. (78/Vic 35382)

140413b THE BEAUTY SHOP records by Raymond Hitchcock of orig cast. "When You're All Dressed Up and No Place to Go" (1916: 78/HMV(E) 02660)(1922: 78/Vocalion 35010)

140420a THE PASSING SHOW contemp records by members of orig (London) prod. MUSIC: Jerome Kern, others. Elsie Janis & Basil Hallam: "You're Here and I'm Here" (LP-158)(LP-430) Gwendoline Brogden: "I'll Make a Man of You" (LP-74)

140601a ZIEGFELD FOLLIES OF 1914 contemp medley by Victor Light Opera Company, (78/Vic 35385)

140601b ZIEGFELD FOLLIES OF 1914 1914 record by Bert Williams of orig cast. "The Darktown Poker Club" (78/Col A-1504)

140610a THE PASSING SHOW OF 1914 contemp medley by Victor Light Opera Compamy, MUSIC: Sigmund Romberg, Harry Carroll. WORDS: Harold Atteridge. (78/Vic 35394)

140824a THE GIRL FROM UTAH contemp medley by Victor Light Opera Company, MUSIC & WORDS: Jerome Kern, Harry B Smith, Paul Rubens, others. (LP-606)

140824b THE GIRL FROM UTAH 1941 records by Julia Sanderson of orig cast. "They Didn't Believe Me" (LP-57) (LP-69) (LP-758) "Same Sort of Girl" (with Frank Crumit) (LP-57)

140824c THE GIRL FROM UTAH 1913 medley by Chappell Light Opera Company. COND: Arthur Wood. (78/Chappell(E) A-I)

140824d THE GIRL FROM UTAH 1938 medley by Victor Light Opera Company. COND: Leonard Joy. (LP-306)

140909a MISS DAISY contemp medley by Victor Light Opera Company. MUSIC: Silvio Hein. WORDS: Philip Bartholomae. (78/Vic 35404)

141010a DANCING AROUND 1914 record by Al Jolson of orig cast. "Sister Susie's Sewing Shirts for Soldiers" (78/Col A-1671)

141020a CHIN-CHIN contemp medley by Columbia Light Opera Company. MUSIC: Ivan Caryll. WORDS: Anne Caldwell, James O'Dea. (78/Col A-5639)

141020b CHIN-CHIN contemp record by members of orig prod. Six Brown Brothers (saxophones): "Pretty Baby/Chin-Chin" (78/Vic 18149)

141020c CHIN-CHIN contemp medley by Victor Light Opera Company. (78/Vic 35440)

141028a THE LILAC DOMINO 1915 record by Eleanor Painter of 1914 New York cast. MUSIC & WORDS: Charles Cuvillier, Robert B Smith, others. "The Lilac Domino" (78/Col A-1937)

141028b THE LILAC DOMINO 1918 records by members of 1918 London prod. COND: Howard Carr. Clara Butterworth, Jamieson Dodds: "Song of the Chimes," "What Is Done You Can Never Undo" (78/ Col(E) L-1238) Butterworth, Dodds, Vincent Sullivan: "The Lilac Domino Waltz Song" Butterworth: "Where Love Is Waiting" (78/ Col(E) L-1239) "For Your Love I Am Waiting" Sullivan, Sybil Westmacott: "True Love Will Find a Way" (78/Col(E) L-1240) Sullivan, Westmacott, Frank Lalor, Edwin Wilson, Stuart Piggott: "Ladies' Day" Lalor, Wilson: "Still We Smile" (78/Col(E) D-1400) Sullivan: "Carnival Night" (78/Col(E) D-1404) Lalor, chorus: "All Line Up in a Queue" Dodds: "Let the Music Play" (78/Col(E) L-1241) Randall Jackson (with Sarah Jones & Ernest Pike not of orig cast): "For Your Love I Am Waiting," "The Lilac Domino" (78/HMV(E) C-848) "What Is Done You Can Never Undo" (78/HMV(E) C-850) Jackson: "Consolation" (78/HMV(E) B-906) Jackson (with Bessie Jones ("Louise Leigh") not of orig cast): "Song of the Chimes," "Where Love Is Waiting" (78/HMV(E) C-849) Orchestra: Medley (78/Col(E) 710)

141028c THE LILAC DOMINO medley by Light Opera Company. (78/ HMV(E) C-1705)

38

141028d THE LILAC DOMINO 1959 album. COND: Michael Collins. VOCALS: Aileen Cochrane, Charles Young, chorus. (45/HMV(E) GES-5778)

141102a THE ONLY GIRL contemp medley by Columbia Light Opera Company. MUSIC: Victor Herbert. WORDS: Henry Blossom. (78/Col A-5639)

141102b THE ONLY GIRL 1916 medley by Light Opera Company. (78/ HMV(E) C-637)

141102c THE ONLY GIRL 1931 medley by Victor Salon Group. COND: Nathaniel Shilkret. (LP-777)

141116a BUSINESS AS USUAL contemp record by Unity More of orig (London) prod. "Mary from Tipperary" (LP-158)

141208a WATCH YOUR STEP contemp records by members of 1915 London cast. MUSIC & WORDS: Irving Berlin. George Graves, Joseph Coyne: "Conversation" (78/HMV(E) B-622) Ethel Levey: "My Bird of Paradise," "Settle Down in a One-Horse Town" (78/HMV(E) C-612) Levey, Coyne: "The Minstrel Parade" Levey, Blanche Tomlin: "The Simple Melody" (78/HMV(E) C-611) Graves, Billie Carleton: "Show Us How to Do the Fox Trot" (78/HMV(E) C-624) Levey, Tomlin, Coyne: "The Syncopated Walk" (78/HMV(E) C-610) Coyne: "They Always Follow Me Around" Levey, Coyne: "Discoveries" (78/HMV(E) B-536)

141208b WATCH YOUR STEP contemp medley by Light Opera Company. (78/HMV(E) C-610)

141208c WATCH YOUR STEP 1916 record by Charles King & Elizabeth Brice of orig cast. "I've Gotta Go Back to Texas" (78/Col A-1944)

141224a TONIGHT'S THE NIGHT contemp records by members of 1915 London prod. MUSIC: Paul Rubens. WORDS: Paul Rubens, Percy Greenbank. George Grossmith (also of orig cast): "Any Old Night Is a Wonderful Night," "Murders" (78/HMV(E) C-574) "The Only Way" (78/HMV(E) C-577) Grossmith, Julia James: "Boots and Shoes" (78/HMV(E) C-584) Grossmith, Haidee de Rance: "They Didn't Believe Me" (by Jerome Kern, Michael E Rourke) (LP-430) Leslie Henson (also of orig cast), Moya Mannering: "I'd Like to Bring My Mother," "Meet Me 'Round the Corner" (78/HMV(E) B-484) Henri Leoni: "Pink and White," "Please Don't Flirt with Me" (78/HMV(E) C-657)

1915

150218a MAID IN AMERICA contemp medley by Victor Light Opera Company. MUSIC: Sigmund Romberg, Harry Carroll. WORDS: Harold Atteridge. (78/Vic 35440)

150322a ROSY RAPTURE, THE PRIDE OF THE BEAUTY CHORUS 1915 records by members of orig (London) cast. MUSIC: Herman Darewski, Jerome Kern, John Crook. WORDS: F W Mark, Jack Norworth: "Which Switch Is the Switch, Miss, for Ipswich?" Norworth, Gertrude Lang: "When I'm with You" (78/Col(E) 524) "Safe in Our Wardrobe for Two" Norworth: "Sally from Calais" (78/Col(E) 525) "The Same Sort of Mother and Same Sort of Child" Lang: "Beauty Chorus" (78/ Col(E) 526)

150420a NOBODY HOME contemp medley by Victor Light Opera Company. MUSIC & WORDS: mostly Jerome Kern, Schuyler Greene. (LP-606)

150424a BETTY 1915 medley by Light Opera Company. MUSIC & WORDS: mostly Paul Rubens, Adrian Ross, Percy Greenbank. (78/HMV(E) C-596)

150424b BETTY 1916 records by Raymond Hitchcock of 1916 New York prod. "Sometime," "Here Comes the Groom" (78/Vic 55080)

150503a A MODERN EVE contemp medley by Victor Light Opera Company. MUSIC: Victor Hollander, Jerome Kern. WORDS: Jean Gilbert, Harry B Smith. (LP-606)

150621a ZIEGFELD FOLLIES OF 1915 1915 record by Bert Williams of orig cast. "I'm Neutral" (78/Col A-1817)

150918a BRIC-A-BRAC contemp records by members of orig (London) prod. Gertie Millar & A Simon-Girard: "Chalk Farm to Camberwell Green" (LP-158) "I'm Simply Crazy over You" Millar: "Toy Town," "Neville Was a Devil" (LP-227)

150929a THE PRINCESS PAT 1915 record by Eleanor Painter of orig cast. MUSIC: Victor Herbert. WORDS: Henry Blossom. "Love Is the Best of All" (78/Col A-1937)

150929b THE PRINCESS PAT contemp medley by Victor Light Opera Company. (78/Vic 35517)

150929c THE PRINCESS PAT 1931 medley by Victor Salon Group. COND: Nathaniel Shilkret. (LP-767)(LP-777)

150930a HIP-HIP-HOORAY 1916 record by chorus girls of orig prod, while being "rehearsed" by Ray Burnside, who wrote & directed the revue. "The Ladder of Roses" (78/Col A-2057)

151223a VERY GOOD EDDIE 1975 prod. MUSIC: Jerome Kern. WORDS: Schuyler Greene, Anne Caldwell, Harry B Smith, others. ORCH: Russell Warner. COND: Lynn Crigler. CAST: David Christmas, Spring Fairbank, Travis Hudson, Charles Repole, Virginia Seidel, Hal Shane, Cynthia Wells, Nicholas Wyman. (DRG Records 6100)

151223b VERY GOOD EDDIE 1938 medley by Victor Light Opera Company. COND: Leonard Joy. (LP-306)

151223c VERY GOOD EDDIE contemp medley by Victor Light Opera Company, (LP-606)

151223*a KATINKA 1916 records by members of orig cast. MUSIC: Rudolf Friml. WORDS: Otto Harbach. May Naudain: "Rackety Coo" (78/Operaphone 1076) Sam Ash: "Rackety Coo" (with Grace Nash, not of orig cast)(78/Col A-1952)(78/Emerson 765)

151223*b KATINKA records by Rudolf Friml (composer) piano. "Allah's Holiday" (Later: LP-733)(1963: LP-354)

151223*c KATINKA 1929 medley by Victor Salon Group. COND: Nathaniel Shilkret. (LP-590)

151225a STOP! LOOK! LISTEN! contemp records by members of 1916 London prod (entitled "Follow the Crowd"). MUSIC & WORDS: Irving Berlin, others. Tom Walls: "Beautiful Honolulu" (78/HMV(E) C-665) Joseph Coyne: "England Every Time for Me" (78/HMV(E) 02647) "The Girl on the Magazine" (78/HMV(E) 02648) Robert Hale: "Father Wanted Me to Learn a Trade" (78/HMV(E) 02646) "The Honolulu Guide" (78/HMV(E) 01132) Hale, Walls: "The Wireless Scene" (78/HMV(E) 01133) Ethel Levey: "I Love a Piano" (78/HMV(E)03476) "That Hula Hula" (78/HMV(E) 03477) "Where Did Robinson Crusoe Go with Friday on Saturday Night?" (LP-158) Blanche Tomlin (with Ernest Pike, not of orig prod): "Teach Me to Love," "Until I Fell in Love with You" (78/HMV(E) C-664) Fay Compton: "Take Off a Little Bit" (LP-158) Compton, Coyne: "I Love to Dance" (78/HMV(E) 04157) Orchestra: Overture (78/HMV(E) C-663)

151225b STOP! LOOK! LISTEN! 1957 record by Blossom Seeley of orig cast. "I Love a Piano" (LP-764)

151225c STOP! LOOK! LISTEN! 1916 medley by Light Opera Company, entitled "Follow the Crowd." COND: Arthur Wood. (LP-583)

1916

160001a ZIEGFELD'S MIDNIGHT FROLIC 1917 record by Frances White of orig cast. "Go-Zin-To" (78/Vic 45149)

160110a SYBIL contemp medley by Victor Light Opera Company. MUSIC: Victor Jacobi. WORDS: Harry Graham, Harry B Smith. (78/Vic 35529)

160110b SYBIL 1916 record by Joseph Cawthorn of orig cast. "I Can Dance with Everybody but My Wife" (by Joseph Cawthorn, John Golden)(78/Vic 55074)

160110c SYBIL contemp records by members of 1921 London prod. Jose Collins: "I Like the Boys" (LP-152) "The Colonel of the Crimson Hussars" Collins, Harry Welchman: "Love May Be A Mystery" (78/Col(E) F-1068) Collins, Noel Leyland: "The Letter Duet" (78/Col(E) F-1069)

160115a BLOSSOM TIME 1947 studio prod. MUSIC: Franz Schubert, arranged by Heinrich Berte & Sigmund Romberg. WORDS: Dorothy Donnelly. COND: Al Goodman. CAST: Earl Wrightson, Donald Dame, Mary Martha Briney, Blanka Peric, Mullen Sisters, chorus. (RCA LK-1018)

160115b BLOSSOM TIME studio prod, entitled "Lilac Time." MUSIC: Franz Schubert, arranged by Heinrich Berte & G H Clutsam. WORDS: Adrian Ross. ORCH: Brian Fahey. COND: Michael Collins. CAST: June Bronhill, Thomas Round, John Cameron, Marion Grimaldi, Elisabeth Osborne, Kenneth Tudor, Eric Wilson-Hyde, Barry Kent. (Angel 35817)

160115c BLOSSOM TIME studio prod. MUSIC: Franz Schubert, arranged by Heinrich Berte, Sigmund Romberg, Henri Rene. WORDS: Dorothy Donnelly. COND: Lehman Engel. CAST: Mary Ellen Pracht, Sara Endich, Richard Fredericks, William Lewis, George Gaynes, Arthur Rubin, Kenneth Smith. (Reader's Digest 40-5, with Rose-Marie)

160115d BLOSSOM TIME 1922 medley by Victor Light Opera Company. (78/Vic 35722)

160115e BLOSSOM TIME records by Richard Tauber of 1942 London prod. 1934: "Love Lost for Evermore," "Once There Lived a Lady Fair" (78/Parlophone(E) RO-20256) 1941: "Love Comes at Blossom Time," "First Love Is Best Love" (78/Parlophone(E) RO-20504) "The Dearest Maiden Waits Me There" (78/Parlophone(E) RO-20506) "The Question," "Laughter and Weeping" (78/Parlophone(E) RO-20507)

160115f BLOSSOM TIME 1935 medley. COND: Nathaniel Shilkret. VOCALS: Milton Watson, Rise Stevens, Helen Marshall, chorus. (LP-307)

160115g BLOSSOM TIME medleys by Columbia Light Opera Company. (1922: 78/Col A-6209)(1929:78/Col(E) 9580)

160115h BLOSSOM TIME 1964 album, entitled "Lilac Time." COND: Johnny Arthey. VOCALS: John Hanson, Mary Bassano, chorus. (Philips(E) SBL-7626, with The Maid of the Mountains)

160115i BLOSSOM TIME 1934 records by Everett Marshall of 1938 prod. "Song of Love" (78/Dec 225) "Lonely Heart" (78/Dec 15002)

160115j BLOSSOM TIME 1923 records by members of 1922 London prod, entitled "Lilac Time." Clara Butterworth, Percy Heming: "When the Lilac Bloom Uncloses," "I Want to Carve Your Name" (78/ Vocalion(E) K-05068) Heming, Courtice Pounds: "Underneath the Lilac Bough" Pounds: "The Golden Song" (78/ Vocalion(E) K-05065) "Dear Flower, Small and Wise" Pounds: "Dream Enthralling" (78/Vocalion(E) K-05067) Heming: "I Am Singing, I, Your Lover" Butterworth: "The Three Little Girls" (78/Vocalion(E) K-05066)

160115k BLOSSOM TIME 1928 medley by Light Opera Company, entitled "Lilac Time." (78/HMV(E) C-1450)

160115l BLOSSOM TIME 1961 studio prod. WORDS: Adrian Ross. COND: John Hollingsworth. CAST: Jacqueline Delman, John Larsen, Peter Glossop, chorus. (World Records(E) SLM-4, entitled "Lilac Time")

160217a ROBINSON CRUSOE JR. records by Al Jolson of orig cast. "Yaaka, Hoola, Hickey, Doola" (1916: LP-758)(1947: LP-331) "You're a Dangerous Girl" (1916: 78/Col A-2041) "Where Did Robinson Crusoe Go With Friday on Saturday Night?" (1916: LP-288)(Later: LP-280) "Tillie Titwillow" (1917: LP-288) "Where the Black-Eyed Susans Grow" (1947: LP-196, LP-244) "Down Where the Swanee River Flows" (1916: 78/Col A-2007)

160228a THE HEART O' TH' HEATHER 1916 records by George MacFarlane of orig (Boston) cast. "Don't Believe All You Hear in the Moonlight," "In Scotland" (78/Vic 45097)

160228*a POM-POM 1916 records by Mizzi Hajos of orig cast. MUSIC: Hugo Felix. WORDS: Anne Caldwell. "Evelyn," "In the Dark" (78/Vic 45091)

160330a MR. MANHATTAN records by Raymond Hitchcock of orig (London) cast. "When You're All Dressed Up and No Place to Go" (1916: 78/HMV(E) 02660)(1922: 78/Vocalion 35010)

160419a THE BING BOYS ARE HERE contemp record by Violet Loraine and George Robey of orig (London) prod. "If You Were the Only Girl in the World" (LP-158)

160513a A HAPPY DAY contemp record by Jose Collins of orig (London) cast. MUSIC & WORDS: Paul Rubens. "Oh, for a Night in Bohemia" (LP-152)

160529a STEP THIS WAY 1916 records by Marguerite Farrell of orig cast. "If I Knock the 'L' Out of Kelly" (78/Col A-2040)(78/Vic 18105) "By the Sad Luana Shore" (78/Vic 18105)

160605a PELL-MELL contemp records by members of orig (London) cast. Alice Delysia: "Summer Days" (LP-128) Nat D Ayer: "You've Got to Do It" (with Bessie Jones) (LP-158)

160831a CHU-CHIN-CHOW 1959 studio prod. MUSIC: Frederic Norton. WORDS: Oscar Asche. ORCH: Brian Fahey. COND: Michael Collins. CAST: Inia Te Wiata, Julie Bryan, Barbara Leigh, Charles Young, chorus. (HMV(E) CLP-1269)

160831b CHU-CHIN-CHOW 1961 studio prod. COND: John Hollingsworth. CAST: Hervey Alan, Marion Grimaldi, Martin Lawrence, John Wakefield, Ian Wallace, Edward Darling, Barbara Elsy, William McCue. (Music for Pleasure(E) 1012)

160831c CHU-CHIN-CHOW 1931 medley by Light Opera Company. (78/ Vic 36138)

160831d CHU-CHIN-CHOW contemp records by members of orig (London) cast. Frank Cochrane: "The Cobbler's Song" (78/Col(E) D-1379) Aileen d'Orme: "Any Time's Kissing Time" (78/Col(E) L-1114) Violet Essex: "I Love You So" (78/HMV(E) 03528) "Cleopatra's Nile" (78/HMV(E) 2-3208) Essex, Courtice Pounds: "Any Time's Kissing Time" (78/HMV(E) 04186) Pounds: "When a Pullet Is Plump" (78/HMV(E) 4-2812) Bryn Gwyn, 1923: "The Cobbler's Song" (78/ Homochord(E) H-530)

160911a FLORA BELLA contemp medley by Victor Light Opera Company. MUSIC: Charles Cuvillier, Milton Schwartzwald. WORDS: Percy Waxman. (78/Vic 35592)

160919a THEODORE AND CO. contemp records by members of orig (London) cast. MUSIC: Jerome Kern. WORDS: Clifford Grey. George Grossmith, Madge Saunders: "All That I Want Is Somebody to Love Me" Leslie Henson, Davy Burnaby: "Three Hundred and Sixty-Five Days" Julie James: "That 'Come Hither' Look" (LP-430)

160919b THEODORE AND CO. 1916 medley by Light Opera Company. (78/HMV(E) C-765)

160925a MISS SPRINGTIME contemp medley by Victor Light Opera Company. MUSIC: Emmerich Kalman. WORDS: Guy Bolton. (78/Vic 35592)

160925b MISS SPRINGTIME 1917 record by George MacFarlane of orig cast. "My Castle in the Air" (LP-784)

161106a VANITY FAIR contemp records by members of orig (London) prod. Teddie Gerard: "The Kirchner Girl" Nelson Keys: "Walkin' the Dog" (LP-158) Regine Flory, Keys: "Some Sort of Somebody"(by Jerome Kern) (LP-430)

161123a HOUP-LA contemp records by members of orig (London) prod. Gertie Millar: "Houp-la," "Pretty Baby," "The Fool of the Family" Millar & Nat D Ayer: "You Can't Love As I Do" (LP-227)

161129a FOLLOW ME 1917 records by Henry Lewis or orig cast. "Oh! Johnny Oh! Johnny Oh!" (78/Emerson 7197) "What Do You Want to Make Those Eyes at Me for?" (78/Emerson 7137)

161206a HER SOLDIER BOY 1918 records by members of 1918 London prod (entitled "Soldier Boy"). MUSIC & WORDS: Sigmund Romberg, Emmerich Kalman, Frederick Chappelle, Rida Johnson Young, others. COND: Leonard Hornsey. Orchestra: Medley (78/Col(E) 717) Winifred Barnes: "The Lonely Princess," "He's Coming Home" (78/Col(E) L-1266) Barnes, Laurence Leonard: "The Kiss Waltz" Laurence Leonard: "Song of Home" (78/Col(E) L-1262) Fred Duprez: "Alone in a City Full of Girls," "The Battle Front at Home" (78/Col(E) L-1263) Duprez, Maisie Gay: "Soldier Boy" (78/Col(E) L-1267) Gay: "I'm Going Home," "March Along" (78/Col(E) L-1264) Gay, Billy Leonard: "The Military Stamp" Dewey Gibson: "Mother" (78/Col(E) L-1265)

1917

170111a HAVE A HEART contemp medley by Victor Light Opera Company. MUSIC: Jerome Kern. WORDS: P G Wodehouse. (LP-606) (LP-784)

170111b HAVE A HEART 1917 record by Billy B Van of orig cast & the Peerless Quartet. "Napoleon" (LP-784)

170115a LOVE O' MIKE contemp medley by Victor Light Opera Company. MUSIC: Jerome Kern. WORDS: Harry B Smith. (LP-606)

170119a DANCE AND GROW THIN 1917 record by Gus Van & Joe Schenck of orig cast. MUSIC & WORDS: Irving Berlin. "Dance and Grow Thin" (78/Vic 18258)

170131a ZIG-ZAG contemp records by members of orig (London) prod. MUSIC: Dave Stamper. WORDS: Gene Buck. Shirley Kellogg: "Beware of Chu-Chin-Chow," "In Grandma's Day" (78/Col(E) L-1144) "Over There" Daphne Pollard: "Thumbs Up" (78/Col(E) L-1222) "Will o' the Wisp," "Somnambulistic Melody" (78/Col (E) L-1139) "I'm a Ragtime Germ," "I Want Someone to Make a Fuss over Me" (78/Col(E) L-1141) George Robey: "Burglar Jim," "I Said Yes, I Would" (78/Col(E) L-1146) "A Deed That Spoke Louder than Words," "She Spoke to Me First" (78/Col(E) L-1223) Kellogg, Robey: "Bye-and-bye You Will Miss Me," "I Can Live without You" (78/Col(E) L-1145) Cicely Debenham, Bertram Wallis: "Hello! My Dearie" Debenham: "Louana Lou" (LP-700) Orchestra of orig prod: "Beware of Chu-Chin-Chow" (78/Col(E) L-1143) "Will-o'-the-Wisp" (78/Col(E) L-1140) "Somnambulistic Melody" (78/Col(E) L-1143)

170206a YOU'RE IN LOVE 1929 medley by Victor Salon Group.

MUSIC: Rudolf Friml. WORDS: Otto Harbach, Edward Clark. COND: Nathaniel Shilkret. (LP-590)

170210a THE MAID OF THE MOUNTAINS contemp records by members of orig (London) prod. MUSIC & WORDS: Harold Fraser-Simson, Harry Graham, others. COND: Merlin Morgan. CAST: Jose Collins, Thorpe Bates, Lauri de Frece, Mark Lester, Mabel Sealby. "Live for Today," "My Life Is Love," "Farewell," "Love Will Find a Way," "Dirty Work," "A Paradise for Two," "Husbands and Wives," "A Bachelor Gay," "I Understood," "Over There and Over Here" (World Record Club(E) 169, with additional songs by Jose Collins) Orchestra: Medley (78/Col(E) L-1160) "Nocturne," "Love Will Find a Way" (78/Col(E) L-1161)

170210b THE MAID OF THE MOUNTAINS medleys by Light Opera Company. (1917: 78/HMV(E) C-814)(1930: HMV(E) C-2063)

170210c THE MAID OF THE MOUNTAINS 1968 studio prod. ORCH & COND: Merrick Farran. CAST: Madge Stephens, Michael Wakeham, Leslie Fyson, Charles Young, Rita Williams, chorus. (Saga(E) EROS-8115)

170210d THE MAID OF THE MOUNTAINS 1972 London prod. ORCH: Ronald Hamner. COND: Derek Taverner, CAST: Jimmy Edwards, Lyn Kennington, Gordon Clyde, Jimmy Thompson, Janet Mahoney, Neville Jason, chorus. (Col(E) SCX-6504)

170210e THE MAID OF THE MOUNTAINS studio prod. WORDS: Frederick Lonsdale. COND: Geoff Harvey. VOCALS: Valda Bagnall, Neil Williams, chorus.(World Record Club(E) 794, with Balalaika)

170210f THE MAID OF THE MOUNTAINS 1964 album. COND: Johnny Arthey. VOCALS: John Hanson, Mary Bassano, chorus. (Philips(E) SBL-7626, with Lilac Time)

170210g THE MAID OF THE MOUNTAINS 1958 album. COND: Michael Collins. VOCALS: Barry Kent, Mary Thomas, chorus. (Encore(E) 178, with No, No, Nanette, The Belle of New York, & others)

170210h THE MAID OF THE MOUNTAINS medley by Light Opera Company. (78/Col(E) DX-81)

170220a OH, BOY! 1919 records by members of 1919 London prod, entitled "Oh, Joy!" MUSIC: Jerome Kern. WORDS: P G Wodehouse. Tom Powers (also of orig cast), Beatrice Lillie: "Till the Clouds Roll By" (LP-430) (LP-784) Billy Leonard: "A Packet of Seeds" Lillie, Powers, Leonard: "March Quarter Day" Dot Temple: "An Old Fashioned Wife" Powers, Temple: "Words Are Not Needed," "You Never Knew about Me" Leonard, Powers, Tom Payne: "Wedding Bells" Powers, Temple, Payne: "Loving by Proxy" Lillie, Leonard: "Nesting Time," "A Pal like You" (LP-430) Lillie: "Rolled into One" (LP-123) (LP-430) Orchestra: Medley (78/Col(E) 729) "Rolled into One" (78/Col(E) L-1290)

170220b OH, BOY! contemp medley by Victor Light Opera Company. (LP-784)

170220c OH, BOY! 1917 records by Anna Wheaton of orig cast. "Rolled into One" (78/Col A-2238) "Till the Clouds Roll By"(with James Harrod)(78/Col A-2261)

170220d OH, BOY! 1938 medley by Victor Light Opera Company. COND: Leonard Joy. (LP-306)(LP-606)

170319a EILEEN 1946 studio prod. MUSIC: Victor Herbert. WORDS: Henry Blossom. COND: Al Goodman. CAST: Frances Greer, Jimmy Carroll, Earl Wrightson. (RCA LK-1019)

170319b EILEEN 1917 medley by Victor Light Opera Company. COND: Victor Herbert (composer). (LP-767)

170319c EILEEN 1917 records by members of orig prod. COND: Victor Herbert (composer). Greek Evans, chorus: "Free Trade and a Misty Moon" Scott Welsh, chorus: "The Irish Have a Great Day To-night" (78/Vic 18285)

170319d EILEEN 1917 records by Vernon Stiles, who was replaced in orig cast by Walter Scanlan before show opened. "The Irish Have a Great Day Tonight" (with quartet), "Ireland, My Sireland" (78/Col A-2247)

170319e EILEEN 1931 medley by Victor Salon Group. COND: Nathaniel Shilkret. (LP-777)

170426a CHEEP contemp records by members of orig (London) cast. Beatrice Lillie: "Shoot the Rabbit" (LP-123) "Julia" (LP-123) (LP-136) Lee White, Clay Smith: "At the Calico Ball" (LP-158)

170426*a THE PASSING SHOW OF 1917 1916 record by Dolly Connolly of orig cast. "'Way Out Yonder in the Golden West" (78/Col A-2084)

170607a HITCHY-KOO 1917 records by Frances White of orig cast. "Six Times Six Is Thirty-Six," "Mississippi" (78/Vic 45137) "I'd Like to Be a Monkey in the Zoo" (78/Vic 45149)

170612a ZIEGFELD FOLLIES OF 1917 records by members of orig cast. Eddie Cantor: "That's the Kind of a Baby for Me" (1917: LP-157, LP-324)(1917: 78/Aeolian Vocalion 1220)(1934: 78/Rex(E) 8389) "The Modern Maiden's Prayer" (1917: LP-324)(1917:78/Aeolian Vocalion 1220) Bert Williams: "No Place Like Home" (1917: 78/Col A-2438)

170612b ZIEGFELD FOLLIES OF 1917 contemp medley by Victor Light Opera Company, (78/Vic 35651)

170719a ROUND THE MAP contemp record by Alfred Lester of orig (London) cast. "A Conscientious Objector" (LP-74)

170816a MAYTIME records by members of 1937 film cast. MUSIC: Sigmund Romberg. WORDS: Rida Johnson Young, Gus Kahn. Jeanette MacDonald & Nelson Eddy: "Will You Remember?" (1936: LP-4, LP-462)(1958: LP-134) "Farewell to Dreams" (dropped before release) (1936: LP-4, LP-462) MacDonald: "Will You Remember?" (1950: LP-77, LP-119) Eddy: "Will You Remember?" (c 1965, with Gale Sherwood: LP-499)

170816b MAYTIME 1944 radio prod with members of 1937 film cast. Nelson Eddy: "Le Regiment" Jeanette MacDonald: "Les Filles de Cadiz," "Air des Bijoux" MacDonald, Eddy: "Carry Me Back to Old Virginny," "Will You Remember?," "Tchaikovsky Airs" (Pelican 121)

170816c MAYTIME 1935 medley. COND: Nathaniel Shilkret. VOCALS: Fred Kuhnly, Helen Marshall, Milton Watson, chorus. (LP-307)

170816d MAYTIME contemp record by John Charles Thomas, who joined orig prod in 1918. "Will You Remember?" (LP-649)

170822a CARMINETTA records by Alice Delysia of orig (London) cast. Contemp: "Cliquot," "Habanera" Later: "The Merry Farewell" (LP-128)

170829a LEAVE IT TO JANE 1959 prod. MUSIC: Jerome Kern. WORDS: Guy Bolton, P G Wodehouse. ORCH: Art Harris. COND: Joseph Stecko. CAST: Kathleen Murray, Art Matthews, Jeanne Allen, Angelo Mango, Dorothy Greener, George Segal, Ray Tudor, Jan Speers. (Strand 1002)

170829b LEAVE IT TO JANE contemp medley by Victor Light Opera Company. (LP-606)(LP-784)

170829c LEAVE IT TO JANE 1938 medley by Victor Light Opera Company, COND: Leonard Joy. (LP-306)

170914a THE BOY 1917 records by members of orig (London) prod. (The show was entitled "Good Morning, Judge" in New York.) MUSIC & WORDS: Lionel Monckton, Howard Talbot, Ad-

rian Ross, Percy Greenbank. W H Berry: "When the Heart Is Young" (78/HMV(E) 4-2944) "I Want to Go Bye-Bye" (with Bessie Jones & Eda Bennie) (78/HMV(E) 02776) Peter Gawthorne: "I'm Sick to Death of Women" (78/HMV(E) B-888) Gawthorne, Nellie Taylor: "I've Always Got Time to Talk to You," "Have a Heart" (78/HMV(E) C-834) Taylor: "Little Miss Melody" (78/HMV(E) C-833)

170914b THE BOY 1919 piano roll by George Gershwin (composer) of a song added to the 1919 New York prod (entitled "Good Morning, Judge"). "I Was So Young (You Were So Beautiful)" (LP-458) (LP-459)

171016a JACK O' LANTERN contemp medley by Victor Light Opera Company. MUSIC: Ivan Caryll. WORDS: Anne Caldwell. (78/Vic 35666)

171101a THE LAND OF JOY 1917 records by Lacalle's Spanish Orchestra of orig prod, MUSIC: Joaquin Valverde. "Alegrias" (Table Dance), "Los Crotalos" (Tambourine Dance) (78/Col A-2475)

171105a MISS 1917 1956 record sung by Irving Caesar, lyricist. MUSIC: George Gershwin. "You-oo, Just You" (LP-353)

171119a ODDS AND ENDS OF 1917 contemp records by Jack Norworth of orig cast. "Fancy You Fancying Me," "The Further It Is from Tipperary" (78/Pathe 29210)

171126a THE STAR GAZER contemp record by John Charles Thomas of 1917 New York prod, MUSIC: Franz Lehar. WORDS: Mathew C Woodward. "If You Only Knew" (78/Vocalion 60053)

171225a GOING UP contemp medley by Columbia Light Opera Company. MUSIC: Louis A Hirsch. WORDS: Otto Harbach. (78/Col A-6055)

171225b GOING UP contemp medley by Victor Light Opera Company. (78/Vic 35672)

171225c GOING UP 1918 records by members of 1918 London prod. Joseph Coyne, Henri de Bray, Marjorie Gordon, Evelyn Laye, Austin Melford: "Going Up" Laye: "Do It for Me" (78/HMV(E) C-860) Coyne, Gordon: "First Act, Second Act, Third Act" (78/ HMV/(E) 04232) Laye, Gordon, others: "If You Look in Her Eyes" (78/HMV(E) 04233) Coyne, Roy Byford, Melford, Franklyn Bellamy: "Down! Up! Left! Right!" (78/HMV(E) 04235) Gordon, deBray: "Kiss Me!"(78/HMV(E) 04234) Gordon, Bellamy: "The Tickle Toe" (78/HMV(E) 03614) Gordon, others: "The Touch of a Woman's Hand" (78/HMV(E) 03613) Orchestra: Medley (78/ HMV(E) C-861) "I'll Bet You/The Touch of a Woman's Hand," "Medley Two-Step" (78/ HMV(E) B-988)

171231a COHAN REVUE OF 1918 record by Nora Bayes of orig cast. "Regretful Blues" (78/Col A-6038)

1918

180201a OH, LADY! LADY!! contemp medley by Victor Light Opera Company, MUSIC: Jerome Kern. WORDS; P G Wodehouse. (LP-784)

180214a SINBAD records by Al Jolson of orig cast. "Rock-a-bye Your Baby" (1918: 78/Col A-2560)(1932: LP-19, LP-42, LP-494, LP-721)(1945: LP-145, LP-244, LP-739)(1947: LP-331, LP-394, LP-478) "Swanee" (1920: LP-38, LP-470)(1945: LP-145, LP-244)(1945: LP-654, LP-,763)(1948: LP-677) "Avalon" (1920: LP-288)(1935: LP-373) (1946: LP-228, LP-244, LP-739)(1946: LP-682) "You Ain't Heard Nothing Yet" (1919: LP-288, LP-470) "'N Everything" (1917: 78/Col A-2519) "Hello Central, Give Me No Man's Land" (1918: LP-548) "I Wonder Why She Kept On Saying 'Si-Si-Si-Si-Senor'" (1918: LP-470) "On the Road to Calais" (1918: LP-288) "I'll Say She Does" (I918: LP-550) "I Gave Her That" (1919: LP-470) "Chloe" (1919: LP-626) "My

Mammy" (1928: LP-82, LP-731)(1946: LP-145, LP-244, LP-739)(1946:LP-682)(1948: LP-677)

180214b SINBAD 1956 record by Irving Caesar, lyricist. MUSIC: George Gershwin. "Swanee" (LP-353)

180214c SINBAD 1920 piano roll by George Gershwin, composer. "Swanee" (LP-458)

180307a OH, LOOK! 1918 record by Harry Fox of orig cast. MUSIC: Harry Carroll. WORDS: Joseph McCarthy. "I'm Always Chasing Rainbows" (78/Col A-2557)

180401a THE RAINBOW GIRL contemp medley by Columbia Light Opera Company. MUSIC: Louis A Hirsch. WORDS: Rennold Wolf. (78/Col A-6055)

180401b THE RAINBOW GIRL contemp medley by Victor Light Opera Company. (78/Vic 35677)

180515a TABS contemp records by members of orig (London) cast. MUSIC & WORDS: Ivor Novello, Ronald Jeans, others. Margaret Campbell: "Goblin Golliwog Trees" Alfred Austin: "Naughty Old Gentleman" (78/Col(E) L-1259) Guy Lefeuvre: "God Gave Me You" Harry Glen: "Mr. Pau-Puk-Keewis" (78/Col(E) L-1260) Beatrice Lillie: "Maryland" Lillie, Campbell: "I Hate to Give Trouble" (78/Col(E) L-1257) Lillie: "I Said Goodbye," "Sammy" (78/Col(E) L-1256) Lillie, Austin: "My River Girl" Ethel Baird: "Something Doing Over There" (78/Col(E) L-1258)

180522a ROCK-A-BYE BABY contemp medley by Victor Light Opera Company. MUSIC: Jerome Kern. WORDS: M E Rourke ("Herbert Reynolds"). (78/Vic 35677)

180803a AS YOU WERE records by Alice Delysia of orig (London) cast. Contemp: "Helen of Troy" Later: "If You Could Care for Me," "Ninon de l'Enclos" (LP-128)

180819a YIP YIP YAPHANK records by Irving Berlin, composer & of orig cast. "Oh, How I Hate to Get Up in the Morning" (1942: Dec 10" 5108, LP-543, LP-321, LP-519)(1940's: 78/V-Disc 780)

180925a HULLO AMERICA 1919 record by Maurice Chevalier, who joined the orig (London) prod in 1919. "On the Level You're a Little Devil" (LP-158)(LP-700)

181004a SOMETIME contemp medley by Victor Light Opera Company. MUSIC: Rudolf Friml. WORDS: Rida Johnson Young. (78/Vic 35694)

181024a LADIES FIRST 1919 records by Nora Bayes of orig cast. "Just like a Gypsy" (78/Col A-6138) "Prohibition Blues" (78/Col A-2823)

181220a BUZZ-BUZZ contemp records by Gertrude Lawrence of orig (London) cast. "Winnie the Window Cleaner" (LP-123) "I've Lost My Heart in Maoriland" (78/Col(E) L-1293) With Walter Williams: "I've Been Waiting for Someone like You" (LP-158)

181223a LISTEN LESTER contemp medley by Victor Light Opera Company. MUSIC: Harold Orlob. WORDS: Harry L Cort, George E Stoddard. (78/Vic 35691)

181223*a SOMEBODY'S SWEETHEART contemp medley by Victor Light Opera Company. MUSIC: Anthony Bafunno. WORDS: Alonzo Price. (78/Vic 35691)

1919

190212a MONTE CRISTO JR 1919 record by Esther Walker of orig cast. MUSIC: Sigmund Romberg, Jean Schwartz. WORDS: Harold Atteridge. "Sahara" (78/Vic 18613)

190419a MONSIEUR BEAUCAIRE 1919 records by members of orig (London) prod. MUSIC: Andre Messager. WORDS: Adrian Ross.

COND: Kennedy Russell. CAST: John Clarke, Marion Green, & Robert Parker, who were also in 1919 New York cast; Alice Moffat, Maggie Teyte. Orchestra: Medley (78/Col(E) 740) "Waltz/Rose Minuet" (78/Col(E) 741) Clarke: "Honour and Love" Clarke, Green, Parker: "Going to the Ball" (78/Col(E) L-1309) Clarke, Moffat: "I Love You a Little," "We Are Not Speaking Now" (78/Col(E) L-1308) Green: "Red Rose," "English Maids" (78/Col(E) L-1306) "Gold and Blue and White," "Under the Moon" (78/Col(E) L-1307) Green, Teyte: "Lightly, Lightly" (78/Col(E) L-1312) "Say No More" (78/Col(E) L-1313) "Finale, Act I" (78/Col(E) L-1314) "What Are Names?" (78/Col(E) L-1315) "Finale, Act II" (78/Col(E) L-1316) Teyte: "Philomel" (78/Col(E) L-1310) "I Do Not Know" (78/Col(E) L-1311)

190419b MONSIEUR BEAUCAIRE 1932 medley by Light Opera Company. (78/HMV C-2443)

190505a SHE'S A GOOD FELLOW records by the Duncan Sisters of orig cast. MUSIC: Jerome Kern. WORDS: Anne Caldwell. "The Bull Frog Patrol" (1922: LP-430)(1924: 78/Vic 19352)(1928:78/Col(E) 5182)

190505b SHE'S A GOOD FELLOW contemp medley by Victor Light Opera Company. (LP-606)

190512a THE LADY IN RED contemp medley by Victor Light Opera Company. MUSIC: Richard Winterberg. WORDS: Anne Caldwell. (78/Vic 35491)

190520a KISSING TIME 1919 records by members of orig (London) prod. MUSIC: Ivan Caryll, Willie Redstone. WORDS: Clifford Grey. COND: Willie Redstone. Orchestra: Medley (78/Col(E) 742) Yvonne Arnaud: "Chiquita," "Cherie, Oh Ma Cherie" (78/Col(E) L-1318) Arnaud, Leslie Henson, George Grossmith: "The Happy Family" (78/Col(E) MC-15) "I Like It" (78/Col(E) MC-16) Phyllis Dare: "Some Day" (78/Col(E) MC-11) "Thousands of Years Ago" (78/Col(E) MC-12) Dare, Grossmith: "Joan and Peter" (78/Col(E) MC-13) "There's a Light in Your Eye" (78/Col(E) MC-14) Grossmith: "Desertion" (78/Col(E) MC-8) Henson, Tom Walls: "A Little Touch of Spring" (78/Col(E) MC-17) Henson: "Motoring" (78/Col(E) MC-9) "Women Haven't Any Mercy on a Man" (78/Col(E) MC-10)

190526a LA LA LUCILLE 1919 piano rolls by George Gershwin, composer. "Tee-Oodle-Um-Bum-Bo" (LP-375)(LP-459) "Nobody but You" (LP-458)

190623a ZIEGFELD FOLLIES OF 1919 records by members of orig cast. Bert Williams, 1919: "When the Moon Shines on the Moonshine" (LP-1)(LP-232)(LP-514)(LP-518)(LP-639) "It's Nobody's Business but My Own" (LP-232)(LP-639) Eddie Cantor, 1919: "You'd Be Surprised" (LP-485)(LP-514) "When They're Old Enough to Know Better" (LP-514)(LP-639)(Pathe 22201) "I've Got My Captain Working for Me Now" (LP-514) "You Don't Need the Wine to Have a Wonderful Time," "Oh, the Last Rose of Summer" (LP-485)(LP-514) (78/Pathe 22163) Cantor, later: "How Ya Gonna Keep 'Em Down on the Farm?" (LP-30)(LP-165)(LP-143)(LP-384) "You'd Be Surprised" (LP-114)(LP-143) "Mandy" (LP-379)(LP-593) John Steel, 1919: "A Pretty Girl is like a Melody" (by Irving Berlin) (LP-157)(LP-514)(LP-519) "Tulip Time," "My Baby's Arms" (LP-514) Steel, 1938: "A Pretty Girl Is like a Melody" (LP-387)(LP-710) Gus Van & Joe Schenck, 1919: "Mandy" (LP-157)(LP-514)(LP-519) (LP-710) "Sweet Kisses" (LP-514)

190715a GREENWICH VILLAGE FOLLIES OF 1919 records by Ted Lewis Orch of orig prod. "When My Baby Smiles at Me" (1920: 78/Col A-2908) (1927: 78/Col 922-D)(1938: LP-167, LP-297, LP-457, LP-491) "I'll See You in C-U-B-A'" (1920: 78/Col A-2927)

190828a BRAN PIE 1919 records by Beatrice Lillie of orig (London) prod. "That Wonderful Lamp" (LP-159) "Someone Else May Be There When I'm Gone" (by Irving Berlin) (LP-583)

190902a BACK AGAIN contemp record by Lee White of orig (London) prod. "A Good Man Is Hard to Find" (LP-159)

190917a AFGAR contemp records by members of orig (London) prod. MUSIC & WORDS: mostly Charles Cuvillier, Douglas Furber. Alice Delysia (also of 1920 New York cast): "Dardanella," "You'd Be Surprised" (by Irving Berlin), "A Garden of Make-Believe" (LP-128) "Live for Love," "No Man's Land" (78/Col(E) F-1027) "Dear Lonely Lover" (78/Col(E) F-1029) Lupino Lane (also of 1920 New York cast): "The Man from Mexico" Harry Welchman: "Give the Devil His Due" (78/Col(E) F-1025) "'Neath Your Casement'" Welchman, Marie Burke: "Ah, Give Me Your Lips" (78/Col(E) F-1026) Welchman, John Humphries: "Antiques" Lane, Humphries: "United We Stand" (78/Col(E) F-1024) Burke: "Rose of Seville," "Sunshine Valley" (78/Col(E) F-1023) Delysia, Welchman: "Night Was Made for Love" (LP-128) Orchestra: Medley (78/Col(E) 781)

191001a BIFF, BING, BANG contemp records by Red Newman of orig (Toronto) cast. "Oh, It's a Lovely War," "Civvies" (78/HMV (C) 216366)

191007a APPLE BLOSSOMS contemp medley by Victor Light Opera Company. MUSIC: Victor Jacobi, Fritz Kreisler. WORDS: William LeBaron. (78/Vic 35697)

191007b APPLE BLOSSOMS contemp records by John Charles Thomas of orig cast. "Little Girls, Goodbye" (78/Vocalion 20001) With Lucille Rene, not of orig cast: "You Are Free" (78/Vocalion 20002)

191007c APPLE BLOSSOMS records by Fritz Kreisler (composer). Fritz Kreisler, violin: "Who Can Tell?" (78/Vic 64902) Fritz Kreisler, piano, & Hugo Kreisler, cello: "The Letter Song," "I'm in Love" (78/Vic 956)

191027a BUDDIES contemp medley by Columbia Light Opera Company. MUSIC & WORDS: B C Hilliam. (78/Col A-6142)

191112a THE ECLIPSE 1919 records by members of orig (London) prod. Nancy Gibbs, F Pope Stamper: "Chelsea," "I Never Realised" (both by Cole Porter) (LP-300) Orchestra: Medley, "I Never Realised" (78/Col(E) 783)

191118a IRENE 1920 records by members of 1920 London prod. MUSIC: Harry Tierney, WORDS: Joseph McCarthy. COND: Frank Tours. Edith Day: "Irene," "Alice Blue Gown," "To Be Worthy of You," "Castle of Dreams," "Sky Rocket" Day, Robert Michaelis: "To Love You" Daisy Hancox: "Hobbies" Winnie Collins, Margaret Campbell, Robert Hale: "We're Getting Away with It," "The Last Part of Every Party," "The Talk of the Town" (Monmouth 7057. Excerpts: Day: "Irene," "Alice Blue Gown" (LP-84).) Orchestra: Medley (78/Col(E) 821) Waltz (78/Col(E) 823)

191118b IRENE 1973 prod with five songs from the orig; additional songs by Charles Gaynor, Otis Clements, others. ORCH: Ralph Burns. COND: Jack Lee, CAST: Debbie Reynolds, Monte Markham, Ruth Warrick George S Irving, Patsy Kelly, Carmen Alvarez, Janie Sell, Ted Pugh. (Col KS-32266)

191118c IRENE records by Edith Day of orig & 1920 London casts. (See also listing for 1920 London prod.) "Alice Blue Gown" (1920: LP-18, LP-711)(1934: LP-56) "Irene" (1920: 78/Vic 45176)

191118d IRENE contemp medley by Victor Light Opera Company. (78/Vic 35697)

191118e IRENE contemp medley by Columbia Light Opera Company. (78/Col A-6142)

191118f IRENE 1976 London prod, based on 1973 New York prod, with additional changes. COND: Michael Reed. CAST: Julie Anthony, Jon Pertwee, Eric Flynn, Jessie Evans, Janet Mahoney, Jenny Logan. (EMI(E) EMC-3139)

191227a MORRIS GEST MIDNIGHT WHIRL 1920 record by George Gershwin, composer. "Limehouse Nights" (LP-458)

1920

200202a THE NIGHT BOAT contemp medley by Victor Light Opera Company. MUSIC: Jerome Kern. WORDS: Anne Caldwell. (LP-606)

200212a THE LAST WALTZ 1922 records by members of 1922 London prod. MUSIC: Oscar Straus. Jose Collins: "Love, the Minstrel," "Just for a While" (LP-152) "The Mirror Song" Collins, Kingsley Lark: "When Life and Love Are Calling" (78/Col(E) 912) "The Magic Waltz Refrain," "The Last Waltz" (78/Col(E) 910) Lark: "Red Roses," "Man Is Master of His Fate" (78/Col(E) 913)

200324a FLY WITH ME 1980 prod, rec live. MUSIC: Richard Rodgers. WORDS: Lorenz Hart, Oscar Hammerstein II, Richard Rodgers. ORCH: Bruce Pomahac. COND: Howard Shanet. CAST: Daniel Frank, Cheryl Suzanne Horowitz, Rod McLucas, Marci Pliskin, Avi Simon, Francis Larson, Annie Laurita. (Original Cast CYM-8023)

200405a ED WYNN CARNIVAL 1920 records by Ray Miller Orch of orig prod. "Rose of Spain" (78/Okeh 4119)(Vocalion 14106)(78/Pathe 22427)(78/Gennett 9075) "I Love the Land of Old Black Joe" (78/Pathe 22425) "Can You Tell?" (78/Vocalion 14106)

200503a HONEY GIRL contemp medley by Victor Light Opera Company. MUSIC: Albert Von Tilzer. WORDS: Neville Fleeson. (78/Vic 35705)

200515a A SOUTHERN MAID contemp records by members of orig (London) cast. MUSIC: Ivor Novello. WORDS: Douglas Furber. Jose Collins: "Every Bit of Loving" Collins, Claude Flemming: "I Want the Sun and Moon" (LP-152)

200528a THE BLUE MAZURKA 1927 medley by Light Opera Company, incl Elisabeth Pechy of 1927 London cast. MUSIC: Franz Lehar. WORDS: Harry Graham. (78/HMV(E) C-1331)

200528b THE BLUE MAZURKA 1927 medley by orchestra of 1927 London prod conducted by Arthur Wood. (78/Col(E) 9216)

200607a GEORGE WHITE'S SCANDALS OF 1920 contemp record by Lester O'Keefe of orig cast. MUSIC: George Gershwin. WORDS: Arthur Jackson. "Songs of Long Ago" (78/Bruns 2046)

200607b GEORGE WHITE'S SCANDALS OF 1920 1920 piano roll by George Gershwin, composer. "On My Mind the Whole Night Long" (LP-375)

200622a ZIEGFELD FOLLIES OF 1920 contemp records by members of orig cast. Fanny Brice: "I'm an Indian" (LP-1)(LP-33) Art Hickman Orch: "Tell Me, Little Gypsy/Bells" (both by Irving Berlin) (78/Col A-2972) "Hold Me" (78/Col A-2899) John Steel: "Tell Me, Little Gypsy" (78/Vic 18687) "The Girls of My Dreams" (by Irving Berlin) (LP-336) "The Love Boat" (by Victor Herbert) (LP-767) Gus Van & Joe Schenck: "All She'd Say Was 'Umh Hum'" (78/Col A-3319) "Marimba" (78/Col A-3336)

200712a THE MIDNIGHT ROUNDERS 1920 record by Jane Green of orig cast. "Wild, Romantic Blues" (78/Pathe 020480)

200715a SILKS AND SATINS 1920 records by Aileen Stanley of orig cast. "My Little Bimbo Down on the Bamboo Isle" (78/Vic 18691)(78/Edison 50707)

200719a COME SEVEN contemp records by Al Bernard, composer. "Read 'Em and Weep" (78/Bruns 4076)(78/Edison 50735)

200830a GREENWICH VILLAGE FOLLIES OF 1920 contemp records by members of orig cast. Frank Crumit: "I'm a Lonesome Little Raindrop" (78/Col A-3332) "Madeline" (78/Col A-3415) Ford Hanford (carpenter's saw): "My Old Kentucky Home" (78/Grey Gull L-7007) "My Old Kentucky Home/Old Black Joe" (78/Vic 18767) Hanford & Pee Wee Myers: "Down in Arkansas" (78/Grey Gull L-7007)(78/Vic 18767)

200918a A NIGHT OUT contemp records by members of orig (London) cast. MUSIC: Cole Porter, WORDS: Clifford Grey. Lily St John: "Looking Around" St John, Leslie Henson: "Why Didn't We Meet Before?" (LP-300)

200929a BROADWAY BREVITIES OF 1920 contemp records by Bert Williams of orig cast. "When the Moon Shines on the Moonshine" (LP-1)(LP-232)(LP-514)(LP-518)(LP-639) "I Want to Know Where Tosti Went" (78/Col A-3305)

201005a TIP TOP 1923 records by members of orig cast. Duncan Sisters: "Baby Sister Blues" (78/Vic 19050) Six Brown Brothers (saxophones): "Wonderful Girl, Wonderful Boy/The Girl I Never Met" (78/Vic 18714)

201018a MARY contemp medley by Victor Light Opera Company. MUSIC: Louis A Hirsch. WORDS: Otto Harbach, Frank Mandel. (78/Vic 35702)

201117a JIMMIE contemp medley by Victor Light Opera Company. MUSIC: Herbert Stothart. WORDS: Otto Harbach, Oscar Hammerstein II. (78/Vic 35705)

201221a SALLY contemp records by members of 1921 London prod. MUSIC: Jerome Kern. WORDS: Clifford Grey, P G Wodehouse, B G DeSylva, Anne Caldwell. Dorothy Dickson: "You Can't Keep a Good Girl Down," "Wild Rose" Gregory Stroud: "Sally" Dickson & Stroud: "Look for the Silver Lining," "Whip-Poor-Will" Leslie Henson: "The Schnitza-Komisski" George Grossmith & Heather Thatcher: "The Church 'Round the Corner" Grossmith, Thatcher, & Seymour Beard: "The Lorelei" Orchestra: Ballet Music (written by Victor Herbert) (Monmouth 7053; LP-430)

201221b SALLY 1942 records by Jessie Matthews of 1942 London prod, entitled "Wild Rose." MUSIC: Jerome Kern. WORDS: B G DeSylva. "Look for the Silver Lining," "Whip-Poor-Will" (LP-64)(LP-173)

201221c SALLY later record by Dorothy Dickson of 1921 London prod. "Wild Rose" (LP-173)

201221d SALLY 1938 medley by Victor Light Opera Company. COND: Leonard Joy. (LP-306)

201221e SALLY album. COND: Geoff Harvey. CAST: Jimmy Parkinson, Betty Parker. (Light Music Club (New Zealand) LZ-7073, with Good News)

201221f SALLY 1932 radio performance by Leon Errol of orig cast. "The Schnitzka Komisska" (LP-566)

201221g SALLY 1929 film soundtrack. Marilyn Miller, Alexander Gray: "If I'm Dreaming," "Look for the Silver Lining" (LP-751)

201227a HER FAMILY TREE 1920 record by Nora Bayes of orig cast. "Why Worry?" (78/Col A-3360)

1921

210205a THE MIDNIGHT ROUNDERS OF 1921 records by Eddie Cantor of orig cast. "Margie" (1920: LP-485)(Later: LP-30, LP-144, LP-165, LP-721) "Ma, He's Making Eyes at Me" (Later: LP-30, LP-38, LP-144, LP-165)

210425a JUNE LOVE later record by Rudolf Friml (composer), piano. "Dear Love, My Love" (LP-733)

210523a SHUFFLE ALONG 1953 album by members of 1952 New York prod. MUSIC: Eubie Blake. WORDS: Noble Sissle. COND:

Eubie Blake. CAST: Avon Long, Thelma Carpenter, Louise Woods, Laurence Watson. (RCA 10" LPM-3154, with Blackbirds of 1928)

210523b SHUFFLE ALONG records by members of orig prod. Eubie Blake (piano) & His Shuffle Along Orch, 1921: "Baltimore Buzz/ In Honeysuckle Time" (LP-422) "Bandana Days/I'm Just Wild about Harry" (LP-431)(LP-587) Noble Sissle (vocal), contemp: "In Honeysuckle Time," "Baltimore Buzz," "On Patrol in No Man's Land" (LP-431) "Ain't Cha Coming Back, Mary Ann, to Maryland" (78/Pathe 22284) "Good Night, Angeline" (78/Pathe 20226) "Low Down Blues," "I'm Just Simply Full of Jazz" (LP-587) Blake piano roll with Edgar Fairchild, 1919: "Good Night, Angeline" (LP-730) Blake, 1921: "Baltimore Buzz/In Honeysuckle Time" (LP-431)(LP-587) Sissle & Blake, contemp: "Love Will Find a Way," "Bandana Days" (LP-422)(LP-431) "If You've Never Been Vamped by a Brownskin" (78/Paramount 12002) "Oriental Blues," "I'm Craving for That Kind of Love" (LP-422) Sissle & Blake, 1969: Medley, including 7 songs (LP-392) Gertrude Saunders, 1921: "I'm Craving for That Kind of Love," "Daddy, Won't You Please Come Home" (LP-431) Contemp sketches by Miller & Lyles: "Fourth of July in Jim Town," "Election Day in Jim Town" (78/Okeh 4766) "Jimtown's Fisticuffs" (LP-431)

210602a SNAPSHOTS OF 1921 1921 record by Nora Bayes of orig cast. "Saturday" (78/Col A-3471)

210621a ZIEGFELD FOLLIES OF 1921 records by members of orig cast. Fanny Brice: "Second-Hand Rose" (1921: LP-18, LP-32, LP-33, LP-230, LP-518, LP-542, LP-710, LP-711) "My Man" (1921: LP-1, LP-148, LP-758)(1927: LP-32, LP-33, LP-44, LP-539, LP-542)(1936: LP-157) John Steel: "Bring Back My Blushing Rose," "Sally, Won't You Come Back?" (1921: 78/Vic 18813) Gus Van & Joe Schenck: "O'Reilly, I'm Ashamed of You" (1921: 78/Col A-3490) "In the Old Town Hall," "What's a-Gonna Be Next?" (1921: 78/Col A-3461) "Wang Wang Blues" (1921: 78/Col A-3427) Schenck: "Sally, Won't You Come Back?" (1921: 78/Col A-3478)

210627a THE CO-OPTIMISTS contemp record by Melville Gideon of orig (London) prod. "When the Sun Goes Down" (LP-159)

210711a GEORGE WHITE'S SCANDALS OF 1921 1921 piano roll by George Gershwin, composer. "Drifting Along with the Tide" (LP-459)

210809a TANGERINE records by members of orig cast. MUSIC: Carlo Sanders, Frank Crumit, Dave Zoob. WORDS: Howard Johnson. Frank Crumit, 1921: "Sweet Lady" (78/Col A-3475) Crumit & Julia Sanderson, 1941: "Sweet Lady," "We'll Never Grow Old" (LP-57)

210823a PUT AND TAKE 1921 records by members of orig cast. Mamie Smith: "Old Time Blues" (78/Okeh 4296) "Stop! Rest a While" (78/Okeh 4471) Edith Wilson (who replaced Smith in the show): "Nervous Blues," "Vampin' Liza Jane" (78/Col A-3479) "Old Time Blues" (78/Col A-3506)

210831a GREENWICH VILLAGE FOLLIES OF 1921 records by Ted Lewis Orch of orig prod. "Down the Old Church Aisle" (1921: 78/Col A-3538)(1927: 78/Col 1207-D)(Later: LP-167, LP-457) "Three O'Clock in the Morning" (1930: 78/Col 2246-D)(1938: LP-167, LP-457) "Georgette" (1922: 78/Col A-3662)

210922a THE MUSIC BOX REVUE OF 1921 records by the Brox Sisters of orig cast. MUSIC & WORDS: Irving Berlin. "School House Blues" (Contemp: LP-336) "Everybody Step" (1938: LP-387)

211004a THE LOVE LETTER contemp record by John Charles Thomas of orig cast. "Canzonetta" (LP-649)

211006a BOMBO records by Al Jolson of orig prod. "April Showers" (1921: LP-516)(1932: LP-41, LP-721)(1945, with Louis Silvers (composer), piano: LP-679)(1945: LP-145, LP-244) (1946: LP-682) (1948: LP-677) "I'm Goin' South" (1923: LP-288)(1924: LP-73, LP-

731) "California, Here I Come" (1924: LP-73, LP-626, LP-731) (1946: LP-145, LP-243, LP-739)(1946: LP-682) "Toot, Toot, Tootsie" (1922: LP-288)(1946: LP-682)(1947: LP-198, LP-244, LP-394, LP-409, LP-739)(1947, with Eddie Cantor: LP-438)(1948: LP-677) "Some Beautiful Morning" (1919: 78/Col A-2940) "Yoo-Hoo" (1921:78/Col A-3513) "Give Me My Mammy" (1921: 78/Col A-3540) "Who Cares?" (1922: 78/Col A-3779) "Morning Will Come" (1923: 78/Col A-3880) "Coo Coo" (1922: 78/Col A-3626)

211011a A TO Z contemp records by members of orig (London) cast. Jack Buchanan: "And Her Mother Came Too" (by Ivor Novello) (LP-61) (LP-97) Buchanan, Trix Sisters: "Dapper Dan" (LP-159) Gertrude Lawrence: "Limehouse Blues" (1931: LP-34)(1936: LP-123, LP-276) (1952: LP-5)

211017a THE FUN OF THE FAYRE 1921 record by Alfred Lester of orig (London) prod. "Germs" (LP-159)

1922

220113a THE BLUE KITTEN 1926 records by members of 1925 London prod. MUSIC & WORDS: Rudolf Friml, Otto Harbach, others. COND: Howard Carr. Ethel Levey, chorus: "Blue Kitten Blues" Levey, Roy Royston: "I'm Head and Heels in Love," "Cutie" Royston, Dorothy Brown: "When I Waltz with You," "I Found a Bud among the Roses," "Down Paradise Way" W H Berry: "Breakfast in Bed," "Summer Is Here" Bobby Howes, Estelle Brody: "Where the Honeymoon Alone Can See," "A Twelve O'Clock Girl in a Nine O'Clock Town" (LP-448)

220220a FOR GOODNESS' SAKE 1923 records by Fred & Adele Astaire of orig & 1923 London prod (entitled "Stop Flirting"). MUSIC & WORDS: Paul Lannin, William Daly. "Oh Gee! Oh Gosh!," "The Whichness of the Whatness" (LP-78)

220302a MADAME POMPADOUR 1924 records by members of 1923 London prod. MUSIC: Leo Fall. WORDS: Harry Graham. COND: Arthur Wood. Evelyn Laye: "Love Me Now" Derek Oldham: "Serenade" (78/Col(E) 966) "Carnival Time" Laye, Oldham: "Reminiscence" (78/Col(E) 3372) "Love's Sentry," "By the Light of the Moon" (78/Col(E) 967) Laye, Huntley Wright: "Joseph" Wright, Elsie Randolph: "Two Little Birds in a Tree" (78/Col(E) 3371) Orchestra: Medley (78/Col(E) 965)

220309a MAYFAIR AND MONTMARTRE 1933 record by Alice Delysia of orig (London) cast. MUSIC: George Gershwin. WORDS: B G DeSylva. "Do It Again" (LP-128)

220413a MAKE IT SNAPPY 1922 records by Eddie Cantor of orig cast. "I'm Hungry for Beautiful Girls," "I Love Her, She Loves Me" (78/Col A-3624) "Sophie" (78/Col A-3754)

220605a ZIEGFELD FOLLIES OF 1922 1922 record by Ed Gallagher & Al Shean of orig cast, "Mr. Gallagher and Mr. Shean" (78/ Vic 18941)(Incomplete: LP-1, LP-18, LP-518, LP-539, LP-711)

220605b ZIEGFELD FOLLIES OF 1922 1941 soundtrack performance by Al Shean of orig cast and Charles Winninger. "Mr. Gallagher and Mr. Shean" (LP-465)

220706a SPICE OF 1922 1956 record sung by Irving Caesar (lyricist with B G DeSylva). MUSIC: George Gershwin. "The Yankee Doodle Blues" (LP-353)

220706b SPICE OF 1922 record sung by J Fred Coots, composer. "In My Little Red Book" (LP-530)

220717a PLANTATION REVUE records by Edith Wilson of orig cast. "He May Be Your Man, but He Comes to See Me Sometimes" (1922: 78/Col A-3653)(1976: LP-723)

220828a GEORGE WHITE'S SCANDALS OF 1922 1922 records by Paul Whiteman Orch of orig prod. MUSIC: George Gershwin.

WORDS: B G DeSylva, E Ray Goetz. "I'll Build a Stairway to Paradise" (LP-49)(LP-518) "I Found a Four-Leaf Clover" (78/Vic 18950)

220828b GEORGE WHITE'S SCANDALS OF 1922 1976 studio prod of "Blue Monday" (a chamber opera later known as "135th Street"), dropped after the opening performance. MUSIC: George Gershwin. WORDS: B G DeSylva. COND: Gregg Smith. CAST: Joyce Andrews, Patrick Mason, Walter Richardson, Thomas Bogdan, Jeffrey Meyer. (Turnabout TV-S-34638, entitled "Gershwin: Blue Monday," with additional material)

220828c GEORGE WHITE'S SCANDALS OF 1922 1968 concert performance of "Blue Monday," a chamber opera later known as "135th Street," rec live. COND: Skitch Henderson. VOCALS: uncredited. (Penzance PR-43, entitled "135th Street," with additional material)

220828d GEORGE WHITE'S SCANDALS OF 1922 contemp piano roll by The Original Piano Trio of orig prod. "I'll Build a Stairway to Paradise" (LP-561)

220904a SALLY, IRENE AND MARY record sung by J Fred Coots, composer. WORDS: Raymond Klages. "Time Will Tell" (LP-530)

220912a GREENWICH VILLAGE FOLLIES OF 1922 1923 records by Savoy & Brennan of orig cast. "You Don't Know the Half of It," "You Must Come Over" (78/Vocalion 14619)

220919a THE CABARET GIRL 1937 records by Dorothy Dickson of orig (London) prod. MUSIC: Jerome Kern. WORDS: Various. "Ka-lu-a," "Dancing Time" (LP-173)

220919b THE CABARET GIRL 1922 medley by orchestra of orig (London) prod conducted by John Ansell. (78/HMV(E) C-1086)

221002a THE YANKEE PRINCESS contemp medley by Victor Light Opera Company, MUSIC: Emmerich Kalman. WORDS: B G DeSylva. (78/Vic 35722)

221010a QUEEN O' HEARTS 1922 records by Nora Bayes of orig prod. "Mammy's Carbon Copy," "You Need Someone, Someone Needs You" (78/Col A-3742)

221023a THE MUSIC BOX REVUE OF 1922 contemp records by John Steel of orig cast. MUSIC & WORDS: Irving Berlin. "Lady of the Evening" (LP-336) "Will She Come from the East?" (78/Vic 18990) "Say It with Music" (78/Vic 18828)

221107a RAIN 1921 record used in the production. Isham Jones Orch: "Wabash Blues" (78/Bruns 5065)

221113a LITTLE NELLIE KELLY 1950 radio prod. MUSIC & WORDS: George M Cohan. Jane Powell: "They're All My Boys" (LP-281)

221127a LIZA 1923 record by Gertrude Saunders of orig cast. "Love Me" (78/Vic 19159)

1923

230105a KATJA, THE DANCER 1925 records by members of 1925 London prod. COND: Arthur Wood. Lilian Davies (also of 1926 New York prod): "Thro' Life We Go Dancing Together" Davies, Gregory Stroud: "Just for a Night" (78/Col(E) 3625) "Those Eyes So Tender" Stroud, Ivy Tresmand: "If You Cared" (78/Col(E) 3627) Stroud: "I've Planned a Rendez-vous" Tresmand, Gene Gerrard: "When We Are Married" (78/Col(E) 3626) "Leander" Bobbie Comber, Rene Mallory: "Love and Duty" (78/Col(E) 3628) Orchestra: Medley (78/Col(E) 9035)

230131a CAROLINE 1923 records by J Harold Murray of orig cast. MUSIC: Charles Kunnecke. WORDS: Harry B Smith. "I'm Only a Pilgrim," "Man in the Moon" (78/Vocalion 14549)

230207a WILDFLOWER contemp records by members of 1926 London prod. MUSIC: Vincent Youmans, Herbert Stothart. WORDS: Otto Harbach, Oscar Hammerstein II. Kitty Reidy: "I Can Always Find Another Partner" Howett Worster: "Wildflower," "Goodbye, Little Rosebud" Reidy, Worster: "Bambalina," "April Blossoms" Evelyn Drewe: "There's Music in Our Hearts" (World Records(E) SH-279, with The Student Prince. Incomplete: Monmouth 7052, with Tip-Toes.)

230322a JACK AND JILL 1923 record by Brooke Johns of orig prod. "I Want a Pretty Girl" (78/Vic 19051)

230618a GEORGE WHITE'S SCANDALS OF 1923 contemp record by Charles Dornberger Orch of orig prod. MUSIC: George Gershwin. "The Life of a Rose" (78/Vic 19151)

230815a LITTLE JESSIE JAMES 1923 record by Paul Whiteman Orch of orig prod. "I Love You" (78/Vic 19151)

230828a LITTLE MISS BLUEBIRD 1923 records by Irene Bordoni of orig & 1925 London casts. "I Won't Say I Will" (by George Gershwin & B G DeSylva), "So This Is Love" (78/Vic 19199)

230904a LONDON CALLING records by members of orig (London) cast. MUSIC & WORDS: Noel Coward, others. Gertrude Lawrence: "Parisian Pierrot" (1931: LP-34) "You Were Meant for Me" (1932: LP-34) (1936: LP-123, LP-276) Noel Coward: "Parisian Pierrot" (1936: LP-28, LP-502) Maisie Gay: "There's Life in the Old Girl Yet" (1924: LP-159, LP-502, LP-524) "What Love Means to Girls like Me" (1924: LP-502)

230922a THE MUSIC BOX REVUE OF 1923 1923 records by members of orig cast. MUSIC & WORDS: Irving Berlin. John Steel: "Little Butterfly," "An Orange Grove in California" (78/Vic 19219) Brox Sisters: "Learn to Do the Strut" (LP-336)

230925a NIFTIES OF 1923 contemp record by Gus Van & Joe Schenck of orig cast. "That Bran' New Gal o' Mine" (78/Col 6-D)

231020a ZIEGFELD FOLLIES OF 1923 records by members of orig cast. Eddie Cantor: "Eddie (Steady)" (1923: 78/Col A-3934) "Oh! Gee, Oh! Gosh, Oh! Golly I'm in Love" (1923: 78/Col A-3934) (1944: LP-143, LP-165, LP-384) Brooke Johns: "Take, Oh Take Those Lips Away" (1923: 78/Vic 19204) Paul Whiteman Orch: "So This Is Venice!" (1924: 78/Vic 19252) "Swanee River Blues," "Shake Your Feet" (1923: 78/Vic 19185) "Chansonette" (by Rudolf Friml) (1923:78/Vic 19145) Olga Steck: "Swanee River Blues" (1924: 78/Okeh 40017)

231020b ZIEGFELD FOLLIES OF 1923 1940 record with vocal by John Olsen & Chic Johnson (lyricists) & girls' quartet. MUSIC: Ernest Breuer. "Oh! Gee, Oh! Gosh, Oh! Golly I'm in Love" (78/Varsity 8308)

231029a RUNNIN' WILD records by members of orig cast. Adelaide Hall: "Old Fashioned Love" (1970: LP-484) Miller & Lyles: Skit "The Fight" (1924: 78/Okeh 40186)

231231a KID BOOTS 1926 medley by orchestra of 1926 London prod. MUSIC: Harry Tierney. WORDS: Joseph McCarthy. (78/Col(E) 9089)

231231b KID BOOTS records by Eddie Cantor of orig cast. "If You Do What You Do" (1924: 78/Col 56-D) "Dinah" (Later: LP-143, LP-144, LP-165, LP-384, LP-542) "Is It True What They Say about Dixie?" (Later: LP-144) "Ma, He's Makin' Eyes at Me" (Later: LP-30, LP-38, LP-144, LP-165) "If You Knew Susie" (1925: LP-379) (Later: LP-30, LP-143, LP-144, LP-165, LP-384, LP-414, LP-758)

231231c KID BOOTS 1924 record by George Olsen Orch of orig prod. "He's the Hottest Man in Town" (78/Vic 19375)

1924

240109a CHARLOT'S REVUE OF 1924 records by Gertrude Lawrence of orig (New York) cast. "Limehouse Blues" (1931: LP-34)(1936: LP-123, LP-276) (1939: LP-766)(1952: LP-5) "You Were Meant for Me" (1932: LP-34)(1936: LP-123, LP-276)

240512a TONI 1924 records by members of orig (London) prod. MUSIC & WORDS: mostly Hugo Hirsch, Douglas Furber. COND: Thomas Tunbridge. Jack Buchanan: "Take a Step" (LP-374)(LP-676) "Blotto" Buchanan, June: "Do It for Me," "For My Friend" Buchanan, Elsie Randolph: "Don't Love You" Orchestra: "Business Is Business" (LP-676)

240520a INNOCENT EYES record sung by J Fred Coots, composer. "Innocent Eyes" (LP-530)

240624a ZIEGFELD FOLLIES OF 1924 1924 record by George Olsen Orch of orig prod. "Biminy" (78/Vic 19429)

240630a GEORGE WHITE'S SCANDALS OF 1924 records by Tom Patricola (banjo & scat vocal) of orig cast. MUSIC: George Gershwin. WORDS: B G DeSylva. "Somebody Loves Me" (With Isabelle Patricola, 1924: 78/Vocalion 14866) (With Sally Sweetland, 1945: LP-654, LP-763)

240901a THE CHOCOLATE DANDIES records by Noble Sissle (vocals) & Eubie Blake (piano) of orig prod. MUSIC: Eubie Blake. WORDS: Noble Sissle. Blake, Sissle, contemp: "Manda" (LP-18)(LP-711) "Dixie Moon" (78/Vic 19494) "You Ought to Know" (78/Edison 51572)(LP-587) "A Jockey's Life for Mine" (78/EBW(E) 4417) "I Wonder Where My Sweetie Can Be" (dropped from the show) (LP-587) Sissle, 1917: "Mammy's Little Choc'late Cullud Chile" (78/Pathe 20210) Blake, 1969: "Dixie Moon" (LP-392)

240902a ROSE-MARIE 1958 studio prod. MUSIC: Rudolf Friml, Herbert Stothart. WORDS: Otto Harbach, Oscar Hammerstein II. COND: Lehman Engel. CAST: Julie Andrews, Giorgio Tozzi, Meier Tzelniker, Frances Day, Marion Keene, Frederick Harvey, John Hauxvell, Tudor Evans. (RCA LOP-1001)

240902b ROSE-MARIE 1954 film soundtrack, with additional songs by Friml, Paul Francis Webster, George Stoll, Herbert Baker. COND: George Stoll. CAST: Ann Blyth, Howard Keel, Bert Lahr, Fernando Lamas, Marjorie Main. (MGM 10" 229)

240902c ROSE-MARIE records by members of 1936 film cast. Jeanette MacDonald & Nelson Eddy: "Indian Love Call" (1936: LP-4, LP-183, LP-242, LP-462)(1948: LP-756)(1958: LP-134) MacDonald: "Indian Love Call" (1944: LP-378)(1950: LP-77) Eddy: "The Mounties" (1935: LP-4, LP-183, LP-242, LP-462) "Rose-Marie" (1935: LP-4, LP-242, LP-462)(1958: LP-134)(c1965: LP-499)

240902d ROSE-MARIE 1925 records by members of 1925 London cast. COND: Herman Finck. Edith Day, Derek Oldham: "Indian Love Call" Day: "Pretty Things," "Door of My Dreams" (LP-84)(LP-127) (LP-448) "The Minuet of the Minute" Billy Merson, Clarice Hardwicke: "Why Shouldn't We?" Merson: "Hard-Boiled Herman" Oldham, chorus: "Rose-Marie" John Dunsmure: "The Mounties" (LP-448) Orchestra: Medley (78/Col(E) 9037)

240902e ROSE-MARIE 1948 studio prod. COND: Al Goodman. CAST: Marion Bell, Charles Fredericks, Christina Lind, chorus, (RCA LK-1012)

240902f ROSE-MARIE studio prod. ORCH: Henri Rene. COND: Lehman Engel. CAST: Anna Moffo, Rosalind Elias, Richard Fredericks, William Chapman. (Reader's Digest 40-5, with Blossom Time)

240902g ROSE-MARIE 1951 album by Nelson Eddy of 1936 film cast & Dorothy Kirsten, chorus. COND: Leon Arnaud. (Col 10" ML-2178. Excerpts: Eddy: "Rose Marie" (LP-268)(LP-432) "The Mounties'' (LP-432) Eddy, Kirsten: "Indian Love Call," "Door of Her Dreams" Kirsten: "Totem Tom Tom" (LP-268)

240902h ROSE-MARIE records by Rudolf Friml (composer), piano. "Indian Love Call" (1929: LP-711)(Later: LP-733)(1963: LP-354) "Rose-Marie," "Totem Tom-Tom," "Door of My Dreams" (Later: LP-733)(1963: LP-354)

240902i ROSE-MARIE 1961 studio prod. COND: Johnny Douglas. CAST: David Croft, David Hughes, Andy Cole, Barbara Leigh, Maggie Fitzgibbon, Barbara Elsy, chorus. (World Records(E) LMP-16)

240902j ROSE-MARIE 1925 medley by Victor Light Opera Company. (78/Vic 35756)

240902k ROSE-MARIE 1961 album, including a song added to 1954 film prod. COND: Paul Conrad. VOCALS: David Whitfield (of 1960 London prod), Janet Waters, chorus. (45/Dec(E) DFE-6669)

240902l ROSE-MARIE 1957 studio prod. ORCH & COND: Tony Osborne. CAST: Andy Cole, Elizabeth Larner, chorus. (HMV(E) CSD-1258, with The New Moon)

240902m ROSE-MARIE 1929 medley by Victor Salon Group. COND: Nathaniel Shilkret. (LP-590)

240902n ROSE-MARIE 1936 film soundtrack, with additional material by Herbert Stothart & Gus Kahn. ORCH & COND: Herbert Stothart. CAST: Jeanette MacDonald, Nelson Eddy, Allan Jones, Gilda Gray, chorus. (Hollywood Soundstage 414)

240904a POPPY 1924 records by W H Berry of orig (London) cast. MUSIC: Stephen Jones, Arthur Samuels. WORDS: Dorothy Donnelly. "Love, Come from Your Hiding-Place," "The Old Army Game" (78/Col(E) 9009)

240911a PRIMROSE 1924 records by members of orig (London) prod. MUSIC: George Gershwin. WORDS: Desmond Carter, Ira Gershwin. COND: John Ansell. Percy Heming: "The Countryside," "Wait a Bit, Susie" Heather Thatcher: "Boy Wanted," "I Make Hay When the Moon Shines" Heming, Margery Hicklin: "Some Far Away Someone" Hicklin, Claude Hulbert: "I'll Have a House in Berkeley Square" Leslie Henson: "That New-Fangled Mother of Mine," "When Toby Is Out of Town" Hicklin: "Naughty Baby" Henson, Hulbert: "Mary, Queen of Scots" Henson, Thatcher, Thomas Weguelen: "The Mophams" Orchestra: "Ballet Music" (World Records(E) SH-214, with additional music) Orchestra: Medley (LP-700)

240916a GREENWICH VILLAGE FOLLIES OF 1924 1934 record by Cole Porter, piano & vocal. MUSIC & WORDS: Cole Porter. "Two Little Babes in the Wood" (LP-182)

241015a ARTISTS AND MODELS OF 1924 record sung by J Fred Coots, composer. "Tomorrow's Another Day" (LP-530)

241201a LADY, BE GOOD! 1926 records by members of 1926 London cast and George Gershwin, piano. MUSIC: George Gershwin. WORDS: Ira Gershwin. CAST: Fred & Adele Astaire (also of orig cast), George Vollaire, William Kent, Buddy Lee. Adele Astaire, Vollaire: "So Am I" Kent: Oh, Lady Be Good!" Fred & Adele Astaire: "Swiss Miss" (LP-14)(LP-512) Fred & Adele Astaire with George Gershwin, piano: "Fascinating Rhythm," "I'd Rather Charleston"(words by Desmond Carter), "Hang On to Me" Fred Astaire with George Gershwin: "The Half of It Dearie Blues" (LP-14)(LP-326)(LP-512)(LP-531) Lee: "Oh, Lady Be Good!," "Fascinating Rhythm" (LP-221)

241201b LADY, BE GOOD! records by members of orig prod. Cliff Edwards: "Fascinating Rhythm" (1924: LP-512) (Later: LP-635) "Insufficient Sweetie" (not by Gershwin) (1924: LP-476, LP-512) "Oh, Lady Be Good!" Victor Arden & Phil Ohman (pianists, with orch): "Fascinating Rhythm/So Am I" (1925: LP-512) Fred Astaire:

"Oh, Lady Be Good!" (1952: LP-348, LP-648)(1959: LP-108) "Fascinating Rhythm" (1952: LP-348, LP-648)

241201c LADY, BE GOOD! radio performances by George Gershwin (composer), piano. "The Man I Love" (dropped from the show) (1934: LP-286, LP-512) "Fascinating Rhythm" (1932: LP-375, LP-512)

241201d LADY, BE GOOD! 1925 piano roll by George Gershwin, composer. "So Am I" (LP-458)(LP-459)(LP-512)

241201e LADY, BE GOOD! soundtrack of 1941 film, with additional songs by Jerome Kern, Oscar Hammerstein II, Arthur Freed, Roger Edens. ORCH & COND: George Stoll, Roger Edens. CAST: Ann Sothern, Eleanor Powell, Connie Russell, Dan Dailey, Red Skelton, John Carroll, Virginia O'Brien, Phil Silvers, Robert Young, Jimmy Dorsey Orch. (Caliban 6010, with Going Places. Excerpts: Russell: "Fascinatin' Rhythm" Sothern, Young, Skelton, Carroll, O'Brien, Powell: "Lady, Be Good" (LP-654)(Incomplete: LP-558).)

241201f LADY, BE GOOD! later record by Ann Sothern of 1941 film cast. "The Last Time I Saw Paris" (LP-614)

241201g LADY, BE GOOD! 1924 piano roll by Victor Arden of orig prod. "Fascinating Rhythm" (LP-621)

241201*a THE MUSIC BOX REVUE OF 1924 records by members of orig prod. MUSIC & WORDS: Irving Berlin. Brox Sisters: "Tokio Blues," "Who?" (1925: 78/Vic 19631) Grace Moore: "Listening," "Tell Her in the Springtime" (1925: LP-336) "Rock-a-bye Baby" (1925: LP-336, LP-519, LP-711)

241202a THE STUDENT PRINCE 1952 studio prod. MUSIC: Sigmund Romberg. WORDS: Dorothy Donnelly. COND: Lehman Engel. CAST: Dorothy Kirsten, Robert Rounseville, Genevieve Warner, Clifford Harvuot, Wesley Dalton, Frank Rogier, Brenda Miller, Jon Geyans, Robert Goss, Robert Holland, Robert Eckles. (Col ML-4592)

241202b THE STUDENT PRINCE 1963 studio prod. ORCH: Hershy Kay. COND: Franz Allers. CAST: Roberta Peters, Jan Peerce, Giorgio Tozzi, Anita Darian, Lawrence Avery. (Col OS-2380)

241202c THE STUDENT PRINCE 1953 studio prod. COND: George Greeley. CAST: Gordon MacRae, Dorothy Warenskjold, Harry Stanton. (Cap 10" L-407)

241202d THE STUDENT PRINCE 1947 album. COND: Robert Armbruster. VOCALS: Nelson Eddy, Rise Stevens, chorus. (Col ML-4060, with The Chocolate Soldier)

241202e THE STUDENT PRINCE studio prod. ORCH: Henri Rene. COND: Lehman Engel. CAST: Jeanette Scovotti, Sara Endich, William Lewis, William Chapman, Lee Cass, Robert Nagy, Peter Palmer, Mallory Walker. (Reader's Digest 40-6, with The Red Mill)

241202f THE STUDENT PRINCE 1947 studio prod. COND: Al Goodman. CAST: Earl Wrightson, Frances Greer, Donald Dame, Mary Martha Briney. (RCA LK-1014)

241202g THE STUDENT PRINCE contemp records by Ann Blyth of 1954 film cast. "Deep in My Heart" (LP-328) "The Students' March Song" (45/MGM K-30853)

241202h THE STUDENT PRINCE 1954 album by Mario Lanza, who sang for Edmund Purdom in 1954 film, and Elizabeth Doubleday. Additional songs by Nicholas Brodszky and Paul Francis Webster. COND: Constantine Callinicos. (RCA LM-1837, with additional songs by Lanza)

241202i THE STUDENT PRINCE 1960 album by Mario Lanza, who sang for Edmund Purdom in 1954 film, and Norma Giusti. Three additional songs by Nicholas Brodszky & Paul Francis Webster. COND: Paul Baron. (RCA LSC-2339)

241202j THE STUDENT PRINCE contemp records by members of 1926 English prods. London prod: John Coast, Raymond Marlowe, Paul Clemon (also of orig prod); Allan Prior (also of New York prod in 1925); Herbert Waterous, Olaf Olson, Lucyenne Herval. English touring prod: Harry Welchman, Rose Hignell. Marlowe, Clemon, Olson: "Students' Entrance," "Drinking Song" Prior: "Memories" Prior, Waterous: "Golden Days" Harvel, Coast: "Just We Two" Welchman: "Serenade" Welchman, Hignell: "Deep in My Heart" Prior, Marlowe, Clemon, Olson: "Serenade" (World Records(E) SH-279, with Wildflower. Incomplete: Monmouth 7054, with The Desert Song.) Cast & orchestra of London prod: Medley (78/Col(E) 9090) Orchestra of London prod: Medley (78/Col(E) 9084)

241202k THE STUDENT PRINCE 1950 studio prod. ORCH & COND: Victor Young. CAST: Lauritz Melchior, Jane Wilson, Lee Sweetland, Gloria Lane. (Dec 10" 7008)

241202l THE STUDENT PRINCE 1925 medley by Victor Light Opera Company. (78/Vic 35757)

241202m THE STUDENT PRINCE 1935 medley. COND: Nathaniel Shilkret. VOCALS: Tom Thomas, Milton Watson, Helen Marshall, Morton Bowe, chorus. (LP-307)

241202n THE STUDENT PRINCE 1940's album. ORCH & COND: Paul Baron. VOCALS: Genevieve Rowe, Glenn Burris, chorus. (Mercury 10" 25001)

241202o THE STUDENT PRINCE 1960 album. COND: Peter Knight. VOCALS: John Hanson, Jane Fyffe, Julie Bryan, Leslie Fyson, chorus. (Pye(E) NPL-18086, with The Vagabond King)

241202p THE STUDENT PRINCE 1949 album. ORCH & COND: Marek Weber. VOCALS: chorus. (Col. 10" CL-6051)

241202q THE STUDENT PRINCE 1968 studio prod by members of 1968 London cast. COND: Johnny Arthey. CAST: John Hanson, Barbara Strathdee, Christine Parker, chorus. (Philips(E) SBL-7850)

241202r THE STUDENT PRINCE 1961 studio prod. COND: John Hollingsworth. CAST: Marion Grimaldi, John Wakefield, William McCue, Christopher Keyte, Robert Bowman, Barbara Elsy, Geoffrey Wall, Edward Brooks. (Cap SN-7510)

241202s THE STUDENT PRINCE 1962 studio prod. COND: Van Alexander. CAST: Dorothy Kirsten, Gordon MacRae, Earle Wilkie, William Felber, Richard Robinson, chorus. (Cap SW-1841)

241202t THE STUDENT PRINCE 1965 studio prod. COND: Colin Beaton. CAST: Mary Thomas, Jamie Phillips, John McNally, chorus. (Fontana(E) SFL-13025, with Naughty Marietta)

241202u THE STUDENT PRINCE 1980 Heidelberg prod, sung in English. COND: Stefan Gyarto. CAST: Erik Geisen, Celia Jeffreys, Dieter Hoenig, chorus. (Kanon(G) 01132)

241223a TOPSY AND EVA records by the Duncan Sisters of orig & 1928 London casts. "I Never Had a Mammy," "Rememb'ring" (1923: 78/Vic 19206) "The Music Lesson " (1922: 78/HMV(E) C-1093) (1923: 78/Vic 19050) (1928: 78/HMV(E) B-2715) "Um-Um-Da-Da" (1924: 78/Vic 19311)

1925

250107a BIG BOY records by Al Jolson of orig prod. "Miami" (1925: LP-274, LP-626, LP-731) "Hello 'Tucky" (1924: LP-274, LP-550, LP-772) (1947: LP-409) "Keep Smiling at Trouble" (1924: LP-274, LP-626) (1947: LP-228, LP-243, LP-394) "It All Depends On You" (1949: LP-243, LP-380)

250107b BIG BOY 1930 film soundtrack. Al Jolson: "Liza Lee," "Hooray for Baby and Me," "Tomorrow Is Another Day" (LP-269)

250113a THE LOVE SONG 1925 medley by Victor Light Opera Company. MUSIC: Jacques Offenbach, arranged by Edward Kunneke. WORDS: Harry B Smith. (LP-772)

250113b THE LOVE SONG contemp medley by Columbia Light Opera Company. (78/Col 50015-D)

250122a BY THE WAY 1928 records by Cicely Courtneidge of orig (London) and 1925 New York prods. MUSIC: Vivian Ellis. WORDS: Graham John. "High Street, Africa," "Three Little Hairs" (78/Bruns(E) 208)

250302a SKY HIGH 1925 records by Willie Howard of orig cast. "Let It Rain," "The Barber of Seville" (78/Col 370-D)

250310a BOODLE 1925 records by members of orig (London) cast. MUSIC: Philip Braham, Max Darewski. WORDS: Douglas Furber. Jack Buchanan, June: "Garden of Lies," "This Year, Next Year" (LP-676)

250311a NO, NO, NANETTE 1969 studio prod. MUSIC: Vincent Youmans WORDS: Irving Caesar, Otto Harbach. ORCH: John McCarthy. COND: Alyn Ainsworth, Geoff Love. CAST: Ann Beach, Vivienne Martin, Tony Adams, Joanna Brown, Leslie Fyson, Charles Young, Alison Chamberlain. (Col(E) TWO-278)

250311b NO,NO, NANETTE 1958 studio prod. ORCH & COND: Johnny Gregory. VOCALS: Bruce Trent, Doreen Hume, chorus. (Epic 3512, with Show Boat)

250311c NO, NO, NANETTE 1925 records by members of orig (London) prod. COND: Percival Mackey. CAST: Binnie Hale, Seymour Beard, Joseph Coyne, George Grossmith, Irene Browne. "I've Confessed to the Breeze," "I Want to Be Happy," "No, No, Nanette," "Take a Little One-Step," "Tea for Two," "Too Many Rings around Rosie," "Where Has My Hubby Gone Blues," "You Can Dance with Any Girl" (World Records(E) 176, with Hit the Deck; Stanyan 10035, with Sunny. Excerpt: "No, No, Nanette" (LP-79).) Orchestra: Medley (78/Col(E) 9036)

250311d NO, NO, NANETTE 1971 New York prod. ORCH: Ralph Burns. COND: Buster Davis. CAST: Ruby Keeler, Jack Gilford, Bobby Van, Helen Gallagher, Susan Watson, Patsy Kelly, Roger Rathburn. (Col S-30563)

250311e NO, NO, NANETTE later medley by Binnie Hale of orig cast. (LP-79)

250311f NO, NO, NANETTE 1950 album by Doris Day & Gene Nelson of 1950 film, entitled "Tea for Two," which had interpolated songs. (Col 10" CL-6149)

250311g NO, NO, NANETTE contemp medley by Columbia Vocal Gem Chorus. (78/Col(E) 9072)

250311h NO, NO, NANETTE 1961 studio prod. ORCH & COND: Alan Braden. CAST: Stephanie Voss, Peter Regan, June Marlow, David Croft, chorus. (World Records(E) TP-88, with Naughty Marietta)

250311i NO, NO, NANETTE 1925 medley by Victor Light Opera Company. (LP-772)

250311j NO, NO, NANETTE studio prod. ORCH: Henri Rene. COND: Lehman Engel. VOCALS: Jeanette Scovotti, William Lewis, John Hauxvell, Bryan Johnson. (Reader's Digest 46-N1, with The Gypsy Baron)

250311k NO, NO, NANETTE 1968 studio prod. COND: Ray Cook. CAST: Margaret Burton, Mary Preston, John Parker, John Dane, Barry Monroe, Betty Winsett, Henrietta Holmes. (Saga(E) EROS-8111)

250311l NO, NO, NANETTE 1973 London prod. ORCH: Ralph Burns. COND: Buster Davis. CAST: Anna Neagle, Anne Rogers,

Thora Hird, Tony Britton, Teddy Green, Barbara Brown, Peter Gale. (CBS(E) 70126)

250311m NO, NO, NANETTE 1958 album. COND: Michael Collins. VOCALS: Pip Hinton, Peter Mander, chorus. (Encore(E) 178, with The Maid of the Mountains, The Belle of New York, & others)

250311n NO, NO, NANETTE 1956 records by Irving Caesar, lyricist. "I Want to Be Happy," "Tea for Two" (LP-353)

250311o NO, NO, NANETTE 1926 piano roll medley by Vincent Youmans, composer. (LP-391)

250311p NO, NO, NANETTE contemp medley by Columbia Light Opera Company. (78/Col 50015-D)

250330a CHARLOT'S REVUE OF 1925 contemp record by Gertrude Lawrence & Beatrice Lillie of orig (London) cast. "Broadway Medley" (78/HMV(E) C-1206. Incomplete: LP-123.)

250404a JOAN OF ARKANSAS 1925 record by Mask & Wig Club Double Male Quartet of orig prod. "Joan of Arkansas" (78/Vic 19626)

250413a MERCENARY MARY 1925 records by members of 1925 London prod. MUSIC & WORDS: Con Conrad, William B Friedlander, others. June & Sonnie Hale: "Honey, I'm in Love with You" (LP-772) "I Am Thinking of You" (78/Col(E) 3807) Peggy O'Neil, A W Bascomb: "I'm a Little Bit Fonder of You" (LP-773) Lew Hearn: "They Still Look Good to Me" O'Neil: "Mercenary Mary" (LP-772) June: "Tie a String around Your Finger" (78/Col(E) 3809) "Over My Shoulder" Bascomb: "There's Nothing Left to Live for" (78/Col(E) 3810)

250413b MERCENARY MARY 1925 medley by Columbia Vocal Gem Chorus. (78/Col(E) 9067)

250413*a TELL ME MORE! records by members of orig cast. MUSIC: George Gershwin. WORDS: Ira Gershwin, B G DeSylva. Alexander Gray: "Three Times a Day," "Tell Me More!" (1925: 78/Col 368-D) Lou Holtz: "Oh, So La Mi" (by Lou Holtz) (1923: 78/Vic 19079 plus 1924: 78/Vic 19403)

250413*b TELL ME MORE! 1925 piano roll by George Gershwin, composer. "Kickin' the Clouds Away" (LP-458) (LP-459)

250430a ON WITH THE DANCE 1925 records by Alice Delysia of orig (London) cast. "Poor Little Rich Girl" (by Noel Coward) (LP-128) (LP-502) "That Means Nothing to Me" (LP-128)

250430b ON WITH THE DANCE 1938 record sung by Noel Coward, composer. "Poor Little Rich Girl" (LP-138) (LP-502)

250624a ARTISTS AND MODELS OF 1925 record sung by J Fred Coots, composer. "The Promenade Walk" (LP-530)

250806a JUNE DAYS record sung by J Fred Coots, composer. "Remembering You" (LP-530)

250918a DEAREST ENEMY 1925 medley by Victor Light Opera Company. MUSIC: Richard Rodgers. WORDS: Lorenz Hart. (78/Vic 35766)

250921a THE VAGABOND KING 1950 studio prod. MUSIC: Rudolf Friml. WORDS: Brian Hooker, W H Post. COND: Paul Weston. CAST: Gordon MacRae, Lucille Norman. (Cap T-219, with The New Moon)

250921b THE VAGABOND KING records by members of 1930 film cast. Dennis King, 1929: "If I Were King" (78/Vic 22263) Jeanette MacDonald, 1950: "Only a Rose" (LP-77)

250921c THE VAGABOND KING studio prod. ORCH: Henri Rene. COND: Lehman Engel. CAST: Rosalind Elias, Sara Endich, William Lewis, William Chapman. (Reader's Digest 40-8, with Porgy and Bess)

250921d THE VAGABOND KING 1950 studio prod. COND: Al Goodman. CAST: Earl Wrightson, Frances Greer, the Guild Choristers. (RCA LK-1010)

250921e THE VAGABOND KING 1951 studio prod. COND: Jay Blackton. CAST: Alfred Drake, Mimi Benzell, Frances Bible. (Dec 10" 7014)

250921f THE VAGABOND KING 1927 records by members of 1927 London prod. Derek Oldham, Winnie Melville: "Love Me Tonight," "Only a Rose" (LP-155) (LP-448) Norah Blaney: "Huguette Waltz," "Love for Sale" (LP-448)

250921g THE VAGABOND KING 1925 records by members of orig cast. Dennis King: "Song of the Vagabonds" (LP-155) (LP-711) (LP-772) Carolyn Thomson: "Only a Rose" (LP-711) (LP-772)

250921h THE VAGABOND KING 1961 album by Mario Lanza & Judith Raskin. COND: Constantine Callinicos. (RCA LSC-2509)

250921i THE VAGABOND KING 1956 album with two new songs written by Rudolf Friml & John Burke for the 1956 film. COND: Henri Rene. VOCALS: Oreste (of 1956 film cast), Jean Fenn, chorus. (RCA LM-2004)

250921j THE VAGABOND KING records by Rudolf Friml (composer), piano, "Song of the Vagabonds" (1925: LP-321) (Later: LP-733) "Huguette Waltz" (1929: 78/Vic 22540) (Later: LP-733) (1963: LP-354) "Someday," "Only a Rose" (Later: LP-733)

250921k THE VAGABOND KING 1960 album. COND: Peter Knight. VOCALS: John Hanson, Jane Fyffe, Julie Bryan, chorus. (Pye(E) NPL-18086, with The Student Prince)

250921l THE VAGABOND KING 1956 film soundtrack. Kathryn Grayson, Oreste: "One, Two, Three, Pause" (dropped before release) Grayson: "A Harp, a Fiddle, and a Flute" (dropped before release), "Some Day" (LP-346)

250921m THE VAGABOND KING 1928 medley by Light Opera Company. (78/HMV(E) C-1346)

250921n THE VAGABOND KING 1929 medley by Victor Salon Group. COND: Nathaniel Shilkret. (45/Camden CAE-253, with High Jinks) (LP-590)

250921o THE VAGABOND KING 1961 studio prod. ORCH: Bobby Richards. COND: Jan Cervenka. CAST: Edwin Steffe, Lissa Gray, Dorothy Dorow, John Larsen, Freda Larsen, chorus. (World Record Club(E) TP-69)

250922a SUNNY 1926 records by members of 1926 London prod. MUSIC: Jerome Kern. WORDS: Oscar Hammerstein II, Otto Harbach. CAST: Jack Buchanan, Binnie Hale, Claude Hulbert, Elsie Randolph, Jack Hobbs. "D'Ye Love Me?," "I Might Grow Fond of You," "I've Looked for Trouble," "Let's Say Goodnight Till It's Morning," "Sunny," "Two Little Bluebirds," "When We Get Our Divorce," "Who?" (World Records(E) SH-240, with Show Boat; Stanyan 10035, with No, No Nanette. Excerpts: "Who?" (LP-61) (LP-79) "D'Ye Love Me?" (LP-79).)

250922b SUNNY 1925 records by members of orig prod. George Olsen Orch: "Who?," "Sunny" (LP-282) "Just a Little Thing Called Rhythm" (78/Vic 19834) Cliff Edwards: "Paddlin' Madeline Home" (1925: 78/Pathe 10904) (Later: LP-635, LP-757)

250922c SUNNY 1926 medley by Victor Light Opera Company. (78/Vic 35769)

250924a MERRY-MERRY 1926 medley by Victor Light Opera Company. MUSIC: Harry Archer. WORDS: Harlan Thompson. (LP-772)

250924b MERRY-MERRY contemp records by Harry Archer Orch of orig prod. "Ev'ry Little Note," "My Own" (78/Bruns 3155) "It Must Be Love," "I Was Blue" (78/Bruns 3003)

251026a THE CITY CHAP 1925 records by George Olsen Orch of orig prod. "Journey's End" (by Jerome Kern & P G Wodehouse) (LP-772) "I'm Knee Deep in Daisies" (78/Vic 19761)

251030a PAGANINI 1937 record by Evelyn Laye of 1937 London cast. MUSIC: Franz Lehar. WORDS: A P Herbert. "My Nicolo" (LP-63)

251102a PRINCESS FLAVIA 1925 medley by Victor Light Opera Company. MUSIC: Sigmund Romberg. WORDS: Harry B Smith. (LP-772)

251109a NAUGHTY CINDERELLA 1926 records by Irene Bordoni of orig prod. "Do I Love You?," "That Means Nothing to Me" (78/Vic 19966)

251110a CHARLOT'S REVUE OF 1926 1925 records by members of orig cast. MUSIC & WORDS: Noel Coward, others. Jack Buchanan, Gertrude Lawrence: "A Cup of Coffee, A Sandwich and You" (LP-518) Lawrence: "Carrie" (78/Col 512-D) "Poor Little Rich Girl" (LP-758) Beatrice Lillie: "Susannah's Squeaking Shoes" (78/Col 513-D) Lawrence: "Russian Blues" Buchanan: "Gigolette" (78/Col 514-D)

251110b CHARLOT'S REVUE OF 1926 later records by members of orig cast. Gertrude Lawrence: "A Cup of Coffee, a Sandwich and You" (1932: LP-34) (1936: LP-123, LP-276) (1939: LP-766) Beatrice Lillie: "Susannah's Squeaking Shoes" (1958: LP-450, LP-680)

251124a MAYFLOWERS record sung by J Fred Coots, composer. "Put Your Troubles in a Candy Box" (LP-530)

251208a THE COCOANUTS 1926 medley by Victor Light Opera Company. MUSIC & WORDS: Irving Berlin. (LP-336)

251208b THE COCOANUTS 1929 film soundtrack, with a new Berlin song ("When My Dreams Come True"), "Florida by the Sea" from orig prod, and the Toreador Song with new words. VOCALS: Oscar Shaw, Mary Eaton, Marx Brothers, chorus. (Sountrak 108)

251228a TIP-TOES contemp records by George Gershwin, piano. MUSIC: George Gershwin. WORDS: Ira Gershwin. "Looking for a Boy," "When Do We Dance"? (LP-78) (LP-433) "That Certain Feeling" (LP-12) (LP-78) (LP-326) (LP-433) "Sweet and Low-Down" (LP-78) (LP-326) (LP-433)

251228b TIP-TOES contemp records by members of 1926 London prod. Allen Kearns (also of orig New York prod), Dorothy Dickson: "That Certain Feeling," "Nightie-Night" Dickson, Laddie Cliff, John Kirby: "These Charming People" Cliff: "It's a Great Little World" Dickson: "Looking for a Boy" Kearns, Peggy Beatty: "When Do We Dance?" Evan Thomas, Vera Bryer: "Nice Baby" Cliff, Beatty: "Sweet and Low-Down" (Monmouth 7052, with Wildflower; LP-221)

251228c TIP-TOES 1926 records by pianists Victor Arden & Phil Ohman of orig prod, with their orch. "That Certain Feeling/When Do We Dance?," "Looking for a Boy/ Sweet and Low Down" (LP-492)

251228d TIP-TOES 1926 medley by the Revelers. (78/Vic 35772)

251228e TIP-TOES 1926 piano rolls by George Gershwin, composer. "That Certain Feeling" (LP-458) "Sweet and Low Down"(LP-459)

251230a SONG OF THE FLAME contemp records by members of orig cast. Russian Art Choir: "I Was There," "The Song of Gold" (78/Col 622-D) "Song of the Field," "Village Pines" (78/Col 581-D) Tessa Kosta & Russian Art Choir: "Song of the Flame," "Cossack Love Song" (both by George Gershwin & Herbert Stothart) (78/Col 618-D)

1926

260223a R.S.V.P. contemp record by Joyce Barbour of orig (London) prod. MUSIC & WORDS: Irving Berlin. "Gentlemen Prefer Blondes" (LP-159)

260317a THE GIRL FRIEND album. MUSIC: Richard Rodgers. WORDS: Lorenz Hart. COND: Johnny Gregory. VOCALS: Doreen Hume, Bruce Trent, chorus. (Epic BN-566, with White Horse Inn & The New Moon)

260317b THE GIRL FRIEND 1926 record by George Olsen Orch of orig prod. "The Girl Friend" (LP-282)

260317c THE GIRL FRIEND contemp medley by Light Opera Company. (78/HMV(E) C-1399)

260317d THE GIRL FRIEND 1927 medley by Columbia Light Opera Company. (78/Col(E) 9267)

260326a COUNTESS MARITZA studio prod. MUSIC: Emmerich Kalman. WORDS: Harry B Smith. COND: Lehman Engel, CAST: Jeanette Scovotti, Patricia Clark, William Lewis, John Hauxvell, Neil Howlett. (Reader's Digest 46-N3, with Bitter Sweet)

260326b COUNTESS MARITZA 1926 medley by Victor Light Opera Company. (78/Vic 35809)

260326c COUNTESS MARITZA 1938 records by members of 1936 London prod, entitled "Maritza." WORDS: Arthur Stanley. Douglas Byng: "I Must Have Everything Hungarian," "I'm the Pest of Budapest" (78/Parlophone(E) F-1200) John Garrick: "Vienna So Gay," "Come, Gipsy, Come" (78/HMV(E) B-8787)

260326d COUNTESS MARITZA contemp record by Walter Woolf of 1926 New York cast. "Play Gypsies, Dance Gypsies" (78/Gennett 6043)

260410a RIVERSIDE NIGHTS 1930 record by Elsa Lanchester of orig (London) cast. "Ladies' Bar" (LP-136) (LP-159)

260425a A SALE AND A SAILOR 1926 medley by Mask & Wig Club chorus of orig prod. (78/Vic 19982)

260522a YVONNE 1926 records by members of orig (London) prod. MUSIC: Vernon Duke. WORDS: Percy Greenbank. COND: Arthur Wood. Ivy Tresmand, chorus: "Day Dreams" Tresmand, Gene Gerrard: "We Always Disagree" Tresmand, Arthur Pusey: "Couleur de Rose" Nita Underwood, chorus: "Magic of the Moon" (LP-700)

260614a GEORGE WHITE'S SCANDALS OF 1926 records by Harry Richman of orig cast. MUSIC: Ray Henderson. WORDS: B G DeSylva, Lew Brown. "The Birth of the Blues" (1926: LP-349) (1930's: LP-414) (1947: LP-113) "Lucky Day" (1926: 78/Vocalion 15412)

260614b GEORGE WHITE'S SCANDALS OF 1926 1966 record by Ray Henderson (composer), piano. "The Birth of the Blues" (LP-671)

260621a MOZART records (in French) by Yvonne Printemps of 1926 London & New York prods. MUSIC: Reynaldo Hahn. WORDS: Sacha Guitry. "Air de la Lettre," "Air des Adieux" (LP-627)

260708a MY MAGNOLIA 1924 record by Eddie Hunter of orig cast. MUSIC: C Luckey Roberts. WORDS: Alex Rogers. "Hard Times" (78/Vic 19359)

260824a EARL CARROLL'S VANITIES OF 1926 1926 records by Don Voorhees & the Earl Carroll Vanities Orch of orig prod. "Hugs and Kisses," "Climbing Up the Ladder of Love" (78/Col 765-D) "Who Do You Love?" (78/Col 881-D)(78/Edison 51919)

260906a CASTLES IN THE AIR 1927 records by members of 1927

London prod. MUSIC: Percy Wenrich. WORDS: Raymond Peck. Helen Gilliland: "Lantern of Love" John Steel: "Latavia," "The Rainbow of Your Smile" Gilliland, Steel: "My Lips, My Love, My Soul" (LP-772)

260908a QUEEN HIGH contemp medley by Gaiety Musical Comedy Chorus with uncredited soloists. MUSIC: Lewis E Gensler, James F Hanley. WORDS: B G DeSylva. (LP-772)

260908b QUEEN HIGH contemp medley by Percival Mackey's Carnival Singers. (78/Col(E) 9183)

260908c QUEEN HIGH 1926 medley by pianists Edgar Fairchild & Ralph Rainger of orig prod. (LP-545)

260908d QUEEN HIGH 1926 records by members of 1926 London prod. Joyce Barbour, A W Bascomb: "Beautiful Baby" (LP-772) Bascomb: "Surplus Women" (78/Col(E) 4204)

260908e QUEEN HIGH 1927 record by Frank Crumit of 1927 touring company. MUSIC & WORDS: Frank Crumit, Ben Jerome. "My Lady" (78/Vic 20486)

260911a BLACKBIRDS 1926 records by the Plantation Orch of orig (London) prod. "Smilin' Joe" (LP-159) (LP-582) "For Baby and Me," "Silver Rose," "Arabella's Wedding Day" (LP-582)

260920a HONEYMOON LANE 1926 records by members of orig cast. MUSIC: James F Hanley. WORDS: Eddie Dowling. Kate Smith: "Mary Dear" (78/Col 810-D) "The Little White House" (LP-434) Johnny Marvin: "Half a Moon" (LP-473) (78/Col 750-D) (78/Edison 51841) (78/Col 832-D) "Jersey Walk" (78/Col 750-D) (78/Edison 51841) (78/Gennett 6011) "The Little White House" (78/Okeh 40704)

260920b HONEYMOON LANE 1926 medley by Victor Light Opera Company. (78/Vic 35811)

261005a THE CHARLOT SHOW OF 1926 1926 records by members of orig (London) prod. MUSIC: Noel Gay, Richard Addinsell. WORDS: Donovan Parsons, Rowland Leigh. Jessie Matthews, Henry Lytton Jr: "Silly Little Hill" Herbert Mundin: "When the 'Ansom Cabs Was Lined Up on the Ranks" (LP-159) Lytton: "Ukulele Liza Brown" Mundin, Hazel Wynne: "The Elevator Belle" (78/Col(E) 4191) Matthews: "The Good Little Girl and the Bad Little Girl" (78/Col(E) 4189) "Journey's End," "Friendly Ghosts" (78/Col(E) 4192) Dick Francis: "Whimiscal Pedlar" (78/Col(E) 4190)

261021a PRINCESS CHARMING contemp records by members of orig (London) prod. MUSIC & WORDS: Various. COND: Percy E Fletcher. Alice Delysia & W H Berry: "Babying You" (LP-128) (LP-700) Berry: "Ninepence a Week," "Not Old Enough to Be Old" (78/Col(E) 4188) John Clarke: "Swords and Sabres" (LP-700) Clarke, Winnie Melville: "Lips May Deny" Melville: "Palace of Dreams" (78/Col(E) 4186)

261021b PRINCESS CHARMING 1934 records by Evelyn Laye of 1935 film cast. MUSIC: Ray Noble. WORDS: Max Kester. "The Princess's Awakening," "Near and Yet So Far," "Love Is a Song" (LP-63)

261108a OH, KAY! 1957 studio prod. MUSIC: George Gershwin. WORDS: Ira Gershwin, Howard Dietz. COND: Lehman Engel. CAST: Barbara Ruick, Jack Cassidy, Allen Case, Roger White. (Col CL-1050)

261108b OH, KAY! 1926 records by pianists Victor Arden & Phil Ohman of orig prod. With vocals by Franklyn Baur & Virginia Rea: "Someone to Watch over Me" (78/Bruns 3381) "Maybe" (78/Bruns 3381) (Excerpt: LP-580) With orch: "Do-Do-Do/ Someone to Watch over Me," "Clap Yo' Hands/Fidgety Feet" (LP-492) (LP-580)

261108c OH, KAY! 1927 records by members of 1927 London prod. COND: Arthur Wood. Gertrude Lawrence (also of orig cast): "Someone to Watch over Me" Lawrence, Harold French: "Maybe," "Do-Do-Do" (LP-29) (LP-221) (LP-276) (LP-580) Claude Hulbert, chorus: "Clap Yo' Hands" (LP-221) (LP-580)

261108d OH, KAY! 1926 records by George Gershwin, piano. "Someone to Watch over Me" (LP-52) (LP-279) (LP-326) (LP-433) (LP-563) (LP-580) "Do-Do-Do" (LP-279) (LP-326) (LP-433) (LP-580) "Maybe" (LP-279) (LP-433) (LP-580) "Clap Yo' Hands" (LP-279) (LP-321) (LP-326) (LP-433) (LP-580)

261108e OH, KAY! 1960 prod with songs interpolated from other Gershwin shows and certain new lyrics by P G Wodehouse. ORCH & COND: Dorothea Freitag. CAST: David Daniels, Marti Stevens, Bernie West, Murray Matheson, Eddie Phillips. (20th Fox 4003)

261108f OH, KAY! records by Gertrude Lawrence of orig cast & 1927 London cast. (See also 261108c.) "Someone to Watch over Me" (1926: LP-580) (1932: LP-34) (1936: LP-123, LP-276) (1952: LP-5) "Do-Do-Do" (1926: LP-456, LP-539, LP-580) (1936: LP-123, LP-276) (1939: LP-766) (1952: LP-5)

261108g OH, KAY! 1938 medley. COND: Nathaniel Shilkret. VOCALS: Jane Froman, Sonny Schuyler, chorus. (LP-303)

261108h OH, KAY! 1927 medley by the Revelers. (78/Vic 35811)

261108i OH, KAY! contemp medley by Columbia Light Opera Company. (78/Col 50031-D) (Excerpt: "Oh, Kay!" (LP-580).)

261130a THE DESERT SONG 1952 studio prod. MUSIC: Sigmund Romberg. WORDS: Otto Harbach, Oscar Hammerstein II. COND: Lehman Engel. CAST: Nelson Eddy, Doretta Morrow, Wesley Dalton, Lee Cass, David Atkinson, Wilton Clary. (Col 10" AAL-37)

261130b THE DESERT SONG 1953 studio prod. ORCH & COND: George Greeley. CAST: Gordon MacRae of 1953 film cast, Lucille Norman, Bob Sands, Thurl Ravenscroft. (Cap 10" L-351)

261130c THE DESERT SONG 1927 records by members of 1927 London prod. COND: Herman Finck. Edith Day: "French Military Marching Song," "The Sabre Song," "Romance" Harry Welchman: "One Alone," "The Riff Song" Day & Welchman: "The Desert Song" Dennis Hoey: "Let Love Go" Sidney Pointer: "One Flower Grows Alone in Your Garden" Gene Gerrard: "It" (World Records(E) SH-254, with The New Moon; Monmouth 7054, with The Student Prince. Excerpts: All Edith Day records are on LP-84.)

261130d THE DESERT SONG 1959 studio prod. ORCH: Brian Fahey. COND: Michael Collins. CAST: Edmund Hockridge, June Bronhill, Julie Dawn, Leonard Weir, Inia Te Wiata, Bruce Forsyth. (Angel 35905)

261130e THE DESERT SONG 1963 studio prod. COND: Van Alexander. CAST: Gordon MacRae of 1953 film cast, Dorothy Kirsten, Gerald Shirkey, Lloyd Bunnell. (Cap SW-1842)

261130f THE DESERT SONG 1958 studio prod. ORCH & COND: Lehman Engel. CAST: Giorgio Tozzi, Kathy Barr, Peter Palmer, Eugene Morgan, Warren Galjour. (RCA LOP-1000)

261130g THE DESERT SONG 1944 album by Dennis Morgan of 1943 film cast. COND: Edgar Roemheid. (Col ML-4272, with My Wild Irish Rose)

261130h THE DESERT SONG 1945 studio prod. COND: Isaac van Grove. CAST: Kitty Carlisle, Wilbur Evans, Felix Knight, Vicki Vola. (Dec 10" 7000)

261130i THE DESERT SONG studio prod. ORCH: Henri Rene. COND: Lehman Engel. CAST: Anna Moffo, Richard Fredericks, William Lewis, Kenneth Smith. (Reader's Digest 40-4, with Naughty Marietta)

261130j THE DESERT SONG 1961 studio prod. COND: Constantine Callinicos. CAST: Mario Lanza, Judith Raskin, Raymond Murcell, Donald Arthur. (RCA LSC-2440)

261130k THE DESERT SONG 1934 record by Edith Day of 1927 London prod. "Romance" (LP-56)

261130l THE DESERT SONG 1926 medley by Victor Light Opera Company. (78/Vic 35809)

261130m THE DESERT SONG contemp medley by Columbia Light Opera Company. (78/ Col 50031-D)

261130n THE DESERT SONG 1958 studio prod. COND: Al Goodman. CAST: Earl Wrightson, Frances Greer, Jimmy Carroll, chorus. (Camden 423)

261130o THE DESERT SONG 1952 album by Kathryn Grayson of 1952 film cast, Tony Martin, & chorus, incl some new lyrics & a new song (not by Romberg) from the 1952 film. COND: Arthur Fiedler. (RCA 10" LPM-3105. Excerpt: Grayson: "One Flower Grows Alone in Your Garden" (LP-636).)

261130p THE DESERT SONG 1935 medley. COND: Nathaniel Shilkret. VOCALS: Helen Marshall, Tom Thomas, Morton Bowe, Milton Watson, chorus. (LP-307)

261130q THE DESERT SONG 1967 album by John Hanson & Patricia Michael of 1957 London prod; chorus. COND: Johnny Arthey. (Philips(E) SBL-7799, with The New Moon)

261130r THE DESERT SONG 1952 film soundtrack. ORCH & COND: Ray Heindorf. CAST: Gordon MacRae, Kathryn Grayson, Allyn McLerie, chorus. (Titania 505, with My Wild Irish Rose. Excerpts: Grayson: "Romance," "Gay Parisienne" (LP-346) Grayson, MacRae: "The Desert Song" (LP-347).)

261130s THE DESERT SONG 1962 album. COND: Paul Conrad. VOCALS: David Whitfield, Janet Waters. (45/Dec(E) DFE-6707)

261130t THE DESERT SONG 1961 studio prod. COND: Bobby Richards. CAST: Peter Grant, Peter Hudson, Olga Gwynne, John Hewer, Diana Landor, Owen Grundy, chorus. (World Record Club(E) T-110)

261130u THE DESERT SONG 1967 studio prod. COND: Ray Cook. VOCALS: Robert Colman, Ivor Danvers, Gordon Trayner, Betty Winsett, Mary Millar, Ted Gilbert, Michael Bretton, Janet Gale. (Saga(E) EROS-8107)

261201a LIDO LADY contemp records by members of orig (London) cast. MUSIC & WORDS: Richard Rodgers, Lorenz Hart, others. COND: Sydney Baynes. Phyllis Dare, Jack Hulbert: "Here in My Arms" Dare: "Atlantic Blues" Cicely Courtneidge, Harold French: "A Tiny Flat Near Soho Square" Courtneidge, Hulbert: "Try Again Tomorrow" (LP-222) "It All Depends on You" (78/Col(E) 4227) Hulbert: "But Not Today" (78/Col(E) 4228)

261217a OH, PLEASE! 1926 records by Beatrice Lillie of orig cast & Vincent Youmans, piano. MUSIC: Vincent Youmans. WORDS: Anne Caldwell. "Like He Loves Me" (LP-18) (LP-473) (LP-563) (LP-711) "Nicodemus" (78/Vic 20361)

261227a PEGGY-ANN contemp records by Dorothy Dickson of 1927 London cast. MUSIC: Richard Rodgers, WORDS: Lorenz Hart. "Tree in the Park," "Where's That Rainbow?"(LP-222)

261227b PEGGY-ANN contemp medley by Light Opera Company. (78/HMV(E) C-1399)

261227c PEGGY-ANN contemp medley by Columbia Light Opera Company. (78/Col(E) 9267)

261227d PEGGY-ANN 1927 medley by Daly's Theatre Orch of 1927 London prod. COND: Charles Prentice. (78/Col(E) 9266)

261228a BETSY 1933 record by Borrah Minnevitch & His Harmonica Rascals of orig prod. MUSIC: George Gershwin. "Rhapsody in Blue" (78/Bruns 6507)

1927

270001a Film THE JAZZ SINGER records by members of orig prod. Al Jolson: "My Mammy" (1928: LP-82, LP-731) (1946:LP-145, LP-244, LP-739) (1946: LP-682) (1948: LP-677) "Dirty Hands, Dirty Face" (1928: LP-82) (1947, with Oscar Levant, piano: LP-478) "Toot, Toot, Tootsie" (1922: LP-288) (1946: LP-682) (1947: LP-198, LP-244, LP-394, LP-409, LP-739) (1947, with Eddie Cantor: LP-438) (1948: LP-677) "Kol Nidre" (1947: LP-372, LP-381) Cantor Josef Rosenblatt: "Kol Nidre" (78/Col E-5126) (78/Vic 35312) (78/Vic 38-1008)

270001b Film THE JAZZ SINGER soundtrack. VOCALS: Al Jolson, Josef Rosenblatt. (Sountrak 102. Excerpts: "Toot, Toot, Tootsie" (LP-269) "Blue Skies," "My Mammy" (LP-595).)

270001c Film THE JAZZ SINGER 1947 radio prod, with other songs added. COND: Louis Silvers. VOCALS: Al Jolson (of orig cast). (Pelican 125) (LP-394)

270101a EARL CARROLL'S VANITIES (INTERNATIONAL EDITION) 1926 records by members of orig prod, who had performed the same material earlier in the Charlot Show of 1926. MUSIC: Noel Gay, Richard Addinsell. WORDS: Donovan Parsons, Rowland Leigh. Jessie Matthews, Henry Lytton Jr: "Silly Little Hill" Herbert Mundin: "When the 'Ansom Cabs Was Lined Up on the Ranks" (LP-159) Lytton: "Ukulele Liza Brown" Mundin, Hazel Wynne: "The Elevator Belle" (78/Col(E) 4191) Matthews: "The Good Little Girl and the Bad Little Girl" (78/Col(E) 4189) "Journey's End," "Friendly Ghosts" (78/Col(E) 4192)

270202a RIO RITA 1929 records by Bebe Daniels of 1929 film cast. MUSIC: Harry Tierney. WORDS: Joseph McCarthy, "You're Always in My Arms" (LP-17) "If You're in Love You'll Waltz" (78/Vic 22132)

270202b RIO RITA 1927 medley by J Harold Murray of orig cast & Victor Light Opera Company. (LP-773. Excerpts: Murray: "Rio Rita," "The Rangers' Song" (LP-18) (LP-710) (LP-711).)

270202c RIO RITA contemp records by members of 1930 London prod, with two additional songs. COND: John Heuvel. Edith Day: "You're Always in My Arms" Edith Day & Geoffrey Gwyther: "If You're in Love You'll Waltz," "I'd Rather Have a Memory of You" (LP-84) (LP-127) "Rio Rita" Gwyther: "The Rangers' Song," "Following the Sun Around" (LP-127)

270202d RIO RITA 1952 album. COND: Al Goodman. VOCALS: Earl Wrightson, Elaine Malbin, chorus. (RCA LK-1026, with A Connecticut Yankee)

270202e RIO RITA contemp medley by Columbia Light Opera Company. (78/Col 50039-D)

270202f RIO RITA album. COND: Geoff Harvey. VOCALS: Neil Williams, Rosalind Keene. (World Record Club(Australia) 7056, with The Great Waltz)

270202g RIO RITA 1927 records by duo-painists Muriel Pollock (of orig prod) & Constance Mering. "Following the Sun Around/ The Kinkajou," "When You're in Love You'll Waltz" (78/Col 952-D)

270322a LUCKY 1927 records by Paul Whiteman Orch of orig prod. "The Same Old Moon," "That Little Something" (78/Vic 20616)

270322b LUCKY contemp medley by Columbia Light Opera Company. (78/Col 50039-D)

270328a RUFUS LEMAIRE'S AFFAIRS contemp records by Ted Lewis Orch of orig prod. "Wandering In Dreamland," "Lily" (78/Col 895-D) "I Can't Get Over a Girl Like You" (78/Col 754-D) "Wah!Wah!" (78/Col 1017-D)

270425a H1T THE DECK 1958 studio prod. MUSIC: Vincent Youmans. WORDS: Leo Robin, Clifford Grey. COND: Johnny Gregory. CAST: Doreen Hume, Denis Quilley, chorus. (Epic 3569, with The Cat and the Fiddle)

270425b HIT THE DECK 1927 record by Louise Groody & Charles King of orig cast. "Sometimes I'm Happy" (LP-18) (LP-711)

270425c HIT THE DECK 1955 film soundtrack with songs interpolated from other Youmans shows. ORCH: Robert Van Eps, Will Beitel. COND: George Stoll. CAST: Jane Powell, Tony Martin, Debbie Reynolds, Vic Damone, Ann Miller, Kay Armen, Russ Tamblyn. (MGM 3163. Excerpt: Chorus: "Hallelujah" (LP-252)

270425d HIT THE DECK contemp records by members of 1927 London prod, which had an additonal Youmans song. COND: Joseph Tunbridge. Orchestral Medley & Vocal Medley (LP-773) Stanley Holloway: "Join the Navy" Ivy Tresmand: "Loo-Loo" Holloway, Tresmand: "Fancy Me Just Meeting You," "Sometimes I'm Happy" Prince Sisters, Barry Twins: "Why, Oh Why?" (World Records(E) SH-176, with No, No, Nanette. Incomplete: LP-773. Excerpt: Holloway: "Join the Navy" (LP-136).)

270425e HIT THE DECK 1959 album. ORCH & COND: Tony Osborne. VOCALS: Millicent Martin, Kevin Scott, chorus, (45/HMV(E) GES-5757)

270425f HIT THE DECK 1956 record by Irving Caesar, lyricist. "Sometimes I'm Happy" (LP-353)

270425g HIT THE DECK 1928 medley by Light Opera Company. (78/HMV(E) C-1433)

270427a LADY LUCK 1927 records by members of orig (London) prod. MUSIC: Richard Rodgers. WORDS: Lorenz Hart. Laddie Cliff: "Sing" Phyllis Monkman, Leslie Henson: "If I Were You" (LP-222)

270427b LADY LUCK contemp medley by Light Opera Company (78/HMV(E) C-1346)

270503a A NIGHT IN SPAIN 1927 records by members of orig prod. "Did You Mean It?" (Marion Harris (vocal) & Phil Baker (accordion): 78/Vic 21116) (Grace Hayes (vocal): HMV(E) B-2688)

270507a HOOT MON 1927 medley by the Mask & Wig Singing Chorus of orig prod. (78/Vic 20524)

270520a ONE DAM' THING AFTER ANOTHER contemp records by members of orig (London) prod. MUSIC: Richard Rodgers. WORDS: Lorenz Hart. "My Heart Stood Still" (Edythe Baker, piano & vocal: LP-159, LP-222; also alternate take of 78/Col(E) 9217 without vocal) (Jessie Matthews: LP-320)

270624a BLUE SKIES 1927 record by Jack Smith of orig (London) prod, piano & vocal. "Blue Skies" (by Irving Berlin) (78/HMV(E) B-2494)

270627a BOTTOMLAND contemp records by Clarence Williams, composer & piano of orig prod. "Any Time" (78/Col 14314-D) "Bottomland" (78/Paramount 12517) (78/Col 14244-D) "Shootin' the Pistol" (78/Paramount 12517) (78/Col 14241-D) "Steamboat Days" (78/Okeh 8672) "When I March in April with May" (78/Col 14241-D) With Eva Taylor (vocal), also of orig prod: "Come on Home" (LP-520)

270711a AFRICANA records by Ethel Waters of orig cast. "I'm Coming Virginia," "Dinah" (1925: LP-15) (1934: LP-236) (1950: LP-361) (c1958: LP-99) "Shake That Thing" (1925: LP-673) "My Special Friend Is Back in Town" (1926: LP-673) "You Can't Do What My Last Man Did" (1923: LP-674) (1925: LP-673) "Weary Feet" (78/Col 14214-D) "Smile" (78/Col 14229-D)

270712a RANG TANG contemp records by Miller & Lyles of orig

prod. Skit "Sam and Steve," Skit "The Fight" (78/Okeh 40186) Skit "The Lost Aviators" (78/Regal 8435)

270816a ZIEGFELD FOLLIES OF 1927 1927 medley by Franklyn Baur & the Brox Sisters of orig prod. MUSIC & WORDS: Irving Berlin. COND: Nathaniel Shilkret. PIANOS: Edgar Fairchild & Ralph Rainger of orig prod. (LP-157) (LP-710)

270816b ZIEGFELD FOLLIES OF 1927 1927 records by members of orig cast. Ruth Etting: "Shakin' the Blues Away" (LP-25)(LP-519)(LP-593) "It All Belongs to Me" (LP-336)(LP-519) Franklyn Baur: "Shakin' the Blues Away" (LP-336) "Ooh! Maybe It's You" (78/Bruns 3639) "It All Belongs to Me" (78/Vic 20900)

270906a GOOD NEWS 1947 film soundtrack. MUSIC & WORDS: Ray Henderson, B G DeSylva, Lew Brown, Hugh Martin, Ralph Blane, Roger Edens, Betty Comden, Adolph Green. COND: Lennie Hayton. CAST: June Allyson, Peter Lawford, Joan McCracken, Patricia Marshall, Mel Torme, Ray McDonald. (Sountrak 111, plus a number dropped before release: Allyson, Marshall: "An Easier Way" (LP-423). Incomplete: MGM 10" 504. Excerpts: Allyson, Lawford: "The Varsity Drag" (LP-252) Allyson: "Just Imagine" (LP-328).)

270906b GOOD NEWS records by authors of songs written for 1947 film prod. Betty Comden & Adolph Green: "The French Lesson" (1955: LP-359) (1958: LP-170) (1977: LP-489) Hugh Martin & Ralph Blane: "Pass That Peace Pipe" (1956: LP-193)

270906c GOOD NEWS 1928 medley by Victor Arden-Phil Ohman Orch. VOCALS: The Revelers. (78/Vic 35918)

270906d GOOD NEWS contemp records by members of orig prod. George Olsen Orch: "Good News" (LP-282) (LP-773) "Varsity Drag" (LP-282) (LP-456) (LP-711) (LP-773) "Lucky in Love," "The Best Things in Life Are Free" (LP-773) Zelma O'Neal (also of 1928 London cast): "Varsity Drag" (78/Bruns 3864)

270906e GOOD NEWS album, including one song written for 1947 film prod. COND: Geoff Harvey. CAST: Jimmy Parkinson, Betty Parker. (Light Music Club(New Zealand) LZ-7073, with Sally)

270906f GOOD NEWS 1974 prod rec live, with interpolated songs by DeSylva, Brown, & Henderson. ORCH: Philip J Lang, COND: Liza Redfield. CAST: Alice Faye, John Payne, Stubby Kaye, Barbara Lail, Wayne Bryan, Jana Robbins, Marti Rolph, Scott Stevensen, Paula Cinko, Tommy Breslin, Rebecca Urich, Timmy Rogers, Gene Nelson. (Unnamed label mx SA-101/4)

270906g GOOD NEWS 1928 records by Abe Lyman Orch of 1927-8 touring prod. Medley (78/Bruns 20063, with uncredited male singer and chorus) "Good News," "Varsity Drag" (78/Bruns 3901) "Just Imagine" (78/Bruns 3837)

270906h GOOD NEWS contemp records by Mel Torme of 1947 film cast. "The Best Things in Life Are Free" (1947: 78/Musicraft 15118) (1950: 78/MGM K-30357)

270906i GOOD NEWS 1966 record by Ray Henderson (composer), piano. "The Best Things in Life Are Free" (LP-671)

270906j GOOD NEWS 1963 Chicago prod. COND: Ken Pierce. CAST: Belleruth Krepon, Ron Inglehart, Cyndee Schwartz, Dave Steinberg, Herb Jones, Jerry Loeb, Susie Workoff, Janie Whitehill. (Unnamed label mx U-17889/90)

270906k GOOD NEWS 1930 film soundtrack. Stanley Smith, Mary Lawlor: "If You're Not Kissing Me" (LP-770)

270912a MY MARYLAND 1927 records by Evelyn Herbert of orig cast & Franklyn Baur. MUSIC: Sigmund Romberg, WORDS: Dorothy Donnelly. Herbert: "Mother" Herbert & Baur: "Silver Moon" (78/Vic 20995)

270912b MY MARYLAND 1927 medley by Victor Light Opera Company. (78/Vic 35816)

270912c MY MARYLAND 1935 medley. COND: Nathaniel Shilkret. VOCALS: Rise Stevens, Tom Thomas, Helen Marshall, chorus. (LP-307)

270926a THE MERRY MALONES 1927 records by Polly Walker of orig cast. MUSIC & WORDS: George M. Cohan. "Roses Understand," "Molly Malone" (78/Bruns 3687)

271103a A CONNECTICUT YANKEE 1943 prod. MUSIC: Richard Rodgers. WORDS: Lorenz Hart. COND: George Hirst. CAST: Vivienne Segal, Dick Foran, Julie Warren, Vera-Ellen, Robert Chisolm, Chester Stratton. (78/Dec album 367; JJA Records 19733, with Inside U.S.A.)

271103b A CONNECTICUT YANKEE 1952 album. COND: Al Goodman. VOCALS: Earl Wrightson, Elaine Malbin, chorus. (RCA LK-1026, with Rio Rita)

271115a ARTISTS AND MODELS OF 1927 contemp records by Ted Lewis of orig cast. "Is Everybody Happy Now?" (78/Col 1207-D) "Start the Band" (78/Col 1391-D)

271122a FUNNY FACE contemp records by members of 1928 London prod. MUSIC: George Gershwin. WORDS: Ira Gershwin. CAST: Fred & Adele Astaire of orig (New York) cast; Leslie Henson, Bernard Clifton, Sydney Howard. "Funny Face," "The Babbit and the Bromide," "He Loves and She Loves," "'S Wonderful," "My One and Only," "High Hat," "Sketch: A Few Drinks," "Tell the Doc" (World Record Club(E) 144 (LP-78), with additonal songs by the Astaires & by George Gershwin, piano) (Smithsonian R-019(LP-727), with additonal material)

271122b FUNNY FACE contemp records by George Gershwin, piano. "Funny Face & 'S Wonderful," "My One and Only" (LP-78) (LP-727)

271122c FUNNY FACE 1952 record by Fred Astaire of orig cast. "'S Wonderful" (LP-125) (LP-358) (LP-567) (LP-648)

271122d FUNNY FACE 1927 records by pianists Victor Arden & Phil Ohman of orig prod, with their orch. VOCALS: Johnny Marvin, "Funny Face," "'S Wonderful" (LP-492) (Incomplete: LP-727)

271122e FUNNY FACE 1928 medley by pianists Victor Arden & Phil Ohman of orig prod, with their orch. VOCALS: Lewis James, The Revelers. (LP-727) (LP-773)

271122f FUNNY FACE 1963 studio prod. ORCH & COND: Bobby Richards. CAST: Scott Peters, Patricia Lynn, Maggie Fitzgibbon, chorus. (World Record Club(E) T-191, with Gigi)

271122*a TAKE THE AIR 1927 records by members of orig prod. MUSIC: Dave Stamper. WORDS: Gene Buck. Kitty O'Connor: "We'll Have a New Home in the Morning," "All I Want Is a Lullaby" (78/Col 1293-D) Max Fisher Orch: "Maybe I'll Baby You," "Lullaby" (78/Col 1226-D)

271130a THE GOLDEN DAWN 1928 record by Robert Chisholm of orig cast. "The Whip" (78/Bruns 3869)

271130b THE GOLDEN DAWN 1930 record by Noah Beery of 1930 film cast, with the Vitaphone Orch. "Whip Song" (78/Bruns 4828)

271130c THE GOLDEN DAWN 1930 film soundtrack. Noah Beery: "The Whip" Walter Woolf: "Here in the Dark" Chorus: "Dawn" (LP-773)

271201a CLOWNS IN CLOVER contemp records by members of orig (London) prod. June Tripp, Bobby Comber, Chick Endor, Dennis Cowles: "Little Boy Blues" Cicely Courtneidge: "Double Damask" (sketch) (LP-159) "The Calinda" (LP-700)

271227a SHOW BOAT 1962 studio prod. MUSIC: Jerome Kern.

WORDS: Oscar Hammerstein II, P G Wodehouse. COND: Franz Allers. CAST: John Raitt, Barbara Cook, William Warfield, Anita Darian, Fay Dewitt, Louise Parker, Jack Dabdoub. (Col OS-2220)

271227b 5HOW BOAT 1956 studio prod. COND: Lehman Engel. CAST: Robert Merrill, Patrice Munsel, Rise Stevens, Katherine Graves, Janet Pavek, Kevin Scott. (RCA LM-2008. Incomplete: LP-435.)

271227c SHOW BOAT 1958 studio prod. ORCH & COND: Johnny Gregory. VOCALS: Bruce Trent, Doreen Hume, chorus. (Epic 3512, with No, No, Nanette)

271227d SHOW BOAT 1928 records by members of orig cast. Helen Morgan: "Bill" (LP-32) (LP-37) (LP-44) (LP-148) (LP-229) (LP-426) (LP-435) (LP-542) (LP-711) (LP-784) "Can't Help Lovin' Dat Man" (LP-32) (LP-37) (LP-229) (LP-230) (LP-435) (LP-539) (LP-542) Tess Gardella ("Aunt Jemima"): "Can't Help Lovin' Dat Man" (LP-52) (LP-710)

271227e SHOW BOAT 1951 film soundtrack. ORCH: Conrad Salinger. COND: Adolph Deutsch. CAST: Kathryn Grayson, Howard Keel, Ava Gardner (although Annette Warren sang for her in the released film), Marge & Gower Champion, William Warfield. (MGM 10" 559. Excerpts edited into a medley, including additional material from the film: LP-252.)

271227f SHOW BOAT 1932 studio prod. COND: Victor Young. CAST: Helen Morgan (of orig, 1932 New York, & 1936 film prods), Paul Robeson (of 1928 London, 1932 New York, & 1936 film prods), Frank Munn, Olga Albani, James Melton. (Col AC-55. Excerpts: Morgan: "Bill" (LP-52) (LP-710) (LP-758) "Can't Help Lovin' That Man" (LP-43) (LP-641) Robeson: "Ol' Man River" (LP-758).)

271227g SHOW BOAT 1928 records by members of 1928 London prod. COND: Herman Finck. Edith Day: "Dance Away the Night" Day, Howett Worster: "You Are Love," "Make Believe," "Why Do I Love You?" (LP-84) (LP-127) (LP-505) Marie Burke: "Bill," "Can't Help Lovin' Dat Man" Mississippi Chorus: "In Dahomey" Paul Robeson, Mississippi Chorus: "Ol' Man River" (LP-505) Norris Smith (Robeson's understudy), Mississippi Chorus: "Ol' Man River" (78/Col(E) 9426) Mississippi Chorus: Medley (78/Col(E) 9426) (Incomplete: LP-505) Orchestra: Medley (78/Col(E) 9430) (78/Regal(E) G-9142)

271227h SHOW BOAT studio prod. ORCH: Henri Rene. COND: Lehman Engel. CAST: Anna Moffo, Mary Ellen Pracht, Rosalind Elias, Richard Fredericks, Valentine Pringle. (Reader's Digest 40-7, with The New Moon)

271227i SHOW BOAT 1941 records by Allan Jones of 1936 film cast. "Make Believe " (LP-126) "Why Do I Love You?" (78/Vic 4555)

271227j SHOW BOAT 1971 London prod, with one interpolated Kern song. ORCH: Keith Amos. COND: Ray Cook, CAST: Lorna Dallas, Andre Jobin, Cleo Laine, Thomas Carey, Kenneth Nelson, Jan Hunt, Ena Cabayo. (Stanyan 10048)

271227k SHOW BOAT 1966 prod. ORCH: Robert Russell Bennett. COND: Franz Allers. CAST: Barbara Cook, William Warfield, Stephen Douglass, Constance Towers, David Wayne, Rosetta LeNoire, Allyn Ann McLerie, Eddie Phillips. (RCA LSO-1126)

271227l SHOW BOAT 1958 studio prod. ORCH & COND: Henri Rene. CAST: Howard Keel of 1951 film cast; Gogi Grant, Anne Jeffreys. (RCA LSO-1505. Excerpts: Keel: "I Have the Room Above" Grant: "Nobody Else but Me" (LP-435).)

271227m SHOW BOAT 1946 prod, with one new Kern/Hammerstein song. COND: Edwin McArthur. CAST: Jan Clayton, Carol Bruce, Colette Lyons, Helen Dowdy, Charles Fredericks, Kenneth Spencer, chorus. (Col ML-4058. Excerpt: Clayton: "Nobody Else but Me" (LP-538).)

271227n SHOW BOAT 1949 album by Dorothy Kirsten & Robert Merrill. COND: John Scott Trotter. (45/RCA album WDM-1341. Excerpt: Kirsten, Merrill: "Why Do I Love You?" (LP-435).)

271227o SHOW BOAT 1936 film soundtrack. ORCH: Robert Russell Bennett. COND: Victor Baravelle. CAST: Irene Dunne (of 1929/30 touring prod), Allan Jones, Helen Morgan (of orig & 1932 New York prods), Paul Robeson (of 1928 London & 1932 New York prods), Hattie McDaniel, Sammy White, Queenie Smith. (Xeno 251. Excerpt: Robeson: "Ol' Man River" (LP-710).)

271227p SHOW BOAT records by Paul Robeson of 1928 London cast, 1932 New York cast, & 1936 film cast. "Ol' Man River" (1928: LP-435, LP-711) (1928: LP-505) (1930: HMV(E) B-3653) (1936: LP-637) (1948: 78/Col 17517-D) "Ah Still Suits Me" (1936, with Elisabeth Welch: LP-638, LP-712) (1948: 78/Col 17518-D)

271227q SHOW BOAT 1936 records by Jules Bledsoe of orig cast & 1929 film cast. "Ol' Man River" (78/Dec(E) K-631) "Lonesome Road" (from 1929 film) (78/Dec(E) F-5939)

271227r SHOW BOAT 1928 medley by Paul Whiteman Orch (of 1929 film prod). VOCALS: Olive Kline, Lambert Murphy, chorus. (78/Vic 35912)

271227s SHOW BOAT records by Kathryn Grayson of 1951 film cast. "Make Believe" (Radio performance: LP-346) "You Are Love" (LP-364)

271227t SHOW BOAT 1938 medley by Victor Light Opera Company. COND: Leonard Joy. (LP-306)

271227u SHOW BOAT 1951 album. VOCALS: Patti Page, Sophie Tucker, Tony Martin, Tony Fontane, Louise Carlisle, Virginia Haskins, Felix Knight. (Mercury 10" 25104)

271227v SHOW BOAT 1949 album. VOCALS: Bing Crosby, Kenny Baker, Frances Langford, Tony Martin, Lee Wiley. (Dec 10" 5060, with another Kern song)

271227w SHOW BOAT 1959 studio prod. ORCH: Brian Fahey. COND: Michael Collins. CAST: Shirley Bassey, Marlys Watters, Don McKay, Inia Te Wiata, Dora Bryan, Isabelle Lucas, Geoffrey Webb, chorus. (Odeon(E) CSD-1279)

271227x SHOW BOAT studio prod. "Ed Sullivan presents Show Boat." No other credits given. (National Academy 3)

271227y SHOW BOAT 1959 studio prod. COND: Hill Bowen. VOCALS: Barbara Leigh, Andy Cole, Bryan Johnson, Maxine Daniels, Patricia Clark, Denis Quilley, Ivor Emmanuel, chorus. (Camden 488)

271227z SHOW BOAT 1953 album. COND: Lehman Engel. VOCALS: Carol Bruce (of 1946 & 1948 prods), Helena Bliss (of 1954 prod), John Tyers, William C Smith (of 1948 & 1954 prods). (RCA 10" LPM-3151, with The Cat and The Fiddle)

271227A SHOW BOAT later records by members of 1928 London prod. Edith Day, 1934, "Why Do I love You?" (LP-56) Marie Burke, 1933: "Bill," "Can't Help Lovin' Dat Man" (78/Col(E) DX-572)

271227B SHOW BOAT 1940 radio prod. COND: Louis Silvers. VOCALS: Irene Dunne & Allan Jones of 1936 film cast, chorus. (Sunbeam P-501)

271227C SHOW BOAT medley. COND: Philip Green. VOCALS: Lizbeth Webb, Steve Conway, Adelaide Hall, Bryan Johnson. (78/Col(E) DX-1771)

271227D SHOW BOAT studio prod. COND: Johnny Douglas. CAST: Martin Lawrence, Isabelle Lucas, Stella Moray, Donald Scott, Janet Waters, Ian Humphris, chorus. (Cap SN-7514)

271227E SHOW BOAT studio prod. COND: Al Goodman. CAST: Richard Torigi, Lee Venora, Audrey Marsh. (Spin-o-rama MK-3044)

271227F SHOW BOAT 1971 studio prod. COND: Johnny Douglas. CAST: June Bronhill, Freddie Williams, Julie Dawn, Fred Lucas, Rita Williams, Joan Brown. (Contour(E) 2870-145)

271227G SHOW BOAT orig prod, rec live for prologue of 1929 film. Tess Gardella, chorus: "Queenie's Ballyhoo" (LP-773)

1928

280001a Film RAMONA 1928 records by Dolores Del Rio of orig cast. In personal appearances to promote this silent film she sang "Ramona" from the film's background music. (English: LP-17) (Spanish: 78/Vic 4054)

280002a Film MY MAN records by Fanny Brice of orig cast. "My Man" (1921: LP-1; LP-148, LP-758) (1927: LP-32, LP-33, LP-44, LP-539, LP-542) (1936: LP-157) "I'd Rather Be Blue Over You" (1928: LP-32, LP-33, LP-230) "If You Want The Rainbow" (1928: LP-33, LP-230)

280002b Film MY MAN soundtrack. Fanny Brice: "My Man" (LP-724) (Incomplete: LP-595) "Second-Hand Rose" (LP-724) "I Was a Florodora Baby" (LP-751)

280003a Film STEAMBOAT WILLIE soundtrack of the Mickey Mouse cartoon (the first musical cartoon). "Turkey in the Straw" (LP-661)

280004a ZIEGFELD'S MIDNIGHT FROLIC 1929 record by Helen Morgan of orig cast. "Who Cares What You Have Been?" (LP-157) (LP-724)

280103a SHE'S MY BABY 1933 record by Beatrice Lillie of orig cast. MUSIC: Richard Rodgers. WORDS: Lorenz Hart. "A Baby's Best Friend" (LP-123) (LP-774)

280130a THE OPTIMISTS records by Melville Gideon, composer. WORDS: Various. (The revue had played in London in 6 editions, all entitled "The Co-Optimists.") "Amapu" (1922: 78/Zonophone(E) 2247, 78/Co(Optimists(E) 2297) "Spare a Little Love" (1923: 78/Zonophone(E) 2434) (1924: 78/Col(E) 3407) "Little Lacquer Lady" (1926: 78/HMV(E) C-1284) "London Town" (1924: 78/Col(E) 3405) "Rolling Stone" (1926: 78/HMV(E) B-2295)

280223a LADY MARY contemp medley by Light Opera Company. MUSIC & WORDS: mostly Albert Sirmay, Harry Graham. COND: Charles Prentice of orig (London) prod. (LP-700)

280227a KEEP SHUFFLIN' 1928 records by members of orig prod. Fats Waller (composer & organ), James P Johnson (composer & piano), Jabbo Smith (cornet): "Willow Tree," " 'Sippi" (78/Vic 21348)

280313a THE THREE MUSKETEERS 1930 records by members of 1930 London prod. MUSIC: Rudolf Friml. WORDS: Clifford Grey, P G Wodehouse. COND: Herman Finck, Dennis King (also of orig New York prod), chorus: "Gascony," "My Sword and I" King, Adrienne Brune: "Your Eyes," "One Kiss" Raymond Newell, chorus: "Ma Belle" (LP-155) (LP-448) King, Newell, Jack Livesey, Robert Woollard, chorus:"March of the Musketeers" (LP-155) (LP-448) (LP-710)

280313b THE THREE MUSKETEERS medley by Light Opera Company. (78/Vic 36097)

280313c THE THREE MUSKETEERS later record by Rudolf Friml (composer), piano. "March of the Musketeers" (LP-733)

280313d THE THREE MUSKETEERS 1930 medley by Columbia Light Opera Company. (78/Col(E) DX-56)

280322a THIS YEAR OF GRACE records by Noel Coward of 1928 New York cast. MUSIC & WORDS: Noel Coward. 1928: "World Weary" (LP-123) (LP-502) "Dance, Little Lady" (LP-218) (LP-136) (LP-

Birnbaum's classic rendering of Fannie Brice, the great comedienne and singer. From *Stage* 1936.

The one, the only "Merrm," Ethel Merman singing up a storm in Cole Porter's RED, HOT BLUE! Co-stars included Jimmy Durante and Bob Hope. 1936.

THE WIZARD OF OZ (1938) MGM
"Joy with Judy" is how the ads read, and it certainly was. A perfect cast singing a wonderful score by Harold Arlen and E.Y. Harburg combined to make one of the all-time favorite films THE WIZARD OF OZ.

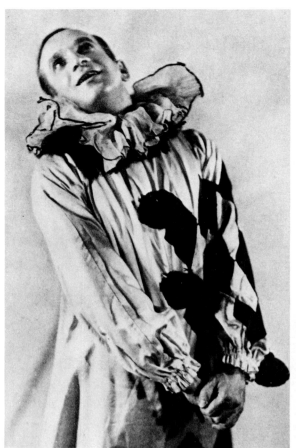

Al Jolson. One of America's greatest troubadours, his singing style influenced generations of singers who followed him. George Jessel played THE JAZZ SINGER on stage, but it was Jolson who became a screen immortal in the film version, the first all singing musical film!

Libby Holman starred in several Broadway revues in the 1930s before a scandal virtually ended her career. She was the quintessential torch singer and made ''Moanin' Low'' and ''Body And Soul'' her very own.

Ethel Waters (1933), one of Broadway's greatest singing stars. In AS THOUSANDS CHEER, she made the most of Irving Berlin's wonderful "Heat Wave."

CAREFREE (1938)

The greatest musical team of them all, Fred Astaire and Ginger Rogers. Virtually every major composer did a film score for them. For CAREFREE it was a reunion with Irving Berlin, who also penned their great success TOP HAT.

EASTER PARADE (1948) MGM

The only time Fred Astaire and Judy Garland got together on screen was in Irving Berlin's hugely successful and golden musical EASTER PARADE. They were to be reteamed in ROYAL WEDDING and THE BARKLEYS OF BROADWAY, but alas, 'twas not to be.

SOUTH PACIFIC (1949) CBS
A triumphant and engrossed trio: Mary Martin, Richard Rodgers, and Ezio Pinza listen to a playback of one of the many songs from a perennial best-selling cast album SOUTH PACIFIC.

KISS ME KATE (1948) CBS
Harold Lang, Patricia Morison, Lisa Kirk, and Alfred Drake sing out a song from one of Cole Porter's greatest successes KISS ME KATE.

MISS LIBERTY (1949) CBS
Mary McCarty and Eddie Albert warble one of the delightful songs from Irving Berlin's musical about the Statute of Liberty MISS LIBERTY.

KISS ME KATE (1953) MGM
Ann Miller chats with a somewhat intimidated Cole Porter during a break in filming KISS ME KATE. Bob Fosse, a dancing member of the supporting cast, joins in.

MY FAIR LADY (1956)
Julie Andrews in rehearsal for one of the plum roles of her career, Eliza in MY FAIR LADY. And loverly it was.

Isabel Bigley and Joan McCracken
of "Me and Juliet"

ME AND JULIET (1953)
Isabel Bigley & Joan McCracken: ME AND JULIET (1953). One of the few Rodgers and Hammerstein musicals which was not a success.

ANKLES AWEIGH

CARNIVAL!

GYPSY

seesaw

THE PAJAMA GAME

HELLO, DOLLY!

Shinbone Alley

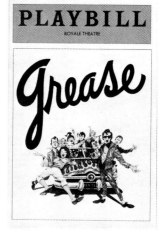

grease

IRMA LA DOUCE

THE GAY LIFE

BELLS ARE RINGING

Sweeney Todd
THE Demon Barber OF FLEET STREET

The King and I

HELLO, DOLLY!

FOLLOW THE GIRLS

A CHORUS LINE

Winter Garden — PLAYBILL — the magazine for theatregoers
FUNNY GIRL

Majestic Theatre — PLAYBILL — a weekly magazine for theatregoers
CAMELOT

Palace Theatre — PLAYBILL — the national magazine for theatregoers
GEORGE M!

Alvin Theatre — PLAYBILL — a weekly magazine for theatregoers
GREENWILLOW

The Broadway Theatre — PLAYBILL — the magazine for theatregoers
The Girl Who Came To Supper

Eugene O'Neill Theatre — PLAYBILL — the magazine for theatregoers
SHE LOVES ME

The Broadhurst Theatre — PLAYBILL — a weekly magazine for theatregoers
SAIL AWAY
CORONIA

The PLAYBILL for the Forty-Sixth Street Theatre
New Girl in Town

The Broadway Theatre
ANNIE GET YOUR GUN

Imperial Theatre — PLAYBILL — the magazine for theatregoers
Fiddler on the Roof

Ethel Barrymore Theatre — PLAYBILL — the national magazine for theatregoers
NOËL COWARD's SWEET POTATO

Lunt-Fontanne Theatre — PLAYBILL — a weekly magazine for theatregoers
GOLDILOCKS

Alvin Theatre — PLAYBILL — the magazine for theatregoers
FLORA THE RED MENACE

Lunt-Fontanne Theatre — PLAYBILL — the national magazine for theatregoers
MARLENE DIETRICH

St. James Theatre — PLAYBILL — the magazine for theatregoers
HELLO, DOLLY!

Phoenix Theatre — PLAYBILL — a weekly magazine for theatregoers
ONCE UPON A MATTRESS

FANNY (1954) RCA
Florence Henderson, William Tabbert, producer David Merrick, and director Joshua Logan rehearsing the Harold Rome musical.

MY FAIR LADY (1956) CBS
Robert Coote, Rex Harrison, and Julie Andrews in the recording session of one of the greatest musical successes of all time. The week before it opened tickets could still be bought for opening night because who wanted to see a musical version of PYGMALION!

SINGIN' IN THE RAIN (1952) MGM
The film musical many people consider the best of them all. Gene Kelly, Donald O'Connor, and Debbie Reynolds starred in this perennially revived film.

SINGIN' IN THE RAIN

Starring

GENE KELLY
DONALD O'CONNOR
DEBBIE REYNOLDS

M-G-M's TECHNICOLOR Musical Treasure!

JEAN HAGEN · MILLARD MITCHELL and CYD CHARISSE

BETTY COMDEN · ADOLPH GREEN · ARTHUR FREED

NACIO HERB BROWN · GENE KELLY · STANLEY DONEN · ARTHUR FREED

HAPPY HUNTING (1956) RCA
Ethel Merman and chorus members. Not one of the big Merman hits, but still the source for her doing the delightful *"New Fangled Tango."*

KISMET (1953) CBS
Alfred Drake is surrounded by chorus members of "A musical Arabian night" KISMET. It opened during a newspaper strike and continued to run anyway.

DAMN YANKEES (1955) RCA
Stephen Douglass, Gwen Verdon, and Ray Walston sing the Adler & Ross score to DAMN YANKEES, the show which proved a musical about baseball could be a hit.

THE GOLDEN APPLE (1954) RCA
Recording director Henri Rene leads cast members (left to right), Patricia Gillette, Bibi Osterwald, Stephen Douglass, and Kaye Ballard in one of the splendid Jerome Moross & John Latouche songs from GOLDEN APPLE.

LADY IN THE DARK (1954) RCA

Ann Sothern and Carleton Carpenter. One of the better 1950s television "spectaculars" was this NBC revival of the Kurt Weill-Ira Gershwin musical about a high fashion editor in psychoanalysis—LADY IN THE DARK.

NEW FACES OF 1956 (1956) RCA

Cast members of one of the best of Leonard Sillman's NEW FACES include (front) T.C. Jones and Maggie Smith (striped blouse second from right).

SILK STOCKINGS (1955) RCA

Hildegarde Neff sings one of the songs from Cole Porter's final Broadway musical, an adaptation of NINOTCHKA.

SILK STOCKINGS (1957) MGM

The cinematic version of Cole Porter's SILK STOCKINGS reteamed Fred Astaire with one of filmland's best dancers, Cyd Charisse.

502) "Try to Learn to Love" (LP-218) (LP-502) "A Room with a View," "Mary Make-Believe," "Lorelei," "The Dream Is Over" (LP-502) 1955: "A Room with a View" (LP-89) "World Weary" (LP-89) (LP-351) Later: "World Weary," "A Room with a View" (LP-138)

280322b THIS YEAR OF GRACE 1928 medley by London Pavillion Orch of orig (London) prod. COND: Ernest Irving. (LP-602)

280404a WILL O' THE WHISPERS 1928 records by Jack Smith of orig (London) prod. MUSIC & WORDS: Various. "Miss Annabelle Lee" (LP-159) "When Day Is Done" (78/HMV(E) B-2666) "Sunshine" (by Irving Berlin), "Whispering" (78/HMV(E) B-2706) "The Song Is Ended" (by Irving Berlin), "My Blue Heaven" (78/HMV(E) B-2665) "I Never Dreamt" (78/HMV/(E) B-2718)

280409a DIAMOND LIL records by Mae West of songs interpolated in 1948 prod. "Frankie and Johnny" (1954: LP-105) (1950s: LP-411, LP-412) "Come Up and See Me Sometime" (1950s: LP-411, LP-412)

280409*a GREENWICH VILLAGE FOLLIES OF 1928 1928 records by Arnold Johnson Orch of orig prod. "Get Your Man," "What's the Reason" (78/Bruns 3914)

280427a BLUE EYES 1928 records by members of orig (London) prod. MUSIC & WORDS: Jerome Kern, Graham John, Guy Bolton, others. COND: Kennedy Russell. Evelyn Laye, Geoffrey Gwyther: "Blue Eyes," "Do I Do Wrong?" Sylvia Cecil, George Vollaire: "Back to the Heather" W H Berry: "Women - Pah!" (LP-173) Orchestra: Medley (LP-700)

280501a HERE'S HOWE 1928 records by Ben Bernie Orch of orig prod. "Crazy Rhythm," "Imagination" (78/Bruns 3913)

280501b HERE'S HOWE 1956 record by Irving Caesar, lyricist. "Crazy Rhythm" (LP-353)

280509a BLACKBIRDS OF 1928 1932/33 studio prod. MUSIC: Jimmy McHugh. WORDS: Dorothy Fields. Orchestras of Duke Ellington, Don Redman. CAST: Bill Robinson & Adelaide Hall of orig cast; Ethel Waters, Cab Calloway, Mills Brothers. (Col OL-6770; Sutton 270. Excerpt: Robinson: "Doin' the New Low-Down" (LP-19) (LP-518) (LP-758).)

280509b BLACKBIRDS OF 1928 1953 album. COND: Lehman Engel. CAST: Cab Calloway, Thelma Carpenter. "I Can't Give You Anything but Love," "Diga-Diga-Doo," "I Must Have That Man," "Doin' the New Low-Down" (RCA 10" LPM-3154, with Shuffle Along) (LP-774)

280509c BLACKBIRDS OF 1928 records by members of orig prod. Lew Leslie's Blackbirds Orch, 1928: "Magnolia's Wedding Day," "Bandanna Babies" (78/Bruns 4030) Adelaide Hall & Lew Leslie's Blackbirds Orch, 1928: "I Must Have That Man, " "Baby" (78/Bruns 4031) Hall, 1938: "I Can't Give You Anything but Love" (LP-582) Hall, 1970: "I Must Have That Man," "Porgy," "Diga Diga Do," "I Can't Give You Anything But Love," "Baby" (LP-484) Elisabeth Welch, 1928: "Diga Diga Do," "Doin' the New Low Down" (78/Bruns 4014) Bill Robinson (tap-dancing), 1929: "Doin' the New Low Down" (78/Bruns 4535)

280509d BLACKBIRDS OF 1928 1928 medley by Warren Mills' Blue Serenaders. COND: Matt Malneck. VOCALS: Sonny Greer, chorus. (78/Vic 35962)

280528a GRAND STREET FOLLIES OF 1928 1928 records by Von Hallberg Trio of orig prod. "Someone to Admire, Someone to Adore," "Tu Sais" (78/Col 1618-D)

280605a THAT'S A GOOD GIRL 1928 records by members of orig (London) cast. MUSIC: Philip Charig, Joseph Meyer. WORDS: Douglas Furber, Ira Gershwin, Desmond Carter. Jack Buchanan: "Sweet So-and-So" Buchanan, Elsie Randolph: "The One I'm Looking For" (LP-61) (LP-676) "Fancy Our Meeting" Randolph:

"Chirp-Chirp" Buchanan, Vera Pearce, Raymond Newell: "Parting Time" Newell: "Marching Song" (LP-676)

280605b THAT'S A GOOD GIRL 1933 records by members of 1934 film cast. Jack Buchanan, Elsie Randolph: "Fancy Our Meeting" (LP-61) (LP-374) "Now That I've Found You" Buchanan: "So Green," "Oh! La! La!" (LP-374)

280605c THAT'S A GOOD GIRL 1929 medley by Light Opera Company. (78/HMV(E) C-1586)

280626a SAY WHEN 1928 records by Henry Busse Orch of orig prod. "How About It?," "One Step to Heaven" (78/Vic 21674)

280702a GEORGE WHITE'S SCANDALS OF 1928 records by members of orig prod. MUSIC: Ray Henderson. WORDS: B G DeSylva, Lew Brown. Harry Richman: "I'm on the Crest of a Wave" (LP-349) (LP-774),Richman, Frances Williams: "What D'Ya Say?" (LP-774) Arnold Johnson Orch: "I'm on the Crest of a Wave," "What D'Ya Say?" (78/Bruns 3909) "Pickin' Cotton" (78/Bruns 4037)

280806a EARL CARROLL'S VANITIES OF 1928 1928 records by Vincent Lopez Orch of orig prod. "Blue Shadows," "Once in a Lifetime" (78/Bruns 4059)

280828a THE THREEPENNY OPERA 1954 New York prod. MUSIC: Kurt Weill. WORDS: Bertolt Brecht, Marc Blitzstein. ORCH: Kurt Weill. COND: Samuel Matlowsky. CAST: Lotte Lenya of orig (Berlin) prod; Scott Merrill, Martin Wolfson, Jo Sullivan, Charlotte Rae, Gerald Price, Beatrice Arthur, George Tyne. (MGM 3121)

280828b The THREEPENNY OPERA 1962 German film soundtrack. WORDS: Bertolt Brecht. COND: Peter Sandloff. CAST: Curt Jurgens, Hildegard Neff, Hilde Hildebrand, Gert Frobe, Maria Korber, Kurt Muhlhardt, June Ritchie, Marlene Warrlich, Adeline Wagner. (London(E) 76004)

280828c THE THREEPENNY OPERA 1964 English soundtrack for 1962 German film. WORDS: Bertolt Brecht, Marc Blitzstein. COND: Samuel Matlowsky. CAST: Sammy Davis, George S Irving, Martha Schlamme, Jo Wilder. (RCA LSO-1086)

280828d THE THREEPENNY OPERA 1930 studio prod by members of orig (Berlin) cast. COND: Theo Mackeben. CAST: Willy Trenk-Trebitsch, Erika Helmke, Kurt Gerron, Lotte Lenya, Erich Ponto. (Telefunken(G) NT-529, with additional material)

280828e THE THREEPENNY OPERA 1930 records by Albert Prejean, Margo Lion, & Jacques Henley of 1931 French film cast. "Chant des canons," "Chant d'amour," "Tango-ballade," "Ballade de la vie agreable" (Telefunken(G) NT-529, with additional material)

280828f THE THREEPENNY OPERA 1962 record by Jerry Orbach of New York prod in 1959. "Mack the Knife" (LP-420)

280828g THE THREEPENNY OPERA 1976 New York prod. WORDS: Bertolt Brecht, Ralph Manheim, John Willett. COND: Stanley Silverman. CAST: C K Alexander, Ellen Greene, Raul Julia, Caroline Kava, David Sabin, Elizabeth Wilson, Roy Brocksmith, Blair Brown. (Col PS-34326)

280828h THE THREEPENNY OPERA 1955 records sung in German by Lotte Lenya of orig (Berlin) & 1954 New York casts. "Moritat," "Barbara-Song," "Seerauber-Jenny" (LP-463)

280828i THE THREEPENNY OPERA 1958 studio prod, sung in German. "Production supervised by Lotte Lenya." COND: Wilhelm Bruckner-Ruggeberg. Cast: Lotte Lenya of orig (Berlin) & 1954 New York casts; Willy Trenk-Trebitsch of orig (Berlin) cast; Wolfgang Neuss, Trude Hesterberg, Erich Schellow, Johanna V Koczian, Wolfgang Grunert, Inge Wolffberg. (Col 02L-257)

280828j THE THREEPENNY OPERA 1963 studio prod. WORDS: Eric Bentley. COND: Alan Braden. CAST: Mike Sammes, John Huw

Davies, Ruth Little, Stella Moray. (World Records(E) ST-253, with Irma la Douce)

280828k THE THREEPENNY OPERA contemp medley. The Dreigroschen Band. VOCALS: Kurt Gerron of orig cast; Carola Neher, A Schroeder. (78/HMV(E) EH-301)

280905a GOOD BOY records by Helen Kane of orig cast. MUSIC & WORDS: Herbert Stothart, Bert Kalmar, Harry Ruby. "I Wanna Be Loved by You" (1928: LP-426, LP-774) (1930s: LP-414)

280915a LUCKEE GIRL 1928 record by the Diplomats of orig prod. "Come On and Make Whoopee" (78/Col 1641-D)

280919a THE NEW MOON 1963 studio prod. MUSIC: Sigmund Romberg. WORDS: Oscar Hammerstein II. ORCH: Van Alexander, Warren Baker. COND: Van Alexander. CAST: Dorothy Kirsten of 1944 prod; Gordon MacRae, Jeannine Wagner, Richard Robinson, Earle Wilkie, James Tippey. (Cap SW-1966)

280919b THE NEW MOON 1950 studio prod. COND: Paul Weston. CAST: Gordon MacRae, Lucille Norman. (Cap 10" H-217)

280919c THE NEW MOON records by members of 1940 film cast. Jeanette MacDonald, contemp: "Lover, Come Back to Me" (LP-4) (LP-71) (LP-137) (LP-242) "One Kiss" (LP-71) (LP-137) Nelson Eddy, 1940: "Lover Come Back to Me," "Stout-Hearted Men" (LP-432) "Softly, as in a Morning Sunrise" (78/Col 4240-M) "Wanting You" (78/Col 4241-M) Eddy, later: "Lover, Come Back to Me" (78/V-Disc 70) MacDonald & Eddy, 1958: "Wanting You" Eddy, 1958: "Stout-Hearted Men" (LP-134)

280919d THE NEW MOON 1929 records by members of 1929 London prod. COND: Herman Finck. CAST: Evelyn Laye, Ben Williams, Howett Worster, Gene Gerrard, Dolores Farris. "Marianne," "The Girl on the Prow," "Gorgeous Alexander," "Softly, As in a Morning Sunrise," "One Kiss," "Stouthearted Men," "Wanting You," "Lover Come Back to Me," "Wedding Chorus," "Try Her Out at Dancing" (World Records(E) SH-254, with the Desert Song; Monmouth 7051.)

280919e THE NEW MOON studio prod. ORCH: Henri Rene. COND: Lehman Engel. CAST: Jeanette Scovotti, Peter Palmer, Arthur Rubin. (Reader's Digest 40-7, with Show Boat)

280919f THE NEW MOON 1953 studio prod. COND: Victor Young. CAST: Thomas Hayward, Jane Wilson, Lee Sweetland. (Dec 10" 5472)

280919g THE NEW MOON 1940 studio prod. COND: Harry Sosnik. CAST: Florence George, Paul Gregory, Frank Forest. (78/Dec album 155)

280919h THE NEW MOON 1950 album by Nelson Eddy of 1940 film cast & Eleanor Steber, chorus. COND: Leon Arnaud. (Col 10" ML-2164. Excerpts: Steber: "One Kiss" Eddy: "Softly as in a Morning Sunrise" Eddy, Steber: "Wanting You," "Lover Come Back to Me" (LP-268).)

280919i THE NEW MOON 1940 film soundtrack. CAST: Jeanette MacDonald, Nelson Eddy. (Pelican 103, with I Married an Angel; plus LP-466.)

280919j THE NEW MOON 1931 records by Lawrence Tibbett of 1930 film cast. "Lover Came Back to Me," "Wanting You" (LP-226) (LP-385)

280919k THE NEW MOON soundtrack of 1930 film, with additional music by Herbert Stothart. CAST: Grace Moore, Lawrence Tibbett, chorus. (Pelican 2020; Raviola BMPB-1929 (entitled "Parisian Belle"), with Broadway Melody. Excerpts: Moore: "Lover Come Back to Me, " "One Kiss" (LP-231).)

280919l THE NEW MOON album. COND: Johnny Gregory. VO-

CALS: Doreen Hume, Bruce Trent, chorus. (Epic BN-566, with White Horse Inn & The Girl Friend)

280919m THE NEW MOON contemp records by members of orig cast. Evelyn Herbert: "Lover Come Back to Me" (LP-711) (LP-774) "One Kiss" William O'Neal: "' Softly, as in a Morning Sunrise," "Stout-Hearted Men" (LP-774)

280919n THE NEW MOON 1929 medley by Victor Light Opera Company. (78/Vic 35969)

280919o THE NEW MOON 1952 studio prod. COND: Al Goodman (of orig & 1944 prods). CAST: Earl Wrightson (of 1944 prod), Frances Greer, Donald Dame, Earl Oxford, chorus. (RCA LK-1011)

280919p THE NEW MOON 1935 medley. COND: Nathaniel Shilkret. VOCALS: Helen Marshall, Milton Watson, Morton Bowe, Helen Oelheim, Tom Thomas, chorus. (LP-307)

280919q THE NEW MOON 1967 album. COND: Johnny Arthey. VOCALS: John Hanson, Patricia Michael, chorus. (Philips(E) SBL-7799, with The Desert Song)

280919r THE NEW MOON 1957 studio prod. ORCH & COND: Tony Osborne. CAST: Andy Cole, Elizabeth Larner, chorus. (HMV(E) CSD-1258, with Rose-Marie)

280919s THE NEW MOON contemp medley by Colonial Club Orch and singers. (78/Bruns 20089)

280919t THE NEW MOON studio prod. COND: Johnny Douglas. CAST: Andy Cole, Barbara Leigh, Denis Quilley, chorus. (Cap SN-7503, with Pal Joey)

280919u THE NEW MOON medley by Columbia Light Opera Company. (78/Col(E) 9831)

280919v THE NEW MOON 1930 records by Perry Askam of 1930 Los Angeles prod. "Lover, Come Back to Me" With male chorus of the prod: "Stout-Hearted Men" (78/Vic 22317)

280925a CHEE-CHEE 1963 album by Betty Comden. PIANO: Richard Lewine. (Ava 26, entitled "Remember These," with Treasure Girl)

281001a BILLIE 1928 records by Polly Walker of orig cast. MUSIC & WORDS: George M Cohan. "Billie" (LP-774) "Where Were You, Where Was I?" (LP-711)

281004a FREDERICA 1930 records by members of 1930 London prod. MUSIC: Franz Lehar. WORDS: Harry S Pepper. Joseph Hislop: "Wonderful, So Wonderful," "Wayside Rose" (78/HMV(E) B-3589) "A Heart as Pure as Gold," "Oh Maiden, My Maiden" (78/HMV(E) B-3590) Lea Seidl: "Love Will Kiss and Ride Away," "Little Roses, Little Flowers" (78/Col(E) DB-269) "Why Did You Kiss My Heart Awake?," "God Has Sent a Lovely Day/I Love Him So" (78/Col(E) DX-131)

281008a PARIS 1934 record by Cole Porter, piano and vocal. MUSIC & WORDS: Cole Porter. "Two Little Babes in the Wood" (LP-182)(LP-340)

281008b PARIS 1928 records by members of orig prod. Irene Bordoni & Irving Aaronson's Commanders: "Don't Look at Me That Way" (by Cole Porter) (LP-426) (LP-774) "The Land of Going to Be" (78/Vic 21742) Aaronson's Commanders: "Let's Do It" (by Cole Porter), "The Land of Going to Be" (78/Vic 21745) "Let's Misbehave" (by Cole Porter, dropped from the show) (LP-426) (LP-711)

281008c PARIS 1929 records by Irene Bordoni of 1930 film cast, with an entirely new score. "My Lover," "I Wonder What Is Really on His Mind" (78/Col 1983-D)

281008*a UPS-A-DAISY 1928 records by pianists Constance Mering & Muriel Pollock of orig prod. MUSIC: Lewis E Gensler. "Hot," "Ups-a-Daisy" (78/Col 1633-D)

281010a HOLD EVERYTHING! 1929 medley by Victor Light Opera Group. MUSIC: Ray Henderson. WORDS: B G DeSylva, Lew Brown. (78/Vic 35970)

281010b HOLD EVERYTHING! contemp medley by Al Goodman Orch. VOCAL: Dick Robertson. (78/Bruns 20090)

281023a ANIMAL CRACKERS later record by Groucho Marx of orig cast & 1930 film cast. MUSIC: Harry Ruby. WORDS: Bert Kalmar. "Hooray for Captain Spalding!" (LP-341)

281030a HELLO, YOURSELF! contemp records by Waring's Pennsylvanians of orig prod. MUSIC: Richard Myers. WORDS Leo Robin. "I Want the World to Know," "Say That You Love Me" (78/Vic 21783) "Jericho" (78/Vic 21870)

281108a TREASURE GIRL records by members of orig prod. MUSIC: George Gershwin. WORDS: Ira Gershwin. Gertrude Lawrence, 1952: "I've Got A Crush On You" (LP-5) Victor Arden & Phil Ohman (pianists), with their orch, 1928: "Feeling I'm Falling," "Got a Rainbow" (LP-492)

281108b TREASURE GIRL 1963 album by Betty Comden. PIANO: Richard Lewine. (Ava 26, entitled "Remember These," with Chee-Chee)

281121a RAINBOW later record by Libby Holman of orig cast. MUSIC: Vincent Youmans. WORDS: Oscar Hammerstein II. "I Want a Man" (LP-51)

281121b RAINBOW 1929 records by John Boles of 1930 film, entitled "Song of the West." "West Wind," "The One Girl" (78/Vic 22229)

281204a WHOOPEE records by members of orig prod. MUSIC & WORDS: Walter Donaldson, Gus Kahn, otthers. Ruth Etting, 1928: "Love Me or Leave Me" (LP-25) (LP-610) "My Blackbirds Are Bluebirds Now" (LP-610) "I'm Bringing a Red, Red Rose" (LP-546) (LP-610) Eddie Cantor, contemp: "Hungry Women" (LP-18) (LP-610) (LP-710) "Makin' Whoopee" (LP-539) (LP-610) "Automobile Horn Song," "I Faw Down an' Go Boom!" (LP-610) Cantor, later: "Makin' Whoopee" (LP-30) (LP-38) (LP-143) (LP-144) (LP-165) (LP-297) (LP-384) (LP-542) George Olsen Orch, 1928: "Makin' Whoopee" (LP-282) (LP-710) (Incomplete: LP-610) "Until You Get Somebody Else" (LP-610) "Come West, Little Girl, Come West," "I'm Bringing a Red, Red Rose" (78/Vic 21808) (Incomplete: LP-610) "I Faw Down an' Go Boom!" (78/Vic 21832) Paul Whiteman Orch (which replaced Olsen Orch on 24 Dec 1928), contemp: "Makin' Whoopee" (LP-540) (Incomplete: LP-610) "I'm Bringing a Red, Red Rose" (LP-541) Ritz Quartet (who joined the show on 24 Dec 1928), contemp: "I'm Bringing a Red, Red Rose" (78/Bruns 4328) "Come West, Little Girl, Come West" (LP-610)

281204b WHOOPEE 1929 medley by Victor Light Opera Company. (LP-774) (Excerpt: LP-610)

281204c WHOOPEE 1930 film soundtrack. COND: Alfred Newman. CAST: Eddie Cantor, Claire Dodd, Betty Grable, Paul Gregory. (Meet-Patti Discs PRW-1930, with Puttin' On the Ritz; plus Cantor: "A Girl Friend of a Boy Friend of Mine" (LP-751). Excerpts: Grable: "Cowboy Number" (LP-284) Gregory: "I'll Still Belong to You" (LP-770).)

281204d WHOOPEE contemp medley by Colonial Club Orch and singers. (78/Bruns 20089) (Incomplete: LP-610)

281204e WHOOPEE medley by New Mayfair Orch of songs from 1930 film prod. Vocals uncredited. (78/HMV(E) C-2058)

281226a HELLO DADDY 1929 records by Jimmy McHugh (composer) conducting the Bostonians. WORDS: Dorothy Fields. "Futuristic Rhythm" (78/Harmony 836-H) "Let's Sit and Talk about You," "In a Great Big Way" (78/Harmony 823-H)

281226b HELLO DADDY contemp records by Ben Pollack Orch

of orig prod. "Futuristic Rhythm" (78/Vic 21858) "Let's Sit and Talk about You" (78/Vic 21858) (Okeh 41189) "In a Great Big Way" (78/Okeh 41189)

1929

290001a Film ON WITH THE SHOW records by Ethel Waters of orig cast. "Am I Blue?" (1929: LP-15, LP-52) (1950: LP-361) (Late 1950's: LP-99) "Birmingham Bertha" (1929: LP-15)

290002a Film HONKY TONK 1929 records by Sophie Tucker of orig cast. "He's a Good Man to Have Around" (LP-17) "I'm the Last of the Red Hot Mammas" (LP-148) (LP-539) "I'm Doin' What I'm Doin' for Love," "I'm Feathering a Nest" (78/Vic 21993) "I don't Want to Get Thin" (78/Vic 21995)

290002b Film HONKY TONK soundtrack. VOCALS: Sophie Tucker. "Some of These Days," "I'm the Last of the Red Hot Mammas," "I'm Feathering a Nest" (LP-751)

290003a Film LUCKY BOY records by George Jessel of orig cast. "My Mother's Eyes" (1929: LP-17, LP-539) (Later: 78/ARA 4515)

290004a Film LADY OF THE PAVEMENTS 1929 record by Lupe Velez of orig cast. MUSIC & WORDS: Irving Berlin. "Where Is the Song of Songs for Me?" (LP-17) (LP-519)

290005a Film BROADWAY MELODY soundtrack. MUSIC & WORDS: Nacio Herb Brown, Arthur Freed, others. COND: Arthur Lange. CAST: Charles King, Bessie Love, Anita Page. (Raviola BMPM-1929, with The New Moon (entitled "Parisian Belle"). Excerpt: King: "Broadway Melody" (LP-252)

290005b Film BROADWAY MELODY 1929 records by Charles King of orig cast. "Broadway Melody" (LP-17) (LP-539) (LP-770) "The Wedding of the Painted Doll," "You Were Meant For Me" (LP-770) "Love Boat" (78/Vic 21965)

290006a Film THE TRESPASSER 1929 records by Gloria Swanson of orig cast. "Love, Your Magic Spell Is Everywhere" (LP-17) (LP-148) (LP-539) "Serenade" (78/Vic 22079)

290007a Film INNOCENTS OF PARIS records by Maurice Chevalier of orig cast. "Wait Till You See Ma Cherie" (1929: LP-102) "It's a Habit of Mine" (1929: 78/Vic 22007) "On Top of the World Alone" (1929: LP-17, LP-72, LP-102, LP-453, LP-539, LP-769) (1947: LP-88, LP-405) (1958: LP-118) "Valentine" (1929: LP-72, LP-148) (1947: LP-88, LP-132, LP-405) (1957: LP-224) (1958: LP-118) "Les Ananas" (1929: LP-72, LP-148)

290008a Film SWEETIES records by Helen Kane of orig cast. "He's So Unusual" (1929: LP-17) (Later(?): LP-699)

290008b Film SWEETIES soundtrack. Helen Kane: "The Prep Step," "I Think You'll Like It" (LP-699)

290009a Film APPLAUSE 1929 record by Helen Morgan of orig cast. "What Wouldn't I Do for That Man!" (LP-17) (LP-32) (LP-37)

290009b Film APPLAUSE soundtrack. Helen Morgan: "What Wouldn't I Do for That Man" (LP-499)

290010a Film GLORIFYING THE AMERICAN GIRL records by members of orig cast. Helen Morgan: "What Wouldn't I Do for That Man!" (1929: LP-17, LP-32, LP-37) Rudy Vallee: "I'm Just a Vagabond Lover" (1929: 78/Vic 21967) (1942: LP-58, LP-96)

290010b Film GLORIFYING THE AMERICAN GIRL soundtrack. Helen Morgan: "What Wouldn't I Do for That Man," "There Must Be Someone Waiting" (LP-499)

290011a Film THE LOVE PARADE records by members of orig cast. MUSIC: Victor Schertzinger. WORDS: Clifford Grey. Jeanette MacDonald, 1929: "Dream Lover" (LP-17) (LP-536) "March of the

Grenadiers'' (LP-536) Maurice Chevalier, 1930: "My Love Parade" (English: LP-62, LP-88) (French: LP-102) "Paris, Stay the Same" (English & French: LP-102, LP-542) (French: LP-62, LP-72) "Nobody's Using It Now" (English: 78/Vic 22285) (French: LP-102) MacDonald, 1944: "March of the Grenadiers" (LP-378) Chevalier, 1954: "Paris, Stay the Same" (French: LP-270)

290011b Film THE LOVE PARADE 1930 medley by Victor Light Opera Company. (78/Vic 36008)

290011c Film THE LOVE PARADE soundtrack. CAST: Maurice Chevalier, Jeanette MacDonald, Lupino Lane, Lillian Roth. (Nadine 260, with The Merry Widow)

290012a Film IT'S A GREAT LIFE 1930 records by members of orig cast. Duncan Sisters: "I'm Following You" (LP-17) "Hoosier Hop" (78/Vic 22269) "It Must Be an Old Spanish Custom" (78/Vic 22345) Lawrence Gray: "I'm Following You," "I'm Sailing on a Sunbeam" (78/Bruns 4631)

290013a Film THE VAGABOND LOVER records by Rudy Vallee of orig cast. 1929: "Heigh Ho, Everybody, Heigh Ho" (LP-58) "I'll Be Reminded by You," "A Little Kiss Each Morning" (78/Vic 22193) "I Love You, Believe Me, I Love You," "If You Were the Only Girl in the World" (78/Vic 22227) 1955: "A Little Kiss Each Morning" (LP-357)

290014a Film THE SINGING FOOL records by Al Jolson of orig cast. "I'm Sitting on Top of the World" (1925: LP-73, LP-731) (1946: LP-682) (1947: LP-198, LP-243, LP-394, LP-739) "Sonny Boy" (1928: LP-82, LP-470, LP-731) (1935: LP-373) (1946: LP-145, LP-243) "There's a Rainbow 'Round My Shoulder" (1928: LP-82, LP-470, LP-626, LP-731) (1947: LP-196, LP-243) "It All Depends on You" (1949: LP-243, LP-380)

290014b Film THE SINGING FOOL soundtrack. Al Jolson: "It All Depends on You" (LP-269) "Sonny Boy" (LP-751)

290015a Film SAY IT WITH SONGS soundtrack. MUSIC & WORDS: Ray Henderson, Lew Brown, B G DeSylva, others. VOCALS: Al Jolson. "Used to You," "Little Pal," "I'm in Seventh Heaven," "Why Can't You?," "One Sweet Kiss" (Subon 1234, with Hallelujah, I'm a Bum; plus "I'm Ka-razy for You" & "Back in Your Own Backyard" (LP-751). Excerpts: "I'm in Seventh Heaven" (LP-269) "Used to You" (LP-269) (LP-751).)

290015b Film SAY IT WITH SONGS records by Al Jolson of orig prod. "Used to You" (1929: LP-73) "One Sweet Kiss" (1929: LP-73, LP-274, LP-626) "I'm in Seventh Heaven" (1929: LP-82) "Little Pal" (1929: LP-82) (Later: LP-370) "Back in Your Own Backyard" (1928: LP-73) (1946: LP-682) (1949: LP-198, LP-243, LP-739) "Why Can't You?" (1929: LP-274, LP-550, LP-731)

290015c Film SAY IT WITH SONGS contemp medley by Brunswick Salon Orch with unidentified vocalist. (78/Bruns 20093)

290016a Film THE PAGAN 1935 record by Ramon Novarro of orig cast. "Pagan Love Song" (LP-124) (LP-136) (LP-770)

290017a Film POINTED HEELS 1929 records by Helen Kane of orig cast. "I Have to Have You" (LP-148) (LP-539) (LP-769) "Aintcha?" (78/Vic 22192)

290017b Film POINTED HEELS soundtrack. Helen Kane: "Ain'tcha?," "I Have to Have You" (LP-699)

290018a Film IS EVERYBODY HAPPY? records by Ted Lewis Orch of orig prod. "I'm the Medecine Man for the Blues" (1929: 78/Col 1882-D) (1938: LP-167, LP-457, LP-491) "Wouldn't It Be Wonderful?" (1929: 78/Col 1882-D) "St. Louis Blues" (1926: 78/Col 697-D) (1938: LP-167, LP-457, LP-491) "Tiger Rag" (1926: LP-168) (1941: LP-167, LP-457) "In the Land of Jazz" (1929: Col(E) CB-5)

290019a Film GOLD DIGGERS OF BROADWAY 1929 records by

Nick Lucas of orig cast. "Tip-Toe through the Tulips" (LP-175) "Painting the Clouds with Sunshine" (78/Bruns 4418)

290019b Film GOLD DIGGERS OF BROADWAY soundtrack. Nick Lucas: "Tip-Toe through the Tulips" (LP-751)

290020a Film HOLLYWOOD REVUE soundtrack. Cliff Edwards: "Singin' in the Rain" (LP-252) (LP-770) Joan Crawford: "I've Got a Feeling for You" (LP-252) (LP-401) (LP-532) Marion Davies: "Tommy Atkins on Parade" (LP-770)

290020b Film HOLLYWOOD REVUE records by Cliff Edwards of orig cast. "Orange Blossom Time" (1929: 78/Col 1869-D) "Singin' in the Rain" (1929: LP-760) (Later: LP-635) (1949: 78/Mercury 5309) (1950s: LP-437)

290021a Film THE SHOW OF SHOWS 1929 records by members of orig prod. Irene Bordoni: "Just an Hour of Love" (78/Col 2027-D) Ted Lewis Orch: "Lady Luck" (78/Col 1999-D) Nick Lucas: "Your Mother and Mine" (78/Bruns 4378)

290022a Film MOTHER'S BOY 1929 records by Morton Downey of orig cast. "I'll Always Be Mother's Boy," "There'll Be You and I" (78/Vic 21940) "There's a Place in the Sun for You," "The World Is Yours and Mine" (78/Vic 21958)

290023a Film LUCKY IN LOVE 1929 records by Morton Downey of orig cast. "Love Is A Dreamer," "When They Sing the Wearin' of the Green" (78/Vic 22048)

290024a Film SYNCOPATION 1929 records by members of orig prod. Morton Downey: "My Inspiration Is You," "I'll Always Be in Love with You" (78/Vic 21860) Waring's Pennsylvanians: "Jericho," "I'll Always Be in Love with You" (78/Vic 21870)

290025a Film SO THIS IS COLLEGE 1929 record by Cliff Edwards of orig cast, "Sophomore Prom" (78/Col 1980-D)

290026a Film MARIANNE records by Cliff Edwards of orig cast. "Hang On to Me" (1929: LP 760) (1950s: LP-437) "Just You, Just Me" (1929: 78/Col 1907-D)

290026b Film MARIANNE soundtrack. Cliff Edwards, Lawrence Gray: "Blondy" (LP-770)

290027a Film HALLELUJAH contemp record by Daniel L Haynes & Dixie Jubilee Singers of orig cast. MUSIC & WORDS: Irving Berlin. "Waiting at the End of the Road" (78/Vic 22097)

290027b Film HALLELUJAH soundtrack. Nina Mae McKinney: "Swanee Shuffle" (LP-336)

290028a Film NOTHING BUT THE TRUTH records by Helen Kane of orig cast. "Do Something" (1929: 78/Vic 21917) (1950s: 45/MGM X-1164)

290029a Film SUNNY SIDE UP 1930 medley by Victor Light Opera Company. MUSIC: Ray Henderson. WORDS: B G DeSylva, Lew Brown. (78/Vic 36008)

290030a Film THE WOLF SONG 1929 record by Lupe Velez of orig cast. "Mi Amado" (78/Vic 21932)

290031a Film WONDER OF WOMEN contemp record by Peggy Wood of orig cast. "At Close of Day" (78/HMV(E)B-3282)

290032a Film THE SONG OF LOVE 1929 records by Belle Baker of orig cast. "I'm Walking with the Moonbeams," "Take Everything but You" (78/Bruns 4558) "I'll Still Go On Wanting You" (78/Bruns 4624)

290033a Film OFFICE BLUES soundtrack. Ginger Rogers: "We Can't Get Along" Rogers, unidentified tenor: "Dear Sir" (LP-402)

290034a Film UNTAMED soundtrack. Joan Crawford, Robert Montgomery: "That Wonderful Something Is Love" (LP-401) Crawford: "Chant of the Jungle" (LP-401) (LP-770)

60

290035a Film FOX MOVIETONE FOLLIES OF 1929 contemp medley by Brunswick Salon Orch with unidentified soloist. (78/Bruns 20093)

290036a Film MASTERS OF MELODY soundtrack. MUSIC: Richard Rodgers. WORDS: Lorenz Hart. Dialogue by Rodgers & Hart, piano by Rodgers. Orchestra with unidentified vocalists. (LP-498)

290037a Film THE SHOPWORN ANGEL record sung by J Fred Coots, composer. "A Precious Little Thing Called Love" (LP-530)

290038a Film ST. LOUIS BLUES soundtrack. Bessie Smith, Hall Johnson Choir: "St Louis Blues" (LP-623)

290039a Film BLACK AND TAN soundtrack, with Duke Ellington Orch. VOCALS: Hall Johnson Choir. (LP-622)

290040a Film THE BATTLE OF PARIS soundtrack. MUSIC & WORDS: Cole Porter. Gertrude Lawrence: "Here Comes the Bandwagon," "They All Fall in Love" (LP-655)

290041a Film MICKEY'S FOLLIES soundtrack of the Mickey Mouse cartoon. Walt Disney (for Mickey Mouse): "Minnie's Yoo-Hoo" (LP-661)

290042a Film DEVIL MAY CARE 1935 records by Ramon Novarro of orig cast. "The Shepherd's Serenade," "Charming" (78/HMV(E) C-2778)

290043a Film CLOSE HARMONY soundtrack, Charles (Buddy) Rogers: "I'm All a-Twitter, I'm All a-Twirl" (LP-769)

290044a Film THE DANCE OF LIFE soundtrack. Hal Skelly: "True Blue Lou" Howard Conrad: "Ladies of the Dance" Marjorie Kane: "The Flippity Flop" (LP-769)

290045a Film THE WAGON MASTER 1930 record by Ken Maynard of orig cast. "Lone Star Trail" (78/Col 2310-D)

290109a FOLLOW THRU records by members of orig prod. MUSIC: Ray Henderson. WORDS: B G DeSylva, Lew Brown. Zelma O'Neal: "I Want to Be Bad" (1929: 78/Bruns 4204) O'Neal & Al Goodman's Follow Thru Orch: "I Want to Be Bad," "Button Up Your Overcoat" (1929: 78/Bruns 4207) Medley (1929: 78/Bruns 20090) Eleanor Powell: "My Lucky Star" (1935: LP-183, LP-474)

290109b FOLLOW THRU 1929 medley by Victor Light Opera Group. (78/Vic 35970)

290109c FOLLOW THRU 1929 medley by Columbia Light Opera Company. (78/Col(E) 9764)

290115a NED WAYBURN'S GAMBOLS records by Libby Holman of orig cast. "There Ain't No Sweet Man That's Worth the Salt of My Tears" (1928: 78/Bruns 3798) (Later: LP-662)

290211a MR. CINDERS contemp records by members of orig (London) cast. MUSIC: Vivian Ellis. WORDS: Clifford Grey, Greatrex Newman. Binnie Hale: "Spread a Little Happiness" (LP-79) Hale, Bobby Howes: "I'm a One-Man Girl," "Every Little Moment" Howes: "On the Amazon" (LP-83)

290218a PLEASURE BOUND 1929 record by the Pleasure Bound Orchestra. COND: Harold Stern. "Just Suppose" (78/Bruns 4357)

290311a SPRING IS HERE 1930 film soundtrack. MUSIC: Richard Rodgers. WORDS: Lorenz Hart. COND: Louis Silvers. Inez Courtney (of orig prod), Lawrence Gray: "Spring Is Here" Alexander Gray, Bernice Claire: "Yours Sincerely" Claire, Frank Albertson: "With a Song in My Heart"(LP-498) Claire, Alexander Gray: "Have a Little Faith in Me" (by Harry Warren) Courtney, Albertson: "What's the Big Idea?" (by Harry Warren) (LP-633)

290327a WAKE UP AND DREAM contemp records by members of orig (London) prod. MUSIC & WORDS: Cole Porter. George Metaxa: "Wake Up and Dream" (LP-159) (LP-300) "What Is This Thing Called Love?" (LP-300) Elsie Carlisle: "Let's Do It," "What Is This Thing Called Love?" (78/Dominion(E) A-125) Leslie Hutchinson, piano: Medley (78/Parlophone(E) E-10869) Hutchinson, piano & vocal: "I'm a Gigolo," "What Is This Thing Called Love?," "Let's Do It," "Looking at You" (LP-477) Medley, including the same 4 songs (78/HMV(E) C-3194)

290327b WAKE UP AND DREAM 1935 record by Cole Porter (composer), piano and vocal. "I'm a Gigolo" (LP-182) (LP-340)

290327c WAKE UP AND DREAM contemp medley by Light Opera Company, probably including George Metaxa of orig cast. (LP-700)

290327d WAKE UP AND DREAM records by Jack Buchanan of 1929 New York prod & Elsie Randolph. "Fancy Our Meeting" (1928: 78/Col(E) 9462) (1933: 78/HMV(E) B-8026)

290422a MESSIN' AROUND records by James P Johnson (piano), composer. WORDS: Perry Bradford. "Put Your Mind Right on It," "Sorry That I Strayed Away from You" (1929: 78/Col 14417-D) "Skiddle-de-Skow" (1927: 78/Col 14247-D)

290430a THE LITTLE SHOW records by Libby Holman of orig cast. "Moanin' Low" (1929: LP-176, LP-518, LP-521, LP-774) (1929: 78/Bruns 4446) (1935 radio performance: LP-556) (Later: LP-662) (Later: LP-51) "Can't We Be Friends?"(1929: 78/Bruns 4506) (Later: LP-662) (Later: LP-51)

290430b THE LITTLE SHOW 1953 album, including one song from the Third Little Show. MUSIC & WORDS: Various. COND:Lehman Engel. VOCALS: Carol Bruce, Sheila Bond, Hiram Sherman. (RCA 10" LPM-3155, with The Band Wagon)

290430c THE LITTLE SHOW 1975 record sung by Arthur Schwartz. MUSIC: Arthur Schwartz. WORDS: Howard Dietz. "I Guess I'll Have to Change My Plan" (LP-418)

290629a HOT CHOCOLATES records by Fats Waller, composer. MUSIC: Thomas (Fats) Waller, Harry Brooks. WORDS: Andy Razaf. "Ain't Misbehavin'" (Piano, 1929: LP-539, LP-581, LP-711) (Pipe organ/vocal, 1938: LP-582) (Piano/vocal, 1938: 78/Bluebird B-10288) (Piano/vocal, 1943: LP-345) (Piano/vocal, later: 78/Vic 40-4003) "Sweet Savannah Sue" (Piano, 1929: LP-581)

290629b HOT CHOCOLATES records by members of orig cast. Louis Armstrong: "Ain't Misbehavin'" (1929: LP-516, LP-581) (1929, with Segar Ellis Orch: LP-52, LP-581) (1938: 78/Dec 2042) (1947: LP-355) "Black and Blue," "That Rhythm Man," "Sweet Savannah Sue" Edith Wilson: "Black and Blue," "My Man Is Good for Nothing but Love" Eddie Green & others of orig cast: Skit "Big Business" (with Fats Waller, piano), Skit "Sending a Wire" (1929: LP-581)

290701a EARL CARROLL'S SKETCH BOOK 1929 records by Don Howard and the Phelps Twins (vocal trio) of orig prod. "Fascinating You," "Like Me Less, Love Me More" (78/Vic 22127)

290702a SHOW GIRL records by members of orig cast. Lou Clayton, Eddie Jackson, & Jimmy Durante: "Can Broadway Do without Me?" (1929: LP-19, LP-42, (LP-494) "So I Ups to Him" (1929: 78/Col 1860-D) Medley "Can Broadway Do without Me?/So I Ups to Him/Because They All Love You" (1949: LP-176) Durante, Jackson: "So I Ups to Him," "Jimmy the Well-Dressed Man" (1944: LP-80) Durante: "Who Will Be With You When I'm Far Away?" (1944: LP-80) (1950's, with Ethel Barrymore: LP-439)

290702b SHOW GIRL 1932 radio performance by George Gershwin (composer), piano, "Liza" (LP-375)

290718a BITTER SWEET studio prod. MUSIC & WORDS: Noel Coward. ORCH: Brian Fahey, Ray Terry. COND: Michael Collins.

CAST: Vanessa Lee, Roberto Cardinali, Julie Dawn, John Hauxvell. (Angel 35814)

290718b BITTER SWEET records by members of 1940 film cast. Nelson Eddy, 1940: "I'll See You Again" (LP-432) "Tokay" (78/Col 4263-M) "Dear Little Cafe," "The Call of Life," "If You Could Only Come with Me" (78/Col 4264-M) Jeanette MacDonald, 1947: "Zigeuner" (LP-65) (LP-71) "I'll See You Again" (LP-4) (LP-65) (LP-71)

290718c BITTER SWEET records sung by Noel Coward, composer. 1929: "Zigeuner" (LP-28) 1938: "I'll See You Again" (LP-28) (LP-710) Later: "I'll See You Again" (LP-138)

290718d BITTER SWEET 1939 records by Evelyn Laye of 1929 New York prod. "Zigeuner," "I'll See You Again" (LP-63)

290718e BITTER SWEET contemp records by members of orig (London) cast. Peggy Wood: "Zigeuner" Wood & George Metaxa: "I'll See You Again," "Dear Little Cafe" Ivy St Helier: "If Love Were All" (LP-174) (LP-308)

290718f BITTER SWEET medley by Jack Hylton Orch. Vocals uncredited. (78/Vic 36098)

290718g BITTER SWEET 1961 studio prod. COND: Kenneth Alwyn. CAST: Susan Hampshire, Adele Leigh, James Pease, the Linden Singers. (Music for Pleasure(E) 1091)

290718h BITTER SWEET 1929 medley by Columbia Light Opera Company. (78/Col(E) 9900)

290718i BITTER SWEET studio prod. COND: Lehman Engel. CAST: Rosalind Elias, Jeanette Scovotti, John Hauxvell. (Reader's Digest 46-N3, with Countess Maritza)

290718j BITTER SWEET studio prod. ORCH & COND: Johnny Douglas. CAST: June Bronhill, Neville Jason, Julia d'Alba, Leslie Fyson, chorus. (Col(E) TWO-273)

290718k BITTER SWEET 1940 film soundtrack. MUSIC & WORDS: mostly Noel Coward. CAST: Jeanette MacDonald, Nelson Eddy, (Bright Tight Discs BIS-1377, with additional material; LP-466. Also a number dropped before release: MacDonald, Eddy: "The Call of Life" (LP-455) Excerpt: MacDonald: "If Love Were All" (LP-588)

290814a MURRAY ANDERSON'S ALMANAC 1929 records by Red Nichols Orch of orig prod. "I May Be Wrong," "The New Yorkers" (78/Bruns 4500) "Wait for the Happy Ending" (78/Bruns 4510)

290903a SWEET ADELINE records by Helen Morgan of orig cast. MUSIC: Jerome Kern. WORDS: Oscar Hammerstein II. "Why Was I Born?" (1929: LP-18, LP-37, LP-229, LP-230) (1932 radio performance: LP-566) (1935: LP-460) "Don't Ever Leave Me" (1929: LP-32, LP-37, LP-229)

290903b SWEET ADELINE records by members of 1935 film cast. Irene Dunne: "Why Was I Born?" (1941: LP-66, LP-607) "Here Am I" (1935 radio performance: LP-592) Phil Regan: "We Were So Young," "Molly O'Donahue" (1934: 78/Col 2990-D)

290903c SWEET ADELINE medley by the New Mayfair Orch, uncredited vocalists. (78/HMV(E) C-2772)

290903d SWEET ADELINE 1938 medley by Victor Light Opera Company. COND: Leonard Joy. (LP-306) (LP-774)

290903e SWEET ADELINE soundtrack of 1935 film. CAST: Irene Dunne, Phil Regan, Joseph Cawthorn, chorus. (Titania 506, with High, Wide and Handsome; LP-335. Excerpt: Dunne: "Here Am I" (LP-669).)

290923a GEORGE WHITE'S SCANDALS OF 1929 1929 records by Frances White of orig cast. MUSIC & WORDS: Cliff Friend, George White. "Bigger and Better Than Ever," "Bottoms Up" (78/Bruns 4503)

291010a THE LAND OF SMILES 1959 London prod. MUSIC: Franz

Lehar. WORDS: Christopher Hassall. COND: Vilem Tausky. CAST: Charles Craig, Elizabeth Fretwell, June Bronhill, Peter Grant, chorus, (HMV(E) CSD-1267)

291010b THE LAND OF SMILES 1935 records by Richard Tauber of 1931 London prod & 1946 New York prod (entitled "Yours Is My Heart"). "You Are My Heart's Delight," "Patiently Smiling" (78/Parlophone(E) RO-20500)

291108a THE HOUSE THAT JACK BUILT contemp record by Jack Hulbert of orig (London) cast. "She's Such a Comfort to Me" (LP-90)

291126a SONS O' GUNS record sung by J Fred Coots, composer. "Why?" (LP-530)

1930

300001a Film THE BLUE ANGEL records by Marlene Dietrich of orig cast. MUSIC & WORDS: Frederick Hollander. 1930 records, Hollander cond: "Falling in Love Again" (English: LP-10, LP-148)(German: LP-81, LP-10, LP-273) "Blonde Women" (English: LP-10)(German: LP-81) "Lola" (English: LP-10)(German: LP-81, LP-129) "This Evening, Children" (English: LP-10)(German: LP-81) Later records: "Falling in Love Again" (LP-54)(LP-175)(LP-178)(LP-191)(LP-332)(LP-521)(German: LP-195) "Lola" (LP-106)(LP-178) (LP-191)(German: LP-195)

300001b Film THE BLUE ANGEL English soundtrack. Marlene Dietrich: "Falling in Love Again" (LP-653)

300002a Film MOROCCO 1931 records by Marlene Dietrich of orig cast. "Give Me the Man," "Quand l'Amour Meurt" (LP-10)

300002b Film MOROCCO soundtrack. Marlene Dietrich: "Quand l'Amour Meurt," "What Am I Bid?" (LP-705)

300003a Film BE YOURSELF 1930 records by Fanny Brice of orig cast. "Cooking Breakfast for the One I Love" (LP-17)(LP-32)(LP-33)(LP-230) "When a Woman Loves a Man" (LP-33)(LP-230)(LP-768)

300003b Film BE YOURSELF soundtrack. Fanny Brice: "When a Woman Loves a Man," "Cooking Breakfast for the One I Love," "Kicking a Hole in the Sky," "It's Gorgeous to Be Graceful"(?) (LP-699)

300004a Film PARAMOUNT ON PARADE 1930 records by members of orig cast. Dennis King: "Nichavo!" (LP-17) Maurice Chevalier: "Sweepin' the Clouds Away" (LP-72)(LP-88) "All I Want Is Just One Girl" (LP-102) Buddy Rogers: "Sweepin' the Clouds Away" (LP-52) "Any Time's the Time to Fall in Love" (78/Col 2143-D)

300004b Film PARAMOUNT ON PARADE soundtrack. Maurice Chevalier: "All I Want Is Just One Girl" (LP-769)

300005a Film THE KING OF JAZZ contemp records by members of orig prod. John Boles: "It Happened in Monterey" (LP-17) "Song of the Dawn" (78/Vic 22372) Rhythm Boys: "A Bench in the Park," "So the Bluebirds and the Blackbirds Got Together" Rhythm Boys, Paul Whiteman Orch: "Happy Feet," "I Like to Do Things for You" Rhythm Boys, Brox Sisters, Whiteman Orch: "A Bench in the Park" Bing Crosby, Whiteman Orch: "Song of the Dawn" Johnny Fulton, Whiteman Orch: "It Happened in Monterey" Jeanie Lang, Whiteman Orch: "Ragamuffin Romeo" (LP-181) Grace Hayes: "My Lover," "I Like to Do Things for You" (78/Vic 22388)

300005b Film THE KING OF JAZZ 1930 medley by the Broadcast Talkie Boys. (78/Broadcast(E) 598)

300005c Film THE KING OF JAZZ contemp medley by Light Opera Company. (78/HMV(E) C-1990)

300006a Film DIXIANA 1930 records by Everett Marshall of orig cast. MUSIC: Harry Tierney. WORDS: Anne Caldwell. "Mr. and Mrs. Sippi" (LP-17) "Goodbye Old Pals" (78/Vic 22471)

300007a Film PLAYBOY OF PARIS records by Maurice Chevalier of orig cast. 1930: "It's a Great Life" (English: LP-769)(French: LP-72, LP-102) "My Ideal" (English: LP-88, LP-769)(French: LP-62, LP-102) 1958: "My Ideal" (LP-118)

300007b Film PLAYBOY OF PARIS soundtrack. VOCALS: Maurice Chevalier. Main Title, "In the Heart of Old Paree," "It's a Great Life" (LP-776)

300008a Film THE BIG POND records by Maurice Chevalier of orig cast. 1930: "Livin' in the Sunlight" (English: LP-62, LP-72, LP-102) "You Brought a New Kind of Love to Me" (English: LP-88, LP-102)(French: LP-62, LP-72) 1958: "Livin' in the Sunlight," "You Brought a New Kind of Love to Me" (English: LP-118)

300008b Film THE BIG POND 1954 record sung by Sammy Fain, composer. "You Brought a New Kind of Love to Me" (LP-707)

300009a Film MONTE CARLO records by Jeanette MacDonald of orig cast. "Beyond the Blue Horizon"(1930: LP-536) (1950: LP-77)(1958: LP-134) "Always in All Ways"(1930: LP-536)

300009b Film MONTE CARLO soundtrack. Jeanette MacDonald: "Beyond the Blue Horizon" MacDonald, Jack Buchanan: "Give Me a Moment, Please," "Whatever It Is, It's Grand!," "Always in All Ways" Buchanan, John Roche, Tyler Brooke: "Trimmin' the Women" Claude Allister, MacDonald: "Love It and Like It" (LP-769)

300010a Film MAMMY records by Al Jolson of orig cast. MUSIC & WORDS: Irving Berlin. "Let Me Sing and I'm Happy" (1930:LP-82, LP-519)(1938: LP-387)(1939: LP-177) (1947: LP-228, LP-243, LP-739) "Looking at You" (1930: LP-175, LP-731) "To My Mammy" (1930: 78/Bruns 4722) "Who Paid the Rent for Mrs. Rip Van Winkle?" (1946: LP-682)

300010b Film MAMMY soundtrack. MUSIC & WORDS: mostly Irving Berlin. COND: Leo F Forbstein. VOCALS: Al Jolson, chorus. (Milloball TMSM-34031 (with Twenty Million Sweethearts) plus Jolson: "Who Paid the Rent for Mrs Rip Van Winkle" (LP-269) & "Yes! We Have No Bananas" (LP-336). Excerpts: Jolson: "Let Me Sing and I'm Happy" (LP-269)(LP-336) "Why Do They Take the Night Boat to Albany?" (LP-269) "To My Mammy" (LP-336).)

300011a Film A SONG OF SOHO 1930 record by Carl Brisson of orig cast. "There's Something about You That's Different" (LP-97)(LP-310)

300012a Film HONEY 1956 record by Lillian Roth of orig cast. "Sing You Sinners!" (LP-104)

300013a Film PUTTIN' ON THE RITZ records by Harry Richman of orig cast. "With You"(by Irving Berlin) (1930: 78/Bruns 4678) "Singing a Vagabond Song" (1930: 78/Bruns 4678)(1930's: LP-414)(1947: LP-113) "Puttin' On the Ritz"(by Irving Berlin) (1930: LP-349, LP-519, LP-593) (1930's: LP-414)(1947: LP-113) "There's Danger in Your Eyes, Cherie" (1930: 78/Bruns 4677)

300013b Film PUTTIN' ON THE RITZ soundtrack, CAST: Harry Richman, Joan Bennett. (Meet-Patti Discs PRW-1930, with Whoopee. Excerpts: Richman, Bennett: "Puttin' on the Ritz" (LP-336) Richman: "Puttin' on the Ritz," "There's Danger in Your Eyes, Cherie" (LP-751).)

300014a Film HER MAJESTY, LOVE soundtrack. Marilyn Miller, Leon Errol: "Baby" (LP-157)(LP-710)

300015a Film CALL OF THE FLESH 1935 record by Ramon Novarro of orig cast. "Lonely" (LP-124)(LP-136)

300016a Film HEADS UP 1930 records by Helen Kane of orig cast.

"My Man Is on the Make" (by Richard Rodgers, Lorenz Hart)(LP-217) "If I Knew You Better," "Readin' Ritin' Rhythm" (78/Vic 22520)

300016b Film HEADS UP soundtrack. MUSIC: Richard Rodgers. WORDS: Lorenz Hart. Buddy Rogers: "A Ship without a Sail" Helen Kane: "My Man Is on the Make" (LP-498) "Readin' Ritin' Rhythm"(by Victor Schertzinger & Don Hartman) (LP-699)

300017a Film THE ROGUE SONG soundtrack. MUSIC: Franz Lehar, Herbert Stothart. WORDS: Clifford Grey. CAST: Lawrence Tibbett, Catherine Dale Owen, Judith Vosselli, Ullrich Haupt, Stan Laurel, Oliver Hardy. (Pelican 2019)

300017b Film THE ROGUE SONG 1930 records by Lawrence Tibbett of orig cast. "The Rogue Song" (LP-226)(LP-385) "The White Dove" (LP-226) "The Narrative" (78/Vic 1446) "When I'm Looking at You" (78/Vic 1447)

300018a Film CAPTAIN OF THE GUARD 1930 records by John Boles of orig cast. "For You," "You, You Alone" (78/Vic 22373)

300019a Film TWO HEARTS IN WALTZ TIME 1934 records by Carl Brisson of 1934 film cast. "Give Her a Little Kiss," "Two Hearts That Beat in Waltz Time" (78/Dec(E) F-3968) "In Old Vienna," "Your Eyes So Tender" (78/Dec(E) F-3969)

300020a Film ROADHOUSE NIGHTS soundtrack. Helen Morgan: "It Can't Go On like This" (LP-499)

300021a Film THE SONG OF THE FLAME 1930 record by Noah Beery of orig cast, with the Vitaphone Orch. "One Little Drink" (78/Bruns 4828)

300021b Film THE SONG OF THE FLAME contemp medley by Van Phillips Concert Band. Vocals uncredited. (78/Col(E) DX-83)

300022a Film CHASING RAINBOWS 1929 records by Charles King of orig cast. "Happy Days Are Here Again," "Love Ain't Nothing But the Blues" (78/Bruns 4615) "Lucky Me, Lovable You," "Everybody Tap" (78/Bruns 4616)

300023a Film CHECK AND DOUBLE CHECK 1930 records by members of orig cast. Rhythm Boys, Duke Ellington Orch: "Three Little Words" Cootie Williams, Ellington Orch: "Ring Dem Bells" (78/Vic 22528) Ellington Orch: "Old Man Blues" (78/Vic 23022)

300024a Film LOVE COMES ALONG 1930 records by Bebe Daniels of orig cast. MUSIC: Oscar Levant. WORDS: Sidney Clare. "Night Winds," "Until Love Comes Along" (78/Vic 22283)

300025a Film MONTANA MOON 1930 record by Cliff Edwards of orig cast. "The Moon Is Low" (78/Col 2169-D)

300025b Film MONTANA MOON soundtrack. Joan Crawford, chorus: "Montana Call" (LP-401)

300026a Film OH! SAILOR BEHAVE 1930 records by Charles King of orig cast. "Love Comes in the Moonlight," "Highway to Heaven" (78/Bruns 4840) "Leave a Little Smile" (78/Bruns 4849)

300027a Film DANGEROUS NAN McGREW 1930 records by Helen Kane of orig cast. "Dangerous Nan McGrew," "I Owe You" (78/Vic 22407)

300028a Film THEY LEARNED ABOUT WOMEN 1929 records by Gus Van & Joe Schenck of orig cast. "Does My Baby Love?," "Dougherty Is the Name" (78/Vic 22352)

300029a Film CHEER UP AND SMILE 1930 records by ("Whispering") Jack Smith of orig cast. "Where Can You Be?," "You May Not Like It" (78/Vic 22443)

300030a Film SAFETY IN NUMBERS 1930 records by Buddy Rogers. "My Future Just Passed," "A Bee in Your Boudoir" (78/Col 2183-D)

300030b Film SAFETY IN NUMBERS soundtrack. Carole Lombard:

"You Appeal to Me" Charles (Buddy) Rogers: "My Future Just Passed" (LP-769)

300031a Film SONG O' MY HEART soundtrack. MUSIC & WORDS: Various. PIANO: Edwin Schneider. VOCALS: John McCormack. (McCormack Association mx S-2707/8)

300031b Film SONG O' MY HEART 1930 records by John Mc-Cormack of orig cast. "Ireland, Mother Ireland," "The Rose of Tralee" (78/Vic 1452) "Little Boy Blue" (78/Vic 1458) "I Feel You Near Me," "A Pair of Blue Eyes" (78/Vic 1453)

300032a Film FOLLOW THE LEADER soundtrack. Ethel Merman: "Satan's Holiday" (LP-334)

300033a Film WAY OUT WEST 1930 record by Cliff Edwards of orig cast. "Singing a Song to the Stars" (LP-760)

300034a Film DIE PRIVATSEKRETAERIN 1932 records by Renate Mueller of orig prod & 1932 English film prod (entitled "Sunshine Susie" in England & "Office Girl" in United States). "Today I Feel So Happy" (LP-310) "Just Because I Lost My Heart to You" (78/Col(E) DB-687)

300035a Film THE CUCKOOS contemp medley by Van Phillips Concert Band. MUSIC & WORDS: Harry Ruby, Bert Kalmar. Vocals uncredited. (78/Col(E) DX-83)

300036a Film SWING HIGH contemp medley by New Mayfair Orch. (78/HMV(E) C-2058)

300037a Film HAPPY DAYS 1929 records by George Olsen Orch of orig prod. "I'm on a Diet of Love," "Mona" (78/Vic 22259)

300038a Film CHILDREN OF PLEASURE 1930 records by Lawrence Gray of orig cast. "Leave It That Way," "The Whole Darned Thing's for You" (78/Bruns 4775)

300039a Film FORWARD MARCH 1930 record by Cliff Edwards of orig cast. "Sing (A Happy Little Thing)" (78/Col 2235-D)

300040a Film ROSELAND soundtrack. Ruth Etting: "Let Me Sing and I'm Happy," "Dancing with Tears in My Eyes" (LP-699)

300041a Film WOMEN EVERYWHERE 1930 records by J Harold Murray of orig cast. "Beware of Love," "Smile, Legionnaire" (78/Bruns 4836)

300042a Film HIGH SOCIETY BLUES contemp medley by Light Opera Company. (78/HMV(E) C-1990)

300043a Film SUNNY SKIES 1930 record by Benny Rubin of orig cast. "The Laugh Song" (78/Bruns 4798)

300044a Film LORD BYRON OF BROADWAY soundtrack. Cliff Edwards, Charles Kaley: "A Bundle of Old Love Letters" Kaley: "Should I?" (LP-770)

300045a Film ONE HEAVENLY NIGHT soundtrack. John Boles, Evelyn Laye: "One Heavenly Night" (LP-770)

300046a Film SEA LEGS soundtrack. Lillian Roth, Jack Oakie: "This Must Be Illegal" (LP-768)

300114a STRIKE UP THE BAND newsreel soundtrack of a 1929 stage rehearsal. MUSIC: George Gershwin. WORDS: Ira Gershwin. Bobby Clark & Paul McCullough, with George Gershwin, piano: "Mademoiselle in New Rochelle" George Gershwin, piano: "Strike Up the Band" (LP-12) (LP-569)

300114b STRIKE UP THE BAND contemp records by Red Nichols & His "Strike Up the Band" Orch of orig prod, with uncredited vocals. "Soon," "Strike Up the Band" (LP-569)

300218a SIMPLE SIMON records by Ruth Etting of orig cast. "Ten Cents a Dance"(by Richard Rodgers & Lorenz Hart) (1930: LP-25, LP-569, LP-710, LP-754) "Love Me or Leave Me" (1928: LP-25)

300220a HERE COMES THE BRIDE 1930 records by members of orig (London) prod. MUSIC: Arthur Schwartz. WORDS: Desmond Carter, Howard Dietz, others. Jean Colin, Clifford Mollison: "High and Low" (LP-728) "I'll Always Remember" (78/Col(E) DB-70) Vera Bryer, Richard Dolman: "I'm like a Sailor," "I Love You and I Like You" (LP-700) Maria Minetti: "Spanish Eyes" Dolman: "Hot" (78/Col(E) DB-72)

300220b HERE COMES THE BRIDE contemp medley by Light Opera Company. (78/HMV(E) C-1871)

300225a LEW LESLIE'S INTERNATIONAL REVUE records by members of orig cast. MUSIC: Jimmy McHugh. WORDS: Dorothy Fields. Gertrude Lawrence, 1952: "Exactly like You," "On the Sunny Side of the Street" (LP-5) Harry Richman: "Exactly like You" (1930: LP-569) "On the Sunny Side of the Street" (1930: LP-349, LP-518, LP-569) (1930's: LP-414)(1947: LP-113, LP-176)

300303a FLYING HIGH contemp records by Al Goodman Orch of orig prod. MUSIC: Ray Henderson. WORDS: B G DeSylva, Lew Brown. "Thank Your Father," "Without Love," "Red Hot Chicago" (LP-569)

300303b FLYING HIGH 1931 film soundtrack. Bert Lahr (also of orig cast), Charlotte Greenwood: "The First Time for Me" (LP-608)

300327a COCHRAN'S 1930 REVUE 1930 records by Leslie Hutchinson, who played piano in orig (London) prod. Piano: Medley (78/Parlophone(E) R-617) Piano & vocal: "With a Song in My Heart"(by Richard Rodgers & Lorenz Hart), "The Things You Do," "The Wind in the Willows" (LP-477)

300604a THE GARRICK GAIETIES (THIRD EDITION) 1971 record sung by Johnny Mercer, lyricist. MUSIC: Everett Miller. "Out of Breath and Scared to Death" (LP-533)

300604b THE GARRICK GAIETIES (THIRD EDITION) record by Nan Blackstone of orig cast. "I've Got It Again" (78/ Liberty Music Shop BL-200)

300821a HOT RHYTHM 1930 records by Edith Wilson of orig cast. "Loving You the Way I Do," "The Penalty of Love" (78/Vic 23010) "I'll Get Even with You" (78/Vic V-38624)

300904a CHARLOT'S MASQUERADE contemp record by Patrick Waddington of orig (London) cast. "Sweet Temptation" (LP-172)

300917a FOLLOW A STAR 1930 records by Sophie Tucker of orig (London) prod. MUSIC: Vivian Ellis, Ted Shapiro. WORDS: Jack Yellen. "Follow a Star," "I Never Can Think of the Words" (78/Broadcast(E) 5195) "That's Where the South Begins" (LP-700) "If Your Kisses Can't Hold The Man You Love" (78/Broadcast(E) 5196)

300917b FOLLOW A STAR 1930 medley by Light Opera Company. (78/HMV(E) C-2057)

300920a NINA ROSA contemp records by members of 1931 London cast. MUSIC: Sigmund Romberg. WORDS: Irving Caesar. Geoffrey Gwyther: "Adored One," "Nina Rosa" (78/Dec(E) F-2467) Helen Gilliland (who replaced Ethelind Terry in the cast): "First Love, Last Love" Gilliland), Robert Chisholm: "The Gaucho's March" (78/Dec(E) F-2468)

300920b NINA ROSA 1956 record by Irving Caesar (lyricist, with Otto Harbach). "My First Love, My Last Love" (LP-353)

300924a PRIVATE LIVES records by members of orig (London) cast. MUSIC & WORDS: Noel Coward. "Someday I'll Find You" (Gertrude Lawrence, 1932: LP-34, LP-542) (Lawrence, 1952: LP-5) (Noel Coward, later: LP-138) Two scenes, incl "Someday I'll Find You," "I Never Realized"(by Cole Porter) & "If You Were the Only Girl in the World"(by Nat D Ayer , Clifford Grey) (Coward & Lawrence, 1930: LP-28, LP-275)

301014a GIRL CRAZY 1951 studio prod. MUSIC: George Gershwin. WORDS: Ira Gershwin. ORCH: Ted Royal, Carol Huxley. COND: Lehman Engel. CAST: Mary Martin, Louise Carlyle, Eddie Chappell. (Col CL-822)

301014b GIRL CRAZY 1943 album by Judy Garland and Mickey Rooney of 1943 film cast, COND: George Stoll (of 1943 film prod). (Dec 10" 5412; LP-640. Incomplete: 45/Dec ED-2022. Excerpts: Garland:"Bidin' My Time" (LP-239) "But Not for Me" (LP-7) "Embraceable You," "I Got Rhythm" (LP-35) Rooney: "Treat Me Rough" (LP-114) Garland, Rooney: "Could You Use Me?" (LP-115).)

301014c GIRL CRAZY 1943 film soundtrack. COND: George Stoll, Tommy Dorsey. CAST: Judy Garland, Mickey Rooney, June Allyson, Rags Ragland. (Curtain Calls 100/9-10, with Strike Up the Band. Excerpt: Garland: "But Not for Me" (LP-8) (LP-289). Also a number dropped before release: Garland, Rooney, Nancy Walker, chorus: "Bronco Busters" (LP-455).)

301014d GIRL CRAZY records by members of orig prod. Ethel Merman: "I Got Rhythm" (1947: LP-68, LP-69) (1955: LP-36) (1961: LP-45) (1962: LP-251) (1972: LP-153) (1977: LP-652) (1979: LP-670) "Embraceable You" (1955: LP-36) "Sam and Delilah," "But Not for Me" (1961: LP-45) The Foursome: "Bidin My Time" (1930: 78/Bruns 4996) (1939: LP-176, LP-569) Red Nichols Orch: "I Got Rhythm," "Embraceable You" (1930: LP-569) Ginger Rogers: "Embraceable You," "But Not for Me" (1965: LP-325) (1978: LP-624)

301014e GIRL CRAZY soundtrack of 1965 film, entitled "When the Boys Meet the Girls," with additional songs by various. ORCH: Fred Karger. COND: Fred Karger, Ernie Freeman. CAST: Connie Francis, Harve Presnell, Louis Armstrong, Sam the Sham and the Pharaohs, Herman's Hermits. (MGM 4334)

301014f GIRL CRAZY 1953 album. COND: Milton Rosenstock. CAST: Lisa Kirk, Helen Gallagher, Edith Adams, male quartet. (RCA 10" LPM-3156, with Porgy and Bess)

301014g GIRL CRAZY performances by George Gershwin (composer), piano. "I Got Rhythm" (1931 newsreel soundtrack: LP-12) (1932 radio performance: LP-375) (1933 radio performance: LP-286, LP-332) (1934 radio performance: LP-286)

301014h GIRL CRAZY 1938 medley. COND: Nathaniel Shilkret. VOCALS: Jane Froman, Felix Knight, chorus. (LP-303)

301014i GIRL CRAZY records by members of 1943 film prod. Judy Garland: "Fascinating Rhythm" (1939: LP-239, LP-490, LP-745) "Embraceable You" (1948, with Bing Crosby: LP-180, LP-718) Tommy Dorsey Orch: "Embraceable You" (1941: 78/Vic 27638)

301014j GIRL CRAZY 1932 film soundtrack. Orchestra: Main Title Male Quartet: "Bidin' My Time" Bert Wheeler, Dixie Lee: "You've Got What Gets Me" Eddie Quillan, Arline Judge, Mitzi Green: "But Not for Me" Kitty Kelly, chorus: "I Got Rhythm/Finale" (LP-654)

301015a THREE'S A CROWD records by Libby Holman of orig cast. "Something To Remember You by" (1930: LP-553, LP-569) (Later: LP-662) (Later: LP-51) "Body and Soul" (1930: LP-569, LP-724, LP-758) (Later: LP-662) (Later: LP-51)

301015b THREE'S A CROWD 1975 record by Arthur Schwartz. MUSIC: Arthur Schwartz. WORDS: Howard Dietz. "Something to Remember You By" (LP-418)

301015c THREE'S A CROWD 1933 record by John Green (composer), piano. "Body and Soul" (LP-589)

301022a BLACKBIRDS OF 1930 1930 records by Ethel Waters of orig cast. MUSIC: Eubie Blake. WORDS: Andy Razaf. "You're Lucky to Me," "Memories of You" (LP-15) (LP-569)

301022b BLACKBIRDS OF 1930 1969 record by Eubie Blake (composer), piano, "Memories of You" (LP-392)

301030a WALTZES FROM VIENNA 1960 studio prod. MUSIC: Johann Strauss. WORDS: Desmond Carter. COND: Michael Collins. CAST: June Bronhill, John Lawrenson, Marion Lowe, Kevin Scott, chorus. (HMV(E) CLP-1330)

301030b WALTZES FROM VIENNA 1965 Los Angeles prod, extensively revised, entitled "The Great Waltz". MUSIC: Johann Strauss, Sr and Jr, arranged by Erich Wolfgang Korngold, Robert Wright, George Forrest. WORDS: Robert Wright, George Forrest, Forman Brown. COND: Karl Kritz. CAST: Giorgio Tozzi, Jean Fenn, Frank Porretta, Anita Gillette, Leo Fuchs, Wilbur Evans, Lynn Fields, Eric Brotherson. (Cap SVAS-2426)

301030c WALTZES FROM VIENNA 1970 London prod based on 1965 Los Angeles prod, entitled "The Great Waltz." COND: Alexander Faris. CAST: Sari Barabas, Walter Cassel, Diane Todd, David Watson, Robert Dorning, Eric Brotherson. (Col(E) SCX-6429)

301030d WALTZES FROM VIENNA soundtrack of 1972 film, entitled "The Great Waltz," with many alterations. ORCH & COND: Roland Shaw. CAST: Mary Costa, Kenneth McKellar, Ken Barrie, Joan Baxter. (MGM 1SE-39)

301030e WALTZES FROM VIENNA album. COND: Geoff Harvey. VOCALS: Neil Williams, Rosalind Keen. (World Record Club (Australia) 7056 (entitled "The Great Waltz"), with Rio Rita)

301030f WALTZES FROM VIENNA 1931 records by members of 1931 London prod. COND: Walford Hyden. Marie Burke (also of 1934 New York prod, entitled "The Great Waltz"): "For We Love You Still" Burke, Dennis Noble: "Love and War" (78/Col(E) DB-620) Orchestra & chorus: Medley (78/Broadcast(E) 3082)

301108a WHITE HORSE INN studio prod. MUSIC: Ralph Benatzky, Robert Stolz. WORDS: Robert Gilbert, Harry Graham. COND: Tony Osborne. CAST: Andy Cole, Mary Thomas, Rita Williams, Charles Young, Peter Regan, Barney Gilbraith. (Angel 35815)

301108b WHITE HORSE INN album. COND: Johnny Gregory. VOCALS: Doreen Hume, Bruce Trent, chorus. (Epic BN-566, with The Girl Friend & The New Moon)

301108c WHITE HORSE INN studio prod. COND: Lehman Engel. NCAST: Jeanette Scovotti, Rosalind Elias, William Lewis, John Haeuxvell. (Reader's Digest 46-2, with The Chocolate Soldier)

301108d WHITE HORSE INN 1961 studio prod. COND: Johnny Douglas. CAST: David Croft, Marion Grimaldi, Jeremy Hawk, Barbara Leigh, Leonard Weir, chorus. (World Records(E) LMP-2)

301108e WHITE HORSE INN 1931 medley by Light Opera Company. COND: Ray Noble. (78/HMV(E) C-2229)

301108f WHITE HORSE INN 1931 medley by Columbia Light Opera Company. COND: Charles Prentice. (78/Col(E) DX-251)

301203a EVER GREEN 1934 records by Jessie Matthews of orig (London) prod & 1935 film prod (entitled "Evergreen"). By Richard Rodgers & Lorenz Hart: "Dancing on the Ceiling" (LP-156) (LP-222) (LP-736) By Harry M Woods (written for film): "Tinkle, Tinkle, Tinkle," "Over My Shoulder" (LP-64) (LP-156) (LP-310) "When You've Got a Little Springtime in Your Heart," "Just by Your Example" (LP-64) (LP-156)

301205a THE WONDER BAR contemp records by members of 1930 London prod. MUSIC & WORDS: Robert Katscher, Rowland Leigh, others. Carl Brisson: "I've Got a Plan about You," "I'll Believe in Love" (78/Dec(E) F-2127) "Wonder Bar" (78/Dec(E) F-2128) "Tell Me I'm Forgiven" (LP-122) Gwen Farrar: "Tell Me I'm Forgiven" (78/Col(E) DB-393) Elsie Randolph: "Turning Night into Day," "Elizabeth" (78/Col(E) DB-394)

301205b THE WONDER BAR records by Al Jolson of 1931 New York prod. "The Cantor" (1932: LP-274) (1935 radio performance: LP-469) (1947: LP-372, LP-381)

301208a THE NEW YORKERS records by members of orig prod. MUSIC & WORDS: Cole Porter. The Three Girl Friends ("The Three Waring Girls") & Waring's Pennsylvanians, 1930: "Love for Sale" (LP-428) (Incomplete: LP-569) "Where Have You Been?" Jimmy Durante, 1934: "Hot Patatta" (by Durante) (LP-569) Elisabeth Welch (who joined the prod in 1931), 1976: "Love for Sale" (LP-415)

1931

310001a Film THE PRODIGAL 1931 records by Lawrence Tibbett of orig cast. "Life Is a Dream," "Without a Song" (LP-226) (LP-774)

310002a Film CUBAN LOVE SONG records by Lawrence Tibbett of orig cast. "Tramps at Sea" (1931: LP-226) "Cuban Love Song" (1931: LP-226) (Later: LP-385)

310003a Film SALLY IN OUR ALLEY records by Gracie Fields of orig cast. "Fall In and Follow the Band" (1931: LP-248) "Sally" (1931: 78/HMV(E) B-3879) (1933: LP-248)

310004a Film A MAN OF MAYFAIR 1931 records by Jack Buchanan of orig cast. "Alone with My Dreams" (LP-374) "You Forgot Your Gloves" (LP-61) (LP-374)

310005a Film PALMY DAYS 1931 record by Eddie Cantor of orig cast. "There's Nothing Too Good for My Baby" (LP-379)

310006a Film INDISCREET 1931 records by Gloria Swanson of orig cast. MUSIC: Ray Henderson. WORDS: B G DeSylva, Lew Brown. "Come to Me" (78/Bruns 6127) "If You Haven't Got Love" (LP-350)

310007a Film THE CONGRESS DANCES contemp records by Lilian Harvey of orig cast. "Just Once for All Time" (LP-310)

310008a Film REACHING FOR THE MOON soundtrack. MUSIC & WORDS: Irving Berlin. Bing Crosby, Bebe Daniels, June McCloy: "When the Folks High Up Do That Mean Low-Down" (LP-336)(LP-506)

310009a Film HOLLYWOOD ON PARADE soundtrack. MUSIC & WORDS: Ginger Rogers. Ginger Rogers, Jack Oakie: "Used to Be You" (LP-402)

310010a Film POSSESSED 1931 record by Joan Crawford of orig cast. "How Long Will It Last?" (LP-401)

310011a Film HOT HEIRESS soundtrack. MUSIC: Richard Rodgers. WORDS: Lorenz Hart. Ben Lyon: "Nobody Loves a Riveter" Lyon, Ona Munson: "You're The Cats" Lyon, Munson, Inez Courtney: "Like Ordinary People Do" (LP-498)

310012a Film I SURRENDER DEAR Soundtrack. Bing Crosby: "I Surrender Dear," "Out of Nowhere," "At Your Command" (LP-506)

310012b Film I SURRENDER DEAR 1931 records by Bing Crosby of orig cast. "I Surrender Dear" (LP-634) "Out of Nowhere" (LP-577)(LP-779) "At Your Command" (LP-576)(LP-779)

310013a Film ONE MORE CHANCE soundtrack. Bing Crosby: "I Surrender Dear" (parody), "Wrap Your Troubles in Dreams," "I'd Climb the Highest Mountain," "Just One More Chance" (LP-506)

310013b Film ONE MORE CHANCE 1931 records by Bing Crosby of orig cast. "Wrap Your Troubles in Dreams" (LP-507) (LP-539) (LP-634) "Just One More Chance" (LP-577) (LP-634) (LP-779) "I Surrender Dear" (LP-634)

310014a Film DELICIOUS soundtrack. MUSIC: George Gershwin. WORDS: Ira Gershwin. Orchestra: Main Title Raul Roulien: "Delishious" Chorus: "Welcome to the Melting Pot" Janet Gaynor: "Somebody from Somewhere" Mischa Auer, Manya Roberti: "Katinkitschka" El Brendel, Manya Roberti: "Blah, Blah, Blah" Orchestra: "New York Rhapsody" (LP-654)

310015a Film DELIVERY BOY soundtrack of the Mickey Mouse cartoon. "In the Shade of the Old Apple Tree" (LP-661)

310016a Film BLUE RHYTHM soundtrack of the Mickey Mouse cartoon. "St Louis Blues" (LP-661)

310017a Film PARDON US soundtrack. Oliver Hardy, chorus: "Lazy Moon" (LP-695) (LP-698)

310018a Film BEAU HUNKS soundtrack. Oliver Hardy: "The Ideal of My Dreams" (LP-698)

310019a Film MONKEY BUSINESS 1954 records sung by Sammy Fain, composer. "When I Take My Sugar to Tea," "You Brought a New Kind Of Love to Me" (LP-707)

310020a Film IRENE soundtrack. Ethel Merman: "Wipe That From Right Off Your Face" (LP-751)

310119a YOU SAID IT 1931 records sung by Harold Arlen, composer. WORDS: Jack Yellen. "You Said It," "Sweet and Hot" (LP-603)

310021a Film NEVER TROUBLE TROUBLE 1931 record by Lupino Lane of orig cast. "Who Could? We Could, We Two" (78/Col(E) DB-465)

310126a GREEN GROW THE LILACS records by Tex Ritter of orig cast. "Blood On the Saddle" (78/Cap 20067) "Chisholm Trail," "Every Day in the Saddle," "Home On the Range" (LP-752) "Green Grow the Lilacs" (LP-753) "Goodbye, Old Paint" (78/Okeh 04911) "A-Ridin' Ole Paint" (78/Conqueror 8144) (LP-752) "Git Along, Little Dogies" (78/Champion 45191) (LP-752) "Sam Hall" (78/Dec 5076)

310305a STAND UP AND SING 1931 records by members of orig (London) prod. MUSIC: Phil Charig. WORDS: Douglas Furber. COND: Harry Perritt, Jack Buchanan: "Stand Up and Sing" (LP-61) (LP-700) "Night Time" (LP-700) "I Would If I Could," "Take It or Leave It" (78/Col(E) DB-486) Buchanan & Elsie Randolph: "There's Always Tomorrow" (LP-61)(LP-700) "It's Not for You" (LP-700)

310319a COCHRAN'S 1931 REVUE records sung by the composer. MUSIC & WORDS: Noel Coward. 1931: "Any Little Fish" (LP-11) (LP-502) "Half-Caste Woman" (LP-28) (LP-502) 1956: "Half-Caste Woman" (LP-89)

310504a RHAPSODY IN BLACK 1931 records by Ethel Waters of orig cast, MUSIC: Alberta Nichols. WORDS: Mann Holiner. "You Can't Stop Me from Lovin' You" (LP-15) (LP-389)

310514a THE GOOD COMPANIONS contemp records by Adele Dixon, John Gielgud, Lawrence Bascomb, Deering Wells of orig (London) prod. "Going Home," "Slipping 'Round the Corner" (LP-310)

310601a THE THIRD LITTLE SHOW records sung by the composer. MUSIC & WORDS: Noel Coward. "Mad Dogs and Englishman" (1932: LP-28, LP-218) (Later: LP-89, LP-138)

310601b THE THIRD LITTLE SHOW records by Beatrice Lillie of orig cast. "There are Fairies at the Bottom of Our Garden" (1934: LP-729) (1955: LP-449, LP-680)

310603a THE BAND WAGON 1931 album by Fred & Adele Astaire of orig cast & Arthur Schwartz (composer), piano. MUSIC: Arthur Schwartz . WORDS: Howard Dietz. Leo Reisman Orch. Accordion on "Sweet Music" by Fred Astaire. (RCA 10" L-24003) RCA(E) RD-

7756 (LP-21),with additional Fred Astaire songs. Nearly complete: Smithsonian R-021 (LP-728), edited and with additional matterial. Incomplete: LP-711. Excerpts: "White Heat," "" Sweet Music," "Hoops," "I Love Louisa" (LP-211).)

310603b THE BAND WAGON records by members of orig cast. Fred & Adele Astaire, 1931: "Hoops" (LP-48)(LP-518) (LP-553)(LP-728) Fred Astaire, 1931: "I Love Louisa," "New Sun in the Sky" (LP-211)(LP-553)(LP-728) "White Heat" (LP-553)(LP-728) Fred Astaire, 1952: "New Sun in the Sky" (LP-125)(LP-552)(LP-648) "I Love Louisa" (LP-648) "Dancing in the Dark" (LP-567)(LP-648)

310603c THE BAND WAGON 1950 album by Mary Martin. ORCH: Ted Royal. COND: Lehman Engel. (Col 10" ML-2160)

310603d THE BAND WAGON 1953 album. COND: Jay Blackton. CAST: Harold Lang, George Britton, Edith Adams. (RCA 10" LPM-3155, with The Little Shows)

310603e THE BAND WAGON records by Arthur Schwartz, composer. "Dancing in the Dark" (1966, piano: LP-671) (1975, vocal: LP-418)

310701a ZIEGFELD FOLLIES OF 1931 1931 records by Ruth Etting of orig cast. "Shine On, Harvest Moon" (LP-25) (LP-518)(LP-564)(LP-710) "Cigarettes, Cigars!," "I'm Good for Nothing but Love" (LP-564)(LP-724)

310814a THE DUBARRY 1932 records by Grace Moore of 1932 New York prod. MUSIC: Karl Millocker. WORDS: Rowland Leigh. "The Dubarry," "I Give My Heart" (LP-443)(LP-565) "Without Your Love"(with Richard Crooks) (LP-526)(LP-565)

310814b THE DUBARRY 1932 records by members of 1932 London prod. COND: Ernest Irving, Anny Ahlers: "I Give My Heart," "The Dubarry," "Beauty," "Happy Little Jeanne," "Today" (45/Parlophone(E) GEP-8623) Heddle Nash: "If I Am Dreaming" (78/Col(E) DB-815) Orchestra: Medley (78/Col(E) DX-349)

310908a FREE FOR ALL 1931 record by Benny Goodman Orch of orig prod. MUSIC: Richard A Whiting. WORDS: Oscar Hammerstein II. "Not That I Care" (78/Col 2542-D)

310914a GEORGE WHITE'S SCANDALS OF 1931 records by members of orig cast. MUSIC: Ray Henderson. WORDS: B G DeSylva, Lew Brown. Rudy Vallee: "Life Is Just a Bowl of Cherries" (1931: LP-58, LP-537, LP-564)(1942: LP-96) (1955: LP-357) "This Is the Missus," "My Song" (1931: LP-564) "The Thrill Is Gone" (1931: 78/Vic 22784) Ethel Merman: "Life Is Just a Bowl of Cherries" (1947: LP-36, LP-45, LP-68)(1977: LP-652) Everett Marshall: "The Thrill Is Gone," "That's Why Darkies Were Born" (1931: LP-564)

310914b GEORGE WHITE'S SCANDALS OF 1931 1931 medley. COND: Victor Young. VOCALS: Bing Crosby, Boswell Sisters, Mills Brothers, Frank Munn. (LP-337)

310914c GEORGE WHITE'S SCANDALS OF 1931 1931 medley by Paul Whiteman Orch. VOCALS: Jack Fulton, Mildred Bailey. (RCA 10" L-16001)

311008a FOR THE LOVE OF MIKE contemp records by Bobby Howes of orig (London) cast. MUSIC: Jack Waller, Joseph Tunbridge. WORDS: Clifford Grey, Sonny Miller. "Got a Date with an Angel," "Who Do You Love?" (LP-83)

311013a CAVALCADE records sung by Noel Coward, composer. MUSIC & WORDS: Noel Coward, others. 1931: Medley (LP-308) "Lover of My Dreams" (LP-174)(LP-218) Medley (Orchestra, with Coward reading Prologue & Epilogue)(78/HMV(E) C-2289) 1956: "Twentieth Century Blues" (LP-89)

311013*a EVERYBODY'S WELCOME 1937 record by Frances Williams of orig cast. "I Shot the Works" (LP-564)

311015a THE CAT AND THE FIDDLE 1958 studio prod. MUSIC: Jerome Kern. WORDS: Otto Harbach. ORCH: Robert Russell Bennett. COND: Johnny Gregory. CAST: Doreen Hume, Denis Quilley, chorus. (Epic 3569, with Hit the Deck)

311015b THE CAT AND THE FIDDLE contemp records by Peggy Wood of 1932 London prod. "She Didn't Say Yes," "Try to Forget," "A New Love Is Old," "The Night Was Made for Love" (LP-173) "She Didn't Say Yes" (78/Col(E) CB-432)

311015c THE CAT AND THE FIDDLE 1953 album. COND: Lehman Engel. CAST: Patricia Neway, Stephen Douglass. (RCA 10" LPM-3151, with Show Boat)

311015d THE CAT AND THE FIDDLE 1932 records by Georges Metaxa of orig cast. "A New Love Is Old" (LP-564) "Try to Forget" (LP-564)(LP-711)

311015e THE CAT AND THE FIDDLE medley by the New Mayfair Orch, uncredited vocalist. (LP-564)

311015f THE CAT AND THE FIDDLE 1932 medley by Light Opera Company. (78/HMV(E) C-2398)

311015g THE CAT AND THE FIDDLE contemp medley by Leo Reisman Orch. VOCALS: Frank Munn, Frances Maddux. (RCA 10" L-16005)

311015h THE CAT AND THE FIDDLE 1938 medley by Victor Light Opera Company. COND: Leonard Joy. (LP-306)

311015i THE CAT AND THE FIDDLE 1932 medley by Savoy Hotel Orpheans. VOCALS: Jessie Matthews, Raymond Newell, Binnie Hale, Jack Plant. (78/Col(E) DX-348)

311015j THE CAT AND THE FIDDLE 1932 medley by Palace Theatre Orch (of 1932 London prod) with unidentified vocalist. COND: Hyam Greenbaum. (LP-602)

311015k THE CAT AND THE FIDDLE 1934 record by Jeanette MacDonald of 1934 film cast. "Try to Forget" (LP-536)

311102a THE LAUGH PARADE contemp medley. MUSIC: Harry Warren. WORDS: Mort Dixon, Joe Young. COND: Abe Lyman. VOCALS: Dick Robertson, Helen Rowland, Phil Neely. (LP-602)

311226a OF THEE I SING 1952 prod, with one interpolated Gershwin song. MUSIC: George Gershwin. WORDS: Ira Gershwin. ORCH: Don Walker. COND: Maurice Levine. CAST: Jack Carson, Paul Hartman, Betty Oakes, Lenore Lonergan, Jonathan Lucas, Florenz Ames (of orig cast), Loring Smith, Jack Whiting, Donald Foster. (Cap S-350)

311226b OF THEE I SING 1972 TV prod, with one interpolated Gershwin song. ORCH & COND: Peter Matz. CAST: Carroll O'Connor, Jack Gilford, Cloris Leachman, Michele Lee, Garrett Lewis. (Col S-31763)

311226c OF THEE I SING 1938 medley. COND: Nathaniel Shilkret. VOCALS: Jane Froman, Sonny Schuyler, chorus. (LP-303)(LP-564)

1932

320001a Film THE KID FROM SPAIN 1932 records by Eddie Cantor of orig cast. "What a Perfect Combination" (LP-16)(LP-643)(LP-721) "Look What You've Done" (LP-379)

320002a Film ONE HOUR WITH YOU soundtrack. MUSIC & WORDS: Oscar Straus, Richard Whiting, Leo Robin. ORCH &

COND: A Franke Harling. CAST: Jeanette MacDonald, Maurice Chevalier, Genevieve Tobin, Donald Novis, Charles Ruggles. (Caliban 6011, with Do You Love Me?; plus Chevalier, Tobin: ''Three Times a Day'' (LP-769). Excerpts: Chevalier: ''What Would You Do?'' Chevalier, Tobin, Novis, Ruggles, MacDonald: ''One Hour with You'' (LP-769).)

320002b Film ONE HOUR WITH YOU records by members of orig cast. Maurice Chevalier, 1932: ''What Would You Do?'' (English: LP-102)(French: LP-102) ''Oh! That Mitzi'' (English: LP-62, LP-72)(French: LP-102) 1958: ''One Hour with You'' (LP-118) Jeanette MacDonald, 1932: ''One Hour with You,'' ''We Will Always Be Sweethearts'' (English & French versions: LP-536)

320003a Film THERE GOES THE BRIDE 1933 record by Jessie Matthews of orig cast. ''I'll Stay with You'' (LP-64)

320004a Film LOVE ME TONIGHT records by members of orig cast. MUSIC: Richard Rodgers. WORDS: Lorenz Hart. Maurice Chevalier, 1932: ''The Poor Apache'' (English: LP-217)(French: LP-72) ''Mimi'' (English: LP-72, LP-88, LP-405)(French: LP-102) Jeanette MacDonald, 1932: ''Love Me Tonight,'' ''Isn't It Romantic?'' (English: LP-217, LP-536)(French: LP-536) Chevalier, later: ''Isn't It Romantic?'' (LP-118) ''Mimi'' (LP-118)(LP-693) MacDonald, 1948: ''Lover'' (LP-756)

320004b Film LOVE ME TONIGHT soundtrack. CAST: Maurice Chevalier, Jeanette MacDonald, Joseph Cawthorn, C Aubrey Smith. (LP-498)

320005a Film JACK'S THE BOY contemp records by Jack Hulbert of orig cast. ''The Flies Crawled Up the Window'' (LP-90) ''I Want to Cling to Ivy'' (78/HMV(E) B-4263)

320006a Film TWO WHITE ARMS 1932 record by Adolphe Menjou of orig cast. ''Two White Arms'' (LP-98)(LP-124)

320007a Film AREN'T WE ALL 1932 record by Gertrude Lawrence of orig cast, ''My Sweet'' (LP-34)

320008a Film GOODNIGHT VIENNA 1932 records by Jack Buchanan of orig cast. ''Goodnight Vienna'' (LP-61) (LP-374) ''Living in Clover'' (LP-374)

320009a Film THE MIDSHIPMAID 1933 record by Jessie Matthews of orig cast. ''One Little Kiss from You'' (LP-64)

320010a Film THE BIG BROADCAST records by members of orig cast. Bing Crosby & Mills Brothers: ''Dinah'' (Contemp: LP-181, LP-337) Crosby: ''Here Lies Love'' (Contemp: LP-181) ''Please'' (Contemp: LP-181, LP-575) (1940: 78/Dec 3450) ''Where the Blue of the Night Meets the Gold of the Day'' (1931: LP-779) (1940: 78/Dec 3354) Kate Smith: ''When the Moon Comes over the Mountain'' (1931: 78/Harmony 1347-H) (1931: LP-434) (1937: LP-539) (1941: LP-42, LP-261) Cab Calloway: ''Minnie the Moocher'' (1931: LP-176) (1933: LP-539) ''Kickin' the Gong Around'' (1931: 78/Bruns 6209) ''Hot Toddy'' (1932: 78/Bruns 6400) Boswell Sisters: ''Crazy People'' (1932: 78/Bruns 6847) Mills Brothers: ''Tiger Rag'' (1931: 78/Bruns 6197) (1934: 78/Dec 167) ''Dinah'' (with Alice Faye, not of orig cast) (1933: LP-488) Arthur Tracy: ''Here Lies Love'' (1933: 78/Dec(E) F-3495)

320010b Film THE BIG BROADCAST soundtrack. VOCALS: Bing Crosby, Mills Brothers, Cab Calloway, Kate Smith, Boswell Sisters, Donald Novis, Arthur Tracy. (Soundtrak 101, plus Tracy: ''Here Lies Love'' on LP-768. Excerpts: Crosby: ''Here Lies Love,'' ''Please'' (LP-768).)

320011a Film DREAM HOUSE soundtrack. Bing Crosby: ''When I Take My Sugar to Tea,'' ''It Must Be True,'' ''Dream House'' (LP-506)

320011b Film DREAM HOUSE 1930 record by Bing Crosby of orig cast. ''It Must Be True'' (LP-507) (LP-634)

320012a Film A WOMAN COMMANDS soundtrack. Pola Negri: ''Paradise'' (LP-350)

320013a Film HORSE FEATHERS soundtrack. Groucho Marx: ''Everyone Says 'I LOVE YOU' '' (LP-350)

320014a Film THE PHANTOM PRESIDENT soundtrack. MUSIC & WORDS: George M Cohan, Richard Rodgers, Lorenz Hart. CAST: George M Cohan, Jimmy Durante, unidentified soloists. (LP-467) (LP-498)

320015a Film BILLBOARD GIRL soundtrack. Bing Crosby: ''Pop Goes the Weasel'' (parody), ''Were You Sincere?,'' ''For You'' (LP-506)

320015b Film BILLBOARD GIRL 1931 record by Bing Crosby of orig cast. ''Were You Sincere?'' (LP-337)

320016a Film SLEEPLESS NIGHTS 1932 records by Stanley Lupino of orig cast & Elsie Carlisle. ''I Don't Want to Go to Bed,'' ''Just One More'' (78/Dec(E) F-3319)

320017a Film RHAPSODY IN BLACK AND BLUE soundtrack. Louis Armstrong, vocal: ''You Rascal You,'' ''Shine'' (LP-623)

320018a Film BLONDE VENUS soundtrack. Marlene Dietrich: ''Hot Voodoo'' (LP-653) (LP-768) ''You Little So-and-So'' (LP-653) (LP-769) ''I Couldn't Be Annoyed'' (LP-769)

320019a Film THE WHOOPEE PARTY soundtrack of the Mickey Mouse cartoon. ''Maple Leaf Rag,'' ''Runnin' Wild'' (LP-661)

320020a Film LOOKING ON THE BRIGHT SIDE 1932 records by Gracie Fields of orig cast. ''After Tonight We Say Goodbye,'' ''I Hate You'' (78/HMV(E) B-4260) ''You're More than All the World to Me'' (78/HMV(E) B-4259) ''He's Dead but He Won't Lie Down,'' ''Looking on the Bright Side of Life'' (78/HMV(E) B-4258)

320021a Film MARRY ME 1932 records by Renate Mueller of orig prod. ''Marry Me'' (in English) With Hermann Thimig (also of orig prod?): ''A Little Sunshine'' (in German) (78/Dec(E) F-3277)

320104a BOW BELLS contemp record by Binnie Hale of orig (London) cast. ''You're Blase'' (LP-79) (LP-172)

320130a HELEN 1932 medley by Columbia Light Opera Company. MUSIC: Jacques Offenbach, arr by E Wolfgang Korngold. WORDS: A P Herbert. (78/Col(E) DX-331)

320209a MAURICE CHEVALIER records by Maurice Chevalier of orig prod. ''Ma Reguliere'' (1926: 78/Pathe(F) 3553) ''Dites-moi, ma Mere'' (1926:78/Pathe(F) 3556) ''Louise'' (1929: LP-17, LP-72, LP-102, LP-453, LP-539) (1947: LP-88, LP-132, LP-405) (1957: LP-224) (1958: LP-118) ''All I Want Is Just One Girl'' (1930: LP-102) ''Sweepin' the Clouds Away'' (1930: LP-72, LP-88, LP-102) ''Hello, Beautiful!'' (1931: LP-72, LP-88) (1958: LP-118) ''What Would You Do?'' (1932: LP-62) ''Oh! That Mitzi'' (1932, English: LP-62, LP-72) (1932, French: LP-102)

320217a FACE THE MUSIC 1932 medley. MUSIC & WORDS: Irving Berlin. COND: Victor Young. VOCALS: Bing Crosby. (LP-593)

320217b FACE THE MUSIC contemp medley by Paul Whiteman Orch. VOCALS: Frank Luther, Red McKenzie, the King's Jesters. (RCA 10'' L-16008, with Hot-Cha!) (LP-336)

320217c FACE THE MUSIC contemp medley by Ben Selvin Orch. VOCALS: Kate Smith, Jack Miller, the Nitecaps. (78/Col(Brazil) 18001-B)

320308a HOT-CHA! contemp medley. MUSIC: Ray Henderson. WORDS: Lew Brown. COND: Paul Whiteman. VOCALS: Mildred Bailey, Red McKenzie. (RCA 10'' L-16008, with Face the Music; LP-602.)

320308b HOT-CHA! 1932 radio performance by Lupe Velez of orig prod. COND: Al Goodman of orig prod. "Conchita" (LP-565) (LP-566)

320308c HOT-CHA! contemp medley by Ben Selvin Orch. VOCALS: Kate Smith, Jack Miller, the Nitecaps. (78/ Col(Brazil) 18001-B)

320611a OUT OF THE BOTTLE 1932 record by Frances Day & Max Kirby of orig (London) cast. MUSIC: Oscar Levant. WORDS: Clifford Grey. "Everything But You" (LP-700)

320614a TELL HER THE TRUTH 1932 records by members of orig (London) prod. MUSIC: Joseph Tunbridge, Jack Waller. WORDS: R P Weston, Bert Lee. Bobby Howes, Wylie Watson, Jack Lambert, Peter Haddon: "The Horrortorio" (LP-83) Howes, Carlyle Cousins: "Happy the Day" Howes, Watson, Haddon, Carlyle Cousins: "Sing, Brothers" (LP-565)

320915a FLYING COLORS records sung by Arthur Schwartz. MUSIC: Arthur Schwartz. WORDS: Howard Dietz. 1932, with the Eva Jessye Choir: "Louisiana Hayride" (LP-553) 1975: "Alone Together," "A Shine on Your Shoes" (LP-418)

320915b FLYING COLORS contemp medley by Waring's Pennsylvanians. VOCALS: Jean Sargent (of orig cast, singing "Alone Together"), Tom Waring, quartet. (RCA 10" L-16016; LP-565. Excerpt, incl Sargent: "Alone Together" (LP-553).)

320915c FLYING COLORS contemp record by Clifton Webb of orig cast. "A Rainy Day" (LP-553)

320916a WORDS AND MUSIC records sung by the composer. MUSIC & WORDS: Noel Coward. 1932: "Let's Say Goodbye" (LP-11) (LP-502) "The Party's Over Now," "Something to Do with Spring" (LP-218) (LP-502) "Mad Dogs and Englishmen" (LP-28) (LP-218) (LP-502) (LP-531) Later: "I Went to a Marvelous Party," "The Party's Over Now" (LP-89) "Mad Dogs and Englishmen" (LP-89) (LP-138) (LP-351) (LP-766)

320916b WORDS AND MUSIC 1932 record by Doris Hare of orig (London) prod. MUSIC & WORDS: Noel Coward. "Three White Feathers" (LP-172) (LP-502)

320927a EARL CARROLL'S VANITIES OF 1932 1932 records by Ray Kavanaugh & the Vanities Orch of orig prod. "My Darling," "Along Came Love" (78/Bruns 6381)

321108a MUSIC IN THE AIR contemp album by Jane Pickens of 1951 prod & the Guild Choristers. MUSIC: Jerome Kern. WORDS: Oscar Hammerstein II. COND: Al Goodman. (RCA LK-1025)

321108b MUSIC IN THE AIR contemp records by Mary Ellis of 1933 London prod. COND: Hyam Greenbaum. "I've Told Ev'ry Little Star," "I'm Alone/The Song Is You" (LP-173)

321108c MUSIC IN THE AIR 1949 radio prod. Jane Powell, Gordon MacRae: "I've Told Every Little Star," "The Song Is You" (LP-281)

321108d MUSIC IN THE AIR 1932 medley. COND: Nathaniel Shilkret. VOCALS: Robert Simmons, Jack Parker, Conrad Thibault, James Stanley, Marjorie Horton. (LP-565)

321108e MUSIC IN THE AIR 1938 medley by Victor Light Opera Company. COND: Leonard Joy. (LP-306)

321108f MUSIC IN THE AIR soundtrack of 1934 film. CAST: Gloria Swanson, John Boles, Betty Hiestand (for June Lang), James O'Brien (for Douglass Montgomery). (LP-335)

321108g MUSIC IN THE AIR studio prod. COND: Alan Braden. CAST: Marion Grimaldi, Andy Cole, Maggie Fitzgibbon, chorus. (World Record Club(E) T-121, with Roberta)

321122a GEORGE WHITE'S MUSIC HALL VARIETIES 1932 record by Harry Richman of orig cast. "I Love a Parade" (by Harold Arlen, Ted Koehler) (LP-447) (LP-565)

321126a TAKE A CHANCE records by Ethel Merman of orig cast. MUSIC: Nacio Herb Brown, Richard Whiting. WORDS: B G DeSylva. 1932, with the Take a Chance Octette: "Eadie Was a Lady" (LP-40) (LP-565) Later: "You're an Old Smoothie" (LP-36) (LP-45) "Eadie Was a Lady" (LP-36) (LP-68) (LP-87) (LP-153)

321126b TAKE A CHANCE 1933 records by Cliff Edwards of 1933 film cast. "It's Only a Paper Moon" (LP-19)(LP-760) "Come Up and See Me Sometime" (LP-16) "Night Owl" (78/ Vocalion 2587)

321126c TAKE A CHANCE 1955 record sung by Harold Arlen, composer (film). "It's Only a Paper Moon" (LP-101)

321126d TAKE A CHANCE 1933 film soundtrack. Lillian Roth, Dorothy Lee: "Eadie Was a Lady" (LP-770)

321129a GAY DIVORCE records by Fred Astaire of orig, 1933 London, & 1934 film casts. MUSIC & WORDS: Cole Porter. "Night and Day" (1932: LP-21, LP-48, LP-211, LP-539, LP-711) (1933: LP-14, LP-300, LP-565, LP-736) (1952: LP-125, LP-358, LP-567, LP-648) (1976: LP-429) Songs from the stage prods only: "After You, Who?" (1933: LP-14, LP-300, LP-565) "I've Got You on My Mind" (1932: LP-21, LP-211, LP-565) Songs from the film prod only, by other composers: "The Continental," "Needle in a Haystack" (1952: LP-348, LP-648)

321129b GAY DIVORCE soundtrack of 1934 film (entitled "The Gay Divorcee"). MUSIC & WORDS: Cole Porter, Con Conrad, Herb Magidson, Mack Gordon, Harry Revel. COND: Max Steiner. CAST: Fred Astaire, Ginger Rogers, Betty Grable, Edward Everett Horton, Erik Rhodes, Lillian Miles. (EMI Records(E) EMTC-101, with Swing Time. Excerpts: Grable, Horton: "Let's K-nock K-nees" (LP-284) (LP-646) Rogers, Rhodes: "The Continental" (incomplete) (LP-558).)

321129c GAY DIVORCE 1978 record by Ginger Rogers of 1934 film cast. "Night and Day" (LP-624)

321212a ALICE IN WONDERLAND studio prod. MUSIC: Richard Addinsell. WORDS: Lewis Carroll. CAST: David Nixon, Juliet Mills, Mick & Montmorency, Doreen Hume. (Rondolette A-12, entitled "Alice in Wonderland & Alice through the Looking-Glass")

321212b ALICE IN WONDERLAND 1947 prod. COND: Tibor Kozma. NARRATOR: Eva Le Gallienne. CAST: Eva Le Gallienne & Richard Waring of orig prod; Bambi Linn, Margaret Webster, William Windom, Hugh Franklin . (78/Vic 12" album K-13)

321222a BALLYHOO contemp record by Zaidee Jackson of orig (London) prod. "I've Got The Wrong Man" (LP-172)

1933

330001a Film GOLD DIGGERS OF 1933 records by members of orig cast. MUSIC: Harry Warren. WORDS: Al Dubin. Dick Powell, 1933: "The Gold Diggers Song" (LP-2) (LP-106) (LP-537) (LP-754) "Pettin' in the Park," "Shadow Waltz," "I've Got to Sing a Torch Song" (LP-2) Powell, 1947: "Shadow Waltz" (LP-133) Ginger Rogers, 1978: "The Gold Diggers Song" (LP-624)

330001b Film GOLD DIGGERS OF 1933 soundtrack. COND: Leo F Forbstein. Orchestra: Main Title. Dick Powell: "I've Got to Sing a Torch Song" Powell, Ruby Keeler, chorus: "Pettin' in the Park" (LP-631) Ginger Rogers, chorus: "We're in the Money" (LP-631) (Incomplete: LP-223) (Excerpt: LP-595) Powell, Keeler, chorus: "Shadow Waltz" Joan Blondell, Etta Moten, chorus: "Remember My Forgotten Man" (LP-631) (Incomplete: LP-154)

330002a Film FOOTLIGHT PARADE records by Dick Powell of orig cast. 1933: "By a Waterfall," "Ah! The Moon Is Here," "Honeymoon Hotel" (LP-2) 1947: "By a Waterfall" (LP-133)

330002b Film FOOTLIGHT PARADE soundtrack. COND: Leo F Forbstein. Dick Powell, Ruby Keeler, chorus: "By a Waterfall"(LP-154) (LP-223) Keeler, James Cagney, chorus: "Shanghai Lil" (LP-631) (Incomplete: LP-154) Powell, Keeler, chorus: "Honeymoon Hotel" (LP-633)

330003a Film THE ROAD IS OPEN AGAIN contemp record by Dick Powell of orig cast. "The Road is Open Again" (LP-2)

330004a Film COLLEGE COACH contemp record by Dick Powell of orig cast. "Lonely Lane" (LP-2)

330005a Film FLYING DOWN TO RIO soundtrack. MUSIC: Vincent Youmans. WORDS: Gus Kahn, Edward Eliscu. ORCH & COND: Max Steiner. CAST: Fred Astaire, Ginger Rogers, Raul Roulien, Etta Moten. (Classic International Filmusicals 3004, with Carefree. Excerpts: Orchestra: "Carioca" (78/Vic 24515) Rogers: "Music Makes Me" (LP-402).)

330005b Film FLYING DOWN TO RIO records by Fred Astaire of orig cast. "Flying Down to Rio" (1933: LP-14) "Music Makes Me" (1933: LP-14, LP-447) "The Carioca" (1952: LP-567, LP-648)

330006a Film HALLELUJAH, I'M A BUM soundtrack. MUSIC: Richard Rodgers. WORDS: Lorenz Hart. CAST: Al Jolson, Frank Morgan, chorus. (LP-498. Incomplete: Subon 1234, labeled "Heart of New York," with Say It with Songs. Excerpt: Jolson: "Sleeping Beauty" (dropped before release) (LP-269).)

330006b Film HALLELUJAH, I'M A BUM 1932 records by Al Jolson of orig prod. "Hallelujah, I'm a Bum" (LP-16) (LP-643) (LP-721) (LP-754) "You Are Too Beautiful" (LP-447)

330007a Film SHE DONE HIM WRONG records by Mae West of orig cast. "A Guy What Takes His Time" (1933: LP-40, LP-141, LP-768)(1954: LP-105, LP-175) (1950s: LP-504) "I Wonder Where My Easy Rider's Gone" (1933: LP-40, LP-43, LP-141, LP-641) "Frankie and Johnny" (1954: LP-105) (1950s: LP-411, LP-412)

330007b Film SHE DONE HIM WRONG soundtrack. Mae West: "Frankie and Johnny" (LP-413)

330008a Film I'M NO ANGEL records by Mae West of orig cast. 1933: "I'm No Angel," "I Found a New Way to Go to Town" (LP-40) (LP-141) "I Want You, I Need You" (LP-40) "They Call Me Sister Honky Tonk" (LP-40) (LP-106) (LP-141) 1955: "I Want You, I Need You," "They Call Me Sister Honky Tonk" (LP-105)

330008b Film I'M NO ANGEL soundtrack. Mae West: "I Want You, I Need You" (LP-413)

330009a Film HELLO, EVERYBODY 1933 records by Kate Smith of orig cast. "Moon Song" (LP-43) (LP-641) "Twenty Million People" (LP-273) "Pickaninnies' Heaven" (78/Bruns 6497) "My Queen of Lullaby Land" (78/Bruns 6496)

330010a Film SONG OF SONGS records by Marlene Dietrich of orig cast. "Jonny" (1931: LP-43, LP-81, LP-139, LP-641) (1955: LP-178) (1965: LP-191)

330011a Film YES! MR. BROWN 1933 records by Jack Buchanan of orig cast, "Yes! Mr. Brown" (LP-61) (LP-374) "Leave a Little Love for Me" (LP-374)

330012a Film THE GOOD COMPANIONS 1933 records by Jessie Matthews of orig cast. "Three Wishes," "Let Me Give My Happiness to You" (LP-64)

330013a Film FALLING FOR YOU contemp record by Jack Hulbert of orig cast. "Sweep" (LP-90)

330014a Film SOLDIERS OF THE KING contemp records by Cicely Courtneidge of orig cast. "The Moment I Saw You" (LP-90) "There's Something about a Soldier" (LP-130) (LP-310)

330015a Film JACK AHOY contemp record by Jack Hulbert of orig cast. "My Hat's on the Side of My Head" (LP-90)

330016a Film AUNT SALLY contemp records by Cicely Courtneidge of orig cast. "Riding on a Rainbow," "If I Had Napoleon's Hat" (LP-90)

330017a Film THE LITTLE DAMOZEL 1933 records by Anna Neagle of orig cast. "What More Can I Ask?" (78/HMV(E) B-4365) "The Dream Is Over" (by Noel Coward) (LP-98) (LP-310)

330018a Film PERFECT UNDERSTANDING 1933 records by Gloria Swanson of orig cast, "Ich Liebe Dich, My Dear" (LP-97) (LP-124) "I Love You So Much That I Hate You" (LP-136)

330019a Film BRITANNIA OF BILLINGSGATE 1933 record by Violet Lorraine of orig cast. "Let the World Go Drifting By" (LP-56)

330020a Film THE BARBARIAN 1937 record by Ramon Novarro of orig cast. "Love Songs of the Nile" (LP-124) (LP-136)

330021a Film 42ND STREET soundtrack. MUSIC: Harry Warren. WORDS: Al Dubin. COND: Leo F Forbstein. Orchestra: Main Title (LP-631) Bebe Daniels: "You're Getting to Be a Habit with Me" Dick Powell, chorus: "Young and Healthy" (LP-333) (LP-631) Powell, Ruby Keeler, chorus: "42nd Street" (LP-631) (Incomplete: LP-154, LP-223) Keeler, Ginger Rogers, Una Merkel, Clarence Nordstrom, chorus: "Shuffle Off to Buffalo" (LP-333) (LP-631) (Incomplete: LP-223)

330021b Film 42ND STREET 1965 record by Ginger Rogers of orig cast. "You're Getting to Be a Habit with Me" (LP-325)

330022a Film GOING HOLLYWOOD contemp records by Bing Crosby and Lennie Hayton Orch of orig prod. MUSIC: mostly Nacio Herb Brown. WORDS: mostly Arthur Freed. "Just an Echo in the Valley," "Beautiful Girl," "After Sundown," "We'll Make Hay While the Sun Shines," "Our Big Love Scene" (LP-181) "Temptation" (LP-181) (LP-578)

330022b Film GOING HOLLYWOOD soundtrack. Bing Crosby, ensemble: Grand Central Station Sequence (LP-770) Crosby: "Going Hollywood" (LP-252) (LP-770) "Just an Echo in the Valley," "After Sundown" Crosby, Marion Davies: "We'll Make Hay While the Sun Shines" Davies: "Cinderella's Fella" (LP-770) "Temptation" (LP-416) (LP-770)

330023a Film COLLEGE HUMOR 1933 records by Bing Crosby of orig cast. MUSIC: Arthur Johnston. WORDS: Sam Coslow. "Learn to Croon" (LP-181) "Down the Old Ox Road"(LP-41) (LP-181) (LP-575) "Moonstruck" (LP-181) (LP-578)

330023b Film COLLEGE HUMOR 1933 records sung by Sam Coslow, lyricist. "Learn to Croon," "Moonstruck" (78/Vic 24386) (78/Vocalion 25001) "Where Have I Heard That Melody?," "Down the Old Ox Road" (78/Vocalion 25002)

330024a Film TOO MUCH HARMONY 1933 records by Bing Crosby of orig cast. "Thanks" (LP-181) (LP-575) "I Guess It Had to Be That Way" (dropped prior to release), "The Day You Came Along" (LP-181) "Black Moonlight" (LP-181) (LP-578)

330024b Film TOO MUCH HARMONY soundtrack. Grace Bradley: "Cradle Me with a Ha-Cha Lullaby" (LP-496)

330025a Film LADIES THEY TALK ABOUT later record by Lillian Roth of orig cast. "If I Could Be with You" (LP-104)

330026a Film THIS WEEK OF GRACE 1933 records by Gracie Fields of orig cast. "Happy Ending," "My Lucky Day," "Heaven Will Protect an Honest Girl" (LP-248) "Mary Rose" (78/HMV(E) B-4471)

330027a Film DANCING LADY soundtrack. Fred Astaire, Joan Crawford, chorus: "Heigh Ho, the Gang's All Here" (LP-252) (LP-401) (LP-532) "Let's Go Bavarian" (LP-401) (LP-532) Art Jarrett, Joan

Crawford: "Everything I Have Is Yours" (LP-401) Nelson Eddy: "Rhythm of the Day" (by Richard Rodgers & Lorenz Hart) (LP-498)

330028a Film ROMAN SCANDALS soundtrack. MUSIC: Harry Warren. WORDS: Al Dubin. ORCH & COND: Alfred Newman. CAST: Eddie Cantor, Ruth Etting, chorus. (Classic International Filmusicals 3007, with Kid Millions)

330028b Film ROMAN SCANDALS 1933 records by Ruth Etting of orig cast. "Build a Little Home," "No More Love" (78/Bruns 6697)

330029a Film SITTING PRETTY records by members of orig cast. MUSIC: Harry Revel. WORDS: Mack Gordon. Pickens Sisters, 1933: "Did You Ever See a Dream Walking?," "Good Morning Glory" (78/Vic 24468) "You're Such a Comfort to Me," "Many Moons Ago" (78/Vic 24471) Ginger Rogers, 1978: "Did You Ever See a Dream Walking?" (LP-624)

330030a Film INTERNATIONAL HOUSE contemp records by members of orig prod. Baby Rose Marie: "My Bluebird's Singing the Blues" (78/Bruns 6570) Rudy Vallee Orch: "Thank Heaven for You" (78/Bluebird B-5098) Cab Calloway Orch: "Reefer Man" (78/Bruns 6340)

330030b Film INTERNATIONAL HOUSE soundtrack. Baby Rose Marie: "My Bluebird's Singing the Blues" (LP-768)

330031a Film PRINCE OF ARCADIA 1933 records by Carl Brisson of orig cast. "Clown Prince of Arcadia/If I Could Only Find Her" (78/Dec(E) F-3759)

330032a Films POPEYE CARTOONS 1935 records by "Popeye" (Billy Costello) & "Olive Oyl." "I'm Popeye the Sailor Man," "Blow the Man Down" (78/Melotone M-13402)

330033a Film F. P. I. contemp record by Conrad Veidt of orig cast. "When the Lighthouse Shines across the Bay" (LP-310)

330034a Film TORCH SINGER soundtrack. Claudette Colbert: "It's a Long, Dark Night" (LP-350)

330035a Film THE THREE LITTLE PIGS combination soundtrack & studio prod. MUSIC & WORDS: Frank Churchill, Ann Ronell. VOCALS: Uncredited. (Disneyland 1310)

330035b Film THE THREE LITTLE PIGS soundtrack of the Walt Disney Silly Symphony cartoon. "Who's Afraid of the Big Bad Wolf?" (LP-661)(78/Vic BK-10)

330036a Film A MAN'S CASTLE soundtrack. Glenda Farrell: "Surprise!" (LP-496)

330037a Film SING, BING, SING records by Bing Crosby of orig cast. "Snuggled on Your Shoulder" (1932: LP-337, LP-643) "Lovable" (1928: LP-634)

330037b Film SING, BING, SING soundtrack. Bing Crosby: "In My Hide-away," "Between the Devil and the Deep Blue Sea," "Lovable," "Snuggled on Your Shoulder" (LP-506)

330038a Film BLUE OF THE NIGHT 1931 record by Bing Crosby of orig cast. "Where the Blue of the Night Meets the Gold of the Day" (LP-576)(LP-779)

330038b Film BLUE OF THE NIGHT soundtrack. Bing Crosby: "My Silent Love," "Auf Wiedersehen My Dear," "Ev'ry Time My Heart Beats," "Where the Blue of the Night Meets the Gold of the Day" (LP-506)

330039a Film FACING THE MUSIC 1933 records by Stanley Lupino of orig cast. "I've Found the Right Girl," "Let Me Gaze" (78/Dec(E) F-3652)

330040a Film BROADWAY THRU A KEYHOLE soundtrack. MUSIC: Harry Revel. WORDS: Mack Gordon. COND: Alfred Newman. CAST: Russ Columbo, Frances Williams, Constance Cummings, Eddie Foy Jr. (LP-557)

330040b Film BROADWAY THRU A KEYHOLE records by members of orig prod. Russ Columbo: "You're My Past, Present and Future" (Contemp radio performance: LP-591) Abe Lyman Orch: "Doin' the Uptown Lowdown," "When You Were the Girl on the Scooter" (1933: 78/Bruns 6674) "You're My Past, Present and Future" (1933: 78/Bruns 6672)

330041a Film THAT GOES DOUBLE soundtrack. Orch: Main Title, End Title. Russ Columbo: "My Love," "Prisoner of Love," "You Call It Madness" (LP-557)

330041b Film THAT GOES DOUBLE records by Russ Columbo of orig cast. "You Call It Madness" (1931: 78/Vic 22802) "Prisoner of Love" (1931: 78/Vic 22867) "My Love" (1932: 78/Vic 24077)

330042a Film LULLABY LAND soundtrack of the Walt Disney Silly Symphony cartoon. (78/Bluebird BK-6)

330043a Film CAB CALLOWAY'S HI-DE-HO soundtrack, with Cab Calloway Orch. Orchestra: "Harlem Camp Meeting," "I Love a Parade" Cab Calloway, vocal: "Zaz-Zuh-Zaz," "The Lady with the Fan" (LP-623)

330044a Film A BUNDLE OF BLUES soundtrack, with Duke Ellington Orch. VOCAL: Ivie Anderson. (LP-622)

330045a Film MICKEY'S GALA PREMIERE soundtrack of the Mickey Mouse cartoon. "Congratulations, Mr. Mickey Mouse" (LP-661)

330046a Film A BEDTIME STORY soundtrack. Maurice Chevalier: "In the Park in Paree," "Home-Made Heaven" (LP-768)

330047a Film THE WAY TO LOVE soundtrack. VOCALS: Maurice Chevalier, Arthur Pierson(?), ensemble. "The Way to Love," "There's a Lucky Guy," "I'm a Lover of Paree," "In a One-Room Flat" (LP-776)

330120a PARDON MY ENGLISH records by Lyda Roberti of orig cast. MUSIC: George Gershwin. WORDS: Ira Gershwin. "My Cousin in Milwaukee" (Contemp: LP-447)(1933 radio performance: LP-556)

330127a MOTHER OF PEARL contemp record by Alice Delysia of orig (London) cast. "Every Woman Thinks She Wants to Wander" (LP-128)

330301a RUN, LITTLE CHILLUN! 1941 record by Hall Johnson Choir of orig prod. "Run, Li'l Chillun" (78/Vic 4547)

330304a STRIKE ME PINK contemp medley by Anson Weeks Orch. MUSIC: Ray Henderson. WORDS: B G DeSylva, Lew Brown. VOCALS: Art Wilson, Harriet Lee. (LP-602)

330908a MURDER AT THE VANITIES 1933 record by John Green (composer) & Ramona Davies, piano & vocals. WORDS: Edward Heyman. "Weep No More, My Baby" (LP-545)

330930a AS THOUSANDS CHEER records by members of orig cast. MUSIC & WORDS: Irving Berlin. Ethel Waters, 1933: "Heat Wave" (LP-15)(LP-389)(LP-519)(LP-593)(LP-758) "Harlem on My Mind" (LP-15)(LP-43)(LP-389)(LP-641) Waters, later: "Supper Time" (1956: LP-393)(Late 1950s: LP-99) Clifton Webb, 1933: "Not for All the Rice in China" (LP-48)(LP-519)(LP-711) "How's Chances?" (LP-336)(LP-519) "Easter Parade" (LP-336)(LP-350)(LP-593)

330930b AS THOUSANDS CHEER 1933 medley by Paul Whiteman Orch. VOCALS: Ramona Davies. (78/Vic 39003)

331006a NYMPH ERRANT 1933 records by members of orig (London) cast. MUSIC & WORDS: Cole Porter. Gertrude Lawrence: "The Physician," "Experiment," "It's Bad for Me," "How Could We Be Wrong?," "Nymph Errant" Elisabeth Welch: "Solomon" (LP-29, LP-276, LP-300. Incomplete: RCA 10" LRT-7001, with Lady in the Dark. Excerpt: Welch: "Solomon" (LP-712).)

331006b NYMPH ERRANT 1935 records by Cole Porter (composer), piano and vocal. "The Cocotte" (LP-182) (LP-340) "The Physician" (LP-182)

331006c NYMPH ERRANT later records by members of orig (London) prod. Gertrude Lawrence: "Experiment" (1936: LP-123, LP-276) Elisabeth Welch: "Solomon" (1976: LP-415)

331021a LET 'EM EAT CAKE 1933 medley by Paul Whiteman Orch. MUSIC: George Gershwin. WORDS: Ira Gershwin. VOCALS: Bob Lawrence, Ramona, the Rhythm Boys. (LP-602)

331116a PLEASE records by Beatrice Lillie of orig (London) cast. "Baby Doesn't Know" (1934: LP-123) "Rhythm" (1955: LP-449, LP-680)

331118a ROBERTA 1952 studio prod. MUSIC: Jerome Kern. WORDS: Otto Harbach, Oscar Hammerstein II, Dorothy Fields, Jimmy McHugh. COND: Lehman Engel. CAST: Joan Roberts, Jack Cassidy, Kaye Ballard, Portia Nelson, Stephen Douglass, Frank Rogier. (Col ML-4765)

331118b ROBERTA records by members of 1935 film cast. Irene Dunne: "Lovely to Look at" (1935: LP-43, LP-322, LP-607, LP-619, LP-642) "Smoke Gets in Your Eyes" (1941: LP-66, LP-109, LP-607) Fred Astaire: "I Won't Dance" (1952: LP-125, LP-358, LP-567, LP-648) "Lovely to Look at" (1952: LP-348, LP-648)

331118c ROBERTA 1952 studio prod. ORCH & COND: George Greeley. CAST: Gordon MacRae, Lucille Norman, Anne Triola. (Cap 10" L-334)

331118d ROBERTA 1944 studio prod. COND: Harry Sosnik, Jeffry Alexander. CAST: Kitty Carlisle, Alfred Drake, Paula Lawrence, Kathryn Meisle. (Dec 8007)

331118e ROBERTA studio prod. "Ed Sullivan presents Roberta." No other credits given. (National Academy 10)

331118f ROBERTA studio prod. ORCH: Henri Rene. COND: Lehman Engel. CAST: Anna Moffo, Jean Sanders, Evelyn Sachs, Stanley Grover, Charles Green. (Reader's Digest 40-9, with Song of Norway)

331118g ROBERTA soundtrack of 1952 film, entitled "Lovely to Look At." ORCH: Leo Arnaud. COND: Carmen Dragon. CAST: Kathryn Grayson, Howard Keel, Red Skelton, Marge & Gower Champion, Ann Miller. (MGM 10" 150. Excerpt: Grayson: "Smoke Gets in Your Eyes" (LP-328) (LP-416).)

331118h ROBERTA 1935 radio prod with members of 1935 film cast. Irene Dunne: "Smoke Gets in Your Eyes," "Lovely to Look at" Fred Astaire: "I Won't Dance" Ginger Rogers: "I'll Be Hard to Handle" (Star-Tone 204, with Top Hat)

331118i ROBERTA 1950 studio prod. COND: Al Goodman. CAST: Ray Charles, Eve Young, Jimmy Carroll, Marion Bell. (RCA LK-1007)

331118j ROBERTA medley by the New Mayfair Orch, uncredited vocalists. (78/HMV(E) C-2772)

331118k ROBERTA 1938 medley by Victor Light Opera Company. COND: Leonard Joy. (LP-306)

331118l ROBERTA soundtrack of 1935 film. COND: Max Steiner. CAST: Fred Astaire, Ginger Rogers, Irene Dunne. (Classic International Filmusicals 3011. Incomplete: LP-335. Excerpt: Astaire, Rogers: "I Won't Dance" (LP-558).)

331118m ROBERTA records by Kathryn Grayson of 1952 film cast. "Yesterdays," "Smoke Gets in Your Eyes" (LP-364)

331118n ROBERTA studio prod. COND: Alan Braden. CAST: Marion Grimaldi, Andy Cole, Maggie Fitzgibbon, chorus. (World Record Club(E) T-121, with Music in the Air)

331118o ROBERTA 1933 record by Tamara of orig cast. COND: Leo Reisman. "Smoke Gets in Your Eyes" (78/Bruns 6715)

331120a SHE LOVES ME NOT contemp records by John Beal of orig cast. MUSIC: Arthur Schwartz. WORDS: Edward Heyman. Leo Reisman Orch. "She Loves Me Not," "After All, You're All I'm After" (LP-554)

1934

340001a Film WONDER BAR soundtrack. MUSIC: Harry Warren. WORDS: Al Dubin. COND: Leo F Forbstein. CAST: Al Jolson, Dick Powell, Dolores Del Rio, Ricardo Cortez, chorus. (Hollywood Soundstage 402, with Go into Your Dance. Excerpts: Jolson: "Goin' to Heaven on a Mule" (LP-269) Powell: "Don't Say Goodnight" (LP-333).)

340001b Film WONDER BAR 1934 records by Dick Powell of orig cast. COND: Ted Fio Rito. "Why Do I Dream Those Dreams?," "Wonder Bar," "Don't Say Goodnight" (LP-2)

340002a Film TWENTY MILLION SWEETHEARTS records by members of orig cast. Dick Powell: "I'll String Along with You" (1934: LP-2)(1947: LP-86, LP-133) "Fair and Warmer" (1934: LP-2) Mills Brothers: "How'm I Doin', Hey-Hey" (1932: 78/Bruns 6269) Powell, Mills Brothers: "Out for No Good" (1934 radio performance: LP-591) Ginger Rogers: "I'll String Along with You" (1978: LP-624)

340002b Film TWENTY MILLION SWEETHEARTS soundtrack. MUSIC & WORDS: mostly Harry Warren, Al Dubin. COND: Leo F Forbstein. CAST: Dick Powell, Ginger Rogers, Mills Brothers, Ted Fio Rito Orch. (Milloball TMSM-34031, with Mammy. Excerpts: Powell, Rogers: "I'll String Along with You" (LP-223) (LP-402) (LP-595) (Incomplete: LP-558) Rogers: "Out for No Good" (LP-273) (LP-402) Mills Brothers: "Out for No Good" (LP-558).)

340003a Film HAPPINESS AHEAD records by Dick Powell of orig cast. 1934: "Pop! Goes Your Heart," "Happiness Ahead," "Beauty Must be Loved" (LP-2) 1947: "Happiness Ahead" (LP-133)

340004a Film FLIRTATION WALK records by Dick Powell of orig cast. 1934: "Mr and Mrs Is the Name" (LP-2) (LP-447) "Flirtation Walk" (LP-2) 1947: "Mr and Mrs Is the Name" (LP-86) (LP-133)

340005a Film GEORGE WHITE'S SCANDALS records by members of orig cast. Alice Faye: "Nasty Man" (1934: LP-9) (1934 radio performance: LP-645) Cliff Edwards: "My Dog Loves Your Dog," "Six Women" (1934: 78/Bruns(E) 01727) Rudy Vallee: "Nasty Man," "Hold My Hand" (1934:78/Vic 24581) "Six Women" (Later: 78/Varsity 8203)

340006a Film SHE LEARNED ABOUT SAILORS 1934 record by Alice Faye of orig cast & Rudy Vallee. "Here's the Key to My Heart" (LP-9)

340006b Film SHE LEARNED ABOUT SAILORS 1934 radio performance by Alice Faye of orig cast. "Here's the Key To My Heart" (LP-645)

340006c Film SHE LEARNED ABOUT SAILORS soundtrack. Alice Faye: "Here's the Key To My Heart" (LP-769)

340007a Film 365 NIGHTS IN HOLLYWOOD 1934 records by Alice Faye of orig cast. "Yes To You" (LP-9) "My Future Star" (78/Melotone M-13220)

340008a Film WAKE UP AND DREAM 1934 records by Russ Columbo of orig cast. "Too Beautiful for Words" (LP-16) (LP-643) "When You're In Love," "Let's Pretend There's a Moon" (78/Bruns 6972)

340008b Film WAKE UP AND DREAM soundtrack. Russ Columbo:

"When You're In Love," "Too Beautiful for Words," "Let's Pretend There's a Moon" (LP-557)

340009a Film FRANKIE & JOHNNY 1934 records by Helen Morgan of orig cast. "Frankie & Johnny" (LP-32) (LP-229) (LP-230) "Give Me a Heart to Sing to" (LP-32) (LP-229)

340010a Film KID MILLIONS 1934 records by members of orig cast. Ethel Merman: "An Earful of Music" (LP-40) Eddie Cantor: "An Earful of Music," "Okay, Toots" (LP-379) "Mandy" (LP-379) (LP-593) "When My Ships Comes In" (LP-379) (LP-754)

340010b Film KID MILLIONS soundtrack. MUSIC & WORDS: Walter Donaldson, Gus Kahn, Burton Lane, Harold Adamson, Irving Berlin. ORCH & COND: Alfred Newman. CAST: Eddie Cantor, Ethel Merman, Ann Sothern, George Murphy, Nicholas Brothers, chorus. (Classic International Filmusicals 3007, with Roman Scandals. Excerpts: Merman: "An Earful of Music" (LP-334) Merman, Cantor, Sothern: "Mandy" (LP-336).)

340011a Film COLLEGE RHYTHM 1934 records by members of orig cast. MUSIC: Harry Revel. WORDS: Mack Gordon. "College Rhythm," "Take a Number From One To Ten" (Lyda Roberti: LP-40) (Jack Oakie: 78/Melotone M-13236) Lanny Ross: "Stay as Sweet as You Are" (LP-447) "Let's Give Three Cheers for Love" (78/Bruns 7318)

340012a Film ONE NIGHT OF LOVE records by members of orig cast. Grace Moore, 1934: "One Night of Love" (LP-43) (LP-231) (LP-322) (LP-641) "Ciribiribin" (LP-231) "Un Bel Di" (LP-235) (LP-247) Moore, later: "Ciribiribin" (LP-443) (LP-526) (LP-539)

340012b Film ONE NIGHT OF LOVE soundtrack. ORCH & COND: Morris Stoloff, Louis Silvers. VOCALS: Grace Moore, Tullio Carminati, chorus. Several operatic selections from the film, but the title song is omitted and two extraneous songs from a radio broadcast are included. (Grapon 15, with I Dream Too Much)

340013a Film BRIGHT EYES soundtrack. Shirley Temple: "On the Good Ship Lollipop" (LP-47) (LP-179) (LP-225) (LP-537) (LP-769)

340014a Film LET'S FALL IN LOVE records sung by Harold Arlen, composer. WORDS: Ted Koehler. "Let's Fall in Love" (1933; LP-321, LP-340, LP-603) (1955: LP-101) "This Is Only the Beginning" (1933: LP-340, LP-603)

340014b Film LET'S FALL IN LOVE later record by Ann Sothern of orig cast. "Let's Fall in Love" (LP-203) (LP-614)

340014c Film LET'S FALL IN LOVE soundtrack. Ann Sothern: "Let's Fall in Love" "Love Is Love Anywhere" (LP-657)

340015a Film SHE LOVES ME NOT 1934 records by Bing Crosby of orig cast. "Straight from the Shoulder" (LP-106) (LP-181) "I'm Hummin'—I'm Whistlin'—I'm Singin'" (LP-181) "Love In Bloom" (LP-181) (LP-768)

340015b Film SHE LOVES ME NOT soundtrack. Miriam Hopkins: "Put a Little Rhythm in Everything You Do" (LP-496)

340016a Film SADIE McKEE records by Gene Austin of orig cast. "All I Do Is Dream of You" (1934: LP-103, LP-453, LP-475, LP-483) "After You've Gone" (1930: LP-103, LP-475, LP-483)

340016b Film SADIE McKEE soundtrack. Gene Raymond: "All I Do Is Dream of You" (LP-770)

340017a Film ROADHOUSE 1934 record by Violet Lorraine of orig cast. "What a Little Moonlight Can Do" (LP-56)

340018a Film STAND UP AND CHEER soundtrack. Shirley Temple, Patricia Lee, James Dunn: "Baby, Take a Bow" (LP-116) (LP-179) (LP-225)

340019a Film BABY TAKE A BOW soundtrack. Shirley Temple:

"On Account-a I Love You" (LP-116) (LP-179) (LP-225) "I'll Always Be Lucky with You" (LP-225)

340020a Film THE CAMELS ARE COMING record by Jack Hulbert of orig cast. "Who's Been Polishing the Sun?" (LP-130)

340021a Film DAMES soundtrack. MUSIC & WORDS: mostly Harry Warren, Al Dubin. ORCH & COND: Leo F Forbstein. CAST: Dick Powell, Ruby Keeler, Joan Blondell, Phil Regan. (Caliban 6014, with St. Louis Blues. Excerpts: Blondell: "The Girl at the Ironing Board" (LP-223) Powell: "Dames" (LP-333) (Incomplete: LP-223) Powell, Keeler: "I Only Have Eyes for You" (LP-632) (Incomplete: LP-154) (Excerpt: LP-223).)

340021b Film DAMES records by members of orig cast. "I Only Have Eyes for You" (Phil Regan, 1934: 78/Col 2942-D) (Dick Powell, 1947: LP-133)

340021c Film DAMES 1966 record by Harry Warren (composer), piano & vocal. "I Only Have Eyes for You" (LP-671)

340022a Film HERE IS MY HEART contemp records by Bing Crosby of orig cast. MUSIC: Ralph Rainger, Lewis Gensler. WORDS: Leo Robin. "Love Is Just Around the Corner," "June in January" (LP-163) "With Every Breath I Take" (LP-163) (LP-768)

340022b Film HERE IS MY HEART soundtrack. Bing Crosby: "June in January" Crosby, Kitty Carlisle: "With Every Breath I Take" (LP-768)

340023a Film PALOOKA records by Jimmy Durante of orig cast. "Inka Dinka Doo" (LP-41) (LP-42) (LP-80) (LP-175) (LP-292) (LP-297)

340024a Film WE'RE NOT DRESSING contemp records by members of orig cast. MUSIC: Harry Revel. WORDS: Mack Gordon. Bing Crosby: "She Reminds Me of You" Crosby, with Nat W Finston & His Paramount Orch: "Love Thy Neighbor," "May I?" "Goodnight, Lovely Little Lady," "Once In a Blue Moon" (LP-181) Ethel Merman: "It's the Animal in Me" (LP-40)

340024b Film WE'RE NOT DRESSING soundtrack. Ethel Merman: "It's Just a New Spanish Custom" (LP-334)

340025a Film THE GIFT OF GAB records by members of orig cast. Ethel Merman: "I Ain't Gonna Sin No More" (Contemp: LP-236) (Later: LP-99) Ruth Etting: "Talkin' to Myself," "Tomorrow, Who Cares?" (1934: 78/Col 2954-D) Gene Austin: "Blue Sky Avenue" (1934: 78/Vic 24725)

340026a Film SING AS WE GO 1934 records by Gracie Fields of orig cast. "Sing as We Go" (LP-248) "In My Little Bottom Drawer" (78/HMV(E) B-8209) "Love," "Just a Catchy Little Tune" (78/HMV(E) B-8208)

340027a Film MOULIN ROUGE contemp records by members of orig cast. Connie Boswell: "Boulevard of Broken Dreams" (LP-273) Boswell Sisters: "Song of Surrender," "Coffee in the Morning" (78/Bruns 6733)

340027b Film MOULIN ROUGE soundtrack. MUSIC: Harry Warren. WORDS: Al Dubin. COND: Alfred Newman. CAST: Russ Columbo, Constance Bennett, Boswell Sisters, Tullio Carminati. (LP-557)

340028a Film MURDER AT THE VANITIES 1934 records by members of orig prod. Carl Brisson: "Cocktails for Two" (LP-447) "Live and Love Tonight" (78/Bruns 6887) Duke Ellington Orch: "Cocktails for Two," "Live and Love Tonight" (78/Vic 24617) "Ebony Rhapsody" (78/Vic 24622)

340029a Film TRANSATLANTIC MERRY-GO-ROUND 1934 records by the Boswell Sisters of orig cast. "Rock and Roll," "If I Had a Million Dollars" (78/Bruns 7302)

340029b Film TRANSATLANTIC MERRY-GO-ROUND soundtrack.

Mitzi Green: "Oh, Leo! It's Love" Green, Boswell Sisters: "Rock and Roll" Frank Parker: "It Was Sweet of You" (LP-769)

340030a Film HIPS, HIPS HOORAY 1934 records by Ruth Etting of orig cast. MUSIC: Harry Ruby. WORDS: Bert Kalmar. "Tired of It All" (78/Bruns 6761) "Keep Romance Alive" (LP-725)

340031a Film STRICTLY DYNAMITE 1934 records by members of orig cast. Jimmy Durante: "Hot Patatta" (78/Bruns 6774) Mills Brothers: "Swing It Sister," "Money in My Clothes" (78/Bruns 6894)

340031b Film STRICTLY DYNAMITE soundtrack. VOCALS: Jimmy Durante, Lupe Velez, Mills Brothers. "Swing It Sister," "Money in My Clothes," "I'm Putty in Your Hands," "Hot Patatta," "Oh Me, Oh My, Oh You" (LP-776)

340032a Film LOVE, LIFE AND LAUGHTER 1934 records by Gracie Fields of orig cast. "Cherie," "Love, Life and Laughter" (78/HMV(E) B-8140) "Riding on the Clouds," "I'm a Failure" (78/HMV(E) B-8141)

340033a Film MARIE GALANTE 1934 records by Helen Morgan of orig cast. "It's Home" (78/Bruns 7329) "Song of a Dreamer" (LP-724)

340034a Film YOU BELONG TO ME 1934 record by Helen Morgan of orig cast. "When He Comes Home to Me" (LP-37)

340035a Film OPERATOR 13 1934 records by the Mills Brothers of orig cast. "Sleepy Head" (78/Bruns 6913) "Jungle Fever" (78/Bruns 6785)

340036a Film BOLERO 1934 record by Nat Finston (cond), Ralph Rainger (piano), & Paramount Studio Orch of orig prod. MUSIC: Ralph Rainger. "Raftero" (LP-768)

340037a Film THE ORPHANS' BENEFIT soundtrack of the Mickey Mouse cartoon. (LP-661)

340038a Film THE GRASSHOPPER AND THE ANTS soundtrack of the Walt Disney Silly Symphony cartoon. (78/Bluebird BK-9)

340039a Film NOW I'LL TELL soundtrack. Alice Faye: "Foolin' with the Other Woman's Man" (LP-283) (LP-645)

340039b Film NOW I'LL TELL 1934 radio performance by Alice Faye of the orig cast. "Foolin' with the Other Woman's Man" (LP-645)

340040a Film FASHIONS OF 1934 soundtrack. Veree Teasdale: "Spin a Little Web of Dreams" (LP-333)

340041a Film UPPER WORLD soundtrack. Ginger Rogers, chorus: "Shake Your Powder Puff" (LP-402)

340042a Film THE BELLE OF THE NINETIES 1934 records by Duke Ellington Orch of orig prod. "My Old Flame," "Troubled Waters" (78/Vic 24651)

340042b Film THE BELLE OF THE NINETIES soundtrack. Mae West, Duke Ellington Orch: "My Old Flame" (78/Biltmore 1014) (Incomplete: LP-413)

340043a Film BIG BUSINESS contemp records by John Green (composer), piano. MUSIC: John Green. WORDS: Various. "An Hour Ago This Minute" (78/Col(E) DB-1379) "Repeal the Blues" (LP-589)

340043b Film BIG BUSINESS 1934 records by Gertrude Lawrence of 1934 English radio prod. "An Hour Ago This Minute," "What Now?" (LP-123)

340044a Film HOLLYWOOD PARTY soundtrack. MUSIC: Richard Rodgers. WORDS: Lorenz Hart. Frances Williams: "Hollywood Party" Jimmy Durante, Jack Pearl: "Hello" Durante: "Reincarnation" (LP-498)

340045a Film MANHATTAN MELODRAMA soundtrack. MUSIC: Richard Rodgers. WORDS: Lorenz Hart. Shirley Ross: "The Bad in Every Man" (LP-498)

340045b Film MANHATTAN MELODRAMA 1937 radio performance by Shirley Ross of orig cast. "Blue Moon" (by Richard Rodgers & Lorenz Hart, originally written as "The Bad in Every Man") (LP-498)

340046a Film HAROLD TEEN soundtrack. Chick Chandler, Rochelle Hudson: "How Do I Know It's Sunday?," "Collegiate Wedding" (LP-558)

340047a Film THE QUEEN'S AFFAIR 1934 records by members of orig cast. MUSIC: Arthur Schwartz. WORDS: Desmond Carter. Anna Neagle, Trefor Jones: "To-Night" (LP-584) Jones: "I Love You So" (78/Col(E) DB-1316)

340048a Film MANY HAPPY RETURNS 1934 records by Guy Lombardo Orch of orig prod. "The Sweetest Music This Side of Heaven," "Fare Thee Well" (78/Bruns 6874)

340049a Film HAPPY 1934 record by Stanley Lupino of orig cast. "Happy" (78/Dec(E) F-3974)

340050a Film JITTERBUG PARTY soundtrack. COND & VOCALS: Cab Calloway. "Hot-cha Razz-Ma-Tazz," "Long about Midnight," "Jitterbug" (LP-623)

340051a Film STUDENT TOUR soundtrack. Betty Grable: "The Snake Dance" (LP-646) Phil Regan: "A New Moon is over My Shoulder" Nelson Eddy: "The Carlo" (LP-770)

340052a Film THE OLD-FASHIONED WAY contemp record by Joe Morrison of orig cast. "Rolling in Love" (78/Bruns 6959)

340053a Film SONS OF THE DESERT soundtrack. Ty Parvis: "Honolulu Baby" Oliver Hardy: "Honolulu Baby" Chorus: "We Are the Sons of the Desert," "Auld Lang Syne" (Mark56 689. Incomplete: LP-695.)

340054a Film LITTLE MISS MARKER soundtrack. Dorothy Dell: "Low-Down LulLaby" Dell, Shirley Temple: "Laugh, You Son-of-a-Gun" (LP-768)

340055a Film BOTTOMS UP soundtrack. John Boles: "Waiting at the Gate for Katie" (LP-769)

340056a Film KISS AND MAKE UP soundtrack. Genevieve Tobin, Edward Everett Horton: "Corned Beef and Cabbage, I Love You" Cary Grant, Helen Mack: "Love Divided by Two" (LP-768)

340104a ZIEGFELD FOLLIES OF 1934 1953 record by Jane Froman of orig cast. MUSIC: Vernon Duke. WORDS: E Y Harburg. "What Is There to Say?" (LP-445)

340104b ZIEGFELD FOLLIES OF 1934 contemp record by Vernon Duke (composer), piano, VOCAL: Bonnie Lake. "Water under the Bridge" (78/Liberty Music Shop L-163)

340112a COME OF AGE contemp records by Ralph Stuart of orig cast. MUSIC: Richard Addinsell. WORDS: Clemence Dane. "I Come Out of a Dream," "I'm Afraid of the Dark" (78/Liberty Music Shop 158)

340201a MR. WHITTINGTON 1933 records by members of orig (London) cast. MUSIC & WORDS: John Green, Edward Heyman, others. Jack Buchanan, Elsie Randolph: Medley, with John Green (composer) & Carroll Gibbons at pianos, with orch (LP-602) "Who You Think You Are?" (LP-61) "Oceans of Time" (78/HMV(E) B-8109) Buchanan: "Weep No More, My Baby" (LP-374) Randolph: "The Sun Is 'Round the Corner" (78/HMV(E)B-8110)

340201b MR. WHITTINGTON 1933 records by John Green (composer) & Ramona Davies, vocals & piano. "Who You Think You Are?," "Weep No More My Baby" (LP-545)

340216a CONVERSATION PIECE contemp records by members of orig (London) prod. MUSIC & WORDS: Noel Coward. COND: Reginald Burston. CAST: Yvonne Printemps, Noel Coward, Louis Hayward, Heather Thatcher, Moya Nugent, Maidie Andrews, Sidney Grammer, George Sanders, Pat Worsley, Antony Brian. "I'll Follow My Secret Heart" (LP-28) (LP-174) (LP-308) "Charming, Charming," "Dear Little Soldiers," "English Lesson," "Nevermore," "Melanie's Aria," "Regency Rakes," "There's Always Something Fishy about the French" (LP-174) (LP-308) Orch Medley (78/HMV(E) C-2654)

340216b CONVERSATION PIECE 1951 studio prod. ORCH: Carol Huxley. COND: Lehman Engel. CAST: Noel Coward of orig (London) prod, Lily Pons, Rosalind Nadell, Ellen Faull, Dorothy Johnson. (Col SL-163)

340315a NEW FACES contemp record by members of orig prod. MUSIC & WORDS: Haven Johnson. PIANO: Cliff Allen. VOCAL: Billie Haywood. "My Last Affair" (78/Unnamed label 501)

340409a THE THREE SISTERS 1934 records by members of orig (London) cast. MUSIC: Jerome Kern. WORDS: Oscar Hammerstein II. Stanley Holloway: "Keep Smiling," "Hand in Hand" (LP-173) The following records "recorded under the personal direction of Jerome Kern": Esmond Knight: "Now That I Have Springtime" Adele Dixon: "Sombody Wants to Go to Sleep" Knight, Victoria Hopper: "Roll On, Rolling Road" (LP-700)

340607a CAVIAR contemp records by members of orig prod. MUSIC & WORDS: Harden Church, Edward Heyman. Jane Winton (who replaced Nanette Guilford): "Gypsy" Winton, George Houston: "Nothing Was Ever like This" (78/Liberty Music Shop L-165)

340827a LIFE BEGINS AT 8:40 1934 records sung by Harold Arlen, composer. WORDS: Ira Gershwin, E Y Harburg. "You're a Builder Upper," "What Can You Say in a Love Song?," "Fun to Be Fooled," "Shoein' the Mare" (LP-603)

340829a KILL THAT STORY 1934 record by Gloria Grafton of orig cast. "Two Cigarettes in the Dark" (78/Vic 24717)

340919a MOONLIGHT IS SILVER 1934 records by Gertrude Lawrence & Douglas Fairbanks Jr of orig (London) cast. MUSIC: Richard Addinsell. WORDS: Clemence Dane. Two scenes, including the song "Moonlight Is Silver" (LP-29) (LP-275)

340927a YES, MADAM contemp records by members of orig (London) cast. MUSIC: Joseph Tunbridge, Jack Waller. WORDS: R P Weston, Bert Lee. Bobby Howes, Binnie Hale: "What Are You Going to Do?," "Sitting Beside o' You" Howes, Hale, Wylie Watson: "Introduction and Cat Duet" Howes, Vera Pearce: "Introduction and Czechoslovakian Love" (LP-83)

340928a STREAMLINE contemp record by Norah Howard of orig (London) cast. "Other People's Babies" (LP-172)

341003a CONTINENTAL VARIETIES records by Lucienne Boyer of orig cast. 1930: "Attends!" (78/Col(F) DF-173) "Parlez-moi d'amour" (LP-442) "Prenez mes roses" (78/Col(F) DF-60) 1932: "Si petite" (LP-442) "Je ne savais pas" (78/Col(F) DFX-146) 1933: "Moi, j'crache dans l'eau" (78/Col(F) DF-1157) "Viens danser quand meme" (78/Col(F) DF-1242) "D'amour en amour" (78/Col(F) DF-1336) "Parle-moi d'autre chose" (LP-442) 1934: "Is It the Singer or Is It the Song?," "Hands across the Table" (78/Col 2971-D) 1936: "Dancing with My Darling" (78/Col 3124-D) Later: "Parlez-moi d'amour" (78/Philips(F) N-72008-H)

341003*a HI DIDDLE DIDDLE contemp record by Douglas Byng of orig (London) cast. "Miss Otis Regrets"(by Cole Porter) (78/Dec(E) F-5249)

341108a SAY WHEN 1934 records by Harry Richman of orig cast.

MUSIC: Ray Henderson. WORDS: Ted Koehler. "Say When," "When Love Comes Swinging Along" (78/Col 2965-D)

341121a ANYTHING GOES contemp records by Cole Porter, vocal & piano. MUSIC & WORDS: Cole Porter. "You're the Top" (LP-18)(LP-182)(LP-513)(LP-539)(LP-711) "Be like the Bluebird" (LP-182)(LP-340)(LP-513) "Anything Goes" (LP-182)(LP-321)(LP-340)(LP-513)(LP-563)

341121b ANYTHING GOES records by members of orig cast. Ethel Merman, 1934: "You're the Top" (LP-3)(LP-40)(LP-93)(LP-160)(LP-513) "I Get a Kick Out of You" (LP-3) (LP-40)(LP-43)(LP-93)(LP-160)(LP-322)(LP-513)(LP-619)(LP-642) Merman, later: "Blow, Gabriel, Blow" (LP-36) (LP-45)(LP-68)(LP-153)(LP-251)(LP-513)(LP-652) "I Get a Kick Out of You" (LP-36)(LP-45)(LP-68)(LP-153)(LP-670) "You're the Top" (LP-36)(LP-45)(LP-68)(LP-109)(LP-153) (LP-176) "Anything Goes" (LP-36)(LP-652) William Gaxton, 1935 radio performance: "You're the Top" (LP-438) Anything Goes Foursome, 1934: "The Gypsy in Me," "There'll Always Be a Lady Fair" (LP-182)(LP-513)

341121c ANYTHING GOES 1954 TV prod, with interpolated Porter songs. COND: Al Goodman. CAST: Ethel Merman of orig cast; Frank Sinatra, Bert Lahr, chorus. (Larynx 567, with Panama Hattie)(LP-407)

341121d ANYTHING GOES 1950 album by Mary Martin. ORCH: Ted Royal. COND: Lehman Engel. (Col 10" CL-2582)

341121e ANYTHING GOES 1962 prod, with songs interpolated from other Porter shows. ORCH: Julian Stein. COND: Ted Simons. CAST: Eileen Rodgers, Hal Linden, Mickey Deems, Margery Gray, Barbara Lang, Kenneth Mars, Kay Norman. (Epic 15100)

341121f ANYTHING GOES contemp records by members of 1935 London prod. Jack Whiting, Jeanne Aubert: "You're the Top" Whiting: "All through the Night" (LP-156) (LP-300)(LP-513) Sydney Howard: "Be Like the Bluebird" Aubert, the Four Admirals: "Blow, Gabriel, Blow" (LP-300) (LP-513) "Anything Goes," "I Get a Kick Out of You" (LP-300)

341121g ANYTHING GOES contemp album (including soundtrack) by members of 1956 film prod. MUSIC & WORDS: Cole Porter, James Van Heusen, Sammy Cahn. COND: Joseph Lilley. CAST: Bing Crosby, Donald O'Connor, Jeanmaire, Mitzi Gaynor. (Dec 8318. Incomplete: LP-26.)

341121h ANYTHING GOES 1953 album. COND: Milton Rosenstock. CAST: Helen Gallagher, Jack Cassidy. (RCA 10" LPM-3157, with Kiss Me Kate)

341121i ANYTHING GOES 1934 medley. COND: Paul Whiteman. VOCALS: Ramona Davies, Peggy Healy, John Hauser, Bob Lawrence. (LP-49)

341121j ANYTHING GOES 1935 records by Bing Crosby of 1936 film cast. MUSIC & WORDS: Various. COND: George Stoll. "Sailor Beware," "My Heart and I," "Moonburn" (Dec 10"6009, with Two for Tonight; LP-319.)

341121k ANYTHING GOES 1936 film soundtrack. Ethel Merman of orig cast, Bing Crosby: "The Shanghai-de-ho"(by Frederick Hollander) (LP-334) Crosby, Merman, Charles Ruggles: "You're the Top" (LP-655)(Incomplete: LP-334) Crosby, uncredited men: "There'll Always Be a Lady Fair" Merman: "I Get a Kick Out of You" (LP-655) Crosby: "Sailor Beware" (LP-769)

341121l ANYTHING GOES medley by Jack Hylton Orch. Vocals uncredited. (78/HMV(E) C-2757)

341121m ANYTHING GOES 1969 London prod. ORCH & COND: Alfred Ralston. CAST: Marian Montgomery, James Kenney, Michael Segal, Michael Malnick, Valerie Verdon, Janet Mahoney, Bernard Sharpe, Peter Honri. (Dec(E) SKL-5031)

341128a REVENGE WITH MUSIC records by Libby Holman of orig cast. MUSIC: Arthur Schwartz. WORDS: Howard Dietz. "You and the Night and the Music" (1934: LP-18, LP-553, LP-711) "When You Love Only One" (1934: LP-553)(1935 radio performance: LP-556)

341128b REVENGE WITH MUSIC 1934 medley. COND: Andre Kostelanetz. VOCALS: The Giesdorf Sisters, quartet, chorus. (LP-553)

341128c REVENGE WITH MUSIC 1975 records sung by Arthur Schwartz, composer. "You and the Night and the Music," "If There Is Someone Lovelier Than You" (LP-418)

341225a FOOLS RUSH IN contemp records by members of orig prod. MUSIC & WORDS: Will Irwin, Norman Zeno, Richard Lewine, June Sillman, others. Billie Haywood & Cliff Allen: "Sixty-Second Romance" (78/Liberty Music Shop L-175) Teddy Lynch, with Irwin & Lewine (composers) at pianos: "Two Get Together/Let's Hold Hands," "Ghost Town/I'm So in Love" (78/Liberty Music Shop L-177)

1935

350001a Film GOLD DIGGERS OF 1935 contemp records by members of orig cast. Dick Powell: "I'm Goin' Shoppin' with You," "The Words Are in My Heart" (LP-2) "Lullaby of Broadway" (LP-2)(LP-19) Winifred Shaw: "Lullaby of Broadway" (LP-175) "I'm Goin' Shoppin' with You" (78/Dec 408)

350001b Film GOLD DIGGERS OF 1935 soundtrack. COND: Leo F Forbstein. Orchestra: Main Title & Opening Scene. Dick Powell, Gloria Stuart: "I'm Going Shopping with You" (LP-632) Powell, Winifred Shaw, chorus: "Lullaby of Broadway" (LP-632)(Incomplete: LP-154)(Excerpts: LP-223, LP-558) Powell, chorus: "The Words Are in My Heart" (LP-632)(Incomplete: LP-333)

350002a Film BROADWAY GONDOLIER records by members of orig cast. Dick Powell, 1935: "Outside of You," "The Rose in Her Hair," "Lonely Gondolier" (LP-2) "Lulu's Back in Town" (LP-2)(LP-16)(LP-644) Powell, 1947: "The Rose in Her Hair" (LP-133) Mills Brothers, 1935: "Lulu's Back in Town," "Sweet and Slow" (78/Bruns(E) 02093)

350002b Film BROADWAY GONDOLIER soundtrack. The Mills Brothers: "Lulu's Back in Town" (LP-558)

350003a Film GEORGE WHITE'S SCANDALS OF 1935 contemp records by members of orig cast. Alice Faye: "According to the Moonlight" (LP-9) "Oh, I Didn't Know" (78/Melotone M-13346) Cliff Edwards: "It's an Old Southern Custom," "Hunkadola" (78/Melotone M-13347) "I Got Shoes, You Got Shoesies," "I Was Born Too Late" (78/Melotone M-13403)

350003b Film GEORGE WHITE'S SCANDALS OF 1935 soundtrack. Alice Faye: "Oh, I Didn't Know" (LP-283)

350003c Film GEORGE WHITE'S SCANDALS OF 1935 1935 radio performance by Alice Faye of orig cast. "Oh, I Didn't Know/According to the Moonlight" (LP-645)

350004a Film EVERY NIGHT AT EIGHT records by members of orig cast. MUSIC & WORDS: Jimmy McHugh, Dorothy Fields. others. Alice Faye: "Speaking Confidentially" (1935: LP-9) Frances Langford: "I'm in the Mood for Love" (1935: LP-43,LP-642)(1939: LP-135, LP-175) "Speaking Confidentially" (1935: 78/Bruns 7513) "I Feel a Song Coming On" (1935: 78/Bruns 7512) "Then You've Never Been Blue" (1935: 78/Bruns 7512)(1938: LP-572)

350004b Film EVERY NIGHT AT EIGHT soundtrack. Alice Faye, Frances Langford, Patsy Kelly: "I Feel a Song Coming On" (LP-283)

350005a Film KING OF BURLESQUE contemp records by members of orig cast. MUSIC: Jimmy McHugh. WORDS: Ted Koehler. Alice Faye: "I've Got My Fingers Crossed," "I'm Shooting High," "Spreadin' Rhythm Around" (LP-9) "I Love to Ride the Horses"(by Lew Pollack & Jack Yellen) (78/Melotone 6-03-09) Fats Waller: "Spreadin' Rhythm Around," "I've Got My Fingers Crossed" (78/Vic 25211)

350005b Film KING OF BURLESQUE soundtrack. Alice Faye "I Love to Ride the Horses" (LP-283) "Whose Big Baby Are You?" (LP-283)(LP-496)

350006a Film TOP HAT records by members of orig cast. MUSIC & WORDS: Irving Berlin. Fred Astaire: "Cheek to Cheek" (1935: LP-23, LP-106, LP-215, LP-277, LP-593) (1952: LP-50, LP-125, LP-648)(1976: LP-429) "Top Hat, White Tie and Tails" (1935: LP-183, LP-215, LP-277)(1952: LP-50, LP-125, LP-358, LP-567, LP-648)(1959: LP-108) (1976: LP-429) "No Strings" (1935: LP-208, LP-215, LP-277)(1952: LP-50, LP-125, LP-567, LP-648) "Isn't This a Lovely Day" (1935: LP-208, LP-215, LP-277)(1952: LP-50, LP-125, LP-358, LP-648)(1959: LP-108)(1976: LP-429) "The Piccolino" (1935: LP-208, LP-215, LP-277) Ginger Rogers: "No Strings," "The Piccolino" (1935: LP-336) "Cheek to Cheek" (1935: LP-336, LP-519) "Isn't This a Lovely Day" (1935: LP-336)(1978: LP-624)

350006b Film TOP HAT 1935 radio prod with members of 1935 film cast. Fred Astaire: "No Strings," "Isn't This a Lovely Day?," "Cheek to Cheek," "Top Hat, White Tie and Tails" Ginger Rogers: "The Piccolino" (Star-Tone 204, with Roberta)

350006c Film TOP HAT 1935 medley. COND: Paul Whiteman. VOCALS: Durelle Alexander, Johnny Hauser, Ramona Davies, the King's Men. (78/Vic 36174)

350006d Film TOP HAT soundtrack. ORCH: Edward Powell. COND: Max Steiner. CAST: Fred Astaire, Ginger Rogers. (EMI Records(E) EMTC-102, with Shall We Dance; LP-468. Excerpts: Astaire: "No Strings," "Isn't This a Lovely Day," "Top Hat, White Tie and Tails" Rogers: "The Piccolino" (LP-669).)

350006e Film TOP HAT 1935 radio performance by Ginger Rogers of orig cast, "Isn't This a Lovely Day?" (LP-592)

350007a Film COME OUT OF THE PANTRY 1936 records by Jack Buchanan of orig cast & Ethel Stewart. Buchanan: "Everything Stops for Tea" Buchanan, Stewart: "From One Minute to Another" (LP-31)

350008a Film WHEN KNIGHTS WERE BOLD 1936 records by Jack Buchanan of orig cast. "Let's Put Some People to Work" (LP-31) "I'm Still Dreaming" (78/Bruns(E) 02153)

350009a Film FIRST A GIRL 1935 records by Jessie Matthews of orig cast. "Everything's in Rhythm with My Heart" (LP-31)(LP-320) "The Little Silk Worm" (78/Dec(E) F-5729) "Say the Word and It's Yours," "I Can Wiggle My Ears" (78/Dec(E) F-5728)

350010a Film THE BIG BROADCAST OF 1936 contemp records by members of orig prod. Ethel Merman: "It's the Animal in Me" (LP-40) Bing Crosby: "I Wished on the Moon" (LP-163) Jack Oakie: "Miss Brown to You," "Why Dream?" (78/Melotone 35-10-01) Ray Noble Orch: "Why Dream?," "I Wished on the Moon" (78/Vic 25104) "Double Trouble," "Why Stars Come Out at Night" (78/Vic 25105)

350010b Film THE BIG BROADCAST OF 1936 soundtrack. Ethel Merman: "It's the Animal in Me" (LP-334) Bing Crosby: "I Wished on the Moon" (LP-768) Lyda Roberti, Jack Oakie, Benny Baker: "Double Trouble" (LP-769)

350011a Film GO INTO YOUR DANCE soundtrack. MUSIC: Harry Warren. WORDS: Al Dubin. COND: Leo F Forbstein. CAST: Al Jolson, Ruby Keeler, Helen Morgan, chorus. (Hollywood Soundstage 402, with Wonder Bar. Excerpts: Jolson: "About a Quarter to Nine'' (LP-223)(LP-269)(LP-595) ''She's a Latin from Manhattan'' (LP-223) ''Mammy, I'll Sing about You,'' ''Go into Your Dance'' (LP-269) Morgan: ''The Little Things You Used to Do'' (LP-499).)

350011b Film GO INTO YOUR DANCE records by members of orig cast. Helen Morgan: ''The Little Things You Used to Do'' (1935: LP-37, LP-273) ''I Was Taken by Storm'' (1935: LP-724) Al Jolson: ''About a Quarter to Nine'' (1947: LP-196, LP-246) ''She's a Latin from Manhattan'' (1935: LP-373)(1947: LP-331)

350012a Film STARS OVER BROADWAY records by members of orig cast. MUSIC: Harry Warren. WORDS: Al Dubin. Kay Thompson, 1935: ''You Let Me Down'' (LP-43)(LP-642) James Melton, 1935: ''Where Am I?,'' ''Carry Me Back to the Lone Prairie''(by Carson Robison) (78/Vic 25185) Melton, 1937: ''September in the Rain'' (LP-175)

350012b Film STARS OVER BROADWAY 1935 radio performances by James Melton of orig cast. ''Where Am I?,'' ''Carry Me Back to the Lone Prairie'' (LP-469)

350013a Film THANKS A MILLION records by members of orig prod. MUSIC: Arthur Johnston. WORDS: Gus Kahn. Dick Powell, 1935: ''Thanks a Million'' (LP-46)(LP-86) ''I've Got a Pocketful of Sunshine'' (78/Dec 612) ''I'm Sitting High on a Hilltop'' (78/Dec 613) Powell, 1936: Medley: ''I've Got a Pocketful of Sunshine/I'm Sitting High on a Hilltop'' (LP-716) Paul Whiteman Orch, 1935: ''New O'leans,'' ''Sugar Plum'' (78/Vic 25150) ''Thanks a Million,'' ''I'm Sittin' High on a Hilltop'' (78/Vic 25151)

350014a Film CURLY TOP soundtrack. Shirley Temple: ''Animal Crackers in My Soup'' (LP-47)(LP-179)(LP-225) ''When I Grow Up'' (LP-116)(LP-179)(LP-225)

350015a Film HYDE PARK CORNER 1935 records by Binnie Hale of orig cast. ''Did You Get That Out of a Book?,'' ''You Don't Know the Half of It'' (LP-56)

350016a Film BREWSTER'S MILLIONS 1934 records by Jack Buchanan of orig cast. ''I Think I Can'' (LP-61)(LP-374) ''One Good Tune Deserves Another'' (LP-374) Medley (78/Col(E) DX-662)

350017a Film THE NIGHT IS YOUNG 1935 records by members of orig cast. MUSIC: Sigmund Romberg. WORDS: Oscar Hammerstein II. Evelyn Laye: ''When I Grow Too Old to Dream'' (LP-63) ''The Night Is Young'' (LP-310) Ramon Novarro: ''The Night Is Young'' (78/HMV(E) C-2778)

350018a Film GOIN' TO TOWN 1950's record by Mae West of orig cast. ''He's a Bad Man'' (LP-504)

350019a Film THE LITTLEST REBEL soundtrack. Shirley Temple: ''Polly-Wolly Doodle'' (LP-47)(LP-225)

350020a Film THINGS ARE LOOKING UP contemp record by Cicely Courtneidge of orig cast. ''Things Are Looking Up'' (LP-90)

350021a Film FOLIES BERGERE records by Maurice Chevalier of orig cast. 1935: ''I Was Lucky'' (English: LP-88) ''Rhythm of the Rain'' (English: LP-88)(French: 78/Vic 24883) ''Singing a Happy Song'' (English: 78/Vic 24882) (French: 78/Vic 24883) ''You Took the Words Right Out of My Mouth'' (78/Vic 24874) 1958: ''I Was Lucky'' (LP-118)

350022a Film A NIGHT AT THE OPERA soundtrack. Allan Jones, Kitty Carlisle: ''Duet from 'Il Trovatore''' (Re-sound 7051) ''Alone'' (LP-770)

350022b Film A NIGHT AT THE OPERA 1949 record by Allan Jones of orig cast. ''Alone'' (LP-129)(LP-453)(LP-539)

350023a Film ALL THE KING'S HORSES records by Carl Brisson of orig cast. MUSIC & WORDS: Sam Coslow. ''A Little White Gardenia'' (1935: LP-122)(Later: 78/Apollo 1051) ''The King Can Do

No Wrong'' (1935: 78/Bruns 7397) ''Dancing the Viennese,'' ''Be Careful, Young Lady'' (1935: 78/Bruns 7398)

350024a Film MISSISSIPPI contemp records by Bing Crosby of orig cast. MUSIC: Richard Rodgers. WORDS: Lorenz Hart. ''It's Easy to Remember,'' ''Soon,'' ''Down By the River,'' ''Swanee River'' (LP-163)

350024b Film MISSISSIPPI contemp records by Richard Rodgers (vocal and piano) of six songs which he and Lorenz Hart wrote for the film. (LP-217)

350024c Film MISSISSIPPI soundtrack. CAST: Bing Crosby, Queenie Smith, chorus. (LP-498)

350025a Film TWO FOR TONIGHT contemp records by Bing Crosby of orig cast. MUSIC: Harry Revel. WORDS: Mack Gordon. Dorsey Brothers Orch. ''Without a Word of Warning,'' ''Two for Tonight,'' ''From the Top of Your Head,'' ''I Wish I Were Aladdin,'' ''Takes Two to Make a Bargain'' (Dec 10'' 6009, with Anything Goes; LP-163.)

350026a Film LOVE ME FOREVER 1935 record by Grace Moore of orig cast. ''Love Me Forever'' (LP-175)(LP-235) (LP-247)

350027a Film BROADWAY MELODY OF 1936 1935 records by Eleanor Powell of orig cast. Tommy Dorsey Orch. ''You Are My Lucky Star'' (LP-183)(LP-474)(LP-770) ''I've Got a Feeling You're Fooling'' (LP-183)(LP-273)(LP-474)(LP-770)

350027b Film BROADWAY MELODY OF 1936 soundtrack. Robert Taylor, June Knight: ''I've Got a Feelin' You're Foolin''' (LP-416) Frances Langford: ''You Are My Lucky Star'' (LP-558) ''Broadway Rhythm'' (LP-770)

350027c Film BROADWAY MELODY OF 1936 contemp rehearsal record by Frances Langford of orig cast, singing a song dropped before release.''Something's Gotta Happen Soon'' (LP-486)

350028a Film THE LITTLE COLONEL soundtrack. Shirley Temple: ''Love's Young Dream,'' ''Parade of the Wooden Soldiers'' (LP-225)

350029a Film OUR LITTLE GIRL soundtrack. Shirley Temple: ''Our Little Girl,'' ''All Aboard the Dreamland Choo-Choo'' (LP-225)

350030a Film METROPOLITAN 1935 records by Lawrence Tibbett of orig cast. ''On the Road to Mandalay'' (LP-226) (LP-385) ''Last Night When We Were Young'' (by Harold Arlen & E Y Harburg) (dropped before release) (78/Vic 11877)

350031a Film RECKLESS soundtrack. Jean Harlow: ''Reckless'' (LP-252) (LP-558)

350031b Film RECKLESS 1935 radio performance by Jean Harlow of orig cast. ''Reckless'' (LP-592)

350032a Film SHIP CAFE 1935 records by Carl Brisson of orig cast. ''A Fatal Fascination,'' ''Change Your Mind'' (78/Dec(E) F-5839)

350033a Film HERE'S TO ROMANCE 1935 records by Nino Martini of orig cast. ''Here's to Romance,'' ''I Carry You in My Pocket,'' ''Midnight in Paris,'' ''Mattinata'' (LP-366)

350034a Film I LIVE FOR LOVE 1935 records by Everett Marshall of orig cast. MUSIC: Jimmy McHugh. WORDS: Harold Adamson. ''Mine Alone,'' ''Silver Wings'' (78/Vic 25164)

350035a Film MAZURKA 1936 records by Pola Negri of orig cast. ''Stay Close to Me,'' ''Mazurka,'' ''Nur eine Stunde'' (LP-625) ''For That One Hour of Passion'' (LP-310) (LP-625)

350036a Film ONE HOUR LATE 1934 records by Joe Morrison of orig cast. ''Me without You,'' ''A Little Angel Told Me So'' (78/Bruns 7347)

350037a Film TO BEAT THE BAND 1935 record by Johnny Mercer of orig cast & Ginger Rogers. MUSIC: Matt Malneck. WORDS: Johnny Mercer. "Eeny, Meeny, Miney, Mo" (78/Dec 638)

350038a Film IN CALIENTE 1935 records by Phil Regan of orig cast. "Muchacha," "To Call You My Own" (78/Col 3035-D)

350038b Film IN CALIENTE soundtrack. Winifred Shaw, Judy Canova: "The Lady in Red" (LP-333) Phil Regan, Dolores Del Rio, chorus: "Muchacha" (LP-633)

350039a Film BROADWAY HOSTESS 1935 records by Phil Regan of orig cast. "Let It Be Me," "Weary" (78/Col 3106-D)

350040a Film SHIPMATES FOREVER 1935 record by Dick Powell of orig cast. MUSIC: Harry Warren. WORDS: Al Dubin. "Don't Give Up the Ship" (78/Dec 613)

350041a Film LIMELIGHT contemp records by Arthur Tracy of orig cast. "Farewell, Sweet Senorita," "The Whistling Waltz" (78/Dec(E) F-5880) "Stay Awhile," "Stranded" (78/Dec(E) F-5882) "Nirewana," "We Were Meant to Meet Again" (78/Dec(E) F-5881)

350042a Film KING SOLOMON OF BROADWAY 1935 record by Pinky Tomlin of orig cast. MUSIC & WORDS: Pinky Tomlin, others. "That's What You Think" (78/Bruns 7502)

350043a Film SANDERS OF THE RIVER 1935 records by Paul Robeson of orig cast, chorus. COND: Muir Mathieson. "Congo Lullaby," "Canoe Song," "Killing Song," "Love Song" (45/HMV(E) 7EG-8185. Excerpts: First 2 songs (LP-637) Last 2 songs (LP-638).)

350044a Film SWEET MUSIC records by members of orig cast. MUSIC & WORDS: Sammy Fain, Irving Kahal. Helen Morgan, contemp: "Winter Overnight" (LP-37) (LP-447) "I See Two Lovers" (LP-37) Rudy Vallee, contemp: "Sweet Music," "Ev'ry Day" (78/Vic 24827) "Fare Thee Well, Annabelle," "There's a Different You in Your Heart" (78/Vic 24833) Vallee, 1955: "Sweet Music" (LP-357)

350044b Film SWEET MUSIC soundtrack. Helen Morgan: "I See Two Lovers" (LP-499)

350045a Film MUSIC IS MAGIC soundtrack. Alice Faye: "Music Is Magic" (LP-283)

350046a Film PADDY O'DAY 1935 record by Pinky Tomlin of orig cast. "Changing My Ambitions" (78/Bruns 7594)

350047a Film CAR OF DREAMS contemp record by John Mills of orig cast. "Goodbye Trouble" (LP-310)

350048a Film I DREAM TOO MUCH records by Lily Pons of orig cast. MUSIC: Jerome Kern. WORDS: Dorothy Fields. "I Dream Too Much," "I'm the Echo, You're the Song," "The Jockey on the Carousel" (LP-607)

350048b Film I DREAM TOO MUCH soundtrack. VOCALS: Lily Pons, chorus. (Grapon 15, with One Night of Love)

350049a Film IN PERSON soundtrack. Ginger Rogers: "I Got a New Lease on Life," "Don't Mention Love to Me," "Out of Sight, Out of Mind" (LP-402)

350050a Film CORONADO 1935 records by Eddy Duchin Orch of orig prod. "How Do I Rate with You?," "You Took My Breath Away" (78/Vic 25178)

350050b Film CORONADO soundtrack. Johnny Downs, Betty Burgess: "How Do I Rate with You?" (LP-769)

350051a Film NAT GONELLA AND HIS GEORGIANS soundtrack. With Nat Gonella & His Georgians. VOCALS: Nat Gonella. (LP-419)

350052a Film PRINCESSE TAM-TAM 1935 radio performance by Josephine Baker of orig cast. "Chemin de Bonheur" (LP-556)

350053a Film WHO KILLED COCK ROBIN? soundtrack. (78/Bluebird BK-5)

350054a Film TIMES SQUARE LADY records sung by Pinky Tomlin (composer) of orig cast. "The Object of My Affection" (1934: 78/Bruns 7308) (1940: 78/Dec 3649) "What's the Reason I'm Not Pleasin' You?" (1934, with Betty Roth: 78/Bruns 7355)

350055a Film PEG OF OLD DRURY 1935 record by Anna Neagle of orig cast. "A Little Dash of Dublin" (78/Dec(E) F-5649)

350056a Film SYMPHONY IN BLACK soundtrack, with Duke Ellington Orch. VOCAL: Billie Holiday. (LP-622)

350057a Film THE BAND CONCERT soundtrack of the Mickey Mouse cartoon. "William Tell Overture" (LP-661)

350058a Film LET'S LIVE TONIGHT 1935 records by Tullio Carminati of orig cast. MUSIC: Victor Schertzinger. WORDS: Jack Scholl. COND: Victor Schertzinger (who also directed the film). "Love Passes By," "I Live in My Dreams" (78/Col 3023-D)

350059a Film LOOK UP AND LAUGH 1935 records by Gracie Fields of orig cast. "Anna from Annacapresi" (with Tommy Fields, Douglas Wakefield, Billy Nelson), "Love Is Everywhere" (with Tommy Fields) (78/Regal Zonophone(E) MR-1793) Gracie Fields, chorus: "Look Up and Laugh" (78/Regal Zonophone(E) MR-1794)

350060a Film MARINELLA 1935 records by Tino Rossi of orig cast. "Marinella," "J'aime les Femmes, c'est ma Folie" (78/Col 4138-M)

350505a GLAMOROUS NIGHT contemp records by members of orig (London) prod. MUSIC: Ivor Novello. WORDS: Christopher Hassall. COND: Charles Prentice. CAST: Mary Ellis, Trefor Jones, Elisabeth Welch. (LP-309, plus orch medley on 78/HMV(E) C-2756. Incomplete: HMV(E) 10" DLP-1095, with Careless Rapture. Excerpts: Welch: "Far Away in Shanty Town," "The Girl I Knew" (LP-712).)

350505b GLAMOROUS NIGHT 1963 studio prod. COND: Kenneth Alwyn. CAST: Patricia Johnson, John Stoddart, Patricia Bartlett, chorus. (World Record Club(E) T-214, with Careless Rapture)

350505c GLAMOROUS NIGHT 1968 radio prod. COND: Marcus Dods. CAST: Rae Woodland, Monica Sinclair, Robert Thomas, John Palmer, chorus. (Col(E) TWO-243)

350505d GLAMOROUS NIGHT 1976 record by Elisabeth Welch of orig (London) prod. "Far Away in Shanty Town" (LP-415)

350505e GLAMOROUS NIGHT contemp medley by Debroy Somers Band. Vocals uncredited. (78/Col(E) DX-687)

350523a GAY DECEIVERS 1935 records by Charlotte Greenwood of orig (London) cast. "It Happened in the Moonlight" (LP-124) (LP-136) (LP-700) "Serenade" (78/HMV(E) B-8324)

350919a AT HOME ABROAD records by members of orig cast. MUSIC: Arthur Schwartz. WORDS: Howard Dietz. Eleanor Powell, 1935: "What a Wonderful World" (LP-18) (LP-474) (LP-711) "Got a Bran' New Suit" (LP-129) (LP-474) (LP-554) "That's Not Cricket" (LP-474) (LP-554) Ethel Waters, 1935: "Hottentot Potentate," "Thief in the Night" (LP-15) (LP-554) Beatrice Lillie: "Get Yourself a Geisha" (1939: LP-112, LP-121, LP-554, LP-729) "Paree" (1935: LP-112, LP-518, LP-554) (1958: LP-450, LP-680, LP-729) Reginald Gardiner (monologue): "Trains" (1934: 78/Dec(E) F-5278) (1941: 78/Dec album 215, entitled "Trains")

350919b AT HOME ABROAD records by Arthur Schwartz, composer. "Love Is a Dancing Thing" (1935 piano: LP-554, LP-589) (1975 vocal: LP-418) "Got a Bran' New Suit" (1935 vocal & piano: LP-589)

351002a PLEASE TEACHER contemp record by Bobby Howes & Sepha Treble of orig (London) cast. MUSIC: Jack Waller, Joseph Tunbridge. WORDS: R P Weston, Bert Lee. "You Give Me Ideas" (LP-83)

351005a THREE WALTZES 1937 album by Yvonne Printemps & Pierre Fresnay of 1937 Paris prod & 1939 film prod, both entitled "Les Trois Valses." MUSIC: Oscar Straus, Johann Strauss Sr, Johann Strauss Jr. ORCH: Oscar Straus. COND: Marcel Cariven. (Pathe(F) OP-3320, entitled "Les Trois Valses," with other songs by Printemps)

351005b THREE WALTZES 1945 records by Evelyn Laye of 1945 London prod. "Forever" (LP-63) "How Can Words Content a Lover?" (78/HMV(E) B-9414)

351010a PORGY AND BESS 1942 prod. MUSIC: George Gershwin. WORDS: Ira Gershwin, DuBose Heyward. ORCH: George Gershwin. COND: Alexander Smallens. CAST: Todd Duncan, Anne Brown, Edward Matthews, Helen Dowdy, & Georgette Harvey of orig prod; William Woolfolk, Avon Long, Harriet Jackson, Gladys Good. (Dec 8042)

351010b PORGY AND BESS 1951 studio prod. COND: Lehman Engel. CAST: Lawrence Winters, Camilla Williams, Inez Matthews, June McMechen, Warren Coleman; Avon Long of 1942 prod; Helen Dowdy & Edward Matthews of orig & 1942 prods. (Col OSL-l62. Excerpts: Col CL-922.)

351010c PORGY AND BESS l959 film soundtrack. ORCH & COND: Andre Previn. CAST: Adele Addison (for Dorothy Dandridge), Robert McFerrin (for Sidney Poitier), Pearl Bailey, Cab Calloway (replacing Sammy Davis Jr of orig cast), Loulie Jean Norman (for Diahann Carroll), Inez Matthews (for Ruth Attaway), Brock Peters, Leslie Scott. (Col OS-2016)

351010d PORGY AND BESS records by members of orig cast. Edward Matthews, 1935: "I Got Plenty o' Nuttin'," "It Ain't Necessarily So" (sung by Duncan & Bubbles respectively in the show) (78/Bruns 7562) John W Bubbles, later: "There's a Boat That's Leaving Soon for New York" (LP-75)

351010e PORGY AND BESS studio prod. ORCH: Henri Rene. COND: Lehman Engel. CAST: Anna Moffo, Urlee Leonardos, Billie Daniels, Valentine Pringle, Avon Long (of 1942 cast), Andrew Frierson. (Reader's Digest 40-8, with The Vagabond King)

351010f PORGY AND BESS 1963 studio prod. COND: Skitch Henderson. CAST: Leontyne Price (of 1952 prod), William Warfield (of 1952 & 1961 prods), McHenry Boatwright, John W Bubbles (of orig cast), Robert Henson, Barbara Webb, Miriam Burton, Alonzo Jones, Berniece Hall, Maeretha Stewart. (RCA LSC-2679)

351010g PORGY AND BESS 1935 album. COND: Alexander Smallens (of orig prod). "Recorded under the supervision of the composer." CAST: Lawrence Tibbett & Helen Jepson; orchestra and chorus of orig prod. (Camden 500. Excerpts: Tibbett, Jepson: "Bess, You Is My Woman Now" Tibbett: "I Got Plenty o' Nuttin'" (LP-436) (LP-711) "Buzzard Song" (LP-436) Jepson: "Summertime" (LP-711).)

351010h PORGY AND BESS 1957 studio prod. COND: Kenneth Alwyn. CAST: Lawrence Winters (of 1962 prod), Isabelle Lucas, Ray Ellington, Barbara Elsy, Pauline Stevens. (Heliodor 25052)

351010i PORGY AND BESS album. COND: Warren Edward Vincent. VOCALS: Avon Long (of 1942 prod), Le Vern Hutcherson (of 1952 prod), Margaret Tynes. (Design 1002)

351010j PORGY AND BESS 1950 album. COND: Robert Russell Bennett. CAST: Rise Stevens, Robert Merrill, chorus. (RCA LM-1124. Excerpts: Merrill: "A Woman Is a Sometime Thing," "Bess, Oh Where's My Bess," "Oh Lawd, I'm on My Way" Chorus: "Gone, Gone, Gone" Stevens: "My Man's Gone Now" (LP-436).)

351010k PORGY AND BESS 1959 album by Harry Belafonte & Lena Horne. ORCH & COND: Lennie Hayton, Robert Corman. (RCA LSO-1507)

351010l PORGY AND BESS 1942 album by Avon Long (of 1942 cast) & Helen Dowdy (of orig & 1942 casts). COND: Leo Reisman. Dowdy: "Summertime" Long: "It Ain't Necessarily So," "A Woman Is a Sometime Thing," "There's a Boat That's Leaving Soon for New York," "I Got Plenty o' Nuttin'" Long, Dowdy: "Bess, You Is My Woman" (78/Dec album 351)

351010m PORGY AND BESS 1938 medley. COND: Nathaniel Shilkret. VOCALS: Jane Froman, Felix Knight, Sonny Schuyler, chorus. (LP-303)

351010n PORGY AND BESS 1953 album by Cab Calloway, Helen Thigpen, & Leslie Scott of 1953 prod. COND: Jay Blackton. (RCA 10" LPM-3156, with Girl Crazy. Excerpt: Calloway: "It Ain't Necessarily So" (LP-436).)

351010o PORGY AND BESS studio prod. COND: Paul Belanger. VOCALS: Brock Peters (of 1959 film cast), Margaret Tynes, Miriam Burton, Charles Colman, Joseph Crawford, William Dillard, Theresa Merritte, chorus. (Musical Masterpiece 2035-OP22)

351010p PORGY AND BESS July 19, 1935 rehearsal by members of orig prod. COND & PIANO: George Gershwin. Abbie Mitchell: "Summertime" Edward Matthews: "A Woman Is a Sometime Thing" Orchestra: Finale, Scene I, Act I Ruby Elzy: "My Man's Gone Now" Todd Duncan, Anne Brown: "Bess, You Is My Woman Now" (LP-375)

351010q PORGY AND BESS 1976 studio prod. COND: Lorin Maazel. CAST: Willard White, Leona Mitchell, McHenry Boatwright, Florence Quivar, Francois Clemmons, Barbara Hendricks, Arthur Thompson, Barbara Conrad. (London(E) OSA-13116)

351010r PORGY AND BESS studio prod. "Ed Sullivan presents Porgy and Bess." No other credits given. (National Academy 7)

351010s PORGY AND BESS 1976 prod. COND: John DeMain. CAST: Donnie Ray Albert, Clamma Dale, Andrew Smith, Wilma Shakesnider, Larry Marshall, Betty Lane, Alexander B Smalls, Carol Brice. (RCA ARL3-2109)

351010t PORGY AND BESS 1959 studio prod. CAST: Fern Susan, Janice Lynne, Gordon Sidney, George Atwell, Paul Francine, chorus. (Lion 70095)

351010u PORGY AND BESS studio prod. COND: Lorenzo Fuller. CAST: Martha Flowers (of 1955 prod), Irving Barnes (of 1953, 1961, & 1964 prods), Joseph Attles (of 1965 prod), Leesa Forster, Lorenzo Fuller, chorus. (Music for Pleasure(E) 1154)

351010v PORGY AND BESS studio prod. COND: Al Goodman. CAST: Lee Carroll, Jene Jones, Bill St Clair, Bob Storm. (Pirouette FM-21)

351010w PORGY AND BESS album of miscellaneous reissues. Cy Walter, piano: Medley. Todd Duncan (of orig cast): "I Got Plenty o' Nuttin'," "Bess, O Where's My Bess?" Mabel Mercer: "Summertime," "My Man's Gone Now," "I Loves You, Porgy" (AEI Records 1107, with Cabin in the Sky. Excerpts: Duncan's records (LP-678)(LP-744).)

351012a JUBILEE l935 records by the composer, vocal and piano. MUSIC & WORDS: Cole Porter. "A Picture of You without her," "Entrance of Eric," "The Kling-Kling Bird on Top of the Divi-Divi Tree," "When Love Comes Your Way," "What a Nice Municipal Park," "When Me, Mowgli, Love," "Ev'rybod-ee Who's Anybod-ee," "Sunday Morning Breakfast Time," "Me and Marie" (LP-160)

351012b JUBILEE 1935 medley. COND: Paul Whiteman. VOCALS: Ramona Davies, Ken Darby, Bud Linn, the King's Men. (LP-182)

351022a Radio show LET'S HAVE FUN soundtrack. MUSIC & WORDS: Richard Rodgers, Lorenz Hart, others. COND: Freddie Rich. VOCALS: Ken Murray, Helen Morgan, chorus.

(Nostalgia(Australia) 002; LP-460. Excerpts: Morgan: "Please Make Me Be Good," "Why Was I Born?" (LP-499).)

351116a JUMBO 1953 album. MUSIC: Richard Rodgers. WORDS: Lorenz Hart. COND: Lehman Engel. CAST: Lisa Kirk, Jack Cassidy, Jordan Bentley. (RCA 10''' LPM-3152, with Babes in Arms)

351116b JUMBO soundtrack of 1962 film (entitled "Billy Rose's Jumbo"), with one song from another Rodgers-Hart show and additional words by Roger Edens. COND: George Stoll. CAST: Doris Day, James Joyce (for Stephen Boyd), Jimmy Durante, Martha Raye. (Col OS-2260)

351116c JUMBO 1936 records by members of orig prod. Paul Whiteman Orch (of orig prod). Gloria Grafton: "Little Girl Blue" Grafton, Donald Novis: "My Romance" (LP-217)

351116d JUMBO contemp radio performance by members of orig prod. Jimmy Durante & Paul Whiteman Orch: "Laugh" (LP-469)

351116e JUMBO TV performance by Martha Raye of 1962 film prod. "Little Girl Blue" (LP-651)

351225a GEORGE WHITE'S SCANDALS OF 1936 1942 record by Willie Howard of orig cast. Skit "French Taught in a Hurry" (LP-630)

351226a CONTINENTAL VARIETIES OF 1936 1936 records by Lucienne Boyer of orig cast. "It's a Thrill All Over Again," "I Found a Bit of Paris in the Heart of Old New York" (78/Col 3123-D) "This Is the Kiss of Romance" (78/Col 3124-D)

1936

360001a Film STOWAWAY soundtrack. Shirley Temple: "Goodnight, My Love" (LP-47)(LP-l79)(LP-225) "That's What I Want for Christmas" (LP-225)

360001b Film STOWAWAY 1936 record by Alice Faye of orig cast. "Goodnight, My Love" (LP-9)

360001c Film STOWAWAY 1956 record by Irving Caesar, lyricist. "That's What I Want for Christmas" (LP-353)

360002a Film SWING TIME records by Fred Astaire of orig cast. MUSIC: Jerome Kern. WORDS: Dorothy Fields. "Bojangles of Harlem" (1936: LP-16, LP-215, LP-277, LP-644) "A Fine Romance" (l936: LP-23, LP-215, LP-277)(1952: LP-125, LP-358, LP-567, LP-648)(1976: LP-429) "Pick Yourself Up" (1936: LP-208, LP-215, LP-277)(1975, with Bing Crosby: LP-396) "The Way You Look Tonight" (1936: LP-208, LP-215, LP-277)(1952: LP-125, LP-552, LP-648) "Never Gonna Dance" (1936: LP-208, LP-215, LP-277)

360002b Film SWING TIME soundtrack. COND: Nathaniel Shilkret. CAST: Fred Astaire, Ginger Rogers, George Metaxa, Victor Moore, Helen Broderick. (EMI Records(E) EMTC-101, with The Gay Divorcee)

360002c Film SWING TIME records by Ginger Rogers of orig cast. "The Way You Look Tonight" (1965: LP-325) "A Fine Romance" (1978: LP-624)

360003a Film THE GREAT ZIEGFELD soundtrack. MUSIC & WORDS: Walter Donaldson, Harold Adamson, Irving Berlin, others. ORCH: Arthur Lange. CAST: Luise Rainer, Allan Jones (for Dennis Morgan), Ray Bolger, Virginia Bruce, Fanny Brice, Harriet Hoctor, Buddy Doyle. (Classic International Filmusicals 3005. Excerpts: Brice: "My Man" (LP-157)(LP-710) Jones: "A Pretty Girl Is like a Melody" (LP-252) Chorus: "You Gotta Pull Strings" Bolger: "She's a Follies Girl" Bruce, chorus: "You Never Looked So Beautiful Before" Rainer: "Won't You Come and Play with Me?" (LP-710).)

360004a Film IT'S LOVE AGAIN 1936 records by Jessie Matthews of orig cast. "Got to Dance My Way to Heaven," "Tony's in Town"

(LP-31)(LP-320) "It's Love Again," "I Nearly Let Love Go Slipping through My Fingers" (LP-320)

360005a Film HEAD OVER HEELS 1937 records by Jessie Matthews of orig cast. "Head over Heels in Love," "May I Have the Next Romance with You?" (LP-31)(LP-320) "There's That Look in Your Eyes Again," "Looking around Corners for You" (LP-320)

360006a Film GOLD DIGGERS OF 1937 soundtrack. MUSIC & WORDS: Harold Arlen, E Y Harburg, Harry Warren, Al Dubin. Dick Powell, Joan Blondell, Rosalind Marquis, Lee Dixon (tap dancing): "All's Fair in Love and War" (LP-632) (Incomplete: LP-333) Powell: "With Plenty of Money and You" (LP-632) Powell, Glenda Farrell, Victor Moore, Lee Dixon: "Let's Put Our Heads Together/Speaking of the Weather" (LP-657)

360006b Film GOLD DIGGERS OF 1937 1936 records by Dick Powell of orig cast. "With Plenty of Money and You" (LP-46)(LP-86)(LP-175) "Speaking of the Weather" (78/Dec 1067) "Let's Put Our Heads Together," "All's Fair in Love and War" (78/Dec 1068)

360007a Film HEARTS DIVIDED contemp records by Dick Powell of orig cast. MUSIC: Harry Warren. WORDS: Al Dubin. "My Kingdom for a Kiss" (LP-46)(LP-86) "Two Hearts Divided" (78/Dec 900)

360008a Film STAGE STRUCK soundtrack. MUSIC: Harold Arlen. WORDS: E Y Harburg. Dick Powell, Jeanne Madden: "Fancy Meeting You" Powell: "In Your Own Quiet Way" (LP-657)

360008b Film STAGE STRUCK 1936 records by Dick Powell of orig cast. "Fancy Meeting You" (LP-46)(LP-86) "In Your Own Quiet Way" (78/Dec(E) F-6293)

360008c Film STAGE STRUCK 1980 record sung by E Y Harburg, lyricist. PIANO: Phil Springer. "Fancy Meeting You" (LP-741)

360009a Film CAPTAIN JANUARY soundtrack. Shirley Temple: "Early Bird" (LP-47) (LP-179)(LP-225) "The Right Someone to Love" Temple & Slim Summerville: "At the Codfish Ball" (LP-116)(LP-225) Temple, Summerville, Guy Kibbee: "Sextet from Lucia" (LP-225)

360010a Film POOR LITTLE RICH GIRL soundtrack. Shirley Temple: "But Definitely" (LP-47)(LP-179)(LP-225) "When I'm with You," "Oh, My Goodness" (LP-116)(LP-179)(LP-225) "Where There's Life There's Soap" (LP-225) Alice Faye: "When I'm with You" (LP-283) Temple, Faye, Jack Haley: "You Gotta Eat Your Spinach, Baby" (LP-283) (Incomplete: LP-116, LP-179, LP-225)

360011a Film DIMPLES soundtrack. MUSIC: Jimmy McHugh. WORDS: Ted Koehler. Shirley Temple: "He Was a Dandy," "Hey! What Did the Bluejay Say?" (LP-47)(LP-225) "Picture Me Without You" (LP-47)(LP-179)(LP-225)

360012a Film FOLLOW THE FLEET records by members of orig cast. MUSIC & WORDS: Irving Berlin. Fred Astaire: "Let's Face the Music and Dance," "Let Yourself Go," "I'd Rather Lead a Band," "We Saw the Sea" (1936: LP-208, LP-215, LP-277) "I'm Putting All My Eggs in One Basket" (1936: LP-208, LP-215, LP-277)(1952: LP-50, LP-348, LP-648) Ginger Rogers: "Let Yourself Go" (1936: LP-109) "I'm Putting All My Eggs in One Basket" (1936: LP-336) (1978: LP-624) Harriet Hilliard: "Get Thee Behind Me, Satan," "But Where Are You?" (1936: LP-336)

360012b Film FOLLOW THE FLEET soundtrack. COND: Max Steiner. CAST: Fred Astaire, Ginger Rogers, Harriet Hilliard, chorus. (Scarce Rarities 5505, with A Damsel in Distress)

360013a Film SAN FRANCISCO 1950 record by Jeanette MacDonald of orig cast. "San Francisco" (LP-77)(LP-119) (LP-242)(LP-453)

360013b Film SAN FRANCISCO soundtrack. Jeanette MacDonald: "Would You?" (LP-770)

360014a Film JACK OF ALL TRADES contemp records by Jack Hulbert of orig cast. "Where There's You There's Me" (LP-90) "You're Sweeter Than I Thought You Were" (78/HMV(E) BD-334) "Tap Your Tootsies" (LP-310)

360015a Film PENNIES FROM HEAVEN records by members of orig cast. MUSIC: Arthur Johnson. WORDS: John Burke. Bing Crosby, 1936: "Pennies from Heaven," "So Do I," "One, Two, Button Your Shoe," "Let's Call a Heart a Heart" (Dec 10" 6010, with Rhythm on the Range; LP-319. Excerpt: "Pennies from Heaven" (LP-175).) Crosby & Louis Armstrong (with Frances Langford, not of orig cast), 1936: "Pennies from Heaven," Medley (78/Dec 15027) Armstrong: "Pennies from Heaven" (1947: LP-355) "The Skeleton in the Closet" (1936: 78/Dec 949)

360016a Film RAINBOW ON THE RIVER 1936 records by Bobby Breen of orig cast. "Rainbow on the River" (LP-175) "Flower Song" (78/Dec 1053)

360017a Film SING, BABY, SING records by members of orig cast. Tony Martin: "When Did You Leave Heaven?" (1936: LP-175, LP-769) Alice Faye: "You Turned the Tables on Me" (1962: LP-100) "Sing, Baby, Sing" (Radio: LP-717)

360017b Film SING, BABY, SING soundtrack. Alice Faye: "You Turned the Tables on Me," "Sing, Baby, Sing" (LP-558)

360018a Film BORN TO DANCE contemp records by members of orig cast. MUSIC & WORDS: Cole Porter. Frances Langford: "Rap Tap on Wood," "I've Got You under My Skin," "Swinging the Jinx Away," "Easy to Love" (LP-182) Virginia Bruce: "Easy to Love," "I've Got You under My Skin" (LP-655)

360018b Film BORN TO DANCE soundtrack. COND: Alfred Newman. CAST: Eleanor Powell, James Stewart, Buddy Ebsen, Frances Langford, Virginia Bruce, Raymond Walburn, Sid Silvers, Una Merkel. (Classic International Filmusicals 3001. Excerpt: Powell, Stewart: "Easy to Love" (LP-252).)

360019a Film JUNGLE PRINCESS 1937 record by Dorothy Lamour of orig cast. "Moonlight and Shadows" (LP-183)

360019b Film JUNGLE PRINCESS soundtrack. Dorothy Lamour: "Moonlight and Shadows" (LP-647)

360020a Film THE SINGING KID soundtrack. MUSIC: Harold Arlen. WORDS: E Y Harburg. ORCH & COND: Leo F. Forbstein. CAST: Al Jolson, Cab Calloway, Sybil Jason, Winifred Shaw, Yacht Club Boys, Edward Everett Horton, Allen Jenkins. Main Title, "My, How This Country's Changed," "Keep That Hi-De-Ho in Your Soul," "Save Me Sister," "Here's Looking at You" (LP-776) "I Love to Sing-a" "You're the Cure for What Ails Me" (LP-657)(LP-776)

360020b Film THE SINGING KID 1936 records by Cab Calloway of orig cast. "I Love to Sing-a," "Save Me Sister" (78/Bruns 7638) "You're the Cure for What Ails Me," "Keep That Hi-De-Ho in Your Soul" (78/Bruns 7639)

360020c Film THE SINGING KID record sung by Harold Arlen, composer. "You're the Cure for What Ails Me" (LP-192)

360021a Film L'HOMME DU JOUR records by Maurice Chevalier of orig cast. "Ma Pomme" (1936: LP-542)(1947, as "Just a Bum": LP-405)(1957: LP-224) "Mon Vieux Paris," "Vous Valez Mieux qu'un Sourire" (1936: 78/Disque Gramophone(F) K-7766)

360022a Film THE KING STEPS OUT records by Grace Moore of orig cast. 1936: "Stars in My Eyes" (LP-231)(LP-247) "The End Begins," "Learn How to Lose," "What Shall Remain" (LP-247) Later: "What Shall Remain" (LP-231) (LP-443)(LP-526)

360023a Film SUZY soundtrack. Cary Grant: "Did I Remember?" (LP-252)

360024a Film LET'S SING AGAIN 1936 record by Bobby Breen of orig cast. "Let's Sing Again" (78/Dec 798)

360025a Film TRAILIN' WEST 1936 record by Dick Foran of orig cast. "Moonlight Valley" (78/Dec 1039)

360026a Film THE BELOVED VAGABOND 1936 records by Maurice Chevalier of orig cast. "You Look So Sweet, Madame," "Tzinga-Doodle-Day" (78/HMV(E) B-8440)

360026b Film BELOVED VAGABOND soundtrack. VOCALS: Maurice Chevalier, chorus. "Loch Lomond," "Tzinga-Doodle-Day," "Quand un Vicomte," "You Look So Sweet, Madame" (LP-776)

360027a Film RHYTHM ON THE RANGE records by members of orig cast. MUSIC & WORDS: Various. Bing Crosby, 1936: "I Can't Escape from You," "I'm an Old Cowhand," "The House Jack Built for Jill," "Empty Saddles" (Dec 10" 6010, with Pennies from Heaven; LP-319. Excerpt: "I Can't Escape from You" (LP-769).) "Round-up Lullaby" (LP-319) Martha Raye, 1939: "You'll Have to Swing It" (LP-6l3)

360027b Film RHYTHM ON THE RANGE soundtrack. Bing Crosby, Frances Farmer: "The House Jack Built for Jill" (LP-455) Martha Raye: "You'll Have to Swing It" (LP-651)

360027c Film RHYTHM ON THE RANGE 1971 records sung by Johnny Mercer, composer & lyricist. "I'm an Old Cowhand" (LP-533)(LP-694)

360028a Film THE HIT PARADE OF 1937 contemp records by members of orig cast. Eddy Duchin Orch: "Love Is Good for Anything That Ails You" (78/Vic 25514) Phil Regan: "Sweet Heartache" (78/Bruns 7869) "Was It Rain?," "Last Night I Dreamed of You" (78/Bruns 7864) Frances Langford: "Sweet Heartache," "Was It Rain?" (78/Dec 1202)

360029a Film COLLEGIATE 1935 record by Frances Langford of orig cast. "You Hit the Spot" (78/Dec 663)

360030a Film PALM SPRINGS contemp records by Frances Langford of orig cast. "Will I Ever Know?" (78/Dec 663) "The Hills of Old Wyomin'," "I Don't Want to Make History" (78/Dec 783)

360030b Film PALM SPRINGS soundtrack. Frances Langford: "I Don't Want to Make History" (LP-768)

360031a Film BANJO ON MY KNEE 1936 records by Tony Martin of orig cast. "Where the Lazy River Goes By," "There's Something in the Air" (78/Bruns 7782)

360032a Film IT'S A GREAT LIFE 1935 records by Joe Morrison of orig cast. "I Lost My Heart," "Lazy Bones Gotta Job Now" (78/Bruns 7574)

360033a Film SING ME A LOVE SONG records by James Melton of orig cast. "The Little House That Love Built," "Summer Night" (1936: 78/Dec 1093) "Your Eyes Have Told Me So" (1934: 78/Bruns 15225)(1936: 78/Dec(E) F-6822)

360034a Film LAUGHING IRISH EYES 1936 records by Phil Regan of orig cast. "Laughing Irish Eyes," "All My Life" (78/Bruns 7623)

360035a Film WITH LOVE AND KISSES contemp records by Pinky Tomlin of orig cast. MUSIC & WORDS: Pinky Tomlin, others. "Sweet" (78/Bruns 7502) "The Trouble with Me Is You" (78/Bruns 7525) "Sittin' on the Edge of My Chair," "With Love and Kisses" (78/Bruns 7897) "I'm Right Back Where I Started" (78/Bruns 7811)

360036a Film THE MUSIC GOES ROUND 1936 records by Harry Richman of orig cast. "Life Begins When You're in Love," "Let's Go" (78/Dec 700) "Suzannah," "There'll Be No South" (78/Dec 701)

360036b Film THE MUSIC GOES ROUND soundtrack. Harry Richman: "Rolling Along" (LP-558)

360037a Film SONG OF FREEDOM 1936 records by Paul Robeson of orig cast. "Sleepy River"(with Elisabeth Welch), "Song of Freedom," "Lonely Road," "The Black Emperor" (45/HMV(E) 7EG-8431. Excerpt: "Sleepy River" (LP-310) (LP-638)(LP-712).)

360038a Film MICKEY'S GRAND OPERA soundtrack of the Mickey Mouse cartoon. "Quartet from Rigoletto" (LP-661)

360039a Film MOVING DAY soundtrack of the Mickey Mouse cartoon. (78/Bluebird BK-9)

360040a Film PIGSKIN PARADE soundtrack. MUSIC: Lew Pollack. WORDS: Sidney Mitchell. CAST: Judy Garland, Tony Martin, Betty Grable, Jack Haley, Dixie Dunbar, Johnny Downs, the Yacht Club Boys. (Pilgrim 4000, with Everybody Sing; plus material dropped before release: Grable, Downs: "It's Love I'm After" (LP-284). Excerpts: Garland: "It's Love I'm After" (LP-284)(LP-726)(LP-759) "Texas Tornado" (LP-558)(LP-726)(LP-759) Garland, Grable, Downs, Company: "The Balboa" (LP-558)(Incomplete: LP-726, LP-759).)

360040b Film PIGSKIN PARADE 1936 records by Tony Martin of orig cast. "It's Love I'm After," "You're Slightly Terrific" (78/Dec 957)

360041a Film THE SMARTEST GIRL IN TOWN 1936 record by Gene Raymond of orig cast. MUSIC & WORDS: Gene Raymond. "Will You?" (78/Bruns 7796)

360042a Film PUBLIC NUISANCE NO. 1 contemp record by Frances Day of orig cast. "For Me and My Dog" (LP-310)

360043a Film STRIKE ME PINK soundtrack. MUSIC: Harold Arlen. WORDS: Lew Brown. Ethel Merman, Eddie Cantor: "Calabash Pipe" Merman: "First You Have Me High, Then You Have Me Low" (LP-334)(LP-657) "Shake It Off with Rhythm" Cantor, Rita Rio (later Dona Drake): "The Lady Dances" (LP-657)

360044a Film THE GAY DESPERADO soundtrack. Nino Martini: "The World Is Mine Tonight" (LP-366)

360045a Film KLONDIKE ANNIE soundtrack. Mae West: "Little Bar Butterfly," "Mister Deep Blue Sea" (LP-413)

360046a Film EVERYTHING IS RHYTHM soundtrack. Harry Roy Orch. VOCALS: Harry Roy, Phyllis Thackery, Ivor Moreton, Mabel Mercer. (LP-419. Excerpt: "Black Minnie's Got the Blues" (LP-715).)

360047a Film THE BIG BROADCAST of 1937 records by Benny Goodman Orch of orig prod. "Here's Love in Your Eyes" (1936: 78/Vic 25391) "Bugle Call Rag" (1936: 78/Vic 25467)(1941: 78/Col 36109)

360047b Film THE BIG BROADCAST OF 1937 soundtrack. Shirley Ross: "I'm Talking through My Heart" (LP-768)

360048a Film AVEC LE SOURIRE contemp records by Maurice Chevalier of orig cast. "Le Chapeau de Zozo" (78/Disque Gramophone(F) K-7767) "Le Bon Systeme," "Je vous Revois, Madame" (78/Disque Gramophone(F) K-7687) "Y'a du Bonheur pour Tout le Monde," "Les Mots qu'on Voudrais Dire" (78/Disque Gramophone(F) K-7816)

360049a Film THE CAPTAIN'S KID 1937 record by Sybil Jason of orig cast. "I'm the Captain's Kid" (LP-487)

360050a Film UNDER YOUR SPELL soundtrack. MUSIC: Arthur Schwartz. WORDS: Howard Dietz. Lawrence Tibbett: "Under Your Spell" (LP-554)

360051a Film THAT GIRL FROM PARIS contemp medley by Geraldo's Orch. VOCALS: Marjorie Steddeford, Cyril Grantham, the Tophatters. (LP-554)

360052a Film DON'T GET PERSONAL records by Pinky Tomlin of orig cast. "I Won't Take No for an Answer," "Barnyard Serenade" (1935: 78/Bruns 7653)

360053a Film MOSKAU-SHANGHAI contemp record by Pola Negri of orig cast. "Mein Herz hat Heimweh" (LP-625)

360054a Film CAIN AND MABEL soundtrack. Chorus: "I'll Sing You a Thousand Love Songs" (LP-633)

360055a Film DESIRE soundtrack. Marlene Dietrich: "Awake in a Dream" (LP-653)

360056a Film COLLEGE HOLIDAY soundtrack. Martha Raye: "So What!," "Who's That Knocking at My Heart?" (LP-651)

360057a Film QUEEN OF HEARTS 1935 records by Gracie Fields of orig cast. "One of the Little Orphans of the Storm," "Queen of Hearts" (78/Rex(E) 8818) "Why Did I Have to Meet You?," "Do You Remember My First Love Song?" (78/Rex(E) 8819)

360058a Film ONE IN A MILLION 1936 radio performances by members of orig cast. Arline Judge: "One in a Million" Ritz Brothers: Specialty Number (LP-716)

360059a Film CHANGING OF THE GUARD 1937 record by Sybil Jason of orig cast. "The Changing of the Guard" (LP-487)

360060a Film EVERY SUNDAY 1935 soundtrack recording (not used in the film). Judy Garland: "Americana" (LP-743)

360061a Film THE THREE LITTLE WOLVES soundtrack of the Walt Disney Silly Symphony cartoon. "Ist Das Nicht ein Sausage Meat?" (78/Vic BK-10)

360062a Film THREE CHEERS FOR LOVE soundtrack. Robert Cummings: "Long Ago and Far Away" (LP-768)

360063a Film COLLEEN soundtrack. MUSIC: Harry Warren. WORDS: Al Dubin. CAST: Dick Powell, Ruby Keeler, Joan Blondell, Jack Oakie, Hugh Herbert. (Caliban 6007, with Variety Girl)

360109a TO-NIGHT AT 8:30 1936 records by Noel Coward & Gertrude Lawrence of orig (London) and 1936 New York casts. MUSIC & WORDS: Noel Coward. From *Shadow Play*: Scene, including "Someday I'll Find You," "Then," "Play, Orchestra, Play," "You Were There." From *Red Peppers*: Scene, including "Has Anybody Seen Our Ship?," "Men about Town." (LP-28)(LP-275) From *Family Album*: Scene, including "Here's a Toast," "Music Box," "Hearts and Flowers." (LP-29)(LP-123)(LP-275) From *We Were Dancing*: Coward: "We Were Dancing" (LP-123)(LP-275)

360109b TO-NIGHT AT 8:30 1935 records by Clifford Greenwood of orig (London) prod conducting the original orchestra. "The Family Album" With vocal by Sam Browne: "You Were There" (78/HMV(E) B-5019)

360204a FOLLOW THE SUN 1936 medley by Jack Jackson Orch. VOCALS: Fred Latham, Florine McKinney. (LP-584)

360204b FOLLOW THE SUN 1935 medley by Arthur Schwartz (composer), piano & vocals. (LP-589)(First side only: LP-554)

360411a ON YOUR TOES 1954 prod, with one interpolated Rodgers/Hart song. MUSIC: Richard Rodgers. WORDS: Lorenz Hart. ORCH: Don Walker. COND: Salvatore Dell'Isola. CAST: Bobby Van, Elaine Stritch, Kay Coulter, Joshua Shelley, Ben Astar, Jack Williams, Eleanor Williams, David Winters. (Dec 9015)

360411b ON YOUR TOES 1952 studio prod. COND: Lehman Engel. CAST: Portia Nelson, Jack Cassidy, Laurel Shelby, Ray Hyson, Robert Eckles, Zamah Cunningham. (Col ML-4645)

360411c ON YOUR TOES contemp records by Jack Whiting of 1937 London prod. "On Your Toes," "There's a Small Hotel," Medley (LP-156)(LP-222)

360411d ON YOUR TOES contemp records by Edgar Fairchild &

Adam Carroll (pianists) of orig prod. "On Your Toes/ The Heart Is Quicker Than the Eye," "There's a Small Hotel/It's Got to Be Love," "Glad to Be Unhappy" (LP-545)

360411e ON YOUR TOES 1958 record by Elaine Stritch of 1954 prod. "You Took Advantage of Me"(an interpolation) (LP-615)

360507a RISE AND SHINE records by Fred Astaire, composer. WORDS: Johnny Mercer. "I'm Building Up to an Awful Letdown" (1936: LP-208, LP-215, LP-277)(1952: LP-125, LP-552, LP-648)(1975: LP-663)

360709a BLACKBIRDS OF 1936 1936 records by members of orig (London) cast. MUSIC: Rube Bloom. WORDS: Johnny Mercer. Nicholas Brothers: "Keep a Twinkle in Your Eye" (LP-172)(LP-582) "Your Heart and Mine" Lavaida Carter: "Dixie Isn't Dixie Any More," "Jo-Jo, the Cannibal Kid" (LP-582)

360911a CARELESS RAPTURE contemp records by members of orig (London) prod. MUSIC: Ivor Novello. WORDS: Christopher Hassall. COND: Charles Prentice. CAST: Dorothy Dickson, Sybil Crawley, Eric Starling, Olive Gilbert, Ivor Novello. (LP-309; plus orch medley on 78/HMV(E) C-2860; plus Dickson & Novello: "Used to You" (dropped from the show) on LP-524. Incomplete: HMV(E) 10" DLP-1095, with Glamorous Night.)

360911b CARELESS RAPTURE 1968 radio prod. COND: Marcus Dods. CAST: Elaine Blighton, Ann Howard, Veronica Lucas, Leslie Fry, Jon Lawrenson, chorus. (Col(E) TWO-260)

360911c CARELESS RAPTURE 1963 studio prod. COND: Kenneth Alwyn. CAST: Patricia Johnson, John Stoddart, Patricia Bartlett, chorus. (World Record Club(E) T-214, with Glamorous Night)

361001a TRANSATLANTIC RHYTHM contemp records by members of orig (London) cast. Buck Washington & John W Bubbles: "Breakfast in Harlem" (LP-172)(LP-582) Ruth Etting: "Holiday Sweetheart," "Who'll Buy My Song of Love?" (78/Rex(E) 8881)

361001b TRANSATLANTIC RHYTHM 1936 medley by Ray Henderson (composer) & Irving Caesar (lyricist) at two pianos. VOCALS: George Scott Wood. (LP-589)

361029a RED, HOT AND BLUE! records by Ethel Merman of orig cast. MUSIC & WORDS: Cole Porter. Contemp: "Red, Hot and Blue!," "Down in the Depths," "Ridin' High," "It's De-lovely" (LP-3)(LP-93)(LP-681) Later: "Ridin' High" (LP-36)(LP-407) "Down in the Depths" (LP-36) (LP-45) "It's De-lovely" (LP-36)(LP-68)(LP-153)

361029b RED, HOT AND BLUE! contemp medley. COND: Leonard Joy. VOCALS: Alan Holt, Rae Giersdorf, chorus. (LP-182)

361029c RED, HOT AND BLUE! later (radio or TV?) performance by Ethel Merman & Bob Hope of orig cast. "It's De-lovely" (LP-295)

361102a FORBIDDEN MELODY contemp medley. MUSIC: Sigmund Romberg. WORDS: Otto Harbach. COND: Leonard Joy. VOCALS: Alan Holt, Dorothy Dreslin, Rae Giersdorf, chorus. (78/Vic 36189)

361117a JOHNNY JOHNSON 1956 studio prod. MUSIC: Kurt Weill. WORDS: Paul Green. ORCH: Kurt Weill. COND: Samuel Matlowsky. CAST: Burgess Meredith, Hiram Sherman, Evelyn Lear, Scott Merrill, Jane Connell, Tom Stewart, Jean Sanders, Bob Shaver, William Malten, Lotte Lenya. (MGM 3447)

361203a O MISTRESS MINE 1936 records by Yvonne Printemps of orig (London) prod. "Goodbye, Little Dream, Goodbye" (by Cole Porter)(LP-182)(LP-300)(LP-681) "When a Woman Smiles" (78/HMV(E) DA-1539)

361218a Radio show HOLLYWOOD HOTEL soundtrack. MUSIC & WORDS: Various. COND: Raymond Paige. VOCALS: Dick Pow-

ell, Frances Langford, Arthur Treacher, Jeannine Love, Igor Gorin, Tony Martin, Arline Judge, Ritz Brothers, chorus. (Medallion 301)(LP-716)

361222a BALALAIKA studio prod. MUSIC: George Posford, Bernard Grun. WORDS: Eric Maschwitz. COND: Geoff Harvey. VOCALS: Valda Bagnall, Neill Williams, chorus. (World Record Club(E) 794, with The Maid of the Mountains)

361225a THE SHOW IS ON 1955 record by Beatrice Lillie of orig cast. "Rhythm" (by Rodgers & Hart) (LP-449)(LP-680)

361225b THE SHOW IS ON TV performance(?) by Bert Lahr of orig cast. "Song of the Woodman"(by Harold Arlen & E Y Harburg) (LP-608)

361225c THE SHOW IS ON 1947 record sung by Hoagy Carmichael (composer). "Little Old Lady" (LP-94)

1937

370001a Film ON THE AVENUE records by members of orig cast. MUSIC & WORDS: Irving Berlin. Alice Faye, contemp: "This Year's Kisses" (LP-9)(LP-106)(Radio: LP-669, LP-592) "Slumming on Park Avenue" (LP-9)(Radio: LP-717) "I've Got My Love to Keep Me Warm" (LP-9)(LP-593)(Radio: LP-7l7) Dick Powell, 1937: "I've Got My Love to Keep Me Warm" (LP-46)(LP-183) "The Girl on the Police Gazette," "This Year's Kisses" (LP-46)(LP-86) "You're Laughing at Me" (LP-336) Faye, 1962: "This Year's Kisses" (LP-100)

370001b Film ON THE AVENUE soundtrack. ORCH: Arthur Lange. CAST: Alice Faye, Dick Powell, Ritz Brothers, chorus. (Hollywood Soundstage 401. Excerpt: Powell: "I've Got My Love to Keep Me Warm" (LP-558).)

370002a Film WAKE UP AND LIVE records by Alice Faye of orig cast. MUSIC: Harry Revel. WORDS: Mack Gordon. "Never in a Million Years" (1937: LP-9)(1962: LP-100) "It's Swell of You" (1937: LP-9) "There's a Lull in My Life" (1937: LP-9)(Radio: LP-717) "Wake Up and Live" (1937: LP-9, LP-43, LP-322, LP-642)

370002b Film WAKE UP AND LIVE soundtrack. COND: Louis Silvers. CAST: Alice Faye, Buddy Clark (for Jack Haley), Grace Bradley, Bobby Baker, Barnett Parker, Leah Ray, Patsy Kelly, Ned Sparks, Ben Bernie, Condos Brothers, Brewster Twins. (Hollywood Soundstage 403)

370003a Film 100 MEN AND A GIRL contemp records by Deanna Durbin of orig cast. "It's Raining Sunbeams" (LP-13)(LP-110)(LP-175)(LP-183) "Alleluja" (LP-91) (LP-404) "Libiamo Ne' Lieti Calici" (LP-110)(LP-404)

370004a Film SHALL WE DANCE? records by members of orig cast. MUSIC: George Gershwin. WORDS: Ira Gershwin. Fred Astaire: "Slap That Bass" (1937: LP-19, LP-23, LP-215, LP-277) "They All Laughed," "They Can't Take That Away from Me" (1937: LP-23, LP-215, LP-277)(1952: LP-125, LP-358, LP-648)(1959: LP-108)(1976: LP-429) "Let's Call the Whole Thing Off" (1937: LP-23, LP-215, LP-277)(1952: LP-125, LP-358, LP-567, LP-648) "I've Got Beginner's Luck," "Shall We Dance?" (1937: LP-208, LP-215, LP-277) Ginger Rogers: "They All Laughed," "Let's Call the Whole Thing Off," "They Can't Take That Away from Me" (1965: LP-325)(1976: LP-654)(1978: LP-624)

370004b Film SHALL WE DANCE? 1937 medley by pianists John Green & Dave Terry. (78/Bruns 7892)

370004c Film SHALL WE DANCE? soundtrack. COND: Nathaniel Shilkret. CAST: Fred Astaire, Ginger Rogers, Mantan Moreland, chorus. (EMI Records(E) EMTC-102, with Top Hat, plus Orchestra: "Walking the Dog" (LP-654).)

370005a Film A DAMSEL IN DISTRESS records by members of orig cast. MUSIC: George Gershwin. WORDS: Ira Gershwin. Fred Astaire, with Ray Noble Orch of orig prod: "A Foggy Day," "I Can't Be Bothered Now," "Things Are Looking Up," "Nice Work If You Can Get It" (1937: LP-23, LP-215, LP-277) Astaire: "A Foggy Day" (1952: LP-125, LP-358, LP-648)(1959: LP-108)(1976: LP-429) "Nice Work If You Can Get It" (1952: LP-348, LP-648)

370005b Film A DAMSEL IN DISTRESS soundtrack. COND: Alfred Newman. CAST: Fred Astaire, Gracie Allen, Mario Berini (for Reginald Gardiner), chorus. (Curtain Calls 100/19, with The Sky's the Limit. Incomplete: Scarce Rarities 5505, with Follow the Fleet.)

370006a Film GANGWAY 1937 records by Jessie Matthews of orig cast. "Gangway," "When You Gotta Sing, You Gotta Sing" (LP-31)(LP-320) "Lord and Lady Whozis" (78/Dec(E) F-6471) "Moon or No Moon" (78/Dec(E) F-6470)

370007a Film BROADWAY MELODY OF 1938 records by members of orig cast. Judy Garland: "Broadway Rhythm" (1935: LP-180, LP-718, LP-726) "You Made Me Love You" (1937: LP-7, LP-183, LP-233)(Later: LP-189, LP-201, LP-240, LP-461, LP-780) "Everybody Sing" (1937: LP-35, LP-183)

370007b Film BROADWAY MELODY OF 1938 soundtrack. Judy Garland: "You Made Me Love You" (LP-8)(LP-252)(LP-289) (LP-511) Garland, Sophie Tucker: "Everybody Sing" George Murphy, Eleanor Powell: "I'm Feelin' like a Million" Tucker: "Your Broadway and My Broadway" Entire cast: Finale (LP-770)

370007c Film BROADWAY MELODY OF 1938 contemp rehearsal record by Judy Garland of orig cast. "I'm Feeling Like a Million" (LP-486)

370008a Film TOP OF THE TOWN 1937 records by Gertrude Niesen of orig cast. "Where Are You?" (LP-43)(LP-322) (LP-619)(LP-642) "Jamboree" (78/Bruns 7837) "Top of the Town," "Blame It on the Rhumba" (78/Bruns 7818)

370009a Film SWING HIGH, SWING LOW contemp records by members of orig cast. Dorothy Lamour: "Panamania" (LP-43) (LP-106)(LP-642) "I Hear a Call to Arms," "Swing High, Swing Low" (LP-647) Carole Lombard: "Then It Isn't Love" (Radio performance: LP-592)

370009b Film SWING HIGH, SWING LOW soundtrack. Carole Lombard: "Then It Isn't Love" (LP-568)(LP-669)

370010a Film VARSITY SHOW 1937 records by Dick Powell of orig cast. MUSIC & WORDS: Richard Whiting, Johnny Mercer. "Have You Got Any Castles, Baby?" (LP-46)(LP-86) (LP-769) "You've Got Something There," "Love Is on the Air Tonight" (78/Dec 1431) "Moonlight on the Campus" (78/Dec 1430)

370011a Film THE SINGING MARINE records by Dick Powell of orig cast. MUSIC & WORDS: Harry Warren, Johnny Mercer, Al Dubin. 1937: "'Cause My Baby Says It's So" (LP-46)(LP-86) "I Know Now" (78/Dec 1310) "You Can't Run Away from Love Tonight," "Song of the Marines" (78/Dec 1311)

370012a Film SNOW WHITE AND THE SEVEN DWARFS soundtrack. MUSIC: Frank Churchill. WORDS: Larry Morey. COND: Leigh Harline, Paul Smith. CAST: Adriana Caselotti, Harry Stockwell, others. (Disneyland 1201)(Edited medley: LP-661)

370012b Film SNOW WHITE AND THE SEVEN DWARFS studio prod. COND: Lyn Murray. CAST: Audrey Marsh, Harrison Knox, Evelyn Knight, Elizabeth Mulliner, chorus. (78/Dec album 368)

370012c Film SNOW WHITE AND THE SEVEN DWARFS 1979 stage prod, with additional music by Jay Blackton & lyrics by Joe Cook. ORCH: Philip J Lang. COND: Donald Pippin. CAST: Mary Joe Salerno, Richard Bowne, chorus. (Vista 5009)

370013a Film TAKE MY TIP contemp record by Jack Hulbert &

Cicely Courtneidge of orig cast. "I Was Anything but Sentimental" (LP-90)

370014a Film YOU CAN'T HAVE EVERYTHING soundtrack. MUSIC & WORDS: mostly Harry Revel, Mack Gordon. ORCH & COND: David Buttolph. CAST: Tony Martin, Alice Faye, the Ritz Brothers, Don Ameche, Louis Prima Orch, Rubinoff. (Titania 508, with The Duchess of Idaho. Excerpt: Faye: "You Can't Have Everything" (LP-273).)

370014b Film YOU CAN'T HAVE EVERYTHING 1962 record by Alice Faye of orig cast. "You Can't Have Everything" (LP-100)

370015a Film YOU'RE A SWEETHEART records by Alice Faye of orig cast. "You're a Sweetheart" (Contemp radio performance: LP-669)(1962: LP-100)

370015b Film YOU'RE A SWEETHEART soundtrack. Alice Faye: "My Fine Feathered Friend" (LP-283)

370016a Film GOOD MORNING, BOYS 1937 record by Lili Palmer of orig cast. "Baby, Whatcha Gonna Do Tonight?" (LP-98)(LP-124)

370017a Film THE HURRICANE records by Dorothy Lamour of orig cast. "The Moon of Manakoora" (1937: LP-271) (1943: LP-109, LP-175)

370018a Film THREE SMART GIRLS contemp records by Deanna Durbin of orig cast. "Someone to Care for Me" (LP-110) "Il Bacio" (LP-110)(LP-404)

370018b Film THREE SMART GIRLS soundtrack. VOCALS: Deanna Durbin. (Caliban 6006, with It Happened in Brooklyn & On Moonlight Bay)

370019a Film THIS'LL MAKE YOU WHISTLE 1936 records by members of orig cast. Jack Buchanan: "Without Rhythm," "There Isn't Any Limit to My Love" Buchanan, Elsie Randolph: "I'm in a Dancing Mood," "This'll Make You Whistle" (LP-31) Randolph: "You've Got the Wrong Rhumba," "My Red Letter Day" (78/Bruns(E) 02349)

370020a Film ROSALIE soundtrack, MUSIC & WORDS: Cole Porter. COND: Herbert Stothart. Chorus, with dancing by Eleanor Powell: "Rosalie" (LP-252) Nelson Eddy: "Rosalie," "In the Still of the Night" Eddy, unidentified woman: "Who Knows?" Powell: "I've a Strange New Rhythm in My Heart" Frank Morgan: "Why Should I Care?" Ilona Massey: "Spring Love Is in the Air" Eddy, Ray Bolger: "It's All Over but the Shouting/To Love or Not to Love" Eddy, chorus: "Wedding Finale" (LP-655)

370020b Film ROSALIE records by Nelson Eddy of orig cast. "Rosalie" (1958: LP-134) "In the Still of the Night" (1948: LP-756)

370021a Film MELODY FOR TWO 1937 records by James Melton of orig cast. MUSIC: Harry Warren. WORDS: Al Dubin. "September in the Rain" (LP-175) "Melody for Two" (78/Dec 1247)

370021b Film MELODY FOR TWO soundtrack. James Melton: "September in the Rain" (LP-223)(LP-633)

370022a Film DOUBLE OR NOTHING contemp records by Bing Crosby of orig cast. MUSIC & WORDS: Arthur Johnson, John Burke, Burton Lane, Ralph Freed. "It's the Natural Thing to Do," "Smarty," "The Moon Got in My Eyes," "All You Want to Do Is Dance" (Dec 10" 6011, with Waikiki Wedding; LP-254. Excerpt: "All You Want to Do Is Dance" (LP-183).)

370022b Film DOUBLE OR NOTHING soundtrack. Bing Crosby: "Smarty" (LP-558) Martha Raye: "Listen, My Children" Crosby, Raye, Frances Faye: "After You" (LP-651)

370023a Film HOLLYWOOD HOTEL soundtrack. MUSIC & WORDS: Richard Whiting, Johnny Mercer, others. ORCH: Ray Heindorf. COND: Leo F Forbstein. CAST: Dick Powell, Rosemary Lane, Frances Langford, Jerry Cooper, Ted Healy, Mabel Todd,

Johnny "Scat" Davis, Benny Goodman Orch, Raymond Paige Orch. (EOH Records 99601. Excerpts: Main Title (LP-333) Powell, Lane: "I'm like a Fish Out of Water" (LP-223)(LP-595)(LP-769) "Silhouetted in the Moonlight" (LP-588) Langford, Davis, Goodman Orch: "Hooray for Hollywood" (LP-333)(LP-769)(Incomplete: LP-223)

370023b Film HOLLYWOOD HOTEL 1937 records by members of orig prod. Dick Powell: "I've Hitched My Wagon to a Star," "I'm Like a Fish Out of Water" (78/Dec 1557) Benny Goodman Orch: "I've Hitched My Wagon to a Star," "Let That Be a Lesson to You" (78/Vic 25708) "Can't Teach My Old Heart New Tricks," "Silhouetted in the Moonlight" (78/Vic 25711) "Sing, Sing, Sing" (78/Vic 36205) Frances Langford: "Silhouetted in the Moonlight," "Can't Teach My Old Heart New Tricks" (78/Dec 1558)

370024a Film HEIDI soundtrack. Shirley Temple: "In Our Little Wooden Shoes" (LP-225)

370025a Film I'LL TAKE ROMANCE soundtrack. Grace Moore: "I'll Take Romance" (LP-231)

370026a Film WHEN YOU'RE IN LOVE 1937 records by Grace Moore of orig cast. MUSIC: Jerome Kern. WORDS: Dorothy Fields. "Our Song," "The Whistling Boy" (LP-247)

370027a Film WAIKIKI WEDDING contemp records by Bing Crosby of orig cast. MUSIC & WORDS: Ralph Rainger, Leo Robin, Harry Owens. "Blue Hawaii," "In a Little Hula Heaven," "Sweet Leilani," "Sweet Is the Word for You," (Dec 10" 6011, with Double or Nothing; LP-254. Excerpt: "Blue Hawaii" (LP-768).)

370028a Film MAKE A WISH 1937 records by Bobby Breen of orig cast. "Make a Wish," "Music in My Heart" (78/Bluebird B-7158)

370028b Film MAKE A WISH soundtrack. Bobby Breen, St Luke Choristers: "My Campfire Dreams" (78/Bluebird B-7168)

370029a Film ARTISTS AND MODELS 1937 records by members of orig prod. Connie Boswell: "Whispers in the Dark" (78/Dec 1420) Louis Armstrong Orch: "Public Melody Number One" (78/Dec 1347)

370029b Film ARTISTS AND MODELS soundtrack. Martha Raye, Louis Armstrong, chorus: "Public Melody Number One" (LP-651)(LP-657)

370030a Film TURN OFF THE MOON 1937 records by Phil Harris & His Orch of orig cast. MUSIC & WORDS: Sam Coslow. "Jammin'," "That's Southern Hospitality" (78/Vocalion 3533)

370031a Film MANHATTAN MERRY-GO-ROUND records by members of orig prod. Phil Regan, 1937: "I Owe You," "Have You Ever Been in Heaven?" (78/Bruns 7984) Cab Calloway Orch, contemp: "Mama, I Wanna Make Rhythm" (78/Variety 644)

370032a Film SWING WHILE YOU'RE ABLE 1937 record by Pinky Tomlin of orig cast. MUSIC & WORDS: Pinky Tomlin, others. "I'm Just a Country Boy at Heart" (78/Bruns 7849)

370033a Film CHAMPAGNE WALTZ 1936 records by Gladys Swarthout of orig cast. "Could I Be in Love?," "Paradise in Waltz Time" (78/Vic 4324)

370034a Film KING SOLOMON'S MINES 1937 records by Paul Robeson of orig cast. "Ho! Ho!," "Climbing Up" (78/HMV(E) B-8586)

370035a Film BIG FELLA 1937 records by members of orig cast. Paul Robeson: "Lazin'," "You Didn't Oughta Do Such Things" (78/HMV(E) B-8607) "Roll Up, Sailorman" (78/HMV(E) B-8591) Elisabeth Welch: "Harlem in My Heart" (LP-582)(LP-712) "One Kiss" (LP-712)

370036a Film JERICHO 1937 records by Paul Robeson of orig cast. "My Way," "Golden River" (78/HMV(E) B-8572) "Deep Desert" (78/HMV(E) B-8621)

370037a Film HIGH, WIDE AND HANDSOME soundtrack. MUSIC: Jerome Kern. WORDS: Oscar Hammerstein II. CAST: Irene Dunne, Dorothy Lamour, William Frawley, chorus. (Titania 506, with Sweet Adeline. Incomplete: LP-335.)

370038a Film THIN ICE soundtrack. Joan Davis: "Olga from the Volga" (LP-350)

370039a Film THE BRIDE WORE RED soundtrack. Joan Crawford: "Who Wants Love?" (LP-401)

370040a Film THE THRILL OF A LIFETIME soundtrack. Betty Grable, Buster Crabbe: "Sweetheart Time" (LP-438)(LP-568) Dorothy Lamour: "The Thrill of a Lifetime" (LP-647)

370041a Film GUNS OF THE PECOS record by Dick Foran of orig cast. "The Prairie Is My Home" (78/Rex(E) 9420)

370042a Film ALI BABA GOES TO TOWN 1937 record by Raymond Scott Orch of orig prod. "Twilight in Turkey" (78/Bruns 7992)

370043a Film TANGO NOTTURNO contemp records by Pola Negri of orig cast. "Kommt das Gluck," "Tango Notturno" (LP-625)

370044a Film THIS WAY PLEASE soundtrack. Betty Grable, Buddy Rogers: "Delighted to Meet You" Grable, chorus: "Is It Love or Infatuation?" (LP-646)

370045a Film MOUNTAIN MUSIC soundtrack. Martha Raye, chorus: "Good Mornin'" (LP-651)

370046a Film HIDEAWAY GIRL soundtrack. Martha Raye: "Beethoven, Mendelssohn and Liszt" (LP-651)

370047a Film NEW FACES OF 1937 1937 record by Harriet Hilliard of orig cast. "Our Penthouse on Third Avenue" (78/Bluebird B-6987)

370048a Film THE LIFE OF THE PARTY 1937 records by Harriet Hilliard of orig cast. "Let's Have Another Cigarette," "Roses in December" (78/Bluebird B-7034)

370049a Film WAY OUT WEST soundtrack. CAST: Stanley Laurel, Oliver Hardy, Rosina Lawrence, Sharon Lynne, Avalon Boys Quartet. "Will Ya Be Ma Lovey-Dovey?," "The Ball at Kokomo," "The Trail of the Lonesome Pine," "Home in Dixieland" (Mark56 Records 688. Excerpts: "The Trail of the Lonesome Pine," "Home in Dixieland" (LP-698).)

370050a Film THE SHOW GOES ON contemp records by Gracie Fields of orig cast. "Smile When You Say Goodbye," "I Never Cried So Much in All My Life" (78/Rex(E) 9095) "We're All Good Pals Together," "The Song in Your Heart" (78/Rex(E) 9096) "My Love for You," "In a Little Lancashire Town" (78/Rex(E) 9097)

370051a Film VOGUES OF 1938 1954 record sung by Sammy Fain, composer. "That Old Feeling" (LP-707)

370052a Film READY, WILLING AND ABLE soundtrack. James Newill (for Ross Alexander), Winifred Shaw, Ruby Keeler, Lee Dixon: "Too Marvelous for Words" (LP-769)

370202a HOME AND BEAUTY contemp records by members of orig (London) cast. Binnie Hale: "A Nice Cup of Tea" (LP-79) Gitta Alpar: "No More" (LP-172)

370414a BABES IN ARMS 1951 studio prod. MUSIC: Richard Rodgers. WORDS: Lorenz Hart. COND: Lehman Engel. CAST: Mary Martin, Mardi Bayne, Jack Cassidy. (Col ML-4488)

370414b BABES IN ARMS 1939 film soundtrack. MUSIC & WORDS: Various. COND: George Stoll. CAST: Judy Garland, Mickey Rooney, Douglas McPhail, Betty Jaynes, with Babes on Broadway. Excerpts: Garland: "I Cried for You" (LP-8)(LP-289)(LP-454) McPhail: "Babes in Arms" (Incomplete: LP-252) Garland, Rooney: "Good Morning" (LP-558)(LP-770) Garland, Rooney, McPhail, Jaynes: "God's Country" (LP-558).)

370414c BABES IN ARMS records by Judy Garland of 1939 film cast. "Broadway Rhythm" (1935: LP-180, LP-718, LP-726) "Figaro" (1939: LP-233, LP-745) "I'm Just Wild about Harry" (1939: 78/Bruns(E) 02969) "I Wish I Were in Love Again"(dropped before release) (1947: LP-217, LP-640) "I Cried for You" Garland, chorus: "God's Country" (1941 radio performances: LP-746)

370414d BABES IN ARMS 1937 records by members of orig prod. Wynn Murray: "Johnny One Note" Ray Heatherton: "Where or When" (78/Vic 25546) Edgar Fairchild & Adam Carroll (pianists): "Johnny One Note/Where or When," "Babes in Arms/I Wish I Were in Love Again," "My Funny Valentine," "All at Once" Fairchild & Carroll with Teddy Lynch (not of orig cast), vocals: "The Lady Is a Tramp," "Way Out West" (LP-545)

370414e BABES IN ARMS 1953 album. COND: Jay Blackton. VOCALS: Lisa Kirk, Bill Tabbert, Sheila Bond. (RCA 10" LPM-3152, with Jumbo)

370414f BABES IN ARMS contemp radio medley by members of orig cast. Wynn Murray: "Way Out West," "Johnny One Note" Ray Heatherton: "Where or When" (LP-217)

370414g BABES IN ARMS 1937 record sung by Harold Arlen, composer, of a song from the 1939 film prod. WORDS: E Y Harburg. "God's Country" (78/Vic 25714)

370623a FLOODLIGHT contemp record by Frances Day & John Mills of orig (London) cast. "A Little White Room" (LP-172)

370901a CREST OF THE WAVE contemp records by members of orig (London) prod. MUSIC: Ivor Novello. WORDS: Christopher Hassall. COND: Charles Prentice. Dorothy Dickson: "If Only You Knew" Dickson, Walter Crisham: "Why Isn't It You?" Edgar Elmes: "Rose of England" Olive Gilbert: "Haven of Your Heart" (LP-342)Orchestra: Selection (78/HMV(E) C-2921)

370916a GOING GREEK 1937 records by Roy Royston & Louise Browne of orig (London) prod. MUSIC & WORDS: Sammy Lerner, Al Goodhart, Al Hoffman. "A Little Cooperation from You," "The Sheep Were in the Meadow" (78/HMV(E) BD-462)

370916b GOING GREEK 1937 medley by Debroy Somers Band with unidentified vocalist. (78/Col(E) DX-790)

371009a THE FIREMAN'S FLAME contemp records by Ben Cutler of orig cast. MUSIC: Richard Lewine. WORDS: Ted Fetter. "I Like the Nose on Your Face," "Do My Eyes Deceive Me?" (78/Liberty Music Shop L-229)

371014a HIDE AND SEEK 1937 records by members of orig (London) cast. MUSIC & WORDS: Vivian Ellis, Sammy Lerner, Al Goodhart, Al Hoffman. Bobby Howes: "She's My Lovely" (LP-83) "Whisper Sweet Nothings/Versatility/I'm Happy When You're Happy" (78/HMV(E) B-8675) Cicely Courtneidge: "Maybelle," "Follow the Bride" (78/HMV(E) B-8674)

371127a PINS AND NEEDLES 1962 studio prod. MUSIC & WORDS: Harold Rome. CAST: Barbra Streisand, Harold Rome, Jack Carroll, Rose Marie Jun, Alan Sokoloff. (Col OS-2210)

371127b PINS AND NEEDLES records by Harold Rome (composer), vocal & piano. "Song of the Ads," "I Wanna Be a G-Man" (Contemp: LP-605) "Sing Me a Song of Social Significance," "One Big Union for Two," "When I Grow Up" (1956: LP-39) "Mene Mene Tekel" (1954: LP-360) (1956: LP-39) "Sunday in the Park" (1954: LP-360) (1956: LP-39, LP-563) "It's Better with a Union Man" (1954: LP-360)

371127c PINS AND NEEDLES contemp records by members of orig prod. Millie Weitz (with Rome & Baldwin Bergerson at pianos): "Nobody Makes a Pass at Me" Ruth Rubinstein (with Rome & Bergerson at pianos): "Chain Store Daisy" The Ensemble: "The Red Mikado"(added April 1939) Clarence Palmer, chorus: "Mene Tekel"(added July 1939) (JJA Records 19783, with additional material; LP-605. Excerpt: Weitz: "Nobody Makes a Pass at Me" (LP-69).)

371127d PINS AND NEEDLES 1966 TV prod soundtrack. VOCALS: Bobby Short, Elaine Stritch, Josephine Premice. (LP-605)

371201a HOORAY FOR WHAT records sung by Harold Arlen, composer. WORDS: E Y Harburg. "In the Shade of the New Apple Tree" (1937: LP-603)(1966: LP-60) "God's Country" (1937: LP-603) "Buds Won't Bud"(dropped from the show), "Moanin' in the Mornin'" (1955: LP-192)

371216a ME AND MY GIRL orig (London) prod rec live in 1938. Lupino Lane, Teddie St Denis: "The Lambeth Walk" (LP-130)

371222a BETWEEN THE DEVIL records by Arthur Schwartz, composer. WORDS: Howard Dietz. "By Myself", composer. (1966, piano: LP-671)(1975, vocal: LP-418) "Triplets" (1975, vocal: LP-418)

371222b BETWEEN THE DEVIL contemp records by the Tune Twisters of orig prod. "I'm Against Rhythm" With Arthur Schwartz (composer), piano: "Triplets" (LP-555)

1938

380001a Film THE GIRL OF THE GOLDEN WEST 1938 records by Nelson Eddy of orig cast. MUSIC: Sigmund Romberg. WORDS: Gus Kahn. COND: Leonard Joy. "Who Are We to Say?" (LP-4) "Sun-Up to Sundown" (78/Vic 4388) "Soldiers of Fortune," "Senorita" (78/Vic 4389)

380002a Film LISTEN DARLING records by Judy Garland of orig cast. "Ten Pins in the Sky" (Contemp: LP-35) "Zing! Went the Strings of My Heart" (1935 radio performance: LP-726, LP-759)(1939: LP-7, LP-490)(Later: LP-188, LP-219, LP-240, LP-461, LP-780)

380003a Film CAREFREE soundtrack. MUSIC & WORDS: Irving Berlin. ORCH & COND: Victor Baravelle. CAST: Fred Astaire, Ginger Rogers. (Classic International Filmusicals 3004, with Flying Down to Rio. Excerpt: Astaire, Rogers: "The Yam" (LP-402).)

380003b Film CAREFREE records by members of orig cast. Fred Astaire: "Change Partners" (1938: LP-23, LP-215, LP-277, LP-593)(1952: LP-50, LP-125, LP-358, LP-648) (1958: LP-338)(1959: LP-108) "I Used to Be Color Blind" (1938: LP-208, LP-215, LP-277)(1952: LP-50, LP-125, LP-552, LP-648) "The Yam," "The Yam Step" (1938: LP-208, LP-215, LP-277) Ginger Rogers: "I Used to Be Color Blind" (1938: LP-129, LP-539)(1978: LP-624) "The Yam" (1938: LP-336)

380004a Film LOVE FINDS ANDY HARDY contemp records by Judy Garland of orig cast. "It Never Rains But What It Pours" (LP-35) "In-Between" (LP-7)(LP-233)(LP-511)

380004b Film LOVE FINDS ANDY HARDY soundtrack. Judy Garland: "Bei Mir Bist Du Schoen" (LP-289) "Easy to Love"(by Cole Porter)(dropped before release) (LP-423) "Meet the Beat of My Heart"(complete version) (LP-486)

380005a Film COWBOY FROM BROOKLYN contemp record by Dick Powell of orig cast. "Ride, Tenderfoot, Ride" (LP-46)(LP-86)(LP-769)

380006a Film JUST AROUND THE CORNER soundtrack. Shirley Temple: "I Love to Walk in the Rain" (LP-47)(LP-179) (LP-225) Temple, Joan Davis, Bert Lahr, Bill Robinson: "A Happy Little Ditty" (LP-116)(LP-179)(LP-225)(LP-608)

380007a Film LITTLE MISS BROADWAY soundtrack. Shirley Temple: "If All the World Were Paper" (LP-47)(LP-225) "Swing Me an Old Fashioned Song" (LP-47)(LP-179) (LP-225) "How Can I Thank You?" (LP-116)(LP-225) "Be Optimistic" (LP-116)(LP-179)(LP-225) "Thank You for the Use of the Hall" (LP-225) Temple, George Murphy: "We Should Be Together" (LP-47)(LP-179)(LP-225)

380008a Film REBECCA OF SUNNYBROOK FARM soundtrack. Shirley Temple: "Come and Get Your Happiness" (LP-47) (LP-179)(LP-225) "An Old Straw Hat," "Happy Ending" (LP-225)

380008b Film REBECCA OF SUNNYBROOK FARM 1937 record by Raymond Scott Orch of orig prod. "The Toy Trumpet" (78/Bruns 7993)

380009a Film ALEXANDER'S RAGTIME BAND soundtrack. MUSIC & WORDS: Irving Berlin. COND: Alfred Newman. CAST: Alice Faye, Ethel Merman, Don Ameche, Jack Haley, Dixie Dunbar, Chick Chandler, Wally Vernon, Donald Douglas, the King's Men. (Hollywood Soundstage 406. Also a number dropped before release: Merman: "Marching Along with Time" (LP-273). Excerpts: Faye: "Now It Can Be Told" (LP-283) "Alexander's Ragtime Band" (LP-558) Faye, Haley, Chandler: "The International Rag" (LP-283) Merman: "Blue Skies," "Pack Up Your Sins and Go to the Devil," "My Walking Stick," "Everybody Step" (LP-334) "Heat Wave" (LP-334)(LP-558) Faye, Ameche: "Remember/The Easter Parade/All Alone" (LP-558).)

380009b Film ALEXANDER'S RAGTIME BAND records by members of orig cast. Alice Faye: "Alexander's Ragtime Band" (1962: LP-100) "Now It Can Be Told" (1938: LP-387, LP-645) Ethel Merman: "How Deep Is the Ocean?" (1932: LP-171, LP-539)(Later: LP-36) "Alexander's Ragtime Band" (Later: LP-36, LP-153, LP-670) "Heat Wave," "My Walking Stick" (1938: LP-387)

380009c Film ALEXANDER'S RAGTIME BAND 1940 radio prod. VOCALS: Alice Faye (of orig cast). (Pelican 132)

380010a Film MAD ABOUT MUSIC contemp records by Deanna Durbin of orig cast. "Ave Maria" (LP-95)

380011a Film THAT CERTAIN AGE contemp records by Deanna Durbin of orig cast. "My Own" (LP-110) "Les Filles de Cadix" (LP-110)(LP-404)(LP-406)

380012a Film THANKS FOR THE MEMORY contemp records by Bob Hope and Shirley Ross of orig cast. "Thanks for the Memory," "Two Sleepy People" (LP-115)

380012b Film THANKS FOR THE MEMORY soundtrack. Bob Hope, Shirley Ross: "Two Sleepy People" (LP-656)

380012c Film THANKS FOR THE MEMORY record by Hoagy Carmichael (composer), vocal. "Two Sleepy People" (LP-750)

380013a Film THE BIG BROADCAST OF 1938 contemp records by members of orig prod. Bob Hope, Shirley Ross: "Thanks for the Memory" (LP-115)(LP-175) Dorothy Lamour: "Thanks for the Memory," "You Took the Words Right Out of My Heart" (LP-271) Shep Fields Orch: "This Little Ripple Had Rhythm," "You Took the Words Right Out of My Heart" (78/Bluebird B-7304) "Thanks for the Memory," "Mama, That Moon Is Here Again" (78/Bluebird B-7318) Martha Raye: "Truckin'" (Contemp radio performance: LP-669, LP-592)

380013b Film THE BIG BROADCAST OF 1938 soundtrack. Shep Fields Orch: "This Little Ripple Had Rhythm" (LP-558) Bob Hope, Shirley Ross: "Thanks for the Memory" (LP-558) (LP-768) Ross, Martha Raye, Robert Cummings: "Two Birdies Up a Tree" Raye: "Truckin'" (LP-651) "Mama, That Moon Is Here Again" Tito Guizar: "Don't Tell a Secret to a Rose" Dorothy Lamour: "You Took the Words Right Out of My Heart" (LP-768)

380014a Film GOLDWYN FOLLIES records by members of orig cast. MUSIC: George Gershwin. WORDS: Ira Gershwin. Kenny Baker: "Love Walked In" (1938: LP-175, LP-537)(1946: 78/Dec 23781) Ella Logan: "I Was Doing All Right," "Love Is Here to Stay" (1937: LP-654)

380014b Film GOLDWYN FOLLIES soundtrack. ORCH: Edward Powell. COND: Alfred Newman. Kenny Baker, Virginia Verrill (for Andrea Leeds): "Love Walked In" Kenny Baker: "Our Love Is Here to Stay" Phil Baker, Edgar Bergen (for Charlie McCarthy): "I Love to Rhyme" Verrill, Kenny Baker, Helen Jepson: "Love Walked In/Finale" (LP-654)

380015a Film GOING PLACES soundtrack. MUSIC: Harry Warren. WORDS: Johnny Mercer. VOCALS: Dick Powell, Louis Armstrong, Maxine Sullivan. (Caliban 6010, with Lady, Be Good!; plus Armstrong, Sullivan, Powell: "Say It with a Kiss" (LP-486). Excerpts: Armstrong: "Jeepers Creepers" (LP-223)(LP-595) Armstrong, Sullivan, Powell: "Mutiny in the Nursery" (LP-633).)

380015b Film GOING PLACES 1938 records by members of orig prod. Louis Armstrong: "Jeepers Creepers" (LP-175) Maxine Sullivan: "Say It with a Kiss" (78/Vic 26124)

380016a Film GARDEN OF THE MOON soundtrack. John Payne, Jerry Colonna: "The Girl Friend of the Whirling Dervish" (LP-223) Payne, Colonna, Ziggy Elman: "The Lady on the 2¢ Stamp" (LP-633)

380017a Film KEEP SMILING contemp records by Gracie Fields of orig cast. "Love Is Everywhere"(with Tommy Fields), "Mrs Binn's Twins" (LP-248) "You've Got to Be Smart in the Army Nowadays," "The Biggest Aspidistra in the World" (78/Regal Zonophone(E) MR-3001) "Giddy-Up," "Swing Your Way to Happiness" (78/Regal Zonophone(E) MR-2950) "Peace of Mind" (78/Regal Zonophone(E) MR-3000)

380018a Film SING YOU SINNERS contemp records by Bing Crosby of orig cast & Johnny Mercer. MUSIC: James V Monaco, Hoagy Carmichael. WORDS: John Burke, Frank Loesser. Crosby: "I've Got a Pocketful of Dreams," "Laugh and Call It Love," "Don't Let That Moon Get Away" Crosby & Mercer: "Small Fry" (Dec 10" 6012, with Paris Honeymoon; LP-254.)

380018b Film SING YOU SINNERS soundtrack. Bing Crosby, Fred MacMurray, Donald O'Connor: "Small Fry" (LP-656)

380018c Film SING YOU SINNERS record by Hoagy Carmichael (composer), vocal. "Small Fry" (LP-750)

380019a Film DOCTOR RHYTHM contemp records by members of orig prod. MUSIC: James V Monaco. WORDS: John Burke. Bing Crosby: "On the Sentimental Side," "My Heart Is Taking Lessons," "This Is My Night to Dream" (Dec 10" 6013, with The Star Maker; LP-264.) Louis Armstrong Orch: "The Trumpet Player's Lament" (78/Dec 1653)

380020a Film BREAKING THE ICE 1938 records by Bobby Breen of orig cast. "Happy as a Lark," "The Sunny Side of Things" (78/Dec 1950) "Put Your Heart in a Song," "Telling My Troubles to a Mule" (78/Dec 1949)

380021a Film HAWAII CALLS soundtrack. Bobby Breen: "Hawaii Calls" (78/Bluebird B-7320) "Down Where the Trade Winds Blow" (78/Bluebird B-7330)

380022a Film START CHEERING 1947 record by Jimmy Durante of orig cast. "I'll Do the Strut-Away in My Cutaway" (LP-142)(LP-454)

380023a Film EVERYBODY SING 1938 records by Allan Jones of orig cast. "The One I Love," "Cosi Cosa" (78/Vic 4381)

380023b Film EVERYBODY SING soundtrack. CAST: Judy Garland, Allan Jones, Reginald Gardiner, Fanny Brice. (Pilgrim 4000, with Pigskin Parade. Excerpt: Garland: "Sweet or Swing" (LP-726).)

380024a Film THE GREAT WALTZ contemp records by Miliza Korjus of orig cast. MUSIC: Johann Strauss II, arranged by Dmitri Tiomkin. WORDS: Oscar Hammerstein II. With Nat W Finston & MGM Orch: "Tales from the Vienna Woods" (LP-529) "There'll Come a Time," "One Day When We Were Young" With European orch, sung in German: "Voices of Spring" (LP-528)

380024b Film THE GREAT WALTZ soundtrack. ORCH & COND: Dmitri Tiomkin. CAST: Miliza Korjus, Fernand Gravet, Christian Rub, George Houston, Al Shean, Curt Bois, Leonid Kinsky, chorus. (Sountrak 109)

380025a Film TROPIC HOLIDAY 1938 records by Dorothy Lamour of orig cast. "On a Tropic Night," "Tonight Will Live" (78/Bruns 8154)

380025b Film TROPIC HOLIDAY soundtrack. Martha Raye: "Havin' Myself a Time" (LP-588) Dorothy Lamour: "Tropic Night" Lamour, chorus: "My First Love" (LP-647)

380026a Film HER JUNGLE LOVE 1938 record by Dorothy Lamour of orig cast. "Lovelight in the Starlight" (78/Bruns 8132)

380026b Film HER JUNGLE LOVE soundtrack. Dorothy Lamour: "Lovelight in the Starlight" (LP-647)

380027a Film SAILING ALONG 1937 records by Jessie Matthews of orig cast. "Trusting My Luck" (LP-320) "My River" (78/Dec(E) F-6672) "Your Heart Skips a Beat," "Souvenir of Love" (78/Dec(E) F-6673)

380028a Film OUTSIDE OF PARADISE 1937 records by Phil Regan of orig cast. "A Sweet Irish Sweetheart of Mine," "Outside of Paradise" (78/Bruns 8051)

380029a Film IN OLD CHICAGO soundtrack. Alice Faye: "In Old Chicago" (LP-283)

380029b Film IN OLD CHICAGO contemp radio performance by Alice Faye of orig cast. "In Old Chicago" (LP-669)

380030a Film BARRICADE soundtrack. Alice Faye: "There'll Be Other Nights"(Dropped before release?) (LP-283)

380031a Film SALLY, IRENE AND MARY soundtrack. Alice Faye: "This Is Where I Came In," "Got My Mind on Music" (LP-283) "Think Twice"(dropped before release) (LP-423) Tony Martin: "Stop Being So Beautiful"(dropped before release) (LP-588)

380031b Film SALLY, IRENE AND MARY contemp radio performance by Alice Faye of orig cast. "Who Stole the Jam?" (LP-669)

380032a Film THE JOY OF LIVING soundtrack. MUSIC: Jerome Kern. WORDS: Dorothy Fields. VOCALS: Irene Dunne. (LP-335)

380033a Film HAPPY LANDING soundtrack. Ethel Merman: "You Are the Music to the Words in My Heart" (dropped before release) (LP-334)(LP-486) "Hot and Happy," "You Appeal to Me" (LP-334)

380034a Film STRAIGHT, PLACE AND SHOW soundtrack. Ethel Merman: "Why Not String Along with Me?" (LP-334) "With You on My Mind" (LP-588)(Incomplete: LP-334)

380035a Film VIVACIOUS LADY soundtrack. Ginger Rogers: "You'll Be Reminded of Me" (LP-402)

380036a Film MANNEQUIN soundtrack. Joan Crawford: "Always and Always" (LP-401)

380037a Film HARD TO GET 1974 record sung by Johnny Mercer, lyricist. MUSIC: Harry Warren. "You Must Have Been a Beautiful Baby" (LP-560)

380038a Film THE COCOANUT GROVE soundtrack. Harriet Hilliard: "Says My Heart" (LP-558)(LP-656)

380038b Film THE COCOANUT GROVE 1938 record by Harriet Hilliard of orig cast. "Says My Heart" (78/Bluebird B-7528)

380039a Film GOLD DIGGERS IN PARIS 1938 records by Rudy Vallee Orch of orig prod. MUSIC: Harry Warren. WORDS: Al Dubin. "The Latin Quarter," "A Stranger in Paree" (78/Vic 25835) "I Wanna Go Back to Bali," "Day Dreaming" (78/Vic 25836)

380039b Film GOLD DIGGERS IN PARIS soundtrack. Rudy Vallee, Rosemary Lane: "Day Dreaming All Night Long" (LP-633)

380040a Film DIE NACHT DER ENTSCHEIDUNG contemp records by Pola Negri of orig cast. "Zeig der Welt," "Siehst du die Sterne" (LP-625)

380041a Film COLLEGE SWING soundtrack. Martha Raye, Bob Hope: "How'dya Like to Love Me?" (LP-651)(LP-656) Gracie Allen: "You're a Natural" (LP-656)

380042a Film GIVE ME A SAILOR soundtrack. Martha Raye: "A Little Kiss at Twilight" (LP-651)(LP-768)

380043a CABARET TAC contemp records by members of orig prod. MUSIC & WORDS: Various. Michael Loring, with Earl Robinson (piano): "Joe Hill"(by Robinson) (78/TAC Records 1) June Havoc, with Albert Arkus (piano): "Swing TAC" Beatrice Kay, with Arkus (piano): "Picket Line Priscilla" (78/TAC Records 2)

380044a Film SWISS MISS soundtrack. Oliver Hardy: "Let Me Call You Sweetheart" (LP-698)

380045a Film ROMANCE IN THE DARK soundtrack. Gladys Swarthout, John Boles: "Tonight We Love" (LP-768)

380103a THE CRADLE WILL ROCK orig prod. MUSIC & WORDS: Marc Blitzstein. NARRATION & PIANO: Marc Blitzstein. CAST: Olive Stanton, Howard Da Silva, Blanche Collins, Edward Fuller, Jules Schmidt, Ralph MacBane, Peggy Coudray, Maynard Holmes, Dulce Fox, Marian Rudley, George Fairchild. (American Legacy T-1001)

380103b THE CRADLE WILL ROCK 1964 prod. ORCH: Marc Blitzstein. COND: Gershon Kingsley. CAST: Jerry Orbach, Lauri Peters, Nancy Andrews, Hal Buckley, Gordon B Clarke, Clifford David, Dean Dittman, Rita Gardner, Micki Grant, Nichols Grimes, Ted Scott, Joseph Bova. (MGM 4289-2)

380105a RIGHT THIS WAY records by Sammy Fain, composer. WORDS: Irving Kahal. "I'll Be Seeing You" (1954, vocal: LP-707)(1971, piano & vocal: LP-694) "I Can Dream, Can't I?" (1954, vocal: LP-707)

380126a 9-SHARP contemp record by Cyril Ritchard, Hermione Baddeley, George Benson, & others of orig (London) prod. Medley: "Pulling Down London," "When Bolonsky Danced Belushka," "Antigua" (LP-172)

380316a OPERETTE contemp records by members of orig (London) prod. MUSIC & WORDS: Noel Coward. COND: Benjamin Frankel. Orchestra: Selection (78/HMV(E) C-2999) Peggy Wood: "Dearest Love," "Where Are the Songs We Sung?" Fritzi Massary: "Countess Mitzi," "Operette" Hugh French, Ross Landon, John Gatrell, Kenneth Carten: "The Stately Homes of England" (LP-174) (LP-308)

380316b OPERETTE 1938 records sung by Noel Coward, composer. "The Stately Homes of England" (LP-11) (LP-218) "Where Are the Songs We Sung?" (LP-218) "Dearest Love" (78/HMV(E) B-8721) (78/HMV(E) B-8740) "Gipsy Melody" (dropped from the show) (LP-174)

380511a I MARRIED AN ANGEL 1942 records by Nelson Eddy of 1942 film cast. MUSIC: Richard Rodgers. WORDS: Lorenz Hart. COND: Robert Armbruster. "Little Work-a-day World" (LP-16) (LP-644) "I Married an Angel" (LP-432) "I'll Tell the Man in the Street," "Spring Is Here" (78/Col 4295-M)

380511b I MARRIED AN ANGEL 1942 radio prod with members of 1942 film cast. CAST: Jeanette MacDonald, Nelson Eddy, Binnie Barnes, Edward Everett Horton. (Pelican 103, with the New Moon)

380511c I MARRIED AN ANGEL contemp records by Audrey Christie of orig prod. "At the Roxy Music Hall," "How to Win Friends and Influence People" (LP-217)

380511d I MARRIED AN ANGEL 1975 record by Phyllis Newman of 1977 Stockbridge (Mass) prod. "A Twinkle in Your Eye" (LP-510)

380511e I MARRIED AN ANGEL 1942 film soundtrack. VOCALS: Jeanette MacDonald, Nelson Eddy, Binnie Barnes, chorus. (Caliban 6004, with Balalaika)

380608a NO SKY SO BLUE 1938 records by Gertrude Niesen of orig (London) cast. MUSIC: Edward Horan. WORDS: Ian Grant. "Rhythm Is My Romeo," "What Is Romance?" (78/Col(E) DB-1779) "In Paree It's Love" (78/Col(E) DB-1780)

380609a THE SUN NEVER SETS 1938 records by Todd Duncan of orig (London) cast. "River God" (by Cole Porter) (LP-300) "Drums" (78/Col(E) DB-1778)

380710a Radio show A TRIBUTE TO GEORGE GERSHWIN soundtrack. MUSIC: George Gershwin. WORDS: mostly Ira Gershwin. COND: Paul Whiteman. PIANOS: Roy Bargy, Walter Gross. VOCALS: Maxine Sullivan, the Modernaires, Lyn Murray Chorus. (Mark56 Records 761)

380803a Radio show AN IRVING BERLIN TRIBUTE soundtrack. MUSIC & WORDS: Irving Berlin, VOCALS: Al Jolson, Ethel Merman, Eddie Cantor, Alice Faye, Irving Berlin, Brox Sisters, John Steel, Sophie Tucker, Lew Lehr, Rudy Vallee, Connie Boswell. (Famous Personality 1001) (LP-387)

380817a THE FLEET'S LIT UP 1938 records by members of orig (London) prod. Frances Day: "It's De-lovely" (by Cole Porter) (LP-300) Orchestra: Medley (78/HMV(E) C-3028)

380924a SING OUT THE NEWS records by Harold Rome, vocal & piano. MUSIC & WORDS: Harold Rome. "PLaza 6-9423" (1938; LP-321) "Yip-Ahoy" (1938: 78/Dec 23078) "F.D.R. Jones, " "One of These Fine Days" (1954: LP-360)(1956: LP-39) "My Heart Is Unemployed" (1956: LP-39)

381007a BOBBY, GET YOUR GUN 1938 record by Gertrude Niesen of orig (London) prod. "La Conga" (78/Col(E) DB-1824)

381019a KNICKERBOCKER HOLIDAY records by Walter Huston of orig cast. MUSIC: Kurt Weill. WORDS: Maxwell Anderson. "September Song"(1938: LP-19)(1944: LP-69, LP-114, LP-164, LP-176) "The Scars" (1938: 78/Bruns 8272)

381019b KNICKERBOCKER HOLIDAY contemp radio prod, CAST: Walter Huston, Jeanne Madden, Richard Kollmar, Ray Middleton, others. (Joey 7243. Excerpts: Huston: "One Touch of Alchemy/All Hail the Political Honeymoon, " "The Scars" (LP-311)

381019c KNICKERBOCKER HOLIDAY contemp radio performance (on "The Fleischmann Hour") by members of orig prod. COND: Maurice d'Abravanel. Walter Huston, Jeanne Madden, chorus: Scene, incl "The Maidens Scrub," "To War!," "September Song" (LP-332)

381019d KNICKERBOCKER HOLIDAY later record by Burl Ives of 1950 touring company. "September Song" (LP-573)

381109a LEAVE IT TO ME records by Mary Martin of orig cast. MUSIC & WORDS: Cole Porter. "Most Gentlemen Don't Like Love" (1938: LP-43, LP-160, LP-642, LP-681) "My Heart Belongs to Daddy" (1938: LP-160, LP-322, LP-619, LP-681) (1940: LP-67, LP-69, LP-109, LP-164, LP-176) (Later: LP-351, LP-652, 45/RCA 47-6694)

381123a THE BOYS FROM SYRACUSE 1963 prod. MUSIC: Richard Rodgers. WORDS: Lorenz Hart. ORCH: Larry Wilcox. COND: Rene Wiegert. CAST: Ellen Hanley, Danny Carroll, Cathryn Damon, Stuart Damon, Clifford David, Julienne Marie, Karen Morrow, Rudy Tronto, Matthew Tobin. (Cap STAO-1933)

381123b THE BOYS FROM SYRACUSE 1953 studio prod. COND:

Lehman Engel. CAST: Portia Nelson, Jack Cassidy, Stanley Prager, Bibi Osterwald, Holly Harris, Bob Shaver. (Col ML-4837)

381123c THE BOYS FROM SYRACUSE records by Allan Jones of 1940 film cast. "Falling in Love with Love" (1940: LP-126)(1951: LP-388) "Who Are You?" (1940: 78/Vic 4525)(1951: LP-388)

381123d THE BOYS FROM SYRACUSE 1938 album by Frances Langford and Rudy Vallee. COND: Harry Sosnik. (78/Dec album 33)

381123e THE BOYS FROM SYRACUSE 1963 London prod. ORCH: Ralph Burns. COND: Robert Lowe. CAST: Bob Monkhouse, Ronnie Corbett, Maggie Fitzgibbon, Denis Quilley, John Adams, John Moore, Lynn Kennington, Pat Turner, Paula Hendrix. (Dec(E) SKL-4564)

381123f THE BOYS FROM SYRACUSE 1940 film soundtrack. Martha Raye: "The Greeks Have No Word for It"(added to film by Rodgers/Hart), "Sing for Your Supper" Raye, Joe Penner: "He and She" (LP-651)

1939

390001a Film THE WIZARD OF OZ soundtrack. MUSIC: Harold Arlen. WORDS: E Y Harburg. COND: Herbert Stothart, George Stoll. CAST: Judy Garland, Ray Bolger, Bert Lahr, Jack Haley, Frank Morgan, Billie Burke, Margaret Hamilton. (MGM 3996. Excerpt: Garland: "Over the Rainbow" (LP-8)(LP-252)(LP-289

390001b Film THE WIZARD OF OZ 1939 studio prod. COND: Victor Young. CAST: Judy Garland of orig cast; uncredited soloists, chorus. (Dec 10" 5152. Excerpt: Garland: "Over the Rainbow" (LP-7)(LP-175)(LP-511).)

390001c Film THE WIZARD OF OZ records sung by Harold Arlen, composer. 1955: "Over the Rainbow" (LP-101) 1966,with Barbra Streisand: "Ding-Dong! The Witch Is Dead" (LP-60)

390001d Film THE WIZARD OF OZ records by Judy Garland of orig cast. "Over the Rainbow" (1939, with Harold Arlen (composer), piano: LP-180, LP-718, LP-726)(Later: LP-188, LP-189, LP-205, LP-219, LP-240, LP-329, LP-461, LP-525, 78/V-Disc 335, LP-547, LP-735, LP-762)

390001e Film THE WIZARD OF OZ 1969 studio prod. ORCH & COND: Marty Gold. VOCALS: chorus. (Camden 1109)

390001f Film THE WIZARD OF OZ studio prod. COND: Joel Herron. VOCALS: Lee Forester, chorus. (78/MGM album L-9)

390001g Film THE WIZARD OF OZ 1950 radio prod. COND: Rudy Schrager. CAST: Judy Garland, unidentified soloists, chorus. (Radiola MR-1109)

390001h Film THE WIZARD OF OZ 1957 studio prod. COND: Mitch Miller. NARRATOR: Art Carney. VOCALS: Anne Lloyd, Dick Byron, Bob Miller, Ralph Nyland, chorus. (Golden A-198-13, with Peter and the Wolf)

390002a Film FIRST LOVE contemp records by Deanna Durbin of orig cast. "Spring in My Heart," "Home, Sweet Home" (LP-13)(LP-95) "Amapola" (LP-91)(LP-406) "One Fine Day" (LP-95)

390002b Film FIRST LOVE soundtrack. Deanna Durbin: "Spring in My Heart" (LP-256)

390003a Film THREE SMART GIRLS GROW UP contemp records by Deanna Durbin of orig cast. "The Last Rose of Summer" (LP-13)(LP-95)(LP-404) "Because" (LP-95)(LP-406)

390004a Film DESTRY RIDES AGAIN records by Marlene Dietrich of orig cast. MUSIC: Frederick Hollander. WORDS: Frank Loesser. "You've Got That Look" (1939: LP-54) "The Boys in the Back Room" (1939: LP-54, LP-521)(Later: LP-151, LP-178)(LP-705)

390004b Film DESTRY RIDES AGAIN soundtrack. Marlene Dietrich, chorus: "Li'l Joe the Wrangler" (LP-656)

390005a Film ROSE OF WASHINGTON SQUARE soundtrack. MUSIC & WORDS: Various. ORCH & COND: Louis Silvers. CAST: Alice Faye, Tyrone Power, Al Jolson, Louis Prima Orch. (Caliban 6002, with Footlight Serenade; plus Faye: "I'll See You in My Dreams"(dropped before release) (LP-486). Excerpt: Faye: "My Man" (LP-283).)

390005b Film ROSE OF WASHINGTON SQUARE later records by members of orig cast. Alice Faye: "Rose of Washington Square" (LP-100)(LP-717) Al Jolson: "California, Here I Come" (LP-145)(LP-243)(LP-682)(LP-739) "My Mammy" (LP-145) (LP-244)(LP-677)(LP-682)(LP-739) "Rock-a-bye Your Baby" (LP-145)(LP-244)(LP-331)(LP-394)(LP-478)(LP-739) "Toot, Toot, Tootsie" (LP-198)(LP-244)(LP-394)(LP-409)(LP-438, with Eddie Cantor)(LP-677)(LP-682)(LP-739) "I'm Just Wild about Harry," "Pretty Baby" (LP-197)(LP-244)(LP-739)

390006a Film THE UNDERPUP 1939 records by Gloria Jean of orig cast. "Annie Laurie," "Penguin Song," "I'm Like a Bird" (LP-234)

390007a Film SHIPYARD SALLY soundtrack. Gracie Fields: "Danny Boy," "Grandfather's Bagpipes/Annie Laurie," "Wish Me Luck as You Wave Me Goodbye" (LP-248) "I've Got the Jitterbugs" (78/Vic 26507)

390007b Film SHIPYARD SALLY 1935 record by Gracie Fields of orig cast. "Grandfather's Bagpipes" (78/Rex 8617)

390008a Film IDIOT'S DELIGHT soundtrack. Clark Gable: "Putting on the Ritz" (LP-252)

390009a Film THE EAST SIDE OF HEAVEN contemp records by Bing Crosby of orig cast. MUSIC: James V Monaco. WORDS: John Burke. "East Side of Heaven," "That Sly Old Gentleman," "Hang Your Heart on a Hickory Limb," "Sing a Song of Sunbeams" (Dec 10" 6014, with Rhythm on the River; LP-264.)

390010a Film PARIS HONEYMOON contemp records by Bing Crosby of orig cast. MUSIC & WORDS: Ralph Rainger, Leo Robin, others. "The Funny Old Hills," "I Have Eyes," "Joobalai," "You're a Sweet Little Headache," "I Ain't Got Nobody" (LP-264. Incomplete: Dec 10" 6012, with Sing You Sinners.)

390010b Film PARIS HONEYMOON soundtrack. Shirley Ross, Bing Crosby: "I Have Eyes" Crosby: "You're a Sweet Little Headache" (LP-768)

390011a Film THE STAR MAKER contemp records by Bing Crosby of orig cast & Connie Boswell. MUSIC & WORDS: James V Monaco, John Burke, Gus Edwards, others. Crosby: "A Man and His Dream," "Medley of Gus Edwards Song Hits," "Still the Bluebird Sings," "Go Fly a Kite" Crosby & Boswell: "An Apple for the Teacher" (Dec 10" 6013, with Doctor Rhythm; LP-262.) Crosby: "In My Merry Oldsmobile" (LP-262)

390012a Film MAN ABOUT TOWN 1939 records by Dorothy Lamour of orig cast. "Strange Enchantment," "That Sentimental Sandwich" (LP-271)

390012b Film MAN ABOUT TOWN soundtrack. Betty Grable: "Fidgety Joe" (LP-284)(LP-646)

390013a Film AT THE CIRCUS 1939 record by Kenny Baker of orig cast. MUSIC: Harold Arlen. WORDS: E Y Harburg. "Two Blind Loves" (78/Vic 26413)

390013b Film AT THE CIRCUS soundtrack. Kenny Baker, Florence Rice: "Two Blind Loves" Groucho Marx:"Lydia the Tattooed Lady" (LP-657)

390014a Film FISHERMAN'S WHARF 1939 records by Bobby Breen of orig cast. "Blue Italian Waters," "Fisherman's Chantie" (78/Dec 2353)

390015a Film SECOND FIDDLE 1939 records by members of orig cast. MUSIC & WORDS: Irving Berlin. Rudy Vallee: "When Winter Comes," "I Poured My Heart into a Song" (LP-336) "I'm Sorry for Myself," "An Old-Fashioned Song Always Is New" (78/Dec 2552) Mary Healy: "I Poured My Heart into a Song" (78/Bruns 8436) "When Winter Comes" (78/Bruns 8437) "The Song of the Metronome," "I'm Sorry for Myself" (LP-336)

390016a Film LET FREEDOM RING 1935 record by Nelson Eddy of orig cast. "Dusty Road" (78/Vic 4313)

390016b Film LET FREEDOM RING soundtrack. Nelson Eddy: "Love Serenade," "Pat Sez He," "Dusty Road," "Where Else but Here" (LP-499)

390017a Film BALALAIKA soundtrack. MUSIC & WORDS: Sigmund Romberg, Gus Kahn, Robert Wright, George Forrest, Herbert Stothart, others. VOCALS: Nelson Eddy, Ilona Massey. (Caliban 6004, with I Married an Angel.)

390017b Film BALALAIKA 1939 records by Nelson Eddy of orig cast. COND: Nathaniel Finston. "Ride, Cossack, Ride" (78/Col 17172-D) "At the Balalaika," "Song of the Volga Boatmen" (LP-432) "The Magic of Your Love" (78/Col 17173-D)

390018a Film THE GREAT VICTOR HERBERT records by Allan Jones of orig cast. MUSIC: Victor Herbert. WORDS: Various. "Someday" (1939: 78/Vic 4447) "Thine Alone," "I'm Falling in Love with Someone" (1939:78/Vic 4446) (1951: LP-388)

390019a Film ST. LOUIS BLUES soundtrack. MUSIC & WORDS: Burton Lane, Frank Loesser, others. CAST: Dorothy Lamour, Maxine Sullivan, Tito Guizar, Lloyd Nolan, the King's Men, Matty Malneck Orch. (Caliban 6014, with Dames. Excerpts: Lamour: "I Go for That," "Blue Nightfall" (LP-647).)

390019b Film ST. LOUIS BLUES records by members of orig cast. Dorothy Lamour, 1938: "I Go for That," "Let's Dream in the Moonlight" (78/Bruns 8291) "Junior," "Kinda Lonesome" (78/Bruns 8304) Maxine Sullivan: "Kinda Lonesome" (1938: 78/Vic 26124) "St Louis Blues" (1938: 78/Vic 25895)(1940: 78/Col 36341)(1941: 78/Dec 4154) "Loch Lomond" (1937: 78/Okeh 3654)(1941: 78/Dec 3954)

390020a Film NAUGHTY BUT NICE 1939 record by Dick Powell of orig cast. "In a Moment of Weakness" (78/ Dec 2387)

390021a Film SOME LIKE IT HOT 1939 records by members of orig prod. MUSIC: Burton Lane. WORDS: Frank Loesser. Bob Hope & Shirley Ross: "The Lady's in Love with You" (78/Dec 2568) Gene Krupa Orch: "The Lady's in Love with You," "Some Like It Hot" (78/Bruns 8340)

390021b Film SOME LIKE IT HOT soundtrack. Shirley Ross, Gene Krupa Orch: "Some Like It Hot" Ross, Bob Hope, Gene Krupa Orch: "The Lady's in Love with You" (LP-656)

390022a Film TAIL SPIN soundtrack. Alice Faye:"Are You in the Mood for Mischief?" (LP-283) Faye, chorus: "Go In and Out the Window" (LP-588)

390023a Film SHE MARRIED A COP 1939 record by Phil Regan of orig cast. "I'll Remember" (78/Dec 2666)

390024a Film FLIGHT AT MIDNIGHT 1939 record by Phil Regan of orig cast. "I Never Thought I'd Fall in Love Again" (78/Dec 2666)

390025a Film ICE FOLLIES OF 1939 1939 record by Joan Crawford of orig cast. "It's All So New to Me" (LP-350) (LP-401)(LP-532)

390026a Film THE GRACIE ALLEN MURDER CASE soundtrack. Gracie Allen: "Snug as a Bug in a Rug" (LP-350)(LP-656)

390027a Film SWANEE RIVER 1950 records by Al Jolson of orig cast. "Old Black Joe," "My Old Kentucky Home," "Beautiful Dreamer," "Old Folks at Home," "Jeanie with the Light Brown Hair," "Oh, Susannah!," "De Camptown Races" (LP-372)(LP-382)

390027b Film SWANEE RIVER 1945 radio prod. CAST: Al Jolson of orig cast; Dennis Morgan, Frances Gifford, chorus. (Totem 1028)(LP-679)

390028a Film PIEGES 1939 records by Maurice Chevalier of orig cast. "Mon Amour," "Il Pleurait" (78/HMV(E) JO-13)

390029a Film HONOLULU soundtrack. Gracie Allen, the Pied Pipers: "Honolulu" (LP-558)

390030a Film DANCING CO-ED 1938 record by Artie Shaw Orch of orig prod. "Jungle Drums" (78/Bluebird B-10091)

390031a Film THAT'S RIGHT, YOU'RE WRONG 1939 records by Kay Kyser Orch of orig prod. "The Little Red Fox," "Fit to Be Tied" (78/Col 35295) "Chatterbox" (78/Col 35307) "Happy Birthday to Love," "The Answer Is Love" (78/Col 35238)

390032a Film NEVER SAY DIE soundtrack. Martha Raye: "The Tra-la-la and Oom-pah-pah" (LP-651)

390033a Film $1000 A TOUCHDOWN soundtrack. Martha Raye: "Love with a Capital 'U'" (LP-651)(LP-768)

390034a Film THE STORY OF VERNON AND IRENE CASTLE soundtrack. MUSIC & WORDS: Various. ORCH & COND: Constantin Bakaleinikoff. VOCALS: Fred Astaire, chorus. (Caliban 6000, with Daddy Long Legs)

390103a MAMBA'S DAUGHTERS contemp record by Ethel Waters of orig cast. MUSIC: Jerome Kern. WORDS: DuBose Heyward. "Lonesome Walls" (78/Bluebird B-10022)

390118a SET TO MUSIC records by members of orig cast. MUSIC & WORDS: Noel Coward. Beatrice Lillie: "Mad about the Boy" (1939: LP-112, LP-121, LP-715, LP-729, LP-758) "Three Whiteee Feathers," "Weary of It All," "I Went to a Marvelous Party" (1939: LP-112, LP-121, LP-715, LP-729) "Weary of It All" (1955: LP-449, LP-680) "The Party's Over Now" (1955: LP-449, LP-680)(1958: LP-450) Richard Haydn (monologue), 1939: "Fish Mimicry" (78/Liberty Music Shop L-285)

390118b SET TO MUSIC records sung by Noel Coward, composer. "The Stately Homes of England" (1938: LP-11, LP-218) "The Party's Over Now" (1932: LP-218, LP-502) (1955: LP-89)(1956: LP-89) "I Went to a Marvelous Party" (1956: LP-89) "Never Again" (1945: LP-502)

390120a MAGYAR MELODY records by Binnie Hale of orig (London) cast. MUSIC: Eric Maschwitz. WORDS: George Posford. "Music for Romance," "Mine Alone" (LP-79)

390209a STARS IN YOUR EYES 1939 album by Ethel Merman of orig prod. MUSIC: Arthur Schwartz. WORDS: Dorothy Fields. COND: Al Goodman of orig prod. "This Is It," "I'll Pay the Check," "Just a Little Bit More," "A Lady Needs a Change" (78/Liberty Music Shop album 255/257, with two dance medleys of songs from the show; LP-3; LP-555.)

390209b STARS IN YOUR EYES later records by members of orig cast. Ethel Merman: "This Is It" (1955: LP-36) (1961: LP-45)(1962: LP-251) "I'll Pay the Check" (1955: LP-36) Dan Dailey: "It's All Yours" (1957: LP-367)

390209c STARS IN YOUR EYES 1935 record by Arthur Schwartz (composer), piano. "I'll Pay the Check"(entitled "Dangerous You") (LP-589)

390323a THE DANCING YEARS orig (London) prod. MUSIC: Ivor Novello. WORDS: Christopher Hassall. ORCH: Charles Prentice. COND: Charles Prentice, Ivor Novello. PIANO: Ivor Novello. CAST: Mary Ellis, Olive Gilbert, Dunstan Hart, Roma Beaumont, Ivor Novello. (HMV(E) 10" DLP-1028; LP-309. Plus orch medley (78/HMV(E) C-3097) & Dickson/ Novello: "Used to You"(dropped from the show) (LP-524).)

390323b THE DANCING YEARS 1968 studio prod. COND: Robert Probst. CAST: June Bronhill & David Knight of 1968 London prod; Moyna Cope, Enrico Giacomini, chorus. (RCA(E) SF-7958)

390323c THE DANCING YEARS 1968 studio prod. COND: Cyril Ornadel, Geoff Love. CAST: Anne Rogers, Ann Howard, Andy Cole, Cheryl Kennedy. (Col(E) TWO-188)

390323d THE DANCING YEARS 1962 studio prod. ORCH: Bobby Richards. COND: Jan Cervenka. VOCALS: Norma Hughes, Andrew Gold, Pamela Woolmore, chorus. (Music for Pleasure(E) 1097, with King's Rhapsody)

390323e THE DANCING YEARS 1950 film soundtrack. Giselle Preville: "Waltz of My Heart," "I Can Give You the Starlight" (78/HMV(E) B-9966)

390323f THE DANCING YEARS orig prod rec live. Mary Ellis & Olive Gilbert: "Wings of Sleep" (LP-524)

390424a SING FOR YOUR SUPPER 1940 studio prod of "Ballad of Uncle Sam," with Paul Robeson & American People's Chorus of 1939 radio prod (entitled "Ballad for Americans"). MUSIC: Earl Robinson. WORDS: John Latouche. COND: Nathaniel Shilkret. CHORAL COND: Earl Robinson (composer). (RCA AVM1-1736, with I Hear America Singing)

390424b SING FOR YOUR SUPPER 1940 studio prod of "Ballad of Uncle Sam." COND: Victor Young. VOCALS: Bing Crosby, chorus. (LP-425)

390424c SING FOR YOUR SUPPER 1944 studio prod of "Ballad of Uncle Sam." Arranged by the composer for chorus a capella. COND: John Finley Williamson. VOCALS: John G Baumgartner, the Westminster Choir. (78/Col album C-49, entitled "Ballad for Americans")

390424d SING FOR YOUR SUPPER 1976 studio prod of "Ballad of Uncle Sam." ORCH: Luther Henderson. COND: Leonard dePaur. VOCALS: Brock Peters, chorus. (United Artists LP-604 entitled "Ballad for Americans," with The Lonesome Train)

390619a THE STREETS OF PARIS records by members of orig prod. Carmen Miranda & Bando da Lua, 1939: "South American Way" (LP-109)(LP-147)(LP-166)(LP-302)(LP-518) (LP-522) "Mama eu Quero" (LP-147)(LP-166)(LP-220)(LP-522) "Touradas em Madrid" (LP-220)(LP-302)(LP-522) "Que e que a Bahiana Tem?" (LP-220) "Co, Co, Co, Co, Co, Co, Ro," "Bambu-Bambu" (LP-220)(LP-522) Miranda, earlier, with Dorival Caymmi (composer): "Que e que a Bahiana Tem?" (78/Dec 23095) Jean Sablon, 1939: "Rendezvous Time in Paree," "We Can Live on Love" (78/Vic 26269) "Is It Possible?" (78/Vic 26286) "South American Way" (LP-596) Hylton Sisters, contemp: "Three Little Maids" (78/Varsity 8071)

390619b THE STREETS OF PARIS contemp radio performance by Carmen Miranda of orig cast. "Mama eu Quero" (LP-311)

390706a YOKEL BOY 1939 record by Judy Canova of orig cast. MUSIC: Sam Stept. WORDS: Lew Brown, Charles Tobias. "Time for Jukin'" (78/Varsity 8094)

390828a GEORGE WHITE'S SCANDALS OF 1939 1939 records by Ella Logan of orig cast. MUSIC: Sammy Fain. WORDS: Jack Yellen, Herb Magidson. "Something I Dreamed Last Night" (LP-43)(LP-322)(LP-642) "Are You Havin' Any Fun?" (LP-518) "Waikiki," "Goodnight, My Beautiful" (78/Col 35243)

390929a THE STRAW HAT REVUE records by members of orig prod. Danny Kaye: "Anatole of Paris" (1942: LP-70, LP-107, LP-518)(1952: LP-6, LP-515) James Shelton (composer & member of cast): "Four Young People," "Our Town" (78/Royale 1782)

391011a THE LITTLE DOG LAUGHED 1939 records by Bud Flanagan & Chesney Allen of orig (London) prod, "F D R Jones" (78/Dec(E) F-7297) "Are You Havin' Any Fun?" (78/Dec(E) F-7343)

391018a TOO MANY GIRLS contemp records by members of orig cast. MUSIC: Richard Rodgers. WORDS: Lorenz Hart. Mary Jane Walsh: "Give It Back to the Indians," "I Didn't Know What Time It Was," "I Like to Recognize the Tune," "Love Never Went to College" Diosa Costello: "She Could Shake the Maracas," "Spic and Spanish" (LP-217)

391018b TOO MANY GIRLS 1940 record by Frances Langford of 1940 film cast. "You're Nearer" (LP-217)

391018c TOO MANY GIRLS 1977 studio prod. ORCH: Dennis Deal. CAST: Anthony Perkins, Estelle Parsons, Nancy Andrews, Johnny Desmond, Nancy Grennan, Jerry Wyatt. (Painted Smiles 1368)

391114a BLACK VELVET contemp records by Pat Kirkwood of orig (London) cast. MUSIC & WORDS: Cole Porter. "Most Gentlemen Don't Like Love" (LP-172) (LP-300) "My Heart Belongs to Daddy" (LP-300)

391129a SWINGIN' THE DREAM records by members of orig prod. MUSIC: James Van Heusen. WORDS: Eddie De Lange. Benny Goodman Quintet, 1938. "Pick-a-Rib" (2 sides) (78/Vic 26166) Benny Goodman Orch, 1939: "Darn That Dream," "Peace, Brother!" (78/Col 35331) "Jumpin' at the Woodside" (78/Col 35210) "Spring Song" (78/Col 35319) Benny Goodman Sextet: "Flying Home" (78/Col 35254)

391206a DUBARRY WAS A LADY records by Ethel Merman of orig cast. MUSIC & WORDS: Cole Porter. "Do I Love You?," "Friendship" (LP-36)(LP-45)

391206b DUBARRY WAS A LADY broadcast performances by members of orig cast. Ethel Merman, Bert Lahr: "Friendship" (Radio, contemp: LP-311, LP-295)(TV, 1954: LP-407) Lahr, chorus: "Friendship" (TV: LP-608)

391206c DUBARRY WAS A LADY 1941 records by members of 1942 London prod. Frances Day, Bud Flanagan: "But in the Morning, No!" (78/Dec(E) F-7951) Day: "Do I Love You?" (78/Dec(E) F-7867)

391206d DUBARRY WAS A LADY soundtrack of 1943 film, with additional material by Burton Lane, Ralph Freed, E Y Harburg, Lew Brown, Roger Edens. ORCH & COND: George Stoll, Roger Edens. CAST: Gene Kelly, Martha Mears (for Lucille Ball), Red Skelton, Virginia O'Brien, Dick Haymes, Jo Stafford, Pied Pipers, Tommy Dorsey Orch. (Titania 509, with Can't Help Singing. Excerpts: Kelly: "Do I Love You?" Skelton, Mears, O'Brien, Tommy Dorsey Orch: "Friendship" Stafford, Haymes, Pied Pipers, Tommy Dorsey Orch: "Katie Went to Haiti" (LP-655) O'Brien: "Salome" (LP-496).)

391206e DUBARRY WAS A LADY contemp record by members of 1943 film prod. Lucille Ball, Red Skelton, Gene Kelly, Virginia O'Brien, Tommy Dorsey Orch: "Friendship" (78/V-Disc 172)

391221a SHEPHARD'S PIE contemp record by Arthur Riscoe of orig (London) prod. "Goodbye Sally" (LP-172)

1940

400001a Film PINOCCHIO soundtrack. MUSIC: Leigh Harline. WORDS: Ned Washington. COND: .Leigh Harline, Paul Smith. CAST: Dickie Jones, Cliff Edwards, Walter Catlett, Christian Rub. (Disneyland 4002)(Edited medley: LP-661)

400001b Film PINOCCHIO 1940 studio prod. COND: Victor Young. CAST: Cliff Edwards of orig cast; Julietta Novis, Harry Stanton, chorus. (Dec 10" 5151)

400002a Film ANDY HARDY MEETS DEBUTANTE records by Judy Garland of orig cast. "I'm Nobody's Baby" (1940: LP-7)(1963: LP-

390, LP-762) Dropped before release: "Buds Won't Bud" (1940: LP-35)

400002b Film ANDY HARDY MEETS DEBUTANTE soundtrack. Judy Garland: "I'm Nobody's Baby" (LP-289)

400003a Film STRIKE UP THE BAND soundtrack. MUSIC & WORDS: Roger Edens, Arthur Freed, George Gershwin, Ira Gershwin. COND: George Stoll, Paul Whiteman. CAST: Mickey Rooney, Judy Garland, chorus. (Curtain Calls 100/9-10, with Girl Crazy. Excerpts: Garland: "I Ain't Got Nobody," "Drummer Boy" (LP-726) Chorus: "Strike Up the Band" (LP-252).)

400003b Film STRIKE UP THE BAND records by members of orig cast. Judy Garland: "Our Love Affair" (1940: LP-7) (1940 radio performance: LP-746) "Nobody" (1940: LP-180, LP-718) Garland, Mickey Rooney: "Our Love Affair" (1958: LP-669)

400004a Film LITTLE NELLIE KELLY soundtrack. MUSIC & WORDS: Various. CAST: Judy Garland, chorus. (Cheerio 5000, with Thousands Cheer, plus Garland: "Danny Boy" (LP-289). Excerpt: "Singin' in the Rain" (LP-8)(LP-252) (LP-289)(LP-558).)

400004b Film LITTLE NELLIE KELLY records by Judy Garland of orig cast. "A Pretty Girl Milking Her Cow" (Contemp: LP-7)(Later: LP-180, LP-201, LP-219, LP-329, LP-461) "It's a Great Day for the Irish" (Contemp: LP-35)(Later: LP-219, LP-547, LP-781)

400005a Film SPRING PARADE soundtrack. MUSIC & WORDS: Various. ORCH & COND: Charles Previn. VOCALS: Deanna Durbin, Robert Cummings, chorus. (Caliban 6005, with Hello, 'Frisco, Hello)

400005b Film SPRING PARADE contemp records by Deanna Durbin of orig cast. COND: Charles Previn (of orig prod). "Waltzing in the Clouds" (LP-13)(LP-131) "When April Sings" (LP-129)(LP-131)(LP-406) "It's Foolish but It's Fun" (LP-131) "Blue Danube Dream" (LP-406)

400006a Film FORTY LITTLE MOTHERS 1940 record by Eddie Cantor of orig cast. "Little Curly Hair in a High Chair" (LP-19)(LP-41)(LP-42)(LP-494)

400007a Film SECOND CHORUS soundtrack. MUSIC & WORDS: Johnny Mercer, others. CAST: Fred Astaire, Paulette Goddard, Artie Shaw Orch. (Hollywood Soundstage 404)

400007b Film SECOND CHORUS contemp records by members of orig prod. Fred Astaire: "Dig It" (LP-23)(LP-277) "Love of My Life," "Me and the Ghost Upstairs," "Poor Mr Chisholm" (LP-208)(LP-277) Artie Shaw Orch: "Concerto for Clarinet" (78/Vic 36383) "Love of My Life" (78/Vic 26790)

400008a Film IT'S A DATE contemp records by Deanna Durbin of orig cast. "Ave Maria," "Loch Lomond," "Love Is All" (LP-91) "Musetta's Waltz Song" (LP-91)(LP-404)(LP-406)

400009a Film DOWN ARGENTINE WAY soundtrack. MUSIC & WORDS: mostly Harry Warren, Mack Gordon. ORCH & COND: Emil Newman. CAST: Betty Grable, Don Ameche, Carmen Miranda, Charlotte Greenwood, Six Hits and a Miss, Nicholas Brothers. (Caliban 6003, with Tin Pan Alley. Excerpt: Grable, Ameche: "Two Dreams Met" (LP-633).)

400009b Film DOWN ARGENTINE WAY contemp radio performance by Carmen Miranda of orig cast. "Mama eu Quero" (LP-311)

400009c Film DOWN ARGENTINE WAY 1939 records by Carmen Miranda of orig cast. "South American Way" (LP-109) (LP-147)(LP-166)(LP-302)(LP-522) "Mama eu Quero" (LP-147)(LP-166)(LP-220)(LP-522)

400010a Film YOUNG PEOPLE soundtrack. Shirley Temple "Fifth Avenue," "Young People" (LP-225) Temple, Jack Oakie, Charlotte

Greenwood: "Tra-la-la-la" (LP-116) (LP-179)(LP-225) "I Wouldn't Take a Million" (LP-633)

400011a Film THE BLUEBIRD soundtrack. Shirley Temple: "Lay-de-o" (LP-116)(LP-179)(LP-225)

400012a Film BROADWAY MELODY OF 1940 1952 records by Fred Astaire of orig cast. MUSIC & WORDS: Cole Porter. "I Concentrate on You" (LP-125)(LP-552)(LP-648) "I've Got My Eyes on You" (LP-348)(LP-358)(LP-648)

400012b Film BROADWAY MELODY OF 1940 soundtrack. COND: Alfred Newman. CAST: Fred Astaire, Eleanor Powell, George Murphy, Douglas McPhail. (Classic International Filmusicals 3002)

400013a Film SEVEN SINNERS records by Marlene Dietrich of orig cast. 1939: "I've Been in Love Before" (LP-54) 1965: "I Can't Give You Anything But Love" (LP-191)

400013b Film SEVEN SINNERS soundtrack. Marlene Dietrich: "I've Been in Love Before" (LP-653) "The Man's in the Navy" (LP-656)

400014a Film SAILORS THREE soundtrack. Tommy Trinder: "All Over the Place" (LP-130) "Happy-Go-Lucky Song" (78/Col(E) FB-2531)

400015a Film TIN PAN ALLEY soundtrack. COND: Alfred Newman. CAST: Alice Faye, Betty Grable, John Payne, Jack Oakie, Roberts Brothers, Brian Sisters, Billy Gilbert. (Sountrak 110; Caliban 6003, with Down Argentine Way. Excerpts: Faye, Payne, Roberts Brothers, Brian Sisters: "America, I Love You" (LP-283) Grable: "Honeysuckle Rose," "Moonlight and Roses" (LP-284) Faye, Payne: "You Say the Sweetest Things" (LP-424) Faye, Payne, Oakie: "You Say the Sweetest Things" (LP-283).)

400015b Film TIN PAN ALLEY 1962 record by Alice Faye of orig cast. "Moonlight Bay" (LP-100)

400016a Film LILLIAN RUSSELL 1962 record by Alice Faye of orig cast. "The Band Played On" (LP-100)

400016b Film LILLIAN RUSSELL soundtrack. MUSIC & WORDS: Various. CAST: Alice Faye, Don Ameche, chorus. (Caliban 6016, with Meet Danny Wilson. Excerpts: Faye: "Blue Lovebird," "After the Ball" (LP-283).)

400017a Film ARGENTINE NIGHTS 1940 records by the Andrews Sisters of orig cast. "Rhumboogie" (LP-265) (LP-266) "Oh, He Loves Me" (78/Dec 3310) "Hit the Road" (78/Dec 3328)

400018a Film IF I HAD MY WAY contemp records by Bing Crosby of orig cast. MUSIC & WORDS: James V Monaco, John Burke, others. "The Pessimistic Character," "Meet the Sun Half-Way," "I Haven't Time to Be a Millionaire," "April Played the Fiddle," "If I Had My Way" (Dec 10" 6015, with The Road to Singapore; LP-262.)

400019a Film THE ROAD TO SINGAPORE contemp records by members of orig cast. MUSIC: James V Monaco, Victor Schertzinger. WORDS: John Burke. Bing Crosby: "Too Romantic," "Sweet Potato Piper," "The Moon and the Willow Tree" (Dec 10" 6015, with If I Had My Way; LP-262.) Dorothy Lamour: "Too Romantic," "Sweet Potato Piper," "The Moon and the Willow Tree" (LP-271)

400020a Film JOHNNY APOLLO 1940 records by Dorothy Lamour of orig cast. "Your Kiss," "This Is the Beginning of the End" (LP-271)

400020b Film JOHNNY APOLLO soundtrack. Dorothy Lamour: "Dancing for Nickels and Dimes" (LP-647)

400021a Film TYPHOON 1939 record by Dorothy Lamour of orig cast. "Palms of Paradise" (LP-271)

400022a Film MOON OVER BURMA 1940 records by Dorothy Lamour of orig cast. "Moon over Burma," "Mexican Magic" (LP-271)

400023a Film BUCK BENNY RIDES AGAIN 1940 record by Eddie Anderson ("Rochester") of orig cast. "My! My!" (78/Col 35442)

400024a Film THE HIT PARADE OF 1941 1940 records by members of orig cast. MUSIC: Jule Styne. WORDS: Walter Bullock. Kenny Baker: "In the Cool of the Evening," "Who Am I?" (78/Vic 26792) Frances Langford: "Who Am I?," "In the Cool of the Evening" (78/Dec 3433)

400025a Film RHYTHM ON THE RIVER 1940 records by members of orig cast. MUSIC: James V Monaco, Victor Schertzinger. WORDS: John Burke. Bing Crosby: "When the Moon Comes over Madison Square," "Only Forever," "Rhythm on the River," "That's for Me" (Dec 10" 6014, with The East Side of Heaven; LP-318.) Mary Martin: "Ain't It a Shame about Mame," "I Don't Want to Cry Any More" (78/Dec 23164)

400026a Film A LITTLE BIT OF HEAVEN 1940 records by Gloria Jean of orig cast. "After Ev'ry Rainstorm," "A Little Bit of Heaven" (78/Dec 3449)

400027a Film DREAMING OUT LOUD 1940 record by Frances Langford of orig cast. "Dreaming Out Loud" (78/Dec 3400)

400028a Film MUSIC IN MY HEART 1939 record by Tony Martin of orig cast. "It's a Blue World" (78/Dec 2932)

400029a Film THE PROUD VALLEY records by Paul Robeson of orig cast. 1939: "Ebenezer," "Land of My Fathers" (78/HMV(E) B-9020) 1927: "Deep River" (78/Vic 20793) 1937: "All Through the Night" (78/HMV(E) B-8668)

400029b Film THE PROUD VALLEY soundtrack. Paul Robeson: "Deep River" (LP-638) "Rehearsal Scene" (78/HMV/(E) B-9024)

400030a Film POT O' GOLD 1941 records by Horace Heidt Orch of orig prod. "Broadway Caballero" (78/Col 36006) "Do You Believe in Fairy Tales?" (78/Col 36026) "Hi Cy, What's a-Cookin?," "When Johnny Toots His Horn" (78/Col 36070) "Pete the Piper," "A Knife, a Fork and a Spoon" (78/Col 36053)

400031a Suite REVEREND JOHNSON'S DREAM orig (record) prod. MUSIC: Harold Arlen. WORDS: Ted Koehler. PIANO: Leon Leonardi. "Produced under the direction of Harold Arlen." VOCALS: William Gillespie, Lois Hodnett, Ruby Elzy, chorus. (78/Dec album 170)

400032a Film DANCE GIRL DANCE soundtrack. Lucille Ball: "Oh Mother, What Do I Do Now?" (LP-496)

400033a Film YOU'LL FIND OUT 1940 records by Kay Kyser Orch of orig prod. MUSIC: Jimmy McHugh. WORDS: Johnny Mercer. "You've Got Me This Way," "I've Got a One-Track Mind" (78/Col 35762) "I'd Know You Anywhere," "The Bad Humor Man" (78/Col 35761)

400034a Film LET'S MAKE MUSIC 1940 records by Bob Crosby of orig cast. "You Forgot about Me" (78/Dec 3417) "The Big Noise from Winnetka" (78/Dec 3611)

400035a Film THE FARMER'S DAUGHTER 1939 record by Martha Raye of orig cast. "Jeanie with the Light Brown Hair" (LP-613)

400035b Film THE FARMER'S DAUGHTER soundtrack. Martha Raye: "Jungle Jingle" (LP-651)

400036a Film STEP LIVELY soundtrack. MUSIC: Jule Styne. WORDS: Sammy Cahn. COND: Constantin Bakaleinikoff. CAST: Frank Sinatra, Gloria de Haven, George Murphy, Anne Jeffreys. (Hollywood Soundstage 412)

400037a Film IT ALL CAME TRUE soundtrack. Ann Sheridan: "Gaucho Serenade" (LP-705)

400209a LIGHTS UP contemp records by Evelyn Laye of orig (London) cast. MUSIC: Noel Gay. WORDS: Ian Grant, Frank Eyton. "Let the People Sing," "All Thro' a Glass of Champagne" (LP-63)(LP-172) "You've Done Something to My Heart" (LP-130)

400404a HIGHER AND HIGHER 1940 records by Shirley Ross of orig prod. MUSIC: Richard Rodgers. WORDS: Lorenz Hart. "It Never Entered My Mind," "Nothing But You," "Ev'ry Sunday Afternoon," "From Another World" (LP-217)

400404b HIGHER AND HIGHER soundtrack of 1943 film prod, with practically all new songs. MUSIC: Jimmy McHugh. WORDS: Harold Adamson. ("Disgustingly Rich" by Rodgers & Hart) COND: Constantin Bakaleinikoff. CAST: Frank Sinatra, Michele Morgan, Marcy Maguire, Mel Torme, Barbara Hale, Dooley Wilson. (Hollywood Soundstage 411)

400404c HIGHER AND HIGHER 1943 records by Frank Sinatra of 1943 film prod. "I Couldn't Sleep a Wink Last Night," "The Music Stopped," "A Lovely Way to Spend an Evening" (LP-250)

400419a UP AND DOING contemp records by members of orig (London) prod. Cyril Ritchard: "I'm One of the Whitehall Warriors" (LP-172) Patricia Burke: "This Can't Be Love" (by Richard Rodgers & Lorenz Hart) (LP-222)

400523a KEEP OFF THE GRASS records by members of orig cast. MUSIC: Jimmy McHugh. WORDS: Howard Dietz, Al Dubin, Harold Adamson. Virginia O'Brien, contemp: "Clear Out of This World," "Two in a Taxi" (78/Col 35578) "Spring," "I'm an Old Jitterbug" (78/Col 35632) Jimmy Durante, later: "A Fugitive from Esquire" (78/MGM(E) 151)

400528a LOUISIANA PURCHASE contemp records by Carol Bruce of orig prod. MUSIC & WORDS: Irving Berlin. "The Lord Done Fixed Up My Soul" (LP-296) "Louisiana Purchase" (LP-296)(LP-519)

400528b LOUISIANA PURCHASE 1951 TV prod. CAST: Irene Bordoni & Victor Moore of orig cast; Sandra Deel, unidentified baritone, chorus. (JJA Records 19746, with additional material)(LP-296)

400528c LOUISIANA PURCHASE 1941 film soundtrack. Orchestra & chorus: Main Title & "It's New to Us" Vera Zorina & Victor Moore (both also of orig cast): "You're Lonely and I'm Lonely" (LP-296)

400827a APPLE SAUCE contemp record by Florence Desmond of orig (London) cast. "Mademoiselle l'Amour" (LP-172)

400911a HOLD ON TO YOUR HATS 1980 studio prod. MUSIC: Burton Lane. WORDS: E Y Harburg. ORCH: Dennis Deal. CAST: Helen Gallagher, Carleton Carpenter, Arthur Siegel, Nancy Grennan, John Hillner, chorus. (LP-741)

401025a CABIN IN THE SKY 1964 prod. MUSIC: Vernon Duke. WORDS: John Latouche. ORCH & COND: Sy Oliver (for this recording). CAST: Rosetta LeNoire, Ketty Lester, Tony Middleton, Sam Laws, Bernard Johnson, Helen Ferguson. (Cap SW-2073)

401025b CABIN IN THE SKY 1940 album. COND: Max Meth (of orig prod). VOCALS: Ethel Waters (of orig prod). Overture, "Taking a Chance on Love," "Honey in the Honeycomb," "Cabin in the Sky," "Love Turned the Light Out" (AEI Records 1107, with Porgy and Bess. Incomplete: LP-15. Excerpt: "Cabin in the Sky" (LP-389).)

401025c CABIN IN THE SKY later records by Ethel Waters of orig cast & 1942 film cast. "Takin' a Chance on Love," "Cabin in the Sky" (1950: LP-361)(Late 1950's: LP-99) From the film: "Happiness Is Just a Thing Called Joe" by Harold Arlen & E Y Harburg (1956: LP-393)(Late 1950's: LP-99)

401025d CABIN IN THE SKY soundtrack of 1942 film, with addi-

tional songs by Harold Arlen & E Y Harburg. ORCH & COND: George Stoll, Roger Edens. CAST: Ethel Waters, Lena Horne, Eddie ("Rochester") Anderson, Buck & Bubbles, Louis Armstrong, Duke Ellington Orch, Hall Johnson Choir. (Hollywood Soundstage 5003; LP-761. Excerpts: Horne: "Ain't It the Truth"(dropped before release) (LP-486) (LP-657) Waters: "Takin' a Chance on Love" (LP-416) "Happiness Is Just a Thing Called Joe," "Li'l Black Sheep" Horne, Anderson: "Dat Ol' Debbil Consequence" (LP-657).)

401030a PANAMA HATTIE contemp album by members of orig cast. MUSIC & WORDS: Cole Porter. COND: Harry Sosnik. Ethel Merman: "Make It Another Old Fashioned, Please," "My Mother Would Love You," "I've Still Got My Health" Merman & Joan Carroll: "Let's Be Buddies" (78/Dec album 203; LP-183. Excerpt: "Let's Be Buddies" (LP-36)(LP-69) (LP-109).)

401030b PANAMA HATTIE later records by Ethel Merman of orig cast. "Make It Another Old Fashioned Please" (LP-36)(LP-251)

401030c PANAMA HATTIE orig prod rec live. Ethel Merman: "I'm Throwing a Ball Tonight," "Make It Another Old Fashioned, Please" (LP-295)

401030d PANAMA HATTIE 1954 TV prod, with interpolated Porter songs. CAST: Ethel Merman of orig cast; Ray Middleton, Jack Leonard, Art Carney, chorus. (Larynx 567, with Anything Goes)(LP-407)

401030e PANAMA HATTIE 1942 film soundtrack. Chorus: Main Title (LP-655) Ann Sothern: "I've Still Got My Health" (LP-496) (LP-655) "Make It Another Old-Fashioned, Please" (dropped before release) Sothern, Virginia O'Brien: "Let's Be Buddies" Lena Horne: "Just One of Those Things" O'Brien, Red Skelton, Ben Blue, Rags Ragland: "Fresh as a Daisy" (LP-655) Sothern: "Salome"(by Roger Edens, dropped before release) (LP-423) Sothern, Skelton, Ragland, Blue: "I'd Do Anything for You"(by Roger Edens, dropped before release) (LP-486)

401030f PANAMA HATTIE later record by Ann Sothern of 1942 film cast. "You'll Never Know" (LP-614)

401225a PAL JOEY 1950 studio prod. MUSIC: Richard Rodgers. WORDS: Lorenz Hart. ORCH: Ted Royal. COND: Lehman Engel. CAST: Vivienne Segal of orig and 1952 casts; Harold Lang of 1952 cast; Barbara Ashley, Beverly Fite, Kenneth Remo, Jo Hurt. (Col ML-4364)

401225b PAL JOEY 1952 prod with Jane Froman and Dick Beavers replacing Vivienne Segal and Harold Lang. ORCH: Don Walker. COND: Max Meth. CAST: Jane Froman, Dick Beavers, Helen Gallagher, Patricia Northrop, Elaine Stritch, Lewis Bolyard. (Cap S-310)

401225c PAL JOEY 1957 film soundtrack, with songs interpolated from other Rodgers shows. ORCH: Nelson Riddle. COND: Morris Stoloff. CAST: Frank Sinatra, Trudi Erwin (for Kim Novak), Jo Ann Greer (for Rita Hayworth). (Cap W-912 plus LP-403, which has a track of "My Funny Valentine" by Greer which was not used in the film. Excerpt: Greer: "Zip" (LP-496).)

401225d PAL JOEY 1963 album by Vivian Blaine. COND: Glenn Osser. (Mercury 60051, with Annie Get Your Gun)

401225e PAL JOEY contemp records by members of 1954 London cast. Carol Bruce: "Bewitched," "What Is a Man?" (78/Philips(E) PB-279) Bruce, Sally Bazely: "Take Him" Jean Brampton: "That Terrific Rainbow" (78/Philips(E) PB-280)

401225f PAL JOEY 1957(?) album, with songs used in 1957 film prod. COND: Eddie Maynard. VOCALS: Bill Sinclair, Jennie Feathers. (Promenade 2089)

401225g PAL JOEY 1957(?) studio prod, with songs used in 1957 film. ORCH & COND: Lew Raymond. VOCALS: Martha Tilton,

Clark Dennis, June Hutton, Bob McKendrick, Curt Massey, Betty Baker, Marilyn Maxwell. (Tops 1607)

401225h PAL JOEY studio prod. "Ed Sullivan presents Pal Joey." No other credits given. (National Academy 9)

401225i PAL JOEY 1972 record by Helen Gallagher of 1952 prod. "Bewitched," "What Is a Man?" (LP-509)

401225j PAL JOEY studio prod. COND: Johnny Douglas. CAST: Joyce Blair, Michael Garson, Stella Moray, chorus. (Cap SN-7503, with The New Moon)

401225k PAL JOEY 1977 record by Gene Kelly of orig cast. "I Could Write a Book" (LP-749)

401225l PAL JOEY contemp records by Sian Phillips of 1980 London prod. "What Is a Man?," "Bewitched, Bothered and Bewildered" (45/Chrysalis CHS-2470)

401225m PAL JOEY 1980 London prod. COND: Trevor York. CAST: Sian Phillips, Denis Lawson, Jane Gurnett, Darlene Johnson, Tracey Perry, Kay Jones, Susan Kyd, Danielle Carson. (That's Entertainment(E) TERX-1005)

1941

410001a Film ZIEGFELD GIRL records by members of orig cast. Judy Garland: "I'm Always Chasing Rainbows" (1940: LP-7)(1963: LP-735, LP-738, LP-762) Tony Martin: "You Stepped Out of a Dream" (1941: LP-612) "Too Beautiful to Last" (dropped before release?) (1941: LP-114)

410001b Film ZIEGFELD GIRL soundtrack. MUSIC & WORDS: Roger Edens, Gus Kahn, Nacio Herb Brown. ORCH: Herbert Stothart. CAST: Judy Garland, Tony Martin, Charles Winninger, Al Shean, chorus. (Classic International Filmusicals 3006; LP-465. Excerpt: Garland, Martin: "We Must Have Music" (dropped before release) (LP-423).)

410002a Film NICE GIRL? contemp records by Deanna Durbin of orig cast. "Beneath the Lights of Home" (LP-13) (LP-131) "Love at Last," "Perhaps," "Thank You America," "Old Folks at Home" (LP-131)

410003a Film YOU'LL NEVER GET RICH records by members of orig cast. MUSIC & WORDS: Cole Porter. Fred Astaire, 1941: "So Near and Yet So Far," "Dream Dancing" Astaire & Delta Rhythm Boys, 1941: "The Wedding Cake Walk" (LP-22)(LP-344) "Since I Kissed My Baby Goodbye" (LP-182) (LP-344) Astaire, 1952: "So Near and Yet So Far" (LP-125) (LP-552)(LP-648) Martha Tilton, contemp: "The Wedding Cake Walk" (LP-182)

410003b Film YOU'LL NEVER GET RICH soundtrack. COND: Morris Stoloff. Fred Astaire, chorus: "Shooting the Works for Uncle Sam" Delta Rhythm Boys: "Since I Kissed My Baby Goodbye" Orchestra: Main Title, "Dream Dancing," "The Boogie Barcarolle," "Astairable Rag" Astaire: "So Near and Yet So Far" Martha Tilton, chorus: "The Wedding Cake Walk/Finale" (Hollywood Soundstage 5001, with Yolanda and the Thief. Incomplete: LP-655.)

410004a Film BABES ON BROADWAY records by members of orig cast. Judy Garland: "How About You?" (1941: LP-35) (1964: LP-205) "F.D.R. Jones" (1941: LP-7) Garland & Mickey Rooney: "How about You?" (1941: LP-398)

410004b Film BABES ON BROADWAY soundtrack. MUSIC & WORDS: Burton Lane, Ralph Freed, E Y Harburg, Roger Edens. COND: George Stoll. CAST: Judy Garland, Mickey Rooney, Ray MacDonald, Richard Quine, Virginia Weidler, Annie Rooney. (Curtain Calls 100/6-7, with Babes in Arms. Excerpts: Garland,

chorus: "Waiting for the Robert E Lee," "Babes on Broadway" (LP-252).)

410005a Film BLUES IN THE NIGHT soundtrack. MUSIC: Harold Arlen. WORDS: Johnny Mercer. COND: Leo F Forbstein. Jimmy Lunceford Orch: "Blues in the Night" Mabel Todd, Will Osborne Orch: "Says Who? Says You, Says I" Priscilla Lane: "This Time the Dream's on Me," "Hang On to Your Lids, Kids" (LP-657)

410005b Film BLUES IN THE NIGHT records sung by Harold Arlen (composer) & Johnny Mercer (lyricist). "Blues in the Night" (Arlen, 1955: LP-101)(Arlen, 1966: LP-60) (Mercer, 1943: LP-559, LP-720)

410006a Film KISS THE BOYS GOODBYE contemp records by members of orig cast. MUSIC: Victor Schertzinger. WORDS: Frank Loesser. Mary Martin: "Kiss the Boys Goodbye" (LP-109) Connie Boswell: "Sand in My Shoes" (78/Dec 3893)

410006b Film KISS THE BOYS GOODBYE soundtrack. Mary Martin: "That's How I Got My Start" (LP-496)(LP-656) Connie Boswell: "Sand in My Shoes" (LP-656)

410007a Film THAT NIGHT IN RIO soundtrack. MUSIC & WORDS: Harry Warren, Mack Gordon, others. COND: Alfred Newman. CAST: Carmen Miranda, Don Ameche, Alice Faye. (Curtain Calls 100/14, with A Week-End in Havana. Excerpts: Faye, Ameche: "Chica, Chica, Boom Chic" Faye: "Boa Noite" (LP-424).)

410007b Film THAT NIGHT IN RIO 1941 records by Carmen Miranda of orig cast. "I, Yi, Yi, Yi, Yi" (LP-109) (LP-147)(LP-166)(LP-199)(LP-302)(LP-522) "Chica Chica Boom Chic" (LP-166)(LP-199)(LP-522) "Cae Cae" (LP-199) (LP-522)

410008a Film THE BIG STORE records by Tony Martin of orig cast. "If It's You" (1941: LP-114) "Tenement Symphony" (1940's: 45/RCA EPA-455)(1965: LP-446)

410009a Film BLOOD AND SAND contemp album by Vincente Gomez (guitar) of orig cast. MUSIC & WORDS: Vincente Gomez. VOCALS: Graciela Parraga. (Dec 10" 5380)

410010a Film A WEEK-END IN HAVANA soundtrack. MUSIC & WORDS: Harry Warren, Mack Gordon, others. COND: Alfred Newman. CAST: Carmen Miranda, Alice Faye, Cesar Romero, John Payne, Natcho Galindo. (Curtain Calls 100/14, with That Night in Rio. Excerpts: Faye: "Tropical Magic" Faye, Galindo: "The Man with the Lollipop Song" (LP-424).)

410010b Film A WEEK-END IN HAVANA 1941 records by Carmen Miranda of orig cast. "A Week-End in Havana," "When I Love I Love" (LP-166)(LP-522) "The Man with the Lollipop Song" (LP-166) "Rebola a Bola" (LP-166)(LP-302)

410011a Film SMILIN' THROUGH 1941 album by Jeanette MacDonald of orig cast. COND: Herbert Stothart. (78/Vic 12" album M-847. Excerpts: "A Little Love, a Little Kiss," "The Kerry Dance" (LP-536).)

410011b Film SMILIN' THROUGH 1944 radio performance by Jeanette MacDonald or orig cast. "Smilin' Through" (LP-378)

410011c Film SMILIN' THROUGH soundtrack. Jeanette MacDonald: "Smiles," "There's a Long, Long Trail" (LP-466)

410012a Film SUN VALLEY SERENADE soundtrack. MUSIC & WORDS: Harry Warren, Mack Gordon, others. COND: Glenn Miller. VOCALS: Tex Beneke, Paula Kelly, the Modernaires. (20th Fox 100-2, entitled "Glenn Miller and His Orchestra," with Orchestra Wives. Incomplete: RCA 10" LPT-3064.)

410012b Film SUN VALLEY SERENADE records by Glenn Miller Orch of orig prod. 1939: "Moonlight Serenade" (78/Bluebird B-10214) "In the Mood" (78/Bluebird B-10416) 1941: "I Know Why," "Chattanooga Choo-Choo" (78/Bluebird B-11230) "The Kiss Polka," "It Happened in Sun Valley" (78/Bluebird B-11263)

410013a Film BUCK PRIVATES 1941 records by the Andrews Sisters of orig cast. "Boogie Woogie Bugle Boy" (LP-265)(LP-266) "Bounce Me Brother with a Solid Four" (78/Dec 3598) "You're a Lucky Fellow, Mr. Smith" (78/Dec 3599) "In Apple Blossom Time" (LP-237)

410014a Film HOLD THAT GHOST 1941 records by the Andrews Sisters of orig cast. "Sleepy Serenade" (78/Dec 3821) "Aurora" (78/Dec 3732)

410015a Film IN THE NAVY 1941 record by the Andrews Sisters of orig cast. "Gimme Some Skin, My Friend" (78/Dec 3871)

410016a Film THE BIRTH OF THE BLUES contemp records by members of orig cast. MUSIC & WORDS: Various. Bing Crosby, Mary Martin, Jack Teagarden: "The Waiter and the Porter and the Upstairs Maid" Crosby: "The Birth of the Blues," "My Melancholy Baby" Crosby, Martin: "Wait Till the Sun Shines, Nellie" (LP-318)

410016b Film THE BIRTH OF THE BLUES 1951 TV performance by Johnny Mercer (lyricist) with Robert Alda & Constance Moore. "The Waiter and the Porter and the Upstairs Maid" (LP-604)

410016c Film THE BIRTH OF THE BLUES 1966 record by Ray Henderson (composer), piano. "The Birth of the Blues" (LP-671)

410017a Film THE ROAD TO ZANZIBAR 1940 records by Bing Crosby of orig cast. MUSIC: James Van Heusen. WORDS: John Burke. "It's Always You," "You Lucky People You," "You're Dangerous," "Birds of a Feather" (LP-318)

410018a Film YOU'RE THE ONE 1940 records by members of orig prod. MUSIC: Jimmy McHugh. WORDS: Johnny Mercer. Jerry Colonna & Orrin Tucker Orch: "The Yogi Who Lost His Will Power" (78/Col 35866) Orrin Tucker Orch: "Strawberry Lane," "I Could Kiss You for That" (78/Col 35858) "You're the One for Me," "Gee! I Wish I'd Listened to My Mother" (78/Col 35848)

410018b Film YOU'RE THE ONE 1971 record sung by Johnny Mercer, lyricist. "The Yogi Who Lost His Will Power" (LP-533)

410019a Film LAS VEGAS NIGHTS records by Frank Sinatra & Tommy Dorsey Orch of orig prod. "I'll Never Smile Again" (1940: 78/Vic 26628) "Dolores" (1941: 78/Vic 27317)

410020a Film KEEP 'EM FLYING 1942 records by members of orig cast. MUSIC: Gene de Paul. WORDS: Don Raye. Martha Raye: "Pig-Foot Pete" (78/Dec 18298) Carol Bruce: "You Don't Know What Love Is," "The Boy with the Wistful Eyes" (78/Col 36471)

410021a Film MOON OVER MIAMI soundtrack. MUSIC & WORDS: mostly Ralph Rainger, Leo Robin. ORCH & COND: Alfred Newman. CAST: Betty Grable, Robert Cummings, Don Ameche, Charlotte Greenwood, Jack Haley, chorus. (Caliban 6001, with Coney Island. Excerpts: Grable: "Kindergarten Conga" (LP-284) Grable, Ameche: "Loveliness and Love" Haley, Greenwood: "Is That Good?" Ameche: "You Started Something" (LP-768).)

410022a Film A YANK IN THE R.A.F. soundtrack. Betty Grable: "Hi'ya, Love," "Another Little Dream Won't Do Us Any Harm" (LP-284)(LP-768)

410023a Film PLAYMATES contemp records by Kay Kyser Orch of orig prod. MUSIC: James Van Heusen. WORDS: John Burke. "How Long Did I Dream?," "Thank Your Lucky Stars and Stripes" (78/Col 36441) "Humpty-Dumpty Heart," "Romeo Smith and Juliet Jones" (78/Col 36433)

410024a Film DUMBO soundtrack. MUSIC & WORDS: Frank Churchill, Oliver Wallace, Ned Washington. ORCH: Ed Plumb. VOCALS: Cliff Edwards, Verna Felton, chorus. (Disneyland 1204) (Incomplete: LP-661)

410025a Film TIME OUT FOR RHYTHM records by members of orig prod. Joan Merrill, 1941: "Twiddlin' My Thumbs," "As If You

Didn't Know" (78/Bluebird B-11149) Glen Gray Orch, 1941: "As If You Didn't Know," "Boogie Woogie Piano Man" (78/Dec 3845)

410026a Film WHEN LADIES MEET soundtrack. Greer Garson, Joan Crawford: "I Love Thee" (LP-401)

410027a Film THE GREAT AMERICAN BROADCAST soundtrack. MUSIC: Harry Warren. WORDS: Mack Gordon. COND: Alfred Newman. Alice Faye: "It's All in a Lifetime," "Long Ago Last Night," "I Take to You" (LP-424) "Where You Are" (LP-424)(LP-633) The Ink Spots: "Alabamy Bound" James Newell: "The Great American Broadcast" (LP-558)

410028a Film FOOTSTEPS IN THE DARK soundtrack. Lee Patrick: "Love Me" (LP-496)

410029a Film NAVY BLUES soundtrack. MUSIC: Arthur Schwartz. WORDS: Johnny Mercer. Martha Raye, Ann Sheridan, chorus: "Navy Blues" (LP-651)(LP-705) Sheridan: "In Waikiki" Sheridan, Warner Anderson: "You're a Natural" (LP-705) Finale medley: "Navy Blues," "When Are We Gonna Land Abroad?," "In Waikiki," "You're a Natural" (LP-555)

410030a Film SIS HOPKINS 1941 record by Bob Crosby of orig cast. MUSIC: Jule Styne. WORDS: Frank Loesser. "Well! Well!" (78/Dec 3762)

410030b Film SIS HOPKINS soundtrack. Judy Canova, Bob Crosby: "Well! Well!" Canova: "That Ain't Hay" (LP-656)

410031a Record prod SCENES FROM "ALICE IN WONDERLAND" AND "THROUGH THE LOOKING GLASS" orig prod. MUSIC: Walter Slaughter. WORDS: Lewis Carroll, S Clark, Walter Slaughter. COND: Clifford Greenwood. CAST: Ann Stephens, Arthur Askey, Florence Desmond, Richard Goolden, Syd Walker, Robertson Hare, Leslie Henson, Stanley Holloway, Ronald Frankau, Nancy Munks, Molly Munks. (Encore(E) 137)

410032a Film DANCING ON A DIME soundtrack. MUSIC: Burton Lane. WORDS: Frank Loesser. Peter Lind Hayes, chorus: "I Hear Music" (LP-656)

410033a Film THE RELUCTANT DRAGON soundtrack. "I'm a Reluctant Dragon" (LP-661)

410034a Film THE SWEETHEART OF THE CAMPUS 1941 record by Harriet Hilliard of orig cast. "Where?" (78/Bluebird B-11155)

410035a Film THEY MET IN ARGENTINA 1941 record by Alberto Vila of orig prod. MUSIC: Richard Rodgers. WORDS: Lorenz Hart. "Lolita" (78/Col 36213)

410036a Film RISE AND SHINE soundtrack. Jack Oakie: "Get Thee Behind Me Clayton" (LP-768)

410037a Film THE FLAME OF NEW ORLEANS soundtrack. Marlene Dietrich: "Sweet Is the Blush of May" (LP-705)

410105a NO FOR AN ANSWER orig prod. MUSIC & WORDS: Marc Blitzstein. PIANO: Marc Blitzstein. CAST: Olive Deering, Lloyd Gough, Carol Channing, Curt Conway, Norma Green, Michael Loring, Coby Ruskin, Hester Sondergaard, Martin Wolfson. (Theme TALP-103)

410123a LADY IN THE DARK 1941 album by Gertrude Lawrence of orig cast & male quartet. MUSIC: Kurt Weill. WORDS: Ira Gershwin. COND: Leonard Joy. "My Ship," "Jenny," "This Is New," "One Life to Live," "O, Fabulous One," "Huxley," "Girl of the Moment," "The Princess of Pure Delight" (RCA 10" LRT-7001, with Nymph Errant. Excerpt: "My Ship" (LP-711).)

410123b LADY IN THE DARK 1954 studio prod based on TV prod. ORCH: Irwin Kostal. COND: Charles Sanford. CAST: Ann Sothern, Carleton Carpenter, chorus. (RCA LM-1882. Excerpt: Sothern: "The Saga of Jenny" (LP-129).)

410123c LADY IN THE DARK 1965 studio prod. ORCH: Kurt Weill. COND: Lehman Engel. CAST: Rise Stevens, Adolph Green, John Reardon, Stephanie Augustine, Kenneth Bridges, Roger White. (Col OS-2390)

410123d LADY IN THE DARK records by members of orig cast. Danny Kaye, 1941: "Jenny," "It's Never Too Late to Mendelssohn," "The Princess of Pure Delight," "The Trial of Liza Elliott/Tschaikowsky" (LP-107)(LP-527) "One Life to Live," "My Ship" (LP-527) Kaye, 1952: "Tschaikowsky" (LP-6)(LP-515) Gertrude Lawrence, 1952: "Jenny" (LP-5)

410123e LADY IN THE DARK 1941 album by Hildegarde and Robert Hannon. COND: Harry Sosnik. (78/Dec album 208)

410123f LADY IN THE DARK 1943 film soundtrack. Chorus: "Girl of the Moment" Ray Milland, Ginger Rogers, chorus: "The Greatest Show on Earth" Rogers, chorus: "The Saga of Jenny" (LP-402) Rogers: "Suddenly It's Spring" (LP-588)

410424a BLACK VANITIES 1941 records by members of orig (London) cast. MUSIC & WORDS: Cole Porter, others. Bud Flanagan, Frances Day: "But in the Morning, No," "It's De-lovely/Underneath the Arches" (78/Dec(E) F-7951) Day: "Much More Lovely," "A Pair of Silver Wings" (78/Dec(E) F-7854) "Do I Love You?," "I L-Love You So" (78/Dec(E) F-7867) Bud Flanagan & Chesney Allen: "Let's Be Buddies" (78/Dec(E) F-7910)

410804a JUMP FOR JOY 1941 records by Duke Ellington Orch of orig (Los Angeles) prod. MUSIC & WORDS: Duke Ellington, Paul Webster, others. Instrumentals: "Take the 'A' Train" (78/Vic 27380) "Just a-Settin' and a-Rockin'," "The Giddybug Gallop," "Subtle Slough" (LP-471) "Clementine" (LP-417) (LP-472) Ivie Anderson: "Chocolate Shake," "I Got It Bad and That Ain't Good," "Jump for Joy" Herb Jeffries: "Jump for Joy," "The Brown Skin Gal" (LP-471) Anderson: "Rocks in My Bed" Ray Nance: "Bli-Blip" (78/Vic 27639) Marie Bryant, Paul White: "Bli-Blip" (LP-472)

411001a BEST FOOT FORWARD 1963 prod with additional Martin & Blane songs, incl 3 songs from 1943 film prod. MUSIC: Hugh Martin. WORDS: Ralph Blane. COND: Buster Davis. CAST: Paula Wayne, Liza Minnelli, Glenn Walken, Karin Wolfe, Grant Walden, Edmund Gaynes, Kay Cole, Ronald Walken. (Cadence 24012; Stet DS-15003.)

411001b BEST FOOT FORWARD records sung by Hugh Martin & Ralph Blane, composers. 1956: "Wish I May," "Ev'ry Time," "That's How I Love the Blues," "Buckle Down, Winsocki" (LP-193) As members of a vocal quartet called "The Martins," 1941: "The Three B's," "Just a Little Joint with a Juke Box" (LP-287)

411001c BEST FOOT FORWARD 1941 records by members of orig & 1943 film casts. Nancy Walker: "What Do You Think I Am?," "Ev'ry Time," "Shady Lady Bird" (LP-287) "Just a Little Joint with a Juke Box" (LP-287)(LP-711) Tommy Dix: "Buckle Down, Winsocki" (78/Col 36429)

411001d BEST FOOT FORWARD records by Liza Minnelli of 1963 cast. COND: Archie Bleyer. "What Do You Think Am?," "You Are for Loving" (45/Cadence 1436)

411029a LET'S FACE IT contemp album by Mary Jane Walsh of orig prod. MUSIC & WORDS: Cole Porter. COND: Max Meth of orig prod. "I Hate You Darling," "Farming," "Everything I Love," "Ace in the Hole" (78/Liberty Music Shop album 343/345, with two dance medleys of songs from the show; LP-182. Incomplete: LP-681.)

411029b LET'S FACE IT records by Danny Kaye of orig cast. "Farming," "Let's Not Talk about Love" (1942: LP-70, LP-160, LP-681) "Melody in 4-F" (1944 film soundtrack: LP-681, LP-701)

411029c LET'S FACE IT 1941 album by Hildegarde. COND: Harry

Sosnik. "Ev'rything I Love," "Ace in the Hole," "You Irritate Me So," "A Little Rhumba Numba," "Farming," "I Hate You Darling" (78/Dec album 291. Excerpts: "You Irritate Me So," "A Little Rhumba Numba" (LP-681).)

411029d LET'S FACE IT 1943 film soundtrack. Bob Hope, chorus: "Let's Face It" Betty Hutton: "Let's Not Talk about Love" (LP-655)

411029e LET'S FACE IT 1954 TV prod soundtrack. Gene Nelson: "You Irritate Me So" Vivian Blaine: "Ace in the Hole" Blaine, Nelson: "Everything I Love" (LP-655)

411031a THE HIGH KICKERS records by Sophie Tucker of orig cast. "Some of These Days" (1911: CYL/Edison 4M-691) (1926: LP-168, LP-185) (1927: LP-52) (1929: 78/Vic 22049) (1930's: LP-332) (1937: LP-187) (1947: LP-186, LP-187, LP-297) (Later: LP-184)

411117a Radio show MERTON OF THE MOVIES orig prod. MUSIC & WORDS: Various. VOCALS: Judy Garland. (Pelican 139) (LP-398)

411201a SONS O' FUN 1941 records by Carmen Miranda of orig cast. MUSIC: Sammy Fain. WORDS: Jack Yellen. "Thank You North America" (78/Dec 23226) "Manuelo" (LP-522)

411225a BANJO EYES 1942 record by Eddie Cantor & June Clyde of orig cast. MUSIC: Vernon Duke. WORDS: Harold Adamson. "We're Having a Baby" (78/Dec 4314)

1942

420001a Film HOLIDAY INN 1942 studio prod. MUSIC & WORDS: Irving Berlin. COND: John Scott Trotter, Bob Crosby. CAST: Bing Crosby & Fred Astaire of orig cast; Margaret Lenhart, chorus. (Dec 4256. Incomplete: Dec 10" 5092. Excerpts: Astaire: "You're Easy to Dance with" (LP-22) (LP-344) "I Can't Tell a Lie" (LP-344).)

420001b Film HOLIDAY INN 1952 record by Fred Astaire of orig cast. "You're Easy to Dance with" (LP-50) (LP-125)(LP-552) (LP-648)

420001c Film HOLIDAY INN soundtrack. COND: Robert Emmett Dolan. CAST: Bing Crosby, Fred Astaire, Marjorie Reynolds, Virginia Dale, chorus. (Sountrak 112)

420001d Film HOLIDAY INN 1943 radio prod. ORCH & COND: Wilbur Hatch. VOCALS: Bing Crosby (of orig prod), Dinah Shore, chorus. (Spokane 15, with The Bells of St. Mary's)

420002a Film FOR ME AND MY GAL records by members of orig cast. Judy Garland, 1937: "Smiles" (LP-180)(LP-718) (LP-726) Garland & Gene Kelly, 1942: "For Me and My Gal," "When You Wore a Tulip" (LP-7) (LP-490) (LP-511) (LP-734) Garland, 1943 radio performance: "After You've Gone," "How Ya Gonna Keep 'Em Down on the Farm?" (LP-746) Garland, later: "For Me and My Gal" (LP-189)(LP-201)(LP-240) (LP-461)(LP-762)(LP-780)(1948, with Bing Crosby: LP-180, LP-693, LP-718) "After You've Gone" (LP-200)(LP-205) (LP-219)(LP-240)(LP-461)(LP-547)(LP-738)(LP-762)(LP-781) Kelly, 1977: "For Me and My Gal" (LP-749)

420002b Film FOR ME AND MY GAL soundtrack. MUSIC & WORDS: Various. COND: George Stoll. CAST: Judy Garland, Gene Kelly, George Murphy, Lucille Norman, Marta Eggerth, Ben Lesey, Ben Blue. (Sountrak 107. Excerpts: Garland, Kelly: "For Me and My Gal" (LP-416)(LP-558) Garland, Kelly, Blue, chorus: World War I Medley (LP-558). Also Garland, Kelly & Murphy in the first version of the Finale, later changed (LP-486).)

420003a Film YOU WERE NEVER LOVELIER contemp album by Fred Astaire of orig cast. MUSIC: Jerome Kern. WORDS: Johnny Mercer. COND: John Scott Trotter. (LP-344. Incomplete: LP-22.)

420003b Film YOU WERE NEVER LOVELIER records by members of orig prod. Fred Astaire, 1959: "Dearly Beloved" (LP-481) Rita

Hayworth, 1971 TV performance with Merv Griffin: "I'm Old Fashioned" (LP-403) Xavier Cugat Orch, 1942: "I'm Old Fashioned," "Dearly Beloved" (78/Col 36637) "You Were Never Lovelier" (78/Col 36660) "Chiu Chiu" (78/Col 36651) "Bim Bam Bum" (78/Col 36681)

420003c Film YOU WERE NEVER LOVELIER soundtrack. MUSIC & WORDS: mostly by Jerome Kern, Johnny Mercer. ORCH & COND: Leigh Harline. CAST: Fred Astaire, Nan Wynn (for Rita Hayworth), Lina Romay, Xavier Cugat Orch. (Curtain Calls 100/24, with Cover Girl)

420004a Film STAR SPANGLED RHYTHM soundtrack. MUSIC: Harold Arlen. WORDS: Johnny Mercer. CAST: Dick Powell, Mary Martin, Betty Hutton, Paulette Goddard, Dorothy Lamour, Martha Mears (for Veronica Lake), Johnny Johnston, Eddie ("Rochester") Anderson, Bing Crosby, Marjorie Reynolds, Betty Rhodes, Dona Drake. (Curtain Calls 100/20)

420004b Film STAR SPANGLED RHYTHM records sung by Harold Arlen, composer. "That Old Black Magic" (LP-101) "Hit the Road to Dreamland" (LP-59)(LP-60)(LP-192)

420005a Film YANKEE DOODLE DANDY soundtrack. MUSIC & WORDS: George M Cohan, Richard Rodgers, Lorenz Hart. CAST: James Cagney, Joan Leslie, Rosemary DeCamp, Jeanne Cagney, Frances Langford, Irene Manning, Walter Huston. (Curtain Calls 100/13. Excerpts: James Cagney: "Off the Record" (LP-217) "Yankee Doodle Boy," "Give My Regards to Broadway" (LP-223)(LP-595) Cagney, Leslie: "Harrigan" (LP-223) Cagney, Langford: "Over There" (LP-595).)

420005b Film YANKEE DOODLE DANDY contemp album. COND: Leonard Joy. VOCALS: Brad Reynolds, Ann Warren, chorus. (78/Vic album P-125)

420005c Film YANKEE DOODLE DANDY 1942 radio prod by members of orig cast. CAST: James Cagney, Joan Leslie, Walter Huston, Jeanne Cagney, chorus. (Radiola 1103, with Strawberry Blonde)

420006a Film PRIVATE BUCKEROO contemp records by members of orig prod. Andrews Sisters: "Don't Sit under the Apple Tree" (LP-237)(LP-265) "Three Little Sisters" (78/Dec 18319) "That's the Moon, My Son" (78/Dec 18398) Harry James Orch: "You Made Me Love You" (78/Col 36296)

420007a Film GIVE OUT SISTERS 1942 record by the Andrews Sisters of orig cast. "Pennsylvania Polka" (LP-237) (LP-265)(LP-266)

420008a Film ORCHESTRA WIVES soundtrack. MUSIC & WORDS: Harry Warren, Mack Gordon, others. COND: Glenn Miller. VOCALS: Marion Hutton, Tex Beneke, Ray Eberle, Pat Friday (for Lynn Bari), the Modernaires. (20th Fox 100-2, entitled "Glenn Miller and His Orchestra," with Sun Valley Serenade. Incomplete: RCA 10" LPT-3065.)

420008b Film ORCHESTRA WIVES contemp records by Glenn Miller Orch of orig prod. "Kalamazoo," "At Last" (78/Vic 27934) "Serenade in Blue," "That's Sabotage" (78/Vic 27935) "Moonlight Serenade" (78/Bluebird B-10214) "American Patrol" (78/Vic 27873) "Chattanooga Choo-Choo" (78/Bluebird B-11230)

420009a Film BAMBI soundtrack. MUSIC: Frank Churchill, Ed Plumb. WORDS: Larry Morey. ORCH: Charles Wolcott, Paul Smith. COND: Alexander Steinert. VOCALS: Unidentified soloists, chorus. (Disneyland 4009)(Incomplete: LP-661)

420010a Film WHAT'S COOKIN'? records by members of orig prod. Andrews Sisters: "What to Do" (1942: 78/Dec 4182) Woody Herman Orch: "Woodchopper's Ball" (1939: 78/Dec 2440)(1947: 78/Col 37238) "Amen" (1942: 78/Dec 18346) "You Can't Hold a Memory in Your Arms" (1942: 78/Dec 4188)

420011a Film SHIP AHOY contemp records by Frank Sinatra &

Tommy Dorsey Orch of orig prod. MUSIC: Burton Lane. WORDS: E Y Harburg. "Poor You," "The Last Call for Love" (78/Vic 27849) "I'll Take Tallulah" (78/Vic 27869)

420011b Film SHIP AHOY soundtrack. Red Skelton, Virginia O'Brien, Tommy Dorsey Orch: "Poor You" Frank Sinatra, Eleanor Powell (tap dancing), the Pied Pipers, Tommy Dorsey Orch: "Moonlight Bay" (LP-558) Bert Lahr, Skelton, Powell, Tommy Dorsey Orch: "I'll Take Tallulah" (LP-608)

420012a Film THE ROAD TO MOROCCO records by members of orig cast. MUSIC: James Van Heusen. WORDS: John Burke. Bing Crosby, 1942: "The Road to Morocco" (78/Dec 18514) "Ain't Got a Dime to My Name," "Moonlight Becomes You," "Constantly" Crosby & Bob Hope, later: "The Road to Morocco" (LP-339) Crosby, Hope, Dorothy Lamour, 1946 parody: "The Road to Morocco" (LP-592)

420013a Film PARDON MY SARONG 1940 record by the Ink Spots of orig cast. "Do I Worry" (78/Dec 23633)

420014a Film SPRINGTIME IN THE ROCKIES soundtrack. MUSIC & WORDS: mostly Harry Warren, Mack Gordon. ORCH & COND: Alfred Newman. CAST: Betty Grable, John Payne, Carmen Miranda, Harry James Orch. (Titania 507, with Sweet Rosie O'Grady. Excerpts: Miranda: "Chattanooga Choo-Choo" (LP-558) Miranda, Payne, Grable: "Pan Americana Jubilee" (LP-633)(Incomplete: LP-558).)

420014b Film SPRINGTIME IN THE ROCKIES 1944 radio prod. CAST: Betty Grable & Carmen Miranda of orig cast; Dick Powell. (Pelican 128)

420014c Film SPRINGTIME IN THE ROCKIES 1942 records by members of orig prod. Carmen Miranda: "Chattanooga Choo-Choo," "Tic-Tac do meu Coracao" (LP-522) Harry James Orch: "A Poem Set to Music," "I Had the Craziest Dream" (78/Col 36659)

420015a Film SONG OF THE ISLANDS soundtrack. MUSIC & WORDS: Harry Owens, Harry Warren, Mack Gordon. ORCH & COND: Alfred Newman. CAST: Betty Grable, Ben Gage (for Victor Mature), Hilo Hattie, Jack Oakie. (Caliban 6009, with Pin-Up Girl; plus Gage, Grable: "Blue Shadows and White Gardenias" (LP-588). Excerpts: Grable: "Sing Me a Song of the Islands" Grable, Hilo Hattie: "Down on Ami-Ami Oni-Oni Isle" (LP-284).)

420016a Film FOOTLIGHT SERENADE soundtrack. MUSIC: Ralph Rainger. WORDS: Leo Robin. ORCH & COND: Charles Henderson. CAST: Betty Grable, John Payne, chorus. (Caliban 6002, with Rose of Washington Square; plus Grable: "I'll Be Marching to a Love Song" (dropped before release) (LP-423). Excerpts: Grable: "I Heard the Birdies Sing" (LP-284)(LP-768) Grable, Payne: "I'm Still Crazy for You" (LP-768).)

420017a Film THE FLEET'S IN soundtrack. MUSIC: Victor Schertzinger. WORDS: Johnny Mercer. COND: Victor Young. CAST: Dorothy Lamour, Betty Hutton, Cass Daley, Bob Eberly, Helen O'Connell, Betty Jane Rhodes, Jimmy Dorsey Orch. (Hollywood Soundstage 405. Excerpts: Hutton: "Arthur Murray Taught Me Dancing in a Hurry" (LP-558) Lamour: "I Remember You," "When You Hear the Time Signal" (LP-647).)

420017b Film THE FLEET'S IN 1971 record sung by Johnny Mercer, lyricist. "Arthur Murray Taught Me Dancing in a Hurry" (LP-533)

420017c Film THE FLEET'S IN contemp records by members of orig prod. Betty Hutton: "Arthur Murray Taught Me Dancing in a Hurry" (LP-285) Jimmy Dorsey Orch: "Tangerine" (LP-480) "I Remember You," "If You Build a Better Mousetrap" (78/Dec 4132) "Not Mine," "Arthur Murray Taught Me Dancing in a Hurry" (78/Dec 4122)

420018a Film SALUDOS AMIGOS contemp album by members

of orig prod and others. MUSIC & WORDS: Charles Wolcott, Aloysio Oliveira, others. COND: Charles Wolcott (of orig prod). VOCALS: Aloysio Oliveira (of orig prod), Kenneth Rundquist. (78/Dec album 369)

420018b Film SALUDOS AMIGOS album. COND: Leo Perachi. VOCALS: chorus. (Disneyland 3039, with The Three Caballeros)

420018c Film SALUDOS AMIGOS soundtrack. Chorus: "Saludos Amigos" (LP-661)

420019a Film YOUTH ON PARADE records sung by Sammy Cahn, lyricist. MUSIC: Jule Styne. "I've Heard That Song Before" (1972: LP-658)(1974: LP-313)(1977: LP-503)

420020a Film SEVEN SWEETHEARTS soundtrack. Kathryn Grayson: "You and the Waltz and I" (LP-346)

420021a Film MY GAL SAL soundtrack. MUSIC & WORDS: Paul Dresser, Ralph Rainger, Leo Robin. Nan Wynn (for Rita Hayworth), chorus: "On the Gay White Way" (LP-403) (LP-768) "Come Tell What's Your Answer," "My Gal Sal" Wynn, Victor Mature: "Oh, the Pity of It All" (LP-403) "Here You Are" (LP-403)(LP-768)

420022a Film NOW, VOYAGER 1975 record by Bette Davis of orig cast. "It Can't Be Wrong" (LP-395)

420023a Film PRESENTING LILY MARS soundtrack. Judy Garland: Medley (complete version, shortened before release)(LP-455)

420024a Film CROSSROADS soundtrack. MUSIC: Arthur Schwartz. WORDS: Howard Dietz. Claire Trevor: "Till You Return" (LP-555)

420025a Film CAIRO soundtrack. MUSIC: Arthur Schwartz, Harold Arlen. WORDS: E Y Harburg, Howard Dietz. Jeanette MacDonald, chorus: "Keep the Light Burning Bright in the Harbor," "Cairo" (LP-555) Ethel Waters: "Buds Won't Bud" (LP-657)

420025b Film CAIRO 1955 record sung by Harold Arlen, composer. "Buds Won't Bud" (LP-192)

420026a Film THIS GUN FOR HIRE soundtrack. Veronica Lake (dubbed): "Now You See It" (LP-568)

420027a Film THE MAYOR OF 44TH STREET 1941 records by Freddy Martin Orch of orig prod. "Heavenly, Isn't It?," "When There's a Breeze on Lake Louise" (78/Bluebird B-11437)

420028a Film SEVEN DAYS' LEAVE 1942 records by Freddy Martin Orch of orig prod. MUSIC: Jimmy McHugh. WORDS: Frank Loesser. "I Get the Neck of the Chicken," "Can't Get Out of This Mood" (78/Vic 20-1515) "A Touch of Texas," "Soft-Hearted" (78/Vic 20-1504)

420029a Film MY FAVORITE SPY 1942 records by Kay Kyser Orch of orig prod. MUSIC: James Van Heusen. WORDS: John Burke. "Just Plain Lonesome," "Got the Moon in My Pocket" (78/Col 36575)

420030a Film ICELAND contemp records by Joan Merrill of orig cast. MUSIC: Harry Warren. WORDS: Mack Gordon. "There Will Never Be Another You," "You Can't Say No to a Soldier" (78/Bluebird B-11574)

420031a Film REAP THE WILD WIND soundtrack. Paulette Goddard: "Sea Chantey" (LP-656)

420032a Film SWEATER GIRL soundtrack. MUSIC: Jule Styne. WORDS: Frank Loesser. Betty Jane Rhodes: "I Don't Want to Walk without You," "I Said 'No'" (LP-656)

420033a Film SYMPHONY HOUR soundtrack of the Mickey Mouse cartoon. "Light Cavalry Overture" (LP-661)

420034a Film STRICTLY IN THE GROOVE 1941 record by Ozzie Nelson Orch of orig prod. "Jersey Jive" (78/Bluebird B-11180)

420035a Film JUKE BOX JENNY 1941 records by Charlie Barnet

Orch of orig prod. "Fifty Million Nickels," "Macumba" (78/Bluebird B-11396)

420602a BY JUPITER 1967 prod. MUSIC: Richard Rodgers. WORDS: Lorenz Hart. ORCH: Abba Bogin. COND: Milton Setzer. CAST: Bob Dishy, Jackie Alloway, Irene Byatt, Rosemarie Heyer, Robert R Kaye, Sheila Sullivan. (RCA LSO-1137)

420602b BY JUPITER 1942 album by Hildegarde. COND: Harry Sosnik. (78/Dec album 326)

420602c BY JUPITER records by Benay Venuta of 1942 prod. "Everything I've Got Belongs to You" (1972: LP-509) (1975: LP-510)

420704a THIS IS THE ARMY orig prod. MUSIC & WORDS: Irving Berlin. COND: Milton Rosenstock. CAST: Irving Berlin, Earl Oxford, Stuart Churchill, Robert Shanley, James Cross, Ezra Stone, Jules Oshins, Philip Truex, chorus. (Dec 10" 5108; CBS Records X-14877, with Call Me Mister; LP-543. Excerpt: Berlin: "Oh, How I Hate to Get Up in the Morning" (LP-321)(LP-519).)

420704b THIS IS THE ARMY 1942 studio prod. CAST: Brad Reynolds, Harvey Harding, Fats Waller. (78/Vic album P-131)

420704c THIS IS THE ARMY contemp records sung by Irving Berlin. With John Scott Trotter Orch: "Oh! How I Hate to Get Up in the Morning" (78/V-Disc 780) From 1943 London prod: "This Is the Army, Mr. Jones," "My British Buddy" (LP-543)(LP-589)

420704d THIS IS THE ARMY records by Kate Smith of 1943 film cast. "God Bless America" (1939: 78/Vic 26198) (1947: 78/MGM 30025)(Later: LP-593)(1970: LP-704)

420704e THIS IS THE ARMY 1943 film soundtrack. COND: Leo F Forbstein. CAST: Irving Berlin, Ezra Stone, Jules Oshins, Philip Truex, Earl Oxford, & Robert Shanley of orig prod; Gertrude Niesen, George Murphy, George Tobias, Kate Smith, Frances Langford, James Burell, Ralph Magelssen, Alan Hale, James Cross. (Hollywood Soundstage 408)

421005a LET FREEDOM SING records sung by Earl Robinson, composer. WORDS: Lewis Allen. "The House I Live In" (78/V-Disc 99)(78/Keynote K-538)

1943

430001a Film HERS TO HOLD contemp record by Deanna Durbin of orig cast. "Say a Prayer for the Boys Over There" (LP-13)

430002a Film THE SKY'S THE LIMIT records sung by Harold Arlen (composer) & Johnny Mercer (lyricist). "One for My Baby" (Arlen, 1955: LP-101)(Mercer, 1944: LP-559, LP-720) "My Shining Hour" (Arlen, 1966: LP-60)

430002b Film THE SKY'S THE LIMIT soundtrack. COND: Leigh Harline. CAST: Fred Astaire, Joan Leslie. (Curtain Calls 100/19, with A Damsel in Distress)

430002c Film THE SKY'S THE LIMIT records by Fred Astaire of orig cast. "One for My Baby" (1945: LP-344)(1976: LP-429)

430003a Film HELLO, 'FRISCO, HELLO soundtrack. MUSIC & WORDS: Various. ORCH & COND: Emil Newman, Charles Henderson. CAST: Alice Faye, John Payne, Jack Oakie, June Havoc. (Caliban 6005, with Spring Parade; plus Havoc: "I Gotta Have You" (dropped before release) (LP-423). Excerpts: Faye: "You'll Never Know" (LP-424) "They Always Pick on Me" Faye, Payne: "Hello, 'Frisco, Hello," "You'll Never Know" Faye, Havoc, Oakie: "The Grizzly Bear" (LP-283).)

430003b Film HELLO, 'FRISCO, HELLO records by Alice Faye of orig cast. "You'll Never Know" (Radio: LP-717)(1962: LP-100) "By the Light of the Silvery Moon," "Ragtime Cowboy Joe" (Radio: LP-717)

430003c Film HELLO,'FRISCO, HELLO 1943 radio prod. VOCALS: Alice Faye, Robert Young. (Pelican 126)

430004a Film THE GANG'S ALL HERE soundtrack. MUSIC & WORDS: mostly by Harry Warren, Leo Robin. ORCH & COND: Alfred Newman, Charles Henderson. CAST: Alice Faye, Carmen Miranda, Phil Baker, Sheila Ryan, Tony De Marco, Benny Goodman Orch. (Classic International Filmusicals 3003. Excerpts: Faye: "A Journey to a Star" Faye, Goodman Orch: "No Love, No Nothing" (LP-424).)

430004b Film THE GANG'S ALL HERE 1962 record by Alice Faye of orig cast. "No Love, No Nothin'" (LP-100)

430005a Film IS EVERYBODY HAPPY? records by Ted Lewis Orch of orig prod. "On the Sunny Side of the Street" (1930: LP-168) "Just around the Corner" (1925: 78/Col 504-D)(1941: LP-167, LP-457, LP-491) "St Louis Blues" (1922: 78/Col A-3790)(1926: 78/Col 697-D)(1938: LP-167, LP-457, LP-491) "Cuddle Up a Little Closer" (1950: LP-457, LP-686)

430006a Film CASABLANCA soundtrack. Dooley Wilson: "As Time Goes By" (LP-223) (Incomplete: LP-595)

430006b Film CASABLANCA contemp records by Dooley Wilson of orig cast. "As Time Goes By, " "Knock on Wood" (78/Dec 40006)

430007a Film STORMY WEATHER soundtrack. MUSIC & WORDS: Various. CAST: Bill Robinson, Lena Horne, Cab Calloway, Fats Waller, Cab Calloway Orch, Zutty Singleton Orch, Ada Brown. (Sountrak 103, plus Waller & Brown: "That Ain't Right" on 78/V-Disc 165)

430007b Film STORMY WEATHER records by members of orig cast. Lena Horne: "Stormy Weather" (1941: LP-241) Fats Waller: "Ain't Misbehavin'" (Piano, 1929: 78/Vic 22108) (Piano/vocal, 1938: 78/Bluebird B-10288)(Piano/vocal, 1943: LP-345)(Piano/vocal, later: 78/Vic 40-4003) Cab Calloway Orch: "Geechee Joe" (1941: 78/Okeh 6147)

430007c Film STORMY WEATHER records sung by Harold Arlen, composer. "Stormy Weather" (1933: LP-48, LP-340, LP-517, LP-603, LP-711)(1955: LP-101)

430008a Film THOUSANDS CHEER soundtrack. MUSIC & WORDS: Various. COND: Herbert Stothart. CAST: Kathryn Grayson, Lena Horne, June Allyson, Gloria DeHaven, Virginia O'Brien, Judy Garland, Jose Iturbi (piano), Kay Kyser Orch, Benny Goodman Orch, Bob Crosby Orch. (Hollywood Soundstage 409. Incomplete: Cheerio 5000, with Little Nellie Kelly. Excerpts: Horne: "Honeysuckle Rose" (LP-252) Grayson: "Daybreak" (LP-346) "Let There Be Music," "Sempre Libera" (LP-347) "Three Letters in the Mailbox" (LP-636).)

430009a Film HIS BUTLER'S SISTER soundtrack. Deanna Durbin: "In the Spirit of the Moment," "When You're Away," "Russian Medley," "The Prince" (LP-256)

430010a Film THE AMAZING MRS. HOLLIDAY soundtrack. Deanna Durbin: "The Old Refrain" (LP-256)

430011a Film HOW'S ABOUT IT? 1942 records by the Andrews Sisters of orig cast. "Here Comes the Navy" (78/Dec 18497) "East of the Rockies" (78/Dec 18533)

430012a Film STAGE DOOR CANTEEN records by members of orig prod. Ethel Merman: "Marching through Berlin" (1942: 78/Vic 20-1521) Peggy Lee, Benny Goodman Orch: "Why Don't You Do Right" (1943: 78/Col 36652) Goodman Orch: "Bugle Call Rag" (1936: 78/Vic 25467)(1941: 78/Col 36109) Peggy Lee: "Why Don't You Do Right" (1951: 78/Cap 1602)

430012b Film STAGE DOOR CANTEEN soundtrack. MUSIC & WORDS: James Monaco, Al Dubin, Richard Rodgers, Lorenz Hart, others. CAST: Gracie Fields, Ethel Merman, Lanny Ross, Ray Bolger, Kenny Baker, Ethel Waters, Ned Sparks, Peggy Lee. (Curtain Calls 100/11-12, with Hollywood Canteen)

430013a Film CONEY ISLAND soundtrack. MUSIC: Ralph Rainger. WORDS: Leo Robin. CAST: Betty Grable, Cesar Romero, Charles Winninger, chorus. (Caliban 6001, with Moon over Miami. Excerpts: Grable: "Take It from There" (LP-284)(LP-768) "Cuddle Up a Little Closer" (LP-284) "There's Danger in a Dance" (LP-768).)

430014a Film SWEET ROSIE O'GRADY soundtrack. MUSIC & WORDS: mostly Harry Warren, Mack Gordon. CAST: Betty Grable, Phil Regan, Robert Young. (Titania 507, with Springtime in the Rockies. Excerpts: Grable, chorus: "Where, Oh Where Is the Groom?," "Waitin' at the Church" (LP-284) Grable, Regan: "My Heart Tells Me" (LP-633) (Incomplete: LP-568).)

430014b Film SWEET ROSIE O'GRADY 1943 radio performance by Betty Grable of orig cast. "My Heart Tells Me" (LP-592) (LP-669)

430014c Film SWEET ROSIE O'GRADY later record by Phil Regan of orig cast. "Sweet Rosie O'Grady" (78/Dec 25482)

430015a Film HAPPY GO LUCKY soundtrack. MUSIC: Jimmy McHugh. WORDS: Frank Loesser. Mary Martin, Dick Powell: "Happy Go Lucky" Betty Hutton: "Murder He Says," "The Fuddy Duddy Watchmaker" (LP-656)

430015b Film HAPPY GO LUCKY 1947 record sung by Frank Loesser, lyricist. "Sing a Tropical Song" (LP-656)

430015c Film HAPPY GO LUCKY contemp record by Betty Hutton of orig cast. "Murder, He Says" (LP-285)

430016a Film THANK YOUR LUCKY STARS soundtrack. MUSIC & WORDS: Arthur Schwartz, Frank Loesser, Harold Arlen, Johnny Mercer. COND: Leo F Forbstein. CAST: Dinah Shore, John Garfield, Dennis Morgan, Joan Leslie, Eddie Cantor, Jack Carson, Alan Hale, Ann Sheridan, Joyce Reynolds, Hattie McDaniel, Errol Flynn, Bette Davis, Olivia de Havilland, Ida Lupino, George Tobias, Spike Jones Orch. (Curtain Calls 100/8. Excerpt: Davis: "They're Either Too Young or Too Old" (LP-595).)

430016b Film THANK YOUR LUCKY STARS records by members of orig prod. Bette Davis: "They're Either Too Young or Too Old" (1975: LP-395) Spike Jones Orch: "Hotcha Cornia" (1942: 78/Bluebird B-30-0818) Dinah Shore: "The Blues in the Night" (1942: 78/Bluebird B-11436)(1966: LP-671)

430017a Film DIXIE contemp records by Bing Crosby of orig cast. MUSIC: James Van Heusen. WORDS: John Burke. "Sunday, Monday or Always," "If You Please" (LP-339)

430018a Film ABOVE SUSPICION soundtrack. Joan Crawford, Fred MacMurray: "A Bird in a Gilded Cage" (LP-401)

430019a Film THEY GOT ME COVERED soundtrack. MUSIC: Harold Arlen. WORDS: Johnny Mercer. Nan Wynn (for Marion Martin): "Palsy Walsy" (LP-496)(LP-657)

430020a Film LADY OF BURLESQUE soundtrack. Barbara Stanwyck: "Take It Off the E-String" (LP-496)

430021a Film SEE HERE, PRIVATE HARGROVE! 1950 record by Frank Loesser (lyricist) & chorus. MUSIC: Ted Grouya. "In My Arms" (78/Col 38964)

430022a Film RIDING HIGH soundtrack. Dorothy Lamour: "Get Your Man," "Injun Gal Heap Hep," "I'm the Secretary to the Sultan," "Whistling in the Light" (LP-647) Cass Daley: "He Loved Me Till the All-Clear Came" (by Harold Arlen) (LP-657)

430023a Film SOMETHING TO SHOUT ABOUT soundtrack. MU-

SIC & WORDS: Cole Porter. COND: Morris Stoloff. Orchestra: Main Title. Janet Blair, Don Ameche: "You'd Be So Nice to Come Home to," "I Always Knew" Blair, Hazel Scott (piano): "Through Thick and Thin" Blair, Jaye Martin: "I Always Knew" Blair: "Something to Shout about," "Lotus Bloom," "Hasta Luego" Ensemble: "Through Thick and Thin/Finale" (LP-655)

430024a Film TRUE TO LIFE records by Hoagy Carmichael (composer) & Johnny Mercer (lyricist). "The Old Music Master" (Mercer, 1944 vocal with Jack Teagarden: LP-720) (Carmichael, vocal & piano, 1947: LP-94)

430107a SOMETHING FOR THE BOYS records by members of orig cast. MUSIC & WORDS: Cole Porter. Paula Laurence, contemp: "Something for the Boys" Laurence, Betty Garrett: "By the Mississinewah" (Contemp: LP-182, LP-301) Garrett: "I'm in Love with a Soldier Boy" (1977: LP-551) Ethel Merman: "He's a Right Guy" (Later: LP-36) "Something for the Boys" (1979: LP-670)

430107b SOMETHING FOR THE BOYS 1943 radio show with Ethel Merman & Bill Johnson of orig cast; chorus. Johnson: "Could It Be You?" Merman: "He's a Right Guy" Merman, Johnson: "Hey, Good Lookin'" Merman, chorus: "Something for the Boys" (LP-182)(LP-301) Chorus: "See That You're Born in Texas" (LP-301)

430107c SOMETHING FOR THE BOYS 1944 records by Evelyn Dall of 1944 London cast. "Hey! Good Lookin'," "Something for the Boys" (78/Dec(E) F-8429)

430107d SOMETHING FOR THE BOYS 1944 film soundtrack. Vivian Blaine: "Something for the Boys" (LP-655)

430107e SOMETHING FOR THE BOYS contemp record by Perry Como of 1944 film prod. "I Wish We Didn't Have to Say Goodnight" (by Jimmy McHugh) (78/Vic 20-1630)

430331a OKLAHOMA! orig prod. MUSIC: Richard Rodgers. WORDS: Oscar Hammerstein II. ORCH: Robert Russell Bennett. COND: Jay Blackton. CAST: Alfred Drake, Joan Roberts, Celeste Holm, Howard da Sylva, Lee Dixon, Joseph Buloff, Betty Garde, Ralph Riggs. (Time/Life P-15590. Incomplete: Dec 8000. Excerpts: Drake, Roberts: "People Will Say We're in Love" (LP-164) Drake: "Lonely Room" Garde, Riggs, chorus: "The Farmer and the Cowman" Joseph Buloff, chorus: "It's a Scandal" (LP-497).)

430331b OKLAHOMA! 1955 film soundtrack. ORCH: Robert Russell Bennett. COND: Jay Blackton. CAST: Gordon MacRae, Gloria Grahame, Gene Nelson, Charlotte Greenwood, James Whitmore, Shirley Jones, Rod Steiger, Jay C Flippen. (Cap SAO-595)

430331c OKLAHOMA! 1952 studio prod. COND: Lehman Engel. CAST: Nelson Eddy, Wilton Clary, Portia Nelson, Virginia Haskins, Kaye Ballard, David Morris, Lee Cass. (Col ML-4598)

430331d OKLAHOMA! 1964 studio prod. ORCH: Philip J Lang. COND: Franz Allers. CAST: Florence Henderson (of 1952 touring prod), John Raitt, Phyllis Newman, Jack Elliott, Ara Berberian, Irene Carroll, Leonard Stokes. (Col OS-2610)

430331e OKLAHOMA! contemp medley by members of 1947 London cast. COND: Reginald Burston. CAST: Howard Keel, Betty Jane Watson, Walter Donahue, Dorothea MacFarland, Henry Clarke, chorus. (World Records(E) SH-393, with Annie Get Your Gun & Carousel. Incomplete: Stanyan SR-10069, with Annie Get Your Gun.)

430331f OKLAHOMA! studio prod. COND: Al Goodman. CAST: Richard Torigi, Susan Shaute, William Reynolds, Dolores Martin, Paula Wayne. (Diplomat 2213. Excerpts: Promenade 2062, with South Pacific.)

430331g OKLAHOMA! 1960 studio prod. CAST: Stuart Foster, Lois Hunt, Fay DeWitt, Leonard Stokes, Keith Booth. (Epic 562)

430331h OKLAHOMA! album. COND: Al Goodman. CAST: James Melton, Eleanor Steber, John Charles Thomas. (78/Vic album M-988)

430331i OKLAHOMA! records by members of orig cast. Alfred Drake: "Oh, What a Beautiful Morning" (1959: LP-294) Celeste Holm: "I Cain't Say No" (1972: LP-509) Joan Roberts: "People Will Say We're in Love," "Many a New Day" (1948: LP-706)

430331j OKLAHOMA! 1953 album. COND: Jay Blackton. VOCALS: John Raitt, Patricia Northrup, chorus. (RCA 10" LPM-3150, with Carousel)

430331k OKLAHOMA! studio prod. ORCH & COND: Thomas M Davis, Hans Hagan. VOCALS: Lloyd Hanna, Irene Cummings, Deeda Patrick, James Cassidy, chorus. (Crown 106)

430331l OKLAHOMA! studio prod. "Ed Sullivan presents Oklahoma!" No other credits given. (National Academy 6)

430331m OKLAHOMA! 1972 records by members of 1955 film prod. Gordon MacRae: Medley. Gene Nelson: "Everything's Up to Date in Kansas City" (LP-509)

430331n OKLAHOMA! album. COND: Johnny Gregory. VOCALS: Elizabeth Larner, Barry Kent, chorus. (Wing(E) SRW-11005, with Annie Get Your Gun)

430331o OKLAHOMA! studio prod. COND: Al Goodman ("Dean Franconi"). VOCALS: Richard Torigi, Susan Shaute, Edgar Powell, Gretchen Rhoads, Paula Wayne. (Hurrah 1037)

430331p OKLAHOMA! 1959 studio prod. COND: Eric Rogers. VOCALS: Bryan Johnson, Eula Parker, Rosalind Page, chorus. (Ace of Clubs(E) 1002, with Carousel)

430331q OKLAHOMA! 1959 studio prod. VOCALS: Kenneth Robert, Jody Kim, Edward Elmer, Steven Donald, chorus. (Lion 70094)

430331r OKLAHOMA! studio prod. COND: Johnny Douglas. CAST: George Romaine, Marion Madden, Barbara Elsy, Barbara Brown, Julian Orchard, Peter Felgate, Fred Lucas, chorus. (Cap SN-7511)

430331s OKLAHOMA! 1966 studio prod. COND: Alyn Ainsworth. VOCALS: Anne Rogers, Tony Adams, Cheryl Kennedy, Betty Winsett, Richard Fox, Fred Lucas, Ted Gilbert, Mike Bretton, chorus. (Music for Pleasure(E) 1084)

430331t OKLAHOMA! 1957 records by Isabel Bigley, who replaced Betty Jane Watson in 1947 London prod. "Out of My Dreams" With Stephen Douglass: "People Will Say We're in Love" (LP-408)

430331u OKLAHOMA! records by uncredited soloists. COND: Robert Russell Bennett (orchestrator of orig & 1955 film prods). "People Will Say We're in Love," "The Surrey with the Fringe on Top," "Oh What a Beautiful Morning," "Many a New Day," "Poor Jud" (45/Royale EP-108)

430331v OKLAHOMA! 1979 prod. ORCH: Robert Russell Bennett. COND: Jay Blackton (of orig prod). CAST: Laurence Guittard, Christine Andreas, Mary Wickes, Martin Vidnovic, Christine Ebersole, Bruce Adler, Philip Rash, Harry Groener, chorus. (RCA CBL1-3572)

430331w OKLAHOMA! 1980 London prod, rec live. COND: John Owen Edwards. CAST: John Diedrich, Rosamund Shelley, Madge Ryan, Alfred Molina, Jillian Mack. (Stiff(E) OAK-1)

430331x OKLAHOMA! 1980 recording of reminiscences and songs by Celeste Holm of orig cast, rec live. ORCH: William Roy. (Original Cast 8129, entitled "Celeste Holm Gives a Very Personal Tribute to Oklahoma")

430414a ZIEGFELD FOLLIES OF 1943 1956 record by the composer, vocal and piano. MUSIC & WORDS: Harold Rome. "The Advertising Song" (LP-316)

430617a EARLY TO BED 1943 records by Thomas (Fats) Waller (composer), piano & vocal. WORDS: George Marion Jr. "Slightly Less Than Wonderful," "There's a Gal in My Life," "This Is So Nice," "Martinique" (45/RCA EPA-449)(LP-345)

430909a MY DEAR PUBLIC 1956 record sung by Irving Caesar, lyricist. "Love Is Such a Cheat" (LP-353)

430909b MY DEAR PUBLIC 1942 record by Willie Howard of orig cast. Skit "Comes the Revolution" (LP-630)

430923a SOMETHING IN THE AIR contemp record by Cicely Courtneidge of orig (London) cast. MUSIC: Manning Sherwin. WORDS: Harold Purcell, Max Kester. "Home" (LP-90)

431007a ONE TOUCH OF VENUS orig prod. MUSIC: Kurt Weill. WORDS: Ogden Nash. ORCH: Kurt Weill. COND: Maurice Abravanel. CAST: Mary Martin, Kenny Baker, chorus. (Dec 9122)

431007b ONE TOUCH OF VENUS 1943 records by Kurt Weill (composer), vocals & piano. "West Wind," "Very Very Very," "Wooden Wedding," "Speak Low," "The Jersey Plunk," "The Trouble with Women," "That's Him" (LP-150)

431007c ONE TOUCH OF VENUS 1977 record by Mary Martin of orig cast. "That's Him" (LP-652)

431109a ARC DE TRIOMPHE contemp records by members of orig (London) prod. MUSIC: Ivor Novello. WORDS: Christopher Hassall, Ivor Novello. COND: Tom Lewis. Elisabeth Welch: "Dark Music" Mary Ellis, Peter Graves: "Easy to Live with" Ellis: "Waking or Sleeping," "Man of My Heart" (LP-342) Orchestra: Medley (78/HMV(E) C-3377)

431120a WINGED VICTORY orig prod. MUSIC & WORDS: David Rose, Moss Hart, others. ORCH: David Rose. COND: Leonard de Paur, David Rose. Winged Victory Chorus & Orchestra, solo by Don Richards. "Winged Victory," "My Dream Book of Memories," "Whiffenpoof Song," "The Army Air Corps" (78/Dec 12" album 363; JJA Records 19782, with Song of Norway & Up in Central Park.)

431202a CARMEN JONES orig prod. MUSIC: Georges Bizet. WORDS: Oscar Hammerstein II. ORCH: Robert Russell Bennett. COND: Joseph Littau, Robert Shaw. CAST: Muriel Smith, Luther Saxon, Carlotta Franzell, Glenn Bryant, June Hawkins. (78/Dec 12" album 366. Incomplete: Dec 80l4.)

431202b CARMEN JONES 1954 film soundtrack. COND: Herschel B Gilbert. CAST: Marilynn Horne (for Dorothy Dandridge), LeVern Hutcherson (for Harry Belafonte), Marvin Hayes (for Joe Adams), Olga James, Pearl Bailey, Broc Peters, Bernice Peterson (for Diahann Carroll), Joe Crawford (for Nick Stewart). (RCA LM-1881)

431202c CARMEN JONES 1967 studio prod. COND: Kenneth Alwyn. CAST: Grace Bumbry, George Webb, Elisabeth Welch, Ena Babb, Thomas Baptiste, Ursula Connors, Edward Darling. (Heliodor 25046)

1944

440001a Film MEET ME IN ST. LOUIS contemp album by Judy Garland of orig cast. MUSIC: Hugh Martin. WORDS: Ralph Blane. COND: George Stoll. (Dec 8498, with The Harvey Girls. Incomplete: LP-7. Excerpts: "The Trolley Song," "Meet Me in St Louis, Louis" (LP-511).)

440001b Film MEET ME IN ST. LOUIS soundtrack. ORCH: Conrad Salinger. COND: George Stoll. Judy Garland: "The Trolley Song" (LP-8)(LP-289) "The Boy Next Door" (LP-8)(LP-289)(LP-454) "Have

Yourself a Merry Little Christmas" (LP-416) Garland, Margaret O'Brien: "Under the Bamboo Tree" (LP-252)

440001c Film MEET ME IN ST. LOUIS 1956 records by Hugh Martin & Ralph Blane, composers. "Have Yourself a Merry Little Christmas," "The Trolley Song," "The Boy Next Door" (LP-193)

440001d Film MEET ME IN ST. LOUIS later records by Judy Garland of orig cast. "The Trolley Song" (LP-189)(LP-201) LP-240)(LP-461)(LP-762)(LP-780) "The Boy Next Door" (LP-201)(LP-738)

440001e Film MEET ME IN ST. LOUIS 1959 TV prod soundtrack. Jane Powell: "The Trolley Song" (LP-281)

440001f Film MEET ME IN ST. LOUIS rehearsal for 1946 radio prod. VOCALS: Judy Garland, Margaret O'Brien. (Pelican 118)

440002a Film CAN'T HELP SINGING 1945 album by Deanna Durbin & Robert Paige of orig cast, with chorus. MUSIC: Jerome Kern. WORDS: E Y Harburg. COND: Edgar Fairchild. (78/Dec 12" album 387; LP-607. Incomplete: Ace of Hearts(E) 60.)

440002b Film CAN'T HELP SINGING soundtrack. ORCH & COND: Hans J. Salter. CAST: Deanna Durbin, Robert Paige. (Titania 509, with Dubarry Was a Lady)

440003a Film I'LL BE SEEING YOU records by Sammy Fain, composer. "I'll Be Seeing You" (1954, vocal: LP-707) (1971, piano & vocal: LP-694)

440004a Film HERE COME THE WAVES contemp records by Bing Crosby of orig cast & the Andrews Sisters. MUSIC: Harold Arlen. WORDS: Johnny Mercer. Crosby: "Let's Take the Long Way Home," "I Promise You" Crosby, the Andrews Sisters: "There's a Fellow Waiting in Poughkeepsie," "Ac-cent-tchu-ate the Positive" (LP-27)

440004b Film HERE COME THE WAVES records sung by Harold Arlen (composer) & Johnny Mercer (lyricist). "Ac-cent-tchu-ate the Positive" (Arlen, 1955: LP-101)(Arlen, 1966: LP-60) (Mercer, 1944: LP-559, LP-720)

440004c Film HERE COME THE WAVES soundtrack. COND: Robert Emmett Dolan. Betty Hutton: "Join the Navy"(duet with self), "There's a Fellow Waiting in Poughkeepsie" Bing Crosby: "Let's Take the Long Way Home" Crosby, Hutton: "I Promise You" Crosby, Sonny Tufts: "Ac-cent-tchu-ate the Positive" Chorus: "Here Come the Waves" (LP-657)

440005a Film UP IN ARMS records by members of orig cast. MUSIC: Harold Arlen. WORDS: Ted Koehler. Dinah Shore: "Now I Know" (78/Vic 20-1562) "Tess's Torch Song" (78/Col 37854) Danny Kaye: "Manic-Depressive Presents" (Lobby Scene, by Sylvia Fine & Max Liebman)(LP-6)(LP-55) (LP-515)

440005b Film UP IN ARMS soundtrack. Orchestra: "Fall Out for Freedom" Dinah Shore: "Now I Know" Shore, Danny Kaye: "Tess's Torch Song," "Greetings, Gates"(the latter number probably by Sylvia Fine) Kaye: "Manic-Depressive Presents," "Malady in 4-F"(both songs by Sylvia Fine & Max Liebman) (Soundtrak 113; LP-701. Excerpt: Shore: "Tess's Torch Song" (LP-657).)

440006a Film GOING MY WAY 1945 album by Bing Crosby of orig cast. MUSIC: James Van Heusen. WORDS: John Burke. COND: John Scott Trotter, Victor Young. (LP-339. Incomplete: Dec 10" 5052, with The Bells of St. Mary's.)

440007a Film TO HAVE AND HAVE NOT records by Hoagy Carmichael (composer) of orig cast. "Hong Kong Blues" (1938: LP-644)(1942: LP-94)(1940s: 78/ARA 123)(1971: LP-694)

440008a Film MOON OVER LAS VEGAS records by Gene Austin of orig cast. "My Blue Heaven" (1927: LP-103, LP-475, LP-516, LP-539)(1942: LP-176)(1954: LP-362)

102

440009a Film MUSIC FOR MILLIONS records by members of orig cast. Jimmy Durante: "Umbriago" (1944: LP-80) Larry Adler, harmonica: "Clair de Lune" (1945: 78/Dec 23467)

440009b Film MUSIC FOR MILLIONS 1956 record sung by Irving Caesar, lyricist. "Umbriago" (LP-353)

440010a Film FOLLOW THE BOYS records by members of orig cast. Jeanette MacDonald: "Beyond the Blue Horizon" (1950: LP-77)(1958: LP-134) Sophie Tucker: "Some of These Days" (1911: CYL/Edison 4M-691)(1926: LP-168, LP-185)(1927: LP-52)(1929: 78/Vic 22049)(1930's: LP-332) (1937: LP-187)(1947: LP-186, LP-187, LP-297)(Later: LP-184) Dinah Shore: "I'll Walk Alone" (1943: 78/Vic 20-1586) "Mad about Him Blues" (1942: 78/Vic 27940) Andrews Sisters: "Shoo-Shoo Baby" (1943: 78/Dec 18572)

440010b Film FOLLOW THE BOYS 1977 record sung by Sammy Cahn, lyricist. MUSIC: Jule Styne. "I'll Walk Alone" (LP-503)

440011a Film TWO GIRLS AND A SAILOR soundtrack. MUSIC & WORDS: Various. CAST: June Allyson, Gloria DeHaven, Van Johnson, Tom Drake, Jimmy Durante, Lina Romay, Lena Horne, Harry James Orch, Xavier Cugat Orch. (Sound/Stage 2307. Excerpt: Durante: "Inka Dinka Doo" (LP-416).)

440011b Film TWO GIRLS AND A SAILOR records by members of orig cast. Jimmy Durante: "Inka Dinka Doo" (LP-41) (LP-42)(LP-80)(LP-175)(LP-292)(LP-297) Gloria DeHaven: "My Mother Told Me" (LP-272) Harry James Orch: "Estrellita" (78/Col 36729)

440012a Film ANCHORS AWEIGH soundtrack. MUSIC & WORDS: Jule Styne, Sammy Cahn, others. COND: George Stoll. PIANO: Jose Iturbi. CAST: Frank Sinatra, Gene Kelly, Kathryn Grayson. (Curtain Calls 100/17, plus Grayson: "Take a Chance on Romance" on LP-347)

440012b Film ANCHORS AWEIGH contemp records by members of orig cast. Frank Sinatra: "I Begged Her," "What Makes the Sunset?" "I Fall in Love Too Easily," "The Charm of You" (LP-250) Kathryn Grayson: "My Heart Sings," "Jealousy" (LP-364)

440013a Film MOONLIGHT AND CACTUS contemp record by the Andrews Sisters of orig cast. "Down in the Valley" (LP-266)

440014a Film SWINGTIME JOHNNY 1941 record by the Andrews Sisters of orig cast. "Boogie Woogie Bugle Boy" (LP-265) (LP-266)

440015a Film HOLLYWOOD CANTEEN soundtrack. MUSIC & WORDS: Cole Porter, Burton Lane, E Y Harburg, Ted Koehler, Vernon Duke, Harold Adamson, others. CAST: Andrews Sisters, Jack Carson, Jane Wyman, Eddie Cantor, Nora Martin, Roy Rogers, Joan Leslie, Kitty Carlisle, Dennis Morgan, Joe E Brown. (Curtain Calls 100/11-12, with Stage Door Canteen)

440015b Film HOLLYWOOD CANTEEN records by members of orig cast. Andrews Sisters, contemp: "Corns for My Country" (78/Dec 18628) Andrews Sisters (with Bing Crosby, not of orig cast), contemp: "Don't Fence Me In" (by Cole Porter)(78/Dec 23364) Eddie Cantor, 1942: "We're Having a Baby" (78/Dec 4314) Roy Rogers, later: "Don't Fence Me In" (LP-278)

440016a Film SHOW BUSINESS records by Eddie Cantor of orig cast. "I Don't Want to Get Well" (1917: 78/Aeolian Vocalion 1233) "Dinah" (1944: LP-143, LP-165, LP-384) (1950: LP-144, LP-542) "Makin' Whoopee" (1928: LP-539) (Later: LP-30, LP-38, LP-143, LP-144, LP-165, LP-297, LP-384, LP-542)

440017a Film CHRISTMAS HOLIDAY 1944 records by Deanna Durbin of orig cast. "Spring Will Be a Little Late This Year"(by Frank Loesser), "Always"(by Irving Berlin) (LP-406)

440018a Film THE YELLOW ROSE OF TEXAS record by Roy Rogers of orig cast. "The Yellow Rose of Texas" (LP-278)

440019a Film SAN FERNANDO VALLEY record by Roy Rogers of orig cast. "San Fernando Valley" (LP-278)

440020a Film THE SONG OF THE OPEN ROAD soundtrack. MUSIC: Walter Kent. WORDS: Kim Gannon. Jane Powell: "Rolling down the Road," "I'm Having Fun in the Sun," "Here It is Monday" (LP-281)

440021a Film AND THE ANGELS SING soundtrack. MUSIC: James Van Heusen. WORDS: John Burke. Dorothy Lamour, Betty Hutton, Diana Lynn, Mimi Chandler: "Knocking on Your Own Front Door," "For the First Hundred Years" Lamour: "It Could Happen to You" (LP-647)

440021b Film AND THE ANGELS SING contemp records by members of orig cast. Betty Hutton: "His Rocking Horse Ran Away" (LP-285) Diana Lynn (piano): "Concerto Theme" (LP-742)

440022a Film FOUR JILLS IN A JEEP soundtrack. MUSIC & WORDS: mostly Jimmy McHugh, Harold Adamson. CAST: Betty Grable, Alice Faye, Dick Haymes, Carole Landis, Carmen Miranda, Martha Raye, Mitzi Mayfair, Jimmy Dorsey Orch. (Hollywood Soundstage 407. Also a number dropped before release: Raye, Landis, Mayfair: "S.N.A.F.U." (LP-588).)

440022b Film FOUR JILLS IN A JEEP records by members of orig prod. Dick Haymes, contemp: "How Blue the Night" (LP-299)(LP-397) "How Many Times Do I Have to Tell You?" (LP-299) Jimmy Dorsey Orch, contemp: "Ohio" (78/Dec 18593) Martha Raye, 1939: "You'll Have to Swing It" (LP-613)

440023a Film THE THREE CABALLEROS contemp album by members of orig prod and others. MUSIC & WORDS: Ray Gilbert, Charles Wolcott, others. COND: Charles Wolcott (of orig prod). VOCALS: Nestor Amaral (of orig cast), Ray Gilbert (composer), chorus. (78/Dec album 373)

440023b Film THE THREE CABALLEROS album. COND: Leo Perachi. VOCALS: chorus. (Disneyland 3039, with Saludos Amigos — and entitled "Saludos Amigos")

440023c Film THE THREE CABALLEROS soundtrack. Jose Oliveira, Joaquin Garay, Clarence Nash: "The Three Caballeros" Dora Luz: "You Belong to My Heart" (LP-661)

440023d Film THE THREE CABALLEROS Spanish soundtrack. VOCALS: Dora Luz, Carlos Ramirez, Aurora Miranda, Clarence Nash, Jose Oliveira, Joaquin Garay. (Disneyland 1239-M, entitled "Los Tres Caballeros," with additional material)

440024a Film THE BELLE OF THE YUKON contemp records by Dinah Shore of orig cast. "I Can't Tell Why I Love You But I Do" (78/Vic 20-1611) "Like Someone in Love" (78/Vic 20-1617) "Sleigh Ride in July" (78/Vic 20-1622)

440025a Film BROADWAY RHYTHM records by members of orig cast. Ginny Simms, 1943: "Irresistible You" (78/Col 36693) Nancy Walker, 1956: "Milkman, Keep Those Bottles Quiet" (LP-293)

440026a Film PIN-UP GIRL soundtrack. MUSIC: James Monaco WORDS: Mack Gordon. ORCH & COND: Alfred Newman. CAST: Betty Grable, Martha Raye, Charlie Spivak Orch. (Caliban 6009, with Song of the Islands. Excerpts: Raye: "Yankee Doodle Hayride," "Red Robins, Bob Whites and Bluebirds" (LP-651).)

440027a Film IRISH EYES ARE SMILING soundtrack. Dick Haymes: "Let the Rest of the World Go By," "Dear Little Boy of Mine," "A Little Bit of Heaven," "I'll Forget You" (LP-386)

440027b Film IRISH EYES ARE SMILING contemp record by Dick Haymes of orig cast. "Let the Rest of the World Go By" (LP-397)

440028a Film COVER GIRL soundtrack. MUSIC & WORDS: mostly by Jerome Kern, Ira Gershwin. ORCH & COND: Morris Stoloff, Carmen Dragon, Saul Chaplin. CAST: Gene Kelly, Nan Wynn (for

Rita Hayworth), Phil Silvers. (Curtain Calls 100/24, with You Were Never Lovelier)

440028b Film COVER GIRL later records by Gene Kelly of orig cast. "Long Ago and Far Away" (1959: LP-481, LP-598) (1977: LP-749)

440029a Film CAROLINA BLUES 1944 records by Kay Kyser Orch of orig prod. MUSIC: Jule Styne. WORDS: Sammy Cahn. "There Goes That Song Again," "I'm Gonna See My Baby" (78/Col 36757)

440030a Film MEET THE PEOPLE soundtrack. MUSIC: Harold Arlen. WORDS: E Y Harburg. Bert Lahr: "Heave Ho!" (LP-608)

440031a Film BATHING BEAUTY 1944 records by members of orig prod. Ethel Smith, organ: "Tico-Tico" (78/Dec 23353) Xavier Cugat Orch: "Tico-Tico" (78/Col 36780)

440032a Film CHAMPAGNE CHARLIE soundtrack. Tommy Trinder: "Champagne Charlie," "Everything Will Be Lovely/The Man on the Flying Trapeze" (78/Col(E) FB-3050)" 'Arf of 'Arf and 'Arf' Betty Warren: "Come on Algernon" (78/Col/(E) FB-3051)

440128a MEXICAN HAYRIDE orig prod. MUSIC & WORDS: Cole Porter. COND: Harry Sosnik. CAST: June Havoc, Wilbur Evans, Corinna Mura, chorus. (Dec 10" 5232; CBS Records X-14878, with Texas, Li'l Darlin'; LP-295.)

440321a Cantata THE LONESOME TRAIN contemp studio prod by members of orig (radio) prod. MUSIC: Earl Robinson. WORDS: Millard Lampell. COND: Lyn Murray. CAST: Burl Ives, Earl Robinson, Richard Huey, Lon Clark. Also Peter Seeger & Raymond Edward Johnson, who were apparently not in orig cast. (Dec 10" 5054)

440321b Cantata THE LONESOME TRAIN 1976 studio prod. ORCH: Luther Henderson. COND: Leonard dePaur. NARRATOR: Brock Peters. VOCALS: Odetta, other uncredited soloists, chorus. (United Artists LA-604, with Ballad for Americans)

440408a FOLLOW THE GIRLS contemp records by Gertrude Niesen of orig cast. MUSIC: Philip Charig. WORDS: Dan Shapiro, Milton Pascal. "I Wanna Get Married" (LP-53)(LP-69)(LP-146)(LP-164) "Twelve O'Clock and All Is Well" (LP-53)

440408b FOLLOW THE GIRLS 1945 record by Evelyn Dall of 1945 London cast. "I Wanna Get Married" (78/Dec(E) F-8587)

440821a SONG OF NORWAY 1944/5 album by Irra Petina of orig cast & Robert Weede. MUSIC: Edvard Grieg, arranged by Robert Wright & George Forrest. WORDS: Robert Wright, George Forrest. ORCH: Alan Shulman. COND: Sylvan Shulman. (78/Col 12" album M-562; JJA Records 19782, with Winged Victory & Up in Central Park.)

440821b SONG OF NORWAY orig prod with Kitty Carlisle replacing Irra Petina. ORCH & COND: Arthur Kay. CAST: Kitty Carlisle (for Irra Petina), Lawrence Brooks, Helena Bliss, Robert Shafer, Sig Arno, Ivy Scott, Walter Kingsford, Kent Edwards, Gwen Jones. (Dec 8002)

440821c SONG OF NORWAY studio prod. ORCH: Henri Rene. COND: Lehman Engel. CAST: Jeanette Scovotti, Patricia Kelly, Evelyn Sachs, Richard Fredericks, William Lewis. (Reader's Digest 40-9, with Roberta)

440821d SONG OF NORWAY 1970 film soundtrack. COND: Roland Shaw. CAST: Florence Henderson, Frank Porretta, Harry Secombe, Toralv Maurstad. (ABC SOC-14)

440821e SONG OF NORWAY 1959 New York (Jones Beach) prod. COND: Lehman Engel. CAST: Brenda Lewis, John Reardon, Helena Scott, Sig Arno, William Olvis, Muriel O'Malley, William Linton, Peryne Anker. (Col CS-8135)

440821f SONG OF NORWAY 1961 studio prod. COND: Michael Collins. CAST: Victoria Elliott, Norma Hughes, Thomas Round, John Lawrenson, Geoffrey Webb, Olwen Price. (Angel 35904)

440821g SONG OF NORWAY contemp records by John Hargreaves & Janet Hamilton-Smith of 1946 London cast. "Strange Music," "Three Loves" (78/HMV(E) B-9479)

441005a BLOOMER GIRL orig prod. MUSIC: Harold Arlen. WORDS: E Y Harburg. ORCH: Robert Russell Bennett. COND: Leon Leonardi. CAST: Celeste Holm, David Brooks, Richard Huey, Joan McCracken, Dooley Wilson, Harold Arlen (for Alan Gilbert), Toni Hart, Mabel Taliaferro, Hubert Dilworth. (78/Dec album 381. Incomplete: Dec 8015, Dec 9126. Excerpt: Wilson: "The Eagle and Me" (LP-164).)

441005b BLOOMER GIRL records by Harold Arlen, composer. Vocal & piano:"Evelina" Vocal: "T'morra', T'morra'" (LP-192)

441207a SEVEN LIVELY ARTS records by members of orig prod. MUSIC & WORDS: Cole Porter. Teddy Wilson Quintet: "Ev'ry Time We Say Goodbye" (1945: LP-182) Benny Goodman Quintet, Jane Harvey vocal: "Only Another Boy and Girl" (1945: LP-182, LP-301, LP-538) Goodman Quintet, Peggy Mann vocal: "Ev'ry Time We Say Goodbye" (1945: LP-301) Dolores Gray: "Is It the Girl?" (1979: LP-703)

441227a SING OUT, SWEET LAND! orig prod. MUSIC & WORDS: Mostly folk music. ORCH & COND: Elie Siegmeister. CAST: Alfred Drake, Burl Ives, Alma Kaye, Bibi Osterwald, Jack McCauley, Juanita Hall, Ted Tiller, Herk Armstrong. (Dec 8023)

441228a ON THE TOWN 1945 studio prod. MUSIC: Leonard Bernstein. WORDS: Betty Comden, Adolph Green. COND: Lyn Murray, Camarata, Leonard Joy. CAST: Nancy Walker, Betty Comden, & Adolph Green of orig cast; Mary Martin. (Dec 8030, with Lute Song)

441228b ON THE TOWN 1960 studio prod. COND: Leonard Bernstein. CAST: Nancy Walker, Betty Comden, Adolph Green, & Cris Alexander of orig cast; John Reardon. (Col S-31005. Incomplete: OS-2028.)

441228c ON THE TOWN 1945 album. Orchestra of orig prod cond by Leonard Bernstein, composer: Ballet music, incl "Lonely Town," "Times Square," "Dance of the Great Lover," "Dream in the Subway," "Dream Sequence" Victor Chorale cond by Robert Shaw: "I Feel like I'm Not Out of Bed Yet/ New York, New York," "Lonely Town," "Some Other Time," "Lucky to Be Me" (78/Vic album DM-995. Ballet music only: 45/Camden CAE-203; LP-617.)

441228d ON THE TOWN 1963 London prod. COND: Lawrence Leonard. CAST: Elliott Gould, Don McKay, Franklin Kiser, Carol Arthur, Gillian Lewis, Meg Walter. (CBS(E) APG-60005)

441228e ON THE TOWN records by Betty Comden & Adolph Green, lyricists and members of orig cast. "New York, New York," "Lonely Town," "Some Other Time," "I Get Carried Away" (1955: LP-359)(1958: LP-170)(1977: LP-489) "Taxi Song" (1955: LP-359) "Lucky to Be Me" (1977: LP-489)

441228f ON THE TOWN 1949 film soundtrack, with additional songs by Roger Edens, Betty Comden, Adolph Green. ORCH: Conrad Salinger. COND: Lennie Hayton. CAST: Frank Sinatra, Gene Kelly, Jules Munshin, Ann Miller, Betty Garrett, Vera-Ellen, Alice Pearce. (Show Biz 5603)

441228g ON THE TOWN 1956 records by Nancy Walker of orig cast. "I Can Cook Too," "Some Other Time" (LP-293)

441228h ON THE TOWN 1959 studio prod using songs of the 1949 film version. COND: Geoff Love. VOCALS: Fred Lucas, Dennis Lotis, Lionel Blair, Shane Rimmer, Noele Gordon, Stella Tanner. (Col(E) SCX-3281)

1945

450001a Film STATE FAIR contemp album by Dick Haymes of orig cast. MUSIC: Richard Rodgers. WORDS: Oscar Hammerstein II. (78/Dec album 412. Incomplete: LP-397. Excerpts: "It's a Grand Night for Singing" (LP-114) (LP-400) "It Might as Well Be Spring" (LP-400).)

450001b Film STATE FAIR soundtrack. ORCH & COND: Alfred Newman, Charles Henderson. VOCALS: Dick Haymes, Louanne Hogan (for Jeanne Crain), Vivian Blaine, William Marshall, Charles Winninger, Fay Bainter, Percy Kilbride. (Classic International Filmusicals 3009, with Centennial Summer. Also LP-497, which includes "We Will Be Together," dropped before release.)

450001c Film STATE FAIR 1962 record by Alice Faye of 1962 film cast. MUSIC & WORDS: Richard Rodgers. "Never Say No" (LP-100)

450001d Film STATE FAIR 1962 film soundtrack, with new songs by Rodgers (words & music). COND: Alfred Newman. CAST: Pat Boone, Anita Gordon (for Pamela Tiffin), Alice Faye, Tom Ewell, Bobby Darin, Ann-Margret, David Street, Bob Smart. (Dot 29011)

450001e Film STATE FAIR 1945 radio prod. CAST: Dick Haymes, Jeanne Crain, Vivian Blaine of orig cast; Elliot Lewis. (EOH Records 99604, with non-musical show I Fly Anything)

450002a Film MASQUERADE IN MEXICO record by Dorothy Lamour of orig cast. "Perfidia" (LP-109)

450003a Film THE DOLLY SISTERS soundtrack. MUSIC & WORDS: Various. ORCH & COND: Alfred Newman, Charles Henderson. CAST: Betty Grable, June Haver, John Payne, chorus. (Classic International Filmusicals 3010)

450003b Film THE DOLLY SISTERS contemp record by Betty Grable of orig cast. "I Can't Begin to Tell You" (LP-106)(LP-493)(LP-646)

450004a Film THRILL OF A ROMANCE contemp album by Lauritz Melchior of orig cast. MUSIC & WORDS: Various. "I Love You," "Lonely Night," "Serenade," "Vive l'Amour," "Please Don't Say No," "I Want What I Want When I Want It" (LP-291)

450004b Film THRILL OF A ROMANCE contemp records by Tommy Dorsey Orch of orig prod. "Please Don't Say No," "I Should Care" (78/Vic 20-1625)

450004c Film THRILL OF A ROMANCE 1977 record sung by Sammy Cahn, lyricist. MUSIC: Axel Stordahl, Paul Weston. "I Should Care" (LP-503)

450005a Film WHERE DO WE GO FROM HERE? 1944 records. MUSIC: Kurt Weill. WORDS: Ira Gershwin. PIANO: Kurt Weill. Ira Gershwin, Kurt Weill: "Opening Sequence," "The Nina, the Pinta, the Santa Maria" Gershwin: "All at Once," "It Happened to Happen to Me," "If Love Remains," "Song of the Rhineland;" "Manhattan" (not used in film). (LP-417. Excerpts: LP-150.)

450006a Film OUT OF THIS WORLD contemp records by Bing Crosby of orig cast. MUSIC & WORDS: Harold Arlen, Johnny Mercer, others. "I'd Rather Be Me," "Out of This World," "June Comes Around Every Year" (LP-l62)

450006b Film OUT OF THIS WORLD 1971 record sung by Johnny Mercer, lyricist. "Out of This World" (LP-533)

450007a Film THE BELLS OF ST. MARY'S 1946 album by Bing Crosby of orig cast. MUSIC & WORDS: Various. COND: John Scott Trotter. (Dec 10" 5052, with Going My Way; LP-27)

450007b Film THE BELLS OF ST. MARY'S 1947 radio prod. VOCALS: Bing Crosby (of orig prod), chorus. (Spokane 15, with Holiday Inn)

450008a Film RHAPSODY IN BLUE soundtrack. MUSIC: George Gershwin. WORDS: mostly Ira Gershwin. ORCH & COND: Leo F Forbstein, Ray Heindorf. CAST: Robert Alda, Sally Sweetland (for Joan Leslie), Al Jolson, Anne Brown, Tom Patricola, Oscar Levant, Hazel Scott, Paul Whiteman Orch. (Titania 512; LP-763. Excerpts: Orchestra: Main Title (LP-654) Jolson, Sweetland, Alda: "Swanee" (LP-654)(Incomplete: LP-223, LP-595) Sweetland, Patricola: "Somebody Loves Me" Uncredited singers: "Blue Monday" Scott (piano & vocal): "The Man I Love/Clap Yo' Hands/Fascinating Rhythm/I Got Rhythm" Sweetland: "Embraceable You," "Delishious" Levant (piano): "Someone to Watch over Me/ I Got Rhythm" Alda, Levant: "Mine/Finale" (LP-654).)

450008b Film RHAPSODY IN BLUE 1945 records by members of orig cast. Al Jolson: "Swanee" (LP-145) Hazel Scott: "The Man I Love," "Fascinating Rhythm" (78/Dec 23429)

450009a Film THE HOUSE I LIVE IN 1945 record by Frank Sinatra of orig cast. MUSIC: Earl Robinson. WORDS: Lewis Allen. "The House I Live In" (LP-250)

450009b Film THE HOUSE I LIVE IN records sung by Earl Robinson, composer. "The House I Live In" (78/V-Disc 99) (78/Keynote K-538)

450010a Film BECAUSE OF HIM soundtrack. Deanna Durbin: "Lover," "Danny Boy" (LP-256)

450011a Film LADY ON A TRAIN soundtrack. MUSIC & WORDS: Cole Porter. Deanna Durbin: "Night and Day" (LP-256)

450012a Film THE STORK CLUB contemp records by members of orig cast. Betty Hutton: "A Square in the Social Circle," "Doctor, Lawyer, Indian Chief" (78/Cap 220) Andy Russell: "Love Me" (78/Cap 221)

450012b Film THE STORK CLUB records sung by Hoagy Carmichael, composer. "Doctor, Lawyer, Indian Chief" (1947: LP-94, LP-771)(Later: 78/ARA 128)

450013a Film ALONG THE NAVAJO TRAIL records by Roy Rogers of orig cast. "Along the Navajo Trail" (Contemp: LP-278)(1975: LP-523)

450014a Film DON'T FENCE ME IN records by Roy Rogers of orig cast. "Don't Fence Me In"(by Cole Porter) (Contemp: LP-278) "Along the Navajo Trail" (Contemp: LP-278)(1975: LP-523)

450015a Film DELIGHTFULLY DANGEROUS soundtrack. MUSIC: Morton Gould. WORDS: Edward Heyman. Jane Powell: "In a Shower of Stars," "Once upon a Song," "Through Your Eyes to Your Heart" (LP-281) Constance Moore: "I'm Only Teasin'" (LP-496)

450016a Film BILLY ROSE'S DIAMOND HORSESHOE soundtrack. Betty Grable: "Welcome to the Diamond Horseshoe," "Acapulco" (LP-284) "I Wish I Knew" Dick Haymes: "The More I See You" (LP-633)

450016b Film BILLY ROSE'S DIAMOND HORSESHOE contemp records by members of orig prod. MUSIC: Harry Warren. WORDS: Mack Gordon. Dick Haymes: "The More I See You" (LP-299)(LP-397) "I Wish I Knew" (LP-397) Carmen Cavallaro Orch: "In Acapulco," "The More I See You" (78/Dec l8671)

450017a Film INCENDIARY BLONDE contemp records by Betty Hutton of orig cast. "It Had to Be You," "What Do You Want to Make Those Eyes at Me for?" (LP-285)

450017b Film INCENDIARY BLONDE soundtrack. MUSIC & WORDS: Various. CAST: Betty Hutton, Arturo de Cordova, chorus. (Athena LM1B-9, with Lucky Me)

450018a Film DUFFY'S TAVERN contemp record by Betty Hutton of orig cast. "Doin' It the Hard Way" (LP-285)

450019a Film DOLL FACE contemp records by Perry Como of orig cast. "Hubba-Hubba-Hubba," "Here Comes Heaven Again" (78/Vic 20-1750)

450020a Film TONIGHT AND EVERY NIGHT soundtrack. Martha Mears (for Rita Hayworth): "What Does an English Girl Think of a Yank?," "You Excite Me" (LP-403)

450021a Film GAY SENORITA records by Corinna Mura of orig cast. "Buenas Noches," "Samba Le Le" (78/ARA 5001)

450022a Film EADIE WAS A LADY soundtrack. MUSIC & WORDS: Nacio Herb Brown, Richard Whiting, B G DeSylva. Ann Miller, chorus: "Eadie Was a Lady" (LP-496)

450023a Film BRING ON THE GIRLS soundtrack. Chorus: "Bring On the Girls" (LP-496)"

450023b Film BRING ON THE GIRLS 1945 record by Spike Jones Orch of orig prod. "Chloe" (78/Vic 20-1654)

450024a Film WEEKEND AT THE WALDORF contemp record by Xavier Cugat Orch of orig prod. "Guadalajara" (78/Col 36694)

450025a Film SUNBONNET SUE contemp records by Phil Regan of orig cast. "Sunbonnet Sue," "By the Light of the Silvery Moon" (78/Majestic 7161)

450026a Film JOHNNY ANGEL record by Hoagy Carmichael of orig cast. MUSIC: Hoagy Carmichael. WORDS: Paul Francis Webster. "Memphis in June" (78/ARA RM-124)

450027a Film YOLANDA AND THE THIEF soundtrack. MUSIC: Harry Warren. WORDS: Arthur Freed. ORCH: Conrad Salinger. COND: Lennie Hayton. Orchestra: Main Title, Dream Ballet. Ludwig Stoessel, children: "This Is a Day for Love" Trudy Erwin (for Lucille Bremmer): "Angel," "Will You Marry Me?" Fred Astaire: "Yolanda" (Hollywood Soundstage 5001, with You'll Never Get Rich. Incomplete: LP-633.) Chorus: "Coffee Time" (LP-633)

450127a UP IN CENTRAL PARK orig prod with cast substitutions. MUSIC: Sigmund Romberg. WORDS: Dorothy Fields. COND: Max Meth. CAST: Wilbur Evans & Betty Bruce of orig cast; Eileen Farrell, Celeste Holm. (78/Dec album 395; JJA Records 19782, with Song of Norway & Winged Victory. Incomplete: Dec 8016, with The Red Mill.)

450127b UP IN CENTRAL PARK album by Jeanette MacDonald & Robert Merrill. COND: Robert Russell Bennett. (78/Vic album M-991. Excerpts: MacDonald: "Carousel in the Park," "It Doesn't Cost You Anything to Dream" MacDonald, Merrill: "Close as Pages in a Book", "The Fireman's Bride" (LP-536).)

450127c UP IN CENTRAL PARK 1948 film soundtrack. Dick Haymes: "When She Walks in the Room" (LP-299)

450215a Radio show DICK TRACY IN B-FLAT soundtrack. CAST: Judy Garland, Bing Crosby, Frank Sinatra, Bob Hope, Jimmy Durante, Dinah Shore, Frank Morgan, Andrews Sisters, Cass Daley, chorus. (Curtain Calls 100/1)

450322a THE FIREBRAND OF FLORENCE 1945 records. MUSIC: Kurt Weill. WORDS: Ira Gershwin. PIANO: Kurt Weill. Ira Gershwin, Kurt Weill: "Prologue Act 1 Scene 1" Gershwin: "You're Far Too Near Me," "Alessandro the Wise," "Sing Me Not a Ballad," "When the Duchess Is Away," "There'll Be Life, Love and Laughter," "Cozy Nook Song," "Soldiers of the Duchy," "Tarantella" (LP-417)

450322b THE FIREBRAND OF FLORENCE later record by Lotte Lenya of orig cast. "Sing Me Not a Ballad" (LP-85)

450419a CAROUSEL orig prod. MUSIC: Richard Rodgers. WORDS: Oscar Hammerstein II. ORCH: Don Walker. COND: Joseph Littau. CAST: John Raitt, Jan Clayton, Jean Darling, Christine Johnson, Eric Mattson, Murvyn Vye, Connie Baxter. (Dec 8003. Excerpt: Raitt: "Soliloquy" (LP-164).)

450419b CAROUSEL 1967 TV prod soundtrack. ORCH & COND: Jack Elliot. CAST: Robert Goulet, Mary Grover, Pernell Roberts, Marlyn Mason, Patricia Neway. (Col CSM-479)

450419c CAROUSEL 1955 studio prod. COND: Lehman Engel. CAST: Robert Merrill, Patrice Munsel, Florence Henderson, Gloria Lane, Herbert Banke, George Irving. (RCA LPM-1048)

450419d CAROUSEL later record by John Raitt of orig cast. "Soliloquy" (LP-149)

450419e CAROUSEL 1956 film soundtrack. ORCH & COND: Alfred Newman. CAST: Gordon MacRae, Shirley Jones, Barbara Ruick, Cameron Mitchell, Claramae Turner, Robert Rounseville. (Cap SW-694)

450419f CAROUSEL 1958 album by Jan Clayton of orig & 1958 Brussels World's Fair prods; chorus. COND: Tutti Camarata. (Disneyland 3036)

450419g CAROUSEL 1962 studio prod. ORCH: Lew Davies. COND: Jay Blackton. CAST: Alfred Drake, Roberta Peters, Claramae Turner, Lee Venora, Norman Treigle, Jon Crain. (Command 843)

450419h CAROUSEL 1965 prod. ORCH: Don Walker. COND: Franz Allers. CAST: John Raitt (of orig prod), Eileen Christy, Susan Watson, Katherine Hilgenberg, Reid Shelton, Jerry Orbach. (RCA LSO-1114)

450419i CAROUSEL 1960 studio prod. CAST: Lois Hunt, Harry Snow, Charmaine Harma, Clifford Young, Helena Seymour, Kay Lande, Charles Green. (Epic 3679)

450419j CAROUSEL 1953 album. COND: Jay Blackton. VOCALS: John Raitt (of orig cast); Doretta Morrow, Brenda Lewis, chorus. (RCA 10" LPM-3150, with Oklahoma!)

450419k CAROUSEL contemp album by members of 1950 London cast. COND: Reginald Burston. CAST: Marion Ross, Margo Moser, Eric Mattson, Iva Withers, Stephen Douglass, Morgan Davies, chorus. (World Records(E) SH-393, with Annie Get Your Gun & Oklahoma!)

450419l CAROUSEL 1961 studio prod. ORCH & COND: Johnny Douglas. CAST: Elizabeth Larner, Barbara Elsy, Barry Kent, John Adams, Diana Landor, Mike Sammes, chorus. (Cap SN-7513)

450419m CAROUSEL studio prod. "Ed Sullivan presents Carousel." No other credits given. (National Academy 11)

450419n CAROUSEL 1959 studio prod. COND: Eric Rogers. VOCALS: Bryan Johnson, Rosalind Page, Eula Parker, chorus. (Ace of Clubs(E) 1002, with Oklahoma!)

450419o CAROUSEL 1965 studio prod. ORCH & COND: Sam Fonteyn. CAST: David Holliday, Shirley Chapman, Matt Zimmerman, chorus. (Music for Pleasure(E) 1009)

450421a PERCHANCE TO DREAM 1945 records by members of orig (London) cast. MUSIC & WORDS: Ivor Novello. COND: Harry Acres (not of orig prod). Muriel Barron: "Love Is My Reason," "This Is My Wedding Day" Olive Gilbert: "Highwayman Love" Barron, Gilbert: "We'll Gather Lilacs" Barron, with Novello at piano: "A Woman's Heart" Roma Beaumont: "Curtsy to the King" (Dec(E) 10" LF-1309)

450421b PERCHANCE TO DREAM 1969 studio prod. COND: Marcus Dods. CAST: Elisabeth Robinson, Ann Howard, Patricia Lambert, Robert Bowman, chorus. (Col(E) TWO-250)

450718a MARINKA 1948 records by Joan Roberts of orig cast.

MUSIC: Emmerich Kalman. WORDS: George Marion Jr. "Sigh by Night," "Treat a Woman like a Drum" (LP-706)

450822a SIGH NO MORE records sung by the composer. MUSIC & WORDS: Noel Coward. 1945: "Nina," "Matelot" (LP-11)(LP-502) "I Wonder What Happened to Him" (LP-11) (LP-218)(LP-502) "Sigh No More" (LP-218)(LP-502) "Never Again," "Wait a Bit, Joe" (LP-502) 1955-56: "Matelot," "I Wonder What Happened to Him," "Wait a Bit, Joe" (LP-89) "Nina" (LP-89)(LP-351) "Loch Lomond"(words by Coward) (LP-351)

450822b SIGH NO MORE records by members of orig cast. Graham Payn: "Sigh No More," "Matelot" (1945: 78/Dec(E) F-8562)(1947: 78/HMV(E) C-3636) Joyce Grenfell: "The End of the News" (1945: 78/Dec(E) F-8561) "Du Maurier" (1945: 78/Dec(E) F-8561)(1964: LP-747)

450927a CARIB SONG contemp album. MUSIC: Baldwin Bergersen. WORDS: William Archibald. COND: Baldwin Bergersen. VOCALS: William Archibald. "Woman Is a Rascal," "Basket, Make a Basket," "Sleep Baby, Don't Cry," "Insect Song," "Washer Woman," "If" (78/International album mx B-401/6)

451006a POLONAISE 1945 studio prod. MUSIC: Frederic Chopin, Bronislaw Kaper. WORDS: John Latouche. ORCH: Bronislaw Kaper. COND: Al Goodman ("Harold Coates"). CAST: Earl Wrightson, Rose Inghram, Mary Martha Briney, chorus. (Camden 210, with Eileen)

451110a ARE YOU WITH IT? records by Joan Roberts of orig cast. MUSIC: Harry Revel. WORDS: Arnold B Horwitt. "Here I Go Again," "This Is My Beloved" (1946: 78/Majestic 1026)(1948: LP-706)

451221a BILLION DOLLAR BABY records by Comden & Green, lyricists. MUSIC: Morton Gould. WORDS: Betty Comden, Adolph Green. "Bad Timing," "Broadway Blossom" (LP-359)

451221b BILLION DOLLAR BABY 1951 record by Morton Gould (composer), piano & conductor. "Bad Timing" (LP-690)

1946

460001a Film ZIEGFELD FOLLIES soundtrack. MUSIC & WORDS: Various. ORCH: Conrad Salinger. COND: Lennie Hayton. CAST: Fred Astaire, Lena Horne, Virginia O'Brien, Judy Garland, Gene Kelly, James Melton, Marion Bell, Kathryn Grayson. (Curtain Calls 100/15-16. Excerpt: Astaire, chorus: "Bring On the Beautiful Girls" (LP-710).)

460001b Film ZIEGFELD FOLLIES 1956 record by Hugh Martin & Ralph Blane, composers. "Love" (LP-193)

460001c Film ZIEGFELD FOLLIES records by members of orig cast. Judy Garland: "Love" (Contemp: LP-7, LP-239) (1945 radio performance: LP-746, LP-759)(1952: LP-329) "This Heart of Mine" (Contemp: LP-35) Fred Astaire: "This Heart of Mine" (Contemp: LP-22, LP-344)

460002a Film TILL THE CLOUDS ROLL BY soundtrack. MUSIC: Jerome Kern. WORDS: Various. ORCH: Conrad Salinger. COND: Lennie Hayton. CAST: Judy Garland, Lena Horne, June Allyson, Kathryn Grayson, Tony Martin, Dinah Shore, Virginia O'Brien, Caleb Peterson. (MGM 10" 501 plus Shore: "The Last Time I Saw Paris" on LP-416. Excerpts: Garland: "Look for the Silver Lining" (LP-8)(LP-259)(LP-782) "Who?" (LP-259)(LP-782) Also four numbers dropped before release: Garland: "D'Ye Love Me?" (LP-423) Horne: "Bill" Grayson: "I've Told Every Little Star" Grayson, Johnny Johnson: "The Song Is You" (LP-455).)

460002b Film TILL THE CLOUDS ROLL BY records by members of orig cast. Tony Martin, 1939: "All The Things You Are" (LP-312) Frank Sinatra, contemp: "Ol' Man River" (78/Col 55037) "All the Things You Are" (LP-696) Judy Garland, 1948: "Who?"(With Bing Crosby: LP-180, LP-718) Kathryn Grayson, contemp: "Make Believe" (LP-346)

460003a Film THE ROAD TO UTOPIA contemp records by members of orig cast. MUSIC: James Van Heusen. WORDS: John Burke. Bing Crosby: "Would You?," "Welcome to My Dream," "It's Anybody's Spring," "Personality" Crosby & Bob Hope: "Put It There, Pal" (LP-27)

460003b Film THE ROAD TO UTOPIA 1970 record by Dorothy Lamour of orig cast. "Personality" (LP-704)

460004a Film BLUE SKIES 1946 album by Bing Crosby & Fred Astaire of orig cast, with Trudy Erwin. MUSIC & WORDS: Irving Berlin. COND: John Scott Trotter. (78/Dec Album 481. Incomplete: Dec 10" 5042; LP-l62. Excerpt: Astaire: "Puttin' on the Ritz" (LP-22)(LP-344)

460004b Film BLUE SKIES records by members of orig cast. Bing Crosby: "How Deep Is the Ocean?" (1932: LP-517, LP-575, LP-593) Fred Astaire: "Puttin' On the Ritz" (1930: LP-14)(1952: LP-50, LP-348, LP-648)(1959: LP-108) Crosby & Astaire: "A Couple of Song and Dance Men" (1975: LP-396)

460004c Film BLUE SKIES soundtrack. COND: Robert Emmett Dolan. CAST: Bing Crosby, Fred Astaire, Joan Caulfield, Olga San Juan. (Sountrak 104)

460005a Film THE JOLSON STORY contemp records by Al Jolson, who sang for Larry Parks in the film. "California, Here I Come" (LP-145)(LP-243)(LP-739) "April Showers," "Swanee," "My Mammy" (LP-145)(LP-244)(LP-739) "Rock-a-bye Your Baby" (LP-145)(LP-244)(LP-331)(LP-394) "About a Quarter to Nine" (LP-196)(LP-246) "Waiting for the Robert E Lee" (LP-198)(LP-245) (LP-739) "When You Were Sweet Sixteen" (LP-198)(LP-245) (LP-409) "I'm Sitting on Top of the World" (LP-198) (LP-243)(LP-394)(LP-682)(LP-739) "Liza" (LP-198)(LP-243) "Anniversary Song" (LP-228)(LP-246) "There's a Rainbow 'Round My Shoulder" (LP-196)(LP-243) "Let Me Sing and I'm Happy" (LP-228)(LP-243)(LP-739) "You Made Me Love You" (LP-145)(LP-245)(LP-409)(LP-739) "Ma Blushin' Rosie" (LP-145)(LP-245)(LP-409) "Toot, Toot, Tootsie!" (LP-198) (LP-244)(LP-409)(LP-438, with Eddie Cantor)(LP-739) "Avalon" (LP-228)(LP-244) "By the Light of the Silvery Moon" (LP-228)(LP-245) "The Spaniard That Blighted My Life" (LP-245)(LP-383) "I Want a Girl" (LP-196)(LP-245)

460005b Film THE JOLSON STORY 1948 radio prod. VOCALS: Al Jolson. (Pelican 129)(LP-677)

460005c Film THE JOLSON STORY soundtrack out-takes & alternate takes. COND: Morris Stoloff. VOCAL: Al Jolson, Rudy Wissler. (Take Two 103)(LP-682)

460006a Film THE HARVEY GIRLS contemp album by members of orig prod. MUSIC: Harry Warren. WORDS: Johnny Mercer. COND: Lennie Hayton. CAST: Judy Garland, Kenny Baker, Virginia O'Brien, Betty Russell (for Cyd Charisse). (Dec 8498, with Meet Me in St. Louis. Excerpts: Garland: "On the Atchison, Topeka and the Santa Fe" Garland, O'Brien, Russell: "It's a Great Big World" (LP-239).)

460006b Film THE HARVEY GIRLS soundtrack. ORCH & COND: Lennie Hayton. CAST: Judy Garland, Virginia O'Brien, Kenny Baker, Marion Doenges (for Cyd Charisse), Virginia Rees (for Angela Lansbury), Ray Bolger, Ben Carter, John Hodiak, Marjorie Main. (Hollywood Soundstage 5002. Excerpts: Garland, chorus: "On the Atchison, Topeka & the Santa Fe" (Incomplete: LP-252, LP-633) "March of the Doagies"(dropped before release) Garland, Hodiak: "My Intuition"(dropped before release) Garland, Bolger: "Hayride"(dropped before release) (LP-423).)

460006c Film THE HARVEY GIRLS records by Judy Garland of orig cast. "On the Atchison, Topeka and the Santa Fe" (1945, with the Merry Macs: LP-7, LP-734)(1963: LP-738)

460006d Film THE HARVEY GIRLS 1945 record sung by Johnny Mercer, lyricist. "On the Atchison, Topeka and the Santa Fe" (LP-559, LP-720)

460007a Film CANYON PASSAGE records by Hoagy Carmichael of orig cast. MUSIC: Hoagy Carmichael. WORDS: Jack Brooks. "Ole Buttermilk Sky" (1946: LP-94)(1966: LP-671) (1971: LP-694)

460008a Film TWO SISTERS FROM BOSTON contemp album by Lauritz Melchior of orig cast and Nadine Connor. MUSIC & WORDS: Various. COND: Charles Previn. "My Country," "Marie Antoinette" (LP-291)

460008b Film TWO SISTERS FROM BOSTON contemp records by Jimmy Durante of orig cast & Eddie Jackson. MUSIC: Sammy Fain. WORDS: Ralph Freed. "G'wan Home, Your Mudder's Callin'," "There's Two Sides to Every Girl" (LP-363)

460009a Film HOLIDAY IN MEXICO contemp album by Jane Powell of orig cast. COND: Carmen Dragon. (78/Col album X-271, entitled "Songs by Jane Powell")

460009b Film HOLIDAY IN MEXICO soundtrack. Jane Powell (vocal) & Jose Iturbi (piano): "I Think of You" (LP-281)

460009c Film HOLIDAY IN MEXICO contemp records by Xavier Cugat Orch of orig prod. "Walter Winchell Rhumba," "Oye Negra" (78/Col 36902) With Dinah Shore (not of orig prod): "You, So It's You!" (78/Col 37090)

460010a Film NIGHT AND DAY records by members of orig cast. MUSIC & WORDS: Cole Porter. Mary Martin: "Let's Do It," "What Is This Thing Called Love?," "My Heart Belongs to Daddy" (1940: LP-67) "I Get a Kick Out of Love" (1940: LP-67)(1955: LP-351) Carlos Ramirez: "Begin the Beguine" (78/SMC 2512)

460010b Film NIGHT AND DAY soundtrack. ORCH & COND: Leo F Forbstein, Ray Heindorf. Mary Martin: "My Heart Belongs to Daddy" (LP-223) Jane Wyman: "I'm in Love Again," "Let's Do It," "You Do Something to Me" Chorus: "Bulldog" Cary Grant, Dorothy Malone, chorus: "In the Still of the Night" Grant, Selena Royle: "An Old-Fashioned Garden" Eve Arden: "I'm Unlucky at Gambling" Monty Woolley: "Miss Otis Regrets" Grant, Ginny Simms: "You're the Top" (LP-655)

460010c Film NIGHT AND DAY contemp album by Ginny Simms of orig cast, "Night and Day," "I've Got You under My Skin," "You're the Top," "My Heart Belongs to Daddy," "What Is This Thing Called Love?," "Just One of Those Things," "I Get a Kick Out of You," "Easy to Love" (Royale 10" VLP-6055, entitled "Ginny Simms: You're the Top")

460011a Film MAKE MINE MUSIC contemp album by Nelson Eddy (of orig prod) of the sequence "The Whale Who Wanted to Sing at the Met." (78/Col album MM-640, entitled "The Whale Who Wanted to Sing at the Met")

460011b Film MAKE MINE MUSIC records by members of orig prod. Benny Goodman Orch: "All the Cats Join In" (1946: 78/Col 36967) "After You've Gone" (1943: 78/Col 36699) (Sextet, 1945: 78/Col 36781)(Trio, 1935: 78/Vic 25115) Andy Russell: "Without You" (1946: 78/Cap 234) Jerry Colonna: "Casey" (1946: 78/Cap 249) Andrews Sisters: "Johnny Fedora" (1945: 78/Dec 23474)

460011c Film MAKE MINE MUSIC soundtrack. Chorus: "Make Mine Music" The King's Men: "The Martins and the Coys" Nelson Eddy: "Shortnin' Bread" (LP-661)

460012a Film ROLL ON TEXAS MOON record by Roy Rogers of orig cast. "Roll On Texas Moon" (LP-278)

460013a Film DO YOU LOVE ME? soundtrack. MUSIC & WORDS:

Various. CAST: Dick Haymes, Harry James Orch. (Caliban 6011, with One Hour with You)

460013b Film DO YOU LOVE ME? contemp records by members of orig prod. Dick Haymes: "As If I Didn't Have Enough on My Mind," "Do You Love Me?" (78/Dec 18792) "The More I See You" (78/Dec 18662) Harry James Orch: "I Didn't Mean a Word I Said" (78/Col 36973) "As If I Didn't Have Enough on My Mind," "Do You Love Me?" (78/Col 36965)

460014a Film CENTENNIAL SUMMER soundtrack. MUSIC: Jerome Kern. WORDS: Leo Robin, E Y Harburg, Oscar Hammerstein II. ORCH & COND: Alfred Newman. VOCALS: Louanne Hogan (for Jeanne Crain), Larry Stevens, Avon Long, Walter Brennan, Cornel Wilde, William Eythe, Kathleen Howard. (Classic International Filmusicals 3009, with State Fair)

460014b Film CENTENNIAL SUMMER contemp records by Louanne Hogan, who sang for Jeanne Crain in orig prod. COND: Alfred Newman (of orig prod). "In Love in Vain," "All through the Day," "Two Hearts Are Better Than One" (dropped before release, words by Johnny Mercer), "The Right Romance" (LP-607)

460015a Film THE SWEETHEART OF SIGMA CHI records sung by Sammy Cahn, lyricist. MUSIC: Jule Styne. "Five Minutes More" (1972: LP-658)(1974: LP-313)

460016a Film LOVER COME BACK 1956 record sung by Irving Caesar, lyricist. "Just a Gigolo" (LP-353)

460017a Film IF I'M LUCKY contemp records by members of orig prod. Perry Como: "If I'm Lucky," "One More Vote" (78/Vic 20-1945) Harry James Orch: "If I'm Lucky," "One More Kiss" (78/Col 37148)

460018a Film GILDA soundtrack. Anita Ellis (for Rita Hayworth): "Put the Blame on Mame"(2 versions, the slower one possibly sung by Rita Hayworth), "Amado Mio" (LP-403)

460018b Film GILDA 1960 record by Anita Ellis, who dubbed for Rita Hayworth in orig prod. "Put the Blame on Mame" (Elektra EKL-179, entitled "Anita Ellis: The World in My Arms," with additional material)

460019a Film SUMMER HOLIDAY soundtrack, including 4 songs dropped before release. MUSIC: Harry Warren. WORDS: Ralph Blane. ORCH: Lennie Hayton. CAST: Mickey Rooney, Gloria DeHaven, Walter Huston, Frank Morgan, Selena Royle, Marilyn Maxwell, Emory Parnell. (Four Jays HW-602. Excerpts: DeHaven: "Wish I Had a Braver Heart" Huston: "Spring Isn't Everything" (LP-455).)

460020a Film SONG OF THE SOUTH soundtrack. MUSIC & WORDS: Various. ORCH & COND: Daniele Amfitheatrof, Paul J Smith. CAST: James Baskett, Johnny Lee, Hattie McDaniel, Nicodemus Stewart, chorus. (Disneyland 1205, entitled "Uncle Remus")(Incomplete: LP-661)

460020b Film SONG OF THE SOUTH contemp album. ORCH & COND: Billy May. VOCALS: James Baskett, Luana Patten, Bobby Driscoll, Nicodemus Stewart, Johnny Lee (all of orig prod); Johnny Mercer, the Pied Pipers. (78/Cap album CC-40, entitled "Tales of Uncle Remus")

460021a Film THE TIME, THE PLACE, AND THE GIRL soundtrack. MUSIC: Arthur Schwartz. WORDS: Leo Robin. ORCH & COND: Leo F Forbstein, Ray Heindorf, Frederick Hollander. CAST: Dennis Morgan, Jack Carson, Martha Vickers, Carmen Cavallaro, Janis Paige. (Titania 511, with The Paleface & Son of Paleface)

460021b Film THE TIME, THE PLACE, AND THE GIRL 1946 record by Carmen Cavallaro Orch of orig prod. "Through a Thousand Dreams" (78/Dec 23747)

460021c Film THE TIME, THE PLACE, AND THE GIRL 1975 records sung by Arthur Schwartz, composer. "A Rainy Night in Rio," "A Gal in Calico" (LP-418)

460022a Film BREAKFAST IN HOLLYWOOD contemp records by members of orig prod. Andy Russell: "If I Had a Wishing Ring" (78/Cap 234) King Cole Trio: "It Is Better to Be by Yourself" (78/Cap 239)

460023a Film THREE LITTLE GIRLS IN BLUE soundtrack. MUSIC: Josef Myrow, Harry Warren. WORDS: Mack Gordon. VOCALS: June Haver, Vivian Blaine, Carol Stewart (for Vera-Ellen), Ben Gage (for George Montgomery), Del Porter (for Charlie Smith), Celeste Holm. (Hollywood Soundstage 410. Excerpt: Haver, Gage: "This Is Always" (LP-588).)

460023b Film THREE LITTLE GIRLS IN BLUE 1971 record by Josef Myrow (composer), piano & vocal. "You Make Me Feel So Young" (LP-694)

460024a Film CUBAN PETE contemp record by Desi Arnaz of orig cast, with Amanda Lane. "Cuban Pete" (78/Vic 25-1058)

460025a Film NO LEAVE, NO LOVE 1946 album by Pat Kirkwood of orig cast. COND: George Stoll. "Love on a Greyhound Bus," "Listen to Me," "Isn't It Wonderful?," "All the Time" (78/Cosmo album DMR-102)

460025b Film NO LEAVE, NO LOVE contemp records by Guy Lombardo Orch of orig prod. "Love on a Greyhound Bus," "All the Time" (78/Dec 18873)

460026a Film THE MAN I LOVE soundtrack. Peg LaCentra (for Ida Lupino): "The Man I Love" (LP-654)

460027a Film LONDON TOWN 1946 records by members of orig prod. MUSIC: James Van Heusen. WORDS: John Burke. COND: Salvador Camarata. Orchestra: Overture. Sid Field: "You Can't Keep a Good Dreamer Down" (78/Dec(E) F-8672) Beryl Davis: "The 'Ampstead Way" (78/Dec(E) F-8676) "My Heart Goes Crazy"(cond by Ted Heath) Ann Sullivan: "If Spring Were Only Here to Stay" (78/Dec(E) F-8674) Davis, Scotty McHarg: "So Would I" (78/Dec(E) F-8675) Orchestra: Daffodil Hill Ballet Music (78/Dec(E) F-8673)

460028a Film THE LISBON STORY records by Richard Tauber of orig cast. "Never Say Goodbye," "Predro the Fisherman" (78/Parlophone(E) RO-20545)

460206a LUTE SONG 1946 album by Mary Martin of orig cast. MUSIC: Raymond Scott. WORDS: Bernard Hanighen. COND: Raymond Scott. (Dec 8030, with On the Town. Excerpt: "Mountain High, Valley Low" (LP-87).)

460330a ST. LOUIS WOMAN orig prod. MUSIC: Harold Arlen. WORDS: Johnny Mercer. COND: Leon Leonardi. CAST: Pearl Bailey, Harold Nicholas, Ruby Hill, June Hawkins, Robert Pope. (Cap 10" L-355)

460330b ST. LOUIS WOMAN records sung by Harold Arlen (composer) & Johnny Mercer (lyricist). Arlen, 1955: "Come Rain or Come Shine" (LP-101) Mercer, 1946: "Li'l Augie Is a Natural Man" (LP-559) "Any Place I Hang My Hat Is Home" (LP-604)

460330c ST. LOUIS WOMAN 1961 records by Pearl Bailey of orig prod. "Come Rain or Come Shine," "Cakewalk Your Lady," "I Had Myself a True Love," "Ridin' on the Moon," "It's a Woman's Prerogative" (LP-260)

460330d ST. LOUIS WOMAN 1957 recording of "Blues Opera" Suite. (Arlen reworked St. Louis Woman into "Blues Opera," which was renamed "Free and Easy" before its December 1959 orig (Amsterdam) prod.) ORCH: Samuel Matlowsky. COND: Andre Kostelanetz. (Col CL-1099, with additional Arlen material)

460418a CALL ME MISTER orig prod. MUSIC & WORDS: Harold Rome. ORCH: Ben Ludlow. COND: Lehman Engel. CAST: Betty Garrett, Lawrence Winters, Paula Bane, Jules Munshin, Danny Scholl, Bill Callahan, Chandler Cowles, Harry Clark, chorus. (Dec 10" 7005; CBS Records X-14877, with This Is the Army; LP-543. Excerpt: Garrett: "South America, Take It Away" (LP-164).)

460418b CALL ME MISTER records by Harold Rome (composer), vocal & piano. "Call Me Mister," "Military Life," "South America, Take It Away" (1954: LP-360)(1956: LP-39) "When We Meet Again," "Along with Me" (1956: LP-39)

460418c CALL ME MISTER soundtrack of 1951 film with additional songs mostly by Sammy Fain, Mack Gordon. CAST: Betty Grable, Dan Dailey, Danny Thomas. (Titania 510, with Starlift)

460516a ANNIE GET YOUR GUN orig prod. MUSIC & WORDS: Irving Berlin. ORCH: Philip J Lang. COND: Jay Blackton. CAST: Ethel Merman, Ray Middleton, John Garth, Clyde Turner, & Leon Bibb of orig cast; Robert Lenn, Kathleen Carnes. (Dec 8001. Excerpts: Merman: "Doin' What Comes Natur'lly" (LP-36)(LP-593) "You Can't Get a Man with a Gun," "I'm an Indian Too," "I Got the Sun in the Morning" Garth, Turner, Bibb: "Moonshine Lullaby" Merman, Middleton: "They Say It's Wonderful" (LP-36) "Anything You Can Do" (LP-593).)

460516b ANNIE GET YOUR GUN 1950 film soundtrack. ORCH: Conrad Salinger. COND: Adolph Deutsch. CAST: Betty Hutton, Howard Keel, Louis Calhern, Keenan Wynn. (MGM 10" 509. Excerpts: Hutton: "I've Got the Sun in the Morning" (LP-328) Hutton, Keel, Wynn, Calhern: "There's No Business Like Show Business" (LP-416). Also a number dropped before release: Hutton, chorus: "Let's Go West Again" (LP-455).)

460516c ANNIE GET YOUR GUN 1966 prod, with a new Berlin song. ORCH: Robert Russell Bennett. COND: Franz Allers. CAST: Ethel Merman, Bruce Yarnell, Benay Venuta, Jerry Orbach, Ronn Carroll, Rufus Smith. (RCA LSO-1124)

460516d ANNIE GET YOUR GUN 1957 TV prod. COND: Louis Adrian. CAST: Mary Martin, John Raitt, chorus. (Cap W-913)

460516e ANNIE GET YOUR GUN records by Ethel Merman of orig prod. "There's No Business like Show Business" (1962: LP-251)(1972: LP-153)(1977, with Mary Martin: LP-652)(1979:LP-670) "They Say It's Wonderful" (1962: LP-251)(1972: LP-153) "I Got Lost in His Arms" (c 1955: LP-36)(1972: LP-153) "You Can't Get a Man with a Gun" (1962: LP-251)

460516f ANNIE GET YOUR GUN 1962 studio prod. ORCH: Philip J Lang. COND: Franz Allers. CAST: Doris Day, Robert Goulet, Renee Winters, Kelly Brown, Leonard Stokes. (Col OS-2360)

460516g ANNIE GET YOUR GUN 1963 album by Vivian Blaine. COND: Glenn Osser. (Mercury 60051, with Pal Joey)

460516h ANNIE GET YOUR GUN soundtrack of original (unreleased) version of 1950 film, with a new Berlin song. ORCH: Conrad Salinger. COND: Adolph Deutsch. CAST: Judy Garland, Howard Keel, Frank Morgan, Keenan Wynn, Benay Venuta. (Sound/Stage 2302. Excerpts: Garland: "You Can't Get a Man with a Gun" (LP-289) "Doin' What Comes Naturally" (LP-588).)

460516i ANNIE GET YOUR GUN 1973 studio prod. COND: Stanley Black. CAST: Ethel Merman (of orig & 1966 casts); Benay Venuta (of 1966 cast and 1950 film cast); Neilson Taylor, Neil Howlett, Leslie Fyson. (London(E) XPS-905)

460516j ANNIE GET YOUR GUN contemp medley by members of 1947 London cast. COND: Lew Stone. CAST: Dolores Gray, Bill Johnson, Irving Davies, Wendy Toye. (World Records(E) SH-393, with Carousel & Oklahoma! Incomplete: Stanyan SR-10069, with Oklahoma!)

460516k ANNIE GET YOUR GUN 1947 studio prod. COND: Al

Goodman ("Harold Coates"). CAST: Jimmy Carroll, Audrey Marsh, Maxine, Earl Oxford, the Mullen Sisters. (Camden 154, with Miss Liberty)

460516l ANNIE GET YOUR GUN album by Judy Lynn & Larry Douglas. COND: Warren Vincent. (Design 1050, with Call Me Madam)

460516m ANNIE GET YOUR GUN studio prod. "Ed Sullivan presents Annie Get Your Gun." No other credits given. (National Academy 8)

460516n ANNIE GET YOUR GUN studio prod. ORCH & COND: Johnny Douglas. VOCALS: Maggie Fitzgibbon, Gordon Boyd, chorus. (Cap SN-7518)

460516o ANNIE GET YOUR GUN album. COND: Johnny Gregory. VOCALS: Elizabeth Larner, Barry Kent, chorus. (Wing(E) SRW-11005, with Oklahoma!)

460516p ANNIE GET YOUR GUN 1961 album. COND: Luther Henderson. VOCALS: Polly Bergen. (Col CS-8432, with Do Re Mi)

460516q ANNIE GET YOUR GUN 1968 studio prod. CAST: Vivienne Martin, Robert Colman, Valentine Palmer, Laurie Webb, chorus. (Saga(E) EROS-8114)

460516r ANNIE GET YOUR GUN 1947 record by Bill Johnson of 1947 London prod. "The Girl That I Marry" (78/Col(E) DB-2373)

460531a AROUND THE WORLD IN EIGHTY DAYS contemp records by Enzo Stuarti ("Larry Laurence") of orig cast. MUSIC & WORDS: Cole Porter. "Should I Tell You I Love You?," "Look What I Found" (78/Real mx 1195-A/B)(LP-295) "If You Smile at Me," "Pipe Dreaming" (78/Real mx 1195-C/D) (LP-295)

460604a SECOND BEST BED later record by Richard Dyer-Bennet of orig cast. "The Tailor's Boy" (Dyer-Bennet Records 1601, entitled "1601")

461219a PACIFIC 1860 contemp records by members of orig (London) prod. MUSIC & WORDS: Noel Coward. CAST: Mary Martin, Grahamm Payn, Daphne Anderson, Pat McGrath, Sylvia Cecil. (AMR Records 300, with additional Pacific 1860 songs sung by Noel Coward)

461219b PACIFIC 1860 records sung by Noel Coward, composer. Contemp: "Uncle Harry," "His Excellency Regrets" (LP-11) "Bright Was the Day," "This Is a Changing World" (LP-216) Later: "Uncle Harry" (LP-89)(LP-138)(LP-351)

1947

470001a Film THE SECRET LIFE OF WALTER MITTY records by Danny Kaye of orig cast. "Anatole of Paris" (1942: LP-70, LP-107, LP-518)(1952: LP-6, LP-515) "The Little Fiddle" (LP-55)

470002a Film THE ROAD TO RIO contemp album by Bing Crosby & the Andrews Sisters of orig cast; Nan Wynn. MUSIC: James Van Heusen. WORDS: John Burke. (LP-263)

470003a Film THE SHOCKING MISS PILGRIM 1946 records by Dick Haymes of orig cast & Judy Garland. MUSIC: George Gershwin. WORDS: Ira Gershwin. "Aren't You Kinda Glad We Did?" (LP-115)(LP-397)(LP-640)(LP-734) "For You, for Me, for Evermore" (LP-397)(LP-640)(LP-734)

470003b Film THE SHOCKING MISS PILGRIM soundtrack. ORCH & COND: Alfred Newman. CAST: Betty Grable, Dick Haymes, Allyn Joslyn, Charles Kemper. (Classic International Filmusicals 3008, with Mother Wore Tights)

470004a Film THIS TIME FOR KEEPS records by members of orig prod. Jimmy Durante: "I'm the Guy Who Found the Lost Chord" (LP-142) "Inka Dinka Doo" (LP-41)(LP-42) (LP-80)(LP-175)(LP-292)(LP-

297) "Little Bit This, Little Bit That" (78/MGM 30035) Xavier Cugat Orch: "Un Poquito de Amor" (78/Col 37829)

470005a Film SOMETHING IN THE WIND 1947 album by Deanna Durbin of orig cast. MUSIC: John Green. WORDS: Leo Robin. ORCH & COND: John Green. "Something in the Wind," "It's Only Love," "You Wanna Keep Your Baby Lookin' Right," "The Turntable Song" (78/Dec album 601. Excerpt: "The Turntable Song" (LP-406).)

470006a Film IT HAPPENED IN BROOKLYN soundtrack. MUSIC: Jule Styne. WORDS: Sammy Cahn. ORCH & COND: John Green. PIANO: Andre Previn. CAST: Frank Sinatra, Jimmy Durante, Kathryn Grayson, Peter Lawford. (Caliban 6006, with On Moonlight Bay & Three Smart Girls. Excerpts: Durante, Sinatra: "The Song's Gotta Come from the Heart" (LP-252) Grayson: "Time after Time" (LP-347) "Bell Song" Grayson, Sinatra: "La ci darem la Mano" (LP-636).)

470006b Film IT HAPPENED IN BROOKLYN records by members of orig cast. Frank Sinatra, 1946: "Time after Time," "It's the Same Old Dream," "The Brooklyn Bridge," "I Believe" (LP-250) Jimmy Durante, 1951: "The Song's Gotta Come from the Heart"(with Helen Traubel, not of orig cast) (45/RCA 49-3229)

470007a Film VARIETY GIRL soundtrack. MUSIC & WORDS: mostly Frank Loesser. CAST: Olga San Juan, Dorothy Lamour, Alan Ladd, Bing Crosby, Bob Hope, Pearl Bailey, Spike Jones Orch. (Caliban 6007, with Colleen. Excerpt: Lamour, Ladd: "Tallahassee" (LP-647).)

470007b Film VARIETY GIRL contemp record by Bing Crosby of orig cast & the Andrews Sisters. "Tallahassee" (LP-263)

470008a Film WELCOME, STRANGER contemp album by Bing Crosby of orig cast. MUSIC: James Van Heusen. WORDS: John Burke. COND: John Scott Trotter. "Smile Right Back at the Sun," "As Long as I'm Dreaming," "My Heart Is a Hobo," "Country Style" (LP-263)

470009a Film MY FAVORITE BRUNETTE contemp records by Bob Hope & Dorothy Lamour of orig cast. MUSIC & WORDS: Jay Livingston, Ray Evans. "Beside You" (78/Cap 381) "My Favorite Brunette" (LP-647)

470010a Film MOTHER WORE TIGHTS soundtrack. MUSIC: Josef Myrow. WORDS: Mack Gordon. ORCH & COND: Alfred Newman. CAST: Dan Dailey, Betty Grable, Mona Freeman, Lee Patrick, Chick Chandler. (Classic International Filmusicals 3008, with The Shocking Miss Pilgrim. Excerpts: Grable: "Burlington Bertie from Bow," "You Do" (LP-284).)

470011a Film THE PERILS OF PAULINE contemp records by Betty Hutton of orig cast. MUSIC & WORDS: Frank Loesser. "Poppa, Don't Preach to Me," "Rumble, Rumble, Rumble," "The Sewing Machine," "I Wish I Didn't Love You So" (LP-285)

470011b Film THE PERILS OF PAULINE soundtrack. Betty Hutton: "Rumble, Rumble, Rumble," "Poppa, Don't Preach to Me" (LP-656)

470012a Film SONG OF SCHEHERAZADE contemp album by Charles Kullman of orig cast. MUSIC: Nicolai Rimsky-Korsakov, arranged by Miklos Rozsa. WORDS: Jack Brooks. COND: Julius Burger. "Song of India," "Hymn to the Sun," "Gypsy Song," "Fandango" (78/Col album X-272)

470013a Film CARNIVAL IN COSTA RICA contemp records by Dick Haymes of orig cast. "Another Night like This" (LP-299)(LP-397) "Mi Vida" (LP-299)

470014a Film THE FABULOUS DORSEYS records by members of orig prod. Jimmy Dorsey Orch: "Green Eyes" (1941: LP-480) Tommy Dorsey Orch: "Marie" (1937: 78/Vic 25523) (1938: LP-387)

"At Sundown," "To Me" (1946: 78/Vic 20-2064) Tommy Dorsey (trombone), Jimmy Dorsey (alto sax & clarinet): "The Dorsey Concerto" (1947: 78/Vic 46-0009)

470015a Film LADIES' MAN contemp records by Spike Jones Orch of orig prod. "Cocktails for Two," "Holiday for Strings" (78/Vic 20-2092)

470016a Film FUN AND FANCY FREE contemp album by Dinah Shore of orig cast. "Lazy Countryside," "Say It with a Slap," "Too Good to Be True" (Col 10" JL-8503 (entitled "Bongo"), with Land of the Lost)

470016b Film FUN AND FANCY FREE 1963 studio prod of "Mickey and the Beanstalk" sequence. MUSIC & WORDS: Various. VOCALS: Clarence Nash, Pinto Colvig, & Jim MacDonald of orig prod; Marilyn Hooven. (Disneyland 1248, entitled "Mickey and the Beanstalk")

470016c Film FUN AND FANCY FREE contemp records by members of orig prod. Dinning Sisters: "Fun and Fancy Free" (78/Cap 466) Dinah Shore: "Lazy Countryside" (78/Col 37884)

470016d Film FUN AND FANCY FREE soundtrack. Chorus: "Fun and Fancy Free" (LP-661)

470016e Film FUN AND FANCY FREE contemp studio prod of "Mickey and the Beanstalk" sequence. NARRATOR: Johnny Mercer. VOCALS: Luana Patten, Jim MacDonald, & Clarence Nash of orig prod; Bobby Driscoll. (78/Cap album CCX-67, entitled "Mickey and the Beanstalk")

470017a Film DOWN TO EARTH soundtrack. Anita Ellis (for Rita Hayworth): "Let's Stay Young Forever," "People Have More Fun Than Anyone" Ellis, Larry Parks: "They Can't Convince Me" (LP-403)

470018a Film NORTHWEST OUTPOST 1947 album by Nelson Eddy of orig cast; chorus. MUSIC: Rudolf Friml. WORDS: Edward Heyman. COND: Robert Armbruster. (78/Col 12" album MM-690)

470019a Film THE UNFINISHED DANCE orig prod. MUSIC & WORDS: Various. COND: Herbert Stothart. Danny Thomas: "Merrily-Merrily," "Minor Melody" (78/MGM album 4)

470020a Film I WONDER WHO'S KISSING HER NOW 1947 album. MUSIC & WORDS: Joseph E Howard, others. COND: Allen Merritt. VOCALS: Joseph E Howard (composer), chorus. (78/DeLuxe album 18)(LP-369)

470020b Film I WONDER WHO'S KISSING HER NOW soundtrack. ORCH & COND: Alfred Newman. CAST: June Haver, Buddy Clark (for Mark Stevens), Martha Stewart. (Titania 502, with Oh, You Beautiful Doll)

470020c Film I WONDER WHO'S KISSING HER NOW records sung by Joseph E Howard, composer & subject of this film biography. "Hello Ma Baby/Goodbye My Lady Love" (1936: LP-321, LP-563) "I Wonder Who's Kissing Her Now/ Honeymoon" (1936: 78/Vocalion 3357) "Honeymoon" (1929: 78/Bruns 4340)

470021a Film NEW ORLEANS records by Louis Armstrong Orch of orig prod. "Endie," "Do You Know What It Means to Miss New Orleans?" (1946: 78/Vic 20-2087) "Dippermouth Blues" (78/ Dec 906) "West End Blues" (1939: 78/Dec 2480) "St Louis Blues" (1933: 78/Vic 24320)(1934: Bruns(F) A-9683) "Where the Blues Were Born in New Orleans" (78/Vic 20-2088)

470022a Film MY WILD IRISH ROSE soundtrack. MUSIC & WORDS: Various. CAST: Dennis Morgan, Andrea King, Arlene Dahl, Alan Hale, chorus. (Titania 505, with The Desert Song)

470022b Film MY WILD IRISH ROSE album by Dennis Day. "My Wild Irish Rose," "By the Light of the Silvery Moon," "Mother Machree," "When Irish Eyes Are Smiling," "My Nellie's Blue Eyes," "A Little Bit of Heaven," "Hush-a-bye, Wee Rose of Killarney" (RCA 10" LPM-3036)

470022c Film MY WILD IRISH ROSE contemp album by Dennis Morgan of orig cast. "Wee Rose of Killarney," "One Little, Sweet Little Girl," "My Wild Irish Rose" (Col ML-4272, with The Desert Song)

470023a Film ON THE OLD SPANISH TRAIL records by Roy Rogers of orig cast. "On the Old Spanish Trail" (Contemp: LP-278)(1975: LP-523)

470024a Film THE TROUBLE WITH WOMEN soundtrack. Iris Adrian: "Trap That Wolf" (LP-496)

470025a Film NORA PRENTISS soundtrack. Ann Sheridan: "Would You Like a Souvenir?" (LP-496)(LP-705) "Who Cares What People Say?" (LP-705)

470026a Film SMASH-UP soundtrack. MUSIC: Jimmy McHugh. WORDS: Harold Adamson. Peg LaCentra (for Susan Hayward): "I Miss That Feeling," "Hush-a-bye Island" (LP-495)

470027a Record prod CINDERELLA orig prod. MUSIC: William Provost. WORDS: Lee Rogow. COND: Russ Case. VOCALS: Jeanette MacDonald. (78/Vic album Y-327)

470028a Film CARNEGIE HALL 1946 record by Vaughn Monroe Orch of orig prod. "Beware, My Heart!" (78/Vic 20-2084)

470029a Film COPACABANA 1947 record by Andy Russell of orig cast. "Je vous aime" (78/Cap 417)

470030a Film NIGHT SONG 1947 record sung by Hoagy Carmichael of orig prod. "Who Killed 'Er?" (LP-771)

470031a Film LIVING IN A BIG WAY 1977 record by Gene Kelly of orig cast. "It Had to Be You" (LP-749)

470032a Film EASY MONEY 1948 record by Greta Gynt of orig cast. "Lady Spiv" (78/Col(E) DB-2395)

470109a STREET SCENE orig prod. MUSIC: Kurt Weill. WORDS: Langston Hughes, Elmer Rice. ORCH: Kurt Weill. COND: Maurice Abravanel. CAST: Anne Jeffreys, Polyna Stoska, Brian Sullivan, Hope Emerson, Remo Lota, Beverly Janis, Creighton Thompson, Don Saxon. (Col OL-4139)

470110a FINIAN'S RAINBOW orig prod. MUSIC: Burton Lane. WORDS: E Y Harburg. ORCH: Robert Russell Bennett, Don Walker. COND: Ray Charles. CAST: Ella Logan, Donald Richards, David Wayne, Delores Martin, Maude Simmons. (Col ML-4062)

470110b FINIAN'S RAINBOW 1968 film soundtrack. COND: Ray Heindorf. CAST: Fred Astaire, Petula Clark, Don Francks, Tommy Steele, Keenan Wynn, Brenda Arnau, Avon Long. (Warner Bros 2550)

470110c FINIAN'S RAINBOW 1960 prod. COND: Max Meth. CAST: Jeannie Carson, Bobby Howes, Howard Morris, Biff McGuire, Carol Brice, Sorrell Booke. (RCA LSO-1057)

470110d FINIAN'S RAINBOW studio prod. ORCH: Various. COND: Morris Stoloff. CAST: Frank Sinatra, Rosemary Clooney, Dean Martin, Sammy Davis Jr. Clark Dennis, Bing Crosby, Debbie Reynolds, Lou Monte. (Reprise 2015)

470110e FINIAN'S RAINBOW 1955 album by Ella Logan of orig prod. COND: George Greeley. (Cap 10" H-561)

470110f FINIAN'S RAINBOW 1947 album. COND: Russ Case. VOCALS: Audrey Marsh, Jimmy Carroll, Jimmy Blair, chorus. (RCA LKT-1000)

470110g FINIAN'S RAINBOW studio prod. "Ed Sullivan presents Finian's Rainbow." No other credits given. (National Academy 12, with Brigadoon)

470110h FINIAN'S RAINBOW 1966 records by Burton Lane (composer), piano & vocal. "How Are Things in Glocca Morra?," "If This Isn't Love" (LP-671)

470310a MAURICE CHEVALIER records by Maurice Chevalier of orig prod. "Bonsoir Messieurs Dames" (1945:78/Voix de son Maitre(F) K-8657) "La Symphonie des Semelles de Bois" (1945: 78/Voix de son Maitre(F) K-8600) "La Lecon de Piano" (1945: 78/Voix de son Maitre(F) K-8630) "Mandarinade" (1945: 78/Voix de son Maitre(F) K-8690) "Weeping Willie," "Vingt Ans" (1947: LP-132) "A Barcelone" (1942: 78/Voix de son Maitre(F) K-8578)(1947: LP-88, LP-405) "Quai de Bercy" (1947: Voix de son Maitre(F) K-8712)(1947: LP-132) "Place Pigalle" (1947: Voix de son Maitre(F) K-8699)(1947: LP-132, LP-405) "Louise" (1929: LP-17, LP-72, LP-102, LP-453)(1947: LP-88, LP-405)(1958: LP-118) "Valentine" (1929: LP-72, LP-148)(1947: LP-88, LP-132, LP-405)(1957: LP-224) (1958: LP-118)

470313a BRIGADOON orig prod. MUSIC: Frederick Loewe. WORDS: Alan Jay Lerner. ORCH: Ted Royal. COND: Franz Allers. CAST: David Brooks, Marion Bell, Pamela Britton, Lee Sullivan, D Anderson. (RCA LOC-1001)

470313b BRIGADOON 1966 TV prod soundtrack. ORCH & COND: Irwin Kostal. CAST: Robert Goulet, Sally Ann Howes, Tommy Carlisle, Marlyn Mason. (Col CSM-385)

470313c BRIGADOON 1957 studio prod. COND: Lehman Engel. CAST: Shirley Jones, Jack Cassidy, Frank Porretta; Susan Johnson (of 1950 prod). (Col OS-2540)

470313d BRIGADOON 1959 studio prod. ORCH: Robert Russell Bennett. COND: John Green. CAST: Jan Peerce, Robert Merrill, Jane Powell. (RCA LSP-2275, with Gigi)

470313e BRIGADOON 1954 film soundtrack. ORCH: Conrad Salinger. COND: John Green, CAST: Gene Kelly, Van Johnson, John Gustafson (for Jimmy Thompson), Carol Richards (for Cyd Charisse). (MGM 3135. Excerpts: Kelly: "The Heather on the Hill," "Almost like Being in Love" (LP-501).)

470313f BRIGADOON 1955 record sung by Alan Jay Lerner, lyricist. "There but for You Go I" (LP-343)

470313g BRIGADOON studio prod. "Ed Sullivan presents Brigadoon." No other credits given. (National Academy 12, with Finian's Rainbow)

470313h BRIGADOON medley from 1953 Ice Capades prod. COND: Jeri Mayhall. VOCALS: Lee Sullivan (of orig cast), Sally Sweetland, chorus. (45/Col 4-50165)

470313i BRIGADOON contemp album. COND: Ted Royal (orchestrator of orig prod). VOCALS: Alfred Drake, Roberta Roberts, Bill Venturo. (78/Rainbow album 309)

470313j BRIGADOON 1977 record by Gene Kelly of 1954 film prod. "Almost like Being in Love" (LP-749)

470313k BRIGADOON studio prod. COND: Johnny Gregory. CAST: Elizabeth Larner, Barry Kent, chorus. (Wing SRW-11006, with Kiss Me Kate)

470426a BLESS THE BRIDE 1947 album by Georges Guetary & Lizbeth Webb of orig (London) prod, chorus. MUSIC: Vivian Ellis. WORDS: A P Herbert. COND: Michael Collins. Guetary: "Table for Two," "La Belle Marguerite" Guetary, Webb: "This Is My Lovely Day," "I Was Never Kissed Before" (45/Col(E) SEG-7551)

470426b BLESS THE BRIDE contemp record by Anona Winn of orig cast. "La Belle Marguerite" (78/HMV(E) BD-1204)

470426c BLESS THE BRIDE contemp medley by Vivian Ellis (composer), piano, COND: Michael Collins. (World Records(E) SH-228, with The Water Gipsies)

470426d BLESS THE BRIDE 1968 studio prod. COND: Geoff Love. CAST: Mary Millar, Roberto Cardinale, Peggy Mount, Charles Young, Leslie Fyson, Joanne Brown, Mary Thomas. (Music for Pleasure(E) 1263)

471009a HIGH BUTTON SHOES orig prod. MUSIC: Jule Styne. WORDS: Sammy Cahn. ORCH: Philip J Lang. COND: Milton Rosenstock. CAST: Phil Silvers, Nanette Fabray, Mark Dawson, Lois Lee, Jack McCauley, Johnny Stewart. (Camden 457. Excerpt: Dawson, Lee: "Can't You Just See Yourself" (LP-538).)

471009b HIGH BUTTON SHOES 1948 records by Joan Roberts, who replaced Nanette Fabray in orig prod. "Papa, Won't You Dance with Me?," "Jealous" (LP-706)

471010a ALLEGRO orig prod. MUSIC: Richard Rodgers. WORDS: Oscar Hammerstein II. ORCH: Robert Russell Bennett. COND: Salvatore Dell'Isola. CAST: Lisa Kirk, John Battles, Gloria Wills, Muriel O'Malley, Annamary Dickey, William Ching, Roberta Jonay, Robert Reeves (understudy to John Conte of orig cast). (RCA LSO-1099)

471015a TUPPENCE COLOURED 1976 record by Elisabeth Welch of orig (London) cast. "La Vie en Rose" (LP-415)

471023a STARLIGHT ROOF 1948 medley by members of orig prod. MUSIC & WORDS: George Melachrino, others. COND: Guy Daines. CAST: Julie Andrews (age 12), Pat Kirkwood, Vic Oliver, chorus. (78/Col(E) DB-2400/1)

471211a ANGEL IN THE WINGS 1978 record by Elaine Stritch of orig cast. MUSIC: Carl Sigman. WORDS: Bob Hilliard. "Civilization" (LP-618)

471226a BONANZA BOUND orig (Philadelphia) prod. MUSIC: Saul Chaplin. WORDS: Betty Comden, Adolph Green. ORCH: Philip J Lang. COND: Lehman Engel. CAST: George Coulouris, Carol Raye, Allyn McLerie, Adolph Green, Hal Hackett, Sid Melton, Betty Lou Barto. (LP-508)

471226b BONANZA BOUND 1977 record by Betty Comden & Adolph Green, lyricists. "Inspiration" (LP-489)

1948

480001a Film WORDS AND MUSIC soundtrack. MUSIC: Richard Rodgers. WORDS: Lorenz Hart. ORCH: Conrad Salinger. COND: Lennie Hayton. CAST: Judy Garland, Mickey Rooney, Lena Horne, Betty Garrett, Ann Sothern, June Allyson. (Metro 580. Incomplete: MGM 10" 505. Excerpts: Garland: "Johnny One Note" (LP-8)(LP-259)(LP-289)(LP-782) Allyson: "Thou Swell" (LP-252) Horne: "Where or When" (LP-328) "The Lady Is a Tramp" (LP-416). Also a number dropped before release: Garrett: "It Never Entered My Mind" (LP-455). Also the complete version of a song abridged before release: Garrett: "Way Out West" (LP-423).)

480001b Film WORDS AND MUSIC records by members of orig cast. Lena Horne: "Where or When" (1941: LP-241) Perry Como: "Blue Room," "With a Song in My Heart" (1948: 45/RCA 47-3229) Mel Torme: "Blue Moon" (1949: 78/Cap 15428) (LP-668) "Mountain Greenery" (78/Coral(E) Q-72150)

480002a Film EASTER PARADE soundtrack. MUSIC & WORDS: Irving Berlin. COND: John Green. CAST: Judy Garland, Fred Astaire, Ann Miller, Peter Lawford. (MGM 10" 502. Excerpts: Astaire: "Steppin' Out with My Baby," "It Only Happens When I Dance with You" (LP-24) Garland: "Better Luck Next Time" (LP-259) Astaire, Garland: "Easter Parade," "A Couple of Swells" (LP-416). Also a number dropped before release: Garland: "Mr. Monotony" (LP-423).)

480002b Film EASTER PARADE later records by members of orig cast. Fred Astaire: "Steppin' Out with My Baby" (1952: LP-50, LP-

125, LP-358, LP-567, LP-648) Judy Garland: "A Couple of Swells" (LP-201)(LP-202)(LP-329, with unidentified man) "Steppin' Out with My Baby" (LP-738)

480003a Film THE PIRATE soundtrack. MUSIC & WORDS: Cole Porter. ORCH: Conrad Salinger. COND: Lennie Hayton. CAST: Judy Garland, Gene Kelly. (MGM 10" 21. Excerpts: Garland: "Love of My Life" (LP-259)(LP-328)(CP-782) Kelly: "Nina" (LP-501). Also a number dropped before release: Garland: "Voodoo" (LP-423).)

480003b Film THE PIRATE 1963 records by Judy Garland of orig cast. "Love of My Life" (LP-201)(LP-738) "Be a Clown" (LP-738)

480004a Film CASBAH records sung by Harold Arlen. MUSIC: Harold Arlen. WORDS: Leo Robin. "For Every Man There's a Woman" (LP-60) "Hooray for Love" (LP-192)

480004b Film CASBAH contemp records by Tony Martin of orig cast. "Hooray for Love" (LP-657) "It Was Written in the Stars" (78/Vic 20-2690) "What's Good about Goodbye?," "For Every Man There's a Woman" (78/Vic 20-2689)

480004c Film CASBAH soundtrack. Tony Martin: "It was Written in the Stars," "What's Good about Goodbye?" Martin, Yvonne DeCarlo: "For Every Man There's a Woman" (LP-657)

480005a Film RACHEL AND THE STRANGER contemp album by Robert Mitchum and Gary Gray of orig cast. MUSIC & WORDS: Waldo Salt & Roy Webb. (78/Dec album 695. Excerpts: Mitchum: "O-He-O-Hi-O-Ho," "Rachel" (LP-114).)

480006a Film A FOREIGN AFFAIR contemp records by Marlene Dietrich of orig cast. MUSIC & WORDS: Frederick Hollander. "Black Market" (LP-109) "Illusions" (78/Bruns(E) 04253)

480006b Film A FOREIGN AFFAIR soundtrack. Marlene Dietrich: "Black Market," "Illusions," "The Ruins of Berlin" (LP-705)

480007a Film THE EMPEROR WALTZ contemp album by Bing Crosby of orig cast. MUSIC & WORDS: Various. COND: Victor Young. (Dec 10" 5272, with Top o' the Morning; LP-263.)

480008a Film BIG CITY contemp album by Lotte Lehmann of orig cast. MUSIC & WORDS: Various. COND: Robert Armbruster. (78/Vic album MO-1226)

480008b Film BIG CITY contemp album. VOCALS: Betty Garrett of orig cast, Art Lund, Kate Smith, Frankie Lester, Hal McIntyre Orch. (78/MGM album 23)

480009a Film IF YOU KNEW SUSIE records by Eddie Cantor of orig prod. "If You Knew Susie" (1925: LP-379)(Later: LP-30, LP-143, LP-144, LP-165, LP-384, LP-414, LP-721, LP-758)

480010a Film ROMANCE ON THE HIGH SEAS soundtrack. MUSIC: Jule Styne. WORDS: Sammy Cahn. ORCH & COND: Ray Heindorf. CAST: Doris Day, Sir Lancelot, Page Cavanaugh Trio. (Caliban 6015, with It's a Great Feeling. Excerpt: Day: "Put 'em in a Box, Tie 'em with a Ribbon" (LP-223).)

480010b Film ROMANCE ON THE HIGH SEAS contemp records by Doris Day of orig cast. "Put 'Em in a Box, Tie 'Em with a Ribbon" (78/Col 38188) "It's Magic" (LP-315) (LP-692) "It's You or No One" With Buddy Clark (not of orig cast): "I'm in Love" (78/Col 38290)

480010c Film ROMANCE ON THE HIGH SEAS 1977 record by Sammy Cahn, lyricist. "It's Magic" (LP-503)

480011a Film THE KISSING BANDIT contemp records by Frank Sinatra of orig cast. "Senorita," "If I Steal a Kiss" (LP-250)

480011b Film THE KISSING BANDIT soundtrack. Kathryn Grayson: "Tomorrow Means Romance" (LP-346) "Love is Where You Find It" (LP-347)(LP-364)(LP-702) "What's Wrong with Me?" (78/MGM 30133)

480012a Film THE MIRACLE OF THE BELLS 1947 record by Frank

Sinatra of orig cast. MUSIC: Jule Styne. WORDS: Sammy Cahn. "Ever Homeward" (LP-250)

480013a Film A DATE WITH JUDY soundtrack. Jane Powell: "It's a Most Unusual Day" (by Jimmy HcHugh, Harold Adamson)(LP-252)(LP-281) "Through the Years," "Love is Where You Find It" Powell, Scotty Beckett: "I'm Strictly on the Corny Side" (LP-281)

480013b Film A DATE WITH JUDY contemp records by members of orig prod. Carmen Miranda: "Cuanto le Gusta"(with Andrews Sisters, not of orig cast) (LP-522) Xavier Cugat Orch: "Cuanto le Gusta" (78/Col 38239)

480014a Record prod MANHATTAN TOWER orig prod. MUSIC & WORDS: Gordon Jenkins. ORCH & COND: Gordon Jenkins. VOCALS: Beverly Mahr, chorus. (Dec 8011, with California)

480015a Film FOR THE LOVE OF MARY soundtrack. Deanna Durbin: "Moonlight Bay," "I'll Take You Home Again Kathleen" (LP-256)

480016a Film THREE DARING DAUGHTERS soundtrack. MUSIC: Sammy Fain. WORDS: Howard Dietz. Jeanette MacDonald, Jane Powell, Ann Todd, Elinor Donahue: "The Dickey Bird Song" (LP-281)

480016b Film THREE DARING DAUGHTERS contemp records by Jeanette MacDonald of orig cast. "Springtide," "Where There's Love" (LP-536)

480017a Film MICKEY 1947 records by Lois Butler of orig cast. "Father Goose," "Dreams in My Heart" (78/Cap 15061)

480018a Film YOU WERE MEANT FOR ME soundtrack. MUSIC & WORDS: Various. CAST: Dan Dailey, Jeanne Crain, Oscar Levant (piano), chorus. (Titania 503, with My Blue Heaven)

480018b Film YOU WERE MEANT FOR ME 1957 record by Dan Dailey of orig cast. "You Were Meant for Me" (LP-367)

480019a Film MELODY TIME contemp records by members of orig prod. Dennis Day: "Johnny Appleseed Overture" (78/Vic 20-2943) Freddy Martin Orch (Jack Fina, piano): "Bumble Boogie" (78/Vic 20-1829) Roy Rogers, Sons of the Pioneers: "Pecos Bill," "Blue Shadows on the Trail" (78/Vic 20-2780) Rogers, 1975: "Blue Shadows on the Trail" (LP-523) Ethel Smith, organ: "Blame It on the Samba" (78/Dec 23828) Buddy Clark: "Melody Time," "Blue Shadows on the Trail" (78/Col 38170)

480019b Film MELODY TIME studio prod of "Johnny Appleseed" sequence. MUSIC: Walter Kent. WORDS: Kim Gannon. COND: Ken Darby. VOCALS: Dennis Day of orig prod, chorus. (Disneyland 1260)

480019c Film MELODY TIME soundtrack. Andrews Sisters: "Little Toot" (LP-661)

480020a Film ONE NIGHT WITH YOU contemp record by Nino Martini of orig cast. "One Night with You," "Roads through the Forest" (78/HMV(E) DA-1882)

480021a Film LADIES OF THE CHORUS soundtrack. Marilyn Monroe: "Anyone Can See I Love You," "Every Baby Needs a Da-Da-Daddy" (LP-452) Chorus: "Ladies of the Chorus" (LP-496)

480022a Film THE PALEFACE soundtrack. MUSIC & WORDS: mostly Jay Livingston, Ray Evans. CAST: Jane Russell, Bob Hope. (Titania 511, with Son of Paleface & The Time, the Place, and the Girl)

480022b Film THE PALEFACE 1948 record by Bob Hope of orig cast. "Buttons and Bows" (78/Cap 15292)

480023a Film THAT LADY IN ERMINE soundtrack. Betty Grable: "There's Something about Midnight" (LP-486)

480024a Film GIVE MY REGARDS TO BROADWAY 1949 record by

Dan Dailey of orig cast with the Andrews Sisters. "Take Me Out to the Ball Game" (78/Dec 24605)

480025a Film A SONG IS BORN 1948 album by members of orig prod. MUSIC & WORDS: Various. Page Cavanaugh Trio: "Daddy-o" Mel Powell Septet: "Muskrat Ramble" Charlie Barnet Orch: "The Redskin Rhumba" Benny Goodman Septet: "Stealin' Apples" Jeri Sullivan (who sang for Virginia Mayo), Golden Gate Quartet, Benny Goodman, Tommy Dorsey, Louis Armstrong, Charlie Barnet, Mel Powell: "A Song Was Born" (2 sides) (78/Cap album CC-106)

480025b Film A SONG IS BORN records by members of orig prod. Benny Goodman Sextet: "Flying Home" (1939: 78/Col 35254) Tommy Dorsey Orch: "Marie" (1937: 78/Vic 25523) (1938: LP-387) "I'm Getting Sentimental over You" (1936: 78/Vic 25236) Lionel Hampton Orch: "Flying Home" (1940: 78/Vic 26595) "Hawk's Nest," "Goldwyn Stomp" (1948: 78/Dec 24505) Louis Armstrong Orch: "A Song Was Born" (1948: 78/Vic 20-3064)

480026a Film GLAMOUR GIRL 1947 record by Gene Krupa Orch of orig prod. "Gene's Boogie" (78/Col 37589)

480027a Film ON AN ISLAND WITH YOU records by member of orig prod. Xavier Cugat Orch: "On an Island with You" (1948:78/Col 38194) Jimmy Durante: "I'll Do the Strut-away in My Cutaway" (1947-LP-142,LP-454)

480028a Film TWO GUYS FROM TEXAS soundtrack. Dennis Morgan, Jack Carson: "I Want to Be a Cowboy in the Movies" (LP-595)

480029a Film SO DEAR TO MY HEART 1949 studio prod. MUSIC & WORDS: Various. ORCH & COND: Billy May. NARRATOR: John Beal (of orig cast). VOCALS: Ken Carson & John Beal of orig cast; unidentified baritone; chorus. (78/Cap album DD-109)

480029b Film SO DEAR TO MY HEART contemp records by Burl Ives of orig cast. "Lavender Blue," "Billy Boy" (78/Dec 24547)

480029c Film SO DEAR TO MY HEART 1964 studio prod. VOCALS: Carl Berg, chorus. (Disneyland 1255)

480030a Film LUXURY LINER contemp records by members of orig prod. Lauritz Melchior: "Spring Came Back to Vienna," "Helan Gar" (78/MGM 30136) Xavier Cugat Orch: "Cugat's Nugats" (78/Col 38185) Pied Pipers: "Yes, We Have No Bananas" (78/Cap 15233)

480031a Film MARY LOU 1945 record by Frankie Carle Orch of orig prod. "Frankie Carle Boogie" (78/Col 36777)

480032a Film LULU BELLE contemp album by Dorothy Lamour of orig cast. MUSIC & WORDS: Various. COND: Henry Russell. "Lulu Belle," "Ace in the Hole," "Sweetie Pie," "I Can't Tell Why I Love You" (78/Coast album C-10)

480032b Film LULU BELLE later record by Dorothy Lamour of orig cast. "Lulu Belle" (LP-737)

480033a Film WHEN MY BABY SMILES AT ME radio performance by Betty Grable of orig cast. "What Did I Do?" (LP-646)

480034a Film A MIRACLE CAN HAPPEN contemp record by Dorothy Lamour of orig cast. "The Queen of the Hollywood Islands" (78/Coast 8036)

480115a MAKE MINE MANHATTAN 1978 studio prod. MUSIC: Richard Lewine. WORDS: Arnold B Horwitt. ORCH: Dennis Deal. CAST: Helen Gallagher, Arthur Siegel, Estelle Parsons, Nancy Grennan, Ken Parks, Bob DeAngelis, Dennis Deal. (Painted Smiles 1369, with additional material) (LP-618)

480129a LOOK MA, I'M DANCIN'! 1947 album by members of orig prod, others. MUSIC & WORDS: Hugh Martin. ORCH: Don Walker. COND: Pembroke Davenport (of orig prod). CAST: Nancy Walker, Harold Lang, & Sandra Deel of orig prod; Hugh Martin, composer; Bill Shirley of pre-Broadway cast; chorus. (Dec 10" 5231; CBS Records X-14879, with Arms and the Girl; LP-287.)

480129b LOOK MA, I'M DANCIN'! 1956 record by Nancy Walker of orig cast. "I'm Tired of Texas" (LP-293)

480229a MAURICE CHEVALIER records by Maurice Chevalier of orig prod. "Mimi" (English, 1932: LP-72, LP-88, LP-405)(French, 1932: LP-102)(English, 1958: LP-118) "A Barcelone" (1942: 78/Voix de son Maitre(F) K-8578)(1947: LP-88, LP-405) "Quai de Bercy" (1947: 78/Voix de son Maitre(F) K-8712)(1947: LP:132) "Place Pigalle" (1947: 78/Voix de son Maitre(F) K-8699)(1947: LP-132, LP-405) "Weeping Willie" (1947: LP-132) "La Symphonie des Semelles de Bois" (1945: 78/Voix de son Maitre(F) K-8600) "Priere" (1947: 78/Voix de son Maitre(F) K-8895) "J'ai du Ciel dans mon Chapeau" (1948: 78/Dec(F) MB-20312)

480430a INSIDE U.S.A. contemp album. MUSIC: Arthur Schwartz. WORDS: Howard Dietz. COND: Russ Case, Irving Miller. VOCALS: Beatrice Lillie & Jack Haley of orig cast; Perry Como, Billy Williams, chorus. (78/Vic album K-14. Incomplete: JJA Records 19733, with A Connecticut Yankee. Excerpt: Lillie: "At the Mardi Gras" (LP-44) (LP-539).)

480430b INSIDE U.S.A. 1948 album by Buddy Clark and Pearl Bailey. COND: Mitchell Ayres. (78/Col album C-162. Excerpts: Bailey: "Blue Grass," "Protect Me" Clark: "Haunted Heart" (LP-209).)

480430c INSIDE U.S.A. 1975 record sung by Arthur Schwartz, composer. "Rhode Island Is Famous for You" (LP-418)

480715a DOWN IN THE VALLEY 1950 TV prod. MUSIC: Kurt Weill. WORDS: Arnold Sundgaard. COND: Peter Herman Adler. CAST: Marion Bell, William McGraw, Kenneth Smith, Ray Jacquemot, Richard Barrows, Robert Holland. (RCA 10" LM-16)

480715b DOWN IN THE VALLEY 1950 studio prod. COND: Maurice Levine. CAST: Alfred Drake, Jane Wilson, John Pettersson, Norman Atkins, Daniel Slick. (Dec 10" 6017)

480924a THAT'S THE TICKET records by Harold Rome, vocal & piano. MUSIC & WORDS: Harold Rome. "The Money Song" (1954: LP-360)(1956: LP-39) "Gin Rummy Rhapsody," "You Never Know What Hit You," "I Shouldn't Love You" (1955: LP-316)

481007a LOVE LIFE 1955 album. MUSIC: Kurt Weill. WORDS: Alan Jay Lerner. ORCH & PIANO: Billy Taylor. COND: Herb Harris. VOCALS: Alan Jay Lerner (lyricist), Kaye Ballard, quartet. (Heritage 0600, entitled "Lyrics by Lerner," with additional material)

481011a WHERE'S CHARLEY? 1958 London prod. MUSIC & WORDS: Frank Loesser. COND: Michael Collins. CAST: Norman Wisdom, Terence Cooper, Pamela Gale, Pip Hinton, Felix Felton, Barry Kent, Marion Grimaldi, Jerry Desmonde. (Col(E) SX-1085)

481011b WHERE'S CHARLEY? records by members of orig cast. Ray Bolger: "Once in Love with Amy" (Contemp: LP-114, LP-164)(Later: 45/Kapp K-180-X) Bolger, Allyn McLerie: "Make a Miracle" (Contemp: 45/Dec 9-40065)

481011c WHERE'S CHARLEY? record by composer Frank Loesser & Lynn Loesser. "Make a Miracle" (78/Mercury 5307)

481011d WHERE'S CHARLEY? 1952 film soundtrack. COND: Robert Farnon. CAST: Ray Bolger, Allyn McLerie, Horace Cooper of orig prod; Mary Germaine, Robert Shackleton. (ECNAD 216, entitled "Charley's Aunt")

481113a AS THE GIRLS GO orig prod. MUSIC: Jimmy McHugh. WORDS: Harold Adamson. COND: Max Meth. Bobby Clark, chorus: "As the Girls Go," "Father's Day" (LP-544)

481116a ICE FOLLIES OF 1949 contemp records by the Ice Follies Ensemble and vocalists of orig prod. MUSIC & WORDS: Larry Morey. Jean Norman, the Woodbury Singers: "Tinkle-Ting-Ting" The Woodbury Singers: "Candy Soldiers on Parade" (78/Unnamed label mx RL-4008/9) Norman, Bill MacArthur: "When You're Young and It's Spring" John Woodbury & Group: "Songbird Singing in a Bamboo Tree" (78/Unnamed label mx RL-4007/4010)

481117a SLINGS AND ARROWS 1972 record by Sandy Wilson (composer), piano & vocal. "Medusa" (LP-755)

481208a GENTLEMEN PREFER BLONDES orig prod. MUSIC: Jule Styne. WORDS: Leo Robin. ORCH: Don Walker. COND: Milton Rosenstock. CAST: Carol Channing, Yvonne Adair, Jack McCauley, Eric Brotherson, George S Irving, Rex Evans, Honi Coles, Cholly Atkins, Alice Pearce. (Col OL-4290)

481208b GENTLEMEN PREFER BLONDES 1953 film soundtrack, with two new songs by Hoagy Carmichael & Harold Adamson. COND: Lionel Newman. CAST: Marilyn Monroe, Eileen Wilson (for Jane Russell). (MGM 10" 208; LP-599; plus additional "Little Girl from Little Rock" material on LP-452. Incomplete: LP-76. Excerpt: Wilson: "Bye-Bye Baby" (LP-328).)

481208c GENTLEMEN PREFER BLONDES later records by Carol Channing of orig cast. "Diamonds Are a Girl's Best Friend," "Little Girl from Little Rock" (LP-111)(LP-377) "Homesick Blues" (LP-204)(LP-377) "Bye Bye Baby" (LP-377)

481208d GENTLEMEN PREFER BLONDES 1973 touring prod entitled "Lorelei" with new songs by Jule Styne, Betty Comden, Adolph Green. ORCH: Philip J Lang, Don Walker. COND: Milton Rosenstock. CAST: Carol Channing of orig prod; Tamara Long, Peter Palmer, Lee Roy Reams, Brandon Maggart, Dody Goodman. (MGM/Verve 5097)

481208e GENTLEMEN PREFER BLONDES 1974 prod entitled "Lorelei" (the end product of the 1973 touring prod) with new songs by Jule Styne, Betty Comden, Adolph Green. ORCH: Philip J Lang, Don Walker. COND: Milton Rosenstock. CAST: Carol Channing of orig prod; Tamara Long, Peter Palmer, Lee Roy Reams, Jack Fletcher, Dody Goodman. (MGM M3G-55)

481208f GENTLEMEN PREFER BLONDES 1962 London prod. ORCH & COND: Alyn Ainsworth. CAST: Dora Bryan, Guy Middleton, Donald Stewart, Anne Hart, Robin Palmer, Valerie Walsh, John Griffin, Gerald Stern. (HMV(E) CSD-1464)

481208g GENTLEMEN PREFER BLONDES record of a song added to the 1953 film prod, sung by Hoagy Carmichael, composer. WORDS: Harold Adamson. "When Love Goes Wrong" (45/Cap F-2593)

481216a LEND AN EAR contemp album by members of orig prod. MUSIC & WORDS: Charles Gaynor. PIANOS: George Bauer & Dorothy Freitag (both of orig prod). "Santa Domingo," "Someone You Love," "Gladiola Girl Medley (Join Us in a Cup of Tea, Boys/Yahoo Step/Teeny, Weeny Nest for Two)," "I'm Not in Love," "Give Your Heart a Chance to Sing" With Beverly Hosier of orig cast (vocal): "Who Hit Me?" (78/Manor album C-3)

481216b LEND AN EAR later records by Carol Channing of orig cast. "Doin' the Old Yahoo Step" (LP-111)(LP-377) "Join Us in a Cup of Tea," "A Little Game of Tennis," "Teeny Little Weeny Nest for Two" (LP-377)

481230a KISS ME KATE orig prod. MUSIC & WORDS: Cole Porter. ORCH: Robert Russell Bennett. COND: Pembroke Davenport. CAST: Alfred Drake, Patricia Morison, Lisa Kirk, Harold Lang, Annabelle Hill, Edwin Clay, Charles Wood, Harry Clark, Jack Diamond, Lorenzo Fuller, Eddie Sledge, Fred Davis. (Col OL-4140)

481230b KISS ME KATE 1959 studio prod. ORCH & COND: Henri Rene. CAST: Howard Keel (of 1953 film cast), Anne Jeffreys (of 1949 touring company & who replaced Patricia Morison in orig prod in 1950), Gogi Grant. (RCA LSP-1984)

481230c KISS ME KATE studio prod. ORCH: Various. COND: Morris Stoloff. CAST: Frank Sinatra, Dean Martin, Keely Smith, Phyllis McGuire, Johnny Prophet, Lou Monte, Dinah Shore, Sammy Davis Jr, Jo Stafford, the Hi-Lo's. (Reprise 2017)

481230d KISS ME KATE 1953 film soundtrack. COND: Andre Previn. CAST: Kathryn Grayson, Howard Keel, Ann Miller, Keenan Wynn, James Whitmore, Tommy Rall, Bobby Van, Bob Fosse. (MGM 3077)

481230e KISS ME KATE 1968 TV prod soundtrack. ORCH & COND: Jack Elliott. CAST: Robert Goulet, Carol Lawrence, Jessica Walter, Michael Callan, Jules Munshin, Marty Ingels. (Col CSS-645)

481230f KISS ME KATE 1959 studio prod. COND: Pembroke Davenport of orig prod. CAST: Alfred Drake, Patricia Morison, Lisa Kirk, Harold Lang, Lorenzo Fuller (all of orig prod); Bob Sands, Ray Drakely. (Cap STAO-1267)

481230g KISS ME KATE 1962 studio prod. CAST: Earl Wrightson, Lois Hunt, Mary Mayo. (Col CS-8568)

481230h KISS ME KATE 1953 album. COND: Lehman Engel. CAST: Lisa Kirk (of orig prod), Helena Bliss (who replaced Patricia Morison in London cast), George Britton, (RCA 10" LPM-3157, with Anything Goes)

481230i KISS ME KATE album by Mimi Benzell & Felix Knight. COND: Warren Vincent. (Design 1009, with Can-Can)

481230j KISS ME KATE records by Lisa Kirk of orig cast "Why Can't You Behave?" (1958: LP-667)(1959: LP-294)

481230k KISS ME KATE contemp records by members of 1951 London prod: COND: Freddie Bretherton. CAST: Patricia Morison (also of orig cast), Bill Johnson, Julie Wilson (also of 1949 US touring company), Archie Savage, Danny Green, Sidney James. (LP-300)

481230l KISS ME KATE studio prod. COND: Hill Bowen. CAST: Ivor Emmanuel (of 1951 London cast), Marie Benson, Patricia Clark, Andy Cole, Bryan Johnson, Denis Quilley, Laurie Cornell. (Camden 482)

481230m KISS ME KATE 1967 studio prod. COND: Geoff Love. VOCALS: Patricia Routledge, David Holliday, Stella Tanner, Geoff Love, chorus. (Music for Pleasure(E) 1126)

481230n KISS ME KATE 1949 album. COND: Paul Weston. VOCALS: Jo Stafford, Gordon MacRae, chorus. (Cap 10" H-157)

481230o KISS ME KATE studio prod. "Ed Sullivan presents Kiss Me Kate." No other credits given. (National Academy 2)

481230p KISS ME KATE contemp album. VOCALS: Madelyn Russell, Patti Page, Dinah Washington, chorus. (Mercury 10" 25002, with South Pacific)

481230q KISS ME KATE 1958 TV prod soundtrack. Alfred Drake (of orig cast): "So in Love" (LP-620)

481230r KISS ME KATE 1951 records by Kathryn Grayson of 1953 film cast. "Were Thine That Special Face" (LP-347) With unidentified baritone: "So in Love," "Wunderbar" (LP-636)

481230s KISS ME KATE studio prod. COND: Johnny Gregory. CAST: Elizabeth Larner, Barry Kent, chorus. (Wing (E) SRW-11006, with Brigadoon)

1949

490001a Film IN THE GOOD OLD SUMMERTIME soundtrack. COND: George Stoll. VOCALS: Judy Garland. (LP-259. Incomplete: MGM 3232, with An American in Paris. Excerpts: "I Don't Care" (LP-8) "Play That Barber Shop Chord," "Last Night When We Were Young" (dropped before release), "Put Your Arms around Me Honey" (LP-782).)

490001b Film IN THE GOOD OLD SUMMERTIME record (piano & vocal) by Harold Arlen, composer, of a song dropped before release. MUSIC: Harold Arlen. WORDS: E Y Harburg. "Last Night When We Were Young" (LP-192)

490001c Film IN THE GOOD OLD SUMMERTIME records by Judy Garland of orig cast. "I Don't Care" (1946: LP-180, LP-718)(Later: LP-390, LP-738) "Last Night When We Were Young"(dropped before release) (Later: LP-188, LP-194, LP-219, LP-738)

490002a Film THE BARKLEYS OF BROADWAY soundtrack. MUSIC: Harry Warren, George Gershwin. WORDS: Ira Gershwin. ORCH: Conrad Salinger. COND: Lennie Hayton. CAST: Fred Astaire, Ginger Rogers, Oscar Levant. (MGM 2-SES-51 (with Silk Stockings & Les Girls) plus Astaire, Rogers, & Levant: " A Weekend in the Country" (LP-402) plus Chorus: "Swing Trot" (LP-588) plus additional material from "Shoes with Wings on," "You'd Be Hard to Replace, " & "My One and Only Highland Fling" (LP-633). Incomplete: LP-24. Excerpts: Astaire: "They Can't Take That Away From Me" (LP-252) "Shoes with Wings On" Astaire, Rogers: "My One and Only Highland Fling" (LP-399).)

490003a Film JOLSON SINGS AGAIN contemp records by Al Jolson, who sang for Larry Parks in the film. "After You've Gone" (LP-197)(LP-244)(LP-370)(LP-739) "I'm Just Wild about Harry," "Pretty Baby" (LP-197)(LP-244)(LP-739) "I Only Have Eyes for You" (LP-197)(LP-246)(LP-381) "Carolina in the Morning" (LP-198)(LP-244) "Toot, Toot, Tootsie!" (LP-198)(LP-244)(LP-394)(LP-409)(LP-438, with Eddie Cantor)(LP-677)(LP-682)(LP-739) "Rock-a-bye Your Baby" (LP-145)(LP-244)(LP-331)(LP-394)(LP-478)(LP-739) "Sonny Boy," "California, Here I Come" (LP-145)(LP-243)(LP-682)(LP-739) "When the Red, Red Robin" (LP-196)(LP-243) "For Me and My Gal" (LP-196)(LP-244)(LP-331)(LP-739) "I'm Looking Over a Four-Leaf Clover" (LP-197)(LP-243) "Baby Face" (LP-197)(LP-243)(LP-409) "Back in Your Own Backyard" (LP-198)(LP-243)(LP-739) "Give My Regards to Broadway" (LP-197)(LP-245)(LP-280)(LP-739) "Chinatown, My Chinatown" (LP-197)(LP-245)(LP-280) "Is It True What They Say about Dixie?" (LP-197)(LP-246)(LP-383)(LP-739)

490004a Film NEPTUNE'S DAUGHTER contemp records by members of orig cast. MUSIC & WORDS: Frank Loesser. COND: George Stoll. Esther Williams, Ricardo Montalban: "Baby, It's Cold Outside" (LP-207) Montalban: "My Heart Beats Faster" (78/MGM 30197)

490004b Film NEPTUNE'S DAUGHTER record by composer Frank Loesser & Lynn Loesser. "Baby It's Cold Outside" (78/Mercury 5307)

490004c Film NEPTUNE'S DAUGHTER soundtrack. Betty Garrett, Red Skelton, Xavier Cugat Orch: "I Love Those Men" Esther Williams, Ricardo Montalban, Garrett, Skelton: "Baby, It's Cold Outside" (LP-656)

490005a Film HOLIDAY IN HAVANA 1955 record by Desi Arnaz of orig cast. "The Straw Hat Song" (LP-207)(LP-702)

490006a Film THAT MIDNIGHT KISS contemp album by Mario Lanza of orig cast. MUSIC & WORDS: Various. COND: Constantine Callinicos, Ray Sinatra. (RCA 10" LM-86, with additional songs by Lanza)

490006b Film THAT MIDNIGHT KISS soundtrack. Kathryn Grayson, Mario Lanza: "They Didn't Believe Me" (LP-347) (LP-665)

490006c Film THAT MIDNIGHT KISS record by Kathryn Grayson of orig cast. "They Didn't Believe Me" (LP-364)

490007a Film TAKE ME OUT TO THE BALL GAME soundtrack, including two songs dropped before release. MUSIC & WORDS: Roger Edens, Betty Comden, Adolph Green, others. COND: Adolph Deutsch. CAST: Gene Kelly, Frank Sinatra, Jules Munshin, Betty Garrett, Esther Williams. (Curtain Calls 100/18. Excerpts: Sinatra: "Boys and Girls like You and Me" Kelly: "Baby Doll" (both dropped before release) (LP-455) Williams, Garrett, Munshin, Kelly: "Strictly U.S.A." (LP-669).)

490007b Film TAKE ME OUT TO THE BALL GAME 1949 records by members of orig cast. Frank Sinatra: "The Right Girl for Me" (LP-250) Betty Garrett, Gene Kelly: "Yes, Indeedy" (78/MGM 30193) "Take Me Out to the Ball Game" (LP-598) "It's Fate, Baby, It's Fate" (78/MGM 30190)

490008a Film TOP O' THE MORNING contemp records by members of orig cast. MUSIC & WORDS: James Van Heusen, John Burke, others. Bing Crosby: "You're in Love with Someone," "The Donovans," "Top o' the Morning" Crosby & Ann Blythe: "Oh, 'Tis Sweet to Think" (Dec 10" 5272, with The Emperor Waltz; LP-253.)

490009a Film A CONNECTICUT YANKEE IN KING ARTHUR'S COURT contemp album by members of orig cast. MUSIC: James Van Heusen. WORDS: John Burke. COND: Victor Young. CAST: Bing Crosby, Rhonda Fleming, Murvyn Vye, William Bendix, Cedric Hardwicke. (78/Dec album 699. Incomplete: LP-253.)

490010a Record prod CALIFORNIA orig prod. MUSIC: Gordon Jenkins. WORDS: Tom Adair. ORCH & COND: Gordon Jenkins. VOCALS: Lee Sweetland, Beverly Mahr, Betty Brewer, Art Gentry. (Dec 8011, with Manhattan Tower)

490011a Film CINDERELLA soundtrack. MUSIC & WORDS: Mack David, Al Hoffman, Jerry Livingston. ORCH: Joseph Dubin. COND: Oliver Wallace, Paul Smith. VOCALS: Ilene Woods, Verna Felton, Don Barclay, chorus. (Disneyland 4007) (LP-661)

490011b Film CINDERELLA studio prod by members of orig cast. COND: Paul Smith. VOCALS: Ilene Woods, Verna Felton, chorus. (Camden 1057, with 20,000 Leagues under the Sea)

490011c Film CINDERELLA contemp records by Ilene Woods of orig cast, with male quartet. COND: Harold Mooney, "Bibbidi-Bobbidi-Boo," "So This Is Love" (78/Vic 30-0019) "A Dream Is a Wish Your Heart Makes," "The Cinderella Work Song" (78/Vic 30-0020)

490012a Film THE GREAT LOVER contemp record by Bob Hope of orig cast & Margaret Whiting. MUSIC & WORDS: Jay Livingston, Ray Evans. "Lucky Us" (45/Cap 54-783)

490013a Film RED, HOT AND BLUE contemp records by Betty Hutton of orig cast. MUSIC & WORDS: Frank Loesser. "That's Loyalty," "I Wake Up in the Morning Feeling Fine," "Hamlet," "Now That I Need You" (LP-285)

490014a Film MY DREAM IS YOURS soundtrack. MUSIC & WORDS: mostly Harry Warren, Ralph Freed. ORCH & COND: Ray Heindorf. VOCALS: Doris Day, Lee Bowman, Frankie Carle (piano). (Titania 501, with The West Point Story)

490014b Film MY DREAM IS YOURS contemp records by members of orig prod. Doris Day: "Someone like You," "My Dream Is Yours" (78/Col 38375) "I'll String Along with You" (with Buddy Clark) (78/Col 38394) "Canadian Capers" (LP-330) Frankie Carle, piano: "Canadian Capers" (78/Col 37315)

490015a Film ICHABOD AND MR. TOAD 1963 album of "The Legend of Sleepy Hollow." MUSIC: Gene de Paul. WORDS: Don

Raye. VOCALS: Uncredited soloists. (Disneyland 1285, entitled "The Legend of Sleepy Hollow," with Rip Van Winkle)

490015b Film ICHABOD AND MR. TOAD contemp album of "The Legend of Sleepy Hollow." NARRATOR: Bing Crosby of orig prod. VOCALS: Bing Crosby, chorus. (Dec 9106, entitled "Ichabod," with Rip Van Winkle)

490016a Film IT'S A GREAT FEELING 1949 records by members of orig cast. MUSIC: Jule Styne. WORDS: Sammy Cahn. Jack Carson: "That Was a Big Fat Lie," "Give Me a Song with a Beautiful Melody" (78/Cap 57-672) Doris Day: "It's a Great Feeling," "At the Cafe Rendezvous" (78/Col(E) DB-2652) "Blame My Absent-Minded Heart" (78/Col(E) DB-2663)

490016b Film IT'S A GREAT FEELING soundtrack. ORCH & COND: Ray Heindorf. CAST: Doris Day, Jack Carson, Dennis Morgan. (Caliban 6015, with Romance on the High Seas)

490017a Film FLAMINGO ROAD soundtrack. Joan Crawford: "If I Could Be with You" (LP-401)

490018a Film LE ROI contemp album by Maurice Chevalier of orig cast. COND: Raymond Legrand. "La Barbe," "Bouquet de Paris," "C'est Fini," "La Cachucha" (78/Dec album DU-758)

490019a Film THE SUN COMES UP contemp records by Jeanette MacDonald of orig cast. "If You Were Mine" (LP-536) "Romance" (LP-756)

490020a Film THE INSPECTOR GENERAL contemp record by Danny Kaye of orig cast. "Happy Times" (78/Dec 24820)

490021a Film ALWAYS LEAVE THEM LAUGHING soundtrack. Milton Berle, Bert Lahr: "By the Light of the Silvery Moon" (LP-608)

490022a Film LOVE HAPPY contemp record by Marion Hutton of orig cast. "Love Happy" (78/MGM 10535)

490023a Film MY FRIEND IRMA contemp records by Dean Martin of orig cast. "Just for Fun," "My Own, My Only, My All" (78/Cap(E) CL-13314)

490024a Film LOOK FOR THE SILVER LINING soundtrack. MUSIC & WORDS: Jerome Kern, others, ORCH & COND: Ray Heindorf. CAST: June Haver, Gordon MacRae, Ray Bolger, chorus. (Titania 504, with I'll Get By)

490024b Film LOOK FOR THE SILVER LINING contemp album by Vaughan Monroe Orch. VOCALS: The Moon Men, chorus. (78/Vic album WP-246, entitled "Silver Lining Songs")

490024c Film LOOK FOR THE SILVER LINING contemp record by Gordon MacRae of orig cast. "A Kiss in the Dark" (78/Cap(E) CL-13207)

490025a Film ADAM'S RIB soundtrack. MUSIC & WORDS: Cole Porter. David Wayne: "Farewell, Amanda" (LP-655)

490026a Film FEUDIN' RHYTHM records by Eddy Arnold of orig cast. "The Cattle Call," "The Nearest Thing to Heaven" (45/RCA 48-0136)

490027a Film OH, YOU BEAUTIFUL DOLL soundtrack. MUSIC: Fred Fisher. WORDS: Various. ORCH & COND: Alfred Newman. CAST: June Haver, Bill Shirley (for Mark Stevens), S Z Sakall. (Titania 502, with I Wonder Who's Kissing Her Now)

490027b Film OH, YOU BEAUTIFUL DOLL 1949 album. COND: Skip Martin, VOCALS: Tony Martin, the Pied Pipers. "Oh, You Beautiful Doll," "I Want You to Want Me," "Peg o' My Heart," "When I Get You Alone Tonight," "There's a Broken Heart for Every Light on Broadway," "Come, Josephine, in My Flying Machine" (45/RCA album WP-252)

490113a ALONG FIFTH AVENUE 1956 record by Nancy Walker of orig cast. "Chant d'Amour" ("Irving") (LP-293)

490407a SOUTH PACIFIC orig prod. MUSIC: Richard Rodgers. WORDS: Oscar Hammerstein II. ORCH: Robert Russell Bennett. COND: Salvatore Dell'Isola. CAST: Mary Martin, Ezio Pinza, Juanita Hall, William Tabbert, Barbara Luna. (Col OL-4180)

490407b SOUTH PACIFIC 1967 prod. ORCH: Robert Russell Bennett. COND: Jonathan Anderson. CAST: Florence Henderson, Giorgio Tozzi (of 1958 film prod), Justin McDonough, Eleanor Cables, Irene Byatt, David Doyle. (Col OS-3100)

490407c SOUTH PACIFIC 1958 film soundtrack, including a song dropped from the stage production. COND: Alfred Newman. CAST: Mitzi Gaynor, Giorgio Tozzi (for Rossano Brazzi), Ray Walston, Bill Lee (for John Kerr), Muriel Smith (for Juanita Hall, who sang the role in orig prod), Thurl Ravenscroft (for Ken Clark). (RCA LOC-1032)

490407d SOUTH PACIFIC 1949 studio prod. COND: Al Goodman. CAST: Sandra Deel, Dickinson Eastham (understudies to the leads of orig cast); Thelma Carpenter, Jimmy Carroll, chorus. (RCA LK-1008)

490407e SOUTH PACIFIC 1951 records by members of 1951 London prod. COND: Reginald Burston. Orchestra: Medley (78/Col(E) DX-1797) Muriel Smith: "Bali Ha'i" Peter Grant: "Younger than Springtime" Mary Martin, Wilbur Evans: "Twin Soliloquies" Evans: "Some Enchanted Evening" (45/Col(E) SEG-7668) Smith: "Happy Talk" Grant: "Carefully Taught" Patricia Lowi, John Levitt: "Dites-moi" Evans: "This Nearly Was Mine" Evans, Martin: "Finale" (45/Col(E) SEG-7688)

490407f SOUTH PACIFIC studio prod. "Ed Sullivan presents South Pacific." No other credits given. (National Academy 5)

490407g SOUTH PACIFIC studio prod. COND: Hans Hagan. VOCALS: Renee Guerin, Bob Stratton, Don Grilley, Patti Steele, Connie Connerly. (Crown 5054)

490407h SOUTH PACIFIC 1959 studio prod. COND: Hill Bowen. VOCALS: Marie Benson, Bryan Johnson, Fred Lucas, Laurie Cornell, Denis Martin. (Camden 494)

490407i SOUTH PACIFIC 1950 album. VOCALS: Peggy Lee, Margaret Whiting, Gordon MacRae, chorus. (Cap 10" H-163)

490407j SOUTH PACIFIC studio prod. COND: Cyril Stapleton. VOCALS: Janet Waters, Andy Cole, Pat Whitworth, chorus. (Richmond B-20074, with Gigi)

490407k SOUTH PACIFIC 1962 studio prod. COND: Al Goodman ("Dean Franconi"). VOCALS: Richard Torigi, Susan Shaute, William Reynolds, Dolores Martin, Paula Wayne, chorus. (Hurrah 1035)

490407l SOUTH PACIFIC studio prod. COND: Al Goodman. VOCALS: Richard Torigi, Susan Shaute, William Reynolds, Dolores Martin, Paula Wayne, chorus. (Promenade 2092)

490407m SOUTH PACIFIC 1952 studio prod. COND: Ivor Slaney. VOCALS: Jean Campbell, Bob Dale, chorus. (Remington 10" 149-54)

490407n SOUTH PACIFIC studio prod. COND: Morris Stoloff. VOCALS: Frank Sinatra, Jo Stafford, McGuire Sisters, Keely Smith, Bing Crosby, Sammy Davis Jr, Dinah Shore, Hi-Lo's, Debbie Reynolds, Rosemary Clooney. (Reprise FS-2018)

490407o SOUTH PACIFIC records by members of orig cast. Mary Martin: "My Girl Back Home," "Loneliness of Evening" (both songs dropped from the show) (LP-497) "I'm in Love with a Wonderful Guy" (1977: LP-652) Medley (1955: LP-351)(1972: LP-509) Ezio Pinza: "Bali Ha'i" (1949: Col 7" 3-397)

490407p SOUTH PACIFIC 1975 record by Ray Walston of 1951

London cast & 1958 film cast. "There Is Nothing like a Dame" (LP-510)

490407q SOUTH PACIFIC 1959 studio prod. VOCALS: Angela Atwell, Louis Massey, Maria Cole, Jim Laine, Elayne Myra, chorus. (Lion 70093)

490407r SOUTH PACIFIC studio prod. COND: Johnny Douglas. CAST: Ian Wallace, Joyce Blair, Peter Grant, Isabelle Lucas, Bernard Martin, chorus. (Cap SN-7501)

490407s SOUTH PACIFIC contemp album. VOCALS: Kitty Kallen, Donald Richards, John Laurenz, Anne Vincent. (Mercury 10" 25002, with Kiss Me Kate)

490407t SOUTH PACIFIC 1965 studio prod. ORCH & COND: Sam Fonteyn. VOCALS: Louie Ramsey, Charles West, Sharon Sefton, Stephen Ayres, Isabel Lucas, Brian Davies, chorus. (Music for Pleasure(E) 1008)

490407u SOUTH PACIFIC 1950 album. VOCALS: Bing Crosby, Danny Kaye, Evelyn Knight, Ella Fitzgerald, chorus, (Dec 10" 5207)

490407v SOUTH PACIFIC 1957 records by Giorgio Tozzi of 1957 Los Angeles prod. ORCH & COND: Irwin Kostal. "Some Enchanted Evening," "Younger Than Springtime," "Bali Ha'i," "This Nearly Was Mine" (45/RCA EPA-4063)

490715a MISS LIBERTY orig prod. MUSIC & WORDS: Irving Berlin. ORCH: Don Walker. COND: Jay Blackton. CAST: Eddie Albert, Allyn McLerie, Mary McCarty, Johnny Thompson, Ethel Griffies. (Col ML-4220)

490715b MISS LIBERTY 1949 studio prod. COND: Al Goodman. CAST: Wynn Murray, Martha Wright, Bob Wright, Sandra Deel, Jimmy Carroll, chorus. (RCA LK-1009)

490715c MISS LIBERTY 1949 album. COND: Fred Waring. VOCALS: Joe Marine, Daisy Bernier, Gordon Goodman, Jane Wilson, Joanne Wheatley, chorus. (Dec 10" 5009)

490915a KING'S RHAPSODY orig (London) cast. MUSIC: Ivor Novello. WORDS: Christopher Hassall. COND: Harry Acres. CAST: Vanessa Lee, Olive Gilbert, Denis Martin, Phyllis Dare, Larry Mandon, Ivor Novello. (LP-309. Incomplete: HMV(E) 10" DLP-1010.)

490915b KING'S RHAPSODY 1962 studio prod. ORCH: Bobby Richards. COND: Jan Cervenka. VOCALS: Pamela Woolmore, Patricia Johnson, Andrew Gold, chorus. (Music for Pleasure(E) 1097, with The Dancing Years)

490915c KING'S RHAPSODY 1968 English radio prod. COND: Vilem Tausky. CAST: Cynthia Glover, Patricia Kern, Marjorie Westbury, Robert Bowman, chorus. (Col(E) TWO-270)

490915d KING'S RHAPSODY 1955 film soundtrack. Anna Neagle: "The Years Together" Patrice Wymore, Edmund Hockridge: "A Violin Began to Play," "If This Were Love" Wymore: "Someday My Heart Will Awake" Orchestra: Selection (45/Parlophone(E) GEP-8553)

490915e KING'S RHAPSODY later record by Vanessa Lee of orig cast. "Some Day My Heart Will Awake" (LP-444)

491013a TOUCH AND GO 1978 records by Nancy Andrews of orig cast. MUSIC: Jay Gorney. WORDS: Jean & Walter Kerr. "This Had Better Be Love" (with Arthur Siegel), "Miss Platt Selects Mate" (LP-618)

491030a LOST IN THE STARS orig prod. MUSIC: Kurt Weill. WORDS: Maxwell Anderson. ORCH: Kurt Weill. COND: Maurice Levine. CAST: Todd Duncan, Inez Matthews, Frank Roane, Sheila Guyse, Herbert Coleman. (Dec 8028)

491125a TEXAS, LI'L DARLIN' orig prod. MUSIC: Robert Emmett

Dolan. WORDS: Johnny Mercer. ORCH: Robert Russell Bennett. COND: Will Irwin. CAST: Kenny Delmar, Danny Scholl, Mary Hatcher, Fredd Wayne, Loring Smith, chorus, (Dec 10" 5188; CBS Records X-14878, with Mexican Hayride; LP-544. Excerpt: "The Big Movie Show in the Sky" (LP-164).)

491125b TEXAS, LI'L DARLIN' records sung by Johnny Mercer, lyricist. "It's Great to Be Alive" (1950's, with Jo Stafford: LP-604)(1974: LP-560) "They Talk a Different Language" (1950's, with Jo Stafford: LP-604)

1950

500001a Film AN AMERICAN IN PARIS soundtrack. MUSIC: George Gershwin. WORDS: Ira Gershwin, B G DeSylva. ORCH: Conrad Salinger, John Green. COND: John Green. PIANO: Oscar Levant. CAST: Gene Kelly, Georges Guetary, Oscar Levant, Benny Carter Orch. (MGM 10" 93, plus Guetary: "Nice Work If You Can Get It" Guetary, Kelly: "By Strauss" Kelly, Levant: "Tra-la-la" Levant: "I Don't Think I'll Fall in Love Today" Benny Carter Orch: "DoDo-Do/Bidin' My Time/I've Got a Crush on You/Our Love is Here to Stay" (LP-654). Also numbers dropped before release: Kelly: "I've Got a Crush on You" (LP-455) Levant: "My Cousin from Milwaukee/A Foggy Day/The Half of It Dearie Blues/But Not for Me," "Bidin' My Time" Guetary: "But Not for Me," "Love Walked In" (LP-654). Excerpts: Kelly, children: "I Got Rhythm" (LP-416)(LP-501) Kelly: "Love Is Here to Stay" Kelly, Guetary: "'S Wonderful" (LP-501) Guetary: "I'll Build a Stairway to Paradise" (LP-416).)

500001b Film AN AMERICAN IN PARIS 1977 records by Gene Kelly of orig cast. "'s Wonderful," "I Got Rhythm," "Love Is Here to Stay" Dropped before release: "I've Got a Crush on You" (LP-749)

500002a Film SUMMER STOCK soundtrack. MUSIC: Harry Warren, Harold Arlen. WORDS: Mack Gordon, Ted Koehler, Saul Chaplin. COND: John Green. CAST: Judy Garland, Gene Kelly, Phil Silvers, Gloria DeHaven, Pete Roberts (for Hans Conried). (MGM 10" 519, plus Main Title (LP-633). Excerpts: Garland: "Get Happy" (LP-8)(LP-252)(LP-259)(LP-782) "If You Feel Like Singing" (LP-8)(LP-259) (LP-399) "Happy Harvest" Kelly: "You, Wonderful You" (LP-399)(LP-501).)

500002b Film SUMMER STOCK records by Judy Garland of orig cast. "Get Happy" (1952: LP-329)(1969: LP-525)

500003a Film MY BLUE HEAVEN soundtrack. MUSIC & WORDS: mostly Harold Arlen, Ralph Blane. CAST: Betty Grable, Dan Dailey, David Wayne, Jane Wyatt, Mitzi Gaynor, chorus. (Titania 503, with You Were Meant for Me)

500004a Film THREE LITTLE WORDS soundtrack. MUSIC: Harry Ruby. WORDS: Bert Kalmar. COND: Andre Previn. CAST: Fred Astaire, Red Skelton, Anita Ellis (for Vera-Ellen), Arlene Dahl, Helen Kane (for Debbie Reynolds), Gloria DeHaven, Gale Robbins. (MGM 10" 516. Excerpt: DeHaven: "Who's Sorry Now?" (LP-272).)

500004b Film THREE LITTLE WORDS contemp records by Phil Regan of orig cast. "You Are My Lucky Star," "Three Little Words" (78/Vic 20-3833)

500005a Film TWO WEEKS WITH LOVE soundtrack. ORCH: Leo Arnaud. COND: George Stoll. CAST: Jane Powell, Debbie Reynolds, Carleton Carpenter. (MGM 10" 530. Excerpt: Reynolds, Carpenter: "Aba Daba Honeymoon" (LP-252).)

500006a Film THE TOAST OF NEW ORLEANS contemp album (of operatic pieces) by Mario Lanza of orig cast and Elaine Malbin. COND: Constantine Callinicos. (RCA 10" LM-75)

500006b Film THE TOAST OF NEW ORLEANS contemp records

(of popular songs) by Mario Lanza of orig cast. MUSIC: Nicholas Brodsky. WORDS: Sammy Cahn. COND: Ray Sinatra. "Be My Love," "I'll Never Love You" (45/RCA 49-1353) "Boom Biddy Boom," "Tina-Lina," "The Bayou Lullaby," "The Toast of New Orleans" (45/RCA album WDM-1417)

500006c Film THE TOAST OF NEW ORLEANS soundtrack. Mario Lanza & Kathryn Grayson: "Be My Love" (LP-252)(LP-665) "Stolta Paura l'Amor" (LP-347) "The Bayou Lullaby" (LP-636)(LP-665)

500006d Film THE TOAST OF NEW ORLEANS 1974 record by Sammy Cahn (lyricist). "Be My Love" (LP-313)

500007a Film STAGE FRIGHT records by Marlene Dietrich of orig cast. MUSIC & WORDS: Cole Porter. "The Laziest Gal in Town" (1955: LP-178)(1965: LP-191)

500008a Film NANCY GOES TO RIO soundtrack. MUSIC & WORDS: Various. COND: George Stoll. CAST: Jane Powell, Carmen Miranda, Ann Sothern, Danny Scholl (for Barry Sullivan). (MGM 2-SES-53, with Royal Wedding & Rich, Young and Pretty. Incomplete: MGM 10" 508.)

500008b Film NANCY GOES TO RIO 1950 records by Carmen Miranda of orig cast with the Andrews Sisters. "Yipsee-i-o," "Ca-room Pa Pa" (78/Dec 24979)

500009a Film PAGAN LOVE SONG soundtrack. MUSIC: Harry Warren, Nacio Herb Brown. WORDS: Arthur Freed. COND: Adolph Deutsch. CAST: Howard Keel, Esther Williams, (MGM 10" 534. Excerpts: Williams: "Sea of the Moon" (LP-328) Keel: "Why Is Love So Crazy?" (LP-633) Also a number dropped before release: Keel: "Music on the Water" (LP-486).)

500010a Film YOUNG MAN WITH A HORN soundtrack. MUSIC: Richard Rodgers. WORDS: Lorenz Hart. Doris Day: "With a Song in My Heart" (LP-223)

500010b Film YOUNG MAN WITH A HORN contemp album by Doris Day (vocals) & Harry James (trumpet) of orig prod. MUSIC & WORDS: Various. (Col CL-582)

500011a Film RIDING HIGH contemp records by members of orig cast. MUSIC: James Van Heusen. WORDS: John Burke. Bing Crosby: "A Sure Thing," "The Horse Told Me," "Someplace on Anywhere Road" Crosby & Carole Richards: "Sunshine Cake" (LP-253)

500012a Film MR. MUSIC contemp album. MUSIC: James Van Heusen. WORDS: John Burke. CAST: Bing Crosby & Dorothy Kirsten of orig cast; the Andrews Sisters. (Dec 10" 5284; LP-255.)

500012b Film MR. MUSIC 1950 radio performance by Bing Crosby of orig cast. "Life Is So Peculiar" (LP-468)

500013a Film FANCY PANTS 1949 records by Bob Hope of orig cast & Margaret Whiting. MUSIC & WORDS: Jay Livingston, Ray Evans. "Home Cookin'" (45/Cap F-1042)

500014a Film THE GREAT RUPERT records by Jimmy Durante of orig cast. "Take an 'L'" (LP-292)(78/MGM(E) 315) "Christmas Comes but Once a Year" (45/MGM K-30257)

500015a Film THE DUCHESS OF IDAHO soundtrack. MUSIC & WORDS: Various. CAST: Van Johnson, Eleanor Powell, Mel Torme, Connie Haines, Lena Horne. (Titania 508, with You Can't Have Everything)

500015b Film THE DUCHESS OF IDAHO contemp records by members of orig cast. Van Johnson: "You Can't Do Wrong Doin' Right," "Let's Choo Choo Choo to Idaho" (78/MGM 10727) Connie Haines: "Let's Choo Choo Choo to Idaho," "Of All Things" (78/Coral 60221)

500016a Film AT WAR WITH THE ARMY contemp records by mem-

bers of orig cast. Dean Martin: "You and Your Beautiful Eyes," "Tanda Wanda Hoy" (45/Cap F-1358) Polly Bergen: "Tanda Wanda Hoy" (45/RCA 47-4022) Jerry Lewis: "The Navy Gets the Gravy" (45/Cap F-1385)

500017a Film WABASH AVENUE soundtrack. Betty Grable: "I Wish I Could Shimmy like My Sister Kate" (LP-284) (LP-646) "May I Tempt You with a Big Red Rosy Apple?" (LP-496)(LP-646) "Wilhelmina," "Baby, Won't You Say You Love Me" (LP-646)

500018a Film GROUNDS FOR MARRIAGE soundtrack. MUSIC & WORDS: Various (operatic). COND: John Green. VOCALS: Kathryn Grayson, Stephen Kemalyan, Richard Atckison, Gilbert Russell. (MGM 10" 536)

500018b Film GROUNDS FOR MARRIAGE soundtrack of a song dropped before release. MUSIC: Richard Rodgers. WORDS: Lorenz Hart. "Wait Till You See Him" (LP-346)

500019a Film I'LL GET BY soundtrack. MUSIC & WORDS: Various. CAST: June Haver, Gloria deHaven, Dennis Day, William Lundigan, Dan Dailey, Harry James Orch. (Titania 504, with Look for the Silver Lining)

500019b Film I'LL GET BY records by members of orig prod. Dennis Day: "There Will Never Be Another You" (1950: 78/Vic 20-3900) Harry James Orch: "I'll Get By" (1941: 78/Col 36285) "It's Been a Long, Long Time" (1945: 78/Col 36838)

500019c Film I'LL GET BY records by composer & lyricist. Sammy Cahn (lyricist), vocal: "It's Been a Long, Long Time"(music by Jule Styne) (1972: LP-658)(1974, incomplete: LP-313)(1977: LP-503) Josef Myrow (composer), piano & vocal: "You Make Me Feel So Young" (words by Mack Gordon) (1971: LP-694)

500020a Film MY FRIEND IRMA GOES WEST contemp records by Dean Martin of orig cast. MUSIC & WORDS: Jay Livingston, Ray Evans. "Baby, Obey Me!," "I'll Always Love You" (45/Cap F-1028)

500021a Film LET'S DANCE contemp record by Betty Hutton of orig cast. MUSIC & WORDS: Frank Loesser. "Can't Stop Talking" (45/RCA 47-3908)

500021b Film LET'S DANCE soundtrack. Orchestra: Main Title Betty Hutton, Fred Astaire: "Can't Help Talking about Him," "Oh, Them Dudes," "The Tunnel of Love" Hutton: "Why Fight the Feeling?" (LP-656)

500022a Film THE TRAVELING SALESWOMAN soundtrack. Adele Jergens: "Ev'ry Baby Needs a Da-Da-Daddy" (LP-496)

500023a Film THE WEST POINT STORY soundtrack. MUSIC: Jule Styne. WORDS: Sammy Cahn. ORCH & COND: Ray Heindorf, Hugh Martin. CAST: Doris Day, Gordon MacRae, James Cagney, Virginia Mayo, Gene Nelson. (Titania 501, with My Dream Is Yours)

500023b Film THE WEST POINT STORY contemp record by Gordon MacRae of orig cast. "You Love Me" (45/Cap F-1214)

500024a Film SINGING GUNS contemp records by Vaughn Monroe of orig cast. "Mule Train," "Singing My Way Back Home" (45/RCA 47-3106)

500025a Film GRANDMA MOSES 1951 suite from the score by Hugh Martin. ARR & ORCH: Alec Wilder. COND: Daniel Saidenberg. (Col 10" ML-2185)

500026a Film HOEDOWN contemp records by Eddy Arnold of orig cast. "I'm Throwing Rice," "Just a Little Lovin'" (45/RCA 48/0138)

500027a Film LA RONDE 1951 record by Anton Walbrook of orig cast. "La Ronde de l'Amour" (45/Parlophone(E) MSP-6002)

500117a ALIVE AND KICKING 1956 records by the composer,

piano and vocal. MUSIC & WORDS: Harold Rome. "Cry, Baby," "French with Tears" (LP-316)

500202a ARMS AND THE GIRL orig prod. MUSIC: Morton Gould. WORDS: Dorothy Fields. ORCH: Morton Gould, Philip J Lang, Allan Small. COND: Frederick Dvonch. CAST: Nanette Fabray, Georges Guetary, Pearl Bailey, Florenz Ames, chorus. (Dec 10" 5200; CBS Records X-14879, with Look Ma, I'm Dancin'!; LP-544.)

500424a PETER PAN orig prod. MUSIC: Leonard Bernstein, Alec Wilder. WORDS: Leonard Bernstein. COND: Ben Steinberg. CAST: Boris Karloff, Marcia Henderson. (Col OL-4312)

500628a MICHAEL TODD'S PEEP SHOW 1956 record by the composer, piano and vocal. MUSIC & WORDS: Harold Rome. "Pocketful of Dreams" (LP-316)

500707a ACE OF CLUBS contemp records by member of orig (London) prod. MUSIC & WORDS: Noel Coward. COND: Mantovani. Pat Kirkwood, Graham Payn, Sylvia Cecil: "Nothing Can Last Forever/I'd Never Know/Something about a Sailor," "My Kind of Man/This Could Be True/Josephine," "Sail Away/Why Does Love Get in the Way/In a Boat on the Lake with My Darling," "Chase Me Charlie/Evening in Summer/I Like America" Peter Tuddenham, Colin Kemball, Norman Warwick: "Three Juvenile Delinquents" (LP-174) (LP-308)

500707b ACE OF CLUBS records sung by the composer, Noel Coward. "Sail Away" (LP-11)(LP-89)(LP-218) "I Like America" (LP-89)(LP-174)(LP-218) "Josephine," "Why Does Love Get in the Way?" (LP-174)(LP-218) "Three Juvenile Delinquents" (LP-218)

501012a CALL ME MADAM orig prod with Dinah Shore replacing Ethel Merman. MUSIC & WORDS: Irving Berlin. ORCH: Don Walker, Joe Glover, Hugo Winterhalter. COND: Jay Blackton. CAST: Dinah Shore, Paul Lukas, Russell Nype, Galina Talva, Pat Harrington, Ralph Chambers, Jay Velie. (RCA LOC-1000)

501012b CALL ME MADAM 1950 album by Ethel Merman of orig cast, with Dick Haymes, Eileen Wilson, chorus. COND: Gordon Jenkins. (Dec 8035. Incomplete: Dec 10" 5304. Excerpts: Merman: "The Hostess with the Mostes' on the Ball," "Washington Square Dance," "The Best Thing for You" Merman, Haymes: "You're Just in Love" (LP-36).)

501012c CALL ME MADAM 1959 film soundtrack, with two additional Berlin songs. COND: Alfred Newman. CAST: Ethel Merman, George Sanders, Donald O'Connor, Carole Richards (for Vera-Ellen), chorus. (Dec 10" 5465)(Stet DS-25001, with Guys and Dolls & I'll Cry Tomorrow)

501012d CALL ME MADAM 1972 record by Ethel Merman of orig cast. "You're Just in Love" (LP-153)

501012e CALL ME MADAM album by Judy Lynn & Larry Douglas. COND: Warren Vincent. (Design 1050, with Annie Get Your Gun)

501012f CALL ME MADAM contemp album by members of 1952 London prod. COND: Cyril Ornadel. CAST: Billie Worth, Anton Walbrook, Jeff Warren, Shani Wallis, Sidney Keith, Arthur Lowe, Launce Maraschal. (Col(E) 1002. Incomplete: Monmouth 7073, with Can-Can.)

501124a GUYS AND DOLLS orig prod. MUSIC & WOODS: Frank Loesser. ORCH: George Bassman, Ted Royal. COND: Irving Actman. CAST: Robert Alda, Vivian Blaine, Sam Levene, Isabel Bigley, Pat Rooney Sr, Stubby Kaye, Johnny Silver, Douglas Deane. (Dec 8036)

501124b GUYS AND DOLLS 1955 film soundtrack. COND: Jay Blackton. CAST: Frank Sinatra, Marlon Brando, Jean Simmons, Vivian Blaine, Stubby Kaye, Johnny Silver, chorus. (LP-656. Excerpts: Brando, Simmons: "A Woman in Love," "I'll Know"

Brando: "Luck Be a Lady" Simmons: "If I Were a Bell" (45/Dec ED-2332)(Stet DS-25001, with Call Me Madam & I'll Cry Tomorrow)

501124c GUYS AND DOLLS studio prod. ORCH: Various. COND: Morris Stoloff. CAST: Frank Sinatra of 1955 film prod; Bing Crosby, Dean Martin, Jo Stafford, Sammy Davis Jr, McGuire Sisters, Dinah Shore, Debbie Reynolds, Allan Sherman, Clark Dennis. (Reprise 2016. Incomplete: Harmony 11374)

501124d GUYS AND DOLLS contemp records by members of 1953 London cast. Edmund Hockridge: "I've Never Been in Love Before," "My Time of Day," "I'll Know," "Luck Be a Lady" (45/Col(E) 8593) Lizbeth Webb: "I've Never Been in Love Before," "If I Were a Bell" (78/HMV(E) B-10508)

501124e GUYS AND DOLLS studio prod. COND: Al Goodman. VOCALS: Audrey Marsh, Ray Charles, Morey Amsterdam, Donald Richards, chorus. (RCA LK-1000)

501124f GUYS AND DOLLS contemp album, including 3 songs by Loesser written for the 1955 film. VOCALS: Rosemary Clooney, Jo Stafford, Frankie Laine, Jerry Vale, Dick Williams, Jan Stewart. (Col 10" CL-2567)

501124g GUYS AND DOLLS 1976 prod. ORCH. Danny Holgate, Horace Ott. COND: Howard Roberts. CAST: Norma Donaldson, Robert Guillaume, Ernestine Jackson, James Randolph, Ken Page, Christophe Pierre, Emett "Babe" Wallace. (Motown M6-876S1)

501124h GUYS AND DOLLS 1962 studio prod. ORCH: Bobby Richards. COND: Kenneth Alwyn. CAST: Adele Leigh, Gordon Boyd, Joyce Blair, chorus. (World Record Club(E) T-177, with West Side Story)

501214a BLESS YOU ALL records by Harold Rome, vocal & piano. MUSIC & WORDS: Harold Rome. "Take Off the Coat" (1954: LP-360)(1956: LP-39) "I Can Hear It Now," "Don't Wanna Write about the South" (1955: LP-316)

501221a OUT OF THIS WORLD orig prod. MUSIC & WORDS: Cole Porter. ORCH: Robert Russell Bennett. COND: Pembroke Davenport. CAST: Charlotte Greenwood, Priscilla Gillette, Barbara Ashley, William Redfield, George Jongeyans, David Burns. (Col OL-4390)

1951

510001a Film ON THE RIVIERA records by Danny Kaye of orig cast. "Ballin' the Jack" (LP-6)(LP-92)(LP-515) "Rhythm of a New Romance," "Happy Ending" (45/Dec 9-27596) "On the Riviera" (45/Dec 9-27597)

510002a Film THE BELLE OF NEW YORK soundtrack. MUSIC: Harry Warren. WORDS: Johnny Mercer. COND: Adolph Deutsch. CAST: Fred Astaire, Anita Ellis (for Vera-Ellen). (Stet DS-15004, with additional Astaire songs; LP-597. Incomplete: MGM 10" 108. Excerpts: Astaire: "Baby Doll," "Seeing's Believing" (LP-24) "I Wanna Be a Dancin' Man" (LP-399).)

510002b Film THE BELLE OF NEW YORK 1976 record by Fred Astaire of orig cast. "I Wanna Be a Dancin' Man" (LP-429)

510003a Film ROYAL WEDDING soundtrack. MUSIC: Burton Lane. WORDS: Alan Jay Lerner. ORCH: Conrad Salinger, Skip Martin. COND: John Green. CAST: Fred Astaire, Jane Powell. (MGM 10" 543. Excerpts: Astaire: "I Left My Hat in Haiti," "Ev'ry Night at Seven" (LP-24).)

510004a Film RICH, YOUNG AND PRETTY soundtrack. MUSIC & WORDS: mostly Nicholas Brodsky & Sammy Cahn. COND: David Rose. Fernando Lamas: "Paris" Lamas, Danielle Darrieux: "We Never Talk Much" Darrieux: "There's Danger in Your Eyes, Cheri," "L'Amour Toujours" Jane Powell: "My Little Nest of Heav-

WEST SIDE STORY (1957) CBS
Carol Lawrence does ''I Feel Pretty'' with a supporting cast including recent Tony Award winner Marilyn Cooper (second from right).

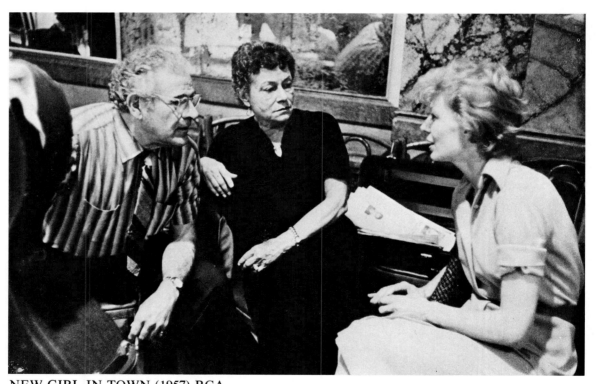

NEW GIRL IN TOWN (1957) RCA
Cameron Prudhomme, Thelma Ritter, and Gwen Verdon in a serious moment during recording of NEW GIRL IN TOWN, the musical version of Eugene O'Neill's ANNA CHRISTIE.

CANDIDE (1956) CBS
A legendary musical failure with a cast including Barbara Cook (front), Robert Rounseville, and Irra Pettina (back to camera).

JAMAICA (1957) RCA
Ricardo Montalban looks on amused as co-star Lena Horne gets into the spirit of "Push de Button," one of the Harold Arlen—E. Y. Harburg songs for JAMAICA.

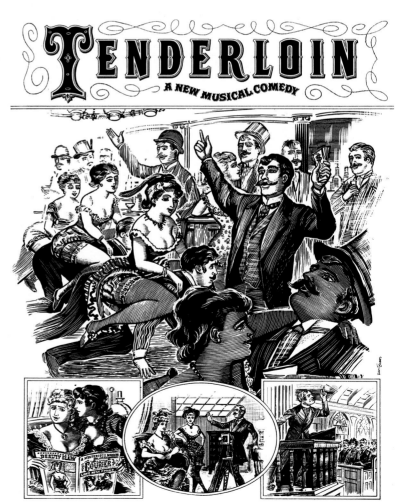

TENDERLOIN (1960) Capitol
Program book cover from TENDERLOIN. The show didn't quite work, but the score by Jerry Bock and Sheldon Harnick remains a delight.

OLIVER (1963) RCA

Georgia Brown and members of the chorus belt out one of Lionel Bart's songs for the tremendous international success OLIVER.

HELLO, DOLLY! (1964) RCA

Carol Channing singing the role of a lifetime, Dolly Levi in HELLO, DOLLY!

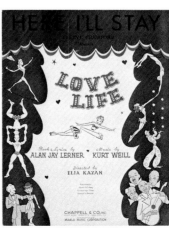

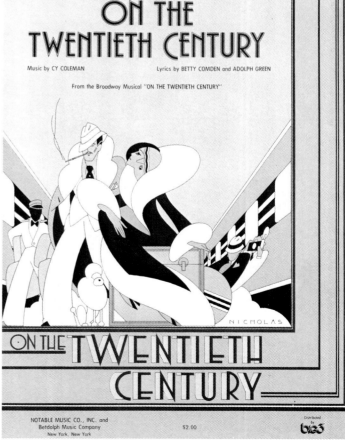

STAR! (1968) RCA
Program cover from the musical biography of Gertrude Lawrence, with Julie Andrews portraying the less than totally lovable star.

THOROUGHLY MODERN MILLIE (1967) Decca
THOROUGHLY MODERN MILLIE had a cast including Julie Andrews, Mary Tyler Moore, Carol Channing, Beatrice Lillie, and James Fox. Nevertheless, the film lost money, proving once again nothing is a sure thing in show business.

HAIR (1968) RCA
The landmark rock musical which reflected and influenced the changing American musical.

ON A CLEAR DAY YOU CAN SEE
FOREVER (1965) RCA
Barbara Harris delivers one of the delightful
songs in Alan Jay Lerner and Burton Lane's
score for ON A CLEAR DAY YOU CAN SEE
FOREVER.

LITTLE ME (1962) RCA
Nancy Andrews, Carolyn Leigh, and Cy Coleman study the score of LITTLE ME.

I DO, I DO (1966) RCA
When does a cast of two seem like thousands? When it is Robert Preston and Mary Martin in the Schmidt-Jones adaptation of THE FOURPOSTER I DO, I DO.

LITTLE ME (1962) RCA
Sid Caesar—star of LITTLE ME.

SWEET CHARITY (1966) CBS
Gwen Verdon chats with cast members while Bob Fosse (director) hovers in the background at recording session of SWEET CHARITY, a musical adaptation of Fellini's THE NIGHTS OF CABIRIA.

CABARET (1966) CBS
Lotte Lenya, Joel Grey, and members of the chorus listen to a playback at the recording
of CABARET.

SWEENEY TODD (1979) RCA
Thomas Z. Shepard (producer of many cast albums), Stephen Sondheim (composer and lyricist), Harold Prince (producer and director).

HELLO, DOLLY! (1975) RCA
Composer and lyricist Jerry Herman chats with one of the best of all Dollies, Pearl Bailey.

SWEENEY TODD (1979) RCA
The Tony Award winning stars of Stephen Sondheim's controversial musical, Len Cariou and Angela Lansbury.

NO, NO, NANETTE (1971) CBS
Ruby Keeler, orchestra, and chorus during a break while recording the "new 1920s musical" NO, NO, NANETTE.

SOPHISTICATED LADIES (1981) RCA
At recording session, Thomas Z. Shepard gives musical advice to the two stars of SOPHISTICATED LADIES, Judith Jamison and Gregory Hines.

42ND STREET (1980) RCA
Lee Roy Reams, Wanda Richert, Jerry Ohrbach, Joseph Bova, and chorus.

Jerry Ohrbach & Tammy Grimes—
42ND STREET (1980). (RCA)

PLAYBILL
a weekly magazine for theatregoers

Sam S. Shubert Theatre

TAKE ME ALONG

Eugene O'Neill Theatre

PLAYBILL
a weekly magazine for theatregoers

SHOW GIRL

Imperial Theatre

PLAYBILL
the national magazine for theatregoers

ZORBÁ

46th St. Theatre

PLAYBILL
a weekly magazine for theatregoers

REDHEAD

THE PLAYBILL

SAM S. SHUBERT THEATRE

John Golden Theatre

PLAYBILL
a weekly magazine for theatregoers

A PARTY
WITH
BETTY COMDEN
AND
ADOLPH GREEN

PLAYBILL
LONGACRE THEATRE

AIN'T MISBEHAVIN'

PLAYBILL
MARK HELLINGER THEATRE

SUGAR BABIES

PLAYBILL
PALACE THEATRE

THE GRAND TOUR

PLAYBILL
PROMENADE THEATRE

GODSPELL

enly Blue" (MGM 10" 86, with additional songs by Powell) Powell, Vic Damone: "How D'Ya Like Your Eggs in the Morning?," "The Old Piano Roll Blues" (LP-281)

510004b Film RICH, YOUNG AND PRETTY contemp records by Jane Powell of orig cast with David Rose Orch. "Wonder Why," "I Can See You," "Dark Is the Night" (MGM 10" 86, with songs from the soundtrack; LP-714.) "We Never Talk Much" (with uncredited baritone), "Paris," "L'Amour Toujours" (LP-714)

510004c Film RICH, YOUNG AND PRETTY contemp records by Vic Damone of orig cast, "Wonder Why?" "I Can See You" (78/Mercury 5669) "How D'Ya Like Your Eggs in the Morning?" (78/Mercury 5670)

510005a Film MR. IMPERIUM 1951 album by Ezio Pinza of orig cast & Fran Warren. MUSIC & WORDS: Harold Arlen, Dorothy Fields, others. COND: John Green. "Andiamo," "My Love and My Mule," "Let Me Look at You," "You Belong to My Heart" (RCA 10" LM-61)

510005b Film MR. IMPERIUM soundtrack. Ezio Pinza, Trudy Erwin (for Lana Turner): "Andiamo" (LP-657)

510006a Film HOTEL SAHARA contemp records by Yvonne De Carlo of orig cast. "I Love a Man" (LP-136) "Say Goodbye, Soldier Boy" (78/Col(E) DB-2850)

510007a Film THE GREAT CARUSO 1958 album by Mario Lanza of original cast. COND: Constantine Callinicos. (RCA LM-1127)

510007b Film THE GREAT CARUSO contemp record by Ann Blyth of orig cast. "The Loveliest Night of the Year" (LP-207)

510008a Film PANDORA AND THE FLYING DUTCHMAN contemp record by Ava Gardner of orig cast. "How Am I to Know?" (LP-207)(LP-328)(LP-702)

510009a Film LULLABY OF BROADWAY soundtrack. MUSIC & WORDS: Various. ORCH & COND: Ray Heindorf. VOCALS: Doris Day, Gene Nelson, Gladys George, Billy DeWolfe, Anne Triola. (Caliban 6008, with I'll See You in My Dreams)

510009b Film LULLABY OF BROADWAY 1951 record by Doris Day (of orig cast) & Harry James Orch. "Lullaby of Broadway" (LP-692)

510009c Film LULLABY OF BROADWAY contemp album by Doris Day (of orig cast) & chorus. COND: Frank Comstock. (Col 10" CL-6168)

510010a Film TWO TICKETS TO BROADWAY contemp album by Tony Martin of orig cast & Dinah Shore. MUSIC & WORDS: Jule Styne, Leo Robin, others. COND: Henri Rene. (RCA 10" LPM-39)

510010b Film TWO TICKETS TO BROADWAY contemp records by Gloria DeHaven of orig cast. "Let the Worry Bird Worry for You, " "The Closer You Are" (LP-272)

510011a Film HERE COMES THE GROOM contemp records by Bing Crosby & Jane Wyman of orig cast. MUSIC: Jay Livingston, Hoagy Carmichael. WORDS: Ray Evans, Johnny Mercer. Crosby: "Your Own Little House," "Bonne Nuit" Crosby, Wyman: "In the Cool, Cool, Cool of the Evening," "Misto Cristofo Columbo" (LP-255)

510011b Film HERE COMES THE GROOM 1975 record by Bing Crosby of orig cast & Fred Astaire. "In the Cool, Cool, Cool of the Evening" (LP-396)

510012a Film ON MOONLIGHT BAY contemp album by Doris Day & Jack Smith of orig cast. MUSIC & WORDS: Various. COND: Paul Weston. (Col 10" CL-6186. Excerpt: Day: "Moonlight Bay" (LP-315).)

510012b Film ON MOONLIGHT BAY soundtrack. ORCH &

COND: Ray Heindorf. VOCALS: Doris Day, Gordon MacRae. (Caliban 6006, with It Happened in Brooklyn & Three Smart Girls)

510013a Film ALICE IN WONDERLAND contemp studio prod. MUSIC & WORDS: Sammy Fain, Bob Hilliard, others. VOCALS: Kathryn Beaumont & Ed Wynn of orig cast; others unidentified. (RCA LBY-1009, with Peter Pan & additional material)

510013b Film ALICE IN WONDERLAND studio prod. COND: Tutti Camarata. VOCALS: Darlene Gillespie, chorus. (Disneyland 1208)

510014a Film ANNA soundtrack. Silvana Mangano: "Anna," "I Loved You" (45/MGM K-11457)

510015a Film DOUBLE DYNAMITE 1950 record by Frank Sinatra & Jane Russell of orig cast. MUSIC: Jule Styne. WORDS: Sammy Cahn. "Kisses and Tears" (78/Col 38790)

510016a Film SUNNY SIDE OF THE STREET contemp album. MUSIC & WORDS: Various. VOCALS: Frankie Laine & Billy Daniels of orig cast; Vic Damone, Tony Fontane. (Mercury 10" 25100)

510016b Film SUNNY SIDE OF THE STREET soundtrack. Billy Daniels: "I Get a Kick Out of You" (by Cole Porter) (LP-481)

510017a Film PAINTING THE CLOUDS WITH SUNSHINE contemp album by Dennis Morgan & Lucille Norman of orig cast, chorus. MUSIC & WORDS: Various. ORCH & COND: George Greeley. (Cap 10" L-291)

510017b Film PAINTING THE CLOUDS WITH SUNSHINE 1956 record by Irving Caesar, lyricist. "Vienna Dreams" (LP-353)

510017c Film PAINTING THE CLOUDS WITH SUNSHINE soundtrack. CAST: Dennis Morgan, Virginia Mayo, Lucille Norman, Gene Nelson, Virginia Gibson. (Caliban 6012, with Meet Me after the Show)

510018a Film GOLDEN GIRL contemp records by Dennis Day of orig cast. "Never," "California Moon" (45/RCA 47-4285)

510019a Film TEXAS CARNIVAL contemp records by Howard Keel of orig cast. "Whoa, Emma!" (78/MGM(E) 444) "Young Folks Should Get Married" (LP-702)

510019b Film TEXAS CARNIVAL soundtrack. Howard Keel, Esther Williams: "Young Folks Should Get Married" (LP-633)

510020a Film THE WILD BLUE YONDER 1950 record by Phil Harris of orig cast. "The Thing" (78/Vic 20-3968)

510021a Film STRICTLY DISHONORABLE contemp records by Ezio Pinza of orig cast. "Everything I Have Is Yours," "I'll See You in My Dreams" (45/RCA 49-3395)

510022a Film ST. BENNY THE DIP contemp record by Dick Haymes of orig cast. "I Believe" (78/Dec 27682)

510023a Film SAILOR BEWARE contemp records by Dean Martin of cast. "Never Before," "Sailor's Polka" (45/Cap F-1901)

510024a Film STARLIFT soundtrack. MUSIC & WORDS: Various. CAST: Doris Day, Gordon MacRae, Virginia Mayo, Gene Nelson, Phil Harris, Patrice Wymore. (Titania 510, with Call Me Mister. Excerpts: Day: "'S Wonderful" Wymore: "Liza" (LP-654).)

510024b Film STARLIFT contemp record by Gordon MacRae. "You're Gonna Lose Your Gal" (45/Cap F-1214)

510025a Film HIS KIND OF WOMAN contemp records by Jane Russell of orig cast. "You'll Know," "Five Little Miles from San Berdoo" (78/London 969)

510026a Film THE STRIP contemp records by members of orig cast. Kay Brown: "A Kiss to Build a Dream on" (78/Mercury 5710) Vic Damone: "Don't Blame Me" (78/Mercury 5744) Monica Lewis: "A Kiss to Build a Dream On" (LP-702) "La Bota" (78/MGM(E) 443)

510027a Film THE WHISTLE AT EATON FALLS 1951 record by Carleton Carpenter of orig cast. MUSIC & WORDS: Carleton Carpenter. "Ev'ry Other Day" (45/MGM K-30424)

510028a Film DISC JOCKEY contemp records by members of orig prod. George Shearing, piano: "Brain Wave" (78/MGM 11046) The Weavers: "The Roving Kind" (78/Dec 27332) Tommy Dorsey Orch: "Oh, Look at Me Now," "Show Me You Love Me" (78/Dec 27733) Russ Morgan Orch: "Nobody Wants Me" (78/Dec 27738)

510029a ICE FOLLIES OF 1951 records by members of orig prod. MUSIC & WORDS: Larry Morey. COND: Stan Myers. Gil Mershon, chorus: "Got a Sunbeam under Me Hat" Bill Reeve, Norma Larson Zimmer: "Me and My Honey" (78/Unnamed label FR-51)

510030a Film MEET ME AFTER THE SHOW soundtrack. MUSIC: Jule Styne. WORDS: Leo Robin. VOCALS: Betty Grable. (Caliban 6012, with Painting the Clouds with Sunshine)

510031a Film COMIN' ROUND THE MOUNTAIN record by Dorothy Shay of orig cast. "Why Don't Someone Marry Mary Anne?" (LP-783)

510215a GAY'S THE WORD 1950 records by members of orig (London) prod. MUSIC: Ivor Novello. WORDS: Alan Melville. COND: Bob Probst. Cicely Courtneidge: "Vitality," "It's Bound to Be Right on the Night" (LP-90)(LP-342) "Gaiety Glad," "If Only He'd Looked My Way," "Bees Are Buzzin'," "Guards on Parade" Thorley Walters: "A Matter of Minutes" Lizbeth Webb: "On Such a Night as This, " "Finder Please Return," "Sweet Thames" Chorus: "Ruritania" (LP-342)

510329a THE KING AND I orig prod. MUSIC: Richard Rodgers. WORDS: Oscar Hammerstein II. ORCH: Robert Russell Bennett. COND: Frederick Dvonch. CAST: Gertrude Lawrence, Yul Brynner, Dorothy Sarnoff, Doretta Morrow, Larry Douglas. (Dec 9008. Excerpt: Lawrence: "Getting to Know You" (LP-164).)

510329b THE KING AND I 1956 film soundtrack. COND: Alfred Newman. CAST: Marni Nixon (for Deborah Kerr), Yul Brynner, Rita Moreno, Terry Saunders, Reuben Fuentes (for Carlos Rivas). (Cap SW-740)

510329c THE KING AND I 1964 studio prod. ORCH: Philip J Lang. COND: Lehman Engel. CAST: Barbara Cook of 1960 prod; Theodore Bikel, Anita Darian, Daniel Ferro, Jeanette Scovotti. (Col OS-2640)

510329d THE KING AND I 1964 prod. ORCH: Robert Russell Bennett. COND: Franz Allers. CAST: Rise Stevens, Darren McGavin, Lee Venora, Frank Porretta, Patricia Neway, James Harvey. (RCA LSO-1092)

510329e THE KING AND I 1960 studio prod. CAST: Lois Hunt, Harry Snow, Samuel Jones, Charmaine Harma, Irene Carroll. (Epic 564)

510329f THE KING AND I 1966 studio prod. COND: Geoff Love. CAST: Jessie Matthews, Fred Lucas, Tony Peters, Mary Mercy, Lorraine Smith. (Music for Pleasure(E) 1257)

510329g THE KING AND I contemp studio prod. COND: Al Goodman, Henri Rene. VOCALS: Patrice Munsel, Robert Merrill, Dinah Shore, Tony Martin. (RCA LK-1022)

510329h THE KING AND I 1953 London prod. ORCH: Robert Russell Bennett. COND: Reginald Burston. CAST: Valerie Hobson, Herbert Lom, Muriel Smith, Jan Mazarus, Doreen Duke. (Philips(E) BBL-7002)

510329i THE KING AND I studio prod. COND: Al Goodman. VOCALS: Susan Shaute, Richard Torigi, Gretchen Rhoads, Edgar Powell. (Diplomat 2211)

510329j THE KING AND I studio prod. "Ed Sullivan presents The King and I." No other credits given. (National Academy 4)

510329k THE KING AND I 1959 studio prod. COND: Hill Bowen. CAST: Patricia Clark, Denis Martin, Pip Hinton, Ivor Emmanuel, chorus. (Camden 502)

510329l THE KING AND I studio prod. ORCH: Robert Russell Bennett. COND: Richard Mueller-Lampertz. CAST: Alberta Hopkins, Tom O'Leary, chorus. (Rondo-lette 863)

510329m THE KING AND I 1964 studio prod. COND: Russ Case. CAST: Eddie Ruhl, Barbara Altman, Alberta Hopkins, Tom O'Leary. (Allegro(E) 727)

510329n THE KING AND I 1977 prod. ORCH: Robert Russell Bennett. COND: Milton Rosenstock. CAST: Yul Brynner (of orig & 1956 film prods), Constance Towers (of orig prod 1952-4), June Angela, Martin Vidnovic, Hye-Young Choi, Alan Amick, Gene Profanato. (RCA ABL1-2610)

510329o THE KING AND I studio prod. COND: Johnny Douglas. CAST: George Pastell, Olga Gwynne, Janet Waters, Peter Regan, Freda Larsen, chorus. (Cap SN-7520)

510329p THE KING AND I 1965 studio prod. COND: Geoff Louis. CAST: June Bronhill, Inia Te Wiata, Mike Hudson, Jennifer West, Ian Burton, chorus. (Music for Pleasure(E) 1064)

510329q THE KING AND I 1979 album by Virginia McKenna of 1979 London prod. ORCH & COND: Richard Holmes. "Hello Young Lovers," "I Whistle a Happy Tune," "Getting to Know You," "Shall We Dance?" (45/Rim(E) 12" 1000)

510329r THE KING AND I broadcast performances by Gertrude Lawrence of orig cast. "I Whistle a Happy Tune," "Getting to Know You" (LP-766)

510418a MAKE A WISH orig prod. MUSIC & WORDS: Hugh Martin. ORCH: Philip J Lang, Allan Small. COND: Milton Rosenstock. CAST: Nanette Fabray, Stephen Douglass, Harold Lang, Helen Gallagher, Dean Campbell. (RCA LOC-1002)

510419a A TREE GROWS IN BROOKLYN orig prod. MUSIC: Arthur Schwartz. WORDS: Dorothy Fields. ORCH: Joe Glover, Robert Russell Bennett. COND: Max Goberman. CAST: Shirley Booth, Johnny Johnston, Marcie Van Dyke, Delbert Anderson, Nomi Mitty, Albert Linville, Nathaniel Frey. (Col ML-4405)

510419b A TREE GROWS IN BROOKLYN studio prod. COND: Malcolm Lockyer. VOCALS: Les Howard, Jean Campbell. (Royale 10" VLP-6080)

510514a FLAHOOLEY orig prod. MUSIC: Sammy Fain. WORDS: E Y Harburg. ORCH: Ted Royal. COND: Maurice Levine. CAST: Yma Sumac, Barbara Cook, Jerome Courtland, Irwin Corey, Fay Dewitt, Marilyn Ross, Lulu Bates. (Cap S-284)

510524a THE LYRIC REVUE 1951 record sung by the composer. MUSIC & WORDS: Noel Coward. "Don't Make Fun of the Fair" (LP-218)(LP-502)

510621a SEVENTEEN orig prod. MUSIC: Walter Kent. WORDS: Kim Gannon. ORCH: Ted Royal. COND: Vincent Travers. CAST: Ann Crowley, Kenneth Nelson, Frank Albertson, Doris Dalton, Ellen McCown, Dick Kallman, Maurice Ellis, Alonzo Bosan, Harrison Muller. (RCA LOC-1003)

510719a TWO ON THE AISLE orig prod. MUSIC: Jule Styne. WORDS: Betty Comden, Adolph Green. ORCH: Philip J Lang. COND: Herbert Greene. CAST: Bert Lahr, Dolores Gray, Kathryne Mylroieee, Fred Bryan. (Dec 8040. Excerpt: Gray: "If You Hadn't, But You Did" (LP-164).)

510719b TWO ON THE AISLE records by Betty Comden & Adolph

Green, lyricists. "If You Hadn't But You Did," "Catch Our Act at the Met" (1955: LP-359)(1958: LP-170) (1977: LP-489) "How Will He Know?" (1955: LP-359)

511003a SEE YOU LATER 1972 records by Sandy Wilson (composer), piano & vocal. "Gaiety Gloom," "1930s Girl," "Don't Be Afraid of the Dark" (LP-755)

511016a JUDY GARLAND AT THE PALACE orig prod, rec live in Feb 1952. MUSIC & WORDS: Various. PIANO: Hugh Martin. CAST: Judy Garland, chorus. (Classic International Theatremusic 2001)(LP-329)

511016b JUDY GARLAND AT THE PALACE album by Judy Garland of orig prod. Reissues of numbers she sang in her Palace show. (Dec 10" 6020)(LP-511)

511101a TOP BANANA orig prod. MUSIC & WORDS: Johnny Mercer. ORCH: Don Walker. COND: Harold Hastings. CAST: Phil Silvers, Rose Marie, Lindy Doherty, Judy Lynn, Bob Scheerer, Jack Albertson, Joey Faye, Herbie Faye, Bradford Hatton, Eddie Hanley. (Cap S-308)

511101b TOP BANANA 1951 TV performance by Johnny Mercer, composer. "O.K. for TV" (LP-604)

511112a PAINT YOUR WAGON orig prod. MUSIC: Frederick Loewe. WORDS: Alan Jay Lerner. ORCH: Ted Royal. COND: Franz Allers. CAST: James Barton, Olga San Juan, Tony Bavaar, Rufus Smith, Robert Penn, Dave Thomas. (RCA LOC-1006)

511112b PAINT YOUR WAGON contemp medley by Bobby Howes, Sally Ann Howes, Ken Cantrill, Joe Leader, & chorus of 1953 London prod. (78/Col(E) 3288/3289. Excerpts: Bobby Howes: "I Still See Elisa," "Wand'rin' Star" (LP-83).)

511112c PAINT YOUR WAGON 1969 film soundtrack with additional songs by Andre Previn & Alan Jay Lerner. ORCH & COND: Nelson Riddle. CAST: Clint Eastwood, Lee Marvin, Harve Presnell, Anita Gordon (for Jean Seberg), Alan Dexter. (Paramount 1001)

511112d PAINT YOUR WAGON 1959 studio prod, COND: John Green. CAST: Jan Peerce, Robert Merrill, Jane Powell. (RCA LSP-6005, with Gigi, Brigadoon, & My Fair Lady)

511112e PAINT YOUR WAGON records sung by Alan Jay Lerner, lyricist. "Wand'rin' Star" (1955: LP-343) "I Talk to the Trees" (1955: LP-343)(1971: LP-534)

511112f PAINT YOUR WAGON 1961 studio prod. ORCH & COND: Michael Adams. CAST: Elizabeth Larner, Andy Cole, Gavin Gordon, Jerry Verno, chorus. (Cap SN-7506, with Can-Can)

511112g PAINT YOUR WAGON records by Burl Ives of later prod."They Call the Wind Maria," "I Talk to the Trees" (LP-573)

511112h PAINT YOUR WAGON records by Tony Bavaar of orig cast. COND: Norman Leyden. "Another Autumn" (45/RCA 47-4420) "I Talk to the Trees," "Carino Mio" (45/RCA 47-4320)

511112i PAINT YOUR WAGON 1970 studio prod, incl songs from the 1969 film. COND: Peter Moore. CAST: Marty Wilde, Lois Lane, Jonathan James, Fred Lucas, chorus. (Fontana(E) SFL-13210)

1952

520001a Film HANS CHRISTIAN ANDERSEN 1953 studio prod. MUSIC & WORDS: Frank Loesser. COND: Gordon Jenkins. CAST: Danny Kaye of orig cast, Jane Wyman. (Dec 10" 5433. Excerpt: Kaye: "Anywhere I Wander" (LP-6).)

520001b Film HANS CHRISTIAN ANDERSEN contemp records narrated & sung by Frank Loesser, composer. "The King's New Clothes," "The Ugly Duckling" (LP-656)

520001c Film HANS CHRISTIAN ANDERSEN 1974 London stage prod, entitled "Hans Andersen," with additional music by Marvin Laird. ORCH: Alyn Ainsworth, Alan Roper, Peter Knight. COND: Michael Reed. CAST: Tommy Steele, Milo O'Shea, Colette Gleeson, Bob Todd, Simon Adams. (Pye(E) NSPL-18451)

520001d Film HANS CHRISTIAN ANDERSEN album. COND: Hugo Winterhalter. VOCALS: Judy Valentine, Stuart Foster, chorus. (RCA 10" LPM-3101, with Peter Pan)

520001e Film HANS CHRISTIAN ANDERSEN 1975 album of songs from 1974 London stage prod entitled "Hans Andersen." COND: Malcolm Lockyer. WORDS: Jon Pertwee, Laura Lee, chorus. (Contour(E) 2870-425, with additional material)

520001f Film HANS CHRISTIAN ANDERSEN 1975 album of songs from 1974 London stage prod entitled "Hans Andersen." ORCH & COND: Dave Gold. VOCALS: Martin Jay, Joanne Browne. (Silverline(E) DJSL-041)

520001g Film HANS CHRISTIAN ANDERSEN 1977 London stage prod, entitled "Hans Andersen," with additional music by Marvin Laird. (Some of the tracks are dubbed from Pye(E) NSPL-18451.) COND: Michael Reed. CAST: Tommy Steele (also of 1974 London prod), Sally Ann Howes, Anthony Valentine, Bob Todd, chorus. (Pye(E) NSPL-18551)

520002a Film SINGIN' IN THE RAIN soundtrack. MUSIC: Nacio Herb Brown. WORDS: Arthur Freed. COND: Lennie Hayton. CAST: Gene Kelly, Debbie Reynolds, Donald O'Connor. (MGM 2-SES-40, with Easter Parade. Incomplete: MGM 10" 113. Excerpts: Kelly: "Singin' in the Rain" (LP-252)(LP-501) "You Were Meant for Me," "All I Do Is Dream of You" (LP-501)"Broadway Ballet"(incomplete) (LP-252) Kelly, Reynolds, O'Connor: "Good Morning" (LP-416). Also a number dropped before release: Reynolds: "You Are My Lucky Star" (LP-423).)

520002b Film SINGIN' IN THE RAIN 1977 records by Gene Kelly of orig cast. "Singin' in the Rain," "You Were Meant for Me" (LP-749)

520003a Film THE FARMER TAKES A WIFE 1966 record sung by Harold Arlen, composer. WORDS: Dorothy Fields. "Today I Love Ev'rybody" (LP-60)

520004a Film WITH A SONG IN MY HEART 1952 album by Jane Froman, who sang for Susan Hayward in the film. MUSIC & WORDS: Various. COND: George Greeley, Sid Feller. (Cap T-309)

520004b Film WITH A SONG IN MY HEART soundtrack (incomplete). ORCH & COND: Alfred Newman. VOCALS: Jane Froman (for Susan Hayward), Richard Allan, chorus. (LP-495)

520004c Film WITH A SONG IN MY HEART 1977 record by Sammy Cahn, lyricist. MUSIC: Jule Styne. "I'll Walk Alone" (LP-503)

520004d Film WITH A SONG IN MY HEART 1952 records by Jane Froman, who sang for Susan Hayward in the film. "With a Song a My Heart," "I'll Walk Alone" (45/Cap F-2044)

520004e Film WITH A SONG IN MY HEART 1954 record sung by Sammy Fain, composer. "That Old Feeling" (LP-707)

520005a Film AARON SLICK FROM PUNKIN CREEK album by members of orig cast. MUSIC & WORDS: Jay Livingston, Ray Evans. COND: Henri Rene, Hugo Winterhalter. CAST: Dinah Shore, Robert Merrill, Alan Young. (RCA 10" LPM-3006)

520006a Film BECAUSE YOU'RE MINE contemp album by Mario Lanza of orig cast. MUSIC & WORDS: Various. COND: Constantine Callinicos. (RCA 10" LM-7015)

520007a Film EVERYTHING I HAVE IS YOURS soundtrack. MUSIC & WORDS: Various. COND: David Rose, John Green. CAST:

Marge & Gower Champion, Monica Lewis. (MGM 10″ 187, with Lili)

520008a Film STARS AND STRIPES FOREVER soundtrack. MUSIC: John Philip Sousa & others. COND: Alfred Newman. No vocals. (MGM 10″ 176)

520009a Film SOMEBODY LOVES ME contemp album by Betty Hutton of orig cast. MUSIC & WORDS: Jay Livingston, Ray Evans, others. COND: Emil Newman. (RCA 10″ LPM-3097. Excerpt: "Somebody Loves Me" (by George Gershwin) (LP-654).)

520009b Film SOMEBODY LOVES ME contemp album by Blossom Seeley & Benny Fields, the subjects of the film. COND: Victor Young. (Dec 10″ 5424)(LP-479)

520010a Film I'LL SEE YOU IN MY DREAMS contemp album by Doris Day & Danny Thomas of orig cast. MUSIC: Various. WORDS: Gus Kahn. COND: Paul Weston. (Col 10″ CL-6198. Excerpt: Day: "I'll See You in My Dreams"(LP-315)

520010b Film I'LL SEE YOU IN MY DREAMS soundtrack. ORCH & COND: Ray Heindorf. VOCALS: Doris Day, Danny Thomas, Patrice Wymore. (Caliban 6008, with Lullaby of Broadway)

520011a Film SKIRTS AHOY contemp record by Debbie Reynolds of orig cast. MUSIC: Harry Warren. WORDS: Ralph Blane. "What Good Is a Gal?" (LP-267)

520011b Film SKIRTS AHOY soundtrack. Billy Eckstine: "Hold Me Close to You" (78/MGM(E) 501)

520012a Film JUST FOR YOU contemp album by Bing Crosby, Jane Wyman, Ben Lessy of orig cast; the Andrews Sisters. MUSIC: Harry Warren. WORDS: Leo Robin. (Dec 10″ 5417 plus LP-161. Neither has all the other has.)

520013a Film THE LAS VEGAS STORY record by Hoagy Carmichael of orig cast. MUSIC: Hoagy Carmichael. WORDS: Harold Adamson. "My Resistance Is Low" (LP-94)

520014a Film SON OF PALEFACE soundtrack. MUSIC & WORDS: Jay Livingston, Ray Evans, others. CAST: Jane Russell, Bob Hope, Roy Rogers. (Titania 511, with The Paleface & The Time, the Place, and the Girl)

520014b Film SON OF PALEFACE contemp records by members of orig cast. Bob Hope, Jane Russell: "Am I in Love?," "Wing Ding Tonight" (78/Cap(E) CL-13781) Roy Rogers: "A Four-Legged Friend," "There's a Cloud in My Valley of Sunshine" (78/HMV(E) BD-1286) "California Rose" (45/RCA 47-4709) Hope with Jimmy Wakely (not of orig cast): "A Four-Legged Friend," "There's a Cloud in My Valley of Sunshine" (45/Cap F-2161)

520015a Film HIGH NOON 1952 record by Tex Ritter of orig prod."High Noon" (78/Cap 2120)

520016a Film RAINBOW 'ROUND MY SHOULDER contemp records by Frankie Laine of orig cast. "Wonderful, Wasn't It?," "The Girl in the Wood," "She's Funny That Way," "Rainbow 'Round My Shoulder" (45/Col B-1512)

520017a Film MEET DANNY WILSON records by Frank Sinatra of orig cast. "All of Me" (1948: 78/Col 38163) "I've Got a Crush on You" (1948: 78/Col 38151) "Lonesome Man Blues" (1952 broadcast performance with Louis Armstrong: LP-669) "How Deep Is the Ocean?," "She's Funny That Way" (1949: LP-696) "That Old Black Magic" (1953: LP-722)

520017b Film MEET DANNY WILSON soundtrack. MUSIC & WORDS: Various. VOCALS: Frank Sinatra. (Caliban 6016, with Lillian Russell)

520018a Film LIMELIGHT soundtrack. Charlie Chaplin: "The Animal Trainer" (LP-350) "The Sardine Song" (78/HMV(Denmark) X-7891)

520019a Film THE STORY OF ROBIN HOOD soundtrack. MUSIC & WORDS: Various. VOCALS: Elton Hayes, James Hayter. (Disneyland DQ-1249)

520019b Film THE STORY OF ROBIN HOOD records by Elton Hayes of orig cast. "Whistle My Love," "Riddle de Diddle de Day" (78/Parlophone(E) R-3509)

520020a Film AFFAIR IN TRINIDAD soundtrack. Jo Ann Greer (for Rita Hayworth): "Trinidad Lady"(with chorus), "I've Been Kissed Before" (LP-403)

520021a Film APRIL IN PARIS contemp records by Doris Day of orig cast. MUSIC: Vernon Duke. WORDS: Sammy Cahn, E Y Harburg. "April in Paris, " "I'm Gonna Ring the Bell Tonight," "I Know a Place," "That's What Makes Paris Paree" (45/Col B-1581)

520021b Film APRIL IN PARIS soundtrack. COND: Ray Heindorf. CAST: Doris Day, Ray Bolger, Claude Dauphin. (Titania 500, with Young at Heart)

520022a Film THE STOOGE contemp album by Dean Martin of orig cast."I Feel a Song Coming On," "A Girl Named Mary and a Boy Named Bill, " "Just One More Chance," "Who's Your Little Who-zis!," "I'm Yours," "I Feel Like a Feather in the Breeze," "Louise," "With My Eyes Wide Open I'm Dreaming" (Cap 10″ H-401)

520023a Film ABOUT FACE contemp records by Gordon MacRae of orig cast. "No Other Girl for Me," "If Someone Had Told Me" (45/Cap F-2047)

520024a Film THE GREATEST SHOW ON EARTH soundtrack. MUSIC & WORDS: John Ringling North, E Ray Goetz. Dorothy Lamour: "Lovely Luawana Lady" (LP-647)

520025a Film STOP, YOU'RE KILLING ME contemp record by Bill Hayes of orig cast. "My Ever Lovin' " (78/MGM(E) 620

520304a PARIS '90 orig prod. MUSIC: Kay Swift, others. WORDS: Kay Swift. ORCH: Robert Russell Bennett. COND: Nathaniel Shilkret. CAST: Cornelia Otis Skinner, chorus. (Col ML-4619)

520321a THREE WISHES FOR JAMIE orig prod. MUSIC & WORDS: Ralph Blane. ORCH: Robert Russell Bennett. COND: Joseph Littau. CAST: Anne Jeffreys, John Raitt, Bert Wheeler, Peter Conlow, Charlotte Rae, Robert Halliday. (Cap S-317)

520516a NEW FACES OF 1952 orig prod. MUSIC & WORDS: Arthur Siegel, June Carroll, Sheldon Harnick, Ronny Graham, Michael Brown, others. ORCH: Ted Royal. COND: Anton Coppola. CAST: Robert Clary, Ronny Graham, Alice Ghostly, Eartha Kitt, June Carroll, Virginia deLuce, Rosemary O'Reilly. (RCA CBM1-2206. Incomplete: RCA LOC-1008.)

520516b NEW FACES OF 1952 records by Eartha Kitt of orig cast & 1954 film cast. From orig prod & 1954 film: "Monotonous" From 1954 film: "Santa Baby" (1954: 45/RCA EPA-557) "C'est Si Bon," "Uska Dara" (1954: 45/RCA EPA-557; LP-685) From orig prod: "Guess Who I Saw Today" (Later: LP-441)

520516c NEW FACES OF 1952 records sung by composers. Michael Brown, composer & lyricist: "Lizzie Borden" (1950s: LP-697)(1962:LP-732) Sheldon Harnick, composer & lyricist: "The Boston Beguine" (1971: LP-535)

520516d NEW FACES OF 1952 records by Robert Clary of orig cast & 1954 film cast. "I'm in Love with Miss Logan," "Lucky Pierre," "C'est si Bon" (LP-666) "Love Is a Simple Thing" (LP-666)(LP-687)

520625a WISH YOU WERE HERE orig prod. MUSIC & WORDS: Harold Rome. ORCH: Don Walker. COND: Jay Blackton. CAST: Sheila Bond, Jack Cassidy, Patricia Marand, Sidney Armus, Paul Valentine, Sammy Smith. (RCA LOC-1007)

520625b WISH YOU WERE HERE records by Harold Rome (composer), vocal & piano. "Wish You Were Here," "Where Did the Night Go?" (1954: LP-360)(1956: LP-39) "Glimpse of Love"(dropped from the show) (1955: LP-316) "Don Jose of Far Rockaway" (1954: LP-360)

520625c WISH YOU WERE HERE contemp records by members of 1953 London prod. ORCH: Don Walker. COND: Cyril Ornadel. CAST: Dickie Henderson, Mark Baker, Shani Wallis, Elizabeth Larner, Bruce Trent, Christopher Hewett, chorus. (Stet DS-15015)

520625d WISH YOU WERE HERE 1975 records by members of orig cast. Sheila Bond: "Shopping Around" Patricia Marand: "Where Did the Night Go?" (LP-510)

520710a GLOBE REVUE 1952 record sung by the composer. MUSIC & WORDS: Noel Coward. "There Are Bad Times Just Around the Corner" (LP-11)(LP-502)

520925a LOVE FROM JUDY contemp medley by members of orig (London) prod. MUSIC: Hugh Martin. WORDS: Timothy Gray. COND: Philip Martell. CAST: Jean Carson, Bill O'Connor, Adelaide Hall, June Whitfield, Johnny Brandon, Audrey Freeman. (78/Col(E) DX-1853/4; LP-287.)

520925b LOVE FROM JUDY record by Adelaide Hall of orig cast. "A Touch of Voodoo" (LP-287)

521002a AN EVENING WITH BEATRICE LILLIE orig prod, rec in 1955 & 1958. MUSIC & WORDS: Various. PIANOS: Eadie & Rack. VOCALS: Beatrice Lillie. (London(E) 5212, entitled "An Evening with Beatrice Lillie," plus London(E) 5471, entitled "Auntie Bea." Incomplete: DRG Records DARC-2-1101, entitled "Queen Bea," with additional material.)

521215a TWO'S COMPANY orig prod. MUSIC: Vernon Duke. WORDS: Ogden Nash, Sammy Cahn, Sheldon Harnick. ORCH: Clare Grundman, Don Walker, Philip J Lang. COND: Milton Rosenstock. CAST: Bette Davis, Hiram Sherman, David Burns, Bill Callahan, Ellen Hanley, Peter Kelley, Sue Hight, Deborah Remsen. (RCA LOC-1009)

521215b TWO'S COMPANY 1971 record sung by Sheldon Harnick, composer & lyricist. "The Merry Little Minuet" (LP-535)

1953

530001a Film THE BAND WAGON soundtrack. MUSIC: Arthur Schwartz. WORDS: Howard Dietz. COND: Adolph Deutsch, CAST: Fred Astaire, Nanette Fabray, Jack Buchanan, India Adams (for Cyd Charisse). (MGM 2-SES-44-ST, with Kiss Me Kate. Incomplete: MGM 3051. Excerpts: Astaire: "I Love Louisa," "A Shine on Your Shoes" (LP-24) "By Myself" (LP-24)(LP-252) Astaire, Buchanan: "I Guess Have to Change My Plan" (LP-252) Astaire, Buchanan, Fabray, Levant: "That's Entertainment" Astaire, Fabray, Buchanan: "Triplets" (LP-416). Also three numbers dropped before release: Fabray, Astaire: "Gotta Bran' New Suit" Orchestra: "You Have Everything" (LP-423) Fabray, Levant: "Sweet Music to Worry the Wolf Away" (LP-455).)

530001b Film THE BAND WAGON 1975 record of a song written for the film, sung by Arthur Schwartz, composer. "That's Entertainment" (LP-418)

530001c Film THE BAND WAGON 1976 record by Fred Astaire of orig cast. "That's Entertainment" (LP-429)

530002a Film MEMBER OF THE WEDDING late 1950's record by Ethel Waters of orig cast. "His Eye Is on the Sparrow" (LP-99)

530003a Film BY THE LIGHT OF THE SILVERY MOON 1953 album by Gordon MacRae of orig cast and June Hutton. ORCH & COND: Axel Stordahl. (Cap 10" H-422)

530003b Film BY THE LIGHT OF THE SILVERY MOON contemp album by Doris Day of orig cast. MUSIC & WORDS: Various. COND: Paul Weston. (Col 10" CL-6248. Excerpts: "By the Light of the Silvery Moon" (LP-315) "Be My Little Baby Bumble Bee" (LP-710).)

530004a Film CALAMITY JANE combination soundtrack and studio prod. MUSIC: Sammy Fain. WORDS: Paul Francis Webster. COND: Ray Heindorf. CAST: Doris Day, Howard Keel. (Col 10" CL-6273. Excerpt: Day: "Secret Love" (LP-223)(LP-315)(LP-692).)

530004b Film CALAMITY JANE 1954 record sung by Sammy Fain, composer. "Secret Love" (LP-707)

530005a Film THE STARS ARE SINGING 1953 album by Rosemary Clooney of orig cast. MUSIC & WORDS: mostly by Jay Livingston, Ray Evans. "I Do, I Do, I Do," "Haven't Got a Worry to My Name," "Lovely Weather for Ducks," "Come on-a My House" (45/Col B-1618)

530006a Film LITTLE BOY LOST 1953 album by Bing Crosby of orig cast. MUSIC: James Van Heusen. WORDS: John Burke. COND: John Scott Trotter. (Dec 10" 5556, with The Country Girl; LP-26)

530007a Film I LOVE MELVIN soundtrack. MUSIC: Josef Myrow. WORDS: Mack Gordon. COND: George Stoll. CAST: Donald O'Connor, Debbie Reynolds, Noreen Corcoran. (MGM 10" 190. Excerpt: Reynolds: " A Lady Loves" (LP-267) .)

530008a Film THREE SAILORS AND A GIRL 1953 studio prod with Jane Powell & Gordon MacRae of orig cast. MUSIC: Sammy Fain. WORDS: Sammy Cahn. ORCH & COND: George Greeley. (Cap 10" L-485)

530009a Film LILI soundtrack. MUSIC: Bronislau Kaper. WORDS: Helen Deutsch. COND: Hans Sommer. Leslie Caron, Mel Ferrer: "Hi-Lili, Hi-Lo" MGM Studio Orch: "Lili and the Puppets," "Adoration" (MGM 10" 187, with Everything I Have Is Yours. Excerpt: "Hi-Lili, Hi-Lo" (LP-416).)

530010a Film PETER PAN soundtrack. MUSIC & WORDS: Sammy Fain, Sammy Cahn, others. ORCH: Ed Plumb. VOCALS: Kathryn Beaumont, Hans Conried, Bobby Driscoll, Bill Thompson, Candy Candido, chorus. (Disneyland 1206, with additional material. Incomplete: LP-661)

530010b Film PETER PAN album. COND: Hugo Winterhalter. VOCALS: Stuart Foster, Judy Valentine, chorus. (RCA 10" LPM-3101, with Hans Christian Andersen)

530011a Film THE ROAD TO BALI contemp album by Bing Crosby & Bob Hope of orig cast, Peggy Lee. MUSIC: James Van Heusen. WORDS: John Burke. (Dec 10" 5444; LP-161.)

530012a Film TORCH SONG contemp album by India Adams, who sang for Joan Crawford in the film. MUSIC & WORDS: Various. Trio with Walter Gross, piano. (MGM 10" 214, with additional songs)

530012b Film TORCH SONG soundtrack. India Adams (for Joan Crawford): "You Won't Forget Me" Adams, chorus: "Two-faced Woman" Adams, Joan Crawford: "Tenderly" (LP-401)

530013a Film SMALL TOWN GIRL soundtrack. MUSIC: Nicholas Brodszky. WORDS: Leo Robin. Jane Powell: "Small Towns," "The Fellow I Follow" (LP-281)

530013b Film SMALL TOWN GIRL records by members of orig cast. Bobby Van, 1977: "Take Me to Broadway" (LP-551) Nat Cole, 1953: "My Flaming Heart" (45/Cap F-2459)

530014a Film THE JAZZ SINGER contemp album by Danny Thomas of orig cast. MUSIC & WORDS: Sammy Fain, Jerry Seelen, others. COND: Frank DeVol. (RCA 10" LPM-3118)

530014b Film THE JAZZ SINGER contemp album by Peggy Lee of orig cast. COND: Gordon Jenkins. "This Is a Very Special Day," "I Hear the Music Now," "Lover," "Just One of Those Things" (45/Dec ED-2003)

530015a Film LET'S DO IT AGAIN contemp records by Jane Wyman of orig cast. "I'm Takin' a Slow Burn," "It Was Great While It Lasted" (78/Dec 28757)

530015b Film LET'S DO IT AGAIN soundtrack. Jane Wyman: "The Call of the Wild" (LP-496)

530016a Film SO THIS IS LOVE soundtrack. MUSIC & WORDS: Various. COND: Ray Heindorf. VOCALS: Kathryn Grayson, chorus. (RCA 10" LOC-3000. Excerpt: Grayson: "I Wish I Could Shimmy like My Sister Kate" (LP-496).)

530016b Film SO THIS IS LOVE contemp record by Merv Griffin of orig cast. "I Kiss Your Hand, Madame" (78/Col 40026)

530017a Film TONIGHT WE SING soundtrack. MUSIC & WORDS: Various (classical). COND: Alfred Newman. CAST: Roberta Peters, Jan Peerce, Edwin Dunning, Ezio Pinza, chorus. (RCA 10" LM-7016)

530018a Film THE CADDY 1953 records by Dean Martin of orig cast. "That's Amore," "You're the Right One" (45/Cap F-2589)

530019a Film MELBA soundtrack. MUSIC & WORDS: Various (classical). COND: Muir Mathieson. CAST: Patrice Munsel, unidentified soloists, chorus. (RCA 10" LM-7012, with additional material)

530019b Film MELBA contemp records by Patrice Munsel of orig cast. COND: Henri Rene. "Is This the Beginning of Love?," "The Melba Waltz" (78/HMV(E) B-10532)

530020a Record prod SEVEN DREAMS orig prod. MUSIC & WORDS: Gordon Jenkins. COND: Gordon Jenkins. VOCALS: Bill Lee, Laurie Carroll, Jeanette Nolan, John McIntire, Beverly Mahr, chorus. (Dec 9011)

530021a Film GIVE A GIRL A BREAK contemp records. MUSIC: Burton Lane. WORDS: Ira Gershwin. PIANO: Burton Lane. Ira Gershwin: "Ach, Du Lieber Oom-Pah-Pah" Lane: "Dream World" (not used in film), "It Happens Every Time" Lane, Gershwin: "Give a Girl a Break," "In Our United State," "Applause, Applause" (LP-417)

530022a Film HOW TO MARRY A MILLIONAIRE soundtrack. Chorus: "New York" (Main Title) (LP-452)

530023a Film NIAGARA soundtrack. Marilyn Monroe & vocal group: "Kiss" (LP-452)

530023b Film NIAGARA 1953 record by Marilyn Monroe of orig cast. "Kiss" (LP-599)

530024a Film MAIN STREET TO BROADWAY soundtrack. MUSIC: Richard Rodgers. WORDS: Oscar Hammerstein II. Mary Martin: "There's Music in You" (LP-497)

530025a Film EASY TO LOVE contemp records by Tony Martin of orig cast. "Look Out, I'm Romantic," "That's What a Rainy Day Is For" (45/RCA 47-5596)

530026a Film OIL TOWN, U.S.A. soundtrack. MUSIC & WORDS: Various. ORCH: Tim Spencer. COND: Ralph Carmichael. VOCALS: Redd Harper, Andy Parker, Cindy Walker, George Beverly Shea. (RCA 10" LFM-3000)

530026b Film OIL TOWN, U.S.A. contemp album. VOCALS: Redd Harper (of orig cast), Georgia Lee, Colleen Townsend Evans, Charles Turner, Vere Raley, Paul Mickelson. (International 10" 10043)

530027a Film WALKING MY BABY BACK HOME records sung by Johnny Mercer, lyricist. "Glow Worm" (1950s: LP-559, LP-720)(1971: LP-533)

530028a Film THE BLUE GARDENIA contemp record by Nat Cole of orig prod. "Blue Gardenia" (45/Cap F-2389)

530029a Film LATIN LOVERS soundtrack. COND: George Stoll. Carlos Ramirez (for Ricardo Montalban): "A Little More of Your Amor," "I Had to Kiss You" (45/MGM K-30836)

530030a Film THE AFFAIRS OF DOBIE GILLIS contemp record by Barbara Ruick of orig cast. "You Can't Do Wrong Doin' Right" (45/MGM K-11555)

530031a Film THOSE REDHEADS FROM SEATTLE contemp records by members of orig prod. Teresa Brewer: "I Guess It Was You All the Time," "Baby Baby Baby" (45/Coral 9-61067) Guy Mitchell: "Chicka-Boom" (45/Col 4-40035) Bell Sisters:"Take Back Your Gold" (45/RCA 47-5433)

530032a Film LAUGHING ANNE contemp records by Margaret Lockwood of orig cast. "I've Fallen in Deep Water," "The World Is Mine on Sunday" (78/Philips(E) PB-186)

530033a Film ESCAPE FROM FORT BRAVO soundtrack. Bill Lee: "Soothe My Lonely Heart," "Shenandoah" (45/MGM K-11620)

530118a DANNY KAYE'S INTERNATIONAL SHOW album of reissues of earlier recordings by Danny Kaye of numbers which he sang in this show. (Dec 10" 6024, entitled "Danny at the Palace") (LP-515)

530128a TV show ARTHUR GODFREY'S TV CALENDAR SHOW orig prod. MUSIC & WORDS: Joan Edwards, Lyn Duddy. COND: Archie Bleyer. CAST: Arthur Godfrey, Janette Davis, Julius La Rosa, Marion Marlowe, Frank Parker, Lu Ann Simms, Haleloke. (Col GL-521)

530211a HAZEL FLAGG orig prod. MUSIC: Jule Styne. WORDS: Bob Hilliard. ORCH: Don Walker. COND: Pembroke Davenport. CAST: Helen Gallagher, Benay Venuta, Jack Whiting, John Howard, Dean Campbell. (RCA LOC-1010)

530214a JOHN BROWN'S BODY orig prod. MUSIC & WORDS: Various, arranged by Walter Schumann. COND: Richard White. READERS: Tyrone Power, Judith Anderson, Raymond Massey. VOCALS: Betty Benson, Roger Miller, chorus. (Col OSL-181)

530226a WONDERFUL TOWN orig prod. MUSIC: Leonard Bernstein. WORDS: Betty Comden, Adolph Green. ORCH: Don Walker. COND: Lehman Engel. CAST: Rosalind Russell, George Gaynes, Edith Adams, Delbert Anderson, Warren Galjour, Albert Linville, Jordan Bentley. (Dec 9010. Excerpt: Russell: "Swing" (LP-164).)

530226b WONDERFUL TOWN 1958 TV prod. COND: Lehman Engel (of orig prod). CAST: Rosalind Russell & Jordan Bentley of orig prod; Sydney Chaplin, Jacquelyn McKeever, Sam Kirkham, Cris Alexander. (Col OS-2008)

530226c WONDERFUL TOWN records by Betty Comden & Adolph Green, lyricists. "A Quiet Girl" (1955: LP-359)(1958: LP-170) "Ohio," "Wrong Note Rag" (1955: LP-359)(1977: LP-489) "It's Love" (1955: LP-359) "100 Easy Ways to Lose a Man" (1977: LP-489)

530226d WONDERFUL TOWN contemp records by members of 1955 London prod. COND: Cyril Ornadel. Pat Kirkwood: "Swing!," "One Hundred Easy Ways" (78/Col(E) DB-3569) Kirkwood, Shani Wallis: "Ohio," "The Wrong Note Rag" (78/Col(E) DB-3568) Dennis Bowers: "A Quiet Girl/It's Love" Wallis: "A Little Bit in Love" (78/Col(E) DB-3570)

530226e WONDERFUL TOWN 1961 Los Angeles prod. COND: Homer R Hummel. CAST: Veronica Lehner, Jerry Lanning, Phyllis Newman. (Location 1261-368)

530507a CAN-CAN orig prod. MUSIC & WORDS: Cole Porter. ORCH: Philip J Lang. COND: Milton Rosenstock. CAST: Lilo, Peter Cookson, Hans Conried, Gwen Verdon, Erik Rhodes. (Cap DW-452)

530507b CAN-CAN 1960 film soundtrack with songs interpolated from other Porter shows. ORCH & COND: Nelson Riddle. CAST: Frank Sinatra, Shirley MacLaine, Maurice Chevalier, Louis Jourdan. (Cap SW-1301)

530507c CAN-CAN album by Mimi Benzell & Felix Knight. COND: Warren Vincent. (Design 1009, with Kiss Me Kate)

530507d CAN-CAN studio prod. COND: Mark Andrews. CAST: Pat O'Day, Dick Ballentine, Bob Mitchell. (Parade 380)

530507e CAN-CAN 1954 London prod. COND; Charles Prentice. CAST: Irene Hilda, Edmund Hockridge, Alfred Marks, George Gee, Gillian Lynne. (Parlophone(E) 10" PMD-1017. Incomplete: Monmouth 7073, with Call Me Madam)

530507f CAN-CAN 1958 album by Genevieve of 1962 prod. COND: Archie Bleyer. (45/Cadence CEP-505)

530507g CAN-CAN studio prod. COND: Eric Rogers. VOCALS: Eula Parker, Bryan Johnson, chorus. (Richmond B-20077, with Kismet)

530507h CAN-CAN studio prod. VOCALS: Glenn Hart, Barbara Newcomb, chorus. (Crown 5148)

530507i CAN-CAN studio prod. COND: Jimmy Warren. CAST: Jennie Gray, Ricky Barker, others unidentified. (Fidelio(E) ATL-4082)

530507j CAN-CAN 1961 studio prod. ORCH & COND: Michael Adams. CAST: Ian Wallace, Elizabeth Larner, Michael Garson, chorus. (Cap SN-7506, with Paint Your Wagon)

530528a ME AND JULIET orig prod. MUSIC: Richard Rodgers. WORDS: Oscar Hammerstein II. ORCH: Don Walker. COND: Salvatore Dell'Isole. CAST: Isabel Bigley, Bill Hayes, Joan Mc-Cracken, Arthur Maxwell, Mark Dawson, Bob Fortier. (RCA LOC-1012)

530528b ME AND JULIET 1957 record by Isabel Bigley of orig cast. "No Other Love" (LP-408)

530615a TV show FORD 50TH ANNIVERSARY TELEVISION SHOW soundtrack (excerpt). ORCH & COND: Jay Blackton. CAST: Ethel Merman, Mary Martin. (Dec 10" 7027, with other songs by Merman and Martin)

530615b TV show FORD 50TH ANNIVERSARY TELEVISION SHOW 1977 medley Mary Martin & Ethel Merman of orig prod. COND: Jay Blackton (of orig prod). (LP-652)

530903a THE WAYWARD WAY 1964 London prod. MUSIC: Lorne Huycke. WORDS: Bill Howe. COND: Ray Cook. CAST: David Holliday, Roberta d'Esti, Jim Dale, John Gower, Stella Courtney, Cheryl Kennedy, Bernard Clifton. (HMV(E) CSD-1587)

530908a THE BUCCANEER 1958 London prod. MUSIC & WORDS: Sandy Wilson. COND: William Small, CAST: Betty Warren, Eliot Makeham, Ronald Radd, John Faassen, Kenneth Williams, Thelma Ruby, Pamela Tearle, Sally Bazely. (HMV(E) CLP-1064)

530908b THE BUCCANEER 1972 record by Sandy Wilson (composer), piano & vocal. "Behind the Times" (LP-755)

531002a COMEDY IN MUSIC orig prod of Victor Borge's show. (Col CL-554, entitled "Comedy in Music," plus Col CL-646, entitled "Caught in the Act")

531203a KISMET orig prod. MUSIC: Alexander Borodin, arranged by Robert Wright & George Forrest. WORDS: Robert Wright,

George Forrest. ORCH: Arthur Kay. COND: Louis Adrian. CAST: Alfred Drake, Doretta Morrow, Joan Diener, Henry Calvin, Richard Kiley, Richard Oneto, Hal Hackett, Lucy Adonian. (Col OL-4850)

531203b KISMET 1955 film soundtrack. COND: Andre Previn. CAST: Howard Keel, Ann Blyth, Dolores Gray, Vic Damone. (MGM 3281)

531203c KISMET 1965 prod. ORCH: Arthur Kay. COND: Franz Allers. CAST: Alfred Drake & Henry Calvin of orig prod; Anne Jeffreys, Lee Venora, Richard Banke, Rudy Vejar, Albert Toigo, Anita Alpert. (RCA LSO-1112)

531203d KISMET 1964 studio prod. ORCH: Van Alexander, Warren Baker. COND: Van Alexander. CAST: Gordon MacRae, Dorothy Kirsten, Salli Terri, Bunny Bishop, Richard Levitt. (Cap SW-2022)

531203e KISMET 1964 studio prod. COND: Mantovani. CAST: Robert Merrill, Regina Resnik, Kenneth McKellar, Adele Leigh, Ian Wallace, chorus. (Dec(E) PFS-4035)

531203f KISMET 1959 record by Doretta Morrow of orig cast. "Baubles, Bangles and Beads" (LP-294)

531203g KISMET studio prod. COND: Eric Rogers. VOCALS: Bryan Johnson, Rosalind Page, Ross Gilmour, chorus. (Richmond B-20077, with Can-Can)

531203h KISMET 1961 studio prod. ORCH: Bobby Richards. COND: Ken Alwyn. CAST: Elizabeth Harwood, Grahame Laver, Peter Grant, Paul Whitsun-Jones, Diana Landor, chorus. (World Record Club(E) TP-68)

531203i KISMET 1978 album incl 2 songs by Eartha Kitt of 1978 prod (entitled "Timbuktu!"): "In the Beginning, Woman" (written by Wright & Forrest for 1978 prod) & "Rahadlakum." VOCALS: Eartha Kitt, Johnny Mathis, Sarah Vaughan, Lena Horne, Della Reese, Isaac Hayes. (April-Blackwood SS-33782-01, entitled "Timbuktu!")

531203j KISMET contemp album. Vic Damone: "Stranger in Paradise" Georgia Gibbs: "Baubles, Bangles and Beads" Ross Bagdasarian: "Not since Nineveh," "Zubbediya" (45/Mercury EP-1-3160)

531210a JOHN MURRAY ANDERSON'S ALMANAC records by members of orig prod. Hermione Gingold: "Which Witch?" (LP-314) Harry Belafonte: "Hold 'Em, Joe" (45/RCA 47-0322) "Acorn in the Meadow" (45/RCA 47-5722) "Mark Twain" (45/RCA album EPB-1022) Elaine Dunn (with Cyril Ritchard, director of orig prod): "You're So Much a Part of Me," "When Am I Gonna Meet Your Mother?" (LP-427)

1954

540001a Film SEVEN BRIDES FOR SEVEN BROTHERS soundtrack. MUSIC: Gene de Paul. WORDS: Johnny Mercer. COND: Adolph Deutsch. CAST: Jane Powell, Howard Keel, Bill Lee (for Matt Mattox), Virginia Gibson. (MGM 10" 244)

540001b Film SEVEN BRIDES FOR SEVEN BROTHERS 1966 studio prod. COND: Geoff Love. CAST: Tony Adams, Mary Millar, Shane Rimmer, Lorraine Smith, Janette Gail, Venetia Fernandez, Betty Winsett. (Music for Pleasure(E) 1316)

540002a Film THE COUNTRY GIRL contemp album by Bing Crosby of orig cast & Patty Andrews. MUSIC: Harold Arlen. WORDS: Ira Gershwin. COND: Joseph Lilley. (Dec 10" 5556, with Little Boy Lost; LP-26)

540002b Film THE COUNTRY GIRL soundtrack. Bing Crosby: "The

Land around Us" Jacqueline Fontaine, Crosby: "Dissertation on the State of Bliss" (LP-657)

540003a Film MISS SADIE THOMPSON soundtrack. COND: Morris Stoloff. VOCALS: Jo Ann Greer (for Rita Hayworth), chorus. (Mercury 10" 25181. Excerpts: Greer: "The Heat Is On," "Blue Pacific Blues," "Hear No Evil" (LP-403).)

540004a Film THERE'S NO BUSINESS LIKE SHOW BUSINESS soundtrack with Dolores Gray replacing Marilyn Monroe. MUSIC & WORDS: Irving Berlin. COND: Alfred Newman, Lionel Newman. CAST: Ethel Merman, Donald O'Connor, Dan Dailey, Johnnie Ray, & Mitzi Gaynor of orig cast; Dolores Gray. (Dec 8091. Excerpt: Merman: "There's No Business like Show Business" (LP-593).)

540004b Film THERE'S NO BUSINESS LIKE SHOW BUSINESS soundtrack. Marilyn Monroe: "Heat Wave" (LP-76)(LP-451) (LP-599)(LP-609) "Lazy," "After You Get What You Want" (LP-76)(LP-451)(LP-609) Monroe, Donald O'Connor: "A Man Chases a Girl" (LP-452)

540004c Film THERE'S NO BUSINESS LIKE SHOW BUSINESS records by members of orig cast. Dan Dailey, 1957: "Alexander's Ragtime Band" (LP-367) Marilyn Monroe, 1954: "You'd Be Surprised" (LP-451)(LP-452)(LP-599) (LP-609) Ethel Merman: "Alexander's Ragtime Band" (1955: LP-36)(1979: LP-670) "There's No Business Like Show Business" (1962: LP-251)(1972: LP-153)(1977, with Mary Martin: LP-652)(1979: LP-670)

540005a Film RIVER OF NO RETURN soundtrack. Marilyn Monroe: "One Silver Dollar" (LP-76) "River of No Return" (LP-76)(LP-451) "I'm Gonna File My Claim" (LP-76) (LP-129)(LP-451) "Down in the Meadow" (LP-452)

540006a Film WHITE CHRISTMAS contemp album by Rosemary Clooney of orig cast and Betty Clooney. MUSIC & WORDS: Irving Berlin. (Col 10" CL-6338. Excerpt: "Love, You Didn't Do Right by Me" (LP-593).)

540006b Film WHITE CHRISTMAS contemp album. COND: Joseph J Lilley. VOCALS: Bing Crosby & Danny Kaye of orig cast; Peggy Lee, Trudy Stevens, chorus. (Dec 8083)

540007a Film THE EDDIE CANTOR STORY soundtrack. MUSIC & WORDS: Various. COND: Ray Heindorf. CAST: Eddie Cantor. (Cap 10" L-467)

540007b Film THE EDDIE CANTOR STORY 1957 records by Keefe Brasselle of orig cast (although Eddie Cantor dubbed for him). "Josephine, Please No Lean on the Bell," "Now's the Time to Fall in Love," "Makin' Whoopee," "How Ya Gonna Keep 'Em Down on the Farm" (LP-317)

540007c Film THE EDDIE CANTOR STORY contemp album of 1940's records by Eddie Cantor, who sang for Keefe Brasselle in the film. "If You Knew Susie," "Ida! Sweet as Apple Cider," "Makin' Whoopee," "How Ya Gonna Keep 'Em Down on the Farm?," "Now's the Time to Fall in Love," "Margie," "Yes Sir, That's My Baby," "Ma (He's Making Eyes at Me)" (Dec 10" 5504, entitled "Eddie Cantor Sings 'The Cantor Story'")

540008a Film THE GLENN MILLER STORY soundtrack. MUSIC: Various. ORCH: mostly Henry Mancini. COND: Joseph Gershenson. No vocals. (Dec 10" 5519)

540009a Film RED GARTERS combination soundtrack and studio prod. MUSIC & WORDS: Jay Livingston, Ray Evans. COND: Joseph J Lilley, Percy Faith, Mitch Miller. CAST: Rosemary Clooney, Guy Mitchell, Joanne Gilbert. (Col 10" CL-6282)

540010a Film DEEP IN MY HEART soundtrack. MUSIC: Sigmund Romberg. WORDS: Various. ORCH & COND: Adolph Deutsch. CAST: Jose Ferrer, Helen Traubel, Gene & Fred Kelly, Jane Powell,

Vic Damone, Ann Miller, Howard Keel, Tony Martin, William Olvis, Rosemary Clooney. (MGM 3153. Excerpt: Gene & Fred Kelly: "I Love to Go Swimmin' with Wimmen" (LP-501). Also 2 numbers dropped before release: Powell: "One Kiss" Traubel: "Dance, My Darlings" (LP-486).)

540010b Film DEEP IN MY HEART contemp album of reissued excerpts from "Gems from Sigmund Romberg Shows." ORCH: Don Walker. COND: Sigmund Romberg. VOCALS: Genevieve Rowe, Lawrence Brooks, Lillian Cornell, Eric Mattson, Stuart Churchill, chorus. (RCA LM-1862, with other Romberg songs)

540011a Film ATHENA soundtrack. MUSIC: Hugh Martin. WORDS: Ralph Blane. COND: George Stoll. CAST: Jane Powell, Vic Damone, Debbie Reynolds. (Mercury 10" 25202 plus Damone: "Faster than Sound" (LP-588).)

540011b Film ATHENA 1956 record by Hugh Martin & Ralph Blane, composers. "Venezia" (LP-193)

540012a Film THE FRENCH LINE soundtrack. MUSIC: Josef Myrow. WORDS: Ralph Blane, Robert Wells. COND: Constantin Bakaleinkoff. CAST: Jane Russell, Gilbert Roland, Mary McCarty. (Mercury 10" 25182)

540013a Film THIS IS MY LOVE contemp record by Connie Russell of orig cast. "This Is My Love" (45/Cap F-2981)

540014a Film THE FLAME AND THE FLESH soundtrack. MUSIC: Nicolas Brodszky. WORDS: Jack Lawrence. COND: George Stoll. VOCALS: Carlos Thompson. "No One but You," "Languida," "Peddler Man," "By Candlelight" (45/MGM X-1080)

540015a Film YOUNG AT HEART contemp album by Doris Day & Frank Sinatra of orig cast. MUSIC & WORDS: Various. COND: Percy Faith, Axel Stordahl. Doris Day: "Till My Love Comes to Me," "Ready, Willing and Able," "Hold Me in Your Arms," "Just One of Those Things," "There's a Rising Moon," "You My Love" Frank Sinatra: "Someone to Watch over Me," "One for My Baby" (Col 10" CL-6339)

540015b Film YOUNG AT HEART soundtrack. ORCH & COND: Ray Heindorf. CAST: Frank Sinatra, Doris Day. (Titania 500, with April in Paris. Excerpt: Sinatra: "Just One of Those Things" (LP-223).)

540015c Film YOUNG AT HEART contemp album by Frank Sinatra of orig cast. "Someone to Watch over Me," "You My Love," "Just One of Those Things," "Young at Heart" (45/Cap EAP-1-571)

540015d Film YOUNG AT HEART 1950 broadcast performance by Frank Sinatra of orig cast. "Just One of Those Things" (LP-669)

540016a Film KNOCK ON WOOD contemp album by Danny Kaye of orig cast. MUSIC & WORDS: Sylvia Fine. COND: Vic Schoen, Victor Young. "Knock on Wood," "All about You," "Monahan, O Han" Instrumental: "End of Spring" (45/Dec ED-2141)

540017a Film 20,000 LEAGUES UNDER THE SEA contemp record by Kirk Douglas of orig cast. "A Whale of a Tale" (45/Dec 9-29355)

540017b Film 20,000 LEAGUES UNDER THE SEA studio prod. COND: Harry Geller. VOCALS: William Clauson. (Camden 1057, with Cinderella)

540017c Film 20,000 LEAGUES UNDER THE SEA studio prod. COND: Tutti Camarata. VOCAL: Unidentified soloist. (Disneyland 1314)

540018a Film LUCKY ME contemp records by Doris Day of orig cast. "I Speak to the Stars" (LP-315) "The Blue Bells of Broadway" (78/Col 40210)

540018b Film LUCKY ME soundtrack. MUSIC: Sammy Fain. WORDS: Paul Francis Webster. CAST: Doris Day, Robert Cummings, Phil Silvers, Nancy Walker. (Athena LM1B-9, with Incendiary Blonde)

540019a Film THREE COINS IN THE FOUNTAIN 1954 record by Frank Sinatra of orig prod. MUSIC: Jule Styne. WORDS: Sammy Cahn. "Three Coins in the Fountain" (LP-562)

540019b Film THREE COINS IN THE FOUNTAIN 1966 record by Jule Styne (composer), piano. "Three Coins in the Fountain" (LP-671)

540020a Film LIVING IT UP soundtrack. MUSIC: Jule Styne. WORDS: Bob Hilliard. ORCH & COND: Walter Scharf. Dean Martin: "Money Burns a Hole in My Pocket," "That's What I Like," "How Do You Speak to an Angel?" Jerry Lewis: "Champagne and Wedding Cake/How Do You Speak to an Angel?" Martin & Lewis: "Ev'ry Street's a Boulevard in Old New York" (45/Cap EAP-1-533)

540021a Film AS LONG AS THEY'RE HAPPY soundtrack. MUSIC & WORDS: Sam Coslow. CAST: Jack Buchanan, Jerry Wayne, Jean Carson, Diana Dors. (HMV(E) 10" DLPC-1)

540022a Film PLAYGIRL soundtrack. Shelley Winters: "Lie to Me" (LP-496)

540023a Film THE HUMAN JUNGLE soundtrack. Jan Sterling: "It Ain't Gonna Be You" (LP-496)

540024a Film THE LAST TIME I SAW PARIS contemp records by Odette of orig cast. "The Last Time I Saw Paris," "Dream, Dream, Dream," "Danse avec moi," "All of a Sudden," "My Heart Sings" (45/MGM X-1124)

540025a Film ABOUT MRS. LESLIE soundtrack. Shirley Booth: "Kiss the Boys Goodbye" (LP-656)

540026a Film SUSAN SLEPT HERE contemp records by members of orig cast. Dick Powell: "Susan Slept Here," "Hold My Hand" (45/Gala(E) XP-1017) Don Cornell: "Hold My Hand" (45/Coral 9-61206)

540114a THE BOY FRIEND orig (London) prod. MUSIC & WORDS: Sandy Wilson. CAST: Anne Rogers, Anthony Hayes, Joan Sterndale Bennett, Violetta, Denise Hirst, Larry Drew, John Rutland, Maria Charles, Hugh Paddick. (HMV(E) 10" DLP-1078)

540114b THE BOY FRIEND 1954 New York prod. ORCH: Ted Royal, Charles L Cooke. COND: Paul McGrane. CAST: Julie Andrews, Ruth Altman, Ann Wakefield, Dilys Lay, John Hewer, Eric Berry, Bob Scheerer, Geoffrey Hibbert. (RCA LOC-1018)

540114c THE BOY FRIEND 1970 New York prod. COND: Jerry Goldberg. CAST: Judy Carne, Barbara Andres, Sandy Duncan, Harvey Evans, Jeanne Beauvais, Leon Shaw, Ronald Young, David Vaughan, Simon McQueen. (Dec 79177)

540114d THE BOY FRIEND 1971 film soundtrack, with two songs by Nacio Herb Brown & Arthur Freed. ORCH & COND: Peter Maxwell Davies. CAST: Twiggy, Christopher Gable, Barbara Windsor, Moyra Fraser, Antonia Ellis, Tommy Tune, Bryan Pringle, Max Adrian, Georgina Hale. (MGM 1SE-32)

540114e THE BOY FRIEND 1965 studio prod. COND: Michael Sammes. VOCALS: Raymond Aske, Joanne Brown, Michael Sammes, Pat Whitmore, chorus. (Society(E) 1014)

540114f THE BOY FRIEND 1967 London prod. COND: Grant Hossack. CAST: Tony Adams, Frances Barlow, Ann Beach, Cheryl Kennedy, Nicholas Bennett, Jacqueline Clarke, Marion Grimaldi, Jeremy Hawk. (Parlophone(E) PCS-7044)

540114g THE BOY FRIEND 1968 Australian prod. COND: Peter Narroway. CAST: Deidre Rubenstein, Kathy Read, Laurel Veitch, Susan Swinford, Julie Day. (Ace of Clubs(E) SCL-1263)

540114h THE BOY FRIEND 1972 records by Sandy Wilson (com-poser), piano and vocal. Medley, "The You-Don't-Want-to-Play-with-Me Blues" (LP-755)

540305a THE GIRL IN PINK TIGHTS orig prod. MUSIC: Sigmund Romberg. WORDS: Leo Robin. ORCH: Don Walker. COND: Sylvan Levin. CAST: Zizi Jeanmaire, Charles Goldner, Brenda Lewis, David Atkinson, Lydia Fredericks, Kalem Kermoyan, John Stamford. (Col ML-4890)

540311a THE GOLDEN APPLE orig prod. MUSIC: Jerome Moross. WORDS: John Latouche. ORCH: Jerome Moross, Hershy Kay. COND: Hugh Ross. CAST: Priscilla Gillette, Stephen Douglass, Kaye Ballard, Jack Whiting, Bibi Osterwald, Portia Nelson, Martha Larrimore, Geraldine Viti, Dean Michener. (RCA LOC-1014) (Elektra EKL-5000)

540311b THE GOLDEN APPLE 1954 record by Kaye Ballard of orig cast. "Lazy Afternoon" (78/Dec 29114)

540408a BY THE BEAUTIFUL SEA orig prod. MUSIC: Arthur Schwartz. WORDS: Dorothy Fields. ORCH: Robert Russell Bennett. COND: Jay Blackton. CAST: Shirley Booth, Wilbur Evans, Richard France, Mae Barnes, Thomas Gleason, Libi Staiger. (Cap S-531)

540513a THE PAJAMA GAME orig prod. MUSIC & WORDS: Richard Adler, Jerry Ross. ORCH: Don Walker. COND: Hal Hastings. CAST: John Raitt, Janis Paige, Eddie Foy Jr, Carol Haney, Reta Shaw, Stanley Prager. (Col OL-4840)

540513b THE PAJAMA GAME 1957 film soundtrack. COND: Ray Heindorf. CAST: Doris Day, John Raitt, Eddie Foy Jr, Carol Haney, Reta Shaw. (Col OL-5210)

540513c THE PAJAMA GAME studio prod. ORCH & COND: Archie Bleyer. CAST: Stephen Douglass, Dorothy Evans, Ray Charles, Arthur Malvin, Doris Hollingsworth. (Cadence 2055)

540513d THE PAJAMA GAME 1955 London prod. ORCH: Don Walker. COND: Robert Lowe. CAST: Max Wall, Joy Nichols, Edmund Hockridge, Elizabeth Seal, Frank Lawless, Joan Emney. (HMV(E) CLP-1062)

540513e THE PAJAMA GAME studio prod. COND: Johnny Douglas. CAST: Joan Heal, Barry Kent, Nicolette Roeg, Mike Sammes, chorus. (Cap SN-7515, with Damn Yankees)

540602a JOYCE GRENFELL REQUESTS THE PLEASURE OF YOUR COMPANY orig (London) prod. MUSIC & WORDS: mostly Richard Addinsell, Joyce Grenfell. COND: William Blezard. VOCALS: Joyce Grenfell, Irving Davies. (Philips(E) BBL-7004; DRG Records SL-5186)

540610a AFTER THE BALL orig (London) prod. MUSIC & WORDS: Noel Coward. COND: Philip Martell. CAST: Vanessa Lee, Mary Ellis, Graham Payn, Irene Browne, Peter Graves, Patricia Cree. (Philips(E) BBL-7005)

540624a ARABIAN NIGHTS orig prod. MUSIC & WORDS: Carmen Lombardo, John Jacob Loeb. ORCH: Joe Glover. COND: Pembroke Davenport. CAST: Lauritz Melchior, Helena Scott, Ralph Herbert, Hope Holiday, William Chapman, James McCracken, Gloria Van Dorp. (Dec 9013)

540624b ARABIAN NIGHTS contemp album by Guy Lombardo (co-producer of orig prod) and His Royal Canadians. VOCALS: Bill Flanagan, Kenny Gardner, the Lombardo Trio. (Dec 10" 5542)

540912a TV show SATINS AND SPURS contemp studio prod. MUSIC & WORDS: Jay Livingston, Ray Evans. ORCH & COND: Nelson Riddle. CAST: Betty Hutton of orig cast, Earl Wrightson. (Cap 10" L-547)

541004a LIBBY HOLMAN'S "BLUES, BALLADS AND SIN-SONGS"

orig prod. PIANO: Gerald Cook. VOCALS: Libby Holman. (MB 102)

541020a PETER PAN orig prod. MUSIC: Moose Charlap, Jule Styne. WORDS: Carolyn Leigh, Betty Comden, Adolph Green. ORCH: Albert Sendrey. COND: Louis Adrian. CAST: Mary Martin, Cyril Ritchard, Kathy Nolan, Robert Harrington, Joseph Stafford, Sondra Lee, Margalo Gillmore. (RCA LOC-1019)

541020b PETER PAN records by Betty Comden & Adolph Green, lyricists. "Mysterious Lady" (1955: LP-359) (1958: LP-170)(1977: LP-489) "Captain Hook's Waltz," "Never Never Land," "Distant Melody" (1955: LP-359) (1977: LP-489)

541020c PETER PAN 1955 record by Cyril Ritchard of a song dropped from the show. "The Old Gavotte" (by Nancy Hamilton & Morgan Lewis) (LP-427)

541104a FANNY orig prod. MUSIC & WORDS: Harold Rome. ORCH: Philip J Lang. COND: Lehman Engel. CAST: Ezio Pinza, Walter Slezak, Florence Henderson, William Tabbert, Gerald Price, Edna Preston, Nejla Ates. (RCA LOC-1015)

541104b FANNY 1960 film soundtrack. MUSIC: Harold Rome. ORCH: Leo Shuken, Jack Hayes. COND: Morris Stoloff. (Warner Bros 1416)

541104c FANNY records by Harold Rome. "Fanny," "Be Kind to Your Parents," "To My Wife" (1956, vocal & piano: LP-39) "Love Is a Very Light Thing," "Be Kind to Your Parents" (1975, vocal: LP-510)

541104d FANNY 1953 album by Harold Rome (composer), piano & vocals. (Heritage 10" 0055)

541129a SANDHOG 1955 album by the composer (vocals & piano) and lyricist (narration). MUSIC: Earl Robinson. WORDS: Waldo Salt. (Vanguard 9001)

541201a MRS. PATTERSON orig prod. MUSIC: James Shelton. WORDS: James Shelton, Charles Sebree, Greer Johnson. ORCH: George Siravo. COND: Abba Bogin. CAST: Eartha Kitt, Enid Markey, Ruth Attaway, Terry Carter, Alonzo Bosan, Helen Dowdy. (RCA LOC-1017)

541215a TV show DAVY CROCKETT contemp records by Fess Parker of orig cast. "I'm Lonely, My Darlin'," "Farewell" (45/Col 4-40450) "The Ballad of Davy Crockett," "I Gave My Love" (45/Col 4-40449) "Old Betsy" (78/Col J-254)

541215b TV show DAVY CROCKETT soundtrack. VOCALS: Fess Parker. (Col CL-666)

541224a TV show A CHRISTMAS CAROL soundtrack. MUSIC: Bernard Herrmann. WORDS: Maxwell Anderson. COND: Bernard Herrmann. VOCALS: Uncredited soloists & chorus. (Unicorn RHS-850)

541230a HOUSE OF FLOWERS orig prod. MUSIC: Harold Arlen. WORDS: Truman Capote, Harold Arlen. ORCH: Ted Royal. COND: Jerry Arlen. CAST: Pearl Bailey, Diahann Carroll, Juanita Hall, Rawn Spearman, Ada Moore, Enid Mosier, Dolores Harper, M Burton. (Col OL-4969)

541230b HOUSE OF FLOWERS 1968 prod. ORCH & COND: Joseph Raposo. CAST: Josephine Premice, Yolande Bavan, Robert Jackson, Thelma Oliver, Hope Clarke, Charles Moore, Novella Nelson, Tom Helmore, Carla Pinza. (United Artists 5180)

541230c HOUSE OF FLOWERS records by Harold Arlen, composer. "Two Ladies in de Shade of de Banana Tree" (Vocal: LP-101) "A Sleepin' Bee" (Vocal: LP-563) "I Never Has Seen Snow" (Piano & vocal: LP-192) "House of Flowers Waltz" (Piano: LP-192) "Can I Leave Off Wearin' My Shoes?" (Vocal with June Ericson: LP-59, LP-352)

541230d HOUSE OF FLOWERS 1961 records by Pearl Bailey of orig prod. "House of Flowers," "A Sleepin' Bee," "Two Ladies in de Shade of de Banana Tree" (LP-260)

541230e HOUSE OF FLOWERS album. COND: Fred Waring. VOCALS: Gordon Goodman, Frank Davis, chorus. (45/Dec ED-2182)

1955

550001a Film A STAR IS BORN soundtrack. MUSIC: Harold Arlen. WORDS: Ira Gershwin. COND: Ray Heindorf. CAST: Judy Garland, chorus. (Col BL-1201. Excerpt: "The Man That Got Away" (LP-106)(LP-223). Also a number dropped before release: "When My Sugar Walks down the Street" (LP-486).)

550001b Film A STAR IS BORN records by Harold Arlen, composer. "The Man That Got Away" (LP-101)(LP-417) "It's a New World" (LP-192)

550001c Film A STAR IS BORN records by Judy Garland of orig cast. "Swanee" (1939: 78/Dec 2881)(Later: LP-188, LP-205, LP-219, LP-240, LP-461, LP-547, LP-738, LP-762, LP-781) "The Peanut Vendor" (1941: LP-398, LP-746) "The Man That Got Away" (Later: LP-188, LP-205, LP-219, LP-240, LP-298, LP-376, LP-525, LP-547, LP-738, LP-762)

550001d Film A STAR IS BORN early draft of "Someone at Last" sequence, sung by Roger Edens (composer) & Judy Garland. (LP-486)

550002a Film GENTLEMEN MARRY BRUNETTES soundtrack. MUSIC & WORDS: Various. COND: Robert Farnon. CAST: Jane Russell, Anita Ellis (for Jeanne Crain), Alan Young, Rudy Vallee, Robert Farnon (for Scott Brady), Johnny Desmond. (Coral 57013)

550003a Film LOVE ME OR LEAVE ME soundtrack. MUSIC & WORDS: Various. COND: Percy Faith. VOCALS: Doris Day. (Col CL-710. Excerpt: "Love Me or Leave Me" (LP-692).)

550004a Film PETE KELLY'S BLUES 1955 album by Peggy Lee and Ella Fitzgerald of orig cast. MUSIC & WORDS: Various. COND: Harold Mooney. (Dec 8166)

550004b Film PETE KELLY'S BLUES soundtrack. Peggy Lee: "He Needs Me," "Sugar" (LP-223)

550004c Film PETE KELLY'S BLUES contemp album by members of orig prod. Matty Matlock's Jazz Band & Ray Heindorf conducting the Warner Bros Orch. (Col CL-690)

550004d Film PETE KELLY'S BLUES 1959 album by combo which recorded soundtrack for TV series. COND: Dick Cathcart. (Warner Bros 1303)

550004e Film PETE KELLY'S BLUES 1955 album by combo which recorded soundtrack. ORCH & COND: Matty Matlock. (RCA LPM-1126)

550005a Film DADDY LONG LEGS soundtrack. MUSIC & WORDS: Johnny Mercer. ORCH & COND: Alfred Newman. CAST: Fred Astaire, Leslie Caron, Ray Anthony Orch, chorus. (Caliban 6000, with The Story of Vernon and Irene Castle)

550005b Film DADDY LONG LEGS records by Fred Astaire of orig cast. "Something's Gotta Give" (1955: LP-129) (1960: LP-108)(1976: LP-429) "Slue Foot" (1955: LP-702)

550005c Film DADDY LONG LEGS 1974 record sung by Johnny Mercer, composer. "Something's Gotta Give" (LP-560)

550005d Film DADDY LONG LEGS contemp records by Ray Anthony Orch of orig prod. "Something's Gotta Give," "Slue Foot," "Dream," "Thunderbird" (45/Cap EAP-1-597)

550006a Film SO THIS IS PARIS soundtrack. MUSIC & WORDS:

Phil Moody, Pony Sherrell. ORCH: Henry Mancini. COND: Joseph Gershenson. CAST: Tony Curtis, Gloria De Haven, Gene Nelson, Paul Gilbert. (Dec 10" 5553)

550006b Film SO THIS IS PARIS contemp records by Gloria De Haven of orig cast. "So This Is Paris," "The Two of Us" (LP-272)

550007a Film IT'S ALWAYS FAIR WEATHER soundtrack. MUSIC: Andre Previn. WORDS: Betty Comden, Adolph Green. ORCH & COND: Andre Previn. CAST: Gene Kelly, Dan Dailey, Dolores Gray, Michael Kidd, Lou Lubin. (MGM 3241. Excerpt: Kelly: "I Like Myself" (LP-501).)

550007b Film IT'S ALWAYS FAIR WEATHER 1955 album, including 2 songs ("I Said Good-Mornin'" & "Love Is Nothing but a Racket") dropped before release. ORCH: Bernie Leighton. VOCALS: Betty Comden & Adolph Green, lyricists. (Heritage 10" 0058)

550007c Film IT'S ALWAYS FAIR WEATHER records by Betty Comden & Adolph Green (lyricists) of a song dropped before release. "I Said Good Morning" (1958: LP-170) (1959: LP-294)(1977: LP-489)

550008a Film THE SEVEN LITTLE FOYS 1955 album by members of orig prod. MUSIC & WORDS: Various. COND: Joseph A Lilley. CAST: Bob Hope, James Cagney, chorus. (RCA 10").) LPM-3275. Excerpt: Cagney: "Mary's a Grand Old Name" (LP-129).)

550009a Film THE GIRL RUSH 1956 record by Hugh Martin & Ralph Blane, composers. "An Occasional Man" (LP-193)

550010a Film THREE FOR THE SHOW soundtrack. MUSIC & WORDS: Various. ORCH: George Duning. COND: Morris Stoloff. CAST: Betty Grable, Jack Lemmon, Marge Champion. (Mercury 10" 25204. Excerpt (alt. take): Grable, Lemmon: "I've Got a Crush on You" (by George Gershwin) (LP-481)(LP-654).)

550011a Film THE BENNY GOODMAN STORY soundtrack. MUSIC & WORDS: Various. COND: Benny Goodman. VOCALS: Martha Tilton. (Dec 8252/8253)

550011b Film THE BENNY GOODMAN STORY 1971 record sung by Johnny Mercer, lyricist. MUSIC: Matt Malneck. "Goody Goody" (LP-694)

550012a Film INTERRUPTED MELODY soundtrack. MUSIC & WORDS: Various. COND: Walter Ducloux. VOCALS: Eileen Farrell (for Eleanor Parker), Heinz Blankenburg, Rudolf Petrak, William Olvis. (MGM 3185)

550013a Film MAN WITHOUT A STAR contemp record by Kirk Douglas of orig cast. "And the Moon Grew Brighter and Brighter" (45/Dec 9-29355)

550014a Film THE TENDER TRAP contemp records by members of orig cast. MUSIC: James Van Heusen. WORDS: Sammy Cahn. "The Tender Trap" (Frank Sinatra: LP-562)(Debbie Reynolds: LP-328)

550014b Film THE TENDER TRAP records sung by Sammy Cahn, lyricist. "The Tender Trap" (1972: LP-658)(1974: LP-313) (1977: LP-503)

550015a FLAME OF THE ISLANDS contemp record by Yvonne DeCarlo of orig cast. "Take It or Leave It" (45/Cap F-3206)

550016a Record prod MY SQUARE LADDIE orig prod. MUSIC: Max Showalter. WORDS: William Howe. ORCH: Billy May, Eddie Dunstedter. COND: Eddie Dunstedter. CAST: Nancy Walker, Reginald Gardiner, Zasu Pitts. (Foremost FMLS-1)

550017a Film ARTISTS AND MODELS contemp album by Dean Martin of orig cast. MUSIC: Harry Warren. WORDS: Jack Brooks. COND: Dick Stabile. "The Lucky Song," "You Look So Familiar," "When You Pretend," "Innamorata" (sic) (45/Cap EAP-1-702. Excerpt: "Innamorata" (LP-562).)

550018a Film LADY AND THE TRAMP orig prod (incl soundtrack). MUSIC: Sonny Burke. WORDS: Peggy Lee. COND: Victor Young (not of orig prod), Oliver Wallace. VOCALS: Peggy Lee, George Givot, chorus. (Dec 10" 5557)

550018b Film LADY AND THE TRAMP soundtrack. ORCH: Ed Plumb, Sidney Fine. COND: Oliver Wallace. VOCALS: Peggy Lee, George Givot, chorus. (LP-661)

550019a Film NOT AS A STRANGER contemp record by Frank Sinatra of orig cast. "Not as a Stranger" (45/Cap F-3130)

550020a Film YOU'RE NEVER TOO YOUNG contemp records by Dean Martin of orig cast. MUSIC: Arthur Schwartz. WORDS: Sammy Cahn. "Simpatico" (LP-562) "Love Is All That Matters" (45/Cap F-3153)

550021a Film REBEL WITHOUT A CAUSE soundtrack. Shirley Harmer: "Secret Doorway" (45/MGM K-12121)

550022a Film SUMMERTIME contemp records by Rossano Brazzi of orig cast. "Summertime in Venice," "Believe in Me" (78/HMV(E) B-10920)

550023a Film LILACS IN THE SPRING contemp record by members of orig cast. Errol Flynn: "Lily of Laguna" Flynn, Patrice Wymore: "We'll Gather Lilacs" (78/Philips(E) PB-380)

550024a Film FOXFIRE 1955 record by Jeff Chandler of orig cast. "Foxfire" (45/Dec 9-29532)

550025a Record prod THE BODY IN THE SEINE orig prod. MUSIC & WORDS: David M Lippincott. ORCH: Joseph Glover, Ralph Norman. COND: Buster Davis. VOCALS: Alice Pearce, Jim Symington, Barbara Ashley, Laurel Shelby, Terry Turner, Pat Wilkes, Don Liberto, George S Irving. (Alden-Shaw VB-001)

550026a Film STRANGE LADY IN TOWN 1955 record by Frankie Laine of orig prod. "Strange Lady in Town" (45/Col 4-40457)

550027a Film KISS ME DEADLY contemp record by Nat Cole of orig prod. "Blues" (78/Cap 3136)

550028a Film FRESH FROM PARIS contemp record by Margaret Whiting of orig cast. "Can This Be Love?" (45/Cap F-2913)

550029a Film LOVE IS A MANY SPLENDORED THING 1971 record by Sammy Fain (composer), piano & vocal. "Love Is a Many Splendored Thing" (LP-694)

550030a Film BRING YOUR SMILE ALONG contemp records by Frankie Laine of orig prod. "Bring Your Smile Along," "Mama Mia," "If Spring Never Comes" (45/Col B-2086)

550031a Film MAD ABOUT MEN 1954 record by Glynis Johns of orig cast. "I Can't Resist Men" (45/Col(E) SCM-5149)

550127a PLAIN AND FANCY orig prod. MUSIC: Albert Hague. WORDS: Arnold B Horwitt. ORCH: Philip J Lang. COND: Franz Allers. CAST: Richard Derr, Barbara Cook, David Daniels, Nancy Andrews, Shirl Conway, Gloria Marlowe, Douglas Fletcher Rodgers, Stefan Schnabel. (Cap S-603)

550127b PLAIN AND FANCY 1956 London prod. COND: Cyril Ornadel. CAST: Joan Hovis & Jack Drummond (both of lesser roles in 1956 London prod, singing here for stars Shirley Conway & Richard Derr); Grace O'Connor, Malcolm Keen, Virginia Somers. (Oriole(E) 10" MG-10009)

550224a SILK STOCKINGS orig prod. MUSIC & WORDS: Cole Porter. ORCH: Don Walker. COND: Herbert Greene. CAST: Hildegarde Neff, Don Ameche, Gretchen Wyler, Leon Belasco, Henry Lascoe, David Opatoshu. (RCA LOC-1016)

550224b SILK STOCKINGS 1957 film soundtrack, with two new Porter songs. COND: Andre Previn, John Green. CAST: Fred Astaire, Carol Richards (for Cyd Charisse), Janis Paige, Peter Lorre, Joseph Buloff, Jules Munshin. (MGM 3542. Excerpt: Astaire: "All of You" (LP-416).)

550228a SHOESTRING REVUE orig prod. MUSIC & WORDS: Mike Stewart, Charles Strouse, Sheldon Harnick, David Baker, Ronny Graham, others. ORCH & COND: Dorothea Freitag. CAST: Bill McCutcheon, Dody Goodman, Dorothy Greener, Beatrice Arthur, Fay deWitt, John Bartis, G Wood. (Painted Smiles 1360 (entitled "Shoestring Revues") plus 1362 (entitled "Shoestring '57"), both of which include additional material. Incomplete: Offbeat 4011.)

550228b SHOESTRING REVUE 1971 record sung by Sheldon Harnick, composer & lyricist. "Garbage" (LP-535)

550406a 3 FOR TONIGHT contemp records by Harry Belafonte of orig cast. "Sylvie," "Noah," "Take My Mother Home," "In That Great Gettin' Up Mornin'," "Matilda," "Scarlet Ribbons," "Troubles" (RCA LSP-1150, entitled "Belafonte") "Mark Twain" (45/RCA album EPB-1022)

550418a ANKLES AWEIGH orig prod. MUSIC: Sammy Fain. WORDS: Dan Shapiro. ORCH: Don Walker. COND: Salvatore dell'Isola. CAST: Betty Kean, Jane Kean, Lew Parker, Mark Dawson, Gabriel Dell, Betty George, Ray Mason. (Dec 9025)

550423a PHOENIX '55 1956 records by Nancy Walker of orig cast. MUSIC: David Baker. WORDS: David Craig. PIANO: David Baker. "Down to the Sea," "A Funny Heart," "The Charade of the Marionettes" (LP-293)

550505a DAMN YANKEES orig prod. MUSIC & WORDS: Richard Adler, Jerry Ross. ORCH: Don Walker. COND: Hal Hastings. CAST: Gwen Verdon, Stephen Douglass, Ray Walston, Shannon Bolin, Robert Shafer, Rae Allen, Eddie Phillips. (RCA LOC-1021)

550505b DAMN YANKEES 1958 film soundtrack with a new song by Richard Adler. COND: Ray Heindorf. CAST: Tab Hunter, Gwen Verdon, Ray Walston, Russ Brown, Shannon Bolin, Rae Allen, Robert Shafer. (RCA LOC-1047)

550505c DAMN YANKEES 1959 record by Ray Walston of orig & 1958 film casts. "Those Were the Good Old Days" (LP-294)

550505d DAMN YANKEES studio prod. COND: Johnny Douglas. CAST: Joan Heal, Barry Kent, Fred Lucas, Robert Nichols, chorus. (Cap SN-7515, with The Pajama Game)

550526a SEVENTH HEAVEN orig prod. MUSIC: Victor Young. WORDS: Stella Unger. ORCH: David Terry. COND: Max Meth. CAST: Gloria DeHaven, Ricardo Montalban, Robert Clary, Chita Rivera, Gerrianne Raphael, Patricia Hammerlee. (Dec 9001. Excerpt: DeHaven: "If It's a Dream" (LP-272).)

550526b SEVENTH HEAVEN contemp record by Gloria DeHaven of orig prod. "Where Is That Someone for Me?" (LP-272)

550727a HEAR! HEAR! orig prod. MUSIC & WORDS: Various. COND: Fred Culley, Jack Best. CAST: Norma Douglas, Dorothy Arms, Leonard Kranendonk, Bob Kranendonk, Eddie Erickson, Bob Sands, Gordon Goodman. (Dec 9031)

550831a THE WATER GIPSIES orig (London) prod. MUSIC: Vivian Ellis. WORDS: A P Herbert. COND: Jack Coles. CAST: Dora Bryan, Roy Godfrey, Pamela Charles, Peter Graves, Laurie Payne, Ernest Butcher, Doris Hare, Jerry Verno. (World Records(E) SH-228, with Bless the Bride. Incomplete: HMV(E) 10" DLP-1097.)

550831b THE WATER GIPSIES 1956(?) studio prod. ORCH & COND: John Gregory, CAST: Vanessa Lee, Harry Dawson, Joan Sims, Bruce Trent. (Dot 3048, with Plain and Fancy)

550919a TV show OUR TOWN contemp album by Frank Sinatra of orig cast. MUSIC: James Van Heusen. WORDS: Sammy Cahn.

COND: Nelson Riddle. "Love and Marriage," "Look to Your Heart," "Our Town," "The Impatient Years" (45/Cap EAP-1-673)

550919b TV show OUR TOWN 1977 record by Sammy Cahn, lyricist. "Love and Marriage" (LP-503)

551020a NO TIME FOR SERGEANTS 1956 record by Andy Griffith of orig & 1958 film casts, chorus. "No Time for Sergeants" (45/Cap F-3498)

551022a TV show TOGETHER WITH MUSIC soundtrack. MUSIC & WORDS: Various. ORCH & COND: Tutti Camarata. PIANO: Peter Matz. VOCALS: Noel Coward, Mary Martin. (DRG Records DARC-2-1103)

551130a PIPE DREAM orig prod. MUSIC: Richard Rodgers. WORDS: Oscar Hammerstein II. ORCH: Robert Russell Bennett. COND: Salvatore Dell'Isola. CAST: Helen Traubel, William Johnson, Judy Tyler, Mike Kellin, G D Wallace. (RCA LOC-1023)

551225a TV show A CHILD IS BORN soundtrack of 1956 TV prod(?). MUSIC: Bernard Herrmann. WORDS: Maxwell Anderson. CAST: Nadine Conner (also of orig cast), Robert Middleton(?), chorus. (Temple 2002, with David and Bathsheba)

551226a THE AMAZING ADELE contemp records by Johnny Desmond of orig (Philadelphia) cast. "Never Again," "Now Is the Time" (45/Coral 9-61570)

1956

560001a Film HIGH SOCIETY soundtrack. MUSIC & WORDS: Cole Porter. ORCH: Conrad Salinger, Nelson Riddle. COND: John Green. CAST: Bing Crosby, Grace Kelly, Frank Sinatra, Louis Armstrong, Celeste Holm. (Cap W-750)

560001b Film HIGH SOCIETY contemp record by Frank Sinatra of orig cast. "You're Sensational" (45/Cap F-3469)

560002a Film YOU CAN'T RUN AWAY FROM IT soundtrack. MUSIC: Gene de Paul. WORDS: Johnny Mercer. COND: Morris Stoloff. CAST: June Allyson, Jack Lemmon, Stubby Kaye, the Four Aces. (Dec 8396, with additional film music. Excerpt: Allyson, Lemmon: "Temporarily" (LP-481).)

560003a Film THAT CERTAIN FEELING contemp records by members of orig cast. Bob Hope: "That Certain Feeling" (LP-129) "Zing! Went the Stings of My Heart" (45/RCA 47-6577) Pearl Bailey: "That Certain Feeling," "Zing! Went the Strings of My Heart" (45/London(E) REU-1104)

560004a Film THE BEST THINGS IN LIFE ARE FREE contemp album by Gordon MacRae of orig cast. MUSIC: Ray Henderson. WORDS: B G DeSylva, Lew Brown. COND: Van Alexander. (Cap T-765)

560004b Film THE BEST THINGS IN LIFE ARE FREE 1957 record by Dan Dailey of orig cast. "Button Up Your Overcoat" (LP-367)

560004c Film THE BEST THINGS IN LIFE ARE FREE contemp album. ORCH: Billy May. COND: Lionel Newman, musical director of the film. (Liberty LRP-3017)

560004d Film THE BEST THINGS IN LIFE ARE FREE 1966 record by Ray Henderson (composer), piano. "The Best Things in Life Are Free" (LP-671)

560005a Film MEET ME IN LAS VEGAS contemp records by Dan Dailey of orig cast. "My Lucky Charm," "The Gal with the Yaller Shoes," "Frankie and Johnny" (45/MGM X-1264). Excerpts: "My Lucky Charm" (LP-207) "The Gal with the Yaller Shoes" (LP-702).)

560005b Film MEET ME IN LAS VEGAS soundtrack. Dan Dailey, George Chakiris, Betty Lynn: "It's Fun to Be in Love" (LP-588) Cara Williams: "I Refuse to Rock and Roll" (dropped before release) (LP-496)

560006a Film SERENADE soundtrack. MUSIC: Nicholas Brodszky, others. WORDS: Sammy Cahn, others. COND: Ray Heindorf. CAST: Mario Lanza, Licia Albanese. (RCA LM-1996)

560007a Film THE EDDY DUCHIN STORY soundtrack. MUSIC & WORDS: Various. COND: Morris Stoloff. PIANO: Carmen Cavallaro (for Tyrone Power). (Dec 8289)

560007b Film THE EDDY DUCHIN STORY contemp album. COND: Harry Geller. PIANOS: Harry Sukman, George Greeley. (Cap T-716)

560007c Film THE EDDY DUCHIN STORY album of Eddy Duchin records of songs used in the film, recorded from 1939 to 1947. PIANO: Eddy Duchin. (Col CL-790)

560008a Film THE COURT JESTER contemp album by Danny Kaye of orig cast. MUSIC & WORDS: Sammy Cahn, Sylvia Fine. COND: Vic Schoen. (Dec 8212)

560009a Film FRIENDLY PERSUASION soundtrack. Pat Boone: "Friendly Persuasion" (45/Dot 45-15490)

560009b Film FRIENDLY PERSUASION 1956 album by Pat Boone, who sang title song on soundtrack. MUSIC: Dmitri Tiomkin. WORDS: Paul Francis Webster. "Coax Me a Little," "The Mocking Bird in the Willow Tree," "Indiana Holiday," "Marry Me, Marry Me" (45/Dot DEP-1054)

560009c Film FRIENDLY PERSUASION contempt record by Anthony Perkins of orig cast. "Friendly Persuasion" (45/Epic 5-9181)

560010a Film BUNDLE OF JOY orig prod. MUSIC: Josef Myrow. WORDS: Mack Gordon. ORCH: Hugo Winterhalter. COND: Hugo Winterhalter, Walter Scharf. CAST: Eddie Fisher, Debbie Reynolds, Nita Talbot, chorus. (RCA LPM-1399)

560011a Film LET'S BE HAPPY 1957 album by Tony Martin of orig cast. MUSIC: Nicolas Brodszky. WORDS: Paul Francis Webster. "The Man from Idaho," "The Rose and the Heather," "One Is a Lonely Number," "Hold On to Love" (45/RCA EPA-4060)

560012a Film I'LL CRY TOMORROW contemp records by Susan Hayward of orig cast. "I'll Cry Tomorrow" (78/MGM(E) 895) "Just One of Those Things" (LP-207)

560012b Film I'LL CRY TOMORROW soundtrack. COND: Charles Henderson. PIANO: John Green. Susan Hayward: "Happiness Is a Thing Called Joe," "Just One of Those Things," "The Vagabond King Waltz," "I'm Sittin' on Top of the World," "When the Red, Red Robin," "Sing You Sinners," "I'll Cry Tomorrow" (LP-495. Incomplete: 45/MGM X-1180; Stet DS-25001, with Call Me Madam & Guys and Dolls. Excerpt: "Happiness Is a Thing Called Joe" (LP-328).)

560013a Film JULIE contemp record by Doris Day of orig cast "Julie" (LP-330)

560014a Film WESTWARD HO THE WAGONS! orig prod. MUSIC & WORDS: Various. COND: George Bruns, Tutti Camarata. VOCALS: Fess Parker, Bill Lee (for Bill Reeve), Kathleen Crowley, chorus. (Disneyland 4008)

560015a Film PARDNERS contemp album by Dean Martin & Jerry Lewis of orig cast. MUSIC: James Van Heusen. WORDS: Sammy Cahn. COND: Dick Stabile. Martin: "Me 'n' You 'n' The Moon," "The Wind, the Wind" Lewis: "Buckskin Beauty" Martin & Lewis: "Pardners" (45/Cap EAP-1-752. Excerpts: "Buckskin Beauty," "Pardners" (LP-562).)

560016a Film HOLLYWOOD OR BUST contemp records by Dean Martin of orig cast. MUSIC: Sammy Fain. WORDS: Paul Francis Webster. "It Looks like Love," "Let's Be Friendly," "A Day in the Country," "Hollywood or Bust" (45/Cap EAP-1-806. Excerpt: "Hollywood or Bust" (LP-562).)

560017a Film LOVE ME TENDER soundtrack. VOCALS: Elvis Presley. "Love Me Tender," "Let Me," "Poor Boy," "We're Gonna Move" (45/RCA EPA-4006)

560018a Film BUS STOP soundtrack. Marilyn Monroe: "That Old Black Magic" (LP-452)

560019a Film THE MAN WHO KNEW TOO MUCH 1956 records by Doris Day of orig cast. MUSIC: Jay Livingston. WORDS: Ray Evans. "Whatever Will Be, Will Be" (LP-692) "We'll Love Again" (45/Col 4-40673)

560020a Film JOHNNY CONCHO contemp record by Frank Sinatra of orig cast. "Wait for Me" (LP-562)

560021a Film THE SECOND GREATEST SEX soundtrack. MUSIC & WORDS: Jay Livingston, Ray Evans. Bert Lahr, chorus: "The Second Greatest Sex" (LP-608)

560021b Film THE SECOND GREATEST SEX contemp records by Kitty Kallen of orig cast. "How Lonely Can I Get?" (45/Dec 9-29708) With Georgie Shaw: "The Second Greatest Sex" (45/Dec 9-29776)

560022a Film THE BIRDS AND THE BEES contemp record by George Gobel of orig cast. "The Birds and the Bees" (45/RCA 47-6483)

560023a Film LIZZIE contemp album by Johnny Mathis of orig prod. "It's Not for Me to Say," "Warm and Tender" (45/Col B-2129, with additional songs)

560024a Film FOREVER DARLING 1955 record by Desi Arnaz of orig cast. "Forever, Darling" (45/MGM K-12144)

560025a Film THE MAVERICK QUEEN contemp record by Joni James of orig cast. "The Maverick Queen" (45/MGM K-12213)

560026a ICE FOLLIES OF 1956 contemp records by the Ice Follies Orch & members of orig prod. Norma Larsen Zimmer, William Reeve: "The Swing Waltz" Ice Follies Ensemble: "Clown Town, U.S.A" (78/Unnamed label mx RR-22268/22929)

560027a Record prod EUROPEAN HOLIDAY orig prod. MUSIC: Lee Thornsby. WORDS: Douglas Lance. COND: Jimmy Carroll. VOCALS: Michael Stewart, Jill Corey, Jerry Vale, chorus. (Col 10" CL-2586, with additional material)

560200a Industrial show W.T. GRANT'S 50TH ANNIVERSARY SHOW orig (White Sulphur Springs, W Va) prod. MUSIC & WORDS: Michael Brown. ORCH: & COND: Norman Paris. CAST: Kenneth Nelson, Marge Redmond, Michael Brown, Ellen Martin. (Fine Sound 935)

560301a CRANKS orig (London) prod. MUSIC: John Addison. WORDS: John Cranko. COND: Anthony Bowles. CAST: Hugh Bryant, Annie Ross, Anthony Newley, Gilbert Vernon (all of whom were also in 1956 New York cast). (HMV(E) CLP-1082)

560304a TV show (Canada) ANNE 1969 London stage prod entitled "Anne of Green Gables." MUSIC: Norman Campbell. WORDS: mostly Donald Harron, Norman Campbell. ORCH: John Fenwick. COND: Martin Goldstein. CAST: Polly James, Barbara Hamilton, Hiram Sherman, Susan Anderson, Pat Starr, Robert Ainslie, Colette Gleeson. (CBS(E) 70053)

560310a TV show HIGH TOR combination soundtrack & studio prod. MUSIC: Arthur Schwartz. WORDS: Maxwell Anderson. ORCH & COND: Joseph J Lilley. CAST: Bing Crosby, Julie Andrews, Everett Sloane. (Dec 8272)

560315a MY FAIR LADY orig prod. MUSIC: Frederick Loewe. WORDS: Alan J Lerner. ORCH: Robert Russell Bennett, Philip J Lang. COND: Franz Allers. CAST: Rex Harrison, Julie Andrews, Stanley Holloway, Robert Coote, Michael King, Philippa Bevans. (Col OL-5090)

560315b MY FAIR LADY 1964 film soundtrack. COND: Andre Previn. CAST: Rex Harrison, Marni Nixon (for Audrey Hepburn), Stanley Holloway, Wilfrid Hyde-White, Bill Shirley (for Jeremy Brett). (Col KOS-2600)

560315c MY FAIR LADY 1959 studio prod. COND: John Green. CAST: Jane Powell, Phil Harris, Jan Peerce, Robert Merrill. (RCA LSP-6005, with Brigadoon, Gigi, & Paint Your Wagon)

560315d MY FAIR LADY 1958 London prod. ORCH: Robert Russell Bennett, Philip J Lang. COND: Cyril Ornadel. CAST: Julie Andrews, Rex Harrison, Stanley Holloway, & Robert Coote of orig prod; Betty Woolfe, Leonard Weir. (Col OS-2015)

560315e MY FAIR LADY studio prod. COND: Lawrence Nash. VOCALS: Julie Jonas, Tex Howard, Margaret Young, chorus. (Silver Seal 104)

560315f MY FAIR LADY 1957 album. COND: Jack Hansen. VOCALS: Lanny Ross, Marcia Neil. (Masterseal 5001)

560315g MY FAIR LADY studio prod. COND: John Gregory. VOCALS: Elizabeth Larner, Hubert Gregg, John Slater, John Harvey, chorus. (Avon(E) 7-3001)

560315h MY FAIR LADY studio prod. "Ed Sullivan presents My Fair Lady." No other credits given. (National Academy 1)

560315i MY FAIR LADY studio prod. COND: Al Goodman ("Dean Franconi"). VOCALS: Lola Fisher (understudy to Julie Andrews in orig prod); Edgar Powell, William Reynolds, Richard Torigi, chorus. (Hurrah 1036)

560315j MY FAIR LADY studio prod. ORCH & COND: Al Goodman. CAST: Lola Fisher (understudy to Julie Andrews in orig prod); Richard Torigi, Edgar Powell, William Reynolds. (Diplomat 2214)

560315k MY FAIR LADY 1965 studio prod. COND: Alyn Ainsworth. CAST: Anne Rogers (who played Eliza both in New York and London), Tony Britton, Jon Pertwee, Clive Rogers, Joe Wise. (Music for Pleasure(E) 1057)

560315l MY FAIR LADY 1976 prod. ORCH: Robert Russell Bennett, Phil Lang. COND: Theodore Saidenberg. CAST: Ian Richardson, Christine Andreas, George Rose, Robert Coote (of orig & 1958 London prods), Jerry Lanning, Sylvia O'Brien. (Col PS-34197)

560315m MY FAIR LADY 1964 album. VOCALS: Mel Torme, Fran Jeffries, Maurice Chevalier. (MGM 4280)

560315n MY FAIR LADY 1958 studio prod. COND: Gordon Fleming. CAST: Evelyn Sharpe, Robert Back, Charles Peck, chorus. (Craftsmen 8020)

560315o MY FAIR LADY studio prod. COND: Richard Mueller-Lampertz. VOCALS: Lawrence Chelsi, Alberta Hopkins, Tom O'Leary, Eddy Ruhl. (Rondo-lette SA-144)

560315p MY FAIR LADY 1959 studio prod. VOCALS: John Ruark, Anna Maria Pallys, chorus. (Lion 70092)

560315q MY FAIR LADY 1971 records sung by Alan Jay Lerner, lyricist. "Oh, Come to the Ball" (dropped from the show); "Why Can't a Woman," "Wouldn't It Be Loverly?," "I've Grown Accustomed to Her Face" (LP-534)

560315r MY FAIR LADY 1956 album. COND: Elliot Everett. VOCALS: chorus. (Allegro 10" 4120)

560317a STRIP FOR ACTION contemp album by Nat Cole. MUSIC: Jimmy McHugh. WORDS: Harold Adamson. ORCH & COND: Nelson Riddle. "Too Young to Go Steady," "I Just Found Out about Love," "Love Me as Though There Were No Tomorrow," "Dame Crazy" (45/Cap EAP-1-709)

560322a MR. WONDERFUL orig prod. MUSIC & WORDS: Jerry Bock, Larry Holofcener, George Weiss. ORCH: Ted Royal, Morton Stevens. COND: Morton Stevens. CAST: Sammy Davis Jr., Jack Carter, Pat Marshall, Olga James, Chita Rivera, Hal Loman, Will Mastin Trio. (Dec 9032)

560322b MR. WONDERFUL records by Sammy Davis Jr of orig prod. "Too Close for Comfort" (1956: 78/Dec 29861) (Later: LP-257) "Jacques d'Iraque" (1956: 78/Dec 29861) "Without You I'm Nothing" (1956: 45/Dec 9-29929)

560325a TV show JOEY 1956 record by Anthony Perkins of orig cast. "A Little Love Can Go a Long, Long Way" (78/Epic 9165)

560400a BARNEY 'N ME orig (Providence, R I) prod. MUSIC: Robert Waldman. WORDS: Alfred Uhry. CAST: The Brownbrokers. (Unnamed label 10" mx G8-OL-4234/5)

560414a TV show THE ADVENTURES OF MARCO POLO orig prod. MUSIC: Nicolai Rimsky-Korsakov, arranged by Clay Warnick & Mel Pahl. WORDS: Edward Eager. ORCH: Irwin Kostal. COND: Charles Sanford. CAST: Alfred Drake, Doretta Morrow, Ray Drakeley, Paul Ukena. (Col ML-5111)

560503a THE MOST HAPPY FELLA orig prod. MUSIC & WORDS: Frank Loesser. ORCH: Don Walker. COND: Herbert Greene. CAST: Robert Weede, Jo Sullivan, Art Lund, Susan Johnson, Shorty Long, Mona Paulee, Keith Kaldenberg, Lee Cass. (Col 03L-240. Excerpts: OS-2330)

560503b THE MOST HAPPY FELLA 1960 London prod. ORCH: Don Walker. COND: Kenneth Alwyn. CAST: Inia Wiata, Art Lund (of orig prod), Helena Scott, Libi Staiger, Jack DeLon, Nina Verushka. (Angel 35887)

560503c THE MOST HAPPY FELLA 1961 studio prod. ORCH: Bobby Richards. COND: Jan Cervenka. CAST: Edwin Steffe, Stella Moray, Marion Grimaldi, Gordon Boyd, Peter Hudson, chorus. (World Record Club(E) SLMP-17)

560503d THE MOST HAPPY FELLA 1960 studio prod. ORCH & COND: Len Stevens. CAST: Ian Paterson, Janet Waters, Dennis MacGregor, Andy Cole, Joyce Blair, chorus. (Ace of Clubs(E) 1035, with West Side Story)

560522a THE LITTLEST REVUE orig prod. MUSIC & WORDS: Vernon Duke, Ogden Nash, John Latouche, Sheldon Harnick, Lee Adams, Charles Strouse, John Strauss, Sammy Cahn, Michael Brown. ORCH: John Strauss. COND: Will Irwin. CAST: Charlotte Rae, Tammy Grimes, Joel Grey, Tommy Morton, George Marcy, Beverly Bozeman. (Painted Smiles 1361. Incomplete: Epic 3275.)

560522b THE LITTLEST REVUE 1955 record by Charlotte Rae of orig cast. "Summer Is a-Comin' In" (LP-464)

560522c THE LITTLEST REVUE record sung by Michael Brown, composer & lyricist. "The Third Avenue El" (LP-697)

5560613a SHANGRI-LA 1960 TV prod. MUSIC: Harry Warren. WORDS: Jerome Lawrence, Robert E Lee. CAST: Alice Ghostley of orig cast; Richard Basehart, Marisa Pavan, Helen Gallagher, Gene Nelson, chorus. (The Sound Of Broadway 300/1, with Shinbone Alley)

560614a NEW FACES OF 1956 orig prod. MUSIC & WORDS: Arthur Siegel, June Carroll, Marshall Barer, Dean Fuller, Murray Grand. ORCH: Ted Royal, Albert Sendry, Joe Glover. COND: Jay Blackton. CAST: John Reardon, Inga Swenson, Virginia Martin, Amru Sani, T C Jones, Jane Connell, Maggie Smith. (RCA LOC-1025)

560917a TV show THE LORD DON'T PLAY FAVORITES contemp records by members of orig prod. MUSIC: Hal Stanley. WORDS: Irving Taylor. Louis Armstrong (vocal): "Rain Rain," "I Never Saw a Better Day" (45/RCA 47-6630) Kay Starr: "Rain Rain," "The Things

I Never Had," "For Better or Worse," "The Good Book" (45/RCA EPA-960)

561107a Industrial show LEAD THE CARE-FREE LIFE...IN THE HOLIDAY MOOD orig prod. MUSIC & WORDS: Michael Brown. ORCH & COND: Norman Paris. CAST: Kenneth Nelson, Ellen Martin, Don Liberto, Elaine Dunn, Joy Williams, Tom Ayre. (Unnamed label OSS-1342)

561112a IRMA LA DOUCE studio prod in French. MUSIC: Marguerite Monnot. WORDS: Alexandre Breffort. ORCH & COND: Andre Popp. CAST: Zizi Jeanmaire, Roland Petit, Luc Davis, les Quatre Barbus. (Philips(F) 842.178-PY; Col WL-177.)

561112b IRMA LA DOUCE 1958 London prod. WORDS: Alexandre Breffort, Julian More, David Heneker, Monty Norman. ORCH: Andre Popp, COND: Alexander Faris. CAST: Elizabeth Seal, Keith Michell, Clive Revill. (Philips(E) BBL-7274)

561112c IRMA LA DOUCE 1960 New York prod. ORCH: Andre Popp, Robert Ginzler. COND: Stanley Lebowsky. CAST: Elizabeth Seal, Keith Michell, Clive Revill, George S Irving, Fred Gwynne, Zack Matalon, Aric Lavie, Osborne Smith, Stuart Damon. (Col OS-2029)

561112d IRMA LA DOUCE 1967 Paris prod. ORCH: Raymond Legrand. COND: Fred Alban. CAST: Colette Renard (of orig prod), Franck Fernandel, Rene Dupuy, Maurice Chevit, Jean Mauvais, Jacques Ferriere. (Vega(F) 16.089/90)

561112e IRMA LA DOUCE 1958 studio prod. ORCH & COND: Jack Dent. VOCALS: Heather Lloyd-Jones, Robert Haber, Siegfried Mynhardt, Harold Lake, chorus. (RCA(E) 30-122)

561112f IRMA LA DOUCE contemp album by Colette Renard of orig (Paris) cast. COND: Raymond Legrand. "Irma la Douce," "Y a qu'Paris pour ca," "Ah! Dis-donc," "Avec les Anges" (Vogue(F) 10" LD-395, with additional material)

561112g IRMA LA DOUCE 1963 studio prod. ORCH & COND: Alan Braden. CAST: Mary Preston, Grahame Laver, chorus. (World Records(E) ST-253, with The Threepenny Opera)

561112*a TV show JACK AND THE BEANSTALK contemp studio prod. MUSIC: Jerry Livingston. WORDS: Helen Deutsch. COND: Joe Leahy. CAST: Bob Graybo, Lynn Roberts, Dave Collyer. (RKO 111)

561115a LI'L ABNER orig prod. MUSIC: Gene de Paul. WORDS: Johnny Mercer. ORCH: Philip J Lang. COND: Lehman Engel. CAST: Edith Adams, Peter Palmer, Howard St John, Stubby Kaye, Charlotte Rae, Carmen Alvarez, Stanley Simmonds. (Col OL-5150)

561115b LI'L ABNER 1959 film soundtrack. ORCH & COND: Nelson Riddle, Joseph J Lilley. CAST: Peter Palmer, Leslie Parrish, Stubby Kaye, Howard St John, Julie Newmar, Stella Stevens. (Col OS-2021)

561121a TV show TOM SAWYER orig prod. MUSIC & WORDS: Frank Luther. ORCH & COND: Ralph Norman Wilkinson. CAST: John Sharpe, Bennye Gatteys, Jimmy Boyd, Rose Bampton, Clarence Cooper. (Dec 8432)

561129a BELLS ARE RINGING orig prod. MUSIC: Jule Styne. WORDS: Betty Comden, Adolph Green. ORCH: Robert Russell Bennett. COND: Milton Rosenstock. CAST: Judy Holliday, Sydney Chaplin, Jean Stapleton, Eddie Lawrence, Peter Gennaro, George Irving. (Col OS-2006)

561129b BELLS ARE RINGING 1960 film soundtrack with two new Styne-Comden-Green songs. ORCH: Alexander Courage, Pete King. COND: Andre Previn. CAST: Judy Holliday, Dean Martin, Eddie Foy Jr, Hal Linden. (Cap SW-1435. Also two numbers

dropped before release: Holliday: "Is It a Crime?" (LP-423) Martin: "My Guiding Star" (45/unnamed label SPO-145).)

561129c BELLS ARE RINGING records by Betty Comden and Adolph Green, lyricists. "Just in Time" (1958: LP-170) (1959, with Andy Williams: LP-294) (1977: LP-489) "The Party's Over" (1958: LP-170) (1977: LP-489)

561129d BELLS ARE RINGING 1966 record by Jule Styne (composer), piano. "Just in Time" (LP-671)

561129e BELLS ARE RINGING record by Judy Holliday (of orig & 1960 film prods) with Gerry Mulligan Orch. "The Party's Over" (45/Col 4-41688)

561201a CANDIDE orig prod. MUSIC: Leonard Bernstein. WORDS: Richard Wilbur, John Latouche, Dorothy Parker. ORCH: Leonard Bernstein, Hershy Kay. COND: Samuel Krachmalnick. CAST: Max Adrian, Robert Rounseville, Barbara Cook, Irra Petina, William Olvis. (Col OS-2350)

561201b CANDIDE 1974 prod with many changes in music & words. MUSIC: Leonard Bernstein. WORDS: Richard Wilbur, Stephen Sondheim, John Latouche. ORCH: Hershy Kay. COND: John Mauceri. CAST: Mark Baker, Maureen Brennan, Sam Freed, June Gable, Deborah St Darr, Lewis J Stadlen. (Col S2X-32923)

561206a HAPPY HUNTING orig prod. MUSIC: Harold Karr. WORDS: Matt Dubey. ORCH: Ted Royal. COND: Jay Blackton. CAST: Ethel Merman, Fernando Lamas, Virginia Gibson, Gordon Polk, Mary Finney, Leon Belasco. (RCA LOC-1026)

561206b HAPPY HUNTING 1977 record by Ethel Merman of orig cast. "Gee, But It's Good to Be Here" (LP-652)

561223a TV show THE STINGIEST MAN IN TOWN orig prod. MUSIC: Fred Spielman. WORDS: Janice Torre. ORCH & COND: Tutti Camarata. CAST: Vic Damone, Johnny Desmond, Patrice Munsel, Basil Rathbone, Robert Weede, Robert Wright, Betty Madigan, Martyn Green. (Col CL-950)

1957

570001a Film FUNNY FACE soundtrack. MUSIC: George Gershwin, Roger Edens. WORDS: Ira Gershwin, Leonard Gershe. ORCH: Conrad Salinger, Alexander Courage, Van Cleave, Skip Martin. COND: Adolph Deutsch. CAST: Fred Astaire, Audrey Hepburn, Kay Thompson. (Verve 15001)

570002a Film LES GIRLS soundtrack. MUSIC & WORDS: Cole Porter. ORCH: Alexander Courage, Skip Martin. COND: Adolph Deutsch. CAST: Gene Kelly, Mitzi Gaynor, Kay Kendall, Taina Elg. (MGM 3590, with additional Porter songs. Excerpt: Kelly, Kendall: "You're Just Too, Too!" (LP-501).)

570003a Record prod ALI BABA AND THE 40 THIEVES 40 orig prod. MUSIC: Mary Rodgers. WORDS: Sammy Cahn. CAST: Bing Crosby, chorus. (Golden Masterpiece GRC-20)

570004a Film THE HELEN MORGAN STORY soundtrack. MUSIC & WORDS: Various. ORCH: Gus Levene, Frank Comstock. COND: Ray Heindorf. VOCALS: Gogi Grant (for Ann Blyth). (RCA LOC-1030)

570005a Record prod FRANKIE AND JOHNNY orig prod. MUSIC: Robert Cobert. WORDS: Dion McGregor. ORCH: Philip J Lang. COND: Herb Harris. CAST: Mary Mayo, Danny Scholl, Joan Coburn, Nathaniel Frey, Jane House. (MGM 3499)

570006a Film THE GIRL MOST LIKELY soundtrack. MUSIC: Hugh Martin. WORDS: Ralph Blane. ORCH & COND: Nelson Riddle.

CAST: Jane Powell, Cliff Robertson, Kaye Ballard, Keith Andes, Tommy Noonan, Kelly Brown. (Cap W-930)

570007a Film APRIL LOVE soundtrack. MUSIC: Sammy Fain. WORDS: Paul Francis Webster. ORCH: Alfred Newman, Cyril J Mockridge. COND: Lionel Newman. CAST: Pat Boone, Shirley Jones. (Dot 9000)

570008a Film TAMMY AND THE BACHELOR soundtrack. MUSIC: Jay Livingston. WORDS: Ray Evans. COND: Joseph Gershenson. Debbie Reynolds: "Tammy" (Coral 57159, with Interlude)

570009a Film BEAU JAMES soundtrack. MUSIC & WORDS: Various. ORCH & COND: Joseph J Lilley. CAST: Bob Hope, Jimmy Durante, Imogene Lynn (for Vera Miles). (Imperial 9041)

570010a Film THE JOKER IS WILD contemp records by Frank Sinatra of orig cast. "Chicago," "All the Way" (LP-562)

570010b Film THE JOKER IS WILD 1972 record by Sammy Cahn, lyricist. MUSIC: James Van Heusen. "All the Way" (LP-658)

570011a Film THE GOOD COMPANIONS soundtrack. Uncredited vocalist: "If Only," "This Kind of Love" (78/Parlophone(E) R-4282)

570012a Film AN AFFAIR TO REMEMBER soundtrack. MUSIC: Harry Warren, Hugo Friedhofer. WORDS: Harold Adamson, Leo McCarey. COND: Lionel Newman. VOCALS: Vic Damone, Marni Nixon (for Deborah Kerr), chorus. (Col CL-1013. Incomplete: LP-633.)

570013a Film RAINTREE COUNTY soundtrack. MUSIC: John Green. WORDS: Paul Francis Webster. COND: John Green. Nat Cole: "The Song of Raintree County" (45/Cap F-3782)

570014a Film THIS COULD BE THE NIGHT soundtrack. MUSIC & WORDS: Various. Ray Anthony Orch. VOCALS: Julie Wilson, Neile Adams. (MGM 3530)

570014b Film THIS COULD BE THE NIGHT records by Sammy Cahn, lyricist. "The Tender Trap" (1972: LP-658) (1974: LP-313) (1977: LP-503)

570015a Film A FACE IN THE CROWD soundtrack. MUSIC: Tom Glazer. WORDS: Budd Schulberg. VOCALS: Andy Griffith, chorus. (Cap W-872)

570016a Film BERNADINE contemp records by Pat Boone of orig cast. "Bernadine," "Love Letters in the Sand" (45/Dot 45-15570) "Technique," "Cathedral in the Pines" (45/Dot DEP-1057, entitled "Four by Pat," with 2 other songs)

570016b Film BERNARDINE record sung by J Fred Coots, composer. "Love Letters in the Sand" (LP-530)

570017a Film ISLAND IN THE SUN contemp records by Harry Belafonte of orig cast. "Island in the Sun," "Lead Man Holler" (45/RCA EPA-4084)

570018a Record prod PINOCCHIO orig prod. MUSIC: Milton Delugg. WORDS: Ira Wallach. COND: Milton Delugg. CAST: Paul Winchell (& "Jerry Mahoney"), Johnny Haymer, Elise Breton, Milton Delugg, chorus. (Dec 8463)

570019a Film AROUND THE WORLD IN EIGHTY DAYS 1958 record prod with lyrics. MUSIC: Victor Young. WORDS: Harold Adamson. ORCH: Leo Shuken. COND: Franz Allers. VOCALS: uncredited soloists, chorus. (Everest SDBR-1020)

570020a Film JAILHOUSE ROCK contemp records by Elvis Presley of orig cast. "Jailhouse Rock," "Young and Beautiful," "I Want to Be Free," "Don't Leave Me Now," "Baby, I Don't Care" (45/RCA EPA-4114)

570020b Film JAILHOUSE ROCK soundtrack. VOCALS: Elvis Presley. (LP-664)

570021a Film TEN THOUSAND BEDROOMS contemp records by Dean Martin of orig cast. MUSIC: Nicholas Brodszky. WORDS: Sammy Cahn. "You I Love," "Money Is a Problem, " "Only Trust Your Heart," "Ten Thousand Bedrooms" (45/Cap EAP-1-840. Excerpt: "Ten Thousand Bedrooms" (LP-562).) "The Man Who Plays the Mandolino" (45/Cap 3648)

570022a Film THE PRINCE AND THE SHOWGIRL soundtrack. Marilyn Monroe: "I Found a Dream" (LP-452)

570023a Film LOVING YOU 1957 album by Elvis Presley of orig cast. MUSIC & WORDS: Various. (RCA LPM-1515, with other songs)

570023b Film LOVING YOU soundtrack. VOCALS: Elvis Presley. (LP-664)

570024a Film SING BOY SING soundtrack. MUSIC & WORDS: Various. COND: Lionel Newman. VOCALS: Tommy Sands, chorus. (Cap T-929)

570025a Film DESIGNING WOMAN 1956 record by Dolores Gray of orig cast. "There'll Be Some Changes Made" (45/Cap F-3719)

570026a Film MAN ON FIRE contemp record by Bing Crosby of orig cast. "Man on Fire" (45/Cap F-3695)

570027a Film THE HAPPY ROAD record by Gene Kelly of orig cast. "The Happy Road" (LP-598)

570028a Film WILD IS THE WIND 1957 record by Johnny Mathis of orig prod. "Wild Is the Wind" (45/Col 4-41060)

570028b Film WILD IS THE WIND soundtrack. Anna Magnani: "Scapricciatiello" (45/Verve V-10113)

570029a Film CHINA GATE contemp record by Nat Cole of orig prod. "China Gate" (45/Cap ST-2340)

570030a Film THE GREAT MAN contemp record by Julie London of orig prod. "The Meaning of the Blues" (45/Liberty F-55052)

570031a Film JEANNE EAGELS contemp record by Jeff Chandler of orig cast. "Half of My Heart" (45/Liberty F-55092)

570032a Film FLIGHT TO HONG KONG contemp records by Rory Calhoun of orig prod. "Flight to Hong Kong," "Kiss of Love" (45/MGM K-12359)

570033a Film FULL OF LIFE contemp record by Judy Holliday of orig prod. "Full of Life" (45/Dec 9-30216)

570034a Film CALYPSO HEAT WAVE contemp record by Johnny Desmond of orig prod. "Consideration" (45/Coral 9-61846)

570035a Film DINO soundtrack. Sal Mineo: "First Love," "Saturday Night," "Death in a Warehouse" (45/Epic EG-7187)

570036a Film THE LONELY MAN contemp record by Tennessee Ernie Ford of orig cast. "The Lonely Man" (78/Cap 3700)

570037a Film BOY ON A DOLPHIN contemp records by members of orig prod. Sophia Loren: "Tin Afto" (45/RCA 53-0133) Julie London: "The Boy on a Dolphin" (45/Liberty F-55052)

570038a Film THE DEVIL'S HAIRPIN contemp record by Jean Wallace of orig prod. "The Touch of Love" (45/Verve 10099)

570039a Film DON'T GO NEAR THE WATER contemp record by the Lancers of orig prod. "Don't Go Near the Water" (45/Coral 9-61899)

570040a Film SEARCH FOR PARADISE contemp album by Robert Merrill of orig prod. MUSIC: Dmitri Tiomkin. WORDS: Ned Washington, Lowell Thomas. ORCH & COND: David Terry. "Search for Paradise," "Kashmir," "Shalimar," "Happy Land of Hunza" (45/RCA EPA-4117)

136

570041a Film THE MONTE CARLO STORY soundtrack. Marlene Dietrich: "Back Home Again in Indiana" (LP-705)

570042a Film WOMAN OF THE RIVER contemp record by Sophia Loren of orig cast. "Mambo Bacan" (45/RCA 47-6385)

570043a Film THE DELICATE DELINQUENT 1957 record by Jerry Lewis of orig cast. MUSIC: Arthur Schwartz. WORDS: Howard Dietz. "By Myself" (45/Dec 9-30370)

570044a Industrial show THIS IS OLDSMOBILITY orig prod. COND: Sherman Frank. CAST: Bill Hayes, Florence Henderson, unidentified soloists, chorus. (Unnamed label HR-118)

570045a Industrial record prod HAVE A HOLIDAY orig prod. MUSIC & WORDS: Michael Brown. ORCH & COND: Norman Paris. CAST: Michael Brown, David Carter, Betty Ann Busch. (Unnamed label OSS-1555)

570124a AT THE DROP OF A HAT orig (London) prod rec live. MUSIC: Donald Swann. WORDS: Michael Flanders. CAST: Michael Flanders, Donald Swann. (Angel 65042)

570124b AT THE DROP OF A HAT 1959 New York prod, with slightly different material, rec live. MUSIC: Donald Swann. WORDS: Michael Flanders. CAST: Michael Flanders, Donald Swann. (Angel 35797)

570124c AT THE DROP OF A HAT album by Michael Flanders & Donald Swann of 4 numbers not on original cast album, (45/Parlophone(E) GEP-8636, entitled "More Out of the Hat")

570203a TV show RUGGLES OF RED GAP orig prod. MUSIC: Jule Styne. WORDS: Leo Robin. ORCH & COND: Buddy Bregman. CAST: Michael Redgrave, Peter Lawford, Imogene Coca, David Wayne, Jane Powell, Joan Holloway. (Verve 15000)

570207a MY FUR LADY orig (Montreal) prod. MUSIC & WORDS: James Domville, Galt MacDermot, Harry Garber, Roy Wolvin, Timothy Porteous. CAST: Ann Golden, Jim Hugessen, Douglas Robertson, Nancy Bacal, Graham Wright, John MacLeod, Sheila McCormick. (McGill(C) MRS-LPM-3)

570207b MY FUR LADY second 1957 Montreal prod. ORCH & COND: Edmund Assaly. CAST: Ann Golden, Jim Hugessen, Nancy Bacal, John MacLeod, & Sheila McCormick of orig prod; Wilfred Hastings, Donald Harvie. (McGill(C) MRS-LPM-5)

570219a THE CRYSTAL HEART orig prod. MUSIC: Baldwin Bergersen. WORDS: William Archibald. COND: Baldwin Bergersen. PIANOS: Eugene Hunt, Baldwin Bergersen. CAST: John Baylis, John Stewart, Jeanne Shea, Mildred Dunnock. (Unnamed label CK-1)

570331a TV show CINDERELLA orig prod. MUSIC: Richard Rodgers. WORDS: Oscar Hammerstein II. ORCH: Robert Russell Bennett. COND: Alfredo Antonini. CAST: Julie Andrews, Alice Ghostley, Kaye Ballard, Jon Cypher, Ilka Chase, Bob Penn, Dorothy Stickney, Howard Lindsay, Edith Adams. (Col OS-2005)

570331b TV show CINDERELLA 1964 TV prod, with a new Rodgers-Hammerstein song. ORCH: Robert Russell Bennett, John Green. COND: John Green. CAST: Lesley Ann Warren, Stuart Damon, Celeste Holm, Barbara Ruick, Jo Van Fleet, Pat Carroll, Don Heitgerd. (Col OS-2730)

570331c TV show CINDERELLA 1958 album by Mary Martin. ORCH: Robert Russell Bennett. COND: Thomas Scherman. (RCA LPM-2012, with Three to Make Music)

570331d TV show CINDERELLA studio prod. ORCH & COND: Gilbert Vinter. CAST: Elizabeth Larner, Denis Quilley, Dudley Rolph, Helen Clare. (Saga(E) 10" STL-9101)

570331e TV show CINDERELLA 1958 London stage prod, with 2 songs interpolated from Me and Juliet. ORCH: Robert Russell Bennett, Ronnie Hanmer. COND: Bobby Howell. CAST: Tommy Steele, Bruce Trent, Yana, Robin Palmer, Kenneth Williams, Ted Durante, Jimmy Edwards, Enid Lowe. (Dec(E) SKL-4050)

570331f TV show CINDERELLA 1959 album. COND: Peter Knight. VOCALS: Elizabeth Humphries, Charles Young, Babs Knight, Patricia Clark. (45/Parlophone(E) GEP-8721)

570331g TV show CINDERELLA "preview" album. PIANO: Richard Rodgers. VOCALS: Julie Andrews, unidentified male singer. "Mother and Daughter March," "In My Own Little Corner," "Ten Minutes Ago," "Do I Love You Because You're Beautiful," "Waltz for a Ball," "A Lovely Night" (Unnamed label 10" mx TV-25822/3)

570331h TV show CINDERELLA contemp album. COND: Henri Rene. VOCALS: Tony Martin, chorus. "A Lovely Night," "Do I Love You," "In Your Own Little Corner," "Ten Minutes Ago" (45/RCA EPA-4056)

570413a SHINBONE ALLEY 1954 record prod. MUSIC: George Kleinsinger. WORDS: Joe Darion, Don Marquis. ORCH & COND: George Kleinsinger. CAST: Eddie Bracken of 1957 stage prod, 1960 TV prod, & 1970 film prod; Carol Channing of 1970 film prod; David Wayne, Percival Dove. (Col ML-4963, entitled "archy and mehitabel," with additional material)

570413b SHINBONE ALLEY contemp records by Eartha Kitt, chorus & orchestra of orig prod. "Toujours Gai," "A Woman Wouldn't Be a Woman" (Sound of Broadway 300/1, with Shangri-La)

570413c SHINBONE ALLEY 1960 TV prod. CAST: Eddie Bracken, Tammy Grimes, chorus. (Sound of Broadway 300/1, with Shangri-La)

570413d SHINBONE ALLEY orig prod, rec live. ORCH: George Kleinsinger, Irwin Kostal. COND: Maurice Levine. CAST: Eartha Kitt, Eddie Bracken, George S Irving, Ross Martin, Erik Rhodes, chorus. (Mastertone 1251)

570421a TV show THE GENE AUSTIN STORY 1957 records by Gene Austin, who sang for George Grizzard in orig prod. "The Sweetheart of Sigma Chi/Sleepy Time Gal/My Blue Heaven," "Ramona/She's Funny That Way/I'm in the Mood for Love" (45/RCA EPA-4057) "That's Love," "Too Late" (45/RCA 47-6880)

570511a TV show MR. BROADWAY contemp album by Mickey Rooney of orig cast. MUSIC & WORDS: George M Cohan. COND: Van Alexander. (RCA LPM-1520, entitled "Mickey Rooney Sings George M Cohan," with other songs by Rooney)

570514a NEW GIRL IN TOWN orig prod. MUSIC & WORDS: Bob Merrill. ORCH: Robert Russell Bennett, Philip J Lang. COND: Hal Hastings. CAST: Gwen Verdon, Thelma Ritter, George Wallace, Cameron Prud'homme, H F Green. (RCA LSO-1027)

570516a TV show THE HELEN MORGAN STORY orig prod. MUSIC & WORDS: Various. ORCH & COND: Luther Henderson. VOCALS: Polly Bergen. (Col CL-994, entitled "Bergen Sings Morgan")

570521a SIMPLY HEAVENLY orig prod, MUSIC: David Martin. WORDS: Langston Hughes. ORCH & COND: David Martin. CAST: Claudia McNeil, Melvin Stewart, Anna English, Marilyn Berry, John Bouie, Brownie McGhee, Duke Williams. (Col OL-5240)

570912a ZIEGFELD FOLLIES OF 1958 contemp record by Kaye Ballard of orig (Toronto) cast. "The Parade Is Passing Me By" (45/Epic 5-9248)

570926a WEST SIDE STORY orig prod. MUSIC: Leonard Bernstein. WORDS: Stephen Sondheim. ORCH: Leonard Bernstein, Sid Ramin, Irwin Kostal. COND: Max Goberman. CAST: Larry Kert, Carol Lawrence, Chita Rivera, Mickey Calin, Reri Grist, Eddie Roll, Grover Dale, Marilyn Cooper. (Col OS-2001)

570926b WEST SIDE STORY 1961 film soundtrack. ORCH: Sid Ramin, Irwin Kostal. COND: John Green. CAST: Marni Nixon (for Natalie Wood), Jim Bryant (for Richard Beymer), Russ Tamblyn, Rita Moreno (with help from Betty Wand & Marni Nixon), George Chakiris, Tucker Smith. (Col OS-2070)

570926c WEST SIDE STORY records by members of orig cast. Carol Lawrence: "Something's Coming," "Tonight" (LP-356) Chita Rivera, 1973, with Pamela Myers (not of orig cast): "America" (LP-169) Larry Kert: "Maria," "Somewhere," "Tonight," "Something's Coming" (LP-616)

570926d WEST SIDE STORY 1966 studio prod. COND: Lawrence Leonard (of 1958 London prod). VOCALS: George Chakiris (of 1958 London & 1961 film casts); Bruce Trent, Lucille Graham, Mary Thomas, Joyce Berry. (Saga(E) EROS-8106)

570926e WEST SIDE STORY contemp album by members of 1958 London prod. COND: Lawrence Leonard. VOCALS: Don McKay, Marlys Watters. "Maria," "I Feel Pretty," "Tonight," "One Hand, One Heart" (45/HMV(E) 7EG-8429)

570926f WEST SIDE STORY 1962 records by George Chakiris of 1961 film cast. "Tonight," "Maria" (LP-482) (LP-562)

570926g WEST SIDE STORY studio prod. "Original London Cast." No credits. (La Brea 8003)

570926h WEST SIDE STORY album of ballet music. COND: Robert Prince. (Stanyan SR-10140, entitled "Bernstein's Broadway," with additional material)

570926i WEST SIDE STORY 1966 studio prod. COND: Alyn Ainsworth. CAST: David Holliday, Diane Todd, Tony Adams, Pat Gogh, Vince Logan, Franklyn Fox, Keith Galloway, Peter Johnson, chorus. (Music for Pleasure(E) 1070)

570926j WEST SIDE STORY 1962 studio prod. ORCH: Bobby Richards. COND: Kenneth Alwyn. CAST: Adele Leigh, Peter Hudson, chorus. (World Record Club(E) T-177, with Guys and Dolls)

570926k WEST SIDE STORY 1960 studio prod. ORCH & COND: Len Stevens. CAST: Janet Waters, Andy Cole, Frances Youles, chorus. (Ace of Clubs(E) 1035, with The Most Happy Fella)

571010a TAKE FIVE orig prod, rec live. MUSIC & WORDS: Bart Howard, Ronny Graham, Carolyn Leigh, Philip Springer, Steven Vinaver, Jonathan Tunick. ORCH: Stan Keen. CAST: Ronny Graham, Jean Arnold, Ceil Cabot, Ellen Hanley, Gerry Matthews. (Offbeat 4013)

571013a TV show PINOCCHIO orig prod. MUSIC: Alec Wilder. WORDS: William Engvick. ORCH & COND: Glenn Osser. CAST: Mickey Rooney, Fran Allison, Jerry Colonna, Stubby Kaye, Martyn Green, Gordon Clarke. (Col CL-1055)

571017a COPPER AND BRASS records by Dick Williams of orig cast. MUSIC: David Baker. WORDS: David Craig. COND: Ralph Burns (of orig prod). "You Walked Out," "Don't Look Now" (45/Dec 9-30476)

571031a JAMAICA orig prod. MUSIC: Harold Arlen. WORDS: E Y Harburg. ORCH: Philip J Lang. COND: Lehman Engel. CAST: Lena Horne, Ricardo Montalban, Adelaide Hall, Josephine Premice, Ossie Davis, Augustine Rios. (RCA LSO-1103 plus RCA LSO-1036. Neither has all the other has.)

571031b JAMAICA 1966 record sung by Harold Arlen, composer. "Little Biscuit" (LP-60)

571031c JAMAICA 1957 demonstration album by Harold Arlen (composer), vocals & piano, & Peter Matz, piano. (Mark 56 Records 683, entitled "Harold Arlen Sings," with additional material)

571031d JAMAICA soundtrack recording of "Ain't It the Truth"

by Lena Horne, dropped from the 1942 film "Cabin in the Sky". (LP-486) (LP-657) (LP-761)

571031e JAMAICA records by Lena Horne of orig cast. COND: Neal Hefti. "Push de Button," "Cocoanut Sweet" (45/RCA 47-7037)

571105a SHOESTRING '57 orig prod. MUSIC & WORDS: Lee Adams, Charles Strouse, Tom Jones, Harvey Schmidt, others. ORCH & COND: Dorothea Freitag. CAST: Beatrice Arthur, Fay deWitt, Dody Goodman, Dorothy Greener, John Bartis, Eddie Hilton, Bill McCutcheon, G Wood. (Offbeat 4012; Painted Smiles 1360 (entitled "Shoestring Revues") plus 1362 (entitled "Shoestring '57"), the latter including three additional songs from a rehearsal tape.)

571105b SHOESTRING '57 1980 record by composer Phil Springer (piano) & lyricist E Y Harburg (vocal). "Saroyan" (LP-741)

571112a TIME REMEMBERED 1958 studio prod. MUSIC & WORDS: Vernon Duke. ORCH: Vernon Duke. Vernon Duke at the piano, COND: Pete Rugolo. VOCALS: Tony Travis. (Mercury 20380)

571117a TV show GENERAL MOTORS 50TH ANNIVERSARY TELEVISION SHOW orig prod. MUSIC & WORDS: Various. COND: Bernard Green, Hugo Winterhalter. CAST: Pat Boone, Steve Lawrence, Dan Dailey, Carol Burnett, Cyril Ritchard, Claudia Crawford, Doretta Morrow, Dinah Shore, Howard Keel. (RCA LOC-1037)

571126a TV show THE PIED PIPER OF HAMELIN 1957 studio prod. MUSIC: Edvard Grieg. WORDS: Hal Stanley, Irving Taylor. COND: Pete King. CAST: Van Johnson of orig prod; a "soloist," quartet, and chorus. (RCA LPM-1563)

571204a TV show COME TO ME contemp records by Julie Wilson of orig cast. "Lilac Chiffon," "Come to Me" (45/Vik 4X-0312)

571219a THE MUSIC MAN orig prod. MUSIC & WORDS: Meredith Willson. COND: Herbert Greene. CAST: Robert Preston, Barbara Cook, Pert Kelton, Paul Reed, the Buffalo Bills, Eddie Hodges, Iggie Wolfington. (Cap SWAO-990)

571219b THE MUSIC MAN 1962 film soundtrack. COND: Ray Heindorf. CAST: Robert Preston, Shirley Jones, Buddy Hackett, Hermione Gingold, Pert Kelton, Ronnie Howard, the Buffalo Bills. (Warner Bros 1459. Excerpt: Preston: "Trouble" (LP-223).)

571219c THE MUSIC MAN 1961 London prod. COND: Gareth Davies. CAST: Van Johnson, Patricia Lambert, Bernard Spear, Denis Waterman, Ruth Kettlewell, Michael Malnick. (HMV(E) CSD-1361)

571219d THE MUSIC MAN contemp album with vocals by Meredith Willson (composer) and Rini Willson (his wife). PIANO: Meredith Willson. (Cap ST-1320)

571219e THE MUSIC MAN 1965 studio prod. COND: Fritz Wallberg. VOCALS: Frances Boyd, Ann Gordon, Rudy Cartier, Paul Mason, chorus. (Saga(E) SOC-1005)

571219f THE MUSIC MAN studio prod. COND: Enoch Light. CAST: Lois Winter, Artie Malvin, Jerry Duane, Willie Winkle, chorus. (Waldorf MHK-33-1248)

571219g THE MUSIC MAN 1958 album. COND: Fred Waring. VOCALS: Gordon Goodman, Chuck Nelson, Jeanne Steel, Patti Beems, Eleanor Forgione, chorus. (Cap T-989)

571219h THE MUSIC MAN studio prod. COND: Thomas M Davis, Hans Hagan. VOCALS: Ken Harp, Donna Cook, Connie Conway, Don Grilley, Patti Steele, Jackie Allen, Barbara Ford, Lucille Smith, Ken Remo, Ray Vasquez, Paul Ely, chorus. (Crown 5062)

571220a TV show JUNIOR MISS contemp album. MUSIC: Burton Lane. WORDS: Dorothy Fields. VOCALS: Vic Damone, Jo Stafford, chorus. "Junior Miss," "Happy Heart," "I'll Buy It," "Let's Make It Christmas All Year 'Round" (45/Col B-2142)

571230a TV show SEE IT NOW: THE LADY FROM PHILADELPHIA soundtrack. PIANO: Franz Rupp. NARRATOR: Edward R Murrow. VOCALS: Marian Anderson. (RCA LM-2212)

1958

580001a Film GIGI soundtrack. MUSIC: Frederick Loewe. WORDS: Alan Jay Lerner. ORCH: Conrad Salinger. COND: Andre Previn. CAST: Maurice Chevalier, Betty Wand (for Leslie Caron), Louis Jourdan, Hermione Gingold. (MGM 3641. Excerpts: Jourdan: "Gigi" Chevalier: "Thank Heaven for Little Girls" (LP-252) Chevalier, Gingold: "I Remember It Well" (LP-416).)

580001b Film GIGI 1959 studio prod. ORCH: Robert Russell Bennett. COND: John Green. CAST: Robert Merrill, Jane Powell, Phil Harris. (RCA LSP-2275, with Brigadoon)

580001c Film GIGI 1973 stage prod with 4 new Lerner-Loewe songs. ORCH: Irwin Kostal. COND: Ross Reimueller. CAST: Alfred Drake, Karin Wolfe, Daniel Massey, Maria Karnilova, Agnes Moorehead, George Gaynes, Howard Chitjian. (RCA ABL-1-0404)

580001d Film GIGI 1958 studio prod. COND: Dennis Farnon. VOCALS: Gogi Grant, Tony Martin, chorus. (RCA LSP-1716)

580001e Film GIGI 1958 French studio prod. WORDS: Alan Jay Lerner, Boris Vian. COND: Paul Baron. CAST: Maurice Chevalier of orig cast, Sacha Distel, Marie-France, Jane Marken. (Col WL-158)

580001f Film GIGI studio prod. COND: Cyril Stapleton. VOCALS: Ray Merril, Bryan Johnson, Joy Worth, chorus. (Richmond B-20074, with South Pacific)

580001g Film GIGI 1971 records sung by Alan Jay Lerner, lyricist. "Gigi," "I'm Glad I'm Not Young Anymore" (LP-534)

580001h Film GIGI 1963 studio prod. ORCH & COND: Bobby Richards. CAST: Ian Wallace, Maggie Fitzgibbon, Laurie Payne, Patricia Lynn, chorus. (World Record Club(E) T-191, with Funny Face)

580001i Film GIGI album. COND: Warren Edward Vincent. VOCALS: Helen Halpin, Jack Searle. (Design DLP-56)

580001j Film GIGI studio prod. COND: Vinny Parle. CAST: Raoul Martin, Margaret Young, George Abel, Dorothy Wilson. (Coronet CXS-68)

580001k Film GIGI 1958 studio prod. COND: Fontanna. CAST: Uncredited. (Masterseal 71)

580002a Industrial show GOOD NEWS ABOUT OLDS orig prod. (Includes 5 songs from "Good News") MUSIC & WORDS: Ray Henderson, B G DeSylva, Lew Brown, others. ORCH: Glen Osser, Luther Henderson. COND: Sherman Frank. CAST: Bill Hayes, Florence Henderson, chorus. (WOR 112272)

580003a Film TOM THUMB soundtrack. MUSIC & WORDS: Peggy Lee, Fred Spielman, Janice Torre, Kermit Goell. COND: Muir Mathieson. CAST: Russ Tamblyn, Ian Wallace, Stan Freberg, Norma Zimmer. (Lion 70084)

580004a COTTON CLUB REVUE 1958 orig prod. MUSIC: Clay Boland. WORDS: Benny Davis. ORCH & COND: Eddie Barefield. CAST: Cab Calloway, Malcolm Dodds, Mauri Leighton. (Gone 101)

580005a Film SEVEN HILLS OF ROME soundtrack. MUSIC & WORDS: Various. COND: George Stoll. VOCALS: Mario Lanza. (RCA LM-2211, with other songs by Lanza)

580006a Film ST. LOUIS BLUES contemp album by Nat Cole of orig cast. MUSIC & WORDS: W C Handy, others. ORCH & COND: Nelson Riddle (of orig prod). (Cap SW-993, with other songs by Handy)

580006b Film ST. LOUIS BLUES 1958 album by Pearl Bailey of orig cast. COND: Don Redman. (Roulette 25037)

580006c Film ST. LOUIS BLUES 1958 album by Eartha Kitt of orig cast. ORCH: Matty Matlock, Jester Hairston. COND: Shorty Rogers. (RCA LSP-1661)

580007a Film MARDI GRAS 1958 studio prod. MUSIC: Sammy Fain. WORDS: Paul Francis Webster. COND: Jimmy Carroll. CAST: Barry Frank, Janet Eden, Ralph Nyland, Lois Winter. (Bell 11)

580007b Film MARDI GRAS contemp album by Pat Boone of orig cast; Steve Allen. ORCH: Milton Rogers. COND: Billy Vaughn. Boone: "Bigger than Texas," "A Fiddle, a Rifle, an Axe, and a Bible," "Bourbon Street Blues" Boone, Allen: "Loyalty" (45/Dot DEP-1075)

580007c Film MARDI GRAS contemp album. VOCALS: Michael Stewart, Loren Becker, Jack Brown, Dottie Evans, chorus. (Waldorf 1405)

580008a Film MERRY ANDREW soundtrack. MUSIC: Saul Chaplin. WORDS: Johnny Mercer. ORCH & COND: Nelson Riddle. CAST: Danny Kaye, Betty Wand (for Pier Angeli), Salvatore Baccaloni, Robert Coote, Rex Evans. (Cap T-1016, with additional circus music)

580009a Film IT STARTED WITH A KISS contemp record by Debbie Reynolds of orig cast. "It Started with a Kiss" (LP-267)

580010a Record prod OMAHA! orig prod. MUSIC & WORDS: Stan Freberg. ORCH & COND: Billy May. CAST: Stan Freberg, Byron Kane, Frances Osborne. "Overture," "Whatta They Got in Omaha?," "Omaha Moon," "Omaha" (45/Cap EAP-1-1101)

580011a Film TUNNEL OF LOVE contemp record by Doris Day of orig cast. "Tunnel of Love" (LP-330)

580012a Film KING CREOLE soundtrack. MUSIC & WORDS: Various. VOCALS: Elvis Presley, chorus. (RCA LPM-1884)

580013a TROPICANA HOLIDAY contemp album of songs from 3 Tropicana Hotel (Las Vegas) shows by members of orig prods. MUSIC & WORDS: Gordon Jenkins. ORCH & COND: Gordon Jenkins. VOCALS: Elaine Dunn, Bill Lee, Dante d'Paulo, Carol Jarvis, Neile Adams, Bob Stevens, Sally Sweetland, George Chakiris, Don Williams. (Cap T-1048)

580014a Film GUNMAN'S WALK contemp record by Tab Hunter of orig cast. "I'm a Runaway" (45/Dot 15767)

580015a Film SOME CAME RUNNING contemp record by Frank Sinatra of orig prod. "To Love and Be Loved" (45/Cap F-4103)

580016a Film THUNDER ROAD contemp record by Robert Mitchum of orig prod. "The Ballad of Thunder Road" (LP-562)

580017a Film ROCK-A-BYE BABY contemp records by Jerry Lewis of orig cast. "Dormi, Dormi, Dormi," "Love Is a Lonely Thing" (45/Dec 9-30664)

580018a Film ANNA LUCASTA contemp record by Sammy Davis Jr of orig cast. "That's Anna" (45/Dec 9-30769)

580019a Record prod NEVER BE AFRAID orig prod. MUSIC: Lew Spence. WORDS: Marilyn Keith, Alan Bergman. NARRATION & VOCALS: Bing Crosby. (Golden A-198-22)

580020a Film WITNESS FOR THE PROSECUTION contemp record by Marlene Dietrich of orig cast. "I May Never Go Home Anymore" (45/Dot 15723)

580021a Film A CERTAIN SMILE contemp record by Johnny Mathis of orig prod. "A Certain Smile" (45/Col 4-33056)

580022a Film KINGS GO FORTH contemp record by Frank Sinatra of orig cast. "Monique" (45/Cap F-2700)

580023a Film MAN OF THE WEST contemp record by Julie London of orig prod. "Man of the West" (45/Liberty F-55157)

580024a Film THE BIG BEAT contemp album by Gogi Grant of orig cast. "Lazy Love," "Call Me," "You've Never Been in Love," "I Waited So Long" (45/RCA EPA-4185)

580025a Film MARACAIBO contemp record by Jean Wallace of orig cast. "Maracaibo Moon" (45/Dec 9-30652)

580026a Film SADDLE THE WIND contemp record by Julie London of orig cast. "Saddle the Wind" (45/Liberty F-55108)

580027a Film PARIS HOLIDAY contemp album (incl soundtrack) by Bob Hope of orig cast. MUSIC & WORDS: Various. ORCH & COND: Joseph Lilley (of orig prod). "April in Paris," "The Last Time I Saw Paris" With Bing Crosby (not of orig cast): "Paris Holiday," "Nothing in Common" (United Artists UAL-40001. The songs only: 45/United Artists UAE-10001.)

580028a Film HOUSEBOAT 1958 records by Sophia Loren of orig cast. MUSIC & WORDS: Jay Livingston, Ray Evans. "Almost in Love," "Bing! Bang! Bong!" (45/Col 4-41200)

580029a Film THE GIFT OF LOVE contemp record by Vic Damone of orig prod. "The Gift of Love" (45/Col 4-41085)

580030a Film HONG KONG AFFAIR contemp record by Ronnie Deauville of orig prod. "Hong Kong Affair" (45/ERA Records 1066)

580031a Film TEACHER'S PET record by Doris Day of orig cast. "Teacher's Pet" (LP-692)

580032a Film THE INN OF THE SIXTH HAPPINESS soundtrack. Children's chorus & Ingrid Bergman: "This Old Man" (45/20th Fox 45-126)

580033a Industrial record prod IT'S HOLIDAY TIME orig prod. MUSIC & WORDS: Michael Brown. ORCH & COND: Norman Paris. CAST: Michael Brown, Hal Linden, Anita Darian. (Unnamed label DC-52258)

580123a THE BODY BEAUTIFUL contemp records by Mindy Carson of orig cast. MUSIC: Jerry Bock. WORDS: Sheldon Harnick. "Hidden in My Heart," "Just My Luck" (45/Col 4-41091)

580204a OH CAPTAIN! orig prod. MUSIC: Jay Livingston. WORDS: Ray Evans, Jay Livingston. COND: Jay Blackton. CAST: Tony Randall, Jacquelyn McKeever, Edward Platt, Susan Johnson, Paul Valentine, Eileen Rodgers (for Abbe Lane). (Col AOS-2002)

580204b OH CAPTAIN! 1958 album sung by Jose Ferrer (director of orig prod) & Rosemary Clooney (his wife); chorus. ORCH & COND: Phil Moore. (MGM 3687)

580204c OH CAPTAIN! contemp records by Abbe Lane of orig cast. "Femininity," "We're Not Children" (45/RCA 47-7169)

580209a TV show HANS BRINKER OR THE SILVER SKATES orig prod. MUSIC & WORDS: Hugh Martin. ORCH & COND: Irwin Kostal, Fred Katz. CAST: Tab Hunter, Peggy King, Jarmila Novotna, Sheila Smith, Vinny Corrod, chorus. (Dot 9001)

580221a TV show ALADDIN orig prod. MUSIC & WORDS: Cole Porter. ORCH: Robert Russell Bennett. COND: Robert Emmett Dolan. CAST: Cyril Ritchard, Dennis King, Anna Maria Alberghetti, Sal Mineo, George Hall. (Col CL-1117)

580221b TV show ALADDIN 1959 London stage prod. COND: Bobby Howell. CAST: Bob Monkhouse, Doretta Morrow, Ronald Shiner, Ian Wallace, Alan Wheatley, chorus. (Col(E) SCX-3296)

580221c TV show ALADDIN "preview" album introduced by Cole Porter, composer. No credits for performers. "Aladdin," "Trust Your Destiny to a Star," "I Adore You," "Opportunity Knocks but Once" (Unnamed label 10" LP-42530)

580312a INTERNATIONAL SOIREE orig prod. MUSIC & WORDS: Various. ACCORDION & COND: Jo Basile. VOCALS: Patachou. (Audio Fidelity 5881)

580403a SAY, DARLING orig prod. MUSIC: Jule Styne. WORDS: Betty Comden, Adolph Green. ORCH & COND: Sid Ramin. CAST: David Wayne, Vivian Blaine, Johnny Desmond, Jerome Cowan, Mitchell Gregg, Steve Condos. (RCA LSO-1045)

580427a TV show HANSEL AND GRETEL orig prod. MUSIC: Alec Wilder. WORDS: William Engvick. ORCH & COND: Glenn Osser. CAST: Red Buttons, Barbara Cook, Rudy Vallee, Paula Lawrence, Stubby Kaye. (MGM 3690, with Suite from Humperdinck's Hansel and Gretel)

580513a CYRANO orig prod. MUSIC: David L Shire. WORDS: Richard Maltby Jr. ORCH & COND: Jay Brower. CAST: John Cunningham, Richard Cavett, Carrie Nye McGeoy, Toni Smith, J Jewett Langdon, Doug Banker, John Jenkins. (RCA unreleased album mx J80P-4263/4264)

580616a THE CROWNING EXPERIENCE contemp album by members of orig (Washington) prod & 1960 film prod. MUSIC & WORDS: Various. ORCH & COND: Paul Dunlap. VOCALS: Muriel Smith, Ann Buckles, Ted Nichols, chorus. (Cap MRA-101)

581002a VALMOUTH orig (London) prod. MUSIC & WORDS: Sandy Wilson. ORCH: Arthur Birkby. COND: Neville Meale. CAST: Cleo Laine, Barbara Couper, Doris Hare, Fenella Fielding, Patsy Rowlands, Denise Hirst, Marcia Ashton, Geoffrey Dunn, Alan Edwards, Peter Gilmore. (Pye(E) NSPL-18029)

581002b VALMOUTH 1972 records by Sandy Wilson (composer), piano & vocal. "Only a Passing Phase," "I Will Miss You" (LP-755)

581011a GOLDILOCKS orig prod. MUSIC: Leroy Anderson. WORDS: Joan Ford, Walter Kerr, Jean Kerr. ORCH: Leroy Anderson, Philip J Lang. COND: Lehman Engel. CAST: Don Ameche, Elaine Stritch, Russell Nype, Pat Stanley, Nathaniel Frey, Margaret Hamilton, Richard Armbruster, Gene Varrone. (Col OS-2007)

581011*a DEMI-DOZEN orig prod. MUSIC & WORDS: Harvey Schmidt, Tom Jones, Cy Coleman, Carolyn Leigh, Portia Nelson, Bud McCreery, others. ORCH: Stan Keen. CAST: Jean Arnold, Ceil Cabot, Jane Connell, Jack Fletcher, George Hall, Gerry Matthews. (Offbeat 4015)

581014a THE WORLD OF SUZIE WONG record used in orig prod. MUSIC: Richard Rodgers. WORDS: Lorenz Hart. Benny Goodman Quartet with Helen Ward, vocal: "How Can You Forget?" (45/BG Records 45-1)

581016a TV show LITTLE WOMEN orig prod. MUSIC & WORDS: Richard Adler. ORCH: Don Walker. COND: Hal Hastings. CAST: Jeanne Carson, Florence Henderson, Rise Stevens, Zina Bethune, Bill Hayes, Roland Winters. (Kapp 1104, with additional material)

581016b TV show LITTLE WOMEN contemp record by Bill Hayes of orig cast. "Love I Mean" (45/Cap K-242X)

581017a TV show AN EVENING WITH FRED ASTAIRE soundtrack. MUSIC & WORDS: Various. ORCH & COND: David Rose. VOCALS: Fred Astaire, Jonah Jones. (Chrysler Corp mx 1/2; DRG Records S3L-5181, entitled "Three Evenings with Fred Astaire," with two other Astaire TV shows; LP-338. Excerpt: LP-213)

581111a LA PLUME DE MA TANTE earlier Paris prod. MUSIC: Gerard Calvi. WORDS: Francis Blanche, Andre Maheux. COND: Gerard Calvi. CAST: Robert Dhery, Colette Brosset, Christian Duvaleix, & Jean Lefebvre of 1958 New York prod; Gerard Calvi (composer), Jean Carmet, Jacqueline Mille. (Vogue(F) LD-691-30)

581201a FLOWER DRUM SONG orig prod. MUSIC: Richard Rodgers. WORDS: Oscar Hammerstein II. ORCH: Robert Russell Bennett. COND: Salvatore Dell'Isola. CAST: Miyoshi Umeki, Pat Suzuki, Larry Blyden, Juanita Hall, Ed Kenney, Keye Luke, Arabella Hong, Pat Adiarte, Anita Ellis, Jack Soo. (Col OS-2009)

581201b FLOWER DRUM SONG 1961 film soundtrack. ORCH & COND: Alfred Newman. CAST: B J Baker (for Nancy Kwan), James Shigeta, Miyoshi Umeki, Juanita Hall, Jack Soo, Marilyn Horne (for Reiko Sato), John Dodson (for Kam Tong). (Dec 79098)

581201c FLOWER DRUM SONG 1960 London prod. ORCH: Robert Russell Bennett. COND: Robert Lowe. CAST: Yama Saki, Tim Herbert, Kevin Scott, Yau Shan Tung, Ida Shepley, Joan Pethers, Ruth Silvestre, Leon Thau, George Minami Jr. (Angel 35886)

581201d FLOWER DRUM SONG studio prod. COND: Al Goodman ("Dean Franconi"). CAST: Bill Hyer, Patricia Wong, Marchicko Lee, Rose Katagiri, Jonathon Hallee, Berea Lum. (Design 1011)

581201e FLOWER DRUM SONG 1959 album by Florence Henderson, chorus. COND: Sid Bass. (Camden 560, with Gypsy)

581201f FLOWER DRUM SONG 1958 studio prod. ORCH & COND: Jimmy Carroll. CAST: Cely Carrillo of orig prod; Edna McGriff, Jean Arnold, Wayne Sherwood, Artie Malvin, June Ericson, chorus. (Bell 13)

581201g FLOWER DRUM SONG 1964 studio prod. COND: Fritz Wallberg. CAST: Frances Boyd, Ann Gordon, Rudy Cartier, Paul Mason, chorus. (Society(E) 949)

581201h FLOWER DRUM SONG 1959 records by Pat Suzuki of orig cast. "I Enjoy Being a Girl," "Love, Look Away," "Sunday" (LP-410)

581201i FLOWER DRUM SONG studio prod. COND: John Benton Cross. VOCALS: Lynn Shizuko, Taruko Taketa, Jodie Elaine Moore, Gwen Richards, Anabell Lake, Jeffrey Lane, Don Vesta. (Crown 5105)

581201j FLOWER DRUM SONG 1960 studio prod. ORCH & COND: Len Stevens. VOCALS; Andy Cole, Janet Waters, Toni Eden, Frances Youles, Dennis MacGregor, Dave Carey, chorus. (Ace of Clubs(E) 1021)

581209a TV show THE GIFT OF THE MAGI orig prod. MUSIC & WORDS: Richard Adler. ORCH: Don Walker. COND: Hal Hastings. CAST: Sally Ann Howes, Allen Case, Bibi Osterwald, Howard St John. (United Artists 5013)

581222a WHOOP-UP orig prod, MUSIC: Moose Charlap. WORDS: Normal Gimbel. ORCH: Philip J Lang. COND: Stanley Lebowsky. CAST: Susan Johnson, Ralph Young, Romo Vincent, Sylvia Syms, Danny Meehan, Julienne Marie, Asia, Tony Gardell, Bobby Shields. (MGM 3745. Excerpt: Johnson: "Men" (LP-206).)

581223a A PARTY WITH BETTY COMDEN AND ADOLPH GREEN orig prod. MUSIC: Various. WORDS: Betty Comden, Adolph Green. COND: Peter Howard. VOCALS: Betty Comden, Adolph Green. (Cap SWAO-1197)(LP-170)

581223b A PARTY WITH BETTY COMDEN AND ADOLPH GREEN 1977 prod, with some new material, rec live 1 May 1977 in Washington. PIANO: Paul Trueblood. CAST: Betty Comden, Adolph Green. (Stet S2L-5177)(LP-489)

581227a THREE TO MAKE MUSIC orig prod. MUSIC: Linda Rodgers Melnick. WORDS: Mary Rodgers. ORCH: Robert Russell Bennett. COND: Thomas Scherman.CAST: Mary Martin, Dirk Sanders. (RCA LPM-2012, with Cinderella)

1959

590001a Industrial show WHO COULD ASK FOR ANYTHING MORE orig prod. (Includes 5 songs from "Girl Crazy") MUSIC & WORDS: George & Ira Gershwin, others. ORCH: Glenn Osser, Luther Henderson. COND: Sherman Frank. CAST: Bill Hayes, Florence Henderson, chorus. (Unnamed label mx CC-1190/1)

590002a Film SOME LIKE IT HOT soundtrack. MUSIC & WORDS: Various. COND: Matty Malneck, Adolph Deutsch. CAST: Marilyn Monroe, the Society Syncopators. (United Artists 4030 plus "Some Like It Hot" (dropped before release) on LP-452. Excerpts: Monroe: "I Wanna Be Loved by You," "I'm Through with Love," "Runnin' Wild" (LP-120).)

590002b Film SOME LIKE IT HOT 1959 album by Jack Lemmon of orig cast. ORCH & COND: Marion Evans. (Epic 3559, with other songs by Lemmon)

590003a Film THE FIVE PENNIES soundtrack. MUSIC & WORDS: Various. ORCH & COND: Leith Stevens. CAST: Danny Kaye, Louis Armstrong, Susan Gordon. (Dot 29500)

590004a Film FOR THF FIRST TIME soundtrack, MUSIC & WORDS: Various. COND: Franco Ferrara. VOCALS: Mario Lanza. (RCA LSC-2338)

590005a Film LA PARISIENNE soundtrack. Christiane Legrand (for Brigitte Bardot): "Paris B. B.," "Un Peu de Toi," "La Parisienne," "Duo du Balcon" (45/United Artists UAE-10002)

590006a Film SAY ONE FOR ME soundtrack. MUSIC: James Van Heusen. WORDS: Sammy Cahn. CAST: Bing Crosby, Debbie Reynolds, Robert Wagner, Judy Harriet. (Col CS-8147)

590006b Film SAY ONE FOR ME contemp album. COND: Tutti Camarata. VOCALS: Rex Allen, Roberta Shore, Tony Paris. (Buena Vista 1302)

590007a Film THE MATING GAME contemp record by Debbie Reynolds of orig cast. MUSIC: Charles Strouse. WORDS: Lee Adams. "The Mating Game" (LP-267)

590008a Film ALIAS JESSE JAMES contemp records by Bob Hope of orig cast & Rosemary Clooney. "Protection," "Ain't a-Hankerin'" (45/RCA 47-7517)

590009a Film PILLOW TALK contemp records by members of orig cast. Doris Day; "Pillow Talk" (LP-330) "Inspiration" (45/Col 4-41463) Rock Hudson: "Pillow Talk," "Roly Poly" (45/Dec 9-30966)

590010a Film SLEEPING BEAUTY soundtrack. MUSIC & WORDS: Various. COND: George Bruns. VOCALS: Mary Costa, Bill Shirley, chorus. (Disneyland 4018) (LP-661)

590011a Film HAPPY ANNIVERSARY contemp records by Mitzi Gaynor of orig cast. "Happy Anniversary," "I Don't Regret a Thing" (45/Laurie 3050) "Play for Keeps" (45/Top Rank(E) JAR-258)

590012a Film TOMMY THE TOREADOR soundtrack. MUSIC & WORDS: Lionel Bart, Michael Pratt, Jimmy Bennett. COND: Stanley Black. Tommy Steele: "Tommy the Toreador," "Take a Ride," "A Little White Bull," "Singing Time," "Amanda" Steele, Sidney James, Bernard Cribbens: "Where's the Birdie?" (45/Dec(E) DFE-6607)

590013a Film SENIOR PROM contemp records by members of orig prod. Louis Prima & Keely Smith: "That Old Black Magic" (by Harold Arlen, Johnny Mercer) (45/Cap F-4063) Paul Hampton: "Love," "The Longer I Love You" Jill Corey: "Big Daddy" (45/Col B-2148)

590014a Film A HOLE IN THE HEAD records by Sammy Cahn, lyricist. MUSIC: James Van Heusen. "High Hopes" (1972: LP-658) (1977: LP-503)

590014b Film A HOLE IN THE HEAD contemp records by Frank Sinatra of orig cast. "High Hopes," "All My Tomorrows" (45/Cap F-4214)

590015a Film IT HAPPENED TO JANE contemp records by Doris Day of orig cast. "Be Prepared," "It Happened to Jane" (45/Col 4-41391) "Twinkle and Shine" (45/Col 4-41993)

590016a Record prod THE NINA, THE PINTA AND THE SANTA MARIA orig prod. MUSIC & WORDS: mostly Ray Gilbert. COND: Neely Plumb. VOCALS Eddie Albert, Joanne Gilbert, Thurl Ravenscroft, Lee Millar. (Dot 29009)

590016b Record prod THE NINA, THE PINTA AND THE SANTA MARIA 1971 record prod. COND: Don Ralke. CAST: Sterling Holloway, Janis Paige, Sidney Miller, Cesar Romero. (Jellybean 1492, entitled "We Think the World Is Round")

590017a Film THE HANGING TREE contemp record by Marty Robbins of orig prod. "The Hanging Tree" (45/Coral 4-41325)

590018a Film GIDGET contemp record by James Darren of orig prod. "Gidget" (45/Good Old Gold 041)

590019a Film CAREER contemp record by Dean Martin of orig cast. "Love Is a Career" (45/Cap 4287)

590020a Film THE BIG CIRCUS 1959 record by Rhonda Fleming of orig cast. "The Big Circus" (LP-702)

590021a Record prod THE LETTER orig prod. MUSIC & WORDS: Gordon Jenkins. ORCH & COND: Gordon Jenkins. NARRATOR: John Ireland. VOCALS: Judy Garland, Charley LaVere, chorus. (Cap STAO-1188; Cap ST-1941, entitled "Our Love Letter")

590022a Film NIGHT OF THE QUARTER MOON contemp records by Nat Cole of orig cast. "Night of the Quarter Moon," "To Whom It May Concern" (45/Cap EAP-1-1211)

590023a MY FAIRFAX LADY orig (Los Angeles) prod. MUSIC & WORDS: Sid Kuller. ORCH & COND: Jerry Fielding. CAST: Billy Gray, Bert Gordon, Carol Shannon, chorus. (Jubilee JGM-2030)

590024a Industrial record prod HOLIDAY IN FASHION orig prod. MUSIC & WORDS: Michael Brown. ORCH & COND: Norman Paris. CAST: Hal Linden, Marlene VerPlanck, Michael Brown. (Unnamed label DC-10158)

590025a Film RIO BRAVO contemp records by Dean Martin of orig cast. "Rio Bravo," "My Rifle, My Pony and Me" (45/Cap F-4174)

590121a BE MY GUEST orig (Winnetka, Illinois) prod. MUSIC & WORDS: Various. COND: Bob Moreen. CAST: Ann-Margret Olson, Bill Ade, Kay Knopf, Linda Ruck, Lois Greenfield, chorus. (Unnamed label mx XCTV-10302/3)

590122a SHE SHALL HAVE MUSIC 1963 Granville, Ohio prod. MUSIC & WORDS: Dede Meyer. COND: Wayne Wentzel, CAST: John Davidson, Don Stickler, Alfred Bonney, Mary Kay Williams, Barbara Daines, Lynne Olsen. (Unnamed label FR-6205)

590201a TV show NO MAN CAN TAME ME orig prod. MUSIC & WORDS: Jay Livingston, Ray Evans. VOCALS: Gisele MacKenzie, Eddie Foy, chorus. (Empire EBC-59-7487)

590205a REDHEAD orig prod. MUSIC: Albert Hague. WORDS: Dorothy Fields. ORCH: Philip J Lang, Robert Russell Bennett. COND: Jay Blackton. CAST: Gwen Verdon, Richard Kiley, Leonard Stone, Doris Rich, Cynthia Latham, Joy Nichols, Pat Ferrier, Bob Dixon. (RCA LSO-1104)

590205b REDHEAD 1959 studio prod. COND: Hill Bowen. CAST: Rita Williams, Bryan Johnson, Fred Lucas. (Camden 521)

590309a JUNO orig prod. MUSIC & WORDS: Marc Blitzstein.

ORCH: Robert Russell Bennett, Marc Blitzstein, Hershy Kay. COND: Robert Emmett Dolan. CAST: Shirley Booth, Melvyn Douglas, Jack MacGowran, Monte Amundsen, Loren Driscoll, Robert Hoyem, Jean Stapleton, Nancy Andrews. (Col OS-2013)

590309b JUNO demonstration album by Marc Blitzstein (composer), vocals & piano. Includes 5 songs dropped from the show. (JJA Records 19772, with No for an Answer)

590319a FIRST IMPRESSIONS orig prod. MUSIC & WORDS: Robert Goldman, Glenn Paxton, George Weiss. ORCH: Don Walker. COND: Frederick Dvonch. CAST: Polly Bergen, Farley Granger, Hermione Gingold, Christopher Hewett, Donald Madden, Phyllis Newman, Lois Bewley, Lynn Ross, Lauri Peters. (Col OS-2014)

590423a DESTRY RIDES AGAIN orig prod. MUSIC & WORDS: Harold Rome. ORCH: Philip J Lang. COND: Lehman Engel. CAST: Andy Griffith, Dolores Gray, Jack Prince, Elizabeth Watts, Rosetta LeNoire. (Dec 79075)

590423b DESTRY RIDES AGAIN 1959 album by Jack Haskell & Louise O'Brien. COND: Norman Leyden. (Camden 540)

590430a GRAND TOUR orig (New Haven) prod. MUSIC & WORDS: Richard Maltby Jr, David L Shire. ORCH: Christopher Porterfield. COND: Arthur Rubinstein. CAST: Gretchen Cryer, Edith Lebok, Robert Driscoll, Bill Hinnant, Mary Jane Wilson, Geoffrey Waddell. (Carillon mx K80P-6075/6)

590511a ONCE UPON A MATTRESS orig prod. MUSIC: Mary Rodgers. WORDS: Marshall Barer. ORCH: Hershy Kay, Arthur Beck. COND: Hal Hastings. CAST: Joe Bova, Carol Burnett, Allen Case, Anne Jones, Matt Mattox, Jane White, Harry Snow, Robert Weil, Jack Gilford. (Kapp 7004)

590511b ONCE UPON A MATTRESS 1960 London prod. COND: Robert Lowe. CAST: Jane Connell, Peter Grant, Patricia Lambert, Bill Newman, Thelma Ruby, Max Wall. (HMV(E) CLP-1410)

590512a THE NERVOUS SET orig prod. MUSIC: Tommy Wolf. WORDS: Fran Landesman. ORCH & COND: Tommy Wolf. CAST: Richard Hayes, Tani Seitz, Larry Hagman, Del Close, Gerald Hiken, Thomas Aldredge. (Col OS-2018)

590521a GYPSY orig prod. MUSIC: Jule Styne. WORDS: Stephen Sondheim. ORCH: Sid Ramin, Robert Ginzler. COND: Milton Rosenstock. CAST: Ethel Merman, Jack Klugman, Sandra Church, Karen Moore, Jacqueline Mayro, Lane Bradbury, Paul Wallace. (Col OS-2017)

590521b GYPSY 1962 film soundtrack. ORCH: Carl Brandt, Frank Perkins. COND: Frank Perkins, Jule Styne. CAST: Rosalind Russell, Lisa Kirk (for Rosalind Russell), Natalie Wood, Karl Malden, Paul Wallace, Ann Jilliann, Suzanne Cupito, Diane Pace. (Warner Bros 1480)

590521c GYPSY records by Ethel Merman of orig prod. "Everything's Coming Up Roses" (1972: LP-153)(1977: LP-652)(1979: LP-670) "Some People" (1979: LP-670)

590521d GYPSY 1973 London prod. COND: Richard Leonard. CAST: Angela Lansbury, Zan Charisse, Barrie Ingham, Andrew Norman, Debbie Bowen, Bonnie Langford. (RCA(E) SER-5686. Remixed, with slight alterations: RCA LBL1-5004.)

590521e GYPSY 1959 album by Florence Henderson, chorus. COND: Sid Bass. (Camden 560, with Flower Drum Song)

590521f GYPSY 1962 album. COND: Bob Sharples. VOCALS: Joyce Blair, Jan Waters, Bryan Johnson. (45/Dec(E) STO-8513)

590521g GYPSY 1969 studio prod. COND: Alyn Ainsworth.CAST: Kay Medford, Lorraine Smith, Sonya Petrie, Jimmy Blackburn, Richard Fox, Janet Webb, Janette Gale, Betty Wimsett. (Music for Pleasure(E) 1308)

590521h GYPSY 1976 South African prod. COND: Boris Cohen. CAST: Libby Morris, Joe Stewardson, Kim Braden, Bonnie Langford, Roz Monat, Hermann Jay Muller. (Philips(South Africa) STO-774)

590521i GYPSY 1966 record by Jule Styne (composer), piano. "Small World" (LP-671)

590528a LOCK UP YOUR DAUGHTERS orig (London) prod. MUSIC: Laurie Johnson. WORDS: Lionel Bart. COND: Laurie Johnson. CAST: Richard Wordsworth, Stephanie Voss, Hy Hazell, Robin Wentworth, Keith Marsh, Frederick Jaeger, Terence Cooper. (Dec(E) SKL-4070)

590609a THE BILLY BARNES REVUE orig prod. MUSIC & WORDS: Billy Barnes. PIANOS: Billy Barnes, Armin Hoffman. CAST: Joyce Jameson, Bert Convy, Jackie Joseph, Ken Berry, Ann Guilbert, Bob Rodgers, Patti Regan, Len Weinrib. (Dec 79076)

590626a THE STEPHEN FOSTER STORY orig(?) (Bardstown, Ky) prod. MUSIC & WORDS: Stephen Foster. ORCH: Isaac van Grove. COND: Ralph Burrier. CAST: Jay Willoughby, Naymond Thomas, Lynn Collner, Jeanette Sallee, Kenn Maxwell. (Audio-Visual Corp GR-3990)

590626b THE STEPHEN FOSTER STORY 1966 Bardstown, Ky, prod. COND: Willis Beckett. CAST: Richard Stilwell, Mitzi Friedlander, William Lathon, Jeanette Sallee, chorus. (Unnamed label mx XSBV-111386/7)

590924a PIECES OF EIGHT orig prod. MUSIC & WORDS: Various. ORCH: William Roy. CAST: Ceil Cabot, Jane Connell, Del Close, Gerry Matthews, Gordon Connell, Estelle Parsons. (Offbeat 4016)

591022a TAKE ME ALONG orig prod. MUSIC & WORDS: Bob Merrill. ORCH: Philip J Lang. COND: Lehman Engel. CAST: Jackie Gleason, Walter Pidgeon, Eileen Herlie, Robert Morse, Una Merkel, Susan Luckey, P Conlow. (RCA LSO-1050)

591022b TAKE ME ALONG studio prod. ORCH: Philip J Lang. COND: Russ Case. VOCALS: Uncredited soloists, chorus. (Rondolette 866)

591102a THE GIRLS AGAINST THE BOYS orig prod, rec live. MUSIC: Richard Lewine. WORDS: Arnold B Horwitt. Bert Lahr: "Old-Fashioned Girl" (LP-608)

591102b THE GIRLS AGAINST THE BOYS contemp album. Dakota Staton: "Where Did We Go? Out." Jonah Jones Orch: "Where Did We Go? Out." King Sisters: "Girls and Boys" Tommy Sands: "I Gotta Have You" (45/Cap PRO-1429)

591104a TV show ANOTHER EVENING WITH FRED ASTAIRE soundtrack. MUSIC & WORDS: Various. ORCH: David Rose. COND: David Rose, Jonah Jones. VOCALS: Fred Astaire, Jonah Jones, chorus. (Chrysler Corp mx K80P-1087/8; DRG Records S3L-5181, entitled "Three Evenings with Fred Astaire," with two other Astaire TV shows. Excerpt: LP-213.)

591113a TV show MUSIC FROM SHUBERT ALLEY orig prod. MUSIC & WORDS: Various. ORCH & COND: Vic Schoen. CAST: Andy Williams, Alfred Drake, Lisa Kirk, Ray Walston, Doretta Morrow, Betty Comden, Adolph Green. (Sinclair 2250)(LP-294)

591116a THE SOUND OF MUSIC orig prod. MUSIC: Richard Rodgers. WORDS: Oscar Hammerstein II. ORCH: Robert Russell Bennett. COND: Frederick Dvonch. CAST: Mary Martin, Theodore Bikel, Patricia Neway, Kurt Kasznar, Marion Marlowe, Lauri Peters, Brian Davies. (Col KOS-2020)

591116b THE SOUND OF MUSIC 1960 album by the Trapp Family Singers. ORCH & COND: Franz Wasner. (RCA LSP-2277)

591116c THE SOUND OF MUSIC 1965 film soundtrack, with additional music and words by Richard Rodgers. ORCH & COND:

Irwin Kostal. CAST: Julie Andrews, Bill Lee (for Christopher Plummer), Dan Truhitte, Charmian Carr, Marjorie McKay (for Peggy Wood). (RCA LSOD-2005)

591116d THE SOUND OF MUSIC 1960 album by Florence Henderson (of 1961 touring prod). COND: Sid Bass. (Camden 599, with Fiorello!)

591116e THE SOUND OF MUSIC 1961 London prod. COND: Robert Lowe. CAST: Jean Bayless, Olive Gilbert, Constance Shacklock, Roger Dann, Barbara Brown, Eunice Gayson, Harold Kasket. (HMV(E) CSD-1365)

591116f THE SOUND OF MUSIC 1961 Australian prod. COND: Eric Clapham. CAST: June Bronhill, Peter Graves, Rosina Raisbeck, Julie Day, Tony Jenkins, Lola Brooks, Eric Reiman. (HMV(Australia) OCSD-7580)

591116g THE SOUND OF MUSIC 1965 album. COND: Robert Lowe. VOCALS: Mary Martin of orig cast, uncredited baritone, chorus. (Disneyland 1296)

591116h THE SOUND OF MUSIC album. COND: Al Goodman ("Dean Franconi"). VOCALS: Bill Heyer, Jane A Johnston, chorus. (Design 135)

591116i THE SOUND OF MUSIC studio prod. "The London Theatre Company." No other credits given. (Richmond(E) 30079)

591116j THE SOUND OF MUSIC 1965 studio prod. ORCH & COND: Sam Fonteyn. VOCALS: Maureen Hartley, Charles West, Shirley Chapman, Richard Loaring, Heather Bishop, chorus. (Music for Pleasure(E) 1007)

591116k THE SOUND OF MUSIC 1966 studio prod. COND: Alyn Ainsworth. CAST: Anne Rogers, Patricia Routledge, Gordon Traynor, Kay Frazer, Ray Cornell, chorus. (Music for Pleasure(E) 1255)

591116l THE SOUND OF MUSIC 1977 record by Mary Martin of orig cast. "My Favorite Things" (LP-652)

591118a LITTLE MARY SUNSHINE orig prod. MUSIC & WORDS: Rick Besoyan. ORCH: Arnold Goland. COND: Glenn Osser. CAST: Eileen Brennan, William Graham, Elmarie Wendel, John McMartin, Mario Siletti, Elizabeth Parrish, John Aniston. (Cap SWAO-1240)

591118b LITTLE MARY SUNSHINE 1962 London prod. COND: Philip Martell. CAST: Patricia Routledge, Bernard Cribbins, Joyce Blair, Terence Cooper, Gita Denise, Erik Chitty. (Pye(E) NPL-18071)

591123a FIORELLO! orig prod. MUSIC: Jerry Bock. WORDS: Sheldon Harnick. ORCH: Irwin Kostal. COND: Hal Hastings. CAST: Tom Bosley, Patricia Wilson, Ellen Hanley, Howard DaSilva, Nathaniel Frey, Pat Stanley, Eileen Rodgers, Bob Holiday. (Cap SWAO-1321)

591123b FIORELLO! 1960 album by Florence Henderson. COND: Sid Bass. (Camden 599, with The Sound of Music)

591123c FIORELLO! 1971 records sung by Sheldon Harnick, lyricist. "'Til Tomorrow" (with Margery Gray, Mary Louise), "Little Tin Box" (LP-535)

591123d FIORELLO! 1961 record by Ron Husmann of orig cast of a song dropped from the show. "Where Do I Go from Here?" (LP-713)

591125a TV show THE GOLDEN CIRCLE contemp album by members of orig prod. MUSIC & WORDS: Various. ORCH & COND: Don Costa. VOCALS: Eydie Gorme, Steve Lawrence. (ABC mx 311)

591207a SARATOGA orig prod. MUSIC: Harold Arlen, Johnny Mercer. WORDS: Johnny Mercer. ORCH: Philip J Lang. COND:

Jerry Arlen. CAST: Howard Keel, Carol Lawrence, Odette Myrtil, Carol Brice. (RCA LSO-1051)

1960

600001a Film LET'S MAKE LOVE soundtrack. MUSIC: James Van Heusen. WORDS: Sammy Cahn. COND: Lionel Newman. CAST: Marilyn Monroe, Yves Montand, Frankie Vaughan. (Col CS-8327)

600002a Film PEPE soundtrack. MUSIC & WORDS: Various. ORCH: John Green. COND: John Green, Andre Previn. CAST: Shirley Jones, Maurice Chevalier, Sammy Davis jr, Bobby Darin, Judy Garland, Bing Crosby. (Colpix 507)

600003a Film CINDERFELLA 1961 studio prod. MUSIC: Harry Warren, Walter Scharf. WORDS: Jack Brooks. ORCH & COND: Walter Scharf. CAST: Jerry Lewis of orig cast; Del Moore, Loulie Jean Norman, Salli Terri, Bill Lee, Max Smith. (Dot 38001)

600004a Film THE GENE KRUPA STORY soundtrack. MUSIC & WORDS: Various. ORCH: Leith Stevens. DRUMS: Gene Krupa. VOCALS: Ruby Lane, Anita O'Day. (Verve 15010)

600005a Film PLEASE DON'T EAT THE DAISIES contemp record by Doris Day of orig cast. "Please Don't Eat the Daisies" (LP-330)

600006a Film JOURNEY TO THE CENTER OF THE EARTH soundtrack. Pat Boone: "The Faithful Heart," "Twice as Tall," "To the Center of the Earth," "My Love Is Like a Red, Red Rose" (45/Dot DEP-1091)

600007a Film FLAMING STAR contemp record by Elvis Presley of orig cast. "Flaming Star" (RCA 7" LPC-128, entitled "Elvis by Request," with 3 other songs)

600008a Film G.I. BLUES soundtrack. MUSIC & WORDS: Various. VOCALS: Elvis Presley, chorus. (RCA LSP-2256)

600009a Film HIGH TIME 1977 record by Sammy Cahn, lyricist. MUSIC: James Van Heusen. "The Second Time Around" (LP-503)

600010a Film OCEAN'S ELEVEN contemp records by Sammy Davis jr of orig cast. "Ain't That a Kick in the Head," "Eee-o Eleven" (45/Verve 10219)

600011a Film POLLYANNA orig prod, incl 3 songs. Hayley Mills: "Pollyanna's Song," "America the Beautiful" Chorus: "The Glad Game" (Disneyland 1307)

600012a Film THE ALAMO contemp records by Frankie Avalon of orig prod. "Ballad of the Alamo," "Tennessee Babe," "The Green Leaves of Summer," "Here's to the Ladies" (45/Chancellor CHLA-303)

600013a Film HOUND-DOG MAN contemp records by Fabian of orig cast. "Hound-Dog Man," "Pretty Little Girl," "This Friendly World," "Single," "I'm Growin' Up" (45/Chancellor CHLA-301)

600014a Film GUNS OF THE TIMBERLAND contemp records by Frankie Avalon of orig prod. "The Faithful Kind," "Gee Whiz - Whilikins - Golly Gee" (45/Chancellor CHLA-302)

600015a Film BECAUSE THEY'RE YOUNG 1961 record by James Darren of orig cast. "Because They're Young" (LP-688)

600016a Film THE SUBTERRANEANS 1959 record by Carmen McRae of orig cast. "Coffee Time" (LP-702)

600103a FOUR BELOW STRIKES BACK orig prod. WORDS & MUSIC: Various. CAST: Jenny Lou Law, Nancy Dussault, George Furth, Cy Young. (Offbeat 4017)

600120a PARADE orig prod. MUSIC & WORDS: Jerry Herman. PIANOS: Jerry Herman, Jack Elliott. CAST: Dody Goodman, Richard Tone, Fia Karin, Charles Nelson Reilly, Lester James. (Kapp 7005)

600201a Industrial show SING A SONG OF SEWING orig prod. MUSIC & WORDS: Michael Brown. ORCH & COND: Norman Paris. CAST: Dorothy Loudon, Marge Redmond, Michael Brown, Ellen Martin, Betty Ann Busch, Walter Farrell. (Unnamed label A&R 1095)

600210a BEG, BORROW OR STEAL 1959 record prod. MUSIC: Leon Pober. WORDS: Bud Freeman. ORCH & COND: Hal Hidey. CAST: Betty Garrett of 1960 stage prod; Jimmie Komack, Johnny Standley, Sid Tomack. (Commentary 02, entitled "Clara")

600211a FINGS AIN'T WOT THEY USED T' BE orig (London) prod. MUSIC & WORDS: Lionel Bart. COND: Ronnie Franklin. CAST: Glynn Edwards, Miriam Karlin, Paddy Joyce, Tom Chatto, Wallas Eaton, Barbara Windsor, James Booth, Edward Caddick. (Dec(E) SKL-4092)

600211b FINGS AIN'T WOT THEY USED T' BE 1960 studio prod. ORCH: Tony Osborne. COND: Tony Osborne, John Barry. CAST: Lionel Bart (composer), Alfie Bass, Adam Faith, Harry Fowler, Joan Heal, Sidney James, Alfred Marks, Marion Ryan, Tony Tanner. (HMV(E) CSD-1298)

600308a GREENWILLOW orig prod. MUSIC & WORDS: Frank Loesser. ORCH: Don Walker. COND: Abba Bogin. CAST: Anthony Perkins, Cecil Kellaway, Pert Kelton, Ellen McCown, William Chapman, Lee Cass, Bruce MacKay, Lynn Brinker. (RCA LSO-2001)

600414a BYE BYE BIRDIE orig prod. MUSIC: Charles Strouse. WORDS: Lee Adams. ORCH: Robert Ginzler. COND: Elliot Lawrence. CAST: Chita Rivera, Dick Van Dyke, Susan Watson, Dick Gautier, Paul Lynde, Marijane Maricle, Johnny Borden. (Col KOS-2025)

600414b BYE BYE BIRDIE soundtrack of 1963 film. ORCH: John Green, Albert Woodbury, Hank Levine. COND: John Green, Hank Levine. CAST: Janet Leigh, Dick Van Dyke, Ann-Margret, Bobby Rydell, Jesse Pearson, Paul Lynde, Maureen Stapleton, Bryan Russell, Mary La Roche. (RCA LSO-1081)

600414c BYE BYE BIRDIE 1961 London prod. ORCH: Robert Ginzler. COND: Alyn Ainsworth. CAST: Chita Rivera, Peter Marshall, Marty Wilde, Sylvia Tysick, Robert Nichol, Mary Laura Wood. (Mercury 17000)

600414d BYE BYE BIRDIE 1962 album by Bobby Rydell of 1963 film cast; chorus. ORCH & COND: Jack Pleis. (Cameo 1043)

600414e BYE BYE BIRDIE album. ORCH & COND: Stu Phillips. VOCALS: James Darren, Shelley Fabares, Paul Petersen, Stu Phillips, the Marcels, chorus. (Colpix SCP-454)

600414f BYE BYE BIRDIE 1963 record by Dick Van Dyke of orig & 1963 film prods. "Put On a Happy Face" (LP-691)

600428a CHRISTINE orig prod. MUSIC: Sammy Fain. WORDS: Paul Francis Webster. ORCH: Philip J Lang. COND: Jay Blackton. CAST: Maureen O'Hara, Morley Meredith, Nancy Andrews, Janet Pavek, Phil Leeds, Leslye Hunter, Barbara Webb, Bhaskar. (Col OS-2026)

600428*a TOM JONES orig (New Haven) prod. MUSIC: Robert Archer. WORDS: Joseph Mathewson, Peter Bergman. ORCH & COND: Arthur Rubinstein. CAST: Philip G Proctor, Winthrop Brainerd, Mary Jane Wilson, Arden Staroba, chorus. (Carillon mx L80P-5436/7)

600503a THE FANTASTICKS orig prod. MUSIC: Harvey Schmidt. WORDS: Tom Jones. ORCH & COND: Julian Stein. CAST: Kenneth Nelson, Jerry Orbach, Rita Gardner, William Larsen, Hugh Thomas. (MGM 3872)

600503b THE FANTASTICKS 1964 records by Ed Ames of 1961 New York cast. "Try to Remember," "They Were You" (LP-212)

600503c THE FANTASTICKS 1962 record by Jerry Orbach of orig cast. "Try to Remember" (LP-420)

600503d THE FANTASTICKS 1964 TV prod soundtrack. Stanley Holloway, Bert Lahr: "Plant a Radish" (LP-608)(LP-620)

600504a ERNEST IN LOVE orig prod. MUSIC: Lee Pockriss. WORDS: Anne Croswell. ORCH: Gershon Kingsley. COND: Liza Redfield. CAST: Leila Martin, John Irving, Louis Edmonds, Gerrianne Raphael, Sara Seegar, Alan Shayne, George Hall, Lucy Landau. (Col OS-2027)

600619a Pageant FREEDOMLAND U.S.A. orig prod. MUSIC: Jule Styne. WORDS: George Weiss. ORCH & COND: Frank DeVol. VOCALS: Johnny Horton, Jill Corey, Richard Hayes, Jimmy Rushing, Cliff Arquette, Earl Wrightson. (Col CS-8275)

600622a CALL IT LOVE 1960 album by members of orig (London) prod. VOCALS: Sandy Wilson. VOCALS: Richard Owens, Penelope Newington, Karin Clair, Jacqueline Guise, Roderick Joyce, Norman Warwick. "Love Play," "Love Song in Rag," "I Know, Know, Know," "Hate Each Other," "Call It Love" (45/Dec(E) DFE-6640)

600630a OLIVER! 1962 studio prod. MUSIC & WORDS: Lionel Bart. COND: Tony Osborne. CAST: Stanley Holloway, Alma Cogan, Violet Carson, Denis Waterman, Tony Tanner, Leslie Fyson, Charles Granville. (Cap ST-1784)

600630b OLIVER! 1968 film soundtrack. ORCH & COND: John Green. CAST: Ron Moody, Harry Secombe, Shani Wallis, Mark Lester, Jack Wild, Sheila White, Peggy Mount. (Colgems 5501)

600630c OLIVER! 1963 New York prod. ORCH: Eric Rogers. COND: Donald Pippin. CAST: Clive Revill, Georgia Brown, Bruce Prochnik, Hope Jackman, Willoughby Goddard, Alice Playten, Danny Sewell; Michael Goodman (of tryout cast but replaced by David Jones before the show opened). (RCA LSOD-2004)

600630d OLIVER! orig (London) prod. ORCH: Eric Rogers. COND: Marcus Dods. CAST: Keith Hamshere, Paul Whitsun-Jones, Hope Jackman, Martin Horsey, Georgia Brown, Ron Moody, Danny Sewell. (Dec(E) SKL-4105)

600630e OLIVER! studio prod. ORCH: Bobby Richards. COND: Kenneth Alwyn. CAST: David Hovell, William Dickey, Rose Hill, Mike Sammes, Ian Carmichael, Stephen Marriott, Joyce Blair, chorus. (World Records(E) TP-151)

600630f OLIVER! 1966 studio prod. COND: Geoff Love. CAST: Tommy Mann (of 1966 English touring prod), Nicolette Roeg (who replaced Georgia Brown in orig London prod), Jim Dale, Blanche Moore, Fred Lucas, Charles Granville, chorus. (Music for Pleasure(E) 1073)

600900a Industrial show A BIRTHDAY GARLAND FOR MR. JAMES CASH PENNEY orig prod. MUSIC & WORDS: Michael Brown. ORCH & COND: Norman Paris. CAST: Michael Brown, Walter Farrell, Ellen Martin, Betty Ann Busch. (Unnamed label A&R 2076)

600912a VINTAGE '60 later record by Fay DeWitt of orig cast. "London Town" (LP-574)

600928a GREENWICH VILLAGE, U.S.A. orig prod. MUSIC: Jeanne Bargy. WORDS: Jeanne Bargy, Frank Gehrecke, Herb Corey. ORCH & COND: Bill Costa. CAST: Jack Betts, Saralou Cooper, James Pompeii, Burke McHugh, Dawn Hampton, Jane A Johnston, Judy Guyll, Pat Finley, James Harwood, Ken Urmston. (20th Fox 105-2. Excerpts: 20th Fox 4005.)

600928*a TV show ASTAIRE TIME soundtrack. MUSIC & WORDS: Various. ORCH: David Rose. COND: David Rose, Count Basie. VOCALS: Fred Astaire, Barrie Chase, Joe Williams, chorus. (Chrysler Corp mx M80P-1003/4; DRG Records S3L-5181, entitled "Three Evenings with Fred Astaire," with two other Astaire TV shows. Excerpts: LP-213.)

600929a DRESSED TO THE NINES orig prod. MUSIC & WORDS: Various. ORCH: William Roy. CAST: Ceil Cabot, Gordon Connell, Bill Hinnant, Gerry Matthews, Pat Ruhl, Mary Louise Wilson. (MGM 3914)

601012a KITTIWAKE ISLAND orig prod. MUSIC: Alec Wilder. WORDS: Arnold Sundgaard. ORCH: Jack Martin. COND: Joseph Stecko. CAST: Joe Lautner, Kathleen Murray, G Wood, Don Liberto, Caroline Worth. (Adelphi mx AD-2015/6)

601017a TENDERLOIN orig prod. MUSIC: Jerry Bock. WORDS: Sheldon Harnick. ORCH: Irwin Kostal. COND: Hal Hastings. CAST: Maurice Evans, Ron Husmann, Wynne Miller, Eileen Rodgers, Lee Becker. (Cap SWAO-1492)

601103a THE UNSINKABLE MOLLY BROWN orig prod. MUSIC & WORDS: Meredith Willson. ORCH: Don Walker. COND: Herbert Greene. CAST: Tammy Grimes, Harve Presnell, Mitchell Gregg, Joseph Sirola, Mony Dalmes. (Cap SWAO-1509)

601103b THE UNSINKABLE MOLLY BROWN 1964 film soundtrack, with a new Willson song. COND: Robert Armbruster. CAST: Debbie Reynolds, Harve Presnell. (MGM 4232)

601103c THE UNSINKABLE MOLLY BROWN 1961 studio prod. ORCH & COND: Elliot Lawrence. VOCALS: Sandy Stewart, Bernie Knee, chorus. (Camden 667)

601103*a Industrial show ONE LITTLE GIRL orig prod. MUSIC & WORDS: Kay Swift. ORCH: Hans Spialek. VOCALS: Louise Carlyle, Stuart Foster. (Campfire Girls LO7P-2300)

601203a CAMELOT orig prod. MUSIC: Frederick Loewe. WORDS: Alan Jay Lerner. ORCH: Robert Russell Bennett, Philip J Lang. COND: Franz Allers. CAST: Richard Burton, Julie Andrews, Roddy McDowall, Robert Goulet, Mary Sue Berry. (Col KOS-2031)

601203b CAMELOT 1967 film soundtrack. ORCH & COND: Alfred Newman. CAST: Richard Harris, Vanessa Redgrave, Gene Merlino (for Franco Nero), David Hemmings, Lionel Jeffries, Laurence Naismith. (Warner Bros 1712. Excerpt: Harris: "How to Handle a Woman" (LP-223).)

601203c CAMELOT 1964 London prod. ORCH: Robert Russell Bennett, Philip J Lang. COND: Kenneth Alwyn. CAST: Laurence Harvey, Elizabeth Larner, Josephine Gordon, Barry Kent, Nicky Henson, Kit Williams. (HMV(E) CSD-1559)

601203d CAMELOT 1967 studio prod. COND: Al Goodman. VOCALS: Richard Torigi, Lois Winters, Earl Rogers, chorus. (Ambassador 98070)

601203e CAMELOT 1967 studio prod. COND: Alyn Ainsworth. CAST: Paul Daneman (of 1962 Australian prod & who replaced Laurence Harvey of London prod in February 1965); Pat Michael, Peter Regan. (Music for Pleasure(E) 50368)

601203f CAMELOT studio prod. COND: Parris Mitchell. VOCALS: Unidentified soloists, chorus. (Pickwick SPC-3103)

601203g CAMELOT 1971 records sung by Alan Jay Lerner, lyricist. "How to Handle a Woman," "Camelot" (LP-534)

601203h CAMELOT 1964 studio prod. COND: Russ Williams. VOCALS: Richard Saunders, Janice Sherwood, Raymond Andrews, Johnny Lang. (Allegro(E) 749)

601203i CAMELOT 1968 studio prod. COND: Gareth Davies. CAST: Patrick Macnee, Madge Stephens, Geoffrey Chard, chorus. (World Record Club(E) ST-851)

601203j CAMELOT 1965 studio prod. COND: Brian Fahey. CAST:

Andy Cole, Mary Thomas, Patricia Lambert, Charles Young. (Society(E) 1011)

601205a SEND ME NO FLOWERS contemp records by David Wayne of orig cast. "Send Me No Flowers," "Jealous Judy" (45/Gulf 45-029)

601205b SEND ME NO FLOWERS contemp record by Doris Day of 1964 film cast. "Send Me No Flowers" (by Burt Bacharach & Hal David) (LP-330)

601215a WILDCAT orig prod. MUSIC: Cy Coleman. WORDS: Carolyn Leigh. ORCH: Robert Ginzler, Sid Ramin. COND: John Morris. CAST: Lucille Ball, Keith Andes, Paula Stewart, Clifford David, Edith King, Don Tomkins. (RCA LSO-1060)

601215b WILDCAT album by Cy Coleman (composer), piano. (Indigo 502)

601215c WILDCAT records sung by Cy Coleman, composer. "Hey, Look Me Over" (1966: LP-238)(1966: LP-671)

601226a DO RE MI orig prod. MUSIC: Jule Styne. WORDS: Betty Comden, Adolph Green. ORCH: Luther Henderson. COND: Lehman Engel. CAST: Phil Silvers, Nancy Walker, John Reardon, Nancy Dussault. (RCA LSOD-2002)

601226b DO RE MI 1961 London prod. CAST: Max Bygraves, Maggie Fitzgibbon, Danny Green, David Lander, Harry Ross, Jan Waters, Steve Arlen. (Dec(E) SKL-4145)

601226c DO RE MI 1961 studio prod. COND: Byron Allison. VOCALS: Randy Williams, Phyllis Cooper, Eileen Carroll, Steve Michaels, Richard Garrett, Ed Francis. (Tops 1720)

601226d DO RE MI 1977 record by Betty Comden & Adolph Green, lyricists. "Make Someone Happy" (LP-489)

601226e DO RE MI 1961 album. COND: Luther Henderson. VOCALS: Polly Bergen. (Col CS-8432, with Annie Get Your Gun)

601226f DO RE MI 1966 record by Jule Styne (composer), piano. "Make Someone Happy" (LP-671)

1961

610001a Film THE ROAD TO HONG KONG soundtrack. MUSIC: James Van Heusen. WORDS: Sammy Cahn. COND: Robert Farnon. CAST: Bing Crosby, Bob Hope, Joan Collins, Dorothy Lamour. (Liberty 17002)

610002a Film THE PARENT TRAP contemp album by members of orig cast. MUSIC & WORDS: Richard M & Robert B Sherman. COND: Tutti Camarata. CAST: Hayley Mills, Maureen O'Hara, Tommy Sands, Annette, chorus. (Buena Vista 3309, with additional material)

610003a Film ALL HANDS ON DECK soundtrack. MUSIC & WORDS: Jay Livingston, Ray Evans. COND: Lionel Newman. Pat Boone: "All Hands on Deck," "There's No One like You," "I've Got It Made," "Somewhere There's Home" (45/Dot DEP-1098)

610004a Film WILD IN THE COUNTRY contemp record by Elvis Presley of orig cast. "Wild in the Country" (RCA 7" 37-7880)

610004b Film WILD IN THE COUNTRY soundtrack. Elvis Presley: "I Slipped, I Stumbled, I Fell" (RCA LSP-2370, entitled "Something for Everybody," with other songs)

610005a Film LOVER COME BACK contemp record by Doris Day of orig cast. "Should I Surrender?" (45/Col 4-42260)

610006a Film BREAKFAST AT TIFFANY'S 1974 record sung by Johnny Mercer, lyricist. MUSIC: Henry Mancini. "Moon River" (LP-560)

610006b Film BREAKFAST AT TIFFANY'S contemp record by Andy Williams of orig prod. "Moon River" (45/Col 13-33049)

610007a Film ALAKAZAM THE GREAT! contemp album. COND: Albert Harris, Ian Freebairn-Smith. VOCALS: Bobby Adano. (Vee-Jay 6000)

610008a Film 101 DALMATIONS soundtrack. Ben Wright: "Cruella de Ville" (LP-661)

610009a Film GIDGET GOES HAWAIIAN 1961 records by James Darren of orig cast. "Gidget Goes Hawaiian," "Wild about That Girl" (LP-688)

610010a Film THE LONG AND THE SHORT AND THE TALL (also entitled "Jungle Fighters") contemp records by Laurence Harvey of orig cast. "The Long and the Short and the Tall," "Hi-Jig-a-Jig" (45/Col 4-42017)

610011a Film THE ABSENT MINDED PROFESSOR contemp record prod. MUSIC & WORDS: Richard M & Robert B Sherman. Chorus: "The Medfield Fight Song" Fred MacMurray of orig cast, chorus: "Flubber Song" (Disneyland 1911)

610112a SHOW GIRL orig prod. MUSIC & WORDS: Charles Gaynor. ORCH: Robert Hunter, Clare Grundman. COND: Robert Hunter. CAST: Carol Channing, Jules Munshin, les Quat' Jeudis. (Roulette 80001)

610112b SHOW GIRL later records by Carol Channing of orig cast. "Doin' the Old Yahoo Step" (LP-111)(LP-377) "Join Us in a Cup of Tea" (LP-377)

610302a 13 DAUGHTERS orig (Honolulu) prod. MUSIC & WORDS: Eaton Magoon Jr. ORCH: Joe Glover, Robert Russell Bennett. COND: Alvina Kaulili. CAST: Richard Kuga, James Kaina, Napua Stevens, Tamara Long, Sherry de Boer, Robin Rankin, Lordie Kaulili, Kam Fong Chun. (Mahalo 3003)

610302*a TV show 25 YEARS OF LIFE soundtrack. MUSIC & WORDS: Various. VOCALS: Bob Hope, Mary Martin, chorus. (Unnamed label 10" mx M8OL-5803/4)

610403a THE HAPPIEST GIRL IN THE WORLD orig prod. MUSIC: Jacques Offenbach. WORDS: E Y Harburg. ORCH: Robert Russell Bennett, Hershy Kay. COND: Robert De Cormier. CAST: Cyril Ritchard, Janice Rule, Dran Seitz, Bruce Yarnell, Nancy Windsor, Lu Leonard. (Col KOS-2050)

610413a CARNIVAL! orig prod. MUSIC & WORDS: Bob Merrill. ORCH: Philip J Lang. COND: Saul Schechtman. CAST: Anna Maria Alberghetti, James Mitchell, Kaye Ballard, Pierre Olaf, Jerry Orbach, Henry Lascoe. (MGM 3946. Excerpt: Ballard, Lascoe: "Humming" (LP-206).)

610413b CARNIVAL! 1964 record by Ed Ames of 1961 national cast & 1962 New York cast. "Her Face" (LP-212)

610413c CARNIVAL! 1963 London prod. COND: Cyril Ornadel. CAST: Sally Logan, Shirley Sands, Michael Maurel, Francis de Wolff, Bob Harris, James Mitchell. (Odeon(E) CSD-1476)

610413d CARNIVAL! 1962 record by Anna Maria Alberghetti of orig cast. "Love Makes the World Go Round" (LP-421)

610419a SMILING THE BOY FELL DEAD orig prod. MUSIC: David Baker. WORDS: Sheldon Harnick. COND: Julian Stein. CAST: Danny Meehan, Louise Larabee, Claiborne Cary, Warren Wade, Phil Leeds, Joseph Macaulay. (Sunbeam mx LB-549/50)

610425a YOUNG ABE LINCOLN orig prod. MUSIC: Victor Ziskin. WORDS: Joan Javits, Arnold Sundgaard. COND: Victor Ziskin. CAST: Darrell Sandeen, Judy Foster, Travis Hudson, Lou Cutell. (Golden 76)

146

610510a BEYOND THE FRINGE orig (London) prod. MUSIC: Dudley Moore. CAST: Alan Bennett, Peter Cook, Jonathan Miller, Dudley Moore. (Parlophone(E) PMC-1145)

610510b BEYOND THE FRINGE 1962 New York prod, with somewhat different material. CAST: Alan Bennett, Peter Cook, Jonathan Miller, Dudley Moore. (Cap SW-1792)

610518a DONNYBROOK! orig prod. MUSIC & WORDS: John Burke. ORCH: Robert Ginzler. COND: Clay Warnick. CAST: Eddie Foy, Art Lund, Joan Fagan, Susan Johnson, Eddie Ericksen, Charles C Welch, Clarence Nordstrom. (Kapp 8500)

610519a THE MAN FROM BROADWAY orig (Detroit) prod. MUSIC & WORDS: Lou Fortunate. CAST: Imogene Wiel, John Lamphier, Ed Connelly, George Pecar, chorus. (Unnamed label mx MOBY-0703/4)

610720a STOP THE WORLD, I WANT TO GET OFF 1962 New York prod. MUSIC & WORDS: Leslie Bricusse, Anthony Newley. ORCH: Various. COND: Milton Rosenstock. CAST: Anthony Newley, Anna Quayle, Jennifer Baker, Susan Baker. (London 88001)

610720b STOP THE WORLD, I WANT TO GET OFF 1966 film prod, with an additional song by Al Ham. ORCH & COND: Al Ham. CAST: Tony Tanner, Millicent Martin, chorus. (Warner Bros 1643)

610720c STOP THE WORLD, I WANT TO GET OFF orig (London) prod. COND: Ian Fraser. CAST: Anthony Newley, Anna Quayle, Susan Baker, Jennifer Baker. (Dec(E) SKL-4142)

610720d STOP THE WORLD, I WANT TO GET OFF 1978 New York prod. ORCH: Billy Byers, Joe Lipman. COND: George Rhodes. CAST: Sammy Davis Jr, Marian Mercer, Shelly Burch, Wendy Edmead, chorus. (Warner Bros HS-3214)

611003a SAIL AWAY orig prod. MUSIC & WORDS: Noel Coward. ORCH: Irwin Kostal. COND: Peter Matz. CAST: Elaine Stritch, James Hurst, Patricia Harty, Grover Dale, Charles Braswell, Paul O'Keefe. (Cap SWAO-1643)

611003b SAIL AWAY 1962 studio prod, all songs sung by Noel Coward, composer. ORCH & COND: Peter Matz. (Cap SW-1667)

611003c SAIL AWAY 1962 London prod, with a new Coward song. COND: Gareth Davies. CAST: Elaine Stritch, Grover Dale of orig cast; David Holliday, Sheila Forbes, John Hewer, Edith Day, Sydney Arnold. (Stanyan 10027)

611003d SAIL AWAY contemp records sung by Noel Coward (composer) & Joe Layton (director) of two songs dropped from the show. "We're the Bronxville Darby and Joan," "This Is a Night for Lovers" (LP-594)

611005a SEVEN COME ELEVEN orig prod. MUSIC & WORDS: William Roy, Jack Holmes, Lesley Davison, Bruce Geller, Jacques Urbont, Michael Brown, others. ORCH: William Roy. CAST: Philip Bruns, Ceil Cabot, Rex Robbins, Steve Roland, Donna Sanders, Mary Louise Wilson. (Col mx 55477/8)

611010a MILK AND HONEY orig prod. MUSIC & WORDS: Jerry Herman. ORCH: Hershy Kay, Eddie Sauter. COND: Max Goberman. CAST: Robert Weede, Mimi Benzell, Molly Picon, Tommy Rall, Juki Arkin. (RCA LSO-1065)

611010b MILK AND HONEY records by members of orig cast. ORCH & COND: Ray Ellis. Robert Weede: "Shalom" Mimi Benzell: "As Simple as That" (45/RCA 47-7937)

611012a LET IT RIDE! orig prod. MUSIC: Jay Livingston. WORDS: Ray Evans, Jay Livingston. ORCH: Raymond Jaimes. COND: Jay Blackton. CAST: George Gobel, Sam Levene, Barbara Nichols, Paula Stewart, Stanley Grover, Larry Alpert, Ted Thurston. (RCA LSO-1064)

611014a HOW TO SUCCEED IN BUSINESS WITHOUT REALLY TRYING orig prod. MUSIC & WORDS: Frank Loesser. ORCH: Robert Ginzler. COND: Elliot Lawrence. CAST: Robert Morse, Rudy Vallee, Bonnie Scott, Virginia Martin, Charles Nelson Reilly, Claudette Sutherland, Sammy Smith, Paul Reed, Ruth Kobart. (RCA LSO-1066)

611014b HOW TO SUCCEED IN BUSINESS WITHOUT REALLY TRYING 1967 film soundtrack. COND: Nelson Riddle. CAST: Robert Morse, Michele Lee, Rudy Vallee, Anthony Teague, John Myhers, Kay Reynolds, Ruth Kobart, Sammy Smith. (United Artists 5151)

611014c HOW TO SUCCEED IN BUSINESS WITHOUT REALLY TRYING 1963 London prod. ORCH: Robert Ginzler. COND: Roy Lowe. CAST: Warren Berlinger, Billy deWolfe, David Knight, Patricia Michael, Eileen Gourlay, Josephine Blake, Olive Lucius. (RCA(E) SF-7564)

611014d HOW TO SUCCEED IN BUSINESS WITHOUT REALLY TRYING 1963 studio prod. ORCH & COND: Alan Braden. CAST: Maggie Fitzgibbon, Louie Ramsay, Mel Todd, Fred Lucas, Bowles Bevan, Charles Granville, Eula Parker. (World Record Club(E) ST-322)

611019a TV show FEATHERTOP orig prod. MUSIC: Mary Rodgers. WORDS: Martin Charnin. CAST: Jane Powell, Hugh O'Brien, Hans Conried, Kathleen Nesbitt, Jackie Joseph, Shirley Mills, Pat Lloyd, Anthony Teague. (Mars Candy Co LB-2931)

611021a BEI MIR BISTU SCHOEN orig prod. MUSIC: Sholom Secunda. WORDS: Jacob Jacobs. COND: Sholom Secunda. CAST: Leo Fuchs, Jacob Jacobs, Miriam Kressyn, Leon Liebgold, Charlotte Cooper, Rebecca Richman, Seymour Rexite. (Dec 79115)

611023a KWAMINA orig prod. MUSIC & WORDS: Richard Adler. ORCH: Sid Ramin, Irwin Kostal. COND: Colin Romoff. CAST: Sally Ann Howes, Terry Carter, Brock Peters, Ethel Ayler, Robert Guillaume, Scott Gibson, Joseph Attles. (Cap SWAO-1645)

611102a KEAN orig prod. MUSIC & WORDS: Robert Wright, George Forrest. ORCH: Philip J Lang. COND: Pembroke Davenport. CAST: Alfred Drake, Lee Venora, Joan Weldon, Truman Smith, Alfred DeSio, Oliver Gray, Christopher Hewett, Robert Penn, Arthur Rubin. (Col KOS-2120)

611110a ALL IN LOVE orig prod. MUSIC: Jacques Urbont. WORDS: Bruce Geller. COND: Jacques Urbont. CAST: David Atkinson, Lee Cass, Gaylea Byrne, Mimi Randolph, Christina Gillespie, Dom deLuise, Michael Davis. (Mercury 6204)

611118a THE GAY LIFE orig prod. MUSIC: Arthur Schwartz. WORDS: Howard Dietz. ORCH: Don Walker. COND: Herbert Greene. CAST: Walter Chiari, Barbara Cook, Jules Munshin, Elizabeth Allen, Jeanne Bal, Loring Smith, Lu Leonard. (Cap SWAO-1560)

611206a SING MUSE! orig prod. MUSIC: Joseph Raposo. WORDS: Erich Segal. ORCH: Joseph Raposo. COND: Jerry Goldberg. CAST: Karen Morrow, Brandon Maggart, Paul Michael, William Pierson, Bob Spencer, Ralph Stantley. (Unnamed label CH-1093)

611211a BLACK NATIVITY orig prod. MUSIC & WORDS: Various. CAST: Marion Williams, Princess Stewart, Prof. Alex Bradford. (Vee Jay 8503)

611227a SUBWAYS ARE FOR SLEEPING orig prod. MUSIC: Jule Styne. WORDS: Betty Comden, Adolph Green. ORCH: Philip J Lang. COND: Milton Rosenstock. CAST: Sydney Chaplin, Carol Lawrence, Orson Bean, Phyllis Newman, Gene Varrone. (Col KOS-2130)

611227b SUBWAYS ARE FOR SLEEPING 1977 record by Betty Comden & Adolph Green, lyricists. "Swing Your Projects" ("Capital Gains")(LP-489)

1962

620001a Film GAY PURR-EE soundtrack. MUSIC: Harold Arlen. WORDS: E Y Harburg. ORCH & COND: Mort Lindsey. CAST: Judy Garland, Robert Goulet, Red Buttons, Hermione Gingold, Paul Frees. (Warner Bros 1479. Exerpts: Garland: "Roses Red, Violets Blue," "Take My Hand, Paree," "Paris Is a Lonely Town," "Little Drops of Rain" (LP-745).)

620001b Film GAY PURR-EE 1963 record by Judy Garland of orig prod. "Paris Is a Lonely Town" (LP-194)

620002a Film JESSICA soundtrack. MUSIC: Marguerite Monnot, M Nascimbene, others. WORDS: Dusty Negulesco. VOCALS: Maurice Chevalier. (United Artists 5096)

620003a Film HOW THE WEST WAS WON soundtrack. MUSIC & WORDS: Alfred Newman, Johnny Mercer, Sammy Cahn, others. VOCALS: Debbie Reynolds, Dave Guard, Ken Darby Singers, Whiskey Hill Singers. (MGM S1E-5. Excerpts: Reynolds: "Raise a Ruckus Tonight," "What Was Your Name in the States," "A Home in the Meadow" (LP-267).)

620003b Film HOW THE WEST WAS WON contemp record by Debbie Reynolds of orig cast. "A House in the Meadow" (45/Dot 16465)

620004a Film SUMMER MAGIC contemp album by members of orig cast. WORDS & MUSIC: Richard M & Robert B Sherman. COND: Tutti Camarata. CAST: Hayley Mills, Marilyn Hooven (for Dorothy McGuire), Eddie Hodges, Burl Ives, Deborah Walley, Wendy Turner. (Buena Vista 4025. Excerpts: Disneyland 1318, with The Parent Trap & In Search of the Castaways)

620005a WAIT A MINIM! orig (South African) prod. MUSIC & WORDS: Jeremy Taylor, others. ORCH & COND: Andrew Tracey. CAST: Andrew Tracey, Paul Tracey, Kendrew Lascelles, Michel Martel, Jeannette James, Zelide Jeppe, Marina Christelis, Jeremy Taylor. (Gallotone(South Africa) GALP-1221)

620005b WAIT A MINIM! 1964 London prod, rec live. ORCH & COND: Andrew Tracey. CAST: Andrew Tracey, Paul Tracey, Jeremy Taylor, Kendrew Lascelles, Michel Martel, Zelide Jeppe, Dana Valery, Jeannette James. (Dec(E) SKL-4610)

620005c WAIT A MINIM! 1966 New York prod. COND: Andrew Tracey. CAST: Andrew Tracey, Paul Tracey, Kendrew Lascelles, Michel Martel, Nigel Pegram, April Olrich, Dana Valery, Sarah Atkinson. (London 88002)

620006a Film DREAMBOAT soundtrack. Ginger Rogers: "You'll Never Know" (LP-402)

620007a Film WHATEVER HAPPENED TO BABY JANE? records by members of orig cast. Bette Davis: "I've Written a Letter to Daddy" (1975: LP-395). Davis, Debbie Burton: "Whatever Happened to Baby Jane?" Burton: "I've Written a Letter to Daddy" (45/MGM K-13107)

620008a Film FOLLOW THAT DREAM soundtrack. Elvis Presley: "Follow That Dream," "Angel," "What A Wonderful Life," "I'm Not the Marrying Kind" (45/RCA EPA-4368)

620009a Film BLUE HAWAII soundtrack. MUSIC & WORDS: Various. VOCALS: Elvis Presley, chorus. (RCA LSP-2426)

620010a Film GIRLS! GIRLS! GIRLS! soundtrack. MUSIC & WORDS: Various. VOCALS: Elvis Presley, chorus. (RCA LSP-2621)

620011a Film DIAMOND HEAD contemp record by James Darren of orig cast. "Diamond Head" (45/Colpix 672)

620012a Film DAYS OF WINE AND ROSES contemp records by Andy Williams of orig prod. "Days of Wine and Roses" (45/Col 4-42674)

620012b Film DAYS OF WINE AND ROSES 1974 record sung by Johnny Mercer, lyricist. "Days of Wine and Roses" (LP-560)

620013a Film THE NOTORIOUS LANDLADY 1962 record by Fred Astaire of orig cast. "The Notorious Landlady" (LP-597)

620014a Record prod THE MIGHTY HERCULES orig prod. MUSIC & WORDS: Winston Sharples, Win Singleton. CAST: uncredited. (Golden 108)

620015a Film MOON PILOT contemp record by Tom Tryon & Dany Saval of orig cast. MUSIC & WORDS: Richard M & Robert B Sherman. "Seven Moons of Beta Lyrae" (45/Vista F-392-P)

620016a Film IF A MAN ANSWERS contemp records by Bobby Darin of orig cast."A True, True Love," "If a Man Answers" (45/Cap 4837)

620127a A FAMILY AFFAIR orig prod. MUSIC & WORDS: John Kander, William Goldman, James Goldman. ORCH: Robert Ginzler. COND: Stanley Lebowsky. CAST: Shelley Berman, Eileen Heckart, Morris Carnovsky, Larry Kert, Rita Gardner, Bibi Osterwald, Beryl Towbin, Jack DeLon, Alice Nunn. (United Artists 5099)

620201a NEW FACES OF 1962 1980 records sung by Arthur Siegel (composer) & June Carroll (lyricist). PIANO: Arthur Siegel. "The Other One," "I Want You to Be the First One to Know" (LP-775)

620205a FLY BLACKBIRD orig prod. MUSIC: C Jackson. WORDS: C Jackson, James Hatch. ORCH & COND: Gershon Kingsley. CAST: Avon Long, Robert Guillaume, Mary Louise, John Anania, Leonard Parker, Helon Blount. (Mercury 6206)

620205b FLY BLACKBIRD 1961 Los Angeles prod. CAST: Loraine Carter, Jack Crowder, Josie Dotson, Russ Ellis, Carl Gipson, Micki Grant, Lee Korf, Thelma Oliver, Paul Palmer, Clarry Smallwood, George Takei. (Imaginate V-13786)

620205*a Industrial show PENNEY PROUD orig (Colorado Springs) prod. MUSIC & WORDS: Michael Brown. ORCH & COND: Norman Paris. CAST: Ellen Martin, Michael Brown, Tom Mixon, Betty Ann Busch, Arthur Arney, Cynthia Wayne, Walter Farrell, Kenneth Nelson. (Unnamed label A&R 2195)

620311a TV show THE PRINCE AND THE PAUPER soundtrack. (Presented in 3 parts on March 11, 18, & 25) MUSIC: George Fischoff. WORDS: Verna Thomasson. CAST: Guy Williams, Sean Scully, Laurence Naismith, Niall MacGuinis, Donald Houston. (Pickwick 3204)

620311b TV show THE PRINCE AND THE PAUPER 1963 stage prod. ORCH & COND: Burt Farber. CAST: Joan Shepard, Robert McHaffey, John Davidson, Carol Blodgett, Joe Bousard, Flora Elkins, Budd Mann. (London 98001)

620315a NO STRINGS orig prod. MUSIC & WORDS: Richard Rodgers, ORCH: Ralph Burns. COND: Peter Matz. CAST: Richard Kiley, Diahann Carroll, Noelle Adam, Bernice Massi, Polly Rowles, Mitchell Gregg, Alvin Epstein. (Cap SO-1695)

620315b NO STRINGS contemp album by the No Strings Sextet. ORCH: Peter Matz. COND: Peter Matz (of orig prod). No vocals. (Col CS-8617)

620315c NO STRINGS 1963 London prod. ORCH: Ralph Burns. COND: Johnnie Spence. CAST: Art Lund, Beverly Todd, Hy Hazell, Ferdy Mayne, Marti Stevens, Erica Rogers, David Holliday, Geoffrey Hutchings. (Dec(E) SKL-4576)

620315d NO STRINGS contemp album with new orchestrations including strings. ORCH: Ralph Burns (of orig prod). COND: Ralph Burns. No vocals. (Epic 3840)

620315e NO STRINGS 1972 record by Richard Kiley of orig cast. "The Sweetest Sounds" (LP-509)

620319a ALL AMERICAN orig prod. MUSIC: Charles Strouse. WORDS: Lee Adams. ORCH: Robert Ginzler. COND: John Morris. CAST: Ray Bolger, Eileen Herlie, Ron Husmann, Anita Gilette, Fritz Weaver. (Col KOS-2160)

620322a I CAN GET IT FOR YOU WHOLESALE orig prod. MUSIC & WORDS: Harold Rome. ORCH: Sid Ramin. COND: Lehman Engel. CAST: Lillian Roth, Jack Kruschen, Harold Lang, Ken LeRoy, Marilyn Cooper, Barbra Streisand, Bambi Linn, Elliott Gould, Sheree North. (Col KOS-2180)

620406a HALF-PAST WEDNESDAY orig prod. MUSIC: Robert Colby. WORDS: Robert Colby, Nita Jonas. ORCH & COND: Julian Stein. CAST: Dom De Luise, Sean Garrison, Andre Johnston, Robert Fitch, David Winters. (Col CS-8717, entitled "Rumpelstiltskin")

620508a A FUNNY THING HAPPENED ON THE WAY TO THE FORUM orig prod. MUSIC & WORDS: Stephen Sondheim. ORCH: Irwin Kostal, Sid Ramin. COND: Harold Hastings. CAST: Zero Mostel, Jack Gilford, Ruth Kobart, David Burns, Brian Davies, Preshy Marker, Ronald Holgate, John Carradine. (Cap SWAO-1717)

620508b A FUNNY THING HAPPENED ON THE WAY TO THE FORUM 1966 film soundtrack. COND: Ken Thorne. CAST: Zero Mostel, Annette Andre, Michael Crawford, Michael Hordern, Jack Gilford, Phil Silvers, Leon Greene. (United Artists 5144)

620508c A FUNNY THING HAPPENED ON THE WAY TO THE FORUM 1963 London prod. ORCH: Irwin Kostal, Sid Ramin. COND: Alyn Ainsworth. CAST: Frankie Howerd, John Rye, Ilsa Blair, Eddie Gray, Kenneth Connor, Leon Greene, Linda Gray. (HMV(E) CSD-1518)

620519a BRAVO GIOVANNI orig prod. MUSIC: Milton Schafer. WORDS: Ronny Graham. ORCH: Robert Ginzler. COND: Anton Coppola. CAST: Cesare Siepi, David Opatoshu, Michele Lee, Maria Karnilova, George S Irving, Gene Varrone. (Col KOS-2200)

620519b BRAVO GIOVANNI 1966 record by Michele Lee of orig cast, "Steady, Steady" (LP-672)

620611a TV show JULIE AND CAROL AT CARNEGIE HALL soundtrack. MUSIC & WORDS: Various. ORCH & COND: Irwin Kostal. CAST: Julie Andrews, Carol Burnett. (Col OS-2240)

620919a A MAN'S A MAN orig prod. MUSIC: Joseph Raposo. WORDS: Bertolt Brecht, Eric Bentley. PIANO: Joseph Raposo. NARRATOR: Eric Bentley. CAST: John Heffernan, Michael Granger, Maurice Edwards, Ralf von Boda, Jenny Egan. (Spoken Arts 870)

621002a EDDIE FISHER AT THE WINTER GARDEN orig prod. MUSIC & WORDS: Various. COND: Eddy Samuels. VOCALS: Eddie Fisher. (Ramrod 1)

621004a THE GOLDEN KNIGHT orig (Orange, Calif) prod. MUSIC & WORDS: Glenn Wescott. CAST: George Dains, Art Sherman, Lorraine Kemp, Betty Peck, Paul Martin, Bob Wentz, Bob Storr, Jeff MacNeill. (Sound Inc 1205)

621008a O SAY CAN YOU SEE! orig prod. MUSIC: Jack Holmes. WORDS: Bill Conklin, Bob Miller. ORCH: Lanny Meyers. COND: Jack Holmes. CAST: Jan Chaney, Elmarie Wendel, Nicolas Coster, Paul B Price, Joel Warfield, Joyce Carey, Thomas Gaines, Richard Neilson. (Sunbeam mx XTV-87195/6)

621010a BILLY BARNES' L.A. orig (Los Angeles) prod. MUSIC & WORDS: Billy Barnes. ORCH & COND: Ray Henderson. CAST: Sylvia Lewis, Ken Berry, Joyce Jameson, Steve Franken, Tom Hatten, Marlyn Mason. (Criterion 1001)

621018a DIME A DOZEN orig prod. MUSIC & WORDS: Various. ORCH: William Roy. CAST: Gerry Matthews, Jack Fletcher, Mary Louise Wilson, Rex Robbins, Fredricka Weber, Susan Browning. (Cadence 26063)

621020a MR. PRESIDENT orig prod. MUSIC & WORDS: Irving Berlin. ORCH: Philip J Lang. COND: Jay Blackton. CAST: Robert Ryan, Nanette Fabray, Anita Gillette, Jack Haskell, Jack Washburn, Wisa d'Orso, Stanley Grover, Jerry Strickler. (Col KOS-2270)

621020b MR. PRESIDENT 1962 studio prod. ORCH: Philip J Lang. COND: Mitchell Ayres. CAST: Perry Como, Kaye Ballard, Sandy Stewart. (RCA LSP-2630)

621117a LITTLE ME orig prod. MUSIC: Cy Coleman. WORDS: Carolyn Leigh. ORCH: Ralph Burns. COND: Charles Sanford. CAST: Sid Caesar, Virginia Martin, Nancy Andrews, Mort Marshall, Joey Faye, Swen Swenson, Peter Turgeon, Mickey Deems. (RCA LSO-1078)

621117b LITTLE ME 1964 London prod. ORCH: Ralph Burns. COND: Ed Coleman. CAST: Bruce Forsyth, Eileen Gourlay, Avril Angers, Bernard Spear, Swen Swenson, David Henderson-Tate, Jack Francois, Laurie Webb. (Pye(E) NSPL-83023)

621117c LITTLE ME records sung by Cy Coleman, composer. "A Real Live Girl" (1966: LP-238)(1966: LP-671) "I've Got Your Number" (1966: LP-238)

621127a NEVER TOO LATE record used in orig prod. MUSIC & WORDS: Jerry Bock, Sheldon Harnick. COND: Joe Quijano. "Never Too Late" (45/Col 4-42636)

621212a RIVERWIND orig prod. MUSIC & WORDS: John Jennings. ORCH & COND: Abba Bogin. CAST: Lawrence Brooks, Elizabeth Parrish, Helon Blount, Dawn Nickerson, Lovelady Powell, Brooks Morton, Martin J Cassidy. (London 78001)

621215a RUGANTINO orig (Rome) prod. MUSIC: Armando Trovaioli. WORDS: Pietro Garinei, Sandro Giovannini. COND: Anton Coppola. CAST: Nino Manfredi, Lea Massari, Aldo Fabrizi, Bice Valori, Lando Fiorini. (Cam(Italy) CMS-30-051)

621215b RUGANTINO 1964 New York prod. COND: Anton Coppola. CAST: Nino Manfredi, Ornella Vanoni, Aldo Fabrizi, Bice Valori, Lando Fiorini. (Warner Bros 1528; Cam(Italy) CMS-30-068)

621215c RUGANTINO 1978 Italian prod. COND: Armando Trovaioli (composer). CAST: Aldo Fabrizi & Bice Valori of orig & 1964 New York prods; Enrico Montesano, Alida Chelli, Aldo Donati, chorus. (Cam(Italy) SAG-9092)

1963

630001a Film I COULD GO ON SINGING soundtrack. MUSIC & WORDS: Various. COND: Mort Lindsey. VOCALS: Judy Garland. (Cap SW-1861)

630001b Film I COULD GO ON SINGING later records by Judy Garland of orig cast. "It Never Was You" (LP-188) (LP-190)(LP-219) "By Myself" (LP-200)(LP-219)

630002a Record prod THREE BILLION MILLIONAIRES orig prod. MUSIC: Robert Allen. WORDS: Diane Lampert, Peter Farrow. ORCH & COND: Ray Ellis. CAST: Jack Benny, Carol Burnett, Wally Cox, Bing Crosby, Sammy Davis Jr, Judy Garland, Danny Kaye, George Maharis, Terry Thomas. (United Artists UXL-4)

630002b Record prod THREE BILLION MILLIONAIRES 1963 studio prod. ORCH & COND: Ray Ellis. CAST: Win Stracke, Rose Marie Jun, Peggy Powers, Lillian Clark, Eric Carlson, Gene Steck, Elise Bretton. (Golden 110)

630003a Film PALM SPRINGS WEEKEND soundtrack. MUSIC &

WORDS: Various. CAST: Troy Donahue, Connie Stevens, Ty Hardin, Jerry Van Dyke, Bob Conrad. (Warner Bros 1519)

630004a Film TWO TICKETS TO PARIS soundtrack. MUSIC & WORDS: Various. ORCH: Marty Manning. CAST: Joey Dee, Gary Crosby, Kay Medford, Jeri Lynne Fraser. (Roulette 25182)

630005a Film MY SIX LOVES contemp record by Debbie Reynolds of orig cast. "My Six Loves" (45/Dot 16465)

630006a Film FOLLOW THE BOYS contemp album by Connie Francis of orig cast. MUSIC & WORDS: Benny Davis, Ted Murry. ORCH & COND: LeRoy Holmes. (MGM 4123, with other songs by Connie Francis)

630007a Film PAPA'S DELICATE CONDITION records sung by Sammy Cahn, lyricist, MUSIC: James Van Heusen. "Call Me Irresponsible" (1972: LP-658) (1974: LP-313)

630008a Film IN SEARCH OF THE CASTAWAYS contemp album by members of orig cast. MUSIC & WORDS: Richard M & Robert B Sherman. COND: Muir Mathieson, CAST: Hayley Mills, Maurice Chevalier. (Disneyland ST-3916)

630009a Film MOVE OVER DARLING contemp records by Doris Day of orig cast. "Move Over Darling" (LP-330) "Twinkle Lullaby" (45/Col 4-42912)

630010a Film SUMMER HOLIDAY soundtrack. Cliff Richard: "Bachelor Boy," "Summer Holiday," "The Next Time," "Dancing Shoes" (Epic 24063)

630011a Industrial show ALL ABOUT LIFE orig prod. MUSIC: Jerry Powell. WORDS: Mike McWhinney. ORCH: Milton Greene. COND: Rod Warren. CAST: Michael Allinson, Gloria Bleezarde, Bill Linton, Eliza Ross, Jay Stuart, Ronny Whyte. (Col mx XTV-89424/5)

630012a Film FUN IN ACAPULCO soundtrack. MUSIC & WORDS: Various. VOCALS: Elvis Presley, chorus. (RCA LSP-2756)

630013a Film IT HAPPENED AT THE WORLD'S FAIR soundtrack. MUSIC & WORDS: Various. VOCALS: Elvis Presley, chorus. (RCA LSP-2697)

630014a Film THE SWORD IN THE STONE studio prod. MUSIC & WORDS: Richard M & Robert B Sherman. VOCALS: uncredited. (Disneyland 1236)

630014b Film THE SWORD IN THE STONE soundtrack. "The Legend of the Sword in the Stone" (LP-661)

630015a Film THE STRIPPER soundtrack. MUSIC & WORDS: Johnny Mercer. Joanne Woodward: "Something's Gotta Give" (LP-496)

630016a Film COME BLOW YOUR HORN 1977 record sung by Sammy Cahn, lyricist. MUSIC: James Van Heusen. "Come Blow Your Horn" (LP-503)

630017a Film WHO'S GOT THE ACTION? contemp record by Dean Martin of orig cast. "Who's Got the Action?" (45/Reprise R-20116)

630018a Film COME FLY WITH ME 1972 record sung by Sammy Cahn, lyricist. MUSIC: James Van Heusen. "Come Fly With Me" (LP-658)

630019a Industrial show THE SAGA OF THE DINGBAT orig prod. MUSIC: Julian Stein. WORDS: Edward Nayor. ORCH: Julian Stein. COND: Rolf Barnes. CAST: Ann Vivian, Mimi Vondra, Carole Woodruff, Arline Woods, Gino Conforte, Don Grilley, Hal Linden, Stan Page. (Herald Tribune mx XCSV-105844/5)

630020a Record prod RAISING THE FAMILY FOR FUN AND PROFIT orig prod. MUSIC: Joseph Raposo. WORDS: John Wolf-

son. CAST: Estelle Parsons, Robert Roman, David Vaughan. (Scarsdale SA-209)

630122a THE ELEPHANT CALF 1967 touring prod, with two additional songs by Black & Bentley. MUSIC: Arnold Black. WORDS: Eric Bentley. COND: Arnold Black. CAST: Logan Ramsey, James Antonio, Beeson Carroll, Frank Groseclose, Hilda Brawner. (Asch 9831)

630318a TOVARICH orig prod. MUSIC: Lee Pockriss. WORDS: Anne Crosswell. ORCH: Philip J Lang. COND: Stanley Lebowsky. CAST: Vivien Leigh, Jean Pierre Aumont, Alexander Scourby, Louise Troy, George S Irving, Louise Kirtland, Byron Mitchell, Margery Gray, Michael Kermoyan. (Cap STAO-1940)

630319a OH WHAT A LOVELY WAR orig (London) prod. MUSIC & WORDS: Various. COND: Alfred Ralston. CAST: Members of the Theatre Workshop. (Dec(E) SKL-4542)

630319b OH WHAT A LOVELY WAR 1969 film soundtrack. ORCH & COND: Alfred Ralston. CAST: Maggie Smith, Jean Pierre Cassel, Penny Allen, Joe Melia, Corin Redgrave, Pia Colombo, Maurice Arthur, Richard Howard, Joanne Brown. (Paramount 5008)

630319c OH WHAT A LOVELY WAR album of contemp records of the World War I songs used in the show. (World Record Club(E) SH-130) (LP-74)

630321a HALF A SIXPENCE 1965 New York prod. MUSIC & WORDS: David Heneker. ORCH: Jim Tyler. COND: Stanley Lebowsky. CAST: Tommy Steele, Polly James, Will MacKenzie, Grover Dale, Norman Allen, Eleonore Treiber, James Grout. (RCA LSO-1110)

630321b HALF A SIXPENCE 1967 film soundtrack, with additional songs by Heneker. ORCH & COND: Irwin Kostal. CAST: Tommy Steele, Marti Webb (of orig London cast, for Julia Foster). (RCA LSO-1146)

630321c HALF A SIXPENCE orig (London) prod. COND: Kenneth Alwyn. CAST: Tommy Steele, Marti Webb, Anna Barry, James Grout. (Dec(E) SKL-4521)

630321d HALF A SIXPENCE 1968 studio prod. COND: Gareth Davies. CAST: Barbara Windson, Marty Wilde, chorus. (World Record Club(E) ST-852)

630321e HALF A SIXPENCE 1967 studio prod, incl 2 songs from 1967 film. COND: Cyril Stapleton. CAST: Roy Sone (of orig cast and who replaced Tommy Steele when he left), Marti Webb (of orig cast), chorus. (Marble Arch(E) MALS-739)

630411a Puppet show MAN IN THE MOON orig prod. MUSIC: Jerry Bock. WORDS: Sheldon Harnick. ORCH & COND: Alvy West. CAST: Bil Baird, Cora Baird, Franz Fazakas, Frank Sullivan of orig cast; Gerald Freedman (director), Eric Carlson, Rosemary Jun. (Golden 104)

630415a SOPHIE demonstration record. MUSIC & WORDS: Steve Allen. ORCH: Sid Ramin. COND: Liza Redfield. CAST: Libi Staiger of orig cast; Steve Allen (composer); Jennie Smith, Mimi Roman, Kathy Keagan, Linda Lavin, Jerry Vale, Sandy Warner, chorus. (AEI Records 1130)

630423a SHE LOVES ME orig prod. MUSIC: Jerry Bock. WORDS: Sheldon Harnick. ORCH: Don Walker. COND: Harold Hastings. CAST: Barbara Cook, Daniel Massey, Barbara Baxley, Jack Cassidy, Nathaniel Frey, Ralph Williams, Ludwig Donath, Wood Romoff. (MGM 4118. Excerpts: Cassidy: "Ilona," "Grand Knowing You" Cook: "Will He Like Me?" (LP-206).)

630423b SHE LOVES ME 1964 London prod. ORCH: Don Walker. COND: Alyn Ainsworth. CAST: Anne Rogers, Gary Raymond, Gary Miller, Rita Moreno, Peter Sallis, Gregory Phillips, Carl Jaffe, Peter Ardran. (HMV(E) CSD-1546)

630423c SHE LOVES ME 1971 records sung by Sheldon Harnick, lyricist. "She Loves Me," "Dear Friend" (LP-535)

630423d SHE LOVES ME 1975 live performances by Barbara Cook of orig cast. "Dear Friend," "Will He Like Me?," "Ice Cream" (LP-689)

630606a THE WORLD OF KURT WEILL IN SONG orig prod. MUSIC: Kurt Weill. WORDS: Bertolt Brecht, Ira Gershwin, Maxwell Anderson, Jacques d'Aval, Marc Blitzstein, Georg Kaiser, Will Holt. ORCH: Samuel Matlovsky. COND: Abraham Stokman. CAST: Will Holt, Martha Schlamme. (MGM 4180, entitled "A Kurt Weill Cabaret")

630704a PICKWICK orig (London) cast. MUSIC: Cyril Ornadel. WORDS: Leslie Bricusse. ORCH: Brian Fahey. COND: Marcus Dodds. CAST: Harry Secombe, Anton Rodgers, Teddy Green, Jessie Evans, Hilda Braid. (Philips(E) SAL-3431)

630816a MY PEOPLE orig (Chicago) prod. MUSIC & WORDS: Duke Ellington. COND: Jimmy Jones. VOCALS: Jimmy McPhail, Joya Sherrill, Jimmy Grissom, Lil Greenwood. (Contact 1)

630930a THE STUDENT GYPSY 1963 instrumental album. MUSIC & WORDS: Rick Besoyan. ORCH & COND: Hill Bowen. "Somewhere," "Romance," "My Love Is Yours," "It's a Wonderful Day to Do Nothing" (Camden CAS-790, with 110 in the Shade & Here's Love)

631002a AT THE DROP OF ANOTHER HAT orig (London) prod rec live. MUSIC: Donald Swann. WORDS: Michael Flanders. CAST: Michael Flanders, Donald Swann. (Angel 36388)

631002b AT THE DROP OF ANOTHER HAT album by Michael Flanders & Donald Swann of 3 numbers not on original cast album. (45/Parlophone(E) GEP-8900, entitled "More Out of the New Hat")

631003a HERE'S LOVE orig prod. MUSIC & WORDS: Meredith Willson. ORCH: Don Walker. COND: Elliot Lawrence. CAST: Janis Paige, Craig Stevens, Laurence Naismith, Valerie Lee, Paul Reed, Fred Gwynne, Kathy Cody. (Col KOS-2400)

631015a BALLAD FOR BIMSHIRE orig prod. MUSIC & WORDS: Irving Burgie. ORCH: Sammy Benskin, Dick Vance. COND: Sammy Benskin. CAST: Ossie Davis, Frederick O'Neal, Christine Spencer, Jimmy Randolph, Alyce Webb, Clebert Ford, Joe Callaway. (London 78002)

631017a JENNIE orig prod. MUSIC: Arthur Schwartz. WORDS: Howard Dietz. ORCH: Philip J Lang, Robert Russell Bennett. COND: John Lesko. CAST: Mary Martin, George Wallace, Robin Bailey, Ethel Shutta, Jack DeLon. (RCA LSO-1083)

631017b JENNIE 1977 record by Mary Martin of orig cast. "Before I Kiss the World Goodbye" (LP-652)

631024a 110 IN THE SHADE orig prod. MUSIC: Harvey Schmidt. WORDS: Tom Jones. ORCH: Hershy Kay. COND: Donald Pippin. CAST: Robert Horton, Inga Swenson, Stephen Douglass, Will Geer, Steve Roland, Scooter Teague, Lesley Warren, George Church. (RCA LSO-1085)

631024b 110 IN THE SHADE 1967 records by members of 1967 London prod. ORCH & COND: Sam Fonteyn. Ivor Emmanuel: "A Man and a Woman," "Gonna Be Another Hot Day" (45/Col(E) DB-8126) Joel Warfield: "110 in the Shade," "The Little Red Hat" (45/Col(E) DB-8131)

631029a THE STREETS OF NEW YORK orig prod. MUSIC: Richard B Chodosh. WORDS: Barry Alan Grael. ORCH & COND: Jack Holmes. CAST: Barbara Williams, Ralston Hill, Gail Johnston, David Cryer, Barry Alan Grael, Margot Hand, Janet Raymond, Don Phelps. (Unnamed label mx SRB-450/1)

631208a THE GIRL WHO CAME TO SUPPER orig (New York) prod. MUSIC & WORDS: Noel Coward. ORCH: Robert Russell Bennett. COND: Jay Blackton. CAST: Jose Ferrer, Florence Henderson, Tessie O'Shea, Roderick Cook, Carey Nairnes, Sean Scully. (Col KOS-2420)

631208b THE GIRL WHO CAME TO SUPPER demonstration records sung by Noel Coward (composer), incl 6 songs dropped from the show. (DRG Records SL-5178)

1964

640001a Film MARY POPPINS soundtrack. MUSIC & WORDS: Richard M & Robert B Sherman. ORCH & COND: Irwin Kostal. CAST: Julie Andrews, Dick Van Dyke, David Tomlinson, Glynis Johns, Ed Wynn, Karen Dotrice, Matthew Garber. (Buena Vista 4026) (LP-661)

640002a Film ROBIN AND THE SEVEN HOODS orig prod. MUSIC: James Van Heusen. WORDS: Sammy Cahn. ORCH & COND: Nelson Riddle. CAST: Frank Sinatra, Bing Crosby, Dean Martin, Sammy Davis Jr, Peter Falk. (Reprise 2021)

640002b Film ROBIN AND THE SEVEN HOODS records sung by Sammy Cahn, lyricist. "My Kind of Town" (1972: LP-658) (1974, incomplete: LP-313) (1977: LP-503) "Style," "I Like to Lead When I Dance" (1977: LP-503)

640003a Film THE UMBRELLAS OF CHERBOURG soundtrack. MUSIC: Michel Legrand. WORDS: Jacques Demy. CAST: Catherine Deneuve, Nino Castelnuovo. (Philips PCC-616)

640003b Film THE UMBRELLAS OF CHERBOURG 1975 record. ORCH, COND, & PIANO: Michel Legrand (composer). Lena Horne: "I Will Wait for You" (LP-675)

640003c Film THE UMBRELLAS OF CHERBOURG 1979 Paris stage prod. COND: Georges Rabol. CAST: Corinne Marchand, Bee Michelin, Daniel Beretta, Jean-Louis Rolland, Anne Forrez, Fabienne Guyon, Marcel Eglin, Mania Mhaidze. (Accord(F) ACV-130011, entitled "Les Parapluies de Cherbourg")

640004a Film FATHER GOOSE records sung by Cy Coleman, composer. WORDS: Carolyn Leigh. "Pass Me By" (1966: LP-238) (1966: LP-671)

640005a Record prod TOM JONES orig prod. MUSIC & WORDS: Bob Roberts, Ruth Batchelor. ORCH & COND: Peter Matz. CAST: Clyde Revill, Bob Roman, Karen Morrow, Iggie Wolfington, Carole Shaw, Darlene Zito. (Theatre Productions 9000)

640006a Record prod HAROLD ROME'S GALLERY orig prod. MUSIC & WORDS: Harold Rome. ORCH: Eddie Sauter. VOCALS: Betty Garrett, Jack Haskell, Rose Marie Jun, Harold Rome. (Col KS-6691)

640007a Film THE LIVELY SET orig prod. MUSIC & WORDS: Bobby Darin, others. ORCH: Billy May, Bill Loose. COND: Joseph Gershenson. CAST: James Darren, Joanie Sommers, Wink Martindale, Ron Wilson. (Dec 79191)

640008a Industrial show THE WONDERFUL WORLD OF CHEMISTRY soundtrack. MUSIC & WORDS: Michael Brown. ORCH & COND: Norman Paris. VOCALS: Chorus. "What's That Ev'ryone's Saying?," "All of Us Were Made for You," "Better Things for Better Living" (Unnamed label 7" mx S4LM-5970/1)

640009a Film HUSH...HUSH, SWEET CHARLOTTE 1975 record by Bette Davis of orig cast. "Hush...Hush, Sweet Charlotte" (LP-395)

640010a Film KID GALAHAD soundtrack. Elvis Presley: "King of the Whole Wide World," "This Is Living," "Riding the Rainbow," "Home Is Where the Heart Is," "I Got Lucky," "A Whistling Tune" (45/RCA EPA-4371)

640011a Film VIVA LAS VEGAS soundtrack. VOCALS: Elvis Presley. (Lucky Records 711. Incomplete: 45/RCA EPA-4382.)

640012a Film ROUSTABOUT soundtrack. MUSIC & WORDS: Various. VOCALS: Elvis Presley, chorus. (RCA LSP-2999)

640013a Film KISSIN' COUSINS soundtrack. MUSIC & WORDS: Various. ORCH & COND: Fred Karger. VOCALS: Elvis Presley, chorus. (RCA LSP-2894)

640014a Film I'D RATHER BE RICH contemp records by members of orig cast. Andy Williams: "Almost There" (45/Col 4-43128) Robert Goulet: "I'd Rather Be Rich" (by Richard Maltby Jr & David Shire) (45/Col 4-43131)

640015a Film YOUR CHEATIN' HEART soundtrack. MUSIC & WORDS: Hank Williams. ORCH: Fred Karger. VOCALS: Hank Williams Jr (for George Hamilton). (MGM 4260)

640016a Film KISS ME, STUPID soundtrack. MUSIC: George Gershwin. WORDS: Ira Gershwin. Dean Martin: "Sophia" (LP-654)

640017a Film A HARD DAY'S NIGHT soundtrack. MUSIC & WORDS: John Lennon, Paul McCartney. CAST: The Beatles. (United Artists UAS-6366)

640018a Film THE INCREDIBLE MR. LIMPET contemp record by Don Knotts of orig cast. "I Wish I Were A Fish" (45/Warner Bros 5431)

640019a Industrial record prod A THOUSAND MILES OF MOUNTAINS orig prod. MUSIC & WORDS: Norman Richards, Bradley G Morison, others. ORCH: Jim Tyler. COND: Norman Richards. NARRATOR: Raymond Massey. VOCALS: Hal Linden, Larry Douglas, Ken Carson, Iggie Wolfington, Stuart Foster, Lynn Roberts, chorus. (Unnamed label KB-4368)

640020a TV show HERE'S PAT O'BRIEN soundtrack. Pat O'Brien: "Harrigan" (by George M Cohan), "Dear Old Donegal" (RIC Records M-1003)

640108a BEYOND THE FRINGE '64 orig (New York) prod. MUSIC & WORDS: Dudley Moore. CAST: Alan Bennett, Peter Cook, Jonathan Miller, Dudley Moore. (Cap SW-2072)

640114a THE ATHENIAN TOUCH orig prod. MUSIC: Willard Straight. WORDS: David Eddy. COND: Glen Clugston. CAST: Marion Marlowe, Butterfly McQueen, Robert Cosden, Peter Sands, Alice Cannon. (Broadway East 101)

640116a HELLO, DOLLY! orig prod. MUSIC & WORDS: Jerry Herman. ORCH: Philip J Lang. COND: Shepard Coleman. CAST: Carol Channing, David Burns, Eileen Brennan, Sondra Lee, Charles Nelson Reilly, Jerry Dodge. (RCA LSO-1087)

640116b HELLO, DOLLY! 1967 prod. COND: Saul Schechtman. CAST: Pearl Bailey, Cab Calloway, Jack Crowder, Emily Yancy, Chris Calloway, Winston DeWitt Hemsley, Roger Lawson. (RCA LSO-1147)

640116c HELLO, DOLLY! 1965 London prod. COND: Alyn Ainsworth. CAST: Mary Martin, Loring Smith, Marilynn Lovell, Garrett Lewis, Coco Ramirez, Beverlee Weir, Johnny Beecher, Mark Alden. (RCA LSOD-2007)

640116d HELLO, DOLLY! 1969 film soundtrack. COND: Lennie Hayton, Lionel Newman. CAST: Barbra Streisand, Walter Matthau, Michael Crawford, Louis Armstrong. (20th Fox 5103)

640116e HELLO, DOLLY! records by Jerry Herman, composer. Piano, 1965: "Hello, Dolly!," "It Only Takes a Moment," "Ribbons Down My Back" (LP-140) Piano & vocal, 1974: "Put On Your Sunday Clothes" (with Joe Masiell), "Hello, Dolly! " (LP-660)

640116f HELLO, DOLLY! 1970 records of two new Herman songs provided for Ethel Merman of 1970 cast. "Love, Look in My Window," "World, Take Me Back" (45/Bar-Mike mx EM-1A-IFA/EM-1B-IFA)

640116g HELLO, DOLLY! contemp records by Carol Channing of orig prod. "Put On Your Sunday Clothes," "So Long, Dearie" (45/RCA 47-8350) "Elegance" (LP-204, with new words by Jerry Herman)

640116h HELLO, DOLLY! 1965 studio prod. COND: Len Stevens. CAST: Rita Cameron, Raymond Cooke, Pat Whitmore, Fred Lucas, David Russell, chorus. (Society(E) 1024)

640116i HELLO, DOLLY! 1966 studio prod. COND: Cyril Ornadel. CAST: Dora Bryan (who replaced Mary Martin in orig London prod); Bernard Spear, Julie Dawn, Mike Bretton, Kay Fraser, Barry Moreland, chorus. (HMV(E) CSD-3545)

640116j HELLO, DOLLY! records by Ginger Rogers, who in August 1965 replaced Carol Channing of orig cast. "Hello, Dolly" (1965: LP-325) "Before the Parade Passes By" (Rec live: LP-402)

640116k HELLO, DOLLY! contemp album. ORCH & COND: Peter Howard (cond of orig prod). No Vocals. (Cameron 7890)

640116l HELLO, DOLLY! 1965 studio prod. COND: Alyn Ainsworth. CAST: Beryl Reid & Arthur Haynes of 1965 London prod; Patricia Routledge, Tony Adams, Richard Fox, Sylvia King. (Music for pleasure(E) 1066)

640116m HELLO, DOLLY! 1970 TV performance by Betty Grable, who played Dolly in the orig prod starting June 1967. "Hello, Dolly!" (LP-284)

640116n HELLO, DOLLY! 1977 record by Ethel Merman of 1970 cast & Mary Martin of 1965 London cast, with chorus. "Hello, Dolly!" (LP-652)

640116o HELLO, DOLLY! 1966 studio prod. ORCH & COND: John Cameron, VOCALS: Jeannie Lambe, Kenny Day, Jo Searle, Barbara Jay, John Cameron, (World Record Club(E) TP-588)

640116p HELLO, DOLLY! 1965 studio prod. COND: Alan Moorhouse. VOCALS: Rita Williams, Joanne Brown, Michael John, Charles Young. (Allegro(E) 802)

640116q HELLO, DOLLY! orig prod rec live after Feb 1967, when Martha Raye replaced Betty Grable. Raye, chorus: "I Put My Hand In," "Before the Parade Passes By," "Hello, Dolly," "So Long, Dearie" (LP-651)

640216a FOXY orig prod rec live. MUSIC: Robert Emmett Dolan. WORDS: Johnny Mercer. ORCH: Edward Sauter, Hal Schaefer. COND: Donald Pippin. CAST: Bert Lahr, Larry Blyden, Cathryn Damon, Julienne Marie, John Davidson, Gerald Hiken. (SPM Records CO-4636. Excerpts (from another tape): Lahr, Blyden: "Many Ways to Skin a Cat" Lahr: "Bon Vivant" (LP-608).)

640216b FOXY records sung by Johnny Mercer, lyricist. "Bon Vivant" (1971: LP-533) "Talk to Me, Baby" (1974: LP-560)

640216c FOXY demonstration record sung by Johnny Mercer, lyricist. (LP-604)

640227a WHAT MAKES SAMMY RUN? orig prod. MUSIC & WORDS: Ervin Drake. ORCH: Don Walker. COND: Lehman Engel. CAST: Steve Lawrence, Sally Ann Howes, Robert Alda, Bernice Massi, Graciela Daniele, Richard France, Barry Newman. (Col KOS-2440)

640319a CINDY orig prod. MUSIC & WORDS: Johnny Brandon. ORCH: Clark McClellan. COND: Sammy Benskin. CAST: Jacqueline Mayro, Sylvia Mann, Johnny Harmon, Lizabeth Pritchett, Joseph Masiell. (ABC SOC-2)

640326a FUNNY GIRL orig prod. MUSIC: Jule Styne. WORDS:

Bob Merrill. ORCH: Ralph Burns. COND: Milton Rosenstock. CAST: Barbra Streisand, Sydney Chaplin, Danny Meehan, Kay Medford, Jean Stapleton, John Lankston. (Cap SVAS-2059)

640326b FUNNY GIRL 1968 film soundtrack, with new songs by Jule Styne, Bob Merrill, others. ORCH: Walter Scharf. COND: Herbert Ross. CAST: Barbra Streisand, Omar Sharif, Kay Medford. (Col BOS-3220)

640326c FUNNY GIRL contemp records by Barbra Streisand of orig & 1968 film casts. "I Am Woman," "People" (45/Col 4-42965) "Funny Girl," "Absent Minded Me" (both dropped from the show) (45/Col 4-43127)

640326d FUNNY GIRL contemp album by Lisa Shane, who replaced Barbra Streisand in the 1966 London prod. COND: Marcus Dodds. "People," "Don't Rain on My Parade," "The Music That Makes Me Dance," "I'm the Greatest Star" (45/Pye(E) NEP-24257)

640326e FUNNY GIRL 1966 studio prod. COND: Alyn Ainsworth. CAST: Julie Dawn, Colin Day, Stella Tanner, Shane Rimmer, chorus. (Music for Pleasure(E) 1077)

640326f FUNNY GIRL 1966 record by Jule Styne (composer), piano. "People" (LP-671)

640326g FUNNY GIRL records by Mimi Hines, who replaced Barbra Streisand in December 1965. "The Music That Makes Me Dance" (LP-709) "People," "I'm the Greatest Star" (LP-708)

640404a ANYONE CAN WHISTLE orig prod. MUSIC & WORDS: Stephen Sondheim. ORCH: Don Walker. COND: Herbert Greene. CAST: Lee Remick, Angela Lansbury, Harry Guardino, Arnold Soboloff, Gabriel Dell, James Frawley. (Col KOS-2480)

640404b ANYONE CAN WHISTLE 1973 records by Members of orig cast. Angela Lansbury, Harvey Evans: "Me and My Town" Lansbury: "A Parade in Town" (LP-169)

640404c ANYONE CAN WHISTLE 1973 record by Stephen Sondheim (composer), piano & vocal. "Anyone Can Whistle" (LP-169)(LP-563)

640407a HIGH SPIRITS orig prod. MUSIC: Hugh Martin. WORDS: Timothy Gray. ORCH: Harry Zimmerman. COND: Fred Werner. CAST: Beatrice Lillie, Tammy Grimes, Edward Woodward, Louise Troy, Timothy Gray. (ABC SOC-1)

640407b HIGH SPIRITS 1964 album by Noel Coward (author of the play on which the musical was based & director of the musical). COND: Peter Knight. "Something Tells Me," "If I Gave You," "Forever and a Day," "Home Sweet Heaven" (45/Pye(E) NEP-24196)(LP-594)

640407c HIGH SPIRITS 1964 London prod. ORCH: Harry Zimmerman. COND: Michael Moores. CAST: Cicely Courtneidge, Marti Stevens, Denis Quilley, Jan Waters. (Pye(E) NPL-18100)

640422a Puppet show LES POUPEES DE PARIS soundtrack. MUSIC: James Van Heusen. WORDS: Sammy Cahn. ORCH: Joe Reisman, Wayne Robinson, Louie Bellson. COND: Joe Reisman. CAST: Pearl Bailey, Milton Berle, Cyd Charisse, Annie Farge, Gene Kelly, Liberace, Jayne Mansfield, Tony Martin, Phil Silvers, Loretta Young, Edie Adams, Janine Forman, Crista Speck, Lance Legault, Joey Forman, Guy Marks, Paul Frees, Jane Kean, Merry Williams. (RCA LSO-1090)

640429a TO BROADWAY WITH LOVE orig prod. MUSIC & WORDS: Sheldon Harnick, Jerry Bock, others. ORCH: Philip J Lang. COND: Franz Allers. CAST: Rod Perry, Don Liberto, Millie Slavin, Patti Karr, Bob Carroll, Guy Rotondo, Miriam Burton, Nancy Leighton. (Col OS-2630)

640526a FADE OUT, FADE IN orig prod. MUSIC: Jule Styne. WORDS: Betty Comden, Adolph Green. ORCH: Ralph Burns, Ray

Ellis. COND: Colin Romoff. CAST: Carol Burnett, Jack Cassidy, Lou Jacobi, Dick Patterson, Tina Louise, Mitchell Jason, Tiger Haynes. (ABC SOC-3)

640602a FOLIES BERGERE orig (New York) prod. MUSIC & WORDS: Various. COND: Jo Basile. VOCALS: Patachou, Georges Ulmer. (Audio Fidelity 6135)

640922a FIDDLER ON THE ROOF orig prod. MUSIC: Jerry Bock. WORDS: Sheldon Harnick. ORCH: Don Walker. COND: Milton Greene. CAST: Zero Mostel, Maria Karnilova, Julia Migenes, Austin Pendleton, Bert Convy, Michael Granger. (RCA LSO-1093)

640922b FIDDLER ON THE ROOF 1966 album by Herschel Bernardi, who replaced Zero Mostel in orig prod. ORCH & COND: Peter Matz. (Col OS-3010)

640922c FIDDLER ON THE ROOF 1971 film soundtrack. ORCH & COND: John Williams. CAST: Topol, Norma Crane, Leonard Frey, Molly Picon, Paul Mann. (United Artists 10900)

640922d FIDDLER ON THE ROOF 1967 London prod. ORCH: Don Walker. COND: Gareth Davies. CAST: Topol, Miriam Karlin, Paul Whitsun-Jones, Sandor Eles, Rosemary Nichols, Linda Gardner, Jonathan Lynn. (Col SX-30742)

640922e FIDDLER ON THE ROOF studio prod. COND: Al Goodman. VOCALS: Phillip Golden, Martha Garry, chorus. (Diplomat 2349)

640922f FIDDLER ON THE ROOF studio prod. ORCH & COND: Peter Moore. VOCALS: Leslie Fyson, Joanna Merlin, Peggy Longo, Martin Meyers, Joan Brown. (Golden 260)

640922g FIDDLER ON THE ROOF 1968 studio prod. COND: Denis Holloway. CAST: Alfie Bass & Avis Bunnage (who assumed leads of London prod in 1968); Patricia Whitmore, Joanne Brown, Marti Webb, Leslie Fyson, Andy Cole, Ken Barrie, chorus. (Hallmark (E) CHM-589)

640922h FIDDLER ON THE ROOF 1969 South African prod. ORCH: Don Walker. COND: Bob Adams. CAST: Shimon Israeli, Lya Dulizkaya, David Matheson, Ferdie Uphof, Jacob Witkin, Carole Gray. (RCA(South Africa) 38-149)

640922i FIDDLER ON THE ROOF 1968 studio prod. COND: Stanley Black. CAST: Robert Merrill, Molly Picon, Mary Thomas, Andy Cole, James Tullett, Robert Bowman, Sylvia King, Barbara Moore, Patricia Whitmore. (London(E) SP-44121)

640922j FIDDLER ON THE ROOF 1971 records sung by Sheldon Harnick, lyricist. "Sunrise, Sunset," "Do You Love Me?" (both with Margery Gray); "When Messiah Comes," "How Much Richer Could One Man Be?" (both dropped from the show); "If I Were a Rich Man" (LP-535).

640922k FIDDLER ON THE ROOF 1967 studio prod. COND: Geoff Love. CAST: Bernard Spear, Stella Moray, Tony Adams, Lorraine Smith, Peter Reeves, Margaret Vickers, Mary Murphy, chorus. (Music for Pleasure(E) 1131)

640922l FIDDLER ON THE ROOF 1967 records by Theodore Bikel of 1967 touring prod. COND: Milton Greene (of orig prod). "If I Were A Rich Man," "Sunrise, Sunset" (45/Elektra EK-632)

640922*a MAGGIE MAY 1964 album by Judy Garland. MUSIC & WORDS: Lionel Bart. COND: Harry Robinson. "Maggie, Maggie May," "There's Only One Union," "The Land of Promises," "It's Yourself" (45/Cap(E) EAP-1-20630)

641020a GOLDEN BOY orig prod. MUSIC: Charles Strouse. WORDS: Lee Adams. ORCH: Ralph Burns. COND: Elliot Lawrence. CAST: Sammy Davis Jr, Billy Daniels, Paula Wayne, Kenneth Tobey, Johnny Brown, Louis Gossett, Terrin Miles. (Cap SVAS-2124 plus Cap STAO-11655. Neither has all the other has.)

153

641020b GOLDEN BOY 1968 album of 4 songs by Sammy Davis Jr of orig cast & 1968 London cast, including 2 songs ("There's a Party Going On Somewhere" & "Yes I Can") not on orig cast album. (45/Reprise(E) 30088)

641026a THE SECRET LIFE OF WALTER MITTY orig prod. MUSIC: Leon Carr. WORDS: Earl Shuman. ORCH: Ray Ellis. COND: Joe Stecko. CAST: Marc London, Cathryn Damon, Eugene Roche, Lorraine Serabian, Rudy Tronto, Charles Rydell, Christopher Norris, Rue McClanahan, Lette Rehnolds. (Col OS-2720)

641027a BEN FRANKLIN IN PARIS orig prod. MUSIC: Mark Sandrich Jr. WORDS: Sidney Michaels. ORCH: Philip J Lang. COND: Donald Pippin. CAST: Robert Preston, Ulla Sallert, Susan Watson, Franklin Kiser, Bob Kaliban, Jack Fletcher. (Cap VAS-2191)

641123a BAJOUR orig prod. MUSIC & WORDS: Walter Marks. ORCH: Mort Lindsey. COND: Lehman Engel. CAST: Chita Rivera, Nancy Dussault, Herschel Bernardi, Robert Burr, Mae Questel, Gus Trikonis, Herbert Edelman. (Col KOS-2700)

641123*a MARLENE DIETRICH orig (London) prod, rec live. MUSIC & WORDS: Various. ORCH & COND: Burt Bacharach. VOCALS: Marlene Dietrich. (Col OL-6430, entitled "Marlene Dietrich in London") (LP-191)

641215a I HAD A BALL orig prod. MUSIC & WORDS: Jack Lawrence, Stan Freeman. ORCH: Philip J Lang. COND: Pembroke Davenport. CAST: Buddy Hackett, Richard Kiley, Karen Morrow, Steve Roland, Luba Lisa, Rosetta LeNoire. (Mercury 6210)

641225a TV show THE DAWN 1966 studio prod. MUSIC: Leslie J Schnierer. WORDS: William O'Malley. CAST: Sheila Cain, Patricia Anzelmo, William Lowry, Patrick Cain. (American Record Society SP-1052)

1965

650001a Film THE PLEASURE SEEKERS soundtrack. MUSIC: James Van Heusen. WORDS: Sammy Cahn. ORCH & COND: Lionel Newman, Alexander Courage. VOCALS: Ann-Margret. (RCA LSO-1101)

650002a Film DO NOT DISTURB contemp record by Doris Day of orig cast. "Do Not Disturb" (LP-330)

650003a Film HOW TO STUFF A WILD BIKINI soundtrack. MUSIC & WORDS: mostly by Guy Hemrick, Jerry Styner. CAST: Annette Funicello, Mickey Rooney, Harvey Lembeck, Brian Donlevy, Lou Ann Simms, the Kingsmen. (Wand 671)

650004a Film TICKLE ME contemp records by Elvis Presley of orig cast. "I Feel That I've Known You Forever," "Night Rider," "Slowly but Surely," "Dirty, Dirty, Feeling," "Put the Blame on Me" (45/RCA EPA-4383)

650005a Film GIRL HAPPY soundtrack. MUSIC & WORDS: Various. VOCALS: Elvis Presley, Nita Talbot, chorus. (RCA LSP-3338 plus Talbot: "I Got News for You" on LP-496)

650006a Film HARUM SCARUM soundtrack. MUSIC & WORDS: Various. VOCALS: Elvis Presley, chorus. (RCA LSP-3468)

650007a Film SEASIDE SWINGERS soundtrack. MUSIC & WORDS: Various. VOCALS: Mike Sarne, John Leyton, Grazina Frame, Freddie & the Dreamers. (Mercury 61031)

650008a Film CAT BALLOU contemp record by Nat Cole of orig prod. "Cat Ballou" (LP-562)

650009a Record prod PASSING FAIR orig prod. MUSIC & WORDS: Jim Chapin. PIANO: Mark Donald. CAST: Jim Chapin, Mary Louise, Valentine Pringle, Dolores Perry, Mark Donald, Bill Dillard. (Proscenium PR-25)

650010a Film HELP! contemp album, incl soundtrack. MUSIC & WORDS: John Lennon, Paul McCartney, George Harrison. CAST: The Beatles. (Cap SMAS-2386)

650010b Film HELP! contemp record by The Beatles of orig prod. "Yes It Is" (45/Cap 5407)

650011a Film THE ART OF LOVE contemp records sung by Cy Coleman, composer. "The Art of Love," "Nikki" (45/Cap 5427)

650012a Film JOHN GOLDFARB, PLEASE COME HOME contemp record by Shirley MacLaine of orig cast. "John Goldfarb, Please Come Home" (45/20th Fox 558)

650013a Film UNCLE TOM'S CABIN soundtrack. MUSIC: Peter Thomas. WORDS: Aldo von Pinelli. ORCH & COND: Peter Thomas. VOCALS: Eartha Kitt, Juliette Greco, George Goodman. (Philips PHS-600-272)

650014a Film BILLIE contemp album. MUSIC & WORDS: Various. ORCH & COND: Arnold Goland. VOCALS: Patty Duke of orig cast. (United Artists UAL-4131)

650202a DIVORCE ME, DARLING! orig (London) prod. MUSIC & WORDS: Sandy Wilson. ORCH & COND: Ian MacPherson. CAST: Patricia Michael, Anna Sharkey, Cy Young, Joan Heal, Jenny Wren, Irlin Hall. (Dec(E) SKL-4675)

650202b DIVORCE ME, DARLING! 1965 album by composer Sandy Wilson (piano & vocals), with Art Greenslade & His Broadcasting Band. "Divorce Me Darling," "What Ever Happened to Love?," "Together Again," "Someone to Dance with" (45/Dec(E) DFE-8614)

650202c DIVORCE ME, DARLING! 1972 record by Sandy Wilson (composer), piano & vocal. "Blondes for Danger" (LP-755)

650206a KELLY 1964 demonstration record. MUSIC: Moose Charlap. WORDS: Eddie Lawrence. PIANO: Moose Charlap (?). VOCALS: Moose Charlap, Eddie Lawrence. (Original Cast 8025)

650216a BAKER STREET orig prod. MUSIC & WORDS: Marian Grudeff, Raymond Jessel. ORCH: Don Walker. COND: Harold Hastings. CAST: Fritz Weaver, Inga Swenson, Martin Gabel, Peter Sallis, Patrick Horgan, Teddy Green, Martin Wolfson, Daniel Keyes, Virginia Vestoff. (MGM 7000)

650216b BAKER STREET 1965 album. COND: Danny Davis. CAST: Richard Burton, Felicia Sanders, Fran Jeffries. (MGM 4293, with songs from other shows)

650222a THE EMPEROR'S NIGHTINGALE orig prod. MUSIC: Philip Fleishman. WORDS: Elsa Rael. CAST: Ken Olfson, Clark Warren, Marisha Vasek, John Joy, Peter Bruni, Bob Lussier, chorus. (Folkways 7588)

650318a DO I HEAR A WALTZ? orig prod. MUSIC: Richard Rodgers. WORDS: Stephen Sondheim. ORCH: Ralph Burns. COND: Frederick Dvonch. CAST: Elizabeth Allen, Sergio Franchi, Carol Bruce, Madeleine Sherwood, Julienne Marie, Stuart Damon, Fleury D'Antonakis, Jack Manning. (Col KOS-2770)

650327a RUMPELSTILTSKIN studio prod. MUSIC: Jacques Urbont. WORDS: David Newburge. CAST: The Peppermint Players, with Jacques Urbont in title role and as narrator. (Peter Pan 8047)

650330a THE DECLINE AND FALL OF THE ENTIRE WORLD AS SEEN THROUGH THE EYES OF COLE PORTER orig prod. MUSIC & WORDS: Cole Porter. ORCH & COND: Skip Redwine. CAST: Kaye Ballard, Harold Lang, Carmen Alvarez, William Hickey, Elmarie Wendel. (Col OS-2810, plus Ballard: "When I Was A Little Cuckoo" (LP-549).)

650511a FLORA, THE RED MENACE orig prod. MUSIC: John Kander. WORDS: Fred Ebb. ORCH: Don Walker. COND: Hal Hastings. CAST: Liza Minnelli, Bob Dishy, Mary Louise Wilson, Dortha

Duckworth, James Cresson, Cathryn Damon, Joe E Marks. (RCA LSO-1111)

650511b FLORA, THE RED MENACE records by Liza Minnelli of orig cast. "A Quiet Thing" (1965: 45/Cap 5411) (1974: LP-327) "All I Need Is One Good Break" (1965: 45/Cap 5411)

650511c FLORA, THE RED MENACE 1973 record by John Kander (composer), piano & vocal. "A Quiet Thing" (LP-659)

650511d FLORA, THE RED MENACE 1965 album. ORCH: Don Walker (of orig prod), Arnold Goland. COND: Hal Hastings (of orig prod). VOCALS: The Showgals. (RCA LSP-3412)

650516a THE ROAR OF THE GREASEPAINT — THE SMELL OF THE CROWD orig (New York) prod. MUSIC & WORDS: Leslie Bricusse, Anthony Newley. ORCH: Philip J Lang. COND: Herbert Grossman. CAST: Anthony Newley, Cyril Ritchard, Sally Smith, Gilbert Price, Joyce Jillson. (RCA LSO-1109)

650516b THE ROAR OF THE GREASEPAINT — THE SMELL OF THE CROWD 1965 album by Anthony Newley (composer and member of orig cast), released before the show opened. COND: Peter Knight. (RCA LSP-3347, entitled "Anthony Newley: Who Can I Turn To?")"

650524a TV show THE YOUNG MAN FROM BOSTON orig prod. MUSIC: Allan J Friedman. WORDS: Paul Francis Webster. VOCALS: Gordon MacRae, Kingston Trio, chorus. (Unnamed label mx WR-4546)

650616a Industrial show MR. WOOLWORTH HAD A NOTION orig prod. MUSIC & WORDS: Michael Brown. COND: Norman Paris. CAST: Ellen Martin, Michael Brown, Joy Franz, Tom Urich, chorus. (Donahue Sales Corp 2686)

650626a MARDI GRAS contemp records by Louis Armstrong (vocal & trumpet) & Guy Lombardo Orch of 1966 Jones Beach prod. "Come Along Down," "Mumbo Jumbo" (45/Cap 5716)

651007a TV show COLE PORTER: A REMEMBRANCE soundtrack. COND & PIANO: Skitch Henderson. VOCALS: William Walker, Sally Ann Howes. (Pontiac mx ST-3-TP-1/2)

651017a ON A CLEAR DAY YOU CAN SEE FOREVER orig prod. MUSIC: Burton Lane. WORDS: Alan Jay Lerner. ORCH: Robert Russell Bennett. COND: Theodore Saidenberg. CAST: Barbara Harris, John Cullum, Titos Vandis, William Daniels, Clifford David, Byron Webster. (RCA LSOD-2006)

651017b ON A CLEAR DAY YOU CAN SEE FOREVER 1970 film soundtrack with additional Lane-Lerner songs. ORCH & COND: Nelson Riddle. CAST: Barbra Streisand, Yves Montand, Jack Nicholson. (Col S-30086. Also two numbers dropped before release: Nicholson: "Who Is There among Us Who Knows?" (LP-423) Streisand, Larry Blyden: "Wait Till You're Sixty-Five" (45/unnamed label SPO-145).)

651017c ON A CLEAR DAY YOU CAN SEE FOREVER 1971 records sung by Alan Jay Lerner, lyricist. "Come Back to Me," "On a Clear Day You Can See Forever" (LP-534)

651017d ON A CLEAR DAY YOU CAN SEE FOREVER 1966 record by Burton Lane (composer), piano & vocal. "On a Clear Day You Can See Forever" (LP-671)

651103a JUST FOR OPENERS orig prod. MUSIC & WORDS: Rod Warren, Alan Friedman, others. CAST: Betty Aberlin, Richard Blair, Stockton Brigel, R G Brown, Fannie Flagg, Madeline Kahn. (Upstairs at the Downstairs 37W56)

651110a THE ZULU AND THE ZAYDA orig prod. MUSIC & WORDS: Harold Rome. ORCH & COND: Meyer Kupferman. CAST: Menasha Skulnik, Ossie Davis, Louis Gossett, Peter DeAnda, Christine Spencer. (Col KOS-2880)

651113a SKYSCRAPER orig prod. MUSIC: James Van Heusen. WORDS: Sammy Cahn. ORCH: Fred Werner. COND: John Lesko. CAST: Julie Harris, Peter L Marshall, Charles Nelson Reilly, Dick O'Neill, Rex Everhart. (Cap SVAS-2422)

651113b SKYSCRAPER records sung by Sammy Cahn, lyricist. "Everybody Has the Right to Be Wrong" (1966: LP-671) (1972: LP-658) (1974: LP-313)

651113c SKYSCRAPER 1966 album. ORCH & COND: Sid Feller. VOCALS: chorus. (Cap T-2411)

651122a MAN OF LA MANCHA orig prod. MUSIC: Mitch Leigh. WORDS: Joe Darion. ORCH: Music Makers Inc. COND: Neil Warner. CAST: Richard Kiley, Irving Jacobson, Ray Middleton, Robert Rounseville, Joan Diener, Harry Theyard, Gino Conforti, Mimi Turque, Eleanor Knapp. (Kapp KS-5505)

651122b MAN OF LA MANCHA 1972 studio prod. ORCH: Music Makers Inc. COND: Paul Weston. CAST: Jim Nabors, Marilyn Horne, Jack Gilford, Richard Tucker, Madeline Kahn, Ron Husmann, Irene Clark, David Bender. (Col S-31237)

651122c MAN OF LA MANCHA 1968 London prod. ORCH: Music Makers Inc. COND: Denys Rawson. CAST: Keith Michell, Joan Diener, Bernard Spear, Olive Gilbert, Alan Crofoot, Patricia Bredin, Peter Gordeno, Edward Atienza, David King. (Dec DXSA-7203)

651122d MAN OF LA MANCHA 1972 film soundtrack. ORCH & COND: Laurence Rosenthal. CAST: Sophia Loren, Peter O'Toole, Simon Gilbert (for Peter O'Toole), James Coco, Harry Andrews, John Castle. (United Artists 9906)

651122e MAN OF LA MANCHA 1972 studio prod. ORCH & COND: Peter Moore. VOCALS: Richard Kiley (of orig cast), Gerianne Raphael, Ed Roll, Shev Rodgers, Fred Williams, Fergus O'Kelly, chorus. (Golden 265)

651122f MAN OF LA MANCHA 1968 Paris prod, entitled "Homme de la Mancha." WORDS: Joe Darion, Jacques Brel. ORCH & COND: Francois Rauber. CAST: Jacques Brel, Joan Diener, Armand Mestral, Louis Navarre, Gerard Clavel, Jean Mauvais, Jean-Claude Calon. (Barclay(F) 80381)

651128a TV show THE DANGEROUS CHRISTMAS OF RED RIDING HOOD orig prod. MUSIC: Jule Styne. WORDS: Bob Merrill. ORCH & COND: Walter Scharf. CAST: Cyril Ritchard, Liza Minnelli, Vic Damone, The Animals. (ABC 536)

651129a ANYA orig prod. MUSIC: Sergei Rachmaninoff, arranged by Robert Wright & George Forrest. WORDS: Robert Wright, George Forrest. ORCH: Don Walker. COND: Harold Hastings. CAST: Constance Towers, Irra Petina, Michael Kermoyan, Lillian Gish, Boris Aplon, George S Irving, Ed Steffe, John Michael King. (United Artists 5133)

651210a THE YEARLING orig prod rec live. MUSIC: Michael Leonard. WORDS: Herbert Martin. ORCH: Larry Wilcox. COND: Julian Stein. CAST: Steve Sanders, David Wayne, Dolores Wilson, Carmen Mathews, Carmen Alvarez, David Hartman. (Unnamed label CA-300)

651214a LA GROSSE VALISE earlier Paris prod entitled "La Grosse Valse." MUSIC: Gerard Calvi. WORDS: Andre Maheux. ORCH: Gerard Calvi. CAST: Louis de Funes, Robert Dhery, Colette Brosset, Liliane Montevecchi, Jacques Legras. (Vogue(F) LD-593-30, entitled "La Grosse Valse")

651218a SNOW WHITE AND THE SEVEN DWARFS 1977 studio prod. MUSIC: Michael Valenti. WORDS: Elsa Rael. ORCH & COND: Michael Valenti. CAST: Christine Andreas, Reid Shelton, Margaret Whiting, John Rivera, Keith Baker, chorus. (Take Home Tunes 775, with Beauty and the Beast)

651223a THE MAD SHOW orig prod. MUSIC: Mary Rodgers. WORDS: Marshall Barer, Larry Siegel, Steven Vinaver, Stephen Sondheim ("Esteban Ria Nido"). ORCH & COND: Sam Pottle. CAST: Linda Lavin, Dick Libertini, Paul Sand, Jo Anne Worley, MacIntyre Dixon. (Col OS-2930)

651226a TV show PINOCCHIO orig prod, with minor replacements. MUSIC: Jim Eiler, Jeanne Bargy. WORDS: Jim Eiler. ORCH: Richard Hayman. COND: Richard Hayman (for Alfredo Antonini of orig prod). CAST: John Joy, David Lile, Fred Grades, Will B Able, Robert Dagny, James Marmon (for Hal Holden of orig prod), Jim Eiler (for Bob Lussier of orig prod), Marcie Stringer, Jodi Williams. (Entertainment Media 999)

1966

660001a Film THE SINGING NUN soundtrack. MUSIC & WORDS: Soeur Sourire. ORCH & COND: Harry Sukman. CAST: Debbie Reynolds. (MGM S1E-7)

660002a Film THE SWINGER 1966 album by Ann-Margret of orig cast. MUSIC & WORDS: Various. COND: Marty Paich. (RCA LSP-3710, with additional material)

660003a Record prod YOU'RE A GOOD MAN, CHARLIE BROWN orig prod. MUSIC & WORDS: Clark Gesner. ORCH & COND: Jay Blackton. CAST: Clark Gesner (composer), Orson Bean, Barbara Minkus, Bill Hinnant. (Leo 900)

660003b Record prod YOU'RE A GOOD MAN, CHARLIE BROWN 7 Mar 1967 New York stage prod. ORCH & COND: Joseph Raposo. CAST: Bill Hinnant (of orig record prod), Reva Rose, Karen Johnson, Bob Balaban, Skip Hinnant, Gary Burghoff (MGM S1E-9)

660003c Record prod YOU'RE A GOOD MAN, CHARLIE BROWN 1973 TV prod. ORCH: Elliot Lawrence, Ralph Burns. COND: Elliot Lawrence. CAST: Bill Hinnant (of orig record & stage prods), Wendell Burton, Ruby Persson, Barry Livingston, Mark Montgomery, Noelle Matlovsky. (Atlantic SD-7252)

660004a Film WINNIE THE POOH AND THE HONEY TREE contemp studio prod. MUSIC & WORDS: Richard M & Robert B Sherman. COND: Tutti Camarata. VOCALS: Sterling Holloway of orig cast, unidentified soloists, chorus. (Disneyland 1277)

660004b Film WINNIE THE POOH AND THE HONEY TREE soundtrack. VOCALS: Sterling Holloway, chorus. "Winnie the Pooh," "Up, Down, Touch the Ground," "Rumbly in My Tumbly," "Little Black Rain Cloud" (LP-661)

660005a Film THE GLASS BOTTOM BOAT contemp records by members of orig cast. Doris Day: "Soft as Starlight," "The Glass Bottom Boat" (45/Col 4-43688) "Whatever Will Be Will Be" (45/Col 4-40704) Arthur Godfrey: "The Glass Bottom Boat" (LP-702)

660006a Film A MAN CALLED ADAM soundtrack. MUSIC & WORDS: Various. VOCALS: Sammy Davis Jr, Louis Armstrong, Mel Torme. (Reprise 6180)

660007a Film SPINOUT soundtrack. MUSIC & WORDS: Various. VOCALS: Elvis Presley, chorus. (RCA LSP-3702)

660008a Film FRANKIE AND JOHNNY soundtrack. MUSIC & WORDS: Various. VOCALS: Elvis Presley, chorus. (RCA LSP-3553)

660009a Film PARADISE, HAWAIIAN STYLE soundtrack. VOCALS: Elvis Presley, chorus. (RCA LSP-3643)

660010a Film CINDERELLA soundtrack. MUSIC & WORDS: Anne & Milton Delugg. COND: Milton Delugg. VOCALS: uncredited soloists, chorus. (Camden 1085)

660107a CIAO, RUDY orig (Rome) prod. MUSIC: Armando Trovaioli. WORDS: Pietro Garinei, Sandro Giovannini. COND: Bruno Nicolai. CAST: Marcello Mastroianni, Giuliana Lojodice, Olga Villi, Giusi Raspani Dandolo. (RCA(Italy) APML-10411)

660107b CIAO, RUDY 1972 Rome Prod. COND: Armando Trovaioli (composer). CAST: Alberto Lionello, Violetta Chiarini, Mita Medici, Marzia Ubaldi, Carmen Scarpitta, Giusy Raspani Dandolo. (RCA(Italy) OLS-13)

660129a SWEET CHARITY orig prod. MUSIC: Cy Coleman. WORDS: Dorothy Fields. ORCH: Ralph Burns. COND: Fred Werner. CAST: Gwen Verdon, John McMartin, Helen Gallagher, Thelma Oliver, James Luisi. (Col KOS-2900)

660129b SWEET CHARITY 1968 film soundtrack with new songs by Coleman & Fields. ORCH: Ralph Burns. COND: Joseph Gershenson. CAST: Shirley Maclaine, Sammy Davis Jr, John McMartin, Stubby Kaye, Chita Rivera, Paula Kelly. (Dec 71502)

660129c SWEET CHARITY contemp records by Cy Coleman, composer. VOCALS: "If My Friends Could See Me Now" (LP-238) (LP-563) "You Wanna Bet" (LP-238) " Where Am I Going?" (LP-238) (LP-671) "Big Spender" Piano: "Baby Dream Your Dream" (LP-671) Piano, with chorus: "Big Spender," "The Rhythm of Life" (45/Cap 5617)

660129d SWEET CHARITY 1968 London prod. ORCH: Ralph Burns. COND: Alyn Ainsworth. CAST: Juliet Prowse, Rod McLennan, John Keston, Paula Kelly, Jospehine Blake. (CBS(E) 70035)

660129e SWEET CHARITY 1976 records by Shirley MacLaine of 1968 film cast. "If My Friends Could See Me Now," "My Personal Property," "Big Spender," "I'm a Brass Band" (LP-500)

660129f SWEET CHARITY 1967 studio prod. COND: Frank Raymond. CAST: Mary Preston, Canna Kendall, June Hunt, Valentine Palmer, John Parker, Craig Hunter, David Weldon Williams, chorus. (Saga(E) EROS-8110)

660207a Industrial show AN EVENING WITH MICHAEL BROWN AND HIS FRIFNDS orig (Colorado Springs) prod. MUSIC & WORDS: Michael Brown. ORCH & COND: Norman Paris. CAST: Michael Brown, Steve Skiles, Gary Sneed, Suzanne Astor, Leo Morrell, Tom Urich, Joel Warfield. (Unnamed label A&R 2758, also entitled "Spirit of '66")

660304a POMEGRANADA orig prod. MUSIC: Al Carmines. WORDS: H M Koutoukas. PIANO: Al Carmines. CAST: Michael Elias, Burton Supree, Margaret Wright, David Vaughan, Julie Kurnitz, Al Carmines. (Patsan 1101)

660325a Industrial show FLUSH LEFT, STAGGER RIGHT orig (Washington) prod. MUSIC: Jerry Powell. WORDS: Michael McWhinney. CAST: Robert Ryan, Hal Linden, Barbara Lang, Charles Goff, Marilyn Cooper, Gloria Bleezarde, Arte Johnson. (Unnamed label LP-1001)

660329a IT'S A BIRD IT'S A PLANE IT'S SUPERMAN orig prod. MUSIC: Charles Strouse. WORDS: Lee Adams. ORCH: Eddie Sauter. COND: Harold Hastings. CAST: Jack Cassidy, Michael O'Sullivan, Patricia Marand, Linda Lavin, Bob Holiday, Don Chastain. (Col KOS-2970)

660330a TV show ALICE IN WONDERLAND orig prod. MUSIC: Charles Strouse. WORDS: Lee Adams. ORCH: Al Capps. CAST: Doris Drew, Don Messick, "Scatman" Crothers, Henry Corden, Mel Blanc, Bill Dana. (HBR 2051)

660501a CUE MAGAZINE'S SALUTE TO ASCAP orig prod, rec live. COND: Luther Henderson. COMPERE: Abe Burrows. PIANO: Cy Coleman, Ray Henderson, James Van Heusen, Arthur Schwartz, Hoagy Carmichael, Burton Lane, Jule Styne, Harry Warren, Jimmy McHugh, Harold Arlen. VOCALS: Cy Coleman, Jack Cassidy, Leslie Uggams, Sammy Cahn, Joan Diener, Hoagy Carmichael, Dinah

Shore, Tony Bennett, Burton Lane, Johnny Desmond, Harry Warren, Sheila MacRae. (Dick Charles 52666)(LP-671)

660521a A TIME FOR SINGING orig prod. MUSIC: John Morris. WORDS: Gerald Freedman, John Morris. ORCH: Don Walker. COND: Jay Blackton. CAST: Ivor Emmanuel, Tessie O'Shea, Shani Wallis, Laurence Naismith, Frank Griso, Elizabeth Hubbard, Brian Avery. (Warner Bros 1639)

660524a MAME orig prod. MUSIC & WORDS: Jerry Herman. ORCH: Philip J Lang. COND: Donald Pippin. CAST: Angela Lansbury, Beatrice Arthur, Jane Connell, Charles Braswell, Jerry Lanning, Frankie Michaels. (Col KOS-3000)

660524b MAME 1974 film soundtrack, with a new song by Jerry Herman. CAST: Lucille Ball, Jane Connell, Beatrice Arthur, Robert Preston, Kirby Furlong, Bruce Davison. (Warner Bros 2773. Excerpt: Ball, Arthur: "Bosom Buddies" (LP-223).)

660524c MAME 1969 studio prod. CAST: Beryl Reid, Joan Turner, Keith Knight, Charles Young, Pat Whitmore, Fred Lucas, chorus. (Major Minor(E) 5005)

660524d MAME 1972 London prod rec live. Ginger Rogers, chorus: "That's How Young I Feel" (LP-402)

660524e MAME album. COND: Joseph Berlingeri. VOCALS: Joe Berl. (Parliament PLPS-901)

660524f MAME 1974 records by Jerry Herman (composer), piano and vocal. "Mame," Medley (LP-660)

660623a BELOW THE BELT orig prod. MUSIC & WORDS: Rod Warren, Michael McWhinney, others. CAST: Richard Blair, Genna Carter, Madeline Kahn, Robert Rovin, Lily Tomlin. (Upstairs 2, with Mixed Doubles)

660627a TV show UP WITH PEOPLE! orig prod. MUSIC & WORDS: Various. VOCALS: Linda Blackmore, Effie Galletly, Charles Woodard, Colwell Brothers, chorus. (Pace 1101)

660914a TV show THE LOVE SONG OF BARNEY KEMPINSKI contemp record by Alan Arkin of orig cast. "Barney's Love Song" (45/Col 4-43787)

660920a Industrial show GO FLY A KITE orig (Williamsburg, Va) prod. MUSIC & WORDS: John Kander, Fred Ebb, Walter Marks. ORCH: Larry Wilcox. COND: Ted Simons. CAST: Dean Stolber, Mary Louise Wilson, Henry Hamilton, Ted Thurston, Nancy Haywood, Valerie Harper, Carole Woodruff, Joel Warfield, Joanna Lester. (General Electric FR-1679)

660921a A HAND IS ON THE GATE orig prod. MUSIC & WORDS: Various. CAST: Leon Bibb, Roscoe Lee Browne, Josephine Premice, Cicely Tyson, Earl Jones, Moses Gunn. (Verve/Folkways 9040-2)

660928a TV show OLYMPUS 7-0000 orig prod. MUSIC & WORDS: Richard Adler. ORCH: Ralph Burns. COND: Philip Della Penna. CAST: Donald O'Connor, Larry Blyden, Phyllis Newman, Eddie Foy Jr. (Command 07)

661018a THE APPLE TREE orig prod. MUSIC: Jerry Bock. WORDS: Sheldon Harnick. ORCH: Eddie Sauter. COND: Elliot Lawrence. CAST: Barbara Harris, Larry Blyden, Alan Alda, Marc Jordan. (Col KOS-3020)

661018b THE APPLE TREE 1973 Toronto prod (Act I only — "The Diary of Adam and Eve"). ORCH & COND: Hank Monis. CAST: Tom Kneebone, Dinah Christie. (Trillium(C) 2000)

661019a MIXED DOUBLES orig prod. MUSIC & WORDS: Rod Warren, Gene Bissell, Michael McWhinney, James Rusk, others. CAST: Judy Graubart, Madeline Kahn, Larry Moss, Robert Rovin, Janie Sell, Gary Sneed. (Upstairs 2, with Below the Belt)

661106a MAN WITH A LOAD OF MISCHIEF orig prod. MUSIC: John Clifton. WORDS: John Clifton, Ben Tarver. COND: Sande Campbell. CAST: Tom Noel, Virginia Vestoff, Reid Shelton, Alice Cannon, Lesslie Nicol, Raymond Thorne. (Kapp 5508)

661106*a TV show ALICE THROUGH THE LOOKING GLASS soundtrack. MUSIC: Moose Charlap. WORDS: Elsie Simmons. ORCH: Don Costa. COND: Harper Mackay. CAST: Judi Rolin, Roy Castle, Robert Coote, Jimmy Durante, Nanette Fabray, Ricardo Montalban, Agnes Moorehead, Jack Palance, the Smothers Brothers. (RCA LSO-1130)

661120a CABARET orig prod. MUSIC: John Kander. WORDS: Fred Ebb. ORCH: Don Walker. COND: Harold Hastings. CAST: Joel Grey, Jill Haworth, Lotte Lenya, Jack Gilford, Bert Convy, Robert Sharp. (Col KOS-3040)

661120b CABARET 1972 film soundtrack, with new songs by Kander and Ebb. ORCH & COND: Ralph Burns. CAST: Liza Minnelli, Joel Grey, Greta Keller, Mark Lambert. (ABC 752)

661120c CABARET records by Liza Minnelli of 1972 film cast. 1972: "Cabaret," "Married" (LP-368) "Cabaret Medley" (LP-258) 1974: "Cabaret" (LP-327)

661120d CABARET 1968 London prod. ORCH: Don Walker. COND: Gareth Davies. CAST: Judi Dench, Lila Kedrova, Peter Sallis, Kevin Colson, Barry Dennen, David Wheldon Williams, Pamela Strong, Richard Owens. (CBS(E) 70039)

661120e CABARET 1970 Vienna prod. WORDS: Fred Ebb, Robert Gilbert. COND: Johannes Fehring. CAST: Blanche Aubry, Lya Dulizkaya, Violetta Ferrari, Harry Fuss, Klaus Wildbolz. (Preiser(Austria) SPR-3220)

661120f CABARET records by Joel Grey of orig cast. Medley incl "Willkommen" & "The Money Song" (1973: LP-440) "Willkommen" (45/Col 4-44095)

661120g CABARET 1973 records sung by the composers. PIANO: John Kander, Fred Ebb: "Cabaret," "Maybe This Time" Kander, Ebb: "Money, Money, Money" (LP-659)

661126a WALKING HAPPY orig prod. MUSIC: James Van Heusen. WORDS: Sammy Cahn. ORCH: Larry Wilcox. COND: Herbert Grossman. CAST: Norman Wisdom, Louise Troy, George Rose, Ed Bakey, Gordon Dilworth. (Cap SVAS-2631)

661205a I DO! I DO! orig prod. MUSIC: Harvey Schmidt. WORDS: Tom Jones. ORCH: Philip J Lang. COND: John Lesko. CAST: Mary Martin, Robert Preston. (RCA LSO-1128)

661205b I DO! I DO! 1968 London prod. ORCH: Philip J Lang. COND: Ian MacPherson. CAST: Ian Carmichael, Anne Rogers. (RCA(E) SF-7938)

661207a TV show ON THE FLIP SIDE orig prod. MUSIC: Burt Bacharach. WORDS: Hal David. ORCH & COND: Peter Matz. CAST: Rick Nelson, Joanie Sommers, Donna Jean Young. (Dec 74836)

661214a BREAKFAST AT TIFFANY'S orig prod rec live during New York previews. MUSIC & WORDS: Bob Merrill. ORCH: Ralph Burns. COND: Stanley Lebowsky. CAST: Mary Tyler Moore, Richard Chamberlain, Art Lund, Larry Kert, Sally Kellerman. (SPM Records CO-4788)

1967

670001a Film THOROUGHLY MODERN MILLIE soundtrack. MUSIC & WORDS: James Van Heusen, Sammy Cahn, others. ORCH & COND: Andre Previn. CAST: Julie Andrews, Carol Channing, Ann Dee. (Dec 71500. Excerpt: Dee: "Rose of Washington Square" (LP-710).)

670001b Film THOROUGHLY MODERN MILLIE records by Carol Channing of orig cast. "Thoroughly Modern Millie," "Jazz Baby" (LP-377)

670001c Film THOROUGHLY MODERN MILLIE 1977 record by Sammy Cahn, lyricist. "Thoroughly Modern Millie" (LP-503)

670001d Film THOROUGHLY MODERN MILLIE contemp album. ORCH & COND: Alan Braden. VOCALS: Millicent Martin, Diana Dors, David Kernan, Valerie Masters. (World Record Club(E) T-849)

670002a Film SMASHING TIME orig prod. MUSIC: John Addison. WORDS: George Melly, John Addison. ORCH: Raymond Jones. COND: John Addison. CAST: Rita Tushingham, Lynn Redgrave. (ABC SOC-6)

670003a Film TELL ME LIES soundtrack. MUSIC: Richard Peaslee. WORDS: Adrian Mitchell. COND: Tony Russell. CAST: Glenda Jackson, Hugh Sullivan, Michael Williams, Margie Lawrence, Robert Lloyd, Mark Jones, John Hussey. (Gre-Gar 5000)

670004a Film THE HAPPIEST MILLIONAIRE soundtrack. MUSIC & WORDS: Richard M & Robert B Sherman. ORCH & COND; Jack Elliott. CAST: Tommy Steele, Lesley Ann Warren, Fred MacMurray, John Davidson, Eddie Hodges, Paul Peterson, Joyce Bulifant, Geraldine Page, Gladys Cooper. (Buena Vista 5001)

670005a Film THE ADVENTURES OF BULLWHIP GRIFFIN soundtrack. MUSIC & WORDS: Richard M & Robert B Sherman; Mel Levin & George Bruns. VOCALS: Suzanne Pleshette, chorus. (Disneyland DQ-1291)

670006a Film DOCTOR DOLITTLE soundtrack. MUSIC & WORDS: Leslie Bricusse. ORCH & COND: Lionel Newman. CAST: Rex Harrison, Anthony Newley, Samantha Eggar, Richard Attenborough, William Dix. (20th Fox 5101)

670006b Film DOCTOR DOLITTLE 1967 album by Anthony Newley of orig cast. (RCA LSP-3839)

670006c Film DOCTOR DOLITTLE 1967 album. ORCH & COND: Marty Paich. VOCALS: Sammy Davis Jr. (Reprise 6264)

670007a Film DOUBLE TROUBLE soundtrack. MUSIC & WORDS: Various. VOCALS: Elvis Presley, chorus. (RCA LSP-3787)

670008a Film EASY COME, EASY GO soundtrack. MUSIC & WORDS: Various. Elvis Presley: "You Gotta Stop," "Sing You Children," "I'll Take Love," "Easy Come, Easy Go," "The Love Machine," "Yoga Is as Yoga Does" (45/RCA EPA-4387)

670009a Film MONKEYS, GO HOME! contemp record by Maurice Chevalier of orig cast. "Joie de Vivre" (LP-600)

670010a Film CLAMBAKE soundtrack. MUSIC & WORDS: Various. VOCALS: Elvis Presley, chorus. (RCA LSP-3893, with additional material)

670110a ICE FOLLIES OF 1967 studio prod. MUSIC & WORDS: Richard A Friesen, others. ORCH: George Hackett. COND: Pete King. VOCALS: Debbie Williams of orig prod; Mike Minor, Sally Sweetland, chorus. (Dot 25757)

670130a THE GOLDEN SCREW orig prod. MUSIC & WORDS: Tom Sankey. VOCALS: Tom Sankey. (ATCO 33-208)

670226a TV show JACK AND THE BEANSTALK soundtrack. MUSIC: James Van Heusen. WORDS: Sammy Cahn. ORCH & COND: Lennie Hayton. CAST: Gene Kelly, Bobby Riha, Marian McKnight, Marni Nixon, Ted Cassidy. (Hanna-Barbera 8511)

670404a HELLO, SOLLY! orig prod. MUSIC & WORDS: Various. COND: Al Hausman. CAST: Mickey Katz, Vivian Lloyd, Stan Porter. (Cap SW-2731)

670411a ILLYA DARLING orig prod. MUSIC: Manos Hadjidakis.

WORDS: Joe Darion. ORCH: Ralph Burns. COND: Karen Gustafson. CAST: Melina Mercouri, Orson Bean, Titos Vandis, Rudy Bond, Ninos Kourkoulos. (United Artists 9901)

670411b ILLYA DARLING 1967 album. ORCH & COND: Ralph Burns, who orchestrated the orig prod. No Vocals. (United Artists 6606)

670426a HALLELUJAH, BABY! orig prod. MUSIC: Jule Styne. WORDS: Betty Comden, Adolph Green. ORCH: Peter Matz. COND: Buster Davis. CAST: Leslie Uggams, Robert Hooks, Allen Case, Lillian Hayman, Barbara Sharma, Winston DeWitt Hemsley, Alan Weeks, (Col KOS-3090)

670731a JUDY GARLAND AT THE PALACE orig prod. MUSIC & WORDS: Various. COND: Bobby Cole. VOCALS: Judy Garland, Lorna Luft, Joe Luft. (ABC 620) (LP-189)

670926a NOW IS THE TIME FOR ALL GOOD MEN orig prod. MUSIC: Nancy Ford. WORDS: Gretchen Cryer. ORCH: Stephen Lawrence, Nancy Ford. COND: Stephen Lawrence. CAST: David Cryer, Sally Niven, Judy Frank, David Sabin, Steve Skiles, Anne Kaye, Art Wallace, John Bennett Perry. (Col OS-3130)

671013a IN CIRCLES orig prod. MUSIC: Al Carmines. WORDS: Gertrude Stein. CAST: Al Carmines, others. (Avant Garde 108)

671023a HENRY, SWEET HENRY orig prod. MUSIC & WORDS: Bob Merrill. ORCH: Eddie Sauter. COND: Shepard Coleman. CAST: Don Ameche, Carol Bruce, Robin Wilson, Neva Small, Louise Lasser, Alice Playten, Laried Montgomery. (ABC SOC-4)

671023b HENRY, SWEET HENRY contemp records by Alice Playten of orig cast. COND: Artie Schroeck. "Poor Little Person," "Henry, Sweet Henry" (45/ABC Records 11014)

671029a HAIR orig prod. MUSIC: Galt MacDermot. WORDS: Gerome Ragni, James Rado. COND: Galt MacDermot. CAST: Gerome Ragni, Walker Daniels, Jill O'Hara, Shelley Plimpton, Suzannah Evans, Linda Compton. (RCA LSO-1143)

671029b HAIR 1968 prod with new songs by same composers. COND: Galt MacDermot. CAST: Gerome Ragni, Steve Curry, Ronald Dyson, Lamont Washington, James Rado, Shelley Plimpton, Jonathan Kramer, Lynn Kellogg. (RCA LSO-1150)

671029c HAIR 1969 album of songs dropped from the show plus new songs, sung by members of orig & other casts. MUSIC: Galt MacDermot. WORDS: Gerome Ragni, James Rado. ORCH & COND: Galt MacDermot. VOCALS: Gerome Ragni, James Rado, Galt MacDermot, George Tipton, Leata Galloway, Donnie Burks, Sakinah. (RCA LSO-1163, entitled "DisinHAIRited")

671029d HAIR 1968 London prod. COND: Derek Wadsworth. CAST: Paul Nicholas, Annabel Leventon, Peter Straker, Vince Edward, Oliver Tobias, Michael Feast, Linda Kendrick, Andy Forray, Sonja Kristina. (ATCO SD-7002)

671029e HAIR 1969 Australian prod. ORCH & COND: Patrick Flynn. CAST: Terry Wilson, Wayne Matthews, Keith Glass, Terry O'Brien, Sharon Redd, Audrey Keyes, Helen Livermore, Berys Marsh. (Spin(Australia) SEL-933544)

671029f HAIR 1970 album of songs dropped from the London prod or the London cast album, plus new songs, sung by members of London cast and others. MUSIC: Galt MacDermot. WORDS: Gerome Ragni, James Rado. COND: Derek Wadsworth. VOCALS: Paul Nicholas, Joyce Rae, Gary Hamilton, Peter Straker, Diane Langton, Paul Burns. (Polydor(E) 2371-066, entitled "Fresh Hair")

671029g HAIR 1979 film soundtrack. ORCH: Galt MacDermot. CAST: John Savage, Treat Williams, Beverly D'Angelo, Annie Golden, Dorsey Wright, Don Dacus, Cheryl Barnes, Melba Moore. (RCA CBL2-3274)

671029h HAIR 1970 Amsterdam prod, sung in English. COND: Del Newman. CAST: Jan Hanson, Oliver Tobias (of 1968 London prod), Ronald Snellenberg, Marius Monkau, chorus. (Polydor(Holland) 2441-002)

671100a THE ECSTASY OF RITA JOE 1973 studio prod. MUSIC: Ann Mortifee, Willie Dunn. WORDS: George Ryga. ORCH: mostly Wolfgang Knittel. VOCALS: Ann Mortifee. (United Artists(C) UALA-126F)

671115a TV show ANDROCLES AND THE LION orig prod. MUSIC & WORDS: Richard Rodgers. ORCH: Robert Russell Bennett. COND: Jay Blackton. CAST: Norman Wisdom, Noel Coward, Ed Ames, Inga Swenson, John Cullum. (RCA LSO-1141)

671118a MATA HARI 1977 record sung by Martin Charnin, lyricist. MUSIC: Edward Thomas. "Maman" (LP-371)

671122a CURLEY McDIMPLE contemp records by Bayn Johnson & Paul Cahill of orig prod. MUSIC & WORDS: Robert Dahdah, Mary Boylan. "Curley McDimple," "I've Got A Little Secret" (45/Cap P-2116)

671207a HOW NOW, DOW JONES orig prod. MUSIC: Elmer Bernstein. WORDS: Carolyn Leigh. ORCH: Philip J Lang. COND: Peter Howard. CAST: Brenda Vaccaro, Marlyn Mason, Anthony Roberts, Hiram Sherman, Sammy Smith, Charlotte Jones, Fran Stevens, Mara Worth. (RCA LSO-1142)

671207b HOW NOW, DOW JONES records conducted by Elmer Bernstein, composer. Chorus: "Music to Their Ears," "Step to the Rear" (45/United Artists 50220)

671218a TV show CRICKET ON THE HEARTH soundtrack. MUSIC: Maury Laws. WORDS: Jules Bass. ORCH & COND: Maury Laws. CAST: Danny Thomas, Marlo Thomas, Ed Ames, Abbe Lane. (RCA LSO-1140)

1968

680001a Film STAR! soundtrack. MUSIC & WORDS: Various. ORCH & COND: Lennie Hayton. CAST: Julie Andrews, Daniel Massey, Garrett Lewis, Bruce Forsyth, Beryl Reid. (20th Fox 5102)

680002a Film WHAT'S NEW PUSSYCAT? orig prod. MUSIC: Burt Bacharach. WORDS: Hal David. CAST: Tom Jones, Manfred Mann, Dionne Warwick. (United Artists 5128)

680003a Film THE ONE AND ONLY GENUINE ORIGINAL FAMILY BAND soundtrack. MUSIC & WORDS: Richard M & Robert B Sherman. ORCH & COND: Jack Elliott. CAST: Walter Brennan, Buddy Ebsen, Lesley Ann Warren, John Davidson, Janet Blair, Wally Cox. (Buena Vista 5002)

680004a Film THE YOUNG GIRLS OF ROCHEFORT soundtrack. MUSIC: Michel Legrand. WORDS: Jacques Demy. COND: Michel Legrand. CAST: Anne Germain (for Catherine Deneuve), Claude Parent (for Francoise Dorleac), Romuald (for George Chakiris), Donald Burke (for Gene Kelly), Danielle Darrieux. (Philips PCC-2-626)

680005a Film CHITTY CHITTY BANG BANG soundtrack. MUSIC & WORDS: Richard M & Robert B Sherman. ORCH & COND: Irwin Kostal. CAST: Dick Van Dyke, Sally Ann Howes, Lionel Jeffries, Gert Frobe, Anna Quayle, Adrian Hall, Heather Ripley. (United Artists 5188)

680006a Film THE NIGHT THEY RAIDED MINSKY'S studio prod based on orig prod. MUSIC: Charles Strouse. WORDS: Lee Adams. ORCH & COND: Philip J Lang, Leroy Holmes. CAST: Jason Robards & Norman Wisdom of orig cast; Rudy Vallee, Lillian Heyman, Dexter Maitland. (United Artists 5191)

680007a Film THE JUNGLE BOOK soundtrack. MUSIC & WORDS: Richard M & Robert B Sherman, Terry Gilkyson. ORCH: Walter Sheets. COND: George Bruns. CAST: Phil Harris, Louis Prima, Darlene Carr, Sterling Holloway, George Sanders, Sebastian Cabot, Bruce Reitherman, J Pat O'Malley. (Buena Vista 4041. Excerpts: LP-661.)

680007b Film THE JUNGLE BOOK 1968 album. VOCALS: Emile Renan, Robin Grean. (Camden 1102)

680008a Film SPEEDWAY soundtrack. MUSIC & WORDS: Various. VOCALS: Elvis Presley, Nancy Sinatra, chorus. (RCA LSP-3989, with additional material)

680009a Film WINNIE THE POOH AND THE BLUSTERY DAY contemp studio prod. MUSIC & WORDS: Richard M & Robert B Sherman. ORCH & COND: Tutti Camarata. VOCALS: Sterling Holloway of orig cast, unidentified soloists, chorus. (Disneyland 1317, entitled "Winnie the Pooh and Tigger," with additional material)

680010a Film A TIME TO SING soundtrack. MUSIC & WORDS: Various. ORCH: Bill McElhiney. VOCALS: Hank Williams Jr, Shelley Fabares. (MGM 4540)

680011a Film VALLEY OF THE DOLLS 1967 album by Patty Duke of orig cast. MUSIC & WORDS: Andre Previn, Dory Previn. (United Artists UAS-6623, with other songs by Duke)

680011b Film VALLEY OF THE DOLLS soundtrack. Judy Garland: "I'll Plant My Own Tree" (dropped before release) (LP-423)

680012a THE LITTLEST CLOWN orig prod. MUSIC: Lew Kesler. WORDS: Christopher Cable. ORCH: Richard Hayman. COND: John Cacavas. CAST: Christopher Cable, Joan Shepard, Pamela Hall, Ronnie Hall, Evan Thompson, Edmund Gaynes, Yvonne Lynn. (Golden GRS-4003)

680013a Film LIVE A LITTLE, LOVE A LITTLE contemp record by Elvis Presley of orig cast. "Wonderful World" (Camden 2304, entitled "Elvis Sings 'Flaming Star'", with other songs)

680014a Film FIVE CARD STUD contemp record by Dean Martin of orig cast. "Five Card Stud" (45/Reprise 0765)

680015a Film YELLOW SUBMARINE contemp album by the Beatles of orig prod. MUSIC & WORDS: John Lennon, Paul McCartney, George Harrison. (Apple SW-153)

680103a LOVE AND LET LOVE orig prod. MUSIC: Stanley J Gelber. WORDS: Don Christopher, John Lollos. ORCH: Arthur Rubinstein. COND: Daniel Paget. CAST: Marcia Rodd, Michael O'Sullivan, Virginia Vestoff, John Cunningham, Michael Hawkins, Tony Hendra, Nic Ullett, Jospeh R Sicari, Tom Lacy. (Sam Fox mx X4RS-0371/2, entitled "Twelfth Night")

680107a HAVE I GOT ONE FOR YOU! orig prod rec live. MUSIC: Jerry Blatt. WORDS: Jerry Blatt, Lonnie Burstein. ORCH & COND: Alan Marlowe, Gloria DeHaven: "Have Got a Girl for You" (LP-272)

680113a YOUR OWN THING orig prod. MUSIC & WORDS: Hal Hester, Danny Apolinar. ORCH: Hayward Morris. COND: Charles Schneider. CAST: Igors Gavon, Rusty Thacker, Leland Palmer, Danny Apolinar, Michael Valenti, John Kuhner, Tom Ligon, Marcia Rodd (who replaced Marian Mercer of orig cast). (RCA LSO-1148)

680113b YOUR OWN THING 1968 album by Hal Hester (composer), piano(?). No vocals. (RCA LSP-3996, entitled "Hal Hester Does His Own Thing")

680113c YOUR OWN THING contemp records sung by Danny Apolinar, composer & of orig cast. ORCH & COND: Don Sebesky. "The Middle Years," "The Flowers" (45/RCA 47-9491)

680118a THE HAPPY TIME orig prod. MUSIC: John Kander. WORDS: Fred Ebb. ORCH: Don Walker. COND: Oscar Kosarin. CAST: Robert Goulet, David Wayne, Mike Rupert, Julie Gregg. (RCA LSO-1144)

680118b THE HAPPY TIME 1973 records by the composers. PIANO: John Kander. VOCALS: Fred Ebb, John Kander. "Tomorrow Morning," "Please Stay" (LP-659)

680122a JACQUES BREL IS ALIVE AND WELL AND LIVING IN PARIS orig prod. MUSIC: Jacques Brel. WORDS: Jacques Brel, Eric Blau, Mort Shuman. ORCH & COND: Wolfgang Knittel. CAST: Elly Stone, Mort Shuman, Shawn Elliott, Alice Whitfield. (Col D2S-779)

680122b JACQUES BREL IS ALIVE AND WELL AND LIVING IN PARIS 1973 Cleveland, Ohio, prod. COND: David Gooding. CAST: Cliff Bemis, David O Frazier, Providence Hollander, Theresa Piteo. (Playhouse Square CLE-2S-101)

680122c JACQUES BREL IS ALIVE AND WELL AND LIVING IN PARIS 1974 Detroit, Mich, prod. COND: Marc Chover. CAST: Barbara Bredius, Charlie Latimer, Mary Ann Paquette, Phil Marcus Esser. (Synchronicity 1306)

680122d JACQUES BREL IS ALIVE AND WELL AND LIVING IN PARIS 1975 film soundtrack. ORCH & COND: Francois Rauber. CAST: Elly Stone & Mort Shuman of orig prod; Jacques Brel (composer); Joe Masiell. (Atlantic SD2-1000)

680122e JACQUES BREL IS ALIVE AND WELL AND LIVING IN PARIS South African prod. COND: Lindsay Heard. CAST: Ann Hamblin, Alain D Woolf, Jean Dell, Ferdie Uphof. (MVN Records(South Africa) MVC-3541)

680127a DARLING OF THE DAY orig prod. MUSIC: Jule Styne. WORDS: E Y Harburg. ORCH: Ralph Burns. COND: Buster Davis. CAST: Vincent Price, Patricia Routledge, Brenda Forbes, Peter Woodthorpe, Teddy Green, Marc Jordan. (RCA LSO-1149)

680204a GOLDEN RAINBOW orig prod. MUSIC & WORDS: Walter Marks. ORCH: Pat Williams, Jack Andrews. COND: Elliot Lawrence. CAST: Steve Lawrence, Eydie Gorme, Scott Jacoby, Joseph Sirola. (Calendar 1001)

680204b GOLDEN RAINBOW records by members of orig cast. COND: Don Kirschner. Eydie Gorme: "He Needs Me Now," "How Could I Be So Wrong?" (45/Calendar 63-1002) Steve Lawrence: "Life's a Gamble," "I've Gotta Be Me" (45/Calendar 63-1001)

680222a THE THIEF OF BAGDAD orig prod. MUSIC: Lew Kesler. WORDS: Christopher Cable. ORCH: Richard Hayman. COND: John Cacavas. CAST: Ronnie Hall, Christopher Cable, Evan Thompson, Donald Westbrook, Bill Tost, Joan Shepard, Sarah Wilson. (Golden GRS-4002)

680222*a PUSS IN BOOTS orig prod. MUSIC: John Clifton. WORDS: Evan Thompson, Joan Shepard. ORCH & COND: John Cacavas. CAST: Joan Shepard, Ronnie Hall, Christopher Cable, David Pursley, Bill Tost, Pamela Hall, Evan Thompson. (Golden GRS-4001)

680305a CATCH MY SOUL 1970 London cast. MUSIC: Ray Pohlman, Emil Dean Zoghby. WORDS: William Shakespeare. ORCH: Basil Elmes. CAST: Lance LeGault, P J Proby, P P Arnold, Sharon Gurney, Dorothy Vernon, Jeffry Wickham. (HMV(E) 2383-035)

680305b CATCH MY SOUL 1973 film soundtrack. MUSIC & WORDS: Various. CAST: Lance LeGault (of 1970 London cast), Richie Havens, Season Hubley, Tony Joe White, Susan Tyrrell, Delaney Bramlett, Bonnie Bramlett. (Metromedia BML-1-0176)

680320a CANTERBURY TALES orig (London) prod. MUSIC: Richard Hill, John Hawkins. WORDS: Nevill Coghill. CAST: Wilfrid Brambell, Jessie Evans, Kenneth J Warren, Martin Starkie, Michael Logan, Nicky Henson, Billy Boyle, Daniel Thorndike, Pamela Charles, Kevin Brennan, Gay Soper. (Dec(E) SKL-4956)

680320b CANTERBURY TALES 1967 record prod, entitled "The Canterbury Pilgrims." MUSIC, ORCH, & COND: Richard Hill, John Hawkins. NARRATOR: Martin Starkie. (Grammophon(G) 139380)

680320c CANTERBURY TALES 1969 New York prod. COND: Oscar Kosarin. CAST: George Rose, Hermione Baddeley, Martyn Green, Ed Evanko, Sandy Duncan, Ann Gardner, Edwin Steffe, Bruce Hyde, Roy Cooper. (Cap SW-229)

680410a GEORGE M! orig prod. MUSIC & WORDS: George M Cohan. ORCH: Philip J Lang. COND: Jay Blackton. CAST: Joel Grey, Bernadette Peters, Jacqueline Alloway, Betty Ann Grove, Jerry Dodge, Jill O'Hara, Loni Ackerman, Harvey Evans, Danny Carroll. (Col KOS-3200)

680410b GEORGE M! records by Joel Grey of orig cast. "I Want to Hear a Yankee Doodle Tune" (Contemp: 45/Col 4-44470) Medley including "Give My Regards to Broadway," "Harrigan," "You're a Grand Old Flag," "Yankee Doodle Boy" (1973: LP-440)

680502a NEW FACES OF 1968 orig prod. MUSIC & WORDS: Various. ORCH: Lanny Meyers. COND: Ted Simons. CAST: Leonard Sillman, Gloria Bleezarde, Brandon Maggart, Michael K Allen, Marilyn Child, Rod Perry, Madeline Kahn, Suzanne Astor, Robert Klein. (Warner Bros 2551)

680509a THE BELIEVERS orig prod. MUSIC & WORDS: Voices, Inc. COND: Brooks Alexander. CAST: Anje Ray, Ron Steward, Barry Hemphill, Don Oliver, Jo Jackson, Jesse DeVore, Veronica Redd, Joseph A Walker, Shirley McKie (RCA LSO-1151)

681013a HOW TO STEAL AN ELECTION orig prod. MUSIC & WORDS: Oscar Brand. ORCH: Bhen Lanzaroni, Jay Dryer. COND: Bhen Lanzaroni. CAST: Ed Crowley, Barbara Anson, Clifton Davis, Beverly Ballard, Carole Demas, D R Allen, Thom Koutsoukos, Bill McCutcheon, Del Hinckley. (RCA LSO-1153)

681020a HER FIRST ROMAN orig prod rec live in Boston during tryout. MUSIC & WORDS: Ervin Drake. ORCH: Don Walker. COND: Peter Howard. CAST: Richard Kiley, Leslie Uggams, Claudia McNeil, Bruce MacKay, Cal Bellini, Brooks Morton. (SPM Records CO-7751)

681020b HER FIRST ROMAN contemp records by members of orig cast. Richard Kiley: "In Vino Veritas," "Come Back to Rome" (45/Atlantic PR-401) Leslie Uggams: "The Wrong Man," "Just for Today" (LP-585)

681023a MAGGIE FLYNN orig prod. MUSIC & WORDS: Hugo Peretti, Luigi Creatore, George David Weiss. ORCH: Philip J Lang. C0ND: John Lesko. CAST: Shirley Jones, Jack Cassidy, Robert Kaye, Jennifer Darling, Sybil Bowan. (RCA LSOD-2009)

681023b MAGGIE FLYNN 1968 album by "Hugo & Luigi Chorus and Orchestra." ORCH: O B Masingill, Marty Gold. (RCA LSP-4083)

681117a ZORBA orig prod. MUSIC: John Kander. WORDS: Fred Ebb. ORCH: Don Walker. COND: Harold Hastings. CAST: Herschel Bernardi, Maria Karnilova, John Cunningham, Carmen Alvarez, Lorraine Serabian. (Cap SO-118)

681117b ZORBA 1973 record by the composers. PIANO: John Kander. VOCALS: Fred Ebb, John Kander. "Life Is" (LP-659)

681117c ZORBA contemp records by Herschel Bernardi of orig cast. ORCH & COND: Frank Hunter. "Zorba Theme," "Only Love" (45/Col 4-44756)

681117*a TV show HEIDI soundtrack. MUSIC: John Williams. WORDS: Rod McKuen. COND: John Williams. VOCAL: Carri Chase. (Cap SKAO-2995)

681201a PROMISES, PROMISES orig prod. MUSIC: Burt Bacharach. WORDS: Hal David. ORCH: Jonathan Tunick. COND: Harold Wheeler. CAST: Jerry Orbach, Jill O'Hara, Edward Winter, Marian Mercer, A Larry Haines. (United Artists 9902)

681201b PROMISES, PROMISES 1969 London prod. ORCH: Jonathan Tunick. COND: Ian MacPherson. CAST: Anthony Roberts, Betty Buckley, James Congdon, Donna McKechnie, Kelly Britt, Jack Kruschen. (United Artists(E) 29075)

681201c PROMISES, PROMISES 1969 studio prod. COND: Keith Roberts. VOCALS: Aimi MacDonald, Ronnie Carroll, Patricia Whitmore. (Fontana(E) SFL-13192)

681203a TV show ELVIS soundtrack. Elvis Presley: "Memories" (45/RCA 47-9731)

681220a DAMES AT SEA orig prod. MUSIC: Jim Wise. WORDS: George Haimsohn, Robin Miller. ORCH: Jonathan Tunick. COND: Richard J Leonard. CAST: Bernadette Peters, David Christmas, Steve Elmore, Tamara Long, Joseph R Sicari, Sally Stark. (Col OS-3330)

681220b DAMES AT SEA 1969 London prod. ORCH: Bill Shepherd. COND: Ray Bishop. CAST: Joyce Blair, Blayne Barrington, Rita Burton, William Ellis, Sheila White, Kevin Scott. (CBS(E) 70063)

681220c DAMES AT SEA 1971 TV prod. ORCH & COND: Elliot Lawrence. CAST: Ann-Margret, Ann Miller, Anne Meara, Fred Gwynne, Dick Shawn, Harvey Evans. (Bell System mx K-4900/1)

1969

690001a Film CAN HEIRONYMUS MERKIN EVER FORGET MERCY HUMPPE AND FIND TRUE HAPPINESS? soundtrack. MUSIC: Anthony Newley. WORDS: Herbert Kretzmer. CAST: Anthony Newley, Joan Collins, Bruce Forsythe, Stubby Kaye, Ron Rubin. (Kapp 5509)

690002a Record prod WHAT IT WAS, WAS LOVE orig prod. MUSIC & WORDS: Gordon Jenkins. ORCH: Peter Matz, Gordon Jenkins. COND: Gordon Jenkins. CAST: Steve Lawrence, Eydie Gorme. (RCA LSP-4115)

690003a Film DARLING LILI orig prod. MUSIC: Henry Mancini. WORDS: Johnny Mercer. ORCH & COND: Henry Mancini. VOCALS: Julie Andrews, Gloria Paul, chorus. (RCA LSPX-1000)

690004a Film GOODBYE, MR. CHIPS soundtrack. MUSIC & WORDS: Leslie Bricusse. ORCH & COND: John Williams. CAST: Petula Clark, Peter O'Toole, chorus. (MGM S1E-19)

690005a Film NORWOOD soundtrack. MUSIC & WORDS: Mac Davis, Mitchell Torok, Ramona Redd. ORCH: Al De Lory, Gus Levene. COND: Al De Lory. VOCALS: Glen Campbell. (Cap SW-475)

690006a Film A BOY NAMED CHARLIE BROWN soundtrack. MUSIC & WORDS: Rod McKuen, others. ORCH: Vince Guaraldi. COND: John Scott Trotter. VOCALS: Rod McKuen, Peter Robbins, Pamelyn Ferdin, Glenn Gilger, chorus. (Col OS-3500)

690007a Film THE ARISTOCATS soundtrack. MUSIC & WORDS: Richard M & Robert B Sherman, others. VOCALS: Robie Lester, Susan Novack, Gregory Novack, Victor Sweier, Phil Harris, chorus. (Disneyland 3995)

690008a Film THE TROUBLE WITH GIRLS contemp record by Elvis Presley of orig cast. "Clean Up Your Own Back Yard" (45/RCA 47-9747)

690009a Film CHARRO! contemp record by Elvis Presley of orig cast. "Charro" (45/RCA 47-9731)

690010a Film THE CHEYENNE SOCIAL CLUB contemp record by Henry Fonda & James Stewart of orig cast. "Rolling Stone" (45/National General 007)

690102a THE FIG LEAVES ARE FALLING 1968 records sung by Allan Sherman, lyricist. MUSIC: Albert Hague. ORCH & COND: Claus Ogerman. "Juggling" (dropped from the show), "The Fig Leaves Are Falling" (45/RCA 47-9693)

690122a CELEBRATION orig prod. MUSIC: Harvey Schmidt. WORDS: Tom Jones. ORCH: Jim Tyler. COND: Rod Derefinko. CAST: Keith Charles, Michael Glenn-Smith, Susan Watson, Ted Thurston. (Cap SW-198)

690127a PEACE orig prod. MUSIC: Al Carmines. WORDS: Tim Reynolds, Al Carmines. PIANO: Al Carmines. CAST: Reathel Bean, Julie Kurnitz, George McGrath, David Vaughan, Arlene Rothlein, Margaret Wright, Marie Santell, David Pursley, David Tice. (Metromedia 33001)

690200a Industrial show PERSPECTIVE FOR THE SEVENTIES orig prod, rec live. MUSIC: Stanley Lebowsky. WORDS: Fred Tobias. CAST: Bob Gorman, Carol Joplin, Barbara Lang, Dell Lewis, Terry O'Mara, Ted Pugh, Virginia Sandifur, Alex Wipf. (RCA mx X4RS-0747/8)

690206a DEAR WORLD orig prod. MUSIC & WORDS: Jerry Herman. ORCH: Philip J Lang. COND: Donald Pippin. CAST: Angela Lansbury, Milo O'Shea, Jane Connell, Carmen Mathews, Kurt Peterson. (Col BOS-3260)

690206b DEAR WORLD 1974 record by Joe Masiell of orig cast. PIANO: Jerry Herman (composer). "I Don't Want to Know" (LP-660)

690316a 1776 orig prod. MUSIC & WORDS: Sherman Edwards. ORCH: Eddie Sauter. COND: Peter Howard. CAST: William Daniels, Paul Hecht, Clifford David, Virginia Vestoff, Ken Howard; Rex Everhart (who replaced Howard Da Silva after the show opened). (Col BOS-3310)

690316b 1776 1972 film soundtrack. ORCH: Eddie Sauter. COND: Ray Heindorf. CAST: William Daniels, Howard Da Silva, Ken Howard, Virginia Vestoff, Blythe Danner, Ronald Holgate, Stephen Nathan, John Cullum, David Ford. (Col S-31741)

690316c 1776 1970 London prod. ORCH: Eddie Sauter. COND: Ray Cook. CAST: Lewis Fiander, Bernard Lloyd, David Kernan, Vivienne Ross, David Morton, Ronald Radd, John Quentin, Cheryl Kennedy, (Col(E) SCX-6424)

690316d 1776 1970 studio prod. COND: Stan Reynolds. VOCALS: chorus. (Marble Arch(E) MALS-1327)

690502a WE'D RATHER SWITCH studio prod. MUSIC & WORDS: Larry Crane. COND: Lorenzo Fuller. CAST: Tricia Sandberg, Yancy Gerber, Martha Wilcox, Howard Lemay, Ron Collins. (Varieties 100)

690604a PROMENADE orig prod with Sandra Schaeffer replacing Madeline Kahn. MUSIC: Al Carmines. WORDS: Maria Irene Fornes. ORCH: Eddie Sauter. COND: Susan Romann. CAST: Sandra Schaeffer, Ty McConnell, Gilbert Price, Margot Albert, Glenn Kezer, Shannon Bolin, Alice Playten, Carrie Wilson, Florence Tarlow, Michael Davis. (RCA LSO-1161)

690617a OH! CALCUTTA! orig prod. MUSIC & WORDS: Peter Schickele, Stanley Walden, Robert Dennis, Jacques Levy. CAST: Nancy Tribush, Boni Enten, Mark Dempsey, Katie Drew-Wilkinson, George Welbes. (Aidart 9903)

690617b OH! CALCUTTA! 1970 Australian prod, which was cancelled before it opened. No credits given. (RCA(E) INTS-1178)

690724a DO WHAT YOU WILL! orig (Lake Oswego, Ore) prod. MUSIC: Alan Wasser. WORDS: Jeffrey Rosen. ORCH: Marc Grafe. COND: Dale Miller. CAST: Rich Frischholz, Steven A Knox, Scott Eckelman, Daryl Smith, Jena Ruchek, Don Robertson, Jan Jacobson, Rod Grafe. (Unnamed label mx 9-348M/9-349M)

690806a MY COUSIN JOSEFA orig (San Diego) prod. MUSIC & WORDS: Robert Austin. ORCH & COND: Richard Braun. CAST: Carla Alberghetti, Jack Ritschel. Leslie Cozzens, Walt Ritter, Asaad Kelada, Graciela Franks. (Harlequin 3270)

690924a SALVATION orig prod. MUSIC & WORDS: Peter Link, C C Courtney. ORCH & COND: Kirk Nurock. CAST: Yolande Bavan, Peter Link, Joe Morton, Chapman Roberts, Marta Heflin, Anne Rachel, C C Courtney. (Cap SO-337)

691021a BUTTERFLIES ARE FREE contemp record by Keir Dullea of orig & 1970(?) London prods. MUSIC & WORDS: Stephen Schwartz. "Butterflies Are Free" (LP-611)

691023a JIMMY orig prod. MUSIC & WORDS: Bill Jacob, Patti Jacob. ORCH: Jack Andrews. COND: Milton Rosenstock. CAST: Frank Gorshin, Anita Gillette, Julie Wilson, Jack Collins, Dorothy Claire, William Griffis, Paul Forrest. (RCA LSO-1162)

691206a TV show THE LITTLEST ANGEL orig prod. MUSIC & WORDS: Lan O'Kun. ORCH: Warren Meyers. CAST: Johnnie Whitaker, Fred Gwynne, Cab Calloway, Connie Stevens, Tony Randall, Corinna Manetto. (Mercury 1-603)

691214a Oratorio CHRISTMAS RAPPINGS 1979 prod. MUSIC: Al Carmines. WORDS: Traditional. COND & PIANO: Al Carmines. VOCALS: members of the Judson Poets' Theater Chorus. (Unnamed label JU-1002)

691215a GERTRUDE STEIN'S FIRST READER orig prod. MUSIC: Ann Sternberg. WORDS: Gertrude Stein. PIANO: Ann Sternberg. CAST: Michael Anthony, Joy Garrett, Frank Giordano, Sandra Thornton. (Polydor 24-7002)

691218a COCO orig prod. MUSIC: Andre Previn. WORDS: Alan Jay Lerner. ORCH: Hershy Kay. COND: Robert Emmett Dolan. CAST: Katherine Hepburn, George Rose, Gale Dixon, David Holliday, Rene Auberjonois, Jack Dabdoub, Jon Cypher. (Paramount 1002)

691230a MAX MORATH AT THE TURN OF THE CENTURY orig (Philadelphia) prod. MUSIC & WORDS: Various. ORCH: Fred Karlin, Ray Wright. COND: Fred Karlin. PIANO & VOCALS: Max Morath. (RCA LSO-1159)

1970

700001a Film SCROOGE soundtrack. MUSIC & WORDS: Leslie Bricusse. ORCH: Herbert W Spencer, Gordon Langford, David Lindup. COND: Ian Fraser. CAST: Albert Finney, Kenneth More, Laurence Naismith, David Collings, Anton Rodgers, Suzanne Neve, Richard Beaumont, Alec Guinness. (Col S-30258)

700002a Film HELLO-GOODBYE record by Genevieve Gilles of orig cast. "Hello-Goodbye" (45/20th Fox 6717)

700003a Film MYRA BRECKINRIDGE soundtrack. Mae West: "You Gotta Taste All the Fruit," "Hard to Handle" (45/20th Fox TK-4580)

700004a Record prod EARL OF RUSTON orig prod. MUSIC & WORDS: Peter Link, C C Courtney, Ragan Courtney. VOCALS: "The Salvation Company," presumably including C C Courtney of May 5, 1971 stage prod. (Cap ST-465)

700005a Film CHANGE OF HABIT contemp record by Elvis Presley of orig cast. "Rubberneckin'" (45/RCA 47-9768)

700006a Film THE MAGIC GARDEN OF STANLEY SWEETHEART soundtrack. MUSIC & WORDS: Various. VOCALS & GROUPS: Bill Medley, Angeline Butler, Michael Greer, Eric Burdon & War, the Mike Curb Congregation, Stilroc, Crow, David Lucas, the Wheel. (MGM 1SE-20ST)

700006b Film THE MAGIC GARDEN OF STANLEY SWEETHEART 1975 record. MUSIC: Michel Legrand. WORDS: Alan & Marilyn Bergman. ORCH, COND, & PIANO: Michel Legrand (composer). Lena Horne: "Nobody Knows" (LP-675)

700103a GONE WITH THE WIND orig (Tokyo) prod, entitled "Scarlett." MUSIC: Harold Rome. WORDS: Harold Rome, Tokiko Iwatani, Ryo Fukui. ORCH: Meyer Kupferman. COND: Lehman Engel. CAST: Sakura Jinguji, Kinya Kitaoji, Jiro Tamiya, Chieko Baisho, Sakura Kamo. (Nivico(J) SJET-9210/9211)

700103b GONE WITH THE WIND 1972 London prod, with several changes in Rome's score. ORCH: Keith Amos. COND: Ray Cook. CAST: Harve Presnell, June Ritchie, Patricia Michael, Robert Swann, Brian Davies, Isabelle Lucas, Marion Ramsey, Bessie Love, Doreen Hermitage, Harry Goodier, Celinda Frediani. (Col(E) SCXA-9252)

700103c GONE WITH THE WIND 1973 album sung by the composer, Harold Rome, accompanied by the Et Tu Brutus ensemble. A few changes in the score. (Chappel(E) 101)

700126a THE LAST SWEET DAYS OF ISAAC orig prod. MUSIC: Nancy Ford. WORDS: Gretchen Cryer. ORCH & COND: Clay Fullum. CAST: Austin Pendleton, Fredericka Weber, Charles Collins, C David Colson, Louise Heath, John Long. (RCA LSO-1169)

700127a JOY orig prod. MUSIC & WORDS: Oscar Brown Jr, Luiz Henrique, Sivuca, others. COND: Sivuca. CAST: Oscar Brown Jr, Jean Pace, Sivuca. (RCA LSO-1166)

700208a EXCHANGE orig prod. MUSIC & WORDS: Mike Brandt, Michael Knight, Robert J Lowery, Susan Kay. VOCALS: Mike Brandt, Michael Knight, Susan Kay, Pamela Talus, Penelope Anne Bodry, Robert J Lowery. (Atlantic SD-8263, entitled "Tamalpais Exchange")

700302a BILLY NONAME orig prod. MUSIC & WORDS: Johnny Brandon. ORCH: Clark McClellan. COND: Sammy Benskin. CAST: Donny Burks, Alan Weeks, Hattie Winston, Urylee Leonardos, Glory Van Scott, Roger Lawson, Marilyn Johnson. (Roulette 11)

700303a TV show GOLDILOCKS 1969 studio prod by members of orig prod. MUSIC & WORDS: Richard M & Robert B Sherman. ORCH: Doug Goodwin. VOCALS: Bing Crosby, Mary Frances Crosby, Kathryn Crosby. (Disneyland 3998)

700315a PURLIE orig prod. MUSIC: Gary Geld. WORDS: Peter Udell. ORCH: Garry Sherman, Luther Henderson. COND: Joyce Brown. CAST: Cleavon Little, Melba Moore, John Heffernan, Sherman Hemsley, Novella Nelson, C David Colson. (Ampex 40101)

700315b PURLIE record by Melba Moore of orig cast. ORCH & COND: Jimmy Wisner. "Purlie" (45/Mercury 73058)

700318a THE HOUSE OF LEATHER orig prod. MUSIC: Dale Menten. WORDS: Dale Menten, Frederick Gaines. ORCH: Dale Menten. Music played by Blackwood Apology. VOCALS: Dennis Craswell, Tom Husting, Dennis Libby, Dale Menten, Bruce Pedalty. (Fontana 67591)

700322a BLOOD RED ROSES 1978 concert performances by Michael Valenti (composer), piano & vocals. WORDS: John Lewin. "The Fair Dissenter Lass," "Blood Red Roses" (LP-650)

700326a MINNIE'S BOYS orig prod. MUSIC: Larry Grossman. WORDS: Hal Hackady. ORCH: Ralph Burns. COND: John Berkman. CAST: Shelly Winters, Mort Marshall, Arny Freeman, Richard B Shull, Daniel Fortus, Lewis J Stadlen, Julie Kurnitz. (Project 3 TS-6002)

700330a APPLAUSE orig prod. MUSIC: Charles Strouse. WORDS: Lee Adams. ORCH: Philip J Lang. COND: Donald Pippin. CAST: Lauren Bacall, Len Cariou, Penny Fuller, Ann Williams, Brandon Maggart, Bonnie Franklin, Robert Mandan, Lee Roy Reams. (ABC SOC-11)

700408a CRY FOR US ALL orig prod. MUSIC: Mitch Leigh. WORDS: William Alfred, Phyllis Robinson. ORCH: Carlyle Hall. COND: Herbert Grossman. CAST: Joan Diener, Robert Weede, Steve Arlen, Helen Gallagher, Tommy Rall, William Griffis, Scott Jacoby, Darel Glaser, Todd Jones. (Project 3 1000)

700426a COMPANY orig prod. MUSIC & WORDS: Stephen Sondheim. ORCH: Jonathan Tunick. COND: Harold Hastings. CAST: Dean Jones, Elaine Stritch, Barbara Barrie, Pamela Myers, Charles Kimbrough, George Coe, Susan Browning, Steve Elmore. (Col OS-3550)

700426b COMPANY 1973 records by members of orig prod. Donna McKechnie, Pamela Myers, Susan Browning: "You Could Drive a Person Crazy" Beth Howland, Steve Elmore, Teri Ralston: "Getting Married Today" Larry Kert (who replaced Dean Jones in orig cast): "Happily Ever After," "Being Alive" (LP-169)

700426c COMPANY orig prod with Larry Kert, who replaced Dean Jones in orig cast. Other credits same as for 700426a. (CBS(E) 70108)

700506a COLETTE orig prod. MUSIC: Harvey Schmidt. WORDS: Tom Jones. PIANO: Harvey Schmidt. Three songs sung by cast in unison. (MIO International 3001)

700518a THE ME NOBODY KNOWS orig prod. MUSIC: Gary William Friedman. WORDS: Will Holt, Herb Schapiro. ORCH & COND: Gary William Friedman. CAST: Melanie Henderson, Northern J Calloway, Jose Fernandez, Gerri Dean, Kevin Lindsay, Beverly Ann Bremers, Hattie Winston. (Atlantic 1566)

700603a WHISPERS ON THE WIND orig prod. MUSIC: Lor Crane. WORDS: John B Kuntz. CAST: David Cryer, Karen Morrow, Joe Ponazecki, Nancy Dussault, Patrick Fox, chorus. (Friends of Lincoln Center SS-492)

701019a THE ROTHSCHILDS orig prod. MUSIC: Jerry Bock. WORDS: Sheldon Harnick. ORCH: Don Walker. COND: Milton Greene. CAST: Paul Hecht, Leila Martin, Keene Curtis, Jill Clayburgh, Hal Linden. (Col S-30337)

701019b THE ROTHSCHILDS 1971 record sung by Sheldon Harnick, lyricist. "In My Own Lifetime" (LP-535)

701026a PAUL SILLS' STORY THEATRE orig prod. MUSIC & WORDS: Bob Dylan, Country Joe McDonald, George Harrison, Hamid Hamilton Camp. Played by the True Brethren. CAST: Hamid Hamilton Camp, Lewis Ross. (Col SG-30415)

701108a TOUCH orig prod. MUSIC & WORDS: Kenn Long, Jim Crozier, Gary Graham. ORCH: Glenn Osser. COND: Jim Crozier. CAST: Phyllis Gibbs, Kenn Long, Gerard Doff, Peter J Mitchell, Barbara Ellis, Ava Rosenblum, Norman Jacob, Dwight Jayne, Susan Rosenblum. (Ampex 50102)

701110a TWO BY TWO orig prod. MUSIC: Richard Rodgers. WORDS: Martin Charnin. ORCH: Eddie Sauter. COND: Jay Blackton. CAST: Danny Kaye, Harry Goz, Madeline Kahn, Michael Karm, Walter Willison, Tricia O'Neil, Joan Copeland, Marilyn Cooper. (Col S-30338)

701215a ISABEL'S A JEZEBEL orig (London) prod. MUSIC: Galt MacDermot. WORDS: William Dumaresq. COND: Steve Gillette. CAST: Peter Farrell, Michele Mowbray, Frank Aiello, Helen Chappell, Maria Popkiewitz, Miguel Sergides, Howard Wakeling. (United Artists(E) 29148)

1971

710001a Film BEDKNOBS AND BROOMSTICKS soundtrack. MUSIC & WORDS: Richard M & Robert B Sherman. ORCH & COND: Irwin Kostal. CAST: Angela Lansbury, David Tomlinson. (Buena Vista 5003)

710002a Film WILLY WONKA & THE CHOCOLATE FACTORY soundtrack. MUSIC & WORDS: Leslie Bricusse, Anthony Newley. ORCH & COND: Walter Scharf. VOCALS: Uncredited. (Paramount 6012)

710003a Record prod PINOCCHIO orig prod. MUSIC & WORDS: "The Charlotte Russe". VOCALS: Uncredited soloists, chorus. (Peter Pan BR-503)

710228a THE SURVIVAL OF ST. JOAN orig prod. MUSIC: Hank & Gary Ruffin. WORDS: James Lineberger. Performed by "Smoke Rise," a vocal-instrumental group. (Paramount 9000)

710404a FOLLIES orig prod. MUSIC & WORDS: Stephen Sondheim. ORCH: Jonathan Tunick. COND: Harold Hastings. CAST: Alexis Smith, Gene Nelson, Dorothy Collins, John McMartin, Yvonne DeCarlo, Fifi D'Orsay, Mary McCarty, Ethel Shutta, Michael Bartlett. (Cap SO-761)

710404b FOLLIES 1973 records by members of orig cast. Justine Johnson, Victoria Mallory: "One More Kiss" Ethel Shutta: "Broadway Baby" Dorothy Collins, John McMartin: "Pleasant Little Kingdom" (cut-out), "Too Many Mornings" Alexis Smith: "Could I Leave You?" Dorothy Collins: "Losing My Mind" (LP-169)

710415a 70, GIRLS, 70, orig prod. MUSIC: John Kander. WORDS: Fred Ebb. ORCH: Don Walker. COND: Oscar Kosarin. CAST: Mildred Natwick, Hans Conried, Lillian Roth, Gil Lamb, Lillian Hayman, Lucie Lancaster, Goldye Shaw, Tommy Breslin, Henrietta Jacobson. (Col S-30589)

710415b 70, GIRLS, 70 1973 record by the composers. PIANO: John Kander. VOCAL: Fred Ebb, John Kander. "Yes" (LP-659)

710517a GODSPELL orig prod. MUSIC: Stephen Schwartz, Peggy Gordon. WORDS: Stephen Schwartz, Jay Hamburger. ORCH & COND: Stephen Schwartz. CAST: Stephen Nathan, David Haskell, Gilmer McCormick, Robin Lamont, Jeffrey Mylett. (Bell 1102)

710517b GODSPELL 1973 film soundtrack, with a new Schwartz song and a song by Peggy Gordon & Jay Hamburger. ORCH: Stephen Reinhardt. CAST: David Haskell, Victor Garber, Robin Lamont, Joanne Jonas, Lynne Thigpen, Merrell Jackson, Katie Hanley. (Bell 1118)

710517c GODSPELL 1972 London prod. COND: Stephen Schwartz. CAST: Jeremy Irons, David Essex, Julie Covington, Verity-Anne Meldrum, Marti Webb, Tom Saffery, Deryk Parkin, Gay Soper, Neil Fitzwilliam. (Bell(E) 203)

710517d GODSPELL 1972 studio prod. No credits. (Music for Pleasure(E) 5271)

710517e GODSPELL Nairobi prod. COND: Kendall Davies. CAST: Tony Rickell, Ray Charmen, Charlene Jones, Grace Waugh, Helen Forbes, Iris Talman, Julie Anderson. (Andrew Crawford(Kenya) ACP-LP-701)

710517f GODSPELL 1971 Australian prod. COND: Rory Thomas. CAST: Christopher Pate, Colleen Hewett, Paul Reid Roman, Jillian

Archer, Chris Sheil, Dominic Luca, Rob Ellis. (Festival(Australia) SFL-934486)

710517g GODSPELL 1976(?) South African prod, CAST: Bruce Millar, Des Lindberg, Jenny Cantan, Graham Clarke. (Cat Records(South Africa) CAL-16000)

710606a A NOTEWORTHY OCCASION orig prod, rec live. PIANO & VOCALS: Josef Myrow, Harry Ruby, Harold Adamson, Sammy Fain, Hoagy Carmichael, Johnny Mercer (vocal only). (Unnamed label R-2658)(LP-694)

710610a SANDY WILSON THANKS THE LADIES rec live in 1972. MUSIC & WORDS: Sandy Wilson. VOCALS & PIANO: Sandy Wilson. (Overtures(E) 1001)(LP-755)

710701a TV show JULIE AND CAROL AT LINCOLN CENTER soundtrack. MUSIC & WORDS: Various. ORCH & COND: Peter Matz. CAST: Julie Andrews, Carol Burnett. (Col S-31153)

710814a TV show ONCE UPON A TOUR soundtrack. MUSIC & WORDS: Various. COND: Jack Elliott. CAST: Dora Hall, Phil Harris, Frank Sinatra Jr, Oliver. (Cozy Records 2000)

711012a JESUS CHRIST SUPERSTAR 1970 record prod. MUSIC: Andrew Lloyd Webber. WORDS: Tim Rice. ORCH: Andrew Lloyd Webber. COND: Alan Doggett. CAST: Yvonne Elliman & Barry Dennen of orig (New York) cast; Ian Gillan, Murray Head, Mike d'Abo, Victor Brox, John Gustafson, Paul Davis, Brian Keith, Paul Raven, Annette Brox. (Dec DXSA-7206)

711012b JESUS CHRIST SUPERSTAR orig (New York) prod. ORCH: Andrew Lloyd Webber. COND: Marc Pressel. CAST: Yvonne Elliman, Barry Dennen, Jeff Fenholt, Ben Vereen, Paul Ainsley, Bob Bingham, Phil Jethro. (MCA 7-1503)

711012c JESUS CHRIST SUPERSTAR 1972 London prod. ORCH: Andrew Lloyd Webber. COND: Anthony Bowles. CAST: Paul Nicholas, Stephen Tate, Dana Gillespie, John Barker, Paul Jabara, George Harris, Richard Barnes, Derek James, Jimmy Cassidy. (MCA MDKS-8008)

711012d JESUS CHRIST SUPERSTAR 1972 Australian prod. COND: Patrick Flynn. CAST: Trevor White, Jon English, Michelle Fawdon, Robin Ramsay, Peter North, John Young, Stevie Wright, Rory O'Donoghue. (MCA(Australia) MAPS-6244)

711012e JESUS CHRIST SUPERSTAR 1973 film soundtrack. ORCH: Andrew Lloyd Webber. COND: Andre Previn. CAST: Ted Neely, Carl Anderson, Yvonne Elliman, Barry Dennen, Bob Bingham, Larry T Marshall. (MCA 2-11000)

711012f JESUS CHRIST SUPERSTAR 1972 studio prod. No credits. (Music for Pleasure(E) 5280)

711019a AMBASSADOR orig (London) prod. MUSIC: Don Gohman. WORDS: Hal Hackady. ORCH: Philip J Lang. COND: Gareth Davies. CAST: Howard Keel & Danielle Darrieux (both also of 1972 New York prod); Margaret Courtenay, Judith Paris, Toni-Sue Burley, Blain Fairman, Isobel Stuart, Neville Jason. (RCA(E) SER-5618)

711020a AIN'T SUPPOSED TO DIE A NATURAL DEATH orig prod. MUSIC & WORDS: Melvin van Peebles. COND: Harold Wheeler. CAST: Various. (A&M Records SP-3510)

711020b AIN'T SUPPOSED TO DIE A NATURAL DEATH album by Melvin van Peebles, composer. ORCH & COND: Warren Smith. (A&M Records SP-4223)

711021a TO LIVE ANOTHER SUMMER, TO PASS ANOTHER WINTER orig New York prod. MUSIC: Dov Seltzer, others. WORDS: Naomi Shemer, Gary McFarland, others. COND: David Krivoshei. CAST: Rivka Raz, Aric Lavie, Yona Atari, Ili Gorlizki, Hanan Goldblatt. (Buddah 95004)

711102a THE GRASS HARP orig prod. MUSIC: Claibe Richardson. WORDS: Kenward Elmslie. ORCH: J (Billy) Ver Planck, Jonathan Tunick, Robert Russell Bennett. COND: Theodore Saidenberg. CAST: Barbara Cook, Carol Brice, Karen Morrow, Ruth Ford, Max Showalter, Russ Thacker. (Painted Smiles 1354)

711201a TWO GENTLEMEN OF VERONA orig prod. MUSIC: Galt MacDermot. WORDS: John Guare. ORCH: Harold Wheeler. CAST: Jonelle Allen, Diana Davila, Clifton Davis, Raul Julia, John Bottoms, Norman Matlock, Frank O'Brien, Alex Elias. (ABC BCSY-1001)

711201b TWO GENTLEMEN OF VERONA 1973 London prod. COND: Clive Chaplin. CAST: Ray C Davis, Jean Gilbert, Derek Griffiths, Benny Lee, Samuel E Wright, Keefe West, B J Arnau, Veronica Clifford, Michael Staniforth, Minoo Golvala. (RSO Records(E) 2394-110)

711201c TWO GENTLEMEN OF VERONA album by Sheila Gibbs & Ken Lowry, understudies of orig prod. COND & PIANO: Galt MacDermot (composer). (Kilmarnock 72004)

711203a TV show SANTA CLAUS IS COMING TO TOWN soundtrack. MUSIC: J Fred Coots, Maury Laws. WORDS: Haven Gillespie, Jules Bass. ORCH: Maury Laws. CAST: Fred Astaire, Mickey Rooney, Keenan Wynn. (MGM 4732)

711219a INNER CITY orig prod. MUSIC: Helen Miller. WORDS: Eve Merriam. ORCH: Gordon Harrell. COND: Clay Fullum. CAST: Allan Nicholls, Linda Hopkins, Carl Hall, Joy Garrett, Delores Hall, Paulette Ellen Jones, Florence Tarlow, Larry Marshall, Fluffer Hirsch. (RCA LSO-1171)

711220a HIS MONKEY WIFE orig (London) prod. MUSIC & WORDS: Sandy Wilson. COND: Richard Holmes. CAST: Robert Swann, Myvanwy Jenn, Bridget Armstrong, Jonathan Elsom, Jeffry Wickham, June Ritchie, Sally Mates, Roland Curram. (President(E) 1051)

711220b HIS MONKEY WIFE 1972 record by Sandy Wilson (composer), piano & vocal. "Marriage" (LP-755)

1972

720001a Film SNOOPY, COME HOME soundtrack. MUSIC & WORDS: Richard M & Robert B Sherman. ORCH & COND: Don Ralke. VOCALS: Thurl Ravenscroft, Shelby Flint, Don Ralke, Ray Pohlman, Linda Ercoli, Guy Pohlman, chorus. (Col S-31541)

720002a Film ALICE'S ADVENTURES IN WONDERLAND soundtrack. MUSIC: John Barry. WORDS: Don Black. ORCH & COND: John Barry. CAST: Fiona Fullerton, Davy Kaye, Michael Crawford, Robert Helpman, Peter Sellers, Dudley Moore, Flora Robson, Peter Bull, Michael Hordern, Spike Mulligan. (Warner Bros(E) BS-2671)

720003a Film MARJOE soundtrack. MUSIC & WORDS: Various. CAST: Marjoe Gortner, Holland Sisters, the Countrymen, June Samuels, The Annointed Ones, Jerry Keller. (Warner Bros BS-2667)

720004a Record prod FREE TO BE ... YOU AND ME orig prod. MUSIC & WORDS: Mary Rodgers, Sheldon Harnick, Carol Hall, others. ORCH & COND: Stephen Lawrence. CAST: Diana Ross, Jack Cassidy, Shirley Jones, Marlo Thomas, Tom Smothers, Alan Alda, Harry Belafonte, Rosey Grier, the New Seekers, Sisters and Brothers. (Arista AL-4003)

720117a TV show 'S WONDERFUL, 'S MARVELOUS, 'S GERSHWIN soundtrack MUSIC: George Gershwin. WORDS: Ira Gershwin, B G DeSylva, DuBose Heyward. ORCH & COND: Elliot Lawrence. CAST: Jack Lemmon, Fred Astaire, Leslie Uggams, Larry Kert, Linda Bennett, Robert Guillaume. (Daybreak DR-2009)

720214a GREASE orig prod. MUSIC & WORDS: Jim Jacobs, Warren Casey. ORCH: Michael Leonard. COND: Louis St Louis. CAST: Carole Demas, Adrienne Barbeau, Barry Bostwick, James Canning, Alan Paul, Walter Bobbie, Marya Small, Garn Stephens. (MGM 1SE-34)

720214b GREASE 1978 film prod. COND: Bill Oakes. CAST: John Travolta, Olivia Newton-John, Frankie Valli, Frankie Avalon, Stockard Channing, Cindy Bullens, Sha-Na-Na, Louis St Louis, Jeff Conaway. (RSO Records RS-2-4002)

720214c GREASE 1978 South African prod. ORCH: Michael Leonard. COND: Josh Sklair. CAST: Bruce Millar, Nigel Daly, Sue Kiel, Leonie Hofmeyr. (Music for Pleasure (South Africa) SRSJ-8079)

720310a DANDELION WINE studio prod. MUSIC: William Goldenberg. WORDS: Larry Alexander. CAST: Art Lund, Penny Fuller, Chris Votos, Scott Jacoby, David Gold, Ronn Carroll, Joseph Macauley, Elaine Swann, Casper Roos, Georgia Heaslip, Peter Falzone. (Unnamed label BS-321)

720326a A CELEBRATION OF RICHARD RODGERS orig prod rec live. MUSIC: Richard Rodgers. WORDS: Lorenz Hart, Oscar Hammerstin II, Richard Rodgers, Martin Charnin. COND: Colin Romoff. CAST: Walter Willison, Tricia O'Neil, Pamela Myers, Tony Randall, Bobby Short, Helen Gallagher, Gene Nelson, Gordon MacRae, Celeste Holm, Joanna Simon, John Reardon, Benay Venuta, John Green (piano), Terry Saunders, Richard Kiley, Leonard Bernstein, Mary Martin. (Friends of the Theatre & Music Collection 545)(LP-509)

720409a SUGAR orig prod. MUSIC: Jule Styne. WORDS: Bob Merrill. ORCH: Philip J Lang. COND: Elliot Lawrence. CAST: Robert Morse, Tony Roberts, Cyril Ritchard, Elaine Joyce, Sheila Smith. (United Artists 9905)

720419a DON'T BOTHER ME, I CAN'T COPE orig prod. MUSIC & WORDS: Micki Grant. ORCH & COND: Danny Holgate. CAST: Alex Bradford, Hope Clarke, Bobby Hill, Arnold Wilkerson, Micki Grant, Alberta Bradford. (Polydor 6013)

720427a CLOWNAROUND orig (Oakland, CA) prod. MUSIC: Moose Charlap. WORDS: Alvin Cooperman. ORCH: Jack Elliott, Allyn Ferguson. COND: Harper MacKay. VOCALS: Uncredited soloists, chorus. Directed by Gene Kelly. (RCA LSP-4741)

720515a HARD JOB BEING GOD orig prod. MUSIC & WORDS: Tom Martel. ORCH: Tom Martel. COND: John O'Reilly. CAST: Tom Martel, Joe Valentine, Tom Troxell, John O'Reilly, Susie Walcher, Dorothy Lerner. (GWP Records 2036)

720516a DON'T PLAY US CHEAP orig prod. MUSIC & WORDS: Melvin van Peebles. ORCH: Harold Wheeler. CAST: Avon Long, Joseph Keyes, Thomas Anderson, Joshie Jo Armstead, Robert Dunn, Rhetta Hughes, Mabel King, George McCurn, Esther Rolle. (Stax 2-3006)

720521a HEATHEN! records by Al Lopaka. MUSIC & WORDS: Eaton Magoon Jr. "More Better Go Easy," "My Sweet Tomorrow," "The Eighth Day," "Christianity," "The Rising Surf" (Lehua SL-7002, entitled "The Isle of Al Lopaka," with additional material)

720522a HARK! orig prod. MUSIC: Dan Goggin, Marvin Solley. WORDS: Robert Lorick. ORCH: John Lissauer. COND: Sande Campbell. CAST: Dan Goggin, Marvin Solley, Jack Blackton, Danny Guerrero, Charron Miller, Elaine Petricoff, chorus. (Ellison mx STK-1015/6/7/8)

720522b HARK! album. VOCALS: Dan Goggin & Marvin Solley (composers & of orig prod & 1973 touring prod); Dianne della Rosa & Ron de Salvo (of 1973 touring prod). From orig prod, sung by all 4: "Hark!," "In a Hundred Years" From 1973 touring prod: "Starsong" (sung by della Rosa),"A Mishandled Tribute to the Nixon Administration" (sung by all 4) (Concert Co JGR-300, entitled "Something for Everybody's Mother," with additional material)

720612a BEAUTY AND THE BEAST 1977 studio prod. MUSIC: Michael Valenti. WORDS: Elsa Rael. ORCH & COND: Michael Valenti. CAST: Reid Shelton, Christine Andreas, Gilbert Price, Sigrid Heath, Diane Tarlton, Steve Sterner, Howard Cutler, chorus. (Take Home Tunes 775, with Snow White and the Seven Dwarfs)

720619a JOAN orig prod. MUSIC & WORDS: Al Carmines. PIANO: Al Carmines. CAST: Lee Guilliatt, others. (Judson 1001)

720710a COWARDY CUSTARD orig (London) prod. MUSIC & WORDS: Noel Coward. ORCH: Keith Amos. COND: John Burrows. CAST: Patricia Routledge, John Moffatt, Derek Waring, Una Stubbs, Peter Gale, Elaine Delmar, Tudor Davies, Jonathan Cecil, Anna Sharkey. (RCA(E) 5656/7)

720910a TV show LIZA WITH A "Z" soundtrack. MUSIC & WORDS: John Kander, Fred Ebb, others. VOCALS: Liza Minnelli, chorus. (Col KC-31762)(LP-258)

720910b TV show LIZA WITH A "Z" 1972 records by Liza Minnelli of orig prod. "Liza with a 'Z'" (sung in French), "God Bless the Child," "My Mammy" (LP-368)

720910c TV show LIZA WITH A "Z" 1973 record by the composers. PIANO: John Kander. VOCAL: Fred Ebb. "Liza with a 'Z'" (LP-659)

721001a BERLIN TO BROADWAY WITH KURT WEILL orig prod. MUSIC: Kurt Weill. WORDS: Various. ORCH: Newton Wayland. COND: Newton Wayland (for Robert Rogers). CAST: Margery Cohen, Ken Kercheval, Judy Lander, Jerry Lanning, Hal Watters. (Paramount PAS-4000)

721004a OH, COWARD! orig prod. MUSIC & WORDS: Noel Coward. ORCH & COND: Rene Wiegert. CAST: Barbara Cason, Roderick Cook, Jamie Ross. (Bell 9001)

721009a DUDE orig prod. MUSIC: Galt MacDermot. WORDS: Gerome Ragni. ORCH: Galt MacDermot, Horace Ott. COND: Thomas Pierson. VOCALS: Salome Bey, Nell Carter, Alan Braunstein, Leta Galloway, Jim Farrell, Nat Morris, David Lasley. (Kilmarnock 72007, entitled "The Highway Life")

721009b DUDE 1972 album by Salome Bey (of orig cast) & chorus. COND & PIANO: Galt MacDermot (composer). (Kilmarnock 72003)

721019a MOTHER EARTH 1971 San Francisco (?) prod. MUSIC: Toni Shearer. WORDS: Ron Thronson. CAST: Patti Austin, Dee Ervin, Carol Christy, Bill Callaway, Indira Danks, Hap Palmer. (Environmental 1001)

721019b MOTHER EARTH 1972 records by Peter Straker of 1972 London prod. "Sail On, Sweet Universe," "God's Country" (45/RCA(E) 2268)

721023a PIPPIN orig prod. MUSIC & WORDS: Stephen Schwartz. ORCH: Ralph Burns. COND: Stanley Lebowsky. CAST: John Rubinstein, Ben Vereen, Jill Clayburgh, Irene Ryan, Eric Berry, Leland Palmer. (Motown 760)

721023b PIPPIN 1973 Australian prod. ORCH: Ralph Burns. COND: Brian Buggy. CAST: Johnny Farnham, Colleen Hewett, Ronne Arnold, David Ravenswood, Nancye Hayes. (EMI(Australia) EMC-2510)

721023c PIPPIN 1975 South African prod. COND: Bill Fairley. CAST: Hal Watters, Sammy Brown, Robin Dolton, Bess Finney, Jo-Ann Pezarro, Andre Hattingh, Taliep Petersen. (Satbel 23008)

721023d PIPPIN 1976 record by Elisabeth Welch of 1973 London prod. "No Time at All" (LP-415)

721023e PIPPIN records by members of orig cast. Irene Ryan, contemp: "No Time at All " (45/Motown M-1221F) Ben Vereen, later: "Good Time Ladies Rag" (dropped from the show) (LP-765)

721106a I AND ALBERT orig (London) prod rec live, plus 4 additional songs from demonstration record. MUSIC: Charles Strouse. WORDS: Lee Adams. ORCH: Gordon Langford. COND: Gareth Davies. CAST: Polly James, Sven-Bertil Taube, Lewis Fiander, Aubrey Woods. (YRS Records 1004)

721106b I AND ALBERT 1981 studio prod. COND: Grant Hossack. CAST: Polly James, Sven-Bertil Taube, Lewis Fiander, & Aubrey Woods of orig (London) prod; Gay Soper, chorus. (That's Entertainment 1004)

721108a JOSEPH AND THE AMAZING TECHNICOLOR DREAMCOAT 1968 record prod. MUSIC: Andrew Lloyd Webber. WORDS: Tim Rice. ORCH: Andrew Lloyd Webber. COND: Alan Doggett. VOCALS: Tim Rice (lyricist), David Daltrey, Terry Saunders, Malcolm Parry, John Cook, Bryan Watson, chorus. (Dec(E) SKL-4973)

721108b JOSEPH AND THE AMAZING TECHNICOLOR DREAMCOAT 1973 studio prod. ORCH: Andrew Lloyd Webber. COND: Chris Hamel-Cooke, Andrew Lloyd Webber. CAST: Peter Reeves & Gary Bond of orig (London) prod; Maynard Williams, Gordon Waller, Roger Watson, chorus. (MCA 399)

721108c JOSEPH AND THE AMAZING TECHNICOLOR DREAMCOAT orig (London) prod. ORCH: Andrew Lloyd Webber. COND: Alan Doggett. CAST: Peter Reeves, Gary Bond, Gavin Reed, Gordon, Joan Heal, Riggs O'Hara, Andrew Robertson, chorus. (RSO Records(E) 2394-103)

721108d JOSEPH AND THE AMAZING TECHNICOLOR DREAMCOAT 1979 studio prod. ORCH: Andrew Lloyd Webber. COND: Geoff Love. CAST: Paul Jones (of 1979 London prod); Tim Rice (lyricist); Gordon Waller, Richard Barnes, Tom Saffery, Mike Sammes, chorus. (Music for Pleasure(E) 50455)

721108e JOSEPH AND THE AMAZING TECHNICOLOR DREAMCOAT contemp album by members of 1975 South African prod. ORCH & COND: Bill Fairley. VOCALS: Richard Loring, Bruce Millar, Avlon Collison. (Music for Pleasure(South Africa) SRSJ-8008)

721108f JOSEPH AND THE AMAZING TECHNICOLOR DREAMCOAT contemp records by members of 1980 London prod. Jess Conrad: "Any Dream Will Do" Dave Mayberry: "Song of the King" Leo Andrew: "Pharoah's Story" Conrad, Andrew: "Jacob and Sons/Joseph's Coat/Go Go Joseph" (45/Kerrysmile(E) KSR-001)

721112a MARY C. BROWN AND THE HOLLYWOOD SIGN contemp album sung by Dory Previn. MUSIC & WORDS: Dory Previn. (United Artists 5657)

721121a BEHIND THE FRIDGE orig (London) prod. MUSIC & WORDS: Dudley Moore. CAST: Dudley Moore, Peter Cook. (Atlantic(E) K-40503)

721121b BEHIND THE FRIDGE 1973 New York prod entitled "Good Evening," with somewhat different material. MUSIC & WORDS: Dudley Moore. CAST: Dudley Moore, Peter Cook. (Island 9298)

721123a DOCTOR SELAVY'S MAGIC THEATRE orig prod. MUSIC: Stanley Silverman. WORDS: Tom Hendry, others. ORCH & COND: Stanley Silverman. CAST: George McGrath, Barry Primus, Jessica Harper, Amy Taubin, Steve Menken, Denise De Lapenha, Robert Schlee, Mary Delson. (United Artists LA-196-G)

721128a VIA GALACTICA 1973 album by members of orig orchestra, incl Billy Butler (guitar) & Galt MacDermot (piano). MUSIC: Galt MaDermot. WORDS: Christopher Gore. ORCH & COND: Galt MacDermot. No vocals. (Kilmarnock 72009)

721220a THE GOOD OLD BAD OLD DAYS orig (London) prod. MUSIC & WORDS: Leslie Bricusse, Anthony Newley. COND: Robert Mandell. CAST: Anthony Newley, Paul Bacon, Julia Sutton, Terry Mitchell. (EMI(E) EMA-751)

1973

730001a Film LOST HORIZON soundtrack. MUSIC: Burt Bacharach. WORDS: Hal David. ORCH: Burt Bacharach, Leo Shuken, Jack Hayes. COND: Burt Bacharach. VOCALS: Shawn Phillips, others. (Bell 1300)

730002a Film TOM SAWYER soundtrack. MUSIC & WORDS: Richard M & Robert B Sherman. ORCH & COND: John Williams. CAST: Celeste Holm, Johnny Whitaker, Jeff East, Warren Oates, Charley Pride. (United Artists LA-057-F)

730003a Film ROBIN HOOD soundtrack. "Oo-de-Lally," "Love Goes On and On" (LP-661)

730117a TV show COLE PORTER IN PARIS soundtrack. MUSIC & WORDS: Cole Porter. VOCALS: Perry Como, Diahann Carroll, Connie Stevens, Louis Jourdan, Twiggy, Charles Aznavour. (Bell System PH-36508)

730125a LEMMINGS orig prod, rec live. MUSIC & WORDS: mostly Paul Jacobs, Christopher Guest, Sean Kelly. COND: Paul Jacobs. CAST: John Belushi, Chevy Chase, Garry Goodrow, Christopher Guest, Paul Jacobs, Mary-Jenifer Mitchell, Alice Playten. (Banana 6006)

730206a SHELTER contemp records by members of orig prod. MUSIC: Nancy Ford. WORDS: Gretchen Cryer. ORCH: Thomas Pierson. COND: Kirk Nurock. Tony Wells: "Run, Little Girl" Wells, Marcia Rodd: "Woke Up Today" (45/Col 4-45812)

730206b SHELTER 1975 record sung by Gretchen Cryer & Nancy Ford, composers. "Changing" (LP-570)

730213a EL COCA-COLA GRANDE orig prod, rec live 1 Sept 1973 in San Francisco. MUSIC & WORDS: Various. CAST: Ron House, Alan Shearman, John Neville-Andrews, Diz White, Sally Willis. (Bottle Cap 7" BC-1001, entitled "El Grande de Coca-Cola")

730225a A LITTLE NIGHT MUSIC orig prod. MUSIC & WORDS: Stephen Sondheim. ORCH: Jonathan Tunick. COND: Harold Hastings. CAST: Glynis Johns, Len Cariou, Hermione Gingold, Mark Lambert, Laurence Guittard, Patricia Elliott, Victoria Mallory, D Jamin-Bartlett. (Col KS-32265)

730225b A LITTLE NIGHT MUSIC 1973 records of songs dropped from the show, sung by members of orig cast. George Lee Andrews: "Silly People" Mark Lambert, Victoria Mallory: "Two Fairy Tales" (LP-169)

730225c A LITTLE NIGHT MUSIC 1975 London prod. ORCH: Jonathan Tunick. COND: Ray Cook. CAST: Jean Simmons, Hermione Gingold, Joss Ackland, David Kernan, Maria Aitken, Veronica Page, Terry Mitchell, Diane Langton, Christine McKenna. (RCA(E) LRL1-5090)

730225d A LITTLE NIGHT MUSIC 1978 film soundtrack. ORCH: Jonathan Tunick. CAST: Elizabeth Taylor, Diana Rigg, Len Cariou (of orig prod), Chloe Franks, Laurence Guittard (of orig prod), Lesley-Anne Down, Christopher Guard. (Col AL-35333)

730311a TV show SONDHEIM: A MUSICAL TRIBUTE soundtrack. MUSIC: Stephen Sondheim, Richard Rodgers, Jule Styne, Leonard Bernstein. WORDS: Stephen Sondheim. COND: Paul Gemignani. VOCALS: Dorothy Collins, Alice Playten, Virginia Sandifur, Chita Rivera, Pamela Myers, Justine Johnson, Victoria Mallory, Ethel Shutta, Donna McKechnie, Susan Browning, Marti Rolph, George Lee Andrews, Mark Lambert, Larry Blyden, Harvey Evans,

Pamela Hall, John McMartin, Angela Lansbury, Tony Stevens, Mary McCarty, Steve Elmore, Teri Ralston, Jack Cassidy, Larry Kert, Laurence Guittard, Ron Hogate, Nancy Walker, Alexis Smith, Stephen Sondheim, Beth Howland. (Warner Bros 2WS-2705)(LP-169)

730316a THE KARL MARX PLAY studio prod. MUSIC: Galt MacDermot. WORDS: Rochelle Owens. COND: Galt Mac-Dermot. CAST: Ralph Carter of orig cast; Phyllis Newman, Harold Gould, Jaime Sanchez of 1973 European tour prod; Norman Matlock of orig & 1973 European tour prod. (Kilmarnock 72010)

730319a SEESAW orig prod. MUSIC: Cy Coleman. WORDS: Dorothy Fields. ORCH: Larry Fallon. COND: Don Pippin. CAST: Michele Lee, Ken Howard, Tommy Tune, Cecelia Norfleet, Giancarlo Esposito, LaMonte DesFontaines. (Buddah 95006-1)

730319b SEESAW contemp record by the "Cy Coleman Co-op." COND: Cy Coleman. "Seesaw" (45/London 193-DJ)

730319*a CYRANO orig prod. MUSIC: Michael J Lewis. WORDS: Anthony Burgess. ORCH: Philip J Lang. COND: Thomas Pierson. CAST: Christopher Plummer, Leigh Berry, Mark Lamos, James Blendick. (A&M 3702)

730404a SMILE, SMILE, SMILE 1973 record by members of orig prod. MUSIC: Hugo Peretti, Luigi Creatore. WORDS: George David Weiss. ORCH: Jack Andrews. COND: Joseph Stecko. Hugo & Luigi Music Machine: "Smile, Smile, Smile" (45/AVCO AV-4615)

730404b SMILE, SMILE, SMILE 1972 record by chorus of 1972 Boston prod (entitled "Comedy"). ORCH: Melvin Marvin. "Comedy" (45/Bell 45-296)

730419a WHAT'S A NICE COUNTRY LIKE YOU DOING IN A STATE LIKE THIS? orig prod. MUSIC: Cary Hoffman. WORDS: Ira Gasman. CAST: Trudy Desmond, Andrea Martin, Martin Short, Claude Tessier, Richard Whelan. (Unnamed label 7" RMSC-747003)

730419b WHAT'S A NICE COUNTRY LIKE YOU DOING IN A STATE LIKE THIS? 1976 London prod, entitled "What's a Nice Country Like U.S. Doing in a State Like This?" CAST: Peter Blake, Billy Boyle, Neil McCaul, Jacquie Toye, Leueen Willoughby. (Galaxy(E) 6004)

730419*a TV show UP WITH PEOPLE! III orig prod. MUSIC & WORDS: Various. COND: Herbert Allen. VOCALS: Frank Fields, Linda Blackmore, Debbie Kirkpatrick, Pat Ektor, Glenn Close, Barbara Jean White, Pam Gearhart, Ken Doran, chorus. (Pace 1104)

730619a THE ROCKY HORROR SHOW orig (London) prod. MUSIC & WORDS: Richard O'Brien. CAST: Jonathan Adams, Tim Curry, Christopher Malcolm, Patricia Quinn, Belinda Sinclair, Richard O'Brien, Rayner Bourton, Paddy O'Hagan. (UK UKAL-1006)

730619b THE ROCKY HORROR SHOW 1974 Los Angeles (& 1975 New York) prod. ORCH: Richard Hartly. COND: D'Vaughn Pershing. CAST: Tim Curry of orig (London) prod, Jamie Donnelly, Boni Enten, Abigale Haness, Meat Loaf, Kim Milford, Bill Miller. (Ode Records SP-77026)

730619c THE ROCKY HORROR SHOW 1975 Australian prod. COND: Roy Ritchie. CAST: Reg Livermore, Kate Fitzpatrick, Arthur Dignam, Jane Harders, John Paramor, Maureen Elkner, Graham Matters, David Cameron, Sal Sharah. (Elephant 7000)

730619d THE ROCKY HORROR SHOW soundtrack of 1975 film, entitled "The Rocky Horror Picture Show." ORCH & COND: Richard Hartley. CAST: Tim Curry (of orig London & 1974 Los Angeles prods), Susan Sarandon, Barry Bostwick, Meat Loaf (of 1974 Los Angeles prod), Richard O'Brien (of orig London prod), Jonathan Adams. (Ode SP-77031)

731019a RAISIN orig prod. MUSIC: Judd Woldin. WORDS: Robert Brittan. ORCH: Al Cohn, Robert Freedman. COND: Howard A Roberts. CAST: Virginia Capers, Joe Morton, Ernestine Jackson, Robert Jackson, Deborah Allen, Helen Martin, Ralph Carter. (Col KS-32754)

731116a TV show GENERAL ELECTRIC PRESENTS SAMMY soundtrack. COND: George Rhodes, Jack Parnell. VOCALS: Sammy Davis Jr. (MGM 4914, entitled "Sammy")

731120a A MIDSUMMER NIGHT'S DREAM 1974 studio prod. MUSIC & WORDS: Randolph Tallman & Steven Mackenroth. ORCH: Jim Abbott. VOCALS: Randolph Tallman & Steven Mackenroth (composers & of orig cast); Adrian Halton, Janet Stover, chorus. (Dada 7801)

731126a RACHAEL LILY ROSENBLOOM records by Paul Jabara of orig cast. MUSIC & WORDS: mostly Paul Jabara. "One Man Ain't Enough" (1975: 45/A&M Records 1741) "Honeymoon," "Foggy Day," "Never Lose Your Sense of Humor" (1979: LP-683)

731217a EARTHQUAKE orig (Los Angeles) prod. MUSIC & WORDS: C Bernard Jackson. COND: Larry Nash. CAST: Bernie Cowens, Karmello Brooks, Rod Perry, Nikki Sanz, Peter Salas, Lupe Zuniga. (Inner City LRS-RT-6075)

1974

740001a Film THAT'S ENTERTAINMENT soundtrack. MUSIC & WORDS: Various. COND: Henry Mancini, others. CAST: Various. (MCA 2-11002)(LP-252)

740002a Film THE LITTLE PRINCE soundtrack. MUSIC: Frederick Loewe. WORDS: Alan Jay Lerner. ORCH: Angela Morley. COND: Douglas Gamley. CAST: Richard Kiley, Donna McKechnie, Bob Fosse, Steven Warner, Gene Wilder. (ABC ABDP-854)

740003a Film LADY SINGS THE BLUES soundtrack. MUSIC & WORDS: Various. ORCH: Michel Legrand. COND: Gil Askey. VOCALS: Diana Ross, Blinky Williams, Michele Aller. (Motown 758-D)

740004a R.S.V.P. THE COLE PORTERS orig (1974 touring) prod. MUSIC & WORDS: Cole Porter. ORCH & COND: Mac Frampton. CAST: Jack & Sally Jenkins. (Respond mx PMS-29913/4)

740005a Film PAPER MOON soundtrack, consisting of records made in the 1930's. (Paramount PAS-1012)

740006a Film PHANTOM OF THE PARADISE soundtrack. MUSIC & WORDS: Paul Williams. ORCH: Paul Williams. COND: Michael Arciaga, Jules Chaikin. VOCALS: Archie Hahn, Bill Finley, Jeffrey Comanor, Jessica Harper, Paul Williams, Harold Oblong, Ray Kennedy. (A&M Records SP-3653)

740007a Film THE DAY OF THE LOCUST soundtrack. MUSIC & WORDS: Various. ORCH & COND: John Barry, Pete King. VOCALS: Louis Armstrong, Michael Dees, Nick Lucas, Paul Jabara, Pamela Myers. (London PS-912)

740008a Film HUCKLEBERRY FINN soundtrack. MUSIC & WORDS: Richard M & Robert B Sherman. ORCH & COND: Fred Werner. VOCALS: Paul Winfield, Jeff East, Harvey Korman, David Wayne, Gary Merrill, Roberta Flack, chorus. (United Artists LA-229-F)

740009a Film JOURNEY BACK TO OZ soundtrack. MUSIC: James Van Heusen. WORDS: Sammy Cahn. ORCH & COND: Walter Scharf. CAST: Liza Minnelli, Herschel Bernardi, Ethel Merman, Danny Thomas, Milton Berle, Jack E Leonard, Rise Stevens, Peter Lawford (replacing Mickey Rooney of orig cast). (RFO 101, entitled "The Return to Oz")

740106a LIZA orig prod. MUSIC & WORDS: John Kander, Fred

Ebb, others. ORCH: Various. COND: Jack French. VOCALS: Liza Minnelli, chorus. (Col PC-32854, entitled "Liza Minnelli Live at the Winter Garden")(LP-327)

740108a LET MY PEOPLE COME orig prod. MUSIC & WORDS: Earl Wilson Jr. ORCH & COND: Billy Cunningham. CAST: Lorraine Davidson, Marty Duffy, Tobie Columbus, Christine Rubens, Larry Paulette, Shezwae Powell, Joe Jones, Peachena. (Libra 1069)

740306a OVER HERE! orig prod. MUSIC & WORDS: Richard M & Robert B Sherman. ORCH: Michael Gibson, Jim Tyler, COND: Joseph Klein. CAST: Patty Andrews, Maxene Andrews, Douglass Watson, Janie Sell, Jim Weston, April Shawhan, John Driver, Samuel E Wright, John Travolta, Phyllis Somerville. (Col KS-32961)

740322a IPI-TOMBI orig (South Africa) prod. MUSIC: Bertha Egnos. WORDS: Gail Lakier. ORCH: Lofty Schultz. CAST: uncredited. (Ashtree(South Africa) 26000)

740322b IPI-TOMBI 1973 record prod, entitled "The Warrior." ORCH: Lofty Schultz. Performed by Ipi 'n Tombia, featuring vocalist Margaret Singana. (Volt(South Africa) STS-5516, entitled "The Warrior")

740325a BRAIN CHILD demonstration record. No performace credits. MUSIC: Michel Legrand. WORDS: Hal David. (Rescued from Oblivion 104)

740325b BRAIN CHILD 1975 records. ORCH, COND, & PIANO: Michel Legrand (composer). Lena Horne: "Let Me Be Your Mirror," "Everything Happens to You Happens to Me," "I've Been Starting Tomorrow All of My Life" (LP-675)

740416a WORDS AND MUSIC 1974 London prod, entitled "The Sammy Cahn Songbook." MUSIC: Various. WORDS: Sammy Cahn. PIANO: Richard Leonard (of orig prod). VOCALS: Sammy Cahn (of orig prod), Lorna Dallas, Terry Mitchell, Laurel Ford. (RCA LRL-1-5079)(LP-313)

740416b WORDS AND MUSIC 1972 preliminary prod, entitled "An Evening with Sammy Cahn," rec live. PIANO: Richard Leonard (of orig & London prods). VOCALS: Sammy Cahn, Shirley Lemmon, Jon Peck of orig prod; Bobbi Baird. (Laureate 604)(LP-658)

740501a BILLY orig (London) prod. MUSIC: John Barry. WORDS: Don Black. ORCH: John Barry, Bobby Richards. COND: Alfred Ralston. CAST: Michael Crawford, Avis Bunnage, Bryan Pringle, Christopher Hancock, Lockwood West, Gay Soper, Diana Quick, Billy Boyle, Elaine Paige, Betty Turner. (CBS(E) 70133)

740528a THE MAGIC SHOW orig prod. MUSIC & WORDS: Stephen Schwartz. COND: Stephen Reinhardt. CAST: Anita Morris, Cheryl Barnes, Dale Soules, David Ogden Stiers, Annie McGreevey, Robert Lu Pone. (Bell 9003)

740702a COLE orig (London) prod. MUSIC & WORDS: Cole Porter. ORCH: Ken Moule. COND: John Burrows. CAST: Ray Cornell, Rod McLennan, Lucy Fenwick, Kenneth Nelson, Peter Gale, Elizabeth Power, Bill Kerr, Andela Richards, Julia McKenzie, Una Stubbs. (RCA(E) LRL2-5054)

740711a THE GOOD COMPANIONS orig (London) prod. MUSIC: Andre Previn. WORDS: Johnny Mercer. ORCH: Herbert W Spencer, Angela Morley. COND: Marcus Dods. CAST: John Mills, Judi Dench, Christopher Gable, Marti Webb, Ray C Davis, Malcolm Rennie. (EMI(E) EMC-3042)

741006a MACK AND MABEL orig prod. MUSIC & WORDS: Jerry Herman. ORCH: Philip J Lang. COND: Donald Pippin. CAST: Robert Preston, Bernadette Peters, Lisa Kirk, Stanley Simmonds. (ABC ABCH-830)

741006b MACK AND MABEL 1974 record by Jerry Herman (composer), piano & vocal. "Movies Were Movies" (LP-660)

741007a MISS MOFFAT 1975 records by members of orig (Philadelphia) prod. MUSIC: Albert Hague. WORDS: Emlyn Williams. Dorian Harewood: "The Debt I Owe" Avon Long; Nell Carter (not of orig cast); chorus: "Peekaboo Jehovah" (LP-510)

741007*a THE JOLSON REVUE orig (Torquay, England) prod. MUSIC & WORDS: Various. ORCH: David Gold. CAST: Dai Francis, Jimmy & Brian Patton, Ann Emery, chorus. (United Artists(E) 29712)

741115a THE KNIGHT OF THE BURNING PESTLE 1979 album. MUSIC: Peter Schickele. WORDS: Brooks Jones, Peter Schickele. ORCH & COND: Peter Schickele. VOCALS: Lucy Shelton, Margo Rose, Frank Hoffmeister, Robert Kuehn, Peter Schickele. (Vanguard VSD-71269, entitled "Music of Peter Schickele," with additional material)

741128a THE JOKER OF SEVILLE orig (Trinidad) prod. MUSIC & WORDS: Derek Walcott, Galt MacDermot. COND: Galt MacDermot. CAST: Hamilton Parris, Syd Skipper, June Nathaniel, Norline Metivier, Errol Jones, Wilbert Holder, Andrew Beddeau. (SEMP CL-2575)

741215a THE INVISIBLE DRAGON orig prod. MUSIC: Jo Adler. WORDS: Hannah Price. ORCH & COND: Jo Adler. CAST: Erwin Kaufman, Beverly Cohen, Joyce Schulman, Justin Paul. (Bag-a-Tale 1000, with Aladd)

1975

750001a Film FUNNY LADY soundtrack. MUSIC & WORDS: John Kander, Fred Ebb, others. ORCH & COND: Peter Matz. VOCALS: Barbra Streisand, Ben Vereen, James Caan. (Arista 9004)

750002a Film AT LONG LAST LOVE soundtrack. MUSIC & WORDS: Cole Porter. ORCH: Gus Levene, Harry Betts, Artie Butler. COND: Lionel Newman, Artie Butler. CAST: Cybill Shepherd, Burt Reynolds, Madeline Kahn, Duilio Del Prete, Eileen Brennan, John Hillerman. (RCA ABL2-0967)

750003a Film NASHVILLE soundtrack. MUSIC & WORDS: Various. ORCH & COND: Richard Baskin. VOCALS: Ronee Blakely, Henry Gibson, Barbara Harris, Karen Black, Keith Carradine. (ABC ABCD-893)

750004a Record prod TURNABOUT! composed of material used in the Turnabout Theatre revues (Los Angeles, 1941-56), performed by members of the original revues. MUSIC & WORDS: Forman Brown. CAST: Elsa Lanchester, Forman Brown, Frances Osborne, Dorothy Neumann, Bill Buck, Harry Burnett. (Pelican 142)

750005a Film LISZTOMANIA soundtrack. MUSIC & WORDS: Various. ORCH: Rick Wakeman. VOCALS: Roger Daltrey, Linda Lewis, Paul Nicholas. (A&M Records SP-4829)

750006a Record prod BIG MAN orig prod. MUSIC: Julian & Nat Adderley. WORDS: Diane Lampert, Peter Farrow. VOCALS: Joe Williams, Randy Crawford, Robert Guillaume, Judy Thames, Lane Smith. (Fantasy 79006)

750105a THE WIZ orig prod. MUSIC & WORDS: mostly by Charlie Smalls. ORCH: Harold Wheeler. COND: Charles H Coleman. CAST: Stephanie Mills, Tiger Haynes, Tedd Ross, Hinton Battle, Clarice Taylor, Andre de Shields, Tasha Thomas, Mabel King, Dee Dee Bridgewater. (Atlantic SD-18137)

750105b THE WIZ soundtrack of 1978 film, with additional music by Quincy Jones, Nick Ashford, Valerie Simpson. ORCH: Quincy Jones. COND: Bobby Tucker. CAST: Diana Ross, Theresa Merritt,

Thelma Carpenter, Michael Jackson, Nipsey Russell, Ted Ross, Mabel King, Lena Horne. (MCA 2-14000)

750107a SHENANDOAH orig prod. MUSIC: Gary Geld. WORDS: Peter Udell. ORCH: Don Walker. COND: Lynn Crigler. CAST: John Cullum, Penelope Milford, Joseph Shapiro, Chip Ford, Donna Theodore, Joel Higgins, Gary Harger. (RCA ARL-1-1019)

750114a DIAMOND STUDS! contemp album. MUSIC: Bland Simpson. WORDS: Jim Wann. VOCALS: Bland Simpson & Jim Wann (composers & of orig cast), Cassandra Morgan (of 1975 Washington cast). (All three also play instruments.) "Jesse James Robbed This Train," "Abiding with You," "Cakewalk into Kansas City," "Sleepy Time Down South," "These Southern States That I Love" (Pasquotank 7" 003)

750127a LOVERS orig prod rec live. MUSIC: Steve Sterner. WORDS: Peter del Valle. CAST: Martin Rivera, Michael Cascone, John Ingle, Robert Sevra, Reathel Bean, Gary Sneed. (Golden Gloves PG-723)

750129a MAN ON THE MOON 1974 records by Genevieve Waite of orig cast. MUSIC & WORDS: John Phillips. "Love Is Coming Back," "American Man on the Moon," "Girls" (LP-601)

750221a STRAWS IN THE WIND 1977 records by Betty Comden & Adolph Green, lyricists. MUSIC: Cy Coleman. "The Lost Word," "Simplified Language" (LP-489)

750226a THE NIGHT THAT MADE AMERICA FAMOUS contemp record by Harry Chapin of orig prod. "The Cat's in the Cradle" (45/Elektra E-45067)

750303a GOODTIME CHARLEY orig prod. MUSIC: Larry Grossman. WORDS: Hal Hackady. ORCH: Jonathan Tunick. COND: Arthur B Rubinstein. CAST: Joel Grey, Ann Reinking, Susan Browning, Richard B Shull, Louis Zorich, Jay Garner. (RCA ARL-1-1011)

750309a THE LIEUTENANT orig prod. MUSIC & WORDS: Gene Curty, Nitra Scharfman, Chuck Strand. ORCH & COND: Chuck Strand. CAST Eddie Mekka, Gene Curty, Walt Hunter, Gordon Grody, Chet D'Elia, Tom Tofel, Burt Rodriguez, Don McGrath. (Unnamed label, unnumbered)

750319a DR. JAZZ 1977 records sung by Bobby Van (of orig cast) & Buster Davis (composer & lyricist). Van: "Everybody Leaves You," "Anywhere the Wind Blows" Davis: "Elgin Watch Movements," "He's Always Ticklin' the Ivories," "Sorry, I've Made Other Arrangements," "Our Medecine Man's a Music Maker Now" (LP-551)

750323a BE KIND TO PEOPLE WEEK 1976 record of "Mad about Manhattan," sponsored by the Citizens Committee for New York City, Inc. MUSIC & WORDS: Jack Bussins, Ellsworth Olin. COND: Skitch Henderson. VOCALS: Naura Hayden of orig cast; Barbara Barrie, Polly Bergen, Angel Cordero jr, Arlene Dahl, Ossie Davis, Ruby Dee, Osborn Elliott, Rocky Graziano, Tammy Grimes, Celeste Holm, Linda Hopkins, Guy Lombardo, Jake LaMotta, Dina Merrill, Robert Merrill, Bess Myerson, Otto Preminger, Cliff Robertson, William B Williams, Henny Youngman. (45/Nutty for You New York Records 1001)

750408a PHILEMON orig prod. MUSIC: Harvey Schmidt. WORDS: Tom Jones. COND: Ken Collins. CAST: Michael Glenn-Smith, Virginia Gregory, Dick Latessa, Leila Martin, Howard Ross, Kathrin King Segal. (Gallery 1)

750422a JEEVES orig (London) prod. MUSIC: Andrew Lloyd Webber. WORDS: Alan Ayckbourn. COND: Anthony Bowles. CAST: David Hemmings, Michael Aldridge, David Wood, Gabrielle Drake, John Turner, Angela Easterling, Debbie Bowen, Gordon Clyde. (MCA(E) MCF-2726)

750502a A GALA TRIBUTE TO JOSHUA LOGAN orig prod rec live. MUSIC & WORDS: Various. COND: Colin Romoff. CAST: Ethel Merman, Harold Rome, Phyllis Newman, Dorian Harewood, Nell Carter, Avon Long, Ray Walston, Diosa Costello, Walter Willison, Dolores Gray, Douglas Fairbanks Jr, Maria Karnilova, Jane Pickens, Benay Venuta, Sheila Bond, Patricia Marand. (Friends of the Theatre & Music Collection mx AC-1/4)(LP-510)

750521a A CHORUS LINE orig prod. MUSIC: Marvin Hamlisch. WORDS: Edward Kleban. ORCH: Bill Byers, Hershy Kay, Jonathan Tunick. COND: Don Pippin. CAST: Wayne Cilento, Priscilla Lopez, Donna McKechnie, Pamela Blair, Renee Baughman, Don Percassi, Carole Bishop, Nancy Lane, Kay Cole. (Col PS-33581)

750603a CHICAGO orig prod. MUSIC: John Kander. WORDS: Fred Ebb. ORCH: Ralph Burns. COND: Stanley Lebowsky. CAST: Gwen Verdon, Chita Rivera, Jerry Orbach, Barney Martin, Mary McCarty, M O'Haughey, chorus. (Arista 9005)

750603b CHICAGO 1975 records by Liza Minnelli, who replaced Gwen Verdon in orig cast during the summer of 1975. "And All That Jazz," "My Own Best Friend" (45/Col 3-10178)

750603c CHICAGO 1973 records by the composers. PIANO: John Kander, VOCALS: Fred Ebb, John Kander. "All That Jazz," "Roxie" (LP-659)

750917a BOY MEETS BOY orig prod. MUSIC & WORDS: Bill Solly. PIANO: David Friedman. CAST: Joe Barrett, David Gallegly, Rita Gordon, Raymond Wood, Paul Ratkevich. (Records & Publishing JO-13)

750917b BOY MEETS BOY 1979 Minneapolis prod. ORCH: Brad Callahan. COND: Brad Callahan, Patti Haigh. CAST: Farrell Batley, Vic Campbell, Mick Isackson, Thomas Freiberg. (Private Editions 37090)

751014a CHRISTY orig prod. MUSIC: Lawrence J Blank. WORDS: Bernie Spiro. COND: Robert Billig. CAST: Jim Elmer, Bette Forsyth, Alexander Sokoloff, Bea Swanson, John Canary. (Original Cast 7913)

751021a TREEMONISHA orig prod. MUSIC & WORDS: Scott Joplin. ORCH & COND: Gunther Schuller. CAST: Carmen Balthrop, Betty Allen, Curtis Rayam, Willard White, Ben Harney, Cora Johnson, Kenneth Hicks, Dorceal Duckens, Dwight Ransom, Raymond Bazemore, Edward Pierson. (Deutsche Grammophone(G) 2707-083)

751022a ME AND BESSIE 1976 album by Linda Hopkins of orig prod. MUSIC & WORDS: Various. ORCH: John Allen. (Col PC-34032)

751113a A MUSICAL JUBILEE 1955 record by Cyril Ritchard of orig cast. "And Her Mother Came Too" (LP-427)

751121a SELMA orig (Los Angeles) prod. MUSIC & WORDS: Tommy Butler. ORCH: Paul Riser. COND: Peggy Long. CAST: Tommy Butler, Jackie Lowe, Denise Erwin, Janice Barnett, Sandra Pitre, Rubert Williams, Fred Tucks, Ernie Banks, Sip Culler, Carlton Williams, Susan Beaubian. (Cotillion SD-2-110)

751201a TUSCALOOSA'S CALLING ME... BUT I'M NOT GOING! orig prod. MUSIC: Hank Beebe. WORDS: Bill Heyer. PIANO: Jeremy Harris. CAST: Len Gochman, Renny Temple, Patti Perkins. (Vanguard VSD-79376)

751209a SNOOPY!!! orig (San Francisco) prod. MUSIC: Larry Grossman, WORDS: Hal Hackady. ORCH: Lawrence J Blank. CAST: Don Potter, James Gleason, Pamela Myers, Jimmy Dodge, Roxann Pyle, Carla Manning. (Power Exchange(E) PXL-015)

751210a MAYFLOWER orig (Washington) prod, in French. MUSIC & WORDS: Eric Charden, Guy Bontempelli, Jean-Claude Petit.

ORCH & COND: Jean-Claude Petit. CAST: Michel Elias, Hubert, Fabienne Waroux, Roland Magdane, Cyril Azzam, Jean-Louis Rolland, Michael Sterling, Pascale Rivaud, Gregory Ken, Mario Dalba, Patrick Topaloff, Gerard Wagner. (CT Records(F) 80-506/7)

751210b MAYFLOWER 1977 Vienna prod, in German. COND: Johannes Fehring. CAST: Wolfgang Mascher, Helge Grau, Marika Lichter, Aniko Benkoe, Savin Sutter, Reginald Evans, Erich Schleyer, Gerard Wagner. (Amadeo(Austria) AVRS-9281)

751219a DOWNRIVER studio prod. MUSIC & WORDS: John Braden. ORCH & COND: Jeff Waxman. CAST: Richard Dunne, Alvin Fields, Donald Arrington, Michael Corbett, Marcia McLain, Robert Price, chorus. (Take Home Tunes 7811)

1976

760001a Film THAT'S ENTERTAINMENT, PART 2 soundtrack. MUSIC & WORDS: Various. COND: Nelson Riddle, others. CAST: Fred Astaire, Gene Kelly, others. (MGM MG-1-5301)(LP-416)

760002a Film LUCKY LADY soundtrack. MUSIC & WORDS: John Kander, Fred Ebb, others. ORCH & COND: Ralph Burns. VOCALS: Liza Minnelli, Burt Reynolds, Vangie Charmichael; also two Bessie Smith records. (Arista AL-4069)

760003a Film THE FIRST NUDIE MUSICAL soundtrack. MUSIC & WORDS: Bruce Kimmel. ORCH & COND: Rene Hall. CAST: Stephen Nathan, Annette O'Toole, Debbie Shapiro. Alexandra Morgan, Diana Canova, Valerie Gillett, Cindy Williams, Bruce Kimmel. (First Musical 1001)

760004a Film BUGSY MALONE soundtrack. MUSIC & WORDS: Paul Williams. ORCH: Paul Williams. CAST: Archie Hahn, Julie McWirder, Liberty Williams, Paul Williams. (RSO Records RS-1-3501)

760005a Film THE BLUE BIRD soundtrack. Elizabeth Taylor: "Wings in the Sky" (45/Col(J) YK-62-MK)

760006a Film THE SLIPPER AND THE ROSE soundtrack. MUSIC & WORDS: Richard M & Robert B Sherman. ORCH & COND: Angela Morley. CAST: Richard Chamberlain, Gemma Craven, Christopher Gable, Michael Hordern, Kenneth More, Peter Graves, Julian Orchard, Annette Crosbie, John Turner. (MCA 2097)

760007a Film A STAR IS BORN contemp album by Barbra Streisand & Kris Kristofferson of orig cast. MUSIC & WORDS: Various. (Col AL-34403)

760008a Film A MATTER OF TIME soundtrack. COND: Bruno Canfora. Liza Minnelli: "A Matter of Time" (by John Kander, Fred Ebb), "Do It Again" (by George Gershwin, B G DeSylva) (Oceania(I) SO-69301, entitled "Nina")

760009a TV show OUR LOVE IS HERE TO STAY soundtrack. MUSIC & WORDS: George & Ira Gershwin. COND: Nick Perito. PIANO: Gerald Robbins. VOCALS: Steve Lawrence, Eydie Gorme. (United Artists(E) UAD-60141/2)

760111a PACIFIC OVERTURES orig prod. MUSIC & WORDS: Stephen Sondheim. ORCH: Jonathan Tunick. COND: Paul Gemignani. CAST: Mako, Sab Shimono, Isao Sato, Alvin Ing, James Dybas, Ernest Harada, Ricardo Tobia, Mark Hsu Syers, Patrick Kinser-Lau, Timm Fujii. (RCA ARL-1-1367)

760111b PACIFIC OVERTURES record arranged for koto and performed by Fusako Yoshida, who played shamisen in orig prod. "Chrysanthemum Tea" (LP-719)

760215a ALADD orig prod. MUSIC: Jo Adler. WORDS: Hannah Price. ORCH & COND: Jo Adler. CAST: Justin Paul, Beverly

Cohen, Joyce Schulman, Larry M Weiner, Kathy DeSalvo. (Bag-a-Tale 1000, with The Dragon)

760217a ROCKABYE HAMLET 1976 album. MUSIC & WORDS: Cliff Jones. VOCALS: Cal Dodd (of 1974 Charlottetown, Canada, prod, entitled "Kronborg: 1582"), Rory Dodd (of 1974 Canadian & 1976 New York prods), Cliff Jones (composer), Lisa Hartt, the Irish Rovers. (Rising(C) 103)

760229a EVERYBODY, EVERYBODY 1974 Wilmington, Del, prod. MUSIC & WORDS: Donald Ashwander. HARPSICHORD: Donald Ashwander. CAST: Irving Burton, Judith Martin, Douglas Norwick, Adrienne Doucette. (Paperbag Players 5, with Grandpa)

760302a BUBBLING BROWN SUGAR orig prod. MUSIC & WORDS: Various. ORCH: Danny Holgate. COND: Danny Holgate. CAST: Avon Long, Josephine Premice, Vivian Reed, Joseph Attles, Carolyn Byrd, Chip Garnett, Ethel Beatty, Barry Preston. (H&L Records 69011-698)

760302b BUBBLING BROWN SUGAR 1977 London prod. ORCH: Danny Holgate. COND: Richard Leonard. CAST: Billy Daniels, Lon Satton, Elaine Delmar, Helen Gelzer, Charles Augins, Miquel Brown. (Pye(E) NSPD-504)

760324a ACROSS AMERICA orig (Washington) prod. MUSIC & WORDS: Shirley Grossman. ORCH: Fred Woolston. COND: Brock Holmes. CAST: Al Witten, Don Blount, Kay McDonald, Roger Day, Tom Satterfield. (Washington Gas 1001)

760400a Industrial show THE SPIRIT OF ACHIEVEMENT orig prod. MUSIC & WORDS: Claibe Richardson. ORCH: Bruce Pomahac. CAST: Virginia Sandifur, Carol Swarbrick, Peter Shawn, David James Carroll, Stanley Grover, Robert Lunny. (Exxon 1886)

760408a ONE STAR RISING orig (New Orleans) prod. MUSIC & WORDS: Robert Moore. COND: Robert Moore. CAST: Robert Moore (not of orig cast), Alyce & Denise Mouledoux, Gia Rabito, Robert Reidy, Ed Cox, Geralyn Grethe, Cheryl Norman. (Rising Star 0001)

760414a BRIGHAM! soundtrack of orig (Provo, Utah) prod. MUSIC: Newell Dayley. WORDS: Arnold Sundgaard. COND: Ralph G Laycock. VOCALS: Harve Presnell, Terry McCombs, Scott Wallace, Clayne Robison, Bryce Ward, Roy Ward, Chyleen Bacon Bluth. (Brigham Young University CO-176M)

760419a SHIRLEY MacLAINE orig prod, rec live. MUSIC & WORDS: Various. ORCH: Cy Coleman. COND: Donn Trenner. CAST: Shirley MacLaine, Adam Grammis, Candy Brown, Gary Flannery, Jo Ann Lehmann, Larry Vickers. (Col PC-34223)(LP-500)

760425a REX orig prod. MUSIC: Richard Rodgers. WORDS: Sheldon Harnick. ORCH: Irwin Kostal. COND: Jay Blackton. CAST: Nicol Williamson, Penny Fuller, Tom Aldredge, Ed Evanko, Barbara Andres, Michael John, Glenn Close, Merwin Goldsmith. (RCA ABL1-1683)

760427a SO LONG, 174TH STREET 1980 studio prod. MUSIC & WORDS: Stan Daniels. ORCH: Jim Tyler. CAST: Robert Morse, Loni Ackerman, George S Irving, Barbara Lang, Jimmy Brennan, & Lawrence John Moss of orig cast; Stan Daniel, composer; Kaye Ballard, Patti Karr, Arthur Rubin, Joy Franz, Jill Cook, chorus. (Original Cast 8131)

760504a SIDE BY SIDE BY SONDHEIM orig (London) prod. MUSIC: Stephen Sondheim, Richard Rodgers, Leonard Bernstein, Mary Rodgers, Jule Styne. WORDS: Stephen Sondheim. CAST: Julia McKenzie, David Kernan, Millicent Martin. (RCA CBL-2-1851)

760504b SIDE BY SIDE BY SONDHEIM 1977 Australian prod. CAST: Jill Perryman, Geraldene Morrow, Bartholomew John. (RCA (Australia) VRL2-0156)

760504c SIDE BY SIDE BY SONDHEIM 1977 Dublin prod, rec live. CAST: Tony Kenny, Loreto O'Connor, Gay Byrne, Gemma Craven. (Ram Records(Ireland) RMLP-1026, entitled "Songs of Sondheim")

760506a ZEN BOOGIE 1978 records produced by Peppy Castro. MUSIC & WORDS: Peppy Castro. Members of 1978 Los Angeles prod(?): "Happy Was the Day We Met," "Mind Boggeleer" (45/Cap 4664)

760511a THE BAKER'S WIFE 1977 album by members of orig prod (opened in Los Angeles, closed in Washington). MUSIC & WORDS: Stephen Schwartz. ORCH: Thomas Pierson, Don Walker. COND: Robert Billig. VOCALS: Paul Sorvino. Patti Lupone, Kurt Peterson, Teri Ralston. (Take Home Tunes 772)

760511b THE BAKER'S WIFE 1977 album sung by members of orig prod, Stephen Schwartz (composer), & Carol Schwartz (his wife). PIANO: Stephen Schwartz. Paul Sorvino: "Perfect Every Time" Sorvino, chorus: "Bread" Sorvino, Portia Nelson, Darlene Conley, Denise Lor: "What's a Man to Do?" Stephen & Carol Schwartz: "A Little Taste of Heaven," "Not in the Market" (Take Home Tunes 7" 773)

760513a LEGEND soundtrack (background music of orig prod). MUSIC: Dan Goggin. ORCH: Bill Brohn. (Theatre Archives 801)

760708a HOUSEWIFE-SUPERSTAR! orig (London) prod, rec live. MUSIC & WORDS: Barry Humphries. PIANO: Iris Mason. VOCALS: Barry Humphries (also of 1977 New York prod). (Charisma(E) CAS-1123)

760709a A 5-6-7-8 orig (Los Angeles) prod. MUSIC & WORDS: Various. ORCH & COND: Jerry Sternbach. CAST: Suzanne Buirgy, John Graham, Valerie Klemow, Gary Kwiatek, Terry Mason, Sue Palladino, Stuart K Robinson. (Spotlight 2222)

761005a LOVESONG 1978 concert performances by Michael Valenti (composer), piano & vocal. WORDS: Various. "Sophia," "Jenny Kiss'd Me," "Song," "So We'll Go No More a-Roving," "An Epitaph" (LP-650)

761005b LOVESONG 1980 studio prod. ORCH, COND & PIANO: Michael Valenti (composer). CAST: Melanie Chartoff, Sigrid Heath, & Jess Richards of orig cast; Robert Manzari. (Original Cast 8022)

761010a THE ROBBER BRIDEGROOM orig prod. MUSIC: Robert Waldman. WORDS: Alfred Uhry. ORCH & COND: Robert Waldman. CAST: Barry Bostwick, Rhonda Coullet, Barbara Lang, Lawrence John Moss, Steven Vinovich, Ernie Sabella, Dennis Warning, Carolyn McCurry, Trip Plymale, Tom Westerman. (CBS P-14589)

761010b THE ROBBER BRIDEGROOM 1976 album, with orchestra & orchestrations of orig prod. Virginia Vestoff: "Nothin' Up," "Sleepy Man" Jerry Orbach: "Love Stolen" Orchestra: "Goodbye Salome" (Take Home Tunes 7" 761)

761202a THE GREAT AMERICAN BACKSTAGE MUSICAL orig (Los Angeles) prod. MUSIC & WORDS: Bill Solly. ORCH & COND: Glen Kelly. CAST: Joe Barrett, Tim Bowman, Jerry Clark, Marsha Kramer, Gaye Kruger, Tamara Long. (AEI Records 1101)

761206a BETJEMANIA 1980 London prod. MUSIC: John Gould. WORDS: John Betjeman. CAST: Rowland Davies, John Gould, Gay Soper, Barry Stokes. (That's Entertainment(E) 1002)

761215a THE SECOND SHEPHERD'S PLAY orig prod. MUSIC & WORDS: Steve Kitsakos. CAST: Greg Cesario, Joel Stevens, Doug Holsclaw, Karen Haas, Richard Woods, Deborah Tilton, Natalia Chuma. (Broadway Baby 774)

761222a YOUR ARMS TOO SHORT TO BOX WITH GOD orig prod. MUSIC & WORDS: Alex Bradford, Micki Grant. ORCH: H

B Barnum. COND: George Broderick. CAST: Salome Bey, Clinton Derricks-Carroll, William Hardy Jr, Sheila Ellis, Delores Hall, Bobby Hill, Alex Bradford, Michael Gray, Vinnette Carroll. (ABC AB-1004)

761222b YOUR ARMS TOO SHORT TO BOX WITH GOD 1980 records by members of 1980 cast. Jennifer-Yvette Holliday: "I Love You So Much Jesus" Sheila Ellis, Holliday: "Too Close to Heaven" (45/JPL 7880)

1977

770001a Film RAGGEDY ANN & ANDY soundtrack. MUSIC & WORDS: Joe Raposo. ORCH: Joe Raposo, Jim Tyler. COND: Joe Raposo. CAST: uncredited. (Col 34686)

770002a Film NEW YORK, NEW YORK orig prod, including material dropped before release. MUSIC & WORDS: John Kander, Fred Ebb, others. ORCH & COND: Ralph Burns. SAXOPHONE: Georgie Auld. CAST: Liza Minnelli, Robert DeNiro, Mary Kay Place, Larry Kert, Diahnne Abbott. (United Artists LA750-L2)

770003a Film OUTLAW BLUES 1977 album including portions of soundtrack. MUSIC & WORDS: Steve Fromholz, Hoyt Axton, others. VOCALS: Peter Fonda & Susan Saint James (of orig cast); Steve Fromholz & Hoyt Axton (composers); chorus. (Cap ST-11691)

770004a Film RECORD CITY soundtrack. MUSIC & WORDS: Freddie Perren, others. VOCALS: Keni St Lewis, James Gadson, Fritz Diego, Rick Dees, Ric & Robyn Wyatt, Gary Starbuck. (Polydor PDI-8002)

770005a Film PETE'S DRAGON soundtrack. MUSIC & WORDS: Al Kasha, Joel Hirschhorn. ORCH & COND: Irwin Kostal. CAST: Helen Reddy, Jim Dale, Mickey Rooney, Red Buttons, Sean Marshall, Shelley Winters. (Cap SW-11704) (Incomplete: LP-661)

770006a Film THE RESCUERS soundtrack. MUSIC & WORDS: Carol Connors, Ayn Robbins, Sammy Fain. "The Journey," "The Rescue Aid Society," "Someone's Waiting for You," "Tomorrow Is Another Day" (LP-661)

770113a THE COCKEYED TIGER contemp album by members of orig prod. MUSIC & WORDS: Nicholas Meyers, Eric Blau, Bert Kalmar, Harry Ruby. CAST: Elly Stone, the C.O.G.S., company. "God Is Good to Me," "Good Times," "Four of the Three Musketeers," "You've Got to Be a Tiger," "A Hell of a Crowd" (Unnamed label 7" 3121)

770123a GRANDPA orig prod. MUSIC & WORDS: Donald Ashwander. HARPSICHORD: Donald Ashwander. CAST: Irving Burton, Judith Martin, Jeanne Michels, Virgil Roberson. (Paperbag Players 5, with Everybody, Everybody)

770207a MADEMOISELLE COLOMBE 1978 concert performances by Michael Valenti (composer), piano & vocals. WORDS: Edwin Dulchin. "Alone," "Years from Now," "Georgie and I," "More Than One Man in Her Life" (LP-650)

770307a STARTING HERE, STARTING NOW orig prod. MUSIC: David Shire. WORDS: Richard Maltby jr. COND: Robert W Preston. CAST: Loni Ackerman, Margery Cohen, George Lee Andrews. (RCA ABL-1-2360)

770307b STARTING HERE, STARTING NOW 1978 South African prod. COND: Bill Fairley. CAST: Richard Loring, Denise Freeman, Andre Hattingh. (EMI(South Africa) EMCJ(L)-11539)

770322a PAGEANT IN EXILE 1979 studio prod. MUSIC & WORDS: Randal Wilson. COND: Jeffrey Olmstead (of 1979 prod, entitled "Duel"). CAST: Thomas Young & Randal Wilson of orig & 1979

prods; Kurt Yahjian, Kate DeZina, & Karen Kraft of orig prod; Bertilla Baker of 1979 prod. (Original Cast 7917, entitled "Duel")

770417a I LOVE MY WIFE orig prod. MUSIC: Cy Coleman. WORDS: Michael Stewart. ORCH: Cy Coleman. COND: John Miller. CAST: Lenny Baker, Joanna Gleason, Ilene Graff, James Naughton. (Atlantic SD-19107)

770417b I LOVE MY WIFE 1978 South African prod. COND: Bill Fairley. CAST: Michael McGovern, Erica Rogers, Jessica Jones, Tobie Cronje. (EMI(South Africa) EMCJ(L)-11552)

770421a ANNIE orig prod. MUSIC: Charles Strouse. WORDS: Martin Charnin. ORCH: Philip J Lang. COND: Peter Howard. CAST: Andrea McArdle, Reid Shelton, Dorothy Loudon, Sandy Faison, Robert Fitch, Barbara Erwin, Donald Craig, Raymond Thorne. (Col PS-34712)

770421b ANNIE 1978 London prod. ORCH: Philip J Lang. COND: John Owen Edwards. CAST: Ann-Marie Gwatkin, Sheila Hancock, Stratford Johns, Kenneth Nelson, Damon Sanders, Judith Paris, Clovissa Newcombe, Matt Zimmerman. (CBS(E) 70160)

770421c ANNIE 1979 Australian prod. COND: Noel Smith. CAST: Sally Anne Bourne, Hayes Gordon, Jill Perryman, Nancye Hayes, Kevan Johnston, Anne Grigg, Ric Hutton, Lance Strauss, Jon Sidney. (Festival(Australia) L-36861)

770515a TOGETHER ON BROADWAY orig prod rec live. MUSIC & WORDS: Various. COND: Eric Knight, John Lasko. Music Director: Jay Blackton. Narrator: Cyril Ritchard. VOCALS: Ethel Merman, Mary Martin, chorus. (Friends of the Theatre & Music Collection AG-77)(LP-652)

770517a TOLLER CRANSTON'S THE ICE SHOW soundtrack. MUSIC & WORDS: Various. COND: Bill Courtney. VOCALS: Uncredited. (Robden RDR-1001)

770531a BEATLEMANIA orig prod. MUSIC & WORDS: John Lennon, Paul McCartney. PERFORMERS: Joe Pecorino, Mitch Weissman, Leslie Fradkin, Justin McNiell, Randy Clark, Reed Kailing, P M Howard, Bobby Taylor. (Arista AL-8501)

770708a CANADA orig (Montville, N J) prod. MUSIC: Bruce Molloy. WORDS: Zachary Morfogen, Bruce Molloy. ORCH & COND: Bruce Molloy. CAST: Bruce Molloy Sr, Carol Lee Gorson, Bridget Coffey, Santiago Patino, chorus. (Broadway Baby 776)

770808a JOSEPH McCARTHY IS ALIVE AND LIVING IN DADE COUNTY orig (Los Angeles) prod. MUSIC & WORDS: Ray Scantlin. CAST: Kim Brassner, Amanda McBroom, Hal James Pederson, Gerrard Wagner, Alfred Wilson. (AEI Records 1103)

770920a NEFERTITI orig (Chicago) prod. MUSIC: David Spangler. WORDS: Christopher Gore. ORCH: Robert Freedman. COND: Robert Billig. CAST: Andrea Marcovicci, Michael V Smartt, Robert LuPone, Michael Nouri, Jane White, chorus. (Take Home Tunes 7810)

771029a THE ACT orig prod. MUSIC: John Kander. WORDS: Fred Ebb. ORCH: Ralph Burns. COND: Stanley Lebowsky. PIANO: John Kander (composer). CAST: Liza Minnelli, Roger Minami, Gayle Crofoot, chorus. (DRG Records 6101)

771201a BEOWULF 1974 Canadian prod. MUSIC: Victor Davies. WORDS: Betty Jane Wylie. ORCH: Victor Davies. CAST: Chad Allan, Doug Mallory, Christine Chandler, Frank A Adamson, Dianne Heatherington, P M Howard, Jayson King, Howard Hicks. (Daffodil(C) 30050)

771221a THE RAGTIME YEARS orig (touring) prod rec live. MUSIC & WORDS: Various. PIANO & VOCALS: Max Morath. (Vanguard VSD-79391, entitled "Living a Ragtime Life")

1978

780001a Record prod THE BLACK EAGLE orig prod. MUSIC & WORDS: Rod McKuen. COND: Arthur Greenslade. CAST: Rod McKuen, Maggie Stredder, Dan Stone, Don Hanmer, Marilyn Child, Ken Barrie, chorus. (Stanyan 2SR-5087)

780002a Film MOVIE MOVIE 1979 album. MUSIC & WORDS: Ralph Burns, Buster Davis, Larry Gelbart, Sheldon Keller. ORCH: John Rodby. COND: Buster Davis. VOCALS: Patricia Marshall, Gene Merlino, Jerry Whitman. (FilmScore 7914, with additional material)

780003a Film WATERSHIP DOWN soundtrack. Art Garfunkel: "Bright Eyes" (by Mike Batt) (Col JS-35707)

780004a Film THE MAGIC OF LASSIE soundtrack. MUSIC & WORDS: Richard M & Robert B Sherman. ORCH & COND: Irwin Kostal. CAST: Mickey Rooney, Pat Boone, Debby Boone, James Stewart, Alice Faye, chorus. (Pickwick(E) SHM-992)

780117a 2 orig prod. MUSIC & WORDS: Julie Mandel. COND & PIANO: Donald Oliver. CAST: Ann Hodapp, Hal Watters. (Take Home Tunes 788)

780219a ON THE TWENTIETH CENTURY orig prod. MUSIC: Cy Coleman. WORDS: Betty Comden, Adolph Green. ORCH: Hershy Kay. COND: Paul Gemignani. CAST: John Cullum, Madeline Kahn, Imogene Coca, George Coe, Dean Dittman, Kevin Kline, chorus. (Col JS-35330)

780219b ON THE TWENTIETH CENTURY 1979 disco records produced & arranged by Cy Coleman (composer) & Larry Fallon. VOCALS: uncredited. "Never," "Our Private World" (Buddah DSC-139)

780300a MONSIEUR DE POURCEAUGNAC orig prod. MUSIC: Howard Harris. WORDS: Tony Schuman. COND: Howard Harris. CAST: Dorian Barth, John Foley, Tony Calabro, Homer Foil, Arthur Erickson, Margaret McGuire, Robert Trebor, Lisa Loomer. (Broadway Baby BBD-789)

780323a A BISTRO CAR ON THE C N R 1979 Vancouver, Canada, prod. MUSIC: Patrick Rose. WORDS: Richard Ouzounian, Merv Campone. ORCH & COND: Edward Henderson. CAST: Patrick Rose (composer) of orig prod; Diane Stapley, Ross Douglas, Nora McClellan. (Berandol 9069)

780323b A BISTRO CAR ON THE C N R 1974 Winnipeg, Canada, prod (entitled "Jubalay"), with quite different material. MUSIC & WORDS: Patrick Rose, Merv Campone. ORCH & COND: Edward Henderson. CAST: Patrick Rose (composer) of orig & 1979 Vancouver casts; Diane Stapley (of 1979 Vancouver cast); Brent Carver, Ruth Nichol. (Unnamed label JP-9001, entitled "Jubalay")

780417a THE BEST LITTLE WHOREHOUSE IN TEXAS orig prod. MUSIC & WORDS: Carol Hall. ORCH & COND: Robert Billig. CAST: Carlin Glynn, Jay Garner, Susan Mansur, Lisa Brown, Henderson Forsythe, Pamela Blair, Delores Hall, Clint Allmon, the Rio Grande Band. (MCA Records MCA-3049)

780509a AIN'T MISBEHAVIN' orig prod. MUSIC: mostly Thomas (Fats) Waller. WORDS: Various. ORCH & COND: Luther Henderson. VOCALS: Nell Carter, Andre DeShields, Armelia McQueen, Ken Page, Charlaine Woodard. (RCA CBL2-2965)

780510a ANGEL orig prod. MUSIC: Gary Geld. WORDS: Peter Udell. ORCH: Don Walker. COND: William Cox. CAST: Frances Sternhagen, Don Scardino, Joel Higgins, Fred Gwynne, Leslie Ann Ray, Patti Allison, Patricia Englund. (Geld-Udell-Abrams GUA-001)

780513a RUNAWAYS orig prod. MUSIC & WORDS: Elizabeth Swados. CAST: David Schechter, Venustra K Robinson, Bernie

Allison, Evan Miranda, Leonard Brown, Ray Contreras, Karen Evans. (Col JS-35410)

780514a WORKING orig prod. MUSIC & WORDS: Stephen Schwartz, James Taylor, Mary Rodgers, Susan Birkenhead, Craig Carnelia, Micki Grant. ORCH: Kirk Nurock. COND: Stephen Reinhardt. CAST: David Langston Smyrl, David Patrick Kelly, Matthew McGrath, Bobo Lewis, Matt Landers, Joe Mantegna, Susan Bigelow, Robin Lamont, Lynne Thigpen, Arny Freeman, Lenora Nemetz, Bob Gunton. (Col JS-35411)

780516a I'M GETTING MY ACT TOGETHER AND TAKING IT ON THE ROAD orig prod. MUSIC: Nancy Ford. WORDS: Gretchen Cryer. CAST: Gretchen Cryer, Don Scardino, Margot Rose, Betty Aberlin, chorus. (CBS X-14885)

780608a PIANO BAR orig prod. MUSIC: Bob Fremont. WORDS: Doris Willens. ORCH: Philip J Lang. PIANO: Joel Silberman. CAST: Kelly Bishop, Karen de Vito, Steve Elmore, Richard Ryder, Joel Silberman, (Original Cast 7812)

780621a EVITA 1976 record prod. MUSIC: Andrew Lloyd Webber. WORDS: Tim Rice. ORCH: Andrew Lloyd Webber. COND: Anthony Bowles. CAST: Julie Covington, Paul Jones, Colm Wilkinson, Tony Christie, Barbara Dickson, Mike Smith, Mike d'Abo, Christopher Neil. (MCA 2-11003. Excerpts: MCA 1170)

780621b EVITA orig (London) prod. ORCH: Hershy Kay. COND: Anthony Bowles. CAST: Elaine Paige, David Essex, Joss Ackland, Siobhan McCarthy, Mark Ryan, chorus. (MCA MCG-3527)

780621c EVITA 1979 New York prod. COND: Rene Wiegert. CAST: Patti LuPone, Mandy Patinkin, Bob Gunton, Mark Syers, Jane Ohringer, chorus. (MCA 2-11007)

780621d EVITA 1979 studio prod. COND: Ramon Boales. CAST: Uncredited. (Pickwick(E) SHM-929)

780621e EVITA 1980 Australian prod. COND: Peter Casey. CAST: Jennifer Murphy, Peter Carroll, John O'May, Tony Alvarez, Laura Mitchell. (MCA(Australia) EVI)

780920a EUBIE! orig prod. MUSIC: Eubie Blake. WORDS: mostly Noble Sissle, Andy Razaf. ORCH: Neal Tate. COND: Vicki Carter. CAST: Ethel Beatty, Terry Burrell, Lynnie Godfrey, Gregory Hines, Maurice Hines, Mel Johnson Jr, Lonnie McNeil, Marion Ramsey, Alaina Reed, Jeffery V Thompson. (Warner Bros HS-3267)

781006a STAGES orig (Los Angeles) prod. MUSIC & WORDS: Bruce Kimmel. COND: Michael Goodrow. CAST: Bruce Kimmel, Randi Kallan, Linden Waddell, Michael Byers. Sammy Williams, Alan Abelew, Philip Clark, Jeffrey Kramer. (Varese Sarabande VC-81083)

781007a THE KING OF THE ENTIRE WORLD orig prod. MUSIC & WORDS: Daniel Pisello. COND: Kit McClure. CAST: uncredited. (Fourth Wall 4)

781022a KING OF HEARTS studio prod by members of orig cast. MUSIC: Peter Link. WORDS: Jacob Brackman. CAST: Don Scardino, Millicent Martin, Pamela Blair, Bob Gunton, Michael McCarty, Gordon Weiss, Rex Hays. (Original Cast 8028)

781031a BAR MITZVAH BOY orig (London) prod. MUSIC: Jule Styne. WORDS: Don Black. ORCH: Irwin Kostal. COND: Alexander Faris. CAST: Barry Angel, Joyce Blair, Harry Towb, Leonie Cosman, Peter Whitman, Vivienne Martin, Ray C Davis, Benny Lee. (CBS Records(E) S-70162)

781109a BEYOND THE RAINBOW orig (London) prod. MUSIC: Armando Travaioli. WORDS: Leslie Bricusse. ORCH: Renato Serio, Armando Travaioli. COND: Michael Reed. CAST: Johnny Dorelli, Roy Kinnear, Janet Mahoney, Lesley Duff, Geoffrey Burridge, Noel Johnson, Dororthy Vernon. (MCA(E) MCF-2874)

781112a PLATINUM orig prod, rec live. MUSIC: Gary William Friedman. WORDS: Will Holt. ORCH: Fred Thaler, Jimmie Haskell. COND: Fred Thaler. CAST: Alexis Smith, Richard Cox, Lisa Mordente, Damita Jo Freeman, Robin Green, Avery Sommers. (Unnamed label CX-335)

781113a LITTLE WILLIE JR'S RESURRECTION orig (London) prod. MUSIC: Johnny Thompson. WORDS: Oscar L Johnson. COND: Johnny Thompson. CAST: The original company. (Glori JC-1044)

781214a BALLROOM orig prod. MUSIC: Billy Goldenberg. WORDS: Alan & Marilyn Bergman. ORCH: Jonathan Tunick. COND: Don Jennings. CAST: Dorothy Loudon, Vincent Gardenia, Bernie Knee, Lynn Roberts. (Col JS-35762)

781222a SCROOGE 1978 album. MUSIC: Mark Holden. WORDS: Jim Bernhard. COND: Mark Holden (composer). VOCALS: Paul Schweiger, Terry Meason, chorus. "Christmas Is Coming," "Ghosts Are People, Too," "Before It's Too Late" (Theatre under the Stars 7" TUTS-78)

1979

790001a Film JUST A GIGOLO soundtrack. VOCALS: Marlene Dietrich, Sydne Rome, others. (Jambo(E) 1. Excerpt: Dietrich: "Just A Gigolo" (45/Col(E) DB-9050).)

790002a Film THE MUPPET MOVIE soundtrack. MUSIC & WORDS: mostly Paul Williams, Kenny Ascher. ORCH & COND: Ian Freebairn-Smith. VOCALS: Jim Henson, Frank Oz, Dave Goelz, Jerry Nelson, Richard Hunt. (Atlantic SD-16001)

790003a Film THE PROMISE soundtrack. MUSIC: David Shire. WORDS: Alan & Marilyn Bergman. ORCH: David Shire. Melissa Manchester: "I'll Never Say Goodbye" (MCA 3082)

790004a Film ALL THAT JAZZ soundtrack. MUSIC & WORDS: Various. ORCH & COND: Ralph Burns. VOCALS: George Benson, Sandahl Bergman, Peter Allen, Leland Palmer, Ann Reinking, Erzsebet Foldi, Ben Vereen, Roy Scheider. (Casablanca NBLP-7198)

790005a A ONE-WAY TICKET TO BROADWAY orig prod. MUSIC: Dan Goggin. WORDS: Robert Lorick. CAST: Katie Anders, Ann Hodapp, Marvin Solley, Elaine Petricoff, Beth Fowler, Dan Goggin. (Theatre Archives 8001)

790111a THE GRAND TOUR orig prod. MUSIC & WORDS: Jerry Herman. ORCH: Philip J Lang. COND: Wally Harper. CAST: Joel Grey, Ron Holgate, Florence Lacey, Stephen Vinovich, Travis Hudson, Gene Varrone, Chevi Colton. (Col JS-35761)

790211a THEY'RE PLAYING OUR SONG orig prod. MUSIC: Marvin Hamlisch. WORDS: Carole Bayer Sager. ORCH: Ralph Burns, Richard Hazard, Gene Page. COND: Larry Blank. CAST: Robert Klein, Lucie Arnaz, chorus. (Casablanca NBLP-7141)

790211b THEY'RE PLAYING OUR SONG 1980 Australian prod. COND: Dale Ringland. CAST: John Waters, Jacki Weaver. (Festival(Australia) L-37356)

790211c THEY'RE PLAYING OUR SONG 1980 London prod. COND: Grant Hossack. CAST: Tom Conti, Gemma Craven. (Chopper(E) E-6)

790211d THEY'RE PLAYING OUR SONG contemp record by Gemma Craven of 1980 London prod. "I Still Believe in Love" (45/Chrysalis(E) CHS-2478)

790213a SARAVA contemp records "produced under the direction of Mitch Leigh." MUSIC: Mitch Leigh. WORDS: N Richard Nash. VOCALS: uncredited. "Sarava," "You Do" (Roadshow YD-11455)(Incomplete: 45/Roadshow YB-11454)

790221a IN TROUSERS orig prod. MUSIC & WORDS: William

Finn. ORCH & COND: Michael Starobin. CAST: Chip Zien, Alison Fraser, Joanna Green, Mary Testa. (Original Cast 7915)

790301a SWEENEY TODD orig prod. MUSIC & WORDS: Stephen Sondheim, ORCH: Jonathan Tunick. COND: Paul Gemignani. CAST: Angela Lansbury, Len Cariou, Victor Garber, Sarah Rice, Merle Louise, Ken Jennings, Joaquin Romaguera, Jack Eric Williams, Edmund Lyndeck. (RCA CBL2-3379)

790328a A DAY IN HOLLYWOOD/A NIGHT IN THE UKRAINE 1980 New York prod. MUSIC & WORDS: Frank Lazarus, Dick Vosburgh, Jerry Herman, Richard Whiting, others. PIANOS: Allen Cohen, Robert Fisher, Frank Lazarus. CAST: Priscilla Lopez, David Garrison, Frank Lazarus, Stephen James, Peggy Hewett, Kate Draper. (DRG Records SBL-12580)

790408a CARMELINA 1980 studio prod. MUSIC: Burton Lane. WORDS: Alan Jay Lerner. ORCH: Philip J Lang. COND: Don Jennings. CAST: Georgia Brown, Grace Keagy, Gordon Ramsey, Howard Ross, & Jossie de Guzman of orig prod; Paul Sorvino, Bernie Knee, chorus. (Original Cast 8019)

790513a THE UTTER GLORY OF MORRISSEY HALL orig prod. MUSIC & WORDS: Clark Gesner. ORCH: Jay Blackton, Russell Warner. COND: John Gordon. CAST: Celeste Holm, Taina Elg, Marilyn Caskey, Becky McSpadden, Mary Saunders, John Gallogly, Karen Gibson. (Original Cast 7918)

790513b THE UTTER GLORY OF MORRISSEY HALL 1976 Santa Maria, Calif prod. ORCH: Jay Blackton. COND: Larry Delinger. CAST: Marilyn Caskey (of New York prod); Thomas M Nahrwold, Jill Tanner, April Harris, Margaret Klenck, Alex Nibley. (Unnamed label 44037)

790517a FESTIVAL orig prod. MUSIC: Stephen Downs. WORDS: Stephen Downs, Randal Martin. COND: David Spear. CAST: Michael Rupert, Bill Hutton, Maureen McNamara, Michael Magnusen, Leon Stewart, John Windsor, Roxann Parker. (Original Cast 7916)

790531a A NEW YORK SUMMER! orig prod. MUSIC: Tom Bahler. WORDS: Mark Bieha. Original cast: "I Thank Heaven," "New York Summer" (45/Radio City Music Hall J3RS-2208)

790611a SCRAMBLED FEET orig prod. MUSIC & WORDS: John Driver, Jeffrey Haddow. ORCH & COND: Jimmy Wisner. CAST: Evalyn Baron, John Driver, Jeffrey Haddow, Roger Neil, Hermione. (DRG Records 6105)

790614a FLOWERS FOR ALGERNON orig (London) prod. MUSIC: Charles Strouse. WORDS: David Rogers. ORCH: Philip J Lang. COND: Alexander Faris. CAST: Michael Crawford, Cheryl Kennedy, Jeanna L'Esty, Betty Benfield, George Harris, Sharon Lee Hill. (Original Cast 8021)

790725a SONGBOOK orig (London) prod. MUSIC: Monty Norman. WORDS: Julian More. COND: Grant Hossack. CAST: Anton Rodgers, Gemma Craven, Diane Langton, Andrew C Wadsworth, David Healy. (Pye(E) NSPL-18609)

790913a DADDY GOODNESS 1979 record by Freda Payne of orig (Washington) cast. MUSIC: Ken Hirsch. WORDS: Ron Miller. "Hungry" (LP-684)

791004a THE ALL NIGHT STRUT! 1976 Cleveland, Ohio, prod. MUSIC & WORDS: Various. ORCH: Gil Leib, Dick Schermesser. COND: Tom Fitt, Dean Hill. VOCALS: Robert Chidsey, Dean Hill, Elaine Psihountas, Laura Robinson. (Playhouse Square 1S-1001)

791020a ONE MO' TIME orig prod, rec live. MUSIC & WORDS: Various. ORCH: Lars Edegran, Orange Kellin. COND: Orange Kellin. CAST: Vernel Bagneris, Topsy Chapman, Thais Clark, Sylvia Williams, John Stell, Jabbo Smith. (Warner Bros HS-3454)

791106a NASHVILLE NEW YORK orig (London) prod, rec live. MUSIC: Vernon Duke, Kurt Weill. WORDS: Ogden Nash. PIANO: David Wykes. CAST: Christopher Benjamin, Robert Cushman, Bryan Murray, Leueen Willoughby. (That's Entertainment(E) 1001)

791127a FIVE AFTER EIGHT orig prod. MUSIC & WORDS: Michael Bitterman. ORCH: Raphe Crystal, Ron Williams. COND: Ron Williams. CAST: Sally Funk, James Handakas, Dena Olstad, Arthur Alan Sorenson, Barbara Walker. (Original Cast 8027)

791221a ALADDIN orig (London) prod. MUSIC & WORDS: Sandy Wilson. ORCH & COND: Colin Sell. CAST: Richard Freeman, Aubrey Woods, Ernest Clark, Elisabeth Welch, Arthur Kohn, Joe Melia, Michael Sadler. (President(E) PTLS-1072)

1980

800128a TELL ME ON A SUNDAY 1980 TV prod. MUSIC: Andrew Lloyd Webber. WORDS: Don Black. VOCALS: Marti Webb. (Polydor(E) PD1-6260)

800228a AN EVENING WITH W. S. GILBERT orig prod. MUSIC: Arthur Sullivan, Osmond Carr, Edward German. WORDS: W S Gilbert. PIANO: Alfred Heller. CAST: Lloyd Harris. (Original Cast 8026)

800430a BARNUM orig prod. MUSIC: Cy Coleman. WORDS: Michael Stewart. ORCH: Hershy Kay. COND: Peter Howard. CAST: Jim Dale, Glenn Close, Marianne Tatum, Terri White, Leonard John Crofoot, William C Witter, chorus. (CBS Masterworks JS-36576)

800430b BARNUM 1980 album by the Cy Coleman Trio. ORCH & PIANO: Cy Coleman. VOCALS: Cy Coleman, Jonathan Miller. (Gryphon 918)

800507a ENCORE BREL orig (South Africa) prod. MUSIC & WORDS: Jacques Brel. ORCH & COND: Lindsay Heard. CAST: Ann Hamblin, Laurika Rauch, Ferdie Uphof. (Nitty Gritty (South Africa) NGC-1025)

800514a MUSICAL CHAIRS orig prod. MUSIC & WORDS: Tom Savage. ORCH: Ada Janik, Dick Lieb. COND: Barry Gordon. CAST: Tom Urich (who replaced Ron Holgate on May 20), Leslie-Anne Wolfe, Brandon Maggart, Joy Franz, Rick Emery, Scott Ellis, Patti Karr, Jess Richards, Enid Blaymore, Helen Blount (who replaced Grace Keagy on May 20), Randall Easterbrook. (Original Cast 8024)

800529a BILLY BISHOP GOES TO WAR orig prod, rec live in Canada in 1979. MUSIC & WORDS: John Gray. PIANO: John Gray. VOCALS: Eric Peterson, John Gray. (Tapestry(C) GD-7372)

800605a TOMFOOLERY orig (London) prod, rec live. MUSIC & WORDS: Tom Lehrer. ORCH & COND: Chris Walker. CAST: Robin Ray, Jonathan Adams, Martin Connor, Tricia George. (Monza(E) MONMT-102)

800622a THE LIFE AND ADVENTURES OF NICHOLAS NICKLEBY orig (London) prod. MUSIC & WORDS: Stephen Oliver. COND: Stephen Oliver. VOCALS: Sharon Bower, Andrew Hawkins, Rose Hill, Lila Kaye, John Woodvine, chorus. (CAS/RSC(E) unnumbered)

800825a 42ND STREET orig prod. MUSIC: Harry Warren. WORDS: mostly Al Dubin. ORCH: Philip J Lang. COND: John Lesko. CAST: Tammy Grimes, Jerry Orbach, Wanda Richert, Lee Roy Reams, Karen Prunczik, Joseph Bova, Carole Cook, James Congdon. (RCA CBL1-3891)

801014a REALLY ROSIE 1975 album (incl soundtrack of 1975 TV prod) by Carole King (composer), piano & vocals. MUSIC: Carole King. WORDS: Maurice Sendak. (Ode SP-77027)

801105a THE FIFTH OF JULY contemp record by Jonathan Hogan (vocal & guitars) of orig cast. MUSIC & WORDS: Jonathan Hogan. "Your Loving Eyes" (45/Penstemon 757)

801111a FRONT STREET GAIETIES orig (Los Angeles) prod. MUSIC: Jeffrey Silverman. WORDS: Walter Willison. CAST: Carol Swarbrick, Charles Ward, Walter Willison, Susan Watson, Lori Milne, Stephanie Stasny. (AEI 1133)

801120a KA-BOOM! orig prod. MUSIC: Joe Ercole. WORDS: Bruce Kluger. ORCH: Joe Ercole. COND: John Lehman. CAST: Ken Ward, Valerie Williams, John Hall, Andrea Wright, Judith Bro, Ben Agresti. (CYM Records 8130)

1981

810001a CAPTAIN CRASH VERSUS THE ZZORG WOMEN orig (Los Angeles) prod. MUSIC: Steve Hammond, Rick Jones, Weston Gavin. WORDS: Dave Pierce. CAST: Weston Gavin, Anna Mathias, Cynthia Zaitz, Laura Loftus, McCall, Rick Jones, Lewis Arquette, Teda Bracci. (WEB Records OC-103)

810201a CHOCALONIA 1976 studio prod. MUSIC & WORDS: Glenn Houle. ORCH & COND: Glenn Houle. CAST: Wade Crookham, Frankie Marshall, Dennis Lybe, Jim Hayes, Ally Ballard, Chris Costello, Alan Jon, Mike Finneran, Gary Fuller. (Crissy 2034)

810301a SOPHISTICATED LADIES orig prod. MUSIC: mostly Duke Ellington. WORDS: Various. ORCH: Al Cohn. COND: Mercer Ellington. CAST: Gregory Hines, Judith Jamison, Phyllis Hyman, P J Benjamin, Hinton Battle, Terri Klausner, Gregg Burge, Priscilla Baskerville. (RCA CBL2-4053)

810328a TINSELTOWN orig (Los Angeles) prod. MUSIC & WORDS: Mark Milner. COND: Steven Applegate. CAST: Diane Benedict, Linda Lyons, David Pavlosky, Mindy Dow, Eddie D'Angelo. (WEB Records OC-102)

810329a WOMAN OF THE YEAR orig prod. MUSIC: John Kander. WORDS: Fred Ebb. ORCH: Michael Gibson. COND: Donald Pippin. CAST: Lauren Bacall, Harry Guardino, Roderick Cook, Eivind Harum, Grace Keagy, Daren Kelly, Marilyn Cooper, Rex Everhart. (Arista AL-8303)

810411a BOY'S OWN McBETH 1979 Australian prod. MUSIC: Grahame Bond. WORDS: Grahame Bond, Jim Burnett. ORCH: Rory O'Donoghue. VOCALS: Grahame Bond, Rory O'Donoghue, Elizabeth Wilder, Paul Johnstone, Bjarne Ohlin, Nick Lyon, Jim Burnett. (Dunsinane(Australia) YPRX-1641)

810511a CATS orig (London) prod. MUSIC: Andrew Lloyd Webber. WORDS: T S Eliot, Trevor Nunn. ORCH: David Cullen, Andrew Lloyd Webber. COND: David Firman, Harry Rabinowitz, CAST: Wayne Sleep, Paul Nicholas, Brian Blessed, Elaine Paige, Finola Hughes, Sharon Lee-Hill, Sarah Brightman, Susan Jane Tanner, Stephen Tate, John Thornton, Bonnie Langford. (Polydor(E) CATX-001)

810605a SPARKLES orig (Los Angeles) prod. MUSIC: Jim Murdock. WORDS: Michael Lewis. ORCH & COND: Jim Murdock. CAST: Michael Lewis, Janell Kerzner, Michael Cascone, Bruce Smith, Robert Kimbrough, Benjamin Lamb, J Michael Raye. (WEB Records OC-105)

Numerical List of "LP" Albums

LP-54 MARLENE DIETRICH SOUVENIR ALBUM Dec 10" 5100

LP-55 DANNY KAYE Dec 10" 5033

LP-56 GREAT STARS OF MUSICAL COMEDY Ace of Clubs(E) 1182

LP-57 JULIA SANDERSON AND FRANK CRUMIT 78/Dec album 245

LP-58 THE YOUNG RUDY VALLEE RCA LPM-2507; THE BEST OF RUDY VALLEE RCA LSP-3816

LP-59 SHOW TUNE TREASURY Walden S-1

LP-60 HAROLD SINGS ARLEN Col OS-2920

LP-61 THE DEBONAIR JACK BUCHANAN Music for Pleasure(E) 1160

LP-62 TOUJOURS MAURICE Camden 579

LP-63 THE ENTRANCING EVELYN LAYE Music for Pleasure(E) 1162

LP-64 THE ORIGINAL RECORDINGS OF JESSIE MATTHEWS Music for Pleasure(E) 1127

LP-65 ROMANTIC MELODIES BY JEANETTE MacDONALD 78/Vic album MO-1217

LP-66 IRENE DUNNE IN SONGS BY JEROME KERN 78/Dec album 484

LP-67 MARY MARTIN IN AN ALBUM OF COLE PORTER SONGS 78/Dec album 123

LP-68 ETHEL MERMAN: SONGS SHE HAS MADE FAMOUS Dec 10" 5053

LP-69 MEMORABLE MOMENTS IN MUSICAL COMEDY Dec 10" 6019

LP-70 DANNY KAYE Col 10" CL-6023

LP-71 JEANETTE MacDONALD: SMILIN' THROUGH Camden 325

LP-72 MAURICE CHEVALIER, VOL. 1 RCA LPV-564

LP-73 AL JOLSON: SAY IT WITH SONGS Ace of Hearts(E) 87

LP-74 OH, WHAT A LOVELY WAR World Record Club(E) 130

LP-75 BUBBLES: JOHN W., THAT IS Vee-Jay 1109

LP-76 THE UNFORGETTABLE MARILYN MONROE Movietone 72016

LP-77 JEANETTE MacDONALD SINGS SAN FRANCISCO RCA VIC-1515

LP-78 FUNNY FACE World Record Club(E) 144

LP-79 BINNIE HALE: SPREAD A LITTLE HAPPINESS World Record Club(E)129

LP-80 JIMMY DURANTE Dec 10" 5116

LP-81 MARLENE DIETRICH Historia(G) 607

LP-82 AL JOLSON: LET ME SING AND I'M HAPPY Ace of Hearts(E) 33

LP-83 BOBBY HOWES: SHE'S MY LOVELY World Record Club(E) 136

LP-84 EDITH DAY World Record Club(E) 138

LP-85 KURT WEILL SUNG BY LOTTE LENYA Col KL-5229

LP-86 THE DICK POWELL SONG BOOK Ace of Hearts(E) 50

LP-87 FORD 50TH ANNIVERSARY TELEVISION SHOW Dec 10" 7027

LP-88 THANK HEAVEN FOR MAURICE CHEVALIER RCA LPM-2076

LP-89 THE NOEL COWARD ALBUM Col MG-30088

LP-90 CICELY COURTNEIDGE AND JACK HULBERT World Record Club(E) 113

LP-91 DEANNA DURBIN SOUVENIR ALBUM NO. 3 78/Dec album 128

LP-92 DANNY KAYE PRESENTED BY YOUR RAMBLER DEALER Dena Pictures mx XTV-92557/92558

LP-93 LEE WILEY & ETHEL MERMAN: TWO CLASSIC INTERPRETATIONS OF COLE PORTER JJC Records 2003

LP-94 HOAGY CARMICHAEL: THE STARDUST ROAD Dec 8588

LP-95 DEANNA DURBIN SOUVENIR ALBUM NO. 2 78/Dec album 75

LP-96 RUDY VALLEE: HEIGH-HO EVERYBODY 78/Vic album P-111

LP-97 A NOSTALGIA TRIP TO THE STARS, 1920-1950, VOL. 1 Monmouth 7030

LP-98 A NOSTALGIA TRIP TO THE STARS, 1920-1950, VOL. 2 Monmouth 7031

LP-99 MISS ETHEL WATERS Monmouth 6812

LP-100 ALICE FAYE SINGS HER GREATEST MOVIE HITS Valiant 122

LP-101 HAROLD ARLEN AND HIS SONGS Cap T-635

LP-102 MAURICE CHEVALIER: YOU BROUGHT A NEW KIND OF LOVE TO ME Monmouth 7028

LP-103 GENE AUSTIN: MY BLUE HEAVEN RCA LPM-2490

LP-104 LILLIAN ROTH: I'LL CRY TOMORROW Epic 3206

LP-105 THE FABULOUS MAE WEST Dec 9016

LP-106 GOLDEN MOMENTS FROM THE SILVER SCREEN Harmony 30549

LP-107 THE BEST OF DANNY KAYE Harmony 7314

LP-108 FRED ASTAIRE: NOW Kapp 3049

LP-109 HOLLYWOOD SINGS: VOL. 1 (THE GIRLS) Ace of Hearts(E) 67

LP-110 DEANNA DURBIN SOUVENIR ALBUM 78/Dec album 35

LP-111 CAROL CHANNING: HER FABULOUS CAFE ACT Vanguard 9056

LP-112 BEATRICE LILLIE SINGS JJC Records 3003

LP-113 HARRY RICHMAN SOUVENIR ALBUM 78/Dec album 632

LP-114 HOLLYWOOD SINGS: VOL. 2 (THE BOYS) Ace of Hearts(E) 68

LP-115 HOLLYWOOD SINGS: VOL. 3 (THE BOYS & GIRLS) Ace of Hearts(E) 69

LP-116 SHIRLEY TEMPLE: CURTAIN CALL Movietone 71012

LP-117 NELSON EDDY FAVORITES Camden 492

LP-118 MAURICE CHEVALIER: YESTERDAY MGM 3702

LP-119 JEANETTE MacDONALD: ROMANTIC MOMENTS 78/Vic album DM-1489

LP-120 MARILYN MONROE Ascot 13008

LP-121 THIRTY MINUTES WITH BEATRICE LILLIE Liberty Music Shop 10" 1002

LP-122 CARL BRISSON SINGS AGAIN Ace of Clubs(E) 1200

LP-123 NOEL AND GERTIE AND BEA Parlophone(E) 7135

LP-124 GREAT MOVIE STARS OF THE 30'S Parlophone(E) 7141

LP-125 FRED ASTAIRE Verve(E) VSP-23/24

LP-126 ALLAN JONES: THE DONKEY SERENADE Camden 2256

LP-127 EDITH DAY IN RIO RITA Monmouth 7058

LP-128 ALICE DELYSIA World Record Club(E) 164

LP-129 HOORAY FOR HOLLYWOOD RCA LPV-579

LP-130 THE HITS OF NOEL GAY Music for Pleasure(E) 1236

LP-131 DEANNA DURBIN SOUVENIR ALBUM NO. 4 78/Dec album 209

LP-132 MAURICE CHEVALIER RETURNS 78/Vic album S-51

LP-133 DICK POWELL SOUVENIR ALBUM 78/Dec album 608

LP-134 JEANETTE MacDONALD & NELSON EDDY: FAVORITES IN HI-FI RCA LPM-1738

LP-135 FRANCES LANGFORD SOUVENIR ALBUM 78/Dec album 87

LP-136 NOSTALGIA'S GREATEST HITS, VOL. 1 Stanyan 10055

LP-137 JEANETTE MacDONALD IN SONG 78/Vic album M-642

LP-138 NOEL COWARD: I'LL SEE YOU AGAIN Philips(E) 10" BBR-8028

LP-139 MARLENE DIETRICH SINGS Vox 10" VL-3040

LP-140 HELLO, JERRY: JERRY HERMAN AND HIS ORCHESTRA United Artists 3432

LP-141 MAE WEST & W. C. FIELDS SIDE BY SIDE Harmony 11405

LP-142 JIMMY DURANTE IN PERSON MGM 10" 542; THE VERY BEST OF JIMMY DURANTE MGM 4207; JIMMY DURANTE IN PERSON Lion 70053

LP-143 EDDIE CANTOR IN SONGS HE MADE FAMOUS 78/Dec album 564

LP-144 EDDIE CANTOR: MY FORTY YEARS IN SHOW BUSINESS Audio Fidelity 702

LP-145 AL JOLSON IN SONGS HE MADE FAMOUS Dec 10" 5026

LP-146 GERTRUDE NIESEN, VOL. 1 45/Dec ED-2045

LP-147 CARMEN MIRANDA, VOL. 1 45/Dec ED-2066

LP-148 OLD CURIOSITY SHOP RCA LCT-1112

LP-149 JOHN RAITT: HIGHLIGHTS OF BROADWAY Cap T-583

LP-150 TRYOUT: KURT WEILL AND IRA GERSHWIN Heritage 0051

LP-151 DIETRICH IN RIO Col WL-164

LP-152 JOSE COLLINS AS THE MAID OF THE MOUNTAINS World Record Club(E) 169

LP-153 MERMAN SINGS MERMAN London(E) XPS-901

LP-154 THE GOLDEN AGE OF THE HOLLYWOOD MUSICAL United Artists(E) 29421

LP-155 THE THREE MUSKETEERS Monmouth 7050

LP-156 JACK WHITING & JESSIE MATTHEWS Monmouth 7049

LP-157 STARS OF THE ZIEGFELD FOLLIES Pelican 102

LP-158 REVUE 1912-1918 Parlophone(E) 7145

LP-159 REVUE 1919-1929 Parlophone(E) 7150

LP-160 COLE Col KS-31456

LP-161 BING CROSBY: ZING A LITTLE ZONG Dec 4263

LP-162 BING CROSBY: BLUE SKIES Dec 4259

LP-163 BING CROSBY: EASY TO REMEMBER Dec 4250

LP-164 THEY STOPPED THE SHOW Dec 79111

LP-165 EDDIE CANTOR: SONGS HE MADE FAMOUS Dec 4431

LP-166 CARMEN MIRANDA: THE BRAZILIAN BOMBSHELL ace of Hearts(E) 99

LP-167 TED LEWIS: THE MEDICINE MAN FOR THE BLUES Dec 8322

LP-168 TED LEWIS: IS EVERYBODY HAPPY 78/Col album C-69

LP-169 SONDHEIM: A MUSICAL TRIBUTE Warner Bros 2WS-2705

LP-170 A PARTY WITH BETTY COMDEN & ADOLPH GREEN Cap WAO-1197

LP-171 ETHEL MERMAN & GERTRUDE NIESEN: ON STAGE, VOL. 1 RCA "X" LVA-1004

LP-172 REVUE 1930-1940 Parlophone(E) 7154

LP-173 JEROME KERN IN LONDON World Record Club(E) 171

LP-174 NOEL COWARD: THE GREAT SHOWS World Records(E) 179/180

LP-175 THOSE WONDERFUL THIRTIES, VOL. 1 Dec DEA-7-1

LP-176 THOSE WONDERFUL THIRTIES, VOL. 2 Dec DEA-7-2

LP-177 THOSE WONDERFUL THIRTIES, VOL. 3 Dec DEA-7-3

LP-178 MARLENE DIETRICH AT THE CAFE DE PARIS Col ML-4975

LP-179 LITTLE MISS SHIRLEY TEMPLE Pickwick 2034

LP-180 JUDY GARLAND 1935 THRU 1952 Star-Tone 201

LP-181 BING CROSBY IN HOLLYWOOD, 1930-1934 Col C2L-43

LP-182 COLE PORTER 1924-1944 JJA Records 19732

LP-183 HOLLYWOOD FILM-MUSIC OF THE THIRTIES Historia(G) 640

LP-184 SOPHIE TUCKER: CABARET DAYS 78/Mercury album 171

LP-185 SOPHIE TUCKER'S GREATEST HITS Col CL-2604

LP-186 SOPHIE TUCKER: A COLLECTION OF SONGS SHE HAS MADE FAMOUS Dec 10" 5371

LP-187 THE GREAT SOPHIE TUCKER Ace of Hearts(E) 115

LP-188 THE JUDY GARLAND DELUXE SET Cap STCL-2988

LP-189 JUDY GARLAND AT HOME AT THE PALACE ABC Records 620

LP-190 JUDY! THAT'S ENTERTAINMENT Cap ST-1467

LP-191 MARLENE DIETRICH IN LONDON Col OL-6430

LP-192 THE MUSIC OF HAROLD ARLEN, VOL. 1 Walden 306; HAROLD ARLEN SINGS Mark 56 Records 683

LP-193 MARTIN & BLANE SING MARTIN & BLANE Harlequin 701

LP-194 UNFORGETTABLE JUDY GARLAND Radiant 711-0105

LP-195 WIEDERSEHEN MIT MARLENE Cap T-10282

LP-196 AL JOLSON, VOL. 3 Dec 10" 5030

LP-197 JOLSON SINGS AGAIN Dec 10" 5006

LP-198 AL JOLSON SOUVENIR ALBUM Dec 10" 5029

LP-199 CARMEN MIRANDA: A NIGHT IN RIO 78/Dec album 210

LP-200 JUDY Radiant 711-0101

LP-201 JUDY IN HOLLYWOOD Radiant 711-0102

LP-202 JUDY'S PORTRAIT IN SONG Radiant 711-0106

LP-203 SONG STYLINGS FEATURING ANN SOTHERN Sutton 317; ANN SOTHERN AND THE BROADWAY BLUES Tiara 531

LP-204 CAROL CHANNING ENTERTAINS Command RS-880

LP-205 JUDY GARLAND & LIZA MINNELLI: "LIVE" AT THE LONDON PALLADIUM Cap ST-11191

LP-206 HIT SONGS FROM BAKER STREET AND OTHER BROADWAY MUSICALS MGM 4293

LP-207 CELEBRITIES Lion 70108

LP-208 FRED ASTAIRE 1935-1940 JJA Records 19731

LP-209 A CONNECTICUT YANKEE & INSIDE U.S.A. JJA Records 19733

LP-210 JEANETTE MacDONALD'S OPERETTA FAVORITES 45/RCA album WMO-1071

LP-211 FRED ASTAIRE RCA "X" LVA-1001

LP-212 OPENING NIGHT WITH ED AMES RCA LSP-2781

LP-213 THREE EVENINGS WITH FRED ASTAIRE Choreo A-1; FRED ASTAIRE—LIVE Pye(E) PKL-5542; AN EVENING WITH FRED ASTAIRE Koala AW-14160

LP-214 GEORGE M. COHAN: YANKEE DOODLE DANDY Olympic 7111

LP-215 STARRING FRED ASTAIRE Col SG-32472

LP-216 NOEL COWARD'S PACIFIC 1860 AMR Records 300

LP-217 RODGERS AND HART 1927-1942 JJA Records 19734

LP-218 NOEL COWARD 1928-1952 JJA Records 1971-2

LP-219 THE MAGIC OF JUDY GARLAND Longines 5217/5221

LP-220 CARMEN MIRANDA: THE SOUTH AMERICAN WAY 78/Dec album 109

LP-221 GEORGE GERSHWIN IN LONDON World Records(E) 185

LP-222 RODGERS & HART IN LONDON World Records(E) 183

LP-223 FIFTY YEARS OF FILM MUSIC Warner Bros 3XX-2736

LP-224 CHEVALIER'S PARIS Col CL-1049

LP-225 THE COMPLETE SHIRLEY TEMPLE SONGBOOK 20th Fox 103-2

LP-226 LAWRENCE TIBBETT Empire 804

LP-227 GERTIE MILLAR World Record Club(E) 186

LP-228 AL JOLSON SOUVENIR ALBUM, VOL. 4 Dec 10" 5031

LP-229 HELEN MORGAN 78/Vic album P-102

LP-230 TORCH SONGS BY HELEN MORGAN & FANNIE BRICE RCA "X" LVA-1006

LP-231 GRACE MOORE Empire 801

LP-232 BERT WILLIAMS 78/Col album C-25

LP-233 JUDY GARLAND SOUVENIR ALBUM 78/Dec 12" album 76

LP-234 GLORIA JEAN SOUVENIR ALBUM 78/Dec 12" album 125

LP-235 GRACE MOORE SOUVENIR ALBUM 78/Dec 12" album 165

LP-236 ETHEL WATERS SOUVENIR ALBUM 78/Dec album 348

LP-237 THE ANDREWS SISTERS' GREATEST HITS Dec 4919

LP-238 CY COLEMAN SINGS Col CS-9378

LP-239 JUDY GARLAND: MISS SHOW-BIZ Ace of Hearts(E) 48

LP-240 JUDY AT CARNEGIE HALL Cap WBO-1569

LP-241 LENA HORNE: MOANIN' LOW 78/Vic album P-118

LP-242 JEANETTE MacDONALD & NELSON EDDY MOVIE MEMORIES 45/RCA EPA-5113

LP-243 AL JOLSON: RAINBOW 'ROUND MY SHOULDER Dec 9036

LP-244 AL JOLSON: ROCK-A-BYE YOUR BABY Dec 9035

LP-245 AL JOLSON: YOU MADE ME LOVE YOU Dec 9034

LP-246 AL JOLSON: YOU AIN'T HEARD NOTHIN' YET Dec 9037

LP-247 GRACE MOORE SINGS Dec 9593

LP-248 GRACIE FIELDS: STAGE AND SCREEN World Record Club(E) 170

LP-249 JEANETTE MacDONALD: OPERA AND OPERETTA FAVORITES RCA LM-2908

LP-250 FRANK SINATRA IN HOLLYWOOD, 1943-1949 Col CL-2913

LP-251 MERMAN IN VEGAS Reprise 6062

LP-252 THAT'S ENTERTAINMENT MCA 2-11002

LP-253 BING CROSBY: SUNSHINE CAKE Dec 4261

LP-254 BING CROSBY: POCKET FULL OF DREAMS Dec 4252

LP-255 BING CROSBY: COOL OF THE EVENING Dec 4262

LP-256 DEANNA DURBIN Dec 75289

LP-257 SAMMY DAVIS JR: WHAT KIND OF FOOL AM I Reprise 6051

LP-258 LIZA WITH A "Z" Col KC-31762

LP-259 THE JUDY GARLAND STORY: THE STAR YEARS MGM 3989

LP-260 PEARL BAILEY SINGS HAROLD ARLEN Roulette 25155

LP-261 KATE SMITH U.S.A. 78/Col album C-50

LP-262 BING CROSBY: THE ROAD BEGINS Dec 4254

LP-263 BING CROSBY: BUT BEAUTIFUL Dec 4260

LP-264 BING CROSBY: EAST SIDE OF HEAVEN Dec 4253

LP-265 THE BEST OF THE ANDREWS SISTERS MCA 2-4024

LP-266 THE ANDREWS SISTERS "IN THE MOOD" Famous Twinsets PAS-2-1023

LP-267 DEBBIE REYNOLDS: RAISE A RUCKUS Metro 535

LP-268 NELSON EDDY: ROMANTIC MOMENTS Col GB-3

LP-269 AL JOLSON: THE VITAPHONE YEARS A-Jay Records 3749

LP-270 MAURICE CHEVALIER Col CL-568

LP-271 DOROTHY LAMOUR West Coast 14002

LP-272 DE HAVEN IN HOLLYWOOD Vedette 8703

LP-273 GIRLS OF THE 30'S Pelican 122

LP-274 THE VINTAGE JOLSON Pelican 111

LP-275 NOEL COWARD & GERTRUDE LAWRENCE: WE WERE DANCING Monmouth 7042

LP-276 GERTRUDE LAWRENCE Monmouth 7043

LP-277 FRED ASTAIRE: ORIGINAL RECORDINGS 1935-40 CBS(F) 66316

LP-278 ROY ROGERS SOUVENIR ALBUM 45/RCA album WP-215

LP-279 GEORGE GERSHWIN: PRIMROSE World Records(E) 214

LP-280 AL JOLSON OVERSEAS Dec 9070

LP-281 JANE POWELL Scarce Rarities 5503

LP-282 GEORGE OLSEN AND HIS MUSIC RCA LPV-549

LP-283 ALICE FAYE Scarce Rarities 5502

LP-284 BETTY GRABLE Scarce Rarities 5501

LP-285 HUTTON IN HOLLYWOOD Vedette 8702

LP-286 GERSHWIN BY GERSHWIN Mark 56 Records 641

LP-287 THREE BY HUGH MARTIN JJA Records 19743

LP-288 AL JOLSON: BROADWAY AL Totem 1010

LP-289 THE JUDY GARLAND STORY: THE HOLLYWOOD YEARS MGM 4005

LP-290 AL JOLSON: THE EARLY YEARS Olympic 7114

LP-291 THE LIGHTER SIDE OF LAURITZ MELCHIOR Camden 424

LP-292 JIMMY DURANTE AT THE PIANO Dec 8884

LP-293 NANCY WALKER: I CAN COOK TOO Dolphin 2

LP-294 MUSIC FROM SHUBERT ALLEY Sinclair OSS-2250

LP-295 COLE PORTER (MUSIC & LYRICS) JJA Records 19745

LP-296 LOUISIANA PURCHASE JJA Records 19746

LP-297 CURTAIN CALL SERIES, VOLUME 1 Dec 10" 7018

LP-298 JUDY GARLAND IN CONCERT: SAN FRANCISCO Mark 56 Records 632

LP-299 HAYMES IN HOLLYWOOD, VOLUME ONE Vedette 8701

LP-300 COLE PORTER IN LONDON World Records(E) SHB-26

LP-301 SOMETHING FOR THE BOYS Sound/Stage 2305

LP-302 CARMEN MIRANDA SOUVENIR ALBUM 78/Dec album 545

LP-303 MEMORIAL ALBUM TO GEORGE GERSHWIN 78/Vic 12" album C-29; MUSIC BY GEORGE GERSHWIN & VICTOR HERBERT Camden 177

LP-304 THE MUSIC OF VICTOR HERBERT 78/Vic 12" album C-1

LP-305 VICTOR HERBERT MELODIES, VOLUME 1 78/Vic 12" album C-33; MUSIC BY GEORGE GERSHWIN & VICTOR HERBERT Camden 177

LP-306 GEMS FROM JEROME KERN MUSICAL SHOWS 78/Vic 12" album C-31

LP-307 THE MUSIC OF SIGMUND ROMBERG Camden 239

LP-308 NOEL COWARD: THE GREAT SHOWS Monmouth 7062/7063

LP-309 IVOR NOVELLO: THE GREAT SHOWS World Records(E) SHB-23

LP-310 MOVIE STAR MEMORIES World Records(E) SH-217

LP-311 STARS OVER BROADWAY Star-Tone 214

LP-312 SHOWBOAT Dec 10" 5060

LP-313 WORDS AND MUSIC RCA LRL-1-5079

LP-314 LA GINGOLD Dolphin 7

LP-315 DORIS DAY: LIGHTS! CAMERA! ACTION! Col 10" CL-2

LP-316 HAROLD ROME: ROME-ANTICS Heritage 0063

LP-317 KEEFE BRASSELLE: THE MODERN MINSTREL RKO 126

LP-318 BING CROSBY: ONLY FOREVER Dec 4255

LP-319 BING CROSBY: PENNIES FROM HEAVEN Dec 4251

LP-320 JESSIE MATTHEWS: OVER MY SHOULDER Dec(E) ECM-2168

LP-321 COMPOSERS DO THEIR OWN THING Pelican 120

LP-322 HERE COME THE GIRLS Epic 3188

LP-323 AMERICAN VAUDE AND VARIETY Rococo(C) 4006

LP-324 AMERICAN VAUDE AND VARIETY, VOL. 2 Rococo(C) 4009

LP-325 HELLO, GINGER! Citel 2201

LP-326 GERSHWIN PLAYS GERSHWIN Audio Rarities 10" 0073

LP-327 LIZA MINNELLI LIVE AT THE WINTER GARDEN Col PC-32854

LP-328 GIRLS AND MORE GIRLS Lion 70118

LP-329 JUDY GARLAND AT THE PALACE Classic International Theatremusic 2001

LP-330 DORIS DAY SINGS HER GREAT MOVIE HITS Harmony 11192

LP-331 THE IMMORTAL AL JOLSON Dec 79063

LP-332 THE FLEISCHMANN'S HOUR STARRING RUDY VALLEE Mark 56 Records 613

LP-333 HOORAY FOR HOLLYWOOD United Artists LA361-H

LP-334 MERMAN IN THE MOVIES: 1930-38 Encore 101

LP-335 JEROME KERN IN HOLLYWOOD: 1934-38 JJA Records 19747

LP-336 IRVING BERLIN 1909-1939 JJA Records 19744

LP-337 BING: THE EARLY THIRTIES, VOL. 1 Ace of Hearts(E) 40

LP-338 AN EVENING WITH FRED ASTAIRE Chrysler Corp mx 1/2; THREE EVENINGS WITH FRED ASTAIRE DRG Records S3L-5181

LP-339 BING CROSBY: SWINGING ON A STAR Dec 4257

LP-340 COMPOSERS AT PLAY: HAROLD ARLEN & COLE PORTER RCA "X" LVA-1003

LP-341 GROUCHO MARX: HOORAY FOR CAPTAIN SPAULDING Dec 10" 5405

LP-342 IVOR NOVELLO World Records(E) SH-216

LP-343 LYRICS BY LERNER Heritage 0600

LP-344 FRED ASTAIRE: EASY TO DANCE WITH MCA(E) MCFM-2698

LP-345 FATS WALLER: 1935 & 1943 Collector's Classics 19

LP-346 KATHRYN GRAYSON: MAKE BELIEVE Azel 101

LP-347 KATHRYN GRAYSON: LET THERE BE MUSIC Azel 102

LP-348 THE SPECIAL MAGIC OF FRED ASTAIRE Verve(E) 2317-082

LP-349 HARRY RICHMAN: ON THE SUNNY SIDE OF THE STREET Pelican 124

LP-350 HOLLYWOOD PARTY Pelican 130

LP-351 TOGETHER WITH MUSIC Unnamed label mx XTV-24162/3

LP-352 THE MUSIC OF HAROLD ARLEN, VOL. 2 Walden 307

LP-353 IRVING CAESAR: AND THEN I WROTE Coral 57083

LP-354 RUDOLF FRIML Nan 4019

LP-355 LOUIS ARMSTRONG TOWN HALL CONCERT 45/RCA EPAT-9

LP-356 CAROL LAWRENCE: TONIGHT AT 8:30 Chancellor 5015

LP-357 RUDY VALLEE: THE KID FROM MAINE Unique 116

LP-358 FRED ASTAIRE: MR. TOP HAT Verve MGV-2010

LP-359 COMDEN AND GREEN Heritage 10" 0057

LP-360 A TOUCH OF ROME Heritage 10" 0053

LP-361 ETHEL WATERS IN SHADES OF BLUE Remington 10" 1025

LP-362 GENE AUSTIN: MY BLUE HEAVEN RCA 10" LPM-3200

LP-363 JIMMY DURANTE PRESENTS TV ON RECORDS Royale 10" 68

LP-364 KATHRYN GRAYSON SINGS MGM 3257

LP-365 A TRIBUTE TO GEORGE M. COHAN Audio Rarities LPA-2295

LP-366 NINO MARTINI IN OPERA AND SONG OASI Records 550

LP-367 DAN DAILEY: MR. MUSICAL COMEDY Tops L-1598

LP-368 LIZA MINNELLI LIVE AT THE OLYMPIA IN PARIS A&M Records SP-4345

LP-369 I WONDER WHO'S KISSING HER NOW 78/Deluxe album 18

LP-370 AL JOLSON: AMONG MY SOUVENIERS Dec 79050

LP-371 MARTIN CHARNIN'S MINI ALBUM Take Home Tunes 7" 771

LP-372 AL JOLSON: MEMORIES Dec 79038

LP-373 AL JOLSON Epitaph 4008

LP-374 JACK BUCHANAN World Records(E) SH-283

LP-375 GEORGE GERSHWIN CONDUCTS EXCERPTS FROM PORGY AND BESS Mark 56 Records 667

LP-376 JUDY GARLAND: THE LONG LOST HOLLAND CONCERT Obligatto GIH-60

LP-377 MEMORIES OF THE ROARING TWENTIES Longines 5100/4

LP-378 SWEETHEARTS Pelican 143

LP-379 EDDIE CANTOR: OL' BANJO EYES IS BACK Pelican 134

LP-380 AL JOLSON SOUVENIR ALBUM, VOL. 5 Dec 10" 5314

LP-381 AL JOLSON SOUVENIR ALBUM, VOL. 6 Dec 10" 5315

LP-382 AL JOLSON: STEPHEN FOSTER SONGS Dec 10" 5303

LP-383 AL JOLSON WITH BING CROSBY, ANDREWS SISTERS, MILLS BROTHERS, GORDON JENKINS Dec 10" 5316

LP-384 EDDIE CANTOR SINGS "THE CANTOR STORY" Dec 10" 5504

LP-385 A LAWRENCE TIBBETT PROGRAM Camden 168

LP-386 DICK HAYMES: THE FABULOUS FORTIES Standing Room Only 1001

LP-387 AN IRVING BERLIN TRIBUTE Famous Personality 1001

LP-388 ALLAN JONES: FALLING IN LOVE RCA 10" LM-95

LP-389 ETHEL WATERS SINGING HER BEST Jay 10" 3010

LP-390 JUDY — THE LEGEND Radiant 711-0103

LP-391 BROADWAY RHYTHMS Biograph 1007

LP-392 THE EIGHTY-SIX YEARS OF EUBIE BLAKE Col C2S-847

LP-393 THE FAVORITE SONGS OF ETHEL WATERS Mercury 20051

LP-394 THE JAZZ SINGER Pelican 125

LP-395 MISS BETTE DAVIS EMI(E) EMA-778

LP-396 BING CROSBY & FRED ASTAIRE: A COUPLE OF SONG & DANCE MEN United Artists(E) 29888

LP-397 THE BEST OF DICK HAYMES MCA(E) MCFM-2720

LP-398 MERTON OF THE MOVIES Pelican 139

LP-399 SONGS BY HARRY WARREN Four Jays HW-601

LP-400 DICK HAYMES: SERENADE Dec 10" 5341

LP-401 JOAN CRAWFORD Curtain Calls 100/23

LP-402 GINGER ROGERS Curtain Calls 100/21

LP-403 RITA HAYWORTH Curtain Calls 100/22

LP-404 DEANNA DURBIN SOUVENIR ALBUM VOLUME ONE 78/Dec album 680

LP-405 MAURICE CHEVALIER RCA 10" LPT-3042

LP-406 DEANNA DURBIN Dec 8785

LP-407 ANYTHING GOES/PANAMA HATTIE Larynx 567

LP-408 ISABEL BIGLEY & STEPHEN DOUGLASS SING RODGERS & HAMMERSTEIN Design 75

LP-409 AL JOLSON: THE WORLD'S GREATEST ENTERTAINER Dec 9074

LP-410 PAT SUZUKI'S BROADWAY '59 RCA LSP-1965

LP-411 MAE WEST SONGS 78/Mezzo Tone album 11

LP-412 W.C. FIELDS & MAE WEST Proscenium 22

LP-413 MAE WEST: THE ORIGINAL VOICE TRACKS FROM HER GREATEST MOVIES Dec 79176

LP-414 CLUB RICHMAN: HARRY RICHMAN & EDDIE CANTOR Torrington JRS-1019

LP-415 ELISABETH WELCH World Records(E) SH-415

LP-416 THAT'S ENTERTAINMENT, PART 2 MGM MG-1-5301

LP-417 IRA GERSHWIN LOVES TO RHYME Mark 56 Records 721

LP-418 FROM THE PEN OF... ARTHUR SCHWARTZ RCA LPL1-5121

LP-419 BANDS ON FILM World Records(E) SH-197

LP-420 JERRY ORBACH OFF BROADWAY MGM 4056

LP-421 ANNA MARIA ALBERGHETTI: LOVE MAKES THE WORLD GO ROUND MGM 4001

LP-422 SISSLE & BLAKE, VOL. 1 Eubie Blake Music 4

LP-423 CUT! OUT TAKES FROM HOLLYWOOD'S GREATEST MUSICALS Out Take Records 1

LP-424 ALICE FAYE AND THE SONGS OF HARRY WARREN Citadel 6004

LP-425 BING CROSBY: THE MAN WITHOUT A COUNTRY & WHAT SO PROUDLY WE HAIL Dec 8020

LP-426 1928 RCA LPV-523

LP-427 CYRIL RITCHARD: ODD SONGS AND A POEM Dolphin 10" 1

LP-428 WARING'S PENNSYLVANIANS RCA LPV-554

LP-429 FRED ASTAIRE: THEY CAN'T TAKE THESE AWAY FROM ME United Artists(E) 29941

LP-430 JEROME KERN IN LONDON, 1914-1923 World Records(E) SHB-34

LP-431 SHUFFLE ALONG New World 260

LP-432 NELSON EDDY'S GREATEST HITS Col CS-9481

LP-433 GERSHWIN PLAYS GERSHWIN RCA AVM1-1740

LP-434 MISS KATE SMITH 1926-31 Sunbeam MCF-13

LP-435 A COLLECTOR'S SHOW BOAT RCA AVM1-1741

LP-436 A COLLECTOR'S PORGY AND BESS RCA AVM1-1742

LP-437 CLIFF EDWARDS: SHAKIN' THE BLUES AWAY Totem 1005

LP-438 CALLING ALL STARS (VOLUME 1) Star-Tone 203

LP-439 THE JIMMY DURANTE SHOW 45/Dec ED-2527

LP-440 JOEL GREY—LIVE! Col KC-32252

LP-441 EARTHA FOR ALWAYS Stanyan 10040

LP-442 SONGS OF LUCIENNE BOYER 78/Col album MM-694

LP-443 THE ART OF GRACE MOORE Camden 519

LP-444 THE FAMED SONGS OF NOEL COWARD AND IVOR NOVELLO Dot 3047

LP-445 JANE FROMAN: YOURS ALONE Cap 10" H-354

LP-446 TONY MARTIN LIVE AT CARNEGIE HALL Movietone MTS-2007

LP-447 ENCORES FROM THE 30'S: VOLUME I, 1930-1935 Epic L2N-6072

LP-448 RUDOLF FRIML IN LONDON World Records(E) SHB-37

LP-449 AN EVENING WITH BEATRICE LILLIE London(E) 5212

LP-450 BEATRICE LILLIE: AUNTIE BEA London(E) 5471

LP-451 MARILYN MONROE: LA VOCE, LE MUSICHE E I FILMS RCA(I) TPL1-7025

LP-452 MARILYN MONROE Legends 1000/1

LP-453 PURE GOLD MOVIES RCA ANL1-1978

LP-454 BROADWAY! BROADWAY! BROADWAY! Longines LW-117

LP-455 CUT! OUT TAKES FROM HOLLYWOOD'S GREATEST MUSICALS, VOL. 2 Out Take Records 2

LP-456 1927 RCA LPV-545

LP-457 THE BEST OF TED LEWIS MCA 2-4101

LP-458 GERSHWIN ... FROM TIN PAN ALLEY TO BROADWAY Mark 56 Records 680

LP-459 GEORGE GERSHWIN PLAYS GERSHWIN & KERN Klavier 122

LP-460 LET'S HAVE FUN Nostalgia(Australia) 002

LP-461 JUDY GARLAND AT THE GROVE Cap T-1118

LP-462 JEANETTE MacDONALD & NELSON EDDY: OPERETTA FAVORITES RCA 10" LCT-16

LP-463 LOTTE LENYA SINGS BERLIN THEATRE SONGS BY KURT WEILL Col ML-5056

LP-464 CHARLOTTE RAE: SONGS I TAUGHT MY MOTHER Vanguard 9004

LP-465 ZIEGFELD GIRL Classic International Filmusicals 3006

LP-466 BITTER SWEET Bright Tight Discs BIS-1377

LP-467 GEORGE M. COHAN: THE ORIGINAL YANKEE DOODLE DANDY Old Shep GMC-1000

LP-468 TOP HAT, WHITE TIE & GOLF SHOES Facit 142

LP-469 BIG BROADCAST OF 1935 Kasha King 1935

LP-470 A TRIBUTE TO AL JOLSON Audio Rarities 2285

LP-471 THE WORKS OF DUKE, VOLUME 16 RCA(F) FXM1-7201

LP-472 THE WORKS OF DUKE, VOLUME 17 RCA(F) FXM1-7274

LP-473 1926 RCA LPV-557

LP-474 THE COMPLETE TOMMY DORSEY, VOL. 1/1935 Bluebird AXM2-5521

LP-475 THIS IS GENE AUSTIN RCA VPM-6056

LP-476 CLIFF EDWARDS: I'M A BEAR IN A LADY'S BOUDOIR Yazoo L-1047

LP-477 HUTCH AT THE PIANO World Records(E) SHB-28

LP-478 AL JOLSON WITH OSCAR LEVANT AT THE PIANO Dec 9095

LP-479 SOMEBODY LOVES ME Dec 10" 5424

LP-480 JIMMY DORSEY'S GREATEST HITS Dec 4853

LP-481 SOUNDTRACKS, VOICES & THEMES FROM GREAT MOVIES Colpix 503

LP-482 GEORGE CHAKIRIS Cap ST-1750

LP-483 GENE AUSTIN SINGS ALL-TIME FAVORITES RCA "X" LVA-1007

LP-484 THAT WONDERFUL ADELAIDE HALL Monmouth 7080

LP-485 EDDIE CANTOR: RARE EARLY RECORDINGS Biograph 12054

LP-486 CUT! OUT TAKES FROM HOLLYWOOD'S GREATEST MUSICALS, VOL. 3 Out Take Records 3

LP-487 SYBIL JASON: CHILDREN'S SONGS 78/Dec album K-11

LP-488 ALICE FAYE ON THE AIR Totem 1011

LP-489 A PARTY WITH BETTY COMDEN AND ADOLPH GREEN Stet S2L-5177

LP-490 JUDY GARLAND: SECOND SOUVENIR ALBUM 78/Dec album 349

LP-491 TED LEWIS AND HIS ORCHESTRA 78/Dec album 353

LP-492 ARDEN & OHMAN (1925-1933) JJA Records 1974-1

LP-493 THE HOT CANARIES Col 10" CL-2534

LP-494 THE GREAT STARS OF VAUDEVILLE Col CSS-1509

LP-495 SUSAN HAYWARD Legends 1000/3

LP-496 LADIES OF BURLESQUE Legends 1000/2

LP-497 RODGERS AND HAMMERSTEIN JJA Records 19761

LP-498 RODGERS AND HART IN HOLLYWOOD JJA Records 19766

LP-499 HELEN MORGAN & NELSON EDDY: THE TORCH SINGER AND THE MOUNTIE Trisklog 4

LP-500 SHIRLEY MacLAINE LIVE AT THE PALACE Col PC-34223

LP-501 THE SPECIAL MAGIC OF GENE KELLY MGM(E) 2353-120

LP-502 NOEL COWARD: THE REVUES World Records(E) SHB-44

LP-503 SAMMY CAHN: I'VE HEARD THAT SONG BEFORE World Records(E) WRS-1002

LP-504 MAE WEST SONGS Mezzo Tone 10" 21

LP-505 SHOW BOAT/SUNNY World Records(E) SH-240

LP-506 BING CROSBY: WHERE THE BLUE OF THE NIGHT MEETS THE GOLD OF THE DAY Biograph BLP-M-1

LP-507 YOUNG BING CROSBY RCA "X" LVA-1000

LP-508 BETTY COMDEN AND ADOLPH GREEN JJA Records 19764

LP-509 A CELEBRATION OF RICHARD RODGERS Friends of the Theatre & Music Collection 545

LP-510 A GALA TRIBUTE TO JOSHUA LOGAN Friends of the Theatre & Music Collection mx AC-1/4

LP-511 JUDY AT THE PALACE Dec 10" 6020

LP-512 LADY, BE GOOD! Smithsonian R-008

LP-513 ANYTHING GOES Smithsonian R-007

LP-514 ZIEGFELD FOLLIES OF 1919 Smithsonian R-009

LP-515 DANNY AT THE PALACE Dec 10" 6024

LP-516 YES SIR, THAT'S MY BABY New World 279

LP-517 THE MUSIC GOES ROUND AND AROUND New World 248

LP-518 FOLLIES, SCANDALS & OTHER DIVERSIONS New World 215

LP-519 THE VINTAGE IRVING BERLIN New World 238

LP-520 WHEN EDISON RECORDED SOUND, VOLUME I Edison mx ZM-473201/4

LP-521 CURTAIN CALL SERIES, VOLUME 4 Dec 10" 7021

LP-522 CARMEN MIRANDA: SOUTH AMERICAN WAY MCA Coral CDLM-8029

LP-523 ROY ROGERS: HAPPY TRAILS TO YOU 20th Century T-467

LP-524 FORTY YEARS OF ENGLISH MUSICAL COMEDY Rococo(C) 4007

LP-525 JUDY. LONDON. 1969. Juno S-1000

LP-526 GRACE MOORE IN OPERA AND SONG RCA 10" LCT-7004

LP-527 DANNY KAYE ENTERTAINS Col 10" CL-6249

LP-528 THE VOICE OF MILIZA KORJUS Camden 279

LP-529 MILIZA KORJUS: VIENNA IN 3/4 TIME Camden 427

LP-530 J. FRED COOTS: AND THEN I WROTE Coral 57084

LP-531 A VOICE TO REMEMBER EMI Records EMSP-75

LP-532 JOAN CRAWFORD: THE DEVIL'S SISTER JOAC X-20

LP-533 AN EVENING WITH JOHNNY MERCER Laureate 601

LP-534 AN EVENING WITH ALAN JAY LERNER Laureate 602

LP-535 AN EVENING WITH SHELDON HARNICK Laureate 603

LP-536 JEANETTE MacDONALD: A TRIBUTE TO JEANETTE OASI Records 594

LP-537 BROTHER, CAN YOU SPARE A DIME? New World 270

LP-538 WHERE HAVE WE MET BEFORE? New World 240

LP-539 THEY STOPPED THE SHOW! RCA R-214175

LP-540 THE BING CROSBY STORY, VOLUME I: 1928-1932 Col CE2E-201

LP-541 PAUL WHITEMAN AND HIS ORCHESTRA Col CL-2830

LP-542 CURTAIN CALLS OF YESTERYEAR Audio Rarities LPA-2300

LP-543 THIS IS THE ARMY/CALL ME MISTER JJA Records 19742

LP-544 FOUR ORIGINAL CAST RECORDINGS JJA Records 19752

LP-545 DUO PIANO 1926-1939 JJA Records 19771

LP-546 RUTH ETTING Biograph C-11

LP-547 JUDY IN LONDON Cap 94407

LP-548 PRAISE THE LORD AND PASS THE AMMUNITION New World 222

LP-549 UNPUBLISHED COLE PORTER Painted Smiles 1358

LP-550 AL JOLSON: STEPPIN' OUT Sunbeam P-503

LP-551 18 INTERESTING SONGS FROM UNFORTUNATE SHOWS Take Home Tunes 777

LP-552 FRED ASTAIRE: EASY TO DANCE WITH Verve MGV-2114

LP-553 THE MUSIC OF ARTHUR SCHWARTZ, VOL. I JJA Records 19756

LP-554 THE MUSIC OF ARTHUR SCHWARTZ, VOL. II JJA Records 19757

LP-555 THE MUSIC OF ARTHUR SCHWARTZ, VOL. III JJA Records 19758

LP-556 THE THIRTIES' GIRLS Totem 1026

LP-557 THE FILMS OF RUSS COLUMBO Golden Legends 2001

LP-558 HOLLYWOOD IS ON THE AIR Radiola mx AAB-1215/8

LP-559 MERCER SINGS MERCER Cap M-11637

LP-560 JOHNNY MERCER SINGS THE SONGS OF JOHNNY MERCER Pye(E) NSPL-18432

LP-561 THE ORIGINAL PIANO TRIO PLAYS NOSTALGIA 20'S STYLE Klavier KS-128

LP-562 THE SINGING ACTORS OF HOLLYWOOD Cap(F) 2C-184

LP-563 AND THEN WE WROTE New World 272

LP-564 THE MUSIC OF BROADWAY: 1931 JJA Records 19778

LP-565 THE MUSIC OF BROADWAY: 1932 JJA Records 19779

LP-566 ZIEGFELD FOLLIES ON THE AIR Mark 56 Records 737

LP-567 THE SPECIAL MAGIC OF FRED ASTAIRE, VOL. 2 Polydor(E) 2489132

LP-568 THOSE BOMBASTIC BLONDE BOMBSHELLS Wallysrite BGMM-42

LP-569 THE MUSIC OF BROADWAY: 1930 JJA Records 19777

LP-570 CRYER & FORD RCA APL1-1235

LP-571 A CENTURY OF SOUND Eva-tone 8" 410782

LP-572 CURTAIN CALL SERIES, VOLUME 6 Dec 10" 7026

LP-573 BURL IVES: BURL'S BROADWAY Dec 4876

LP-574 FAY DeWITT: THROUGH SICK & SIN Epic BN-596

LP-575 CROSBY CLASSICS Col 10" CL-6027

LP-576 BING CROSBY, VOLUME 2 78/Bruns album B-1015

LP-577 BING CROSBY, VOLUME 1 78/Bruns album B-1012

LP-578 CROSBY CLASSICS, VOLUME 2 Col 10" CL-6105

LP-579 A LAST CURTAIN CALL B&B Documentary Records 2

LP-580 OH, KAY! Smithsonian R-011

LP-581 SOUVENIRS OF HOT CHOCOLATES Smithsonian R-012

LP-582 HARLEM COMES TO LONDON World Records(E) SH-265

LP-583 THE YOUNG IRVING BERLIN World Records(E) SH-275

LP-584 THE GREAT BRITISH DANCE BANDS PLAY THE MUSIC OF ARTHUR SCHWARTZ World Records(E) SH-274

LP-585 LESLIE UGGAMS: WHAT'S AN UGGAMS? Atlantic SD-8196

LP-586 ALLAN JONES SINGS FOR A MAN AND A WOMAN Scepter SPS-566

LP-587 SISSLE & BLAKE, VOL. 2 Eubie Blake Music 7

LP-588 CHOICE CUTS, VOLUME 1 Choice Cuts ST-500/1

LP-589 ALL OUR OWN WORK World Records(E) SH-273

LP-590 THE MUSIC OF RUDOLF FRIML Camden 252

LP-591 SINGING TROUBADOURS ON THE AIR Star-Tone 206

LP-592 THE FEMININE TOUCH Star-Tone 205

LP-593 THE MAGICAL SONGS OF IRVING BERLIN Book of the Month Records 60-5256

LP-594 NOEL COWARD: A SPECIAL EVENT DRG Records SL-5180

LP-595 THE GOLDEN AGE OF THE HOLLYWOOD STARS United Artists(E) USD-311

LP-596 JEAN SABLON'S BEST RCS "X" LXA-1021

LP-597 FRED ASTAIRE: THE BELLE OF NEW YORK Stet DS-15004

LP-598 GENE KELLY: SONG AND DANCE MAN Stet DS-15010

LP-599 MARILYN MONROE: NEVER BEFORE AND NEVER AGAIN Stet DS-15005

LP-600 A MUSICAL TOUR OF FRANCE WITH MAURICE CHEVALIER Disneyland 3940

LP-601 GENEVIEVE WAITE: ROMANCE IS ON THE RISE Paramour 5088

LP-602 MUSICAL COMEDY MEDLEYS, 1928-1934 JJA Records 1977-6

LP-603 HAROLD ARLEN SINGS, 1930-1937 JJA Records 1975-9

LP-604 JOHNNY MERCER SINGS JJA Records 19775

LP-605 PINS AND NEEDLES JJA Records 19783

LP-606 JEROME KERN GEMS JJA Records 19781

LP-607 JEROME KERN IN HOLLYWOOD, VOLUME 2 JJA Records 19784

LP-608 BERT LAHR ON STAGE, SCREEN AND RADIO JJA Records 19765

LP-609 MARILYN MONROE: THERE'S NO BUSINESS LIKE SHOW BUSINESS 45/RCA EPA-593

LP-610 WHOOPEE Smithsonian R-012

LP-611 KEIR DULLEA Platypus 5001

LP-612 TONY MARTIN Vocalion VL-3610

LP-613 HERE'S MARTHA RAYE Epic LG-3061

LP-614 SOTHERN EXPOSURE Tops L-1611

LP-615 ELAINE STRITCH: STRITCH Dolphin 3; Stet SOT-2001

LP-616 LARRY KERT SINGS LEONARD BERNSTEIN Seeco 4670

LP-617 BERNSTEIN CONDUCTS BERNSTEIN Camden 196

LP-618 MAKE MINE MANHATTAN & GREAT REVUES REVISITED Painted Smiles 1369

LP-619 HERE COME THE GIRLS Epic 10" 1114

LP-620 GREAT MOMENTS FROM THE HALLMARK HALL OF FAME RCA PRM-202

LP-621 THE MUSIC OF GEORGE GERSHWIN Biograph 1022

LP-622 DUKE ELLINGTON'S BAND SHORTS Biograph M-2

LP-623 LEGENDARY BLACK JAZZ STARS IN THEIR FIRST FILMS Biograph M-3

LP-624 MISS GINGER ROGERS EMI(E) ODN-1002

LP-625 POLA NEGRI Discophilia(G) UG-N-1

LP-626 AL JOLSON: CALIFORNIA, HERE I COME Sunbeam P-505

LP-627 SELECTIONS FROM THE REPERTOIRE OF YVONNE PRINTEMPS AND SACHA GUITRY 78/Vic 12" album C-8

LP-628 THE EARLY VICTOR HERBERT Smithsonian R-017

LP-629 VICTOR HERBERT & HIS ORCHESTRA Mark56 Records 795

LP-630 WILLIE HOWARD: A GALA RECORD REVUE Gala 10" 104

LP-631 THE CLASSIC MOVIE MUSICALS OF HARRY WARREN, VOL. 1 JJA Records 19792

LP-632 THE CLASSIC MOVIE MUSICALS OF HARRY WARREN, VOL. 2 JJA Records 19793

LP-633 THE HOLLYWOOD YEARS OF HARRY WARREN, 1930-57 JJA Records 19791

LP-634 BING CROSBY: WRAP YOUR TROUBLES IN DREAMS RCA LPV-584

LP-635 CLIFF EDWARDS: "UKELELE IKE" Glendale 6011

LP-636 KATHRYN GRAYSON: OPERA AND SONG Azel 103

LP-637 THE BEST OF PAUL ROBESON Starline(E) SRS-5041

LP-638 THE BEST OF PAUL ROBESON, VOL. 2 Starline(E) SRS-5127

LP-639 BERT WILLIAMS: SONGS & SAYINGS Sunbeam P-506

LP-640 JUDY GARLAND: THE BEGINNING DRG Records SL-5187

LP-641 THOSE LEGENDARY LEADING LADIES OF STAGE, SCREEN & RADIO Harmony KH-32422

LP-642 THOSE LEGENDARY LEADING LADIES OF STAGE, SCREEN & RADIO, VOL. 2 Harmony KH-32423

LP-643 THOSE LEGENDARY LEADING MEN OF STAGE, SCREEN & RADIO Harmony KH-32424

LP-644 THOSE LEGENDARY LEADING MEN OF STAGE, SCREEN & RADIO, VOL. 2 Harmony KH-32430

LP-645 ALICE FAYE ON THE AIR, VOL. 2 Totem 1032

LP-646 BETTY GRABLE Star-Tone 219

LP-647 DOROTHY LAMOUR Legends 1000/4

LP-648 THE ASTAIRE STORY Mercury MG-C-1001/4; DRG Records DARC3-1102

LP-649 JOHN CHARLES THOMAS: THE YOUNG THOMAS IN OPERA AND SONG OASI Records 527

LP-650 MICHAEL VALENTI IN CONCERT Unnamed label HR-13

LP-651 MARTHA RAYE Legends 1000/5-6

LP-652 TOGETHER ON BROADWAY Friends of the Theatre & Music Collection AG-77

LP-653 DIETRICH LIVE 1932-52 Wildebeest-Maclon 5290

LP-654 THE GERSHWINS IN HOLLYWOOD, 1931-1964 JJA Records 19773

LP-655 COLE PORTER IN HOLLYWOOD, 1929-1956 JJA Records 19767

LP-656 FRANK LOESSER IN HOLLYWOOD, 1937-1955 JJA Records 19762

LP-657 HAROLD ARLEN IN HOLLYWOOD, 1934-1954 JJA Records 19763

LP-658 AN EVENING WITH SAMMY CAHN Laureate 604

LP-659 AN EVENING WITH FRED EBB AND JOHN KANDER Laureate 605

LP-660 AN EVENING WITH JERRY HERMAN Laureate 606

LP-661 THE MAGICAL MUSIC OF WALT DISNEY Ovation 5000

LP-662 LIBBY HOLMAN SINGS MB Records 10" 101

LP-663 FRED ASTAIRE: ATTITUDE DANCING United Artists(E) 29885

LP-664 ELVIS PRESLEY: GOT A LOT O' LIVIN' TO DO Party Records 101

LP-665 KATHRYN GRAYSON & MARIO LANZA: LOVE IS MUSIC Azel 104

LP-666 ROBERT CLARY LIVES IT UP AT THE PLAYBOY CLUB Atlantic 8053

LP-667 LISA KIRK SINGS AT THE PLAZA MGM 3737

LP-668 THE BEST OF MEL TORME Verve 8593

LP-669 HOLLYWOOD STORY Festival(F) 214

LP-670 THE ETHEL MERMAN DISCO ALBUM A&M Records SP-4775

LP-671 CUE MAGAZINE'S "SALUTE TO ASCAP" Dick Charles 52666

LP-672 MICHELE LEE: A TASTE OF THE FANTASTIC Col CS-9286

LP-673 ETHEL WATERS' GREATEST YEARS Col KG-31571

LP-674 ETHEL WATERS: OH DADDY Biograph 12022

LP-675 LENA (HORNE) AND MICHEL (LEGRAND) RCA BGL1-1026

LP-676 JACK BUCHANAN: ORIGINAL LONDON CAST RECORDINGS World Records(E) SH-329

LP-677 THE JOLSON STORY Pelican 129

LP-678 TODD DUNCAN Sutton 285

LP-679 SWANEE RIVER Totem 1028

LP-680 BEATRICE LILLIE: QUEEN BEA DRG Records DARC-2-1101

LP-681 LET'S FACE IT/RED HOT AND BLUE LEAVE IT TO ME Smithsonian R-016

LP-682 THE JOLSON STORY Take Two 103

LP-683 PAUL JABARA: THE THIRD ALBUM Casablanca NBLP-7163

LP-684 FREDA PAYNE: HOT Cap ST-12003

LP-685 RCA VICTOR PRESENTS EARTHA KITT RCA 10" LPM-3062

LP-686 TED LEWIS, VOLUME 2 Dec 10" 5233

LP-687 ROBERT CLARY: HOORAY FOR LOVE Epic LN-3281

LP-688 JAMES DARREN: GIDGET GOES HAWAIIAN Colpix 418

LP-689 BARBARA COOK AT CARNEGIE HALL Col M-33438

LP-690 CURTAIN TIME Col ML-4451

LP-691 DICK VAN DYKE: SONGS I LIKE Command RS-860

LP-692 DORIS DAY'S GREATEST HITS Col CL-1210

LP-693 THE BING CROSBY RADIO SHOWS Golden Age 5023

LP-694 A NOTEWORTHY OCCASION Unnamed label R-2658

LP-695 LAUREL & HARDY: ANOTHER FINE MESS United Artists(E) UAG-30010

LP-696 SONGS BY SINATRA, VOLUME 1 Col 10" CL-6087

LP-697 MICHAEL BROWN SINGS HIS OWN SONGS Trio 10" 1001

LP-698 LAUREL & HARDY Mark56 Records 575

LP-699 THREE OF A KIND Fanett 146

LP-700 BRITISH MUSICAL COMEDIES BY AMERICAN COMPOSERS (1912-1935) JJA Records 19794

LP-701 UP IN ARMS Sountrak 113

LP-702 25 YEARS OF RECORDED SOUND DRG Records DARC-2-2100

LP-703 COLE PORTER REVISITED, VOL. IV Painted Smiles 1371

LP-704 PROUDLY THEY CAME... TO HONOR AMERICA Landmark 101

LP-705 ANN SHERIDAN/MARLENE DIETRICH Marsher 201

LP-706 JOAN ROBERTS Quality 10" 719-26

LP-707 I'LL BE SEEING YOU: THE MUSIC OF SAMMY FAIN MGM 10" 241

LP-708 MIMI HINES IS A HAPPENING Dec 4834

LP-709 MIMI HINES SINGS Dec 4709

LP-710 MUSIC FROM THE 1973 EXHIBITION "ZIEGFELD" Friends of the Theatre & Music Collection mx AC-731/4

LP-711 FIRST EDITION RCA DMM4-0407

LP-712 MISS ELISABETH WELCH, 1933-1940 World Records(E) SH-328

LP-713 RON HUSMANN Cap ST-1624

LP-714 JANE POWELL: SOMETHING WONDERFUL MGM 3451; JANE POWELL SINGS Lion 70111

LP-715 COMMAND PERFORMANCE DRG Records DARC-1-1106

LP-716 HOLLYWOOD HOTEL Medallion 301

LP-717 MISS ALICE FAYE SINGS THE RARE ONES Wong 087

LP-718 JUDY GARLAND: THE RARE EARLY BROADCAST PERFORMANCES Accessor Pro 1001

LP-719 FUSAKO YOSHIDA: KOTO RECITAL Major mx TJV-FY-1/2

LP-720 JOHNNY MERCER SINGS JOHNNY MERCER Cap(E) OU-2081

LP-721 JOLSON & CANTOR: THE IMMORTALS Epic 10" LN-1128

LP-722 SING AND DREAM WITH FRANK SINATRA Col 10" CL-6143

LP-723 EDITH WILSON: HE MAY BE YOUR MAN Delmark 637

LP-724 THE ORIGINAL TORCH SINGERS Take Two 207

LP-725 RUTH ETTING: REFLECTIONS, 1927-1935 Take Two 203

LP-726 JUDY GARLAND: BORN IN A TRUNK, 1935-1940 AEI Records 2108

LP-727 FUNNY FACE Smithsonian R-019

LP-728 THE BANDWAGON Smithsonian R-021

LP-729 A MARVELOUS PARTY WITH BEATRICE LILLIE AEI Records 2103

LP-730 EUBIE BLAKE: BLUES AND RAGS, VOLUME 1 Biograph 1011Q

LP-731 AL JOLSON: SITTING ON TOP OF THE WORLD Vocalion(E) VLP-3

LP-732 MICHAEL BROWN: ALARUMS & EXCURSIONS Impulse(C) AS-24

LP-733 THE GENIUS OF RUDOLF FRIML Golden Crest CRS-4200

LP-734 JUDY GARLAND SINGS WITH DICK HAYMES, GENE KELLY, THE MERRY MACS, GORDON JENKINS 78/Dec album 682

LP-735 JUDY GARLAND: OVER THE RAINBOW CAS/Radiant 212-0116

LP-736 THE SONGS AND STARS OF THE THIRTIES World Records(E) SH-370

LP-737 DOROTHY LAMOUR: THE ROAD TO ROMANCE Design 45

LP-738 JUDY GARLAND COLLECTOR'S REMEMBRANCE ALBUM Compusonic 734786

LP-739 THE GREATEST OF AL JOLSON Tele House CD-2036

LP-740 WILL ROGERS Murray Hill 51220

LP-741 E. Y. HARBURG REVISITED Painted Smiles 1372

LP-742 DIANA LYNN: PIANO PORTRAITS 78/Cap album CC-38

LP-743 THE WIT & WONDER OF JUDY GARLAND DRG Records SL-5179

LP-744 TODD DUNCAN RECITAL 78/Musicraft album 82

LP-745 THE UNCOLLECTED JUDY GARLAND Stanyan SR-10095

LP-746 JUDY GARLAND: BORN IN A TRUNK, 1940-1945 AEI Records 2109

LP-747 JOYCE GRENFELL HMV(E) CLP-1810

LP-748 ERNESTINE SCHUMANN-HEINK, VOLUME III Rococo(C) 5335

LP-749 GENE KELLY: SINGIN' IN THE RAIN AGAIN Dec(E) SKL-5265

LP-750 HOAGY CARMICHAEL'S HAVIN' A PARTY Golden 198:18

LP-751 LEGENDS OF THE MUSICAL STAGE Take Two 104

LP-752 TEX RITTER: CHUCK WAGON DAYS Cap ST-213

LP-753 THE BEST OF TEX RITTER Cap DT-2595

LP-754 SONGS OF THE DEPRESSION Book-of-the-Month 21-5406

LP-755 SANDY WILSON THANKS THE LADIES Overtures(E) 1001

LP-756 NELSON EDDY: ON THE AIR Totem 1035

LP-757 CLIFF EDWARDS: I WANT A GIRL Totem(C) 1014

LP-758 LEGENDARY MUSICAL STARS Time/Life P-15637

LP-759 THE JUDY GARLAND MUSICAL SCRAPBOOK Star-Tone 208

LP-760 THE VINTAGE RECORDINGS OF CLIFF EDWARDS Take Two 205

LP-761 CABIN IN THE SKY Hollywood Soundstage 5003

LP-762 JUDY'S GREATEST HITS CAS/Radiant 211-0113

LP-763 RHAPSODY IN BLUE Titania 512

LP-764 BENNY FIELDS & BLOSSOM SEELEY: TWO-A-DAY AT THE PALACE Mercury 20224

LP-765 BEN VEREEN OFF-STAGE Buddah BDS-5627

LP-766 A BROADCAST TRIBUTE TO BRITISH STAGE AND SCREEN ROYALTY Magna ZZ89

LP-767 THE OPERETTA WORLD OF VICTOR HERBERT (1895-1924) JJA Records 1980-5

LP-768 THE CLASSIC MOVIE MUSICALS OF RALPH RAINGER (1930-43) JJA Records 1981-1

LP-769 THE CLASSIC MOVIE MUSICALS OF RICHARD A. WHITING (1929-38) JJA Records 1980-6

LP-770 THE CLASSIC MOVIE MUSICALS OF NACIO HERB BROWN (1929-39) JJA Records 19802

LP-771 HOAGY CARMICHAEL JJA Records 19774

LP-772 MUSIC OF BROADWAY: THE TWENTIES, VOLUME 1 (1925-26) JJA Records 19796

LP-773 MUSIC OF BROADWAY: THE TWENTIES, VOLUME 2 (1927) JJA Records 1980-3

LP-774 MUSIC OF BROADWAY: THE TWENTIES, VOLUME 3 (1928-29) JJA Records 1980-4

LP-775 EVERYONE ELSE REVISITED Painted Smiles 1374

LP-776 PLAYBOY OF PARIS, THE WAY TO LOVE, BELOVED VAGABOND, STRICTLY DYNAMITE, THE SINGING KID Caliban 6013

LP-777 THE MUSIC OF VICTOR HERBERT, VOLUME 2 78/Vic 12'' album C-11

LP-778 FIRST DISC RECORDINGS Mark56 Records 828

LP-779 BING: THE EARLY THIRTIES, VOL. 2 Ace of Hearts(E) 88

LP-780 JUDY GARLAND IN HOLLAND, VOL. 2 Obligato GIH-610

LP-781 JUDY GARLAND IN HOLLAND, VOL. 3 Obligato GIH-6100

LP-782 JUDY GARLAND SINGS MGM 10'' 82

LP-783 DOROTHY SHAY: COMING 'ROUND THE MOUNTAIN Col 10'' CL-6089

LP-784 THE THEATRE LYRICS OF P.G. WODEHOUSE Folkways RFS-601

Artist Albums

ALBERGHETTI, ANNA MARIA "Anna Maria Alberghetti: Love Makes the World Go Round" ORCH & COND: Luther Henderson. Rec 1962. (MGM 4001)(LP-421)

AMES, ED "Opening Night with Ed Ames" (RCA LSP-2781) (LP-212)

ANDREWS SISTERS "The Andrews Sisters 'In the Mood' "(Famous Twinsets PAS-21023)(LP-266)

ANDREWS SISTERS "The Andrews Sisters' Greatest Hits" (Dec 4919)(LP-237)

ANDREWS SISTERS "The Best of the Andrews Sisters" (MCA Records 2-4024)(LP-265)

ANDREWS, JULIE See 620611 TV show "Julie and Carol at Carnegie Hall"

ANDREWS, JULIE See 710701 TV show "Julie and Carol at Lincoln Center"

ARDEN & OHMAN "Arden and Ohman (1925-1933)" (JJA Records 1974-1)(LP-492)

ARDEN & OHMAN "Arden and Ohman (Volume 2)" (JJA Records 1975-3)

ARLEN, HAROLD "Harold Arlen Sings, 1930-1937" From original 78's. (JJA Records 1975-9)(LP-603)

ARLEN, HAROLD "Composers at Play: Harold Arlen and Cole Porter" (RCA "X" LVA-1003)(LP-340)

ARLEN, HAROLD "Harold Arlen in Hollywood, 1934-1954" Mostly soundtrack recordings. (JJA Records 19763)(LP-657)

ARLEN, HAROLD "The Music of Harold Arlen, Volume 1" ORCH & COND: Peter Matz. PIANO: Harold Arlen, Peter Matz. VOCALS: Harold Arlen. 1955 album. (Walden 306; Mark 56 Records 683, entitled "Harold Arlen Sings," with additional material)(LP-192)

ARLEN, HAROLD "The Music of Harold Arlen, Volume 2" ORCH & COND: Peter Matz. VOCALS: Louise Carlyle, Bob Shaver, Warren Galjour, Miriam Burton, June Ericson, Harold Arlen. 1955 album. (Walden 307)(LP-352)

ARLEN, HAROLD "Harold Arlen and His Songs" 1955 album. (Cap T-635)(LP-101)

ARLEN, HAROLD "Harold Sings Arlen" 1966 album. (Col OS-2920)(LP-60)

ARLEN, HAROLD "Pearl Bailey Sings Harold Arlen" 1961 album.(Roulette 25155)(LP-260)

ARLEN, HAROLD "Harold Arlen Revisited" ORCH & COND: Ralph Burns, Dick Hyman. VOCALS: Nancy Andrews, David Burns, Blossom Dearie, Gloria DeHaven, Phyllis Diller, Estelle Parsons, Charles Rydell. (Painted Smiles 1345)

ARMSTRONG, LOUIS "Louis Armstrong Town Hall Concert" Rec April 24, 1947. (45/RCA EPAT-9)(LP-355)

ASTAIRE, FRED "Fred Astaire" VOCALS: Fred & Adele Astaire. PIANO: Arthur Schwartz. COND: Leo Reisman. (RCA "X" LVA-1001)(LP-211)

ASTAIRE, FRED "Fred Astaire 1935-1940" (JJA Records 19731)(LP-208)

ASTAIRE, FRED "Starring Fred Astaire" The 1935-1938 Brunswick recordings. (Col SG-32472)(LP-215)

ASTAIRE, FRED "Fred Astaire: Original Recordings 1935-40" (CBS(F) 66316)(LP-277)

ASTAIRE, FRED "Fred Astaire: Nothing Thrilled Us Half As Much" (Epic 13103)(LP-23)

ASTAIRE, FRED "Fred Astaire" (Vocalion 3716)(LP-22)

ASTAIRE, FRED "Fred Astaire: Easy to Dance With" (MCA(E) MCFM-2698)(LP-344)

ASTAIRE, FRED "Fred Astaire" MGM soundtracks. (Lion 70121; reissued as "Fred Astaire: A Shine on Your Shoes" on MGM(E) 2353-112)(LP-24)

ASTAIRE, FRED "Fred Astaire: The Belle of New York" Includes 8 additional songs by Astaire. (Stet DS-15004) (LP-597)

ASTAIRE, FRED "The Astaire Story" VOCALS & TAP DANCING: Fred Astaire. JAZZ ENSEMBLE: Oscar Peterson, Barney Kessel, Charlie Shavers, Flip Phillips, Ray Brown, Alvin Stoller. Rec 1952. (Mercury MG-C-1001/4)(DRG Records DARC-3-1102)(LP-648)

ASTAIRE, FRED "Fred Astaire Sings and Swings Irving Berlin" Excerpts from The Astaire Story (rec 1952). (MGM PR-1)(LP-50)

ASTAIRE, FRED "Fred Astaire: Mr. Top Hat" Excerpts from The Astaire Story (rec 1952). (Verve MGV-2010)(LP-358)

ASTAIRE, FRED "The Special Magic of Fred Astaire" Rec 1952. (Verve(E) 2317-082)(LP-348)

ASTAIRE, FRED "The Special Magic of Fred Astaire, Vol. 2) Rec 1952, 1956, & 1957. (Polydor(E) 2489132)(LP-567)

Astaire, FRED "Fred Astaire" Rec 1953 & 1958. (Verve(E) VSP-23/24)(LP-125)

ASTAIRE, FRED "Fred Astaire: Easy to Dance With" Rec 1952 & 1958. (Verve MGV-2114)(LP-552)

ASTAIRE, FRED "Fred Astaire: Now" ORCH: Pete King, Marty Paich. COND: Pete King. Rec 1959. (Kapp KS-3049) (LP-108)

ASTAIRE, FRED See 581017 TV show "An Evening with Fred Astaire," 591104 TV show "Another Evening with Fred Astaire," & 600928 TV show "Astaire Time"

ASTAIRE, FRED "Three Evenings with Fred Astaire" Excerpts from TV soundtracks of "An Evening with Fred Astaire" (1959), "Another Evening with Fred Astaire" (1960), & "Astaire Time" (1961). (Choreo A-1; reissued as "Fred Astaire -- Live" on Pye(E) PKL-5542 and as "An Evening with Fred Astaire" on Koala AW-14160; LP-213.)

ASTAIRE, FRED "Fred Astaire: Attitude Dancing" ORCH & COND: Pete Moore. 1975 album. (United Artists(E) 29885) (LP-663)

ASTAIRE, FRED "Bing Crosby & Fred Astaire: A Couple of Song & Dance Men" ORCH & COND: Pete Moore. 1975 album. (United Artists(E) 29888)(LP-396)

ASTAIRE, FRED "Fred Astaire: They Can't Take These Away

from Me'' ORCH: Pete Moore, Dave Lindup. COND: Pete Moore. 1976 album. (United Artists(E) 29941)(LP-429)

AUSTIN, GENE See 570421 TV show ''The Gene Austin Story''

AUSTIN, GENE ''Gene Austin Sings All-Time Favorites'' Reissues of 1927-34 records. (RCA ''X'' LVA-1007)(LP-483)

AUSTIN, GENE ''Gene Austin: My Blue Heaven'' 1954 album. (RCA 10'' LPM-3200)(LP-362)

AUSTIN, GENE ''Gene Austin: My Blue Heaven'' (RCA LPM-2490)(LP-103)

AUSTIN, GENE ''This Is Gene Austin'' (RCA VPM-6056) (LP-475)

BAILEY, PEARL ''Pearl Bailey Sings Harold Arlen'' 1961 album. (Roulette 25155)(LP-260)

BENNETT, RICHARD RODNEY ''Special Occasions: Richard Rodney Bennett Plays Ballet Music'' Arranged for 2 pianos & played by Bennett. ''Civil War Ballet'' (Harold Arlen: Bloomer Girl, 1944), ''Within the Quota'' (Cole Porter, 1923), ''Ghost Town'' (Richard Rodgers, 1939). (DRG Records 6102)

BENNETT, ROBERT RUSSELL ''By Special Arrangement: Robert Russell Bennett ... Conducts His Original Broadway Orchestrations'' Rec c. 1944. (AEI Records 2106, reissued from 78/Sonora albums 468 & 475, the latter of which has 2 songs not on the LP)

BERGEN, POLLY See 570516 TV show ''The Helen Morgan Story''

BERLIN, IRVING See 380803 Radio show ''An Irving Berlin Tribute''

BERLIN, IRVING ''Irving Berlin 1909-1939'' (JJA Records 19744)(LP-336)

BERLIN, IRVING ''The Vintage Irving Berlin'' Reissues of 78's. (New World 238)(LP-579)

BERLIN, IRVING ''The Young Irving Berlin'' Reissues of English 78's from 1910 to 1921. (World Records(E) SH-275)(LP-583)

BERLIN, IRVING ''The Magical Songs of Irving Berlin: There's No Business like Show Business'' (Book of the Month Records 60-5256)(LP-593)

BERLIN, IRVING ''Irving Berlin: All By Myself, Vol. 1'' ORCH & COND: Rusty Dedrick. VOCALS: Annette Sanders, Steve Clayton, the Jack Manno Singers. (Monmouth 6809)

BERLIN, IRVING ''Irving Berlin: All By Myself, Vol. 2'' ORCH & COND: Rusty Dedrick. VOCALS: Annette Sanders, Steve Clayton, the Jack Manno Singers. (Monmouth 6810)

BERLIN, IRVING ''Irving Berlin: All By Myself, Vol. 3'' ORCH & COND: Rusty Dedrick. VOCALS: Annette Sanders'' Steve Clayton, the Jack Manno Singers. (Monmouth 6811)

BERLIN, IRVING ''Fred Astaire Sings and Swings Irving Berlin'' (MGM PR-1)(LP-50)

BERLIN, IRVING ''Irving Berlin Revisited'' ORCH & COND: Norman Paris. VOCALS: Richard Chamberlain, Blossom Dearie, Dorothy Loudon, Bobby Short. (MGM 4435)

BERNSTEIN, LEONARD ''Bernstein Conducts Bernstein'' Includes ''On the Town'' ballet music. (Camden 196)(LP-617)

BERNSTEIN, LEONARD ''Larry Kert Sings Leonard Bernstein'' ORCH & COND: Richard Wess. 1959 album. (Seeco 4670) (LP-616)

BIGLEY, ISABEL ''Isabel Bigley & Stephen Douglass Sing Rodgers & Hammerstein'' ORCH & COND: Warren Vincent. 1957 album. (Design 75) (LP-408)

BLAKE, EUBIE ''Eubie Blake: Blues and Rags, Volume 1'' Piano rolls from 1917 to 1921. (Biograph 1011Q)(LP-730)

BLAKE, EUBIE ''Sissle & Blake, Vol. 1'' MUSIC & PIANO: Eubie Blake. WORDS & VOCALS: Noble Sissle. A reissue of early acoustic records. (Eubie Blake Music 4)(LP-422)

BLAKE, EUBIE ''Sissle & Blake, Vol. 2'' PIANO: Eubie Blake. VOCALS: Noble Sissle. Reissue of 78's. (Eubie Blake Music 7)(LP-587)

BLAKE, EUBIE ''The Eighty-Six Years of Eubie Blake'' PIANO: Eubie Blake. VOCALS: Noble Sissle, Eubie Blake. Rec 1968/9. (Col C2S-847)(LP-392)

BLANE, RALPH ''Martin & Blane Sing Martin & Blane'' COND: Ralph Burns. 1956 album. (Harlequin 701)(LP-193)

BLITZSTEIN, MARC ''Marc Blitzstein'' Blitzstein discusses The Cradle Will Rock, No for an Answer, and Regina. 1951 album. VOCALS: Roddy McDowall, Evelyn Lear, Jane Connell, Alvin Epstein, Joshua Shelley, Brenda Lewis, George Gaynes. (Spoken Arts 717)

BOCK, JERRY ''New Songs We Sing in School'' MUSIC & WORDS: Jerry Bock. COND: Jim Timmens. VOCALS: Jerry Bock, others. 1962 album. (Golden 97)

BOCK, JERRY ''Songs about Animals'' MUSIC & WORDS: Jerry Bock. COND: Jim Timmens. VOCALS: Jerry Bock, children's chorus. (Golden 162)

BORGE, VICTOR See 531002 ''Comedy in Music''

BORGE, VICTOR ''Victor Borge Live at the London Palladium'' 1972 album. (Pye(E) NSPL-18394)

BOYER, LUCIENNE ''Songs of Lucienne Boyer'' (78/Col album MM-694)(LP-442)

BRASSELLE, KEEFE ''Keefe Brasselle: The Modern Minstrel'' 1957 album. (RKO ULP-126)(LP-317)

BRICE, FANNY See ''The Original Torch Singers''

BRICE, FANNY See ''Three of a Kind''

BRICE, FANNY ''Torch Songs by Helen Morgan & Fanny Brice'' (RCA ''X'' LVA-1006)(LP-230)

BRICE, FANNY ''Fanny Brice & Helen Morgan'' (RCA LPV-561)(LP-32)

BRICE, FANNY ''Fanny Brice Sings the Songs She Made Famous'' (Audio Fidelity 707)(LP-33)

BRISSON, CARL ''Carl Brisson Sings Again'' (Ace of Clubs(E) 1200)(LP-122)

BROWN, MICHAEL ''Michael Brown Sings His Own Songs'' With the Norman Paris Trio. (Trio 10'' 1001)(LP-697)

BROWN, MICHAEL ''Michael Brown: Alarums & Excursions'' MUSIC & WORDS: Michael Brown. ORCH & COND: Arnold Goland. VOCALS: Michael Brown, chorus. 1962 album. (Impluse(C) AS-24) (LP-732)

BROWN, NACIO HERB ''The Classic Movie Musicals of Nacio Herb Brown (1929-39)'' (JJA Records 19802)(LP-770)

BUBBLES, JOHN W. ''Bubbles: John W., that is'' (Vee-Jay 1109)(LP-75)

BUCHANAN, JACK ''The Debonair Jack Buchanan'' (Music for Pleasure(E) 1160)(LP-61)

BUCHANAN, JACK ''Jack Buchanan'' (World Records(E) SH-283) (LP-374)

BUCHANAN, JACK ''Jack Buchanan: Original London Cast Recordings'' Songs from That's a Good Girl, Boodle, & Toni. (World Records(E) SH-329)(LP-676)

BUCHANAN, JACK ''Jack Buchanan & Jessie Matthews'' (Ace of Clubs(E) 1140)(LP-31)

BURNETT, CAROL See 620611 TV show ''Julie and Carol at Carnegie Hall''

BURNETT, CAROL See 710701 TV show ''Julie and Carol at Lincoln Center''

CAESAR, IRVING ''Irving Caesar: And Then I Wrote'' WORDS: Irving Caesar. VOCALS: Irving Caesar. 1956 album.(Coral 57083)(LP-353)

CAHN, SAMMY See 740416 ''Words and Music''

CAHN, SAMMY ''An Evening with Sammy Cahn'' Rec live 12 & 14 March 1972. MUSIC: Various.WORDS: Sammy Cahn. PIANO: Richard Leonard. VOCALS: Sammy Cahn, Shirley Lemmon, Jon Peck, Bobbi Baird. (Laureate 604)(LP-658)

CAHN, SAMMY ''Sammy Cahn: ''I've Heard That Song Before'' MUSIC: Various. WORDS; Sammy Cahn. ORCH: Neil

Richardson. PIANO: Richard Leonard. VOCALS: Sammy Cahn, chorus. (World Records(E) WRS-1002)(LP-503)

CANTOR, EDDIE "Eddie Cantor: Rare Early Recordings" Reissues of 1919-21 records. (Biograph 12054)(LP-485)

CANTOR, EDDIE "Eddie Cantor: Ol' Banjo Eyes Is Back" (Pelican 134)(LP-379)

CANTOR, EDDIE "Jolson & Cantor: The Immortals" Reissues of 78s.(Epic 10" LN-1128)(LP-721)

CANTOR, EDDIE "Club Richman: Harry Richman & Eddie Cantor" From radio broadcasts of 1930's and 1940's. (Torrington JRS-1019)(LP-414)

CANTOR, EDDIE "Eddie Cantor Sings "The Cantor Story" A reissue of 1940's records. (Dec 10" 5504)(LP-384)

CANTOR, EDDIE "Eddie Cantor: Songs He Made Famous" 1944 album. (78/Dec album 564)(LP-143)

CANTOR, EDDIE "Cantor: Songs He Made Famous" (Dec 4431)(LP-165)

CANTOR, EDDIE "Eddie Cantor: My Forty Years in Show Business" orig prod. Concert at Carnegie Hall, March 21,1950. (Audio Fidelity 702)(LP-144)

CANTOR, EDDIE "The Best of Eddie Cantor" ORCH & COND: Henri Rene. Rec 1957. (Vik LX-1119; reissued as "Eddie Cantor Sings 'Ida, Sweet as Apple Cider' " on Camden 870.)(LP-30)

CARMICHAEL, HOAGY "Hoagy Carmichael: The Stardust Road" MUSIC,VOCALS, & PIANO: Hoagy Carmichael. (Dec 8588) (LP-94)

CARMICHAEL, HOAGY "Hoagy Carmichael: The Stardust Road" MUSIC, VOCALS, & PIANO: Hoagy Carmichael. (Dec 8588)(LP-94)

CARMICHAEL, HOAGY "Hoagy Carmichael's Havin' a Party" VOCALS: Hoagy Carmichael, chorus. COND: Arthur Norman. (Golden 198:18)(LP-750)

CHAKIRIS, GEORGE "George Chakiris" 1962 album. (Cap ST-1750)(LP-482)

CHANNING, CAROL See "Memories of the Roaring Twenties"

CHANNING, CAROL "Carol Channing Entertains" 1965 album. (Command RS-880)(LP-204)

CHANNING, CAROL "Carol Channing" Her cafe act rec live on tour. (Vanguard 9056)(LP-111)

CHARNIN, MARTIN "Martin Charnin's Mini Album: 5 Great Songs from Not-so-Great Shows" MUSIC: Elliot Lawrence, Edward Thomas, Harold Arlen. WORDS: Martin Charnin. COND & PIANO: David Lewis. VOCALS: Laurie Beechman, Robert Guillaume, Larry Kert, Martin Charnin. Rec 1977. (Take Home Tunes 7" 771)(LP-371)

CHEVALIER, MAURICE See 320209 "Maurice Chevalier"

CHEVALIER, MAURICE See 470310 "Maurice Chevalier"

CHEVALIER, MAURICE See 480229 "Maurice Chevalier"

CHEVALIER, MAURICE "Maurice Chevalier, Vol 1" (RCA LPV-564)(LP-72)

CHEVALIER, MAURICE "Maurice Chevalier" (RCA 10" LPT-3042)(LP-405)

CHEVALIER, MAURICE "Toujours Maurice" (Camden 579) (LP-62)

CHEVALIER, MAURICE "Maurice Chevalier Returns" 1947 album of songs from his 1947 one-man show. COND: Henri Rene. (78/Vic album S-51)(LP-132)

CHEVALIER, MAURICE "Thank Heaven for Maurice Chevalier" (RCA LPM-2076)(LP-88)

CHEVALIER, MAURICE "Maurice Chevalier: You Brought a New Kind of Love to Me" (Monmouth 7028)(LP-102)

CHEVALIER, MAURICE "Maurice Chevalier" 1954 album, sung in French. (Col CL-568)(LP-270)

CHEVALIER, MAURICE "Chevalier's Paris" Rec 1957 live in Paris. COND: Michel Legrand. (Col CL-1049)(LP-224)

CHEVALIER, MAURICE "Maurice Chevalier: Yesterday" Rec 1958. (MGM 3702)(LP-118)

CHEVALIER, MAURICE "A Musical Tour of France with Maurice Chevalier" 1966 album. VOCALS: Maurice Chevalier, children's chorus. (Disneyland 3940)(LP-600)

CLARY, ROBERT "Robert Clary: Hooray for Love" COND: Neal Hefti. 1956 album. (Epic LN-3281)(LP-687)

CLARY, ROBERT "Robert Clary Lives It Up at the Playboy Club" Rec live. (Atlantic 8053)(LP-666)

COHAN, GEORGE M "A Tribute to George M Cohan" Includes all but two of Cohan's 1911 records (several excerpted), his 1938 curtain speech, the 1941 ASCAP radio broadcast, & additional material. NARRATOR: Chamberlain Brown. (Audio Rarities LPA-2295)(LP-365)

COHAN, GEORGE M "George M Cohan: Yankee Doodle Dandy" (Olympic 7111)(LP-214)

COHAN, GEORGE M "George M Cohan: The Original Yankee Doodle Dandy" MUSIC & WORDS: mostly George M Cohan. VOCALS: mostly George M Cohan. Includes soundtrack of 1932 film The Phantom President. (Old Shep GMC-1000) (LP-467)

COHAN, GEORGE M "George M Cohan Songs Sung by George M Cohan, Jr." COND: Thomas Lender Jones. 1948 album. (Camden 167, with Guys and Dolls)

COLEMAN, CY "Cy Coleman Sings" 1966 album. (Col CS-9378) (LP-238)

COLUMBO, RUSS "The Films of Russ Columbo" Soundtracks of Broadway thru a Keyhole, Moulin Rouge, Wake Up and Dream, & That Goes Double. (Golden Legends 2001)(LP-557)

COMDEN, BETTY See 570007b Film "It's Always Fair Weather"

COMDEN, BETTY See 581223 "A Party with Betty Comden and Adolph Green"

COMDEN, BETTY See artist album listing for "The Revuers"

COMDEN, BETTY "Betty Comden and Adolph Green" (JJA Records 19764)(LP-508)

COMDEN, BETTY "Comden and Green: Show Music at Its Best, Vol. 1" 1955 album. Vocals, with Adolph Green, of songs they wrote lyrics for. (Heritage 0057)(LP-359)

COOK, BARBARA "Barbara Cook at Carnegie Hall" ORCH: Bill Brohn. COND: Wally Harper. Rec live 26 January 1975. (Col M-33438)(LP-689)

COOTS, J FRED "J Fred Coots ... And Then I Wrote" MUSIC: J Fred Coots. WORDS: Various. VOCALS: J Fred Coots. (Coral 57084)(LP-530)

COURTNEIDGE, CICELY "Cicely Courtneidge and Jack Hulbert" (World Record Club(E) SH-113)(LP-90)

COWARD, NOEL See 551022 TV show "Together with Music"

COWARD, NOEL See 720710 "Cowardy Custard"

COWARD, NOEL See 721004 "Oh, Coward!"

COWARD, NOEL "Noel Coward: The Great Shows" (World Records(E) SH-179/80)(LP-174)

COWARD, NOEL "Noel Coward: The Great Shows" (Monmouth 7062/3)(LP-308)

COWARD, NOEL "Noel Coward: The Revues" MUSIC & WORDS: Noel Coward. VOCALS: Noel Coward, Maisie Gay, Alice Delysia, Doris Hare. (World Records(E) SHB-44)(LP-502)

COWARD, NOEL "Noel Coward 1928-1952" (JJA Records 1971-2)(LP-218)

COWARD, NOEL "Noel Coward: The Master Sings" (Music for Pleasure(E) 1111)(LP-11)

COWARD, NOEL "Noel Coward & Gertrude Lawrence: We Were Dancing" (Monmouth 7042)(LP-275)

COWARD, NOEL "Noel and Gertie" (RCA LCT-1156)(Odeon(E) PCLP-1050)(LP-28)

COWARD, NOEL "Noel and Gertie and Bea" (Parlophone(E) PMC-7135)(LP-123)

COWARD, NOEL "Noel Coward: I'll See You Again" VOCALS: Noel Coward. COND: Wally Stott. (Philips(E) 10" BBR-8028) (LP-138)

COWARD, NOEL "The Noel Coward Album" Noel Coward at Las Vegas (1955) and Noel Coward in New York (1956). (Col MG-30088)(LP-89)

COWARD, NOEL "Noel Coward: A Special Event" Songs from "High Spirits" (sung by Noel Coward) & "Sail Away" (sung by Coward & Joe Layton) and the score for "London Morning." (DRG Records SL-5180)(LP-594)

COWARD, NOEL "Joan Sutherland Sings Noel Coward, with Guest Appearance of Noel Coward" (London 25992)

COWARD, NOEL "The Famed Songs of Noel Coward and Ivor Novello" COND: John Gregory. VOCALS: John Hanson, Doreen Hume, Dick Bentley, Jean Campbell, Vanessa Lee, Bruce Trent. (Dot 3047)(LP-444)

COWARD, NOEL "Noel Coward Revisited" ORCH & COND: Norman Paris. VOCALS: Laurence Harvey, Hermione Gingold, Nancy Andrews, Edward Earle. (MGM 4430)

CRAWFORD, JOAN "Joan Crawford" (Curtain Calls 100/23) (LP-401)

CRAWFORD, JOAN "Joan Crawford: The Devil's Sister" (JOAC X-20)(LP-532)

CROSBY, BING "Bing Crosby: Wrap Your Troubles in Dreams" Reissues of 1927-31 records. (RCA LPV-584)(LP-634)

CROSBY, BING "Young Bing Crosby" With Paul Whiteman & Gus Arnheim Orchs. (RCA "X" LVA-1000)(LP-507)

CROSBY, BING "Bing Crosby: Where the Blue of the Night Meets the Gold of the Day" 1930/31 soundtracks. (Biograph BLP-M-1)(LP-506)

CROSBY, BING "The Bing Crosby Story, Volume I: The Early Jazz Years, 1928-1932" (Col CE2E-201)(LP-540)

CROSBY, BING "Bing Crosby in Hollywood, 1930-1934" (Col C2L-43)(LP-181)

CROSBY, BING "Bing Crosby, Volume 1" Reissues of 1931 records. (78/Bruns album B-1012)(LP-577)

CROSBY, BING "Bing Crosby, Volume 2" Reissues of 1931 records. (78/Bruns album B-1015)(LP-576)

CROSBY, BING "Crosby Classics" Reissues of 1932/3 records. (Col 10" CL-6027)(LP-575)

CROSBY, BING "Crosby Classics, Volume 2" Reissues of 1932/3 records. (Col 10" CL-6105)(LP-578)

CROSBY, BING "Paul Whiteman and His Orchestra Featuring Bing Crosby" (Col CL-2830)(LP-541)

CROSBY, BING "Bing: The Early Thirties, Vol. 1" (Ace of Hearts(E) 40)(LP-337)

CROSBY, BING "Bing: The Early Thirties, Vol. 2" (Ace of Hearts(E) 88)(LP-779)

CROSBY, BING "Bing Crosby: The Man without a Country & What So Proudly We Hail" Includes 1940 studio prod of "Ballad for Americans." (Dec 8020)(LP-425)

CROSBY, BING "The Bing Crosby Radio Shows" With Maurice Chevalier, Judy Garland, Jimmy Durante, Bob Hope, others. (Golden Age 5023)(LP-693)

CROSBY, BING "Judy Garland in Holland, Vol. 3" Includes 1951(?) radio show with Garland and Crosby. (Obligato GIH-6100)(LP-781)

CROSBY, BING "Bing Crosby: Easy to Remember" (Dec 4250)(LP-163)

CROSBY, BING "Bing Crosby: Pennies from Heaven" (Dec 4251)(LP-319)

CROSBY, BING: "Bing Crosby: Pocket Full of Dreams" (Dec 4252)(LP-254)

CROSBY, BING "Bing Crosby: East Side of Heaven" (Dec 4253)(LP-264)

CROSBY, BING "Bing Crosby: The Road Begins" (Dec 4254) (LP-262)

CROSBY, BING "Bing Crosby: Only Forever" (Dec 4255) (LP-318)

CROSBY, BING "Bing Crosby: Swinging on a Star" (Dec 4257)(LP-339)

CROSBY, BING "Bing Crosby: Accentuate the Positive" (Dec 4258)(LP-27)

CROSBY, BING "Bing Crosby: Blue Skies" (Dec 4259) (LP-162)

CROSBY, BING "Bing Crosby: But Beautiful" (Dec 4260) (LP-263)

CROSBY, BING "Bing Crosby: Sunshine Cake" (Dec 4261) (LP-253)

CROSBY, BING "Bing Crosby: Cool of the Evening" (Dec 4262)(LP-255)

CROSBY, BING "Bing Crosby: Zing a Little Zong" (Dec 4263)(LP-161)

CROSBY, BING "Bing Crosby: Anything Goes" (Dec 4264) (LP-26)

CROSBY, BING "Bing Crosby & Fred Astaire: A Couple of Song & Dance Men" ORCH & COND: Pete Moore. 1975 album. (United Artists(E) 29888)(LP-396)

CRUMIT, FRANK "Julia Sanderson and Frank Crumit" 1940 album. (78/Dec album 245)(LP-57)

CRYER, GRETCHEN "Cryer & Ford" MUSIC & WORDS: Gretchen Cryer, Nancy Ford. VOCALS: Cryer & Ford. ORCH: Ken Ascher, Mike Zager. 1975 album. This is basically the material used in their Manhattan Theatre Club engagement which opened 23 January 1975. (RCA APL1-1235)(LP-570)

DAILEY, DAN "Dan Dailey: Mr. Musical Comedy" ORCH & COND: Ernie Felice. 1957 album. (Tops L-1598)(LP-367)

DARREN, JAMES "James Darren: Gidget Goes Hawaiian" 1961 album. (Colpix 418)(LP-688)

DAVIS, BETTE "Miss Bette Davis" ORCH & COND: Roger Webb. VOCALS: Bette Davis, chorus. (EMI(E) EMA-778) (LP-395)

DAVIS, BUSTER "Buster Davis: Doin' the Obscuriana" PIANO & VOCALS: Buster Davis. Obscure songs by well-known composers. 1979 album. (FilmScore 7914, with Movie Movie)

DAVIS, SAMMY, JR See 731116 TV show "General Electric Presents Sammy"

DAVIS, SAMMY, JR "Sammy Davis Jr: What Kind of Fool Am I?" ORCH & COND: Marty Paich. Rec 1961. (Reprise 6051)(LP-257)

DAY, DORIS "Doris Day: Lights! Camera! Action!" (Col 10" CL-2)(LP-315)

DAY, DORIS "Doris Day's Greatest Hits" (Col CL-1210) (LP-692)

DAY, DORIS "Doris Day Sings Her Great Movie Hits" (Harmony 11192)(LP-330)

DAY, EDITH "Edith Day" (World Record Club(E) SH-138) (LP-84)

DeHAVEN, GLORIA "DeHaven in Hollywood" (Vedette 8703) (LP-272)

DELYSIA, ALICE " Alice Delysia" (World Record Club(E) SH-164)(LP-128)

DeWITT, FAY "Fay DeWitt: Through Sick & Sin" ORCH & COND: Joe Harnell. (Epic BN-596)(LP-574)

DIETRICH, MARLENE See 641123 "Marlene Dietrich"

DIETRICH, MARLENE "The Legendary Marlene Dietrich" (Music for Pleasure(E) 1172)(LP-10)

DIETRICH, MARLENE "Marlene Dietrich" (Historia(G) 607) (LP-81)

DIETRICH, MARLENE "Marlene Dietrich Sings" 1950 reissue of records made about 1930. COND: Peter Kreuder. (Vox 10" 3040)(LP-139)

DIETRICH, MARLENE "Dietrich Live 1932-52" Includes soundtracks. (Wildebeest-Maclon 5290)(LP-653)

DIETRICH, MARLENE "Ann Sheridan/Marlene Dietrich" Mostly soundtracks. (Marsher 201)(LP-705)

DIETRICH, MARLENE "Marlene Dietrich Souvenir Album" Rec 1939. (78/Dec album 115; Dec 10" 5100, with 2 extra songs recorded later.)(LP-54)

DIETRICH, MARLENE "Marlene Dietrich at the Cafe de Paris" Rec live in 1954 in London. Introduction by Noel Coward. (Col ML-4975)(LP-178)

DIETRICH, MARLENE "Dietrich in Rio" Rec live in 1959 at Rio de Janiero. ORCH & COND: Burt Bacharach. (Col WL-164)(LP-151)

DIETRICH, MARLENE "Wiedersehen mit Marlene" Rec live in 1960 in Germany. ORCH & COND: Burt Bacharach. (Cap T-10282)(LP-195)

DISNEY, WALT See anthology "The Magical Music of Walt Disney"

DORSEY, JIMMY "Jimmy Dorsey's Greatest Hits" (Dec 4853) (LP-480)

DORSEY, TOMMY "The Complete Tommy Dorsey, Vol. 1/1935" Includes the 5 Eleanor Powell recordings. (Bluebird AXM2-5521)(LP-474)

DOUGLASS, STEPHEN "Isabel Bigley & Stephen Douglass Sing Rodgers & Hammerstein" ORCH & COND: Warren Vincent. 1957 album. (Design 75)(LP-408)

DUKE, VERNON "Hildegarde: Vernon Duke Songs" PIANO: Vernon Duke. Rec 1940. (78/Dec album 149)

DUKE, VERNON "Vernon Duke Plays Vernon Duke" PIANO: Vernon Duke. VOCALS: Dorothy Richards, Huguette Ferly. (Atlantic 10" ALS-407)

DUKE, VERNON "Vernon Duke Revisited" ORCH & COND: Norman Paris. VOCALS: Blossom Dearie, Gloria DeHaven, Tammy Grimes, Anthony Perkins, Rex Reed, Joan Rivers. (Crewe 1342)

DULLEA, KEIR "Keir Dullea" (Platypus 5001)(LP-611)

DUNCAN, TODD "Todd Duncan Recital" PIANO: William Allen. (78/Musicraft album 82)(LP-744)

DUNCAN, TODD "Todd Duncan" With Sister Rosetta Tharpe, King Odom, & the Gospel Singers. (Sutton 285)(LP-678)

DUNHAM, KATHERINE "Katherine Dunham: Afro-Caribbean Songs and Rhythms" VOCALS: Katherine Dunham, Jean Leon Destine, LaRosa Estrada, Julio Mendez. Rec 1947. (Dec 10" 5251)

DUNNE, IRENE "Irene Dunne in Songs by Jerome Kern" Rec 1941. (78/Dec album 484)(LP-66)

DURANTE, JIMMY "Jimmy Durante" Rec 1944 & 1946. (Dec 10" 5116)(LP-80)

DURANTE, JIMMY "Jimmy Durante in Person" 1951 album. COND: Roy Bargy. (MGM 10" 542; LP-142. Reissued with 4 additional songs as "The Very Best of Jimmy Durante" (MGM 4207) and "Jimmy Durante in Person" (Lion 70053).)

DURANTE, JIMMY "Jimmy Durante Presents TV on Records" With Paul Douglas, Eddie Jackson, Louis Prima Orch, Lily Ann Carol. (Royale 10" 68)(LP-363)

DURANTE, JIMMY "Jimmy Durante at the Piano" (Dec 8884) (LP-292)

DURANTE, JIMMY "The Jimmy Durante Show" Starring Jimmy Durante, Ethel Barrymore, Helen Traubel. From 1950's radio and TV shows. (45/Dec ED-2527)(LP-439)

DURANTE, JIMMY "Jimmy Durante at the Copacabana" With Eddie Jackson. Rec 1960. (Roulette 25123)

DURBIN, DEANNA "Deanna Durbin Souvenir Album" (78/Dec album 35)(LP-110)

DURBIN, DEANNA "Deanna Durbin Souvenir Album No. 2" (78/Dec 12" album 75)(LP-95)

DURBIN, DEANNA "Deanna Durbin Souvenir Album No. 3" (78/Dec album 128)(LP-91)

DURBIN, DEANNA "Deanna Durbin Souvenir Album No. 4" (78/Dec album 209)(LP-131)

DURBIN, DEANNA "Deanna Durbin Souvenir Album No. Five" Reissues, released in 1941. (78/Dec album 280)

DURBIN, DEANNA "Deanna Durbin Souvenir Album Volume One" Reissues, released in 1948. (78/Dec album 680)(LP-404)

DURBIN, DEANNA "Deanna Durbin" Soundtracks from her films. (Dec 75289)(LP-256)

DURBIN, DEANNA "Deanna Durbin" (Dec 8785)(LP-406)

DURBIN, DEANNA "Deanna Durbin: Can't Help Singing" Ace of Hearts(E) 60)(LP-13)

EBB, FRED "An Evening with Fred Ebb and John Kander" Rec live 8 & 10 April 1973. MUSIC: John Kander. WORDS: Fred Ebb. PIANO: John Kander. VOCALS: Fred Ebb, John Kander. (Laureate 605)(LP-659)

EDDY, NELSON "Jeanette MacDonald and Nelson Eddy" (RCA LPV-526)(LP-4)

EDDY, NELSON "Jeanette MacDonald & Nelson Eddy: Operetta Favorites" 1935/6 recordings. (RCA 10" LCT-16)(LP-462)

EDDY, NELSON "Nelson Eddy Favorites" (Camden 492) (LP-117)

EDDY, NELSON "Jeanette MacDonald & Nelson Eddy: Movie Memories" (45/RCA EPA-5113)(LP-242)

EDDY, NELSON "Helen Morgan & Nelson Eddy: The Torch Singer and the Mountie" (Trisklog 4)(LP-499)

EDDY, NELSON "Nelson Eddy: On the Air" 1948 radio broadcasts. VOCALS: Nelson Eddy, Jeanette MacDonald. (Totem 1035)(LP-756)

EDDY, NELSON "Jeanette MacDonald & Nelson Eddy: Favorites in Hi-Fi" Rec 1958. (RCA LPM-1738)(LP-134)

EDDY, NELSON "Nelson Eddy's Greatest Hits" (Col CS-9481)(LP-432)

EDDY, NELSON "Nelson Eddy: Romantic Moments" Songs from Rose-Marie, The New Moon, & Naughty Marietta, with Nadine Conner, Dorothy Kirsten, & Eleanor Steber. (Col GB-3)(LP-268)

EDWARDS, CLIFF "Cliff Edwards: I'm a Bear in a Lady's Boudoir" Reissues of 1924-30 records. (Yazoo L-1047) (LP-476)

EDWARDS, CLIFF "The Vintage Recordings of Cliff Edwards" (Take Two 205)(LP-760)

EDWARDS, CLIFF "Cliff Edwards: 'Ukelele Ike'" Rec in 1940's & 1950's. (Glendale 6011)(LP-635)

EDWARDS, CLIFF "Cliff Edwards: Shakin' the Blues Away" Transcription library records from 1950's. (Totem 1005) (LP-437)

EDWARDS, CLIFF "Cliff Edwards: I Want a Girl" Rec 1950s(?). (Totem(C) 1014)(LP-757)

ELLINGTON, DUKE "Duke Eillington's Band Shorts (1929-1935)" Complete soundtracks of "Black and Tan" (1929), "A Bundle of Blues" (1933), & "Symphony in Black" (1935). (Biograph M-2)(LP-622)

ELLINGTON, DUKE "The Works of Duke, Volume 16" Reissues of 78rpm records. (RCA(F) FXM1-7201)(LP-471)

ELLINGTON, DUKE "The Works of Duke, Volume 17" Reissues of 78rpm records. (RCA(F) FXM1-7274)(LP-472)

ETTING, RUTH See anthology "The Original Torch Singers"

ETTING, RUTH See anthology "Three of a Kind"

ETTING, RUTH "The Original Recordings of Ruth Etting" (Col ML-5050)(LP-25)

ETTING, RUTH "Ruth Etting" Reissues of 78's. (Biograph C-11)(LP-546)

ETTING, RUTH "Ruth Etting: Reflections, 1927-1935" (Take Two 203)(LP-725)

FAIN, SAMMY "I'll Be Seeing You: The Music of Sammy Fain as

Sung by the Composer" COND: Van Alexander. 1954 album. (MGM 10" 241)(LP-707)

FAYE, ALICE "Alice Faye in Hollywood (1934-1937)" (Col CL-3068)(LP-9)

FAYE, ALICE "Alice Faye on the Air" Songs from 1932/4 radio broadcasts. (Totem 1011)(LP-488)

FAYE, ALICE "Alice Faye on the Air, Vol.2" Rec 1930-39. (Totem 1032)(LP-645)

FAYE, ALICE "Miss Alice Faye Sings the Rare Ones" Radio performances. (Wong 087)(LP-717)

FAYE, ALICE "Alice Faye " Film soundtracks. (Curtain Calls 100/3)(LP-283)

FAYE, ALICE "Alice Faye and the Songs of Harry Warren" Soundtracks from films of the early 1940's. (Citadel 6004)(LP-424)

FAYE, ALICE "Alice Faye Sings Her Famous Movie Hits" ORCH & COND: Neal Hefti. 1962 album. (Reprise 9-6029; Valiant(E) 122 (entitled "Alice Faye Sings Her Greatest Movie Hits"); Stanyan 10072 (entitled "Alice Faye's Greatest Hits"); LP-100.)

FIELDS, BENNY "Benny Fields & Blossom Seeley: Two-a-Day at the Palace" 1957 album. (Mercury 20224)(LP-764)

FIELDS, GRACIE "Gracie Fields: Stage and Screen" (World Record Club(E) SH-170)(LP-248)

FISHER, EDDIE See 621002 "Eddie Fisher at the Winter Garden"

FORD, NANCY "Cryer & Ford" MUSIC & WORDS: Gretchen Cryer, Nancy Ford. VOCALS: Cryer & Ford. ORCH: Ken Ascher, Mike Zager. 1975 album. This is basically the material used in their Manhattan Theatre Club engagement which opened 23 January 1975. (RCA APL1-1235)(LP-570)

FRIML, RUDOLF "Rudolf Friml in London" (World Records(E) SHB-37)(LP-448)

FRIML, RUDOLF "Friml Presents Friml" COND & PIANO: Rudolf Firml. No vocals. (Westminster 15008)

FRIML, RUDOLF "The Genius of Rudolf Friml" MUSIC & PIANO: Rudolf Friml. Rec 1950s and 1960s. (Golden Crest CRS-4200)(LP-733)

FRIML, RUDOLF "Rudolf Friml" Friml plays his songs on the piano. Rec 1963. (Nan 4019)(LP-354)

FRIML, RUDOLF "The Music of Rudolf Friml" COND: Nathaniel Shilkret. VOCALS: Victor Salon Group. Rec 1929. (Camden 252)(LP-590)

FROMAN, JANE "Jane Froman: Yours Alone" ORCH & COND: Sid Feller. 1953 album. (Cap 10" H-354)(LP-445)

GARLAND, JUDY See 511016 "Judy Garland at the Palace"

GARLAND, JUDY See 590021 Record prod "The Letter"

GARLAND, JUDY See 630005 Record prod "Our Love Letter"

GARLAND, JUDY See 670731 "Judy Garland at the Palace"

GARLAND, JUDY "Judy Garland Souvenir Album" (78/Dec 12" album 76)(LP-233)

GARLAND, JUDY "Judy Garland: Second Souvenir Album" (78/Dec album 349)(LP-490)

GARLAND, JUDY "Judy Garland Sings with Dick Haymes, Gene Kelly, the Merry Macs, Gordon Jenkins" (78/Dec album 682)(LP-734)

GARLAND, JUDY "Judy Garland 'Collector's Items' (1936-1945)" (Dec DEA-7-5)(LP-35)

GARLAND, JUDY "The Best of Judy Garland" (Dec DXB-172) (LP-7)

GARLAND, JUDY "Judy Garland: Miss Show-Biz" (Ace of Hearts(E) 48)(LP-239)

GARLAND, JUDY "Judy Garland: Born in a Trunk, 1935-1940) Soundtrack & radio material. (AEI Records 2108)(LP-726)

GARLAND, JUDY "Judy Garland: Born in a Trunk, 1940-1945" Soundtrack material. (AEI Records 2109)(LP-746)

GARLAND, JUDY "Judy Garland: The Beginning" Reissues of 78's. (DRG Records SL-5187)(LP-640)

GARLAND, JUDY "Judy Garland 1935 thru 1952" Identical to LP-718, but with 5 more numbers. (Star-Tone 201)(LP-180)

GARLAND, JUDY "The Judy Garland Musical Scrapbook" Performances from 1935 through 1949. (Star-Tone 208)(LP-759)

GARLAND, JUDY "Judy Garland: The Rare Early Broadcast Performances" Identical to LP-180, but with 5 fewer numbers. (Accessor Pro 1001)(LP-718)

GARLAND, JUDY "The Uncollected Judy Garland" Reissues of 78s & her songs from Gay Purr-ee. (Stanyan SR-10095) (LP-745)

GARLAND, JUDY "The Magic of Judy Garland" (also titled "The Immortal Judy Garland") (Longines 5217/5221) (LP-219)

GARLAND, JUDY "The Judy Garland Story: The Star Years" Soundtracks from her films. (MGM 3989)(LP-259)

GARLAND, JUDY "The Judy Garland Story: The Hollywood Years" Soundtracks from her films. (MGM 4005)(LP-289)

GARLAND, JUDY "Judy Garland Sings" Soundtrack recordings. (MGM 10" 82)(LP-782)

GARLAND, JUDY "The Very Best of Judy Garland" Soundtracks from her films. (MGM 4204)(LP-8)

GARLAND, JUDY "Judy! That's Entertainment!" (Cap ST-1467)(LP-190)

GARLAND, JUDY "The Judy Garland Deluxe Set" (Cap STCL-2988)(LP-188)

GARLAND, JUDY "Judy Garland at the Grove" 1959 album, rec live in Los Angeles. COND: Freddy Martin. (Cap T-1118)(LP-461)

GARLAND, JUDY "Judy in London" Rec August 1960. COND: Norrie Paramor. (Cap 94407)(LP-547)

GARLAND, JUDY "Judy at Carnegie Hall" Rec Apr 23,1961. COND: Mort Lindsey. (Cap WBO-1569)(LP-240)

GARLAND, JUDY "Judy Garland & Liza Minnelli: 'Live' at the London Palladium" Rec Nov 8, 1964. (Cap ST-11191) (LP-205)

GARLAND, JUDY "Judy. London. 1969." Rec live. (Juno S-1000)(LP-525)

GARLAND, JUDY "The Wit & Wonder of Judy Garland" Rec from radio, TV, and stage performances. (DRG Records SL-5179)(LP-743)

GARLAND, JUDY "Judy Garland in Concert: San Franciso" Rec live. (Mark 56 Records 632)(LP-298)

GARLAND, JUDY "Judy Garland: The Long Lost Holland Concert" Rec 1961(?). (Obligato GIH-60)(LP-376)

GARLAND, JUDY "Judy Garland in Holland, Vol. 2" Rec 1961(?). (Obligato GIH-610)(LP-780)

GARLAND, JUDY "Judy Garland in Holland, Vol. 3" Live performance rec 1961(?). Also 1951(?) radio show with Bing Crosby. (Obligato GIH-6100)(LP-781)

GARLAND, JUDY "Judy" 1963 TV show soundtrack. (Radiant 711-0101)(LP-200)

GARLAND, JUDY "Judy in Hollywood" 1963 TV show soundtrack. (Radiant 711-0102)(LP-201)

GARLAND, JUDY "Judy--the Legend" 1963 TV show soundtrack. (Radiant 711-0103)(LP-390)

GARLAND, JUDY "Judy's Greatest Hits" 1963 TV show soundtrack. (CAS/Radiant 212-0113)(LP-762)

GARLAND, JUDY "Unforgettable Judy Garland" 1963 TV show soundtrack. (Radiant 711-0105)(LP-194)

GARLAND, JUDY "Judy's Portrait in Song" 1963 TV show soundtrack. (Radiant 711-0106)(LP-202)

GARLAND, JUDY "Judy Garland: Over the Rainbow" 1963 TV show soundtrack. (CAS/Radiant 212-0116)(LP-735)

GARLAND, JUDY "Judy Garland Collector's Remembrance Album" 1963/4 TV show soundtracks. (Compusonic 734786) (LP-738)

GAY, NOEL "The Hits of Noel Gay" (Music for Pleasure(E) 1236)(LP-130)

GERSHWIN, GEORGE See 380710 Radio show "A Tribute to George Gershwin"

GERSHWIN, GEORGE "Gershwin Plays Gershwin" (RCA AVM1-1740)(LP-433)

GERSHWIN, GEORGE "George Gershwin Plays Gershwin & Kern" Piano rolls made by Gershwin from 1919-1925. (Klavier 122)(LP-459)

GERSHWIN, GEORGE "George Gershwin Plays Rhapsody in Blue and His Other Favorite Compositions" (Movietone 1009)(LP-12)

GERSHWIN, GEORGE "Gershwin Plays Gershwin" VOCALS: Fred & Adele Astaire. (Audio Archives 10" 0073)(LP-326)

GERSHWIN, GEORGE "George Gershwin Conducts Excerpts from Porgy and Bess" Gershwin conducts a Porgy and Bess rehearsal; also 3 Gershwin piano rolls and a radio broadcast. (Mark 56 Records 667)(LP-375)

GERSHWIN, GEORGE "Gershwin ... from Tin Pan Alley to Broadway" Piano rolls made by Gershwin from 1916-1926. (Mark 56 Records 680)(LP-458)

GERSHWIN, GEORGE "George Gershwin: Primrose" Includes Gershwin piano solos. (World Records(E) SH-214)(LP-279)

GERSHWIN, GEORGE "Gershwin: Blue Monday" (A chamber opera, also known as "135th Street," briefly used in George White's Scandals of 1922) Rec 1976. WORDS: B G DeSylva. COND: Gregg Smith. VOCALS: Joyce Andrews, Patrick Mason, Walter Richardson, Thomas Bogdan, Jeffrey Meyer, chorus. Other Gershwin songs by Rosalind Rees, Catherine Aks, Priscilla Magdamo. (Turnabout 34638, with additional Gershwin material)

GERSHWIN, GEORGE "Gershwin: 135th Street" (A chamber opera originally known as "Blue Monday," briefly used in George White's Scandals of 1922) 1968 concert performance, rec live. COND: Skitch Henderson. VOCALS: uncredited. Also includes "I Got Rhythm" Variations (1944, cond Rodzinski), Rhapsody in Blue (1942, cond Toscanini, piano Earl Wild), & "Mischa, Jascha, Toscha, Sascha" (1971, vocal & piano Bobby Short). (Penzance PR-43)

GERSHWIN, GEORGE "Memorial Album to George Gershwin" Rec from the RCA Magic Key Gershwin Memorial Program of July 10, 1938. COND: Nathaniel Shilkret. VOCALS: Jane Froman, Sonny Schuyler, Felix Knight, chorus. (78/Vic 12" album C-29. Incomplete: Camden 177, entitled "Music by George Gershwin & Victor Herbert," with additional material.)(LP-303)

GERSHWIN, GEORGE "The Gershwin Years" ORCH & COND: George Bassman. VOCALS: Richard Hayes, Paula Stewart, Lynn Roberts. (Dec DX-160. Excerpts: Dec 4468, entitled "Gershwin from Broadway to Hollywood.")

GERSHWIN, GEORGE "Gershwin on Broadway" Overtures to six Gershwin shows by the Buffalo Philharmonic cond by Michael Tilson Thomas. (Col M-34542)

GERSHWIN, GEORGE "Gershwin Rarities, Vol 1" 1953 album. VOCALS: Kaye Ballard, David Craig, Betty Gillett. (Walden 302)

GERSHWIN, GEORGE "Gershwin Rarities, Vol. 2" 1953 album. VOCALS: Louise Carlyle, Warren Galjour. (Walden 303)

GERSHWIN, GEORGE "The Music of George Gershwin" From piano rolls, incl "Facinating Rhythm" played by Victor Arden (of orig prod). (Biograph 1022)(LP-621)

GERSHWIN, GEORGE "Gershwin Specials" VOCALS: George Byron. PIANO: Bobby Tucker. (78/General album 14)

GERSHWIN, GEORGE "Rediscovered Gershwin" VOCALS: George Byron. PIANO: Dick Hyman. (Atlantic 10" 410)

GERSHWIN, GEORGE "George Gershwin Revisited" ORCH &

COND: Norman Paris. VOCALS: Barbara Cook, Bobby Short, Elaine Stritch, Anthony Perkins. (MGM 4375)

GERSHWIN, GEORGE & IRA "Gershwin by Gershwin" (Mark 56 Records 641)(LP-286)

GERSHWIN, GEORGE & IRA "The Gershwins in Hollywood, 1931-1964" Mostly soundtrack recordings. (JJA Records 19773)(LP-654)

GERSHWIN, GEORGE & IRA "Frances Gershwin: For George and Ira" VOCALS: Frances Gershwin. PIANO: Alfred Simon & Jack Easton. (Monmouth 7060)

GERSHWIN, GEORGE & IRA "Gershwin Rarities" Excerpts from the 1952/3 Walden albums 300, 302, & 303. VOCALS: Kaye Ballard, David Craig, Nancy Walker, Louise Carlyle, Warren Galjour, Betty Gillett. (Citadel 7017)

GERSHWIN, IRA "Kurt Weill and Ira Gershwin: Tryout" PIANO: Kurt Weill. VOCALS: Ira Gershwin, Kurt Weill. (Heritage 0051)(LP-150)

GERSHWIN, IRA "Ira Gershwin Loves to Rhyme" WORDS: Ira Gershwin. MUSIC & PIANO: Kurt Weill, Harold Arlen, Burton Lane. VOCALS: Ira Gershwin, Burton Lane, Kurt Weill, Harold Arlen. (Mark 56 Records 721)(LP-417)

GERSHWIN, IRA "Lyrics by Ira Gershwin" 1952 album. VOCALS: Nancy Walker, Louise Carlyle, David Craig. (Walden 300)

GERSHWIN, IRA "Ira Gershwin Revisited" ORCH & COND: Dick Hyman. VOCALS: Blossom Dearie, Mary McCarty, Danny Meehan, Charles Rydell, Ethel Shutta, Margaret Whiting. (Painted Smiles 1353)

GINGOLD, HERMIONE "La Gingold" (Dolphin 7) (LP-314)

GRABLE, BETTY "Betty Grable" Film & TV soundtracks. (Curtain Calls 100/5) (LP-284)

GRABLE, BETTY "Betty Grable" Soundtracks & radio performances. (Star-Tone 219)(LP-646)

GRAYSON, KATHRYN "Kathryn Grayson Sings" (MGM 3257) (LP-364)

GRAYSON, KATHRYN "Kathryn Grayson: Make Believe" (Azel 101)(LP-346)

GRAYSON, KATHRYN "Kathryn Grayson: Let There Be Music" (Azel 102)(LP-347)

GRAYSON, KATHRYN "Kathryn Grayson: Opera and Song" (Azel 103)(LP-636)

GRAYSON, KATHRYN "Kathryn Grayson & Mario Lanza: Love Is Music" (Azel 104)(LP-665)

GREEN, ADOLPH See 570007b Film "It's Always Fair Weather"

GREEN, ADOLPH See 581223 "A Party with Betty Comden and Adolph Green"

GREEN, ADOLPH See artist album listing for "The Revuers"

GREEN, ADOLPH "Comden and Green: Show Music at Its Best, Vol. 1" 1955 album. Vocals, with Betty Comden, of songs they wrote lyrics for. (Heritage 0057)(LP-359)

GREEN, ADOLPH "Betty Comden and Adolph Green" (JJA Records 19764)(LP-508)

GRENFELL, JOYCE See 540602 "Joyce Grenfell Requests the Pleasure of Your Company"

GRENFELL, JOYCE "Joyce Grenfell" 1964 album. (HMV(E) CLP-1810)(LP-747)

GREY, JOEL "Joel Grey -- Live!" Rec live in 1973 at the Waldorf Astoria Hotel, New York. ORCH: Peter Matz, Billy Byers, Alan Copeland. COND: Everett Gordon. (Col KC-32252)(LP-440)

HALE, BINNIE "Binnie Hale: Spread a Little Happiness" (World Record Club(E) SH-129)(LP-79)

HALL, ADELAIDE "That Wonderful Adelaide Hall" Rec 1970. (Monmouth 7080)(LP-484)

HAMMERSTEIN, OSCAR, II "Oscar Hammerstein Revisited" ORCH & COND: Norman Paris. VOCALS: Gloria Swanson, Blossom Dearie, Cab Calloway, Patrice Munsel, Elaine

Stritch, E Y Harburg, Dorothy Loudon, Alfred Drake. (Painted Smiles 1365)
HARBURG, E Y "E Y Harburg Revisited" MUSIC: Burton Lane, Harold Arlen, Dana Suesse, Sammy Fain, Vernon Duke, Phil Springer. ORCH: Dennis Deal, Albert Evans. PIANO: Phil Springer. VOCALS: Helen Gallagher, Carleton Carpenter, Arthur Siegel, Nancy Grennan, John Hillner, E Y Harburg, Tammy Grimes, Patrice Munsel, Blossom Dearie. (Painted Smiles 1372)(LP-741)
HARNICK, SHELDON "An Evening with Sheldon Harnick" Rec live 14 February 1971. MUSIC: Jerry Bock, Sheldon Harnick. WORDS: Sheldon Harnick. PIANO: Richard Leonard. VOCALS: Sheldon Harnick, Margery Gray, Mary Louise. (Laureate 603)(LP-535)
HAYMES, DICK "The Best of Dick Haymes" (MCA(E) MCFM-2720)(LP-397)
HAYMES, DICK "Dick Haymes: Serenade" (Dec 10" 5341) (LP-400)
HAYMES, DICK "Dick Haymes: The Fabulous Forties" Reissues from V-Discs. (Standing Room Only 1001) (LP-386)
HAYMES, DICK "Haymes in Hollywood, Volume One" (Vedette 8701)(LP-299)
HAYWARD, SUSAN "Susan Hayward" Soundtrack material from films "With a Song in My Heart," "I'll Cry Tomorrow," & "Smash-up." VOCALS: Susan Hayward, Jane Froman, Peg LaCentra. (Legends 1000/3)(LP-495)
HAYWORTH, RITA "Rita Hayworth" (Curtain Calls 100/22) (LP-403)
HENDERSON, RAY "DeSylva, Brown & Henderson Revisited" ORCH & COND: Norman Paris. VOCALS: Cab Calloway, Blossom Dearie, Gloria DeHaven, Dorothy Loudon, Charles Rydell. (Painted Smiles 1351)
HERBERT, VICTOR "The Early Victor Herbert" From the Gay Nineties to the First World War. Reissues of early recordings. (Smithsonian R-017)(LP-628)
HERBERT, VICTOR "Victor Herbert & His Orchestra" From 1909/10 cylinders. (Mark 56 Records 795)(LP-629)
HERBERT, VICTOR "The Operetta World of Victor Herbert (1895-1924)" (JJA Records 1980-5)(LP-767)
HERBERT, VICTOR "The Music of Victor Herbert, Volume 1" COND: Nathaniel Shilkret. Victor Light Opera Company. Rec c. 1930. (78/Vic 12" album C-1)(LP-304)
HERBERT, VICTOR "The Music of Victor Herbert, Volume 2" COND: Nathaniel Shilkret. Victor Salon Group & Victor Salon Orch. Rec 1931. (78/Vic 12" album C-11)(LP-777)
HERBERT, VICTOR "Victor Herbert Melodies, Volume 1" COND: Nathaniel Shilkret. VOCALS: Anne Jamison, Thomas L Thomas, Jan Peerce, Gladys Rice, chorus. Rec 1938. (78/Vic 12" album C-33. Incomplete: Camden 177, entitled "Music by George Gershwin & Victor Herbert," with additional material.)(LP-305)
HERMAN, JERRY "Hello, Jerry: Jerry Herman and His Orchestra" ORCH: Leroy Holmes. 1965 album. (United Artists 3432)(LP-140)
HERMAN, JERRY "An Evening with Jerry Herman" Rec live 24 November 1974. MUSIC & WORDS: Jerry Herman. PIANO: Jerry Herman. VOCALS: Jerry Herman, Lisa Kirk, Joe Masiell, Carol Dorian. (Laureate 606)(LP-660)
HINES, MIMI "Mimi Hines Sings" COND: Richard Marx. (Dec 4709)(LP-709)
HINES, MIMI "Mimi Hines Is a Happening" COND: Phil Ford. (Dec 74834)(LP-708)
HOLM, CELESTE See 430331x "Oklahoma!"
HOLMAN, LIBBY See 541004 "Libby Holman's 'Blues, Ballads, and Sin-Songs'"
HOLMAN, LIBBY See anthology "The Original Torch Singers"

HOLMAN, LIBBY "Libby Holman Sings" COND: Gerald Cook. (MB Records 10" 101)(LP-662)
HOLMAN, LIBBY "The Legendary Libby Holman" (Monmouth 6501)(LP-51)
HORNE, LENA "Lena Horne: Moanin' Low" Rec 1941. (78/Vic album P-118)(LP-241)
HORNE, LENA "Lena and Michel" ORCH, COND, & PIANO: Michel Legrand. VOCALS: Lena Horne. Rec 1975. (RCA BGL1-1026)(LP-675)
HOWARD, JOE See 470020b Film "I Wonder Who's Kissing Her Now"
HOWARD, WILLIE "Willie Howard: A Gala Record Revue" 1942 album of comedy and songs. COND: Harley Dainger. (Gala 10" 104)(LP-630)
HOWES, BOBBY "Bobby Howes: She's My Lovely" (World Record Club(E) SH-136)(LP-83)
HULBERT, JACK "Cicely Courtneidge and Jack Hulbert" (World Record Club(E) SH-113)(LP-90)
HUSMANN, RON "Ron Husmann" COND: Arnold Goland. 1961 album. (Cap ST-1624)(LP-713)
HUTCHINSON, LESLIE "Hutch at the Piano" Reissues of 78s. (World Records(E) SHB-28)(LP-477)
HUTTON, BETTY "Hutton in Hollywood" (Vedette 8702) (LP-285)
IVES, BURL "Burl Ives: Burl's Broadway" ORCH & COND: Charles Albertine. (Dec 4876)(LP-573)
JABARA, PAUL "Paul Jabara: The Third Album" MUSIC & WORDS: mostly Paul Jabara. ORCH & COND: Greg Mathieson. VOCALS: Paul Jabara. Includes material from Rachael Lily Rosenbloom. 1979 album. (Casablanca NBLP-7163)(LP-683)
JASON, SYBIL "Sybil Jason: Children's Songs" (78/Dec album K-11)(LP-487)
JEAN, GLORIA "Gloria Jean Souvenir Album" Rec 1939. (78/Dec 12" album 125)(LP-234)
JESSEL, GEORGE "George Jessel: Songs My Pals Sang" (Audio Fidelity AFSD-1708), packaged with "The Actual Voices of My Pals" (45/Audio Fidelity 45-708)(LP-38).
JOLSON, AL "Al Jolson: California, Here I Come" Reissues of 78's from 1911 to 1929. (Sunbeam P-505)(LP-626)
JOLSON, AL "Al Jolson: The Early Years" (Olympic 7114) (LP-290)
JOLSON, AL "Broadway Al" Reissues of early Columbia records. (Totem 1010)(LP-288)
JOLSON, AL "Al Jolson: Steppin' Out" Reissues of 78's. (Sunbeam P-503)(LP-550)
JOLSON, AL "A Tribute to Al Jolson" Re-issues of early Jolson records. Narrated by Chamberlain Brown. (Audio Rarities 2285)(LP-470)
JOLSON, AL "Jolson & Cantor: The Immortals" Reissues of 78s. (Epic 10" LN-1128)(LP-721)
JOLSON, AL "Al Jolson: Sitting on Top of the World" Reissues of 78s from 1924 to 1931. (Vocalion(E) VLP-3) (LP-731)
JOLSON, AL "The Vintage Jolson" Reissues of 78's from 1924 to 1932. (Pelican 111)(LP-274)
JOLSON, AL "Al Jolson: Let Me Sing and I'm Happy" (Ace of Hearts(E) 33)(LP-82)
JOLSON, AL "Al Jolson: Say It with Songs" (Ace of Hearts(E) 87)(LP-73)
JOLSON, AL "Al Jolson: The Vitaphone Years" (A-Jay Records 3749)(LP-269)
JOLSON, AL "Al Jolson" 1935/6(?) radio performances. (Epitaph 4008)(LP-373)
JOLSON, AL "Al Jolson in Songs He Made Famous" Rec 1945/6. (Dec 10" 5026)(LP-145)
JOLSON, AL "Al Jolson Souvenir Album" Rec 1947. (Dec 10" 5029)(LP-198)

JOLSON, AL "Al Jolson, Volume Three" Rec 1947. (Dec 10"
5030)(LP-196)
JOLSON, AL "Al Jolson, Souvenir Album, Vol. 4" Rec 1946/7.
(Dec 10" 5031)(LP-228)
JOLSON, AL "Jolson Sings Again" Rec 1949. (Dec 10" 5006)(LP-
197)
JOLSON, AL "Al Jolson: Stephen Foster Songs" Rec 1950. (Dec
10" 5303)(LP-382)
JOLSON, AL "Al Jolson Souvenir Album, Vol. 5" Rec 1949/50.
(Dec 10" 5314)(LP-380)
JOLSON, AL "Al Jolson Souvenir Album, Vol. 6" Rec 1947/50.
(Dec 10" 5315)(LP-381)
JOLSON, AL "Al Jolson and Bing Crosby" Also with the
Andrews Sisters & the Mills Brothers. Rec 1947/50. (Dec 10"
5316)(LP-383)
JOLSON, AL "Al Jolson: You Made Me Love You" (Dec
79034)(LP-245)
JOLSON, AL "Al Jolson: Rock-a-bye Your Baby" (Dec 79035)(LP-
244)
JOLSON, AL "Al Jolson: Rainbow 'round My Shoulder" (Dec
79036)(LP-243)
JOLSON, AL "Al Jolson: You Ain't Heard Nothin' Yet" (Dec
79037)(LP-246)
JOLSON, AL "Al Jolson: Memories" (Dec 79038)(LP-372)
JOLSON, AL "Al Jolson: Among My Souvenirs" Radio
performances. COND: Lou Bring. (Dec 79050)(LP-370)
JOLSON, AL "The Immortal Al Jolson" Selections originally
recorded for the Kraft Music Hall broadcasts. COND: Lou
Bring. Rec 1947, (Dec 79063)(LP-331)
JOLSON, AL "Al Jolson Overseas" (Dec 9070)(LP-280)
JOLSON, AL "Al Jolson: The World's Greatest Entertainer"
COND: Lou Bring. Selections originally recorded in 1947
for the Kraft Music Hall broadcasts. (Dec 9074)(LP-409)
JOLSON, AL "Al Jolson with Oscar Levant at the Piano"
Selections originally recorded in 1947 for Kraft Music Hall
broadcasts. (Dec 9095)(LP-478)
JOLSON, AL "The Greatest of Al Jolson" Reissues of his Decca
records. (Tele House CD-2036)(LP-739)
JONES, ALLAN "Allan Jones: The Donkey Serenade" (Camden
2256)(LP-126)
JONES, ALLAN "Allan Jones: Falling in Love" COND: Robert
Armbruster. 1951 album. (RCA 10" LM-95)(LP-388)
JONES, ALLAN "Allan Jones Sings for a Man and a Woman"
1966 album. (Scepter SPS-566)(LP-586)
JONES, ALLAN "Cole Porter: Night and Day" COND: Ray
Sinatra. VOCALS: Allan Jones. (RCA LM-1140)
KANDER, JOHN "An Evening with Fred Ebb and John Kander"
Rec live 8 & 10 April 1973. MUSIC: John Kander. WORDS:
Fred Ebb. PIANO: John Kander. VOCALS: Fred Ebb, John
Kander. (Laureate 605)(LP-659)
KANE, HELEN See anthology "Three of a Kind"
KAYE, DANNY See 530118 "Danny Kaye's International Show"
KAYE, DANNY "The Best of Danny Kaye" (Dec DXB-175) (LP-6)
KAYE, DANNY "Danny Kaye" (Dec 10" 5033)(LP-55)
KAYE, DANNY "Danny Kaye" 1942 album. (Col 10" CL-6023) (LP-
70)
KAYE, DANNY "Danny Kaye Entertains" Includes all of his
records from Lady in the Dark. (Col 10" CL-6249)(LP-527)
KAYE, DANNY "The Best of Danny Kaye" (Harmony 7314) (LP-
107)
KAYE, DANNY "Danny Kaye -- Presented by Your Rambler
Dealer" (Dena Pictures mx XTV-92557/8)(LP-92)
KELLY, GENE "Gene Kelly: Song and Dance Man" His
interpretations (rec 1947) of George M Cohan, George
Primrose, Pat Rooney, Fred Astaire, Eddie Leonard, & Bill
Robinson, with additional Kelly songs. (Stet DS-15010; LP-
598. The 1947 interpretations only: MGM 10" 30.)

KELLY, GENE "The Special Magic of Gene Kelly" Soundtrack
recordings. (MGM(E) 2353-120)(LP-501)
KELLY, GENE "Gene Kelly: Singin' in the Rain Again" ORCH &
COND: Pete Moore. Rec 1977. (Dec(E) SKL-5265)(LP-749)
KERN, JEROME "Jerome Kern in London, 1914-1923" (World
Records(E) SHB-34)(LP-430)
KERN, JEROME "Jerome Kern in London" (World Record
Club(E) SH-171)(LP-173)
KERN, JEROME "Jerome Kern in Hollywood: 1934-38"
Soundtrack recordings. (JJA Records 19747)(LP-335)
KERN, JEROME "Jerome Kern in Hollywood, Volume 2" Reissue
of 78's. (JJA Records 19784)(LP-607)
KERN, JEROME "Jerome Kern Gems" From early 78's. (JJA
Records 19781)(LP-606)
KERN, JEROME "The Theatre Lyrics of P. G. Wodehouse"
MUSIC: mostly Jerome Kern. Reissues of early 78s.
(Folkways RFS-601)(LP-784)
KERN, JEROME "The Melodies of Jerome Kern, Vol. 1" ORCH &
COND: John Morris. VOCALS: June Ericson, Warren
Galjour, Jay Harnick. 1955 album. (Walden 308)
KERN, JEROME "The Melodies of Jerome Kern, Vol. 2" ORCH &
COND: Ben Ludlow. VOCALS: David Daniels, Christina
Lind. 1955 album. (Walden 309)
KERN, JEROME "Gems from Jerome Kern Musical Shows"
ORCH: Leonard Joy, Sydney Green. COND: Leonard Joy.
VOCALS: Dorothy Chapman, Marie Louise Quevli, Felix
Knight, Alan Holt. 1938 album. (78/Vic 12" album C-31) (LP-
306)
KERN, JEROME "Irene Dunne in Songs by Jerome Kern" (78/
Dec album 484)(LP-66)
KERN, JEROME "Jerome Kern: All the Things You Are"
VOCALS: Reid Shelton, Susan Watson, Danny Carroll.
(Monmouth 6808)
KERN, JEROME "Jerome Kern Favorites" VOCALS: George
Byron. PIANO: Bobby Tucker. (78/General album 19)
KERN, JEROME "Jerome Kern Songs, Personally Selected (by
Kern) for George Byron" 1952 album. VOCALS: George
Byron. PIANO: William Roy. (Atlantic 10" 409)
KERN, JEROME "Premiere Performance: George Byron Sings
New and Rediscovered Jerome Kern Songs" ORCH,
COND, PIANO: Andre Previn. 1958 album. (Atlantic 1293)
KERN, JEROME "Jerome Kern Revisisted" ORCH & COND:
Norman Paris. PIANO: Judd Woldin. VOCALS: Nancy
Andrews, Barbara Cook, Harold Lang, Bobby Short, Cy
Young, George Reinholt. (Painted Smiles 1363. Incomplete:
Col OS-2840.)
KERT, LARRY "Larry Kert Sings Leonard Bernstein" ORCH &
COND: Richard Wess. 1959 album. (Seeco 4670)(LP-616)
KIRK, LISA "Lisa Kirk Sings at the Plaza" COND: Don Pippin.
Rec live in 1958. (MGM 3737)(LP-667)
KITT, EARTHA "RCA Victor Presents Eartha Kitt" (RCA 10" LPM-
3062)(LP-685)
KITT, EARTHA "Eartha for Always" (Stanyan 10040)(LP-441)
KORJUS, MILIZA "The Voice of Miliza Korjus" (Camden 279)
(LP-528)
KORJUS, MILIZA "Miliza Korjus: Vienna in 3/4 Time" (Camden
427)(LP-529)
LAHR, BERT "Bert Lahr on Stage, Screen and Radio" (JJA
Records 19765)(LP-608)
LAMOUR, DOROTHY "Dorothy Lamour" (Legends 1000/4)(LP-
647)
LAMOUR, DOROTHY "Dorothy Lamour" (West Coast 14002)
(LP-271)
LAMOUR, DOROTHY "Dorothy Lamour: The Road to
Romance" COND: Henry Russell. (Design 45)(LP-737)
LANGFORD, FRANCES "Frances Langford Souvenir Album"
1940 album. (78/Dec album 87)(LP-135)

197

LANZA, MARIO "Kathryn Grayson & Mario Lanza: Love Is Music" (Azel 104)(LP-665)
LAUREL & HARDY "Laurel & Hardy" Soundtracks. (Mark56 Records 575)(LP-698)
LAUREL & HARDY "Laurel & Hardy: Another Fine Mess" Soundtrack material. (United Artists(E) UAG-30010)(LP-695)
LAWRENCE, CAROL "Carol Lawrence: Tonight at 8:30" ORCH & COND: Peter Matz. (Chancellor 5015)(LP-356)
LAWRENCE, GERTRUDE "Gertrude Lawrence" (Monmouth 7043)(LP-276)
LAWRENCE, GERTRUDE "The Star Gertrude Lawrence" (Audio Fidelity 709)(LP-34)
LAWRENCE, GERTRUDE "Gertrude Lawrence: The Star Herself" (Music for Pleasure(E) 1245)(LP-29)
LAWRENCE, GERTURDE "Noel Coward & Gertrude Lawrence: We Were Dancing" (Monmouth 7042)(LP-275)
LAWRENCE, GERTRUDE "Noel and Gertie" (RCA LCT-1156; Odeon(E) PCLP-1050)(LP-28)
LAWRENCE, GERTRUDE "Noel and Gertie and Bea" (Parlophone(E) PMC-7135)(LP-123)
LAWRENCE, GERTRUDE "Gertrude Lawrence Souvenir Album" Rec 1952. COND: Jay Blackton. (Dec 10" 5418; reissued, with 3 additional songs not from her shows, as "Gertrude Lawrence: A Remembrance" on Dec 8673 and as "Gertrude Lawrence: A Bright, Particular Star" on Dec 74940.)(LP-5)
LAYE, EVELYN "The Entrancing Evelyn Laye" (Music for Pleasure(E) 1162)(LP-63)
LEE, GYPSY ROSE "Gypsy Rose Lee Remembers Burlesque" MUSIC: Bobby Kroll. WORDS: Eli Basse. ORCH: Bobby Kroll. 1962 album. CAST: Gypsy Rose Lee, others uncredited. (StereOddities CG-1)
LEE, MICHELE "Michele Lee: A Taste of the Fantastic" ORCH & COND: Ray Ellis. 1966 album. (Col CS-9286)(LP-672)
LEGRAND, MICHEL "Lena and Michel" ORCH, COND, & PIANO: Michel Legrand. VOCALS: Lena Horne. Rec 1975. (RCA BGL1-1026)(LP-675)
LERNER, ALAN JAY "Lyrics by Lerner" 1955 album. MUSIC: Kurt Weill, Frederick Loewe. WORDS: Alan Jay Lerner. ORCH & PIANO: Billy Taylor. COND: Herb Harris. VOCALS: Alan Jay Lerner (lyricist), Kaye Ballard, quartet. (Heritage 0600)(LP-343)
LERNER, ALAN JAY "An Evening with Alan Jay Lerner" Rec live 12 December 1971. MUSIC: Frederick Loewe, Burton Lane. WORDS: Alan Jay Lerner. PIANO: Richard Leonard. VOCALS: Alan Jay Lerner, Bobbi Baird, J T Cromwell, Barbara Williams. (Laureate 602)(LP-534)
LERNER, ALAN JAY "Alan Jay Lerner Revisited" ORCH & COND: Norman Paris. VOCALS: Blossom Dearie, Dorothy Loudon, Roddy McDowell, Jerry Orbach, Nancy Walker. (Crewe 1337)
LEWIS, TED "Ted Lewis and His Orchestra" Reissues of earlier records. (78/Dec album 353)(LP-491)
LEWIS, TED "Ted Lewis, Volume 2" Reissues of earlier records. (Dec 10" 5233)(LP-686)
LEWIS, TED "Ted Lewis: The Medicine Man for the Blues" (Dec 8322)(LP-167)
LEWIS, TED "The Best of Ted Lewis" (MCA Records 2-4101) (LP-457)
LEWIS, TED "Ted Lewis: Is Everybody Happy?" Reissues of earlier records. (78/Col album C-69)(LP-168)
LILLIE, BEATRICE See 521002 "An Evening with Beatrice Lillie"
LILLIE, BEATRICE "Beatrice Lillie Sings" (JJC Records 3003)(LP-112)
LILLIE, BEATRICE "Thirty Minutes with Beatrice Lillie" (Liberty Music Shops 10" 1002)(LP-121)
LILLIE, BEATRICE "A Marvelous Party with Beatrice Lillie" Reissues of 1930s records. (AEI Records 2103)(LP-729)

LILLIE, BEATRICE "Noel and Gertie and Bea" (Parlophone(E) PMC-7135)(LP-123)
LOESSER, FRANK "Frank Loesser in Hollywood, 1937-1955" MUSIC: Frank Loesser, others. WORDS: Frank Loesser. Mostly soundtrack recordings. (JJA Records 19762)(LP-656)
LOESSER, FRANK "Frank Loesser Revisited" ORCH: Dick Hyman. VOCALS: Gloria Swanson, Rhonda Fleming, Johnny Desmond, Madeline Kahn, Bibi Osterwald, Margaret Whiting, Blossom Dearie. (Painted Smiles 1359)
LOGAN, JOSHUA See 750502 "A Gala Tribute to Joshua Logan"
LYNN, DIANA "Diana Lynn: Piano Portraits" PIANO: Diana Lynn. COND: Paul Weston. Rec 1945. (78/Cap album CC-38) (LP-742)
MacDONALD, JEANETTE "Jeanette MacDonald and Nelson Eddy" (RCA LPV-526)(LP-4)
MacDONALD, JEANETTE "Jeanette MacDonald & Nelson Eddy: Operetta Favorites" 1935/6 recordings. (RCA 10" LCT-16) (LP-462)
MacDONALD, JEANETTE "Jeanette MacDonald & Nelson Eddy: Movie Memories" (45/RCA EPA-5113)(LP-242)
MacDONALD, JEANETTE "Jeanette MacDonald in Song" 1939 album. COND: Giuseppe Bamboschek. (78/Vic album M-642) (LP-137)
MacDONALD, JEANETTE "Jeanette MacDonald Sings San Francisco and Other Silver Screen Favorites" (Victrola 1515)(LP-77)
MacDONALD, JEANETTE "Jeanette MacDonald: Opera and Operetta Favorites" (RCA LM-2908)(LP-249)
MacDONALD, JEANETTE "Jeanette MacDonald's Operetta Favorites" 1946 album. COND: Russ Case. (45/RCA album WMO-1071)(LP-210)
MacDONALD, JEANETTE "Romantic Melodies by Jeanette MacDonald" 1947 album. COND: Robert Armbruster. (78/Vic album MO-1217)(LP-65)
MacDONALD, JEANETTE "Jeanette MacDonald: Romantic Moments" 1950 album. COND: Robert Russell Bennett. (RCA 10" LM-62)(LP-119)
MacDONALD, JEANETTE "Jeanette MacDonald: Smilin' Through" (Camden 325)(LP-71)
MacDONALD, JEANETTE "Jeanette MacDonald & Nelson Eddy: Favorites in Hi-Fi" 1958 album. (RCA LPM-1738)(LP-134)
MacDONALD, JEANETTE "Jeanette MacDonald: A Tribute to Jeanette" (OASI Records 594)(LP-536)
MacLAINE, SHIRLEY See 760419 "Shirley MacLaine"
MARTIN, HUGH "Martin & Blane Sing Martin & Blane" COND: Ralph Burns. 1956 album. (Harlequin 701)(LP-193)
MARTIN, HUGH "Three by Hugh Martin" (JJA Records 19743) (LP-287)
MARTIN, MARY See 551022 TV show "Together with Music"
MARTIN, MARY See 770515 "Together on Broadway"
MARTIN, MARY "Mary Martin in an Album of Cole Porter Songs" 1940 album. COND: Ray Sinatra. (78/Dec album 123)(LP-67)
MARTIN, MARY "Mary Martin Sings, Richard Rodgers Plays" MUSIC: Richard Rodgers. ORCH: Robert Russell Bennett. COND: John Lesko. (RCA LPM-1539)
MARTIN, TONY "Tony Martin" Reissues of 78's from 1939-1942. (Vocalion VL-3610)(LP-612)
MARTIN, TONY "Tony Martin Live at Carnegie Hall" Rec live in 1965. (Movietone MTS-2007)(LP-446)
MARTINI, NINO "Nino Martini in Opera and Song" (OASI Records 550)(LP-366)
MARX, GROUCHO "Groucho Marx: Hooray for Captain Spaulding" With other Kalmar-Ruby songs. (Dec 10" 5405)(LP-341)
MATTHEWS, JESSIE "Jessie Matthews: Over My Shoulder" (Dec(E) ECM-2168)(LP-320)

MATTHEWS, JESSIE "The Original Recordings of Jessie Matthews" (Music for Pleasure)(E) 1127)(LP-64)

MATTHEWS, JESSIE "Jack Buchanan & Jessie Matthews" (Ace of Clubs(E) 1140)(LP-31)

MATTHEWS, JESSIE "Jack Whiting & Jessie Matthews" (Monmouth 7049)(LP-156)

MELCHIOR, LAURITZ "The Lighter Side of Lauritz Melchior" (Camden 424)(LP-291)

MERCER, JOHNNY "Mercer Sings Mercer" Reissues. (Cap M-11637)(LP-559)

MERCER, JOHNNY "Johnny Mercer Sings Johnny Mercer" Reissues of 78s. (Cap(E) OU-2081)(LP-720)

MERCER, JOHNNY "Johnny Mercer Sings" Includes 10 songs from Foxy. (JJA Records 19775)(LP-604)

MERCER, JOHNNY "An Evening with Johnny Mercer" Rec live 14 March 1971. MUSIC: Various. WORDS: Johnny Mercer. PIANO: Richard Leonard. VOCALS: Johnny Mercer, Margaret Whiting, Robert Sands. (Laureate 601)(LP-533)

MERCER, JOHNNY "Johnny Mercer Sings the Songs of Johnny Mercer" ORCH & COND: Pete Moore. 1974 album. (Pye(E) NSPL-18432)(LP-560)

MERMAN, ETHEL See 770515 "Together on Broadway"

MERMAN, ETHEL "Ethel Merman and Gertrude Niesen: On Stage, Volume 1" (RCA "X" LVA-1004)(LP-171)

MERMAN, ETHEL "Ethel Merman (1932-1935), Lyda Roberti (1934), Mae West (1933)" (Col CL-2751)(LP-40)

MERMAN, ETHEL "Ethel Merman Sings Cole Porter" (JJC Records 3004)(LP-3)

MERMAN, ETHEL "Lee Wiley and Ethel Merman: Two Classic Interpretations of the Immortal Cole Porter" (JJC Records 2003)(LP-93)

MERMAN, ETHEL "Merman in the Movies: 1930-38" Soundtrack recordings. (Encore 101)(LP-334)

MERMAN, ETHEL "Ethel Merman: Songs She Has Made Famous" Rec 1947. (Dec 10" 5053)(LP-68)

MERMAN, ETHEL "Ethel Merman: A Musical Autobiography" Issued c. 1955. (Dec DX-153)(LP-36)

MERMAN, ETHEL "Merman: Her Greatest!" ORCH & COND: Billy May. 1961 album. (Reprise 6032; Stanyan 10070, entitled "Ms. Ethel Merman - Her Greatest Hits.") (LP-45)

MERMAN, ETHEL "Merman in Vegas" Rec live. Show opened Oct 25, 1962. ORCH: Billy May. COND: Russ Black. (Reprise 9-6062)(LP-251)

MERMAN, ETHEL "Merman Sings Merman" 1972 record. COND: Stanley Black. (London(E) XPS-901)(LP-153)

MERMAN, ETHEL "The Ethel Merman Disco Album" ORCH & COND: Peter Matz. 1979 album. (A&M Records SP-4775) (LP-670)

MILLAR, GERTIE "Gertie Millar" (World Record Club(E) SH-186)(LP-227)

MINNELLI, LIZA See 720910 TV Show "Liza with a Z"

MINNELLI, LIZA See 740106 "Liza"

MINNELLI, LIZA "Judy Garland & Liza Minnelli: 'Live' at the London Palladium" Rec Nov 8, 1964. (Cap ST-11191)(LP-205)

MINNELLI, LIZA "Liza Minnelli Live at the Olympia in Paris" Rec 1972. (A&M Records SP-4345)(LP-368)

MIRANDA, CARMEN "Carmen Miranda: The South American Way" Six songs, all of them from "Streets of Paris." Rec 1939. (78/Dec album 109)(LP-220)

MIRANDA, CARMEN "Carmen Miranda: A Night in Rio" (78/ Dec album 210)(LP-199)

MIRANDA, CARMEN "Carmen Miranda Souvenir Album" (78/ Dec album 545)(LP-302)

MIRANDA, CARMEN "Carmen Miranda, Vol. 1" (45/Dec ED-2066)(LP-147)

MIRANDA, CARMEN "Carmen Miranda: South American Way" Reissues of 78's. (MCA Coral(E) CDLM-8029)(LP-522)

MIRANDA, CARMEN "Carmen Miranda: The Brazilian Bombshell" (Ace of Hearts(E) 99)(LP-166)

MONROE, MARILYN "Marilyn Monroe" (Ascot 13008)(LP-120)

MONROE, MARILYN "Marilyn Monroe" (Legends 1000/1) (LP-452)

MONROE, MARILYN "Marilyn Monroe: Never Before and Never Again" Includes Gentlemen Prefer Blondes soundtrack. (Stet DS-15005)(LP-599)

MONROE, MARILYN "Marilyn Monroe: There's No Business like Show Business" (45/RCA EPA-593)(LP-609)

MONROE, MARILYN "Marilyn Monroe: la voce, le musiche e i films" (RCA(I) TPL1-7025)(LP-451)

MONROE, MARILYN "The Unforgettable Marilyn Monroe" (Movietone 72016)(LP-76)

MOORE, GRACE "Grace Moore Souvenir Album" (78/Dec 12" album 165)(LP-235)

MOORE, GRACE "Grace Moore Sings" (Dec 9593)(LP-247)

MOORE, GRACE "Grace Moore in Opera and Song" Reissues of 78's. (RCA 10" LCT-7004)(LP-526)

MOORE, GRACE "The Art of Grace Moore" (Camden 519)(LP-443)

MOORE, GRACE "Grace Moore" (Empire 801)(LP-231)

MORGAN, HELEN See anthology "The Original Torch Singers"

MORGAN, HELEN "Helen Morgan" (78/Vic album P-102) (LP-229)

MORGAN, HELEN "Helen Morgan Sings" (Audio Rarities LPA-2330)(LP-37)

MORGAN, HELEN "Torch Songs by Helen Morgan & Fanny Brice" (RCA "X" LVA-1006)(LP-230)

MORGAN, HELEN "Fanny Brice & Helen Morgan" (RCA LPV-561)(LP-32)

MORGAN, HELEN "Helen Morgan & Nelson Eddy: The Torch Singer and the Mountie" (Trisklog 4)(LP-499)

MORSE, ROBERT "A Jolly Theatrical Season" ORCH & COND: Elliot Lawrence. VOCALS: Robert Morse, Charles Nelson Reilly. 1963 album. (Cap T-1862)

NEGRI, POLA "Pola Negri" Reissues of 78's. (Discophilia(G) UG-N-1)(LP-625)

NIESEN, GERTRUDE "Ethel Merman and Gertrude Niesen: On Stage, Volume 1" (RCA "X" LVA-1004)(LP-171)

NIESEN, GERTRUDE "Gertrude Niesen Souvenir Album" (Dec 10" 5138)(LP-53)

NIESEN, GERTRUDE "Gertrude Niesen, Vol. 1" (45/Dec ED-2045)(LP-146)

NOVELLO, IVOR "Ivor Novello: The Great Shows" (World Records(E) SHB-23)(LP-309)

NOVELLO, IVOR "Ivor Novello" Original cast recordings of Crest of the Wave, Arc de Triomphe, Gay's the Word. (World Records(E) SH-216)(LP-342)

NOVELLO, IVOR "The Famed Songs of Noel Coward and Ivor Novello" COND: John Gregory. VOCALS: John Hanson, Doreen Hume, Dick Bentley, Jean Campbell, Vanessa Lee, Bruce Trent. (Dot 3047)(LP-444)

NOVELLO, IVOR "Ivor Novello: His Greatest Songs" 1959 album. ORCH: Brian Fahey, Ray Terry. COND: Michael Collins. VOCALS: Vanessa Lee, Julie Bryan, Marion Grimaldi, Ivor Emmanuel. (HMV(E) CLP-1258)

OLSEN, GEORGE "George Olsen and His Music" (RCA LPV-549)(LP-282)

ORBACH, JERRY "Jerry Orbach Off Broadway" ORCH & COND: Norman Paris. Rec 1962. (MGM 4056)(LP-420)

PAYNE, FREDA "Freda Payne: Hot" 1979 album. (Cap ST-12003)(LP-684)

PORTER, COLE See 651007 TV show "Cole Porter: A Remembrance"

PORTER, COLE "Harold Arlen and Cole Porter: Composers at Play" (RCA "X" LVA-1003)(LP-340)

PORTER, COLE "Cole" (Col KS-31456)(LP-160)

PORTER, COLE "Ethel Merman Sings Cole Porter" (JJC Records 3004)(LP-3)

PORTER, COLE "Lee Wiley & Ethel Merman: Two Classic Interpretations of the Immortal Cole Porter" (JJC Records 2003)(LP-93)

PORTER, COLE "Cole Porter in London" (World Records(E) SHB-26)(LP-300)

PORTER, COLE "Cole Porter 1924-1944" (JJA Records 19732)(LP-182)

PORTER, COLE "Cole Porter in Hollywood, 1929-1956" Mostly soundtrack recordings. (JJA Records 19767)(LP-655)

PORTER, COLE "Cole Porter (Music & Lyrics)" (JJA Records 19745)(LP-295)

PORTER, COLE "Mary Martin in an Album of Cole Porter Songs" 1940 album. COND: Ray Sinatra. (78/Dec album 123)(LP-67)

PORTER, COLE "Cole Porter Songs" VOCALS: Louise Carlyle, Bob Shaver. 1953 album. (Walden 301)

PORTER, COLE "Cole" 1974 album. MUSIC & WORDS: Cole Porter. COND: Mike Sammes. CAST: Elaine Stritch, Patricia Routledge, Ian Carmichael, Susannah McCorkle, chorus. (EMI(E) EMC-3049)

PORTER, COLE "Cole Porter: Night and Day" COND: Ray Sinatra. VOCALS: Allan Jones. (RCA LM-1140)

PORTER, COLE "Cole Porter Revisited" ORCH & COND: Norman Paris. VOCALS: David Allen, Kaye Ballard, Ronny Graham, Bibi Osterwald, Bobby Short. (Recording Industries Corp 3002)

PORTER, COLE "Unpublished Cole Porter" ORCH & COND: Judd Woldin. VOCALS: Carmen Alvarez, Edward Earle, Laura Kenyon, Karen Morrow, Alice Playten, Charles Rydell, Kaye Ballard. (Painted Smiles 1358 -- 1977 edition)(LP-549)

PORTER, COLE "Cole Porter Revisited, Vol. III" ORCH: Dennis Deal. Arthur Siegel. COND: Dennis Deal. VOCALS: Georgia Engel, Helen Gallagher, Dolores Gray, Lynn Redgrave, Arthur Siegel, Elaine Stritch, Nancy Grennan, chorus. (Painted Smiles 1370)

PORTER, COLE "Cole Porter Revisited, Vol IV" ORCH: Dennis Deal. VOCALS: Dolores Gray, Katherine Hepburn, Helen Gallagher, Arthur Siegel, Blossom Dearie, Patrice Munsel. 1979 album. (Painted Smiles 1371)(LP-703)

POWELL, DICK "Dick Powell in Hollywood (1933-1935)" (Col C2L-44)(LP-2)

POWELL, DICK "Dick Powell Souvenir Album" 1947 album. COND: Victor Young. (78/Dec album 608)(LP-133)

POWELL, DICK "The Dick Powell Song Book" (Dec 8837) (LP-46)

POWELL, DICK "The Dick Powell Song Book" (Ace of Hearts(E) 50)(LP-86)

POWELL, JANE "Jane Powell: Something Wonderful" ORCH & COND: David Rose. Includes 6 songs from Rich, Young and Pretty. (MGM 3451)(LP-714)

POWELL, JANE "Jane Powell" (Curtain Calls 100/4)(LP-281)

PRESLEY, ELVIS "Elvis Presley: Got a Lot o' Livin' to Do" Soundtracks of Loving You & Jailhouse Rock, plus additional material. (Party Records 101)(LP-664)

PRINTEMPS, YVONNE "Selections from the Repertoire of Yvonne Printemps and Sacha Guitry" Rec 1930. (78/Vic 12" album C-8)(LP-627)

RAE, CHARLOTTE "Charlotte Rae: Songs I Taught My Mother" MUSIC & WORDS: Marc Blitzstein, Cole Porter, Ogden Nash, Sheldon Harnick, John Latouche, Richard Rodgers, Lorenz Hart, Vernon Duke. ORCH & COND: John Strauss. 1955 album. (Vanguard 9004)(LP-464)

RAINGER, RALPH "The Classic Movie Musicals of Ralph Rainger (1930-43)" (JJA Records 1980-1)(LP-768)

RAITT, JOHN "John Raitt: Highlights of Broadway" ORCH & COND: George Bassman. (Cap T-583)(LP-149)

RAYE, MARTHA "Here's Martha Raye" Reissues of 78's from 1939. (Epic LG-3061)(LP-613)

RAYE, MARTHA "Martha Raye" From soundtracks, television and theatre (live). (Legends 1000/5-6)(LP-651)

REILLY, CHARLES NELSON "A Jolly Theatrical Season" ORCH & COND: Elliot Lawrence. VOCALS: Charles Nelson Reilly, Robert Morse. 1963 album. (Cap T-1862)

REISMAN, LEO "Leo Reisman, Volume 1" (RCA LPV-565) (LP-48)

REVUERS, THE "Night Life in New York" Includes the sketches "The Girl with the Two Left Feet" and "Joan Crawford Fan Club." 1944(?) album. MUSIC & WORDS: The Revuers. PIANO: Leonard Bernstein. CAST: Betty Comden, Judy Holliday ("Judith Tuvim"), John Frank, Adolph Green, Alvin Hammer. (78/Musicraft 12" album N-2; LP-508.)

REYNOLDS, DEBBIE "Debbie Reynolds: Raise a Ruckus" (Metro 535)(LP-267)

RICHMAN, HARRY "Harry Richman Souvenir Album" Rec 1947. (78/Dec album 632)(LP-113)

RICHMAN, HARRY "Harry Richman: On the Sunny Side of the Street" (Pelican 124)(LP-349)

RICHMAN, HARRY "Club Richman: Harry Richman & Eddie Cantor" From radio boadcasts of 1930's and 1940's. (Torrington JRS-1019)(LP-414)

RITCHARD, CYRIL "Cyril Ritchard: Odd Songs and a Poem" With Elaine Dunn. PIANO: Stuart Ross. 1955 album. (Dolphin 10" 1)(LP-427)

RITTER, TEX "The Best of Tex Ritter" (Cap DT-2595)(LP-753)

RITTER, TEX "Tex Ritter: Chuck Wagon Days" (Cap ST-213) (LP-752)

ROBERTI, LYDA "Ethel Merman (1932-1935), Lyda Roberti (1934), Mae West (1933)" (Col CL-2751)(LP-40)

ROBERTS, JOAN "Joan Roberts" 1948 album. COND: Johnny Lytell. (Quality 10" 719-26)(LP-706)

ROBESON, PAUL "The Best of Paul Robeson" (Starline(E) SRS-5041)(LP-637)

ROBESON, PAUL "The Best of Paul Robeson, Vol. 2" (Starline(E) SRS-5127)(LP-638)

RODGERS, RICHARD See 720326 "A Celebration of Richard Rodgers"

RODGERS, RICHARD "Richard Rodgers & Oscar Hammerstein II: A Recorded Portrait" In conversation with Arnold Michaelis. (MGM 2E4-RP)

RODGERS, RICHARD "Rodgers and Hart 1927-1942" (JJA Records 19734)(LP-217)

RODGERS, RICHARD "Rodgers and Hart in Hollywood, Vol.1 (1929-1935)" (JJA Records 19766)(LP-498)

RODGERS, RICHARD "Rodgers and Hammerstein" (JJA Records 19761)(LP-497)

RODGERS, RICHARD "A Rodgers-Hart Production" 1940 album. COND & PIANO: Richard Rodgers. VOCALS: Lee Sullivan, Deane Janis. (COL 10" CL-6074)

RODGERS, RICHARD "Mary Martin Sings, Richard Rodgers Plays" MUSIC & PIANO: Richard Rodgers. ORCH: Robert Russell Bennett. COND: John Lesko. (RCA LPM-1539)

RODGERS, RICHARD "Rodgers and Hart Selections" COND: Lehman Engel. VOCALS: Milton Berle, Betty Garrett, Vic Damone, Marie Greene, chorus. 1947 album. (78/Vic album P-170)

RODGERS, RICHARD "Rodgers and Hart" 1953 album. VOCALS: Louise Carlyle, Bob Shaver. (Walden 304)

RODGERS, RICHARD "Rodgers and Hart Revisited" ORCH & COND: Norman Paris. VOCALS: Dorothy Loudon, Charlotte Rae, Danny Meehan, Cy Young. (Recording Industries Corp 3001)

RODGERS, RICHARD "Rodgers and Hart Revisited, Vol. II"

ORCH & COND: Norman Paris. VOCALS: Blossom Dearie, Gloria DeHaven, Dorothy Loudon, Bibi Osterwald, Charles Rydell, Bobby Short. (Painted Smiles 1343)

RODGERS, RICHARD "Rodgers and Hart Revisited, Vol. III" ORCH: Dennis Deal. VOCALS: Nancy Andrews, Blossom Dearie, Johnny Desmond, Estelle Parsons, Anthony Perkins, Lynn Redgrave, Arthur Siegel. (Painted Smiles 1366)

RODGERS, RICHARD "Rodgers and Hart Revisited, Vol. IV" ORCH: Dennis Deal. VOCALS: Nancy Andrews, Blossom Dearie, Johnny Desmond, Anthony Perkins, Lynn Redgrave, Elaine Stritch. (Painted Smiles 1367)

ROGERS, GINGER "Ginger Rogers" (Curtain Calls 100/21) (LP-402)

ROGERS, GINGERS "Hello, Ginger!" 1965 album. ORCH & COND: Jack Marshall. (Citel 2201)(LP-325)

ROGERS, GINGER "Miss Ginger Rogers" Rec 1978. (EMI(E) ODN-1002)(LP-624)

ROGERS, ROY "Roy Rogers Souvenir Album" (45/RCA album WP-215)(LP-278)

ROGERS, ROY "Roy Rogers: Happy Trails to You" ORCH & COND: Stephen Hartley Dorff. 1975 album. (20th Century T-467)(LP-523)

ROGERS, WILL "Will Rogers" 1933-1935 radio broadcasts, incl 2 duets with Fred Stone. (Murray Hill 51220)(LP-740)

ROMBERG, SIGMUND "Gems from Sigmund Romberg Shows, Vol. 1" COND: Sigmund Romberg. VOCALS: Genevieve Rowe, Lawrence Brooks, Lillian Cornell, Eric Mattson, chorus. (45/RCA album WDM-1051)

ROMBERG, SIGMUND "Gems from Sigmund Romberg Shows, Vol. 2" COND: Sigmund Romberg. VOCALS: Lillian Cornell, Genevieve Rowe, Lawrence Brooks. (45/RCA album WDM-1256)

ROMBERG, SIGMUND "Gems from Sigmund Romberg Shows, Vol. 3" COND: Sigmund Romberg. VOCALS: Warren Galjour, Shirlee Emmons, Richard Wright, chorus. (45/RCA album WDM-1422)

ROMBERG, SIGMUND "Gems from Sigmund Romberg Shows, Vol. 4" ORCH: Don Walker. COND: Sigmund Romberg. VOCALS: Jean Carlton, Lois Hunt, Jo Cameron, Stuart Churchill, William Diehl, Larry Douglas. (45/RCA album WDM-1529)

ROMBERG, SIGMUND "Gems from Sigmund Romberg Shows, Vol. 5" ORCH: Don Walker. COND: Sigmund Romberg. VOCALS: Lois Hunt, Jean Carlton, Stuart Churchill, Jo Cameron, Warren Galjour, William Diehl. (45/RCA album WDM-1600)

ROMBERG, SIGMUND "The Music of Sigmund Romberg" COND: Nathaniel Shilkret. VOCALS: Helen Marshall, Helen Oelheim, Rise Stevens, Morton Bowe, Thomas L Thomas, Fred Kuhnly, Milton Watson, chorus. 1935 album. (Camden 239)(LP-307)

ROME, HAROLD See 640006 Record prod "Harold Rome's Gallery"

ROME, HAROLD "A Touch of Rome" Harold Rome plays and sings his own songs. 1954 album. (Heritage 10" 0053) (LP-360)

ROME, HAROLD "Rome-Antics" Harold Rome plays and sings his own songs. 1955 album. (Heritage 0063)(LP-316)

ROME, HAROLD "Harold Rome: And Then I Wrote" (Coral 57082)(LP-39)

ROTH, LILLIAN "Lillian Roth: I'll Cry Tomorrow" (Epic 3206)(LP-104)

SABLON, JEAN "Jean Sablon's Best" Reissues of 78's. (RCA "X" LXA-1021)(LP-596)

SANDERSON, JULIA "Julia Sanderson and Frank Crumit" 1940 album. (78/Dec album 245)(LP-57)

SCHUMANN-HEINK "Ernestine Schumann-Heink, Volume III" (Rococo(C) 5335)(LP-748)

SCHWARTZ, ARTHUR "From the Pen of...Arthur Schwartz" MUSIC: Arthur Schwartz. WORDS: Howard Dietz, Leo Robin. ORCH & COND: Tony Osborne. VOCALS: Arthur Schwartz. Rec 1975. (RCA LPL1-5121)(LP-418)

SCHWARTZ, ARTHUR "The Music of Arthur Schwartz, Vol. I: 1929-1934" (JJA Records 19756)(LP-553)

SCHWARTZ, ARTHUR "The Music of Arthur Schwartz: Vol. II: 1933-1937" (JJA Records 19757)(LP-554)

SCHWARTZ, ARTHUR "The Music of Arthur Schwartz, Vol. III: 1937-1943" (JJA Records 19758)(LP-555)

SCHWARTZ, ARTHUR "The Great British Dance Bands Play the Music of Arthur Schwartz" Reissues of 78's from 1930 to 1936. (World Records(E) SH-274)(LP-584)

SCHWARTZ, ARTHUR "Alone Together: 32 of the Greatest Songs by Dietz & Schwartz" VOCALS: Nancy Dussault, Karen Morrow, Clifford David, Neal Kenyon. (Monmouth 6604/5)

SCHWARTZ, ARTHUR "Jonathan Schwartz Sings Arthur Schwartz" Vocals by Arthur's son Jonathan. Rec 1977. (Muse 5143)

SCHWARTZ, ARTHUR "Songs by Arthur Schwartz, Vol 1" ORCH & COND: Art Wagner. VOCALS: Bob Shaver, Laurel Shelby. 1954 album. (Walden 305)

SCHWARTZ, ARTHUR "Arthur Schwartz Revisited" ORCH & COND: Norman Paris. VOCALS: Cab Calloway, Blossom Dearie, Gloria DeHaven, Phyllis Diller, Warde Donovan, Charles Rydell. (Painted Smiles 1350)

SEELEY, BLOSSOM "Benny Fields & Blossom Seeley: Two-a-Day at the Palace" 1957 album. (Mercury 20224)(LP-764)

SHAY, DOROTHY "Dorothy Shay: Coming 'Round the Mountain" COND: Mitchell Ayres. (Col 10" CL-6089)(LP-783)

SHERIDAN, ANN "Ann Sheridan/Marlene Dietrich" Mostly soundtracks. (Marsher 201)(LP-705)

SIMMS, GINNY See 460010c Film "Night and Day"

SINATRA, FRANK "Frank Sinatra in Hollywood, 1943-1949" (Col CL-2913)(LP-250)

SINATRA, FRANK "Songs by Sinatra, Volume 1" COND: Axel Stordahl. 1949 album. (Col 10" CL-6087)(LP-696)

SINATRA, FRANK "Sing and Dream with Frank Sinatra" 1953 album. (Col 10" CL-6143)(LP-722)

SISSLE, NOBLE "Sissle & Blake, Vol. 1" MUSIC & PIANO: Eubie Blake. WORDS & VOCALS: Noble Sissle. A reissue of early acoustic records. (Eubie Blake Music 4)(LP-422)

SISSLE, NOBLE "Sissle & Blake, Vol 2" PIANO: Eubie Blake. VOCALS: Noble Sissle. Reissues of 78's. (Eubie Blake Music 7)(LP-587)

SMITH, KATE "Kate Smith U.S.A." COND: Jack Miller. Rec 1941. (78/Col album C-50)(LP-261)

SMITH, KATE "Miss Kate Smith 1926-31" (Sunbeam MCF-13) (LP-434)

SONDHEIM, STEPHEN See 730311 TV show "Sondheim: A Musical Tribute"

SOTHERN, ANN "Sothern Exposure" ORCH & COND: Ian Bernard. (Tops L-1611)(LP-614)

SOTHERN, ANN "Songs Stylings Featuring Ann Sothern" (Sutton 317; also issued as "Ann Sothern and the Broadway Blues" on Tiara 531.)(LP-203)

STRITCH, ELAINE "Stritch" ORCH: Portia Nelson. COND: Deane Kincaide. 1958 album. (Dolphin 3)(Stet SOT-2001, with an extra song)(LP-615)

STYNE, JULE "My Name Is Jule" MUSIC: Jule Styne. WORDS: Various. PIANO: Jule Styne, with orchestra. (United Artists 6469)

SUZUKI, PAT "Pat Suzuki's Broadway '59" ORCH & COND: George Siravo. 1959 album. (RCA LSP-1965)(LP-410)

SWIFT, KAY "'Fine and Dandy': The Music of Kay Swift" Miscellaneous compositions. VOCALS: Louise Carlyle, Kay Swift. Swift also plays piano. (Mark 56 Records 700)

TEMPLE, SHIRLEY "Shirley Temple; On the Good Ship Lollipop" (Movietone 1001)(LP-47)

TEMPLE, SHIRLEY "Shirley Temple: Curtain Call" (Movietone 71012)(LP-116)

TEMPLE, SHIRLEY "The Complete Shirley Temple Songbook" (20th Fox 103-2)(LP-225)

TEMPLE, SHIRLEY "Little Miss Shirley Temple" (Pickwick PTP-2034)(LP-179)

THOMAS, JOHN CHARLES "John Charles Thomas: The Young Thomas in Opera and Song" (OASI 527)(LP-649)

TIBBETT, LAWRENCE "A Lawrence Tibbett Program" (Camden 168)(LP-385)

TIBBETT, LAWRENCE "Lawrence Tibbett" (Empire 804) (LP-226)

TORME, MEL "The Best of Mel Torme" (Verve 8593)(LP-668)

TUCKER, SOPHIE "Sophie Tucker's Greatest Hits" (Col CL-2604)(LP-185)

TUCKER, SOPHIE "Sophie Tucker: A Collection of Songs She Has Made Famous" (Dec 10" 5371)(LP-186)

TUCKER, SOPHIE "The Great Sophie Tucker" (Ace of Hearts(E) 115)(LP-187)

TUCKER, SOPHIE "Sophie Tucker: Cabaret Days" (Mercury 20046)(LP-184)

UGGAMS, LESLIE "Leslie Uggams: What's an Uggams?" 1968 album. (Atlantic SD-8196)(LP-585)

VALENTI, MICHAEL "Michael Valenti in Concert" Rec live in 1978. (Unnamed label HR-13)(LP-650)

VALLEE, RUDY "Rudy Vallee: Heigh-Ho, Everybody" 1942 album. (78/Vic album P-111)(LP-96)

VALLEE, RUDY "The Best of Rudy Vallee," formerly entitled "The Young Rudy Vallee" (RCA LSP-3816)(LP-58)

VALLEE, RUDY "The Fleischmann's Hour Starring Rudy Vallee" With guests George Gershwin, Sophie Tucker, John Barrymore, Walter Huston, Bert Lahr, & Marlene Dietrich. Rec 1930's. (Mark 56 Records 613)(LP-332)

VALLEE, RUDY "Rudy Vallee: The Kid from Maine" 1955 album. (Unique 116)(LP-357)

VAN DYKE, DICK "Dick Van Dyke: Songs I Like" MUSIC & WORDS: Various. ORCH: Lew Davies. COND: Enoch Light. VOCALS: Dick Van Dyke, chorus. 1963 album. (Command RS-860)(LP-691)

VAN HEUSEN, JAMES "Jimmy Van Heusen Plays Jimmy Van Heusen" PIANO: James Van Heusen. With orchestra. Rec 1966. (United Artists 3494)

VEREEN, BEN "Ben Vereen Off-Stage" (Buddah BDS-5627) (LP-765)

WAITE, GENEVIEVE "Genevieve Waite: Romance Is on the Rise" 1974 album. MUSIC & WORDS: mostly John Phillips. (Paramour 5088)(LP-601)

WALKER, NANCY "Nancy Walker: I Can Cook Too" PIANO: David Baker. 1956 album. (Dolphin 2)(LP-293)

WALLER, THOMAS ("FATS") "Fats Waller: 1935 & 1943" (Collector's Classics 19)(LP-345)

WARING'S PENNSYLVANIANS "Waring's Pennsylvanians" (RCA LPV-554)(LP-428)

WARREN, HARRY "The Hollywood Years of Harry Warren, 1930-57" Soundtrack recordings. (JJA Records 19791) (LP-633)

WARREN, HARRY "The Classic Movie Musicals of Harry Warren, Vol. 1" Soundtracks from Forty-Second Street, Gold Diggers of 1933, & Footlight Parade. (JJA Records 19792)(LP-631)

WARREN, HARRY "The Classic Movie Musicals of Harry Warren, Vol. 2", Soundtracks from Gold Diggers of 1935, Gold Diggers of 1937, & Dames. (JJA Records 19793) (LP-632)

WARREN, HARRY "Alice Faye and the Songs of Harry Warren" Soundtracks from films of the early 1940's. (Citadel 6004)(LP-424)

WARREN, HARRY "Songs by Harry Warren" Reissues of records (soundtracks & other) by MGM, Capitol, & Decca. (Four Jays HW-601)(LP-399)

WATERS, ETHEL "Ethel Waters: Oh Daddy" (Biograph 12022) (LP-674)

WATERS, ETHEL "Ethel Waters" (Col CL-2792)(LP-15)

WATERS, ETHEL "Ethel Waters' Greatest Years" (Col KG-31571)(LP-673)

WATERS, ETHEL "Ethel Waters Souvenir Album" (78/Dec album 348)(LP-236)

WATERS, ETHEL "Ethel Waters Singing Her Best" Reissues of 78rpm records. (Jay 10" 3010)(LP-389)

WATERS, ETHEL "Ethel Waters in Shades of Blue" COND: J C Heard. Rec 1950. (Remington 10" 1025)(LP-361)

WATERS, ETHEL "The Favorite Songs of Ethel Waters" 1956 album. (Mercury 20051)(LP-393)

WATERS, ETHEL "Miss Ethel Waters" Rec c. 1958. (Monmouth MES-6812)(LP-99)

WEILL, KURT See 630606 "The World of Kurt Weill in Song"

WEILL, KURT See 721001 "Berlin to Broadway with Kurt Weill"

WEILL, KURT "Kurt Weill and Ira Gershwin: Tryout" PIANO: Kurt Weill. VOCALS: Ira Gershwin, Kurt Weill. (Heritage 0051)(LP-150)

WEILL, KURT "Recollections of Kurt Weill" by Ira Gershwin, Ogden Nash, Langston Hughes, & Morton Gould. (RCA 7" LL-201) Included with "The Two Worlds of Kurt Weill," orch & cond by Morton Gould. (RCA LSC-2863)

WEILL, KURT "Lotte Lenya Sings Berlin Theatre Songs by Kurt Weill" COND: Roger Bean. Rec 1955. (Col ML-5056) (LP-463)

WEILL, KURT "September Song and Other American Theatre Songs of Kurt Weill Sung by Lotte Lenya" COND: Maurice Levine. Rec 1957. (Col KL-5229)(LP-85)

WEILL, KURT "The World of Kurt Weill in Song" 1962 album. ORCH & COND: Samuel Matlovsky. VOCALS: Martha Schlamme. (MGM 4052)

WELCH, ELISABETH "Elisabeth Welch" Rec 1976. (World Records(E) SH-233)(LP-415)

WELCH, ELISABETH "Miss Elisabeth Welch, 1933-1940" Reissue of 78's. (World Records(E) SH-328)(LP-712)

WEST, MAE "Ethel Merman (1932-1935), Lyda Roberti (1934), Mae West (1933)" (Col CL-2751)(LP-40)

WEST, MAE "Mae West and W.C. Fields Side by Side" (Harmony 11405)(LP-141)

WEST, MAE "The Fabulous Mae West" Rec 1954. (Dec 9016) (LP-105)

WEST, MAE "Mae West: The Original Voice Tracks from Her Greatest Movies" (Dec 79176)(LP-413)

WEST, MAE "Mae West Songs" COND: Josef Chernivasky. (78/Mezzo Tone album 11)(LP-411)

WEST, MAE "Mae West Songs" COND: Lenny Marvin. (Mezzo Tone 10" 21)(LP-504)

WEST, MAE "W. C. Fields & Mae West" (Proscenium 22) (LP-412)

WHITEMAN, PAUL "Paul Whiteman, Volume 1" (RCA LPV-555)(LP-49)

WHITEMAN, PAUL "Paul Whiteman and His Orchestra Featuring Bing Crosby" (Col CL-2830)(LP-541)

WHITING, JACK "Jack Whiting & Jessie Matthews" (Monmouth 7049)(LP-156)

WHITING, RICHARD A "The Classic Movie Musicals of Richard A Whiting (1929-38)" (JJA Records 1980-6)(LP-769)

WILLIAMS, BERT "The Famous Songs of Bert Williams" (78/Col album C-25)(LP-232)

WILLIAMS, BERT "Bert Williams: Songs & Sayings" (Sunbeam P-506)(LP-639)

WILSON, EDITH "Edith Wilson: He May Be Your Man" 1976 album. (Delmark 637)(LP-723)

WILSON, SANDY See 710610 "Sandy Wilson Thanks the Ladies"

WODEHOUSE, P G "The Theatre Lyrics of P.G. Wodehouse" MUSIC: mostly Jerome Kern. Reissues of early 78s. (Folkways RFS-601)(LP-784)

WRIGHT, MARTHA "Martha Wright: Censored" The original versions of 12 songs presented on Broadway, not cleared for broadcasting. With the Joe Harnell Trio. (Jubilee 1028)

YOSHIDA, FUSAKO "Fusako Yoshida: Koto Recital" (Major mx TJV-FY-1/2)(LP-719)

YOUMANS, VINCENT "Through the Years with Vincent Youmans" VOCALS: Ellie Quint, Millie Slavin, Bob Quint, Nolan Van Way. (Monmouth 6401/2)

YOUMANS, VINCENT "Vincent Youmans Revisited" ORCH & COND: Norman Paris, Dick Hyman. VOCALS: Cab Calloway, Blossom Dearie, Gloria DeHaven, Dorothy Loudon, Mary McCarty, Charles Rydell, Maureen Stapleton. (Painted Smiles 1352)

Anthologies

ALL OUR OWN WORK Reissues of performances by composers & lyricists. (World Records(E) SH-273)(LP-589)

THE AMERICAN MUSICAL THEATER Twenty-eight numbers selected by Lehman Engel to accompany his book of the same title. (CBS Legacy 32-B5-0004)

AMERICAN VAUDE AND VARIETY (Rococo(C) 4006)(LP-323)

AMERICAN VAUDE AND VARIETY, VOL. 2 (Rococo(C) 4009) (LP-324)

AND THEN WE WROTE American composers and lyricists sing, play, and conduct their own songs. Reissues. (New World 272)(LP-563)

BALLET ON BROADWAY COND: Lehman Engel. Rec 1959. (RCA LPM-1865; Painted Smiles 1364, with additional material.)

BANDS ON FILM Soundtracks of films "Everything Is Rhythm" and "Nat Gonella and His Georgians" (World Records(E) SH-197)(LP-419)

BIG BROADCAST OF 1935 1935 radio broadcasts. (Kasha King 1935)(LP-469)

BRITISH MUSICAL COMEDIES BY AMERICAN COMPOSERS (1912-1935) Reissues of 78's. (JJA Records 19794)(LP-700)

A BROADCAST TRIBUTE TO BRITISH STAGE AND SCREEN ROYALTY VOCALS: Gertrude Lawrence, Noel Coward, others. (Magna ZZ89)(LP-766)

BROADWAY! BROADWAY! BROADWAY! (Longines LW-117)(LP-454)

BROADWAY RHYTHMS Piano rolls from the 20's and 30's. (Biograph 1007)(LP-391)

BROADWAY SHOWCASE A 10-record American box set of English studio prods issued in 1962, incl South Pacific, Carousel, Can-Can, Paint Your Wagon, The Student Prince, Pal Joey, The New Moon, The King and I, The Pajama Game, Damn Yankees, Show Boat, Oklahoma!, Annie Get Your Gun. (Capitol)

BROTHER, CAN YOU SPARE A DIME? "American Song during the Great Depression" Reissues. (New World 270)(LP-537)

CALLING ALL STARS (VOLUME 1) Previously unreleased performances, mostly from radio broadcasts. (Star-Tone 203)(LP-438)

CELEBRITIES (Lion 70108)(LP-207)

A CENTURY OF SOUND Cylinders from the collection of the "Antique Phonograph Monthly." (Eva-tone 8" 410782) (LP-571)

A CHILD'S INTRODUCTION TO JAZZ MUSIC: Linda Melnick. WORDS: Mary Rodgers, Marshall Barer. COND: Don Elliott, Jim Timmens. VOCALS: Bob Keeshan, the Honey Dreamers. (Golden GLP-29)

CHOICE CUTS, VOLUME 1 "Soundtracks from Hollywood's cutting room floor" (Choice Cuts ST-500/1)(LP-588)

COMMAND PERFORMANCE "Night of 100 Stars at the London Palladium, June 28, 1956" With additional material. (DRG Records DARC-1-1106)(LP-715)

COMPOSERS DO THEIR OWN THING (Pelican 120)(LP-321)

CURTAIN CALL SERIES, VOLUME 1 Vocals by Ted Lewis, Eddie Cantor, Jimmy Durante, Sophie Tucker. (Dec 10" 7018)(LP-297)

CURTAIN CALL SERIES, VOLUME 4 Records by Marlene Dietrich, Libby Holman, George Jessel, & Ben Bernie Orch. (Dec 10" 7021)(LP-521)

CURTAIN CALL SERIES, VOLUME 6 Vocals by Ella Fitzgerald, Mildred Bailey, Frances Langford, Connie Boswell. (Dec 10" 7026)(LP-572)

CURTAIN CALLS OF YESTERYEAR Reissues of 78's. (Audio Rarities LPA-2300)(LP-542)

CURTAIN GOING UP Overtures of Broadway's Hit Shows. Rec 1958. COND: Lehman Engel. (Col CL-1279)

CURTAIN TIME MUSIC & WORDS: Various. ORCH, COND: PIANO: Morton Gould. 1951 album. Includes one of Gould's songs from Billion Dollar Baby. (Col ML-4451)(LP-690)

CUT! OUT TAKES FROM HOLLYWOOD'S GREATEST MUSICALS (Out Take Records 1)(LP-423)

CUT! OUT TAKES FROM HOLLYWOOD'S GREATEST MUSICALS, VOL. 2 (Out Take Records 2)(LP-455)

CUT! OUT TAKES FROM HOLLYWOOD'S GREATEST MUSICALS, VOL. 3 (Out Take Records 3)(LP-486)

DISCOVERY First recordings of music by Gershwin, Porter, Kern, Rodgers, Arlen, Gould. Harmonica: Larry Adler. COND: Morton Gould. 1968 album. (RCA LSC-2986)

DON'T GIVE THE NAME A BAD PLACE "Types and Sterotypes in American Musical Theater 1870 -1900" COND & PIANO: Dick Hyman. VOCALS: Max Morath, Danny Barker, Clifford Jackson, chorus. 1978 album. (New World 265)

DUO PIANO 1926-1939 Music from Broadway & Hollywood, including piano teams from orig prods. (JJA Records 19771)(LP-545)

18 INTERESTING SONGS FROM UNFORTUNATE SHOWS MUSIC & WORDS: Various. ORCH & COND: Buster Davis. VOCALS: Bobby Van, Betty Garrett, Susan Watson, Buster Davis. Rec 1977. (Take Home Tunes 777)(LP-551)

ENCORES FROM THE 30's: VOLUME I, 1930-1935 (Epic L2N-6072)(LP-447)

EVERYONE ELSE REVISTED MUSIC & WORDS: Various. ORCH: Dennis Deal, Albert Evans. PIANO: Arthur Siegel. VOCALS: Nell Carter, Arthur Siegel, Patti Wyss, Su-La Haska, June Carroll. 1980 album. (Painted Smiles 1374)(LP-775)

THE FEMININE TOUCH (Star-Tone 205)(LP-592)

FIFTY YEARS OF FILM MUSIC Soundtracks from Warner Bros films. (Warner Bros 3XX-2736)(LP-223)

FIRST DISC RECORDINGS (Mark 56 Records 828)(LP-778)

FIRST EDITION Produced by RCA for Neiman-Marcus. Reissues of 78's. (RCA DMM4-0407)(LP-711)

FOLLIES, SCANDALS & OTHER DIVERSIONS FROM ZIEGFELD

TO THE SHUBERTS Reissues of 78's. (New World 215)(LP-518)

FORTY YEARS OF ENGLISH MUSICAL COMEDY (Rococo(C) 4007) (LP-524)

FOUR ORIGINAL CAST RECORDINGS Arms and the Girl (1950), As the Girls Go (1948), Texas, Li'l Darlin' (1949), Meet the People (1940) (JJA Records 19752)(LP-544)

GIRLS AND MORE GIRLS (Lion 70118)(LP-328)

GIRLS OF THE 30's (Pelican 122)(LP-273)

THE GOLDEN AGE OF THE HOLLYWOOD MUSICAL Original soundtracks. (United Artists UAG-29421)(LP-154)

THE GOLDEN AGE OF THE HOLLYWOOD STARS Original soundtrack dialogue, music & songs from 50 Warner Bros productions, 1926-1949. (United Artists(E) USD-311)(LP-595)

GOLDEN MOMENTS FROM THE SILVER SCREEN (Harmony 30549) (LP-106)

GREAT MEMORIES FROM OLD TIME RADIO (Columbia Musical Treasuries DS-515)(LP-41)

GREAT MOMENTS FROM OLD TIME RADIO (Harmony 11353) (LP-42)

GREAT MOMENTS FROM THE HALMARK HALL OF FAME Issued in celebration of the television show's 15th anniversary. (RCA PRM-202)(LP-620)

GREAT MOMENTS IN SHOW BUSINESS (Epic 15105)(LP-19)

GREAT MOVIE STARS OF THE 30's (Parlophone(E) PMC-7141)(LP-124)

GREAT PERSONALITIES OF BROADWAY (Camden 745)(LP-44)

GREAT STARS OF MUSICAL COMEDY (Ace of Clubs(E) 1182) (LP-56)

THE GREAT STARS OF VAUDEVILLE (Col CSS-1509)(LP-494)

HARLEM COMES TO LONDON Reissues of 78's from 1926 to 1938. (World Records(E) SH-265)(LP-582)

HERE COME THE GIRLS (Epic 10" LN-1114)(LP-619)

HERE COME THE GIRLS (Epic LN-3188)(LP-322)

HOLLYWOOD FILM-MUSIC OF THE THIRTIES (Historia(G) 640)(LP-183)

HOLLYWOOD IS ON THE AIR Soundtracks of 1934-1942 films from promotional radio programs. (Radiola mx AAB-1215/8) (LP-558)

HOLLYWOOD PARTY (Pelican 130)(LP-350)

HOLLYWOOD SINGS: VOL. 1 (THE GIRLS) (Ace of Hearts(E) 67)(LP-109)

HOLLYWOOD SINGS: VOL. 2 (THE BOYS) (Ace of Hearts(E) 68)(LP-114)

HOLLYWOOD SINGS: VOL. 3 (THE BOYS & THE GIRLS) (Ace of Hearts(E) 69)(LP-115)

HOLLYWOOD STORY Reissues of songs sung by Hollywood stars. (Festival(F) 214)(LP-669)

HOORAY FOR HOLLYWOOD Original soundtracks. (United Artists LA361-H)(LP-333)

HOORAY FOR HOLLYWOOD (RCA LPV-579)(LP-129)

THE HOT CANARIES One vocal each by Betty Grable, Peggy Lee, Doris Day, Rosemary Clooney, Kitty Kallen, Jane Russell. (Col 10" CL-2534)(LP-493)

I WANTS TO BE A ACTOR LADY Hits from early musical comedies (1866-1905). COND: Earl Rivers. VOCALS: Cincinnati's University Singers. 1978 album. (New World 221)

LADIES OF BURLESQUE Songs from soundtracks. (Legends 1000/2)(LP-496)

A LAST CURTAIN CALL "The Voices of Bygone Stars of Stage and Screen" (B&B Documentary Records 2)(LP-579)

LEGENDARY BLACK JAZZ STARS IN THEIR FIRST FILMS Soundtracks of "St Louis Blues" (1929), "Rhapsody in Black and Blue" (1932), "Cab Calloway's HI-De-Ho" (1933), "Jitterbug Party" (1934). (Biograph M-3)(LP-623)

LEGENDARY MUSICAL STARS Reissues of original cast 78s. (Time/Life P-15637)(LP-758)

LEGENDS OF THE MUSICAL STAGE 1929-1931 soundtrack recordings. (Take Two 104)(LP-751)

THE MAGICAL MUSIC OF WALT DISNEY 50 Years of Original Motion Picture Sound Tracks. (Ovation 5000)(LP-661)

MAKE MINE MANHATTAN & GREAT REVUES REVISITED ORCH: Dennis Deal, Judd Woldin. CAST: Nancy Andrews, Carleton Carpenter, Helen Gallagher, Dolores Gray, Estelle Parsons, Lynn Redgrave, Arthur Siegel, Elaine Stritch. Includes orig cast performances. (Painted Smiles 1369) (LP-618)

MEMORABLE MOMENTS IN MUSICAL COMEDY (Dec 10" 6019) (LP-69)

MEMORIES OF THE ROARING TWENTIES Featuring Carol Channing, the Ragtime Rascals, & the Collegians. (Longines 5100/4)(LP-377)

THE MGM YEARS Soundtracks of MGM Musicals -- 4 LP's of songs and 2 LP's of background music, accompanied by a book of the same title. (MGM P6S-5878)

MOVIE STAR MEMORIES (World Records(E) SH-217)(LP-310)

MUSIC FROM THE 1973 EXHIBITION "ZIEGFELD" Reissues of records and soundtracks. (Friends of the Theatre & Music Collection mx AC-731/4)(LP-710)

THE MUSIC GOES ROUND AND AROUND "The Golden Years of Tin Pan Alley: 1930-1939" Reissues of 78's. (New World 248)(LP-517)

MUSIC OF BROADWAY: THE TWENTIES, VOLUME 1 (1925-26) Reissues of 78s. (JJA Records 19796)(LP-772)

MUSIC OF BROADWAY: THE TWENTIES, VOLUME 2 (1927) Mostly reissues of 78s. (JJA Records 1980-3)(LP-773)

MUSIC OF BROADWAY: THE TWENTIES, VOLUME 3 (1928-29) Reissues of 78s. (JJA Records 1980-4)(LP-774)

THE MUSIC OF BROADWAY: 1930 Reissues of 78's. (JJA Records 19777)(LP-569)

THE MUSIC OF BROADWAY: 1931 Reissues of 78's (JJA Records 19778)(LP-564)

THE MUSIC OF BROADWAY: 1932 Reissues of 78's (JJA Records 19779)(LP-565)

MUSICAL COMEDY MEDLEYS, 1928-1934 From original 78's. (JJA Records 1977-6)(LP-602)

NIGHT LIFE IN NEW YORK See artist album listing for "The Revuers"

1926 (RCA LPV-557)(LP-473)

1927 (RCA LPV-545)(LP-456)

1928 (RCA LPV-523)(LP-426)

NOSTALGIA'S GREATEST HITS, VOLUME 1 (Stanyan 10055) (LP-136)

OLD CURIOSITY SHOP (RCA LCT-1112)(LP-148)

ORIGINAL PIANO TRIO "The Original Piano Trio Plays Nostalgia 20's Style" From piano rolls. (Klavier KS-128)(LP-561)

THE ORIGINAL SOUND OF THE TWENTIES (Col C3L-35)(LP-52)

THE ORIGINAL TORCH SINGERS VOCALS: Fanny Brice, Ruth Etting, Libby Holman, Helen Morgan. (Take Two 207) (LP-724)

ORIGINALS: MUSICAL COMEDY 1909-1935 (RCA LPV-560) (LP-18)

PLAYBOY OF PARIS, THE WAY TO LOVE, BELOVED VAGABOND, STRICTLY DYNAMITE, THE SINGING KID Soundtracks. (Caliban 6013)(LP-776)

PRAISE THE LORD AND PASS THE AMMUNITION Songs of World Wars I & II. Reissues of 78's. (New World 222)(LP-548)

PROUDLY THEY CAME... TO HONOR AMERICA Rec live at Washington 4 July 1970. VOCALS: Pat Boone, Kate Smith,

Dinah Shore, Bob Hope, Glen Campbell, Dorothy Lamour. (Landmark 101)(LP-704)
PURE GOLD MOVIES (RCA ANL1-1978)(LP-453)
RADIO CITY MUSIC HALL SOUVENIR ALBUM MUSIC & WORDS: Various. COND: Erno Rapee. VOCALS: Kenneth Schon, John Brooks McCormick, Irene Hill, chorus. 1946 album. (Dec 10'' 7001)
REVUE 1912-1918 (Parlophone(E) PMC-7145)(LP-158)
REVUE 1919-1929 (Parlophone(E) PMC-7150)(LP-159)
REVUE 1930-1940 (Parlophone(E) PMC-7154)(LP-172)
SHOW BIZ Narrated by George Jessel. (RCA LOC-1011)
SHOW TUNE TREASURY (Walden S-1)(LP-59)
THE SINGING ACTORS OF HOLLYWOOD Reissues. (Cap(F) 2C-184)(LP-562)
SINGING TROUBADOURS ON THE AIR (Star-Tone 206)(LP-591)
SOMETHING FOR THE BOYS (Sound/Stage 2305)(LP-301)
THE SONGS & STARS OF THE THIRTIES Reissues of 78s. (World Records(E) SH-370)(LP-736)
SONGS OF THE DEPRESSION Reissues of 78s. (Book-of-the-Month Records 21-5406)(LP-754)
SOUNDTRACKS, VOICES & THEMES FROM GREAT MOVIES Includes re-recorded material. Released in 1959. (Colpix 503) (LP-481)
STARS OF THE SILVER SCREEN, 1929-1930 (RCA LPV-538) (LP-17)
STARS OF THE ZIEGFELD FOLLIES (Pelican 102)(LP-157)
STARS OVER BROADWAY (Star-Tone 214)(LP-311)
THEY STOPPED THE SHOW (Audio Rarities 2290)(LP-20)
THEY STOPPED THE SHOW! "The original performances by the legendary stars of show business" (RCA R-214175)(LP-539)
THEY STOPPED THE SHOW (Dec 79111)(LP-164)
THE THIRTIES' GIRLS Performances from radio broadcasts. (Totem 1026)(LP-556)
THIS IS BROADWAY'S BEST (Col B2W-1)
THIS IS MY SHOW BUSINESS Narrated by George Jessel. (ShowBiz 1003)
THOSE BOMBASTIC BLONDE BOMBSHELLS (Wallysrite BGMM-42) (LP-568)
THOSE LEGENDARY LEADING LADIES OF STAGE, SCREEN & RADIO Reissues of 78's. (Harmony KH-32422)(LP-641)
THOSE LEGENDARY LEADING LADIES OF STAGE, SCREEN & RADIO, VOL. 2 Reissues of 78's. (Harmony KH-32423)(LP-642)
THOSE LEGENDARY LEADING MEN OF STAGE, SCREEN & RADIO Reissues of 78's. (Harmony KH-32424)(LP-643)
THOSE LEGENDARY LEADING MEN OF STAGE, SCREEN & RADIO, VOL. 2 Reissues of 78's. (Harmony KH-32430)(LP-644)
THOSE WONDERFUL GIRLS OF STAGE, SCREEN & RADIO (Epic BSN-159)(LP-43)
THOSE WONDERFUL GUYS OF STAGE, SCREEN & RADIO (Epic B2N-164)(LP-16)
THOSE WONDERFUL THIRTIES, VOL I (Dec DEA-7-1)(LP-175)
THOSE WONDERFUL THIRTIES, VOL. II Dec DEA-7-2)(LP-176)
THOSE WONDERFUL THIRTIES, VOL III (Dec DEA-7-3)(LP-177)
THREE OF A KIND Soundtracks. VOCALS: Helen Kane, Ruth Etting, Fanny Brice. (Fanett 146)(LP-699)
TO THE MEMORIES 1980 album of highlights from 50 years of Waa-Mu Shows. MUSIC & WORDS: Various, incl Sheldon Harnick. PIANO: Lloyd B Norlin. VOCALS: Members of past Waa-Mu Shows. (Northwestern University 010044X)
TOP HAT, WHITE TIE & GOLF SHOES A 1950 radio broadcast with Bing Crosby & Fred Astaire plus soundtrack of 1935 film Top Hat. (Facit 142)(LP-468)
25 YEARS OF RECORDED SOUND From the Vaults of M-G-M Records. (DRG Records DARC-2-2100)(LP-702)
VAUDEVILLE Songs of the Great Ladies of the Musical Stage. PIANO: William Bolcom. VOCALS: Joan Morris. 1976 album. (Nonesuch H-71330)
A VOICE TO REMEMBER "The sounds of 75 years on EMI records 1898-1973 recalled by Alistair Cooke" (EMI(E) EMSP-75)(LP-531)
WHEN EDISON RECORDED SOUND, VOLUME I Reissues of 78's. (Edison mx ZM-473201/4)(LP-520)
WHERE HAVE WE MET BEFORE? "Forgotten Songs from Broadway, Hollywood and Tin Pan Alley" Reissues. (New World 240) (LP-538)
YES SIR, THAT'S MY BABY "The Golden Years of Tin Pan Alley: 1920-1929" Reissues of 78's. (New World 279) (LP-516)
ZIEGFELD FOLLIES (Veritas 107)(LP-1)
ZIEGFELD FOLLIES ON THE AIR (Also titled "Florenz Ziegfeld and the Ziegfeld Follies") Two March 1932 radio programs. (Mark 56 Records 737)(LP-566)

Index

060421a
Anderson, Carl 711012e
Anderson, D 470313a
Anderson, Daphne 461219a
Anderson, Delbert 931223a
   510419a 530226a
Anderson, Eddie 400023a
   401025d 420004a
Anderson, Ivie 330044a
   410804a
Anderson, Jonathan 490407b
Anderson, Judith 530214a
Anderson, Julie 710517e
Anderson, Leroy 581011a
Anderson, Marian 571230a
Anderson, Maxwell 381019a
   491030a 541224a 551225a
   560310a 630606a
Anderson, Susan 560304a
Anderson, Thomas 720516a
Anderson, Warner 410029a
Andes, Keith 570006a
   601215a
Andre, Annette 620508b
Andreas, Christine 430331v
   560315l 651218a 720612a
Andres, Barbara 540114c
   760425a
Andrew, Leo 721108f
Andrews Sisters 400017a
   410013a 410014a 410015a
   420006a 420007a 420010a
   430011a 440004a 440010a
   440013a 440014a 440015a
   440015b 450215a 460011b
   470002a 470007b 480013b
   480019c 480024a 500008b
   500012a 520012a
Andrews, George Lee 730225b
   730311a 770307a
Andrews, Harry 651122d
Andrews, Jack 680204a
   691023a 730404a
Andrews, Joyce 220828b
Andrews, Julie 240902a
   471023a 540114b 560310a
   560315a 560315b 560315i
   560315j 570331a 570331g
   591116c 601203a 620611a
   640001a 670001a 680001a
   690003a 710701a
Andrews, Maidie 340216a
Andrews, Mark 530507d
Andrews, Maxene 740306a
Andrews, Nancy 380103b
   391018c 491013a 550127a
   590309a 600428a 621117a
Andrews, Patty 540002a
   740306a
Andrews, Raymond 601203h
Angel, Barry 781031a
Angela, June 510329n
Angeli, Pier 580008a
Angers, Avril 621117b
Animals 651128a
Aniston, John 591118a
Anker, Peryne 440821e
Ann-Margret 450001d 590121a

600414b 650001a 660002a
   681220c
Annette 610002a
Ansell, John 220919b 240911a
Anson, Barbara 681013a
Anthony, Julie 191118f
Anthony, Michael 691215a
Anthony, Ray 550005a
   550005d 570014a
Antonini, Alfredo 570331a
   651226a
Antonio, James 630122a
Anzelmo, Patricia 641225a
Aplon, Boris 651129a
Apolinar, Danny 680113a
   680113c
Applegate, Steven 810328a
Archer, Harry 250924a
   250924b
Archer, Jillian 710517f
Archer, Robert 600428*a
Archibald, William 450927a
   570219a
Arciaga, Michael 740006a
Arden, Eve 460010b
Arden, Victor 241201b
   241201g 251228c 261108b
   270906c 271122d 271122e
   281108a
Ardran, Peter 630423b
Arkin, Alan 660914a
Arkin, Juki 611010a
Arkus, Albert 380043a
Arlen, Harold 310119a
   321122a 321126c 340014a
   340827a 350030a 360006a
   360008a 360020a 360020c
   360043a 361225b 370414g
   371201a 390001a 390001c
   390001d 390013a 400031a
   401025c 401025d 410005a
   410005b 420004a 420004b
   420025a 420025b 430002a
   430007c 430016a 430019a
   430022a 440004a 440004b
   440005a 440030a 441005a
   441005b 450006a 460330a
   460330b 460330d 480004a
   490001b 500002a 500003a
   510005a 520003a 540002a
   541230a 541230c 550001a
   550001b 571031a 571031b
   571031c 590013a 591207a
   620001a 660501a
Arlen, Jerry 541230a 591207a
Arlen, Steve 601226b 700408a
Armbruster, Richard 581011a
Armbruster, Robert 081114c
   101107e 241202d 380511a
   470018a 480008a 601103b
Armen, Kay 270425c
Arms, Dorothy 550727a
Armstead, Joshie Jo 720516a
Armstrong, Bridget 711220a
Armstrong, Herk 441227a
Armstrong, Louis 290629b
   301014e 320017a 360015a
   370029a 370029b 380015a

380015b 380019a 401025d
   470021a 480025a 480025b
   520017a 560001a 560917a
   590003a 640116d 650626a
   660006a 740007a
Armus, Sidney 520625a
Arnau, B J 711201b
Arnau, Brenda 470110b
Arnaud, Leo 331118g 500005a
Arnaud, Leon 240902g
   280919h
Arnaud, Yvonne 190520a
Arnaz, Desi 460024a 490005a
   560024a
Arnaz, Lucie 790211a
Arney, Arthur 620205*a
Arno, Sig 051230k 440821b
   440821e
Arnold, Eddy 490026a
   500026a
Arnold, Jean 571010a
   581011*a 581201f
Arnold, P P 680305a
Arnold, Ronne 721023b
Arnold, Sydney 611003c
Arquette, Cliff 600619a
Arquette, Lewis 810001a
Arrington, Donald 751219a
Arthey, Johnny 160115h
   170210f 241202q 261130q
   280919q
Arthur, Beatrice 280828a
   550228a 571105a 660524a
   660524b
Arthur, Carol 441228d
Arthur, Donald 261130j
Arthur, Maurice 630319b
Arthurs, George 080425a
Asche, Oscar 160831a
Ascher, Kenny 790002a
Ash, Sam 151223*a
Ashford, Nick 750105b
Ashley, Barbara 401225a
   501221a 550025a
Ashton, Marcia 581002a
Ashwander, Donald 760229a
   770123a
Asia 581222a
Askam, Perry 280919v
Aske, Raymond 540114e
Askey, Arthur 410031a
Askey, Gil 740003a
Assaly, Edmund 570207b
Astaire, Adele 220220a
   241201a 271122a 310603a
   310603b
Astaire, Fred 220220a 241201a
   241201b 271122a 271122c
   310603a 310603b 321129a
   321129b 330005a 330005b
   330027a 331118b 331118h
   331118l 350006a 350006b
   350006d 360002a 360002b
   360012a 360012b 360507a
   370004a 370004c 370005a
   370005b 380003a 380003b
   390034a 400007a 400007b
   400012a 400012b 410003a

410003b 420001a 420001b
   420001c 420003a 420003b
   420003c 430002b 430002c
   450027a 460001a 460001c
   460004a 460004b 460004c
   470110b 480002a 480002b
   490002a 500004a 500021b
   510002a 510002b 510003a
   510011b 530001a 530001c
   550005a 550005b 550224b
   570001a 581017a 591104a
   600928*a 620013a 711203a
   720117a 760001a
Astar, Ben 360411a
Astor, Suzanne 660207a
   680502a
Atari, Yona 711021a
Atckison, Richard 500018a
Ates, Nejla 541104a
Atienza, Edward 651122c
Atkins, Cholly 481208a
Atkins, Norman 480715b
Atkinson, David 261130a
   540305a 611110a
Atkinson, Sarah 620005c
Attaway, Ruth 351010c
   541201a
Attenborough, Richard
   670006a
Atteridge, Harold 121223a
   140610a 150218a 190212a
Attles, Joseph 351010u
   611023a 760302a
Atwell, Angela 490407q
Atwell, George 351010t
Atwell, Roy 140130b
Auberjonois, Rene 691218a
Aubert, Jeanne 341121f
Aubry, Blanche 661120e
Audran, Edmond 791113a
   801229a
Auer, Mischa 051230k
   310014a
Augarde, Amy 081114j
Augins, Charles 760302b
Augustine, Stephanie 410123c
Auld, Georgie 770002a
Aumont, Jean Pierre 630318a
Aunt Jemima 271227d
Austin, Alfred 180515a
Austin, Gene 340016a
   340025a 440008a 570421a
Austin, Patti 721019a
Austin, Robert 690806a
Avalon, Frankie 600012a
   600014a 720214b
Avery, Brian 660521a
Avery, Lawrence 241202b
Axton, Hoyt 770003a
Ayars, Ann 081114a
Ayckbourn, Alan 750422a
Ayer, Nat D 160605a 161123a
   300924a
Ayler, Ethel 611023a
Ayre, Tom 561107a
Ayres, Mitchell 480430b
   621020b
Ayres, Stephen 490407t

Azito, Tony 791231a
Aznavour, Charles 730117a
Azzam, Cyril 751210a

Babb, Ena 431202c
Babbitt, Dick 951104b
Baby Rose Marie 330030a
  330030b
Bacal, Nancy 570207a
  570207b
Bacall, Lauren 700330a
  810329a
Baccaloni, Salvatore 580008a
Bacharach, Burt 601205b
  641123*a 661207a 680002a
  681201a 730001a
Back, Robert 560315n
Bacon, Paul 721220a
Baddeley, Hermione 380126a
  680320c
Bafunno, Anthony 181223*a
Bagdasarian, Ross 531203j
Bagnall, Valda 170210e
  361222a
Bagneris, Vernel 791020a
Bahler, Tom 790531a
Bailey, Mildred 310914c
  320308a
Bailey, Pearl 351010c 431202b
  460330a 460330c 470007a
  480430b 500202a 541230a
  541230d 560003a 580006b
  640116b 640422a
Bailey, Robin 631017a
Bainter, Fay 450001b
Baird, Bil 630411a
Baird, Bobbi 740416b
Baird, Cora 630411a
Baird, Ethel 180515a
Baisho, Chieko 700103a
Bakaleinikoff, Constantin
  390034a 400036a 400404b
  540012a
Baker, B J 581201b
Baker, Belle 290032a
Baker, Benny 350010b
Baker, Bertilla 770322a
Baker, Betty 401225g
Baker, Bobby 370002b
Baker, David 550228a
  550423a 571017a 610419a
Baker, Edythe 270520a
Baker, Herbert 240902b
Baker, Jennifer 610720a
  610720c
Baker, Josephine 350052a
Baker, Keith 651218a
Baker, Kenny 031013b
  271227v 380014a 380014b
  390013a 390013b 400024a
  430012b 431007a 460006a
  460006b 770417a 520625c
  561201b
Baker, Phil 270503a 380014b
  430004a
Baker, Susan 610720a
  610720c
Baker, Warren 280919a

531203d
Bakey, Ed 661126a
Bal, Jeanne 611118a
Balaban, Bob 660003b
Balfe, William Michael
  431127a
Ball, Ernest 110130a 120205a
  130127a
Ball, Lucille 391206d 391206e
  400032a 601215a 660524b
Ballard, Ally 810201a
Ballard, Beverly 681013a
Ballard, Kaye 331118a
  430331c 481007a 540311a
  540311b 570006a 570331a
  570912a 610413a 621020b
  650330a 760427a
Ballentine, Dick 530507d
Balthrop, Carmen 751021a
Bampton, Rose 561121a
Bane, Paula 460418a
Banke, Herbert 450419c
Banke, Richard 531203c
Banker, Doug 580513a
Banks, Ernie 751121a
Baptiste, Thomas 431202c
Barabas, Sari 301030c
Baravelle, Victor 271227o
  380003a
Barbeau, Adrienne 720214a
Barbour, Joyce 260223a
  260908d
Barclay, Don 490011a
Bardot, Brigitte 590005a
Barefield, Eddie 580004a
Barer, Marshall 560614a
  590511a 651223a
Bargy, Jeanne 600928a
  651226a
Bargy, Roy 380710a
Bari, Lynn 420008a
Barker, John 711012c
Barker, Ricky 530507i
Barlow, Frances 540114f
Barnes, Billy 590609a 621010a
Barnes, Binnie 380511b
  380511e
Barnes, Cheryl 671029g
  740528a
Barnes, Irving 351010u
Barnes, Mae 540408a
Barnes, Richard 711012c
  721108d
Barnes, Rolf 630019a
Barnes, Winifred 161206a
Barnet, Charlie 420035a
  480025a
Barnet, Robert Ayres 930515a
Barnett, Janice 751121a
Barnum, H B 761222a
Baron, Evalyn 790611a
Baron, Paul 241202i 241202n
  580001e
Barr, Kathy 261130f
Barrett, Joe 750917a 761202a
Barrie, Barbara 700426a
  750323a
Barrie, Ken 301030d 640922g

780001a
Barrington, Blayne 681220b
Barron, Muriel 450421a
Barrows, Richard 480715a
Barry Twins 270425d
Barry, Anna 630321c
Barry, John 600211b 720002a
  740007a 740501a
Barry, Marilyn 570521a
Barrymore, Ethel 290702a
Bart, Lionel 590012a 590528a
  600211a 600211b 600630a
  640922*a
Barth, Dorian 780300a
Bartholomae, Philip 130818a
  140909a
Bartis, John 550228a 571105a
Bartlett, Michael 710404a
Bartlett, Patricia 350505b
  360911c
Bartley, Betty 051230a
Barto, Betty Lou 471226a
Barton, James 511112a
Bascomb, A W 250413a
  260908d
Bascomb, Lawrence 310514a
Basehart, Richard 560613a
Basie, Count 600928*a
Basile, Jo 580312a 640602a
Baskerville, Priscilla 810301a
Baskett, James 460020a
  460020b
Baskin, Richard 750003a
Bass, Alfie 600211b 640922g
Bass, Jules 671218a 711203a
Bass, Sid 581201e 590521e
  591116d 591213b
Bassano, Mary 160115h
  170210f
Bassey, Shirley 271227w
Bassman, George 501124a
Batchelor, Ruth 640005a
Bates, Lulu 510514a
Bates, Thorpe 170210a
Batley, Farrell 750917b
Batt, Mike 780003a
Battle, Hinton 750105a
  810301a
Battles, John 471010a
Bauer, George 481216a
Baughman, Renee 750521a
Baumgartner, John G 390424c
Baur, Franklyn 261108b
  270816a 270816b 270912a
Bavaar, Tony 511112a 511112h
Bavan, Yolande 541230b
  690924a
Baxley, Barbara 630423a
Baxter, Connie 450419a
Baxter, Joan 301030d
Bayes, Nora 100106a 110403a
  171231a 181024a 201227a
  210602a 221010a
Bayless, Jean 591116e
Baylis, John 570219a
Bayne, Mardi 370414a
Baynes, Sidney 261201a
Bazely, Sally 401225e

530908a
Bazemore, Raymond 751021a
Beach, Ann 250311a 540114f
Beal, John 331120a 480029a
Bean, Orson 611227a 660003a
  670411a
Bean, Reathel 690127a
  750127a
Beard, Seymour 201221a
  250311c
Beatles 640017a 650010a
  650010b 680015a
Beaton, Colin 101107n
  241202t
Beaton, Norman 850314d
Beatty, Ethel 760302a
  780920a
Beatty, Peggy 251228b
Beaubian, Susan 751121a
Beaumont, Kathryn 510013a
  530010a
Beaumont, Richard 700001a
Beaumont, Roma 390323a
  450421a
Beauvais, Jeanne 540114c
Beavers, Dick 401225b
  401225b
Beck, Arthur 590511a
Becker, Lee 601017a
Becker, Loren 580007c
Beckett, Scotty 480013a
Beckett, Willis 590626b
Beddeau, Andrew 741128a
Beebe, Hank 751201a
Beecher, Johnny 640116c
Beems, Patti 571219g
Beery, Noah 271130b 271130c
  300021a
Beitel, Will 270425c
Belafonte, Harry 351010k
  431202b 531210a 550406a
  570017a 720004a
Belanger, Paul 351010o
Belasco, Leon 550224a
  561206a
Bell Sisters 530031a
Bell, Marion 240902e 331118i
  460001a 470313a 480715a
Bellamy, Franklyn 171225c
Bellini, Cal 681020a
Bellson, Louie 640422a
Belushi, John 730125a
Bemis, Cliff 680122b
Benatzky, Ralph 301108a
Bender, David 651122b
Bendix, William 490009a
Benedict, Diane 810328a
Benedict, Julius 620208a
Beneke, Tex 410012a 420008a
Benfield, Betty 790614a
Benjamin, Christopher
  791106a
Benjamin, P J 810301a
Benkoe, Aniko 751210b
Bennett, Alan 610510a
  610510b 640108a
Bennett, Constance 340027b
Bennett, Jimmy 590012a

Bennett, Joan 300013b
Bennett, Joan Sterndale
540114a
Bennett, Linda 720117a
Bennett, Nicholas 540114f
Bennett, Robert Russell
271227k 271227o 311015a
351010j 430331a 430331b
430331u 430331v 431202a
441005a 450127b 460516c
470110a 470313d 471010a
481230a 490407a 490407b
491125a 501221a 510329a
510329d 510329h 510329l
510329n 510419a 520304a
520321a 540408a 551130a
560315a 560315d 560315l
561129a 570331a 570331b
570331c 570331e 570514a
580001b 580221a 581201a
581201c 581227a 590205a
590309a 591116a 601203a
601203c 610302a 610403a
631017a 631208a 651017a
671115a 711102a
Bennett, Tony 660501a
Bennie, Eda 170914a
Benny, Jack 630002a
Benskin, Sammy 631015a
640319a 700302a
Benson, Betty 530214a
Benson, George 380126a
790004a
Benson, Marie 481230l
490407h
Bentley, Eric 280828j 620919a
630122a
Bentley, Jordan 351116a
530226a 530226b
Benzell, Mimi 250921e
481230i 530507c 611010a
611010b
Berberian, Ara 430331d
Beretta, Daniel 640003c
Berg, Carl 480029c
Bergen, Edgar 380014b
Bergen, Polly 460516p
500016a 570516a 590319a
601226e 750323a
Bergersen, Baldwin 371127c
450927a 570219a
Bergman, Alan 580019a
700006b 781214a 790003a
Bergman, Ingrid 580032a
Bergman, Marilyn 700006b
781214a 790003a
Bergman, Peter 600428*a
Bergman, Sandahl 790004a
Berini, Mario 370005b
Berkman, John 700326a
Berl, Joe 660524e
Berle, Milton 490021a
640422a 740009a
Berlin, Irving 110626a
120214a 141208a 151225a
170119a 180819a 190623a
190828a 190917a 200622a
210922a 221023a 230922a

241201*a 251208a 251208b
260223a 270624a 270816a
280404a 290004a 290027a
300010a 300010b 300013a
310008a 320217a 330930a
340010b 350006a 360003a
360012a 370001a 380003a
380009a 380803a 390015a
400528a 420001a 420704a
420704c 420704e 440017a
460004a 460516a 460516c
460516h 480002a 490715a
540004a 540006a 621020a
Berlinger, Warren 611014c
Berlingeri, Joseph 660524e
Berman, Shelley 620127a
Bernard, Al 200719a
Bernardi, Herschel 640922b
641123a 681117a 681117c
740009a
Bernhard, Jim 781222a
Bernie, Ben 280501a 370002b
Bernier, Daisy 490715c
Bernstein, Elmer 671207a
671207b
Bernstein, Leonard 441228a
441228b 441228c 500424a
530226a 561201a 561201b
570926a 720326a 730311a
760504a
Berry, Eric 540114b 721023a
Berry, Joyce 570926d
Berry, Ken 590609a 621010a
Berry, Leigh 730319*a
Berry, Mary Sue 601203a
Berry, W H 091112d 131210b
170914a 220113a 240904a
261021a 280427a
Berry, Walter 740405b
Berte, Heinrich 160115a
160115b 160115c
Besoyan, Rick 591118a
630930a
Best, Jack 550727a
Bethune, Zina 581016a
Betjeman, John 761206a
Betts, Harry 750002a
Betts, Jack 600928a
Bevan, Bowles 611014d
Bevans, Philippa 560315a
Bewley, Lois 590319a
Bey, Salome 721009a 721009b
761222a
Beymer, Richard 570926b
Bhaskar 600428a
Bibb, Leon 460516a 660921a
Bible, Frances 250921e
Bieha, Mark 790531a
Bigelow, Susan 780514a
Bigley, Isabel 430331t
501124a 530528a 530528b
Bikel, Theodore 510329c
591116a 640922l
Billig, Robert 751014a
760511a 770920a 780417a
Billings, James 051230s
Bingham, Bob 711012b
711012e

Birkby, Arthur 581002a
Birkenhead, Susan 780514a
Bishop, Bunny 531203d
Bishop, Carole 750521a
Bishop, Heather 591116j
Bishop, Kelly 780608a
Bishop, Ray 681220b
Bissell, Gene 661019a
Bitterman, Michael 791127a
Bizet, George 431202a
Black, Arnold 630122a
Black, Don 720002a 740501a
781031a 800128a
Black, Karen 750003a
Black, Stanley 460516i
590012a 640922i
Blackburn, Jimmy 590521g
Blackmore, Linda 660627a
730419*a
Blackstone, Nan 300604b
Blackton, Jack 720522a
Blackton, Jay 051225b
051230d 060924d 101107f
250921e 310603d 351010n
370012c 370414e 430331a
430331b 430331j 430331v
450419g 450419j 460516a
490715a 501012a 501124b
520625a 530615a 530615b
540408a 560614a 561206a
580204a 590205a 600428a
611012a 621020a 631208a
660003a 660521a 671115a
680410a 701110a 760425a
770515a 790513a 790513b
Blackwood Apology 700318a
Blaine, Vivian 401225d
411029e 430107d 450001b
450001e 460023a 460516g
501124a 501124b 580403a
Blair, Ilsa 620508c
Blair, Janet 430023a 680003a
Blair, Jimmy 470110f
Blair, Joyce 401225j 490407r
501124h 560503d 590521f
591118b 600630e 681220b
781031a
Blair, Lionel 441228h
Blair, Pamela 750521a
780417a 781022a
Blair, Richard 651103a
660623a
Blake, Eubie 210523a 210523b
240901a 301022a 301022b
780920a
Blake, Josephine 611014c
660129d
Blake, Peter 730419b
Blakely, Ronee 750003a
Blanc, Jonny 051230t
Blanc, Mel 660330a
Blanche, Francis 581111a
Blanche, Marie 131210b
Blane, Ralph 270906a
270906b 411001a 411001b
440001a 440001c 460001b
460019a 500003a 520011a
520321a 540011a 540011b

540012a 550009a 570006a
Blaney, Norah 250921f
Blank, Larry 790211a
Blank, Lawrence J 751014a
751209a
Blankenburg, Heinz 550012a
Blatt, Jerry 680107a
Blau, Eric 680122a 770113a
Blaymore, Enid 800514a
Bledsoe, Jules 271227q
Bleezarde, Gloria 630011a
660325a 680502a
Blendick, James 730319*a
Blessed, Brian 810511a
Bleyer, Archie 411001d
530128a 530507f 540513c
Blezard, William 540602a
Blighton, Elaine 360911b
Bliss, Helena 271227z
440821b 481230h
Blitzstein, Marc 280828a
280828c 380103a 380103b
410105a 590309a 590309b
630606a
Blodgett, Carol 620311b
Blondell, Joan 330001b
340021a 360006a 360063a
Bloom, Rube 360709a
Blossom, Henry 040222a
051225a 060924a 141102a
150929a 170319a
Blount, Don 760324a
Blount, Helen 800514a
Blount, Helon 620205a
621212a
Blue, Ben 401030e 420002b
Bluth, Chyleen Bacon
760414a
Blyden, Larry 581201a
640216a 651017b 660928a
661018a 730311a
Blyth, Ann 240902a 241202g
490008a 510007b 531203b
570004a
Blyth, Violet 131210b
Boales, Ramon 780621d
Boatwright, Helen 931223a
Boatwright, McHenry 351010f
351010q
Bobbie, Walter 720214a
Bock, Jerry 560322a 580123a
591123a 601017a 621127a
630411a 630423a 640429a
640922a 661018a 701019a
Bodry, Penelope Anne
700208a
Bogdan, Thomas 220828b
Bogin, Abba 420602a 541201a
600308a 621212a
Bois, Curt 380024b
Boland, Clay 580004a
Boles, John 281121b 300005a
300018a 300045a 321108f
340055a 380045a
Bolger, Ray 031013c 360003a
370020a 390001a 430012b
460006b 481011b 481011d
490024a 520021b 620319a

Bolin, Shannon 550505a
550505b 690604a
Bolton, Guy 160925a 170829a
280427a
Bolyard, Lewis 401225b
Bond, Gary 721108b 721108c
Bond, Grahame 810411a
Bond, Rudy 670411a
Bond, Sheila 290430b
370414e 520625a 520625d
750502a
Bonita 121223a
Bonney, Alfred 590122a
Bontempelli, Guy 751210a
Booke, Sorrell 470110c
Boone, Debby 780004a
Boone, Pat 450001d 560009a
560009b 570007a 570016a
571117a 580007b 600006a
610003a 780004a
Booth, James 600211a
Booth, Keith 430331g
Booth, Shirley 510419a
540025a 540408a 590309a
Borden, Johnny 600414a
Bordoni, Irene 230828a
251109a 281008b 281008c
290021a 400528b
Borge, Victor 531002a
Borodin, Alexander 531203a
Bosan, Alonzo 510621a
541201a
Bosley, Tom 591123a
Bostwick, Barry 720214a
730619d 761010a
Boswell Sisters 310914b
320010a 320010b 340027a
340027b 340029a 340029b
Boswell, Connie 340027a
370029a 380803a 390011a
410006a 410006b
Bottoms, John 711201a
Boucicault, Dion 620208a
Bouie, John 570521a
Bourne, Sally Anne 770421c
Bourton, Rayner 730619a
Bousard, Joe 620311b
Bova, Joe 590511a
Bova, Joseph 380103b
800825a
Bovill, C H 110304a
Bowan, Sybil 681023a
Bowe, Morton 241202m
261130p 280919p
Bowen, Debbie 590521d
750422a
Bowen, Hill 271227y 481230l
490407h 510329k 590205b
630930a
Bower, Sharon 800622a
Bowers, Dennis 530226d
Bowles, Anthony 560301a
711012c 750422a 780621a
780621b
Bowman, Lee 490014a
Bowman, Robert 051230p
090428a 241202r 450421b
490915c 640922i

Bowman, Tim 761202a
Bowne, Richard 370012c
Boyd, Frances 571219e
581201g
Boyd, Gordon 460516n
501124h 560503c
Boyd, Jimmy 561121a
Boyd, Stephen 351116b
Boyer, Lucienne 341003a
351226a
Boylan, Mary 671122a
Boyle, Billy 680320a 730419b
740501a
Bozeman, Beverly 560522a
Bracci, Teda 810001a
Bracken, Eddie 570413a
570413c 570413d
Brackman, Jacob 781022a
Bradbury, Lane 590521a
Braden, Alan 081114f 101107l
121202e 250311h 280828j
321108g 331118n 561112g
611014d 670001d
Braden, John 751219a
Braden, Kim 590521h
Bradfield, Louis 971116a
991111g 010601a 021115a
040305a
Bradford, Alberta 720419a
Bradford, Alex 611211a
720419a 761222a
Bradford, Perry 290422a
Bradley, Grace 330024b
370002b
Brady, Scott 550002a
Braham, Philip 250310a
Braid, Hilda 630704a
Brainerd, Winthrop 600428*a
Brambell, Wilfrid 680320a
Bramlett, Bonnie 680305a
Bramlett, Delaney 680305b
Brampton, Jean 401225e
Brand, Oscar 681013a
Brando, Marlon 501124b
Brandon, Johnny 520925a
640319a 700302a
Brandt, Carl 590521b
Brandt, Mike 700208a
Brasselle, Keefe 540007b
540007c
Brassner, Kim 770808a
Braswell, Charles 611003a
660524a
Braun, Richard 690806a
Braunstein, Alan 721009a
Brawner, Hilda 630122a
Brazzi, Rossano 490407c
550022a
Brecht, Bertolt 280828a
280828b 280828c 280828g
620919a 630606a
Bredin, Patricia 651122c
Bredius, Barbara 680122c
Bredschneider, Willy 130405a
Breen, Bobby 360016a
360024a 370028a 370028b
380020a 380021a 390014a
Breffort, Alexandre 561112a

561112b
Bregman, Buddy 570203a
Brel, Jacques 651122f 680122a
680122d 800507a
Bremers, Beverly Ann
700518a
Bremmer, Lucille 450027a
Brendel, El 310014a
Brennan, Eileen 591118a
640116a 750002a
Brennan, Jimmy 760427a
Brennan, Kevin 680320a
Brennan, Maureen 561201b
Brennan, Walter 460014a
680003a
Breslin, Tommy 270906f
710415a
Bretherton, Freddie 481230k
Breton, Elise 570018a
Brett, Jeremy 051230o
560315b
Bretton, Elise 630002b
Bretton, Michael 261130u
Bretton, Mike 430331s
640116i
Breuer, Ernest 231020b
Brewer, Betty 490010a
Brewer, Teresa 530031a
Brewster Twins 370002b
Brian Sisters 400015a
Brian, Antony 340216a
Brice, Carol 351010s 470110c
591207a 711102a
Brice, Elizabeth 110102a
141208c
Brice, Fanny 200622a 210621a
280002a 280002b 300003a
300003b 360003a 380023b
Bricusse, Leslie 610720a
630704a 650516a 670006a
690004a 700001a 710002a
721220a 781109a
Bridges, Kenneth 410123c
Bridgewater, Dee Dee
750105a
Brigel, Stockton 651103a
Brigham, Constance 931223a
Brightman, Sarah 810511a
Briney, Mary Martha 060924b
160115a 241202f 451006a
Brinker, Lynn 600308a
Briquet, Jean 100926a
130828a 140223a
Brisson, Carl 051230j 300011a
300019a 301205a 330031a
340028a 350023a 350032a
Britt, Kelly 681201b
Brittan, Robert 731019a
Britten, Paul 101107k 121202c
Britton, George 310603d
481230h
Britton, Pamela 470313a
Britton, Tony 250311l 560315k
Bro, Judith 801120a
Brocksmith, Roy 280828g
Broderick, George 761222a
Broderick, Helen 360002b
Brodszky, Nicholas 241202h

241202i 500006b 510004a
530013a 540014a 560006a
560011a 570021a
Brody, Estelle 220113a
Brogden, Gwendoline 140420a
Brohn, Bill 760513a
Bronhill, June 051230l
051230o 070302b 090428c
091112b 160115b 261130d
271227F 290718j 291010a
301030a 390323b 510329p
591116f
Brooke, Tyler 300009b
Brooks, David 441005a
470313a
Brooks, Edward 051230p
241202r
Brooks, Harry 290629a
Brooks, Jack 460007a 470012a
550017a 600003a
Brooks, Karmello 731217a
Brooks, Lawrence 440821b
540010b 621212a
Brooks, Lola 591116f
Brosset, Colette 581111a
651214a
Brotherson, Eric 301030b
301030c 481208a
Broughton, Jessie 080425b
Brower, Jay 580513a
Brown, Ada 430007a
Brown, Anne 351010a
351010p 450008a
Brown, Barbara 250311l
430331r 591116e
Brown, Blair 280828g
Brown, Candy 760419a
Brown, Dorothy 220113a
Brown, Forman 051230k
301030b 750004a
Brown, Georgia 600630c
600630d 600630f 790408a
Brown, Jack 580007c
Brown, Joan 271227F 640922f
Brown, Joanna 250311a
Brown, Joanne 470426d
540114e 630319b 640116p
640922g
Brown, Joe E 440015a
Brown, Johnny 641020a
Brown, Joyce 700315a
Brown, Kay 510026a
Brown, Kelly 460516f 570006a
Brown, Leonard 780513a
Brown, Lew 260614a 270906a
280702a 281010a 290015a
290029a 290109a 300303a
310006a 310914a 320308a
330304a 360043a 390706a
391206d 560004a 580002a
Brown, Lisa 780417a
Brown, Michael 520516a
520516c 560200a 560522a
560522c 561107a 570045a
580033a 590024a 600201a
600900a 611005a 620205*a
640008a 650616a 660207a
Brown, Miquel 760302b

Brown, Nacio Herb 290005a
321126a 330022a 410001b
450022a 500009a 520002a
540114d
Brown, Oscar, Jr 700127a
Brown, R G 651103a
Brown, Rose 850314b
Brown, Russ 550505b
Brown, Sammy 721023c
Browne, Irene 250311c
540610a
Browne, Joanne 520001f
Browne, Louise 370916a
Browne, Roscoe Lee 660921a
Browne, Sam 360109b
Browning, Susan 621018a
700426a 700426b 730311a
750303a
Brownlee, John 740405c
740405f
Brox Sisters 210922a 230922a
241201*a 270816a 300005a
380803a
Brox, Annette 711012a
Brox, Victor 711012a
Bruce, Betty 450127a
Bruce, Carol 271227m
271227z 290430b 400528a
401225e 410020a 650318a
671023a
Bruce, Virginia 360003a
360018a 360018b
Bruckner-Ruggeberg,
Wilhelm 280828i
Bruins, Charles 101107o
Brune, Adrienne 280313a
Bruni, Peter 650222a
Bruns, George 031013c
560014a 590010a 670005a
680007a
Bruns, Philip 611005a
Bryan, Dora 271227w 481208f
550831a 640116i
Bryan, Fred 510719a
Bryan, Julie 160831a 241202o
250921k
Bryan, Wayne 270906f
Bryant, Glenn 431202a
Bryant, Hugh 560301a
Bryant, Jim 570926b
Bryant, Marie 410804a
Bryer, Vera 251228b
Brynner, Yul 510329a 510329b
510329n
Bubbles, John W 351010d
351010f 361001a
Buchanan, Jack 211011a
240512a 250310a 250922a
251110a 280605a 280605b
290327d 300009b 310004a
310305a 320008a 330011a
340201a 350007a 350008a
350016a 370019a 530001a
540021a
Buck & Bubbles 401025d
Buck, Bill 750004a
Buck, Gene 170131a 271122*a
Buckles, Ann 580616a

Buckley, Betty 681201b
Buckley, Hal 380103b
Buffalo Bills 571219a 571219b
Buggy, Brian 721023b
Buirgy, Suzanne 760709a
Bulifant, Joyce 670004a
Bull, Peter 720002a
Bullens, Cindy 720214b
Bullock, Walter 400024a
Buloff, Joseph 430331a
550224b
Bumbry, Grace 431202c
Bunn, Alfred 431127a
Bunnage, Avis 640922g
740501a
Bunnell, Lloyd 261130e
Burch, Shelly 610720d
Burdon, Eric 700006a
Burell, James 420704e
Burge, Gregg 810301a
Burger, Julius 470012a
Burgess, Anthony 730319*a
Burgess, Betty 350050b
Burgess, Michael 090428c
Burghoff, Gary 660003b
Burgie, Irving 631015a
Burke, Billie 390001a
Burke, Donald 680004a
Burke, John 250921i 360015a
370022a 380018a 380019a
390009a 390011a 400018a
400019a 400025a 410017a
410023a 420012a 420029a
430017a 440006a 440021a
460003a 460027a 470002a
470008a 490008a 490009a
500011a 500012a 530006a
530011a 610518a
Burke, Marie 190917a
271227A 271227g 301030f
Burke, Patricia 400419a
Burke, Sonny 550018a
Burks, Donnie 671029c
Burks, Donny 700302a
Burley, Toni-Sue 711019a
Burnaby, Davy 160919a
Burnett, Carol 571117a
590511a 620611a 630002a
640526a 710701a
Burnett, Harry 750004a
Burnett, Jim 810411a
Burns, David 501221a
521215a 620508a 640116a
Burns, Paul 671029f
Burns, Ralph 191118b 250311d
250311l 381123e 571017a
620315a 620315c 620315d
621117a 621117b 640326a
640526a 641020a 650318a
660003c 660129a 660129b
660129d 660928a 661120b
661214a 670411a 670411b
680127a 700326a 721023a
721023b 750603a 760002a
770002a 771029a 780002a
790004a 790211a
Burnside, Ray 150930a
Burr, Robert 641123a

Burrell, Terry 780920a
Burridge, Geoffrey 781109a
Burrier, Ralph 590626a
Burris, Glenn 241202n
Burrows, Abe 660501a
Burrows, John 720710a
740702a
Burstein, Lonnie 680107a
Burston, Reginald 340216a
430331e 450419k 490407e
510329h
Burton, Debbie 620007a
Burton, Ian 510329p
Burton, Irving 760229a
770123a
Burton, M 541230a
Burton, Margaret 250311k
Burton, Miriam 351010f
351010o 640429a
Burton, Richard 601203a
650216b
Burton, Rita 681220b
Burton, Wendell 660003c
Busch, Betty Ann 570045a
600201a 600900a 620205*a
Busse, Henry 280626a
Bussins, Jack 750323a
Butcher, Ernest 550831a
Butler, Angeline 700006a
Butler, Artie 750002a
Butler, Billy 721128a
Butler, Lois 480017a
Butler, Tommy 751121a
Butterworth, Clara 141028b
160115j
Buttolph, David 370014a
Buttons, Red 580427a
620001a 770005a
Byatt, Irene 420602a 490407b
Byers, Bill 750521a
Byers, Billy 610720d
Byers, Michael 781006a
Byford, Roy 171225c
Bygraves, Max 601226b
Byng, Douglas 260326c
341003*a
Byrd, Carolyn 760302a
Byrne, Gay 760504c
Byrne, Gaylea 611110a
Byron, Dick 390001h

Caan, James 750001a
Cabayo, Ena 271227j
Cable, Christopher 680012a
680222*a 680222a
Cables, Eleanor 490407b
Cabot, Ceil 571010a 581011*a
590924a 600929a 611005a
Cabot, Sebastian 680007a
Cacavas, John 680012a
680222*a 680222a
Caddick, Edward 600211a
Caesar, Irving 171105a
180214b 220706a 250311a
250311n 270425f 280501b
300920a 300920b 360001c
361001b 430909a 440009b
460016a 510017b

Caesar, Sid 621117a
Cagney, James 330002b
420005a 420005c 500023a
550008a
Cagney, Jeanne 420005a
420005c
Cahill, Marie 020829a
030216a
Cahill, Paul 671122a
Cahn, Sammy 341121g
400036a 420019a 440010b
440012a 440029a 450004c
460015a 470006a 471009a
480010a 480010c 480012a
490016a 500006b 500006d
500019c 500023a 510004a
510015a 520004c 520021a
521215a 530008a 530010a
540019a 550014a 550014b
550020a 550919a 550919b
560006a 560008a 560015a
560522a 570003a 570010b
570014b 570021a 590006a
590014a 600001a 600009a
610001a 620003a 630007a
630016a 630018a 640002a
640002b 640422a 650001a
651113a 651113b 660501a
661126a 670001a 670001c
670226a 740009a 740416a
740416b
Cain, Patrick 641225a
Cain, Sheila 641225a
Calabro, Tony 780300a
Caldwell, Anne 141020a
151223a 160228*a 171016a
190505a 190512a 200202a
201221a 261217a 300006a
Calhern, Louis 460516b
Calhoun, Rory 570032a
Calin, Mickey 570926a
Callahan, Bill 460418a
521215a
Callahan, Brad 750917b
Callan, Michael 481230e
Callaway, Bill 721019a
Callaway, Joe 631015a
Callinicos, Constantine
241202h 250921h 261130j
490006a 500006a 510007a
520006a
Calloway, Cab 280509a
280509b 320010a 320010b
330030a 330043a 340050a
351010c 351010n 360020a
360020b 370031a 430007a
430007b 580004a 640116b
691206a
Calloway, Chris 640116b
Calloway, Northern J 700518a
Calon, Jean-Claude 651122f
Calvi, Gerard 581111a
651214a
Calvin, Henry 031013c
531203a 531203c
Camarata 441228a
Camarata, Salvador 460027a
Camarata, Tutti 450419f

510013b 540017c 551022a
560014a 561223a 590006b
610002a 620004a 660004a
680009a
Cameron, David 730619c
Cameron, Grace 081203a
Cameron, John 160115b
640116o
Cameron, Rita 640116h
Camp, Hamid Hamilton
701026a
Campbell, Craig 121202f
Campbell, Dean 510418a
530211a
Campbell, Glen 690005a
Campbell, Jean 490407m
510419b
Campbell, Margaret 180515a
191118a
Campbell, Norman 560304a
Campbell, Sande 661106a
720522a
Campbell, Vic 750917b
Campone, Merv 780323a
780323b
Canary, John 751014a
Candido, Candy 530010a
Canfora, Bruno 760008a
Canning, James 720214a
Cannon, Alice 640114a
661106a
Canova, Diana 760003a
Canova, Judy 350038b
390706a 410030b
Cantan, Jenny 710517g
Cantor, Eddie 170612a
190623a 210205a 211006a
220413a 231020a 231231b
270001a 281204a 281204c
310005a 320001a 330028a
340010a 340010b 360043a
380803a 390005b 400006a
411225a 430016a 440015a
440015b 440016a 460005a
480009a 490003a 540007a
540007b 540007c
Cantrill, Ken 511112b
Capers, Virginia 731019a
Capote, Truman 541230a
Capps, Al 660330a
Cardinale, Roberto 470426d
290718a
Carey, Dave 581201j
Carey, Joyce 621008a
Carey, Thomas 271227j
Cariou, Len 700330a 730225a
730225d 790301a
Cariven, Marcel 351005a
Carle, Frankie 480031a
490014a 490014b
Carleton, Billie 141208a
Carlisle, Elsie 290327a
320016a
Carlisle, Kitty 051230g
261130h 331118d 340022b
350022a 440015a 440821b
Carlisle, Louise 271227u
Carlisle, Tommy 470313b

Carlson, Eric 630002b 630411a
Carlyle Cousins 320614a
Carlyle, Louise 301014a
601103*a
Carmet, Jean 581111a
Carmichael, Hoagy 361225c
380012c 380018a 380018c
430024a 440007a 450012b
450026a 460007a 470030a
481208b 481208g 510011a
520013a 660501a 710606a
Carmichael, Ian 600630e
661205b
Carmichael, Ralph 530026a
Carminati, Tullio 340012b
340027b 350058a
Carmines, Al 660304a
671013a 690127a 690604a
691214a 720619a
Carne, Judy 540114c
Carnelia, Craig 780514a
Carnes, Kathleen 460516a
Carney, Art 390001h 401030d
Carnovsky, Morris 620127a
Caron, Leslie 530009a
550005a 580001a
Carpenter, Carleton 400911a
410123b 500005a 510027a
Carpenter, Thelma 210523a
280509b 490407d 750105b
Carr, Charmian 591116c
Carr, Darlene 680007a
Carr, Howard 141028b
220113a
Carr, Leon 641026a
Carr, Osmond 800228a
Carradine, John 620508a
Carradine, Keith 750003a
Carrillo, Cely 581201f
Carroll, Adam 360411d
370414d
Carroll, Beeson 630122a
Carroll, Bob 640429a
Carroll, Danny 381123a
680410a
Carroll, David James 760400a
Carroll, Diahann 351010c
431202b 541230a 620315a
730117a
Carroll, Earl 260824a
Carroll, Eileen 601226c
Carroll, George 020510a
Carroll, Harry 140610a
150218a 180307a
Carroll, Irene 430331d
510329e
Carroll, Jack 371127a
Carroll, Jimmy 081114a
101107c 130908b 170319a
261130n 331118i 460516k
470110f 490407d 490715b
560027a 580007a 581201f
Carroll, Joan 401030a
Carroll, John 241201e
Carroll, June 520516a 560614a
620201a
Carroll, Laurie 530020a
Carroll, Lee 351010v

Carroll, Lewis 321212a
410031a
Carroll, Pat 570331b
Carroll, Peter 780621e
Carroll, Ronn 460516c
720310a
Carroll, Ronnie 681201c
Carroll, Vinnette 761222a
Carson, Danielle 401225m
Carson, Jack 311226a 430016a
440015a 460021a 480028a
490016a 490016b
Carson, Jean 470110c 520925a
540021a 581016a
Carson, Ken 480029a 640019a
Carson, Mindy 580123a
Carson, Violet 600630a
Carten, Kenneth 380316a
Carter, Ben 460006b
Carter, Benny 500001a
Carter, David 570045a
Carter, Desmond 240911a
241201a 280605a 300220a
301030a 340047a
Carter, Frank 131223a
Carter, Genna 660623a
Carter, Jack 560322a
Carter, Lavaida 360709a
Carter, Loraine 620205b
Carter, Nell 721009a 741007a
750502a 780509a
Carter, Ralph 730316a
731019a
Carter, Terry 541201a 611023a
Carter, Vicki 780920a
Cartier, Rudy 571219e
581201g
Carver, Brent 780323b
Cary, Claiborne 610419a
Caryll, Ivan 941124a 980521a
000203a 021115a 031017a
031210a 090123a 110313a
120930a 131110a 141020a
171016a 190520a
Cascone, Michael 750127a
810605a
Case, Allen 261108a 581209a
590511a 670426a
Case, Russ 470027a 470110f
480430a 510329m 591022b
Caselotti, Adriana 370012a
Casey, Peter 780621e
Casey, Warren 720214a
Caskey, Marilyn 790513a
790513b
Cason, Barbara 721004a
Cass, Lee 740405a 241202e
261130a 430331c 560503a
600308a 611110a
Cassel, Jean Pierre 630319b
Cassel, Walter 301030c
Cassidy, Jack 261108a
331118a 341121h 351116a
360411b 370414a 381123b
470313c 520625a 630423a
640526a 660329a 660501a
681023a 720004a 730311a
Cassidy, James 430331k

Cassidy, Jimmy 711012c
Cassidy, Martin J 621212a
Cassidy, Ted 670226a
Castelnuovo, Nino 640003a
Castle, John 651122d
Castle, Roy 661106*a
Castro, Peppy 760506a
Cathcart, Dick 550004d
Catlett, Walter 400001a
Caulfield, Joan 460004c
Cavalieri, Deena 051230i
Cavallaro, Carmen 450016b
460021a 460021b 560007a
Cavanaugh, Page 480010a
480025a
Cavett, Richard 580513a
Cawthorn, Joseph 120224b
160110b 290903e 320004b
Caymmi, Dorival 390619a
Cecil, Jonathan 720710a
Cecil, Sylvia 280427a 461219a
500707a
Cellier, Alfred 860925a
Cervenka, Jan 250921o
390323d 490915b 560503c
Cesario, Greg 761215a
Chaikin, Jules 740006a
Chakiris, George 560005b
570926b 570926d 570926f
580013a 680004a
Chamberlain, Alison 250311a
Chamberlain, Richard 661214a
760006a
Chambers, Ralph 501012a
Chambers, Robert W 131229a
Champion, Gower 271227e
331118g 520007a
Champion, Marge 271227e
331118g 520007a 550010a
Chandler, Chick 340046a
380009a 470010a
Chandler, Christine 771201a
Chandler, Jeff 550024a
570031a
Chandler, Mimi 440021a
Chaney, Jan 621008a
Channing, Carol 410105a
481208a 481208c 481208d
481208e 481216b 570413a
610112a 610112b 640116a
640116g 640116j 670001a
670001b
Channing, Stockard 720214b
Chapin, Harry 750226a
Chapin, Jim 650009a
Chaplin, Charlie 520018a
Chaplin, Clive 711201b
Chaplin, Saul 440028a
471226a 500002a 580008a
Chaplin, Sydney 530226b
561129a 611227a 640326a
Chapman, Shirley 450419o
591116j
Chapman, Topsy 791020a
Chapman, William 740405a
070302a 240902f 241202e
250921c 540624a 600308a
060924c

Chappell, Eddie 301014a
Chappell, Helen 701215a
Chappelle, Frederick 161206a
Chard, Geoffrey 601203i
Charden, Eric 751210a
Charig, Phil 310305a
Charig, Philip 280605a
  440408a
Charisse, Cyd 460006a
  460006b 470313e 530001a
  550224b 640422a
Charisse, Zan 590521d
Charlap, Moose 541020a
  581222a 650206a 661106*a
  720427a
Charles, Keith 690122a
Charles, Maria 540114a
Charles, Pamela 550831a
  680320a
Charles, Ray 331118i 470110a
  501124e 540513c
Charmen, Ray 710517e
Charmichael, Vangie 760002a
Charnin, Martin 611019a
  671118a 701110a 720326a
  770421a
Chartoff, Melanie 761005b
Chase, Barrie 600928*a
Chase, Carri 681117*a
Chase, Chevy 730125a
Chase, Ilka 570331a
Chastain, Don 660329a
Chatto, Tom 600211a
Chelli, Alida 621215c
Chelsi, Lawrence 560315o
Chevalier, Maurice 051230v
  180925a 290007a 290011a
  290011c 300004a 300004b
  300007a 300007b 300008a
  320002a 320002b 320004a
  320004b 320209a 330046a
  330047a 350021a 360021a
  360026a 360026b 360048a
  390028a 470310a 480229a
  490018a 530507b 560315m
  580001a 580001e 600002a
  620002a 630008a 670009a
Chevit, Maurice 561112d
Chiari, Walter 611118a
Chiarini, Violetta 660107b
Chidsey, Robert 791004a
Child, Marilyn 680502a
  780001a
Chin, Tsai 850314c
Ching, William 471010a
Chisholm, Robert 271103a
  271130a 300920a
Chitjian, Howard 580001c
Chitty, Erik 591118b
Chivot, Henri 791113a
  801229a
Chodosh, Richard B 631029a
Choi, Hye-Young 510329n
Chopin, Frederic 451006a
Chover, Marc 680122c
Christelis, Marina 620005a
Christianson, Bob 031013k
Christie, Audrey 380511c

Christie, Dinah 661018b
Christie, Tony 780621a
Christmas, David 151223a
  681220a
Christopher, Don 680103a
Christy, Carol 721019a
Christy, Eileen 450419h
Chuma, Natalia 761215a
Chun, Kam Fong 610302a
Church, George 631024a
Church, Harden 340607a
Church, Sandra 590521a
Churchill, Frank 330035a
  370012a 410024a 420009a
Churchill, Stuart 420704a
  540010b
Cilento, Wayne 750521a
Cinko, Paula 270906f
Clair, Karin 600622a
Claire, Bernice 051230u
  290311a
Claire, Dorothy 691023a
Clapham, Eric 591116f
Clare, Helen 570331d
Clare, Sidney 300024a
Clark, Bobby 300114a
  481113a
Clark, Buddy 370002b
  470020b 480010b 480019a
  480430b 490014b
Clark, Edward 170206a
Clark, Ernest 791221a
Clark, Harry 460418a 481230a
Clark, Irene 651122b
Clark, Jerry 761202a
Clark, Ken 490407c
Clark, Lillian 630002b
Clark, Lon 440321a
Clark, Patricia 260326a
  271227y 481230l 510329k
  570331f
Clark, Petula 470110b
  690004a
Clark, Philip 781006a
Clark, Randy 770531a
Clark, S 410031a
Clark, Thais 791020a
Clarke, Gordon 571013a
Clarke, Gordon B 380103b
Clarke, Graham 710517g
Clarke, Henry 430331e
Clarke, Hope 541230b
  720419a
Clarke, Jacqueline 540114f
Clarke, John 190419a 261021a
Clary, Robert 520516a
  520516d 550526a
Clary, Wilton 261130a
  430331c
Clauson, William 540017b
Clavel, Gerard 651122f
Clay, Edwin 481230a
Clayburgh, Jill 701019a
  721023a
Clayton, Jan 271227m
  450419a 450419f
Clayton, Lou 290702a
Cleather, E Gordon 060421a

Cleave, Van 570001a
Clements, Otis 191118b
Clemmons, Francois 351010q
Clemon, Paul 241202j
Cliff, Laddie 251228b 270427a
Clifford, Veronica 711201b
Clifton, Bernard 271122a
  530903a
Clifton, John 661106a
  680222*a
Clooney, Betty 540006a
Clooney, Rosemary 470110d
  490407n 501124f 530005a
  540006a 540009a 540010a
  580204b 590008a
Close, Del 590512a 590924a
Close, Glenn 730419*a
  760425a 800430a
Clugston, Glen 640114a
Clutsam, G H 160115b
Clyde, Gordon 170210d
  750422a
Clyde, June 411225a
Coast, John 241202j
Coates, Harold See Al
  Goodman
Cobert, Robert 570005a
Coburn, Joan 570005a
Coca, Imogene 570203a
  780219a
Cochrane, Aileen 141028d
Cochrane, Frank 160831d
Coco, James 651122d
Cody, Kathy 631003a
Coe, George 700426a 780219a
Coe, Peggy 951104b
Coffey, Bridget 770708a
Cogan, Alma 600630a
Coghill, Nevill 680320a
Cohan, George M 031202a
  041107a 060212a 080203a
  111120a 221113a 270926a
  281001a 320014a 420005a
  570511a 640020a 680410a
Cohen, Allen 790328a
Cohen, Beverly 741215a
  760215a
Cohen, Boris 590521h
Cohen, Margery 721001a
  770307a
Cohn, Al 731019a 810301a
Colbert, Claudette 330034a
Colby, Robert 620406a
Cole, Andy 090428c 240902i
  240902l 271227y 280919r
  280919t 301108a 321108g
  331118n 390323c 481230l
  490407j 511112f 560503d
  570926k 581201j 601203j
  640922g 640922i
Cole, Bobby 670731a
Cole, Kay 411001a 750521a
Cole, Maria 490407q
Cole, Nat 530013b 530028a
  550027a 560317a 570013a
  570029a 580006a 590022a
  650008a
Coleman, Charles H 750105a

Coleman, Cy 581011*a
  601215a 601215b 601215c
  621117a 621117c 640004a
  650011a 660129a 660129b
  660129c 660501a 730319a
  730319b 750221a 760419a
  770417a 780219a 780219b
  800430a 800430b
Coleman, Ed 621117b
Coleman, Herbert 491030a
Coleman, Shepard 640116a
  671023a
Coleman, Warren 351010b
Coles, Honi 481208a
Coles, Jack 550831a
Colin, Jean 300220a
Collings, David 700001a
Collins, Blanche 380103a
Collins, Charles 700126a
Collins, Dorothy 710404a
  710404b 730311a
Collins, Jack 691023a
Collins, Joan 610001a 690001a
Collins, Jose 130616a 160110c
  160513a 170210a 200212a
  200515a
Collins, Ken 750408a
Collins, Michael 970928c
  070302b 141028d 160115b
  160831a 170210g 250311m
  261130d 271227w 290718a
  301030a 440821f 470426a
  470426c 481011a
Collins, Ron 690502a
Collins, Winnie 191118a
Collison, Avlon 721108e
Collner, Lynn 590626a
Collyer, Dave 561112*a
Colman, Charles 351010o
Colman, Robert 261130u
  460516q
Colombo, Pia 630319b
Colonna, Jerry 380016a
  410018a 460011b 571013a
Colson, C David 700126a
  700315a
Colson, Kevin 661120d
Colton, Chevi 790111a
Colum, Padraic 931223a
Columbo, Russ 330040a
  330040b 330041a 330041b
  340008a 340008b 340027b
Columbus, Tobie 740108a
Colvig, Pinto 470016b
Colwell Brothers 660627a
Comanor, Jeffrey 740006a
Comber, Bobbie 230105a
Comber, Bobby 271201a
Comden, Betty 270906a
  270906b 280925a 281108b
  441228a 441228b 441228e
  441228f 451221a 471226a
  471226b 481208d 481208e
  490007a 510719a 510719b
  530226a 530226c 541020a
  541020b 550007a 550007b
  550007c 561129a 561129b
  561129c 580403a 581223a

581223b 591113a 601226a
601226d 611227a 611227b
640526a 670426a 750221a
780219a
Como, Perry 430107e 450019a
460017a 480001b 480430a
621020b 730117a
Compton, Fay 151225a
Compton, Linda 671029a
Comstock, Frank 510009c
570004a
Conaway, Jeff 720214b
Condos Brothers 370002b
Condos, Steve 580403a
Conforti, Gino 630019a
651122a
Congdon, James 681201b
800825a
Conklin, Bill 621008a
Conley, Darlene 760511b
Conlow, P 591022a
Conlow, Peter 520321a
Connell, Gordon 590924a
600929a
Connell, Jane 361117a
560614a 581011*a 590511b
590924a 660524a 660524b
690206a
Connelly, Ed 610519a
Conner, Nadine 101107e
551225a
Connerly, Connie 490407g
Conners, Jane 031013i
Connolly, Dolly 170426*a
Connor, Kenneth 620508c
Connor, Martin 800605a
Connor, Nadine 460008a
Connors, Carol 770006a
Connors, Ursula 431202c
Conrad, Barbara 351010q
Conrad, Bob 630003a
Conrad, Con 250413a 321129b
Conrad, Howard 290044a
Conrad, Jess 721108f
Conrad, Paul 240902k
261130s
Conried, Hans 500002a
530010a 530507a 611019a
710415a
Conte, John 471010a
Conti, Tom 790211c
Contreras, Ray 780513a
Convy, Bert 590609a 640922a
661120a
Conway, Connie 571219h
Conway, Curt 410105a
Conway, Shirl 550127a
550127b
Conway, Steve 271227C
Cook, Barbara 271227a
271227k 510329c 510514a
550127a 561201a 571219a
580427a 611118a 630423a
630423d 711102a
Cook, Carole 800825a
Cook, Donna 571219h
Cook, Gerald 541004a
Cook, Jill 760427a

Cook, Joe 370012c
Cook, John 721108a
Cook, Peter 610510a 610510b
640108a 721121a 721121b
Cook, Ray 250311k
261130u 271227j 530903a
690316c 700103b 730225c
Cook, Roderick 631208a
721004a 810329a
Cooke, Charles L 540114b
Cooke, Raymond 640116h
Cookson, Peter 530507a
Cooney, M 770419a
Cooper, Charlotte 611021a
Cooper, Clarence 561121a
Cooper, Gladys 670004a
Cooper, Horace 481011d
Cooper, Jerry 370023a
Cooper, Marilyn 570926a
620322a 660325a 701110a
810329a
Cooper, Phyllis 601226c
Cooper, Roy 680320c
Cooper, Saralou 600928a
Cooper, Terence 481011a
590528a 591118b
Cooperman, Alvin 720427a
Coote, Robert 560315a
560315d 560315l 580008a
661106*a
Coots, J Fred 220706b
220904a 240520a 241015a
250624a 250806a 251124a
290037a 291126a 570016b
711203a
Cope, Moyna 390323b
Copeland, Joan 701110a
Coppola, Anton 520516a
620519a 621215a 621215b
Corbett, Michael 751219a
Corbett, Ronnie 381123e
Corcoran, Noreen 530007a
Corden, Henry 660330a
Cordero, Angel, Jr 750323a
Corey, Herb 600928a
Corey, Irwin 510514a
Corey, Jill 560027a 590013a
600619a
Corman, Robert 351010k
Cornell, Don 540026a
Cornell, Laurie 481230l
490407h
Cornell, Lillian 540010b
Cornell, Ray 591116k 740702a
Corrod, Vinny 580209a
Cort, Harry L 181223a
Cortez, Ricardo 340001a
Cosden, Robert 640114a
Coslow, Sam 330023a
330023b 350023a 370030a
540021a
Cosman, Leonie 781031a
Costa, Bill 600928a
Costa, Don 591125a 661106*a
Costa, Mary 301030d 590010a
Costello, Billy 330032a
Costello, Chris 810201a
Costello, Diosa 391018a

750502a
Coster, Nicolas 621008a
Coudray, Peggy 380103a
Coullet, Rhonda 761010a
Coulouris, George 471226a
Coulter, Kay 360411a
Countrymen 720003a
Couper, Barbara 581002a
Courage, Alexander 561129b
570001a 570002a 650001a
Courtenay, Margaret 711019a
Courtland, Jerome 510514a
Courtneidge, Cicely 250122a
261201a 271201a 330014a
330016a 350020a 370013a
371014a 430923a 510215a
640407c
Courtney, Bill 770517a
Courtney, C C 690924a
700004a
Courtney, Inez 290311a
310011a
Courtney, Ragan 700004a
Courtney, Stella 530903a
Covington, Julie 710517c
780621a
Cowan, Jerome 580403a
Coward, Noel 230904a
250430a 250430b 251110a
280322a 290718a 290718c
290718k 300924a 310319a
310601a 311013a 320916a
320916b 330017a 340216a
340216b 360109a 380316a
380316b 390118a 390118b
450822a 461219a 461219b
500707a 500707b 510524a
520710a 540610a 551022a
611003a 611003b 611003c
611003d 631208a 631208b
640407b 671115a 720710a
721004a
Cowens, Bernie 731217a
Cowles, Chandler 460418a
Cowles, Dennie 271201a
Cowles, Eugene 910928a
980926a
Cox, Ed 760408a
Cox, Richard 781112a
Cox, Wally 630002a 680003a
Cox, William 780510a
Coyne, Joseph 101105a
141208a 151225a 171225c
250311c
Cozzens, Leslie 690806a
Crabbe, Buster 370040a
Craig, Charles 291010a
Craig, David 550423a 571017a
Craig, Donald 770421a
Crain, Jeanne 450001b
450001e 460014a 460014b
480018a 550002a
Crain, Jon 450419g
Crane, Larry 690502a
Crane, Lor 700603a
Crane, Norma 640922c
Cranko, John 560301a
Craswell, Dennis 700318a

Craven, Gemma 760006a
760504c 790211c 790211d
790725a
Crawford, Claudia 571117a
Crawford, Joan 290020a
290034a 300025b 310010a
330027a 370039a 380036a
390025a 410026a 430018a
490017a 530012a 530012b
Crawford, Joe 431202b
Crawford, Joseph 351010o
Crawford, Michael 620508b
640116d 720002a 740501a
790614a
Crawford, Randy 750006a
Crawley, Sybil 360911a
Creatore, Luigi 681023a
730404a
Cree, Patricia 540610a
Cresson, James 650511a
Cribbens, Bernard 590012a
591118b
Crichton, Madge 020510a
Crigler, Lynn 151223a
750107a
Crisham, Walter 370901a
Crispi, Ida 120214a
Crofoot, Alan 651122c
Crofoot, Gayle 771029a
Crofoot, Leonard John
800430a
Croft, David 240902i 250311h
301108d
Cronje, Tobie 770417b
Crook, John 150322a
Crookham, Wade 810201a
Crooks, Richard 310814a
Crosbie, Annette 760006a
Crosby, Bing 271227v 300005a
301014i 310008a 310012a
310012b 310013a 310013b
310914b 320010a 320010b
320011a 320011b 320015a
320015b 320217a 330022a
330022b 330023a 330024a
330037a 330037b 330038a
330038b 340015a 340022a
340022b 340024a 341121g
341121j 341121k 350010a
350010b 350024a 350024c
350025a 360002a 360015a
360027a 360027b 370022a
370022b 370027a 380018a
380018b 380019a 390009a
390010a 390010b 390011a
390424b 400018a 400019a
400025a 410016a 410017a
420001a 420001c 420001d
420002a 420004a 420012a
430017a 440004a 440004c
440006a 440015b 450006a
450007a 450007b 450215a
460002b 460003a 460004a
460004b 460004c 470002a
470007a 470007b 470008a
470110d 480007a 490008a
490009a 490015a 490407n
490407u 500011a 500012a

500012b 501124c 510011a
510011b 520012a 530006a
530011a 540002a 540002b
540006b 560001a 560310a
570003a 570026a 580019a
580027a 590006a 600002a
610001a 630002a 640002a
700303a
Crosby, Bob 400034a 410030a
410030b 420001a 430008a
Crosby, Gary 630004a
Crosby, Kathryn 700303a
Crosby, Mary Frances
700303a
Cross, James 420704a 420704e
Cross, John Benton 581201i
Croswell, Anne 600504a
630318a
Crothers, Scatman 660330a
Crowder, Jack 620205b
640116b
Crowley, Ann 510621a
Crowley, Ed 681013a
Crowley, Kathleen 560014a
Crozier, Jim 701108a
Crumit, Frank 140824b
200830a 210809a 260908e
Cryer, David 631029a 670926a
700603a
Cryer, Gretchen 590430a
670926a 700126a 730206a
730206a 780516a
Crystal, Raphe 791127a
Cugat, Xavier 420003b
420003c 440011a 440031a
450024a 460009c 470004a
480013b 480027a 480030a
490004c
Cullen, David 810511a
Culler, Sip 751121a
Culley, Fred 550727a
Cullum, John 651017a
671115a 690316b 750107a
780219a
Cummings, Constance
330040a
Cummings, Irene 430331k
Cummings, Robert 360062a
380013b 400005a 410021a
540018b
Cunningham, Billy 740108a
Cunningham, John 580513a
680103a 681117a
Cunningham, Zamah 360411b
Cupito, Suzanne 590521b
Curb, Mike 700006a
Curram, Roland 711220a
Curry, Ed 951104b
Curry, Steve 671029b
Curry, Tim 730619a 730619b
730619d
Curtis, Keene 701019a
Curtis, Tony 550006a
Curty, Gene 750309a
Cushing, C C S 121010a
Cushman, Robert 791106a
Cutell, Lou 610425a
Cutler, Ben 371009a

Cutler, Howard 720612a
Cutler, Kate 991111g
Cuvillier, Charles 141028a
160911a 190917a
Cypher, Jon 570331a 691218a

d'Abo, Mike 711012a 780621a
d'Abravanel, Maurice 381019c
d'Alba, Julia 290718j
d'Alroy, Evelyn 081114j
D'Angelo, Beverly 671029g
D'Angelo, Eddie 810328a
D'Antonakis, Fleury 650318a
d'Armond, Isobell 131223a
d'Aval, Jacques 630606a
D'Elia, Chet 750309a
d'Esti, Roberta 530903a
d'Orme, Aileen 160831d
D'Orsay, Fifi 710404a
d'Orso, Wisa 621020a
d'Paulo, Dante 580013a
Da Silva, Howard 380103a
591123a 690316a 690316b
430331a
Dabdoub, Jack 271227a
691218a
Dacus, Don 671029g
Dagny, Robert 651226a
Dahdah, Robert 671122a
Dahl, Arlene 470022a 500004a
750323a
Dailey, Dan 241201e 390209b
460418c 470010a 480018a
480018b 480024a 500003a
500019a 540004a 540004c
550007a 560004b 560005a
560005b 571117a
Daines, Barbara 590122a
Daines, Guy 471023a
Dains, George 621004a
Dainton, Marie 011005a
Dalba, Mario 751210a
Dale, Bob 490407m
Dale, Clamma 351010s
Dale, Grover 570926a
611003a 611003c 630321c
Dale, Jim 530903a 600630f
770005a 800430a
Dale, Virginia 420001c
Daley, Cass 420017a 430022a
450215a
Dall, Evelyn 430107c 440408b
Dallas, Lorna 271227j 740416a
Dalmes, Mony 601103a
Dalton, Doris 510621a
Dalton, Wesley 051230a
241202a 261130a
Daltrey, David 721108a
Daltrey, Roger 750005a
Daly, Nigel 720214c
Daly, William 220220a
Dam, H J 941124a
Dame, Donald 060924b
160115a 241202f 280919o
Damon, Cathryn 381123a
640216a 641026a 650511a
Damon, Stuart 381123a
561112c 570331b 650318a

Damone, Vic 270425c
510004a 510004c 510016a
510026a 531203b 531203j
540010a 540011a 561223a
570012a 571220a 580029a
651128a
Dana, Bill 660330a
Dance, George 011005a
Dandolo, Giusi Raspani
660107a 660107b
Dandridge, Dorothy 351010c
431202b
Dane, Clemence 340112a
340919a
Dane, John 250311k
Daneman, Paul 601203e
Daniele, Graciela 640227a
Daniels, Bebe 270202a
300024a 310008a 330021a
Daniels, Billie 351010e
Daniels, Billy 510016a
510016b 641020a 760302b
Daniels, David 261108e
550127a
Daniels, Maxine 271227y
Daniels, Stan 760427a
Daniels, Walker 671029a
Daniels, William 651017a
690316a 690316b
Danks, Indira 721019a
Dann, Roger 591116e
Danner, Blythe 690316b
Danon, Oscar 740405g
Danvers, Ivor 261130u
Darby, Ken 351012b 480019b
Dare, Phyllis 081223b
090428e 110304a 190520a
261201a 490915a
Darewski, Herman 150322a
Darewski, Max 250310a
Darian, Anita 241202b
271227a 510329c 580033a
Darin, Bobby 450001d
600002a 620016a 640007a
Darion, Joe 570413a 651122a
651122f 670411a
Darling, Edward 160831b
431202c
Darling, Jean 450419a
Darling, Jennifer 681023a
Darren, James 590018a
600015a 600414e 610009a
620011a 640007a
Darrieux, Danielle 510004a
680004a 711019a
Dauphin, Claude 520021b
Davenport, Pembroke 480129a
481230a 481230f 501221a
530211a 540624a 611102a
641215a
David, Clifford 380103b
381123a 601215a 651017a
690316a
David, Hal 601205b 661207a
680002a 681201a 730001a
740325a
David, Mack 490011a
Davidson, John 590122a

620311b 640216a 670004a
680003a
Davidson, Lorraine 740108a
Davies, Brian 490407t
591116a 620508a 700103b
Davies, Gareth 571219c
601203i 611003c 630321d
640922d 661120d 711019a
721106a
Davies, Irving 460516j
Davies, John Huw 280828j
Davies, Kendall 710517e
Davies, Lew 450419g
Davies, Lilian 230105a
Davies, Marion 290020a
330022b
Davies, Morgan 450419k
Davies, Peter Maxwell
540114d
Davies, Ramona 330908a
330930b 331021a 340201b
341121i 350006c 351012b
Davies, Rowland 761206a
Davies, Tudor 720710a
Davies, Victor 771201a
Davila, Diana 711201a
Davis, Benny 580004a
630006a
Davis, Beryl 460027a
Davis, Bette 420022a 430016a
430016b 521215a 620007a
640009a
Davis, Buster 250311d
250311l 411001a 550025a
670426a 680127a 750319a
780002a
Davis, Charles K L 051230i
Davis, Clifton 681013a
711201a
Davis, Danny 650216b
Davis, Frank 541230e
Davis, Fred 481230a
Davis, Irving 540602a
Davis, Janette 530128a
Davis, Jessie Bartlett 910928a
970316c
Davis, Joan 370038a 380006a
Davis, Johnny "Scat" 370023a
Davis, Luc 561112a
Davis, Mac 690005a
Davis, Michael 611110a
690604a
Davis, Ossie 571031a 631015a
651110a 750323a
Davis, Paul 711012a
Davis, Ray C 711201b
740711a 781031a
Davis, Sammy 280828c
Davis, Sammy, Jr 351010c
470110d 481230c 490407n
501124c 560322a 560322b
580018a 600002a 600010a
610720d 630002a 640002a
641020a 641020b 660006a
660129b 670006c 731116a
Davis, Thomas M 430331k
571219h
Davison, Bruce 660524b

Davison, Lesley 611005a
Dawn, Julie 261130d 271227F
 290718a 640116i 640326e
Dawson, Harry 550831b
Dawson, Mark 471009a
 530528a 550418a
Dawson, Peter 090906b
Day, Colin 640326e
Day, Dennis 470022b 480019a
 480019b 500019a 500019b
 510018a
Day, Doris 250311f 351116b
 460516f 480010a 480010b
 490014a 490014b 490016a
 490016b 500010a 500010b
 500023a 510009a 510009b
 510009c 510012a 510012b
 510024a 520010a 520010b
 520021a 520021b 530004a
 540015a 540015b 540018a
 540018b 540513b 550003a
 560013a 560019a 580011a
 580031a 590009a 590015a
 600005a 601205b 610005a
 630009a 650002a 660005a
Day, Edith 191118a 191118c
 240902d 261130c 261130k
 270202c 271227A 271227g
 611003c
Day, Frances 240902a
 320611a 360042a 370623a
 380817a 391206c 410424a
Day, Julie 540114g 591116f
Day, Kenny 640116o
Day, Roger 760324a
Dayley, Newell 760414a
de Boer, Sherry 610302a
de Bray, Henri 171225c
de Carlo, Yvonne 480004c
 510006a 550015a 710404a
de Cordova, Arturo 450017b
De Cormier, Robert 610403a
de Frece, Lauri 170210a
de Funes, Louis 651214a
de Guzman, Jossie 790408a
de Haven, Gloria 400036a
 430008a 440011a 440011b
 460019a 500002a 500004a
 500019a 510010b 550006a
 550006b 550526a 550526b
 680107a
de Havilland, Olivia 430016a
De Lange, Eddie 391129a
De Lapenha, Denise 721123a
De Lory, Al 690005a
de Luise, Dom 611110a
 620406a
De Marco, Tony 430004a
de Paul, Gene 410020a
 490015a 540001a 560002a
 561115a
de Paur, Leonard 390424d
 431120a 440321b
de Rance, Haidee 141224a
de Salvo, Ron 720522b
De Shields, Andre 750105a
 780509a
de Sousa, May 091112d

de Vito, Karen 780608a
de Wolff, Francis 610413c
Deal, Dennis 391018c
 400911a 480115a
Dean, Gerri 700518a
DeAnda, Peter 651110a
Deane, Douglas 501124a
Deane, Uel 431127a 451115a
 620208a
DeAngelis, Bob 480115a
Deauville, Ronnie 580030a
Debenham, Cicely 170131a
DeCamp, Rosemary 420005a
Dee, Ann 670001a
Dee, Joey 630004a
Dee, Ruby 750323a
Deel, Sandra 400528b
 480129a 490407d 490715b
Deems, Mickey 341121e
 621117a
Deering, Olive 410105a
Dees, Michael 740007a
Dees, Rick 770004a
DeKoven, Reginald 910928a
 941029a 090410a
Del Prete, Duilio 750002a
Del Rio, Dolores 280001a
 340001a 350038b
del Valle, Peter 750127a
Delinger, Larry 790513b
Dell'Isola, Salvatore 360411a
 471010a 490407a 530528a
 550418a 551130a 581201a
Dell, Dorothy 340054a
Dell, Gabriel 550418a
 640404a
Dell, Jean 680122e
Della Casa, Lisa 051230i
della Rosa, Dianne 720522b
Delman, Jacqueline 051230p
 160115l
Delmar, Elaine 720710a
 760302b
Delmar, Kenny 491125a
DeLon, Jack 560503b 620127a
 631017a
Delson, Mary 721123a
Delta Rhythm Boys 410003a
 410003b
deLuce, Virginia 520516a
Delugg, Anne 660010a
Delugg, Milton 570018a
 660010a
Delysia, Alice 160605a
 170822a 180803a 190917a
 220309a 250430a 261021a
 330127a
DeMain, John 351010s
Demas, Carole 681013a
 720214a
Dempsey, Mark 690617a
Demy, Jacques 640003a
 680004a
Dench, Judi 661120d 740711a
Deneuve, Catherine 640003a
 680004a
DeNiro, Robert 770002a
Denise, Gita 591118b

Denison, Michael 850314d
Dennen, Barry 661120d
 711012a 711012b 711012e
Dennis, Clark 401225g
 470110d 501124c
Dennis, Robert 690617a
Dent, Jack 561112e
Derefinko, Rod 690122a
Derr, Richard 550127a
 550127b
Derricks-Carroll, Clinton
 761222a
DeSalvo, Kathy 760215a
DesFontaines, LaMonte
 730319a
DeSio, Alfred 611102a
Desmond, Florence 400827a
 410031a
Desmond, Johnny 391018c
 550002a 551226a 561223a
 570034a 580403a 660501a
Desmond, Trudy 730419a
Desmonde, Jerry 481011a
DeSylva, B G 201221a
 201221b 220309a 220706a
 220828a 220828b 221002a
 230828a 240630a 250413*a
 260614a 260908a 270906a
 280702a 281010a 290015a
 290029a 290109a 300303a
 310006a 310914a 321126a
 330304a 450022a 500001a
 560004a 580002a 720117a
 760008a
Deutsch, Adolph 271227e
 460516b 460516h 490007a
 500009a 510002a 530001a
 540001a 540010a 570001a
 570002a 590002a
Deutsch, Helen 530009a
 561112*a
DeVol, Frank 530014a
 600619a
DeVore, Jesse 680509a
Dewitt, Fay 271227a 430331g
 510514a 550228a 571105a
 600912a
DeWolfe, Billy 510009a
 611014c
Dexter, Alan 511112c
DeZina, Kate 770322a
Dhery, Robert 581111a
 651214a
Diamond, Jack 481230a
Dickey, Annamary 471010a
Dickey, William 600630e
Dickson, Barbara 780621a
Dickson, Dorothy 201221a
 201221c 220919a 251228b
 261227a 360911a 370901a
Diedrich, John 430331w
Diego, Fritz 770004a
Diener, Joan 531203a 651122a
 651122c 651122f 660501a
 700408a
Dietrich, Marlene 300001a
 300001b 300002a 300002b
 320018a 330010a 360055a

390004a 390004b 400013a
 400013b 410037a 480006a
 480006b 500007a 570041a
 580020a 641123*a 790001a
Dietz, Howard 740405c
 740405f 261108a 290430c
 300220a 301015b 310603a
 320915a 341128a 350919a
 360050a 371222a 400523a
 420024a 420025a 480016a
 480430a 530001a 570043a
 611118a 631017a
Dignam, Arthur 730619c
Dillard, Bill 650009a
Dillard, William 351010o
Dilworth, Gordon 661126a
Dilworth, Hubert 441005a
Dinning Sisters 470016c
Dishy, Bob 420602a 650511a
Disney, Walt 290041a
 330035b 330042a 340038a
 360061a
Distel, Sacha 580001e
Dittman, Dean 380103b
 780219a
Dix, Tommy 411001c
Dix, William 670006a
Dixon, Adele 310514a
 340409a
Dixon, Bob 590205a
Dixon, Conway 960425a
 991021b
Dixon, Gale 691218a
Dixon, Lee 360006a 370052a
 430331a
Dixon, MacIntyre 651223a
Dixon, Mort 311102a
Dodd, Cal 760217a
Dodd, Claire 281204c
Dodd, Rory 760217a
Dodds, Jamieson 141028b
Dodds, Malcolm 580004a
Dodge, Jerry 640116a 680410a
Dodge, Jimmy 751209a
Dods, Marcus 350505c
 360911b 450421b 600630d
 630704a 640326d 740711a
Dodson, John 581201b
Doenges, Marion 460006b
Doff, Gerard 701108a
Doggett, Alan 711012a
 721108a 721108c
Doherty, Lindy 511101a
Dolan, Robert Emmett
 420001c 440004c 460004c
 491125a 580221a 590309a
 640216a 691218a
Dolman, Richard 300220a
Dolton, Robin 721023c
Domville, James 570207a
Donahue, Elinor 480016a
Donahue, Troy 630003a
Donahue, Walter 430331e
Donald, Mark 650009a
Donald, Steven 430331q
Donaldson, Norma 501124g
Donaldson, Walter 281204a
 340010b 360003a

Elias, Michel 751210a
Elias, Rosalind 740405a
  851024a 101107d 240902f
  250921c 271227h 290718i
  301108c
Eliot, T S 810511a
Eliscu, Edward 330005a
Elkins, Flora 620311b
Elkner, Maureen 730619c
Elliman, Yvonne 711012a
  711012b 711012e
Ellington, Duke 280509a
  290039a 300023a 330044a
  340028a 340042a 340042b
  350056a 401025d 410804a
  630816a 810301a
Ellington, Mercer 810301a
Ellington, Ray 351010h
Elliott, Jack 430331d 450419b
  481230e 600120a 670004a
  680003a 710814a 720427a
Elliott, Osborn 750323a
Elliott, Patricia 730225a
Elliott, Shawn 680122a
Elliott, Victoria 740405h
  440821f
Elliott, William 791231a
Ellis, Anita 460018a 460018b
  470017a 500004a 510002a
  550002a 581201a
Ellis, Antonia 540114d
Ellis, Barbara 701108a
Ellis, Mary 321108b 350505a
  390323a 390323f 431109a
  540610a
Ellis, Maurice 510621a
Ellis, Ray 611010b 630002a
  630002b 640526a 641026a
Ellis, Rob 710517f
Ellis, Russ 620205b
Ellis, Scott 800514a
Ellis, Segar 290629b
Ellis, Sheila 761222a 761222b
Ellis, Vivian 250122a 290211a
  300917a 371014a 470426a
  470426c 550831a
Ellis, William 681220b
Elman, Ziggy 380016a
Elmassian, Zaruhi 101107o
Elmer, Edward 430331q
Elmer, Jim 751014a
Elmes, Basil 680305a
Elmes, Edgar 370901a
Elmore, Steve 681220a
  700426a 700426b 730311a
  780608a
Elmslie, Kenward 711102a
Elsom, Jonathan 711220a
Elson, Louis C 801001a
Elsy, Barbara 051230p
  081114f 160831b 240902i
  241202r 351010h 430331r
  450419l
Ely, Paul 571219h
Elzy, Ruby 351010p 400031a
Emerson, Hope 470109a
Emery, Ann 741007*a
Emery, Rick 800514a

Emmanuel, Ivor 271227y
  481230l 510329k 631024b
  660521a
Emney, Joan 540513d
Endich, Sara 031013a 051225a
  160115c 241202e 250921c
Endor, Chick 271201a
Engel, Lehman 740405a
  831003b 851024a 031013a
  051225a 051230a 051230e
  060924c 070302a 081114b
  081114e 101107d 160115c
  240902a 240902f 241202a
  241202e 250311j 250921c
  260326a 261108a 261130a
  261130f 261130i 271227b
  271227h 271227z 280509b
  280919e 290430b 290718i
  301014a 301108c 310603c
  311015c 331118a 331118f
  340216b 341121d 351010b
  351010e 351116a 360411b
  370414a 381123b 401225a
  410123c 430331c 440821c
  440821e 450419c 460418a
  470313c 471226a 481230h
  510329c 530226a 530226b
  541104a 561115a 571031a
  581011a 590423a 591022a
  601226a 620322a 640227a
  641123a 700103a
Englander, Ludwig 000319a
English, Anna 570521a
English, Jon 711012d
Englund, Patricia 780510a
Engvick, William 571013a
  580427a
Enten, Boni 690617a 730619b
Epstein, Alvin 620315a
Ercole, Joe 801120a
Ercoli, Linda 720001a
Ericksen, Eddie 550727a
  610518a
Erickson, Arthur 780300a
Ericson, June 541230c
  581201f
Errol, Leon 201221f 300014a
Ervin, Dee 721019a
Erwin, Barbara 770421a
Erwin, Denise 751121a
Erwin, Trudy 051230d 401225c
  450027a 460004a 510005b
Esposito, Giancarlo 730319a
Esser, Phil Marcus 680122c
Essex, David 710517c
Essex, Violet 120224a 160831d
Etting, Ruth 270816b 281204a
  300040a 300218a 310701a
  330028a 330028b 340025a
  340030a 361001a
Evanko, Ed 680320c
Evans, Colleen Townsend
  530026b
Evans, Dorothy 540513c
Evans, Dottie 580007c
Evans, Greek 170319c
Evans, Harvey 540114c
  640404b 680410a 681220c

  730311a
Evans, Jessie 191118f 630704a
  680320a
Evans, Marion 590002b
Evans, Maurice 601017a
Evans, Ray 470009a 480022a
  490012a 500013a 500020a
  510011a 520005a 520009a
  520014a 530005a 540009a
  540912a 560019a 560021a
  570008a 580028a 580204a
  590201a 610003a 611012a
Evans, Rex 481208a 580008a
Evans, Suzannah 671029a
Evans, Tudor 240902a
Evans, Wilbur 051230g
  060924d 261130h 301030b
  440128a 450127a 490407e
  540408a
Everett, Elliot 560315r
Everhart, Rex 651113a
  690316a
Evett, Robert 971116a
  051230q 070302c
Ewell, Tom 450001d
Eysler, Edmund 090906a
  131002a
Eythe, William 460014a
Eyton, Frank 400209a

Faassen, John 530908a
Fabares, Shelley 600414e
  680010a
Fabian 600013a
Fabray, Nanette 471009a
  471009b 500202a 510418a
  530001a 621020a 661106*a
Fabrizi, Aldo 621215a
  621215b 621215c
Fagan, Joan 610518a
Fahey, Brian 160115b 160831a
  261130d 271227w 290718a
  601203j 630704a
Fain, Sammy 300008b
  310019a 350044a 370051a
  380105a 390828a 411201a
  440003a 460008b 460418c
  480016a 510013a 510514a
  520004e 530004a 530004b
  530008a 530010a 530014a
  540018b 550029a 550418a
  560016a 570007a 580007a
  600428a 710606a 770006a
Fairbank, Spring 151223a
Fairbanks, Douglas, Jr
  340919a 750502a
Fairbanks, Nola 831003a
Fairchild, Edgar 210523b
  260908c 270816a 360411d
  370414d 440002a
Fairchild, George 380103a
Fairley, Bill 721023c 721108e
  770307b 770417b
Fairman, Blain 711019a
Faison, Sandy 770421a
Faith, Adam 600211b
Faith, Percy 540009a 540015a
  550003a

Falk, Peter 640002a
Fall, Leo 081223a 120203a
  130825a 220302a
Fallon, Larry 730319a 780219b
Falzone, Peter 720310a
Farber, Burt 620311b
Farge, Annie 640422a
Faris, Alexander 301030c
  561112b 781031a 790614a
Farkoa, Maurice 950202a
  010907a 041217a
Farmer, Frances 360027b
Farnham, Johnny 721023b
Farnon, Dennis 580001d
Farnon, Robert 481011d
  550002a 610001a
Farran, Merrick 170210c
Farrar, Gwen 301205a
Farrell, Eileen 060924d
  450127a 550012a
Farrell, Glenda 330036a
  360006a
Farrell, Jim 721009a
Farrell, Marguerite 160529a
Farrell, Peter 701215a
Farrell, Walter 600201a
  600900a 620205*a
Farris, Dolores 280919d
Farrow, Peter 630002a
  750006a
Faull, Ellen 340216b
Favor, Edward M 930515a
Fawdon, Michelle 711012d
Faye, Alice 270906f 320010a
  340005a 340006a 340006b
  340006c 340007a 340039a
  340039b 350003a 350003b
  350003c 350004a 350004b
  350005a 350005b 350045a
  360001b 360010a 360017a
  360017b 370001a 370001b
  370002a 370002b 370014a
  370014b 370015a 370015b
  380009a 380009b 380009c
  380029a 380029b 380030a
  380031a 380031b 380803a
  390005a 390005b 390022a
  400015a 400015b 400016a
  400016b 410007a 410010a
  410027a 430003a 430003b
  430003c 430004a 430004b
  440022a 450001c 450001d
  780004a
Faye, Frances 370022b
Faye, Herbie 511101a
Faye, Joey 511101a 621117a
Fazakas, Franz 630411a
Feast, Michael 671029a
Feathers, Jennie 401225f
Fehring, Johannes 661120e
  751210b
Felber, William 241202s
Felgate, Peter 430331r
Felix, Hugo 160228*a
Feller, Sid 520004a 651113c
Felton, Felix 481011a
Felton, Verna 410024a
  490011a 490011b

Fenholt, Jeff 711012b
Fenn, Jean 250921i 301030b
Fenwick, John 560304a
Fenwick, Lucy 740702a
Ferdin, Pamelyn 690006a
Ferguson, Allyn 720427a
Ferguson, Helen 401025a
Fernandel, Franck 561112d
Fernandez, Jose 700518a
Fernandez, Venetia 540001b
Ferrara, Franco 590004a
Ferrari, Violetta 661120e
Ferrer, Jose 540010a 580204b
    631208a
Ferrer, Mel 740405b 530009a
Ferrier, Pat 590205a
Ferriere, Jacques 561112d
Ferro, Daniel 510329c
Fetter, Ted 371009a
Fiander, Lewis 690316c
    721106a 721106b
Fiedler, Arthur 261130o
Field, Sid 460027a
Fielding, Fenella 581002a
Fielding, Jerry 590023a
Fields, Alvin 751219a
Fields, Benny 520009b
Fields, Dorothy 280509a
    281226a 300225a 331118a
    350004a 350048a 360002a
    370026a 380032a 390209a
    450127a 500202a 510005a
    510419a 520003a 540408a
    571220a 590205a 660129a
    660129b 730319a
Fields, Frank 730419*a
Fields, Gracie 310003a
    320020a 330026a 340026a
    340032a 350059a 360057a
    370050a 380017a 390007a
    390007b 430012b
Fields, Lynn 301030b
Fields, Shep 380013a 380013b
Fields, Tommy 350059a
    380017a
Fina, Jack 480019a
Finck, Herman 240902d
    261130c 271227g 280313a
    280919d
Fine, Sidney 550018b
Fine, Sylvia 440005a 440005b
    540016a 560008a
Finley, Bill 740006a
Finley, Pat 600928a
Finn, William 790221a
Finneran, Mike 810201a
Finney, Albert 700001a
Finney, Bess 721023c
Finney, Mary 561206a
Finston, Nathaniel W 340024a
    340036a 380024a 390017b
Fio Rito, Ted 340001b
    340002b
Fiorini, Lando 621215a
    621215b
Firman, David 810511a
Firth, Elizabeth 051230q
Fischoff, George 620311a

Fisher, Eddie 560010a
    621002a
Fisher, Fred 490027a
Fisher, Lola 560315i 560315j
Fisher, Max 271122*a
Fisher, Robert 790328a
Fitch, Robert 620406a
    770421a
Fite, Beverly 401225a
Fitt, Tom 791004a
Fitzball, Edward 451115a
Fitzgerald, Ella 490407u
    550004a
Fitzgibbon, Maggie 240902i
    271122f 321108g 331118n
    381123e 460516n 580001h
    601226b 611014d
Fitzpatrick, Kate 730619c
Fitzwilliam, Neil 710517c
Flack, Roberta 740008a
Flagg, Fannie 651103a
Flanagan, Bill 540624b
Flanagan, Bud 391011a
    391206c 410424a
Flanders, Michael 570124a
    570124b 570124c 631002a
    631002b
Flannery, Gary 760419a
Fleeson, Neville 200503a
Fleet, Edgar 051230o
Fleishman, Philip 650222a
Fleming, Gordon 560315n
Fleming, Rhonda 490009a
    590020a
Flemming, Claude 200515a
Fletcher, Jack 481208e
    581011*a 621018a 641027a
Fletcher, Percy E 261021a
Flint, Shelby 720001a
Flippen, Jay C 430331b
Flory, Regine 161106a
Flowers, Martha 351010u
Flynn, Eric 191118f
Flynn, Errol 430016a 550023a
Flynn, Patrick 671029e
    711012d
Foil, Homer 780300a
Foldi, Erzsebet 790004a
Foley, John 780300a
Fonda, Henry 690010a
Fonda, Peter 770003a
Fontaine, Jacqueline 540002b
Fontane, Tony 271227u
    510016a
Fontanna 580001k
Fonteyn, Sam 450419o
    490407t 591116j 631024b
Foran, Dick 271103a 360025a
    370041a
Forbes, Brenda 680127a
Forbes, Helen 710517e
Forbes, Sheila 611003c
Forbstein, Leo F 300010b
    330001b 330002b 330021a
    340001a 340002b 340021a
    350001b 350011a 360020a
    370023a 410005a 420704e
    430016a 450008a 460010b

    460021a
Ford, Barbara 571219h
Ford, Chip 750107a
Ford, Clebert 631015a
Ford, David 690316b
Ford, Joan 581011a
Ford, Laurel 740416a
Ford, Nancy 670926a 700126a
    730206a 730206a 780516a
Ford, Ruth 711102a
Ford, Tennessee Ernie
    570036a
Forest, Frank 280919g
Forester, Lee 390001f
Forgione, Eleanor 571219g
Forman, Janine 640422a
Forman, Joey 640422a
Fornes, Maria Irene 690604a
Forray, Andy 671029d
Forrest, George 121202a
    301030b 390017a 440821a
    531203a 531203i 611102a
    651129a
Forrest, Paul 691023a
Forrez, Anne 640003c
Forster, Leesa 351010u
Forsyth, Bette 751014a
Forsyth, Bruce 261130d
    621117b 680001a
Forsythe, Bruce 690001a
Forsythe, Henderson 780417a
Fortier, Bob 530528a
Fortunate, Lou 610519a
Fortus, Daniel 700326a
Fosse, Bob 481230d 740002a
Foster, Donald 311226a
Foster, Judy 610425a
Foster, Julia 630321b
Foster, Stephen 590626a
Foster, Stuart 430331g
    520001d 530010b 601103*a
    640019a
Four Aces 560002a
Foursome, The 301014d
Fowler, Beth 790005a
Fowler, Harry 600211b
Fowles, Glenys 051230s
Fox, Dulce 380103a
Fox, Franklyn 570926i
Fox, Harry 180307a
Fox, Patrick 700603a
Fox, Richard 430331s 590521g
    640116l
Foy, Eddie, Jr 330040a
    540513a 540513b 561129b
    590201a 610518a 660928a
Fradkin, Leslie 770531a
Frame, Grazina 650007a
Frampton, Mac 740004a
France, Richard 540408a
    640227a
Franchi, Sergio 740405g
    650318a
Francine, Paul 351010t
Francis, Connie 301014e
    630006a
Francis, Dai 741007*a
Francis, Dick 261005a

Francis, Ed 601226c
Francks, Don 470110b
Francois, Jack 621117b
Frank, Adams 090208a
Frank, Barry 580007a
Frank, Daniel 200324a
Frank, Judy 670926a
Frank, Sherman 570044a
    580002a 590001a
Frankau, Ronald 410031a
Franke, Paul 051230i
Frankel, Benjamin 380316a
Franken, Steve 621010a
Franklin, Bonnie 700330a
Franklin, Hugh 321212b
Franklin, Irene 100604a
Franklin, Ronnie 600211a
Franks, Chloe 730225d
Franks, Graciela 690806a
Franz, Joy 650616a 760427a
    800514a
Franzell, Carlotta 431202a
Fraser, Alison 790221a
Fraser, Ian 610720c 700001a
Fraser, Jeri Lynne 630004a
Fraser, Kay 640116i
Fraser, Moyra 540114d
Fraser-Simson, Harold
    170210a
Frawley, James 640404a
Frawley, William 370037a
Frazer, Kay 591116k
Frazier, David O 680122b
Freberg, Stan 580003a
    580010a
Fredericks, Charles 081114a
    240902e 271227m
Fredericks, Lydia 540305a
Fredericks, Richard 060924c
    160115c 240902f 261130i
    271227h 440821c
Frediani, Celinda 700103b
Freear, Louie 011005a
Freebairn-Smith, Ian 610007a
    790002a
Freed, Arthur 241201e
    290005a 330022a 400003a
    450027a 500009a 520002a
    540114d
Freed, Ralph 370022a 391206d
    410004b 460004b 490014a
Freed, Sam 561201b
Freedman, Gerald 630411a
    660521a
Freedman, Robert 731019a
    770920a
Freeman, Arny 700326a
    780514a
Freeman, Audrey 520925a
Freeman, Bud 600210a
Freeman, Damita Jo 781112a
Freeman, Denise 770307b
Freeman, Ernie 301014e
Freeman, Mona 470010a
Freeman, Richard 791221a
Freeman, Stan 641215a
Frees, Paul 620001a 640422a
Freiberg, Thomas 750917b

790513a
Geyans, Jon 241202a
Ghostley, Alice 520516a
   560613a 570331a
Giacomini, Enrico 390323b
Gibbons, Carroll 340201a
Gibbs, Georgia 531203j
Gibbs, Nancy 191112a
Gibbs, Phyllis 701108a
Gibbs, Sheila 711201c
Gibson, Alexander 051230t
Gibson, Dewey 161206a
Gibson, Henry 750003a
Gibson, Karen 790513a
Gibson, Michael 740306a
   810329a
Gibson, Scott 611023a
Gibson, Virginia 510017c
   540001a 561206a
Gideon, Melville 210627a
   280130a
Gielgud, John 310514a
Giersdorf, Rae 361029b
   361102a
Giesdorf Sisters 341128b
Gifford, Frances 390027b
Gilbert, Alan 441005a
Gilbert, Billy 400015a
Gilbert, Herschel B 431202b
Gilbert, Jean 140112a 150503a
   711201b
Gilbert, Joanne 540009a
   590016a
Gilbert, Olive 360911a
   370901a 390323a 390323f
   450421a 490915a 591116e
   651122c
Gilbert, Paul 550006a
Gilbert, Ray 440023a 440023a
   590016a
Gilbert, Robert 301108a
   661120e
Gilbert, Simon 651122d
Gilbert, Ted 261130u 430331s
Gilbert, William S 791231a
   850314a 800228a
Gilbraith, Barney 301108a
Gilette, Anita 620319a
Gilford, Jack 250311d 311226b
   590511a 620508a 620508b
   651122b 661120a
Gilger, Glenn 690006a
Gilkyson, Terry 680007a
Gillan, Ian 711012a
Gilles, Genevieve 700002a
Gillespie, Christina 611110a
Gillespie, Dana 711012c
Gillespie, Darlene 510013b
Gillespie, Haven 711203a
Gillespie, William 400031a
Gillett, Valerie 760003a
Gillette, Anita 301030b
   621020a 691023a
Gillette, Priscilla 501221a
   540311a
Gillette, Steve 701215a
Gilliland, Helen 260906a
   300920a

Gillmore, Margalo 541020a
Gilmore, Peter 581002a
Gilmour, Ross 531203g
Gimbel, Normal 581222a
Gingold, Hermione 531210a
   571219b 580001a 590319a
   620001a 730225a 730225c
Ginzler, Robert 561112c
   590521a 600414a 600414c
   601215a 610518a 611014a
   611014c 620127a 620319a
   620519a
Giordano, Frank 691215a
Giovannini, Sandro 621215a
   660107a
Gipson, Carl 620205b
Gish, Lillian 651129a
Giusti, Norma 241202i
Givot, George 550018a
   550018b
Glaser, Darel 700408a
Glass, Keith 671029e
Glazer, Tom 570015a
Gleason, Jackie 591022a
Gleason, James 751209a
Gleason, Joanna 770417a
Gleason, Thomas 540408a
Gleeson, Colette 520001c
   560304a
Glen, Harry 180515a
Glenn, Wilfred 910928d
Glenn-Smith, Michael 690122a
   750408a
Glossop, Peter 160115l
Glover, Cynthia 070417a
   090428a 490915c
Glover, Joe 501012a 510419a
   540624a 550025a 560614a
   610302a
Glynn, Carlin 780417a
Glynne, Howell 051230l
Gobel, George 560022a
   611012a
Goberman, Max 510419a
   570926a 611010a
Gochman, Len 751201a
Goddard, Paulette 400007a
   420004a 420031a
Goddard, Willoughby 600630c
Godfrey, Arthur 530128a
   660005a
Godfrey, Lynnie 780920a
Godfrey, Roy 550831a
Goell, Kermit 580003a
Goelz, Dave 790002a
Goetz, E Ray 220828a
   520024a
Goff, Charles 660325a
Goggin, Dan 720522a 720522b
   760513a 790005a
Gogh, Pat 570926i
Gohman, Don 711019a
Goland, Arnold 591118a
   650014a 650511d
Gold, Andrew 390323d
   490915b
Gold, Dave 520001f
Gold, David 720310a 741007*a

Gold, Marty 390001e 681023b
Goldberg, Jerry 540114c
   611206a
Goldblatt, Hanan 711021a
Golden, Ann 570207a
   570207b
Golden, Annie 671029g
Golden, John 120224b
   160110b
Golden, Phillip 640922e
Goldenberg, Billy 720310a
   781214a
Goldman, James 620127a
Goldman, Robert 590319a
Goldman, William 620127a
Goldner, Charles 540305a
Goldsmith, Merwin 760425a
Goldstein, Martin 560304a
Golvala, Minoo 711201b
Gomez, Vincente 410009a
Gonella, Nat 350051a
Good, Gladys 351010a
Goodhart, Al 370916a
   371014a
Goodier, Harry 700103b
Gooding, David 680122b
Goodman, Al 051230c
   060924b 081114a 101107c
   121202a 130908b 160115a
   170319a 240902e 241202f
   250921d 261130n 270202d
   271103b 271227E 280919o
   281010b 290109a 300303a
   320308b 321108a 331118i
   341121c 351010v 390209a
   430331f 430331h 430331o
   451006a 460516k 490407d
   490407k 490407l 490715b
   501124e 510329g 510329i
   560315i 560315j 581201d
   591116h 601203d 640922e
Goodman, Benny 310908a
   360047a 370023a 370023b
   391129a 430004a 430008a
   430012a 441207a 460011b
   480025a 480025b 550011a
   581014a
Goodman, Dody 481208d
   481208e 550228a 571105a
   600120a
Goodman, George 650013a
Goodman, Gordon 490715c
   541230e 550727a 571219g
Goodman, Michael 600630c
Goodrow, Garry 730125a
Goodrow, Michael 781006a
Goodwin, Doug 700303a
Goolden, Richard 410031a
Gordeno, Peter 651122c
Gordon 721108c
Gordon, Anita 450001d
   511112c
Gordon, Ann 571219e
   581201g
Gordon, Barry 800514a
Gordon, Bert 590023a
Gordon, Gavin 511112f
Gordon, Hayes 121202a

770421c
Gordon, John 790513a
Gordon, Josephine 601203c
Gordon, Mack 321129b
   330029a 330040a 340011a
   340024a 350025a 370002a
   370014a 400009a 410007a
   410010a 410012a 410027a
   420008a 420014a 420015a
   420030a 430014a 440026a
   450016b 460023a 460418c
   470010a 500002a 500019c
   530007a 560010a
Gordon, Marjorie 171225c
Gordon, Noele 441228h
Gordon, Peggy 710517a
   710517b
Gordon, Rita 750917a
Gordon, Susan 590003a
Gore, Christopher 721128a
   770920a
Gorin, Igor 361218a
Gorlizki, Ili 711021a
Gorman, Bob 690200a
Gorme, Eydie 591125a
   680204a 680204b 690002a
   760009a
Gorney, Jay 491013a
Gorshin, Frank 691023a
Gorson, Carol Lee 770708a
Gortner, Marjoe 720003a
Goss, Robert 051230k
   241202a
Gossett, Louis 641020a
   651110a
Gough, Lloyd 410105a
Gould, Elliott 441228d
   620322a
Gould, Harold 730316a
Gould, John 761206a
Gould, Morton 450015a
   451221a 451221b 500202a
Goulet, Robert 450419b
   460516f 470313b 481230e
   601203a 620001a 640014a
   680118a
Gourlay, Eileen 611014c
   621117b
Gower, John 530903a
Goz, Harry 701110a
Grable, Betty 281204c
   321129b 340051a 360040a
   370040a 370044a 390012b
   400009a 400015a 410021a
   410022a 420014a 420014b
   420015a 420016a 430013a
   430014a 430014b 440022a
   440026a 450003a 450003b
   450016a 460418c 470003b
   470010a 480023a 480033a
   500003a 500017a 510030a
   550010a 640116m 640116q
Grades, Fred 651226a
Grael, Barry Alan 631029a
Grafe, Marc 690724a
Grafe, Rod 690724a
Graff, George 130127a
Graff, Ilene 770417a

730619d
Hartman, David 651210a
Hartman, Don 300016b
Hartman, Paul 311226a
Hartt, Lisa 760217a
Harty, Patricia 611003a
Harum, Eivind 810329a
Harvey, Frederick 070417a
240902a
Harvey, Geoff 170210e
201221e 270202f 270906e
301030e 361222a
Harvey, Georgette 351010a
Harvey, James 510329d
Harvey, Jane 441207a
Harvey, John 560315g
Harvey, Laurence 601203c
601203e 610010a
Harvey, Lilian 310007a
Harvey, Morris 131223a
Harvie, Donald 570207b
Harvuot, Clifford 740405c
051230a 241202a
Harwood, Elizabeth 531203h
Harwood, James 600928a
Haskell, David 710517a
710517b
Haskell, Jack 590423b
621020a 640006a
Haskell, Jimmie 781112a
Haskins, Virginia 271227u
430331c
Hassall, Christopher 740405h
051230l 051230o 051230p
291010a 350505a 360911a
370901a 390323a 431109a
490915a
Hastings, Hal 511101a
540513a 550505a 570514a
581016a 581209a 590511a
591123a 601017a 620508a
630423a 650216a 650511a
650511d 651129a 660329a
661120a 681117a 700426a
710404a 730225a
Hastings, Wilfred 570207b
Hatch, James 620205a
Hatch, Wilbur 420001d
Hatcher, Mary 491125a
Hatfield, Edward J, Jr 951104b
Hatten, Tom 621010a
Hattie, Hilo 420015a
Hattingh, Andre 721023c
770307b
Hatton, Bradford 511101a
Haupt, Ullrich 300017a
Hauser, John 341121i 350006c
Hausman, Al 670404a
Hauxvell, John 740405g
851024a 081114e 240902a
250311j 260326a 290718a
290718i 301108c
Havens, Richie 680305b
Haver, June 450003a 460023a
470020b 490024a 490027a
500019a 380043a 430003a
440128a
Hawk, Jeremy 301108d

540114f
Hawkins, Andrew 800622a
Hawkins, John 680320a
680320b
Hawkins, June 431202a
460330a
Hawkins, Michael 680103a
Haworth, Jill 661120a
Hay, Patricia 051230t
Hayden, Carl 100108b
Hayden, Naura 750323a
Haydn, Richard 051230d
390118a
Hayes, Anthony 540114a
Hayes, Bill 520025a 530528a
570044a 580002a 581016a
581016b 590001a
Hayes, Elton 520019a 520019b
Hayes, Grace 270503a
300005a
Hayes, Isaac 531203i
Hayes, Jack 541104b 730001a
Hayes, Jim 810201a
Hayes, Marvin 431202b
Hayes, Nancye 721023b
770421c
Hayes, Peter Lind 410032a
Hayes, Richard 590512a
600619a
Hayman, Lillian 670426a
710415a
Hayman, Richard 651226a
680012a 680222a
Haymer, Johnny 570018a
Haymes, Dick 391206d
440022a 440022b 440027a
440027b 450001a 450001b
450001e 450016a 450016b
450127c 460013a 460013b
470003a 470003b 470013a
501012b 510022a
Haynes, Arthur 640116l
Haynes, Daniel L 290027a
Haynes, Tiger 640526a
750105a
Hays, Rex 781022a
Hayter, James 520019a
Hayton, Lennie 270906a
330022a 351010k 441228f
450027a 460001a 460002a
460006a 460006b 460019a
480001a 480003a 490002a
520002a 640116d 670226a
680001a
Hayward, Louis 340216a
Hayward, Susan 470026a
520004a 520004b 520004d
560012a 560012b
Hayward, Thomas 740405c
280919f
Hayward, Thomas Tibbett
831003a
Haywood, Billie 340315a
341225a
Haywood, Nancy 660920a
Hayworth, Rita 401225c
420003b 420003c 420021a
440028a 450020a 460018a

460018b 470017a 520020a
540003a
Hazard, Richard 790211a
Hazell, Hy 590528a 620315c
Head, Murray 711012a
Heal, Joan 540513e 550505d
600211b 650202a 721108c
Healy, David 790725a
Healy, Mary 390015a
Healy, Peggy 341121i
Healy, Ted 370023a
Heard, Lindsay 680122e
800507a
Hearn, Lew 121223a 250413a
Heaslip, Georgia 720310a
Heath, E P 121010a
Heath, Louise 700126a
Heath, Sigrid 720612a
761005b
Heath, Ted 460027a
Heatherington, Dianne
771201a
Heatherton, Ray 370414d
370414f
Hecht, Paul 690316a 701019a
Heckart, Eileen 620127a
Heffernan, John 620919a
700315a
Heflin, Marta 690924a
Hefti, Neal 571031e
Heidt, Horace 400030a
Hein, Silvio 130818a 140909a
Heindorf, Ray 261130r
370023a 450008a 460010b
460021a 470110b 480010a
490014a 490016b 490024a
500023a 510009a 510012b
520010b 520021b 530004a
530016a 540007a 540015b
540513b 550001a 550004c
550505b 560006a 570004a
571219b 690316b
Heitgerd, Don 570331b
Heller, Alfred 800228a
Helmke, Erika 280828d
Helmore, Tom 541230b
Helpman, Robert 720002a
Heming, Percy 160115j
240911a
Hemmings, David 601203b
750422a
Hemphill, Barry 680509a
Hemrick, Guy 650003a
Hemsley, Sherman 700315a
Hemsley, Winston DeWitt
640116b 670426a
Henderson, Charles 420016a
430003a 430004a 450001b
450003a 560012b
Henderson, Dickie 520625c
Henderson, Edward 780323a
780323b
Henderson, Florence 430331d
440821d 450419c 490407b
541104a 570044a 580002a
581016a 581201e 590001a
590521e 591116d 591123b
631208a

Henderson, Luther 390424d
440321b 460516p 570516a
580002a 590001a 601226a
601226e 660501a 700315a
780509a
Henderson, Marcia 500424a
Henderson, Melanie 700518a
Henderson, Ray 260614a
260614b 270906a 270906i
280702a 281010a 290015a
290029a 290109a 300303a
310006a 310914a 320308a
330304a 341108a 361001b
410016c 560004a 560004d
580002a 621010a 660501a
Henderson, Skitch 220828c
351010f 651007a 750323a
Henderson-Tate, David
621117b
Hendra, Tony 680103a
Hendricks, Barbara 351010q
Hendrix, Paula 381123e
Hendry, Tom 721123a
Heneker, David 561112b
630321a 630321b
Henley, Jacques 280828e
Henri, Louie 940101b
Henrique, Luiz 700127a
Henry, Charlotte 031013g
Henson, Jim 790002a
Henson, Leslie 141224a
160919a 190520a 200918a
201221a 240911a 270427a
271122a 410031a
Henson, Nicky 601203c
680320a
Henson, Robert 351010f
Hepburn, Audrey 560315b
570001a
Hepburn, Katherine 691218a
Herbert, A P 251030a 320130a
470426a 550831a
Herbert, Evelyn 270912a
280919m
Herbert, Hugh 360063a
Herbert, Joseph W 090410a
Herbert, Ralph 540624a
Herbert, Tim 581201c
Herbert, Victor 951104a
970316a 971025a 980926a
980926c 991023a 991023b
031013a 031013c 031013h
031116a 041205a 041205b
051225a 051225d 060924a
060924h 070218a 080831a
090920a 091122a 101107a
101107m 121028a 130908a
130908g 131111a 141102a
150929a 170319a 170319b
170319c 200622a 201221a
390018a
Herlie, Eileen 591022a
620319a
Herman's Hermits 301014e
Herman, Jerry 600120a
611010a 640116a 640116e
640116f 640116g 660524a
660524b 660524f 690206a

227

Jewkes, Delos 101107o
Jilliann, Ann 031013c 590521b
Jillson, Joyce 650516a
Jinguji, Sakura 700103a
Jobin, Andre 271227j
John, Bartholomew 760504b
John, Graham 250122a
280427a
John, Michael 640116p
760425a
Johns, Brooke 230322a
231020a
Johns, Glynis 550031a
640001a 730225a
Johns, Stratford 770421b
Johnson, Arnold 280409*a
280702a
Johnson, Arte 660325a
Johnson, Arthur 360015a
370022a
Johnson, Bayn 671122a
Johnson, Bernard 401025a
Johnson, Bill 430107b
460516j 460516r 481230k
551130a
Johnson, Bryan 250311j
271227C 271227y 430331p
450419n 481230l 490407h
530507g 531203g 580001f
590205b 590521f
Johnson, Chic 231020b
Johnson, Christine 450419a
Johnson, Cora 751021a
Johnson, Darlene 401225m
Johnson, Dorothy 340216b
Johnson, Greer 541201a
Johnson, Hall 290038a
290039a 330301a 401025d
Johnson, Haven 340315a
Johnson, Howard 210809a
Johnson, James P 280227a
290422a
Johnson, Justine 710404b
730311a
Johnson, Karen 660003b
Johnson, Laurie 590528a
Johnson, Marilyn 700302a
Johnson, Mel, Jr 780920a
Johnson, Noel 781109a
Johnson, Oscar L 781113a
Johnson, Patricia 350505b
360911c 490915b
Johnson, Peter 570926i
Johnson, Raymond Edward
440321a
Johnson, Susan 470313c
560503a 580204a 581222a
610518a
Johnson, Van 440011a
470313e 500015a 500015b
571126a 571219c
Johnston, Andre 620406a
Johnston, Arthur 330023a
350013a
Johnston, Gail 631029a
Johnston, Jane A 591116h
600928a
Johnston, Johnny 420004a

Johnston, Kevan 770421c
Johnstone, Paul 810411a
Jolson, Al 110320a 111120a
130206a 141010a 160217a
180214a 211006a 250107a
250107b 270001a 270001b
270001c 290014a 290014b
290015a 290015b 300010a
300010b 301205b 330006a
330006b 340001a 350011a
350011b 360020a 380803a
390005a 390005b 390027a
390027b 450008a 450008b
460005a 460005b 460005c
490003a
Jon, Alan 810201a
Jonas, Joanne 710517b
Jonas, Julie 560315e
Jonas, Nita 620406a
Jonay, Roberta 471010a
Jones, Allan 121202a 121202b
240902n 271227B 271227i
271227o 350022a 350022b
360003a 380023a 380023b
381123c 390018a
Jones, Alonzo 351010f
Jones, Anne 590511a
Jones, Bessie 141028b
160605a 170914a
Jones, Brooks 741115a
Jones, Charlene 710517e
671207a
Jones, Cliff 760217a
Jones, David 600630c
Jones, Dean 700426a 700426b
700426c
Jones, Dickie 400001a
Jones, Earl 660921a
Jones, Errol 741128a
Jones, Gwen 440821b
Jones, Herb 270906j
Jones, Isham 221107a
Jones, Jacqueline 850314c
Jones, Jene 351010v
Jones, Jessica 770417b
Jones, Jimmy 630816a
Jones, Joe 740108a
Jones, Jonah 581017a 591102b
591104a
Jones, Kay 401225m
Jones, Mark 670003a
Jones, Paul 721108d 780621a
Jones, Paulette Ellen 711219a
Jones, Quincy 750105b
Jones, Raymond 670002a
Jones, Rick 810001a
Jones, Rowland 740405h
Jones, Samuel 510329e
Jones, Sarah 141028b
Jones, Shirley 430331b
450419e 470313c 570007a
571219b 600002a 681023a
720004a
Jones, Sidney 960425a
980608a 991021a 030314a
Jones, Spike 430016a 430016b
450023b 470007a 470015a

Jones, Stephen 240904a
Jones, T C 560614a
Jones, Todd 700408a
Jones, Tom 571105a 581011*a
600503a 631024a 661205a
680002a 690122a 700506a
750408a
Jones, Trefor 340047a 350505a
Jones, Walter 020605a
Jones-Hudson, Eleanor
090906b
Jongeyans, George 501221a
Joplin, Carol 690200a
Joplin, Scott 751021a
Jordan, Marc 661018a
680127a
Joseph, Jackie 590609a
611019a
Joslyn, Allyn 470003b
Jourdan, Louis 530507b
580001a 730117a
Joy, John 650222a 651226a
Joy, Leonard 140824d
151223b 170220d 170829c
201221d 271227t 290903d
311015h 321108e 331118k
361029b 361102a 380001a
410123a 420005b 441228a
Joyce, Elaine 720409a
Joyce, James 351116b
Joyce, Paddy 600211a
Joyce, Roderick 600622a
Judge, Arline 301014j 360058a
361218a
Julia, Raul 280828g 711201a
Jun, Rose Marie 371127a
630002b 630411a 640006a
June 240512a 250310a
250413a
Jurgens, Curt 280828b

Kahal, Irving 350044a
380105a
Kahl, Howard 051230i
Kahn, Gus 051230v 081114c
101107o 121202a 170816a
240902n 281204a 330005a
340010b 350013a 380001a
390017a 410001b 520010a
Kahn, Madeline 651103a
651122b 660623a 661019a
680502a 690604a 701110a
750002a 780219a
Kaiawe, S M 120108a
Kailing, Reed 770531a
Kaina, James 610302a
Kaiser, Georg 630606a
Kaldenberg, Keith 560503a
Kaley, Charles 300044a
Kaliban, Bob 641027a
Kallan, Randi 781006a
Kallen, Kitty 490407s 560021b
Kallman, Dick 510621a
Kalman, Emmerich 121010a
160925a 161206a 221002a
260326a 450718a
Kalmar, Bert 280905a 281023a
300035a 340030a 500004a

770113a
Kamo, Sakura 700103a
Kander, John 620127a
650511a 650511c 660920a
661120a 661120b 661120g
680118a 680118b 681117a
681117b 710415a 710415b
720910a 720910c 740106a
750001a 750603a 750603c
760002a 760008a 770002a
771029a 810329a
Kane, Byron 580010a
Kane, Helen 280905a 290008a
290008b 290017a 290017b
290028a 300016a 300016b
300027a 500004a
Kane, Marjorie 290044a
Kaper, Bronislau 081114c
530009a 451006a
Karger, Fred 301014e 640013a
640015a
Karin, Fia 600120a
Karlin, Fred 691230a
Karlin, Miriam 600211a
640922d
Karloff, Boris 500424a
Karm, Michael 701110a
Karnilova, Maria 580001c
620519a 640922a 681117a
750502a
Karr, Harold 561206a
Karr, Patti 640429a 760427a
800514a
Kasha, Al 770005a
Kasket, Harold 591116e
Kasznar, Kurt 591116a
Katagiri, Rose 581201d
Katscher, Robert 301205a
Katz, Fred 580209a
Katz, Mickey 670404a
Kaufman, Erwin 741215a
Kaulili, Alvina 610302a
Kaulili, Lordie 610302a
Kava, Caroline 280828g
Kavanaugh, Ray 320927a
Kay, Arthur 440821b 531203a
531203c
Kay, Beatrice 380043a
Kay, Hershy 241202b 540311a
561201a 561201b 590309a
590511a 610403a 611010a
631024a 691218a 750521a
780219a 780621b 800430a
Kay, Susan 700208a
Kaye, Alma 441227a
Kaye, Anne 670926a
Kaye, Danny 390929a
410123d 411029b 440005a
440005b 470001a 490020a
490407u 510001a 520001a
530118a 540006b 540016a
560008a 580008a 590003a
630002a 701110a
Kaye, Davy 720002a
Kaye, Lila 800622a
Kaye, Robert 420602a
681023a
Kaye, Stubby 850314c

230

301030b 320130a
Kosarin, Oscar 680118a
680320c 710415a
Kosta, Tessa 251230a
Kostal, Irwin 410123b
470313b 490407v 560414a
570413d 570926a 570926b
580001c 580209a 591116c
591123a 601017a 611003a
611023a 620508a 620508c
620611a 630321b 640001a
680005a 710001a 760425a
770005a 780004a 781031a
Kostelanetz, Andre 341128b
460330d
Kourkoulos, Ninos 670411a
Koutoukas, H M 660304a
Koutsoukos, Thom 681013a
Kozma, Tibor 740405c
321212b
Krachmalnick, Samuel
561201a
Kraft, Karen 770322a
Krall, Heidi 740405c
Kramer, Jeffrey 781006a
Kramer, Jonathan 671029b
Kramer, Marsha 761202a
Kranendonk, Bob 550727a
Kranendonk, Leonard 550727a
Kreisler, Fritz 191007a
191007c
Kreisler, Hugo 191007c
Krepon, Belleruth 270906j
Kressyn, Miriam 611021a
Kretzmer, Herbert 690001a
Kristina, Sonja 671029d
Kristofferson, Kris 760007a
Kritz, Karl 301030b
Krivoshei, David 711021a
Kruger, Gaye 761202a
Krupa, Gene 390021a 390021b
480026a 600004a
Kruschen, Jack 620322a
681201b
Kuehn, Robert 741115a
Kuga, Richard 610302a
Kuhner, John 680113a
Kuhnly, Fred 170816c
Kuller, Sid 590023a
Kullman, Charles 740405f
470012a
Kunnecke, Charles 230131a
Kunneke, Edward 250113a
Kuntz, John B 700603a
Kupferman, Meyer 651110a
700103a
Kurlan, David 831003a
Kurnitz, Julie 660304a
690127a 700326a
Kwan, Nancy 581201b
Kwiatek, Gary 760709a
Kyd, Susan 401225m
Kyser, Kay 390031a 400033a
410023a 420029a 430008a
440029a

L'Esty, Jeanna 790614a
La Roche, Mary 600414b

La Rosa, Julius 530128a
Lacalle's Spanish Orch
171101a
LaCentra, Peg 460026a
470026a
Lacey, Florence 790111a
Lacy, Tom 680103a
Ladd, Alan 470007a
Lahr, Bert 240902b 300303b
341121c 361225b 380006a
390001a 391206b 420011b
440030a 490021a 510719a
560021a 591102a 600503d
640216a
Lail, Barbara 270906f
Laine, Cleo 271227j 581002a
Laine, Frankie 501124f
510016a 520016a 550026a
550030a
Laine, Jim 490407q
Laird, Marvin 520001c
520001g
Lake, Anabell 581201i
Lake, Bonnie 340104b
Lake, Harold 561112e
Lake, Veronica 420004a
420026a
Lakier, Gail 740322a
Lalor, Frank 141028b
Lamas, Fernando 051230d
240902b 510004a 561206a
Lamb, Benjamin 810605a
Lamb, Gil 710415a
Lambe, Jeannie 640116o
Lambert, Jack 320614a
Lambert, Mark 661120b
730225a 730225b 730311a
Lambert, Patricia 450421b
571219c 590511b 601203j
Lamont, Robin 710517a
710517b 780514a
Lamos, Mark 730319*a
LaMotta, Jake 750323a
Lamour, Dorothy 360019a
360019b 370009a 370017a
370037a 370040a 380013a
380031b 380025a 380025b
380026a 380026b 390012a
390019a 390019b 400019a
400020a 400020b 400021a
400022a 420004a 420012a
420017a 430022a 440021a
450002a 460003b 470007a
470009a 480032a 480032b
480034a 520024a 610001a
Lampell, Millard 440321a
Lampert, Diane 630002a
750006a
Lamphier, John 610519a
Lancaster, Lucie 710415a
Lance, Douglas 560027a
Lancelot, Sir 480010a
Lancers 570039a
Lanchester, Elsa 260410a
750004a
Landau, Lucy 600504a
Lande, Kay 450419i
Lander, David 601226b

Lander, Judy 721001a
Landers, Matt 780514a
Landesman, Fran 590512a
Landis, Carole 440022a
Landon, Ross 380316a
Landor, Diana 261130t
450419l 531203h
Lane, Abbe 580204a 580204c
671218a
Lane, Amanda 460024a
Lane, Betty 351010s
Lane, Burton 340010b
370022a 390019a 390021a
391206d 400911a 410004b
410032a 420011a 440015a
470110a 470110h 510003a
530021a 571220a 651017a
651017b 651017d 660501a
790408a
Lane, Gloria 241202k 450419c
Lane, Jeffrey 581201i
Lane, Lois 511112i
Lane, Lupino 190917a
290011c 310021a 371216a
Lane, Nancy 750521a
Lane, Priscilla 410005a
Lane, Rosemary 370023a
380039b
Lane, Ruby 600004a
Lang, Barbara 341121e
660325a 690200a 760427a
761010a
Lang, Gertrude 150322a
Lang, Harold 310603d
401225a 401225b 480129a
481230a 481230f 510418a
620322a 650330a
Lang, Jeanie 300005a
Lang, Johnny 601203h
Lang, June 321108f
Lang, Philip J 270906f
370012c 430331d 460516a
460516f 471009a 471226a
481208d 481208e 500202a
510329c 510418a 510719a
521215a 530507a 541104a
550127a 560315a 560315d
560315l 561115a 570005a
570514a 571031a 581011a
581222a 590205a 590423a
591022a 591022b 591207a
600428a 601203a 601203c
610413a 611102a 611227a
621020a 621020b 630318a
631017a 640116a 640429a
641027a 641215a 650516a
660524a 661205a 661205b
671207a 680006a 680410a
681023a 690206a 700330a
711019a 720409a 730319*a
741006a 770421a 770421b
780608a 790111a 790408a
790614a 800825a
Langdon, J Jewett 580513a
Lange, Arthur 290005a
360003a 370001b
Langford, Bonnie 590521d
590521h 810511a

Langford, Frances 271227v
350004a 350004b 350027b
350027c 360015a 360018a
360018b 360028a 360029a
360030a 360030b 361218a
370023a 370023b 381123d
391018b 400024a 400027a
420005a 420704e
Langford, Gordon 700001a
721106a
Langton, Diane 671029f
730225c 790725a
Lankston, John 640326a
Lannin, Paul 220220a
Lanning, Jerry 530226e
560315l 660524a 721001a
Lansbury, Angela 460006b
590521d 640404a 640404b
660524a 690206a 710001a
730311a 790301a
Lanza, Mario 241202h
241202i 250921h 261130j
490006a 490006b 500006a
500006b 500006c 510007a
520006a 560006a 580005a
590004a
Lanzaroni, Bhen 681013a
Larabee, Louise 610419a
Lark, Kingsley 200212a
Larner, Elizabeth 240902l
280919r 430331n 450419l
460516o 470313k 481230s
511112f 520625c 530507j
560315g 570331d 601203c
Larrimore, Martha 540311a
Larsen, Freda 250921o
510329o
Larsen, John 051230p 160115l
250921o
Larsen, William 600503a
Larson, Francis 200324a
Lascelles, Kendrew 620005a
620005b 620005c
Lascoe, Henry 550224a
610413a
Lasko, John 770515a
Lasley, David 721009a
Lasser, Louise 671023a
Latessa, Dick 750408a
Latham, Cynthia 590205a
Latham, Fred 360204a
Lathon, William 590626b
Latimer, Charlie 680122c
Latouche, John 390424a
401025a 451006a 540311a
560522a 561201a 561201b
Laurel, Stan 300017a 370049a
Laurence, Larry See Enzo
Stuarti
Laurence, Paula 331118d
430107a 580427a
Laurenz, John 490407s
Laurita, Annie 200324a
Lautner, Joe 601012a
Laver, Grahame 531203h
561112g
LaVere, Charley 590021a
Lavie, Aric 561112c 711021a

Lavin, Linda 630415a 651223a
  660329a
Law, Jenny Lou 600103a
Lawford, Peter 270906a
  470006a 480002a 570203a
  740009a
Lawless, Frank 540513d
Lawlor, Mary 270906k
Lawrence, Bob 331021a
  341121i
Lawrence, Carol 481230e
  570926a 570926c 591207a
  611227a
Lawrence, Eddie 561129a
  650206a
Lawrence, Elliot 600414a
  601103c 611014a 631003a
  641020a 660003c 661018a
  680204a 681220c 720117a
  720409a
Lawrence, Gertrude 181220a
  211011a 230904a 240109a
  250330a 251110a 251110b
  261108c 261108f 281108a
  290040a 300225a 300924a
  320007a 331006a 331006c
  340043b 340919a 360109a
  410123a 410123d 510329a
  510329r
Lawrence, Jack 540014a
  641215a
Lawrence, Jerome 560613a
Lawrence, Margie 670003a
Lawrence, Martin 160831b
  271227D
Lawrence, Rosina 370049a
Lawrence, Stephen 670926a
  720004a
Lawrence, Steve 571117a
  591125a 640227a 680204a
  680204b 690002a 760009a
Lawrenson, John 090428a
  301030a 440821f
Lawrenson, Jon 360911b
Laws, Maury 671218a 711203a
Laws, Sam 401025a
Lawson, Denis 401225m
Lawson, Roger 640116b
  700302a
Lawton, Frank 970928a
Lay, Dilys 540114b
Laycock, Ralph G 760414a
Laye, Evelyn 171225c 220302a
  251030a 261021b 280427a
  280919d 290718d 300045a
  350017a 351005b 400209a
Layton, Joe 611003d
Lazarus, Frank 790328a
Le Gallienne, Eva 321212b
Leachman, Cloris 311226b
Leader, Joe 511112b
Leahy, Joe 561112*a
Lear, Evelyn 361117a
LeBaron, William 191007a
Lebok, Edith 590430a
Lebowsky, Stanley 561112c
  581222a 620127a 630318a
  630321a 661214a 690200a

721023a 750603a 771029a
Lecocq, Charles 741111a
Lee, Benny 711201b 781031a
Lee, Bert 320614a 340927a
  351002a
Lee, Bill 490407c 530020a
  530033a 540001a 560014a
  580013a 591116c 600003a
Lee, Buddy 241201a
Lee, Dixie 301014j
Lee, Dorothy 321126d
Lee, Georgia 530026b
Lee, Harriet 330304a
Lee, Jack 191118b
Lee, Johnny 460020a 460020b
Lee, Laura 520001e
Lee, Lois 471009a
Lee, Marchicko 581201d
Lee, Michele 311226b
  611014b 620519a 620519b
  730319a
Lee, Patricia 340018a
Lee, Peggy 430012a 430012b
  490407i 530011a 530014b
  540006b 550004a 550004b
  550018a 550018b 580003a
Lee, Robert E 560613a
Lee, Sondra 541020a 640116a
Lee, Valerie 631003a
Lee, Vanessa 290718a
  490915a 490915e 540610a
  550831b
Lee-Hill, Sharon 810511a
Leeds, Andrea 380014b
Leeds, Phil 600428a 610419a
Lefebvre, Jean 581111a
Lefeuvre, Guy 180515a
LeGault, Lance 640422a
  680305a 680305b
Legrand, Christiane 590005a
Legrand, Michel 640003a
  640003b 680004a 700006b
  740003a 740325a 740325b
Legrand, Raymond 490018a
  561112d 561112f
Legras, Jacques 651214a
Lehar, Franz 051230a 080121a
  091112a 100108a 140130a
  171126a 200528a 251030a
  281004a 291010a 300017a
Lehman, John 801120a
Lehman, Liza 040614a
Lehmann, Jo Ann 760419a
Lehmann, Lotte 480008a
Lehner, Veronica 530226e
Lehr, Lew 380803a
Lehrer, Tom 800605a
Leib, Gil 791004a
Leigh, Adele 290718g 501124h
  531203e 570926j
Leigh, Barbara 160831a
  240902i 271227y 280919t
  301108d
Leigh, Carolyn 541020a
  571010a 581011*a 601215a
  621117a 640004a 671207a
Leigh, Gracie 101105a
Leigh, Janet 600414b

Leigh, Louise 141028b
Leigh, Mitch 651122a 700408a
  790213a
Leigh, Rowland 261005a
  270101a 301205a 310814a
Leigh, Vivien 630318a
Leighton, Bernie 550007b
Leighton, Mauri 580004a
Leighton, Nancy 640429a
Leisten, Annette 031013k
Lemay, Howard 690502a
Lembeck, Harvey 650003a
Lemmon, Jack 550010a
  560002a 590002b 720117a
Lemmon, Shirley 740416b
Lenhart, Margaret 420001a
Lenn, Robert 460516a
Lennon, John 640017a
  650010a 680015a 770531a
LeNoire, Rosetta 271227k
  401025a 590423a 641215a
Lenya, Lotte 280828a 280828d
  280828h 280828i 361117a
  450322b 661120a
Leon, Joseph 051230k
Leonard, Billy 161206a
  170220a
Leonard, Jack 401030d
Leonard, Jack E 740009a
Leonard, Laurence 161206a
  441228d 570926d 570926e
Leonard, Lu 610403a 611118a
Leonard, Michael 651210a
  720214a 720214c
Leonard, Richard 590521d
  681220a 740416a 740416b
  760302b
Leonardi, Leon 400031a
  441005a 460330a
Leonardos, Urylee 351010e
  700302a
Leoni, Henri 061127a 141224a
Lerner, Alan Jay 470313a
  470313f 481007a 510003a
  511112a 511112c 511112e
  560315a 560315q 580001a
  580001c 580001e 580001g
  601203a 601203g 651017a
  651017b 651017c 691218a
  740002a 790408a
Lerner, Dorothy 720515a
Lerner, Sammy 370916a
  371014a
LeRoy, Ken 620322a
Lesey, Ben 420002b
Lesko, John 631017a 651113a
  661205a 681023a 800825a
Leslie, Joan 420005a 420005c
  430002b 430016a 440015a
  450008a
Leslie, Lew 280509c
Lessy, Ben 520012a
Lester, Alfred 090428e
  170719a 211017a
Lester, Frankie 480008b
Lester, Joanna 660920a
Lester, Ketty 401025a
Lester, Mark 170210a 600630b

Lester, Robie 690007a
Levant, Oscar 270001a
  300024a 320611a 450008a
  480018a 490002a 500001a
Leven, Mel 031013c
Levene, Gus 570004a 690005a
  50002a
Levene, Sam 501124a 611012a
Leventon, Annabel 671029d
Levey, Ethel 121223a 131223a
  141208a 151225a 220113a
Levin, Mel 670005a
Levin, Sylvan 540305a
Levine, Hank 600414b
Levine, Maurice 311226a
  480715b 491030a 510514a
  570413d
Levitt, John 490407e
Levitt, Richard 531203d
Levy, Jacques 690617a
Lewin, John 700322a
Lewine, Richard 280925a
  281108b 341225a 371009a
  480115a 591102a
Lewington, James 091112b
Lewis, Bobo 780514a
Lewis, Brenda 440821e
  450419j 540305a
Lewis, Dell 690200a
Lewis, Elliot 450001e
Lewis, Garrett 311226b
  640116c 680001a
Lewis, Gillian 441228d
Lewis, Henry 161129a
Lewis, Jerry 500016a 540020a
  560015a 570043a 580017a
  600003a
Lewis, Linda 750005a
Lewis, Michael 730319*a
  810605a
Lewis, Monica 510026a
  520007a
Lewis, Morgan 541020c
Lewis, Richard 740405g
Lewis, Sylvia 621010a
Lewis, Ted 190715a 210831a
  270328a 271115a 290018a
  290021a 430005a
Lewis, Tom 431109a
Lewis, William 740405a
  831003b 851024a 051230e
  081114e 101107d 160115c
  241202e 250311j 250921c
  260326a 261130i 301108c
  440821c
Leyden, Norman 511112h
  590423b
Leyland, Noel 160110c
Leyton, John 650007a
Libby, Dennis 700318a
Liberace 640422a
Libertini, Dick 651223a
Liberto, Don 550025a 561107a
  601012a 640429a
Licette, Miriam 451115e
Lichter, Marika 751210b
Lieb, Dick 800514a
Liebgold, Leon 611021a

Liebman, Max 440005a
440005b
Light, Enoch 571219f
Ligon, Tom 680113a
Lile, David 651226a
Lilley, Joseph J 341121g
540002a 540006b 540009a
550008a 560310a 561115b
570009a 580027a
Lillie, Beatrice 170220a
170426a 180515a 190828a
250330a 251110a 251110b
261217a 280103a 331116a
350919a 361225a 390118a
480430a 521002a 640407a
Lilo 530507a
Lind, Christina 130908b
240902e
Lindberg, Des 710517g
Linden, Hal 341121e 561129b
580033a 590024a 630019a
640019a 660325a 701019a
Lindsay, Howard 570331a
Lindsay, Kevin 700518a
Lindsey, Mort 620001a
630001a 641123a
Lindup, David 700001a
Lineberger, James 710228a
Link, Peter 690924a 700004a
781022a
Linn, Bambi 321212b 620322a
Linn, Bud 351012b
Linton, Bill 630011a
Linton, William 440821e
Linville, Albert 510419a
530226a
Lion, Margo 280828e
Lionello, Alberto 660107b
Lipman, Joe 610720d
Lippincott, David M 550025a
Lipton, Martha 740405f
Lisa, Luba 641215a
Lissauer, John 720522a
Littau, Joseph 431202a
450419a 520321a
Little, Beatrice 310601b
Little, Cleavon 700315a
Little, Ruth 280828j
Livermore, Helen 671029e
Livermore, Reg 730619c
Livesey, Jack 280313a
Livingston, Barry 660003c
Livingston, Jay 470009a
480022a 490012a 500013a
500020a 510011a 520005a
520009a 520014a 530005a
540009a 540912a 560019a
560021a 570008a 580028a
580204a 590201a 610003a
611012a
Livingston, Jerry 490011a
561112*a
Lloyd, Anne 390001h
Lloyd, Bernard 690316c
Lloyd, Pat 611019a
Lloyd, Robert 670003a
Lloyd, Vivian 670404a
Lloyd-Jones, Heather 561112e

Loaring, Richard 591116j
Lockwood, Margaret 530032a
Lockyer, Malcolm 510419b
520001e
Loeb, Jerry 270906j
Loeb, John Jacob 540624a
Loesser, Frank 380018a
390004a 390019a 390021a
410006a 410030a 410032a
420028a 420032a 430015a
430015b 430016a 430021a
440017a 470007a 470011a
481011a 481011c 490004a
490004b 490013a 500021a
501124a 501124f 520001a
520001b 560503a 600308a
611014a
Loesser, Lynn 481011c
490004b
Loewe, Frederick 470313a
511112a 560315a 580001a
580001c 601203a 740002a
Loftus, Laura 810001a
Logan, Ella 380014a 390828a
470110a 470110e
Logan, Jenny 191118f
Logan, Michael 680320a
Logan, Sally 610413c
Logan, Vince 570926i
Lojodice, Giuliana 660107a
Lollos, John 680103a
Lom, Herbert 510329h
Loman, Hal 560322a
Lombard, Carole 300030b
370009a 370009b
Lombard, Carmen 540624a
Lombardo, Guy 340048a
460025b 540624b 650626a
750323a
London, George 740405g
London, Julie 570030a
570037a 580023a 580026a
London, Marc 641026a
Lonergan, Lenore 311226a
Long, Avon 210523a 351010a
351010b 351010e 351010i
351010l 460014a 470110b
620205a 720516a 741007a
750502a 760302a
Long, John 700126a
Long, Kenn 701108a
Long, Peggy 751121a
Long, Shorty 560503a
Long, Tamara 481208d
481208e 610302a 681220a
761202a
Longo, Peggy 640922f
Lonsdale, Frederick 170210e
Loomer, Lisa 780300a
Loose, Bill 640007a
Lopaka, Al 720521a
Lopez, Priscilla 750521a
790328a
Lopez, Vincent 280806a
Lor, Denise 760511b
Loren, Sophia 570037a
570042a 580028a 651122d
Lorick, Robert 720522a

790005a
Loring, Michael 380043a
410105a
Loring, Richard 721108e
770307b
Lorraine, Violet 160419a
330019a 340017a
Lorre, Peter 550224b
Lota, Remo 470109a
Lotis, Dennis 441228h
Loudon, Dorothy 600201a
770421a 781214a
Louis, Geoff 510329p
Louise, Mary 591123c
620205a 650009a
Louise, Merle 790301a
Louise, Tina 640526a
Love, Bessie 290005a 700103b
Love, Geoff 250311a 390323c
441228h 470426d 481230m
510329f 540001b 600630f
640922k 721108d
Love, Jeannine 361218a
Lovell, Marilynn 640116c
Lowe, Arthur 501012f
Lowe, Enid 570331e
Lowe, Jackie 751121a
Lowe, Marion 051230l
301030a
Lowe, Robert 381123e
540513d 581201c 590511b
591116e 591116g
Lowe, Roy 611014c
Lowery, Robert J 700208a
Lowi, Patricia 490407e
Lowry, Ken 711201c
Lowry, William 641225a
Lubin, Lou 550007a
Luca, Dominic 710517f
Lucas, David 700006a
Lucas, Fred 271227F 430331r
430331s 441228h 490407h
510329f 511112i 550505d
590205b 600630f 611014d
640116h 660524c
Lucas, Isabelle 271227D
271227w 351010h 490407r
490407t 700103b
Lucas, Jonathan 311226a
Lucas, Nick 290019a 290019b
290021a 740007a
Lucas, Veronica 360911b
Lucius, Olive 611014c
Luckey, Susan 591022a
Luders, Gustav 020512a
030317a
Ludlow, Ben 460418a
Luft, Joe 670731a
Luft, Lorna 670731a
Luisi, James 660129a
Lukas, Paul 501012a
Luke, Keye 581201a
Lum, Berea 581201d
Luna, Barbara 490407a
Lunceford, Jimmy 410005a
Lund, Art 480008b 560503a
560503b 610518a 620315c
661214a 720310a

Lundigan, William 500019a
Lunny, Robert 760400a
Lupino, Ida 430016a 460026a
Lupino, Stanley 320016a
330039a 340049a
LuPone, Patti 760511a
780621c
LuPone, Robert 740528a
770920a
Lussier, Bob 650222a 651226a
Luther, Frank 320217b
561121a
Luz, Dora 440023c 440023d
Lybe, Dennis 810201a
Lyman, Abe 270906g 311102a
330040b
Lynch, Teddy 341225a
370414d
Lynde, Paul 600414a 600414b
Lyndeck, Edmund 790301a
Lynn, Betty 560005b
Lynn, Diana 440021a 440021b
Lynn, Imogene 570009a
Lynn, Jonathan 640922d
Lynn, Judy 460516l 501012e
511101a
Lynn, Patricia 271122f
580001h
Lynn, Yvonne 680012a
Lynne, Gillian 530507e
Lynne, Janice 351010t
Lynne, Sharon 370049a
Lyon, Ben 310011a
Lyon, Nick 810411a
Lyons, Colette 271227m
Lyons, Linda 810328a
Lytton, Henry 940101b
031210a
Lytton, Henry, Jr 261005a
270101a

Maazel, Lorin 351010q
MacArthur, Bill 481116a
Macaulay, Joseph 610419a
720310a
MacBane, Ralph 380103a
MacDermot, Galt 570207a
671029a 671029b 671029c
671029f 671029g 701215a
711201a 711201c 721009a
721009a 721128a 730316a
741128a
MacDonald, Aimi 681201c
MacDonald, Christie 090123*a
130908a
MacDonald, Glen 080831a
MacDonald, Jeanette 051230b
051230v 101107b 101107h
101107o 121202b 130908c
130908e 170816a 170816b
240902c 240902n 250921b
280919c 280919i 290011a
290011c 290718b 290718k
300009a 300009b 311015k
320002a 320002b 320004a
320004b 360013a 360013b
380511b 380511e 410011a
410011b 410011c 420025a

270425c 271227u 271227v
360017a 360031a 360040a
360040b 361218a 370014a
380031a 400028a 410001a
410001b 410008a 460002a
460002b 480004b 480004c
490027b 510010a 510329g
530025a 540010a 560011a
570331h 580001d 640422a
Martin, Virginia 560614a
611014a 621117a
Martin, Vivienne 250311a
460516q 781031a
Martindale, Wink 640007a
Martini, Nino 350033a
360044a 480020a
Marvin, Johnny 260920a
271122d
Marvin, Lee 511112c
Marvin, Melvin 730404b
Marx Brothers 251208b
Marx, Groucho 850314a
281023a 320013a 390013b
Marx, Melinda 850314a
Mascher, Wolfgang 751210b
Maschwitz, Eric 361222a
390120a
Masiell, Joe 640116e 640319a
680122d 690206b
Masingill, O B 681023b
Mask & Wig Club 250404a
260425a 270507a
Mason, Delia 041217a
Mason, Iris 760708a
Mason, Marlyn 450419b
470313b 621010a 671207a
Mason, Patrick 220828b
Mason, Paul 571219e 581201g
Mason, Ray 550418a
Mason, Terry 760709a
Massari, Lea 621215a
Massary, Fritzi 380316a
Massey, Curt 401225g
Massey, Daniel 580001c
630423a 680001a
Massey, Ilona 370020a
390017a
Massey, Louis 490407q
Massey, Raymond 530214a
640019a
Massi, Bernice 620315a
640227a
Masters, Valerie 670001d
Mastin, Will 560322a
Mastroianni, Marcello
660107a
Matalon, Zack 561112c
Mates, Sally 711220a
Matheson, David 640922h
Matheson, Murray 261108e
Mathews, Carmen 651210a
690206a
Mathewson, Joseph 600428*a
Mathias, Anna 810001a
Mathieson, Muir 350043a
530019a 580003a 630008a
Mathis, Johnny 531203i
560023a 570028a 580021a

Matlock, Matty 550004c
550004e 580006c
Matlock, Norman 711201a
730316a
Matlovsky, Noelle 660003c
Matlovsky, Samuel 630606a
280828a 280828c 361117a
460330d
Matters, Graham 730619c
Matthau, Walter 640116d
Matthews, Art 170829a
Matthews, Edward 351010a
351010b 351010d 351010p
Matthews, Gerry 571010a
581011*a 590924a 600929a
621018a
Matthews, Inez 351010b
351010c 491030a
Matthews, Jessie 201221b
261005a 270101a 270520a
301203a 311015i 320003a
320009a 330012a 350009a
360004a 360005a 370006a
380027a 510329f
Matthews, Wayne 671029e
Mattox, Matt 540001a
590511a
Mattson, Eric 450419a
450419k 540010b
Mature, Victor 420015a
420021a
Matz, Peter 311226b 551022a
571031c 611003a 611003b
620315a 620315b 640005a
640922b 661207a 670426a
690002a 710701a 750001a
Mauceri, John 561201b
Maurel, Michael 610413c
Maurstad, Toralv 440821d
Mauvais, Jean 561112d
651122f
Maxine 460516k
Maxwell, Arthur 530528a
Maxwell, Kenn 590626a
Maxwell, Marilyn 401225g
460019a
May, Billy 460020b 480029a
550016a 560004c 580010a
640007a
May, Edna 961228a 970928a
May, Olive 110304a
Mayberry, Dave 721108f
Mayfair, Mitzi 440022a
Mayhall, Jeri 470313h
Mayhew, Stella 040502a
051016a 100106a 120305a
Maynard, Eddie 401225f
Maynard, Ken 290045a
Mayne, Ferdy 620315c
Mayo, Mary 481230g 570005a
Mayo, Virginia 480025a
500023a 510017c 510024a
Mayro, Jacqueline 590521a
640319a
Mazarus, Jan 510329h
McAlpine, William 051230l
McArdle, Andrea 770421a
McArthur, Edwin 271227m

McBroom, Amanda 770808a
McCall 810001a
McCarey, Leo 570012a
McCarthy, Charlie 380014b
McCarthy, John 250311a
McCarthy, Joseph 180307a
191118a 231231a 270202a
McCarthy, Justin 131111a
McCarthy, Mary 031013c
McCarthy, Siobhan 780621b
McCartney, Paul 640017a
650010a 680015a 770531a
McCarty, Mary 490715a
540012a 710404a 730311a
750603a
McCarty, Michael 781022a
McCaul, Neil 730419b
McCauley, Jack 441227a
471009a 481208a
McClanahan, Rue 641026a
McClellan, C M S 110313a
120930a 131110a
McClellan, Clark 640319a
700302a
McClellan, Nora 780323a
McCloy, June 310008a
McClure, Kit 781007a
McCollum, Sadie 081114b
McCombs, Terry 760414a
McConnell, Ty 690604a
McCormack, John 300031a
300031b
McCormick, Gilmer 710517a
McCormick, Sheila 570207a
570207b
McCown, Ellen 510621a
600308a
McCracken, James 540624a
McCracken, Joan 270906a
441005a 530528a
McCreery, Bud 581011*a
McCue, William 160831b
241202r
McCullough, Paul 300114a
McCurn, George 720516a
McCurry, Carolyn 761010a
McCutcheon, Bill 550228a
571105a 681013a
McDaniel, Hattie 271227o
430016a 460020a
McDonald, Country Joe
701026a
McDonald, Kay 760324a
McDonald, Ray 270906a
McDonough, Justin 490407b
McDowall, Roddy 601203a
McElhiney, Bill 680010a
McFarland, Gary 711021a
McFerrin, Robert 351010c
McGavin, Darren 510329d
McGeoy, Carrie Nye 580513a
McGhee, Brownie 570521a
McGovern, Michael 770417b
McGrane, Paul 540114b
McGrath, Don 750309a
McGrath, George 690127a
721123a
McGrath, Matthew 780514a

McGrath, Pat 461219a
McGraw, William 480715a
McGreevey, Annie 740528a
McGregor, Dion 570005a
McGriff, Edna 581201f
McGuire Sisters 490407n
501124c
McGuire, Biff 470110c
McGuire, Dorothy 620004a
McGuire, Margaret 780300a
McGuire, Phyllis 481230c
McHaffey, Robert 620311b
McHarg, Scotty 460027a
McHugh, Burke 600928a
McHugh, Jimmy 280509a
281226a 300225a 331118a
350004a 350005a 350034a
360011a 400033a 400404b
400523a 410018a 420028a
430015a 430107e 440022a
470026a 480013a 481113a
560317a 660501a
McIntire, John 530020a
McIntyre, Hal 480008b
McKay, Don 271227w
441228d 570926e
McKay, Marjorie 591116c
McKechnie, Donna 681201b
700426b 730311a 740002a
750521a
McKeever, Jacquelyn 530226b
580204a
McKellar, Kenneth 301030d
531203e
McKendrick, Bob 401225g
McKenna, Christine 730225c
McKenna, Virginia 510329q
McKenzie, Julia 740702a
760504a
McKenzie, Red 320217b
320308a
McKie, Shirley 680509a
McKinney, Florine 360204a
McKinney, Nina Mae 290027b
McKnight, Marian 670226a
McKuen, Rod 681117*a
690006a 780001a
McLain, Marcia 751219a
McLellan, C M S 961228a
970928a
McLennan, Rod 660129d
740702a
McLerie, Allyn 261130r
271227k 471226a 481011b
481011d 490715a
McLucas, Rod 200324a
McMartin, John 591118a
660129a 660129b 710404a
710404b 730311a
McMechen, June 351010b
McNally, John 101107n
241202t
McNamara, Maureen 790517a
McNaughton, Tom 090123*a
McNeil, Claudia 570521a
681020a
McNeil, Lonnie 780920a
McNiell, Justin 770531a

Mitchell, Leona 351010q
Mitchell, Mary-Jenifer 730125a
Mitchell, Parris 601203f
Mitchell, Peter J 701108a
Mitchell, Sidney 360040a
Mitchell, Terry 721220a 730225c 740416a
Mitchum, Robert 480005a 580016a
Mitty, Nomi 510419a
Mixon, Tom 620205*a
Mockridge, Cyril J 570007a
Modernaires 410012a 420008a
Moffat, Alice 190419a
Moffatt, John 720710a
Moffo, Anna 740405a 740405g 831003b 051230e 101107d 240902f 261130i 271227h 331118f 351010e
Molina, Alfred 430331w
Mollison, Clifford 300220a
Molloy, Bruce 770708a
Molloy, Bruce, Sr 770708a
Monaco, James V 380018a 380019a 390009a 390011a 400018a 400019a 400025a 430012b 440026a
Monat, Roz 590521h
Monckton, Lionel 940101a 941124a 980521a 991021a 000203a 010907a 040305a 090123a 090428a 101105a 170914a
Monis, Hank 661018b
Monkau, Marius 671029h
Monkhouse, Bob 381123e 580221b
Monkman, Phyllis 270427a
Monnot, Marguerite 561112a 620002a
Monroe, Barry 250311k
Monroe, Marilyn 480021a 481208b 530023a 530023b 540004a 540004b 540004c 540005a 560018a 570022a 590002a 600001a
Monroe, Vaughn 470028a 490024b 500024a
Montalban, Ricardo 490004a 490004c 530029a 550526a 571031a 661106*a
Montand, Yves 600001a 651017b
Monte, Lou 470110d 481230c
Montesano, Enrico 621215c
Montevecchi, Liliane 651214a
Montgomery, David 100110a
Montgomery, Douglass 321108f
Montgomery, George 460023a
Montgomery, Laried 671023a
Montgomery, Marian 341121m
Montgomery, Mark 660003c
Montgomery, Robert 290034a
Moody, Phil 550006a
Moody, Ron 600630b 600630d
Mooney, Harold 490011c

550004a
Moore, Ada 541230a
Moore, Barbara 640922i
Moore, Blanche 600630f
Moore, Charles 541230b
Moore, Constance 410016b 450015a
Moore, Del 600003a
Moore, Dudley 610510a 610510b 640108a 720002a 721121a 721121b
Moore, Grace 241201*a 280919k 310814a 340012a 340012b 350026a 360022a 370025a 370026a
Moore, Jodie Elaine 581201i
Moore, John 381123e
Moore, Karen 590521a
Moore, Mary Tyler 661214a
Moore, Melba 671029g 700315a 700315b
Moore, Peter 511112i 640922f 651122e
Moore, Phil 580204b
Moore, Robert 760408a
Moore, Victor 360002b 360006a 400528b 400528c
Moorehead, Agnes 580001c 661106*a
Moores, Michael 640407c
Moorhouse, Alan 640116p
Morath, Max 691230a 771221a
Moray, Stella 271227D 280828j 401225j 560503c 640922k
Mordente, Lisa 781112a
More, Julian 561112b 790725a
More, Kenneth 700001a 760006a
More, Unity 141116a
Moreen, Bob 590121a
Moreland, Barry 640116i
Moreland, Mantan 370004c
Moreno, Rita 510329b 570926b 630423b
Moreton, Ivor 360046a
Morey, Larry 370012a 420009a 481116a 510029a
Morfogen, Zachary 770708a
Morgan, Alexandra 760003a
Morgan, Cassandra 750114a
Morgan, Dennis 051230h 261130g 360003a 390027b 430016a 440015a 460021a 470022a 470022c 480028a 490016b 510017a 510017c
Morgan, Eugene 081114b 261130f
Morgan, Frank 330006a 370020a 390001a 450215a 460019a 460516h
Morgan, Helen 271227d 271227f 271227o 280004a 290009a 290009b 290010a 290010b 290903a 300020a 340009a 340033a 340034a 350011a 350011b 350044a

350044b 351022a 570516a
Morgan, Merlin 170210a
Morgan, Michele 400404b
Morgan, Russ 510028a
Morison, Bradley G 640019a
Morison, Patricia 481230a 481230b 481230f 481230h 481230k
Morley, Angela 740002a 740711a 760006a
Moross, Jerome 540311a
Morrell, Leo 660207a
Morrell, Olive 040614a
Morris, Anita 740528a
Morris, David 430331c
Morris, Hayward 680113a
Morris, Howard 470110c
Morris, John 601215a 620319a 660521a
Morris, Libby 590521h
Morris, Nat 721009a
Morrison, Joe 340052a 350036a 360032a
Morrow, Doretta 051225b 101107f 261130a 450419j 510329a 531203a 531203f 560414a 571117a 580221b 591113a
Morrow, Geraldene 760504b
Morrow, Karen 381123a 611206a 640005a 641215a 700603a 711102a
Morse, Robert 591022a 611014a 611014b 720409a 760427a
Mortifee, Ann 671100a
Morton, Brooks 621212a 681020a
Morton, David 690316c
Morton, Hugh 961228a 970928a
Morton, Joe 690924a 731019a
Morton, Tommy 560522a
Moser, Margo 450419k
Mosier, Enid 541230a
Moss, Larry 661019a
Moss, Lawrence John 760427a 761010a
Mostel, Zero 620508a 620508b 640922a 640922b
Moten, Etta 330001b 330005a
Moule, Ken 740702a
Mouledoux, Alyce 760408a
Mouledoux, Denise 760408a
Mount, Peggy 470426d 600630b
Mowbray, Michele 701215a
Mueller, Renate 300034a 320021a
Mueller-Lampertz, Richard 510329l 560315o
Muhlhardt, Kurt 280828b
Mullen Sisters 060924b 160115a 460516k
Muller, Harrison 510621a
Muller, Hermann Jay 590521h
Mulligan, Gerry 561129e
Mulligan, Spike 720002a

Mulliner, Elizabeth 370012b
Mundin, Herbert 261005a 270101a
Munks, Molly 410031a
Munks, Nancy 410031a
Munn, Frank 271227f 310914b 311015g
Munsel, Patrice 051230k 271227b 450419c 510329g 530019a 530019b 561223a
Munshin, Jules 441228f 460418a 481230e 490007a 550224b 610112a 611118a
Munson, Ona 310011a
Mura, Corinna 440128a 450021a
Murcell, Raymond 261130j
Murdock, Jim 810605a
Murphy, George 340010b 370007b 380007a 400012b 400036a 420002b 420704e
Murphy, Jennifer 780621e
Murphy, Lambert 271227r
Murphy, Mary 640922k
Murray, Bryan 791106a
Murray, J Harold 230131a 270202b 300041a
Murray, Kathleen 170829a 601012a
Murray, Ken 351022a
Murray, Lyn 370012b 380710a 440321a 441228a
Murray, Wynn 370414d 370414f 490715b
Murrow, Edward R 571230a
Murry, Ted 630006a
Myers, Pamela 570926c 700426a 700426b 720326a 730311a 740007a 751209a
Myers, Pee Wee 200830a
Myers, Richard 281030a
Myers, Stan 510029a
Myerson, Bess 750323a
Myhers, John 611014b
Mylett, Jeffrey 710517a
Mylroie, Kathryne 510719a
Mynhardt, Siegfried 561112e
Myra, Elayne 490407q
Myrow, Josef 460023a 460023b 470010a 500019c 530007a 540012a 560010a 710606a
Myrtil, Odette 591207a

Nabors, Jim 651122b
Nadell, Rosalind 340216b
Nagy, Robert 740405a 051225a 051230e 241202e
Nahrwold, Thomas M 790513b
Nairnes, Carey 631208a
Naismith, Laurence 601203b 620311a 631003a 660521a 700001a
Nance, Ray 410804a
Narroway, Peter 540114g
Nascimbene, M 620002a
Nash, Clarence 440023c

Oakes, Bill 720214b
Oakie, Jack 300046a 310009a
340011a 350010a 350010b
360063a 400010a 400015a
410036a 420015a 430003a
Oates, Warren 730002a
Oblong, Harold 740006a
Odetta 440321b
Odette 540024a
Oelheim, Helen 280919p
Offenbach, Jacques 250113a
320130a 610403a
Ogerman, Claus 690102a
Ohlin, Bjarne 810411a
Ohman, Phil 241201b
251228c 261108b 270906c
271122d 271122e 281108a
Ohringer, Jane 780621c
Olaf, Pierre 610413a
Olcott, Chauncey 910928*a
970125a 990109a 100124a
110130a 120205a 130127a
140202a
Oldham, Derek 220302a
240902d 250921f
Olfson, Ken 650222a
Olin, Ellsworth 750323a
Oliveira, Aloysio 420018a
Oliveira, Jose 440023c
440023d
Oliver 710814a
Oliver, Don 680509a
Oliver, Donald 780117a
Oliver, Stephen 800622a
Oliver, Sy 401025a
Oliver, Thelma 541230b
620205b 660129a
Oliver, Vic 471023a
Olmstead, Jeffrey 770322a
Olrich, April 620005c
Olsen, George 231231c
240624a 250922b 251026a
260317b 270906d 281204a
300037a
Olsen, John 231020b
Olsen, Lynne 590122a
Olson, Olaf 241202j
Olstad, Dena 791127a
Olvis, William 440821e
540010a 550012a 561201a
Omeron, Guen 831003a
Oneto, Richard 531203a
Opatoshu, David 550224a
620519a
Orbach, Jerry 280828f
380103b 450419h 460516c
600503a 600503c 610413a
681201a 750603a 761010b
800825a
Orchard, Julian 430331r
760006a
Oreste 250921i 250921l
Original Piano Trio 220828d
Orlob, Harold 090208a
181223a
Ormandy, Eugene 740405f
Orme, Denise 971116a
Ornadel, Cyril 390323c

501012f 520625c 530226d
550127b 560315d 610413c
630704a 640116i
Osborne, Elisabeth 160115b
Osborne, Frances 580010a
750004a
Osborne, Tony 240902l
270425e 280919r 301108a
600211b 600630a
Osborne, Will 410005a
Oshins, Jules 420704a
420704e
Osser, Glenn 401225d
460516g 571013a 580002a
580427a 590001a 591118a
701108a
Osterwald, Bibi 381123b
441227a 540311a 581209a
620127a
Ott, Horace 501124g 721009a
Ouzounian, Richard 780323a
Owen, Catherine Dale
300017a
Owens, Harry 370027a
420015a
Owens, Richard 600622a
661120d
Owens, Rochelle 730316a
Oxenford, John 620208a
Oxford, Earl 280919o 420704a
420704e 460516k
Oz, Frank 790002a

Pace, Diane 590521b
Pace, Jean 700127a
Paddick, Hugh 540114a
Page, Anita 290005a
Page, Gene 790211a
Page, Geraldine 670004a
Page, Ken 501124g 780509a
Page, Patti 271227u 481230p
Page, Rosalind 430331p
450419n 531203g
Page, Stan 630019a
Page, Veronica 730225c
Paget, Daniel 680103a
Pahl, Mel 560414a
Paich, Marty 660002a
670006c
Paige, Elaine 740501a
780621b 810511a
Paige, Janis 460021a 540513a
550224b 590016b 631003a
Paige, Raymond 361218a
370023a
Paige, Robert 440002a
440002b
Painter, Eleanor 141028a
150929a
Palance, Jack 661106*a
Palladino, Sue 760709a
Pallys, Anna Maria 560315p
Palmer, Clarence 371127c
Palmer, Hap 721019a
Palmer, John 350505c
Palmer, Leland 680113a
721023a 790004a
Palmer, Lili 370016a

Palmer, Paul 620205b
Palmer, Peter 831003b
031013a 081114b 241202e
261130f 280919e 481208d
481208e 561115a 561115b
Palmer, Robin 481208f
570331e
Palmer, Valentine 460516q
660129f
Paquette, Mary Ann 680122c
Paramor, John 730619c
Parent, Claude 680004a
Paris, Judith 711019a 770421b
Paris, Norman 560200a
561107a 570045a 580033a
590024a 600201a 600900a
620205*a 640008a 650616a
660207a
Paris, Tony 590006b
Parker, Andy 530026a
Parker, Barnett 370002b
Parker, Betty 201221e
270906e
Parker, Christine 241202q
Parker, Dorothy 561201a
Parker, Eleanor 550012a
Parker, Eula 430331p 450419n
530507g 611014d
Parker, Fess 541215a 541215b
560014a
Parker, Frank 340029b
530128a
Parker, Jack 321108d
Parker, John 250311k 660129f
Parker, Leonard 620205a
Parker, Lew 550418a
Parker, Louise 271227a
Parker, Robert 190419a
Parker, Roxann 790517a
Parkin, Deryk 710517c
Parkinson, Jimmy 201221e
270906e
Parks, Ken 480115a
Parks, Larry 460005a 470017a
490003a
Parle, Vinny 580001j
Parnell, Emory 460019a
Parnell, Jack 731116a
Parraga, Graciela 410009a
Parris, Hamilton 741128a
Parrish, Elizabeth 591118a
621212a
Parrish, Leslie 561115b
Parrish, Robert 850314b
Parry, Malcolm 721108a
Parsons, Donovan 261005a
270101a
Parsons, Estelle 791231a
391018c 480115a 590924a
630020a
Parvis, Ty 340053a
Pascal, Milton 440408a
Pastell, George 510329o
Patachou 580312a 640602a
Pate, Christopher 710517f
Paterson, Ian 560503d
Patinkin, Mandy 780621c
Patino, Santiago 770708a

Patrick, Deeda 430331k
Patrick, Lee 410028a 470010a
Patricola, Isabelle 240630a
Patricola, Tom 240630a
450008a
Patten, Luana 460020b
470016e
Patterson, Dick 640526a
Patton, Brian 741007*a
Patton, Jimmy 741007*a
Paul, Alan 720214a
Paul, Gloria 690003a
Paul, Justin 741215a 760215a
Paulee, Mona 560503a
Paulette, Larry 740108a
Paulton, Edward 130828a
140223a
Paulton, Harry 851109a
Pavan, Marisa 560613a
Pavek, Janet 271227b 600428a
Pavlosky, David 810328a
Paxton, Glenn 590319a
Payn, Graham 450822b
461219a 500707a 540610a
Payne, Edmund 110304a
Payne, Freda 790913a
Payne, John 270906f 380016a
400015a 410010a 420014a
420016a 430003a 450003a
Payne, Laurie 081114f
121202e 550831a 580001h
Payne, Tom 170220a
Peachena 740108a
Pearce, Alice 441228f
481208a 550025a
Pearce, Vera 280605a 340927a
Pearl, Jack 340044a
Pearson, Jesse 600414b
Pease, James 290718g
Peaslee, Richard 670003a
Pecar, George 610519a
Pechy, Elisabeth 200528a
Peck, Betty 621004a
Peck, Charles 560315n
Peck, Jon 740416b
Peck, Raymond 260906a
Pecorino, Joe 770531a
Pedalty, Bruce 700318a
Pederson, Hal James 770808a
Peerce, Jan 060924g 101107j
130908f 241202b 470313d
511112d 530017a 560315c
Pegram, Nigel 620005c
Pendleton, Austin 640922a
700126a
Penn, Bob 570331a
Penn, Robert 511112a 611102a
Penna, Philip Della 660928a
Penner, Joe 381123f
Pepper, Harry S 281004a
Peppermint Players 650327a
Perachi, Leo 420018b 440023b
Percassi, Don 750521a
Percival, John 081114a
Peretti, Hugo 681023a
730404a
Peric, Blanka 160115a
Perito, Nick 760009a

Perkins, Anthony 391018c 560009c 560325a 600308a
Perkins, Frank 590521b
Perkins, Patti 751201a
Perren, Freddie 770004a
Perritt, Harry 310305a
Perry, Dolores 650009a
Perry, John Bennett 670926a
Perry, Rod 640429a 680502a 731217a
Perry, Tracey 401225m
Perryman, Jill 760504b 770421c
Pershing, D'Vaughn 730619b
Persson, Ruby 660003c
Pertwee, Jon 090428c 191118f 520001e 560315k
Peters, Bernadette 680410a 681220a 741006a
Peters, Broc 431202b
Peters, Brock 351010c 351010o 390424d 440321b 611023a
Peters, Lauri 380103b 590319a 591116a
Peters, Roberta 241202b 450419g 530017a
Peters, Scott 271122f
Peters, Tony 510329f
Peters, William F 131229a
Petersen, Paul 600414e
Petersen, Taliep 721023c
Peterson, Bernice 431202b
Peterson, Caleb 460002a
Peterson, Eric 800529a
Peterson, Kurt 690206a 760511a
Peterson, Paul 670004a
Pethers, Joan 581201c
Petina, Irra 440821a 440821b 561201a 651129a
Petit, Jean-Claude 751210a
Petit, Roland 561112a
Petrak, Rudolf 550012a
Petricoff, Elaine 720522a 790005a
Petrie, Sonya 590521g
Pettersson, John 480715b
Pezarro, Jo-Ann 721023c
Pflueger, Carl 930515a
Phelps Twins 290701a
Phelps, Don 631029a
Philipp, Adolph 130828a 140223a
Phillips, Eddie 261108e 271227k 550505a
Phillips, Gregory 630423b
Phillips, Jamie 241202t
Phillips, John 750129a
Phillips, Shawn 730001a
Phillips, Sian 401225l 401225m
Phillips, Stu 600414e
Phillips, Van 300021b 300035a
Piazza, Marguerite 101107a
Pickens Sisters 330029a
Pickens, Jane 931223c 321108a 750502a
Picon, Molly 611010a 640922c

640922i
Pidgeon, Walter 591022a
Pied Pipers 390029a 391206d 420011b 460020b 480030a 490027b
Pierce, Dave 810001a
Pierce, Ken 270906j
Pierre, Christophe 501124g
Pierson, Arthur 330047a
Pierson, Edward 751021a
Pierson, Thomas 721009a 730206a 730319*a 760511a
Pierson, William 611206a
Piggott, Stuart 141028b
Pike, Ernest 090906b 141028b 151225a
Pinza, Carla 541230b
Pinza, Ezio 490407a 490407o 510005a 510005b 510021a 530017a 541104a
Pippin, Donald 370012c 600630c 631024a 640216a 641027a 660524a 690206a 700330a 730319a 741006a 750521a 810329a
Pisello, Daniel 781007a
Piteo, Theresa 680122b
Pitre, Sandra 751121a
Pitts, Zasu 550016a
Pixley, Frank 020512a 030317a
Place, Mary Kay 770002a
Planquette, Robert Jean 770419a
Plant, Jack 311015i
Platt, Edward 580204a
Playten, Alice 600630c 671023a 671023b 690604a 730125a 730311a
Pleis, Jack 600414d
Pleshette, Suzanne 670005a
Plimpton, Shelley 671029a 671029b
Pliskin, Marci 200324a
Plumb, Ed 410024a 420009a 530010a 550018b
Plumb, Neely 590016a
Plummer, Christopher 591116c 730319*a
Plymale, Trip 761010a
Pober, Leon 600210a
Pockriss, Lee 600504a 630318a
Pohlman, Guy 720001a
Pohlman, Ray 680305a 720001a
Pointer, Sidney 261130c
Poitier, Sidney 351010c
Polk, Gordon 561206a
Pollack, Ben 281226b
Pollack, Lew 350005a 360040a
Pollak, Anna 740405h
Pollard, Daphne 170131a
Pollock, Frank 941029b
Pollock, Muriel 270202g 281008*a
Pomahac, Bruce 200324a

760400a
Pompeii, James 600928a
Ponazecki, Joe 700603a
Pons, Lily 740405f 340216b 350048a 350048b
Ponto, Erich 280828d
Pope, Robert 460330a
Popkiewitz, Maria 701215a
Popp, Andre 561112a 561112b 561112c
Porretta, Frank 051230k 301030b 440821d 470313c 510329d
Porteous, Timothy 570207a
Porter, Cole 191112a 200918a 240916a 281008a 281008b 290040a 290327a 290327b 300924a 301208a 321129a 321129b 331006a 331006b 341003*a 341121a 341121g 351012a 360018a 361029a 361203a 370020a 380004b 380609a 380817a 381109a 391114a 391206a 400012a 401030a 401030d 410003a 410424a 411029a 430023a 430107a 440015a 440015b 440128a 441207a 450011a 450014a 460010a 460531a 480003a 481230a 490025a 500007a 501221a 510016b 530507a 530507b 550224a 550224b 560001a 570002a 580221a 580221c 650330a 730117a 740004a 740702a 750002a
Porter, Del 460023a
Porter, Stan 670404a
Porterfield, Christopher 590430a
Posford, George 361222a 390120a
Post, W H 250921a
Potter, Don 751209a
Pottle, Sam 651223a
Pounds, Courtice 160115j 160831a
Powell, Dick 330001a 330001b 330002a 330002b 330003a 330004a 330021a 340001a 340001b 340002a 340002b 340003a 340004a 340021a 340021b 350001a 350001b 350002a 350013a 350040a 360006a 360006b 360007a 360008a 360008b 360063a 361218a 370001a 370001b 370010a 370011a 370023a 370023b 380005a 380015a 390020a 420004a 420014b 430015a 540026a
Powell, Edgar 430331o 510329i 560315i 560315j
Powell, Edward 350006d 380014b
Powell, Eleanor 241201e 290109a 350027a 350919a 360018b 370007b 370020a

400012b 420011b 500015a
Powell, Jane 931223b 221113a 270425c 321108c 440001e 440020a 450015a 460009a 460009b 470313d 480013a 480016a 500005a 500008a 510003a 510004a 510004b 511112d 530008a 530013a 540001a 540010a 540011a 560315c 570006a 570203a 580001b 611019a
Powell, Jerry 630011a 660325a
Powell, Lovelady 621212a
Powell, Mel 480025a
Powell, Shezwae 740108a
Powell, William 060924i
Power, Elizabeth 740702a
Power, Tyrone 390005a 530214a 560007a
Powers, Peggy 630002b
Powers, Tom 170220a
Pracht, Mary Ellen 031013a 051230e 060924c 070302a 160115c 271227h
Prager, Stanley 381123b 540513a
Pratt, Michael 590012a
Prejean, Albert 280828e
Premice, Josephine 371127d 541230b 571031a 660921a 760302a
Preminger, Otto 750323a
Prentice, Charles 261227d 280223a 301108f 350505a 360911a 370901a 390323a 530507e
Presley, Elvis 560017a 570020a 570020b 570023a 570023b 580012a 600007a 600008a 610004a 610004b 620008a 620009a 620010a 630012a 630013a 640010a 640011a 640012a 640013a 650004a 650005a 650006a 660007a 660008a 660009a 670007a 670008a 670010a 680008a 680013a 681203a 690008a 690009a 700005a
Presnell, Harve 301014e 511112c 601103a 601103b 700103b 760414a
Pressel, Marc 711012b
Preston, Barry 760302a
Preston, Edna 541104a
Preston, Mary 250311k 561112g 660129f
Preston, Robert 571219a 571219b 641027a 660524b 661205a 741006a
Preston, Robert W 770307a
Preston, Walter 051230u
Preville, Giselle 390323e
Previn, Andre 351010c 470006a 481230d 500004a 511112c 531203b 550007a 550224b 560315b 561129b 580001a 600002a 670001a 680011a 691218a 711012e

060924c 070302a 101107d
160115c 240902f 241202e
250311j 250921c 250921i
261130i 271227h 271227l
280919e 331118f 351010e
440821c 481230b 510010a
510329g 520005a 530019b
570331h
Rene, Lucille 191007b
Rennie, Malcolm 740711a
Repole, Charles 151223a
Resnik, Regina 531203e
Revel, Harry 321129b 330029a
330040a 340011a 340024a
350025a 370002a 370014a
451110a
Revill, Clive 561112b 561112c
600630c 640005a
Rexite, Seymour 611021a
Reynolds, Brad 420005b
420704b
Reynolds, Burt 750002a
760002a
Reynolds, Debbie 191118b
270425c 470110d 490407n
500004a 500005a 501124c
520002a 520011a 530007a
540011a 550014a 560010a
570008a 580009a 590006a
590007a 601103b 620003a
620003b 630004a 660001a
Reynolds, Herbert 180522a
Reynolds, Joyce 430016a
Reynolds, Kay 611014b
Reynolds, Marjorie 420001c
420004a
Reynolds, Stan 690316d
Reynolds, Tim 690127a
Reynolds, William 430331f
490407k 490407l 560315i
560315j
Rhoads, Gretchen 430331o
510329i
Rhodes, Betty Jane 420004a
420017a 420032a
Rhodes, Erik 321129b 530507a
570413d
Rhodes, George 610720d
731116a
Rhythm Boys 300005a
300023a 331021a
Rice, Elmer 470109a
Rice, Florence 390013b
Rice, Gladys 031013f
Rice, Sarah 790301a
Rice, Tim 711012a 721108a
721108d 780621a
Rich, Doris 590205a
Rich, Freddie 351022a
Richard, Cliff 630010a
Richards, Andela 740702a
Richards, Bobby 250921o
261130t 271122f 390323d
490915b 501124h 531203h
560503c 570926j 580001h
600630e 740501a
Richards, Carol 470313e
500011a 501012c 550224b

Richards, Donald 051230c
431120a 470110a 490407s
501124e
Richards, Gwen 581201i
Richards, Jess 761005b
800514a
Richards, Norman 640019a
Richards, Paul 051230i
Richardson, Claibe 711102a
760400a
Richardson, Ian 560315l
Richardson, Walter 060924i
220828b
Richert, Wanda 800825a
Richman, Harry 260614a
280702a 300013a 300013b
300225a 321122a 341108a
360036a 360036b
Richman, Rebecca 611021a
Rickell, Tony 710517e
Riddle, Nelson 401225c
511112c 530507b 540912a
550919a 560001a 560317a
561115b 570006a 580006a
580008a 611014b 640002a
651017b 760001a
Rigg, Diana 730225d
Riggs, Ralph 430331a
Riha, Bobby 670226a
Riley, Stanley 070417a
090428a
Rimmer, Shane 441228h
540001b 640326e
Rimsky-Korsakov, Nicolai
470012a 560414a
Ring, Blanche 090118a
090522a 100210a
Ringland, Dale 790211b
Rio, Rita 360043a
Rios, Augustine 571031a
Ripley, Heather 680005a
Riscoe, Arthur 391221a
Riser, Paul 751121a
Risque, W H 010601a
Ritchard, Cyril 380126a
400419a 531210a 541020a
541020c 571117a 580221a
610403a 650516a 651128a
720409a 751113a 770515a
Ritchie, June 280828b
700103b 711220a
Ritchie, Roy 730619c
Ritschel, Jack 690806a
Ritter, Tex 310126a 520015a
Ritter, Thelma 570514a
Ritter, Walt 690806a
Ritz Brothers 360058a
361218a 370001b 370014a
Ritz Quartet 281204a
Rivas, Carlos 510329b
Rivaud, Pascale 751210a
Rivera, Chita 550526a
560322a 570926a 570926c
600414a 600414c 641123a
660129b 730311a 750603a
Rivera, John 651218a
Rivera, Martin 750127a
Roane, Frank 491030a

Robards, Jason 680006a
Robbins, Ayn 770006a
Robbins, Gale 500004a
Robbins, Gerald 760009a
Robbins, Jana 270906f
Robbins, Marty 590017a
Robbins, Peter 690006a
Robbins, Rex 611005a
621018a
Roberson, Virgil 770123a
Robert, Kenneth 430331q
Roberti, Lyda 330120a
340011a 350010b
Roberti, Manya 310014a
Roberts Brothers 400015a
Roberts, Anthony 671207a
681201b
Roberts, Bob 640005a
Roberts, C Luckey 260708a
Roberts, Chapman 690924a
Roberts, Gladys 971116a
Roberts, Howard 501124g
731019a
Roberts, Joan 331118a
430331a 430331i 450718a
451110a 471009b
Roberts, Keith 681201c
Roberts, Lynn 561112*a
640019a 781214a
Roberts, Pernell 450419b
Roberts, Pete 500002a
Roberts, Roberta 470313i
Roberts, Tony 720409a
Robertson, Andrew 721108c
Robertson, Cliff 570006a
750323a
Robertson, Dick 281010b
311102a
Robertson, Don 690724a
Robertson, Douglas 570207a
Robeson, Paul 271227f
271227g 271227o 271227p
350043a 360037a 370034a
370035a 370036a 390424a
400029a 400029b
Robey, George 160419a
170131a
Robin, Leo 270425a 281030a
320002a 340022a 370027a
390010a 410021a 420016a
420021a 430004a 430013a
460014a 460021a 470005a
480004a 481208a 510010a
510030a 520012a 530013a
540305a 570203a
Robinson, Bill 850314b
280509a 280509c 380006a
430007a
Robinson, Earl 380043a
390424a 421005a 440321a
440321a 450009a 450009b
541129a
Robinson, Elisabeth 450421b
Robinson, Harry 640922*a
Robinson, Laura 791004a
Robinson, Phyllis 700408a
Robinson, Richard 241202s
280919a

Robinson, Stuart K 760709a
Robinson, Venustra K
780513a
Robinson, Wayne 640422a
Robison, Carson 350012a
Robison, Clayne 760414a
Robson, Flora 720002a
Robyn, Alfred G 040222a
070812a
Roche, Eugene 641026a
Roche, John 300009b
Rodby, John 780002a
Rodd, Marcia 680103a
680113a 730206a
Rodgers, Anton 630704a
700001a 790725a
Rodgers, Bob 590609a
Rodgers, Douglas Fletcher
550127a
Rodgers, Eileen 341121e
580204a 591123a 601017a
Rodgers, Mary 570003a
581227a 590511a 611019a
651223a 720004a 760504a
780514a
Rodgers, Richard 200324a
250918a 260317a 261201a
261227a 270427a 270520a
271103a 280103a 290036a
290311a 300016a 300016b
300218a 300327a 301203a
310011a 320004a 320014a
330006a 330027a 340044a
340045a 340045b 350024a
350024b 351022a 351116a
360411a 361225a 370414a
380511a 381123a 381123f
391018a 400404a 400404b
400419a 401225a 410035a
420005a 420602a 430012b
430331a 450001a 450001c
450001d 450419a 471010a
480001a 490407a 500010a
500018b 510329a 530024a
530528a 551130a 570331a
570331b 570331g 581014a
581201a 591116a 591116c
620315a 650318a 671115a
701110a 720326a 730311a
760425a 760504a
Rodgers, Shev 651122e
Rodriguez, Burt 750309a
Roecker, Robert 051225b
Roeg, Nicolette 540513e
600630f
Roemheid, Edgar 261130g
Rogers, Alex 260708a
Rogers, Anne 250311l 390323c
430331s 540114a 560315k
591116k 630423b 661205b
Rogers, Charles (Buddy)
290043a 300004a 300016b
300030a 300030b 370044a
Rogers, Clive 560315k
Rogers, David 790614a
Rogers, Earl 601203d
Rogers, Eric 430331p 450419n
530507g 531203g 600630c

600630d
Rogers, Erica 620315c
770417b
Rogers, Ginger 290033a
301014d 310009a 321129b
321129c 330001a 330001b
330005a 330021a 330021b
330029a 331118h 331118l
340002a 340002b 340041a
350006a 350006b 350006d
350006e 350037a 350049a
360002b 360002c 360012a
360012b 370004a 370004c
380003a 380003b 380035a
410123f 490002a 620006a
640116j 660524d
Rogers, Milton 580007b
Rogers, Robert 721001a
Rogers, Roy 440015a 440015b
440018a 440019a 450013a
450014a 460012a 470023a
480019a 520014a 520014b
Rogers, Shorty 580006c
Rogers, Timmy 270906f
Rogers, Will 100110b
Rogier, Frank 931223a
241202a 331118a
Rogow, Lee 470027a
Roland, Gilbert 540012a
Roland, Jean-Louis 751210a
Roland, Steve 611005a
631024a 641215a
Rolin, Judi 661106*a
Roll, Eddie 570926a 651122e
Rolland, Jean-Louis 640003c
Rolle, Esther 720516a
Rolph, Dudley 570331d
Rolph, Marti 270906f 730311a
Romaguera, Joaquin 790301a
Romaine, George 430331r
Romaine, Margaret 140223a
Roman, Mimi 630415a
Roman, Paul Reid 710517f
Roman, Robert 630020a
640005a
Romann, Susan 690604a
Romay, Lina 420003c 440011a
Romberg, Sigmund 140610a
150218a 160115a 160115c
161206a 170816a 190212a
241202a 251102a 261130a
270912a 280919a 300920a
350017a 361102a 380001a
390017a 450127a 540010a
540010b 540305a
Rome, Harold 371127a
371127b 371127c 380924a
430414a 460418a 460418b
480924a 500117a 500628a
501214a 520625a 520625b
541104a 541104b 541104c
541104d 590423a 620322a
640006a 651110a 700103a
700103b 700103c 750502a
Rome, Sydne 790001a
Romero, Cesar 410010a
430013a 590016b
Romoff, Colin 611023a

640526a 720326a 750502a
Romoff, Wood 630423a
Romuald 680004a
Ronell, Ann 330035a
Ronstadt, Linda 791231a
Rooney, Annie 410004b
Rooney, Mickey 301014b
301014c 370414b 400003a
400003b 410004a 410004b
460019a 480001a 570511a
571013a 650003a 711203a
740009a 770005a 780004a
Rooney, Pat, Sr 501124a
Roos, Casper 720310a
Roper, Alan 520001c
Roper, Eric 131223a
Rose Marie 511101a
Rose, Billy 351116b
Rose, David 431120a 510004a
510004b 520007a 581017a
591104a 600928*a
Rose, E K 120108a
Rose, George 791231a
560315l 661126a 680320c
691218a
Rose, Margot 741115a
780516a
Rose, Patrick 780323a
780323b
Rose, Reva 660003b
Rosen, Jeffrey 690724a
Rosenblatt, Josef 270001a
270001b
Rosenblum, Ava 701108a
Rosenblum, Susan 701108a
Rosenfeld, Sydney 021110a
Rosenstock, Milton 301014f
341121h 420704a 471009a
481208a 481208d 481208e
510329n 510418a 521215a
530507a 561129a 590521a
610720a 611227a 640326a
691023a
Rosenthal, Laurence 651122d
Ross, Adrian 940101a 941124a
980608a 991021a 000203a
010907a 021115a 040305a
051230a 070302b 070302c
080425a 081223a 090123a
090906a 091112a 100108a
101105a 130405a 150424a
160115b 160115l 170914a
190419a
Ross, Annie 560301a
Ross, Diana 720004a 740003a
750105b
Ross, Eliza 630011a
Ross, Harry 601226b
Ross, Herbert 640326b
Ross, Howard 750408a
790404a
Ross, Hugh 540311a
Ross, Jamie 721004a
Ross, Jerry 540513a 550505a
Ross, Lanny 340011a 430012b
560315f
Ross, Lewis 701026a
Ross, Lynn 590319a

Ross, Marilyn 510514a
Ross, Marion 450419k
Ross, Shirley 340045a 340045b
360047b 380012a 380012b
380013a 380013b 390010b
390021a 390021b 400404a
Ross, Ted 750105a 750105b
Ross, Vivienne 690316c
Rossi, Tino 350060a
Roth, Betty 350054a
Roth, Lillian 290011c 300012a
300046a 321126d 330025a
620322a 710415a
Rothenberger, Annelise
740405b
Rothlein, Arlene 690127a
Rotondo, Guy 640429a
Roulien, Raul 310014a
330005a
Round, Thomas 051230l
160115b 440821f
Rounseville, Robert 850314a
051230a 241202a 450419e
561201a 651122a
Rourke, Michael E 120203b
141224a 180522a
Routledge, Patricia 481230m
591116k 591118b 640116l
680127a 720710a
Rovin, Robert 660623a
661019a
Rowe, Genevieve 241202n
540010b
Rowland, Helen 311102a
Rowlands, Patsy 581002a
Rowles, Polly 620315a
Roy, Harry 360046a
Roy, William 430331x
590924a 600929a 611005a
621018a
Royal, Ted 301014a 310603c
341121d 401225a 470313a
470313i 501124a 510514a
510621a 511112a 520516a
540114b 541230a 560322a
560614a 561206a
Royle, Selena 460010b
460019a
Royston, Roy 220113a
370916a
Rozsa, Miklos 470012a
Ruark, John 560315p
Rub, Christian 380024b
400001a
Rubens, Christine 740108a
Rubens, Paul 940101a
020510a 040305a 041217a
070131a 100219a 120224a
140824a 141224a 150424a
160513a
Rubenstein, Deidre 540114g
Rubin, Arthur 051225a
051230e 160115c 280919e
611102a 760427a
Rubin, Benny 300043a
Rubin, Ron 690001a
Rubinoff 370014a
Rubinstein, Arthur 590430a

600428*a 680103a 750303a
Rubinstein, John 721023a
Rubinstein, Ruth 371127c
Ruby, Harry 280905a 281023a
300035a 340030a 500004a
710606a 770113a
Ruby, Thelma 530908a
590511b
Ruchek, Jena 690724a
Ruck, Linda 590121a
Rudel, Julius 051230s
Rudley, Marian 380103a
Rudolf, Max 051230h
Ruffin, Gary 710228a
Ruffin, Hank 710228a
Ruggles, Charles 320002a
341121k
Rugolo, Peter 571112a
Ruhl, Eddy 510329m 560315o
Ruhl, Pat 600929a
Ruick, Barbara 261108a
450419e 530030a 570331b
Rule, Janice 610403a
Rundquist, Kenneth 420018a
Rupert, Michael 790517a
Rupert, Mike 680118a
Rupp, Franz 571230a
Rushing, Jimmy 600619a
Rusk, James 661019a
Ruskin, Coby 410105a
Russell, Andy 450012a
460011b 460022a 470029a
Russell, Anna 931223a
Russell, Betty 460006a
Russell, Bryan 600414b
Russell, Connie 241201e
540013a
Russell, David 640116h
Russell, Gilbert 500018a
Russell, Henry 480032a
Russell, Jack 831003a
Russell, Jane 480022a 481208b
510015a 510025a 520014a
520014b 540012a 550002a
Russell, Kennedy 190419a
280427a
Russell, Lillian 020911a
120208a 520017b
Russell, Madelyn 481230p
Russell, Nipsey 750105b
Russell, Rosalind 530226a
530226b 590521b
Russell, Scott 980608a
991021b
Russell, Tony 670003a
Russian Art Choir 251230a
Rutland, John 540114a
Ryan, Irene 721023a 721023e
Ryan, Madge 430331w
Ryan, Marion 600211b
Ryan, Mark 780621b
Ryan, Robert 621020a
660325a
Ryan, Sheila 430004a
Rydell, Bobby 600414b
600414d
Rydell, Charles 641026a
Ryder, Richard 780608a

Shafer, Robert 440821b
  550505a 550505b
Shakesnider, Wilma 351010s
Shakespeare, William 680305a
Shale, Tom 081114j
Shane, Hal 151223a
Shane, Lisa 640326d
Shanet, Howard, 200324a
Shanley, Robert 420704a
  420704e
Shannon, Carol 590023a
Shapiro, Dan 440408a
  550418a
Shapiro, Debbie 760003a
Shapiro, Joseph 750107a
Shapiro, Ted 300917a
Sharah, Sal 730619c
Sharif, Omar 640326b
Sharkey, Anna 650202a
  720710a
Sharma, Barbara 670426a
Sharp, Frederick 740405h
Sharp, Robert 661120a
Sharpe, Bernard 341121m
Sharpe, Evelyn 560315n
Sharpe, John 561121a
Sharples, Bob 590521f
Sharples, Winston 620014a
Shattuck, Truly 100926a
Shaute, Susan 430331f
  430331o 490407k 490407l
  510329i
Shaver, Bob 361117a 381123b
Shaw, Artie 390030a 400007a
  400007b
Shaw, Carole 640005a
Shaw, Geoffrey 051230p
Shaw, Georgie 560021b
Shaw, Goldye 710415a
Shaw, Leon 540114c
Shaw, Marcie 791231a
Shaw, Oscar 251208b
Shaw, Reta 540513a 540513b
Shaw, Robert 431202a
  441228c
Shaw, Roland 301030d
  440821d
Shaw, Winifred 350001a
  350001b 350038b 360020a
  370052a
Shawhan, April 740306a
Shawn, Dick 681220c
Shawn, Peter 760400a
Shay, Dorothy 510031a
Shayne, Alan 600504a
Shea, George Beverly 530026a
Shea, Jeanne 570219a
Shean, Al 220605a 220605b
  380024b 410001b
Shearer, Toni 721019a
Shearing, George 510028a
Shearman, Alan 730213a
Sheets, Walter 680007a
Sheil, Chris 710517f
Shelby, Laurel 360411b
  550025a
Shelley, Joshua 360411a
Shelley, Rosamund 430331w

Shelton, James 390929a
  541201a
Shelton, Lucy 741115a
Shelton, Reid 450419h
  651218a 661106a 720612a
  770421a
Shemer, Naomi 711021a
Shepard, Joan 620311b
  680012a 680222*a 680222a
Shepherd, Bill 681220b
Shepherd, Cybill 750002a
Shepley, Ida 581201c
Sheridan, Ann 400037a
  410029a 430016a 470025a
Sherman, Allan 501124c
  690102a
Sherman, Art 621004a
Sherman, Garry 700315a
Sherman, Hiram 290430b
  361117a 521215a 560304a
  671207a
Sherman, Richard M &
  Robert B 610002a 610011a
  620004a 620015a 630008a
  630014a 640001a 660004a
  670004a 670005a 680003a
  680005a 680007a 680009a
  690007a 700303a 710001a
  720001a 730002a 740008a
  740306a 760006a 780004a
Sherrell, Pony 550006a
Sherrill, Joya 630816a
Sherwin, Manning 430923a
Sherwood, Gale 081114h
  170816a
Sherwood, Janice 601203h
Sherwood, Madeleine 650318a
Sherwood, Wayne 581201f
Shields, Bobby 581222a
Shigeta, James 581201b
Shilkret, Nathanial 031013f
  151223*c 031013e 031116a
  060924f 060924g 090920a
  101107j 121202g 130908f
  131210d 141102c 150929c
  160115f 170206a 170319e
  170816c 240902m 241202m
  250921n 261108g 261130p
  270816a 270912c 280919p
  301014h 311226c 321108d
  351010m 360002b 370004c
  390424a 520304a
Shimono, Sab 760111a
Shiner, Ronald 580221b
Shire, David 580513a 590430a
  640014a 770307a 790003a
Shirk, Julie 951104b
Shirkey, Gerald 261130e
Shirley, Bill 480129a 490027a
  560315b 590010a
Shizuko, Lynn 581201i
Shope, Henry M 051230u
Shore, Dinah 420001d
  430016a 430016b 440005a
  440005b 440010a 440024a
  450215a 460002a 460009c
  470016a 470016c 481230c
  490407n 501012a 501124c

  510010a 510329g 520005a
  571117a 660501a
Shore, Roberta 590006b
Short, Bobby 371127d
  720326a
Short, Martin 730419a
Showalter, Max 550016a
  711102a
Shuken, Leo 541104b 570019a
  730001a
Shull, Richard B 700326a
  750303a
Shulman, Alan 440821a
Shulman, Sylvan 440821a
Shuman, Earl 641026a
Shuman, Mort 680122a
  680122a
Shutta, Ethel 631017a
  710404a 710404b 730311a
Sicari, Joseph R 680103a
  681220a
Sidney, Gordon 351010t
Sidney, Jon 770421c
Siegel, Arthur 400911a
  480115a 491013a 520516a
  560614a 620201a
Siegel, Larry 651223a
Siegmeister, Elie 441227a
Siepi, Cesare 620519a
Sigman, Carl 471211a
Silberman, Joel 780608a
Siletti, Mario 591118a
Sillman, June 341225a
Sillman, Leonard 680502a
Sills, Beverly 051230s
Silver, Johnny 501124a
  501124b
Silverman, Jeffrey 801111a
Silverman, Stanley 280828g
  721123a
Silvers, Louis 211006a
  270001c 271227B 290311a
  340012b 370002b 390005a
Silvers, Phil 241201e 440028a
  471009a 500002a 511101a
  540018b 601226a 620508b
  640422a
Silvers, Sid 360018b
Silvestre, Ruth 581201c
Simmonds, Stanley 561115a
  741006a
Simmons, Elsie 661106*a
Simmons, Jean 501124b
  730225c
Simmons, Maude 470110a
Simmons, Robert 321108d
Simms, Ginny 440025a
  460010b 460010c
Simms, Lou Ann 530128a
  650003a
Simon, Avi 200324a
Simon, Joanna 720326a
Simon-Girard, A 150918a
Simons, Ted 341121e 660920a
  680502a
Simpson, Bland 750114a
Simpson, Valerie 750105b
Sims, Joan 550831b

Sinatra, Frank 341121c
  400036a 400404b 400404c
  401225c 410019a 420011a
  420011b 440012a 440012b
  441228f 450009a 450215a
  460002b 470006a 470006b
  470110d 480011a 480012a
  481230c 490007a 490007b
  490407n 501124b 501124c
  510015a 520017a 520017b
  530507b 540015a 540015b
  540015c 540015d 540019a
  550014a 550019a 550919a
  560001a 560001b 560020a
  570010a 580015a 580022a
  590014b 640002a
Sinatra, Frank, Jr 710814a
Sinatra, Nancy 680008a
Sinatra, Ray 490006a 500006b
Sinclair, Belinda 730619a
Sinclair, Bill 401225f
Sinclair, Monica 350505c
Singana, Margaret 740322b
Singleton, Win 620014a
Singleton, Zutty 430007a
Siravo, George 541201a
Sirmay, Albert 130405a
  280223a
Sirola, Joseph 601103a
  680204a
Sissle, Noble 210523a
  210523b 240901a 780920a
Sivuca 700127a
Six Brown Brothers 141020b
  201005a
Skelly, Hal 290044a
Skelton, Red 241201e 331118g
  391206d 391206e 401030e
  420011b 490004c 500004a
Skiles, Steve 660207a 670926a
Skinner, Cornelia Otis
  520304a
Skipper, Syd 741128a
Sklair, Josh 720214c
Skulnik, Menasha 651110a
Slaney, Ivor 490407m
Slater, John 560315g
Slaughter, Walter 410031a
Slavin, Martin 850314c
Slavin, Millie 640429a
Sledge, Eddie 481230a
Sleep, Wayne 810511a
Slezak, William 541104a
Slick, Daniel 480715b
Sloane, A Baldwin 021110a
Sloane, Everett 560310a
Small, Allan 500202a 510418a
Small, Marya 720214a
Small, Neva 671023a
Small, William 530908a
Smallens, Alexander 031013b
  351010a 351010g
Smalls, Alexander B 351010s
Smalls, Charlie 750105a
Smallwood, Clarry 620205b
Smart, Bob 450001d
Smartt, Michael V 770920a
Smith, Alexis 710404a

710404b 730311a 781112a
Smith, Andrew 351010s
Smith, Bessie 290038a
760002a
Smith, Bruce 810605a
Smith, C Aubrey 320004b
Smith, Charlie 460023a
Smith, Clay 170426a
Smith, Daryl 690724a
Smith, David Rae 051230s
Smith, Edgar 120203a
Smith, Emerson 951104a
Smith, Ethel 440031a 480019a
Smith, Gregg 060924i 220828b
Smith, Harry B 741111a
910928a 941029a 951104a
970316a 980926a 991023a
000319a 031116a 090123*a
130825a 131002a 131030a
140824a 150503a 151223a
160110a 170115a 230131a
250113a 251102a 260326a
Smith, Jabbo 280227a
791020a
Smith, Jack 270624a 280404a
300029a 510012a
Smith, Jennie 630415a
Smith, Kate 260920a 320010a
320010b 320217c 320308c
330009a 420704d 420704e
480008b
Smith, Keely 481230c 490407n
590013a
Smith, Kenneth 051225a
051230e 160115c 261130i
480715a
Smith, Lane 750006a
Smith, Loring 311226a
491125a 611118a 640116c
Smith, Lorraine 510329f
540001b 590521g 640922k
Smith, Lucille 571219h
Smith, Maggie 560614a
630319b
Smith, Mamie 210823a
Smith, Max 600003a
Smith, Mike 780621a
Smith, Muriel 431202a
490407c 490407e 510329h
580616a
Smith, Noel 770421c
Smith, Norris 271227g
Smith, Norwood 831003a
Smith, Osborne 561112c
Smith, Paul 370012a 400001a
420009a 460020a 490011a
490011b
Smith, Queenie 271227o
350024c
Smith, Rex 791231a
Smith, Robert B 090123*a
130908a 141028a
Smith, Rufus 460516c
511112a
Smith, Sally 650516a
Smith, Sammy 520625a
611014a 611014b 671207a
Smith, Sheila 580209a

720409a
Smith, Stanley 270906k
Smith, Toni 580513a
Smith, Truman 611102a
Smith, Tucker 570926b
Smith, Warren 711020b
Smith, William C 271227z
Smithson, Florence 090428e
Smothers Brothers 661106*a
Smothers, Tom 720004a
Smyrl, David Langston
780514a
Sneed, Gary 660207a 661019a
750127a
Snellenberg, Ronald 671029h
Snow, Harry 450419i 510329e
590511a
Soboloff, Arnold 640404a
Sokoloff, Alan 371127a
Sokoloff, Alexander 751014a
Solley, Marvin 720522a
720522b 790005a
Solly, Bill 750917a 761202a
Somers, Debroy 350505e
370916b
Somers, Virginia 550127b
Somerville, Phyllis 740306a
Sommer, Hans 530009a
Sommers, Avery 781112a
Sommers, Joanie 640007a
661207a
Sondergaard, Hester 410105a
Sondheim, Stephen 561201b
570926a 590521a 620508a
640404a 640404c 650318a
651223a 700426a 710404a
730225a 730311a 760111a
760504a 790301a
Sone, Roy 630321e
Sons of the Pioneers 480019a
Soo, Jack 581201a 581201b
Soper, Gay 680320a 710517c
721106b 740501a 761206a
Sorenson, Arthur Alan
791127a
Sorvino, Paul 760511a
760511b 790408a
Sosnik, Harry 931223c
280919g 331118d 381123d
401030a 410123e 411029c
420602b 440128a
Sothern, Ann 241201e
241201f 340010b 340014b
340014c 401030e 401030f
410123b 480001a 500008a
Soules, Dale 740528a
Sourire, Soeur 660001a
Sousa, John Philip 520008a
Spangler, David 770920a
Sparks, Ned 370002b 430012b
Spear, Bernard 571219c
621117b 640116i 640922k
651122c
Spear, David 790517a
Spearman, Rawn 541230a
Speck, Crista 640422a
Speers, Jan 170829a
Spence, Johnnie 620315c

Spence, Lew 580019a
Spencer, Bob 611206a
Spencer, Christine 631015a
651110a
Spencer, Herbert W 700001a
740711a
Spencer, Kenneth 271227m
Spencer, Tim 530026a
Spialek, Hans 601103*a
Spielman, Fred 561223a
580003a
Spiro, Bernie 751014a
Spitalny, H Leopold 051230u
Spivak, Charlie 440026a
Springer, Phil 360008c
571010a 571105b
St Clair, Bill 351010v
St Darr, Deborah 561201b
St Denis, Teddie 371216a
St Helier, Ivy 290718e
St John, Florence 991111g
St John, Howard 561115a
561115b 581209a
St John, Lily 200918a
St Lewis, Keni 770004a
St Louis, Louis 720214a
720214b
Stabile, Dick 550017a
560015a
Stadlen, Lewis J 561201b
700326a
Stafford, Jo 391206d 481230c
481230n 490407n 491125b
501124c 501124f 571220b
Stafford, Joseph 541020a
Staiger, Libi 540408a 560503b
630415a
Stamford, John 540305a
Stamper, Dave 170131a
271122*a
Stamper, F Pope 191112a
Standley, Johnny 600210a
Stanford, Charles 960302a
Stange, Stanislaus 041003a
081114a
Staniforth, Michael 711201b
Stanley, Aileen 200715a
Stanley, Arthur 260326c
Stanley, Hal 560917a 571126a
Stanley, James 321108d
Stanley, Pat 581011a 591123a
Stantley, Ralph 611206a
Stanton, Harry 241202c
400001b
Stanton, Olive 380103a
Stanwyck, Barbara 430020a
Stapleton, Cyril 490407j
580001f 630321e
Stapleton, Jean 561129a
590309a 640326a
Stapleton, Maureen 600414b
Stapley, Diane 780323a
780323b
Starbuck, Gary 770004a
Stark, Sally 681220a
Starkie, Martin 680320a
680320b
Starling, Eric 360911a

Staroba, Arden 600428*a
Starobin, Michael 790221a
Starr, Kay 560917a
Starr, Pat 560304a
Stasny, Stephanie 801111a
Staton, Dakota 591102b
Steber, Eleanor 280919h
430331h
Steck, Gene 630002b
Steck, Olga 231020a
Stecko, Joseph 170829a
601012a 641026a 730404a
Steddeford, Marjorie 360051a
Steel, Jeanne 571219g
Steel, John 190623a 200622a
210621a 221023a 230922a
260906a 380803a
Steele, Patti 490407g 571219h
Steele, Tommy 470110b
520001c 520001g 570331e
590012a 630321a 630321b
630321c 630321e 670004a
Steffe, Edwin 250921o
560503c 651129a 680320c
Steiger, Rod 430331b
Stein, Gertrude 671013a
691215a
Stein, Julian 341121e 600503a
610419a 620406a 630019a
651210a
Steinberg, Ben 500424a
Steinberg, Dave 270906j
Steiner, Max 321129b 330005a
331118l 350006d 360012b
Steinert, Alexander 420009a
Stell, John 791020a
Stephens, Ann 410031a
Stephens, Garn 720214a
Stephens, Madge 170210c
601203i
Stephenson, B C 860925a
Stept, Sam 390706a
Sterling, Jan 540023a
Sterling, Michael 751210a
Stern, Gerald 481208f
Stern, Harold 290218a
Sternbach, Jerry 760709a
Sternberg, Ann 691215a
Sterner, Steve 720612a
750127a
Sternhagen, Frances 780510a
Stevens, Bob 580013a
Stevens, Connie 630003a
691206a 730117a
Stevens, Craig 631003a
Stevens, Davis 131111a
Stevens, Fran 671207a
Stevens, James 910928f
Stevens, Joel 761215a
Stevens, Larry 460014a
Stevens, Leith 590003a
600004a
Stevens, Len 560503d 570926k
581201j 640116h
Stevens, Mark 470020b
490027a
Stevens, Marti 261108e
620315c 640407c

Stevens, Morton 560322a
Stevens, Napua 610302a
Stevens, Pauline 081114f
    351010h
Stevens, Rise 740405g
    051230h 081114b 081114c
    160115f 241202d 270912c
    271227b 351010j 410123c
    510329d 581016a 740009a
Stevens, Stella 561115b
Stevens, Tony 730311a
Stevens, Trudy 540006b
Stevensen, Scott 270906f
Steward, Ron 680509a
Stewardson, Joe 590521h
Stewart, Carol 460023a
Stewart, Donald 481208f
Stewart, Ethel 350007a
Stewart, James 360018b
    690010a 780004a
Stewart, Jan 501124f
Stewart, John 570219a
Stewart, Johnny 471009a
Stewart, Leon 790517a
Stewart, Maeretha 351010f
Stewart, Martha 470020b
Stewart, Melvin 570521a
Stewart, Michael 560027a
    580007c 770417a 800430a
Stewart, Mike 550228a
Stewart, Nick 431202b
Stewart, Nicodemus 460020a
    460020b
Stewart, Paula 601215a
    611012a
Stewart, Princess 611211a
Stewart, Sandy 601103c
    621020b
Stewart, Tom 361117a
Stickler, Don 590122a
Stickney, Dorothy 570331a
Stiers, David Ogden 740528a
Stiles, Vernon 170319d
Stilwell, Richard 590626b
Stockwell, Harry 370012a
Stoddard, George E 181223a
Stoddart, John 350505b
    360911c
Stoessel, Ludwig 450027a
Stokes, Barry 761206a
Stokes, Leonard 430331d
    430331g 460516f
Stokman, Abraham 630606a
Stolber, Dean 660920a
Stoll, George 240902b
    241201e 270425c 301014b
    301014c 341121j 351116b
    370414b 390001a 391206d
    400003a 401025d 410004b
    420002b 440001a 440001b
    440012a 460025a 490001a
    490004a 500005a 500008a
    530007a 530029a 540011a
    540014a 580005a
Stoloff, Morris 340012b
    401225c 410003b 430023a
    440028a 460005c 470110d
    481230e 490407n 501124c

540003a 541104b 550010a
    560002a 560007a
Stolz, Robert 301108a
Stone, Dan 780001a
Stone, Elly 680122a 680122d
    770113a
Stone, Ezra 420704a 420704e
Stone, Fred 100110a 100110b
Stone, Leonard 590205a
Stone, Lew 460516j
Stordahl, Axel 450004c
    530003a 540015a
Storm, Bob 351010v
Storr, Bob 621004a
Stoska, Polyna 470109a
Stothart, Herbert 051230v
    101107o 201117a 230207a
    240902a 240902n 251230a
    280905a 280919k 300017a
    370020a 390001a 390017a
    410001b 410011a 430008a
    470019a
Stover, Janet 731120a
Stracke, Win 630002b
Straight, Willard 640114a
Straker, Peter 671029d
    671029f 721019b
Strand, Chuck 750309a
Strathdee, Barbara 241202q
Stratton, Bob 490407g
Stratton, Chester 271103a
Straus, Oscar 070302a
    081114a 200212a 320002a
    351005a
Strauss, Johann 740405e
    801001a 831003a 301030a
Strauss, Johann, Jr 740405a
    851024a 301030b 351005a
    380024a
Strauss, Johann, Sr 301030b
    351005a
Strauss, John 560522a
Strauss, Lance 770421c
Stredder, Maggie 780001a
Street, David 450001d
Streisand, Barbra 371127a
    390001c 620322a 640116d
    640326a 640326b 640326c
    640326d 640326g 651017b
    750001a 760007a
Strickler, Jerry 621020a
Stringer, Marcie 651226a
Stritch, Elaine 360411a
    360411e 371127d 401225b
    471211a 581011a 611003a
    611003c 700426a
Strong, Pamela 661120d
Stroud, Gregory 201221a
    230105a
Strouse, Charles 550228a
    560522a 571105a 590007a
    600414a 620319a 641020a
    660329a 660330a 680006a
    700330a 721106a 770421a
    790614a
Stuart, Gloria 350001b
Stuart, Isobel 711019a
Stuart, Jay 630011a

Stuart, Leslie 991111a 010601a
    080425a 110304a
Stuart, Ralph 340112a
Stuarti, Enzo 831003a
    460531a
Stubbs, Una 720710a 740702a
Studholme, Marion 740405h
Style, Jule 500023a 400024a
    400036a 410030a 420019a
    420032a 440010b 440012a
    440029a 460015a 470006a
    471009a 480010a 480012a
    481208a 481208d 481208e
    490016a 500019c 510010a
    510015a 510030a 510719a
    520004c 530211a 540019a
    540019b 540020a 541020a
    561129a 561129b 561129d
    570203a 580403a 590521a
    590521b 590521i 600619a
    601226a 601226f 611227a
    640326a 640326b 640326f
    640526a 651128a 660501a
    670426a 680127a 720409a
    730311a 760504a 781031a
Styner, Jerry 650003a
Sukman, Harry 560007b
    660001a
Sullivan, Ann 460027a
Sullivan, Arthur 791231a
    850314a 991129a 800228a
Sullivan, Barry 500008a
Sullivan, Brian 740405c
    470109a
Sullivan, Ed 271227x 331118e
    351010r 401225h 430331l
    450419m 460516m 470110g
    470313g 481230o 490407f
    510329j 560315h
Sullivan, Frank 630411a
Sullivan, Hugh 670003a
Sullivan, Jeri 480025a
Sullivan, Jo 081114b 280828a
    560503a
Sullivan, Lee 470313a
    470313h
Sullivan, Maxine 380015a
    380015b 380710a 390019a
    390019b
Sullivan, Sheila 420602a
Sullivan, Vincent 141028b
Sumac, Yma 510514a
Summerville, Slim 360009a
Sundgaard, Arnold 480715a
    601012a 610425a 760414a
Supree, Burton 660304a
Susan, Fern 351010t
Sutherland, Claudette 611014a
Sutter, Savin 751210b
Sutton, Julia 721220a
Suzuki, Pat 581201a 581201h
Swados, Elizabeth 780513a
Swann, Donald 570124a
    570124b 570124c 631002a
    631002b
Swann, Elaine 720310a
Swann, Robert 700103b
    711220a

Swanson, Bea 751014a
Swanson, Gloria 290006a
    310006a 321108f 330018a
Swarbrick, Carol 760400a
    801111a
Swarthout, Gladys 370033a
    380045a
Sweetland, Lee 241202k
    280919f 490010a
Sweetland, Sally 240630a
    450008a 470313h 580013a
    670110a
Sweier, Victor 690007a
Swenson, Inga 560614a
    631024a 650216a 671115a
Swenson, Swen 621117a
    621117b
Swift, Kay 520304a 601103*a
Swinford, Susan 540114g
Syers, Mark 780621c
Syers, Mark Hsu 760111a
Sylva, Marguerite 100108b
Symington, Jim 550025a
Syms, Sylvia 581222a

Tabbert, William 370414e
    490407a 541104a
Takei, George 620205b
Taketa, Taruko 581201i
Talbot, Howard 010907a
    011005a 060421a 090428a
    170914a
Talbot, Nita 560010a 650005a
Taliaferro, Mabel 441005a
Tallman, Randolph 731120a
Tally, Harry 050828a
Talman, Iris 710517e
Talus, Pamela 700208a
Talva, Galina 501012a
Tamara 331118o
Tamblyn, Russ 270425c
    570926b 580003a
Tamiya, Jiro 700103a
Tanguay, Eva 090614a
Tanner, Jill 790513b
Tanner, Stella 441228h
    481230m 640326e
Tanner, Susan Jane 810511a
Tanner, Tony 600211b
    600630a 610720b
Tarlow, Florence 690604a
    711219a
Tarlton, Diane 720612a
Tarver, Ben 661106a
Tate, Neal 780920a
Tate, Stephen 711012c
    810511a
Tatum, Marianne 800430a
Taube, Sven-Bertil 721106a
    721106b
Tauber, Richard 740405d
    160115e 291010b 460028a
Taubin, Amy 721123a
Tausky, Vilem 740405h
    051230o 090428c 091112b
    291010a 490915c
Taverner, Derek 170210d
Taylor, Billie 120305a

Turner, Charles 530026b
Turner, Claramae 450419e
450419g
Turner, Clyde 460516a
Turner, Joan 660524c
Turner, John 750422a 760006a
Turner, Lana 051230d 510005b
Turner, Pat 381123e
Turner, Terry 550025a
Turner, Wendy 620004a
Turque, Mimi 651122a
Tushingham, Rita 670002a
Twiggy 540114d 730117a
Tyers, John 271227z
Tyler, Jim 630321a 640019a
690122a 740306a 760427a
770001a Tyler, Judy 551130a
Tyne, George 280828a
Tynes, Margaret 351010i
351010o
Tyrrell, Susan 680305b
Tysick, Sylvia 600414c
Tyson, Cicely 660921a
Tzelniker, Meier 240902a

Ubaldi, Marzia 660107b
Udell, Peter 700315a 750107a
780510a
Uggams, Leslie 660501a
670426a 681020a 681020b
720117a
Uhry, Alfred 560400a 761010a
Ukena, Paul 560414a
Ullett, Nic 680103a
Ulmer, Georges 640602a
Umeki, Miyoshi 581201a
581201b
Underwood, Nita 260522a
Unger, Stella 550526a
Uphof, Ferdie 640922h
680122e 800507a
Urbont, Jacques 611005a
611110a 650327a
Urich, Rebecca 270906f
Urich, Tom 650616a 660207a
800514a
Urmston, Ken 600928a

Vaccaro, Brenda 671207a
Vale, Jerry 501124f 560027a
630415a
Valenti, Michael 651218a
680113a 700322a 720612a
761005a 761005b 770207a
Valentine, Anthony 520001g
Valentine, Joe 720515a
Valentine, Judy 520001d
530010b
Valentine, Paul 520625a
580204a
Valery, Dana 620005b
620005c
Vallee, Rudy 290010a 290013a
310914a 330030a 340005a
340006a 350044a 380039a
380039b 380803a 381123d
390015a 550002a 580427a
611014a 611014b 680006a

Valli, Frankie 720214b
Valori, Bice 621215a 621215b
621215c
Valverde, Joaquin 171101a
Van Alstyne, Egbert 090816a
Van Camp, Leonard 060924i
Van Dorp, Gloria 540624a
Van Dyke, Dick 600414a
600414b 600414f 640001a
680005a
Van Dyke, Jerry 630003a
Van Dyke, Marcie 510419a
Van Eps, Robert 270425c
Van Fleet, Jo 570331b
van Grove, Isaac 051230g
261130h 590626a
Van Heusen, James 341121g
391129a 410017a 410023a
420012a 420029a 430017a
440006a 440021a 460003a
460027a 470002a 470008a
490008a 490009a 500011a
500012a 530006a 530011a
550014a 550919a 560015a
570010b 590006a 590014a
600001a 600009a 610001a
630007a 630016a 630018a
640002a 640422a 650001a
651113a 660501a 661126a
670001a 670226a 740009a
van Peebles, Melvin 711020a
711020b 720516a
Van Scott, Glory 700302a
Van, Billy B 170111b
Van, Bobby 250311d 360411a
481230d 530013b 750319a
Van, Gus 170119a 190623a
200622a 210621a 230925a
300028a
Vance, Dick 631015a
Vandis, Titos 651017a
670411a
Vanoni, Ornella 621215b
Varrone, Gene 581011a
611227a 620519a 790111a
Vasek, Marisha 650222a
Vasquez, Ray 571219h
Vaughan, David 540114c
630020a 660304a 690127a
Vaughan, Frankie 600001a
Vaughan, Sarah 531203i
Vaughn, Billy 580007b
Veidt, Conrad 330033a
Veitch, Laurel 540114g
Vejar, Rudy 051230k 531203c
Velez, Lupe 290004a 290030a
320308b 340031b
Velie, Jay 501012a
Venora, Lee 271227E 450419g
510329d 531203c 611102a
Ventura, Nino 051230c
Venturo, Bill 470313i
Venuta, Benay 420602c
460516c 460516h 460516i
530211a 720326a 750502a
Ver Planck, J (Billy) 711102a
Vera-Ellen 271103a 441228f
460023a 500004a 501012c

510002a
Verdon, Gwen 530507a
550505a 550505b 570514a
590205a 660129a 750603a
750603b
Verdon, Valerie 341121m
Verea, Lisette 051230g
Vereen, Ben 711012b 721023a
721023e 750001a 790004a
Verno, Jerry 511112f 550831a
Vernon, Dorothy 680305a
781109a
Vernon, Gilbert 560301a
Vernon, Wally 380009a
VerPlanck, Marlene 590024a
Verrill, Virginia 380014b
Verushka, Nina 560503b
Vesta, Don 581201i
Vestoff, Virginia 650216a
661106a 680103a 690316a
690316b 761010b
Vian, Boris 580001e
Vickers, Larry 760419a
Vickers, Margaret 640922k
Vickers, Martha 460021a
Vidnovic, Martin 430331v
510329n
Vila, Alberto 410035a
Villi, Olga 660107a
Vinaver, Steven 571010a
651223a
Vincent, Anne 490407s
Vincent, Romo 581222a
Vincent, Ruth 070417b
Vincent, Warren 351010i
460516l 481230i 501012e
530507c 580001i
Vinovich, Stephen 761010a
790111a
Vinter, Gilbert 070417a
090428a 570331d
Violetta 540114a
Viti, Geraldine 540311a
Vivian, Ann 630019a
Vola, Vicki 261130h
Vollaire, George 241201a
280422a
von Boda, Ralf 620919a
Von Hallberg Trio 280528a
von Pinelli, Aldo 650013a
Von Tilzer, Albert 200503a
Vondra, Mimi 630019a
Voorhees, Don 850314a
260824a
Vosburgh, Dick 790328a
Voss, Stephanie 081114f
101107l 121202e 250311h
590528a
Vosselli, Judith 300017a
Votos, Chris 720310a
Vye, Murvyn 450419a
490009a

Waddell, Geoffrey 590430a
Waddell, Linden 781006a
Waddington, Patrick 300904a
Wade, Warren 610419a
Wadsworth, Andrew C

790725a
Wadsworth, Derek 671029d
671029f
Wagner, Adeline 280828b
Wagner, Gerard 751210a
751210b
Wagner, Gerrard 770808a
Wagner, Jeannine 280919a
Wagner, Robert 590006a
Waiaiole, Ben 120108a
Waite, Genevieve 750129a
Wakefield, Ann 540114b
Wakefield, Douglas 350059a
Wakefield, Henrietta 941029b
Wakefield, John 051230p
160831b 241202r
Wakeham, Michael 170210c
Wakeling, Howard 701215a
Wakely, Jimmy 520014b
Wakeman, Rick 750005a
Walbrook, Anton 740405b
500027a 501012f
Walburn, Raymond 360018b
Walcher, Susie 720515a
Walcott, Derek 741128a
Walden, Grant 411001a
Walden, Stanley 690617a
Waldman, Robert 560400a
761010a
Walken, Glenn 411001a
Walken, Ronald 411001a
Walker, Barbara 791127a
Walker, Chris 800605a
Walker, Cindy 530026a
Walker, Don 311226a 360411a
401225b 450419a 450419h
470110a 480129a 481208a
481208d 481208e 490715a
501012a 511101a 520625a
520625c 521215a 530211a
530226a 530528a 540010b
540305a 540513a 540513d
550224a 550418a 550505a
560503a 560503b 571219a
581016a 581209a 590319a
600308a 601103a 611118a
630423a 630423b 631003a
640227a 640404a 640922a
640922d 640922h 650216a
650511a 650511d 651129a
660521a 661120a 661120d
680118a 681020a 681117a
701019a 710415a 750107a
760511a 780510a
Walker, Esther 190212a
Walker, George 020303a
060220a
Walker, Joseph A 680509a
Walker, Mallory 031013a
070302a 241202e
Walker, Nancy 301014c
411001c 440025a 441228a
441228b 441228g 480129a
480129b 490113a 540018b
550016a 550423a 601226a
730311a
Walker, Polly 270926a
281001a

Walker, Syd 410031a
Walker, William 651007a
Wall, Geoffrey 241202r
Wall, Max 540513d 590511b
Wallace, Art 670926a
Wallace, Emett "Babe"
  501124g
Wallace, G D 551130a
Wallace, George 570514a
  631017a
Wallace, Ian 160831b 490407r
  530507j 531203e 580001h
  580003a 580221b
Wallace, Jean 570038a
  580025a
Wallace, Oliver 410024a
  490011a 550018a 550018b
Wallace, Paul 590521a
  590521b
Wallace, Scott 760414a
Wallace, William Vincent
  451115a
Wallach, Ira 570018a
Wallberg, Fritz 571219e
  581201g
Waller, Fats 280227a 290629a
  290629b 350005a 420704b
  430007a 430007b 430617a
  780509a
Waller, Gordon 721108b
  721108d
Waller, Jack 311008a 320614a
  340927a 351002a
Walley, Deborah 620004a
Wallis, Bertram 170131a
Wallis, Shani 501012f 520625c
  530226d 600630b 660521a
Walls, Geoffrey 051230p
Walls, Tom 151225a 190520a
Walsh, Mary Jane 391018a
  411029a
Walsh, Valerie 481208f
Walston, Ray 490407c
  490407p 550505a 550505b
  550505c 591113a 750502a
Walter, Cy 351010w
Walter, Jessica 481230e
Walter, Meg 441228d
Walters, Thorley 510215a
Wand, Betty 570926b 580001a
  580008a
Wann, Jim 750114a
Ward, Bryce 760414a
Ward, Charles 801111a
Ward, Helen 581014a
Ward, Ken 801120a
Ward, Roy 760414a
Warenskjold, Dorothy
  241202c
Warfield, Joel 621008a
  631024b 660207a 660920a
Warfield, William 271227a
  271227e 271227k 351010f
Waring, Derek 720710a
Waring, Fred 301208a
  490715c 541230e 571219g
Waring, Richard 321212b
Waring, Tom 320915b

Warner, Genevieve 051230a
  241202a
Warner, Neil 651122a
Warner, Russell 151223a
  790513a
Warner, Sandy 630415a
Warner, Steven 740002a
Warnick, Clay 560414a
  610518a
Warning, Dennis 761010a
Waroux, Fabienne 751210a
Warren, Ann 420005b
Warren, Annette 271227e
Warren, Betty 440032a
  530908a
Warren, Clark 650222a
Warren, Fran 510005a
Warren, Harry 290311a
  311102a 330001a 330021a
  330028a 340001a 340002b
  340021a 340021c 340027b
  350011a 350012a 350040a
  360006a 360007a 360063a
  370011a 370021a 380015a
  380037a 380039a 400009a
  410007a 410010a 410012a
  410027a 420008a 420014a
  420015a 420030a 430004a
  430014a 450016b 450027a
  460006a 460019a 460023a
  490002a 490014a 500002a
  500009a 510002a 520011a
  520012a 550017a 560613a
  570012a 600003a 660501a
  800825a
Warren, Jeff 501012f
Warren, Jimmy 530507i
Warren, Julie 271103a
Warren, Kenneth J 680320a
Warren, Lesley Ann 570331b
  631024a 670004a 680003a
Warren, Rod 630011a 651103a
  660623a 661019a
Warrick, Ruth 191118b
Warrlich, Marlene 280828b
Warwick, Dionne 680002a
Warwick, Norman 500707a
  600622a
Washburn, Jack 621020a
Washington, Buck 361001a
Washington, Dinah 481230p
Washington, Lamont 671029b
Washington, Ned 400001a
  410024a 570040a
Wasner, Franz 591116b
Wasser, Alan 690724a
Waterman, Denis 571219c
  600630a
Waterous, Herbert 910928f
  241202j
Waters, Ethel 270711a
  280509a 290001a 301022a
  310504a 330930a 350919a
  390103a 401025b 401025c
  401025d 420025a 430012b
  530002a
Waters, Jan 590521f 601226b
  640407c

Waters, Janet 240902k
  261130s 271227D 490407j
  510329o 560503d 570926k
  581201j
Waters, John 790211b
Wathall, Alfred G 021229a
Watson, Betty Jane 430331e
  430331t
Watson, Bryan 721108a
Watson, David 301030c
Watson, Douglass 740306a
Watson, Laurence 210523a
Watson, Milton 160115f
  170816c 241202m 261130p
  280919p
Watson, Roger 721108b
Watson, Susan 250311d
  450419h 600414a 641027a
  690122a 801111a
Watson, Wylie 320614a
  340927a
Watters, Hal 721001a 721023c
  780117a
Watters, Marlys 271227w
  570926e
Watts, Elizabeth 590423a
Waugh, Grace 710517e
Waxman, Jeff 751219a
Waxman, Percy 160911a
Wayland, Newton 721001a
Wayne, Cynthia 620205*a
Wayne, David 271227k
  470110a 490025a 500003a
  570203a 570413a 580403a
  601205a 651210a 680118a
  740008a
Wayne, Fredd 491125a
Wayne, Jerry 540021a
Wayne, Paula 411001a
  430331f 430331o 490407k
  490407l 641020a
Weaver, Fritz 620319a
  650216a
Weaver, Jacki 790211b
Weavers 510028a
Webb, Alyce 631015a
Webb, Barbara 351010f
  600428a
Webb, Clifton 320915c
  330930a
Webb, Geoffrey 271227w
  440821f
Webb, George 431202c
Webb, Janet 590521g
Webb, Laurie 460516q
  621117b
Webb, Lizbeth 271227C
  470426a 501124d 510215a
Webb, Marti 630321b 630321c
  630321e 640922g 710517c
  740711a 800128a
Webb, Roy 480005a
Webber, Andrew Lloyd
  711012a 711012b 711012c
  711012e 721108a 721108b
  721108c 721108d 750422a
  780621a 800128a 810511a
Weber & Fields 971202a

  980908a 990921a 120208a
Weber, Fredericka 700126a
Weber, Fredricka 621018a
Weber, Marek 241202p
Webster, Byron 651017a
Webster, Margaret 321212b
Webster, Paul 410804a
Webster, Paul Francis
  051230d 240902b 241202h
  241202i 450026a 530004a
  540018b 560009b 560011a
  560016a 570007a 570013a
  580007a 600428a 650524a
Weede, Robert 440821a
  560503a 561223a 611010a
  611010b 700408a
Weeks, Alan 670426a 700302a
Weeks, Anson 330304a
Weguelen, Thomas 240911a
Weidler, Virginia 410004b
Weil, Robert 590511a
Weill, Kurt 280828a 361117a
  381019a 410123a 410123c
  431007a 431007b 450005a
  450322a 470109a 480715a
  481007a 491030a 630606a
  721001a 791106a
Weiner, Larry M 760215a
Weinrib, Len 590609a
Weir, Beverlee 640116c
Weir, Leonard 261130d
  301108d 560315d
Weiss, George David 560322a
  590319a 600619a 681023a
  730404a
Weiss, Gordon 781022a
Weissman, Mitch 770531a
Weitz, Millie 371127c
Welbes, George 690617a
Welch, Charles C 610518a
Welch, Elisabeth 271227p
  280509c 301208a 331006a
  331006c 350505a 350505d
  360037a 370035a 431109a
  431202c 471015a 721023d
  791221a
Welchman, Harry 160110c
  190917a 241202j 261130c
Weldon, Joan 051230k
  611102a
Welitch, Ljuba 740405f
Wells, Cynthia 151223a
Wells, Deering 310514a
Wells, Robert 540012a
Wells, Tony 730206a
Welsh, Scott 170319c
Wendel, Elmarie 591118a
  621008a 650330a
Wenrich, Percy 260906a
Wentworth, Robin 590528a
Wentz, Bob 621004a
Wentzel, Wayne 590122a
Werner, Fred 640407a
  651113a 660129a 740008a
Werrenrath, Reinald 090123*a
  130908a
Wescott, Glenn 621004a
West, Alvy 630411a

West, Bernie 261108e
West, Charles 490407t
　591116j
West, Jennifer 510329p
West, Keefe 711201b
West, Lockwood 740501a
West, Mae 280409a 330007a
　330007b 330008a 330008b
　340042b 350018a 360045a
　700003a
Westbrook, Donald 680222a
Westbury, Marjorie 490915c
Westerman, Tom 761010a
Westmacott, Sybil 141028b
Weston, Jim 740306a
Weston, Paul 250921a
　280919b 450004c 481230n
　510012a 520010a 530003b
　651122b
Weston, R P 320614a 340927a
　351002a
Wette, Adelheid 931223a
Wheatley, Alan 580221b
Wheatley, Joanne 490715c
Wheaton, Anna 170220c
Wheeler, Bert 301014j
　520321a
Wheeler, Harold 681201a
　711020a 711201a 720516a
　750105a
Wheeler, Kimball 060924i
Whelan, Richard 730419a
Whitaker, Johnny 691206a
　730002a
White, Barbara Jean 730419*a
White, Diz 730213a
White, Frances 160001a
　170607a 290923a
White, George 290923a
White, Jane 590511a 770920a
White, Lee 170426a 190902a
White, Paul 410804a
White, Richard 530214a
White, Roger 261108a
　410123c
White, Sammy 271227o
White, Sheila 600630b
　681220b
White, Terri 800430a
White, Tony Joe 680305b
White, Trevor 711012d
White, Willard 351010q
　751021a
Whitehill, Janie 270906j
Whiteman, Paul 220828a
　230815a 231020a 270322a
　271227r 281204a 300005a
　310914c 320217b 320308a
　330930b 331021a 341121i
　350006c 350013a 351012b
　351116c 351116d 380710a
　400003a 450008a
Whitfield, Alice 680122a
Whitfield, David 240902k
　261130s
Whitfield, June 520925a
Whiting, Jack 311226a
　341121f 360411c 530211a

540311a
Whiting, Margaret 490012a
　490407i 500013a 550028a
　651218a
Whiting, Richard 310908a
　320002a 321126a 370010a
　370023a 450022a 790328a
Whitman, Jerry 780002a
Whitman, Peter 781031a
Whitmore, James 430331b
　481230d
Whitmore, Pat 540114e
　640116h 660524c
Whitmore, Patricia 640922g
　640922i 681201c
Whitsun-Jones, Paul 531203h
　600630d 640922d
Whitworth, Pat 490407j
Whyte, Ronny 630011a
Wiata, Inia Te 160831a
　261130d 271227w 510329p
　560503b
Wickes, Mary 430331v
Wickham, Jeffry 680305a
　711220a
Wiegert, Rene 381123a
　721004a 780621c
Wiel, Imogene 610519a
Wilbur, Richard 561201a
　561201b
Wilcox, Larry 381123a
　651210a 660920a 661126a
Wilcox, Martha 690502a
Wild, Jack 600630b
Wildbolz, Klaus 661120e
Wilde, Cornel 460014a
Wilde, Harold 090906b
Wilde, Marty 511112i 600414c
　630321d
Wilder, Alec 500025a 500424a
　571013a 580427a 601012a
Wilder, Elizabeth 810411a
Wilder, Gene 740002a
Wilder, Jo 280828c
Wiley, Lee 271227v
Wilkerson, Arnold 720419a
Wilkes, Pat 550025a
Wilkie, Earle 241202s 280919a
Wilkinson, Colm 780621a
Wilkinson, Ralph Norman
　561121a
Willams, Randy 601226c
Willens, Doris 780608a
Willett, John 280828g
Williams, Andy 561129c
　591113a 610006b 620012a
　640014a
Williams, Ann 700330a
Williams, Barbara 631029a
Williams, Ben 280919d
Williams, Bert 000402a
　020303a 060220a 100620a
　110626a 121021a 140601b
　150621a 170612a 190623a
　200929a
Williams, Billy 480430a
Williams, Blinky 740003a
Williams, Camilla 351010b

Williams, Cara 560005b
Williams, Carlton 751121a
Williams, Cindy 760003a
Williams, Clarence 270627a
Williams, Cootie 300023a
Williams, David Wheldon
　660129f 661120d
Williams, Debbie 670110a
Williams, Dick 501124f
　571017a
Williams, Don 580013a
Williams, Duke 570521a
Williams, Eleanor 360411a
Williams, Emlyn 741007a
Williams, Esther 490004a
　490004c 490007a 500009a
　510019b
Williams, Frances 280702a
　311013*a 330040a 340044a
Williams, Fred 651122e
Williams, Freddie 271227F
Williams, Guy 620311a
Williams, Hank 640015a
Williams, Hank, Jr 640015a
　680010a
Williams, Harry 090816a
Williams, Jack 360411a
Williams, Jack Eric 790301a
Williams, Jodi 651226a
Williams, Joe 600928*a
　750006a
Williams, John 640922c
　681117*a 690004a 730002a
Williams, Joy 561107a
Williams, Kenneth 530908a
　570331e
Williams, Kit 601203c
Williams, Liberty 760004a
Williams, Marion 611211a
Williams, Mary Kay 590122a
Williams, Maynard 721108b
Williams, Merry 640422a
Williams, Michael 670003a
Williams, Neil 170210e
　270202f 301030e 361222a
Williams, Pat 680204a
Williams, Paul 740006a
　760004a 790002a
Williams, Ralph 630423a
Williams, Rita 081114e
　170210c 271227F 301108a
　590205b 640116p
Williams, Ron 791127a
Williams, Rubert 751121a
Williams, Russ 601203h
Williams, Sammy 781006a
Williams, Sylvia 791020a
Williams, Treat 671029g
Williams, Valerie 801120a
Williams, Walter 181220a
Williams, William B 750323a
Williamson, John Finley
　390424c
Williamson, Nicol 760425a
Willis, Sally 730213a
Willison, Walter 701110a
　720326a 750502a 801111a
Willoughby, Jay 590626a

Willoughby, Leueen 730419b
　791106a
Wills, Gloria 471010a
Wills, Nat M 130616a
Willson, Meredith 571219a
　571219d 601103a 601103b
　631003a
Willson, Rini 571219d
Wilson, Alfred 770808a
Wilson, Art 330304a
Wilson, Carrie 690604a
Wilson, Catherine 051230t
Wilson, Dolores 651210a
Wilson, Dooley 400404b
　430006a 430006b 441005a
Wilson, Dorothy 580001j
Wilson, Earl, Jr 740108a
Wilson, Edith 210823a
　220717a 290629b 300821a
Wilson, Edwin 141028b
Wilson, Eileen 481208b
　501012b
Wilson, Elizabeth 280828g
Wilson, Jane 241202k 280919f
　480715b 490715c
Wilson, Julie 481230k
　570014a 571204a 691023a
Wilson, Mary Jane 590430a
　600428*a
Wilson, Mary Louise 600929a
　611005a 621018a 650511a
　660920a
Wilson, Michael 060924i
Wilson, Patricia 591123a
Wilson, Randal 770322a
Wilson, Robin 671023a
Wilson, Ron 640007a
Wilson, Sandy 481117a
　511003a 530908a 530908b
　540114a 540114h 581002a
　581002b 600622a 650202a
　650202b 650202c 710610a
　711220a 711220b 791221a
Wilson, Sarah 680222a
Wilson, Teddy 441207a
Wilson, Terry 671029e
Wilson-Hyde, Eric 160115b
Wimperis, Arthur 090428a
　100219a 120224a 131002a
Wimsett, Betty 590521g
Winchell, Paul 570018a
Windom, William 321212b
Windson, Barbara 630321d
　540114d 600211a
Windsor, John 790517a
Windsor, Nancy 610403a
Winfield, Paul 740008a
Winkle, Willie 571219f
Winn, Anona 470426b
Winninger, Charles 220605b
　410001b 430013a 450001b
Winsett, Betty 250311k
　261130u 430331s 540001b
Winston, Hattie 700302a
　700518a
Winter, Edward 681201a
Winter, Lois 571219f 580007a
Winterberg, Richard 190512a

Winterhalter, Hugo 501012a
520001d 520005a 530010b
560010a 571117a
Winters, David 360411a
620406a
Winters, Lawrence 351010b
351010h 460418a
Winters, Lois 601203d
Winters, Renee 460516f
Winters, Roland 581016a
Winters, Shelley 540022a
700326a 770005a
Winton, Jane 340607a
Wipf, Alex 690200a
Wisdom, Norman 481011a
661126a 671115a 680006a
Wise, Jim 681220a
Wise, Joe 560315k
Wisner, Jimmy 700315b
790611a
Wissler, Rudy 460005c
Withers, Iva 450419k
Witkin, Jacob 640922h
Witten, Al 760324a
Witter, William C 800430a
Wodehouse, P G 170111a
170220a 170829a 180201a
201221a 251026a 261108e
271227a 280313a
Wolcott, Charles 420009a
420018a 440023a
Woldin, Judd 731019a
Wolf, Rennold 140413a
180401a
Wolf, Tommy 590512a
Wolfe, Karin 411001a 580001c
Wolfe, Leslie-Anne 800514a
Wolffberg, Inge 280828i
Wolfington, Iggie 571219a
640005a 640019a
Wolfson, John 630020a
Wolfson, Martin 280828a
410105a 650216a
Wolvin, Roy 570207a
Wong, Patricia 581201d
Wood, Arthur 140824c
151225c 200528b 220302a
230105a 260522a 261108c
Wood, Charles 481230a
Wood, David 750422a
Wood, G 550228a 571105a
601012a
Wood, George Scott 361001b
Wood, J Hickory 040614a
Wood, Mary Laura 600414c
Wood, Natalie 570926b
590521b
Wood, Peggy 290031a
290718e 311015b 380316a
591116c
Wood, Raymond 750917a
Woodard, Charlaine 780509a
Woodard, Charles 660627a
Woodbury, Albert 600414b
Woodbury, John 481116a
Woodland, Rae 350505c
Woodruff, Carole 630019a
660920a

Woods, Arline 630019a
Woods, Aubrey 721106a
721106b 791221a
Woods, Harry M 301203a
Woods, Ilene 490011a
490011b 490011c
Woods, Louise 210523a
Woods, Richard 761215a
Woodthorpe, Peter 680127a
Woodvine, John 800622a
Woodward, Edward 640407a
Woodward, Joanne 630015a
Woodward, Matthew 140130a
171126a
Woolf, Alain D 680122e
Woolf, Walter 260326d
271130c
Woolfe, Betty 560315d
Woolfolk, William 351010a
Woollard, Robert 280313a
Woolley, Monty 460010b
Woolmore, Pamela 390323d
490915b
Woolston, Fred 760324a
Wordsworth, Richard 590528a
Workman, C H 991129a
081114j
Workoff, Susie 270906j
Worley, Jo Anne 651223a
Worsley, Pat 340216a
Worster, Howett 230207a
271227g 280919d
Worth, Billie 501012f
Worth, Caroline 601012a
Worth, Joy 580001f
Worth, Mara 671207a
Wren, Jenny 650202a
Wright, Andrea 801120a
Wright, Ben 610008a
Wright, Bob 051230k 490715b
Wright, Dorsey 671029g
Wright, Fred, Jr 000203a
031026a
Wright, Graham 570207a
Wright, Huntley 220302a
Wright, Margaret 660304a
690127a
Wright, Martha 121202a
490715b
Wright, Ray 691230a
Wright, Robert 121202a
301030b 390017a 440821a
531203a 531203i 561223a
611102a 651129a
Wright, Samuel E 711201b
740306a
Wright, Stevie 711012d
Wrightson, Earl 060924b
101107c 130908b 160115a
170319a 241202f 250921d
261130n 270202d 271103b
280919o 451006a 481230g
540912a 600619a
Wyatt, Jane 500003a
Wyatt, Jerry 391018c
Wyatt, Ric 770004a
Wyatt, Robin 770004a
Wykes, David 791106a

Wyler, Gretchen 550224a
Wylie, Betty Jane 771201a
Wyman, Jane 440015a
460010b 510011a 520001a
520012a 530015a 530015b
Wyman, Nicholas 151223a
Wymore, Patrice 490915d
510024a 520010b 550023a
Wynn, Ed 031013c 510013a
640001a
Wynn, Keenan 460516b
460516h 470110b 481230d
711203a
Wynn, Nan 420003c 420021a
430019a 440028a 470002a
Wynne, Hazel 261005a
270101a

Yacht Club Boys 360020a
360040a
Yahjian, Kurt 770322a
Yana 570331e
Yancy, Emily 640116b
Yarnell, Bruce 460516c
610403a
Yellen, Jack 300917a 310119a
350005a 390828a 411201a
York, Trevor 401225m
Yoshida, Fusako 760111b
Youles, Frances 570926k
581201j
Youmans, Vincent 230207a
250311a 250311o 261217a
270425a 281121a 330005a
Young, Alan 520005a 550002a
Young, Alexander 740405b
740405h
Young, Charles 141028d
160831a 170210c 250311a
301108a 470426d 570331f
601203j 640116p 660524c
Young, Clifford 450419i
Young, Cy 600103a 650202a
Young, Donna Jean 661207a
Young, Eve 331118i
Young, Joe 311102a
Young, John 711012d
Young, Loretta 640422a
Young, Margaret 560315e
580001j
Young, Ralph 581222a
Young, Rida Johnson 101107a
101107o 120205a 161206a
170816a 181004a
Young, Robert 241201e
430003c 430014a
Young, Ronald 540114c
Young, Thomas 770322a
Young, Victor 241202k
271227f 280919f 310914b
320217a 390001b 390424b
400001b 420017a 440006a
480007a 490009a 520009a
540016a 550018a 550526a
570019a
Youngman, Henny 750323a

Zaitz, Cynthia 810001a

Zeno, Norman 341225a
Zien, Chip 790221a
Zimmer, Norma 580003a
Zimmer, Norma Larsen
510029a 560026a
Zimmerman, Harry 640407a
640407c
Zimmerman, Matt 450419o
770421b
Ziskin, Victor 610425a
Zito, Darlene 640005a
Zoghby, Emil Dean 680305a
Zoob, Dave 210809a
Zorich, Louis 750303a
Zorina, Vera 400528c
Zuniga, Lupe 731217a